From Modernism to Postmodernism

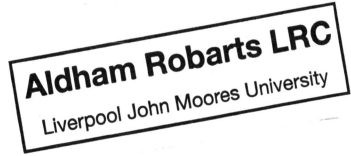

BLACKWELL PHILOSOPHY ANTHOLOGIES

Each volume in this outstanding series provides an authoritative and comprehensive collection of the essential primary readings from philosophy's main fields of study. Designed to complement the *Blackwell Companions to Philosophy* series, each volume represents an unparalleled resource in its own right, and will provide the ideal platform for course use.

From Modernism to Postmodernism

An Anthology

Expanded Second Edition

Edited by

Lawrence Cahoone

Blackwell
Publishing

Editorial material and organization © 2003 by Blackwell Publishing Ltd

350 Main Street, Malden, MA 02148-5018, USA
108 Cowley Road, Oxford OX4 1JF, UK
550 Swanston Street, Carlton South, Melbourne, Victoria 3053, Australia
Kurfürstendamm 57, 10707 Berlin, Germany

First published 1996
This expanded second edition published 2003 by Blackwell Publishing Ltd

Library of Congress Cataloging-in-Publication Data

From modernism to postmodernism: an anthology / edited by Lawrence Cahoone – 2nd ed.
    p. cm. – (Blackwell philosophy anthologies; 2)
  Includes bibliographical references and index.
  ISBN 0-631-23212-5 (alk. paper) – ISBN 0-631-23213-3 (pbk. : alk. paper)
  1. Postmodernism. I. Cahoone, Lawrence E., 1954 –II. Series.

B831.2.F76 2002
149′.97 – dc 21   2002071051

A catalogue record for this title is available from the British Library.

Set in 9 on 11pt Ehrhardt
by Kolam Information Services Pvt Ltd, Pondicherry, India
Printed and bound in the United Kingdom
by TJ International, Padstow, Cornwall

For further information on
Blackwell Publishing, visit our website:
http://www.blackwellpublishing.com

Contents

Contents

Contents

Preface

This expanded edition attempts to fill the same function as its earlier self, to provide teachers and students with a useful selection of postmodern and related writings in a broad historical context. The problem with introducing students to any discussion of postmodernism is not merely the notorious difficulties of the meaning of the term. It is that most students do not adequately understand what is *modern*, what it is whose obsolescence the term "postmodern" presumably announces. Any discussion of postmodernism assumes a great deal of knowledge about modernism, or modernity, or the modern world, without which the distinctive and polemical import of the postmodern cannot be understood. The purpose of the present volume is to fill that void by putting postmodernism in context. Certainly this is a task to which no anthology can be adequate, yet some attempt in that direction is, I believe, better than none.

The revised edition presents 14 new authors and 20 new selections, most of them recent writers either expressing or criticizing postmodernism. In making the selections I have tried to include primary texts that are either of historical importance, or that represent an historically important perspective. I have preferred exemplifications of modernism and postmodernism to commentaries on them. My introductions, to the volume and each part, have been revised. Though primarily a philosophical anthology, enough work in literature, sociology, and the arts has been included to at least show the relation of philosophical to nonphilosophical modernism and postmodernism.

Every effort has been made to render the anthology convenient for use by faculty and students: a brief introductory essay begins each of its three parts; headers introduce each writer; and the source of each selection is clearly given on the first page, the preposition "from" indicating that not all of the named text is reproduced, with ellipses in the text to mark deletions. My annotations appear as footnotes, while author's notes are always endnotes [with my interpolations bracketed] or in rare cases asterisked below the text (authors' notes have been renumbered to be continuous). Parts I and II are arranged chronologically. Since the expanded Part III is now organized into four thematic sections, chronological order does not hold across them.

The original impetus for this project came from Stephan Chambers. Steve Smith ably took it over, and made this new edition possible. Jeffrey Dean and Beth Remmes have been utterly helpful in ushering it into print. Anthony Grahame has saved me from numerous typographical embarrassments. I have benefited from the advice and comments of Al Anderson, Elizabeth Baeten, Bettina Bergo, Jeffrey Bloechl, Tian-yu Cao, Tina Chanter, Fred Evans, Lewis Gordon, Peter Kaufman, Frank Kirkland, Len Lawlor, Tommy Lott, Michael Naas, Lucius Outlaw, Robin Reisenfeld, Margaret Rose, Denise Schaeffer, Jacqueline Scott, James Schmidt, Brian Seitz, Fred Tauber, Tom Thorp, and Jack Weinstein. They are guilty only of offering information and suggestions, not all of which I have followed. The final choices, hence misjudgments and errors, are mine alone.

Acknowledgments

The authors and publishers gratefully acknowledge the following for permission to reproduce copyright material:

1 Descartes, René, *Meditations on First Philosophy*, Meditations One and Two, pp. 144–57 from *The Philosophical Works of Descartes*, vol. I (trans. Elizabeth Haldane and G. R. T. Ross). Cambridge: Cambridge University Press, 1975;

2 Hume, David, Conclusion to Book One, pp. 263–74 from *A Treatise of Human Nature*, Book 1, Part IV (ed. L. A. Selby-Bigge). Oxford: Oxford University Press, 1975. © Oxford University Press 1975, reprinted by permission of Oxford University Press;

3 Rousseau, Jean-Jacques, pp. 3–10 from Part One of "Discourse on the Sciences and the Arts" in *The Basic Political Writings of Jean-Jacques Rousseau* (trans. Donald Cress). Indianapolis: Hackett Publishing Company Inc., 1987. Reprinted by permission of Hackett Publishing Company, Inc. All rights reserved;

4 Smith, Adam, from *The Theory of Moral Sentiments*, Part IV, chapter 1, pp. 179–87 and Part VI, section 2, chapter 2, paras. 15–18, pp. 232–4. Glasgow Edition. Oxford: Oxford University Press, 1976. Paperback by Indianapolis: Liberty Fund, 1984. © Oxford University Press 1984, reprinted by permission of Oxford University Press;

5 Kant, Immanuel: [A] "An Answer to the Question: What is Enlightenment?" (trans. H. B. Nisbet, ed. Hans Reiss), pp. 54–60 from Kant's Political Writings. Cambridge: Cambridge University Press, 1970; [B] from "Preface to the Second Edition" of *Critique of Pure Reason* (trans. Norman Kerry Smith), New York: St. Martin's Press, 1965, Bvii–Bxxii, pp. 17–25;

6 Burke, Edmund, a selection of unmarked sections, in each case separated by space in the text, from *Reflections on the Revolution in France* (ed. J. G. A. Pocock), pp. 12–19, 25–6, 29–31, 51–2, 76–7, 216–18. Indianapolis: Hackett Publishing Company Inc., 1987. Reprinted by permission of Hackett Publishing Company, Inc. All rights reserved;

7 Caritat, Marie Jean Antoine Nicolas, marquis de Condorcet, from "The Ninth Stage: From Descartes to the Foundation of the French Republic" from *Sketch for an Historical Picture of the Progress of the Human Mind* (trans. June Barraclough), pp. 124–37. New York: Hyperion Press, rpt of 1955 Noonday Press edition. Reprinted by permission of Hyperion Press;

8 Hegel, Georg Wilhelm Friedrich, "Absolute Freedom and Terror," paras. 582–95, pp. 355–63 from *Phenomenology of Spirit* (trans. A. V. Miller). Oxford: Oxford University Press, 1977. © Oxford University Press 1977, reprinted by permission of Oxford University Press;

9 Marx, Karl, with Friedrich Engels, "Bourgeois and Proletarians," section 1 of *Manifesto of the Communist Party* (trans. Samuel Moore),

reproduced in Robert C. Tucker (ed.), *The Marx–Engels Reader* (second edition), pp. 473–83. New York: Norton, 1978. Copyright © 1978, 1972 by W.W. Norton & Company, Inc. Used by permission of W.W. Norton & Company, Inc.;

10 Darwin, Charles, from chapter 3 ("Struggle for Existence"), pp. 51–4, 62–6; from chapter 4 ("Natural Selection"), pp. 67–73; and from chapter 14 ("Recapitulation and Conclusion"), pp. 371, 389, and 394–6 in *The Origin of Species*. Oxford: Oxford University Press, 1996. © Oxford University Press 1996, reprinted by permission of Oxford University Press;

11 Baudelaire, Charles, from "The Painter of Modern Life" (trans. P. E. Charvet) in *Baudelaire: Selected Writings on Art and Literature*, London: Penguin, 1992, sections 3–4, pp. 395–406. Reproduced by permission of Penguin Books Ltd.;

12 Peirce, Charles S., section II (pp. 289–93) and section IV (pp. 297–302) from "How to Make Our Ideas Clear," second paper of the series "Illustrations of the Logic of Science," *Popular Science Monthly*, vol. XII, January 1878. New York: D. Appleton and Co.;

13 Nietzsche, Friedrich: [A] "On Truth and Lies in a Nonmoral Sense," pp. 79–91 from *Philosophy and Truth* (ed. Daniel Brazeale). New York: Humanities Press, 1979; [B] "The Madman" from *The Gay Science* (trans. and ed. Walter Kaufmann), Part Three, section 125, pp. 181–2. New York: Vintage, 1974. Copyright © 1974 by Random House, Inc. Used by permission of Random House, Inc.; [C] "How the True World Finally Became a Fable," from *Twilight of the Idols*, reproduced in *The Portable Nietzsche* (trans. and ed. Walter Kaufmann), pp. 485–6. New York: Viking, 1968. Copyright © 1954 by The Viking Press, renewed © 1982 by Viking Penguin Inc. Used by permission of Viking Penguin, a division of Penguin Putnam Inc.; [D] The Dionysian World,* para. 1067, pp. 449–50 from *The Will to Power* (trans. Walter Kaufmann and R. J. Hollingdale, edited with commentary by Walter Kaufmann). New York: Random House, 1967). Copyright © 1967 by Walter Kaufmann. Used by permission of Random House, Inc. * Note that the title given to this fourth section is this volume editor's not Nietzsche's;

14 Marinetti, Filippo Tommaso, "The Founding and Manifesto of Futurism" (trans. R. W. Flint and Arthur W. Coppotelli) from *Marinetti: Selected Writings* (ed. R. W. Flint), pp. 39–44. New York: Farrar, Straus, Giroux, 1972. Copyright © 1971, 1972 by Farrar, Straus & Giroux, Inc. Reprinted by permission of Farrar, Straus & Giroux, Inc.;

15 de Saussure, Ferdinand, from *Course in General Linguistics* (trans. Wade Baskin), Part One, chapter 1, pp. 65–70. New York: McGraw-Hill, 1966. Reprinted by permission of McGraw-Hill Inc.;

16 Weber, Max, from "Science as a Vocation," pp. 138–40, 143–9, 155–6 in *From Max Weber: Essays in Sociology* (trans. and ed. H. H. Gerth and C. Wright Mills). New York: Oxford University Press, 1946. Copyright © 1946, 1958 by H. H. Gerth and C. Wright Mills, used by permission of Oxford University Press, Inc.;

17 Le Corbusier, from "Argument," pp. 1–8; "First Reminder: Mass," pp. 29–31; and "Third Reminder: Mass," pp. 47–64 in *Towards a New Architecture* (trans. Frederick Etchells). New York: Dover Publications, 1986;

18 Wittgenstein, Ludwig: [A] "Lecture on Ethics," *The Philosophical Review* 74, no. 1 (January 1965), pp. 3–12, reproduced with permission; [B] from *Tractatus Logico-Philosophicus* (trans. D. F. Pears and B. F. McGuinness), paras. 6.53–6.57, pp. 73–4. London: Routledge and Kegan Paul, 1961. Reprinted by permission of Taylor & Francis Books Ltd.;

19 Freud, Sigmund, chapters 6 and 7, pp. 64–80, from *Civilization and its Discontents* (trans. James Strachey). New York: Norton, 1961. Copyright © 1961 by James Strachey, renewed 1989 by Alix Strachey. Used by permission of W.W. Norton & Company, Inc.;

20 Husserl, Edmund, Part One, section 3–5, pp. 7–14 and Part Two, section 9h–9l, pp. 48–59 from *The Crisis of European Sciences and Transcendental Phenomenology* (trans. David Carr). Evanston: Northwestern University Press, 1970. Reprinted by permission of Northwestern University Press;

21 Horkheimer, Max and Theodor Adorno, from "The Concept of Enlightenment," pp. 23–9, and from "Juliette, or Enlightenment and Morality," pp. 81–93, in *Dialectic of Enlightenment* (trans. John Cumming). New York: Seabury, 1972. Copyright © The Continuum Publishing Group;

22 Sartre, Jean-Paul, from "Existentialism" (trans. Bernard Frechtman) in *Existentialism and Human Emotions*, pp. 15–24 and 46–51. New York: Citadel 1985. Copyright © 1957, 1985 by Philosophical Library, Inc. Published by arrangement with Carol Publishing Group;

23 Heidegger, Martin, "Letter on Humanism" from *Martin Heidegger: Basic Writings* (trans. Frank A. Capuzzi, with J. Glenn Gray and David Farrell Krell, ed. David Farrell Krell), pp. 193–242. New York: Harper & Row, 1977. English translation copyright © 1977 by Harper & Row, Publishers, Inc. General introduction and introductions to each selection copyright © 1977 by David Farrell Krell. Reprinted by permission of Harper-Collins Publishers, Inc.;

24 Jacques Lacan, "The Mirror Stage as Formative of the Function of the I as Revealed in Psychoanalytic Experience," in *Écrits: A Selection*, trans. by Alan Sheridan, New York: W.W. Norton & Company, 1977, chapter one, pp. 1–7;

25 Kuhn, Thomas, "The Nature and Necessity of Scientific Revolutions," chapter IX, pp. 92–110, from *The Structure of Scientific Revolutions*. Chicago: University of Chicago Press, 1962. Copyright © 1962, 1970 The University of Chicago. Reprinted by permission of University of Chicago Press;

26 Bell, Daniel, "Foreword: 1976" from *The Coming of Post-Industrial Society*, pp. ix–xxii. New York: Basic Books, 1976. Copyright © 1976 by Daniel Bell. Reprinted by permission of Basic Books, a division of HarperCollins Publishers, Inc.;

27 Derrida, Jacques, "Differance," pp. 129–60 in *Speech and Phenomena and Other Essays on Husserl's Theory of Signs* (trans. David B. Allison). Evanston: Northwestern University Press, 1973. Reprinted by permission of Northwestern University Press. This translation includes the introduction to the original 1968 lecture by Derrida (the first five paragraphs);

28 Foucault, Michel: [A] "Nietzsche, Genealogy, History" (trans. Donald F. Bouchard and Sherry Simon), from *Language, Counter-Memory, Practise: Selected Essays and Interviews* (ed. Donald F. Bouchard), pp. 139–64. Ithaca: NY: Cornell University Press, 1977. Copyright © 1977 Cornell University. Used by permission of the publisher, Cornell University Press; [B] from "Truth and Power," pp. 131–3, answer to final question of interview by Alessandro Fontana and Pasquale Pasquino (trans. Colin Gordon) in *Power/Knowledge: Selected Interviews and Other Writings 1972–77* (ed. Colin Gordon). Copyright © 1972, 1975, 1976, 1977 by Michel Foucault. This collection © 1980 by The Harvester Press. Used by permission of Pantheon Books, a division of Random House, Inc.;

29 Irigaray, Luce, "The Sex Which is Not One" (trans. Claudia Reeder) from *New French Feminisms* (ed. Elaine Marks and Isabelle de Courtivron), New York: Schoken, 1981, pp. 99–106. Copyright © Editions de Minuit, Paris;

30 Lyotard, Jean-François, Introduction (pp. xxiii–xxv), Sections 9–11 (pp. 31–47), and Section 14 (pp. 64–7) from *The Postmodern Condition: A Report on Knowledge* (trans. Geoff Bennington and Brian Massumi). Minneapolis: University of Minnesota Press, 1984. Originally published in France as *La condition postmoderne: rapport sur le savoir*. Copyright © 1979 by Les Editions de Minuit, Paris. English translation and foreword copyright © 1984 by the University of Minnesota. Reprinted by permission of the University of Minnesota and by kind permission of Manchester University Press;

31 Deleuze, Gilles, and Félix Guattari, from "1227: Treatise on Nomadology – The War Machine," chapter 12 of *A Thousand Plateaus* (trans. Brian Massumi), pp. 351–5, 361–2, 366–7, 369–71, 380–9, 416–18, 420–3. Minneapolis: University of Minnesota Press, 1987. Copyright © 1987 by the University of Minnesota Press. Originally published as *Mille Plateaux*, volume 2 of *Capitalisme et Schizophrenie*. Copyright © 1980 by Les Editions de Minuit, Paris and Athlone Press, London;

32 Cornel West, "A Genealogy of Modern Racism," chapter four of his *Prophesy Deli-*

verance! An Afro-American Revolutionary Christianity, Philadelphia: Westminster Press, 1982, pp. 47–65. Copyright © 1982 by Cornel West. Used by permission of Westminster John Knox Press;

33 Foster, Hal, "Subversive Signs" from *Recodings: Art, Spectacle, Cultural Politics*, pp. 99–115. New York: The New Press, 1985. Note that illustrations have not been reproduced here;

34 Spivak, Gayatri Chakravorty, pp. 279–89, 292–4, 294–313 from "Can the Subaltern Speak?" in *Marxism and the Interpretation of Culture* (ed. Cary Nelson and Lawrence Grossberg). Champaign: University of Illinois Press, 1988;

35 Harding, Sandra, "From Feminist Empiricism to Feminist Standpoint Epistemologies," chapter 6, pp. 141–61 from *The Science Question in Feminism*. Ithaca, NY: Cornell University Press, 1986. Copyright © 1986 by Cornell University. Published in the United Kingdom by Open University Press 1986. Reprinted by permission of Cornell University Press, Open University Press, and the author;

36 Bordo, Susan, "The Cartesian Masculinization of Thought and the Seventeenth-Century Flight from the Feminine," chapter 6, pp. 97–118 from *The Flight to Objectivity: Essays on Cartesianism and Culture*. Albany: State University of New York Press, 1987. Copyright © 1987 State University of New York. Reprinted by permission of State University of New York and the author;

37 Young, Iris Marion, pp. 122–4, 136–48, 152–5 from "The Scaling of Bodies and the Politics of Identity," chapter 5 in *Justice and the Politics of Difference*. Princeton: Princeton University Press, 1990. Copyright © 1990 by Princeton University Press. Reprinted by permission of Princeton University Press;

38 Giroux, Henry A., "Towards a Postmodern Pedagogy," section of the Introduction to *Postmodernism, Feminism and Cultural Politics*, pp. 45–55. Albany: State University of New York Press, 1991. Copyright © 1991 State University of New York. Reprinted by permission of State University of New York Press;

39 Butler, Judith, "Contingent Foundations: Feminism and the Question of Postmodernism" from Judith Butler and Joan Scott, *Fem-*

inists Theorize the Political, pp. 3–21. London and New York: Routledge, 1992. Reprinted by permission of Taylor & Francis Group;

40 Venturi, Robert, pp. 16–17, 23–5, 38–41, 88, and 102–4 from *Complexity and Contradiction in Architecture*. New York: The Museum of Modern Art, 1966, 1977. Reprinted by permission of The Museum of Modern Art;

41 Hassan, Ihab, "POSTmodernISM: A Paracritical Bibliography," from *Paracriticisms: Seven Speculations of the Times*, pp. 39–59. Urbana: University of Illinois Press, 1975. Copyright © 1975 by the Board of Trustees of the University of Illinois. Used with permission of the University of Illinois Press;

42 Baudrillard, Jean, *Symbolic Exchange and Death* (trans. Iain H. Grant), from chapter 1 (pp. 6–12) and from chapter 2 (pp. 50, 55–61, and 70–6). London: Sage Publications, 1993. English translation copyright © Sage Publications, 1993. Introduction and Bibiliography copyright © Mike Gane 1993. Originally published as *L'échange symbolique et la mort* copyright © Editions Gallimard, Paris. Reprinted by permission of Sage Publications Ltd.;

43 Taylor, Mark C., from *Erring: A Postmodern A/theology*, pp. 6–13, 103–7, and 115–20. Chicago: University of Chicago Press, 1984. Copyright © 1984 by the University of Chicago, reprinted by permission of The University of Chicago Press;

44 Rorty, Richard, "Solidarity or Objectivity?" pp. 3–19, from *Post-Analytic Philosophy* (ed. John Rajchman and Cornel West). New York: Columbia University Press, 1985;

45 Jencks, Charles: [A] "The Death of Modern Architecture," pp. 9–10 from *The Language of Post-Modern Architecture*. New York: Rizzoli, 1986; [B] from chapter 2 (pp. 14–20) and from chapter 7 (pp. 57–9) of *What is Post-Modernism?* London: Academy Editions, 1986. Reproduced by permission of John Wiley & Sons Limited;

46 Haraway, Donna, pp. 190–6, 203–7, and 212–33 from "A Manifesto for Cyborgs: Science, Technology and Socialist Feminism in the 1980s" in *Feminism/Postmodernism* (ed. Linda Nicholson). London and New York: Routledge, 1990. Reprinted by permission of Taylor & Francis Group;

47 Griffin, David Ray, from "Introduction: The Reenchantment of Science," section 1, pp. 2–8

and section 3, 22–30 in *The Reenchantment of Science* (ed. David Ray Griffin). Albany: State University of New York Press, 1988. Copyright © 1988 State University of New York. Reprinted by permission of State University of New York Press;

48   Luhmann, Niklas, "The Cognitive Program of Constructivism and a Reality that Remains Unknown" from *Selforganization: Portrait of a Scientific Revolution* (ed. Wolfgang Krohn, Guenter Kueppers, and Helga Nowotny), pp. 64–85. Dordrecht: Kluwer Academic Publishers, 1990. Reprinted with kind permission of Kluwer Academic Publishers;

49   Hall, David, "Modern China and the Postmodern West" from *Culture and Modernity: East–West Philosophic Perspective*s (ed. Eliot Deutsch), fourth through sixth editions, pp. 57–67. Honolulu: University of Hawaii Press, 1991;

50   Levinas, Emmanuel, "Meaning and Sense" (trans. Alphonso Lingis) from *Collected Philosophical Papers*, pp. 75–107 (Amsterdam: Nijhoff, 1987);

51   Quine, W. V., "Epistemology Naturalized," chapter 3 (pp. 69–90) from *Ontological Relativity and Other Essays*. New York: Columbia University Press, 1969;

52   MacIntyre, Alasdair, "The Virtues, the Unity of a Human Life and the Concept of a Tradition," chapter 15 (pp. 204–25) from *After Virtue: A Study in Moral Theory*. Notre Dame, Ind.: University of Notre Dame Press, 1984. Copyright © 1984 University of Notre Dame Press. Used by permission;

53   Jameson, Fredric, pp. 1–6, 32–8, 45–51, and 54 from "The Cultural Logic of Late Capitalism," chapter 1 in *Postmodernism, Or, The Cultural Logic of Late Capitalism*. Durham: Duke University Press, 1991. Copyright © 1991 Duke University Press. All rights reserved. Reprinted with permission;

54   Habermas, Jürgen, "An Alternative Way out of the Philosophy of the Subject: Communicative versus Subject-Centered Reason," pp. 294–326 from *The Philosophical Discourse of Modernity* (trans. Frederick Lawrence). Cambridge, Mass: The MIT Press, 1987. Copyright © 1986 by the Massachusetts Institute of Technology. Original publication copyright © 1985 Suhrkamp Verlag, Frankfurt am Main. Reprinted by permission of The MIT Press and the author;

55   Putnam, Hilary, "Is There Still Anything to Say About Reality and Truth," Lecture One, pp. 3–21 from *The Many Faces of Realism*. LaSalle, Ill.: Open Court Publishing Inc., 1987.

Every effort has been made to trace copyright holders and to obtain their permission for the use of copyright material. The publisher apologizes for any errors or omissions in the above list and would be grateful if notified of any corrections that should be incorporated in future reprints or editions of this book.

For my Son,
Harrison Baeten Cahoone

Introduction

The term "postmodern" has become a popular label for something about the life and thought of recent decades in the most developed societies. It both refers to phenomena in the real world, and to an intellectual movement, or rather, a not very happy family of intellectual movements. But to paraphrase Tolstoy, dysfunctional families are the most interesting ones. The members of the postmodern family not only express conflicting views, but are interested in barely overlapping subject matters: art, communications media, history, economics, politics, ethics, cosmology, theology, methodology, literature, education. Some of the most important members of the family refuse to be called by the family name. And there are distant relations who deny that they are related at all.

Philosophical opinion regarding the postmodern family is deeply divided. For some, postmodernism connotes the final escape from the stultifying legacy of modern European theology, metaphysics, authoritarianism, colonialism, patriarchy, racism, and domination. To others it represents the attempt by disgruntled left-wing intellectuals to destroy Western civilization. To yet others it labels a goofy collection of hermetically obscure writers who are really talking about nothing at all.

All three reactions are misguided. Certainly the term "postmodern," like any slogan widely used, has been attached to so many different kinds of intellectual, social, and artistic phenomena that it can be subjected to easy ridicule as hopelessly ambiguous or empty. This shows only that it is a mistake to seek a single, essential meaning applicable to all the term's instances. As one of the inspirers of postmodernism would say, the members of the postmodern clan resemble each other in the overlapping way that family members do; two members may share the same eye color, one of these may have the same shape ears as a third, the third may have the same hair color as a fourth, and so on. More important than discovering an essential commonality is recognizing that there are some important new developments in the world that deserve examination, that 'postmodern' labels some of them, and that there are some very important works, raising deep questions, that are likewise labeled. Neither members of the family, nor their critics, ought to be too concerned with the name. Theoretical labels are nothing to be feared, they have a purpose as long as they are thought's servant, rather than its master. Postmodernism deserves careful, sober scrutiny, devoid of trendy enthusiasm, indignant condemnation, or reactionary fear. Its appearance is unlikely either to save the Western world or destroy it.

When philosophers use the word "postmodernism" they usually mean to refer to a movement that developed in France in the 1960s, which could more precisely be called "post-structuralism," along with subsequent and related developments. They have in mind that this movement denies the possibility of "realist" knowledge, objective knowledge of the world independent of the knower, "univocal" (single or primary) meaning of words and texts, the unity of the human self, even the very notion of truth, as well as the cogency of the distinctions between rational inquiry and political action, literal and metaphorical meaning, and science and art. Simply put, they regard it as rejecting most of the fundamental intellectual pillars of modern Western civilization. They may further associate this rejection with political movements like multiculturalism, feminism, and the critique of Eurocentrism, which regard the rejected notions as the ideology of a privileged sexual, ethnic, cultural and economic group, and aim to subvert their privilege in favor of the disenfranchised.

This view is neither entirely right nor entirely wrong. There are writers who make the philosophical denials listed above, and there is a connection between some of them and the political aims of feminists, multiculturalists, and critics of Eurocentrism. But not everyone who engages in the postmodern critique of truth or meaning can be politically characterized; and certainly not all feminists or multiculturalists accept postmodernism. Postmodernism, multiculturalism, feminism, and the critique of Eurocentrism represent overlapping but different intellectual tendencies.

At a minimum, "postmodern" implies that something about recent society or thought in the "advanced" societies since, let us say, the 1960s, reveals a discontinuity with earlier phases of the modern period, hence with the socio-cultural forms, or ideas and methods, characteristic of modern Western culture. This discontinuity may cut so deep as to signal the "end" of the modern, or may indicate merely a novel phase *within* the modern. Those who affirm that these changes are inescapable facts, or who affirm the implied critique of older principles, are thus in some sense "postmodernists," adherents of "postmodernism." In this way, postmodernism is the latest wave in the critique of the Enlightenment, the criticism of the principles characteristic of modern Western society that trace their legacy to the eighteenth century. Such critique is nothing new; modernity has been criticizing itself all its life. Some postmodernists are concerned only to make the historical claim that modernity is at an end, or has entered a new phase, while others argue normatively that it *ought* to end, that it was wrong or unsupportable. Some reject modernity, while some only question it, problematize it, without advocating any alternative. And some never speak of "the modern" or "modernism" at all, but instead criticize certain principles that most would regard as essential to the modern world.

Facing all this diversity, the sincere observer of the debate may be understandably confused. The present volume attempts to lift some of the confusion. The aim is to arm the reader with most of the background that is necessary to participate in the current debate over postmodernism among philosophers. That means knowing something about:

the modern period, or the characteristic doctrines of modern philosophy that postmodernism is criticizing; the wide variety of criticisms of modern thought that are current today, which are by no means exhausted by postmodernism, and postmodernism as it is expressed in a number of fields – architecture, literature, sociology – not just philosophy. The effect of this contextualization will be to render postmodernism less mysterious and less frightening, which may also make it less exciting. Whether the last effect is for good or ill will be up to the reader.

I The History of Postmodernism

The term "postmodern," understood as distinguishing the contemporary scene from the modern, seems first to have been used in 1917 by the German philosopher Rudolf Pannwitz to describe the "nihilism" of twentieth-century Western culture, a theme he took from Friedrich Nietzsche.[1] It resurfaced in the work of the Spanish literary critic Federico de Onis in 1934 to refer to the backlash against literary modernism.[2] It first appeared in English in 1939, used in two very different ways, by the theologian Bernard Iddings Bell, signifying the recognition of the failure of secular modernism and a return to religion,[3] and by the historian Arnold Toynbee to refer to the post-World War I rise of mass society, in which the working class surpasses the capitalist class in importance.[4] It was then employed in literary criticism in the 1950s and 1960s, referring to the reaction against literary modernism, and in the 1970s was pressed into analogous use in architecture. Also in the 1970s it began to be connected with analysis of "post-

---

[1] See Rudolf Pannwitz, *Die Krisis der Europaeischen Kultur* (Nuremberg: Hans Carl, 1917), p. 64.
[2] See Federico de Onis, *Antologia de la Poesia española e hispanoamericana: 1882–1932* (Madrid, 1934), pp. xviii–xix. For the best historical discussion of the term, and the best bibliographical account of postmodernism in general, see Margaret Rose's *The Post-Modern and the Post-Industrial: A Critical Analysis* (Cambridge: Cambridge University, 1991).
[3] Bernard Iddings Bell, *Religion For Living: A Book for Postmodernists* (London: The Religious Book Club, 1939). I thank Margaret Rose for bringing this reference to my attention.
[4] Arnold Toynbee, *A Study of History* (London: Oxford University, 1939), vol. 5, p. 43. Toynbee referred to postmodernism again in volume 8, published 1954, p. 338.

industrial" society, the increasingly service- or knowledge-dominated economies of the most advanced societies after World War II. In philosophy it came in the 1980s to refer primarily to French post-structuralist philosophy, and secondarily to a general reaction against modern rationalism, utopianism, and what came to be called "foundationalism," the traditional philosophical attempt to justify knowledge by rooting it in uncriticizable first principles or sense-data or both. Eventually, "postmodern" burst into popular usage as a term for everything from rock videos to the demographics of Los Angeles to the whole cultural style and mood of recent decades.

Despite the divergence among these usages of "postmodern" one could find some commonality centering on: a recognition of pluralism and indeterminacy in the world that modern or modernist thought had evidently sought to disavow, hence a renunciation of intellectual hopes for simplicity, completeness and certainty; a new focus on representation or images or information or cultural signs as occupying a dominant position in social life; and an acceptance of play and fictionalization in cultural fields that had earlier sought a serious, realist truth. This is a vague commonality, to be sure. In order to gain some finer resolution in our picture, let us focus on the development of the most famous strain of postmodernism in philosophy. For this we must travel to France.

In the 1960s philosophy in France underwent a major change. A new group of young intellectuals emerged who were not only deeply critical of the French academic and political establishment – a rebelliousness not new in French intellectual circles – but also critical of the very forms of radical philosophy that had given the establishment headaches in the past, primarily, Marxism and existentialism, and to some extent phenomenology and psychoanalysis as well.[5] Marxism, existentialism, and phenomenology had been, perhaps awkwardly, combined by the great French philosophers of the middle of the century, especially Jean-Paul Sartre and Maurice Merleau-Ponty, along with a dash of Freudian psychoanalysis. These intellectual movements had pictured the individual human subject or consciousness as alienated in contemporary society, estranged from his or her authentic modes of experience and being – whether the source of that

estrangement was capitalism (for Marxism), the scientific naturalism pervading modern Western culture (for phenomenology), excessively repressive social mores (for Freud), bureaucratically organized social life and mass culture (for existentialism), or religion (for all of them). Methodologically, they rejected the belief that the study of humanity could be modeled on or reduced to the physical sciences, hence they avoided behaviorism and naturalism. Unlike physics, chemistry, or biology the human sciences must understand the experience, the first person point of view, of their objects of study: they are concerned not merely with facts but with the *meaning* of facts for human subjects.[6] To diagnose contemporary alienation they produced an historical analysis of how human society and the human self develop over time, in order to see how and why modern civilization had gone wrong. What was needed, it seemed, was a return to the true, or authentic, or free, or integrated human self as the center of lived experience. This meant not an abandonment of modern industry, technology, and secularism, but some reconstruction of society (for Marx), or of moral culture (for Freud), or of our openness to the vicissitudes of our own authentic experience (for phenomenology and existentialism).

Now, Marxism, existentialism, phenomenology, and psychoanalysis never ruled the academic roost in France or anywhere else (exempting of course the case of Marxism in communist societies, where it had official status). They represented the major theoretical opposition to the status quo in the first half of the century. Young intellectuals dissatisfied with the neo-Scholastic, rationalistic, neo-Kantian, theologically- or scientifically-oriented forms of thought dominant in the academy – all of which seemed well-suited to endorsing institutional and political authorities – tended to see these movements as the main alternatives. In the post-World War II period they constituted a major intellectual subculture in Europe, gradually influencing American thought as well.

The new French philosophers of the 1960s – including Gilles Deleuze, Luce Irigary, Jean-

---

[5] For some of this story, see Vincent Descombes, *Modern French Philosophy*, trans. L. Schott-Fox and J. M. Harding (New York: Cambridge University, 1980).

[6] Marxism, under some interpretations, is an exception to this trend. Some, emphasizing Marx's aspirations to historical determinism, have aspired to the model of the sciences, while others, more concerned with individualism and alienation (sometimes called "Western Marxists"), have rejected pretensions to scientific methodology.

François Lyotard, and above all, Jacques Derrida and Michel Foucault – also wanted to fight the political and academic establishment. But their approach was different from that of Sartre and Merleau-Ponty. They had been schooled by another theoretical movement, structuralism, developed by linguists Ferdinand de Saussure and Roman Jakobson, and championed in mid-century by the French anthropologist Claude Lévi-Strauss. Structuralism rejected the centrality of the self and its historical development that had characterized Marxism, existentialism, phenomenology, and psychoanalysis. The social or human sciences, like anthropology, linguistics, and philosophy, needed to focus instead on the supra-individual structures of language, ritual, and kinship which make the individual what he or she is. Simply put, it is not the self that creates culture, it is culture that creates the self. The study of abstract relations within systems or "codes" of cultural signs (words, family relations, etc.) is the key to understanding human existence. Structuralism seemed to offer the student of humanity a way of avoiding reduction to the natural sciences, while yet retaining objective, scientific methods, unlike the apparently subjective orientation of phenomenology, existentialism, and psychoanalysis. At the same time, it also implied that nothing is "authentic," that there is no fundamental, original nature of the human self against which we could judge a culture.

The new philosophers of the 1960s accepted structuralism's refusal to worship at the altar of the self. But they rejected its scientific pretensions. They saw deep self-reflexive philosophical problems in the attempt by human beings to be "objective" about themselves. They applied the structural–cultural analysis of human phenomena to the human sciences themselves, which are, after all, human cultural constructions. Hence they are commonly named "post-structuralists," meaning not that they rejected, but radicalized, structuralism. The import of their work appeared radical indeed. They seemed to announce the end of rational inquiry into truth, the illusory nature of any unified self, the impossibility of clear and unequivocal meaning, and the oppressive nature of all modern Western institutions. They appeared critically to undermine any and all positive philosophical and political positions, to exhibit hidden paradoxes and modes of social domination operating within all products of reason. Whether they were really as radical as they appeared is less clear, as we shall see. In the 1960s and 1970s, however, their critique had a patently political meaning. It served to undermine the claims to legitimacy by academic authorities and the State, and was connected to the critique of Western imperialism and racism, especially American involvement in Indochina, and eventually to the feminist critique of male power as well.

One other factor in the development of postmodernism since the early 1970s deserves special mention: the decline of Marxism. The new left of the 1960s, and some of the new French philosophers, reinterpreted their Marxism through Freud and Ferdinand de Saussure, and so had already begun to shake off Marxist–Leninist orthodoxy. But a deeper disenchantment can be traced to the 1973 publication, in Paris, of the first volume of Alexander Solzhenitsyn's *The Gulag Archipelago*, a monumental recounting of Stalinist atrocities in the Soviet Union. After this, it was no longer possible for people of the left to look to the Soviet Union as a free society in any sense. The Western European and North American academy became increasingly unsympathetic with Marxism and to some extent with socialism over the next decade. This coincided with the popular turn to the right in many Western societies during the 1980s. Then came the dismantling of the Soviet empire and the eclipse of communism in the home of the revolution, Russia, beginning in 1989. In the last decade of the twentieth century the modern competitor to liberal capitalism – the qualifier "modern" functioning here to exempt rejuvenated premodern competitors, like Islamic fundamentalism – utterly collapsed. The result of this change was profound, and not limited to yet another swing in the pendulum of popular opinion between the demand for a freer market and the demand for greater government control over capitalism (a pendulum that will no doubt continue to swing). Marxism had provided a philosophy of history that served for a sizable segment of the secularized Western intelligentsia as a promise of worldly salvation, a fulfillment of that great modernist hope in progress, what Christopher Lasch called the "True and Only Heaven."[7] For many irreligious intellectuals, the hope for a utopian so-

---

[7] A phrase Lasch took from Nathaniel Hawthorne. See Christopher Lasch, *The True and Only Heaven: Progress and its Critics* (New York: Norton, 1991). I must add here my posthumous appreciation for Professor Lasch's having many years ago taken seriously the work of a graduate student that he had never met, and responding sensitively and intelligently.

cialist future gave badly needed significance to a life lived after the "death of God." The loss of hope struck a sizable portion of this group much as the loss of religion had already struck traditional society: absent a historical *telos* or goal, it seemed that the world had become centerless and pointless once again. Hence Ernest Gellner dubbed it the "second secularization." Postmodernism in its French origins is a wayward stepchild of Marxism, and in this sense a generation's realization that it is orphaned.

Simultaneously, in British and American philosophy, where phenomenology, existentialism, Marxism, and psychoanalysis had been far less influential, related, albeit quieter, changes were taking place.

Logical empiricism, also called positivism, which had by mid-century swept aside the indigenous American pragmatist philosophical tradition (of Charles Sanders Peirce, William James, George Herbert Mead, Josiah Royce, and John Dewey) as well as English idealism and empiricism (especially of F. H. Bradley and John Stuart Mill, respectively), pursued a systematization of human knowledge based in the certainties of a recently revolutionized logic combined with a scientific explanation of "sense data." Philosophy had traditionally been hoodwinked by a failure to employ a perfectly clear "ideal language," which the logical revolution – rooted in Gottlob Frege's 1879 *Begriffsschrift* ("concept notation") and Bertrand Russell's and Alfred North Whitehead's reduction of mathematics to logic in their *Principia Mathematica* (1910–13) – had made possible. Ludwig Wittgenstein's attempt to undercut traditional philosophy by distinguishing all that could be said clearly from what is "nonsense" in his *Tractatus Logico-Philosophicus* (1921) had a powerful effect. Philosophy was to shed its metaphysical musings and ethical pretensions and concern itself with logic, the clarification of science's method and results, and the dismissal of traditional philosophical questions through a careful analysis of linguistic errors. Positivism was only one of a wide variety of philosophical movements of the first half of the twentieth century – including much of Continental thought – that attacked the very possibility of philosophical inquiry into the ultimate nature of reality, the existence of God, or a universally valid ethics.

But subsequent philosophers of language, logic, and science began to cast doubt on the adequacy of the positivist picture. A complete and consistent logic complex enough to include arithmetic was shown by Kurt Gödel to be impossible, rendering unrealizable not only the complete axiomatization of mathematics, but the greatest hopes of an ideal language philosophy as well. The distinction between analytic or logical statements and synthetic or empirical statements, and the distinction between statements of observed sense data and theoretical explanations of those data – oppositions crucial to positivism – appeared more and more to be porous: there seemed no way to say what we sense without already using some unverified theoretical language in order to say it. But that implied that verification in a strict sense is impossible, since any statement of "fact" (sense experience) must presuppose the theoretical perspective it might be offered to verify. Wittgenstein's own later philosophy, most famously his 1953 *Philosophical Investigations*, suggested that the attempt to discover the foundations of knowledge was as senseless as that of speculative metaphysics. Even science itself, the model of knowledge for so many Anglo-American, and European, philosophers, came to be seen after Thomas Kuhn's 1962 *The Structure of Scientific Revolutions* as partly non-systematic, hence perhaps non-rational, in its development. By no means did most English and American philosophers feel kinship with the French poststructuralists, but by the 1960s they were becoming equally dubious about the canonical aims of modern philosophy and the ultimate hopes of rational inquiry. On both sides of the Atlantic, the study of language and, in effect, *culture*, was superseding the study of the previously alleged *source* of culture in logic, in nature, or in the self.[8]

Here we may add that throughout the twentieth century the novel *content* of certain scientific discoveries generated new kinds of theories that eventually, since 1970, have contributed to the development of what may be called a *scientific postmodernism*. This arguably began with quantum theory in the 1920s, which was forced by the nature of its objects to abandon determinism as an ideal of

---

[8]   Not that these aims disappeared entirely. Indeed, the search for a naturalistic basis for language and thought through the use of advances in the study of artificial intelligence and linguistics has become in the last decade an increasingly powerful philosophical program under the name of "cognitive science." Some of the new naturalists are indeed "non-foundationalist" – hence like postmodernists, chastened of hopes of ultimate justification, as in the Quine selection below – while others seem to have unlearned the lessons of Wittgenstein in order to reprise a naive version of positivism.

explanation and to accept the inescapable effect of observation on the phenomena observed. In the last decades of the century developments in the theory of self-regulating systems in biology and cybernetics (e.g. in the work of Humberto Maturana), chaos theory (Edward Lorenz and Benoit Mandelbroit), and catastrophe theory (René Thom) have been exploited as part of a "new science" with postmodern implications, expressed for example in Ilya Prigogine's and Isabelle Stenger's *Order Out of Chaos: Man's New Dialogue with Nature* (1984). This approach breaks down the epistemic superiority, hence the distinction, of the natural sciences over the "hermeneutic" social and humanistic disciplines, thereby serving as a kind of successor to structuralism in opening the possibility of a "Third Wave" of scientific yet humanistic theory. All this remains controversial; many scientists and philosophers of science would counter that while recent scientific changes may undermine a cultural and philosophical picture of *what* science tells us – i.e. a "modernist" or Newtonian deterministic system in which all phenomena are fully describable in terms of the observable traits of their constituent, sub-atomic parts – they do not indicate a fundamental change in scientific *method* or *aims*. Nevertheless, whereas French post-structuralism and its associated thinkers have remained virtually anti-naturalistic and anti-scientific, these naturalistic, scientific developments constitute another strain of postmodernism.

Returning to the early post-World War II period, outside philosophical and scientific inquiry, new tendencies in art, literature, music, and especially architecture were critically superseding movements that had earlier been considered radical. Through the first half of the century modernist art and literature had seemed to critique the bourgeois, capitalist social order that carried the economic load of modernity. Dissonant and atonal music, impressionism, surrealism, and expressionism in painting, literary realism, the stream of consciousness novel, to name only a few developments, seemed to open the imagination to a subjective world of experience and to seamy realities ignored by the official cultures of societies in a mad rush to modernize technologically and economically, to absorb the natural scientific view of the world, while yet trying to hold onto traditional religious imagery and morality. Often in league with the philosophies of alienated subjectivity (phenomenology, existentialism, Marxism, psychoanalysis), they became identified with an "oppositionist,"

"avant-garde" subculture. This may seem odd in the case of architecture, since modernist architecture embraced the new technologies of construction and eventually became the official architecture of the advanced industrial world. Nevertheless, its radically "truthful," de-ornamented style and utopian egalitarianism opposed what it regarded as the official culture's refusal to recognize the reality and problems of modern industrial life.

By the time of the 1960s, a new generation of writers, painters, and architects began to react against aesthetic modernism. The "end" of modernism in literature was recognized as early as the 1950s by Irving Howe and in the 1960s by Leslie Fiedler.[9] Literary irony and camp seemed to capture the sensibility of the time more than the seriousness of the modernist search for the alienated soul and the essence of reality. This period saw the development of art that seemingly renounced unity of style for pastiche and threatened to break down the very notion of the "aesthetic," hence the distinctiveness of the art-object. Some embraced eclecticism, chaos and discontinuity, laughed at (or with?) alienation rather than complaining of it, while others produced a critical form of art that mixed media, performance, and discourse. The heroic distinction between high and low, fine and commercial art, the truth-seeking modern avant-garde and the superficial, hedonistic marketplace was being superseded by an anti-heroic embrace of pop culture, most famously by Pop Art in the work of Andy Warhol.

It was in the most socially consequential of arts, architecture, that postmodernism had its most widespread influence in the 1960s and 1970s.[10] The groundwork had been laid in 1961 by Jane Jacob's devastating book, *The Death and Life of Great American Cities*.[11] Jacobs lashed out at the

---

9   See Irving Howe, "Mass Society and Postmodern Fiction," in *The Decline of the New* (New York: Harcourt, Brace and World, 1970), pp. 190–207, and Leslie Fiedler, "The New Mutants," in *The Collected Essays of Leslie Fiedler*, vol. II (New York: Stein and Day, 1971), pp. 379–99.

10   The term had been used in architecture by Joseph Hudnut in the 1940s to mean extreme- or *ultra*-modern architecture. See his "The Post-Modern House," *Architectural Record*, vol. 97, May 1945, pp. 70–5. Charles Jencks, in the 1970s, was the first architectural writer to use the word to mean the end or transformation of modernism.

11   Jane Jacobs, *The Death and Life of Great American Cities* (New York: Vintage, 1961).

orthodox urban reform movement of the day, in which modernism had been joined with welfare state policy to create vast "single use" housing complexes for the poor. She exposed the virtually anti-urban, anti-human impulses of this alleged humanitarian policy, whose abstract grids undercut the social mechanisms by which urban neighborhoods had traditionally maintained themselves as viable communities. Then in 1966 in his *Complexity and Contradiction in Architecture* Robert Venturi insisted that architectural communication requires not simplicity but complexity and even contradiction. Modernism's search for a simplified univocal style had been summarized by Mies van der Rohe's slogan "less is more," to which Venturi replied "less is a bore." In the decade to come both the modernist style and the idea of social reform through uniform, technocratic, top-down solutions increasingly fell out of favor. Alternately, other architectural theorists, including Peter Eisenman and Bernard Tschumi, explicitly employed post-structuralist methods to transcend modernism while avoiding what they regarded as Venturi's capitulation to the popular building trends of mass capitalism.

Not to mention that society was undergoing other radical changes almost too numerous to recount: the end of the last vestiges of European colonialism after World War II, the development of mass communications and a media culture in the advanced industrial countries, the rapid modernization of much of the non-Western world, and the shrinking of the globe by international marketing, telecommunications, and intercontinental missiles. In many Western nations there was a significant delegitimation of authority, most prominently seen in the political explosion of students virtually around the world, culminating in 1968 in the USA, Paris, Prague, and China (towards different ends, to be sure). The revolt against authority among the young educated, or about-to-be-educated, classes was profound. It was in this highly charged university setting, within an increasingly complex social context, that postmodernism in the strictest sense was born in France among some younger professors. The attack of Parisian students on the French government, on the university that was literally one of its arms, on capitalism, and on the American war in Vietnam, all seemed to resonate with the post-structuralist critique of Reason and Authority.

In the late 1970s, three books galvanized postmodernism as a movement: Charles Jencks's *The Language of Post-Modern Architecture* (1977); Jean-François Lyotard's *La Condition Postmoderne: rapport sur le savoir* (1979; English translation: *The Postmodern Condition: A Report on Knowledge*, 1984); and Richard Rorty's *Philosophy and the Mirror of Nature* (1979). The last, while not employing the term "postmodern," argued that the developments of post-Heideggerian Continental philosophy and post-Wittgensteinian analytic philosophy were converging on a kind of pragmatic anti-foundationalism. Rorty thereby became an American representative of postmodernism, albeit in pragmatic garb, giving "postmodern" a meaning for philosophers outside the European tradition.

We must caution, of course, that postmodernism is not the only philosophical *ism* recently to rebel against what might be considered the dominant strains of modern thought. As postmodernism developed, others responded to the problems of late twentieth-century society and culture with a call for a return to traditional cultural forms. This "pre-modernism" can be seen in the widespread political conservatism that first emerged in the 1980s, the call for moral regeneration, for a return to community and religion, the re-emergence of nationalism and ethnic tribalism, and religious fundamentalism (especially Islamic, Hindu, and Christian). Alasdair MacIntyre put the issue starkly: if Enlightenment ideals are suspect, then we are left with the choice "Nietzsche or Aristotle," a leap into postmodernism or a reincoporation of premodern principles, which in the West means either ancient Greek or Judeo-Christian notions. In political theory, the "premodernist" elements of conservatism and communitarianism echoed, in far milder tones, the global resurgence of nativism, nationalism, and militant fundamentalism that began with the Iranian Revolution of 1980 and was accelerated in the Balkans and Central Asia after the fall of the Soviet empire. MacIntyre's philosophical choice "Nietzsche or Aristotle" is thus matched (albeit in reverse order) by political theorist Benjamin Barber's geo-political opposition, "Jihad versus McWorld," the postmodern global service economy and mass culture versus an anti-modern traditionalism, fundamentalism, and/or nationalism. At the same time, of course, other intellectuals, like Jürgen Habermas, continue to defend the modern legacy of rationalism and liberal individualism by developing a non-foundational version of Enlightenment thought. Their reformed "promodernism" seeks to obviate either a fearful return to the premodern past or an impulsive leap into the postmodern future.

Thus ends our brief history lesson. But, as postmodernists would insist, how postmodernism developed and what it *means* are two separate questions. In order to examine the meaning of postmodernism, we must first understand what it is whose decline postmodernism announces. We must gain some understanding of what is meant by *modernity*.

II What is Modern?

The term "modern," derived from the Latin *modo*, simply means "of today" or what is current, as distinguished from earlier times. It has been used in various periods and places to distinguish contemporary from traditional ways, and in principle can refer to any sphere of life and any period in history. It is still used in this local, contextual sense, hence "modern English" and "modern dance" do not imply that the historical period of these two phenomena are the same. Likewise, the invention of writing was certainly "modern" in comparison to pre-literate society.

"Modernity" on the other hand, has a fixed reference in contemporary intellectual discussion. It refers to the new civilization that developed in Europe and North America over the last several centuries, fully evident by the early twentieth century. "Modernity" implies that this civilization is modern in the non-relative sense that it is unique in human history. Exactly what makes this civilization unique is to some extent uncontroversial. Everyone admits that Europe and North America developed and applied a new, powerful technique for the study of nature, and new machine technologies and modes of industrial production that have led to an unprecedented rise in material living standards. It is this form of modernity that is today described as "modernization" or simply "development" in the non-Western world. In the West it is arguably characterized as well by other traits: free markets, a largely secular culture, liberal democracy, individualism, rationalism, humanism, etc. Whether these traits are unique in human history is more controversial. Many historical societies have, in a limited sphere, had relatively free markets, respected individuality, engaged in rational planning and rational inquiry, created secular or profane zones of culture, etc. While the modern Western *combination* of science, technology, and industrial production, with capitalism, liberal democracy, individualism, etc., is certainly unprecedented, the complex and interpretive nature of the latter makes the precise definition of the modern consciousness rather difficult.

One may be tempted to say, "Who cares about the non-technological components of modernity? What makes modernity modern is science, machines, industrialization, advanced living standards and expanded life expectancy; the rest is unimportant." Certainly we should never lose sight of these essential practical and material advances. But here the American sociologist Peter Berger asks the right question: are we simply ancient Egyptians in airplanes? That is, is the sole important shift in modernity a difference in tools and material conditions, rather than a difference in the human beings themselves, their worldview, their sense of self? If only the tools matter, then the sole significant difference between a corporate executive in a Boeing 747 and an astrologer in the Pharaoh's court is the 747. This would imply that the modernization of undeveloped countries is a purely technical affair, having nothing to do with culture and psychology. But, as the complex cultural and social problems arising from modernization have shown, this is not the case. The difference between executive and astrologer lies not only in the airplane, but in the human mind, or, in what might be the same thing, human culture. But because minds and cultures are harder to understand and specify than airplanes, this recognition makes the specification of what makes modernity modern controversial.

The debate is complicated by the question of the historical parameters of modernity. The decision as to when modernity started is entangled with the question of what is modernity; your answer to the second decides the first. Did modernity in the West begin in the sixteenth century with the Protestant reformation, the rejection of the universal power of the Roman Catholic Church, and the development of a humanistic skepticism epitomized by Erasmus and Montaigne? Or was it in the seventeenth century with the scientific revolution of Galileo, Harvey, Hobbes, Descartes, Boyle, Leibniz, and Newton? Was it caused by the first development of a market economy in eighteenth-century England? Or the republican political theories and revolutions of the United States and France in the late eighteenth century? What about the industrial revolution of the nineteenth century? Much can be learned about the pieces of the puzzle from these disparate views. There is no non-circular way to decide among them. Fortunately, at least for the philosopher, there is also no need to decide. Our primary question is not, When did modernity begin? but, What is the inner nature, the probable destiny, and the validity of this new way of life? It is enough to know that some new form of human society evolved in Europe and North America, fully evident by, say, 1914, whose various pieces had fallen into place gradually over several centuries.

The positive self-image modern Western culture has most often given to itself, a picture born in the Enlightenment, is of a civilization founded on scientific knowledge of the world and rational knowledge of value, which places the highest premium on individual human life and freedom, and believes that such freedom and rationality will lead to social progress through virtuous, self-controlled work, creating a better material, political, and intellectual life for all. (The complexity of the eighteenth century, rightfully attested by historians, does not belie the enduring efficacy of this self-image, cobbled-together from the multiple legacies of that most fecund of centuries.) This combination of science, reason, individuality, freedom, truth, and social progress has, however, been questioned and criticized by many. Some critics see modernity instead as a movement of ethnic and class domination, European imperialism, anthropocentrism, the destruction of nature, the dissolution of community and tradition, the rise of alienation, the death of individuality in bureaucracy. More benign critics have argued skeptically that modernity cannot achieve what it hopes, e.g. that objective truth or freedom is unavailable, or that modernity's gains are balanced by losses, even if there is no alternative either to modernity or to its discontents. This is not the place to debate the relative truth of these claims; nevertheless, it can at least be said that while there is some truth in each of them, the whole truth is more complex. More than any other topic, the evaluation of modernity brings to mind the story of the elephant and the blind men, each of whom grasped one part of the beast – trunk, side, tail, leg, ear, tusk – leading to an interminable argument among their utterly dissimilar, fantastic conclusions about its nature – "It's a snake," "No, a wall," "No, a rope," "No, a tree," "No, a fan," "No, a spear." Contemporary theorists often take one part of modernity to be the whole.

There is one last ambiguity to unfurl. While "modernism" has been used by some philosophers and social analysts as synonymous with "modern" or "modernity," hence to refer to the whole period

since the seventeenth or eighteenth century, its most common use is specific to visual art, architecture, literature and music, where it refers to movements that thrived from the second half of the nineteenth century through the first half of the twentieth century. As mentioned above, this period saw unprecedented experimentation in the arts: in painting, from the realism of Gustav Courbet and the impressionism of Claude Monet to the abstract expression of Jackson Pollack; in literature, the modernist abandonment of objective narrative in Virginia Woolf and James Joyce, and of idealized treatment of subject matter in Ernest Hemingway; in music, Albert Schönberg's and Alban Berg's atonality, and Igor Stravinsky's dissonance and non-thematic structure, to name but a few examples. In architecture, the modernism of Le Corbusier, Mies van der Rohe, and Walter Gropius has played a particularly important role. One way of understanding the relation of this aesthetic modernism to modernity in the broader sense is that modernism is a form of art characteristic of high or actualized modernity, that is, of that period in which social, economic, and cultural life in the widest sense were revolutionized by modern ideas. This does not, by itself, imply that modernist art endorses modernization or expresses the aims of social modernity. But it does mean that modernist art is scarcely thinkable outside the context of the modernized society of the late nineteenth and twentieth centuries. Social modernity is the home of modernist art, even where that art rebels against it.

III What Postmodernism Means

It is difficult – some would say, impossible – to summarize what postmodernism means, not only because there is much disagreement among writers labeled postmodern, but also because many deny having any doctrines or theories at all. The very idea of a summary may be antithetical to postmodernism. Still, understanding must begin somewhere. Let us try to be a bit more systematic and doctrinal, even if thereby inevitably superficial, remembering how foreign such an attempt is to postmodernism.[12]

---

[12] "Superficial" being, for some postmodernists, a term of praise, if "deep" philosophical claims have been discredited. Nietzsche's remark that the ancient Greeks were "superficial out of profundity" could be a postmodern slogan.

First, it is often said that postmodernists, being concerned only with signs and never with things, have nothing to say about objectivity. That is not true. Postmodernists do have a characteristic attitude toward whatever is under their consideration – whether physical, social, psychological, semiotic (concerning signs), or epistemological – namely, that every object is incorrigibly, dynamically *complex*. The complexity of the phenomenon is not capable of exhaustion, and is *generative*, that is, capable of growth. In traditional metaphysical language, this is the denial of *simples*, the constitution of phenomena by ultimate irreducible parts. Any conceptual scheme, any fundamental distinction, any law or rule, is prone to violation, not just because of limits on representation and cognition, but because of the *nature of what is to be known*. Completeness and consistency of a system of phenomena, and of its representation, are impossible. Analysis never ends. As a result postmodernists are critics of unity wherever it is claimed to appear: the unity of the world, of knowledge, of society, of the self, of the meaning of a word. In the case of the human self, this leads to a *post-humanist* denial of unified human agency, contrary to the modern humanism that was still active in the philosophies of the subject. Thus, if anything is fundamental for the postmodernist, it could only be *difference* (*différance* in Derrida's terminology), the production of differences, underwritten by no unitary agency or origin. Applying this complexity to inquiry itself, postmodernism tends not to respect the barriers between particular disciplines. Methodological *pluralists*, they are sensitive to the ways philosophy, literature, politics, and science overlap and interweave.

The second claim of postmodernism is the *denial of presence* or the immediate relation of human judgments to what they judge. What is directly, immediately given in experience has traditionally been contrasted both with *representation*, the sphere of linguistic signs and concepts, and *construction*, the products of human invention, hence in either case whatever is mediated by the human factor. For example, philosophers have often distinguished perception or sensation or sense data, as immediate conduits for reality, from judgment, thought, conception, interpretation, theory, hence symbolization. Postmodernism rejects this distinction. It denies that anything is "immediately present," hence independent of signs, language, or interpretation. *Presentation presupposes representation*. Thus at one point Derrida literally denies that there is

such a thing as "perception" (understood as immediate, transparent reception of the given). This denial shows up as well in arguments about interpretation. The saying "Every author is a dead author" denies that the meaning of a text can be "authoritatively" revealed through reference to authorial intentions or regarded as immediately valid due to the text's immediate presence to the author's consciousness. On the contrary, an author's intentions are not immediately available, nor more relevant to understanding the text than any other set of considerations; they are not the *origin* of the text and so have no *privilege* over other factors. This denial of presence is crucial; if there *were* valid immediate judgments, then postmodern doubts about and criticisms of standard modern conceptions of knowing could not even get started. Postmodernism must in consequence reject *foundationalism*, the attempt to justify realist knowledge through recourse to "basic" or fundamental or incorrigible cognition. In this denial postmodernists are not alone; many other recent philosophical movements, like pragmatism and ordinary language philosophy, have likewise denied presence or immediacy. Postmodernists are more radically *antifoundationalist* than others, however, in denying the legitimacy of the whole enterprise of epistemology or the attempt to justify human knowledge. They are utterly skeptical of the three great Western sources of cognitive norms: God, Nature, and Reason.

Third, postmodernists are *constructivists* about knowledge; knowledge is something humanly made. This was Kant's point at the end of the eighteenth century, that cognition is an active, structure-imposing process. "Construction" does not need to imply a creation *ex nihilo*; one may say more modestly that knowledge is always a *selection* from a phenomenal or semiotic complexity too great to exhaust. But that amounts to the same thing: what we take to be real is significantly the product of human cognitive activity. Postmodernists often take from this constructivism a particularly radical point, that *meaning is repression*. If complexity is too great to be grasped, any discrete act of meaning or knowing must actively suppress, or ignore, complexity, the act and fact of suppression being itself covered up. Every semiotic act or judgment obscures, represses, mystifies; if it did not, it could not mean. Contentiously put, if "truth" is understood as correspondence to reality, then postmodernists argue that all experienced reality, the world as we know it, including ourselves, is the product of error, misrecognition, a necessary misreading.

The denial of presence and the acceptance of constructivism occasionally leads postmodernists to substitute the analysis of *representations of* a thing for discussion of *the thing*. For example, in a debate over whether to use intelligence tests in a local school system, a postmodernist might produce a long analysis of how the term "intelligence" has been used by the test's proponents, implying that its object or referent is never present to us, and so it is the history of those representations and their political use which is really at issue. In another example, early in his career Foucault wrote that "man" was invented in the modern period; what he meant was that the modern social sciences for the first time made "man" or "humankind" an object of scientific attention, thereby constituting a new concept of "man." The most famous global expression of this approach was Derrida's claim that, "There is nothing outside the text." As Derrida himself latter clarified, this did not mean that there is no real world, but that we only encounter real referents through texts, representations, mediation. The *world we know* is, or is constructed by, representations. We can never say what is independent of all saying.

Fourth, what is implicit in the foregoing but worthy of distinct mention, is the *immanence of norms,* including reason itself. This is in effect a denial of dualism, not only metaphysical but methodological. Beyond obvious cases of the former, like Descartes' mind–body metaphysics, dualism often functions in a philosophical system to put the means by which we know and judge things *outside* the things judged, e.g. by making the validity of the rules of reason or morality *independent* of nature or human convention. Normative immanence in contrast asserts that the norms we use to judge processes are *themselves products of the processes they judge.* There is no access to an "outside." For example, where most philosophers might use an idea of justice independently derived from a philosophical argument to judge a social order, postmodernism regards that idea as itself the product of the social relations that it serves to judge; the idea of justice was created at a certain time and place, to serve certain interests, is dependent on a certain intellectual and social context, etc. Norms are not independent of nature or semiosis (sign production and interpretation) or experience or social interests. This leads postmodernists to respond to the normative claims of others by displaying the processes of thought, writing, negotiation, and power which produced those normative claims. Whether or not this implies that postmodernists themselves cannot consistently make their own normative claims, it clearly unleashes a form of critical analysis which makes all such claims problematic, including their own.

Fifth, there is a characteristic *analytic strategy* which is the complex application of the four themes just mentioned, and which is central to the politics of postmodernism. The apparent identity of what appear to be cultural units – human beings, words, meanings, ideas, philosophical systems, social organizations – are maintained only through *constitutive repression*, an active process of *exclusion, opposition*, and *hierarchization.* A phenomenon maintains its identity in semiotic systems only if other units are represented as foreign or "*other*" through a hierarchical dualism in which the first is *privileged* or favored while the other is *deprivileged* or devalued in some way. This process must itself be hidden or covered up, so that the hierarchy can be *assumed inherent* in the nature of the phenomena, rather than a motivated construction. Thus, the privileged term's actual dependence on the demoted other, and on the process of semiotic construction, must be, as already noted, *repressed.* For example, in examining a social system characterized by a class or ethnic division, postmodernists will discover that the privileged group must actively produce and maintain its position by representing or picturing itself – in theory, in literature, in law, in art – as not having the properties ascribed to the under-privileged group(s) *by nature*, while representing those groups as *intrinsically* lacking the properties of the privileged group. In a human psyche, the self may be compelled to represent itself as excluding sexual or aggressive feelings, which, however, cannot simply be obliterated, and so must be ascribed to chance situations, to idiosyncratic events (e.g. "I was not myself today"), etc. In a philosophical system, the dualism of "reality" and "appearance" involves the construction of a kind of waste-basket into which phenomena that the system does not want to sanctify with the privileged term "real" can be tossed ("mere appearances"). Only in this way can the pristine integrity of the idealized or privileged term be maintained.[13]

---

[13] This strategic mode of analysis is partly inspired by the dialectical method of the great German philosopher G. W. F. Hegel (1770–1831).

Metaphorically, this can be expressed by saying that it is the *margins that constitute the text*. The postmodernist will attend to the apparently excluded or *marginalized* elements of any system or text, because therein lies the key to its structure. Just as in psychoanalysis excessive repression creates neurotic symptoms like jokes, dreams, and seemingly unimportant conversational mistakes, postmodernists will turn their attention away from the well-known, openly announced themes in a text to discover tell-tale marks of the hidden act of constitutive repression in seldom mentioned, virtually absent, presumably accidental marginalia. Linguistic tropes, such as metaphors, which other readers may take as secondary or peripheral to the meaning of a text, are read by postmodernists as crucial to the constitution of the text's privileged theme. Pulling on these threads *deconstructs* the text, in Derrida's famous term. Such deconstruction is the making explicit of the way the text *undermines its own meaning*.

Sometimes implicit and sometimes explicit in this kind of analysis through constitutive repression is the claim that the process of exclusion is false, unstable, and/or immoral: false in that it is mendacious, a lie; unstable in that the repression must sooner or later be admitted, forcing an acceptance of the excluded factors into the representation of the privileged unit (the "return of the repressed" in Freud); immoral when it takes the form of social oppression. Social disenfranchisement, marginalization of sexual and racial groups, is the moral and political case of this pattern. This is at the heart of *every* postmodernist intervention in politics. Some postmodernists wish to remove such repression, while others, seeing in that wish a longing for an impossible authenticity, admit that there is no escape from repression and hope only to render repressive forces more diverse and fluid, so that none becomes monopolistic and hence excessively onerous.

One might, as a postscript, own up to a last, particularly troublesome feature of postmodernism, namely, its notoriously difficult writing style. No doubt some of this is due to the fashions characteristic of the location of postmodernism's birth (that is, the Parisians who invented it just happened to write in a difficult style). But there is a more substantive reason as well. Postmodernists are bound to write in a way that reflects the self-conscious application of the preceding points to their *own* writing. They must write while conscious of constructivism, the disruption of authorial privilege, the undecidability of meaning, the absence of presence, the ubiquity of difference. They must write while recognizing that all *writing is lying*. Indeed, taken far enough their method must question the very distinction of inquiry (e.g. philosophy, science, history, etc.), from practical and productive disciplines, like politics and art. Once those lines are crossed or blurred, it is no longer clear whether a sentence written by a postmodern writer is intended to be a proposition aiming at truth, or a practical utterance offered for its effects on the reader, or an aesthetic performance. No one who tries to write in a way that would be "consistent" with these commitments could help but become a hermeneutic pretzel.

IV Putting Postmodernism in Context

This volume is structured chronologically around three phases in the development of the modern West's philosophical evaluation of itself.

Part I presents the reader with a small selection of some of the most influential statements of modernity from the seventeenth through the nineteenth centuries, as well as some of the most famous criticisms of that evolving civilization. Throughout these centuries most human beings in Europe and North America continued to live and think as they had for the thousand years preceding: in small towns and agricultural communities, imagining the world in more or less religious terms, uninfluenced by the scientific and secular ideas emerging in educated circles in the great cities. It was not until the beginnings of the market economy and the republican political revolutions of the eighteenth century that modern ideas had widespread concrete effect. But even then, daily life for most people continued relatively unchanged until almost the twentieth century. Each new element of modern thought was opposed by cultural inertia, political and religious leaders, and intellectuals, several of whom are included here. It is crucial to understand that what we have called modernity was always under attack.

Part II presents the critical analysis of modern art, society, and philosophy that came with the triumph of modernity, the full establishment of a society unique in human history. It is in this period, roughly from 1860 to 1950, that Western modernity ceased to be a primarily intellectual and political phenomenon and dramatically remade the everyday socio–economic world in which people live. It is also the period in which Western modernity became the dominant geopolitical force in the world. This actualization of modernity provoked a new reaction from intellectuals and artists, instigating a debate over bourgeois values and mass culture, resulting in a period of unprecedented aesthetic and intellectual experimentation. The artistic modernism that resulted is both a critique of bourgeois modernity and an expression of it. Of the authors in this section Friedrich Nietzsche is the most influential for later postmodernism. The final four selections of Part II – from Heidegger, Lacan, Kuhn, and Bell – constitute the historical transition to the postmodern.

The selections in Part III are from the post-World War II period, and are broken into four categories: French post-structuralism; critical appropriations of post-structuralism; postmodernists who move beyond critique; and finally alternatives and resistances to postmodernism. These will all be further discussed in the Introduction to Part III.

It may be well to conclude this Introduction with a general comment about the validity of postmodernism. Some philosophers dismiss postmodernism for using intentionally elusive rhetoric, in part to avoid self-contradiction. If, they say, postmodernists literally and explicitly undermine truth, objectivity, and the univocal meanings of words, then this would undermine their own writing as well, undercutting their meaning or truth. Postmodernists would then be in the position of denying the validity of their own denials. To avoid this, the critics continue, postmodernists write in a coy, ironic, or convoluted fashion, unwilling to make explicit methodological or philosophical claims. Hence they dodge criticism by a subterfuge unbefitting an inquirer.

Rhetorical flourishes on both sides notwithstanding, postmodernism raises crucial questions to which philosophy is bound by its own commitments to respond. The charge of self-contradiction is an important one. Nevertheless, it is a purely negative argument that does nothing to blunt the criticisms postmodernism makes of traditional inquiry. The sometimes obscure rhetorical strategies of postmodernism make sense if one accepts its critique of the latter. To say then that the postmodern critique is invalid because the kind of theory it produces does not meet the standards of traditional or normal inquiry is a rather weak counter-attack. It says in effect that whatever critique does not advance the interests of normal or traditional inquiry is invalid. The same charge was made against the very patron saint of philosophy, Socrates, whose infernal questioning, it was said in Plato's *Apology*, led to nothing positive and practical, undermined socially important beliefs, and could not justify itself except for his eccentric claim to a divine mission. So, while the threat of self-contradiction does raise a serious problem for postmodernism, one that would prevent postmodernism from regarding itself as valid in the way traditional philosophies hope to be, that fact does nothing to show that normal inquiry is immune to its critique. Postmodernism raises serious challenges which cannot be so easily dismissed. Whether it is *right*, is, of course, another matter, and one that is up to the reader to decide.

Modern Civilization and its Critics

Introduction to Part I

It is impossible to recount the dramatic changes that stimulated European modernity. Certainly the voyages of discovery of the fifteenth century, the Protestant Reformation of the sixteenth, and the scientific revolution of the seventeenth had a profound effect on the European mind. By the eighteenth century momentum began to gather behind a new *view* of the world, which would eventually create a new *world*, the modern world of science and industry and business and cities and cosmopolitanism and republicanism, where the rhythm of life was to be increasingly dictated by machines rather than by nature, where the Rights of Man would replace the Divine Right of Kings, where the merchant would displace the landed aristocrat, where cities would become home to pragmatic strangers who had left their local communities, where beliefs were increasingly generated from the printing press, the laboratory, and the street, not parents, princes or pulpit. It meant the beginning of an accelerating process of change whereby modes of living that had altered little in thousands of years would eventually be turned upside down.

Philosophically, the novelty of the age centered on the idea of reason. It signified above all the belief that humans more or less universally possess the faculty of rational thought, less a body of truths than a capacity and a method for grasping them, perhaps endowed to us by God as the essence of humanity; that this reason is the ultimate and legitimate earthly judge of truth, beauty, moral goodness and political right independent of the dictates of tradition and authority; that it is at war with ignorance and superstition; that, despite its universality, it is individually possessed and applied,

hence the individual's autonomous employment of reason is to be encouraged; and that the meaning of human existence is in some measure to be fulfilled by using this reason to grasp a larger share of truth that will enable the reconstruction of human society for the better, materially and politically – all this is largely a product of the eighteenth century. While this set of ideas is not the *sole* meaning of the Enlightenment – there are in fact many "Enlightenments," many versions of that century's contribution – it remains its most effective legacy. We have ever since imbibed the conviction that Reason, Freedom, and social Progress naturally imply one another, as if with our mother's milk.

Even if we have come to find the milk a bit sour, and demand a more varied diet, as some European intellectuals did almost from the start. European modernity was never without critics from within its own house. The impression that a universal naive acceptance of Enlightenment rationalism dominated early modernity, to be upset only by the sophistication of the twentieth century, is the result of historical ignorance. It was always plain to anyone with eyes and mind that modernity meant the exchange of one kind of life for another, hence a very real loss: community, tradition, religion, familiar political authority, customs and manners – all were at the very least to be transformed, if not displaced. This sense of loss was reflected by some of the greatest thinkers of the eighteenth and nineteenth centuries.

In our brief selection, just as Descartes, Kant, Smith, and Condorcet are formulating and celebrating the new rationality, Hume presses it to its skeptical conclusions, and Rousseau and Burke warn against it. Then in the nineteenth century,

Hegel's objection to a one-sided Enlightenment inspired Marx to offer the most influential critique of the emerging market economy. But however much these thinkers criticize modernity in one respect, they are entangled in it in others. Such is forever the fate of the critics of modernity, who oppose a force so encompassing that even its enemies must borrow its power to fight against it.

1

From *Meditations on First Philosophy*

René Descartes

Frenchman René Descartes (1596–1650) is often considered the father of modern philosophy. Scientist, mathematician, and philosopher, he recognized the problems raised for traditional Scholastic thought – the dominant medieval synthesis of Aristotle's logic and science with Christian theology – by the scientific revolution of his century. Spending much of his productive life in Holland, he sought an absolutely certain foundation from which he could prove the existence of God, the proper method of science, and the existence of the material world, thereby harmonizing theology and the new science. His aptly named *Meditations on First Philosophy* (1641) is virtually a personal diary tracing his journey from the despair of doubt to the peace of certainty. In the following selection, he begins his *Meditations* by attempting to doubt all his beliefs in order to discover whether any are indubitable. He famously found his indubitable starting point in consciousness, the individual human mind's certainty of its own existence in absolute distinction from matter and from all other minds. The effect was to shift subjectivity to the center of philosophy.

Meditation I

Of the things which may be brought within the sphere of the doubtful.

It is now some years since I detected how many were the false beliefs that I had from my earliest youth admitted as true, and how doubtful was everything I had since constructed on this basis;

and from that time I was convinced that I must once for all seriously undertake to rid myself of all the opinions which I had formerly accepted, and commence to build anew from the foundation, if I wanted to establish any firm and permanent structure in the sciences. But as this enterprise appeared to be a very great one, I waited until I had attained an age so mature that I could not hope that at any later date I should be better fitted to execute my design. This reason caused me to delay so long that I should feel that I was doing wrong were I to occupy in deliberation the time that yet remains to me for action. To-day, then, since very opportunely for the plan I have in view I have delivered my mind from every care [and am happily agitated by no passions][i] and since I have procured for myself an assured leisure in a peaceable retirement, I shall at last seriously and freely address myself to the general upheaval of all my former opinions.

Now for this object it is not necessary that I should show that all of these are false – I shall perhaps never arrive at this end. But inasmuch as reason already persuades me that I ought no less carefully to withhold my assent from matters which

[i] Passages in square brackets are from a French translation of the *Meditations* which Descartes himself corrected, and which the translators from the Latin text have included for the sake of their greater clarity.

René Descartes, *Meditations on First Philosophy*, Meditations One and Two, pp. 144–57 from *The Philosophical Works of Descartes*, vol. I (trans. Elizabeth Haldane and G. R. T. Ross). Cambridge: Cambridge University Press, 1975.

are not entirely certain and indubitable than from those which appear to me manifestly to be false, if I am able to find in each one some reason to doubt, this will suffice to justify my rejecting the whole. And for that end it will not be requisite that I should examine each in particular, which would be an endless undertaking; for owing to the fact that the destruction of the foundations of necessity brings with it the downfall of the rest of the edifice, I shall only in the first place attack those principles upon which all my former opinions rested.

All that up to the present time I have accepted as most true and certain I have learned either from the senses or through the senses; but it is sometimes proved to me that these senses are deceptive, and it is wiser not to trust entirely to any thing by which we have once been deceived.

But it may be that although the senses sometimes deceive us concerning things which are hardly perceptible, or very far away, there are yet many others to be met with as to which we cannot reasonably have any doubt, although we recognise them by their means. For example, there is the fact that I am here, seated by the fire, attired in a dressing gown, having this paper in my hands and other similar matters. And how could I deny that these hands and this body are mine, were it not perhaps that I compare myself to certain persons, devoid of sense, whose cerebella are so troubled and clouded by the violent vapours of black bile, that they constantly assure us that they think they are kings when they are really quite poor, or that they are clothed in purple when they are really without covering, or who imagine that they have an earthenware head or are nothing but pumpkins or are made of glass. But they are mad, and I should not be any the less insane were I to follow examples so extravagant.

At the same time I must remember that I am a man, and that consequently I am in the habit of sleeping, and in my dreams representing to myself the same things or sometimes even less probable things, than do those who are insane in their waking moments. How often has it happened to me that in the night I dreamt that I found myself in this particular place, that I was dressed and seated near the fire, whilst in reality I was lying undressed in bed! At this moment it does indeed seem to me that it is with eyes awake that I am looking at this paper; that this head which I move is not asleep, that it is deliberately and of set purpose that I extend my hand and perceive it; what happens in sleep does not appear so clear nor so distinct as does all this. But in thinking over this I remind myself that on many occasions I have in sleep been deceived by similar illusions, and in dwelling carefully on this reflection I see so manifestly that there are no certain indications by which we may clearly distinguish wakefulness from sleep that I am lost in astonishment. And my astonishment is such that it is almost capable of persuading me that I now dream.

Now let us assume that we are asleep and that all these particulars, e.g. that we open our eyes, shake our head, extend our hands, and so on, are but false delusions; and let us reflect that possibly neither our hands nor our whole body are such as they appear to us to be. At the same time we must at least confess that the things which are represented to us in sleep are like painted representations which can only have been formed as the counterparts of something real and true, and that in this way those general things at least, i.e. eyes, a head, hands, and a whole body, are not imaginary things, but things really existent. For, as a matter of fact, painters, even when they study with the greatest skill to represent sirens and satyrs by forms the most strange and extraordinary cannot give them natures which are entirely new, but merely make a certain medley of the members of different animals; or if their imagination is extravagant enough to invent something so novel that nothing similar has ever before been seen, and that then their work represents a thing purely fictitious and absolutely false, it is certain all the same that the colours of which this is composed are necessarily real. And for the same reason, although these general things, to wit, [a body], eyes, a head, hands, and such like, may be imaginary, we are bound at the same time to confess that there are at least some other objects yet more simple and more universal, which are real and true; and of these just in the same way as with certain real colours, all these images of things which dwell in our thoughts, whether true and real or false and fantastic, are formed.

To such a class of things pertains corporeal nature in general, and its extension,[ii] the figure of extended things, their quantity or magnitude and number, as also the place in which they are, the time which measures their duration, and so on.

That is possibly why our reasoning is not unjust when we conclude from this that Physics, Astronomy, Medicine and all other sciences which have as their end the consideration of composite things, are very dubious and uncertain; but that Arithmetic, Geometry and other sciences of that kind which

---

[ii] "Extension" means the space the thing takes up, i.e. its size or volume.

only treat of things that are very simple and very general, without taking great trouble to ascertain whether they are actually existent or not, contain some measure of certainty and an element of the indubitable. For whether I am awake or asleep, two and three together always form five, and the square can never have more than four sides, and it does not seem possible that truths so clear and apparent can be suspected of any falsity [or uncertainty].

Nevertheless I have long had fixed in my mind the belief that an all-powerful God existed by whom I have been created such as I am. But how do I know that He has not brought it to pass that there is no earth, no heaven, no extended body, no magnitude, no place, and that nevertheless [I possess the perceptions of all these things and that] they seem to me to exist just exactly as I now see them? And, besides, as I sometimes imagine that others deceive themselves in the things which they think they know best, how do I know that I am not deceived every time that I add two and three, or count the sides of a square, or judge of things yet simpler, if anything simpler can be imagined? But possibly God has not desired that I should be thus deceived, for He is said to be supremely good. If, however, it is contrary to His goodness to have made me such that I constantly deceive myself, it would also appear to be contrary to His goodness to permit me to be sometimes deceived, and nevertheless I cannot doubt that He does permit this.

There may indeed be those who would prefer to deny the existence of a God so powerful, rather than believe that all other things are uncertain. But let us not oppose them for the present, and grant that all that is here said of a God is a fable; nevertheless in whatever way they suppose that I have arrived at the state of being that I have reached – whether they attribute it to fate or to accident, or make out that it is by a continual succession of antecedents, or by some other method – since to err and deceive oneself is a defect, it is clear that the greater will be the probability of my being so imperfect as to deceive myself ever, as is the Author to whom they assign my origin the less powerful. To these reasons I have certainly nothing to reply, but at the end I feel constrained to confess that there is nothing in all that I formerly believed to be true, of which I cannot in some measure doubt, and that not merely through want of thought or through levity, but for reasons which are very powerful and maturely considered so that henceforth I ought not the less carefully to refrain from giving credence to these opinions than to that

which is manifestly false, if I desire to arrive at any certainty [in the sciences].

But it is not sufficient to have made these remarks, we must also be careful to keep them in mind. For these ancient and commonly held opinions still revert frequently to my mind, long and familiar custom having given them the right to occupy my mind against my inclination and rendered them almost masters of my belief; nor will I ever lose the habit of deferring to them or of placing my confidence in them, so long as I consider them as they really are, i.e. opinions in some measure doubtful, as I have just shown, and at the same time highly probable, so that there is much more reason to believe in than to deny them. That is why I consider that I shall not be acting amiss, if, taking of set purpose a contrary belief, I allow myself to be deceived, and for a certain time pretend that all these opinions are entirely false and imaginary, until at last, having thus balanced my former prejudices with my latter [so that they cannot divert my opinions more to one side than to the other], my judgment will no longer be dominated by bad usage or turned away from the right knowledge of the truth. For I am assured that there can be neither peril nor error in this course, and that I cannot at present yield too much to distrust, since I am not considering the question of action, but only of knowledge.

I shall then suppose, not that God who is supremely good and the fountain of truth, but some evil genius not less powerful than deceitful, has employed his whole energies in deceiving me; I shall consider that the heavens, the earth, colours, figures, sound, and all other external things are nought but the illusions and dreams of which this genius has availed himself in order to lay traps for my credulity; I shall consider myself as having no hands, no eyes, no flesh, no blood, nor any senses, yet falsely believing myself to possess all these things; I shall remain obstinately attached to this idea, and if by this means it is not in my power to arrive at the knowledge of any truth, I may at least do what is in my power [i.e. suspend my judgment], and with firm purpose avoid giving credence to any false thing, or being imposed upon by this arch deceiver, however powerful and deceptive he may be. But this task is a laborious one, and insensibly a certain lassitude leads me into the course of my ordinary life. And just as a captive who in sleep enjoys an imaginary liberty, when he begins to suspect that his liberty is but a dream, fears to awaken, and conspires with these agreeable illusions that the deception may be prolonged, so insensibly of my own accord I fall back into my former opinions, and I dread awakening from this slumber, lest the laborious wakefulness which would follow the tranquillity of this repose should have to be spent not in daylight, but in the excessive darkness of the difficulties which have just been discussed.

Meditation II

Of the Nature of the Human Mind; and that it is more easily known than the Body.

The Meditation of yesterday filled my mind with so many doubts that it is no longer in my power to forget them. And yet I do not see in what manner I can resolve them; and, just as if I had all of a sudden fallen into very deep water, I am so disconcerted that I can neither make certain of setting my feet on the bottom, nor can I swim and so support myself on the surface. I shall nevertheless make an effort and follow anew the same path as that on which I yesterday entered, i.e. I shall proceed by setting aside all that in which the least doubt could be supposed to exist, just as if I had discovered that it was absolutely false; and I shall ever follow in this road until I have met with something which is certain, or at least, if I can do nothing else, until I have learned for certain that there is nothing in the world that is certain. Archimedes, in order that he might draw the terrestrial globe out of its place, and transport it elsewhere, demanded only that one point should be fixed and immoveable; in the same way I shall have the right to conceive high hopes if I am happy enough to discover one thing only which is certain and indubitable.[iii]

I suppose, then, that all the things that I see are false; I persuade myself that nothing has ever existed of all that my fallacious memory represents to me. I consider that I possess no senses; I imagine that body, figure, extension, movement and place are but the fictions of my mind. What, then, can be esteemed as true? Perhaps nothing at all, unless that there is nothing in the world that is certain.

But how can I know there is not something different from those things that I have just considered, of which one cannot have the slightest doubt? Is there not some God, or some other being by whatever name we call it, who puts these

reflections into my mind? That is not necessary, for is it not possible that I am capable of producing them myself? I myself, am I not at least something? But I have already denied that I had senses and body. Yet I hesitate, for what follows from that? Am I so dependent on body and senses that I cannot exist without these? But I was persuaded that there was nothing in all the world, that there was no heaven, no earth, that there were no minds, nor any bodies: was I not then likewise persuaded that I did not exist? Not at all; of a surety I myself did exist since I persuaded myself of something [or merely because I thought of something]. But there is some deceiver or other, very powerful and very cunning, who ever employs his ingenuity in deceiving me. Then without doubt I exist also if he deceives me, and let him deceive me as much as he will, he can never cause me to be nothing so long as I think that I am something. So that after having reflected well and carefully examined all things, we must come to the definite conclusion that this proposition: I am, I exist, is necessarily true each time that I pronounce it, or that I mentally conceive it.

But I do not yet know clearly enought what I am, I who am certain that I am; and hence I must be careful to see that I do not imprudently take some other object in place of myself, and thus that I do not go astray in respect of this knowledge that I hold to be the most certain and most evident of all that I have formerly learned. That is why I shall now consider anew what I believed myself to be before I embarked upon these last reflections; and of my former opinions I shall withdraw all that might even in a small degree be invalidated by the reasons which I have just brought forward, in order that there may be nothing at all left beyond what is absolutely certain and indubitable.

What then did I formerly believe myself to be? Undoubtedly I believed myself to be a man. But what is a man? Shall I say a reasonable animal? Certainly not; for then I should have to inquire what an animal is, and what is reasonable; and thus from a single question I should insensibly fall into an infinitude of others more difficult; and I should not wish to waste the little time and leisure remaining to me in trying to unravel subtleties like these. But I shall rather stop here to consider the thoughts which of themselves spring up in my mind, and which were not inspired by anything beyond my own nature alone when I applied myself to the consideration of my being. In the first place, then, I considered myself as having a face, hands,

---

[iii] Greek mathematician Archimedes (287–212 BC) boasted that with a lever long enough and the right place to stand, he could move the Earth.

arms, and all that system of members composed of bones and flesh as seen in a corpse which I designated by the name of body. In addition to this I considered that I was nourished, that I walked, that I felt, and that I thought, and I referred all these actions to the soul: but I did not stop to consider what the soul was, or if I did stop, I imagined that it was something extremely rare and subtle like a wind, a flame, or an ether, which was spread throughout my grosser parts. As to body I had no manner of doubt about its nature, but thought I had a very clear knowledge of it; and if I had desired to explain it according to the notions that I had then formed of it, I should have described it thus: By the body I understand all that which can be defined by a certain figure: something which can be confined in a certain place, and which can fill a given space in such a way that every other body will be excluded from it; which can be perceived either by touch, or by sight, or by hearing, or by taste, or by smell: which can be moved in many ways not, in truth, by itself, but by something which is foreign to it, by which it is touched [and from which it receives impressions]: for to have the power of self-movement, as also of feeling or of thinking, I did not consider to appertain to the nature of body: on the contrary, I was rather astonished to find that faculties similar to them existed in some bodies.

But what am I, now that I suppose that there is a certain genius which is extremely powerful, and, if I may say so, malicious, who employs all his powers in deceiving me? Can I affirm that I possess the least of all those things which I have just said pertain to the nature of body? I pause to consider, I revolve all these things in my mind, and I find none of which I can say that it pertains to me. It would be tedious to stop to enumerate them. Let us pass to the attributes of soul and see if there is any one which is in me? What of nutrition or walking [the first mentioned]? But if it is so that I have no body it is also true that I can neither walk nor take nourishment. Another attribute is sensation. But one cannot feel without body, and besides I have thought I perceived many things during sleep that I recognised in my waking moments as not having been experienced at all. What of thinking? I find here that thought is an attribute that belongs to me; it alone cannot be separated from me. I am, I exist, that is certain. But how often? Just when I think; for it might possibly be the case if I ceased entirely to think, that I should likewise cease altogether to exist. I do not now admit anything which is not necessarily true: to speak accurately I am not more

than a thing which thinks, that is to say a mind or a soul, or an understanding, or a reason, which are terms whose significance was formerly unknown to me. I am, however, a real thing and really exist; but what thing? I have answered: a thing which thinks.

And what more? I shall exercise my imagination [in order to see if I am not something more]. I am not a collection of members which we call the human body: I am not a subtle air distributed through these members, I am not a wind, a fire, a vapour, a breath, nor anything at all which I can imagine or conceive; because I have assumed that all these were nothing. Without changing that supposition I find that I only leave myself certain of the fact that I am somewhat. But perhaps it is true that these same things which I supposed were non-existent because they are unknown to me, are really not different from the self which I know. I am not sure about this, I shall not dispute about it now; I can only give judgment on things that are known to me. I know that I exist, and I inquire what I am, I whom I know to exist. But it is very certain that the knowledge of my existence taken in its precise significance does not depend on things whose existence is not yet known to me; consequently it does not depend on those which I can feign in imagination. And indeed the very term *feign* in imagination proves to me my error, for I really do this if I image myself a something, since to imagine is nothing else than to contemplate the figure or image of a corporeal thing. But I already know for certain that I am, and that it may be that all these images, and, speaking generally, all things that relate to the nature of body are nothing but dreams [and chimeras]. For this reason I see clearly that I have as little reason to say, 'I shall stimulate my imagination in order to know more distinctly what I am,' than if I were to say, 'I am now awake, and I perceive somewhat that is real and true: but because I do not yet perceive it distinctly enough, I shall go to sleep of express purpose, so that my dreams may represent the perception with greatest truth and evidence.' And, thus, I know for certain that nothing of all that I can understand by means of my imagination belongs to this knowledge which I have of myself, and that it is necessary to recall the mind from this mode of thought with the utmost diligence in order that it may be able to know its own nature with perfect distinctness.

But what then am I? A thing which thinks. What is a thing which thinks? It is a thing which doubts, understands, conceives, affirms, denies, wills refuses, which also imagines and feels.

Certainly it is no small matter if all these things pertain to my nature. But why should they not so pertain? Am I not that being who now doubts nearly everything, who nevertheless understands certain things, who affirms that one only is true, who denies all the others, who desires to know more, is averse from being deceived, who imagines many things, sometimes indeed despite his will, and who perceives many likewise, as by the intervention of the bodily organs? Is there nothing in all this which is as true as it is certain that I exist, even though I should always sleep and though he who has given me being employed all his ingenuity in deceiving me? Is there likewise any one of these attributes which can be distinguished from my thought, or which might be said to be separated from myself? For it is so evident of itself that it is I who doubts, who understands, and who desires, that there is no reason here to add anything to explain it. And I have certainly the power of imagining likewise; for although it may happen (as I formerly supposed) that none of the things which I imagine are true, nevertheless this power of imagining does not cease to be really in use, and it forms part of my thought. Finally, I am the same who feels, that is to say, who perceives certain things, as by the organs of sense, since in truth I see light, I hear noise, I feel heat. But it will be said that these phenomena are false and that I am dreaming. Let it be so; still it is at least quite certain that it seems to me that I see light, that I hear noise and that I feel heat. That cannot be false; properly speaking it is what is in me called feeling; and used in this precise sense that is no other thing than thinking.

From this time I begin to know what I am with a little more clearness and distinction than before; but nevertheless it still seems to me, and I cannot prevent myself from thinking, that corporeal things, whose images are framed by thought, which are tested by the senses, are much more distinctly known than that obscure part of me which does not come under the imagination. Although really it is very strange to say that I know and understand more distinctly these things whose existence seems to me dubious, which are unknown to me, and which do not belong to me, than others of the truth of which I am convinced, which are known to me and which pertain to my real nature, in a word, than myself. But I see clearly how the case stands: my mind loves to wander, and cannot yet suffer itself to be retained within the just limits of truth. Very good, let us once more give it the

freest rein, so that, when afterwards we seize the proper occasion for pulling up, it may the more easily be regulated and controlled.

Let us begin by considering the commonest matters, those which we believe to be the most distinctly comprehended, to wit, the bodies which we touch and see; not indeed bodies in general, for these general ideas are usually a little more confused, but let us consider one body in particular. Let us take, for example, this piece of wax: it has been taken quite freshly from the hive, and it has not yet lost the sweetness of the honey which it contains; it still retains somewhat of the odour of the flowers from which it has been culled; its colour, its figure, its size are apparent; it is hard, cold, easily handled, and if you strike it with the finger, it will emit a sound. Finally all the things which are requisite to cause us distinctly to recognise a body, are met with in it. But notice that while I speak and approach the fire what remained of the taste is exhaled, the smell evaporates, the colour alters, the figure is destroyed, the size increases, it becomes liquid, it heats, scarcely can one handle it, and when one strikes it, no sound is emitted. Does the same wax remain after this change? We must confess that it remains, none would judge otherwise. What then did I know so distinctly in this piece of wax? It could certainly be nothing of all that the senses brought to my notice, since all these things which fall under taste, smell, sight, touch, and hearing, are found to be changed, and yet the same wax remains.

Perhaps it was what I now think, viz. that this wax was not that sweetness of honey, nor that agreeable scent of flowers, nor that particular whiteness, nor that figure, nor that sound, but simply a body which a little while before appeared to me as perceptible under these forms, and which is now perceptible under others. But what, precisely, is it that I imagine when I form such conceptions? Let us attentively consider this, and, abstracting from all that does not belong to the wax, let us see what remains. Certainly nothing remains excepting a certain extended thing which is flexible and movable. But what is the meaning of flexible and movable? Is it not that I imagine that this piece of wax being round is capable of becoming square and of passing from a square to a triangular figure? No, certainly it is not that, since I imagine it admits of an infinitude of similar changes, and I nevertheless do not know how to compass the infinitude by my imagination, and consequently this conception which I have of the wax is not brought about by the faculty of imagination. What now is this extension? Is it not also unknown? For it becomes greater when the wax is melted, greater when it is boiled, and greater still when the heat increases; and I should not conceive [clearly] according to truth what wax is, if I did not think that even this piece that we are considering is capable of receiving more variations in extension than I have ever imagined. We must then grant that I could not even understand through the imagination what this piece of wax is, and that it is my mind alone which perceives it. I say this piece of wax in particular, for as to wax in general it is yet clearer. But what is this piece of wax which cannot be understood excepting by the [understanding or] mind? It is certainly the same that I see, touch, imagine, and finally it is the same which I have always believed it to be from the beginning. But what must particularly be observed is that its perception is neither an act of vision, nor of touch, nor of imagination, and has never been such although it may have appeared formerly to be so, but only an intuition of the mind, which may be imperfect and confused as it was formerly, or clear and distinct as it is at present, according as my attention is more or less directed to the elements which are found in it, and of which it is composed.

Yet in the meantime I am greatly astonished when I consider [the great feebleness of mind] and its proneness to fall [insensibly] into error; for although without giving expression to my thoughts I consider all this in my own mind, words often impede me and I am almost deceived by the terms of ordinary language. For we say that we see the same wax, if it is present, and not that we simply judge that it is the same from its having the same colour and figure. From this I should conclude that I knew the wax by means of vision and not simply by the intuition of the mind; unless by chance I remember that, when looking from a window and saying I see men who pass in the street, I really do not see them, but infer that what I see is men, just as I say that I see wax. And yet what do I see from the window but hats and coats which may cover automatic machines? Yet I judge these to be men. And similarly solely by the faculty of judgment which rests in my mind, I comprehend that which I believed I saw with my eyes.

A man who makes it his aim to raise his knowledge above the common should be ashamed to derive the occasion for doubting from the forms of speech invented by the vulgar; I prefer to pass on and consider whether I had a more evident and perfect conception of what the wax was when I first perceived it, and when I believed I knew it by means of the external senses or at least by the common sense as it is called, that is to say by the imaginative faculty, or whether my present conception is clearer now that I have most carefully examined what it is, and in what way it can be known. It would certainly be absurd to doubt as to this. For what was there in this first perception which was distinct? What was there which might not as well have been perceived by any of the animals? But when I distinguish the wax from its external forms, and when, just as if I had taken from it its vestments, I consider it quite naked, it is certain that although some error may still be found in my judgment, I can nevertheless not perceive it thus without a human mind.

But finally what shall I say of this mind, that is, of myself, for up to this point I do not admit in myself anything but mind? What then, I who seem to perceive this piece of wax so distinctly, do I not know myself, not only with much more truth and certainty, but also with much more distinctness and clearness? For if I judge that the wax is or exists from the fact that I see it, it certainly follows much more clearly that I am or that I exist myself from the fact that I see it. For it may be that what I see is not really wax, it may also be that I do not possess eyes with which to see anything; but it cannot be that when I see, or (for I no longer take account of the distinction) when I think I see, that I myself who think am nought. So if I judge that the wax exists from the fact that I touch it, the same thing will follow, to wit, that I am; and if I judge that my imagination, or some other cause, whatever it is, persuades me that the wax exists, I shall still conclude the same. And what I have here remarked of wax may be applied to all other things which are external to me [and which are met with outside of me]. And further, if the [notion or] perception of wax has seemed to me clearer and more distinct, not only after the sight or the touch, but also after many other causes have rendered it quite manifest to me, with how much more [evidence] and distinctness must it be said that I now know myself, since all the reasons which contribute to the knowledge of wax, or any other body whatever, are yet better proofs of the nature of my mind! And there are so many other things in the mind itself which may contribute to the elucidation of its nature, that those which depend on body such as these just mentioned, hardly merit being taken into account.

But finally here I am, having insensibly reverted to the point I desired, for, since it is now manifest to me that even bodies are not properly speaking known by the senses or by the faculty of imagination, but by the understanding only, and since they are not known from the fact that they are seen or touched, but only because they are understood, I see clearly that there is nothing which is easier for me to know than my mind. But because it is difficult to rid oneself so promptly of an opinion to which one was accustomed for so long, it will be well that I should halt a little at this point, so that by the length of my meditation I may more deeply imprint on my memory this new knowledge.

2

From *A Treatise on Human Nature*

David Hume

While Descartes and other epistemological "rationalists" held that there is some source of knowledge beyond, or prior to, experience (e.g. "innate ideas"), modern "empiricist" philosophers, starting with John Locke (1632–1704), insisted that all mental contents, hence all knowledge, derived solely from experience. Such a view might seem tailor made for modern science. But David Hume (1711–76), member of the Scottish Enlightenment and the greatest skeptic of modern philosophy, radicalized empiricism to the point of undermining science itself, at least as it is normally understood. For experience, stripped of preconceptions, is nothing but a series of impressions among which we can note "conjunctions" or correlations. There is then no reason, or evidence, for claiming that these impressions "inhere" in "substances" that endure when we do not perceive them, or for belief in "necessary connection" among impressions. Nothing in experience *must* be as it is. Hence any prediction of the future based on past experience is merely a projection of mental habit or custom, even though, as Hume recognizes, we cannot live without making such predictions. Likewise, there can be no reason or evidence for asserting the necessary existence of something altogether beyond experience, that is, God. The Conclusion to the first part of his greatest work, *A Treatise of Human Nature* (1739), is the most poignant and disturbing expression of skepticism in the history of Western philosophy.

But before I launch out into those immense depths of philosophy, which lie before me, I find myself inclin'd to stop a moment in my present station,

and to ponder that voyage, which I have undertaken, and which undoubtedly requires the utmost art and industry to be brought to a happy conclusion. Methinks I am like a man, who having struck on many shoals, and having narrowly escap'd shipwreck in passing a small frith, has yet the temerity to put out to sea in the same leaky weather-beaten vessel, and even carries his ambition so far as to think of compassing the globe under these disadvantageous circumstances. My memory of past errors and perplexities, makes me diffident for the future. The wretched condition, weakness, and disorder of the faculties, I must employ in my enquiries, encrease my apprehensions. And the impossibility of amending or correcting these faculties, reduces me almost to despair, and makes me resolve to perish on the barren rock, on which I am at present, rather than venture myself upon that boundless ocean, which runs out into immensity. This sudden view of my danger strikes me with melancholy; and as 'tis usual for that passion, above all others, to indulge itself; I cannot forbear feeding my despair, with all those desponding reflections, which the present subject furnishes me with in such abundance.

I am first affrighted and confounded with that forelorn solitude, in which I am plac'd in my philosophy, and fancy myself some strange uncouth monster, who not being able to mingle and unite in

David Hume, Conclusion to Book One, pp. 263–74 from *A Treatise of Human Nature*, Book 1, Part IV (ed. L. A. Selby-Bigge). Oxford: Oxford University Press, 1975.

society, has been expell'd all human commerce, and left utterly abandon'd and disconsolate. Fain wou'd I run into the crowd for shelter and warmth; but cannot prevail with myself to mix with such deformity. I call upon others to join me, in order to make a company apart; but no one will hearken to me. Every one keeps at a distance, and dreads that storm, which beats upon me from every side. I have expos'd myself to the enmity of all metaphysicians, logicians, mathematicians, and even theologians; and can I wonder at the insults I must suffer? I have declar'd my dis-approbation of their systems; and can I be surpriz'd, if they shou'd express a hatred of mine and of my person? When I look abroad, I foresee on every side, dispute, contradiction, anger, calumny and detraction. When I turn my eye inward, I find nothing but doubt and ignorance. All the world conspires to oppose and contradict me; tho' such is my weakness, that I feel all my opinions loosen and fall of themselves, when unsupported by the approbation of others. Every step I take is with hesitation, and every new reflection makes me dread an error and absurdity in my reasoning.

For with what confidence can I venture upon such bold enterprizes, when beside those numberless infirmities peculiar to myself, I find so many which are common to human nature? Can I be sure, that in leaving all establish'd opinions I am following truth; and by what criterion shall I distinguish her, even if fortune shou'd at last guide me on her foot-steps? After the most accurate and exact of my reasonings, I can give no reason why I shou'd assent to it; and feel nothing but a *strong* propensity to consider objects *strongly* in that view, under which they appear to me. Experience is a principle, which instructs me in the several conjunctions of objects for the past. Habit is another principle, which determines me to expect the same for the future; and both of them conspiring to operate upon the imagination, make me form certain ideas in a more intense and lively manner, than others, which are not attended with the same advantages. Without this quality, by which the mind enlivens some ideas beyond others (which seemingly is so trivial, and so little founded on reason) we cou'd never assent to any argument, nor carry our view beyond those few objects, which are present to our senses. Nay, even to these objects we cou'd never attribute any existence, but what was dependent on the senses; and must comprehend them entirely in that succession of perceptions, which constitutes our self or person. Nay farther, even with relation to that succession, we cou'd only admit of those perceptions, which are immediately present to our consciousness, nor cou'd those lively images, with which the memory presents us, be ever receiv'd as true pictures of past perceptions. The memory, senses, and understanding are, therefore, all of them founded on the imagination, or the vivacity of our ideas.

No wonder a principle so inconstant and fallacious shou'd lead us into errors, when implicitly follow'd (as it must be) in all its variations. 'Tis this principle, which makes us reason from causes and effects; and 'tis the same principle, which convinces us of the continu'd existence of external objects, when absent from the senses. But tho' these two operations be equally natural and necessary in the human mind, yet in some circumstances they are directly contrary, nor is it possible for us to reason justly and regularly from causes and effects, and at the same time believe the continu'd existence of matter. How then shall we adjust those principles together? Which of them shall we prefer? Or in case we prefer neither of them, but successively assent to both, as is usual among philosophers, with what confidence can we afterwards usurp that glorious title, when we thus knowingly embrace a manifest contradiction?

This contradiction wou'd be more excusable, were it compensated by any degree of solidity and satisfaction in the other parts of our reasoning. But the case is quite contrary. When we trace up the human understanding to its first principles, we find it to lead us into such sentiments, as seem to turn into ridicule all our past pains and industry, and to discourage us from future enquiries. Nothing is more curiously enquir'd after by the mind of man, than the causes of every phænomenon; nor are we content with knowing the immediate causes, but push on our enquiries, till we arrive at the original and ultimate principle. We wou'd not willingly stop before we are acquainted with that energy in the cause, by which it operates on its effect; that tie which connects them together; and that efficacious quality, on which the tie depends. This is our aim in all our studies and reflections: And how must we be disappointed, when we learn, that this connexion, tie, or energy lies merely in ourselves, and is nothing but that determination of the mind, which is acquir'd by custom, and causes us to make a transition from an object to its usual attendant, and from the impression of one to the lively idea of the other? Such a discovery not only cuts off all hope of ever attaining satisfaction, but even prevents our very wishes; since it appears that when we say we desire to know the ultimate and operating principle, as something, which resides in the external object, we either contradict ourselves, or talk without a meaning.

This deficiency in our ideas is not, indeed, perceiv'd in common life, nor are we sensible, that in the most usual conjunctions of cause and effect we are as ignorant of the ultimate principle, which binds them together, as in the most unusual and extraordinary. But this proceeds merely from an illusion of the imagination; and the question is, how far we ought to yield to these illusions. This question is very difficult, and reduces us to a very dangerous dilemma, whichever way we answer it. For if we assent to every trivial suggestion of the fancy; beside that these suggestions are often contrary to each other; they lead us into such errors, absurdities, and obscurities, that we must at last become asham'd of our credulity. Nothing is more dangerous to reason than the flights of the imagination, and nothing has been the occasion of more mistakes among philosophers. Men of bright fancies may in this respect be compar'd to those angels, whom the scripture represents as covering their eyes with their wings. This has already appear'd in so many instances, that we may spare ourselves the trouble of enlarging upon it any farther.

But on the other hand, if the consideration of these instances makes us take a resolution to reject all the trivial suggestions of the fancy, and adhere to the understanding, that is, to the general and more establish'd properties of the imagination; even this resolution, if steadily executed, wou'd be dangerous, and attended with the most fatal consequences. For I have already shewn, that the understanding, when it acts alone, and according to its most general principles, entirely subverts itself, and leaves not the lowest degree of evidence in any proposition, either in philosophy or common life. We save ourselves from this total scepticism only by means of that singular and seemingly trivial property of the fancy, by which we enter with difficulty into remote views of things, and are not able to accompany them with so sensible an impression, as we do those, which are more easy and natural. Shall we, then, establish it for a general maxim, that no refin'd or elaborate reasoning is ever to be receiv'd? Consider well the consequences of such a principle. By this means you cut off entirely all science and philosophy: You proceed upon one singular quality of the imagination, and by a parity of reason must embrace all of them: And you expresly contradict yourself; since this maxim must be built on the preceding reasoning, which will be allow'd to be sufficiently

refin'd and metaphysical. What party, then, shall we choose among these difficulties? If we embrace this principle, and condemn all refin'd reasoning, we run into the most manifest absurdities. If we reject it in favour of these reasonings, we subvert entirely the human understanding. We have, therefore, no choice left but betwixt a false reason and none at all. For my part, I know not what ought to be done in the present case. I can only observe what is commonly done; which is, that this difficulty is seldom or never thought of; and even where it has once been present to the mind, is quickly forgot, and leaves but a small impression behind it. Very refin'd reflections have little or no influence upon us; and yet we do not, and cannot establish it for a rule, that they ought not to have any influence; which implies a manifest contradiction.

But what have I here said, that reflections very refin'd and metaphysical have little or no influence upon us? This opinion I can scarce forbear retracting, and condemning from my present feeling and experience. The *intense* view of these manifold contradictions and imperfections in human reason has so wrought upon me, and heated my brain, that I am ready to reject all belief and reasoning, and can look upon no opinion even as more probable or likely than another. Where am I, or what? From what causes do I derive my existence, and to what condition shall I return? Whose favour shall I court, and whose anger must I dread? What beings surround me? and on whom have I any influence, or who have any influence on me? I am confounded with all these questions, and begin to fancy myself in the most deplorable condition imaginable, inviron'd with the deepest darkness, and utterly depriv'd of the use of every member and faculty.

Most fortunately it happens, that since reason is incapable of dispelling these clouds, nature herself suffices to that purpose, and cures me of this philosophical melancholy and delirium, either by relaxing this bent of mind, or by some avocation, and lively impression of my senses, which obliterate all these chimeras. I dine, I play a game of backgammon, I converse, and am merry with my friends; and when after three or four hours' amusement, I wou'd return to these speculations, they appear so cold, and strain'd, and ridiculous, that I cannot find in my heart to enter into them any farther.

Here then I find myself absolutely and necessarily determin'd to live, and talk, and act like other people in the common affairs of life. But notwithstanding that my natural propensity, and the course of my animal spirits and passions reduce me to this indolent belief in the general maxims of the world, I still feel such remains of my former disposition, that I am ready to throw all my books and papers into the fire, and resolve never more to renounce the pleasures of life for the sake of reasoning and philosophy. For those are my sentiments in that splenetic humour, which governs me at present. I may, nay I must yield to the current of nature, in submitting to my senses and understanding; and in this blind submission I shew most perfectly my sceptical disposition and principles. But does it follow, that I must strive against the current of nature, which leads me to indolence and pleasure; that I must seclude myself, in some measure, from the commerce and society of men, which is so agreeable; and that I must torture my brain with subtilties and sophistries, at the very time that I cannot satisfy myself concerning the reasonableness of so painful an application, nor have any tolerable prospect of arriving by its means at truth and certainty. Under what obligation do I lie of making such an abuse of time? And to what end can it serve either for the service of mankind, or for my own private interest? No: If I must be a fool, as all those who reason or believe any thing *certainly* are, my follies shall at least be natural and agreeable. Where I strive against my inclination, I shall have a good reason for my resistance; and will no more be led a wandering into such dreary solitudes, and rough passages, as I have hitherto met with.

These are the sentiments of my spleen and indolence; and indeed I must confess, that philosophy has nothing to oppose to them, and expects a victory more from the returns of a serious good-humour'd disposition, than from the force of reason and conviction. In all the incidents of life we ought still to preserve our scepticism. If we believe, that fire warms, or water refreshes, 'tis only because it costs us too much pains to think otherwise. Nay if we are philosophers, it ought only to be upon sceptical principles, and from an inclination, which we feel to the employing ourselves after that manner. Where reason is lively, and mixes itself with some propensity, it ought to be assented to. Where it does not, it never can have any title to operate upon us.

At the time, therefore, that I am tir'd with amusement and company, and have indulg'd a *reverie* in my chamber, or in a solitary walk by a river-side, I feel my mind all collected within itself, and am naturally *inclin'd* to carry my view into all those subjects, about which I have met with so many disputes in the course of my reading and conversation. I cannot forbear having a curiosity to be acquainted with the principles of moral good and evil, the nature and foundation of government, and the cause of those several passions and inclinations, which actuate and govern me. I am uneasy to think I approve of one object, and disapprove of another; call one thing beautiful, and another deform'd; decide concerning truth and falshood, reason and folly, without knowing upon what principles I proceed. I am concern'd for the condition of the learned world, which lies under such a deplorable ignorance in all these particulars. I feel an ambition to arise in me of contributing to the instruction of mankind, and of acquiring a name by my inventions and discoveries. These sentiments spring up naturally in my present disposition; and shou'd I endeavour to banish them, by attaching myself to any other business or diversion, I *feel* I shou'd be a loser in point of pleasure; and this is the origin of my philosophy.

But even suppose this curiosity and ambition shou'd not transport me into speculations without the sphere of common life, it wou'd necessarily happen, that from my very weakness I must be led into such enquiries. Tis certain, that superstition is much more bold in its systems and hypotheses than philosophy; and while the latter contents itself with assigning new causes and principles to the phænomena, which appear in the visible world, the former opens a world of its own, and presents us with scenes, and beings, and objects, which are altogether new. Since therefore 'tis almost impossible for the mind of man to rest, like those of beasts, in that narrow circle of objects, which are the subject of daily conversation and action, we ought only to deliberate concerning the choice of our guide, and ought to prefer that which is safest and most agreeable. And in this respect I make bold to recommend philosophy, and shall not scruple to give it the preference to superstition of every kind or denomination. For as superstition arises naturally and easily from the popular opinions of mankind, it seizes more strongly on the mind, and is often able to disturb us in the conduct of our lives and actions. Philosophy on the contrary, if just, can present us only with mild and moderate sentiments; and if false and extravagant, its opinions are merely the objects of a cold and general speculation, and seldom go so far as to interrupt the course of our natural propensities. The CYNICS are an extraordinary instance of philosophers, who from reasonings purely philosophical ran into as great extravagancies of conduct as any *Monk* or *Dervise* that ever was in the world.[i] Generally speaking, the errors in religion are dangerous; those in philosophy only ridiculous.

I am sensible, that these two cases of the strength and weakness of the mind will not comprehend all mankind, and that there are in *England*, in particular, many honest gentlemen, who being always employ'd in their domestic affairs, or amusing themselves in common recreations, have carried their thoughts very little beyond those objects, which are every day expos'd to their senses. And indeed, of such as these I pretend not to make philosophers, nor do I expect them either to be associates in these researches or auditors of these discoveries. They do well to keep themselves in their present situation; and instead of refining them into philosophers, I wish we cou'd communicate to our founders of systems, a share of this gross earthy mixture, as an ingredient, which they commonly stand much in need of, and which wou'd serve to temper those fiery particles, of which they are compos'd. While a warm imagination is allow'd to enter into philosophy, and hypotheses embrac'd merely for being specious and agreeable, we can never have any steady principles, nor any sentiments, which will suit with common practice and experience. But were these hypotheses once remov'd, we might hope to establish a system or set of opinions, which if not true (for that, perhaps, is too much to be hop'd for) might at least be satisfactory to the human mind, and might stand the test of the most critical examination. Nor shou'd we despair of attaining this end, because of the many chimerical systems, which have successively arisen and decay'd away among men, wou'd we consider the shortness of that period, wherein these questions have been the subjects of enquiry and reasoning. Two thousand years with such long interruptions, and under such mighty discouragements are a small space of time to give any tolerable perfection to the sciences; and perhaps we are still in too early an age of the world to discover any principles, which will bear the examination of the latest posterity. For my part, my only hope is, that I may contribute a little to the advancement of knowledge, by giving in some particulars a different turn to the speculations of philosophers, and pointing out to them more distinctly those subjects, where alone they can expect assurance and conviction. Human Nature is the only science of man; and yet has been hitherto the most neglected. 'Twill be sufficient for me, if I can bring it a little more into fashion; and the hope of this serves to compose my temper from that spleen, and invigorate it from that indolence, which sometimes prevail upon me. If the reader finds himself in the same easy disposition, let him follow me in my future speculations. If not, let him follow his inclination, and wait the returns of application and good humour. The conduct of a man, who studies philosophy in this careless manner, is more truly sceptical than that of one, who feeling in himself an inclination to it, is yet so over-whelm'd with doubts and scruples, as totally to reject it. A true sceptic will be diffident of his philosophical doubts, as well as of his philosophical conviction; and will never refuse any innocent satisfaction, which offers itself, upon account of either of them.

Nor is it only proper we shou'd in general indulge our inclination in the most elaborate philosophical researches, notwithstanding our sceptical principles, but also that we shou'd yield to that propensity, which inclines us to be positive and certain in *particular points*, according to the light, in which we survey them in any *particular instant*. 'Tis easier to forbear all examination and enquiry, than to check ourselves in so natural a propensity, and guard against that assurance, which always arises from an exact and full survey of an object. On such an occasion we are apt not only to forget our scepticism, but even our modesty too; and make use of such terms as these, *'tis evident, 'tis certain, 'tis undeniable*; which a due deference to the public ought, perhaps, to prevent. I may have fallen into this fault after the example of others; but I here enter a *caveat* against any objections, which may be offer'd on that head; and declare that such expressions were extorted from me by the present view of the object, and imply no dogmatical spirit, nor conceited idea of my own judgment, which are sentiments that I am sensible can become no body, and a sceptic still less than any other.

---

[i] "Derise" means dervish. The Cynics were an ancient philosophical school that advocated the violation of social conventions.

3

From *Discourse on the Sciences and the Arts*

Jean-Jacques Rousseau

Jean-Jacques Rousseau (1712–78) was virtually alone among eighteenth-century intellectuals, the first great critic of the new Enlightenment faith in science and progress. A native of his beloved Geneva, he led an emotionally complex and troubled life. Rousseau felt uncomfortable in the emerging cosmopolitan world, which he believed made genuine selfhood impossible. He established his reputation in 1750 by arguing in the essay excerpted here that modern learning does not improve, but on the contrary harms, human morals. In a later work, his *Discourse on the Origins of Inequality among Men* (1754), he revealed his concern for social equality, foreshadowing the views of Marx, and roundly condemned modern culture. He was chastised by the great Voltaire, who wrote to Rousseau: "no one has ever been so witty as you are in trying to turn us into brutes: to read your book makes one long to go on all fours. Since, however, it is now some sixty years since I gave up the practice, I feel that it is unfortunately impossible for me to resume it." Voltaire's wit to the contrary notwithstanding, Rousseau never argued for an actual return to primitive existence; rather, he sought a new egalitarian way of life that would be just as authentic in the modern context as was primitive existence in its context.

We are deceived by the appearance of right.[i]

Has the restoration of the sciences and the arts contributed to the purification of mores, or to their corruption? That is what is to be examined. Which

---

[i]   Horace, *On the Art of Poetry*, v. 25.

side should I take in this question? The one, gentlemen, that is appropriate to an honest man who knows nothing and who thinks no less of himself for it.

It will be difficult, I feel, to adapt what I have to say to the tribunal before which I appear. How can I dare to blame the sciences before one of Europe's most learned societies, praise ignorance in a famous Academy, and reconcile contempt for study with respect for the truly learned? I have seen these points of conflict, and they have not daunted me. I am not abusing science, I told myself; I am defending virtue before virtuous men. Integrity is even dearer to good men than erudition is to the studious. What then have I to fear? The enlightenment of the assembly that listens to me? I admit it; but this is owing to the composition of the discourse and not to the sentiment of the speaker. Fair-minded sovereigns have never hesitated to pass judgments against themselves in disputes whose outcomes are uncertain; and the position most advantageous for a just cause is to have to defend oneself against an upright and enlightened opponent who is judge in his own case.

To this motive which heartens me is joined another which determines me, namely that, having upheld, according to my natural light, the side of truth, whatever my success, there is a prize which I cannot fail to receive; I will find it within the depths of my heart.

Jean-Jacques Rousseau, pp. 3–10 from Part One of "Discourse on the Sciences and the Arts" in *The Basic Political Writings of Jean-Jacques Rousseau* (trans. Donald Cress). Indianapolis: Hackett Publishing Company Inc., 1987.

It is a grand and beautiful sight to see man emerge somehow from nothing by his own efforts; dissipate, by the light of his reason, the shadows in which nature had enveloped him; rise above himself; soar by means of his mind into the heavenly regions; traverse, like the sun, the vast expanse of the universe with giant steps; and, what is even grander and more difficult, return to himself in order to study man and know his nature, his duties, and his end. All of these marvels have been revived in the past few generations.

Europe had relapsed into the barbarism of the first ages. A few centuries ago the peoples of that part of the world, who today live such enlightened lives, lived in a state worse than ignorance. Some nondescript scientific jargon, even more contemptible than ignorance, had usurped the name of knowledge, and posed a nearly invincible obstacle to its return. A revolution was needed to bring men back to common sense; it finally came from the least expected quarter. It was the stupid Moslem, the eternal scourge of letters, who caused them to be reborn among us. The fall of the throne of Constantinople[ii] brought into Italy the debris of ancient Greece. France in turn was enriched by these precious spoils. Soon the sciences followed letters. To the art of writing was joined the art of thinking – a sequence of events that may seem strange, but which perhaps is only too natural. And the chief advantage of commerce with the Muses began to be felt, namely, that of making men more sociable by inspiring in them the desire to please one another with works worthy of their mutual approval.

The mind has its needs, as does the body. The needs of the latter are the foundations of society; the needs of the former make it pleasant. While the government and the laws see to the safety and well-being of assembled men, the sciences, letters and the arts, less despotic and perhaps more powerful, spread garlands of flowers over the iron chains with which they are burdened, stifle in them the sense of that original liberty for which they seem to have been born, make them love their slavery, and turn them into what is called civilized peoples. Need raised up thrones; the sciences and the arts have strengthened them. Earthly powers, love talents and protect those who cultivate them![1] Civilized peoples, cultivate them! Happy slaves, you owe them that delicate and refined taste on which you pride yourselves; that sweetness of character and

that urbanity in mores which make relationships among you so cordial and easy; in a word, the appearances of all the virtues without having any.

By this sort of civility, all the more agreeable as it puts on fewer airs, Athens and Rome once distinguished themselves in the much vaunted days of their magnificence and splendor. By it our century and our nation will doubtlessly surpass all times and all peoples. A philosophic tone without pedantry, manners natural yet engaging, equally removed from Teutonic rusticity as from Italian pantomine. These are the fruits of the taste acquired by good schooling and perfected in social interaction.

How sweet it would be to live among us, if outer appearances were always the likeness of the heart's dispositions, if decency were virtue, if our maxims served as our rules, if true philosophy were inseparable from the title of philosopher! But so many qualities are all too rarely found in combination, and virtue seldom goes forth in such great pomp. Expensive finery can betoken a wealthy man, and elegance a man of taste. The healthy and robust man is recognized by other signs. It is in the rustic clothing of the fieldworker and not underneath the gilding of the courtier that one will find bodily strength and vigor. Finery is no less alien to virtue, which is the strength and vigor of the soul. The good man is an athlete who enjoys competing in the nude. He is contemptuous of all those vile ornaments which would impair the use of his strength, most of which were invented merely to conceal some deformity.

Before art had fashioned our manners and taught our passions to speak an affected language, our mores were rustic but natural, and, differences in behavior heralded, at first glance, differences of character. At base, human nature was no better, but men found their safety in the ease with which they saw through each other, and that advantage, which we no longer value, spared them many vices.

Today, when more subtle inquiries and a more refined taste have reduced the art of pleasing to established rules, a vile and deceitful uniformity reigns in our mores, and all minds seem to have been cast in the same mold. Without ceasing, politeness makes demands, propriety gives orders; without ceasing, common customs are followed, never one's own lights. One no longer dares to seem what one really is; and in this perpetual constraint, the men who make up this herd we call society will, if placed in the same circumstances, do all the same things unless stronger motives deter them. Thus no one will ever really know those with whom he is dealing. Hence in order to know one's friend, it would be necessary to wait for critical occasions, that is, to wait until it is too late, since it is for these very occasions that it would have been essential to know him.

What a retinue of vices must attend this incertitude! No more sincere friendships, no more real esteem, no more well-founded confidence. Suspicions, offenses, fears, coldness, reserve, hatred, betrayal will unceasingly hide under that uniform and deceitful veil of politeness, under that much vaunted urbanity that we owe to the enlightenment of our century. The name of the master of the universe will no longer be profaned with oaths; rather it will be insulted with blasphemies without our scrupulous ears being offended by them. No one will boast of his own merit, but will disparage that of others. No one will crudely wrong his enemy, but will skillfully slander him. National hatreds will die out, but so will love of country. Scorned ignorance will be replaced by a dangerous Pyrrhonism.[iii] Some excesses will be forbidden, some vices held in dishonor, but others will be adorned with the name of virtues. One must either have them or affect them. Let those who wish extoll the sobriety of the wise men of the present. For my part, I see in it merely a refinement of intemperance as unworthy of my praise as their artful simplicity.[2]

Such is the purity that our mores have acquired. Thus have we become decent men. It is for letters, the sciences, and the arts to claim their part in so wholesome an achievement. I will add but one thought: an inhabitant of some distant lands who sought to form an idea of European mores on the basis of the state of the sciences among us, the perfection of our arts, the seemliness of our theatrical performances, the civilized quality of our manners, the affability of our speech, our perpetual displays of goodwill, and that tumultuous competition of men of every age and circumstance who, from morning to night, seem intent on being obliging to one another; that foreigner, I say, would guess our mores to be exactly the opposite of what they are.

Where there is no effect, there is no cause to seek out. But here the effect is certain, the depravation real, and our souls have become corrupted in proportion as our sciences and our arts have advanced toward perfection. Will it be said that this is a misfortune peculiar to our age? No, gentlemen, the evils caused by our vain curiosity are as old as the world. The daily rise and fall of the ocean's

waters have not been more unvaryingly subjected to the star which provides us with light during the night, than has the fate of mores and integrity been to the progress of the sciences and the arts. Virtue has been seen taking flight in proportion as their light rose on our horizon, and the same phenomenon has been observed in all times and in all places.

Consider Egypt, that first school of the universe, that climate so fertile beneath a brazen sky, that famous country from which Sesostris[iv] departed long ago to conquer the world. She became the mother of philosophy and the fine arts, and soon thereafter was conquered by Cambyses,[v] then by Greeks, Romans, Arabs, and finally Turks.

Consider Greece, formerly populated by heroes who twice conquered Asia, once at Troy and once on their own home ground. Nascent letters had not yet brought corruption into the hearts of her inhabitants; but the progress of the arts, the dissolution of mores and the Macedonian's yoke followed closely upon one another; and Greece, ever learned, ever voluptuous, and ever the slave, experienced nothing in her revolutions but changes of masters. All the eloquence of Demosthenes could never revive a body which luxury and the arts had enervated.

It is at the time of the likes of Ennius and Terence[vi] that Rome, founded by a shepherd and made famous by fieldworkers, began to degenerate. But after the likes of Ovid, Catullus, Martial,[vii] and that crowd of obscene writers whose names alone offend modesty, Rome, formerly the temple of virtue, became the theater of crime, the disgrace of nations, and the plaything of barbarians. Finally, that capital of the world falls under the yoke which she had imposed on so many peoples, and the day of her fall was the eve of the day when one of her citizens was given the title of Arbiter of Good Taste.[viii]

What shall I say about that capital of the Eastern Empire, which, by virtue of its location, seemed destined to be the capital of the entire world, that

---

[iii] An ancient school of skeptical philosophers.

[iv] A legendary pharoah.

[v] King of Persia in 6th century BC.

[vi] Quintus Ennius (239–ca. 170 BC) was the father of Roman poetry, and Publius Terentius Afer (ca. 190–ca. 159 BC) was a Roman playwright.

[vii] Publius Ovidus Naso (93 BC–AD 18) was one of the greatest Roman writers. Caius Valerius Catullus (ca. 84–ca. 54 BC) was a famous Roman lyric poet. Marcus Valerius Martialis (ca. 40–ca. AD 104) was a Roman satirist.

[viii] Tacitus claims that the Roman Emperor Nero made the idler Petronius (d. AD 66) "Arbiter of Good Taste."

refuge of the sciences and the arts banished from the rest of Europe – more perhaps out of wisdom than barbarism. All that is most shameful about debauchery and corruption; blackest in betrayals, assassinations, and poisons; most atrocious in the coexistence of every sort of crime: that is what constitutes the fabric of the history of Constantinople. That is the pure source whence radiates to us the enlightenment on which our century prides itself.

But why seek in remote times proofs of a truth for which we have existing evidence before our eyes? In Asia there is an immense country where acknowledgement in the field of letters leads to the highest offices of the state. If the sciences purified mores, if they taught men to shed their blood for their country, if they enlivened their courage, the peoples of China should be wise, free and invincible. But if there is not a single vice that does not have mastery over them; not a single crime that is unfamiliar to them; if neither the enlightenment of the ministers, nor the alleged wisdom of the laws, nor the multitude of the inhabitants of that vast empire have been able to shield her from the yoke of the ignorant and coarse Tartar, what purpose has all her learned men served? What benefit has been derived from the honors bestowed upon them? Could it be to be peopled by slaves and wicked men?

Contrast these scenes with that of the mores of the small number of peoples who, protected against this contagion of vain knowledge, have by their virtues brought about their own happiness and the model for other nations. Such were the first Persians, a singular nation in which virtue was learned just as science is among us, which subjugated Asia so easily, and which alone has enjoyed the distinction of having the history of its institutions taken for a philosophical novel.[ix] Such were the Scythians, about whom we have been left such magnificent praises. Such were the Germans, whose simplicity, innocence, and virtues a pen – weary of tracing the crimes and atrocities of an educated, opulent and voluptuous people – found relief in depicting. Such had been Rome herself in the times of her poverty and ignorance. Such, finally, has that rustic nation shown herself to this day – so vaunted for her courage which adversity could not overthrow, and for her faithfulness which example could not corrupt.[3]

It is not out of stupidity that these people have preferred other forms of exercise to those of the mind. They were not unaware of the fact that in other lands idle men spent their lives debating about the sovereign good, about vice and about virtue; and that arrogant reasoners, bestowing on themselves the highest praises, grouped other peoples under the contemptuous name of barbarians. However, they considered their mores and learned to disdain their teaching.[4]

Could I forget that it was in the very bosom of Greece that there was seen to arise that city as famous for her happy ignorance as for the wisdom of her laws, that republic of demi-gods rather than men, so superior to humanity did their virtues seem? O Sparta! Eternal shame to a vain doctrine! While the vices, led by the fine arts, intruded themselves together into Athens, while a tyrant there gathered so carefully the works of the prince of poets,[x] you drove out from your walls the arts and artists, the sciences and scientists.

The event confirmed this difference. Athens became the abode of civility and good taste, the country of orators and philosophy. The elegance of her buildings paralleled that of the language. Marble and canvas, animated by the hands of the most capable masters, were to be seen everywhere. From Athens came those astonishing works that will serve as models in every corrupt age. The picture of Lacedaemon is less brilliant. "There," said the other peoples, "men are born virtuous, and the very air of the country seems to inspire virtue." Nothing of her inhabitants is left to us except the memory of their heroic actions. Are such monuments worth less to us than the curious marbles that Athens has left us?

Some wise men, it is true, had resisted the general torrent and protected themselves from vice in the abode of the Muses. But listen to the judgement that the first and unhappiest of them made of the learned men and artists of his time.

"I have," he says, "examined the poets, and I view them as people whose talent makes an impression on them and on others who claim to be wise, who are taken to be such, and who are nothing of the sort.

"From poets," continues Socrates, "I moved on to artists. No one knew less about the arts than I; no one was more convinced that artists possessed some especially fine secrets. Still, I perceived that their

---

[ix] Probably Xenophon's (430–354 BC) *Education of Cyrus.*

[x] Peisistratus (ca. 600–527 BC) allegedly directed the collection of Homer's works.

condition is no better than that of the poets, and that they are both laboring under the same prejudice. Because the most skillful among them excel in their specialty, they view themselves as the wisest of men. To my way of thinking, this presumption has completely tarnished their knowledge. From this it follows that, as I put myself in the place of the oracle and ask myself whether I would prefer to be what I am or what they are, to know what they have learned or to know that I know nothing. I answered myself and God: I want to remain what I am.

"We do not know – neither the sophists, nor the poets, nor the orators, nor the artists, nor I – what is the true, the good, and the beautiful. But there is this difference between us: that although these people know nothing, they all believe they know something. I, however, if I know nothing, at least am not in doubt about it. Thus all that superiority in wisdom accorded me by the oracle, reduces to being convinced that I am ignorant of what I do not know."

Here then is the wisest of men in the judgment of the gods, and the most learned of Athenians in the opinion of all Greece, Socrates, speaking in praise of ignorance! Does anyone believe that, were he to be reborn among us, our learned men and our artists would make him change his mind? No, gentlemen, this just man would continue to hold our vain sciences in contempt. He would not aid in the enlargement of that mass of books which inundate us from every quarter, and the only precept he would leave is the one left to his disciples and to our descendants: the example and the memory of his virtue. Thus is it noble to teach men!

Socrates had begun in Athens, Cato[xi] the Elder continued in Rome to rail against those artful and subtle Greeks who seduced the virtue and enervated the courage of his fellow citizens. But the sciences, the arts, and dialectic prevailed once again. Rome was filled with philosophers and orators; military discipline was neglected, agriculture scorned, sects embraced, and the homeland forgotten. The sacred names of liberty, disinterestedness, obedience to the laws were replaced by the names of Epicurus, Zeno, Arcesilaus.[xii] "Ever since

learned men have begun to appear in our midst," their own philosophers said, "good men have vanished." Until then the Romans had been content to practice virtue; all was lost when they began to study it.

O Fabricius![xiii] What would your great soul have thought, if, had it been your misfortune to be returned to life, you had seen the pompous countenance of that Rome saved by your arm and honored more by your good name than by all her conquests? "Gods!" you would have said, "what has become of those thatched roofs and those rustic hearths where moderation and virtue once dwelt? What fatal splendor has followed upon Roman simplicity? What is this strange speech? What are these effeminate mores? What is the meaning of these statues, these paintings, these buildings? Fools, what have you done? You, the masters of nations, have you made yourselves the slaves of the frivolous men you conquered? Do rhetoricians govern you? Was it to enrich architects, painters, sculptors, and actors that you soaked Greece and Asia with your blood? Are the spoils of Carthage the prey of a flute player? Romans make haste to tear down these amphitheaters; shatter these marbles; burn these paintings; drive out these slaves who subjugate you and whose fatal arts corrupt you. Let others achieve notoriety by vain talents; the only talent worthy of Rome is that of conquering the world and making virtue reign in it. When Cineas[xiv] took our Senate for an assembly of kings, he was dazzled neither by vain pomp nor by studied elegance. There he did not hear that frivolous eloquence, the focus of study and delight of futile men. What then did Cineas see that was so majestic? O citizens! He saw a sight which neither your riches nor all your arts could ever display; the most beautiful sight ever to have appeared under the heavens, the assembly of two hundred virtuous men, worthy of commanding in Rome and of governing the earth."

But let us leap over the distance of place and time and see what has happened in our countries and before our eyes; or rather, let us set aside odious pictures that offend our delicate sensibilities, and spare ourselves the trouble of repeating the same things under different names. It was not in vain that I summoned the shade of Fabricius; and what did I make that great man say that I could not have

---

[xi] Marcus Porcius Cato "the Elder" (243–149 BC) was a highly respected Roman general and statesman, famous for simplicity of virtue.

[xii] Epicurus (341–270 BC), founder of Epicureanism; Zeno of Citium (336–264 BC), founder of Stoicism; and Arcesilaus (316–241 BC), a famous Skeptic.

[xiii] Caius Fabricius Luscinus (d. 250 BC) was a great Roman general.

[xiv] An ambassador of the Thessalian king Pyrrhus.

placed in the mouth of Louis XII or Henry IV? Among us, it is true, Socrates would not have drunk the hemlock; but he would have drunk from a cup more bitter still: the insulting ridicule and scorn that are a hundred times worse than death.

That is how luxury, dissolution and slavery have at all times been the punishment for the arrogant efforts that we have made to leave the happy ignorance where eternal wisdom had placed us. The heavy veil with which she had covered all her operations seemed to give us sufficient warning that she had not destined us for vain inquiries. But is there even one of her lessons from which we have learned to profit, or which we have neglected with impunity? Peoples, know then once and for all that nature wanted to protect you from science just as a mother wrests a dangerous weapon from the hands of her child; that all the secrets she hides from you are so many evils from which she is

protecting you, and that the difficulty you find in teaching yourselves is not the least of her kindnesses. Men are perverse; they would be even worse if they had had the misfortune of being born learned.

How humiliating are these reflections for humanity! How mortified our pride must be! What! Could probity be the daughter of ignorance? Science and virtue incompatible? What consequences might not be drawn from these prejudices? But to reconcile these apparent points of conflict, one need merely examine at close range the vanity and the emptiness of those proud titles which overpower us and which we so gratuitously bestow upon human knowledge. Let us then consider the sciences and the arts in themselves. Let us see what must result from their progress; and let us no longer hesitate to be in agreement on all the points where our reasoning will be found to be in accord with historical inductions.

Author's Notes

1   Princes always view with pleasure the spread, among their subjects, of the taste for pleasant arts and luxuries not resulting in the exporting of money. For, in addition to nurturing in them that pettiness of soul so appropriate to servitude, they know very well that all the needs the populace imposes on itself are so many chains which burden it. Alexander, wishing to keep the Ichthyophagi in a state of dependency, forced them to renounce fishing and to eat foods common to other peoples. And the savages of America who go totally naked and who live off the fruit of their hunting have never been tamed. Indeed, what yoke could be imposed upon men who need nothing?

2   "I love," says Montaigne, "to debate and discuss, but only with a few men and for my own sake. For I find it an especially unworthy profession for a man of honor to serve as a spectacle to the great and shamelessly parade one's mind and one's prattling." It is the profession of all our wits, save one.

3   I dare not speak of those happy nations which do not know even by name the vices that we have so much

trouble repressing, those savages in America whose simple and natural polity Montaigne unhesitatingly prefers not only to Plato's *Laws* but even to everything philosophy could ever imagine as most perfect for the government of peoples. He cites a number of examples that are striking for someone who would know how to admire them. "What!" he says, "why they don't wear pants!" Montaigne, "Of Cannibals," *Essays*, Book I, chapter 31.

4   Will someone honestly tell me what opinion the Athenians themselves must have held regarding eloquence, when they were so fastidious about banning it from that upright tribunal whose judgments the gods themselves did not appeal? What did the Romans think of medicine, when they banished it from their republic? And when a remnant of humanity led the Spanish to forbid their lawyers to enter America, what idea must they have had of jurisprudence? Could it not be said that they believed that by this single act they had made reparation for all the evils they had brought upon those unfortunate Indians?

4

From *The Theory of Moral Sentiments*

Adam Smith

In the same year that Hume died one of the defining works of the modern age was published, *An Inquiry into the Nature and Causes of the Wealth of Nations* (1776), by Hume's fellow Scotsman, Adam Smith (1723–90). The most famous defense of free market capitalism ever written, after two centuries it continues to be at the center of philosophical and social debate. Its central idea, which had been suggested by earlier writers such as Bernard Mandeville, was that the economic progress of society is promoted not by the design of authorities but by the uncoordinated, largely self-interested activities of independent agents, whose competition will tend toward higher and better production at lower prices. Important as it has been to capitalism, this claim supersedes even economics, for the notion of what would later be called "emergent" or "spontaneous order" is arguably central to modernity in general. Contrary to not only classical and medieval thought, but even the Age of Reason (the seventeenth century), Smith accepted that order, even beneficent or virtuous order, need not be the result of planning. The Good is *not* the product of design. In the following selection from his earlier work on moral philosophy, *The Theory of Moral Sentiments* (1759), Smith argues, as did Hume, for the moral importance of "utility" or usefulness, and presented his famous figure of the "invisible hand," through which society, without design, is nevertheless guided toward betterment.

That utility is one of the principal sources of beauty has been observed by every body, who has considered with any attention what constitutes the nature of beauty. The conveniency of a house gives pleasure to the spectator as well as its regularity, and he is as much hurt when he observes the contrary defect, as when he sees the correspondent windows of different forms, or the door not placed exactly in the middle of the building. That the fitness of any system or machine to produce the end for which it was intended, bestows a certain propriety and beauty upon the whole, and renders the very thought and contemplation of it agreeable, is so very obvious that nobody has overlooked it.

The cause too, why utility pleases, has of late been assigned by an ingenious and agreeable philosopher,[i] who joins the greatest depth of thought to the greatest elegance of expression, and possesses the singular and happy talent of treating the abstrusest subjects not only with the most perfect perspicuity, but with the most lively eloquence. The utility of any object, according to him, pleases the master by perpetually suggesting to him the pleasure or conveniency which it is fitted to promote. Every time he looks at it, he is put in mind of this pleasure; and the object in this manner becomes a source of perpetual satisfaction and enjoyment. The spectator enters by sympathy into the sentiments of the master, and necessarily views the object under the same agreeable aspect. When we

[i] David Hume.

Adam Smith, from *The Theory of Moral Sentiments*, Part IV, chapter 1, pp. 179–87 and Part VI, section 2, chapter 2, paras. 15–18, pp. 232–4. Glasgow Edition. Oxford: Oxford University Press, 1976. Paperback by Indianapolis: Liberty Fund, 1984.

visit the palaces of the great, we cannot help conceiving the satisfaction we should enjoy if we ourselves were the masters, and were possessed of so much artful and ingeniously contrived accommodation. A similar account is given why the appearance of inconveniency should render any object disagreeable both to the owner and to the spectator.

But that this fitness, this happy contrivance of any production of art, should often be more valued, than the very end for which it was intended; and that the exact adjustment of the means for attaining any conveniency or pleasure, should frequently be more regarded, than that very conveniency or pleasure, in the attainment of which their whole merit would seem to consist, has not, so far as I know, been yet taken notice of by any body. That this however is very frequently the case, may be observed in a thousand instances, both in the most frivolous and in the most important concerns of human life.

When a person comes into his chamber, and finds the chairs all standing in the middle of the room, he is angry with his servant, and rather than see them continue in that disorder, perhaps takes the trouble himself to set them all in their places with their backs to the wall. The whole propriety of this new situation arises from its superior conveniency in leaving the floor free and disengaged. To attain this conveniency he voluntarily puts himself to more trouble than all he could have suffered from the want of it; since nothing was more easy, than to have set himself down upon one of them, which is probably what he does when his labour is over. What he wanted therefore, it seems, was not so much this conveniency, as that arrangement of things which promotes it. Yet it is this conveniency which ultimately recommends that arrangement, and bestows upon it the whole of its propriety and beauty.

A watch, in the same manner, that falls behind above two minutes in a day, is despised by one curious in watches. He sells it perhaps for a couple of guineas, and purchases another at fifty, which will not lose above a minute in a fortnight. The sole use of watches however, is to tell us what o'clock it is, and to hinder us from breaking any engagement, or suffering any other inconveniency by our ignorance in that particular point. But the person so nice with regard to this machine, will not always be found either more scrupulously punctual than other men, or more anxiously concerned upon any other account, to know precisely what time of day it is. What interests him is not so much the attainment of this piece of knowledge, as the perfection of the machine which serves to attain it.

How many people ruin themselves by laying out money on trinkets of frivolous utility? What pleases these lovers of toys is not so much the utility, as the aptness of the machines which are fitted to promote it. All their pockets are stuffed with little conveniencies. They contrive new pockets, unknown in the clothes of other people, in order to carry a greater number. They walk about loaded with a multitude of baubles, in weight and sometimes in value not inferior to an ordinary Jew's-box,[ii] some of which may sometimes be of some little use, but all of which might at all times be very well spared, and of which the whole utility is certainly not worth the fatigue of bearing the burden.

Nor is it only with regard to such frivolous objects that our conduct is influenced by this principle; it is often the secret motive of the most serious and important pursuits of both private and public life.

The poor man's son, whom heaven in its anger has visited with ambition, when he begins to look around him, admires the condition of the rich. He finds the cottage of his father too small for his accommodation, and fancies he should be lodged more at his ease in a palace. He is displeased with being obliged to walk a-foot, or to endure the fatigue of riding on horseback. He sees his superiors carried about in machines, and imagines that in one of these he could travel with less inconveniency. He feels himself naturally indolent, and willing to serve himself with his own hands as little as possible; and judges, that a numerous retinue of servants would save him from a great deal of trouble. He thinks if he had attained all these, he would sit still contentedly, and be quiet, ejoying himself in the thought of the happiness and tranquillity of his situation. He is enchanted with the distant idea of this felicity. It appears in his fancy like the life of some superior rank of beings, and, in order to arrive at it, he devotes himself for ever to the pursuit of wealth and greatness. To obtain the conveniencies which these afford, he submits in the first year, nay in the first month of his application, to more fatigue of body and more uneasiness of mind than he could have suffered through the whole of his life from the want of them. He studies to distinguish himself in some laborious profession. With the most unrelenting industry he labours night and day to acquire talents superior to all his competitors. He endeavours next to bring those talents into public view, and with equal assiduity solicits every opportunity of employment. For this purpose he makes his

---

[ii] Probably a Jewish pedlar's box of goods.

court to all mankind; he serves those whom he hates, and is obsequious to those whom he despises. Through the whole of his life he pursues the idea of a certain artificial and elegant repose which he may never arrive at, for which he sacrifices a real tranquillity that is at all times in his power, and which, if in the extremity of old age he should at last attain to it, he will find to be in no respect preferable to that humble security and contentment which he had abandoned for it. It is then, in the last dregs of life, his body wasted with toil and diseases, his mind galled and ruffled by the memory of a thousand injuries and disappointments which he imagines he has met with from the injustice of his enemies, or from the perfidy and ingratitude of his friends, that he begins at last to find that wealth and greatness are mere trinkets of frivolous utility, no more adapted for procuring ease of body or tranquillity of mind than the tweezer-cases of the lover of toys; and like them too, more troublesome to the person who carries them about with him than all the advantages they can afford him are commodious. There is no other real difference between them, except that the conveniencies of the one are somewhat more observable than those of the other. The palaces, the gardens, the equipage, the retinue of the great, are objects of which the obvious conveniency strikes every body. They do not require that their masters should point out to us wherein consists their utility. Of our own accord we readily enter into it, and by sympathy enjoy and thereby applaud the satisfaction which they are fitted to afford him. But the curiosity of a tooth-pick, of an ear-picker, of a machine for cutting the nails, or of any other trinket of the same kind, is not so obvious. Their conveniency may perhaps be equally great, but it is not so striking, and we do not so readily enter into the satisfaction of the man who possesses them. They are therefore less reasonable subjects of vanity than the magnificence of wealth and greatness; and in this consists the sole advantage of these last. They more effectually gratify that love of distinction so natural to man. To one who was to live alone in a desolate island it might be a matter of doubt, perhaps, whether a palace, or a collection of such small conveniencies as are commonly contained in a tweezer-case, would contribute most to his happiness and enjoyment. If he is to live in society, indeed, there can be no comparison, because in this, as in all other cases, we constantly pay more regard to the sentiments of the spectator, than to those of the person principally concerned, and consider rather how his situation will appear to other people, than how it will appear to himself. If we examine, however, why the spectator distinguishes with such admiration the condition of the rich and the great, we shall find that it is not so much upon account of the superior ease or pleasure which they are supposed to enjoy, as of the numberless artificial and elegant contrivances for promoting this ease or pleasure. He does not even imagine that they are really happier than other people: but he imagines that they possess more means of happiness. And it is the ingenious and artful adjustment of those means to the end for which they were intended, that is the principal source of his admiration. But in the languor of disease and the weariness of old age, the pleasures of the vain and empty distinctions of greatness disappear. To one, in this situation, they are no longer capable of recommending those toilsome pursuits in which they had formerly engaged him. In his heart he curses ambition, and vainly regrets the ease and the indolence of youth, pleasures which are fled for ever, and which he has foolishly sacrificed for what, when he has got it, can afford him no real satisfaction. In this miserable aspect does greatness appear to every man when reduced either by spleen or disease to observe with attention his own situation, and to consider what it is that is really wanting to his happiness. Power and riches appear then to be, what they are, enormous and operose machines[iii] contrived to produce a few trifling conveniencies to the body, consisting of springs the most nice and delicate, which must be kept in order with the most anxious attention, and which in spite of all our care are ready every moment to burst into pieces, and to crush in their ruins their unfortunate possessor. They are immense fabrics, which it requires the labour of a life to raise, which threaten every moment to overwhelm the person that dwells in them, and which while they stand, though they may save him from some smaller inconveniencies, can protect him from none of the severer inclemencies of the season. They keep off the summer shower, not the winter storm, but leave him always as much, and sometimes more exposed than before, to anxiety, to fear, and to sorrow; to diseases, to danger, and to death.

But though this splenetic philosophy, which in time of sickness or low spirits is familiar to every man, thus entirely depreciates those great objects of human desire, when in better health and in better humour, we never fail to regard them under a more

---

[iii]   "Operose" means laborious.

agreeable aspect. Our imagination, which in pain and sorrow seems to be confined and cooped up within our own persons, in times of ease and prosperity expands itself to every thing around us. We are then charmed with the beauty of that accommodation which reigns in the palaces and economy of the great; and admire how every thing is adapted to promote their ease, to prevent their wants, to gratify their wishes, and to amuse and entertain their most frivolous desires. If we consider the real satisfaction which all these things are capable of affording, by itself and separated from the beauty of that arrangement which is fitted to promote it, it will always appear in the highest degree contemptible and trifling. But we rarely view it in this abstract and philosophical light. We naturally confound it in our imagination with the order, the regular and harmonious movement of the system, the machine or oeconomy by means of which it is produced. The pleasures of wealth and greatness, when considered in this complex view, strike the imagination as something grand and beautiful and noble, of which the attainment is well worth all the toil and anxiety which we are so apt to bestow upon it.

And it is well that nature imposes upon us in this manner. It is this deception which rouses and keeps in continual motion the industry of mankind. It is this which first prompted them to cultivate the ground, to build houses, to found cities and commonwealths, and to invent and improve all the sciences and arts, which ennoble and embellish human life; which have entirely changed the whole face of the globe, have turned the rude forests of nature into agreeable and fertile plains, and made the trackless and barren ocean a new fund of subsistence, and the great high road of communication to the different nations of the earth. The earth by these labours of mankind has been obliged to redouble her natural fertility, and to maintain a greater multitude of inhabitants. It is to no purpose, that the proud and unfeeling landlord views his extensive fields, and without a thought for the wants of his brethren, in imagination consumes himself the whole harvest that grows upon them. The homely and vulgar proverb, that the eye is larger than the belly, never was more fully verified than with regard to him. The capacity of his stomach bears no proportion to the immensity of his desires, and will receive no more than that of the meanest peasant. The rest he is obliged to distribute among those, who prepare, in the nicest manner, that little which he himself makes use of, among those who fit up the palace in which this

little is to be consumed, among those who provide and keep in order all the different baubles and trinkets, which are employed in the oeconomy of greatness; all of whom thus derive from his luxury and caprice, that share of the necessaries of life, which they would in vain have expected from his humanity or his justice. The produce of the soil maintains at all times nearly that number of inhabitants which it is capable of maintaining. The rich only select from the heap what is most precious and agreeable. They consume little more than the poor, and in spite of their natural selfishness and rapacity, though they mean only their own conveniency, though the sole end which they propose from the labours of all the thousands whom they employ, be the gratification of their own vain and insatiable desires, they divide with the poor the produce of all their improvements. They are led by an invisible hand to make nearly the same distribution of the necessaries of life, which would have been made, had the earth been divided into equal portions among all its inhabitants, and thus without intending it, without knowing it, advance the interest of the society, and afford means to the multiplication of the species. When Providence divided the earth among a few lordly masters, it neither forgot nor abandoned those who seemed to have been left out in the partition. These last too enjoy their share of all that it produces. In what constitutes the real happiness of human life, they are in no respect inferior to those who would seem so much above them. In ease of body and peace of mind, all the different ranks of life are nearly upon a level, and the beggar, who suns himself by the side of the highway, possesses that security which kings are fighting for.

The same principle, the same love of system, the same regard to the beauty of order, of art and contrivance, frequently serves to recommend those institutions which tend to promote the public welfare. When a patriot exerts himself for the improvement of any part of the public police, his conduct does not always arise from pure sympathy with the happiness of those who are to reap the benefit of it. It is not commonly from a fellow-feeling with carriers and waggoners that a public-spirited man encourages the mending of high roads. When the legislature establishes premiums and other encouragements to advance the linen or woollen manufactures, its conduct seldom proceeds from pure sympathy with the wearer of cheap or fine cloth, and much less from that with the manufacturer or merchant. The perfection of police, the extension of trade and manufactures, are noble and magnificent objects. The contemplation of them pleases us, and we are interested in whatever can tend to advance them. They make part of the great system of government, and the wheels of the political machine seem to move with more harmony and ease by means of them. We take pleasure in beholding the perfection of so beautiful and grand a system, and we are uneasy till we remove any obstruction that can in the least disturb or encumber the regularity of its motions. All constitutions of government, however, are valued only in proportion as they tend to promote the happiness of those who live under them. This is their sole use and end. From a certain spirit of system, however, from a certain love of art and contrivance, we sometimes seem to value the means more than the end, and to be eager to promote the happiness of our fellow-creatures, rather from a view to perfect and improve a certain beautiful and orderly system, than from any immediate sense or feeling of what they either suffer or enjoy. There have been men of the greatest public spirit, who have shown themselves in other respects not very sensible to the feelings of humanity. And on the contrary, there have been men of the greatest humanity, who seem to have been entirely devoid of public spirit. Every man may find in the circle of his acquaintance instances both of the one kind and the other. Who had ever less humanity, or more public spirit, than the celebrated legislator of Muscovy?[iv] The social and well-natured James the First of Great Britain seems, on the contrary, to have had scarce any passion, either for the glory or the interest of his country. Would you awaken the industry of the man who seems almost dead to ambition, it will often be to no purpose to describe to him the happiness of the rich and the great; to tell him that they are generally sheltered from the sun and the rain, that they are seldom hungry, that they are seldom cold, and that they are rarely exposed to weariness, or to want of any kind. The most eloquent exhortation of this kind will have little effect upon him. If you would hope to succeed, you must describe to him the conveniency and arrangement of the different apartments in their palaces; you must explain to him the propriety of their equipages, and point out to him the number, the order, and the different offices of all their attendants. If any thing is capable of making impression upon

him, this will. Yet all these things tend only to keep off the sun and the rain, to save them from hunger and cold, from want and weariness. In the same manner, if you would implant public virtue in the breast of him who seems heedless of the interest of his country, it will often be to no purpose to tell him, what superior advantages the subjects of a well-governed state enjoy; that they are better lodged, that they are better clothed, that they are better fed. These considerations will commonly make no great impression. You will be more likely to persuade, if you describe the great system of public police which procures these advantages, if you explain the connexions and dependencies of its several parts, their mutual subordination to one another, and their general subserviency to the happiness of the society; if you show how this system might be introduced into his own country, what it is that hinders it from taking place there at present, how those obstructions might be removed, and all the several wheels of the machine of government be made to move with more harmony and smoothness, without grating upon one another, or mutually retarding one another's motions. It is scarce possible that a man should listen to a discourse of this kind, and not feel himself animated to some degree of public spirit. He will, at least for the moment, feel some desire to remove those obstructions, and to put into motion so beautiful and so orderly a machine. Nothing tends so much to promote public spirit as the study of politics, of the several systems of civil government, their advantages and disadvantages, of the constitution of our own country, its situation, and interest with regard to foreign nations, its commerce, its defence, the disadvantages it labours under, the dangers to which it may be exposed, how to remove the one, and how to guard against the other. Upon this account political disquisitions, if just, and reasonable, and practicable, are of all the works of speculation the most useful. Even the weakest and the worst of them are not altogether without their utility. They serve at least to animate the public passions of men, and rouse them to seek out the means of promoting the happiness of the society.

Amidst the turbulence and disorder of faction, a certain spirit of system is apt to mix itself with that public spirit which is founded upon the love of humanity, upon a real fellow-feeling with the inconveniencies and distresses to which some of our fellow-citizens may be exposed. This spirit of system commonly takes the direction of that more

---

[iv] Peter the Great (1672–1725), Russian Czar (from 1682).

gentle public spirit; always animates it, and often inflames it even to the madness of fanaticism. The leaders of the discontented party seldom fail to hold out some plausible plan of reformation which, they pretend, will not only remove the inconveniencies and relieve the distresses immediately complained of, but will prevent, in all time coming, any return of the like inconveniencies and distresses. They often propose, upon this account, to new-model the constitution, and to alter, in some of its most essential parts, that system of government under which the subjects of a great empire have enjoyed, perhaps, peace, security, and even glory, during the course of several centuries together. The great body of the party are commonly intoxicated with the imaginary beauty of this ideal system, of which they have no experience, but which has been represented to them in all the most dazzling colours in which the eloquence of their leaders could paint it. Those leaders themselves, though they originally may have meant nothing but their own aggrandisement, become many of them in time the dupes of their own sophistry, and are as eager for this great reformation as the weakest and foolishest of their followers. Even though the leaders should have preserved their own heads, as indeed they commonly do, free from this fanaticism, yet they dare not always disappoint the expectation of their followers; but are often obliged, though contrary to their principle and their conscience, to act as if they were under the common delusion. The violence of the party, refusing all palliatives, all temperaments, all reasonable accommodations, by requiring too much frequently obtains nothing; and those inconveniencies and distresses which, with a little moderation, might in a great measure have been removed and relieved, are left altogether without the hope of a remedy.

The man whose public spirit is prompted altogether by humanity and benevolence, will respect the established powers and privileges even of individuals, and still more those of the great orders and societies, into which the state is divided. Though he should consider some of them as in some measure abusive, he will content himself with moderating, what he often cannot annihilate without great violence. When he cannot conquer the rooted prejudices of the people by reason and persuasion, he will not attempt to subdue them by force; but will religiously observe what, by Cicero, is justly called the divine maxim of Plato, never to use violence to his country no more than to his parents.[v] He will

accommodate, as well as he can, his public arrangements to the confirmed habits and prejudices of the people; and will remedy as well as he can, the inconveniencies which may flow from the want of those regulations which the people are averse to submit to. When he cannot establish the right, he will not disdain to ameliorate the wrong; but like Solon, when he cannot establish the best system of laws, he will endeavour to establish the best that the people can bear.[vi]

The man of system, on the contrary, is apt to be very wise in his own conceit; and is often so enamoured with the supposed beauty of his own ideal plan of government, that he cannot suffer the smallest deviation from any part of it. He goes on to establish it completely and in all its parts, without any regard either to the great interests, or to the strong prejudices which may oppose it. He seems to imagine that he can arrange the different members of a great society with as much ease as the hand arranges the different pieces upon a chess-board. He does not consider that the pieces upon the chess-board have no other principle of motion besides that which the hand impresses upon them; but that, in the great chess-board of human society, every single piece has a principle of motion of its own, altogether different from that which the legislature might chuse to impress upon it. If those two principles coincide and act in the same direction, the game of human society will go on easily and harmoniously, and is very likely to be happy and successful. If they are opposite or different, the game will go on miserably, and the society must be at all times in the highest degree of disorder.

Some general, and even systematical, idea of the perfection of policy and law, may no doubt be necessary for directing the views of the statesman. But to insist upon establishing, and upon establishing all at once, and in spite of all opposition, every thing which that idea may seem to require, must often be the highest degree of arrogance. It is to erect his own judgment into the supreme standard of right and wrong. It is to fancy himself the only wise and worthy man in the commonwealth, and that his fellow-citizens should accommodate themselves to him and not he to them. It is upon this account, that of all political speculators, sovereign princes are by far the most dangerous. This

---

[v] Marcus Tullius Cicero (106–143 BC), the great Roman writer, citing Plato's remark from the *Crito* (51C) that country is to be honored even above parents.
[vi] Solon (630–560 BC), Athenion statesman.

Adam Smith

arrogance is perfectly familiar to them. They entertain no doubt of the immense superiority of their own judgment. When such imperial and royal reformers, therefore, condescend to contemplate the constitution of the country which is committed to their government, they seldom see any thing so wrong in it as the obstructions which it may sometimes oppose to the execution of their own will. They hold in contempt the divine maxim of Plato, and consider the state as made for themselves, not themselves for the state. The great object of their reformation, therefore, is to remove those obstructions; to reduce the authority of the nobility; to take away the privileges of cities and provinces, and to render both the greatest individuals and the greatest orders of the state, as incapable of opposing their commands, as the weakest and most insignificant.

5

"An Answer to the Question: 'What is Enlightenment?' "
From the Preface to *Critique of Pure Reason*

Immanuel Kant

Immanuel Kant (1724–1804), perhaps the greatest modern philosopher, was deeply inspired by Rousseau. What Kant took from Rousseau was not the latter's critique of modernity, but his notion of freedom as autonomy or self-legislation, the belief that human dignity requires humans to make the laws that they themselves must obey. In the famous 1784 essay that follows he defines the meaning of the Enlightenment with the Horatian motto, *Sapere Aude*, "Think for yourself." Characteristic of the German Enlightenment (the *Aufklärung*), he recognized the threat that the modern scientific view of the world posed to morality and religion. His solution in the *Critique of Pure Reason* (1781) changed philosophy forever: just as Copernicus shifted the Sun to the center of our universe, displacing the Earth from its Ptolemaic, geocentric home, Kant argued that rather than our knowledge conforming to objects, experienced objects conform to our ways of knowing. The order of our reality is constructed, contributed, by our own minds. Thus *a priori* knowledge *of appearances* is safe from Hume's critique, since experience *necessarily* conforms to our cognitive apparatus. But this also means, following Hume, that knowledge of "things in themselves," independent of how they appear to our senses, is permanently unavailable. Thus could contemporary Moses Mendelsohn call Kant "the great destroyer."

"An Answer to the Question: 'What is Enlightenment?' "

Enlightenment is man's emergence from his self-incurred immaturity. Immaturity is the inability to use one's own understanding without the guidance of another. This immaturity is *self-incurred* if its cause is not lack of understanding, but lack of resolution and courage to use it without the guidance of another. The motto of enlightenment is therefore: *Sapere aude!*[i] Have courage to use your *own* understanding!

Laziness and cowardice are the reasons why such a large proportion of men, even when nature has long emancipated them from alien guidance (*naturaliter maiorennes*),[ii] nevertheless gladly remain immature

---

[i] From Horace, literally, "Dare to be wise."
[ii] "Those who have come of age by virtue of nature."

Immanuel Kant: [A] "An Answer to the Question: What is Enlightenment?" (trans. H. B. Nisbet, ed. Hans Reiss), pp. 54–60 from *Kant's Political Writings*. Cambridge: Cambridge University Press, 1970; [B] from "Preface to the Second Edition" of *Critique of Pure Reason* (trans. Norman Kerry Smith), New York: St. Martin's Press, 1965, Bvii–Bxxii, pp. 17–25.

for life. For the same reasons, it is all too easy for others to set themselves up as their guardians. It is so convenient to be immature! If I have a book to have understanding in place of me, a spiritual adviser to have a conscience for me, a doctor to judge my diet for me, and so on, I need not make any efforts at all. I need not think, so long as I can pay; others will soon enough take the tiresome job over for me. The guardians who have kindly taken upon themselves the work of supervision will soon see to it that by far the largest part of mankind (including the entire fair sex) should consider the step forward to maturity not only as difficult but also as highly dangerous. Having first infatuated their domesticated animals, and carefully prevented the docile creatures from daring to take a single step without the leading-strings to which they are tied, they next show them the danger which threatens them if they try to walk unaided. Now this danger is not in fact so very great, for they would certainly learn to walk eventually after a few falls. But an example of this kind is intimidating, and usually frightens them off from further attempts.

Thus it is difficult for each separate individual to work his way out of the immaturity which has become almost second nature to him. He has even grown fond of it and is really incapable for the time being of using his own understanding, because he was never allowed to make the attempt. Dogmas and formulas, those mechanical instruments for rational use (or rather misuse) of his natural endowments, are the ball and chain of his permanent immaturity. And if anyone did throw them off, he would still be uncertain about jumping over even the narrowest of trenches, for he would be unaccustomed to free movement of this kind. Thus only a few, by cultivating their own minds, have succeeded in freeing themselves from immaturity and in continuing boldly on their way.

There is more chance of an entire public enlightening itself. This is indeed almost inevitable, if only the public concerned is left in freedom. For there will always be a few who think for themselves, even among those appointed as guardians of the common mass. Such guardians, once they have themselves thrown off the yoke of immaturity, will disseminate the spirit of rational respect for personal value and for the duty of all men to think for themselves. The remarkable thing about this is that if the public, which was previously put under this yoke by the guardians, is suitably stirred up by some of the latter who are incapable of enlightenment, it may subsequently compel the guardians themselves to remain under the yoke. For it is very harmful to propagate prejudices, because they finally avenge themselves on the very people who first encouraged them (or whose predecessors did so). Thus a public can only achieve enlightenment slowly. A revolution may well put an end to autocratic despotism and to rapacious or power-seeking oppression, but it will never produce a true reform in ways of thinking. Instead, new prejudices, like the ones they replaced, will serve as a leash to control the great unthinking mass.

For enlightenment of this kind, all that is needed is *freedom*. And the freedom in question is the most innocuous form of all – freedom to make *public use* of one's reason in all matters. But I hear on all sides the cry: *Don't argue!* The officer says: Don't argue, get on parade! The tax-official: Don't argue, pay! The clergyman: Don't argue, believe! (Only one ruler in the world says: *Argue* as much as you like and about whatever you like, *but obey!*)[iii] All this means restrictions on freedom everywhere. But which sort of restriction prevents enlightenment, and which, instead of hindering it, can actually promote it? I reply: The *public* use of man's reason must always be free, and it alone can bring about enlightenment among men; the *private use* of reason may quite often be very narrowly restricted, however, without undue hindrance to the progress of enlightenment. But by the public use of one's own reason I mean that use which anyone may make of it *as a man of learning* addressing the entire *reading public*. What I term the private use of reason is that which a person may make of it in a particular *civil* post or office with which he is entrusted.

Now in some affairs which affect the interests of the commonwealth, we require a certain mechanism whereby some members of the commonwealth must behave purely passively, so that they may, by an artificial common agreement, be employed by the government for public ends (or at least deterred from vitiating them). It is, of course, impermissible to argue in such cases; obedience is imperative. But in so far as this or that individual who acts as part of the machine also considers himself as a member of a complete commonwealth or even of cosmopolitan society, and thence as a man of learning who may through his writings address a public in the truest sense of the word, he may indeed argue without harming the affairs in which he is employed for some of the time in a passive capacity. Thus it would be very harmful if an officer receiving an

---

iii Frederick II, also called "the Great" (1712–86), King of Prussia from 1740 to 1786.

order from his superiors were to quibble openly, while on duty, about the appropriateness or usefulness of the order in question. He must simply obey. But he cannot reasonably be banned from making observations as a man of learning on the errors in the military service, and from submitting these to his public for judgement. The citizen cannot refuse to pay the taxes imposed upon him; presumptuous criticisms of such taxes, where someone is called upon to pay them, may be punished as an outrage which could lead to general insubordination. Nonetheless, the same citizen does not contravene his civil obligations if, as a learned individual, he publicly voices his thoughts on the impropriety or even injustice of such fiscal measures. In the same way, a clergyman is bound to instruct his pupils and his congregation in accordance with the doctrines of the church he serves, for he was employed by it on that condition. But as a scholar, he is completely free as well as obliged to impart to the public all his carefully considered, well-intentioned thoughts on the mistaken aspects of those doctrines, and to offer suggestions for a better arrangement of religious and ecclesiastical affairs. And there is nothing in this which need trouble the conscience. For what he teaches in pursuit of his duties as an active servant of the church is presented by him as something which he is not empowered to teach at his own discretion, but which he is employed to expound in a prescribed manner and in someone else's name. He will say: Our church teaches this or that, and these are the arguments it uses. He then extracts as much practical value as possible for his congregation from precepts to which he would not himself subscribe with full conviction, but which he can nevertheless undertake to expound, since it is not in fact wholly impossible that they may contain truth. At all events, nothing opposed to the essence of religion is present in such doctrines. For if the clergyman thought he could find anything of this sort in them, he would not be able to carry out his official duties in good conscience, and would have to resign. Thus the use which someone employed as a teacher makes of his reason in the presence of his congregation is purely *private*, since a congregation, however large it is, is never any more than a domestic gathering. In view of this, he is not and cannot be free as a priest, since he is acting on a commission imposed from outside. Conversely, as a scholar addressing the real public (i.e. the world at large) through his writings, the clergyman making *public use* of his reason enjoys unlimited freedom to use his own reason and to speak in his own person. For to maintain that the guardians of the people in spiritual matters should themselves be immature, is an absurdity which amounts to making absurdities permanent.

But should not a society of clergymen, for example an ecclesiastical synod or a venerable presbytery (as the Dutch call it), be entitled to commit itself by oath to a certain unalterable set of doctrines, in order to secure for all time a constant guardianship over each of its members, and through them over the people? I reply that this is quite impossible. A contract of this kind, concluded with a view to preventing all further enlightenment of mankind for ever, is absolutely null and void, even if it is ratified by the supreme power, by Imperial Diets[iv] and the most solemn peace treaties. One age cannot enter into an alliance on oath to put the next age in a position where it would be impossible for it to extend and correct its knowledge, particularly on such important matters, or to make any progress whatsoever in enlightenment. This would be a crime against human nature, whose original destiny lies precisely in such progress. Later generations are thus perfectly entitled to dismiss these agreements as unauthorised and criminal. To test whether any particular measure can be agreed upon as a law for a people, we need only ask whether a people could well impose such a law upon itself. This might well be possible for a specified short period as a means of introducing a certain order, pending, as it were, a better solution. This would also mean that each citizen, particularly the clergyman, would be given a free hand as a scholar to comment publicly, i.e. in his writings, on the inadequacies of current institutions. Meanwhile, the newly established order would continue to exist, until public insight into the nature of such matters had progressed and proved itself to the point where, by general consent (if not unanimously), a proposal could be submitted to the crown. This would seek to protect the congregations who had, for instance, agreed to alter their religious establishment in accordance with their own notions of what higher insight is, but it would not try to obstruct those who wanted to let things remain as before. But it is absolutely impermissible to agree, even for a single lifetime, to a permanent religious constitution which no-one might publicly question. For this would virtually nullify a phase in man's upward progress, thus making it fruitless and even detrimental to subsequent generations. A man may for his own person, and even then only for a

iv A diet is a legislative assembly.

limited period, postpone enlightening himself in matters he ought to know about. But to renounce such enlightenment completely, whether for his own person or even more so for later generations, means violating and trampling underfoot the sacred rights of mankind. But something which a people may not even impose upon itself can still less be imposed on it by a monarch; for his legislative authority depends precisely upon his uniting the collective will of the people in his own. So long as he sees to it that all true or imagined improvements are compatible with the civil order, he can otherwise leave his subjects to do whatever they find necessary for this salvation, which is none of his business. But it is his business to stop anyone forcibly hindering others from working as best they can to define and promote their salvation. It indeed detracts from his majesty if he interferes in these affairs by subjecting the writings in which his subjects attempt to clarify their religious ideas to governmental supervision. This applies if he does so acting upon his own exalted opinions – in which case he exposes himself to the reproach: *Caesar non est supra Grammaticos*[v] – but much more so if he demeans his high authority so far as to support the spiritual despotism of a few tyrants within his state against the rest of his subjects.

If it is now asked whether we at present live in an *enlightened* age, the answer is: No, but we do live in an age of *enlightenment*. As things are at present, we still have a long way to go before men as a whole can be in a position (or can even be put into a position) of using their own understanding confidently and well in religious matters, without outside guidance. But we do have distinct indications that the way is now being cleared for them to work freely in this direction, and that the obstacles to universal enlightenment, to man's emergence from his self-incurred immaturity, are gradually becoming fewer. In this respect our age is the age of enlightenment, the century, of *Frederick*.[vi]

A prince who does not regard it as beneath him to say that he considers it his duty, in religious matters, not to prescribe anything to his people, but to allow them complete freedom, a prince who thus even declines to accept the presumptuous title of *tolerant*, is himself enlightened. He deserves to be praised by a grateful present and posterity as the man who first liberated mankind from immaturity (as far as government is concerned), and who left all men free to use their own reason in all matters of

conscience. Under his rule, ecclesiastical dignitaries, notwithstanding their official duties, may in their capacity as scholars freely and publicly submit to the judgement of the world their verdicts and opinions, even if these deviate here and there from orthodox doctrine. This applies even more to all others who are not restricted by any official duties. This spirit of freedom is also spreading abroad, even where it has to struggle with outward obstacles imposed by governments which misunderstand their own function. For such governments can now witness a shining example of how freedom may exist without in the least jeopardising public concord and the unity of the commonwealth. Men will of their own accord gradually work their way out of barbarism so long as artificial measures are not deliberately adopted to keep them in it.

I have portrayed *matters of religion* as the focal point of enlightenment, i.e. of man's emergence from his self-incurred immaturity. This is firstly because our rulers have no interest in assuming the role of guardians over their subjects so far as the arts and sciences are concerned, and secondly, because religious immaturity is the most pernicious and dishonourable variety of all. But the attitude of mind of a head of state who favours freedom in the arts and sciences extends even further, for he realises that there is no danger even to his *legislation* if he allows his subjects to make *public* use of their own reason and to put before the public their thoughts on better ways of drawing up laws, even if this entails forthright criticism of the current legislation. We have before us a brilliant example of this kind, in which no monarch has yet surpassed the one to whom we now pay tribute.

But only a ruler who is himself enlightened and has no fear of phantoms, yet who likewise has at hand a well-disciplined and numerous army to guarantee public security, may say what no republic would dare to say: *Argue as much as you like and about whatever you like, but obey!* This reveals to us a strange and unexpected pattern in human affairs (such as we shall always find if we consider them in the widest sense, in which nearly everything is paradoxical). A high degree of civil freedom seems advantageous to a people's *intellectual* freedom, yet it also sets up insuperable barriers to it. Conversely, a lesser degree of civil freedom gives intellectual freedom enough room to expand to its fullest extent. Thus once the germ on which nature has lavished most care – man's inclination and vocation to *think freely* – has developed within this hard shell, it gradually reacts upon the mentality of the

---

[v] "Caesar is not above the grammarians."
[vi] Again, Frederick the Great.

people, who thus gradually become increasingly able to *act freely*. Eventually, it even influences the principles of governments, which find that

they can themselves profit by treating man, who is *more than a machine*, in a manner appropriate to his dignity.[1]

Author's Note

1 I read today on the 30th September in Büsching's *Wöchentliche Nachrichten* of 13th September a notice concerning this month's *Berlinische Monatsschrift*. The notice mentions Mendelssohn's answer to the same question as that which I have answered. I have not yet seen this journal, otherwise I should have held back the above reflections. I let them stand only as a means of finding out by comparison how far the thoughts of two individuals may coincide by chance. [Moses Mendelssohn (1729–86) published an essay, "*über die Frage: was heisst Aufklärung?*" ("On the Question: What is Enlightenment"), in 1784.]

Preface to *Critique of Pure Reason*

Whether the treatment of such knowledge as lies within the province of reason does or does not follow the secure path of a science, is easily to be determined from the outcome. For if after elaborate preparations, frequently renewed, it is brought to a stop immediately it nears its goal; if often it is compelled to retrace its steps and strike into some new line of approach; or again, if the various participants are unable to agree in any common plan of procedure, then we may rest assured that it is very far from having entered upon the secure path of a science, and is indeed a merely random groping. In these circumstances, we shall be rendering a service to reason should we succeed in discovering the path upon which it can securely travel, even if, as a result of so doing, much that is comprised in our original aims, adopted without reflection, may have to be abandoned as fruitless.

That logic has already, from the earliest times, proceeded upon this sure path is evidenced by the fact that since Aristotle it has not required to retrace a single step, unless, indeed, we care to count as improvements the removal of certain needless subtleties or the clearer exposition of its recognised teaching, features which concern the elegance rather than the certainty of the science. It is remarkable also that to the present day this logic has not been able to advance a single step, and is thus to all appearance a closed and completed body of doctrine. If some of

the moderns have thought to enlarge it by introducing *psychological* chapters on the different faculties of knowledge (imagination, wit, etc.), *metaphysical* chapters on the origin of knowledge or on the different kinds of certainty according to difference in the objects (idealism, scepticism, etc.), or *anthropological* chapters on prejudices, their causes and remedies, this could only arise from their ignorance of the peculiar nature of logical science. We do not enlarge but disfigure sciences, if we allow them to trespass upon one another's territory. The sphere of logic is quite precisely delimited; its sole concern is to give an exhaustive exposition and a strict proof of the formal rules of all thought, whether it be *a priori* or empirical, whatever be its origin or its object, and whatever hindrances, accidental or natural, it may encounter in our minds.[i]

That logic should have been thus successful is an advantage which it owes entirely to its limitations, whereby it is justified in abstracting – indeed, it is under obligation to do so – from all objects of knowledge and their differences, leaving the understanding nothing to deal with save itself and its form. But for reason to enter on the sure path of science is, of course, much more difficult, since it has to deal not with itself alone but also with objects. Logic, therefore, as a propaedeutic, forms, as it were, only the vestibule of the sciences; and when we are concerned with specific modes of knowledge, while logic is indeed presupposed in any critical estimate of them, yet for the actual acquiring of them we have to look to the sciences properly and objectively so called.

Now if reason is to be a factor in these sciences, something in them must be known *a priori*, and this knowledge may be related to its object in one or other of two ways, either as merely *determining* it and its concept (which must be supplied from elsewhere) or as also *making it actual*. The former is *theoretical*, the latter *practical* knowledge of reason. In both, that part in which reason determines its

---

i   *A priori* knowledge is justified independent of experience ("prior" to it), hence is universally and necessarily true, unlike *a posteriori* or "empirical" knowledge whose justification is experiential ("after" experience).

object completely *a priori*, namely, the *pure* part – however much or little this part may contain – must be first and separately dealt with, in case it be confounded with what comes from other sources. For it is bad management if we blindly pay out what comes in, and are not able, when the income falls into arrears, to distinguish which part of it can justify expenditure, and in which line we must make reductions.

Mathematics and physics, the two sciences in which reason yields theoretical knowledge, have to determine their objects *a priori*, the former doing so quite purely, the latter having to reckon, at least partially, with sources of knowledge other than reason.

In the earliest times to which the history of human reason extends, *mathematics*, among that wonderful people, the Greeks, had already entered upon the sure path of science. But it must not be supposed that it was as easy for mathematics as it was for logic – in which reason has to deal with itself alone – to light upon, or rather to construct for itself, that royal road. On the contrary, I believe that it long remained, especially among the Egyptians, in the groping stage, and that the transformation must have been due to a *revolution* brought about by the happy thought of a single man, the experiment which he devised marking out the path upon which the science must enter, and by following which, secure progress throughout all time and in endless expansion is infallibly secured. The history of this intellectual revolution – far more important than the discovery of the passage round the celebrated Cape of Good Hope – and of its fortunate author, has not been preserved. But the fact that Diogenes Laertius,[ii] in handing down an account of these matters, names the reputed author of even the least important among the geometrical demonstrations, even of those which, for ordinary consciousness, stand in need of no such proof, does at least show that the memory of the revolution, brought about by the first glimpse of this new path, must have seemed to mathematicians of such outstanding importance as to cause it to survive the tide of oblivion. A new light flashed upon the mind of the first man (be he Thales or some other)[iii] who demonstrated the properties of the isosceles triangle. The true method, so he found, was not to

inspect what he discerned either in the figure, or in the bare concept of it, and from this, as it were, to read off its properties; but to bring out what was necessarily implied in the concepts that he had himself formed *a priori*, and had put into the figure in the construction by which he presented it to himself. If he is to know anything with *a priori* certainty he must not ascribe to the figure anything save what necessarily follows from what he has himself set into it in accordance with his concept.

Natural science was very much longer in entering upon the highway of science. It is, indeed, only about a century and a half since Bacon, by his ingenious proposals, partly initiated this discovery, partly inspired fresh vigour in those who were already on the way to it. In this case also the discovery can be explained as being the sudden outcome of an intellectual revolution. In my present remarks I am referring to natural science only in so far as it is founded on *empirical* principles.

When Galileo caused balls, the weights of which he had himself previously determined, to roll down an inclined plane; when Torricelli made the air carry a weight which he had calculated beforehand to be equal to that of a definite volume of water; or in more recent times, when Stahl changed metals into oxides, and oxides back into metal, by withdrawing something and then restoring it,[1] a light broke upon all students of nature.[iv] They learned that reason has insight only into that which it produces after a plan of its own, and that it must not allow itself to be kept, as it were, in nature's leading-strings, but must itself show the way with principles of judgment based upon fixed laws, constraining nature to give answer to questions of reason's own determining. Accidental observations, made in obedience to no previously thought-out plan, can never be made to yield a necessary law, which alone reason is concerned to discover. Reason, holding in one hand its principles, according to which alone concordant appearances can be admitted as equivalent to laws, and in the other hand the experiment which it has devised in conformity with these principles, must approach nature in order to be taught by it. It must not, however, do so in the character of a pupil who listens to everything that the teacher chooses to say, but of an appointed judge who compels the witnesses to answer questions which he has himself formulated. Even physics, therefore, owes the

---

[ii]   The third century AD Greek author of *Lives, Teachings, and Sayings of Famous Philosophers*.
[iii]   Thales of Miletus, 6th century BC Greek philosopher.

[iv]   George Ernst Stahl (1660–1734), German chemist and physician who developed the "phlogiston" theory.

beneficent revolution in its point of view entirely to the happy thought, that while reason must seek in nature, not fictitiously ascribe to it, whatever as not being knowable through reason's own resources has to be learnt, if learnt at all, only from nature, it must adopt as its guide, in so seeking, that which it has itself put into nature. It is thus that the study of nature has entered on the secure path of a science, after having for so many centuries been nothing but a process of merely random groping.

Metaphysics is a completely isolated speculative science of reason, which soars far above the teachings of experience, and in which reason is indeed meant to be its own pupil. Metaphysics rests on concepts alone – not, like mathematics, on their application to intuition.[v] But though it is older than all other sciences, and would survive even if all the rest were swallowed up in the abyss of an all-destroying barbarism, it has not yet had the good fortune to enter upon the secure path of a science. For in it reason is perpetually being brought to a stand, even when the laws into which it is seeking to have, as it professes, an *a priori* insight are those that are confirmed by our most common experiences. Ever and again we have to retrace our steps, as not leading us in the direction in which we desire to go. So far, too, are the students of metaphysics from exhibiting any kind of unanimity in their contentions, that metaphysics has rather to be regarded as a battle-ground quite peculiarly suited for those who desire to exercise themselves in mock combats, and in which no participant has ever yet succeeded in gaining even so much as an inch of territory, not at least in such manner as to secure him in its permanent possession. This shows, beyond all questioning, that the procedure of metaphysics has hitherto been a merely random groping, and, what is worst of all, a groping among mere concepts.

What, then, is the reason why, in this field, the sure road to science has not hitherto been found? Is it, perhaps, impossible of discovery? Why, in that case, should nature have visited our reason with the restless endeavour whereby it is ever searching for such a path, as if this were one of its most important concerns? Nay, more, how little cause have we to place trust in our reason, if, in one of the most important domains of which we would fain have knowledge, it does not merely fail us, but lures us on by deceitful promises, and in the end betrays us! Or if it be only that we have thus far failed to find the true path, are there any indications to justify the hope that by renewed efforts we may have better fortune than has fallen to our predecessors?

The examples of mathematics and natural science, which by a single and sudden revolution have become what they now are, seem to me sufficiently remarkable to suggest our considering what may have been the essential features in the changed point of view by which they have so greatly benefited. Their success should incline us, at least by way of experiment, to imitate their procedure, so far as the analogy which, as species of rational knowledge, they bear to metaphysics may permit. Hitherto it has been assumed that all our knowledge must conform to objects. But all attempts to extend our knowledge of objects by establishing something in regard to them *a priori*, by means of concepts, have, on this assumption, ended in failure. We must therefore make trial whether we may not have more success in the tasks of metaphysics, if we suppose that objects must conform to our knowledge. This would agree better with what is desired, namely, that it should be possible to have knowledge of objects *a priori*, determining something in regard to them prior to their being given. We should then be proceeding precisely on the lines of Copernicus' primary hypothesis.[vi] Failing of satisfactory progress in explaining the movements of the heavenly bodies on the supposition that they all revolved round the spectator, he tried whether he might not have better success if he made the spectator to revolve and the stars to remain at rest. A similar experiment can be tried in metaphysics, as regards the *intuition* of objects. If intuition must conform to the constitution of the objects, I do not see how we could know anything of the latter *a priori*; but if the object (as object of the senses) must conform to the constitution of our faculty of intuition, I have no difficulty in conceiving such a possibility. Since I cannot rest in these intuitions if they are to become known, but must relate them as representations to something as their object, and determine this latter through them, either I must assume that the *concepts*, by means of which I obtain this determination, conform to the object, or else I

---

[v]   Intuition is the faculty of sensibility, which receives sensations, while the understanding (*Verstand*) thinks them through concepts.

[vi]   Nicholas Copernicus (1473–1543), Polish astronomer who proposed the modern heliocentric model of the solar system. Kant is comparing his own reversal of the accepted roles of knower and the known to Copernicus' reversal of Sun and Earth.

assume that the objects, or what is the same thing, that the *experience* in which alone, as given objects, they can be known, conform to the concepts. In the former case, I am again in the same perplexity as to how I can know anything *a priori* in regard to the objects. In the latter case the outlook is more hopeful. For experience is itself a species of knowledge which involves understanding; and understanding has rules which I must presuppose as being in me prior to objects being given to me, and therefore as being *a priori*. They find expression in *a priori* concepts to which all objects of experience necessarily conform, and with which they must agree. As regards objects which are thought solely through reason, and indeed as necessary, but which can never – at least not in the manner in which reason thinks them – be given in experience, the attempts at thinking them (for they must admit of being thought) will furnish an excellent touchstone of what we are adopting as our new method of thought, namely, that we can know *a priori* of things only what we ourselves put into them.[2]

This experiment succeeds as well as could be desired, and promises to metaphysics, in its first part – the part that is occupied with those concepts *a priori* to which the corresponding objects, commensurate with them, can be given in experience – the secure path of a science. For the new point of view enables us to explain how there can be knowledge *a priori*; and, in addition, to furnish satisfactory proofs of the laws which form the *a priori* basis of nature, regarded as the sum of the objects of experience – neither achievement being possible on the procedure hitherto followed. But this deduction of our power of knowing *a priori*, in the first part of metaphysics, has a consequence which is startling, and which has the appearance of being highly prejudicial to the whole purpose of metaphysics, as dealt with in the second part. For we are brought to the conclusion that we can never transcend the limits of possible experience, though that is precisely what this science is concerned, above all

else, to achieve. This situation yields, however, just the very experiment by which, indirectly, we are enabled to prove the truth of this first estimate of our *a priori* knowledge of reason, namely, that such knowledge has to do only with appearances, and must leave the thing in itself[3] as indeed real *per se*, but as not known by us. For what necessarily forces us to transcend the limits of experience and of all appearances is the *unconditioned*, which reason, by necessity and by right, demands in things in themselves, as required to complete the series of conditions. If, then, on the supposition that our empirical knowledge conforms to objects as things in themselves, we find that the unconditioned *cannot be thought without contradiction*, and that when, on the other hand, we suppose that our representation of things, as they are given to us, does not conform to these things as they are in themselves, but that these objects, as appearances, conform to our mode of representation, *the contradiction vanishes*; and if, therefore, we thus find that the unconditioned is not to be met with in things, so far as we know them, that is, so far as they are given to us, but only so far as we do not know them, that is, so far as they are things in themselves, we are justified in concluding that what we at first assumed for the purposes of experiment is now definitely confirmed.[4] But when all progress in the field of the supersensible has thus been denied to speculative reason, it is still open to us to enquire whether, in the practical knowledge of reason, data may not be found sufficient to determine reason's transcendent concept of the unconditioned, and so to enable us, in accordance with the wish of metaphysics, and by means of knowledge that is possible *a priori*, though only from a practical point of view, to pass beyond the limits of all possible experience. Speculative reason has thus at least made room for such an extension; and if it must at the same time leave it empty, yet none the less we are at liberty, indeed we are summoned, to take occupation of it, if we can, by practical data of reason. . . .

Author's Notes

[These Author's Notes appear unnumbered at the bottom of the page in the original.]

1 I am not, in my choice of examples, tracing the exact course of the history of the experimental method; we have indeed no very precise knowledge of its first beginnings.

2 This method, modelled on that of the student of nature, consists in looking for the elements of pure reason in *what admits of confirmation or refutation by experiment*. Now the propositions of pure reason, especially if they venture out beyond all limits of possible experience, cannot be brought to the test through any experiment with their *objects*, as in nat-

ural science. In dealing with those *concepts* and *principles* which we adopt *a priori*, all that we can do is to contrive that they be used for viewing objects from two different points of view – on the one hand, in connection with experience, as objects of the senses and of the understanding, and on the other hand, for the isolated reason that strives to transcend all limits of experience, as objects which are thought merely. If, when things are viewed from this twofold standpoint, we find that there is agreement with the principle of pure reason, but that when we regard them only from a single point of view reason is involved in unavoidable self-conflict, the experiment decides in favour of the correctness of this distinction.

3 This experiment of pure reason bears a great similarity to what in chemistry is sometimes entitled the experiment of *reduction*, or more usually the *synthetic* process. The *analysis of the metaphysician* separates pure *a priori* knowledge into two very heterogeneous elements, namely, the knowledge of things as appearances, and the knowledge of things in themselves; his *dialectic* combines these two again, in *harmony* with the necessary idea of the *unconditioned* demanded by reason, and finds that this harmony can never be obtained except through the above distinction, which must therefore be accepted.

4 Similarly, the fundamental laws of the motions of the heavenly bodies gave established certainty to what Copernicus had at first assumed only as an hypothesis, and at the same time yielded proof of the invisible force (the Newtonian attraction), which holds the universe together. The latter would have remained for ever undiscovered if Copernicus had not dared, in a manner contradictory of the senses, but yet true, to seek the observed movements, not in the heavenly bodies, but in the spectator. The change in point of view, analogous to this hypothesis, which is expounded in the *Critique*, I put forward in this preface as an hypothesis only, in order to draw attention to the character of these first attempts at such a change, which are always hypothetical. But in the *Critique* itself it will be proved, apodeictically not hypothetically, from the nature of our representations of space and time and from the elementary concepts of the understanding.

6

From *Reflections on the Revolution in France*

Edmund Burke

The French Revolution seemed to many to embody the new ideals of modern, Enlightened culture, while to others it threatened a new barbarism. Edmund Burke (1729–97), Irish by birth and a member of the English Parliament, provides us with the most famous critique of revolutionary modernity. His *Reflections on the Revolution in France* (1790), a letter to a French correspondent, was inspired by several events: the arrest of the royal family of France by a mob on October 6, 1789; the seizure of all Church property by the French republic; and closer to home, a sermon by an Englishman, Dr Richard Price of the Revolution Society, endorsing the principles of the French Revolution for England. (All of this was years before the worst revolutionary violence in France, the "Terror.") Critical of the modern attempt to replace traditional social arrangements with abstract principles like equality and individual rights, Burke's work remains the classical source of true conservatism. But his traditionalism is no simple authoritarianism; Burke supported Irish and American independence from Great Britain because he felt that the Crown had abused the traditionally recognized rights of Ireland and the American colonies. He likewise approved the 1688 revolution of the English Parliament against James II as a conservative revolution aimed at restoring the traditional distribution of power which the King had disturbed.

But I may say of our preacher "*utinam nugis tota illa dedisset tempora saevitiae*".[i] – All things in this his fulminating bull are not of so innoxious a tendency. His doctrines affect our constitution in its vital parts.

He tells the Revolution Society in this political sermon that this Majesty "is almost the *only* lawful king in the world because the *only* one who owes his crown to the *choice of his people*". As to the kings of *the world*, all of whom (except one) this archpontiff of the *rights of men*, with all the plenitude and with more than the boldness of the papal deposing power in its meridian fervor of the twelfth century, puts into one sweeping clause of ban and anathema and proclaims usurpers by circles of longitude and latitude, over the whole globe, it behooves them to consider how they admit into their territories these apostolic missionaries who are to tell their subjects they are not lawful kings. That is their concern. It is ours, as a domestic interest of some moment, seriously to consider the solidity of the *only* principle upon which these gentlemen acknowledge a king of Great Britain to be entitled to their allegiance.

This doctrine, as applied to the prince now on the British throne, either is nonsense and therefore neither true nor false, or it affirms a most unfounded, dangerous, illegal, and unconstitutional position. According to this spiritual doctor of politics, if his Majesty does not owe his crown to the choice of his people, he is no *lawful king*. Now

[i] "Would that he had devoted to trifles all the time he spent in violence." Juvenal, *Satires*, IV, 150–1. The preacher is Dr Richard Price.

Edmund Burke, a selection of unmarked sections, in each case separated by space in the text, from *Reflections on the Revolution in France* (ed. J. G. A. Pocock), pp. 12–19, 25–6, 29–31, 51–2, 76–7, 216–18. Indianapolis: Hackett Publishing Company Inc., 1987.

nothing can be more untrue than that the crown of this kingdom is so held by his Majesty. Therefore, if you follow their rule, the king of Great Britain, who most certainly does not owe his high office to any form of popular election, is in no respect better than the rest of the gang of usurpers who reign, or rather rob, all over the face of this our miserable world without any sort of right or title to the allegiance of their people. The policy of this general doctrine, so qualified, is evident enough. The propagators of this political gospel are in hopes that their abstract principle (their principle that a popular choice is necessary to the legal existence of the sovereign magistracy) would be overlooked, whilst the king of Great Britain was not affected by it. In the meantime the ears of their congregations would be gradually habituated to it, as if it were a first principle admitted without dispute. For the present it would only operate as a theory, pickled in the preserving juices of pulpit eloquence, and laid by for future use. *Condo et compono quae mox depromere possim.*[ii] By this policy, whilst our government is soothed with a reservation in its favor, to which it has no claim, the security which it has in common with all governments, so far as opinion is security, is taken away.

Thus these politicians proceed whilst little notice is taken of their doctrines; but when they come to be examined upon the plain meaning of their words and the direct tendency of their doctrines, then equivocations and slippery constructions come into play. When they say the king owes his crown to the choice of his people and is therefore the only lawful sovereign in the world, they will perhaps tell us they mean to say no more than that some of the king's predecessors have been called to the throne by some sort of choice, and therefore he owes his crown to the choice of his people. Thus, by a miserable subterfuge, they hope to render their proposition safe by rendering it nugatory. They are welcome to the asylum they seek for their offense, since they take refuge in their folly. For if you admit this interpretation, how does their idea of election differ from our idea of inheritance?

And how does the settlement of the crown in the Brunswick line derived from James the First come to legalize our monarchy rather than that of any of the neighboring countries? At some time or other, to be sure, all the beginners of dynasties were chosen by those who called them to govern. There is ground enough for the opinion that all the king-

doms of Europe were, at a remote period, elective, with more or fewer limitations in the objects of choice. But whatever kings might have been here or elsewhere a thousand years ago, or in whatever manner the ruling dynasties of England or France may have begun, the king of Great Britain is, at this day, king by a fixed rule of succession according to the laws of his country; and whilst the legal conditions of the compact of sovereignty are performed by him (as they are performed), he holds his crown in contempt of the choice of the Revolution Society, who have not a single vote for a king amongst them, either individually or collectively, though I make no doubt they would soon erect themselves into an electoral college if things were ripe to give effect to their claim. His Majesty's heirs and successors, each in his time and order, will come to the crown with the same contempt of their choice with which his Majesty has succeeded to that he wears.

Whatever may be the success of evasion in explaining away the gross error of *fact*, which supposes that his Majesty (though he holds it in concurrence with the wishes) owes his crown to the choice of his people, yet nothing can evade their full explicit declaration concerning the principle of a right in the people to choose; which right is directly maintained and tenaciously adhered to. All the oblique insinuations concerning election bottom in this proposition and are referable to it. Lest the foundation of the king's exclusive legal title should pass for a mere rant of adulatory freedom, the political divine[iii] proceeds dogmatically to assert that, by the principles of the Revolution, the people of England have acquired three fundamental rights, all which, with him, compose one system and lie together in one short sentence, namely, that we have acquired a right:

1   to choose our own governors.
2   to cashier them for misconduct.
3   to frame a government for ourselves.

This new and hitherto unheard-of bill of rights, though made in the name of the whole people, belongs to those gentlemen and their faction only. The body of the people of England have no share in it. They utterly disclaim it. They will resist the practical assertion of it with their lives and fortunes. They are bound to do so by the laws of their country made at the time of that very Revolution which is appealed to in favor of the fictitious rights claimed by the Society which abuses its name.

[ii]   "I concoct and compound what soon I may bring forth." Horace, *Epistles*, I, 1, 12.

[iii]   Dr Price.

These gentlemen of the Old Jewry, in all their reasonings on the Revolution of 1688,[iv] have a revolution which happened in England about forty years before and the late French revolution, so much before their eyes and in their hearts that they are constantly confounding all the three together. It is necessary that we should separate what they confound. We must recall their erring fancies to the *acts* of the Revolution which we revere, for the discovery of its true *principles*. If the *principles* of the Revolution of 1688 are anywhere to be found, it is in the statute called the *Declaration of Right*. In that most wise, sober, and considerate declaration, drawn up by great lawyers and great statesmen, and not by warm and inexperienced enthusiasts, not one word is said, nor one suggestion made, of a general right "to choose our own *governors*, to cashier them for misconduct, and to *form* a government for *ourselves*."

This Declaration of Right (the act of the 1st of William and Mary, sess. 2, ch. 2) is the cornerstone of our constitution as reinforced, explained, improved, and in its fundamental principles for ever settled. It is called, "An Act for declaring the rights and liberties of the subject, and for *settling* the *succession* of the crown." You will observe that these rights and this succession are declared in one body and bound indissolubly together.

A few years after this period, a second opportunity offered for asserting a right of election to the crown. On the prospect of a total failure of issue from King William, and from the Princess, afterwards Queen Anne, the consideration of the settlement of the crown and of a further security for the liberties of the people again came before the legislature. Did they this second time make any provision for legalizing the crown on the spurious revolution principles of the Old Jewry? No. They followed the principles which prevailed in the Declaration of Right, indicating with more precision the persons who were to inherit in the Protestant line. This act also incorporated, by the same policy, our liberties and an hereditary succession in the same act. Instead of a right to choose our own governors, they declared that the *succession* in that line (the Protestant line drawn from James the

First), was absolutely necessary "for the peace, quiet, and security of the realm," and that it was equally urgent on them "to maintain a *certainty in the succession* thereof, to which the subjects may safely have recourse for their protection." Both these acts, in which are heard the unerring, unambiguous oracles of revolution policy, instead of countenancing the delusive, gipsy predictions of a "right to choose our governors," prove to a demonstration how totally adverse the wisdom of the nation was from turning a case of necessity into a rule of law.

Unquestionably, there was at the Revolution, in the person of King William, a small and a temporary deviation from the strict order of a regular hereditary succession; but it is against all genuine principles of jurisprudence to draw a principle from a law made in a special case and regarding an individual person. *Privilegium non transit in exemplum.*[v] If ever there was a time favorable for establishing the principle that a king of popular choice was the only legal king, without all doubt it was at the Revolution. Its not being done at that time is a proof that the nation was of opinion it ought not to be done at any time. There is no person so completely ignorant of our history as not to know that the majority in parliament of both parties were so little disposed to anything resembling that principle that at first they were determined to place the vacant crown, not on the head of the Prince of Orange, but on that of his wife Mary, daughter of King James, the eldest born of the issue of that king, which they acknowledged as undoubtedly his. It would be to repeat a very trite story, to recall to your memory all those circumstances which demonstrated that their accepting King William was not properly a *choice*; but to all those who did not wish, in effect, to recall King James or to deluge their country in blood and again to bring their religion, laws, and liberties into the peril they had just escaped, it was an act of *necessity*, in the strictest moral sense in which necessity can be taken.

In the very act in which for a time, and in a single case, parliament departed from the strict order of inheritance in favor of a prince who, though not next, was, however, very near in the line of succession, it is curious to observe how Lord Somers, who drew the bill called the Declaration of Right, has comported himself on that delicate occasion. It is curious to observe with what address this tempor-

---

[iv] Dr Price's lecture was delivered in the Old Jewry, a district of London. In the "Glorious Revolution" of 1688, Parliament successfully ousted Catholic James II and installed William III. Burke approved this revolution as having reinstated the traditional rights of Parliament which James had threatened.

[v] "A privilege does not become a precedent."

ary solution of continuity is kept from the eye, whilst all that could be found in this act of necessity to countenance the idea of an hereditary succession is brought forward, and fostered, and made the most of, by this great man and by the legislature who followed him. Quitting the dry, imperative style of an act of parliament, he makes the Lords and Commons fall to a pious, legislative ejaculation and declare that they consider it "as a marvellous providence and merciful goodness of God to this nation to preserve their said Majesties' *royal* persons most happily to reign over us *on the throne of their ancestors*, for which, from the bottom of their hearts, they return their humblest thanks and praises." – The legislature plainly had in view the act of recognition of the first of Queen Elizabeth, chap. 3rd, and of that of James the First, chap. 1st, both acts strongly declaratory of the inheritable nature of the crown; and in many parts they follow, with a nearly literal precision, the words and even the form of thanksgiving which is found in these old declaratory statutes.

The two Houses, in the act of King William, did not thank God that they had found a fair opportunity to assert a right to choose their own governors, much less to make an election the *only lawful* title to the crown. Their having been in a condition to avoid the very appearance of it, as much as possible, was by them considered as a providential escape. They threw a politic, well-wrought veil over every circumstance tending to weaken the rights which in the meliorated order of succession they meant to perpetuate, or which might furnish a precedent for any future departure from what they had then settled forever. Accordingly, that they might not relax the nerves of their monarchy, and that they might preserve a close conformity to the practice of their ancestors, as it appeared in the declaratory statutes of Queen Mary and Queen Elizabeth, in the next clause they vest, by recognition, in their Majesties *all* the legal prerogatives of the crown, declaring "that in them they are most *fully*, rightfully, and *entirely* invested, incorporated, united, and annexed." In the clause which follows, for preventing questions by reason of any pretended titles to the crown, they declare (observing also in this the traditionary language, along with the traditionary policy of the nation, and repeating as from a rubric the language of the preceding acts of Elizabeth and James,) that on the preserving "a *certainty* in the SUCCESSION thereof, the unity, peace, and tranquillity of this nation doth, under God, wholly depend."

They knew that a doubtful title of succession would but too much resemble an election, and that an election would be utterly destructive of the "unity, peace, and tranquillity of this nation," which they thought to be considerations of some moment. To provide for these objects and, therefore, to exclude for ever the Old Jewry doctrine of "a right to choose our own governors," they follow with a clause containing a most solemn pledge, taken from the preceding act of Queen Elizabeth, as solemn a pledge as ever was or can be given in favor of an hereditary succession, and as solemn a renunciation as could be made of the principles by this Society imputed to them: The Lords spiritual and temporal, and Commons, do, in the name of all the people aforesaid, most humbly and faithfully submit *themselves, their heirs and posterities for ever*, and do faithfully promise that they will stand to maintain, and defend their said Majesties, and also the *limitation of the crown*, herein specified and contained, to the utmost of their powers, etc. etc.

So far is it from being true that we acquired a right by the Revolution to elect our kings that, if we had possessed it before, the English nation did at that time most solemnly renounce and abdicate it, for themselves and for all their posterity forever. These gentlemen may value themselves as much as they please on their whig[vi] principles, but I never desire to be thought a better whig than Lord Somers, or to understand the principles of the Revolution better than those by whom it was brought about, or to read in the Declaration of Right any mysteries unknown to those whose penetrating style has engraved in our ordinances, and in our hearts, the words and spirit of that immortal law.

It is true that, aided with the powers derived from force and opportunity, the nation was at that time, in some sense, free to take what course it pleased for filling the throne, but only free to do so upon the same grounds on which they might have wholly abolished their monarchy and every other part of their constitution. However, they did not think such bold changes within their commission. It is indeed difficult, perhaps impossible, to give limits to the mere *abstract* competence of the supreme power, such as was exercised by parliament at that time, but the limits of a *moral* competence subjecting, even in powers more indisputably sovereign, occasional will to permanent reason and

---

vi   The Whigs were the party that advocated the removal of James II from the English throne in 1688. They were opposed by the Tories.

to the steady maxims of faith, justice, and fixed fundamental policy, are perfectly intelligible and perfectly binding upon those who exercise any authority, under any name or under any title, in the state. The House of Lords, for instance, is not morally competent to dissolve the House of Commons, no, nor even to dissolve itself, nor to abdicate, if it would, its portion in the legislature of the kingdom. Though a king may abdicate for his own person, he cannot abdicate for the monarchy. By as strong, or by a stronger reason, the House of Commons cannot renounce its share of authority. The engagement and pact of society, which generally goes by the name of the constitution, forbids such invasion and such surrender. The constituent parts of a state are obliged to hold their public faith with each other and with all those who derive any serious interest under their engagements, as much as the whole state is bound to keep its faith with separate communities. Otherwise competence and power would soon be confounded and no law be left but the will of a prevailing force. On this principle the succession of the crown has always been what it now is, an hereditary succession by law; in the old line it was a succession by the common law; in the new, by the statute law operating on the principles of the common law, not changing the substance, but regulating the mode and describing the persons. Both these descriptions of law are of the same force and are derived from an equal authority emanating from the common agreement and original compact of the state, *communi sponsione reipublicae*,[vii] and as such are equally binding on king and people, too, as long as the terms are observed and they continue the same body politic.

I should have considered all this as no more than a sort of flippant, vain discourse, in which, as in an unsavory fume, several persons suffer the spirit of liberty to evaporate, if it were not plainly in support of the idea and a part of the scheme of "cashiering kings for misconduct." In that light it is worth some observation.

Kings, in one sense, are undoubtedly the servants of the people because their power has no other rational end than that of the general advantage; but it is not true that they are, in the ordinary sense (by our constitution, at least), anything like servants; the essence of whose situation is to obey the commands of some other and to be removable at pleasure. But the king of Great Britain obeys no

other person; all other persons are individually, and collectively too, under him and owe to him a legal obedience. The law, which knows neither to flatter nor to insult, calls this high magistrate not our servant, as this humble divine calls him, but "*our sovereign Lord the king*"; and we, on our parts, have learned to speak only the primitive language of the law, and not the confused jargon of their Babylonian pulpits.[viii]

As he is not to obey us, but as we are to obey the law in him, our constitution has made no sort of provision toward rendering him, as a servant, in any degree responsible. Our constitution knows nothing of a magistrate like the *Justicia* of Aragon,[ix] nor of any court legally appointed, nor of any process legally settled, for submitting the king to the responsibility belonging to all servants. In this he is not distinguished from the Commons and the Lords, who, in their several public capacities, can never be called to an account for their conduct, although the Revolution Society chooses to assert, in direct opposition to one of the wisest and most beautiful parts of our constitution, that "a king is no more than the first servant of the public, created by it, *and responsible to it*."

Ill would our ancestors at the Revolution have deserved their fame for wisdom if they had found no security for their freedom but in rendering their government feeble in its operations, and precarious in its tenure; if they had been able to contrive no better remedy against arbitrary power than civil confusion. Let these gentlemen state who that *representative* public is to whom they will affirm the king, as a servant, to be responsible. It will then be time enough for me to produce to them the positive statute law which affirms that he is not.

You will observe that from Magna Charta to the Declaration of Right it has been the uniform policy of our constitution to claim and assert our liberties as an *entailed inheritance* derived to us from our forefathers, and to be transmitted to our posterity – as an estate specially belonging to the people of this kingdom, without any reference whatever to any other more general or prior right. By this means our constitution preserves a unity in so great a diversity of its parts. We have an inheritable crown, an inheritable peerage, and a House of

---

[vii] "By the common volition of the Commonwealth."

[viii] Perhaps a reference to the confusion of tongues preceding the fall of the Tower of Babel in the Hebrew Bible.
[ix] Chief magistrate of Aragón, an historical autonomous region of Spain.

Commons and a people inheriting privileges, franchises, and liberties from a long line of ancestors.

This policy appears to me to be the result of profound reflection, or rather the happy effect of following nature, which is wisdom without reflection, and above it. A spirit of innovation is generally the result of a selfish temper and confined views. People will not look forward to posterity, who never look backward to their ancestors. Besides, the people of England well know that the idea of inheritance furnishes a sure principle of conservation and a sure principle of transmission, without at all excluding a principle of improvement. It leaves acquisition free, but it secures what it acquires. Whatever advantages are obtained by a state proceeding on these maxims are locked fast as in a sort of family settlement, grasped as in a kind of mortmain[x] forever. By a constitutional policy, working after the pattern of nature, we receive, we hold, we transmit our government and our privileges in the same manner in which we enjoy and transmit our property and our lives. The institutions of policy, the goods of fortune, the gifts of providence are handed down to us, and from us, in the same course and order. Our political system is placed in a just correspondence and symmetry with the order of the world and with the mode of existence decreed to a permanent body composed of transitory parts, wherein, by the disposition of a stupendous wisdom, molding together the great mysterious incorporation of the human race, the whole, at one time, is never old or middle-aged or young, but, in a condition of unchangeable constancy, moves on through the varied tenor of perpetual decay, fall, renovation, and progression. Thus, by preserving the method of nature in the conduct of the state, in what we improve we are never wholly new; in what we retain we are never wholly obsolete. By adhering in this manner and on those principles to our forefathers, we are guided not by the superstition of antiquarians, but by the spirit of philosophic analogy. In this choice of inheritance we have given to our frame of polity the image of a relation in blood, binding up the constitution of our country with our dearest domestic ties, adopting our fundamental laws into the bosom of our family affections, keeping inseparable and cherishing with the warmth of all their combined and mutually reflected charities our state, our hearths, our sepulchres, and our altars.

<hr>

[x] Literally "deadhand," a legal means making possession perpetual in a corporation.

Through the same plan of a conformity to nature in our artificial institutions, and by calling in the aid of her unerring and powerful instincts to fortify the fallible and feeble contrivances of our reason, we have derived several other, and those no small, benefits from considering our liberties in the light of an inheritance. Always acting as if in the presence of canonized forefathers, the spirit of freedom, leading in itself to misrule and excess, is tempered with an awful gravity. This idea of a liberal descent inspires us with a sense of habitual native dignity which prevents that upstart insolence almost inevitably adhering to and disgracing those who are the first acquirers of any distinction. By this means our liberty becomes a noble freedom. It carries an imposing and majestic aspect. It has a pedigree and illustrating ancestors. It has its bearings and its ensigns armorial. It has its gallery of portraits, its monumental inscriptions, its records, evidences, and titles. We procure reverence to our civil institutions on the principle upon which nature teaches us to revere individual men: on account of their age and on account of those from whom they are descended. All your sophisters cannot produce anything better adapted to preserve a rational and manly freedom than the course that we have pursued, who have chosen our nature rather than our speculations, our breasts rather than our inventions, for the great conservatories and magazines of our rights and privileges.

Far am I from denying in theory, full as far is my heart from withholding in practice (if I were of power to give or to withhold) the real rights of men. In denying their false claims of right, I do not mean to injure those which are real, and are such as their pretended rights would totally destroy. If civil society be made for the advantage of man, all the advantages for which it is made become his right. It is an institution of beneficence; and law itself is only beneficence acting by a rule. Men have a right to live by that rule; they have a right to do justice, as between their fellows, whether their fellows are in public function or in ordinary occupation. They have a right to the fruits of their industry and to the means of making their industry fruitful. They have a right to the acquisitions of their parents, to the nourishment and improvement of their offspring, to instruction in life, and to consolation in death. Whatever each man can separately do, without trespassing upon others, he has a right to do for himself; and he has a right to a fair portion of all which society, with all its combinations of skill and force, can do in his favor. In this partnership all men have equal rights, but not to equal things. He that has but five shillings in the partnership has as good a right to it as he that has five hundred pounds has to his larger proportion. But he has not a right to an equal dividend in the product of the joint stock; and as to the share of power, authority, and direction which each individual ought to have in the management of the state, that I must deny to be amongst the direct original rights of man in civil society; for I have in my contemplation the civil social man, and no other. It is a thing to be settled by convention.

If civil society be the offspring of convention, that convention must be its law. That convention must limit and modify all the descriptions of constitution which are formed under it. Every sort of legislative, judicial, or executory power are its creatures. They can have no being in any other state of things; *and how can any man claim under the conventions of civil society rights which do not so much as suppose its existence – rights which are absolutely repugnant to it?* One of the first motives to civil society, and which becomes one of its fundamental rules, is *that no man should be judge in his own cause.* By this each person has at once divested himself of the first fundamental right of unconvenanted man, that is, to judge for himself and to assert his own cause. He abdicates all right to be his own governor. He inclusively, in a great measure, abandons the right of self-defense, the first law of nature. Men cannot enjoy the rights of an uncivil and of a civil state together. That he may obtain justice, he gives up his right of determining what it is in points the most essential to him. That he may secure some liberty, he makes a surrender in trust of the whole of it.

You see, Sir, that in this enlightened age I am bold enough to confess that we are generally men of untaught feelings, that, instead of casting away all our old prejudices, we cherish them to a very considerable degree, and, to take more shame to ourselves, we cherish them because they are prejudices; and the longer they have lasted and the more generally they have prevailed, the more we cherish them. We are afraid to put men to live and trade each on his own private stock of reason, because we suspect that this stock in each man is small, and that the individuals would do better to avail themselves of the general bank and capital of nations and of ages. Many of our men of speculation, instead of

exploding general prejudices, employ their sagacity to discover the latent wisdom which prevails in them. If they find what they seek, and they seldom fail, they think it more wise to continue the prejudice, with the reason involved, than to cast away the coat of prejudice and to leave nothing but the naked reason; because prejudice, with its reason, has a motive to give action to that reason, and an affection which will give it permanence. Prejudice is of ready application in the emergency; it previously engages the mind in a steady course of wisdom and virtue and does not leave the man hesitating in the moment of decision skeptical, puzzled, and unresolved. Prejudice renders a man's virtue his habit, and not a series of unconnected acts. Through just prejudice, his duty becomes a part of his nature.

The effects of the incapacity shown by the popular leaders in all the great members of the commonwealth are to be covered with the "all-atoning name" of liberty. In some people I see great liberty indeed; in many, if not in the most, an oppressive, degrading servitude. But what is liberty without wisdom and without virtue? It is the greatest of all possible evils; for it is folly, vice, and madness, without tuition or restraint. Those who know what virtuous liberty is cannot bear to see it disgraced by incapable heads on account of their having high-sounding words in their mouths. Grand, swelling sentiments of liberty I am sure I do not despise. They warm the heart; they enlarge and liberalize our minds; they animate our courage in a time of conflict. Old as I am, I read the fine raptures of Lucan and Corneille with pleasure.[xi] Neither do I wholly condemn the little arts and devices of popularity. They facilitate the carrying of many points of moment; they keep the people together; they refresh the mind in its exertions; and they diffuse occasional gaiety over the severe brow of moral freedom. Every politician ought to sacrifice to the graces, and to join compliance with reason. But in such an undertaking as that in France, all these subsidiary sentiments and artifices are of little avail. To make a government requires no great prudence. Settle the seat of power, teach obedience, and the work is done. To give freedom is still more easy. It is not necessary to guide; it only requires to let go the rein. But to form a *free*

[xi] Marcus Annaeus Lucanus (AD 39–65), a Roman who wrote a famous historical epic poem, and Pierre Corneille (1606–84), father of French classical tragic drama.

government, that is, to temper together these opposite elements of liberty and restraint in one consistent work, requires much thought, deep reflection, a sagacious, powerful, and combining mind. This I do not find in those who take the lead in the National Assembly. Perhaps they are not so miserably deficient as they appear. I rather believe it. It would put them below the common level of human understanding. But when the leaders choose to make themselves bidders at an auction of popularity, their talents, in the construction of the state, will be of no service. They will become flatterers instead of legislators, the instruments, not the guides, of the people. If any of them should happen to propose a scheme of liberty, soberly limited and defined with proper qualifications, he will be immediately outbid by his competitors who will produce something more splendidly popular. Suspicions will be raised of his fidelity to his cause. Moderation will be stigmatized as the virtue of cowards, and compromise as the prudence of traitors, until, in hopes of preserving the credit which may enable him to temper and moderate, on some occasions, the popular leader is obliged to become active in propagating doctrines and establishing powers that will afterwards defeat any sober purpose at which he ultimately might have aimed.

But am I so unreasonable as to see nothing at all that deserves commendation in the indefatigable labors of this Assembly? I do not deny that, among an infinite number of acts of violence and folly, some good may have been done. They who destroy everything certainly will remove some grievance. They who make everything new have a chance that they may establish something beneficial. To give them credit for what they have done in virtue of the authority they have usurped, or which can excuse them in the crimes by which that authority has been acquired, it must appear that the same things could not have been accomplished without producing such a revolution. Most assuredly they might, because almost every one of the regulations made by them which is not very equivocal was either in the cession of the king, voluntarily made at the meeting of the states, or in the concurrent instructions to the orders. Some usages have been abolished on just grounds, but they were such that if they had stood as they were to all eternity, they would little detract from the happiness and prosperity of any state. The improvements of the National Assembly are superficial, their errors fundamental.

Whatever they are, I wish my countrymen rather to recommend to our neighbours the example of the British constitution than to take models from them for the improvement of our own. In the former, they have got an invaluable treasure. They are not, I think, without some causes of apprehension and complaint, but these they do not owe to their constitution but to their own conduct. I think our happy situation owing to our constitution, but owing to the whole of it, and not to any part singly, owing in a great measure to what we have left standing in our several reviews and reformations as well as to what we have altered or superadded. Our people will find employment enough for a truly patriotic, free, and independent spirit in guarding what they possess from violation. I would not exclude alteration neither, but even when I changed, it should be to preserve. I should be led to my remedy by a great grievance. In what I did. I should follow the example of our ancestors. I would make the reparation as nearly as possible in the style of the building. A politic caution, a guarded circumspection, a moral rather than a complexional timidity were among the ruling principles of our forefathers in their most decided conduct. Not being illuminated with the light of which the gentlemen of France tell us they have got so abundant a share, they acted under a strong impression of the ignorance and fallibility of mankind. He that had made them thus fallible rewarded them for having in their conduct attended to their nature. Let us imitate their caution if we wish to deserve their fortune or to retain their bequests. Let us add, if we please, but let us preserve what they have left; and, standing on the firm ground of the British constitution, let us be satisfied to admire rather than attempt to follow in their desperate flights the aeronauts of France.

I have told you candidly my sentiments. I think they are not likely to alter yours. I do not know that they ought. You are young; you cannot guide but must follow the fortune of your country. But hereafter they may be of some use to you, in some future form which your commonwealth may take. In the present it can hardly remain; but before its final settlement it may be obliged to pass, as one of our poets says, "through great varieties of untried being",[xii] and in all its transmigrations to be purified by fire and blood.

I have little to recommend my opinions but long observation and much impartiality. They

---

[xii] Addison, *Cato*, Act V, scene i.

come from one who has been no tool of power, no flatterer of greatness; and who in his last acts does not wish to belie the tenor of his life. They come from one almost the whole of whose public exertion has been a struggle for the liberty of others; from one in whose breast no anger, durable or vehement, has ever been kindled but by what he considered as tyranny; and who snatches from his share in the endeavors which are used by good men to discredit opulent oppression the hours he has employed on your affairs; and who in so doing persuades himself he has not departed from his usual office; they come from one who desires honors, distinctions, and emoluments but little, and who expects them not at all; who has no contempt for fame, and no fear of obloquy; who shuns contention, though he will hazard an opinion; from one who wishes to preserve consistency, but who would preserve consistency by varying his means to secure the unity of his end, and, when the equipoise of the vessel in which he sails may be endangered by overloading it upon one side, is desirous of carrying the small weight of his reasons to that which may preserve its equipoise.

7

From *Sketch for an Historical Picture of the Progress of the Human Mind*

Marquis de Condorcet

Marie Jean Antoine Nicolas Caritat, the marquis de Condorcet (1743–94), was one of *les philosophes*, philosophers who led the French Enlightenment. He was associated with that characteristic Enlightenment project, the composition of the *Encyclopédie* of all knowledge. A journalist and supporter of the initial phase of the French Revolution, he became a member of the Legislative Assembly during its radical phase, but his constitutional and non-violent views led him publicly to attack the 1793 Jacobin Constitution. He was forced into hiding for nine months, during which he wrote his *Sketch*. Subsequently arrested, he died in his cell, presumably a suicide. Condorcet distills in his book what would become the canonical self-interpretation of the modern European world, in which rational inquiry spurs progress not only in science, but in society and politics. He foresaw a coming era of "reason, tolerance, humanity."

We have watched man's reason being slowly formed by the natural progress of civilization; we have watched superstition seize upon it and corrupt it, and tyranny degrade and deaden the minds of men under the burden of misery and fear.

One nation alone escapes the two-fold influence of tyranny and superstition. From that happy land where freedom had only recently kindled the torch of genius, the mind of man, released from the leading-strings of its infancy, advances with firm steps towards the truth.[i] But this triumph soon encourages tyranny to return, followed by its faith-

ful companion superstition, and the whole of mankind is plunged once more into darkness, which seems as if it must last for ever. Yet, little by little, day breaks again; eyes long condemned to darkness catch a glimpse of the light and close again, then slowly become accustomed to it, and at last gaze on it without flinching; once again genius dares to walk abroad on the earth, from which fanaticism and barabarism had exiled it.

We have already seen reason lift her chains, shake herself free from some of them, and, all the time regaining strength, prepare for and advance the moment of her liberation. It remains for us to study the stage in which she finally succeeds in breaking these chains, and when, still compelled to drag their vestiges behind her, she frees herself from them one by one; when at last she can go forward unhindered, and the only obstacles in her path are those that are inevitably renewed at every fresh advance because they are the necessary consequence of the very constitution of our understanding – of the connection, that is, between our means of discovering the truth and the resistance that it offers to our efforts.

Religious intolerance had forced seven of the Belgian provinces to throw off the yoke of Spain and form a federal republic. Religious intolerance alone had aroused the spirit of English liberty,

---

[i] "That happy land" is presumably France.

Marie Jean Antoine Nicolas Caritat, marquis de Condorcet, from "The Ninth Stage: From Descartes to the Foundation of the French Republic" from *Sketch for an Historical Picture of the Progress of the Human Mind* (trans. June Barraclough), pp. 124–37. New York: Hyperion Press, rpt. of 1955 Noonday Press edition.

which, exhausted by a protracted and bloody civil war, was finally embodied in a constitution that was for long the admiration of philosophers, but owes its preservation merely to the superstition of the English nation and the hypocrisy of their politicians. And, finally, it was also through priestly persecution that the Swedish nation found courage to reclaim a portion of their rights.

However, in the midst of all these advances, which owed their origin to theological disputes, France, Spain, Hungary and Bohemia saw their feeble liberties extinguished, or so at least it seemed.

It would be vain to look, in those countries which we call free, for that liberty which infringes none of the natural rights of man; a liberty which not only allows man to possess these rights but allows him to exercise them. For the liberty we find there is based on a system of positive rights, unequally distributed among men, and grants them different privileges according to the town in which they live, the class into which they have been born, the means of which they can dispose, and the profession that they follow. A comparative sketch of the curious inequalities to be found in different countries is the best retort that we can make to those who still uphold their virtue or necessity.

But in these same countries the law guarantees individual and civil liberty, so that if man has not there reached a state of perfection, his natural dignity is not degraded; some at least of his rights are recognized; he can no longer be said to be a slave though he can be said to be not truly free.

In those nations where at this time there was, to a greater or less extent, a genuine loss of liberty, the political rights enjoyed by the great mass of the people had been confined within such narrow limits that the destruction of the virtually arbitrary power of the aristocracy under which man had groaned, seems to have more than compensated for their loss. Man lost the title of citizen, which inequality had rendered little more than a name, but the quality of man was accorded greater respect; royal despotism saved him from feudal oppression, and relieved him from a state of humiliation all the more painful because the awareness of his condition was constantly kept alive in him by the number and actual presence of his tyrants. The system of laws tended to improve, both in those states whose constitution was partly free, and in those ruled by despots: in the former because the interests of those who exercised the real power did not invariably conflict with the interests of the people; in the latter because the interests of the despot were often

indistinguishable from those of public prosperity, or because the despot's endeavours to destroy the vestiges of feudal or clerical power had imparted to the law a spirit of equality, whose inspiration may have been the desire to establish equality in slavery, but whose effects were often salutary.

We shall give a detailed exposition of the causes that have produced in Europe a kind of despotism for which there is no precedent in earlier ages or in other parts of the world, a despotism in which an all but arbitrary authority, restrained by public opinion, controlled by enlightenment, tempered by self-interest, has often contributed to the progress of wealth, industry, and education, and sometimes even to that of liberty.

Manners have become less violent through the weakening of the prejudices that had maintained their savagery, through the influence of the spirit of industry and commerce which is inimical to unrest and violence as the natural enemies of wealth, through the sense of horror inspired by the none too distant picture of the barbarism of the preceding stage, through a wider diffusion of the philosophical ideas of equality and humanity, and, finally, through the influence, slow but sure, of the general progress of enlightenment.

Religious intolerance remains, but more as an instrument of human prudence, as a tribute to popular prejudice, or as a precaution against popular unrest. Its fury abates; the fires at the stake are seldom lit, and have been replaced by a form of oppression that, if it is often more arbitrary, is less barbarous; and of recent years the persecutions have become much rarer, and the result rather of complacency or habit. Everywhere, and in every respect, governmental practice has slowly and regretfully followed the progress of public opinion and even of philosophy.

Indeed, if in the moral and political sciences there is always a large interval between the point to which philosophers have carried the progress of enlightenment and the degree of enlightenment attained by the average man of education (and it is the body of beliefs held in common by such men that constitutes the generally accepted creed known as public opinion), those who direct public affairs and who immediately influence the fate of the common people, under whatever constitution they may hold their powers, are very far from rising to the level of public opinion; they follow its advance, without ever overtaking it and are always many years behind it and therefore always ignorant of many of the truths that it has learned.

This sketch of the progress of philosophy and of the dissemination of enlightenment, whose more general and more evident effects we have already examined, brings us up to the stage when the influence of progress upon public opinion, of public opinion upon nations or their leaders, suddenly ceases to be a slow, imperceptible affair, and produces a revolution in the whole order of several nations, a certain earnest of the revolution that must one day include in its scope the whole of the human race.

After long periods of error, after being led astray by vague or incomplete theories, publicists have at last discovered the true rights of man and how they can all be deduced from the single truth, that *man is a sentient being, capable of reasoning and of acquiring moral ideas.*

They have seen that the maintenance of these rights was the sole object of men's coming together in political societies, and that the social art is the art of guaranteeing the preservation of these rights and their distribution in the most equal fashion over the largest area. It was felt that in every society the means of assuring the rights of the individual should be submitted to certain common rules, but that the authority to choose these means and to determine these rules could belong only to the majority of the members of the society itself; for in making this choice the individual cannot follow his own reason without subjecting others to it, and the will of the majority is the only mark of truth that can be accepted by all without loss of equality.

Each man can in fact genuinely bind himself in advance to the will of the majority which then becomes unanimous; but he can bind only himself; and he cannot engage even himself towards this majority when it fails to respect the rights of the individual, after having once recognized them.

Here we see at once the rights of the majority over society or its members, and the limits of these rights. Here we see the origin of that unanimity which allows the decisions taken by the majority alone to impose an obligation upon all; an obligation which ceases to be legitimate when, with a change in the individuals constituting the majority, the sanction of unanimity no longer exists. Doubtless there are issues on which the decision of the majority is likely to be in favour of error and against the interests of all; but it is still this majority that must decide which issues are not to be subjected to its own direct decision; it is the majority that must appoint those persons whose judgment it considers to be more reliable than its own; it is the majority

that must lay down the procedure that it considers most likely to conduct them to the truth; and it may not abdicate its authority to decide whether the decisions they take on its behalf do or do not infringe the rights that are common to all.

So, in the face of such simple principles, we see the disappearance of the belief in the existence of a contract between the people and their lawgivers, which can be annulled only by mutual consent or by the defection of one of the parties; and along with it there disappeared the less servile but no less absurd opinion according to which a nation was for ever chained to its constitution once this constitution had been established – as though the right to change it were not the guarantee of every other right, and as though human institutions, which are necessarily defective and capable of perfection as men become more enlightened, could be condemned to remain for ever in their infancy. Man was thus compelled to abandon that astute and false policy, which, forgetful of the truth that all men possess equal rights by nature, would seek to apportion those rights unequally between countries, according to the character or prosperity of a country, the conditions of its industry and commerce, and unequally between men, according to a man's birth, fortune, or profession, and which then calls into being conflicting interests and opposing forces to restore the balance, measures which would have been unnecessary without this policy and which are in any event impotent to control its more dangerous tendencies.

Nor did men any longer dare to divide humanity into two races, the one fated to rule, the other to obey, the one to deceive, the other to be deceived. They had to recognize that all men have an equal right to be informed on all that concerns them, and that none of the authorities established by men over themselves has the right to hide from them one single truth.

These principles, which the noble Sydney paid for with his blood and on which Locke set the authority of his name, were later developed by Rousseau with greater precision,[ii] breadth and energy, and he deserves renown for having established them among the truths that it is no longer permissible to forget or to combat. Man has certain needs and also certain faculties with which to satisfy them; from

---

[ii] Three republican political writers: the English philosopher John Locke (1632–1704); Jean-Jacques Rousseau; and presumably Algernon Sidney (1622–89), a Whig martyr who was exiled during the Restoration of the English monarchy in 1660, eventually returned to England, and was executed.

these faculties and from their products, modified and distributed in different ways, there results an accumulation of wealth out of which must be met the common needs of mankind. But what are the laws according to which this wealth is produced or distributed, accumulated or consumed, increased or dissipated? What, too, are the laws governing that general tendency towards an equilibrium between supply and demand from which it follows that, with any increase in wealth, life becomes easier and men are happier, until a point is reached when no further increase is possible; or that, again, with any decrease in wealth, life becomes harder, suffering increases, until the consequent fall in population restores the balance? How, with all the astonishing multifariousness of labour and production, supply and demand, with all the frightening complexity of conflicting interests that link the survival and well-being of one individual to the general organization of societies, that make his well-being dependent on every accident of nature and every political event, his pain and pleasure on what is happening in the remotest corner of the globe, how, with all this seeming chaos, is it that, by a universal moral law, the efforts made by each individual on his own behalf minister to the welfare of all, and that the interests of society demand that everyone should understand where his own interests lie, and should be able to follow them without hindrance?

Men, therefore, should be able to use their faculties, dispose of their wealth and provide for their needs in complete freedom. The common interest of any society, far from demanding that they should restrain such activity, on the contrary, forbids any interference with it; and as far as this aspect of public order is concerned, the guaranteeing to each man his natural rights is at once the whole of social utility, the sole duty of the social power, the only right that the general will can legitimately exercise over the individual.

But it is not enough merely that this principle should be acknowledged by society; the public authority has specific duties to fulfil. It must establish by law recognized measures for the determination of the weight, volume, size and length of all articles of trade; it must create a coinage to serve as a common measure of value and so to facilitate comparison between the value of one article of trade and that of another, so that having a value itself, it can be exchanged against anything else that can be given one; for without this common measure trade must remain confined to barter, and can acquire very little activity or scope.

The wealth produced each year provides a portion for disposal which is not required to pay for either the labour that has produced it or the labour required to ensure its replacement by an equal or greater production of wealth. The owner of this disposable portion does not owe it directly to his work; he possesses it independently of the use to which he puts his faculties in order to provide for his needs. Hence it is out of this available portion of the annual wealth that the public authority, without violating anyone's rights, can establish the funds required for the security of the State, the preservation of peace within its borders, the protection of individual rights, the exercise of those powers established for the formation or execution of the law, and, finally, the maintenance of public prosperity.

There are certain undertakings and institutions which are beneficial to society in general, and which it therefore ought to initiate, control and supervise; these provide services which the wishes and interests of individuals cannot provide by themselves, and which advance the progress of agriculture, industry or trade or the prevention or alleviation of inevitable natural hardships or unforeseen accidents.

Up to the stage of which we speak and even for a long time afterwards, these various undertakings were left to chance, to the greed of governments, to the skill of charlatans or to the prejudices or self-interest of powerful sections of the community. A disciple of Descartes, however, the famous and ill-starred John de Witt,[iii] felt that political economy ought like every other science to submit itself to the principles of philosophy and the rigour of calculation.

Political economy made little progress until the Peace of Utrecht[iv] gave Europe the promise of lasting peace. From then onwards one notices an increasing intellectual interest taken in this hitherto neglected subject; and the new science was advanced by Stewart, Smith[v] and more particularly the French economists, at least as far as precision and the purity of its principles are involved, to a point that one could hardly have hoped to reach so soon after such a long period of indifference.

[iii] Presumably Johan de Witt (1625–72), Dutch statesman.
[iv] Of 1713, which ended the War of the Spanish Succession.
[v] The Scottish philosophers Dugald Stewart (1753–1828) and Adam Smith (1723–90).

But this progress in politics and political economy was caused primarily by the progress in general philosophy and metaphysics, if we take the latter word in its broadest sense.

Descartes had brought philosophy back to reason; for he had understood that it must be derived entirely from those primary and evident truths which we can discover by observing the operations of the human mind. Soon, however, his impatient imagination snatched it from the path that he had traced for it, and for a time it seemed that philosophy had regained her independence only to be led astray by new errors.

At last, Locke grasped the thread by which philosophy should be guided; he showed that an exact and precise analysis of ideas, which reduces them step by step to other ideas of more immediate origin or of simpler composition, is the only way to avoid being lost in that chaos of incomplete, incoherent and indeterminate notions which chance presents to us at hazard and we unthinkingly accept.

By this same analysis he proved that all ideas are the result of the operations of our minds upon sensations we have received, or, to put it more exactly, that they are the combinations of these sensations presented to us simultaneously by the faculty of memory in such a way that our attention is arrested and our perception is thereby limited to no more than a part of such compound sensations.

He showed that if we attach a word to each idea after analysing it and circumscribing it, we shall succeed in remembering the idea ever afterwards in a uniform fashion; that is to say, the idea will always be formed of the same simple ideas, it will always be enclosed within the same limits, and it can in consequence be used in a chain of reasoning without any risk of confusion. On the other hand, if a word is used in such a way that it does not correspond to a determinate idea, it can at different times arouse different ideas in the same person's mind, and this is the most fecund source of error in reasoning.

Locke, finally, was the first man who dared to set a limit to the human understanding, or rather to determine the nature of the truths that it can come to know and of the objects it can comprehend.

This method was soon adopted by all philosophers and, by applying it to moral science, to politics and to social economy, they were able to make almost as sure progress in these sciences as they had in the natural sciences. They were able to admit only proven truths, to separate these truths from whatever as yet remained doubtful and uncertain,

and to ignore whatever is and always will be impossible to know.

Similarly the analysis of our feelings, leads to our finding, in the development of our capacity to feel pleasure and pain, the origin of our moral ideas, the foundation of those general truths which, resulting from these ideas, determine the necessary and immutable laws of justice and injustice, and, finally, the motives that we have for conforming to them, motives which spring from the very nature of our sensibility, from what might be called our moral constitution.

This metaphysical method became virtually a universal instrument. Men learnt to use it in order to perfect the methods of the physical sciences, to throw light on their principles and to examine the validity of their proofs; and it was extended to the examination of facts and to the rules of taste.

Thus it was applied to all the various undertakings of the human understanding, and by means of it the operations of the mind in every branch of knowledge were subjected to analysis, and the nature of the truths and the kind of certainty we can expect to find from each of these branches of knowledge was thereby revealed. It is this new step in philosophy that has for ever imposed a barrier between mankind and the errors of its infancy, a barrier that should save it from relapsing into its former errors under the influence of new prejudices, just as it should assure the eventual eradication of those that still survive unrecognized, and should make it certain that any that may take their place will exercise only a faint influence and enjoy only an ephemeral existence.

In Germany, however, a man of vast and profound genius laid the foundations of a new doctrine.[vi] His ardent and passionate imagination could not rest satisfied with a modest philosophy and leave unsolved those great questions about the spirituality or the survival of the human soul, about man's freedom or the freedom of God, about the existence of pain and evil in a universe governed by an all-powerful intelligence whose wisdom, justice and loving-kindness ought, it would seem, to exclude the possibility of their existence. He cut the knot which the most skilful analysis would never have been able to untie and constructed the universe from simple, indestructible, entities equal by their very nature. The relations of each of these entities with all the others, which with it form part

[vi] German philosopher and mathematician G. W. Leibniz (1646–1716).

of the system of the universe, determine those qualities of it whereby it differs from every other. The human soul and the least atom of a block of stone are, each of them, one of these monads, and they differ only in the different place assigned to them in the universal order. Out of all the possible combinations of these beings an infinite intelligence has preferred one, and could have preferred one only, the most perfect of all. If that which exists offends us by the misery and crime that we see in it, it is still true that any other combination would have had more painful results.

We shall explain this system which, being adopted, or at least upheld, by Leibniz's compatriots, has retarded the progress of philosophy amongst them. One entire school of English philosophers enthusiastically embraced and eloquently defended the doctrine of optimism, but they were less subtle and less profound than Leibniz, for whereas he based his doctrine on the belief that an all-powerful intelligence, by the very necessity of its nature, could choose only the best of all possible worlds, the English philosophers sought to prove their doctrine by appealing to observation of the particular world in which we live and, thereby sacrificing all the advantages possessed by this system so long as it remains abstract and general; they lost themselves in details, which were too often either revolting or ridiculous.

In Scotland, however, other philosophers finding that the analysis of the development of our actual faculties led to no principle that could provide a sufficiently pure or solid basis for the morality of our actions, thought to attribute a new faculty to the human soul,[vii] distinct from but associated with those of feeling or thinking, a faculty whose existence they proved only by showing that they could not do without it. We shall recount the history of these opinions and shall show how, if they have retarded the progress of philosophy, they have advanced the dissemination of philosophical ideas.

Up till now we have shown the progress of philosophy only in the men who have cultivated, deepened and perfected it. It remains for us to show what have been its effects on public opinion; how reason, while it learnt to safeguard itself against the errors into which the imagination and respect for authority had so often led it, at last found a sure method of discovering and recognizing truth; and how at the same time it destroyed the

prejudices of the masses which had for so long afflicted and corrupted the human race.

At last man could proclaim aloud his right, which for so long had been ignored, to submit all opinions to his own reason and to use in the search for truth the only instrument for its recognition that he has been given. Every man learnt with a sort of pride that nature had not for ever condemned him to base his beliefs on the opinions of others; the superstitions of antiquity and the abasement of reason before the transports of supernatural religion disappeared from society as from philosophy.

Soon there was formed in Europe a class of men who were concerned less with the discovery or development of the truth than with its propagation, men who whilst devoting themselves to the tracking down of prejudices in the hiding places where the priests, the schools, the governments and all long-established institutions had gathered and protected them, made it their life-work to destroy popular errors rather than to drive back the frontiers of human knowledge – an indirect way of aiding its progress which was not less fraught with peril, nor less useful.

In England Collins and Bolingbroke, in France Bayle, Fontenelle, Voltaire, Montesquieu and the schools founded by these famous men,[viii] fought on the side of truth, using in turn all the weapons with which learning, philosophy, wit and literary talent can furnish reason; using every mood from humour to pathos, every literary form from the vast erudite encyclopædia to the novel or the broadsheet of the day; covering truth with a veil that spared weaker eyes and excited one to guess what lay beyond it; skilfully flattering prejudices so as to attack them the better; seldom threatening them, and then always either only one in its entirety or several partially; sometimes conciliating the enemies of reason by seeming to wish only for a half-tolerance in religious matters, only for a half-freedom in politics; sparing despotism when tilting against the absurdities of religion, and religion when abusing tyranny; yet always attacking the principles of these two scourges even when they seemed to be against only their more revolting or ridiculous

---

[vii]   Presumably the faculty of "commonsense."

[viii]   Philosopher Arthur Collins (1680–1732), statesman Henry Bolingbroke (1678–1751), philosopher Pierre Bayle (1647–1706), writer Bernard de Fontenelle (1657–1757), influential Enlightenment intellectual François de Voltaire (1694–1778), and political philosopher Charles de Secondat, Baron de Montesquieu (1689–1755).

abuses, and laying their axes to the very roots of these sinister trees when they appeared to be lopping off a few stray branches; sometimes teaching the friends of liberty that superstition is the invincible shield behind which despotism shelters and should therefore be the first victim to be sacrificed, the first chain to be broken, and sometimes denouncing it to the despots as the real enemy of their power, and frightening them with stories of its secret machinations and its bloody persecutions; never ceasing to demand the independence of reason and the freedom of the press as the right and the salvation of mankind; protesting with indefatigable energy against all the crimes of fanaticism and tyranny; pursuing, in all matters of religion, administration, morals and law, anything that bore the marks of tyranny, harshness or barbarism; invoking the name of nature to bid kings, captains, magistrates and priests to show respect for human life; laying to their charge, with vehemence and severity, the blood their policy or their indifference still spilled on the battlefield or on the scaffold; and finally, taking for their battle cry – *reason, tolerance, humanity*....

8

"Absolute Freedom and Terror"

G. W. F. Hegel

The most influential European philosopher of the first half of the nineteenth century was the German thinker Georg Wilhelm Friedrich Hegel (1770–1831). His idealistic system saw all reality as *Geist* or Spirit developing through a dialectical process of self-opposition and higher incorporation, a process embodied in the actual stages and events of human history. He endorsed Enlightenment ideals – the idea of consciousness as individual freedom, and of the objects of consciousness as value-neutral objects of potential utility – as a necessary but incomplete stage through which the human spirit must pass in its journey to complete self-understanding. In this excerpt from his most beautiful work, *Phenomenology of Spirit* (1807), Hegel characterizes what is wrong with the Enlightened consciousness: it is one-sided and unbalanced, the freedom of a solipsistic, empty individual who sees others as mere objects for use. Hence it led to the worst violence of the French Revolution, the Terror of 1793–4, during which the French ruling "Committee of Public Safety" executed about 40,000 alleged enemies of the fledgling republic. For true freedom, Spirit must await its further development, when it discovers that real, concrete freedom can only be achieved in the context of membership in a moral community under the institutions of the State.

Consciousness has found its Notion in Utility.[i] But it is partly still an *object*, and partly, for that very reason, still an *End* to be attained, which conscious-

ness does not find itself to possess immediately. Utility is still a predicate of the object, not itself a subject or the immediate and sole *actuality* of the object. It is the same thing that appeared before, when being-for-self had not yet shown itself to be the substance[ii] of the other moments, a demonstration which would have meant that the Useful was directly nothing else but the self of consciousness and that this latter was thereby in possession of it. This withdrawal from the form of objectivity of the Useful has, however, already taken place in principle and from this inner revolution there emerges the actual revolution of the actual world, the new shape of consciousness, *absolute freedom*.

In fact, what we have here is no more than an empty show of objectivity separating self-consciousness from possession. For, partly, all existence and validity of the specific members of the organization of the actual world and the world of faith[iii] have, in general, returned into this simple determination as into their ground and spiritual principle; partly, however, this simple determination no longer possesses anything of its own, it is rather pure metaphysic, pure Notion, or a pure knowing by self-consciousness. That is to say, of

---

[ii] "Substance" refers to the underlying reality, the true being, of a thing.
[iii] The world beyond the actual world, as pictured by religious faith.

---

[i] "Notion" refers to the pure, comprehensive understanding of a thing. Hegel is claiming that the Enlightenment regards the essence of reality as mere utility.

Georg Wilhelm Friedrich Hegel, "Absolute Freedom and Terror," paras. 582–95, pp. 355–63 from *Phenomenology of Spirit* (trans. A. V. Miller). Oxford: Oxford University Press, 1977.

the *being-in-and-for-itself* of the Useful *qua* object, consciousness recognizes that its *being-in-itself*, is essentially a *being-for-an-other*; being-in-itself, as *devoid of self*, is in truth a passive self, or that which is a self for another self.[iv] The object, however, exists for consciousness in this abstract form of pure being-in-itself, for consciousness is pure *insight* whose distinctions are in the pure form of Notions. But the *being-for-self* into which being-for-an-other returns, i.e. the self, is not a self belonging exclusively to what is called object and distinct from the "I"; for consciousness, *qua* pure insight, is not a *single* self which could be confronted by the object as equally having a self of its own, but is pure Notion, the gazing of the self into the self, the absolute seeing of *itself* doubled; the certainty of itself is the universal Subject, and its conscious Notion is the essence of all actuality. If, then, the Useful was merely the alternation of the moments, an alternation which did not return into its own *unity*, and hence was still an object for knowing, it now ceases to be this. For knowing is itself the movement of those abstract moments, it is the universal self, the self of itself as well as of the object and, as universal, is the self-returning unity of this movement.

Spirit thus comes before us as *absolute freedom*. It is self-consciousness which grasps the fact that its certainty of itself is the essence of all the spiritual 'masses', or spheres, of the real as well as of the supersensible world, or conversely, that essence and actuality are consciousness's knowledge of *itself*. It is conscious of its pure personality and therein of all spiritual reality, and all reality is solely spiritual; the world is for it simply its own will, and this is a general will.[v] And what is more, this will is not the empty thought of will which consists in silent assent, or assent by a representative, but a real general will, the will of all *individuals* as such. For will is in itself the consciousness of personality, or of each, and it is as this genuine actual will that it ought to be, as the *self-conscious* essence of each and every personality, so that each, undivided from the whole, always does everything, and what appears as done by the whole is the direct and conscious deed of each.

This undivided Substance of absolute freedom ascends the throne of the world without any power

being able to resist it. For since, in truth, consciousness alone is the element in which the spiritual beings or powers have their substance, their entire system which is organized and maintained by division into 'masses' or spheres has collapsed, now that the individual consciousness conceives the object as having no other essence than self-consciousness itself, or as being absolutely Notion. What made the Notion into an existent *object* was its diremption into separate *subsistent* spheres, but when the object becomes a Notion, there is no longer anything in it with a continuing existence; negativity has permeated all its moments. It comes into existence in such a way that each individual consciousness raises itself out of its allotted sphere, no longer finds its essence and its work in this particular sphere, but grasps itself as the *Notion* of will, grasps all spheres as the essence of this will, and therefore can only realize itself in a work which is a work of the whole. In this absolute freedom, therefore, all social groups or classes which are the spiritual spheres into which the whole is articulated are abolished; the individual consciousness that belonged to any such sphere, and willed and fulfilled itself in it, has put aside its limitation; its purpose is the general purpose, its language universal law, its work the universal work.

The object and the [moment of] *difference* have here lost the meaning of *utility*, which was the predicate of all real being; consciousness does not begin its movement in the object as if this were something *alien* from which it first had to return into itself; on the contrary, the object is for it consciousness itself. The antithesis, consists, therefore, solely in the difference between the *individual* and the *universal* consciousness; but the individual consciousness itself is directly in its own eyes that which had only the *semblance* of an antithesis; it is universal consciousness and will. The *beyond* of this its actual existence hovers over the corpse of the vanished independence of real being, or the being of faith, merely as the exhalation of a stale gas, of the vacuous *Être suprême*.[vi]

After the various spiritual spheres and the restricted life of the individual have been done away with, as well as his two worlds, all that remains, therefore, is the immanent movement of universal self-consciousness as a reciprocity of self-consciousness in the form of *universality* and of *personal* consciousness: the universal will goes *into* *itself* and is a *single*, *individual* will to which univer-

---

[iv] Being "in-itself" simply is; being "for- another" is an object for consciousness; being "in-and-for- itself" both is and is an object for itself, as in a self-aware human being.

[v] A reference to Rousseau's concept of the general will of a free society, which was influential during the French Revolution.

[vi] Supreme Being.

sal law and work stand opposed. But this *individual* consciousness is no less directly conscious of itself as universal will; it is aware that its object is a law given by that will and a work accomplished by it; therefore, in passing over into action and in creating objectivity, it is doing nothing individual, but carrying out the laws and functions of the state.

This movement is thus the interaction of consciousness with itself in which it lets nothing break loose to become a *free object* standing over against it. It follows from this that it cannot achieve anything positive, either universal works of language or of reality, either of laws and general institutions of *conscious* freedom, or of deeds and works of a freedom that *wills* them. The work which *conscious* freedom might accomplish would consist in that freedom, *qua universal* substance, making itself into an *object* and into an *enduring being*. This otherness would be the moment of difference in it whereby it divided itself into stable spiritual 'masses' or spheres and into the members of various powers. These spheres would be partly the 'thought-things' of a *power* that is separated into legislative, judicial, and executive powers; but partly, they would be the *real essences* we found in the real world of culture, and, looking more closely at the content of universal action, they would be the particular spheres of labour which would be further distinguished as more specific 'estates' or classes. Universal freedom, which would have separated itself in this way into its constituent parts and by the very fact of doing so would have made itself into an *existent* Substance, would thereby be free from *particular* individuality, and would apportion the *plurality* of individuals to its various constituent parts. This, however, would restrict the activity and the being of the personality to a branch of the whole, to one kind of activity and being; when placed in the element of *being*, personality would have the significance of a specific personality; it would cease to be in truth universal self-consciousness. Neither by the mere idea of obedience to *self-given* laws which would assign to it only a part of the whole, nor by its being *represented* in law-making and universal action, does self-consciousness let itself be cheated out of *reality*, the reality of *itself* making the law and accomplishing, not a particular work, but the universal work itself. For where the self is merely *represented* and is present only as an idea, there it is not *actual*; where it is represented by proxy, it *is not*.

Just as the individual self-consciousness does not find itself in this *universal work* of absolute freedom *qua* existent Substance, so little does it find itself in

the *deeds* proper and *individual* actions of the will of this freedom. Before the universal can perform a deed it must concentrate itself into the One of individuality and put at the head an individual self-consciousness; for the universal will is only an *actual* will in a self, which is a One. But thereby all other individuals are excluded from the entirety of this deed and have only a limited share in it, so that the deed would not be a deed of the *actual universal* self-consciousness. Universal freedom, therefore, can produce neither a positive work nor a deed; there is left for it only *negative* action; it is merely the *fury* of destruction.

But the supreme reality and the reality which stands in the greatest antithesis to universal freedom, or rather the sole object that will still exist for that freedom, is the freedom and individuality of actual self-consciousness itself. For that universality which does not let itself advance to the reality of an organic articulation, and whose aim is to maintain itself in an unbroken continuity, at the same time creates a distinction within itself, because it is movement or consciousness in general. And, moreover, by virtue of its own abstraction, it divides itself into extremes equally abstract, into a simple, inflexible cold universality, and into the discrete, absolute hard rigidity and self-willed atomism of actual self-consciousness. Now that it has completed the destruction of the actual organization of the world, and exists now just for itself, this is its sole object, an object that no longer has any content, possession, existence, or outer extension, but is merely this knowledge of itself as an absolutely pure and free individual self. All that remains of the object by which it can be laid hold of is solely its *abstract* existence as such. The relation, then, of these two, since each exists indivisibly and absolutely for itself, and thus cannot dispose of a middle term which would link them together, is one of wholly *unmediated* pure negation, a negation, moreover, of the individual as a being *existing* in the universal. The sole work and deed of universal freedom is therefore *death*, a death too which has no inner significance or filling, for what is negated is the empty point of the absolutely free self. It is thus the coldest and meanest of all deaths, with no more significance than cutting off a head of cabbage or swallowing a mouthful of water.[vii]

[vii] During the Terror thousands died on the guillotine, and thousands more on boats that were floated into the Loire river, then sunk. I thank James Schmidt for the latter reference.

In this flat, commonplace monosyllable is contained the wisdom of the government, the abstract intelligence of the universal will, in the fulfilling of itself. The government is itself nothing else but the self-established focus, or the individuality, of the universal will. The government, which wills and executes its will from a single point, at the same time wills and executes a specific order and action. On the one hand, it excludes all other individuals from its act, and on the other hand, it thereby constitutes itself a government that is a specific will, and so stands opposed to the universal will; consequently, it is absolutely impossible for it to exhibit itself as anything else but a *faction*. What is called government is merely the *victorious* faction, and in the very fact of its being a faction lies the direct necessity of its overthrow; and its being government makes it, conversely, into a faction, and [so] guilty. When the universal will maintains that what the government has actually done is a crime committed against it, the government, for its part, has nothing specific and outwardly apparent by which the guilt of the will opposed to it could be demonstrated; for what stands opposed to it as the *actual* universal will is only an unreal pure will, *intention. Being suspected*, therefore, takes the place, or has the significance and effect, of *being guilty*; and the external reaction against this reality that lies in the simple inwardness of intention, consists in the cold, matter-of-fact annihilation of this existent self, from which nothing else can be taken away but its mere being.

In this its characteristic *work*, absolute freedom becomes explicitly objective to itself, and self-consciousness learns what absolute freedom in effect is. *In itself*, it is just this *abstract self-consciousness*, which effaces all distinction and all continuance of distinction within it. It is as such that it is objective to itself; the *terror* of death is the vision of this negative nature of itself. But absolutely free self-consciousness finds this its reality quite different from what its own Notion of itself was, viz. that the universal will is merely the *positive* essence of personality, and that this latter knows itself in it only positively, or as preserved therein. Here, however, this self-consciousness which, as pure insight, completely separates its positive and its negative nature – completely separates the predicateless Absolute as pure *Thought* and as pure *Matter* – is confronted with the absolute *transition* of the one into the other as a present reality. The universal will, *qua* absolutely *positive*, actual self-consciousness, because it is this self-conscious reality heightened to the level of *pure* thought or of *abstract* matter, changes round into its negative nature and shows itself to be equally that which *puts an end to the thinking of oneself*, or to self-consciousness.

Absolute freedom as *pure* self-identity of the universal will thus has within it *negation*; but this means that it contains *difference* in general, and this again it develops as an *actual* difference. For pure *negativity* has in the self-identical universal will the element of subsistence, or the *Substance* in which its moments are realized; it has the matter which it can utilize in accordance with its own determinateness; and in so far as this Substance has shown itself to be the negative element for the individual consciousness, the organization of spiritual 'masses' or spheres to which the plurality of individual consciousnesses are assigned thus takes shape once more. These individuals who have felt the fear of death, of their absolute master, again submit to negation and distinctions, arrange themselves in the various spheres, and return to an apportioned and limited task, but thereby to their substantial reality.

Out of this tumult, Spirit would be thrown back to its starting-point, to the ethical and real world of culture, which would have been merely refreshed and rejuvenated by the fear of the lord and master which has again entered men's hearts. Spirit would have to traverse anew and continually repeat this cycle of necessity if the result were only the complete interpenetration of self-consciousness and Substance – an interpenetration in which self-consciousness, which has experienced the negative power of its universal essence acting on it, would desire to know and find itself, not as this particular individual, but only as a universal, and therefore, too, would be able to endure the objective reality of universal Spirit, a reality excluding self-consciousness *qua* particular. But in absolute freedom there was no reciprocal action between a consciousness that is immersed in the complexities of existence, or that sets itself specific aims and thoughts, and a valid *external* world, whether of reality or thought; instead, the world was absolutely in the form of consciousness as a universal will, and equally self-consciousness was drawn together out of the whole expanse of existence or manifested aims and judgements, and concentrated into the simple self. The culture to which it attains in interaction with that essence is, therefore, the grandest and the last, is that of seeing its pure, simple reality immediately vanish and pass away into empty nothingness. In the world of culture itself it does not get as far as to behold its negation or alienation in this form of pure abstraction; on the contrary, its negation is filled with a content, either honour or wealth, which it gains in place of the self that it has alienated from itself; or the language of Spirit and insight which the disrupted consciousness acquires; or it is the heaven of faith, or the Utility of the Enlightenment. All these determinations have vanished in the loss suffered by the self in absolute freedom; its negation is the death that is without meaning, the sheer terror of the negative that contains nothing positive, nothing that fills it with a content. At the same time, however, this negation in its real existence is not something alien; it is neither the universal inaccessible *necessity* in which the ethical world perishes, nor the particular accident of private possession, nor the whim of the owner on which the disrupted consciousness sees itself dependent; on the contrary, it is the *universal will* which in this its ultimate abstraction has nothing positive and therefore can give nothing in return for the sacrifice. But for that very reason it is immediately one with self-consciousness, or it is the pure positive, because it is the pure negative; and the meaningless death, the unfilled negativity of the self, changes round in its inner Notion into absolute positivity. For consciousness, the immediate unity of itself with the universal will, its demand to know itself as this specific point in the universal will, is changed round into the absolutely opposite experience. What vanishes for it in that experience is abstract *being* or the immediacy of that insubstantial point, and this vanished immediacy is the universal will itself which it now knows itself to be in so far as it is a pure knowing or pure will. Consequently, it knows that will to be itself, and knows itself to be essential being; but not essential being as

an *immediate existence*, not will as revolutionary government or anarchy striving to establish anarchy, nor itself as the centre of this faction or the opposite faction; on the contrary, the *universal will* is its *pure knowing and willing* and *it* is the universal will *qua* this pure knowing and willing. It does not lose *itself* in that will, for pure knowing and willing is much more *it* than is that atomic point of consciousness. It is thus the interaction of pure knowing with itself; pure *knowing qua essential being* is the universal will; but this essential being is absolutely nothing else but pure knowing. Self-consciousness is, therefore, the pure knowing of essential being *qua* pure knowing. Further, as an *individual self*, it is only the form of the subject or of real action, a form which is known by it as *form*. Similarly, *objective* reality, *being*, is for it simply a selfless form; for that reality would be something that is not known. This knowing, however, knows knowing to be essential being.

Absolute freedom has thus removed the antithesis between the universal and the individual will. The self-alienated Spirit, driven to the extreme of its antithesis in which pure willing and the agent of that pure willing are still distinct, reduces the antithesis to a transparent form and therein finds itself. Just as the realm of the real world passes over into the realm of faith and insight, so does absolute freedom leave its self-destroying reality and pass over into another land of self-conscious Spirit where, in this unreal world, freedom has the value of truth. In the thought of this truth Spirit refreshes itself, in so far as *it is* and remains *thought*, and knows this being which is enclosed within self-consciousness to be essential being in its perfection and completeness. There has arisen the new shape of Spirit, that of the *moral* Spirit.

9

"Bourgeois and Proletarians"

Karl Marx and Friedrich Engels

Marxism is the most important criticism of the dominant Western form of economic modernity, capitalism. Among the various forms of socialism and anti-industrialism common in the nineteenth century, the German thinkers Karl Marx (1818–83) and his collaborator Friedrich Engels (1820–95) uniquely devised what they regarded as a "scientific" socialism. Borrowing Hegel's notion of dialectical development, they formulated a comprehensive theory of human history in which capitalism is a necessary but temporary stage whose industrial development would prepare the way for the eventual communist abolition of private property. They did not object to modern industry, science, technology, and secularism, but only to the restriction of ownership and benefits to the capitalist or "bourgeois" class. The following excerpt from their famous pamphlet, *Manifesto of the Communist Party* (1848), represents one of the most moving and prescient depictions of modern society. Capitalism is itself an ongoing economic revolution that continually builds and demolishes society, in the process demystifying all non-monetary forms of authority, thereby making class struggle naked and shameless. However abhorrent this capitalism is to the authors, it is hard not to hear in their words a hostile awe at the monumental changes it was working on the human condition.

The history of all hitherto existing society is the history of class struggles.[i]

[i] In capitalism, the most important classes are the bourgeoisie, that is, the owners of modern industry, and the proletariat, the class of industrial workers.

Freeman and slave, patrician and plebeian, lord and serf, guild-master and journeyman, in a word, oppressor and oppressed, stood in constant opposition to one another, carried on an uninterrupted, now hidden, now open fight, a fight that each time ended, either in a revolutionary re-constitution of society at large, or in the common ruin of the contending classes.

In the earlier epochs of history, we find almost everywhere a complicated arrangement of society into various orders, a manifold gradation of social rank. In ancient Rome we have patricians, knights, plebeians, slaves; in the Middle Ages, feudal lords, vassals, guild-masters, journeymen, apprentices, serfs; in almost all of these classes, again, subordinate gradations.

The modern bourgeois society that has sprouted from the ruins of feudal society has not done away with class antagonisms. It has but established new classes, new conditions of oppression, new forms of struggle in place of the old ones.

Our epoch, the epoch of the bourgeoisie, possesses, however, this distinctive feature: it has simplified the class antagonisms: Society as a whole is more and more splitting up into two great hostile camps, into two great classes directly facing each other: Bourgeoisie and Proletariat.

From the serfs of the Middle Ages sprang the

Karl Marx, with Friedrich Engels, "Bourgeois and Proletarians," section 1 of *Manifesto of the Communist Party* (trans. Samuel Moore), reproduced in Robert C. Tucker (ed.), *The Marx–Engels Reader* (second edition), pp. 473–83. New York: Norton, 1978.

chartered burghers of the earliest towns.[ii] From these burgesses the first elements of the bourgeoisie were developed.

The discovery of America, the rounding of the Cape, opened up fresh ground for the rising bourgeoisie. The East-Indian and Chinese markets, the colonisation of America, trade with the colonies, the increase in the means of exchange and in commodities generally, gave to commerce, to navigation, to industry, an impulse never before known, and thereby, to the revolutionary element in the tottering feudal society, a rapid development.

The feudal system of industry, under which industrial production was monopolised by closed guilds, now no longer sufficed for the growing wants of the new markets. The manufacturing system took its place. The guild-masters were pushed on one side by the manufacturing middle class; division of labour between the different corporate guilds vanished in the face of division of labour in each single workshop.[iii]

Meantime the markets kept ever growing, the demand ever rising. Even manufacture no longer sufficed. Thereupon, steam and machinery revolutionised industrial production. The place of manufacture was taken by the giant, Modern Industry, the place of the industrial middle class, by industrial millionaires, the leaders of whole industrial armies, the modern bourgeois.

Modern industry has established the world-market, for which the discovery of America paved the way. This market has given an immense development to commerce, to navigation, to communication by land. This development has, in its turn, reacted on the extension of industry; and in proportion as industry, commerce, navigation, railways extended, in the same proportion the bourgeoisie developed, increased its capital, and pushed into the background every class handed down from the Middle Ages.

We see, therefore, how the modern bourgeoisie is itself the product of a long course of development, of a series of revolutions in the modes of production and of exchange.

Each step in the development of the bourgeoisie was accompanied by a corresponding political advance of that class. An oppressed class under the

sway of the feudal nobility, an armed and self-governing association in the mediaeval commune,[iv] here independent urban republic (as in Italy and Germany), there taxable "third estate" of the monarchy (as in France), afterwards, in the period of manufacture proper, serving either the semi-feudal or the absolute monarchy as a counterpoise against the nobility, and, in fact, corner-stone of the great monarchies in general, the bourgeoisie has at last, since the establishment of Modern Industry and of the world-market, conquered for itself, in the modern representative State, exclusive political sway. The executive of the modern State is but a committee for managing the common affairs of the whole bourgeoisie.

The bourgeoisie, historically, has played a most revolutionary part.

The bourgeoisie, wherever it has got the upper hand, has put an end to all feudal, patriarchal, idyllic relations. It has pitilessly torn asunder the motley feudal ties that bound man to his "natural superiors," and has left remaining no other nexus between man and man than naked self-interest, than callous "cash payment." It has drowned the most heavenly ecstasies of religious fervour, of chivalrous enthusiasm, of philistine sentimentalism, in the icy water of egotistical calculation. It has resolved personal worth into exchange value, and in place of the numberless indefeasible chartered freedoms, has set up that single, unconscionable freedom – Free Trade. In one word, for exploitation, veiled by religious and political illusions, it has substituted naked, shameless, direct, brutal exploitation.

The bourgeoisie has stripped of its halo every occupation hitherto honoured and looked up to with reverent awe. It has converted the physician, the lawyer, the priest, the poet, the man of science, into its paid wage-labourers.

The bourgeoisie has torn away from the family its sentimental veil, and has reduced the family relation to a mere money relation.

The bourgeoisie has disclosed how it came to pass that the brutal display of vigour in the Middle Ages, which Reactionists so much admire, found its fitting complement in the most slothful indolence. It has been the first to show what man's activity can bring about. It has accomplished wonders far surpassing Egyptian pyramids, Roman aqueducts, and Gothic cathedrals; it has conducted expeditions

---

[ii] Burghers were the residents of legally independent towns, whose lands (borough) had been freed from the control of the rural, feudal lords, ultimately by a royal charter granting their freedoms. Later, charters would primarily grant trading and commercial rights.

[iii] Guilds were trade associations of medieval craftsmen.

[iv] "Commune" was an early term for the independent town, unowned by rural lords.

that put in the shade all former Exoduses of nations and crusades.

The bourgeoisie cannot exist without constantly revolutionising the instruments of production, and thereby the relations of production, and with them the whole relations of society. Conservation of the old modes of production in unaltered form, was, on the contrary, the first condition of existence for all earlier industrial classes. Constant revolutionising of production, uninterrupted disturbance of all social conditions, everlasting uncertainty and agitation distinguish the bourgeois epoch from all earlier ones. All fixed, fast-frozen relations, with their train of ancient and venerable prejudices and opinions, are swept away, all new-formed ones become antiquated before they can ossify. All that is solid melts into air, all that is holy is profaned, and man is at last compelled to face with sober senses, his real conditions of life, and his relations with his kind.

The need of a constantly expanding market for its products chases the bourgeoisie over the whole surface of the globe. It must nestle everywhere, settle everywhere, establish connexions everywhere.

The bourgeoisie has through its exploitation of the world-market given a cosmopolitan character to production and consumption in every country. To the great chagrin of Reactionists, it has drawn from under the feet of industry the national ground on which it stood. All old-established national industries have been destroyed or are daily being destroyed. They are dislodged by new industries, whose introduction becomes a life and death question for all civilised nations, by industries that no longer work up indigenous raw material, but raw material drawn from the remotest zones; industries whose products are consumed, not only at home, but in every quarter of the globe. In place of the old wants, satisfied by the productions of the country, we find new wants, requiring for their satisfaction the products of distant lands and climes. In place of the old local and national seclusion and self-sufficiency, we have intercourse in every direction, universal inter-dependence of nations. And as in material, so also in intellectual production. The intellectual creations of individual nations become common property. National one-sidedness and narrow-mindedness become more and more impossible, and from the numerous national and local literatures, there arises a world literature.

The bourgeoisie, by the rapid improvement of all instruments of production, by the immensely facilitated means of communication, draws all, even the most barbarian, nations into civilisation. The cheap prices of its commodities are the heavy artillery with which it batters down all Chinese walls, with which it forces the barbarians' intensely obstinate hatred of foreigners to capitulate. It compels all nations, on pain of extinction, to adopt the bourgeois mode of production; it compels them to introduce what it calls civilisation into their midst, i.e., to become bourgeois themselves. In one word, it creates a world after its own image.

The bourgeoisie has subjected the country to the rule of the towns. It has created enormous cities, has greatly increased the urban population as compared with the rural, and has thus rescued a considerable part of the population from the idiocy of rural life. Just as it has made the country dependent on the towns, so it has made barbarian and semi-barbarian countries dependent on the civilised ones, nations of peasants on nations of bourgeois, the East on the West.

The bourgeoisie keeps more and more doing away with the scattered state of the population, of the means of production, and of property. It has agglomerated population, centralised means of production, and has concentrated property in a few hands. The necessary consequence of this was political centralisation. Independent, or but loosely connected provinces, with separate interests, laws, governments and systems of taxation, became lumped together into one nation, with one government, one code of laws, one national class-interest, one frontier and one customs-tariff.

The bourgeoisie, during its rule of scarce one hundred years, has created more massive and more colossal productive forces than have all preceding generations together. Subjection of Nature's forces to man, machinery, application of chemistry to industry and agriculture, steam-navigation, railways, electric telegraphs, clearing of whole continents for cultivation, canalisation of rivers, whole populations conjured out of the ground – what earlier century had even a presentiment that such productive forces slumbered in the lap of social labour?

We see then: the means of production and of exchange, on whose foundation the bourgeoisie built itself up, were generated in feudal society. At a certain stage in the development of these means of production and of exchange, the conditions under which feudal society produced and exchanged, the feudal organisation of agriculture and manufacturing industry, in one word, the feudal relations of property became no longer compatible with the already developed productive forces; they became so many fetters. They had to be burst asunder; they were burst asunder.

Into their place stepped free competition, accompanied by a social and political constitution adapted to it, and by the economical and political sway of the bourgeois class.

A similar movement is going on before our own eyes. Modern bourgeois society with its relations of production, of exchange and of property, a society that has conjured up such gigantic means of production and of exchange, is like the sorcerer, who is no longer able to control the powers of the nether world whom he has called up by his spells. For many a decade past the history of industry and commerce is but the history of the revolt of modern productive forces against modern conditions of production, against the property relations that are the conditions for the existence of the bourgeoisie and of its rule. It is enough to mention the commercial crises that by their periodical return put on its trial, each time more threateningly, the existence of the entire bourgeois society. In these crises a great part not only of the existing products, but also of the previously created productive forces, are periodically destroyed. In these crises there breaks out an epidemic that, in all earlier epochs, would have seemed an absurdity – the epidemic of over-production. Society suddenly finds itself put back into a state of momentary barbarism; it appears as if a famine, a universal war of devastation had cut off the supply of every means of subsistence; industry and commerce seem to be destroyed; and why? Because there is too much civilisation, too much means of subsistence, too much industry, too much commerce. The productive forces at the disposal of society no longer tend to further the development of the conditions of bourgeois property; on the contrary, they have become too powerful for these conditions, by which they are fettered, and so soon as they overcome these fetters, they bring disorder into the whole of bourgeois society, endanger the existence of bourgeois property. The conditions of bourgeois society are too narrow to comprise the wealth created by them. And how does the bourgeoisie get over these crises? On the one hand by enforced destruction of a mass of productive forces; on the other, by the conquest of new markets, and by the more thorough exploitation of the old ones. That is to say, by paving the way for more extensive and more destructive crises, and by diminishing the means whereby crises are prevented.

The weapons with which the bourgeoisie felled feudalism to the ground are now turned against the bourgeoisie itself.

But not only has the bourgeoisie forged the weapons that bring death to itself; it has also called into existence the men who are to wield those weapons – the modern working class – the proletarians.

In proportion as the bourgeoisie, i.e., capital, is developed, in the same proportion is the proletariat, the modern working class, developed – a class of labourers, who live only so long as they find work, and who find work only so long as their labour increases capital. These labourers, who must sell themselves piece-meal, are a commodity, like every other article of commerce, and are consequently exposed to all the vicissitudes of competition, to all the fluctuations of the market.

Owing to the extensive use of machinery and to division of labour, the work of the proletarians has lost all individual character, and consequently, all charm for the workman. He becomes an appendage of the machine, and it is only the most simple, most monotonous, and most easily acquired knack, that is required of him. Hence, the cost of production of a workman is restricted, almost entirely, to the means of subsistence that he requires for his maintenance, and for the propagation of his race. But the price of a commodity, and therefore also of labour, is equal to its cost of production. In proportion, therefore, as the repulsiveness of the work increases, the wage decreases. Nay more, in proportion as the use of machinery and division of labour increases, in the same proportion the burden of toil also increases, whether by prolongation of the working hours, by increase of the work exacted in a given time or by increased speed of the machinery, etc.

Modern industry has converted the little workshop of the patriarchal master into the great factory of the industrial capitalist. Masses of labourers, crowded into the factory, are organised like soldiers. As privates of the industrial army they are placed under the command of a perfect hierarchy of officers and sergeants. Not only are they slaves of the bourgeois class, and of the bourgeois State; they are daily and hourly enslaved by the machine, by the over-looker, and, above all, by the individual bourgeois manufacturer himself. The more openly this despotism proclaims gain to be its end and aim, the more petty, the more hateful and the more embittering it is.

The less the skill and exertion of strength implied in manual labour, in other words, the more modern industry becomes developed, the more is the labour of men superseded by that of women. Differences of age and sex have no longer any distinctive social validity for the working class. All are instruments of labour, more or less expensive to use, according to their age and sex.

No sooner is the exploitation of the labourer by the manufacturer, so far, at an end, that he receives his wages in cash, than he is set upon by the other portions of the bourgeoisie, the landlord, the shop-keeper, the pawnbroker, etc.

The lower strata of the middle class – the small tradespeople, shopkeepers, and retired tradesmen generally, the handicraftsmen and peasants – all these sink gradually into the proletariat, partly because their diminutive capital does not suffice for the scale on which Modern Industry is carried on, and is swamped in the competition with the large capitalists, partly because their specialised skill is rendered worthless by new methods of production. Thus the proletariat is recruited from all classes of the population.

The proletariat goes through various stages of development. With its birth begins its struggle with the bourgeoisie. At first the contest is carried on by individual labourers, then by the workpeople of a factory, then by the operatives of one trade, in one locality, against the individual bourgeois who directly exploits them. They direct their attacks not against the bourgeois conditions of production, but against the instruments of production themselves; they destroy imported wares that compete with their labour, they smash to pieces machinery, they set factories ablaze, they seek to restore by force the vanished status of the workman of the Middle Ages.

At this stage the labourers still form an incoher-ent mass scattered over the whole country, and broken up by their mutual competition. If any-where they unite to form more compact bodies, this is not yet the consequence of their own active union, but of the union of the bourgeoisie, which class, in order to attain its own political ends, is compelled to set the whole proletariat in motion, and is moreover yet, for a time, able to do so. At this stage, therefore, the proletarians do not fight their enemies, but the enemies of their enemies, the remnants of absolute monarchy, the landowners, the non-industrial bourgeois, the petty bourgeoisie. Thus the whole historical movement is concen-trated in the hands of the bourgeoisie; every victory so obtained is a victory for the bourgeoisie.

But with the development of industry the prole-tariat not only increases in number; it becomes concentrated in greater masses, its strength grows, and it feels that strength more. The various inter-ests and conditions of life within the ranks of the proletariat are more and more equalised, in propor-tion as machinery obliterates all distinctions of labour, and nearly everywhere reduces wages to the same low level. The growing competition among the bourgeois, and the resulting commercial crises, make the wages of the workers ever more fluctuating. The unceasing improvement of ma-chinery, ever more rapidly developing, makes their livelihood more and more precarious; the collisions between individual workmen and indi-vidual bourgeois take more and more the character of collisions between two classes. Thereupon the workers begin to form combinations (Trades Unions) against the bourgeois; they club together in order to keep up the rate of wages; they found permanent associations in order to make provision beforehand for these occasional revolts. Here and there the contest breaks out into riots.

Now and then the workers are victorious, but only for a time. The real fruit of their battles lies, not in the immediate result, but in the ever-expanding union of the workers. This union is helped on by the improved means of communica-tion that are created by modern industry and that place the workers of different localities in contact with one another. It was just this contact that was needed to centralise the numerous local struggles, all of the same character, into one national struggle between classes. But every class struggle is a polit-ical struggle. And that union, to attain which the burghers of the Middle Ages, with their miserable highways, required centuries, the modern proletar-ians, thanks to railways, achieve in a few years.

This organisation of the proletarians into a class, and consequently into a political party, is continu-ally being upset again by the competition between the workers themselves. But it ever rises up again, stronger, firmer, mightier. It compels legislative recognition of particular interests of the workers, by taking advantage of the divisions among the bourgeoisie itself. Thus the ten-hours' bill in Eng-land was carried.[v]

Altogether collisions between the classes of the old society further, in many ways, the course of development of the proletariat. The bourgeoisie finds itself involved in a constant battle. At first with the aristocracy; later on, with those portions of

---

[v]   Passed in 1847, the bill limited the work day to ten hours, but only for women and children.

the bourgeoisie itself, whose interests have become antagonistic to the progress of industry; at all times, with the bourgeoisie of foreign countries. In all these battles it sees itself compelled to appeal to the proletariat, to ask for its help, and thus, to drag it into the political arena. The bourgeoisie itself, therefore, supplies the proletariat with its own elements of political and general education, in other words, it furnishes the proletariat with weapons for fighting the bourgeoisie.

Further, as we have already seen, entire sections of the ruling classes are, by the advance of industry, precipitated into the proletariat, or are at least threatened in their conditions of existence. These also supply the proletariat with fresh elements of enlightenment and progress.

Finally, in times when the class struggle nears the decisive hour, the process of dissolution going on within the ruling class, in fact within the whole range of society, assumes such a violent, glaring character, that a small section of the ruling class cuts itself adrift, and joins the revolutionary class, the class that holds the future in its hands. Just as, therefore, at an earlier period, a section of the nobility went over to the bourgeoisie, so now a portion of the bourgeoisie goes over to the proletariat, and in particular, a portion of the bourgeois ideologists, who have raised themselves to the level of comprehending theoretically the historical movement as a whole.

Of all the classes that stand face to face with the bourgeoisie today, the proletariat alone is a really revolutionary class. The other classes decay and finally disappear in the face of Modern Industry; the proletariat is its special and essential product.

The lower middle class, the small manufacturer, the shopkeeper, the artisan, the peasant, all these fight against the bourgeoisie, to save from extinction their existence as fractions of the middle class. They are therefore not revolutionary, but conservative. Nay more, they are reactionary, for they try to roll back the wheel of history. If by chance they are revolutionary, they are so only in view of their impending transfer into the proletariat, they thus defend not their present, but their future interests, they desert their own standpoint to place themselves at that of the proletariat.

The "dangerous class," the social scum, that passively rotting mass thrown off by the lowest layers of old society, may, here and there, be swept into the movement by a proletarian revolution; its conditions of life, however, prepare it far more for the part of a bribed tool of reactionary intrigue.

In the conditions of the proletariat, those of old society at large are already virtually swamped. The proletarian is without property; his relation to his wife and children has no longer anything in common with the bourgeois family-relations; modern industrial labour, modern subjection to capital, the same in England as in France, in America as in Germany, has stripped him of every trace of national character. Law, morality, religion, are to him so many bourgeois prejudices, behind which lurk in ambush just as many bourgeois interests.

All the preceding classes that got the upper hand, sought to fortify their already acquired status by subjecting society at large to their conditions of appropriation. The proletarians cannot become masters of the productive forces of society, except by abolishing their own previous mode of appropriation, and thereby also every other previous mode of appropriation. They have nothing of their own to secure and to fortify; their mission is to destroy all previous securities for, and insurances of, individual property.

All previous historical movements were movements of minorities, or in the interests of minorities. The proletarian movement is the self-conscious, independent movement of the immense majority, in the interests of the immense majority. The proletariat, the lowest stratum of our present society, cannot stir, cannot raise itself up, without the whole superincumbent strata of official society being sprung into the air.

Though not in substance, yet in form, the struggle of the proletariat with the bourgeoisie is at first a national struggle. The proletariat of each country must, of course, first of all settle matters with its own bourgeoisie.

In depicting the most general phases of the development of the proletariat, we traced the more or less veiled civil war, raging within existing society, up to the point where that war breaks out into open revolution, and where the violent overthrow of the bourgeoisie lays the foundation for the sway of the proletariat.

Hitherto, every form of society has been based, as we have already seen, on the antagonism of oppressing and oppressed classes. But in order to oppress a class, certain conditions must be assured to it under which it can, at least, continue its slavish existence. The serf, in the period of serfdom, raised himself to membership in the commune, just as the petty bourgeois, under the yoke of feudal absolutism, managed to develop into a bourgeois. The modern labourer, on the contrary, instead of rising with the progress of industry, sinks deeper and deeper below the conditions of existence of his own class. He becomes a pauper, and pauperism develops more rapidly than population and wealth. And here it becomes evident, that the bourgeoisie is unfit any longer to be the ruling class in society, and to impose its conditions of existence upon society as an over-riding law. It is unfit to rule because it is incompetent to assure an existence to its slave within his slavery, because it cannot help letting him sink into such a state, that it has to feed him, instead of being fed by him. Society can no longer live under this bourgeoisie, in other words, its existence is no longer compatible with society.

The essential condition for the existence, and for the sway of the bourgeois class, is the formation and augmentation of capital; the condition for capital is wage-labour. Wage-labour rests exclusively on competition between the labourers. The advance of industry, whose involuntary promoter is the bourgeoisie, replaces the isolation of the labourers, due to competition, by their revolutionary combination, due to association. The development of Modern Industry, therefore, cuts from under its feet the very foundation on which the bourgeoisie produces and appropriates products. What the bourgeoisie, therefore, produces, above all, is its own grave-diggers. Its fall and the victory of the proletariat are equally inevitable.

PART II

Modernity Realized

Introduction to Part II

The century from 1860 to 1950 brought the triumph of modernity, and simultaneously its greatest crises, both intellectual and social. It is in this period that the new science and the industrial revolution actually changed the lives of most human beings living in Europe, North America, and indirectly, much of the world. Peoples bound to a local agrarian lifestyle were thrown, either by choice or necessity, into the cities and a new industrial world market. Waves of scientific revolution, in cosmology, physics, geology, chemistry, and biology deeply altered our view of the world, unleashing new technologies of awesome power. The conditions of life changed, and the mere fact of change seemed to make traditional wisdom and religion less relevant to everyday life. Liberal democracy became widespread, then was challenged by fascism and communism, themselves modernist reactions against features of modernity. Two world wars, employing new communications and military technologies, devastated Europe and much of the developed world, and closed with the terrifying first act of the atomic age. Throughout the period there was a cultural response to the new conditions of life, in which some artists and thinkers embraced the new, fluid, non-traditional environment, while others were revolted by it.

Western philosophy reflected this transformation by regarding itself as in crisis. Many of the most important philosophers of the period claimed that *all* earlier thought had suffered from some deep flaw requiring radical revision, a break with the past. This is historically distinctive; philosophers in every era usually think other philosophers are wrong about something, but the claim that *all* past philosophy was *fundamentally* wrong-headed was a particularly radical critique. When radicalism appears it is usually the purview of a few cranks at the margins, but in the late nineteenth and early twentieth centuries *the* most prominent philosophical schools – analytical and logical philosophy, phenomenology and existentialism, pragmatism, Marxism – radically rejected the speculative, metaphysical, and quasi-theological tendencies of earlier thought from the Greeks through the mid-nineteenth century. Historically speaking, in twentieth-century philosophy, radicalism became the *norm*.

It is this period that created most of the philosophical schools and divisions prevalent among Western (and a large percentage of non-Western) philosophers to this day: pragmatism (in the work of Charles Sanders Peirce, George Hebert Mead, William James, Josiah Royce, and John Dewey), existentialism (Friedrich Nietzsche, Søren Kierkegaard, Paul Tillich, Jean-Paul Sartre, Simone de Beauvoir); phenomenology (Edmund Husserl, Martin Heidegger, and Maurice Merleau-Ponty); logic, logical positivism, and analytic philosophy (Gottlob Frege, G. E. Moore, Bertrand Russell, the early Ludwig Wittgenstein, Rudolf Carnap, Kurt Gödel, and Alfred Tarski); ordinary language philosophy (the later Wittgenstein, J. L. Austin); and process philosophy (Henri Bergson and Alfred North Whitehead). In their rejection of philosophical tradition these movements also diverged from each other, leaving Western philosophy fragmented into divergent styles or sub-cultures, each denying the legitimacy of the others. To be sure, some remained faithful to the older speculative–metaphysical tradition, but it was the new methods that defined the era. To a very large degree we philosophers of the new millennium are still looking back to the creativity of the late nineteenth and early twentieth century for inspiration.

During the same early twentieth-century period, art, politics, and science were being revolutionized. Modernism in painting initially took the form of a new realism that renounced the idealization of subject matter, but more prominently it was the age of abstraction, of the liberation of artistic imagination by Impressionism, Cubism, Expressionism, Futurism, Surrealism, Symbolism, Dada, and ultimately Abstract Expressionism. In other arts as well it was a period of explosive waves of experimentation: the poetry of Ezra Pound and T. S. Eliot, the stream of consciousness novels of James Joyce and Virginia Woolf, the existential realism of Hemingway; the atonal music of Albert Schönberg and Alban Berg, the non-thematic dissonance of Igor Stravinsky; and the architectural modernism of Le Corbusier, Mies van der Rohe, Walter Gropius, and the Bauhaus school. Simultaneously new forms of social radicalism developed in response to the coming of mass, industrial society: socialism, Marxist–Leninist bolshevism, futurism, syndicalism, fascism, Nazism, anarchism. Discontents and intellectuals sought new alternatives to the juggernaut of modernization and mass culture. Scientifically, Charles Darwin and Sigmund Freud recast our picture of human beings, while in physics the greatest revolution in our picture of the universe since the seventeenth century was led by Neils Bohr, Max Planck, Wolfgang Pauli, Louis de Broglie, Albert Einstein, Erwin Schrödinger, Werner Heisenberg, and Paul Dirac. Particularly important for understanding modernity, the field of sociology established itself in this period as an independent discipline, largely through providing theories of modernization. Besides Marx and Weber, the work of Émile Durkheim, Henry Sumner Maine, Georg Simmel, Ferdinand Tönnies, Walter Benjamin, Talcott Parsons and Arnold Gehlen, to name but a few, are central for later studies of modernization.

The following selections illustrate these movements, and auger the later shift to postmodernity. Darwin's denial of the fixity of species would become the dominant paradigm for the life sciences, and put the distinction of human and non-human in question. Baudelaire was the first to employ the term *modernité* in describing the new nineteenth-century urban aesthetic. Peirce was the inventor of pragmatism, which would eventually form the basis for Rorty's postmodernism as well as the attempt of more moderate "non-foundationalists" to counter postmodernism. Through his radical critique of the idealism of the Western tradition, both moral (i.e. Judeo-Christian) and epistemic, Nietzsche is the godfather of postmodernism, crucial especially for Derrida, Deleuze, and Foucault. De Saussure's structuralist linguistics set the stage for French post-structuralism. Marinetti and later Le Corbusier extolled new forms of literature and architecture, respectively, that reflect the utopian social theories characteristic of the period between the world wars. Weber, one of the most influential theorists of modernity, presented an historically informed, yet incipiently existentialist account of the modern age. Wittgenstein's radical assertion of the limits of philosophy became the most prominent form of twentieth-century anti-foundationalism, and his later view of language as pluralistic "language-games" inspired the postmodernism of Rorty and Lyotard. Freud, whose psychoanalytic theory was hugely influential in the humanities and social sciences, warned of the mounting "discontent" inherent in the progress of civilization. Husserl diagnosed the "crisis" of modernity with his new philosophy of phenomenology, which formed the basis both for Heidegger's thought and the French post-structuralists' critique. Adorno's and Horkheimer's classic *Dialectic of Enlightenment* was crucial for the debate over the fate of modernity, and, with Weber, forms the basis for Habermas's work. Sartre's existentialism was an important mid-century response to the problem of modern alienation, and a prime target for Heidegger.

The final four selections, which follow World War II, represent the transition to postmodernism. Heidegger's attack on Western humanism and the technological domination of nature by the "subject," a project with which he believed Western philosophy to have been complicit, is crucial to postmodernism, as well as his willingness to bend philosophical language in an attempt to say the unsayable. Lacan's structuralist version of psychoanalysis had a major impact on the French post-structuralists. Thomas Kuhn's famous analysis of scientific progress through revolutions and non-rational decisions, rather than a purely rational and cumulative process, was crucial for Rorty and other anti-foundationalists, as well as for the widespread uncertainty about the limits of rationalism and realism in science. Daniel Bell authored the most well-known version of the thesis that advanced, post-World War II Western societies were passing out of the modern industrial period into a post-industrial information age, with profound cultural and political implications.

From *The Origin of Species*

Charles Darwin

Perhaps the most momentous scientific advance of the nineteenth century, and certainly the one that most profoundly affected philosophy and the human sciences, was Charles Darwin's theory of evolution. In *The Origin of Species* (1859), Darwin (1809–82) argued that biological species are not fixed, but are the result of a process of "natural selection." In its way, this argument reconceived biology in light of emergent or spontaneous order by claiming that the formation of species is the undesigned outcome of random mutations and the complex interactions of species with their environment. The philosophical implications were vast, since natural selection cleared the way for understanding the distinction of human from non-human, crucial to notions of morality and rationality, as the contingent product of a natural process. Darwin himself applied his argument to the case of humans in *The Descent of Man* (1871).

Struggle for Existence

Before entering on the subject of this chapter, I must make a few preliminary remarks, to show how the struggle for existence bears on Natural Selection. It has been seen in the last chapter that amongst organic beings in a state of nature there is some individual variability: indeed I am not aware that this has ever been disputed. It is immaterial for us whether a multitude of doubtful forms be called species or sub-species or varieties; what rank, for instance, the two or three hundred doubtful forms of British plants are entitled to hold, if the existence of any well-marked varieties be admitted. But the mere existence of individual variability and of some few well-marked varieties, though necessary as the foundation for the work, helps us but little in understanding how species arise in nature. How have all those exquisite adaptations of one part of the organisation to another part, and to the conditions of life, and of one distinct organic being to another being, been perfected? We see these beautiful co-adaptations most plainly in the woodpecker and mistletoe; and only a little less plainly in the humblest parasite which clings to the hairs of a quadruped or feathers of a bird; in the structure of the beetle which dives through the water; in the plumed seed which is wafted by the gentlest breeze; in short, we see beautiful adaptations everywhere and in every part of the organic world.

Again, it may be asked, how is it that varieties, which I have called incipient species, become ultimately converted into good and distinct species, which in most cases obviously differ from each other far more than do the varieties of the same species? How do those groups of species, which constitute what are called distinct genera, and which differ from each other more than do the species of the same genus, arise? All these results, as we shall more fully see in the next section, follow from the struggle for life. Owing to this struggle for

Charles Darwin, from chapter 3 ("Struggle for Existence"), pp. 51–4, 62–6; from chapter 4 ("Natural Selection"), pp. 67–73; and from chapter 14 ("Recapitulation and Conclusion"), pp. 371, 389, and 394–6, in *The Origin of Species*. Oxford: Oxford University Press, 1996.

life, any variation, however slight, and from what-ever cause proceeding, if it be in any degree profit-able to an individual of any species, in its infinitely complex relations to other organic beings and to external nature, will tend to the preservation of that individual, and will generally be inherited by its offspring. The offspring, also, will thus have a better chance of surviving, for, of the many individ-uals of any species which are periodically born, but a small number can survive. I have called this principle, by which each slight variation, if useful, is preserved, by the term of Natural Selection, in order to mark its relation to man's power of selec-tion. We have seen that man by selection can cer-tainly produce great results, and can adapt organic beings to his own uses, through the accumulation of slight but useful variations, given to him by the hand of Nature. But Natural Selection, as we shall hereafter see, is a power incessantly ready for action, and is as immeasurably superior to man's feeble efforts, as the works of Nature are to those of Art.

We will now discuss in a little more detail the struggle for existence. In my future work this sub-ject shall be treated, as it well deserves, at much greater length. The elder de Candolle and Lyell have largely and philosophically shown that all organic beings are exposed to severe competition.[i] In regard to plants, no one has treated this subject with more spirit and ability than W. Herbert, Dean of Manchester, evidently the result of his great horticultural knowledge.[ii] Nothing is easier than to admit in words the truth of the universal struggle for life, or more difficult – at least I have found it so – than constantly to bear this conclusion in mind. Yet unless it be thoroughly engrained in the mind, I am convinced that the whole economy of nature, with every fact on distribution, rarity, abundance, extinction, and variation, will be dimly seen or quite misunderstood. We behold the face of nature bright with gladness, we often see superabundance of food; we do not see, or we forget that the birds which are idly singing round us mostly live on insects or seeds, and are thus constantly destroying life; or we forget how largely these songsters, or their eggs, or their nestlings, are destroyed by birds and beasts of prey; we do not always bear in mind, that though food may be now superabundant, it is not so at all seasons of each recurring year.

I should premise that I use the term Struggle for Existence in a large and metaphorical sense, includ-ing dependence of one being on another, and in-cluding (which is more important) not only the life of the individual, but success in leaving progeny. Two canine animals in a time of dearth, may be truly said to struggle with each other which shall get food and live. But a plant on the edge of a desert is said to struggle for life against the drought, though more properly it should be said to be dependent on the moisture. A plant which annually produces a thousand seeds, of which on an average only one comes to maturity, may be more truly said to struggle with the plants of the same and other kinds which already clothe the ground. The mistle-toe is dependent on the apple and a few other trees, but can only in a far-fetched sense be said to struggle with these trees, for if too many of these parasites grow on the same tree, it will languish and die. But several seedling mistletoes, growing close together on the same branch, may more truly be said to struggle with each other. As the mistletoe is disseminated by birds, its existence depends on birds; and it may metaphorically be said to struggle with other fruit-bearing plants, in order to tempt birds to devour and thus disseminate its seeds rather than those of other plants. In these several senses, which pass into each other, I use for convenience' sake the general term of struggle for existence.

A struggle for existence inevitably follows from the high rate at which all organic beings tend to increase. Every being, which during its natural lifetime produces several eggs or seeds, must suffer destruction during some period of its life, and during some season or occasional year, otherwise, on the principle of geometrical increase, its numbers would quickly become so inordinately great that no country could support the product. Hence, as more individuals are produced than can possibly survive, there must in every case be a struggle for existence, either one individual with another of the same species, or with the individuals of distinct species, or with the physical conditions of life. It is the doctrine of Malthus applied with manifold force to the whole animal and vegetable kingdoms; for in this case there can be no artificial increase of food, and no prudential restraint from marriage.[iii] Although some species may be now

---

[i] Augustin de Candolle (1778–1841), botanist, and Charles Lyell (1797–1875), whose *Principles of Geology* (1833) influenced Darwin.
[ii] William Herbert (1778–1847), botanist.

[iii] Thomas Robert Malthus (1766–1834), a political economist, argued that uncontrolled growth of the human population will proceed exponentially, hence exceed natural resources.

increasing, more or less rapidly, in numbers, all cannot do so, for the world would not hold them.

There is no exception to the rule that every organic being naturally increases at so high a rate, that if not destroyed, the earth would soon be covered by the progeny of a single pair. Even slow-breeding man has doubled in twenty-five years, and at this rate, in a few thousand years, there would literally not be standing room for his progeny. Linnæus has calculated that if an annual plant produced only two seeds – and there is no plant so unproductive as this – and their seedlings next year produced two, and so on, then in twenty years there would be a million plants.[iv] The elephant is reckoned the slowest breeder of all known animals, and I have taken some pains to estimate its probable minimum rate of natural increase: it will be under the mark to assume that it breeds when thirty years old, and goes on breeding till ninety years old, bringing forth three pair of young in this interval; if this be so, at the end of the fifth century there would be alive fifteen million elephants, descended from the first pair. . . .

In the case of every species, many different checks, acting at different periods of life, and during different seasons or years, probably come into play; some one check or some few being generally the most potent, but all concur in determining the average number or even the existence of the species. In some cases it can be shown that widely-different checks act on the same species in different districts. When we look at the plants and bushes clothing an entangled bank, we are tempted to attribute their proportional numbers and kinds to what we call chance. But how false a view is this! Every one has heard that when an American forest is cut down, a very different vegetation springs up; but it has been observed that ancient Indian ruins in the Southern United States, which must formerly have been cleared of trees, now display the same beautiful diversity and proportion of kinds as in the surrounding virgin forests. What a struggle between the several kinds of trees must here have gone on during long centuries, each annually scattering its seeds by the thousand; what war between insect and insect – between insects, snails, and other animals with birds and beasts of prey – all striving to increase, and all feeding on each other or on the trees or their seeds and seedlings, or on the other plants which first clothed the ground and thus checked the growth of the trees! Throw up a handful of feathers, and all must fall to the ground according to definite laws; but how simple is this problem compared to the action and reaction of the innumerable plants and animals which have determined, in the course of centuries, the proportional numbers and kinds of trees now growing on the old Indian ruins!

The dependency of one organic being on another, as of a parasite on its prey, lies generally between beings remote in the scale of nature. This is often the case with those which may strictly be said to struggle with each other for existence, as in the case of locusts and grass-feeding quadrupeds. But the struggle almost invariably will be most severe between the individuals of the same species, for they frequent the same districts, require the same food, and are exposed to the same dangers. In the case of varieties of the same species, the struggle will generally be almost equally severe, and we sometimes see the contest soon decided: for instance, if several varieties of wheat be sown together, and the mixed seed be resown, some of the varieties which best suit the soil or climate, or are naturally the most fertile, will beat the others and so yield more seed, and consequently in a few years quite supplant the other varieties. To keep up a mixed stock of even such extremely close varieties as the variously coloured sweet-peas, they must be each year harvested separately, and the seed then mixed in due proportion, otherwise the weaker kinds will steadily decrease in numbers and disappear. So again with the varieties of sheep: it has been asserted that certain mountain-varieties will starve out other mountain-varieties, so that they cannot be kept together. The same result has followed from keeping together different varieties of the medicinal leech. It may even be doubted whether the varieties of any one of our domestic plants or animals have so exactly the same strength, habits, and constitution, that the original proportions of a mixed stock could be kept up for half-a-dozen generations, if they were allowed to struggle together, like beings in a state of nature, and if the seed or young were not annually sorted.

As species of the same genus have usually, though by no means invariably, some similarity in habits and constitution, and always in structure, the struggle will generally be more severe between species of the same genus, when they come into competition with each other, than between species of distinct genera. We see this in the recent extension over parts of the United States of one species of swallow having caused the decrease of another

[iv] Linnæus (Carl von Linné, 1708–79), who produced the modern 'taxonomy', or classification of living things.

species. The recent increase of the misselthrush in parts of Scotland has caused the decrease of the songthrush. How frequently we hear of one species of rat taking the place of another species under the most different climates! In Russia the small Asiatic cockroach has everywhere driven before it its great congener. One species of charlock will supplant another, and so in other cases. We can dimly see why the competition should be most severe between allied forms, which fill nearly the same place in the economy of nature; but probably in no one case could we precisely say why one species has been victorious over another in the great battle of life.

A corollary of the highest importance may be deduced from the foregoing remarks, namely, that the structure of every organic being is related, in the most essential yet often hidden manner, to that of all other organic beings, with which it comes into competition for food or residence, or from which it has to escape, or on which it preys. This is obvious in the structure of the teeth and talons of the tiger; and in that of the legs and claws of the parasite which clings to the hair on the tiger's body. But in the beautifully plumed seed of the dandelion, and in the flattened and fringed legs of the water-beetle, the relation seems at first confined to the elements of air and water. Yet the advantage of plumed seeds no doubt stands in the closest relation to the land being already thickly clothed by other plants; so that the seeds may be widely distributed and fall on unoccupied ground. In the water-beetle, the structure of its legs, so well adapted for diving, allows it to compete with other aquatic insects, to hunt for its own prey, and to escape serving as prey to other animals.

The store of nutriment laid up within the seeds of many plants seems at first sight to have no sort of relation to other plants. But from the strong growth of young plants produced from such seeds (as peas and beans), when sown in the midst of long grass, I suspect that the chief use of the nutriment in the seed is to favour the growth of the young seedling, whilst struggling with other plants growing vigorously all around.

Look at a plant in the midst of its range, why does it not double or quadruple its numbers? We know that it can perfectly well withstand a little more heat or cold, dampness or dryness, for elsewhere it ranges into slightly hotter or colder, damper or drier districts. In this case we can clearly see that if we wished in imagination to give the plant the power of increasing in number, we should have to give it some advantage over its competitors, or over the animals which preyed on it. On the confines of its geographical range, a change of constitution with respect to climate would clearly be an advantage to our plant; but we have reason to believe that only a few plants or animals range so far, that they are destroyed by the rigour of the climate alone. Not until we reach the extreme confines of life, in the Arctic regions or on the borders of an utter desert, will competition cease. The land may be extremely cold or dry, yet there will be competition between some few species, or between the individuals of the same species, for the warmest or dampest spots.

Hence, also, we can see that when a plant or animal is placed in a new country amongst new competitors, though the climate may be exactly the same as in its former home, yet the conditions of its life will generally be changed in an essential manner. If we wished to increase its average numbers in its new home, we should have to modify it in a different way to what we should have done in its native country; for we should have to give it some advantage over a different set of competitors or enemies.

It is good thus to try in our imagination to give any form some advantage over another. Probably in no single instance should we know what to do, so as to succeed. It will convince us of our ignorance on the mutual relations of all organic beings; a conviction as necessary, as it seems to be difficult to acquire. All that we can do, is to keep steadily in mind that each organic being is striving to increase at a geometrical ratio; that each at some period of its life, during some season of the year, during each generation or at intervals, has to struggle for life, and to suffer great destruction. When we reflect on this struggle, we may console ourselves with the full belief, that the war of nature is not incessant, that no fear is felt, that death is generally prompt, and that the vigorous, the healthy, and the happy survive and multiply.

Natural Selection

How will the struggle for existence, discussed too briefly in the last section, act in regard to variation? Can the principle of selection, which we have seen is so potent in the hands of man, apply in nature? I think we shall see that it can act most effectually. Let it be borne in mind in what an endless number of strange peculiarities our domestic productions, and, in a lesser degree, those under nature, vary; and how strong the hereditary tendency is. Under domestication, it may be truly said that the whole organisation becomes in some degree plastic. Let it be borne in mind how infinitely complex and close-fitting are the mutual relations of all organic beings to each other and to their physical conditions of life. Can it, then, be thought improbable, seeing that variations useful to man have undoubtedly occurred, that other variations useful in some way to each being in the great and complex battle of life, should sometimes occur in the course of thousands of generations? If such do occur, can we doubt (remembering that many more individuals are born than can possibly survive) that individuals having any advantage, however slight, over others, would have the best chance of surviving and of procreating their kind? On the other hand, we may feel sure that any variation in the least degree injurious would be rigidly destroyed. This preservation of favourable variations and the rejection of injurious variations, I call Natural Selection. Variations neither useful nor injurious would not be affected by natural selection, and would be left a fluctuating element, as perhaps we see in the species called polymorphic.

We shall best understand the probable course of natural selection by taking the case of a country undergoing some physical change, for instance, of climate. The proportional numbers of its inhabitants would almost immediately undergo a change, and some species might become extinct. We may conclude, from what we have seen of the intimate and complex manner in which the inhabitants of each country are bound together, that any change in the numerical proportions of some of the inhabitants, independently of the change of climate itself, would seriously affect many of the others. If the country were open on its borders, new forms would certainly immigrate, and this also would seriously disturb the relations of some of the former inhabitants. Let it be remembered how powerful the influence of a single introduced tree or mammal has been shown to be. But in the case of an island, or of a country partly surrounded by barriers, into which new and better adapted forms could not freely enter, we should then have places in the economy of nature which would assuredly be better filled up, if some of the original inhabitants were in some manner modified; for, had the area been open to immigration, these same places would have been seized on by intruders. In such case, every slight modification, which in the course of ages chanced to arise, and which in any way favoured the individuals of any of the species, by better adapting them to their altered conditions, would tend to be preserved; and natural selection would thus have free scope for the work of improvement.

We have reason to believe, as stated in the first chapter, that a change in the conditions of life, by specially acting on the reproductive system, causes or increases variability; and in the foregoing case the conditions of life are supposed to have undergone a change, and this would manifestly be favourable to natural selection, by giving a better chance of profitable variations occurring; and unless profitable variations do occur, natural selection can do nothing. Not that, as I believe, any extreme amount of variability is necessary; as man can certainly produce great results by adding up in any given direction mere individual differences, so could Nature, but far more easily, from having incomparably longer time at her disposal. Nor do I believe that any great physical change, as of climate, or any unusual degree of isolation to check immigration, is actually necessary to produce new and unoccupied places for natural selection to fill up by modifying and improving some of the varying inhabitants. For as all the inhabitants of each country are struggling together with nicely balanced forces, extremely slight modifications in the structure or habits of one inhabitant would often give it an advantage over others; and still further modifications of the same kind would often still further increase the advantage. No country can be named in which all the native inhabitants are now so perfectly adapted to each other and to the physical conditions under which they live, that none of them could anyhow be improved; for in all countries, the native have been so far conquered by naturalised productions, that they have allowed foreigners to take firm possession of the land. And as foreigners have thus everywhere beaten some of the natives, we may safely conclude that the natives might have been modified with advantage, so as to have better resisted such intruders.

As man can produce and certainly has produced a great result by his methodical and unconscious means of selection, what may not Nature effect? Man can act only on external and visible characters: Nature cares nothing for appearances, except in so far as they may be useful to any being. She can act on every internal organ, on every shade of constitutional difference, on the whole machinery of life. Man selects only for his own good; Nature only for that of the being which she tends. Every selected character is fully exercised by her; and the being is placed under well-suited conditions of life. Man keeps the natives of many climates in the same country; he seldom exercises each selected character in some peculiar and fitting manner; he feeds a long and a short beaked pigeon on the same food; he does not exercise a long-backed or long-legged quadruped in any peculiar manner; he exposes sheep with long and short wool to the same climate. He does not allow the most vigorous males to struggle for the females. He does not rigidly destroy all inferior animals, but protects during each varying season, as far as lies in his power, all his productions. He often begins his selection by some half-monstrous form; or at least by some modification prominent enough to catch his eye, or to be plainly useful to him. Under nature, the slightest difference of structure or constitution may well turn the nicely-balanced scale in the struggle for life, and so be preserved. How fleeting are the wishes and efforts of man! how short his time! and consequently how poor will his products be, compared with those accumulated by Nature during whole geological periods. Can we wonder, then, that Nature's productions should be far 'truer' in character than man's productions; that they should be infinitely better adapted to the most complex conditions of life, and should plainly bear the stamp of far higher workmanship?

It may metaphorically be said that natural selection is daily and hourly scrutinising, throughout the world, every variation, even the slightest; rejecting that which is bad, preserving and adding up all that is good; silently and insensibly working, whenever and wherever opportunity offers, at the improvement of each organic being in relation to its organic and inorganic conditions of life. We see nothing of these slow changes in progress, until the hand of time has marked the long lapse of ages, and then so imperfect is our view into long past geological ages, that we only see that the forms of life are now different from what they formerly were.

Although natural selection can act only through and for the good of each being, yet characters and structures, which we are apt to consider as of very trifling importance, may thus be acted on. When we see leaf-eating insects green, and bark-feeders mottled-grey; the alpine ptarmigan white in winter, the red-grouse the colour of heather, and the black-grouse that of peaty earth, we must believe that these tints are of service to these birds and insects in preserving them from danger. Grouse, if not destroyed at some period of their lives, would increase in countless numbers; they are known to suffer largely from birds of prey; and hawks are

guided by eyesight to their prey – so much so, that on parts of the Continent persons are warned not to keep white pigeons, as being the most liable to destruction. Hence I can see no reason to doubt that natural selection might be most effective in giving the proper colour to each kind of grouse, and in keeping that colour, when once acquired, true and constant. Nor ought we to think that the occasional destruction of an animal of any particular colour would produce little effect: we should remember how essential it is in a flock of white sheep to destroy every lamb with the faintest trace of black. In plants the down on the fruit and the colour of the flesh are considered by botanists as characters of the most trifling importance: yet we hear from an excellent horticulturist, Downing, that in the United States smooth-skinned fruits suffer far more from a beetle, a curculio, than those with down; that purple plums suffer far more from a certain disease than yellow plums; whereas another disease attacks yellow-fleshed peaches far more than those with other coloured flesh.[v] If, with all the aids of art, these slight differences make a great difference in cultivating the several varieties, assuredly, in a state of nature, where the trees would have to struggle with other trees and with a host of enemies, such differences would effectually settle which variety, whether a smooth or downy, a yellow or purple fleshed fruit, should succeed.

In looking at many small points of difference between species, which, as far as our ignorance permits us to judge, seem quite unimportant, we must not forget that climate, food, etc., probably produce some slight and direct effect. It is, however, far more necessary to bear in mind that there are many unknown laws of correlation of growth, which, when one part of the organisation is modified through variation, and the modifications are accumulated by natural selection for the good of the being, will cause other modifications, often of the most unexpected nature.

As we see that those variations which under domestication appear at any particular period of life, tend to reappear in the offspring at the same period; – for instance, in the seeds of the many varieties of our culinary and agricultural plants; in the caterpillar and cocoon stages of the varieties of the silkworm; in the eggs of poultry, and in the colour of the down of their chickens; in the horns of

[v] Andrew Downing (1815–52), American botanist of fruit trees.

our sheep and cattle when nearly adult; – so in a state of nature, natural selection will be enabled to act on and modify organic beings at any age, by the accumulation of variations profitable at that age, and by their inheritance at a corresponding age. If it profit a plant to have its seeds more and more widely disseminated by the wind, I can see no greater difficulty in this being effected through natural selection, than in the cotton-planter increasing and improving by selection the down in the pods on his cotton-trees. Natural selection may modify and adapt the larva of an insect to a score of contingencies, wholly different from those which concern the mature insect. These modifications will no doubt affect, through the laws of correlation, the structure of the adult; and probably in the case of those insects which live only for a few hours, and which never feed, a large part of their structure is merely the correlated result of successive changes in the structure of their larvæ. So, conversely, modifications in the adult will probably often affect the structure of the larva; but in all cases natural selection will ensure that modifications consequent on other modifications at a different period of life, shall not be in the least degree injurious: for if they became so, they would cause the extinction of the species.

Natural selection will modify the structure of the young in relation to the parent, and of the parent in relation to the young. In social animals it will adapt the structure of each individual for the benefit of the community; if each in consequence profits by the selected change. What natural selection cannot do, is to modify the structure of one species, without giving it any advantage, for the good of another species; and though statements to this effect may be found in works of natural history, I cannot find one case which will bear investigation. A structure used only once in an animal's whole life, if of high importance to it, might be modified to any extent by natural selection; for instance, the great jaws possessed by certain insects, used exclusively for opening the cocoon – or the hard tip to the beak of nestling birds, used for breaking the egg. It has been asserted, that of the best short-beaked tumbler-pigeons more perish in the egg than are able to get out of it; so that fanciers assist in the act of hatching. Now, if nature had to make the beak of a full-grown pigeon very short for the bird's own advantage, the process of modification would be very slow, and there would be simultaneously the most rigorous selection of the young birds within the egg, which had the most powerful and hardest beaks, for all with weak beaks would inevitably perish: or, more delicate and more easily broken shells might be selected, the thickness of the shell being known to vary like every other structure. . . .

Recapitulation and Conclusion

As this whole volume is one long argument, it may be convenient to the reader to have the leading facts and inferences briefly recapitulated.

That many and serious objections may be advanced against the theory of descent with modification through natural selection, I do not deny. I have endeavoured to give to them their full force. Nothing at first can appear more difficult to believe than that the more complex organs and instincts should have been perfected, not by means superior to, though analogous with, human reason, but by the accumulation of innumerable slight variations, each good for the individual possessor. Nevertheless, this difficulty, though appearing to our imagination insuperably great, cannot be considered real if we admit the following propositions, namely, – that gradations in the perfection of any organ or instinct which we may consider, either do now exist or could have existed, each good of its kind, – that all organs and instincts are, in ever so slight a degree, variable, – and, lastly, that there is a struggle for existence leading to the preservation of each profitable deviation of structure or instinct. The truth of these propositions cannot, I think, be disputed. . . .

Although I am fully convinced of the truth of the views given in this volume under the form of an abstract, I by no means expect to convince experienced naturalists whose minds are stocked with a multitude of facts all viewed, during a long course of years, from a point of view directly opposite to mine. It is so easy to hide our ignorance under such expressions as the 'plan of creation', 'unity of design', etc., and to think that we give an explanation when we only restate a fact. Any one whose disposition leads him to attach more weight to unexplained difficulties than to the explanation of a certain number of facts will certainly reject my theory. A few naturalists, endowed with much flexibility of mind, and who have already begun to doubt on the immutability of species, may be influenced by this volume; but I look with confidence to the future, to young and rising naturalists, who will be able to view both sides of the question with impartiality. Whoever is led to believe that species are mutable will do good service by conscientiously expressing his conviction; for only thus can the load of prejudice by which this subject is overwhelmed be removed. . . .

Authors of the highest eminence seem to be fully satisfied with the view that each species has been independently created. To my mind it accords better with what we know of the laws impressed on matter by the Creator, that the production and extinction of the past and present inhabitants of the world should have been due to secondary causes, like those determining the birth and death of the individual. When I view all beings not as special creations, but as the lineal descendants of some few beings which lived long before the first bed of the Silurian system was deposited, they seem to me to become ennobled.[vi] Judging from the past, we may safely infer that not one living species will transmit its unaltered likeness to a distant futurity. And of the species now living very few will transmit progeny of any kind to a far distant futurity; for the manner in which all organic beings are grouped, shows that the greater number of species of each genus, and all the species of many genera, have left no descendants, but have become utterly extinct. We can so far take a prophetic glance into futurity as to foretell that it will be the common and widely-spread species, belonging to the larger and dominant groups, which will ultimately prevail and procreate new and dominant species. As all the living forms of life are the lineal descendants of those which lived long before the Silurian epoch, we may feel certain that the ordinary succession by generation has never once been broken, and

that no cataclysm has desolated the whole world. Hence we may look with some confidence to a secure future of equally inappreciable length. And as natural selection works solely by and for the good of each being, all corporeal and mental endowments will tend to progress towards perfection.

It is interesting to contemplate an entangled bank, clothed with many plants of many kinds, with birds singing on the bushes, with various insects flitting about, and with worms crawling through the damp earth, and to reflect that these elaborately constructed forms, so different from each other, and dependent on each other in so complex a manner, have all been produced by laws acting around us. These laws, taken in the largest sense, being Growth with Reproduction; Inheritance, which is almost implied by reproduction; Variability, from the indirect and direct action of the external conditions of life, and from use and disuse; a Ratio of Increase so high as to lead to a Struggle for Life, and as a consequence to Natural Selection, entailing Divergence of Character and the Extinction of less-improved forms. Thus, from the war of nature, from famine and death, the most exalted object which we are capable of conceiving, namely, the production of the higher animals, directly follows. There is grandeur in this view of life, with its several powers, having been originally breathed by the Creator into a few forms or into one; and that, whilst this planet has gone cycling on according to the fixed law of gravity, from so simple a beginning endless forms most beautiful and most wonderful have been, and are being, evolved.

[vi]   The Silurian system is an early Palaeozoic stratum of fossil-containing rocks.

11

From "The Painter of Modern Life"

Charles Baudelaire

Charles Baudelaire (1821–67), controversial Parisian poet and critic of the arts, was the first to use the term "modernity" (*modernité*), in the essay "The Painter of Modern Life" (1863). For Baudelaire modernity is the attitude or sensibility of the urban *flâneur* or idler, the non-productive aesthete who embodies the sensibility of the outdoor café, that vantage point from which the passing carnival of city life can be observed. Most famous for the collection of poems, *The Flowers of Evil*, for which he was legally charged with offending public morality, Baudelaire revolutionized French poetry with his realistic attention to the disorder and depravity of urban life, in which he nevertheless saw a characteristically modern beauty.

An Artist, Man of the World, Man of Crowds, and Child

Today I want to talk to my readers about a singular man, whose originality is so powerful and clear-cut that it is self-sufficing, and does not bother to look for approval. None of his drawings is signed, if by signature we mean the few letters, which can be so easily forged, that compose a name, and that so many other artists grandly inscribe at the bottom of their most carefree sketches. But all his works are signed with his dazzling soul, and art-lovers who have seen and liked them will recognize them easily from the description I propose to give of them. M. C. G.[i] loves mixing with the crowds, loves being incognito, and carries his originality to the point of modesty. M. Thackeray, who, as is well known, is very interested in all things to do with art, and who draws the illustrations for his own novels, one day spoke of M. G. in a London review, much to the irritation of the latter who regarded the matter as an outrage to his modesty. And again quite recently, when he heard that I was proposing to make an assessment of his mind and talent, he begged me, in a most peremptory manner, to suppress his name, and to discuss his works only as though they were the works of some anonymous person. I will humbly obey this odd request. The reader and I will proceed as though M. G. did not exist, and we will discuss his drawings and his water-colours, for which he professes a patrician's disdain, in the same way as would a group of scholars faced with the task of assessing the importance of a number of precious historical documents which chance has brought to light, and the author of which must for ever remain unknown. And even to reassure my conscience completely, let my readers assume that all the things I have to say about the artist's nature, so strangely and mysteriously dazzling, have been more or less accurately suggested by the works in question; pure poetic hypothesis, conjecture, or imaginative reconstructions.

[i] Constantin Guys (1802–92), Parisian painter and journalist.

Charles Baudelaire, from "The Painter of Modern Life" (trans. P. E. Charvet) in *Baudelaire: Selected Writings on Art and Literature*, London: Penguin, 1992, sections 3–4, pp. 395–406.

M. G. is an old man. Jean-Jacques[ii] began writing, so they say, at the age of forty-two. Perhaps it was at about that age that M. G., obsessed by the world of images that filled his mind, plucked up courage to cast ink and colours on to a sheet of white paper. To be honest, he drew like a barbarian, like a child, angrily chiding his clumsy fingers and his disobedient tool. I have seen a large number of these early scribblings, and I admit that most of the people who know what they are talking about, or who claim to, could, without shame, have failed to discern the latent genius that dwelt in these obscure beginnings. Today, M. G., who has discovered unaided all the little tricks of the trade, and who has taught himself, without help or advice, has become a powerful master in his own way; of his early artlessness he has retained only what was needed to add an unexpected spice to his abundant gift. When he happens upon one of these efforts of his early manner, he tears it up or burns it, with a most amusing show of shame and indignation.

For ten whole years I wanted to make the acquaintance of M. G., who is by nature a great traveller and very cosmopolitan. I knew that he had for a long time been working for an English illustrated paper and that in it had appeared engravings from his travel sketches (Spain, Turkey, the Crimea). Since then I have seen a considerable mass of these on-the-spot drawings from life, and I have thus been able to 'read' a detailed and daily account, infinitely preferable to any other, of the Crimean campaign. The same paper had also published (without signature, as before) a large quantity of compositions by this artist from the new ballets and operas. When at last I ran him to ground I saw at once that I was not dealing exactly with an artist but rather with a man of the world. In this context, pray interpret the word 'artist' in a very narrow sense, and the expression 'man of the world' in a very broad one. By 'man of the world', I mean a man of the whole world, a man who understands the world and the mysterious and legitimate reasons behind all its customs; by 'artist', I mean a specialist, a man tied to his palette like a serf to the soil. M. G. does not like being called an artist. Is he not justified to a small extent? He takes an interest in everything the world over, he wants to know, understand, assess everything that happens on the surface of our spheroid. The artist moves little, or even not at all, in intellectual and political circles. If he lives in the Bréda quarter he knows nothing of

ii   Rousseau.

iii   A less, and a more, posh quarter of Paris, respectively.

what goes on in the Faubourg Saint-Germain.[iii] With two or three exceptions, which it is unnecessary to name, the majority of artists are, let us face it, very skilled brutes, mere manual labourers, village pub-talkers with the minds of country bumpkins. Their talk, inevitably enclosed within very narrow limits, quickly becomes a bore to the man of the world, to the spiritual citizen of the universe.

Thus to begin to understand M. G., the first thing to note is this: that curiosity may be considered the starting point of his genius.

Do you remember a picture (for indeed it is a picture!) written by the most powerful pen of this age and entitled *The Man of the Crowd*?[iv] Sitting in a café, and looking through the shop window, a convalescent is enjoying the sight of the passing crowd, and identifying himself in thought with all the thoughts that are moving around him. He has only recently come back from the shades of death and breathes in with delight all the spores and odours of life; as he has been on the point of forgetting everything, he remembers and passionately wants to remember everything. In the end he rushes out into the crowd in search of a man unknown to him whose face, which he had caught sight of, had in a flash fascinated him. Curiosity had become a compelling, irresistible passion.

Now imagine an artist perpetually in the spiritual condition of the convalescent, and you will have the key to the character of M. G.

But convalescence is like a return to childhood. The convalescent, like the child, enjoys to the highest degree the faculty of taking a lively interest in things, even the most trivial in appearance. Let us hark back, if we can, by a retrospective effort of our imaginations, to our youngest, our morning impressions, and we shall recognize that they were remarkably akin to the vividly coloured impressions that we received later on after a physical illness, provided that illness left our spiritual faculties pure and unimpaired. The child sees everything as a novelty; the child is always 'drunk'. Nothing is more like what we call inspiration than the joy the child feels in drinking in shape and colour. I will venture to go even further and declare that inspiration has some connection with congestion, that every sublime thought is accompanied by a more or less vigorous nervous impulse that reverberates in the cerebral cortex. The man of genius has strong nerves; those of the child are weak. In the one, reason has assumed an important role; in the other, sensibility occupies almost the whole being. But genius is no more than childhood recaptured at will, childhood equipped now with man's physical means to express itself, and with the analytical mind that enables it to bring order into the sum of experience, involuntarily amassed. To this deep and joyful curiosity must be attributed that stare, animal-like in its ecstasy, which all children have when confronted with something new, whatever it may be, face or landscape, light, gilding, colours, watered silk, enchantment of beauty, enhanced by the arts of dress. A friend of mine was telling me one day how, as a small boy, he used to be present when his father was dressing, and how he had always been filled with astonishment, mixed with delight, as he looked at the arm muscle, the colour tones of the skin tinged with rose and yellow, and the bluish network of the veins. The picture of the external world was already beginning to fill him with respect, and to take possession of his brain. Already the shape of things obsessed and possessed him. A precocious fate was showing the tip of its nose. His damnation was settled. Need I say that, today, the child is a famous painter.

I was asking you just now to think of M. G. as an eternal convalescent; to complete your idea of him, think of him also as a man-child, as a man possessing at every moment the genius of childhood, in other words a genius for whom no edge of life is blunted.

I told you that I was unwilling to call him a pure artist, and that he himself rejected this title, with a modesty tinged with aristocratic restraint. I would willingly call him a dandy, and for that I would have a sheaf of good reasons; for the word 'dandy' implies a quintessence of character and a subtle understanding of all the moral mechanisms of this world; but, from another aspect, the dandy aspires to cold detachment, and it is in this way that M. G., who is dominated, if ever anyone was, by an insatiable passion, that of seeing and feeling, parts company trenchantly with dandyism. *Amabam amare*, said St Augustine. 'I love passion, passionately,' M. G. might willingly echo. The dandy is blasé, or affects to be, as a matter of policy and class attitude. M. G. hates blasé people. Sophisticated minds will understand me when I say that he possesses that difficult art of being sincere without being ridiculous. I would willingly confer on him the title of philosopher, to which he has a right for more than one reason; but his excessive love of visible, tangible things, in their most plastic form, inspires him

with a certain dislike of those things that go to make up the intangible kingdom of the metaphysician. Let us therefore reduce him to the status of the pure pictorial moralist, like La Bruyère.[v]

The crowd is his domain, just as the air is the bird's, and water that of the fish. His passion and his profession is to merge with the crowd. For the perfect idler, for the passionate observer it becomes an immense source of enjoyment to establish his dwelling in the throng, in the ebb and flow, the bustle, the fleeting and the infinite. To be away from home and yet to feel at home anywhere; to see the world, to be at the very centre of the world, and yet to be unseen of the world, such are some of the minor pleasures of those independent, intense and impartial spirits, who do not lend themselves easily to linguistic definitions. The observer is a prince enjoying his incognito wherever he goes. The lover of life makes the whole world into his family, just as the lover of the fair sex creates his from all the lovely women he has found, from those that could be found, and those who are impossible to find, just as the picture-lover lives in an enchanted world of dreams painted on canvas. Thus the lover of universal life moves into the crowd as though into an enormous reservoir of electricity. He, the lover of life, may also be compared to a mirror as vast as this crowd; to a kaleidoscope endowed with consciousness, which with every one of its movements presents a pattern of life, in all its multiplicity, and the flowing grace of all the elements that go to compose life. It is an ego athirst for the non-ego, and reflecting it at every moment in energies more vivid than life itself, always inconstant and fleeting. 'Any man', M. G. once said, in one of those talks he rendered memorable by the intensity of his gaze, and by his eloquence of gesture, 'any man who is not weighed down with a sorrow so searching as to touch all his faculties, and who is bored in the midst of the crowd, is a fool! A fool! and I despise him!'

When, as he wakes up, M. G. opens his eyes and sees the sun beating vibrantly at his window-panes, he says to himself with remorse and regret: 'What an imperative command! What a fanfare of light! Light everywhere for several hours past! Light I have lost in sleep! and endless numbers of things bathed in light that I could have seen and have failed to!' And off he goes! And he watches the flow of life move by, majestic and dazzling. He admires the eternal beauty and the astonishing harmony of life in the

[v] Jean La Bruyère (1645–96), French moralist.

capital cities, a harmony so providentially maintained in the tumult of human liberty. He gazes at the landscape of the great city, landscapes of stone, now swathed in the mist, now struck in full face by the sun. He enjoys handsome equipages, proud horses, the spit and polish of the grooms, the skilful handling by the page boys, the smooth rhythmical gait of the women, the beauty of the children, full of the joy of life and proud as peacocks of their pretty clothes; in short, life universal. If in a shift of fashion, the cut of a dress has been slightly modified, if clusters of ribbons and curls have been dethroned by rosettes, if bonnets have widened and chignons have come down a little on the nape of the neck, if waist-lines have been raised and skirts become fuller, you may be sure that from a long way off his eagle's eye will have detected it. A regiment marches by, maybe on its way to the ends of the earth, filling the air of the boulevard with its martial airs, as light and lively as hope; and sure enough M. G. has already seen, inspected and analysed the weapons and the bearing of this whole body of troops. Harness, highlights, bands, determined mien, heavy and grim mustachios, all these details flood chaotically into him; and within a few minutes the poem that comes with it all is virtually composed. And then his soul will vibrate with the soul of the regiment, marching as though it were one living creature, proud image of joy and discipline!

But evening comes. The witching hour, the uncertain light, when the sky draws its curtains and the city lights go on. The gaslight stands out on the purple background of the setting sun. Honest men or crooked customers, wise or irresponsible, all are saying to themselves: 'The day is done at last!' Good men and bad turn their thoughts to pleasure, and each hurries to his favourite haunt to drink the cup of oblivion. M. G. will be the last to leave any place where the departing glories of daylight linger, where poetry echoes, life pulsates, music sounds; any place where a human passion offers a subject to his eye where natural man and conventional man reveal themselves in strange beauty, where the rays of the dying sun play on the fleeting pleasure of the 'depraved animal!'[vi] 'Well, there, to be sure, is a day well filled,' murmurs to himself a type of reader well-known to all of us; 'each one of us has surely enough genius to fill it in the same way.' No! few men have the gift of seeing; fewer still have the power to express themselves. And now, whilst others are sleeping, this man is leaning over his table, his steady gaze on a sheet of paper, exactly the same gaze as he directed just now at the things about him, brandishing his pencil, his pen, his brush, splashing water from the glass up to the ceiling, wiping his pen on his shirt, hurried, vigorous, active, as though he was afraid the images might escape him, quarrelsome though alone, and driving himself relentlessly on. And things seen are born again on the paper, natural and more than natural, beautiful and better than beautiful, strange and endowed with an enthusiastic life, like the soul of their creator. The weird pageant has been distilled from nature. All the materials, stored higgledypiggledy by memory, are classified, ordered, harmonized, and undergo that deliberate idealization, which is the product of a childlike perceptiveness, in other words a perceptiveness that is acute and magical by its very ingenuousness.

Modernity

And so, walking or quickening his pace, he goes his way, for ever in search. In search of what? We may rest assured that this man, such as I have described him, this solitary mortal endowed with an active imagination, always roaming the great desert of men, has a nobler aim than that of the pure idler, a more general aim, other than the fleeting pleasure of circumstance. He is looking for that indefinable something we may be allowed to call 'modernity', for want of a better term to express the idea in question. The aim for him is to extract from fashion the poetry that resides in its historical envelope, to distil the eternal from the transitory. If we cast our eye over our exhibitions of modern pictures, we shall be struck by the general tendency of our artists to clothe all manner of subjects in the dress of the past. Almost all of them use the fashions and the furnishings of the Renaissance, as David used Roman fashions and furnishings, but there is this difference, that David, having chosen subjects peculiarly Greek or Roman, could not do otherwise than present them in the style of antiquity, whereas the painters of today, choosing, as they do, subjects of a general nature, applicable to all ages, will insist on dressing them up in the fashion of the Middle Ages, of the Renaissance, or of the East.[vii]

[vi] Rousseau's phrase: "The man who meditates is a depraved animal" (*Discourse on the Origin and Foundations of Inequality Among Men*, Part One).

[vii] Jacques Louis David (1748–1825), French neo-classical painter.

This is evidently sheer laziness; for it is much more convenient to state roundly that everything is hopelessly ugly in the dress of a period than to apply oneself to the task of extracting the mysterious beauty that may be hidden there, however small or light it may be. Modernity is the transient, the fleeting, the contingent; it is one half of art, the other being the eternal and the immovable. There was a form of modernity for every painter of the past; the majority of the fine portraits that remain to us from former times are clothed in the dress of their own day. They are perfectly harmonious works because the dress, the hairstyle, and even the gesture, the expression and the smile (each age has its carriage, its expression and its smile) form a whole, full of vitality. You have no right to despise this transitory fleeting element, the metamorphoses of which are so frequent, nor to dispense with it. If you do, you inevitably fall into the emptiness of an abstract and indefinable beauty, like that of the one and only woman of the time before the Fall. If for the dress of the day, which is necessarily right, you substitute another, you are guilty of a piece of nonsense that only a fancy-dress ball imposed by fashion can excuse. Thus the goddesses, the nymphs, and sultanas of the eighteenth century are portraits in the spirit of their day.

No doubt it is an excellent discipline to study the old masters, in order to learn how to paint, but it can be no more than a superfluous exercise if your aim is to understand the beauty of the present day. The draperies of Rubens or Veronese will not teach you how to paint watered silk *à l'antique*, or satin *à la reine* or any other fabric produced by our mills, supported by a swaying crinoline, or petticoats of starched muslin. The texture and grain are not the same as in the fabrics of old Venice, or those worn at the court of Catherine.[viii] We may add that the cut of the skirt and bodice is absolutely different, that the pleats are arranged into a new pattern, and finally that the gesture and carriage of the woman of today give her dress a vitality and a character that are not those of the woman of former ages. In short, in order that any form of modernity may be worthy of becoming antiquity, the mysterious beauty that human life unintentionally puts into it must have been extracted from it. It is this task that M. G. particularly addresses himself to.

I have said that every age has its own carriage, its expression, its gestures. This proposition may be easily verified in a large portrait gallery (the one at

Versailles, for example). But it can be yet further extended. In a unity we call a nation, the professions, the social classes, the successive centuries, introduce variety not only in gestures and manners, but also in the general outlines of faces. Such and such a nose, mouth, forehead, will be standard for a given interval of time, the length of which I shall not claim to determine here, but which may certainly be a matter of calculation. Such ideas are not familiar enough to portrait painters; and the great weakness of M. Ingres, in particular, is the desire to impose on every type that sits for him a more or less complete process of improvement, in other words a despotic perfecting process, borrowed from the store of classical ideas.

In a matter such as this, *a priori* reasoning would be easy and even legitimate. The perpetual correlation between what is called the soul and what is called the body is a quite satisfactory explanation of how what is material or emanates from the spiritual reflects and will always reflect the spiritual force it derives from. If a painter, patient and scrupulous but with only inferior imaginative power, were commissioned to paint a courtesan of today, and, for this purpose, were to get his inspiration (to use the hallowed term) from a courtesan by Titian or Raphael, the odds are that his work would be fraudulent, ambiguous, and difficult to understand. The study of a masterpiece of that date and of that kind will not teach him the carriage, the gaze, the come-hitherishness, or the living representation of one of these creatures that the dictionary of fashion has, in rapid succession, pigeonholed under the coarse or light-hearted rubric of unchaste, kept women, Lorettes.[ix]

The same remark applies precisely to the study of the soldier, the dandy, and even animals, dogs or horses, and of all things that go to make up the external life of an age. Woe betide the man who goes to antiquity for the study of anything other than ideal art, logic and general method! By immersing himself too deeply in it, he will no longer have the present in his mind's eye; he throws away the value and the privileges afforded by circumstance; for nearly all our originality comes from the stamp that time impresses upon our sensibility. The reader will readily understand that I could easily verify my assertions from innumerable objects other than women. What would you say, for example, of a marine painter (I take an extreme case) who, having to represent the sober and elegant

---

[viii] Russian Empress, Catherine the Great (1684–1727).

[ix] Women of suspect "virtue".

beauty of a modern vessel, were to tire out his eyes in the study of the overloaded, twisted shapes, the monumental stern, of ships of bygone ages, and the complex sails and rigging of the sixteenth century? And what would you think of an artist you had commissioned to do the portrait of a thorough-bred, celebrated in the solemn annals of the turf, if he were to restrict his studies to museums, if he were to content himself with looking at equine studies of the past in the picture galleries, in Van Dyck, Bourguignon, or Van der Meulen.[x]

M. G., guided by nature, tyrannized over by circumstance, has followed a quite different path.

He began by looking at life, and only later did he contrive to learn how to express life. The result has been a striking originality, in which whatever traces of untutored simplicity may still remain take on the appearance of an additional proof of obedience to the impression, of a flattery of truth. For most of us, especially for businessmen, in whose eyes nature does not exist, unless it be in its strict utility relationship with their business interests, the fantastic reality of life becomes strangely blunted. M. G. registers it constantly; his memory and his eyes are full of it.

[x] Seventeenth-century Flemish painters Anthony Van Dyck and Adam Van der Meulen, with French contemporary Jacques Courtois (nicknamed *Il Bourguignon*).

12

From "How to Make Our Ideas Clear"

Charles S. Peirce

America's most original philosophic genius,
Charles S. Peirce (1839–1914) is the inventor of
pragmatism, America's most famous contribution to world philosophy. His career was marked
by brilliance in a variety of mathematical, scientific and philosophical pursuits, and by the tragedy
of unfulfilled promise. He was fired from Johns
Hopkins University at the age of forty-five, never
held another regular academic appointment, and
lived his later life in abject poverty. In its critique
of metaphysics pragmatism is consonant with
much of twentieth-century philosophy – like
logical positivism and phenomenology – but it
has more recently served the radical purposes of
antifoundationalism and postmodernism. Peirce,
however, regarded pragmatism as perfectly compatible with metaphysics and cosmology; his was
a truly systematic philosophy. In "How to Make
Our Ideas Clear" (1878) Peirce explains pragmatism for the first time, although he does not use
the term, which would not appear in print until William James introduced it in 1898. In fact, in order
to distinguish his views from those that James
and others were promoting as pragmatism,
Peirce later changed the name of his doctrine to
"pragmaticism," which, he said, was "ugly enough
to be safe from kidnappers."

Section II

The principles set forth in the first of these papers[i]
lead, at once, to a method of reaching a clearness of

thought of a far higher grade than the "distinctness" of the logicians. We have there found that the
action of thought is excited by the irritation of
doubt, and ceases when belief is attained; so that
the production of belief is the sole function of
thought. All these words, however, are too strong
for my purpose. It is as if I had described the
phenomena as they appear under a mental micro-
scope. Doubt and Belief, as the words are commonly employed, relate to religious or other grave
discussions. But here I use them to designate the
starting of any question, no matter how small or
how great, and the resolution of it. If, for instance,
in a horse-car, I pull out my purse and find a five-
cent nickel and five coppers, I decide, while my
hand is going to the purse, in which way I will pay
my fare. To call such a question Doubt, and my
decision Belief, is certainly to use words very dis-
proportionate to the occasion. To speak of such a
doubt as causing an irritation which needs to be
appeased, suggests a temper which is uncomfortable to the verge of insanity. Yet, looking at the
matter minutely, it must be admitted that, if there
is the least hesitation as to whether I shall pay the
five coppers or the nickel (as there will be sure to
be, unless I act from some previously contracted
habit in the matter), though irritation is too strong a
word, yet I am excited to such small mental activity
as may be necessary to deciding how I shall act.

[i] "The Fixation of Belief," *Popular Science Monthly*,
November 1877.

Charles S. Peirce, section II (pp. 289–93) and
section IV (pp. 297–302) from "How to Make Our
Ideas Clear," second paper of the series "Illustrations
of the Logic of Science," *Popular Science Monthly*, vol.
XII, January 1878. New York: D. Appleton and Co.

Most frequently doubts arise from some indecision, however momentary, in our action. Sometimes it is not so. I have, for example, to wait in a railway-station, and to pass the time I read the advertisements on the walls, I compare the advantages of different trains and different routes which I never expect to take, merely fancying myself to be in a state of hesitancy, because I am bored with having nothing to trouble me. Feigned hesitancy, whether feigned for mere amusement or with a lofty purpose, plays a great part in the production of scientific inquiry. However the doubt may originate, it stimulates the mind to an activity which may be slight or energetic, calm or turbulent. Images pass rapidly through consciousness, one incessantly melting into another, until at last, when all is over – it may be in a fraction of a second, in an hour, or after long years – we find ourselves decided as to how we should act under such circumstances as those which occasioned our hesitation. In other words, we have attained belief.

In this process we observe two sorts of elements of consciousness, the distinction between which may best be made clear by means of an illustration. In a piece of music there are the separate notes, and there is the air.[ii] A single tone may be prolonged for an hour or a day, and it exists as perfectly in each second of that time as in the whole taken together; so that, as long as it is sounding, it might be present to a sense from which everything in the past was as completely absent as the future itself. But it is different with the air, the performance of which occupies a certain time, during the portions of which only portions of it are played. It consists in an orderliness in the succession of sounds which strike the ear at different times; and to perceive it there must be some continuity of consciousness which makes the events of a lapse of time present to us. We certainly only perceive the air by hearing the separate notes; yet we cannot be said to directly hear it, for we hear only what is present at the instant, and an orderliness of succession cannot exist in an instant. These two sorts of objects, what we are *immediately* conscious of and what we are *mediately* conscious of, are found in all consciousness. Some elements (the sensations) are completely present at every instant so long as they last, while others (like thought) are actions having beginning, middle, and end, and consist in a congruence in the succession of sensations which flow through the mind. They cannot be immediately

[ii] Melody.

present to us, but must cover some portion of the past or future. Thought is a thread of melody running through the succession of our sensations.

We may add that just as a piece of music may be written in parts, each part having its own air, so various systems of relationship of succession subsist together between the same sensations. These different systems are distinguished by having different motives, ideas, or functions. Thought is only one such system, for its sole motive, idea, and function, is to produce belief, and whatever does not concern that purpose belongs to some other system of relations. The action of thinking may incidentally have other results; it may serve to amuse us, for example, and among *dilettanti* it is not rare to find those who have so perverted thought to the purposes of pleasure that it seems to vex them to think that the questions upon which they delight to exercise it may ever get finally settled; and a positive discovery which takes a favorite subject out of the arena of literary debate is met with ill-concealed dislike. This disposition is the very debauchery of thought. But the soul and meaning of thought, abstracted from the other elements which accompany it, though it may be voluntarily thwarted, can never be made to direct itself toward anything but the production of belief. Thought in action has for its only possible motive the attainment of thought at rest; and whatever does not refer to belief is no part of the thought itself.

And what, then, is belief? It is the demi-cadence which closes a musical phrase in the symphony of our intellectual life. We have seen that it has just three properties: First, it is something that we are aware of; second, it appeases the irritation of doubt; and, third, it involves the establishment in our nature of a rule of action, or, say for short, a *habit*. As it appeases the irritation of doubt, which is the motive for thinking, thought relaxes, and comes to rest for a moment when belief is reached. But, since belief is a rule for action, the application of which involves further doubt and further thought, at the same time that it is a stopping-place, it is also a new starting-place for thought. That is why I have permitted myself to call it thought at rest, although thought is essentially an action. The *final* upshot of thinking is the exercise of volition, and of this thought no longer forms a part; but belief is only a stadium of mental action, an effect upon our nature due to thought, which will influence future thinking.

The essence of belief is the establishment of a habit, and different beliefs are distinguished by the different modes of action to which they give rise. If beliefs do not differ in this respect, if they appease the same doubt by producing the same rule of action, then no mere differences in the manner of consciousness of them can make them different beliefs, any more than playing a tune in different keys is playing different tunes. Imaginary distinctions are often drawn between beliefs which differ only in their mode of expression; – the wrangling which ensues is real enough, however. To believe that any objects are arranged as in figure 12.1, and to believe that they are arranged as in figure 12.2, are one and the same belief; yet it is conceivable that a man should assert one proposition and deny the other. Such false distinctions do as much harm as the confusion of beliefs really different, and are among the pitfalls of which we ought constantly to beware, especially when we are upon metaphysical ground. One singular deception of this sort, which often occurs, is to mistake the sensation produced by our own unclearness of thought for a character of the object we are thinking. Instead of perceiving that the obscurity is purely subjective, we fancy that we contemplate a quality of the object

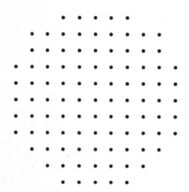

Figure 12.1

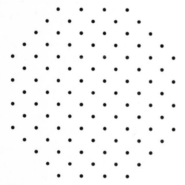

Figure 12.2

which is essentially mysterious; and if our conception be afterward presented to us in a clear form we do not recognize it as the same, owing to the absence of the feeling of unintelligibility. So long as this deception lasts, it obviously puts an impassable barrier in the way of perspicuous thinking; so that it equally interests the opponents of rational thought to perpetuate it, and its adherents to guard against it.

Another such deception is to mistake a mere difference in the grammatical construction of two words for a distinction between the ideas they express. In this pedantic age, when the general mob of writers attend so much more to words than to things, this error is common enough. When I just said that thought is an *action*, and that it consists in a *relation*, although a person performs an action but not a relation, which can only be the result of an action, yet there was no inconsistency in what I said, but only a grammatical vagueness.

From all these sophisms we shall be perfectly safe so long as we reflect that the whole function of thought is to produce habits of action; and that whatever there is connected with a thought, but irrelevant to its purpose, is an accretion to it, but no part of it. If there be a unity among our sensations which has no reference to how we shall act on a given occasion, as when we listen to a piece of music, why we do not call that thinking. To develop its meaning, we have, therefore, simply to determine what habits it produces, for what a thing means is simply what habits it involves. Now, the identity of a habit depends on how it might lead us to act, not merely under such circumstances as are likely to arise, but under such as might possibly occur, no matter how improbable they may be. What the habit is depends on *when* and *how* it causes us to act. As for the *when*, every stimulus to action is derived from perception; as for the *how*, every purpose of action is to produce some sensible result. Thus, we come down to what is tangible and practical, as the root of every real distinction of thought, no matter how subtle it may be; and there is no distinction of meaning so fine as to consist in anything but a possible difference of practice.

To see what this principle leads to, consider in the light of it such a doctrine as that of transubstantiation. The Protestant churches generally hold that the elements of the sacrament are flesh and blood only in a tropical sense; they nourish our souls as meat and the juice of it would our bodies. But the Catholics maintain that they are literally just that; although they possess all the sensible qualities of wafer-cakes and diluted wine. But we can have no conception of wine except what may enter into a belief, either –

1   That this, that, or the other, is wine; or,
2   That wine possesses certain properties.

Such beliefs are nothing but self-notifications that we should, upon occasion, act in regard to such things as we believe to be wine according to the qualities which we believe wine to possess. The occasion of such action would be some sensible perception, the motive of it to produce some sensible result. Thus our action has exclusive reference to what affects the senses, our habit has the same bearing as our action, our belief the same as our habit, our conception the same as our belief; and we can consequently mean nothing by wine but what has certain effects, direct or indirect, upon our senses; and to talk of something as having all the sensible characters of wine, yet being in reality blood, is senseless jargon. Now, it is not my object to pursue the theological question; and having used it as a logical example I drop it, without caring to anticipate the theologian's reply. I only desire to point out how impossible it is that we should have an idea in our minds which relates to anything but conceived sensible effects of things. Our idea of anything *is* our idea of its sensible effects; and if we fancy that we have any other we deceive ourselves, and mistake a mere sensation accompanying the thought for a part of the thought itself. It is absurd to say that thought has any meaning unrelated to its only function. It is foolish for Catholics and Protestants to fancy themselves in disagreement about the elements of the sacrament, if they agree in regard to all their sensible effects, here or hereafter.

It appears, then, that the rule for attaining the third grade of clearness of apprehension is as follows: Consider what effects, which might conceivably have practical bearings, we conceive the object of our conception to have. Then, our conception of these effects is the whole of our conception of the object.

Section IV

Let us now approach the subject of logic, and consider a conception which particularly concerns it, that of *reality*. Taking clearness in the sense of familiarity, no idea could be clearer than this. Every child uses it with perfect confidence, never dreaming that he does not understand it. As for clearness in its second grade, however, it would probably puzzle most men, even among those of a reflective turn of mind, to give an abstract definition of the real. Yet such a definition may perhaps be reached by considering the points of difference between reality and its opposite, fiction. A figment is a product of somebody's imagination; it has such characters as his thought impresses upon it. That whose characters are independent of how you or I think is an external reality. There are, however, phenomena within our own minds, dependent upon our thought, which are at the same time real in the sense that we really think them. But though their characters depend on how we think, they do not depend on what we think those characters to be. Thus, a dream has a real existence as a mental phenomenon, if somebody has really dreamt it; that he dreamt so and so, does not depend on what anybody thinks was dreamt, but is completely independent of all opinion on the subject. On the other hand, considering, not the fact of dreaming, but the thing dreamt, it retains its peculiarities by virtue of no other fact than that it was dreamt to possess them. Thus we may define the real as that whose characters are independent of what anybody may think them to be.

But, however satisfactory such a definition may be found, it would be a great mistake to suppose that it makes the idea of reality perfectly clear. Here, then, let us apply our rules. According to them, reality, like every other quality, consists in the peculiar sensible effects which things partaking of it produce. The only effect which real things have is to cause belief, for all the sensations which they excite emerge into consciousness in the form of beliefs. The question therefore is, how is true belief (or belief in the real) distinguished from false belief (or belief in fiction). Now, as we have seen in the former paper, the ideas of truth and falsehood, in their full development, appertain exclusively to the scientific method of settling opinion. A person who arbitrarily chooses the propositions which he will adopt can use the word truth only to emphasize the expression of his determination to hold on to his choice. Of course, the method of tenacity never prevailed exclusively; reason is too natural to men for that. But in the literature of the dark ages we find some fine examples of it. When Scotus Erigena is commenting upon a poetical passage in which hellebore is spoken of as having caused the death of Socrates, he does not hesitate to inform the inquiring reader that Helleborus and Scorates were two eminent Greek philosophers, and that the latter having been overcome in argument by the former took the matter to heart and died of it![iii] What sort of an idea of truth could a man have who could adopt and teach, without the qualification of a perhaps, an opinion taken so entirely at random? The real spirit of Socrates, who I hope would have been delighted to have been "overcome in argument," because he would have learned something by it, is in curious contrast with the naïve idea of the glossist, for whom discussion would seem to have been simply a struggle. When philosophy began to awake from its long slumber, and before theology completely dominated it, the practice seems to have been for each professor to seize upon any philosophical position he found unoccupied and which seemed a strong one, to intrench himself in it, and to sally forth from time to time to give battle to the others. Thus, even the scanty records we possess of those disputes enable us to make out a dozen or more opinions held by different teachers at one time concerning the question of nominalism and realism. Read the opening part of the "Historia Calamitatum" of Abelard, who was certainly as philosophical as any of his contemporaries, and see the spirit of combat which it breathes.[iv] For him, the truth is simply his particular stronghold. When the method of authority prevailed, the truth meant little more than the Catholic faith. All the efforts of the scholastic doctors are directed toward harmonizing their faith in Aristotle and their faith in the Church, and one may search their ponderous folios through without finding an argument which goes any further. It is noticeable that where different faiths flourish side by side, renegades are looked upon with contempt even by the party whose belief they adopt; so completely has the idea of loyalty replaced that of truth-seeking. Since the time of Descartes, the defect in the conception of truth has been less apparent. Still, it will sometimes strike a scientific man that the philosophers have been less intent on finding out what the facts are, than on inquiring what belief is most in harmony with their system. It is hard to convince a follower of the *a priori* method by adducing facts; but show him that an opinion he is defending is inconsistent with what he has laid down elsewhere, and he will be very apt

to retract it. These minds do not seem to believe that disputation is ever to cease; they seem to think that the opinion which is natural for one man is not so for another, and that belief will, consequently, never be settled. In contenting themselves with fixing their own opinions by a method which would lead another man to a different result, they betray their feeble hold of the conception of what truth is.

On the other hand, all the followers of science are fully persuaded that the processes of investigation, if only pushed far enough, will give one certain solution to every question to which they can be applied. One man may investigate the velocity of light by studying the transits of Venus and the aberration of the stars; another by the oppositions of Mars and the eclipses of Jupiter's satellites; a third by the method of Fizeau; a fourth by that of Foucault; a fifth by the motions of the curves of Lissajoux; a sixth, a seventh, an eighth, and a ninth, may follow the different methods of comparing the measures of statical and dynamical electricity.[v] They may at first obtain different results, but, as each perfects his method and his processes, the results will move steadily together toward a destined centre. So with all scientific research. Different minds may set out with the most antagonistic views, but the progress of investigation carries them by a force outside of themselves to one and the same conclusion. This activity of thought by which we are carried, not where we wish, but to a foreordained goal, is like the operation of destiny. No modification of the point of view taken, no selection of other facts for study, no natural bent of mind even, can enable a man to escape the predestinate opinion. This great law is embodied in the conception of truth and reality. The opinion which is fated[1] to be ultimately agreed to by all who investigate, is what we mean by the truth, and the object represented in this opinion is the real. That is the way I would explain reality.

But it may be said that this view is directly opposed to the abstract definition which we have given of reality, inasmuch as it makes the characters of the real to depend on what is ultimately thought about them. But the answer to this is that, on the one hand, reality is independent, not necessarily of thought in general, but only of what you or I or any finite number of men may think about it; and that,

---

[iii] "Hellebore" refers to a plant of the lily family; Socrates actually died from drinking a potion made from hemlock; John Scotus Erigena (born AD 810) was a medieval philosopher.
[iv] Peter Abelard (1079–1142), medieval theologian and logician.

[v] Armand-Hippolyte Louis Fizeau (1819–96) and Jean-Bernard-Léon Foucault (1819–68) were French physicists; Jules-Antoine Lissajoux (1822–80) was a French mathematician.

on the other hand, though the object of the final opinion depends on what that opinion is, yet what that opinion is does not depend on what you or I or any man thinks. Our perversity and that of others may indefinitely postpone the settlement of opinion; it might even conceivably cause an arbitrary proposition to be universally accepted as long as the human race should last. Yet even that would not change the nature of the belief, which alone could be the result of investigation carried sufficiently far; and if, after the extinction of our race, another should arise with faculties and disposition for investigation, that true opinion must be the one which they would ultimately come to. "Truth crushed to earth shall rise again," and the opinion which would finally result from investigation does not depend on how anybody may actually think. But the reality of that which is real does depend on the real fact that investigation is destined to lead, at last, if continued long enough, to a belief in it.

But I may be asked what I have to say to all the minute facts of history, forgotten never to be recovered, to the lost books of the ancients, to the buried secrets.

Full many a gem of purest ray serene
  The dark, unfathomed caves of ocean bear;
Full many a flower is born to blush unseen,
  And waste its sweetness on the desert air.[vi]

Do these things not really exist because they are hopelessly beyond the reach of our knowledge? And then, after the universe is dead (according to the prediction of some scientists), and all life has ceased forever, will not the shock of atoms continue though there will be no mind to know it? To this I reply that, though in no possible state of knowledge can any number be great enough to express the relation between the amount of what rests unknown to the amount of the known, yet it is unphilosophical to suppose that, with regard to any given question (which has any clear meaning), investigation would not bring forth a solution of it, if it were carried far enough. Who would have said, a few years ago, that we could ever know of what substances stars are made whose light may have been longer in reaching us than the human race has existed? Who can be sure of what we shall not know in a few hundred years? Who can guess what would be the result of continuing the pursuit of science for ten thousand years, with the activity of the last hundred? And if it were to go on for a million, or a billion, or any number of years you please, how is it possible to say that there is any question which might not ultimately be solved?

But it may be objected, "Why make so much of these remote considerations, especially when it is your principle that only practical distinctions have a meaning?" Well, I must confess that it makes very little difference whether we say that a stone on the bottom of the ocean, in complete darkness, is brilliant or not – that is to say, that it *probably* makes no difference, remembering always that that stone *may* be fished up to-morrow. But that there are gems at the bottom of the sea, flowers in the untraveled desert, etc., are propositions which, like that about a diamond being hard when it is not pressed, concern much more the arrangement of our language than they do the meaning of our ideas.

It seems to me, however, that we have, by the application of our rule, reached so clear an apprehension of what we mean by reality, and of the fact which the idea rests on, that we should not, perhaps, be making a pretension so presumptuous as it would be singular, if we were to offer a metaphysical theory of existence for universal acceptance among those who employ the scientific method of fixing belief. However, as metaphysics is a subject much more curious than useful, the knowledge of which, like that of a sunken reef, serves chiefly to enable us to keep clear of it, I will not trouble the reader with any more Ontology at this moment. I have already been led much further into that path than I should have desired; and I have given the reader such a dose of mathematics, psychology, and all that is most abstruse, that I fear he may already have left me, and that what I am now writing is for the compositor and proof-reader exclusively. I trusted to the importance of the subject. There is no royal road to logic, and really valuable ideas can only be had at the price of close attention. But I know that in the matter of ideas the public prefer the cheap and nasty; and in my next paper I am going to return to the easily intelligible, and not wander from it again. The reader who has been at the pains of wading through this month's paper, shall be rewarded in the next one by seeing how beautifully what has been developed in this tedious way can be applied to the ascertainment of the rules of scientific reasoning.[vii]

[vi] Thomas Grey (1716–71), *Elegy Written in a Country Churchyard*, II, 53–6.

[vii] "The Doctrine of Chances," *Popular Science Monthy*, March 1878.

We have, hitherto, not crossed the threshold of scientific logic. It is certainly important to know how to make our ideas clear, but they may be ever so clear without being true. How to make them so, we have next to study. How to give birth to those vital and procreative ideas which multiply into a thousand forms and diffuse themselves everywhere, advancing civilization and making the dignity of man, is an art not yet reduced to rules, but of the secret of which the history of science affords some hints.

Author's Note

1   Fate means merely that which is sure to come true, and can nohow be avoided. It is a superstition to suppose that a certain sort of events are ever fated, and it is another to suppose that the word fate can never be freed from its superstitious taint. We are all fated to die.

13

"On Truth and Lies in a Nonmoral Sense"
"The Madman"
"How the 'True World' Finally Became a Fable"
The Dionysian World*

Friedrich Nietzsche

A student of ancient languages by trade and a philosopher by predilection, Friedrich Nietzsche (1844–1900) was a unique and misunderstood genius. Retiring in ill health from his only university post aged 34, he wrote feverishly in relative isolation until becoming insane eleven years later. Nietzsche's concern was nothing less than the conditions of health, greatness, and sickness in human cultures. He was deeply critical of Judeo-Christian civilization, which he saw as destroying the health of Western humanity by undermining human instincts through a slavish, nihilistic belief in the unreality of this world and the promise of happiness in the next. Nietzsche was one of the first to foresee the waning of Christianity in an increasingly secular Europe, and famously coined the phrase "God is dead." He pressed this critique to a remarkable denial of the very concept of truth – "truthfulness" being a prime Christian value. Nietzsche's notion of a future "overman," the authentic individual of the post-Christian era, was later embraced by the Nazis (although nothing could be more foreign to Nietzsche than a mass, collectivist movement). Nietzsche's radical critique of metaphysics, the unity of the self, and of truth, make him the godfather of postmodernism.

"On Truth and Lies in a Nonmoral Sense"[i]

1

Once upon a time, in some out of the way corner of that universe which is dispersed into numberless

[i] The German term in the title translated here as "nonmoral," *aussermoralischen*, could be, and has been, also translated as "super-" or "extra-" moral.

Friedrich Nietzsche: [A] "On Truth and Lies in a Nonmoral Sense," pp. 79–91 from *Philosophy and Truth* (ed. Daniel Brazeale). New York: Humanities Press, 1979; [B] "The Madman" from *The Gay Science* (trans. and ed. Walter Kaufmann), Part Three, section 125, pp. 181–2. New York: Vintage, 1974; [C] "How the True World Finally Became a Fable," from *Twilight of the Idols*, reproduced in *The Portable Nietzsche* (trans. and ed. Walter Kaufmann), pp. 485–6. New York: Viking, 1968; [D] The Dionysian World,* para. 1067, pp. 449–50 from *The Will to Power* (trans. Walter Kaufmann and R. J. Hollingdale, edited with commentary by Walter Kaufmann). New York: Random House, 1967. * Note that the title given to this fourth section is this volume editor's not Nietzsche's.

twinkling solar systems, there was a star upon which clever beasts invented knowing. That was the most arrogant and mendacious minute of "world history," but nevertheless, it was only a minute. After nature had drawn a few breaths, the star cooled and congealed, and the clever beasts had to die. – One might invent such a fable, and yet he still would not have adequately illustrated how miserable, how shadowy and transient, how aimless and arbitrary the human intellect looks within nature. There were eternities during which it did not exist. And when it is all over with the human intellect, nothing will have happened. For this intellect has no additional mission which would lead it beyond human life. Rather, it is human, and only its possessor and begetter takes it so solemnly – as though the world's axis turned within it. But if we could communicate with the gnat, we would learn that he likewise flies through the air with the same solemnity, that he feels the flying center of the universe within himself. There is nothing so reprehensible and unimportant in nature that it would not immediately swell up like a balloon at the slightest puff of this power of knowing. And just as every porter wants to have an admirer, so even the proudest of men, the philosopher, supposes that he sees on all sides the eyes of the universe telescopically focused upon his action and thought.

It is remarkable that this was brought about by the intellect, which was certainly allotted to these most unfortunate, delicate, and ephemeral beings merely as a device for detaining them a minute within existence. For without this addition they would have every reason to flee this existence as quickly as Lessing's son.[ii] The pride connected with knowing and sensing lies like a blinding fog over the eyes and senses of men, thus deceiving them concerning the value of existence. For this pride contains within itself the most flattering estimation of the value of knowing. Deception is the most general effect of such pride, but even its most particular effects contain within themselves something of the same deceitful character.

As a means for the preserving of the individual, the intellect unfolds its principal powers in dissimulation, which is the means by which weaker, less robust individuals preserve themselves – since they have been denied the chance to wage the battle for existence with horns or with the sharp teeth of beasts of prey. This art of dissimulation reaches its peak in man. Deception, flattering, lying, deluding, talking behind the back, putting up a false front, living in borrowed splendor, wearing a mask, hiding behind convention, playing a role for others and for oneself – in short, a continuous fluttering around the *solitary* flame of vanity – is so much the rule and the law among men that there is almost nothing which is less comprehensible than how an honest and pure drive for truth could have arisen among them. They are deeply immersed in illusions and in dream images; their eyes merely glide over the surface of things and see "forms." Their senses nowhere lead to truth; on the contrary, they are content to receive stimuli and, as it were, to engage in a groping game on the backs of things. Moreover, man permits himself to be deceived in his dreams every night of his life. His moral sentiment does not even make an attempt to prevent this, whereas there are supposed to be men who have stopped snoring through sheer will power. What does man actually know about himself? Is he, indeed, ever able to perceive himself completely, as if laid out in a lighted display case? Does nature not conceal most things from him – even concerning his own body – in order to confine and lock him within a proud, deceptive consciousness, aloof from the coils of the bowels, the rapid flow of the blood stream, and the intricate quivering of the fibers! She threw away the key. And woe to that fatal curiosity which might one day have the power to peer out and down through a crack in the chamber of consciousness and then suspect that man is sustained in the indifference of his ignorance by that which is pitiless, greedy, insatiable, and murderous – as if hanging in dreams on the back of a tiger. Given this situation, where in the world could the drive for truth have come from?

Insofar as the individual wants to maintain himself against other individuals, he will under natural circumstances employ the intellect mainly for dissimulation. But at the same time, from boredom and necessity, man wishes to exist socially and with the herd; therefore, he needs to make peace and strives accordingly to banish from his world at least the most flagrant *bellum omni contra omnes*.[iii] This peace treaty brings in its wake something which appears to be the first step toward acquiring that puzzling truth drive: to wit, *that* which shall count as "truth" from now on is established. That is to say, a uniformly valid and binding designation is invented for things, and this legislation of language

[ii] Gotthold Ephraim Lessing (1729–81), German dramatist and philosopher, whose son died the day he was born.

[iii] War of each against all.

likewise establishes the first laws of truth. For the contrast between truth and lie arises here for the first time. The liar is a person who uses the valid designations, the words, in order to make something which is unreal appear to be real. He says, for example, "I am rich," when the proper designation for his condition would be "poor." He misuses fixed conventions by means of arbitrary substitutions or even reversals of names. If he does this in a selfish and moreover harmful manner, society will cease to trust him and will thereby exclude him. What men avoid by excluding the liar is not so much being defrauded as it is being harmed by means of fraud. Thus, even at this stage, what they hate is basically not deception itself, but rather the unpleasant, hated consequences of certain sorts of deception. It is in a similarly restricted sense that man now wants nothing but truth: he desires the pleasant, life-preserving consequences of truth. He is indifferent toward pure knowledge which has no consequences; toward those truths which are possibly harmful and destructive he is even hostilely inclined. And besides, what about these linguistic conventions themselves? Are they perhaps products of knowledge, that is, of the sense of truth? Are designations congruent with things? Is language the adequate expression of all realities?

It is only by means of forgetfulness that man can ever reach the point of fancying himself to possess a "truth" of the grade just indicated. If he will not be satisfied with truth in the form of tautology, that is to say, if he will not be content with empty husks, then he will always exchange truths for illusions. What is a word? It is the copy in sound of a nerve stimulus. But the further inference from the nerve stimulus to a cause outside of us is already the result of a false and unjustifiable application of the principle of sufficient reason.[iv] If truth alone had been the deciding factor in the genesis of language, and if the standpoint of certainty had been decisive for designations, then how could we still dare to say "the stone is hard," as if "hard" were something otherwise familiar to us, and not merely a totally subjective stimulation! We separate things according to gender, designating the tree as masculine and the plant as feminine.[v] What arbitrary assignments! How far this oversteps the canons of certainty! We speak of a "snake": this designation touches only upon its ability to twist itself and could therefore also fit a worm. What arbitrary differentiations! What one-sided preferences, first for this, then for that property of a thing! The various languages placed side by side show that with words it is never a question of truth, never a question of adequate expression; otherwise, there would not be so many languages. The "thing in itself" (which is precisely what the pure truth, apart from any of its consequences, would be) is likewise something quite incomprehensible to the creator of language and something not in the least worth striving for. This creator only designates the relations of things to men, and for expressing these relations he lays hold of the boldest metaphors. To begin with, a nerve stimulus is transferred into an image: first metaphor. The image, in turn, is imitated in a sound; second metaphor. And each time there is a complete overleaping of one sphere, right into the middle of an entirely new and different one. One can imagine a man who is totally deaf and has never had a sensation of sound and music. Perhaps such a person will gaze with astonishment at Chladni's sound figures:[vi] perhaps he will discover their causes in the vibrations of the string and will now swear that he must know what men mean by "sound." It is this way with all of us concerning language: we believe that we know something about the things themselves when we speak of trees, colors, snow, and flowers; and yet we possess nothing but metaphors for things – metaphors which correspond in no way to the original entities. In the same way that the sound appears as a sand figure, so the mysterious X of the thing in itself first appears as a nerve stimulus, then as an image, and finally as a sound. Thus the genesis of language does not proceed logically in any case, and all the material within and with which the man of truth, the scientist, and the philosopher later work and build, if not derived from never-never land, is at least not derived from the essence of things.

In particular, let us further consider the formation of concepts. Every word instantly becomes a concept precisely insofar as it is not supposed to serve as a reminder of the unique and entirely individual original experience to which it owes its origin; but rather, a word becomes a concept insofar as it simultaneously has to fit countless more or less

---

[iv]   The "principle of sufficient reason," formulated by Gottfried Wilhelm Leibniz (1646–1716), held that every factual truth must be supported by a sufficient reason.

[v]   Nietzsche is referring to the German language's gender assignment of nouns.

[vi]   Ernst Chladni, German physicist who studied the speed of sound with vibrating rods in the late eighteenth century.

similar cases – which means, purely and simply, cases which are never equal and thus altogether unequal. Every concept arises from the equation of unequal things. Just as it is certain that one leaf is never totally the same as another, so it is certain that the concept "leaf" is formed by arbitrarily discarding these individual differences and by forgetting the distinguishing aspects. This awakens the idea that, in addition to the leaves, there exists in nature the "leaf": the original model according to which all the leaves were perhaps woven, sketched, measured, colored, curled, and painted – but by incompetent hands, so that no specimen has turned out to be a correct, trustworthy, and faithful likeness of the original model. We call a person "honest," and then we ask "why has he behaved so honestly today?" Our usual answer is, "on account of his honesty." Honesty! This in turn means that the leaf is the cause of the leaves. We know nothing whatsoever about an essential quality called "honesty"; but we do know of countless individualized and consequently unequal actions which we equate by omitting the aspects in which they are unequal and which we now designate as "honest" actions. Finally we formulate from them a *qualitas occulta*[vii] which has the name "honesty." We obtain the concept, as we do the form, by overlooking what is individual and actual; whereas nature is acquainted with no forms and no concepts, and likewise with no species, but only with an X which remains inaccessible and undefinable for us. For even our contrast between individual and species is something anthropomorphic and does not originate in the essence of things; although we should not presume to claim that this contrast does not correspond to the essence of things: that would of course be a dogmatic assertion and, as such, would be just as indemonstrable as its opposite.

What then is truth? A movable host of metaphors, metonymies, and anthropomorphisms: in short, a sum of human relations which have been poetically and rhetorically intensified, transferred, and embellished, and which, after long usage, seem to a people to be fixed, canonical, and binding. Truths are illusions which we have forgotten are illusions; they are metaphors that have become worn out and have been drained of sensuous force, coins which have lost their embossing and are now considered as metal and no longer as coins.

We still do not yet know where the drive for truth comes from. For so far we have heard only of the duty which society imposes in order to exist: to be truthful means to employ the usual metaphors. Thus, to express it morally, this is the duty to lie according to a fixed convention, to lie with the herd and in a manner binding upon everyone. Now man of course forgets that this is the way things stand for him. Thus he lies in the manner indicated, unconsciously and in accordance with habits which are centuries' old; and precisely *by means of this unconsciousness* and forgetfulness he arrives at his sense of truth. From the sense that one is obliged to designate one thing as "red," another as "cold," and a third as "mute," there arises a moral impulse in regard to truth. The venerability, reliability, and utility of truth is something which a person demonstrates for himself from the contrast with the liar, whom no one trusts and everyone excludes. As a "*rational*" being, he now places his behavior under the control of abstractions. He will no longer tolerate being carried away by sudden impressions, by intuitions. First he universalizes all these impressions into less colorful, cooler concepts, so that he can entrust the guidance of his life and conduct to them. Everything which distinguishes man from the animals depends upon this ability to volatilize perceptual metaphors in a schema, and thus to dissolve an image into a concept. For something is possible in the realm of these schemata which could never be achieved with the vivid first impressions: the construction of a pyramidal order according to castes and degrees, the creation of a new world of laws, privileges, subordinations, and clearly marked boundaries – a new world, one which now confronts that other vivid world of first impressions as more solid, more universal, better known, and more human than the immediately perceived world, and thus as the regulative and imperative world. Whereas each perceptual metaphor is individual and without equals and is therefore able to elude all classification, the great edifice of concepts displays the rigid regularity of a Roman columbarium[viii] and exhales in logic that strength and coolness which is characteristic of mathematics. Anyone who has felt this cool breath will hardly believe that even the concept – which is as bony, foursquare, and transposable as a die – is nevertheless merely the *residue of a metaphor*, and that the illusion which is involved in the artistic transference of a nerve stimulus into images is, if not the mother, then the grandmother of every single concept. But in this concep-

---

[vii]   Occult quality.

[viii]   Roman vault for funeral urns.

tual crap game "truth" means using every die in the designated manner, counting its spots accurately, fashioning the right categories, and never violating the order of caste and class rank. Just as the Romans and Etruscans cut up the heavens with rigid mathematical lines and confined a god within each of the spaces thereby delimited, as within a *templum*,[ix] so every people has a similarly mathematically divided conceptual heaven above themselves and henceforth thinks that truth demands that each conceptual god be sought only within *his own* sphere. Here one may certainly admire man as a mighty genius of construction, who succeeds in piling up an infinitely complicated dome of concepts upon an unstable foundation, and, as it were, on running water. Of course, in order to be supported by such a foundation, his construction must be like one constructed of spiders' webs: delicate enough to be carried along by the waves, strong enough not to be blown apart by every wind. As a genius of construction man raises himself far above the bee in the following way: whereas the bee builds with wax that he gathers from nature, man builds with the far more delicate conceptual material which he first has to manufacture from himself. In this he is greatly to be admired, but not on account of his drive for truth or for pure knowledge of things. When someone hides something behind a bush and looks for it again in the same place and finds it there as well, there is not much to praise in such seeking and finding. Yet this is how matters stand regarding seeking and finding "truth" within the realm of reason. If I make up the definition of a mammal, and then, after inspecting a camel, declare "look, a mammal," I have indeed brought a truth to light in this way, but it is a truth of limited value. That is to say, it is a thoroughly anthropomorphic truth which contains not a single point which would be "true in itself" or really and universally valid apart from man. At bottom, what the investigator of such truths is seeking is only the metamorphosis of the world into man. He strives to understand the world as something analogous to man, and at best he achieves by his struggles the feeling of assimilation. Similar to the way in which astrologers considered the stars to be in man's service and connected with his happiness and sorrow, such an investigator considers the entire universe in connection with man: the entire universe as the infinitely fractured echo of one original sound – man; the entire

universe as the infinitely multiplied copy of one original picture – man. His method is to treat man as the measure of all things but in doing so he again proceeds from the error of believing that he has these things [which he intends to measure] immediately before him as mere objects. He forgets that the original perceptual metaphors are metaphors and takes them to be the things themselves.

Only by forgetting this primitive world of metaphor can one live with any repose, security, and consistency: only by means of the petrification and coagulation of a mass of images which originally streamed from the primal faculty of human imagination like a fiery liquid, only in the invincible faith that *this* sun, *this* window, *this* table is a truth in itself, in short, only by forgetting that he himself is an *artistically creating* subject, does man live with any repose, security, and consistency. If but for an instant he could escape from the prison walls of this faith, his "self consciousness" would be immediately destroyed. It is even a difficult thing for him to admit to himself that the insect or the bird perceives an entirely different world from the one that man does, and that the question of which of these perceptions of the world is the more correct one is quite meaningless, for this would have to have been decided previously in accordance with the criterion of the *correct perception*, which means, in accordance with a criterion which is *not available*. But in any case it seems to me that "the correct perception" – which would mean "the adequate expression of an object in the subject" – is a contradictory impossibility. For between two absolutely different spheres, as between subject and object, there is no causality, no correctness, and no expression; there is, at most, an *aesthetic* relation: I mean, a suggestive transference, a stammering translation into a completely foreign tongue – for which there is required, in any case, a freely inventive intermediate sphere and mediating force. "Apearance" is a word that contains many temptations, which is why I avoid it as much as possible. For it is not true that the essence of things "appears" in the empirical world. A painter without hands who wished to express in song the picture before his mind would, by means of this substitution of spheres, still reveal more about the essence of things than does the empirical world. Even the relationship of a nerve stimulus to the generated image is not a necessary one. But when the same image has been generated millions of times and has been handed down for many generations and finally appears on the same occa-

---

[ix] A religiously distinct, e.g. holy, space.

sion every time for all mankind, then it acquires at last the same meaning for men it would have if it were the sole necessary image and if the relationship of the original nerve stimulus to the generated image were a strictly causal one. In the same manner, an eternally repeated dream would certainly be felt and judged to be reality. But the hardening and congealing of a metaphor guarantees absolutely nothing concerning its necessity and exclusive justification.

Every person who is familiar with such considerations has no doubt felt a deep mistrust of all idealism of this sort: just as often as he has quite clearly convinced himself of the eternal consistency, omnipresence, and infallibility of the laws of nature. He has concluded that so far as we can penetrate here – from the telescopic heights to the microscopic depths – everything is secure, complete, infinite, regular, and without any gaps. Science will be able to dig successfully in this shaft forever, and all the things that are discovered will harmonize with and not contradict each other. How little does this resemble a product of the imagination, for if it were such, there should be some place where the illusion and unreality can be divined. Against this, the following must be said: if each of us had a different kind of sense perception – if we could only perceive things now as a bird, now as a worm, now as a plant, or if one of us saw a stimulus as red, another as blue, while a third even heard the same stimulus as a sound – then no one would speak of such a regularity of nature, rather, nature would be grasped only as a creation which is subjective in the highest degree. After all, what is a law of nature as such for us? We are not acquainted with it in itself, but only with its effects, which means in its relation to other laws of nature – which, in turn, are known to us only as sums of relations. Therefore all these relations always refer again to others and are thoroughly incomprehensible to us in their essence. All that we actually know about these laws of nature is what we ourselves bring to them – time and space, and therefore relationships of succession and number. But everything marvelous about the laws of nature, everything that quite astonishes us therein and seems to demand our explanation, everything that might lead us to distrust idealism: all this is completely and solely contained within the mathematical strictness and inviolability of our representations of time and space. But we produce these representations in and from ourselves with the same necessity with which the spider spins. If we are forced to comprehend all things only under these forms, then it ceases to be amazing that in all things we actually comprehend nothing but these forms. For they must all bear within themselves the laws of number, and it is precisely number which is most astonishing in things. All that conformity to law, which impresses us so much in the movement of the stars and in chemical processes, coincides at bottom with those properties which we bring to things. Thus it is we who impress ourselves in this way. In conjunction with this, it of course follows that the artistic process of metaphor formation with which every sensation begins in us already presupposes these forms and thus occurs within them. The only way in which the possibility of subsequently constructing a new conceptual edifice from metaphors themselves can be explained is by the firm persistence of these original forms. That is to say, this conceptual edifice is an imitation of temporal, spatial, and numerical relationships in the domain of metaphor.

2

We have seen how it is originally *language* which works on the construction of concepts, a labor taken over in later ages by *science*. Just as the bee simultaneously constructs cells and fills them with honey, so science works unceasingly on this great columbarium of concepts, the graveyard of perceptions. It is always building new, higher stories and shoring up, cleaning, and renovating the old cells; above all, it takes pains to fill up this monstrously towering framework and to arrange therein the entire empirical world, which is to say, the anthropomorphic world. Whereas the man of action binds his life to reason and its concepts so that he will not be swept away and lost, the scientific investigator builds his hut right next to the tower of science so that he will be able to work on it and to find shelter for himself beneath those bulwarks which presently exist. And he requires shelter, for there are frightful powers which continuously break in upon him, powers which oppose scientific "truth" with completely different kinds of "truths" which bear on their shields the most varied sorts of emblems.

The drive toward the formation of metaphors is the fundamental human drive which one cannot for a single instant dispense with in thought, for one would thereby dispense with man himself. This drive is not truly vanquished and scarcely subdued by the fact that a regular and rigid new world is constructed as its prison from its own ephemeral products, the concepts. It seeks a new realm and another channel for its activity, and it finds this in *myth* and in *art* generally. This drive continually confuses the conceptual categories and cells by bringing forward new transferences, metaphors, and metonymies. It continually manifests an ardent desire to refashion the world which presents itself to waking man, so that it will be as colorful, irregular, lacking in results and coherence, charming, and eternally new as the world of dreams. Indeed, it is only by means of the rigid and regular web of concepts that the waking man clearly sees that he is awake; and it is precisely because of this that he sometimes thinks that he must be dreaming when this web of concepts is torn by art. Pascal is right in maintaining that if the same dream came to us every night we would be just as occupied with it as we are with the things that we see every day. "If a workman were sure to dream for twelve straight hours every night that he was king," said Pascal, "I believe that he would be just as happy as a king who dreamt for twelve hours every night that he was a workman."[x] In fact, because of the way that myth takes it for granted that miracles are always happening, the waking life of a mythically inspired people – the ancient Greeks, for instance – more closely resembles a dream than it does the waking world of a scientifically disenchanted thinker. When every tree can suddenly speak as a nymph, when a god in the shape of a bull can drag away maidens, when even the goddess Athena herself is suddenly seen in the company of Peisistratus driving through the market place of Athens with a beautiful team of horses[xi] – and this is what the honest Athenian believed – then, as in a dream, anything is possible at each moment, and all of nature swarms around man as if it were nothing but a masquerade of the gods, who were merely amusing themselves by deceiving men in all these shapes.

But man has an invincible inclination to allow himself to be deceived and is, as it were, enchanted with happiness when the rhapsodist tells him epic fables as if they were true, or when the actor in the theater acts more royally than any real king. So long as it is able to deceive without *injuring*, that master of deception, the intellect, is free; it is released from its former slavery and celebrates its Saturnalia. It is never more luxuriant, richer, prouder, more clever and more daring. With creative pleasure it throws

metaphors into confusion and displaces the boundary stones of abstractions, so that, for example, it designates the stream as "the moving path which carries man where he would otherwise walk." The intellect has now thrown the token of bondage from itself. At other times it endeavors, with gloomy officiousness, to show the way and to demonstrate the tools to a poor individual who covets existence; it is like a servant who goes in search of booty and prey for his master. But now it has become the master and it dares to wipe from its face the expression of indigence. In comparison with its previous conduct, everything that it now does bears the mark of dissimulation, just as that previous conduct did of distortion. The free intellect copies human life, but it considers this life to be something good and seems to be quite satisfied with it. That immense framework and planking of concepts to which the needy man clings his whole life long in order to preserve himself is nothing but a scaffolding and toy for the most audacious feats of the liberated intellect. And when it smashes this framework to pieces, throws it into confusion, and puts it back together in an ironic fashion, pairing the most alien things and separating the closest, it is demonstrating that it has no need of these makeshifts of indigence and that it will now be guided by intuitions rather than by concepts. There is no regular path which leads from these intuitions into the land of ghostly schemata, the land of abstractions. There exists no word for these intuitions; when man sees them he grows dumb, or else he speaks only in forbidden metaphors and in unheard-of combinations of concepts. He does this so that by shattering and mocking the old conceptual barriers he may at least correspond creatively to the impression of the powerful present intuition.

There are ages in which the rational man and the intuitive man stand side by side, the one in fear of intuition, the other with scorn for abstraction. The latter is just as irrational as the former is inartistic. They both desire to rule over life: the former, by knowing how to meet his principal needs by means of foresight, prudence, and regularity; the latter, by disregarding these needs and, as an "overjoyed hero," counting as real only that life which has been disguised as illusion and beauty. Whenever, as was perhaps the case in ancient Greece, the intuitive man handles his weapons more authoritatively and victoriously than his opponent, then, under favorable circumstances, a culture can take shape and art's mastery over life can be established. All the manifestations of such a life will be accompanied by this dissimulation, this disavowal of indigence, this

---

[x] Blaise Pascal (1623–62), *Pensées*, number 386.
[xi] According to Herodotus, the tyrant Peisistratus (600–527 BC) entered Athens accompanied by a woman dressed as the goddess Athena.

glitter of metaphorical intuitions, and, in general, this immediacy of deception: neither the house, nor the gait, nor the clothes, nor the clay jugs give evidence of having been invented because of a pressing need. It seems as if they were all intended to express an exalted happiness, an Olympian cloudlessness, and, as it were, a playing with seriousness. The man who is guided by concepts and abstractions only succeeds by such means in warding off misfortune, without ever gaining any happiness for himself from these abstractions. And while he aims for the greatest possible freedom from pain, the intuitive man, standing in the midst of a culture, already reaps from his intuition a harvest of continually inflowing illumination, cheer, and redemption – in addition to obtaining a defense against misfortune. To be sure, he suffers more intensely, *when* he suffers; he even suffers more frequently, since he does not understand how to learn from experience and keeps falling over and over again into the same ditch. He is then just as irrational in sorrow as he is in happiness: he cries aloud and will not be consoled. How differently the stoical man who learns from experience and governs himself by concepts is affected by the same misfortunes! This man, who at other times seeks nothing but sincerity, truth, freedom from deception, and protection against ensnaring surprise attacks, now executes a masterpiece of deception: he executes his masterpiece of deception in misfortune, as the other type of man executes his in times of happiness. He wears no quivering and changeable human face, but, as it were, a mask with dignified, symmetrical features. He does not cry; he does not even alter his voice. When a real storm cloud thunders above him, he wraps himself in his cloak, and with slow steps he walks from beneath it.

"The Madman"

Have you not heard of that madman who lit a lantern in the bright morning hours, ran to the market place, and cried incessantly: "I seek God! I seek God!" – As many of those who did not believe in God were standing around just then, he provoked much laughter. Has he got lost? asked one. Did he lose his way like a child? asked another. Or is he hiding? Is he afraid of us? Has he gone on a voyage? emigrated? – Thus they yelled and laughed.

The madman jumped into their midst and pierced them with his eyes. "Whither is God?" he cried; "I will tell you. *We have killed him* – you and I. All of us are his murderers. But how did we do this? How could we drink up the sea? Who gave us the sponge to wipe away the entire horizon? What were we doing when we unchained this earth from its sun? Whither is it moving now? Whither are we moving? Away from all suns? Are we not plunging continually? Backward, sideward, forward, in all directions? Is there still any up or down? Are we not straying as through an infinite nothing? Do we not feel the breath of empty space? Has it not become colder? Is not night continually closing in on us? Do we not need to light lanterns in the morning? Do we hear nothing as yet of the noise of the gravediggers who are burying God? Do we smell nothing as yet of the divine decomposition? Gods, too, decompose. God is dead. God remains dead. And we have killed him.

"How shall we comfort ourselves, the murderers of all murderers? What was holiest and mightiest of all that the world has yet owned has bled to death under our knives: who will wipe this blood off us? What water is there for us to clean ourselves? What festivals of atonement, what sacred games shall we have to invent? Is not the greatness of this deed too great for us? Must we ourselves not become gods simply to appear worthy of it? There has never been a greater deed; and whoever is born after us – for the sake of this deed he will belong to a higher history than all history hitherto."

Here the madman fell silent and looked again at his listeners; and they, too, were silent and stared at him in astonishment. At last he threw his lantern on the ground, and it broke into pieces and went out. "I have come too early," he said then; "my time is not yet. This tremendous event is still on its way, still wandering; it has not yet reached the ears of men. Lightning and thunder require time; the light of the stars requires time; deeds, though done, still require time to be seen and heard. This deed is still more distant from them than the most distant stars – *and yet they have done it themselves*."

It has been related further that on the same day the madman forced his way into several churches and there struck up his *requiem aeternam deo*.[i] Led out and called to account, he is said always to have replied nothing but: "What after all are these churches now if they are not the tombs and sepulchers of God?"

---

[i] A "requiem" is a Latin prayer for the dead, in which eternal rest (*requiem aeternam*) is asked for the deceased. Here it is being asked for God (*deo*).

"How the 'True World' Finally Became a Fable"

The History of an Error

1. The true world – attainable for the sage, the pious, the virtuous man; he lives in it, *he is it*.

(The oldest form of the idea, relatively sensible, simple, and persuasive. A circumlocution for the sentence, "I, Plato, *am* the truth.")

2. The true world – unattainable for now, but promised for the sage, the pious, the virtuous man ("for the sinner who repents").

(Progress of the idea: it becomes more subtle, insidious, incomprehensible – *it becomes female*, it becomes Christian.)[i]

3. The true world – unattainable, indemonstrable, unpromisable; but the very thought of it – a consolation, an obligation, an imperative.

(At bottom, the old sun, but seen through mist and skepticism. The idea has become elusive, pale, Nordic, Königsbergian.)[ii]

4. The true world – unattainable? At any rate, unattained. And being unattained, also *unknown*. Consequently, not consoling, redeeming, or obligating: how could something unknown obligate us?

(Gray morning. The first yawn of reason. The cockcrow of positivism.)

5. The "true" world – an idea which is no longer good for anything, not even obligating – an idea which has become useless and superfluous – *consequently*, a refuted idea: let us abolish it!

(Bright day; breakfast; return of *bon sens*[iii] and cheerfulness; Plato's embarrassed blush; pandemonium of all free spirits.)

6. The true world – we have abolished. What world has remained? The apparent one perhaps? But no! *With the true world we have also abolished the apparent one.*

(Noon; moment of the briefest shadow; end of the longest error; high point of humanity; INCIPIT ZARATHUSTRA.)[iv]

[i] Nietzsche regarded women as fundamentally mendacious.
[ii] Kant lived in Königsberg, Prussia.
[iii] Good sense.
[iv] "Zarathustra begins," referring to Nietzsche's own book *Thus Spoke Zarathustra*.

The Dionysian World[i]

And do you know what "the world" is to me? Shall I show it to you in my mirror? This world: a monster of energy, without beginning, without end; a firm, iron magnitude of force that does not grow bigger or smaller, that does not expend itself but only transforms itself; as a whole, of unalterable size, a household without expenses or losses, but likewise without increase or income; enclosed by "nothingness" as by a boundary; not something blurry or wasted, not something endlessly extended, but set in a definite space as a definite force, and not a space that might be "empty" here or there, but rather as force throughout, as a play of forces and waves of forces, at the same time one and many, increasing here and at the same time decreasing there; a sea of forces flowing and rushing together, eternally changing, eternally flooding back, with tremendous years of recurrence, with an ebb and a flood of its forms; out of the simplest forms striving toward the most complex, out of the stillest, most rigid, coldest forms toward the hottest, most turbulent, most self-contradictory, and then again returning home to the simple out of this abundance, out of the play of contradictions back to the joy of concord, still affirming itself in this uniformity of its courses and its years, blessing itself as that which must return eternally,[ii] as a becoming that knows no satiety, no disgust, no weariness: this, my *Dionysian* world of the eternally self-creating, the eternally self-destroying, this mystery world of the twofold voluptuous delight, my "beyond good and evil," without goal, unless the joy of the circle is itself a goal; without will, unless a ring feels good-will toward itself – do you want a *name* for this world? A *solution* for all its riddles? A *light* for you, too, you best-concealed, strongest, most intrepid, most midnightly men? – *This world is the will to power – and nothing besides*! And you yourselves are also this will to power – and nothing besides!

[i] The title – The Dionysian World – is mine, not Nietzsche's.
[ii] A reference to Nietzsche's idea of the "eternal recurrence," that in our finite material universe all events must be endlessly repeated. "Dionysian" below refers to Dionysus, the Greek god of intoxication and sexuality.

14

"The Founding and Manifesto of Futurism"

Filippo Tommaso Marinetti

The cosmopolitan writer Filippo Tommaso Marinetti (1876–1944) founded the movement of Futurism in 1909 by publishing "The Manifesto of Futurism" in a Paris newspaper. Marinetti's Futurism is a prime example of the artistic and social movements that exploded in the period between the world wars. Utopian, modern, intense, Marinetti wants an art that can re-make the world by recognizing the novel possibilities of industrial, mass society. This is not a purely aesthetic view, nor is it benign in its implications. Marinetti urged Italian involvement in World War I and later became an enthusiastic supporter of Benito Mussolini, arguing that fascism was an expression of Futurism. Like Mussolini, Marinetti regarded war as an heroic intensification of life.

We had stayed up all night, my friends and I, under hanging mosque lamps with domes of filigreed brass, domes starred like our spirits, shining like them with the prisoned radiance of electric hearts. For hours we had trampled our atavistic ennui into rich oriental rugs, arguing up to the last confines of logic and blackening many reams of paper with our frenzied scribbling.

An immense pride was buoying us up, because we felt ourselves alone at that hour, alone, awake, and on our feet, like proud beacons or forward sentries against an army of hostile stars glaring down at us from their celestial encampments. Alone with stokers feeding the hellish fires of great ships, alone with the black specters who grope in the red-hot bellies of locomotives launched down their crazy courses, alone with drunkards reeling like wounded birds along the city walls.

Suddenly we jumped, hearing the mighty noise of the huge double-decker trams that rumbled by outside, ablaze with colored lights, like villages on holiday suddenly struck and uprooted by the flooding Po and dragged over falls and through gorges to the sea.

Then the silence deepened. But, as we listened to the old canal muttering its feeble prayers and the creaking bones of sickly palaces above their damp green beards, under the windows we suddenly heard the famished roar of automobiles.

"Let's go!" I said. "Friends, away! Let's go! Mythology and the Mystic Ideal are defeated at last. We're about to see the Centaur's birth and, soon after, the first flight of Angels!...We must shake the gates of life, test the bolts and hinges. Let's go! Look there, on the earth, the very first dawn! There's nothing to match the splendor of the sun's red sword, slashing for the first time through our millennial gloom!"

We went up to the three snorting beasts, to lay amorous hands on their torrid breasts. I stretched out on my car like a corpse on its bier, but revived at once under the steering wheel, a guillotine blade that threatened my stomach.

The raging broom of madness swept us out of ourselves and drove us through streets as rough and deep as the beds of torrents. Here and there, sick

Filippo Tommaso Marinetti, "The Founding and Manifesto of Futurism" (trans. R. W. Flint and Arthur W. Coppotelli) from *Marinetti: Selected Writings* (ed. R. W. Flint), pp. 39–44. New York: Farrar, Straus, Giroux, 1972.

lamplight through window glass taught us to distrust the deceitful mathematics of our perishing eyes.

I cried, "The scent, the scent alone is enough for our beasts."

And like young lions we ran after Death, its dark pelt blotched with pale crosses as it escaped down the vast violet living and throbbing sky.

But we had no ideal Mistress raising her divine form to the clouds, nor any cruel Queen to whom to offer our bodies, twisted like Byzantine rings! There was nothing to make us wish for death, unless the wish to be free at last from the weight of our courage!

And on we raced, hurling watchdogs against doorsteps, curling them under our burning tires like collars under a flatiron. Death, domesticated, met me at every turn, gracefully holding out a paw, or once in a while hunkering down, making velvety caressing eyes at me from every puddle.

"Let's break out of the horrible shell of wisdom and throw ourselves like pride-ripened fruit into the wide, contorted mouth of the wind! Let's give ourselves utterly to the Unknown, not in desperation but only to replenish the deep wells of the Absurd!!"

The words were scarcely out of my mouth when I spun my car around with the frenzy of a dog trying to bite its tail, and there, suddenly, were two cyclists coming toward me, shaking their fists, wobbling like two equally convincing but nevertheless contradictory arguments. Their stupid dilemma was blocking my way – damn! Ouch!...
I stopped short and to my disgust rolled over into a ditch with my wheels in the air....

Oh! Maternal ditch, almost full of muddy water! Fair factory drain! I gulped down your nourishing sludge; and I remembered the blessed black breast of my Sudanese nurse.... When I came up – torn, filthy, and stinking – from under the capsized car, I felt the white-hot iron of joy deliciously pass through my heart!

A crowd of fishermen with handlines and gouty naturalists were already swarming around the prodigy. With patient, loving care those people rigged a tall derrick and iron grapnels to fish out my car, like a big beached shark. Up it came from the ditch, slowly, leaving in the bottom like scales its heavy framework of good sense and its soft upholstery of comfort.

They thought it was dead, my beautiful shark, but a caress from me was enough to revive it; and there it was, alive again, running on its powerful fins!

And so, faces smeared with good factory muck – plastered with metallic waste, with senseless sweat, with celestial soot – we, bruised, our arms in slings, but unafraid, declared our high intentions to all the *living* of the earth:

Manifesto of Futurism

1. We intend to sing the love of danger, the habit of energy and fearlessness.

2. Courage, audacity, and revolt will be essential elements of our poetry.

3. Up to now literature has exalted a pensive immobility, ecstasy, and sleep. We intend to exalt aggressive action, a feverish insomnia, the racer's stride, the mortal leap, the punch and the slap.

4. We say that the world's magnificence has been enriched by a new beauty; the beauty of speed. A racing car whose hood is adorned with great pipes, like serpents of explosive breath – a roaring car that seems to ride on grapeshot – is more beautiful than the *Victory of Samothrace*.[i]

5. We want to hymn the man at the wheel, who hurls the lance of his spirit across the Earth, along the circle of its orbit.

6. The poet must spend himself with ardor, splendor, and generosity, to swell the enthusiastic fervor of the primordial elements.

7. Except in struggle, there is no more beauty. No work without an aggressive character can be a masterpiece. Poetry must be conceived as a violent attack on unknown forces, to reduce and prostrate them before man.

8. We stand on the last promontory of the centuries!... Why should we look back, when what we want is to break down the mysterious doors of the Impossible? Time and Space died yesterday. We already live in the absolute, because we have created eternal, omnipresent speed.

9. We will glorify war – the world's only hygiene – militarism, patriotism, the destructive gesture of freedom-bringers, beautiful ideas worth dying for, and scorn for woman.

10. We will destroy the museums, libraries, academies of every kind, will fight moralism, feminism, every opportunistic or utilitarian cowardice.

11. We will sing of great crowds excited by work, by pleasure, and by riot; we will sing of the multi-colored, polyphonic tides of revolution in the modern capitals; we will sing of the vibrant nightly fervor of arsenals and shipyards blazing

---

[i] A second century BC Greek sculpture.

with violent electric moons; greedy railway stations that devour smoke-plumed serpents; factories hung on clouds by the crooked lines of their smoke; bridges that stride the rivers like giant gymnasts, flashing in the sun with a glitter of knives; adventurous steamers that sniff the horizon; deep-chested locomotives whose wheels paw the tracks like the hooves of enormous steel horses bridled by tubing; and the sleek flight of planes whose propellers chatter in the wind like banners and seem to cheer like an enthusiastic crowd.

It is from Italy that we launch through the world this violently upsetting, incendiary manifesto of ours. With it, today, we establish *Futurism* because we want to free this land from its smelly gangrene of professors, archaeologists, ciceroni, and antiquarians.[ii] For too long has Italy been a dealer in second hand clothes. We mean to free her from the numberless museums that cover her like so many graveyards.

Museums: cemeteries!... Identical, surely, in the sinister promiscuity of so many bodies unknown to one another. Museums: public dormitories where one lies forever beside hated or unknown beings. Museums; absurd abattoirs of painters and sculptors ferociously macerating each other with color-blows and line-blows, the length of the fought-over walls!

That one should make an annual pilgrimage, just as one goes to the graveyard on All Souls' Day – that I grant. That once a year one should leave a floral tribute beneath the *Gioconda*,[iii] I grant you that.... But I don't admit that our sorrows, our fragile courage, our morbid restlessness should be given a daily conducted tour through the museums. Why poison ourselves? Why rot?

And what is there to see in an old picture except the laborious contortions of an artist throwing himself against the barriers that thwart his desire to express his dream completely?... Admiring an old picture is the same as pouring our sensibility into a funerary urn instead of hurling it far off, in violent spasms of action and creation.

Do you, then, wish to waste all your best powers in this eternal and futile worship of the past, from which you emerge fatally exhausted, shrunken, beaten down?

In truth I tell you that daily visits to museums, libraries, and academies (cemeteries of empty exer-

tion, calvaries of crucified dreams, registries of aborted beginnings!) is, for artists, as damaging as the prolonged supervision by parents of certain young people drunk with their talent and their ambitious wills. When the future is barred to them, the admirable past may be a solace for the ills of the moribund, the sickly, the prisoner.... But we want no part of it, the past, we the young and strong *Futurists*!

So let them come, the gay incendiaries with charred fingers! Here they are! Here they are!... Come on! set fire to the library shelves! Turn aside the canals to flood the museums!... Oh, the joy of seeing the glorious old canvases bobbing adrift on those waters, discolored and shredded!... Take up your pickaxes, your axes and hammers, and wreck, wreck the venerable cities, pitilessly!

The oldest of us is thirty: so we have at least a decade for finishing our work. When we are forty, other younger and stronger men will probably throw us in the wastebasket like useless manuscripts – we want it to happen!

They will come against us, our successors, will come from far away, from every quarter, dancing to the winged cadence of their first songs, flexing the hooked claws of predators, sniffing doglike at the academy doors the strong odor of our decaying minds, which already will have been promised to the literary catacombs.

But we won't be there.... At last they'll find us – one winter's night – in open country, beneath a sad roof drummed by a monotonous rain. They'll see us crouched beside our trembling airplanes in the act of warming our hands at the poor little blaze that our books of today will give out when they take fire from the flight of our images.

They'll storm around us, panting with scorn and anguish, and all of them, exasperated by our proud daring, will hurtle to kill us, driven by hatred: the more implacable it is, the more their hearts will be drunk with love and admiration for us.

Injustice, strong and sane, will break out radiantly in their eyes.

Art, in fact, can be nothing but violence, cruelty, and injustice.

The oldest of us is thirty: even so we have already scattered treasures, a thousand treasures of force, love, courage, astuteness, and raw will power; have thrown them impatiently away, with fury, carelessly, unhesitatingly, breathless and unresting.... Look at us! We are still untired! Our hearts know no weariness because they are fed

---

ii   Ciceroni are guides who explain antiquities to tourists.
iii   Leonardo da Vinci's painting *Mona Lisa*.

with fire, hatred, and speed! ... Does that amaze you? It should, because you can never remember having lived! Erect on the summit of the world, once again we hurl our defiance at the stars!

You have objections? – Enough! Enough! We know them ... we've understood! ... Our fine deceitful intelligence tells us that we are the revival and extension of our ancestors – perhaps! ... If only it were so! – But who cares? We don't want to understand! ... Woe to anyone who says those infamous words to us again!

Lift up your heads!

Erect on the summit of the world, once again we hurl defiance to the stars!

15

From *Course in General Linguistics*

Ferdinand de Saussure

Genevan linguist Ferdinand de Saussure (1857–1913) presented a new approach to the study of language, and hence implicitly to all cultural phenomena, which not only revolutionized linguistics but had a great impact on structuralism and the poststructuralism that succeeded it. His influence lay in his *Course in General Linguistics* (1906–11), a reconstruction of his lectures from the notes of students. Of particular importance was his attempt to analyze language (or *langue*, rather than *parole*, or speech) as a system in which each element is dependent on relations to other elements. For Saussure the meaning of a word is determined, not by any natural or preconventional relation of word to object, but by the word's relation to other words. Meaning rests on the differences among elements in a linguistic system. This is summarized in his famous phrase: "in language there are only differences."

Sign, Signified, Signifier

Some people regard language, when reduced to its elements, as a naming-process only – a list of words, each corresponding to the thing that it names. For example, see figure 15.1.

This conception is open to criticism at several points. It assumes that ready-made ideas exist before words; it does not tell us whether a name is vocal or psychological in nature (*arbor*, for instance, can be considered from either viewpoint); finally, it lets us assume that the linking of a name and a thing is a very simple operation – an assumption that is anything but true. But this rather naïve approach can bring us near the truth by showing us that the

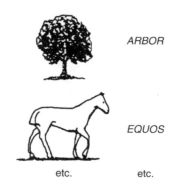

Figure 15.1

linguistic unit is a double entity, one formed by the associating of two terms.

We have seen in considering the speaking-circuit that both terms involved in the linguistic sign are psychological and are united in the brain by an associative bond. This point must be emphasized.

The linguistic sign unites, not a thing and a name, but a concept and a sound-image. The latter is not the material sound, a purely physical thing, but the psychological imprint of the sound, the impression that it makes on our senses. The sound-image is sensory, and if I happen to call it "material," it is only in that sense, and by way of opposing it to the other term of the association, the concept, which is generally more abstract.

Ferdinand de Saussure, from *Course in General Linguistics* (trans. Wade Baskin), Part One, chapter 1, pp. 65–70. New York: McGraw-Hill, 1966.

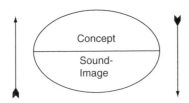

Figure 15.2

The psychological character of our sound-images becomes apparent when we observe our own speech. Without moving our lips or tongue, we can talk to ourselves or recite mentally a selection of verse. Because we regard the words of our language as sound-images, we must avoid speaking of the "phonemes" that make up the words. This term, which suggests vocal activity, is applicable to the spoken word only, to the realization of the inner image in discourse. We can avoid that misunderstanding by speaking of the *sounds* and *syllables* of a word provided we remember that the names refer to the sound-image.

The linguistic sign is then a two-sided psychological entity that can be represented by the drawing in figure 15.2.

The two elements are intimately united, and each recalls the other. Whether we try to find the meaning of the Latin word *arbor* or the word that Latin uses to designate the concept "tree," it is clear that only the associations sanctioned by that language appear to us to conform to reality, and we disregard whatever others might be imagined.

Our definition of the linguistic sign poses an important question of terminology. I call the combination of a concept and a sound-image a *sign*, but in current usage the term generally designates only a sound-image, a word, for example (*arbor*, etc.). One tends to forget that *arbor* is called a sign only because it carries the concept "tree," with the result that the idea of the sensory part implies the idea of the whole [figure 15.3].

Ambiguity would disappear if the three notions involved here were designated by three names, each suggesting and opposing the others. I propose to retain the word *sign* to designate the whole and to replace *concept* and *sound-image* respectively by *signified* and *signifier;*[i] the last two terms have the advantage of indicating the opposition that separates them from each other and from the whole of

---
[i] The French terms are *signifié* (signified) and *signifiant* (signifier). Note that for Saussure the signified is the *concept* of an object, not the object itself.

which they are parts. As regards *sign*, if I am satisfied with it, this is simply because I do not know of any word to replace it, the ordinary language suggesting no other.

The linguistic sign, as defined, has two primordial characteristics. In enunciating them I am also positing the basic principles of any study of this type.

Principle I: The Arbitrary Nature of the Sign

The bond between the signifier and the signified is arbitrary. Since I mean by sign the whole that results from the associating of the signifier with the signified, I can simply say: *the linguistic sign is arbitrary*.

The idea of "sister" is not linked by any inner relationship to the succession of sounds *s-ö-r* which serves as its signifier in French; that it could be represented equally by just any other sequence is proved by differences among languages and by the very existence of different languages: the signified "ox" has as its signifier *b-ö-f* on one side of the border and *O-k-s* (*Ochs*) on the other.

No one disputes the principle of the arbitrary nature of the sign, but it is often easier to discover a truth than to assign to it its proper place. Principle I dominates all the linguistics of language; its consequences are numberless. It is true that not all of them are equally obvious at first glance; only after many detours does one discover them, and with them the primordial importance of the principle.

One remark in passing: when semiology becomes organized as a science, the question will arise whether or not it properly includes modes of expression based on completely natural signs, such as pantomime. Supposing that the new science welcomes them, its main concern will still be the whole group of systems grounded on the arbitrariness of the sign. In fact, every means of expression used in society is based, in principle, on collective behavior or – what amounts to the same thing – on convention. Polite formulas, for instance, though often imbued with a certain natural expressiveness (as in the case of a Chinese who greets his emperor by bowing down to the ground nine times), are nonetheless fixed by rule; it is this rule and not the intrinsic value of the gestures that obliges one to use them. Signs that are wholly arbitrary realize better than the others the ideal of the semiological process; that is why language, the most complex and universal of all systems of expression, is also the most characteristic; in this sense linguistics can become the master-pattern for

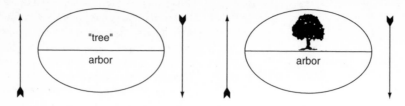

Figure 15.3

all branches of semiology although language is only one particular semiological system.

The word *symbol* has been used to designate the linguistic sign, or more specifically, what is here called the signifier. Principle I in particular weighs against the use of this term. One characteristic of the symbol is that it is never wholly arbitrary; it is not empty, for there is the rudiment of a natural bond between the signifier and the signified. The symbol of justice, a pair of scales, could not be replaced by just any other symbol, such as a chariot.

The word *arbitrary* also calls for comment. The term should not imply that the choice of the signifier is left entirely to the speaker (we shall see below that the individual does not have the power to change a sign in any way once it has become established in the linguistic community); I mean that it is unmotivated, i.e. arbitrary in that it actually has no natural connection with the signified.

In concluding let us consider two objections that might be raised to the establishment of Principle I:

(1) *Onomatopoeia*[ii] might be used to prove that the choice of the signifier is not always arbitrary. But onomatopoeic formations are never organic elements of a linguistic system. Besides, their number is much smaller than is generally supposed. Words like French *fouet* "whip" or *glas* "knell" may strike certain ears with suggestive sonority, but to see that they have not always had this property we need only examine their Latin forms (*fouet* is derived from *fāgus* "beech-tree," *glas* from *classicum* "sound of a trumpet"). The quality of their present sounds, or rather the quality that is attributed to them, is a fortuitous result of phonetic evolution.

As for authentic onomatopoeic words (e.g. *glug-glug*, *tick-tock*, etc.), not only are they limited in number, but also they are chosen

somewhat arbitrarily, for they are only approximate and more or less conventional imitations of certain sounds (cf. English *bow-wow* and French *ouaoua*). In addition, once these words have been introduced into the language, they are to a certain extent subjected to the same evolution – phonetic, morphological, etc. – that other words undergo (cf. *pigeon*, ultimately from Vulgar Latin *pīpiō*, derived in turn from an onomatopoeic formation): obvious proof that they lose something of their original character in order to assume that of the linguistic sign in general, which is unmotivated.

(2) *Interjections*, closely related to onomatopoeia, can be attacked on the same grounds and come no closer to refuting our thesis. One is tempted to see in them spontaneous expressions of reality dictated, so to speak, by natural forces. But for most interjections we can show that there is no fixed bond between their signified and their signifier. We need only compare two languages on this point to see how much such expressions differ from one language to the next (e.g. the English equivalent of French *aie!* is *ouch!*). We know, moreover, that many interjections were once words with specific meanings (cf. French *diable!* 'darn!' *mordieu!* 'golly!' from *mort Dieu* 'God's death,' etc.).

Onomatopoeic formations and interjections are of secondary importance, and their symbolic origin is in part open to dispute.

Principle II: The Linear Nature of the Signifier

The signifier, being auditory, is unfolded solely in time from which it gets the following characteristics: (a) it represents a span, and (b) the span is measurable in a single dimension; it is a line.

While Principle II is obvious, apparently linguists have always neglected to state it, doubtless

---

[ii] Words that, when spoken, make the sound they refer to (e.g. "buzz" to describe the activity of a bee).

because they found it too simple; nevertheless, it is fundamental, and its consequences are incalculable. Its importance equals that of Principle I; the whole mechanism of language depends upon it. In contrast to visual signifiers (nautical signals, etc.) which can offer simultaneous groupings in several dimensions, auditory signifiers have at their command only the dimension of time. Their elements are presented in succession; they form a chain. This feature becomes readily apparent when they are represented in writing and the spatial line of graphic marks is substituted for succession in time.

Sometimes the linear nature of the signifier is not obvious. When I accent a syllable, for instance, it seems that I am concentrating more than one significant element on the same point. But this is an illusion; the syllable and its accent constitute only one phonational act. There is no duality within the act but only different oppositions to what precedes and what follows.

The Sign Considered in Its Totality

Everything that has been said up to this point boils down to this: in language there are only differences. Even more important: a difference generally implies positive terms between which the difference is set up; but in language there are only differences *without positive terms*. Whether we take the signified or the signifier, language has neither ideas nor sounds that existed before the linguistic system but only conceptual and phonic differences that have issued from the system. The idea or phonic substance that a sign contains is of less importance than the other signs that surround it. Proof of this is that the value of a term may be modified without either its meaning or its sound being affected, solely because a neighboring term has been modified.

But the statement that everything in language is negative is true only if the signified and the signifier are considered separately; when we consider the sign in its totality, we have something that is positive in its own class. A linguistic system is a series of differences of sound combined with a series of differences of ideas; but the pairing of a certain number of acoustical signs with as many cuts made from the mass of thought engenders a system of values; and this system serves as the effective link between the phonic and psychological elements within each sign. Although both the signified and the signifier are purely differential and negative when considered separately, their combination is a positive fact; it is even the sole type of facts that language has, for maintaining the parallelism between the two classes of differences is the distinctive function of the linguistic institution.

Certain diachronic facts are typical in this respect. Take the countless instances where alteration of the signifier occasions a conceptual change and where it is obvious that the sum of the ideas distinguished corresponds in principle to the sum of the distinctive signs. When two words are confused through phonetic alteration (e.g. French *décrépit* from *dēcrepitus* and *décrépi* from *crispus*), the ideas that they express will also tend to become confused if only they have something in common. Or a word may have different forms (cf. *chaise* 'chair' and *chaire* 'desk'). Any nascent difference will tend invariably to become significant but without always succeeding or being successful on the first trial. Conversely, any conceptual difference perceived by the mind seeks to find expression through a distinct signifier, and two ideas that are no longer distinct in the mind tend to merge into the same signifier.

When we compare signs – positive terms – with each other, we can no longer speak of difference; the expression would not be fitting, for it applies only to the comparing of two sound-images, e.g. *father* and *mother*, or two ideas, e.g. the idea "father" and the idea "mother"; two signs, each having a signified and signifier, are not different but only distinct. Between them there is only *opposition*. The entire mechanism of language, with which we shall be concerned later, is based on oppositions of this kind and on the phonic and conceptual differences that they imply.

What is true of value is true also of the unit. A unit is a segment of the spoken chain that corresponds to a certain concept; both are by nature purely differential.

Applied to units, the principle of differentiation can be stated in this way: the characteristics of the unit blend with the unit itself. In language, as in any semiological system, whatever distinguishes one sign from the others constitutes it. Difference makes character just as it makes value and the unit.

Another rather paradoxical consequence of the same principle is this: in the last analysis what is commonly referred to as a "grammatical fact" fits the definition of the unit, for it always expresses an opposition of terms; it differs only in that the opposition is particularly significant (e.g. the formation of German plurals of the type *Nacht:*

Nächte).[iii] Each term present in the grammatical fact (the singular without umlaut or final *e* in opposition to the plural with umlaut and *e*) consists of the interplay of a number of oppositions within the system. When isolated, neither *Nacht* nor *Nächte* is anything: thus everything is opposition. Putting it another way, the *Nacht: Nächte* relation can be expressed by an algebraic formula a/b in which a and b are not simple terms but result from a set of relations. Language, in a manner of speaking, is a type of algebra consisting solely of complex terms. Some of its oppositions are more significant than others; but units and grammatical facts are only different names for designating diverse aspects of the same general fact: the functioning of linguistic oppositions. This statement is so true that we might very well approach the problem of units by starting from grammatical facts. Taking an opposition like

Nacht: Nächte, we might ask what are the units involved in it. Are they only the two words, the whole series of similar words, *a* and *ä*, or all singulars and plurals, etc.?

Units and grammatical facts would not be confused if linguistic signs were made up of something besides differences. But language being what it is, we shall find nothing simple in it regardless of our approach; everywhere and always there is the same complex equilibrium of terms that mutually condition each other. Putting it another way, *language is a form and not a substance*. This truth could not be overstressed, for all the mistakes in our terminology, all our incorrect ways of naming things that pertain to language, stem from the involuntary supposition that the linguistic phenomenon must have substance.

[iii] *Nacht* means night.

16

From "Science as a Vocation"

Max Weber

Max Weber (1864–1920), giant of the great age of German sociology, stands with Freud and Marx as one of the quintessential theorists of modernity. A supporter of liberal republicanism in imperialist, quasi-feudal Germany, Weber famously opposed the politicization of science, arguing for the need for dispassionate objectivity, a stance directly connected to his view of modernity. In the Introduction to his most famous book, *The Protestant Ethic and the Spirit of Capitalism*, he described Euro-American modernization as an expanding "rationalism," by which he meant an increasing subjection of spheres of life to instrumental rationality (*Zweckrationalität*), the analysis, planning, and manipulation of phenomena in order to serve worldly goals. The development of Protestantism, he then theorized, was an example; unlike Catholicism, it announced an individualistic, calculative form of salvation through disciplined work, an *innerweltliche Askese* or "this-worldly asceticism." Christianity thereby evolved a form of belief that sanctified the character traits required by modern capitalism. For Weber, modernity comes at a price: it buys individual liberty, rational thought, and material progress in exchange for a "disenchantment of the world," a permanent state of dissatisfaction, and an "iron cage" of bureaucratic alienation. There is no way around this bargain, Weber argued in his marvelous 1918 lecture "Science as a Vocation." He concludes that one must either "bear the fate of the times like a man," or sacrifice rational intelligence and "return [to] the arms of the old churches..." There is no third option.

Scientific progress is a fraction, the most important fraction, of the process of intellectualization which we have been undergoing for thousands of years and which nowadays is usually judged in such an extremely negative way. Let us first clarify what this intellectualist rationalization, created by science and by scientifically oriented technology, means practically.

Does it mean that we, today, for instance, everyone sitting in this hall, have a greater knowledge of the conditions of life under which we exist than has an American Indian or a Hottentot?[i] Hardly. Unless he is a physicist, one who rides on the streetcar has no idea how the car happened to get into motion. And he does not need to know. He is satisfied that he may 'count' on the behaviour of the streetcar, and he orients his conduct according to this expectation; but he knows nothing about what it takes to produce such a car so that it can move. The savage knows incomparably more about his tools. When we spend money today I bet that even if there are colleagues of political economy here in the hall, almost every one of them will hold a different answer in readiness to the question: How does it happen that one can buy something for money – sometimes more and sometimes less? The savage knows what he does in order to get his daily food and which institutions serve him in this

i   A southern African people.

Max Weber, from "Science as a Vocation," pp. 138–40, 143–9, 155–6 in *From Max Weber: Essays in Sociology* (trans. and ed. H. H. Gerth and C. Wright Mills). New York: Oxford University Press, 1946.

pursuit. The increasing intellectualization and rationalization do *not*, therefore, indicate an increased and general knowledge of the conditions under which one lives.

It means something else, namely, the knowledge or belief that if one but wished one *could* learn it at any time. Hence, it means that principally there are no mysterious incalculable forces that come into play, but rather that one can, in principle, master all things by calculation. This means that the world is disenchanted. One need no longer have recourse to magical means in order to master or implore the spirits, as did the savage, for whom such mysterious powers existed. Technical means and calculations perform the service. This above all is what intellectualization means.

Now, this process of disenchantment, which has continued to exist in Occidental culture for millennia, and, in general, this "progress," to which science belongs as a link and motive force, do they have any meanings that go beyond the purely practical and technical? You will find this question raised in the most principled form in the works of Leo Tolstoi.[ii] He came to raise the question in a peculiar way. All his broodings increasingly revolved around the problem of whether or not death is a meaningful phenomenon. And his answer was: for civilized man death has no meaning. It has none because the individual life of civilized man, placed into an infinite "progress," according to its own imminent meaning should never come to an end; for there is always a further step ahead of one who stands in the march of progress. And no man who comes to die stands upon the peak which lies in infinity. Abraham, or some peasant of the past, died "old and satiated with life" because he stood in the organic cycle of life; because his life, in terms of its meaning and on the eve of his days, had given to him what life had to offer; because for him there remained no puzzles he might wish to solve; and therefore he could have had "enough" of life. Whereas civilized man, placed in the midst of the continuous enrichment of culture by ideas, knowledge, and problems, may become "tired of life" but not "satiated with life." He catches only the most minute part of what the life of the spirit brings forth ever anew, and what he seizes is always something provisional and not definitive, and therefore death for him is a meaningless occurrence. And because death is meaningless, civilized life as such is meaningless; by its very "progressiveness" it gives death

the imprint of meaninglessness. Throughout his late novels one meets with this thought as the keynote of the Tolstoyan art.

What stand should one take? Has "progress" as such a recognizable meaning that goes beyond the technical, so that to serve it is a meaningful vocation? The question must be raised. But this is no longer merely the question of man's calling *for* science, hence, the problem of what science as a vocation means to its devoted disciples. To raise this question is to ask for the vocation of science within the total life of humanity. What is the value of science? . . .

Today one usually speaks of science as "free from presuppositions." Is there such a thing? It depends upon what one understands thereby. All scientific work presupposes that the rules of logic and method are valid; these are the general foundations of our orientation in the world; and, at least for our special question, these presuppositions are the least problematic aspect of science. Science further presupposes that what is yielded by scientific work is important in the sense that it is "worth being known." In this, obviously, are contained all our problems. For this presupposition cannot be proved by scientific means. It can only be *interpreted* with reference to its ultimate meaning, which we must reject or accept according to our ultimate position towards life.

Furthermore, the nature of the relationship of scientific work and its presuppositions varies widely according to their structure. The natural sciences, for instance, physics, chemistry, and astronomy, presuppose as self-evident that it is worth while to know the ultimate laws of cosmic events as far as science can construe them. This is the case not only because with such knowledge one can attain technical results but for its own sake, if the quest for such knowledge is to be a "vocation." Yet this presupposition can by no means be proved. And still less can it be proved that the existence of the world which these sciences describe is worth while, that it has any "meaning," or that it makes sense to live in such a world. Science does not ask for the answers to such questions.

Consider modern medicine, a practical technology which is highly developed scientifically. The general "presupposition" of the medical enterprise is stated trivially in the assertion that medical science has the task of maintaining life as such and of diminishing suffering as such to the greatest possible degree. Yet this is problematical. By his means the medical man preserves the life of the mortally ill man, even if the patient implores us to relieve him

[ii] A great Russian writer (1828–1910).

of life, even if his relatives, to whom his life is worthless and to whom the costs of maintaining his worthless life grow unbearable, grant his redemption from suffering. Perhaps a poor lunatic is involved, whose relatives, whether they admit it or not, wish and must wish for his death. Yet the presuppositions of medicine, and the penal code, prevent the physician from relinquishing his therapeutic efforts. Whether life is worth while living and when – this question is not asked by medicine. Natural science gives us an answer to the question of what we must do if we wish to master life technically. It leaves quite aside, or assumes for its purposes, whether we should and do wish to master life technically and whether it ultimately makes sense to do so.

Consider a discipline such as aesthetics. The fact that there are works of art is given for aesthetics. It seeks to find out under what conditions this fact exists, but it does not raise the question whether or not the realm of art is perhaps a realm of diabolical grandeur, a realm of this world, and therefore, in its core, hostile to God and, in its innermost and aristocratic spirit, hostile to the brotherhood of man. Hence, aesthetics does not ask whether there *should* be works of art.

Consider jurisprudence. It establishes what is valid according to the rules of juristic thought, which is partly bound by logically compelling and partly by conventionally given schemata. Juridical thought holds when certain legal rules and certain methods of interpretations are recognized as binding. Whether there should be law and whether one should establish just these rules – such questions jurisprudence does not answer. It can only state: If one wishes this result, according to the norms of our legal thought, this legal rule is the appropriate means of attaining it.

Consider the historical and cultural sciences. They teach us how to understand and interpret political, artistic, literary, and social phenomena in terms of their origins. But they give us no answer to the question, whether the existence of these cultural phenomena has been and is *worth while*. And they do not answer the further question, whether it is worth the effort required to know them. They presuppose that there is an interest in partaking, through this procedure, of the community of "civilized men." But they cannot prove "scientifically" that this is the case; and that they presuppose this interest by no means proves that it goes without saying. In fact it is not at all self-evident.

Finally, let us consider the disciplines close to me: sociology, history, economics, political science, and those types of cultural philosophy that make it their task to interpret these sciences. It is said, and I agree, that politics is out of place in the lecture-room. It does not belong there on the part of the students. If, for instance, in the lecture-room of my former colleague Dietrich Schäfer in Berlin, pacifist students were to surround his desk and make an uproar, I should deplore it just as much as I should deplore the uproar which anti-pacifist students are said to have made against Professor Förster, whose views in many ways are as remote as could be from mine. Neither does politics, however, belong in the lecture-room on the part of the docents, and when the docent is scientifically concerned with politics, it belongs there least of all.

To take a practical political stand is one thing, and to analyze political structures and party positions is another. When speaking in a political meeting about democracy, one does not hide one's personal standpoint; indeed, to come out clearly and take a stand is one's damned duty. The words one uses in such a meeting are not means of scientific analysis but means of canvassing votes and winning over others. They are not plow-shares to loosen the soil of contemplative thought; they are swords against the enemies: such words are weapons. It would be an outrage, however, to use words in this fashion in a lecture or in the lecture-room. If, for instance, "democracy" is under discussion, one considers its various forms, analyzes them in the way they function, determines what results for the conditions of life the one form has as compared with the other. Then one confronts the forms of democracy with non-democratic forms of political order and endeavors to come to a position where the student may find the point from which, in terms of his ultimate ideals, he can take a stand. But the true teacher will beware of imposing from the platform any political position upon the student, whether it is expressed or suggested. "To let the facts speak for themselves" is the most unfair way of putting over a political position to the student.

Why should we abstain from doing this? I state in advance that some highly esteemed colleagues are of the opinion that it is not possible to carry through this self-restraint and that, even if it were possible, it would be a whim to avoid declaring oneself. Now one cannot demonstrate scientifically what the duty of an academic teacher is. One can only demand of the teacher that he have the intellectual integrity to see that it is one thing to state facts, to determine mathematical or logical relations or the internal structure of cultural values, while it is another thing to answer questions of the *value* of culture and its individual contents and the question of how one should act in the cultural community and in political associations. These are quite heterogeneous problems. If he asks further why he should not deal with both types of problems in the lecture-room, the answer is: because the prophet and the demagogue do not belong on the academic platform....

Thus far I have spoken only of practical reasons for avoiding the imposition of a personal point of view. But these are not the only reasons. The impossibility of "scientifically" pleading for practical and interested stands – except in discussing the means for a firmly given and presupposed end – rests upon reasons that lie far deeper.

"Scientific" pleading is meaningless in principle because the various value spheres of the world stand in irreconcilable conflict with each other. The elder Mill,[iii] whose philosophy I will not praise otherwise, was on this point right when he said: If one proceeds from pure experience, one arrives at polytheism. This is shallow in formulation and sounds paradoxical, and yet there is truth in it. If anything we realize again today that something can be sacred not only in spite of its not being beautiful, but rather because and in so far as it is not beautiful. You will find this documented in the fifty-third chapter of the book of Isaiah and in the twenty-first Psalm. And, since Nietzsche, we realize that something can be beautiful, not only in spite of the aspect in which it is not good, but rather in that very aspect. You will find this expressed earlier in the *Fleurs du mal*, as Baudelaire named his volume of poems.[iv] It is commonplace to observe that something may be true although it is not beautiful and not holy and not good. Indeed it may be true in precisely those aspects. But all these are only the most elementary cases of the struggle that the gods of the various orders and values are engaged in. I do not know how one might wish to decide "scientifically" the value of French and German culture; for here, too, different gods struggle with one another, now and for all times to come.

[iii] Scottish utilitarian philosopher James Mill (1773–1836), father of philosopher John Stuart Mill.
[iv] "Flowers of Evil," by Charles Baudelaire (1821–67). See the editor's headnote to the Baudelaire selection in the present volume (Chapter 11).

We live as did the ancients when their world was not yet disenchanted of its gods and demons, only we live in a different sense. As Hellenic man at times sacrificed to Aphrodite and at other times to Apollo, and, above all, as everybody sacrificed to the gods of his city, so do we still nowadays, only the bearing of man has been disenchanted and denuded of its mystical but inwardly genuine plasticity. Fate, and certainly not "science," holds sway over these gods and their struggles. One can only understand what the godhead is for the one order or for the other, or better, what godhead is in the one or in the other order. With this understanding, however, the matter has reached its limit so far as it can be discussed in a lecture-room and by a professor. Yet the great and vital problem that is contained therein is, of course, very far from being concluded. But forces other than university chairs have their say in this matter.

What man will take upon himself the attempt to "refute scientifically" the ethic of the Sermon on the Mount? For instance, the sentence, "resist no evil," or the image of turning the other cheek? And yet it is clear, in mundane perspective, that this is an ethic of undignified conduct; one has to choose between the religious dignity which this ethic confers and the dignity of manly conduct which preaches something quite different; "resist evil – lest you be co-responsible for an overpowering evil." According to our ultimate standpoint, the one is the devil and the other the God, and the individual has to decide which is God for him and which is the devil. And so it goes throughout all the orders of life.

The grandiose rationalism of an ethical and methodical conduct of life which flows from every religious prophecy has dethroned this polytheism in favor of the "one thing that is needful." Faced with the realities of outer and inner life, Christianity has deemed it necessary to make those compromises and relative judgments, which we all know from its history. Today the routines of everyday life challenge religion. Many old gods ascend from their graves; they are disenchanted and hence take the form of impersonal forces. They strive to gain power over our lives and again they resume their eternal struggle with one another. What is hard for modern man, and especially for the younger generation, is to measure up to *workaday* existence. The ubiquitous chase for "experience" stems from this weakness; for it is weakness not to be able to countenance the stern seriousness of our fateful times....

The fate of our times is characterized by rationalization and intellectualization and, above all, by the "disenchantment of the world." Precisely the ultimate and most sublime values have retreated from public life either into the transcendental realm of mystic life or into the brotherliness of direct and personal human relations. It is not accidental that our greatest art is intimate and not monumental, nor is it accidental that today only within the smallest and intimate circles, in personal human situations, in *pianissimo*,[v] that something is pulsating that corresponds to the prophetic *pneuma*,[vi] which in former times swept through the great communities like a firebrand, welding them together. If we attempt to force and to "invent" a monumental style in art, such miserable monstrosities are produced as the many monuments of the last twenty years. If one tries intellectually to construe new religions without a new and genuine prophecy, then, in an inner sense, something similar will result, but with still worse effects. And academic prophecy, finally, will create only fanatical sects but never a genuine community.

To the person who cannot bear the fate of the times like a man, one must say: may he rather return silently, without the usual publicity build-up of renegades, but simply and plainly. The arms of the old churches are opened widely and compassionately for him. After all, they do not make it hard for him. One way or another he has to bring his "intellectual sacrifice" – that is inevitable. If he can really do it, we shall not rebuke him. For such an intellectual sacrifice in favor of an unconditional religious devotion is ethically quite a different matter than the evasion of the plain duty of intellectual integrity, which sets in if one lacks the courage to clarify one's own ultimate standpoint and rather facilitates this duty by feeble relative judgments. In my eyes, such religious return stands higher than the academic prophecy, which does not clearly realize that in the lecture-rooms of the university no other virtue holds but plain intellectual integrity. Integrity, however, compels us to state that for the many who today tarry for new prophets and saviors, the situation is the same as resounds in the beautiful Edomite watchman's song of the period of exile that has been included among Isaiah's oracles:[vii]

> He calleth to me out of Seir, Watchman, what of the night? The watchman said, The morning cometh, and also the night; if ye will enquire, enquire ye: return, come.

The people to whom this was said has enquired and tarried for more than two millennia, and we are shaken when we realize its fate. From this we want to draw the lesson that nothing is gained by yearning and tarrying alone, and we shall act differently. We shall set to work and meet the "demands of the day," in human relations as well as in our vocation. This, however, is plain and simple, if each finds and obeys the demon who holds the fibers of his very life.

[v] Very softly or quietly.
[vi] Spirit.

[vii] The Edomites were the descendants of Esau, Jacob's brother, who lived in the land of Edom. In the following Oracle from Isaiah 21: 11–12 "Seir" is another name for Edom and its people.

17

From *Towards a New Architecture*

Le Corbusier

Charles-Édouard Jeanneret, a.k.a. Le Corbusier (1887–1965), was a Swiss architect whose 1923 collection of magazine articles *Vers une Architecture* (translated as *Towards a New Architecture*) is perhaps the most important architectural book of the twentieth-century. Le Corbusier took it as his generation's task fundamentally to rethink architecture's meaning for a new technological and socially egalitarian age. De-ornamentation and geometrical simplicity are not only functional and egalitarian, but they reveal the truth of a building, naked and essential. When his innovative design for the first League of Nations center in Geneva in 1927 was disqualified (because it had not been drawn using India ink!), the International Congress of Modern Architecture (CIAM) was formed, largely to defend his kind of avant-garde work. His architectural style was based on a vision of a future society that would be true to its own industrial nature.

The Engineer's Æsthetic and Architecture

The Engineer's Æsthetic, and Architecture, are two things that march together and follow one from the other: the one being now at its full height, the other in an unhappy state of retrogression.

The Engineer, inspired by the law of Economy and governed by mathematical calculation, puts us in accord with universal law. He achieves harmony.

The Architect, by his arrangement of forms, realizes an order which is a pure creation of his spirit; by forms and shapes he affects our senses to an acute degree and provokes plastic emotions; by the relationships which he creates he wakes profound echoes in us, he gives us the measure of an order which we feel to be in accordance with that of our world, he determines the various movements of our heart and of our understanding; it is then that we experience the sense of beauty.

Three Reminders to Architects

MASS

Our eyes are constructed to enable us to see forms in light.

Primary forms are beautiful forms because they can be clearly appreciated.

Architects to-day no longer achieve these simple forms.

Working by calculation, engineers employ geometrical forms, satisfying our eyes by their geometry and our understanding by their mathematics; their work is on the direct line of good art.

SURFACE

A mass is enveloped in its surface, a surface which is divided up according to the directing and generating lines of the mass; and this gives the mass its individuality.

Le Corbusier, from "Argument," pp. 1–8; "First Reminder: Mass," pp. 29–31; and "Third Reminder: Mass," pp. 47–64 in *Towards a New Architecture* (trans. Frederick Etchells). New York: Dover Publications, 1986.

Architects to-day are afraid of the geometrical constituents of surfaces.

The great problems of modern construction must have a geometrical solution.

Forced to work in accordance with the strict needs of exactly determined conditions, engineers make use of generating and accusing lines in relation to forms. They create limpid and moving plastic facts.

PLAN

The Plan is the generator.

Without a plan, you have lack of order, and wilfulness.

The Plan holds in itself the essence of sensation.

The great problems of to-morrow, dictated by collective necessities, put the question of "plan" in a new form.

Modern life demands, and is waiting for, a new kind of plan, both for the house and for the city.

Regulating Lines

An inevitable element of Architecture.

The necessity for order. The regulating line is a guarantee against wilfulness. It brings satisfaction to the understanding.

The regulating line is a means to an end; it is not a recipe. Its choice and the modalities of expression given to it are an integral part of architectural creation.

Eyes Which Do Not See

LINERS[i]

A great epoch has begun.

There exists a new spirit.

There exists a mass of work conceived in the new spirit; it is to be met with particularly in industrial production.

Architecture is stifled by custom.

The "styles" are a lie.

Style is a unity of principle animating all the work of an epoch, the result of a state of mind which has its own special character.

Our own epoch is determining, day by day, its own style.

Our eyes, unhappily, are unable yet to discern it.

[i] Ocean liners.

AIRPLANES

The airplane is the product of close selection.

The lesson of the airplane lies in the logic which governed the statement of the problem and its realization.

The problem of the house has not yet been stated.

Nevertheless there do exist standards for the dwelling house.

Machinery contains in itself the factor of economy, which makes for selection.

The house is a machine for living in.

AUTOMOBILES

We must aim at the fixing of standards in order to face the problem of perfection.

The Parthenon is a product of selection applied to a standard.

Architecture operates in accordance with standards.

Standards are a matter of logic, analysis and minute study; they are based on a problem which has been well "stated." A standard is definitely established by experiment.

Architecture

THE LESSON OF ROME

The business of Architecture is to establish emotional relationships by means of raw materials.

Architecture goes beyond utilitarian needs.

Architecture is a plastic thing.

The spirit of order, a unity of intention.

The sense of relationships; architecture deals with quantities.

Passion can create drama out of inert stone.

THE ILLUSION OF PLANS

The Plan proceeds from within to without; the exterior is the result of an interior.

The elements of architecture are light and shade, walls and space.

Arrangement is the gradation of aims, the classification of intentions.

Man looks at the creation of architecture with his eyes, which are 5 feet 6 inches from the ground. One can only deal with aims which the eye can appreciate, and intentions which take into account architectural elements. If there come into play intentions which do not speak the language of architecture, you arrive at the illusion of plans, you transgress the rules of the Plan through an error in conception, or through a leaning towards empty show.

PURE CREATION OF THE MIND

Contour and profile are the touchstone of the architect.

Here he reveals himself as artist or mere engineer.

Contour is free of all constraint.

There is here no longer any question of custom, nor of tradition, nor of construction nor of adaptation to utilitarian needs.

Contour and profile are a pure creation of the mind; they call for the plastic artist.

Mass-production Houses

A great epoch has begun.

There exists a new spirit.

Industry, overwhelming us like a flood which rolls on towards its destined ends, has furnished us with new tools adapted to this new epoch, animated by the new spirit.

Economic law inevitably governs our acts and our thoughts.

The problem of the house is a problem of the epoch. The equilibrium of society to-day depends upon it. Architecture has for its first duty, in this period of renewal, that of bringing about a revision of values, a revision of the constituent elements of the house.

Mass-production is based on analysis and experiment.

Industry on the grand scale must occupy itself with building and establish the elements of the house on a mass-production basis.

We must create the mass-production spirit.

The spirit of constructing mass-production houses.

The spirit of living in mass-production houses.

The spirit of conceiving mass-production houses.

If we eliminate from our hearts and minds all dead concepts in regard to the house, and look at the question from a critical and objective point of view, we shall arrive at the "House-Machine," the mass-production house, healthy (and morally so too) and beautiful in the same way that the working tools and instruments which accompany our existence are beautiful.

Beautiful also with all the animation that the artist's sensibility can add to severe and pure functioning elements.

Architecture or Revolution

In every field of industry, new problems have presented themselves and new tools have been created capable of resolving them. If this new fact be set against the past, then you have revolution.

In building and construction, mass-production has already been begun; in face of new economic needs, mass-production units have been created both in mass and detail; and definite results have been achieved both in detail and in mass. If this fact be set against the past, then you have revolution, both in the method employed and in the large scale on which it has been carried out.

The history of Architecture unfolds itself slowly across the centuries as a modification of structure and ornament, but in the last fifty years steel and concrete have brought new conquests, which are the index of a greater capacity for construction, and of an architecture in which the old codes have been overturned. If we challenge the past, we shall learn that "styles" no longer exist for us, that a style belonging to our own period has come about; and there has been a Revolution.

Our minds have consciously or unconsciously apprehended these events and new needs have arisen, consciously or unconsciously.

The machinery of Society, profoundly *out of gear*, oscillates between an amelioration, of historical importance, and a catastrophe.

The primordial instinct of every human being is to assure himself of a shelter. The various classes of workers in society to-day *no longer have dwellings adapted to their needs; neither the artizan nor the intellectual.*

It is a question of building which is at the root of the social unrest of to-day: architecture or revolution.

First Reminder: Mass

Architecture is the masterly, correct and magnificent play of masses brought together in light. Our eyes are made to see forms in light; light and shade reveal these forms; cubes, cones, spheres, cylinders or pyramids are the great primary forms which light reveals to advantage; the image of these is distinct and tangible within us and without ambiguity. It is for that reason that these are *beautiful forms, the most beautiful forms.* Everybody is agreed as to that, the child, the savage and the metaphysician. It is of the very nature of the plastic arts.

Egyptian, Greek or Roman architecture is an architecture of prisms, cubes and cylinders, pyramids or spheres: the Pyramids, the Temple of Luxor, the Parthenon, the Coliseum, Hadrian's Villa.

Gothic architecture is not, fundamentally, based on spheres, cones and cylinders. Only the nave is an expression of a simple form, but of a complex geometry of the second order (intersecting arches). It is for that reason that a cathedral is not very beautiful and that we search in it for compensations of a subjective kind outside plastic art. A cathedral interests us as the ingenious solution of a difficult problem, but a problem of which the postulates have been badly stated because they do not proceed from the great primary forms. *The cathedral is not a plastic work; it is a drama; a fight against the force of gravity, which is a sensation of a sentimental nature.*

The Pyramids, the Towers of Babylon, the Gates of Samarkand, the Parthenon, the Coliseum, the Pantheon, the Pont du Gard, Santa Sophia, the Mosques of Stamboul, the Tower of Pisa, the Cupolas of Brunelleschi and of Michael Angelo, the Pont-Royal, the Invalides – all these belong to Architecture.

The Gare du Quai d'Orsay, the Grand Palais do not belong to Architecture.[ii]

The *architects* of to-day, lost in the sterile backwaters of their plans, their foliage, their pilasters and their lead roofs, have never acquired the conception of primary masses. They were never taught that at the Schools.

Not in pursuit of an architectural idea, but simply guided by the results of calculation (derived from the principles which govern our universe) and the conception of A LIVING ORGANISM, *the* ENGINEERS *of to-day make use of the primary elements and, by co-ordinating them in accordance with the rules, provoke in us architectural emotions and thus make the work of man ring in unison with universal order.*

[ii] In the preceding two paragraphs Le Corbusier is contrasting mammoth, geometrical, and relatively non-ornamented buildings, most of them built for religious or practical purposes (e.g. the Parisian hospital, *Les Invalides*; the *Santa Sophia*, a Greek Christian cathedral in Istanbul), with the neo-classically ornamented style to which he denies even the title "Architecture."

Thus we have the American grain elevators and factories, the magnificent FIRST-FRUITS *of the new age.* THE AMERICAN ENGINEERS OVERWHELM WITH THEIR CALCULATIONS OUR EXPIRING ARCHITECTURE.

Third Reminder: The Plan

The plan is the generator.

The eye of the spectator finds itself looking at a site composed of streets and houses. It receives the impact of the masses which rise up around it. If these masses are of a formal kind and have not been spoilt by unseemly variations, if the disposition of their grouping expresses a clean rhythm and not an incoherent agglomeration, if the relationship of mass to space is in just proportion, the eye transmits to the brain co-ordinated sensations and the mind derives from these satisfactions of a high order: this is architecture.

The eye observes, in a large interior, the multiple surfaces of walls and vaults; the cupolas determine the large spaces; the vaults display their own surfaces; the pillars and the walls adjust themselves in accordance with comprehensible reasons. The whole structure rises from its base and is developed in accordance with a rule which is written on the ground in the plan: noble forms, variety of form, unity of the geometric principle. A profound projection of harmony: this is architecture.

The plan is at its basis. Without plan there can be neither grandeur of aim and expression, nor rhythm, nor mass, nor coherence. Without plan we have the sensation, so insupportable to man, of shapelessness, of poverty, of disorder, of wilfulness.

A plan calls for the most active imagination. It calls for the most severe discipline also. The plan is what determines everything; it is the decisive moment. A plan is not a pretty thing to be drawn, like a Madonna face; it is an austere abstraction; it is nothing more than an algebrization and a dry-looking thing. The work of the mathematician remains none the less one of the highest activities of the human spirit.

Arrangement is an appreciable rhythm which reacts on every human being in the same way.

The plan bears within itself a primary and predetermined rhythm: the work is developed in extent and in height following the prescriptions of the plan, with results which can range from the simplest to the most complex, all coming within the same law. Unity of law is the law of a good plan: a simple law capable of infinite modulation.

Rhythm is a state of equilibrium which proceeds either from symmetries, simple or complex, or from delicate balancings. Rhythm is an equation; Equalization (symmetry, repetition) (*Egyptian and Hindoo temples*); compensation (movement of contrary parts) (*the Acropolis at Athens*); modulation (the development of an original plastic invention) (*Santa Sophia*). So many reactions, differing in the main for every individual, in spite of the unity of aim which gives the rhythm, and the state of equilibrium. So we get the astonishing diversity found in great epochs, a diversity which is the result of architectural principle and not of the play of decoration.

The plan carries in itself the very essence of sensation.

But the sense of the plan has been lost for the last hundred years. The great problems of to-morrow, dictated by collective necessities, based upon statistics and realized by mathematical calculation, once more revive the problem of the plan. When once the indispensable breadth of vision, which must be brought to town planning, has been realized, we shall enter upon a period that no epoch has yet known. Towns must be conceived and planned throughout their entire extent in the same way as were planned the temples of the East and as the Invalides or the Versailles of Louis XIV were laid out.

The technical equipment of this epoch – the technique of finance and the technique of construction – is ready to carry out this task.

Tony Garnier, backed by Herriot at Lyons, planned his "industrial quarter" (*Cité*).[iii] It is an attempt at an ordered scheme and a fusion of utilitarian and plastic solutions. One fixed rule governing the units employed gives, in every quarter of the town, the same choice of essential masses and determines the intervening spaces in accordance with practical necessities and the biddings of a poetical sense peculiar to the architect. Though we may reserve our judgment as to the relationship of the various zones of this industrial city, one experiences here the beneficent results of order. Where order reigns, well-being begins. By the happy creation of a system of arrangement of the various plots, even the residential quarters for artisans take

on a high architectural significance. Such is the result of a plan.

In the present state of marking time (for modern town planning is not yet born), the most noble quarters of our towns are inevitably the manufacturing ones where the basis of grandeur and style – namely, geometry – results from the problem itself. The plan has been a weak feature, and is still so to-day. True, an admirable order reigns in the interior of markets and workshops, has dictated the structure of machines and governs their movements, and conditions each gesture of a gang of workmen; but dirt infects their surroundings, and incoherence ran riot when the rule and square dictated the placing of the buildings, spreading them about in a crazy, costly and dangerous way.

It would have been enough if there had been a plan. And one day we shall have a plan for our needs. The extent of the evil will bring us to this.

One day Auguste Perret created the phrase: "The City of Towers."[iv] A glittering epithet which aroused the poet in us. A word which struck the note of the moment because the fact itself is imminent! Almost unknown to us, the "great city" is engendering its plan. This plan may well be a gigantic affair, since the great city is a rising tide. It is time that we should repudiate the existing lay-out of our towns, in which the congestion of buildings grows greater, interlaced by narrow streets full of noise, petrol fumes and dust; and where on each storey the windows open wide on to this foul confusion. The great towns have become too dense for the security of their inhabitants and yet they are not sufficiently dense to meet the new needs of "modern business."

If we take as our basis the vital constructional event which the American sky-scraper has proved to be, it will be sufficient to bring together at certain points (relatively distant) the great density of our modern populations and to build at these points enormous constructions of 60 storeys high. Reinforced concrete and steel allow of this audacity and lend themselves in particular to a certain development of the façade by means of which all the windows have an uninterrupted view: in this way, in the future, inside courts and "wells" will no longer exist. Starting from the fourteenth storey you have absolute calm and the purest air.

[iii] French architect Tony Garnier (1869–1948) devised a plan ("*Cité Industrielle*") for an "ideal" industrial city of 35,000 people, first exhibited in Paris in 1904.

[iv] French architect Auguste Perret (1874–1954) was a pioneer in the use of modern reinforced-concrete materials and techniques.

In these towers which will shelter the worker, till now stifled in densely packed quarters and congested streets, all the necessary services, following the admirable practice in America, will be assembled, bringing efficiency and economy of time and effort, and as a natural result the peace of mind which is so necessary. These towers, rising up at great distances from one another, will give by reason of their height the same accommodation that has up till now been spread out over the superficial area; they will leave open enormous spaces in which would run, well away from them, the noisy arterial roads, full of a traffic which becomes increasingly rapid. At the foot of the towers would stretch the parks: trees covering the whole town. The setting out of the towers would form imposing avenues; there indeed is an architecture worthy of our time.

Auguste Perret set forth the principle of the City of Towers; but he has not produced any designs. On the other hand he allowed himself to be interviewed by a reporter of the "Intransigeant" and to be so far carried away as to swell out his conception beyond reasonable limits. In this way he threw a veil of dangerous futurism over what was a sound idea. The reporter noted that enormous bridges would link each tower to the next; for what purpose? The arteries for traffic would be placed far away from the houses; and the inhabitants, free to disport themselves in the parks among trees planted in ordered patterns, or on the grass or in the places of amusement, would never have the slightest desire to take their exercise on giddy bridges, with nothing at all to do when they got there! The reporter would have it also that the town would be raised on innumerable piles of reinforced concrete carrying the streets at a height of 65 feet (6 storeys if you please!) and linking the towers one to another. These piles would leave an immense space underneath the town in which would be placed the gas and water mains and the sewers, the viscera of the city. Perret had never set out his plan, and the idea could not be carried further without a plan.

I had myself put forward this idea of using piles a long time before Auguste Perret, and it was a conception of a much less grandiose character; but it was capable of meeting a genuine need. I applied it to the existing type of town such as the Paris of to-day. Instead of forming foundations by excavating and constructing thick foundation walls, instead of digging up and digging up again the roadways in order to bury in them (a labour of Sisyphus) the gas and water mains, the sewers and the Tubes,[v] with constant repairs to execute, it would be agreed that any new districts should be constructed at ground level, the foundations being replaced by the necessary number of concrete piles; these would have carried the ground floor of the houses and, by a system of corbelling, the pavements and the roadways.

Within this space so gained, of a height of from 12 to 18 feet, would run heavy lorries, and the Tubes replacing the encumbrance of tramways, and so on, with a direct service to points immediately below the buildings. This complete network of traffic, working independently of that reserved for pedestrians and quick-moving vehicles, would be a pure gain and would have its own geography independent of any obstruction due to the houses: an ordered forest of pillars in the midst of which the town would exchange its merchandise, bring in its food supplies, and perform all the slow and clumsy tasks which to-day impede the speed of traffic.

Cafes and places for recreation would no longer be that fungus which eats up the pavements of Paris: they would be transferred to the flat roofs, as would be all commerce of a luxury kind (for is it not really illogical that one entire superficies of a town should be unused and reserved for a flirtation between the tiles and the stars?). Short passageways in the shape of bridges above the ordinary streets would enable foot traffic to get about among these newly gained quarters consecrated to leisure amidst flowers and foliage.

The result of this conception would be nothing less than a triplication of the traffic area of a town; it was capable of realization *since it corresponded to a need, was less costly and more rational than the aberrations of to-day*. It was a reasonable notion, given the old framework of our towns, just as the conception of the City of Towers will prove a reasonable idea, as regards the towns of to-morrow.

Here, then, we have a lay-out of streets which would bring about an entirely new system of town planning and would provide a radical reform in the tenanted house or apartment; this imminent reform, necessitated by the transformation of domestic economy, demands a new type of plan for dwelling-houses, and an entirely new organization of services corresponding to modern life in a great

---

[v] The Greek mythological character Sisyphus was condemned by the gods repeatedly to roll a boulder up a hill, only to see it roll back down, for eternity. "Tubes" refers to subways.

city. Here again the plan is the generator; without it poverty, disorder, wilfulness reign supreme.

Instead of our towns being laid out in massive quadrangles, with the streets in narrow trenches walled in by seven-storeyed buildings set perpendicular on the pavement and enclosing unhealthy courtyards, airless and sunless wells, our new layout, employing the same area and housing the same number of people, would show great blocks of houses with successive set-backs, stretching along arterial avenues. No more courtyards, but flats opening on every side to air and light, and looking, not on the puny trees of our boulevards of to-day, but upon green sward, sports grounds and abundant plantations of trees.

The jutting prows of these great blocks would break up the long avenues at regular intervals. The various set-backs would promote the play of light and shade, so necessary to architectural expression.

Reinforced concrete has brought about a revolution in the æsthetics of construction. By suppressing the roof and replacing it by terraces, reinforced concrete is leading us to a new æsthetic of the plan, hitherto unknown. These set-backs and recessions are quite possible and will, in the future, lead to a play of half-lights and of heavy shade with the accent running not from top to bottom, but horizontally from left to right.

This is a modification of the first importance in the æsthetic of the plan; it has not yet been realized; but we shall be wise to bear this in our minds, in considering projects for the extension of our towns.

* * *

We are living in a period of reconstruction and of adaptation to new social and economic conditions. In rounding this Cape Horn the new horizons before us will only recover the grand line of tradition by a complete revision of the methods in vogue and by the fixing of a new basis of construction established in logic.

In architecture the old bases of construction are dead. We shall not rediscover the truths of architecture until new bases have established a logical ground for every architectural manifestation. A period of 20 years is beginning which will be occupied in creating these bases. A period of great problems, a period of analysis, of experiment, a period also of great æsthetic confusion, a period in which a new æsthetic will be elaborated.

We must study the *plan*, the key of this evolution.

18

"Lecture on Ethics"
From *Tractatus Logico-Philosophicus*

Ludwig Wittgenstein

Austrian philosopher Ludwig Wittgenstein (1889–1953) was perhaps the most influential Western philosopher of the twentieth century. Brilliant and unhappy, Wittgenstein struggled all his life against the "bewitchment" of his mind by philosophical questions. Having studied with Bertrand Russell (1872–1970), his early work on fundamental issues in the philosophy of mathematics, logic, and the nature of philosophy gave major impetus to logical positivism. Wittgenstein then declared that he had put all philosophical questions to rest and left academia. Years later, after a major change in outlook, he returned and gave rise to "ordinary language" philosophy, presented in his posthumous but hugely influential *Philosophical Investigations* (1953). Its notion that meaning is determined by social contexts of practical activity, or "language-games," would later play an important role in postmodernism. Most of the following excerpt is his lesser known "Lecture on Ethics" (1929), in which he explains the limits of human inquiry. Following this is the famous conclusion to his first book, *Tractatus Logico-Philosophicus* (1921), in which Wittgenstein announced the end of traditional philosophical reflection.

"Lecture on Ethics"

Before I begin to speak about my subject proper let me make a few introductory remarks. I feel I shall have great difficulties in communicating my thoughts to you and I think some of them may be diminished by mentioning them to you beforehand. The first one, which almost I need not mention, is that English is not my native tongue and my expression therefore often lacks that precision and subtlety which would be desirable if one talks about a difficult subject. All I can do is to ask you to make my task easier by trying to get at my meaning in spite of the faults which I will constantly be committing against the English grammar. The second difficulty I will mention is this, that probably many of you come up to this lecture of mine with slightly wrong expectations. And to set you right in this point I will say a few words about the reason for choosing the subject I have chosen: When your former secretary honoured me by asking me to read a paper to your society, my first thought was that I would certainly do it and my second thought was that if I was to have the opportunity to speak to you I should speak about something which I am keen on communicating to you and that I should not misuse this opportunity to give you a lecture about, say, logic. I call this a misuse, for to explain a scientific matter to you it would need a course of lectures and not an hour's paper. Another alternative would have been to give you what's called a popular-scientific lecture, that is a lecture intended to make you believe that you understand a thing which actually you don't

Ludwig Wittgenstein: [A] "Lecture on Ethics," *The Philosophical Review* 74, no. 1 (January 1965), pp. 3–12; [B] from *Tractatus Logico-Philosophicus* (trans. D. F. Pears and B. F. McGuinness), paras. 6.53–6.57, pp. 73–4. London: Routledge and Kegan Paul, 1961.

understand, and to gratify what I believe to be one of the lowest desires of modern people, namely the superficial curiosity about the latest discoveries of science. I rejected these alternatives and decided to talk to you about a subject which seems to me to be of general importance, hoping that it may help to clear up your thoughts about this subject (even if you should entirely disagree with what I will say about it). My third and last difficulty is one which, in fact, adheres to most lengthy philosophical lectures and it is this, that the hearer is incapable of seeing both the road he is led and the goal which it leads to. That is to say: he either thinks: "I understand all he says, but what on earth is he driving at" or else he thinks "I see what he's driving at, but how on earth is he going to get there." All I can do is again to ask you to be patient and to hope that in the end you may see both the way and where it leads to.

I will now begin. My subject, as you know, is Ethics and I will adopt the explanation of that term which Professor Moore has given in his book *Principia Ethica*.[i] He says: "Ethics is the general enquiry into what is good." Now I am going to use the term Ethics in a slightly wider sense, in a sense in fact which includes what I believe to be the most essential part of what is generally called Aesthetics. And to make you see as clearly as possible what I take to be the subject matter of Ethics I will put before you a number of more or less synonymous expressions each of which could be substituted for the above definition, and by enumerating them I want to produce the same sort of effect which Galton produced when he took a number of photos of different faces on the same photographic plate in order to get the picture of the typical features they all had in common. And as by showing to you such a collective photo I could make you see what is the typical – say – Chinese face; so if you look through the row of synonyms which I will put before you, you will, I hope, be able to see the characteristic features they all have in common and these are the characteristic features of Ethics. Now instead of saying "Ethics is the enquiry into what is good" I could have said Ethics is the enquiry into what is valuable, or, into what is really important, or I could have said Ethics is the enquiry into the meaning of life, or into what makes life worth living, or into the right way of living. I believe if you look at all these phrases you will get a rough idea as to what it is that Ethics is

concerned with. Now the first thing that strikes one about all these expressions is that each of them is actually used in two very different senses. I will call them the trivial or relative sense on the one hand and the ethical or absolute sense on the other. If for instance I say that this is a *good* chair this means that the chair serves a certain predetermined purpose and the word good here has only meaning so far as this purpose has been previously fixed upon. In fact the word good in the relative sense simply means coming up to a certain predetermined standard. Thus when we say that this man is a good pianist we mean that he can play pieces of a certain degree of difficulty with a certain degree of dexterity. And similarly if I say that it is *important* for me not to catch cold I mean that catching a cold produces certain describable disturbances in my life and if I say that this is the *right* road I mean that it's the right road relative to a certain goal. Used in this way these expressions don't present any difficult or deep problems. But this is not how Ethics uses them. Supposing that I could play tennis and one of you saw me playing and said "Well, you play pretty badly" and suppose I answered "I know, I'm playing badly but I don't want to play any better," all the other man could say would be "Ah then that's all right." But suppose I had told one of you a preposterous lie and he came up to me and said "You're behaving like a beast" and then I were to say "I know I behave badly, but then I don't want to behave any better," could he then say "Ah, then that's all right"? Certainly not; he would say "Well, you *ought* to want to behave better." Here you have an absolute judgment of value, whereas the first instance was one of a relative judgment. The essence of this difference seems to be obviously this: Every judgment of relative value is a mere statement of facts and can therefore be put in such a form that it loses all the appearance of a judgment of value: Instead of saying "This is the right way to Granchester," I could equally well have said, "This is the right way you have to go if you want to get to Granchester in the shortest time"; "This man is a good runner" simply means that he runs a certain number of miles in a certain number of minutes, etc. Now what I wish to contend is that, although all judgments of relative value can be shown to be mere statements of facts, no statement of fact can ever be, or imply, a judgment of absolute value. Let me explain this: Suppose one of you were an omniscient person and therefore knew all the movements of all the bodies in the world dead or alive and that he also knew all the states of mind of all

[i] G. E. Moore (1873–1958), English philosopher who, with Bertrand Russell, invented twentieth-century "analytic" philosophy.

human beings that ever lived, and suppose this man wrote all he knew in a big book, then this book would contain the whole description of the world; and what I want to say is, that this book would contain nothing that we would call an *ethical* judgment or anything that would logically imply such a judgment. It would of course contain all relative judgments of value and all true scientific propositions and in fact all true propositions that can be made. But all the facts described would, as it were, stand on the same level and in the same way all propositions stand on the same level. There are no propositions which, in any absolute sense, are sublime, important, or trivial. Now perhaps some of you will agree to that and be reminded of Hamlet's words: "Nothing is either good or bad, but thinking makes it so." But this again could lead to a misunderstanding. What Hamlet says seems to imply that good and bad, though not qualities of the world outside us, are attributes to our states of mind. But what I mean is that a state of mind, so far as we mean by that a fact which we can describe, is in no ethical sense good or bad. If for instance in our world-book we read the description of a murder with all its details physical and psychological, the mere description of these facts will contain nothing which we could call an *ethical* proposition. The murder will be on exactly the same level as any other event, for instance the falling of a stone. Certainly the reading of this description might cause us pain or rage or any other emotion, or we might read about the pain or rage caused by this murder in other people when they heard of it, but there will simply be facts, facts, and facts but no Ethics. And now I must say that if I contemplate what Ethics really would have to be if there were such a science, this result seems to me quite obvious. It seems to me obvious that nothing we could ever think or say should be *the* thing. That we cannot write a scientific book, the subject matter of which could be intrinsically sublime and above all other subject matters. I can only describe my feeling by the metaphor, that, if a man could write a book on Ethics which really was a book on Ethics, this book would, with an explosion, destroy all the other books in the world. Our words used as we use them in science, are vessels capable only of containing and conveying meaning and sense, *natural* meaning and sense. Ethics, if it is anything, is supernatural and our words will only express facts; as a teacup will only hold a teacup full of water and if I were to pour out a gallon over it. I said that so far as facts and propositions are con-

cerned there is only relative value and relative good, right, etc. And let me, before I go on, illustrate this by a rather obvious example. The right road is the road which leads to an arbitrarily predetermined end and it is quite clear to us all that there is no sense in talking about the right road apart from such a predetermined goal. Now let us see what we could possibly mean by the expression, "*the* absolutely right road." I think it would be the road which *everybody* on seeing it would, *with logical necessity*, have to go, or be ashamed for not going. And similarly the *absolute good*, if it is a describable state of affairs, would be one which everybody, independent of his tastes and inclinations, would *necessarily* bring about or feel guilty for not bringing about. And I want to say that such a state of affairs is a chimera. No state of affairs has, in itself, what I would like to call the coercive power of an absolute judge. Then what have all of us who, like myself, are still tempted to use such expressions as "absolute good," "absolute value," etc., what have we in mind and what do we try to express? Now whenever I try to make this clear to myself it is natural that I should recall cases in which I would certainly use these expressions and I am then in the situation in which you would be if, for instance, I were to give you a lecture on the psychology of pleasure. What you would do then would be to try and recall some typical situation in which you always felt pleasure. For, bearing this situation in mind, all I should say to you would become concrete and, as it were, controllable. One man would perhaps choose as his stock example the sensation when taking a walk on a fine summer's day. Now in this situation I am, if I want to fix my mind on what I mean by absolute or ethical value. And there, in my case, it always happens that the idea of one particular experience presents itself to me which therefore is, in a sense, my experience *par excellence* and this is the reason why, in talking to you now, I will use this experience as my first and foremost example. (As I have said before, this is an entirely personal matter and others would find other examples more striking.) I will describe this experience in order, if possible, to make you recall the same or similar experiences, so that we may have a common ground for our investigation. I believe the best way of describing it is to say that when I have it *I wonder at the existence of the world.* And I am then inclined to use such phrases as "how extraordinary that anything should exist" or "how extraordinary that the world should exist." I will mention another experience straight away which I also know and which others of you might be acquainted with: it is, what one might call, the experience of feeling *absolutely* safe. I mean the state of mind in which one is inclined to say "I am safe, nothing can injure me whatever happens." Now let me consider these experiences, for, I believe, they exhibit the very characteristics we try to get clear about. And there the first thing I have to say is, that the verbal expression which we give to these experiences is nonsense! If I say "I wonder at the existence of the world" I am misusing language. Let me explain this: It has a perfectly good and clear sense to say that I wonder at something being the case, we all understand what it means to say that I wonder at the size of a dog which is bigger than anyone I have ever seen before or at any thing which, in the common sense of the word, is extraordinary. In every such case I wonder at something being the case which I *could* conceive *not* to be the case. I wonder at the size of this dog because I could conceive of a dog of another, namely the ordinary size, at which I should not wonder. To say "I wonder at such and such being the case" has only sense if I can imagine it not to be the case. In this sense one can wonder at the existence of, say, a house when one sees it and has not visited it for a long time and has imagined that it had been pulled down in the meantime. But it is nonsense to say that I wonder at the existence of the world, because I cannot imagine it not existing. I could of course wonder at the world round me being as it is. If for instance I had this experience while looking into the blue sky, I could wonder at the sky being blue as opposed to the case when it's clouded. But that's not what I mean. I am wondering at the sky being *whatever it is*. One might be tempted to say that what I am wondering at is a tautology, namely at the sky being blue or not blue. But then it's just nonsense to say that one is wondering at a tautology. Now the same applies to the other experience which I have mentioned, the experience of absolute safety. We all know what it means in ordinary life to be safe. I am safe in my room, when I cannot be run over by an omnibus. I am safe if I have had whooping cough and cannot therefore get it again. To be safe essentially means that it is physically impossible that certain things should happen to me and therefore it's nonsense to say that I am safe *whatever* happens. Again this is a misuse of the word "safe" as the other example was of a misuse of the word "existence" or "wondering." Now I want to impress on you that a certain characteristic misuse of our language runs

through *all* ethical and religious expressions. All these expressions *seem*, prima facie, to be just *similes*. Thus it seems that when we are using the word *right* in an ethical sense, although, what we mean, is not right in its trivial sense, it's something similar, and when we say "This is a good fellow," although the word good here doesn't mean what it means in the sentence "This is a good football player" there seems to be some similarity. And when we say "This man's life was valuable" we don't mean it in the same sense in which we would speak of some valuable jewelry but there seems to be some sort of analogy. Now all religious terms seem in this sense to be used as similes or allegorically. For when we speak of God and that he sees everything and when we kneel and pray to him all our terms and actions seem to be parts of a great and elaborate allegory which represents him as a human being of great power whose grace we try to win, etc., etc. But this allegory also describes the experience which I have just referred to. For the first of them is, I believe, exactly what people were referring to when they said that God had created the world; and the experience of absolute safety has been described by saying that we feel safe in the hands of God. A third experience of the same kind is that of feeling guilty and again this was described by the phrase that God disapproves of our conduct. Thus in ethical and religious language we seem constantly to be using similes. But a simile must be the simile for *something*. And if I can describe a fact by means of a simile I must also be able to drop the simile and to describe the facts without it. Now in our case as soon as we try to drop the simile and simply to state the facts which stand behind it, we find that there are no such facts. And so, what at first appeared to be a simile now seems to be mere nonsense. Now the three experiences which I have mentioned to you (and I could have added others) seem to those who have experienced them, for instance to me, to have in some sense an intrinsic, absolute value. But when I say they are experiences, surely, they are facts; they have taken place then and there, lasted a certain definite time and consequently are describable. And so from what I have said some minutes ago I must admit it is nonsense to say that they have absolute value. And I will make my point still more acute by saying "It is the paradox that an experience, a fact, should seem to have supernatural value." Now there is a way in which I would be tempted to meet this paradox. Let me first consider, again, our first experience of wondering at the existence of the world and let me describe it in a slightly different way; we all know what in ordinary life would be called a miracle. It obviously is simply an event the like of which we have never yet seen. Now suppose such an event happened. Take the case that one of you suddenly grew a lion's head and began to roar. Certainly that would be as extraordinary a thing as I can imagine. Now whenever we should have recovered from our surprise, what I would suggest would be to fetch a doctor and have the case scientifically investigated and if it were not for hurting him I would have him vivisected. And where would the miracle have got to? For it is clear that when we look at it in this way everything miraculous has disappeared; unless what we mean by this term is merely that a fact has not yet been explained by science which again means that we have hitherto failed to group this fact with others in a scientific system. This shows that it is absurd to say "Science has proved that there are no miracles." The truth is that the scientific way of looking at a fact is not the way to look at it as a miracle. For imagine whatever fact you may, it is not in itself miraculous in the absolute sense of that term. For we see now that we have been using the word "miracle" in a relative and an absolute sense. And I will now describe the experience of wondering at the existence of the world by saying: it is the experience of seeing the world as a miracle. Now I am tempted to say that the right expression in language for the miracle of the existence of the world, though it is not any proposition *in* language, is the existence of language itself. But what then does it mean to be aware of this miracle at some times and not at other times? For all I have said by shifting the expression of the miraculous from an expression *by means of* language to the expression *by the existence* of language, all I have said is again that we cannot express what we want to express and that all we *say* about the absolute miraculous remains nonsense. Now the answer to all this will seem perfectly clear to many of you. You will say: Well, if certain experiences constantly tempt us to attribute a quality to them which we call absolute or ethical value and importance, this simply shows that by these words we *don't* mean nonsense, that after all what we mean by saying that an experience has absolute value *is just a fact like other facts* and that all it comes to is that we have not yet succeeded in finding the correct logical analysis of what we mean by our ethical and religious expressions. Now when this is urged against me I at once see clearly, as it were in a flash of light, not only that no description that I can think

of would do to describe what I mean by absolute value, but that I would reject every significant description that anybody could possibly suggest, *ab initio*, on the ground of its significance. That is to say: I see now that these nonsensical expressions were not nonsensical because I had not yet found the correct expressions, but that their non-sensicality was their very essence. For all I wanted to do with them was just *to go beyond* the world and that is to say beyond significant language. My whole tendency and I believe the tendency of all men who ever tried to write or talk Ethics or Religion was to run against the boundaries of language. This running against the walls of our cage is perfectly, absolutely hopeless. Ethics so far as it springs from the desire to say something about the ultimate meaning of life, the absolute good, the absolute valuable, can be no science. What it says does not add to our knowledge in any sense. But it is a document of a tendency in the human mind which I personally cannot help respecting deeply and I would not for my life ridicule it.

Tractatus Logico-Philosophicus

6.53   The correct method in philosophy would really be the following: to say nothing except what can be said, i.e. propositions of natural science – i.e. something that has nothing to do with philosophy – and then, whenever someone else wanted to say something metaphysical, to demonstrate to him that he had failed to give a meaning to certain signs in his propositions. Although it would not be satisfying to the other person – he would not have the feeling that we were teaching him philosophy – *this* method would be the only strictly correct one.

6.54   My propositions serve as elucidations in the following way: anyone who understands me eventually recognizes them as nonsensical, when he has used them – as steps – to climb up beyond them. (He must, so to speak, throw away the ladder after he has climbed up it.)

He must transcend these propositions, and then he will see the world aright.

7   What we cannot speak about we must pass over in silence.

19

From *Civilization and its Discontents*

Sigmund Freud

Sigmund Freud (1856–1939), Moravian-born Austrian neurologist and founder of psychoanalysis, is the most influential psychological theorist of the twentieth century, despite the continuing reaction against his work. He saw unconscious instincts of sexuality and aggression behind all human life and culture, including the behavior of infants. In a later speculative work, *Civilization and its Discontents* (1930), he used psychoanalytic theory to explore the inherent discomfort human instinctual nature must always feel in the confines of a civilized society. Freud concluded that the more well organized society becomes, the more discomfort or guilt its members must feel, even if they obey its strictures. Freud is, however, no utopian; he does not want to unshackle human instincts. Human beings are innately aggressive, and this aggression must be controlled. His account is poignant in its historical context, written as it was during the rise of Nazism, and preceding a period of violence that perhaps even he could not have imagined. Forced as a Jew into emigration by Hitler's annexation of Austria in 1938, he died in London in exile. The Nazis burned his books as a prime representative of "Jewish science."

The assumption of the existence of an instinct of death or destruction has met with resistance even in analytic circles; I am aware that there is a frequent inclination rather to ascribe whatever is dangerous and hostile in love to an original bipolarity in its own nature. To begin with it was only tentatively that I put forward the views I have developed here, but in the course of time they have gained such a hold upon me that I can no longer think in any other way. To my mind, they are far more serviceable from a theoretical standpoint than any other possible ones; they provide that simplification, without either ignoring or doing violence to the facts, for which we strive in scientific work. I know that in sadism and masochism we have always seen before us manifestations of the destructive instinct (directed outwards and inwards), strongly alloyed with erotism; but I can no longer understand how we can have overlooked the ubiquity of non-erotic aggressivity and destructiveness and can have failed to give it its due place in our interpretation of life. (The desire for destruction when it is directed *inwards* mostly eludes our perception, of course, unless it is tinged with erotism.) I remember my own defensive attitude when the idea of an instinct of destruction first emerged in psychoanalytic literature, and how long it took before I became receptive to it. That others should have shown, and still show, the same attitude of rejection surprises me less. For 'little children do not like it'[i] when there is talk of the inborn human inclination to 'badness', to aggressiveness and destructiveness, and so to cruelty as well. God has made them in the image of His own perfection; nobody wants to be reminded how hard it is to reconcile the undeniable existence of evil – despite the protestations

---

[i]   A quotation from a poem of Goethe's.

Sigmund Freud, chapters 6 and 7, pp. 64–80 from *Civilization and its Discontents* (trans. James Strachey). New York: Norton, 1961.

of Christian Science – with His all-powerfulness or His all-goodness. The Devil would be the best way out as an excuse for God; in that way he would be playing the same part as an agent of economic discharge as the Jew does in the world of the Aryan ideal. But even so, one can hold God responsible for the existence of the Devil just as well as for the existence of the wickedness which the Devil embodies. In view of these difficulties, each of us will be well advised, on some suitable occasion, to make a low bow to the deeply moral nature of mankind; it will help us to be generally popular and much will be forgiven us for it.[1]

The name 'libido'[ii] can once more be used to denote the manifestations of the power of Eros in order to distinguish them from the energy of the death instinct.[2] It must be confessed that we have much greater difficulty in grasping that instinct; we can only suspect it, as it were, as something in the background behind Eros, and it escapes detection unless its presence is betrayed by its being alloyed with Eros. It is in sadism, where the death instinct twists the erotic aim in its own sense and yet at the same time fully satisfies the erotic urge, that we succeed in obtaining the clearest insight into its nature and its relation to Eros. But even where it emerges without any sexual purpose, in the blindest fury of destructiveness, we cannot fail to recognize that the satisfaction of the instinct is accompanied by an extraordinarily high degree of narcissistic enjoyment, owing to its presenting the ego with a fulfilment of the latter's old wishes for omnipotence. The instinct of destruction, moderated and tamed, and, as it were, inhibited in its aim, must, when it is directed towards objects, provide the ego with the satisfaction of its vital needs and with control over nature. Since the assumption of the existence of the instinct is mainly based on theoretical grounds, we must also admit that it is not entirely proof against theoretical objections. But this is how things appear to us now, in the present state of our knowledge; future research and reflection will no doubt bring further light which will decide the matter.

In all that follows I adopt the standpoint, therefore, that the inclination to aggression is an original, self-subsisting instinctual disposition in man, and I return to my view that it constitutes the greatest impediment to civilization. At one point in the course of this enquiry I was led to the idea that

civilization was a special process which mankind undergoes, and I am still under the influence of that idea. I may now add that civilization is a process in the service of Eros, whose purpose is to combine single human individuals, and after that families, then races, peoples and nations, into one great unity, the unity of mankind. Why this has to happen, we do not know; the work of Eros is precisely this. These collections of men are to be libidinally bound to one another. Necessity alone, the advantages of work in common, will not hold them together. But man's natural aggressive instinct, the hostility of each against all and of all against each, opposes this programme of civilization. This aggressive instinct is the derivative and the main representative of the death instinct which we have found alongside of Eros and which shares world-dominion with it. And now, I think, the meaning of the evolution of civilization is no longer obscure to us. It must present the struggle between Eros and Death, between the instinct of life and the instinct of destruction, as it works itself out in the human species. This struggle is what all life essentially consists of, and the evolution of civilization may therefore be simply described as the struggle for life of the human species. And it is this battle of the giants that our nurse-maids try to appease with their lullaby about Heaven. . . .

Another question concerns us more nearly. What means does civilization employ in order to inhibit the aggressiveness which opposes it, to make it harmless, to get rid of it, perhaps? We have already become acquainted with a few of these methods, but not yet with the one that appears to be the most important. This we can study in the history of the development of the individual. What happens in him to render his desire for aggression innocuous? Something very remarkable, which we should never have guessed and which is nevertheless quite obvious. His aggressiveness is introjected, internalized; it is, in point of fact, sent back to where it came from – that is, it is directed towards his own ego. There it is taken over by a portion of the ego, which sets itself over against the rest of the ego as super-ego, which now, in the form of 'conscience', is ready to put into action against the ego the same harsh aggressiveness that the ego would have liked to satisfy upon other, extraneous individuals. The tension between the harsh super-ego and the ego that is subjected to it, is called by us the sense of guilt; it expresses itself as a need for punishment. Civilization, therefore, obtains mastery over the individual's dangerous

---

[ii] "Libido" refers more simply and narrowly to the sexual instinct which Freud is here interpreting broadly as "Eros".

desire for aggression by weakening and disarming it and by setting up an agency within him to watch over it, like a garrison in a conquered city....

Thus we know of two origins of the sense of guilt: one arising from fear of an authority, and the other, later on, arising from fear of the super-ego. The first insists upon a renunciation of instinctual satisfactions; the second, as well as doing this, presses for punishment, since the continuance of the forbidden wishes cannot be concealed from the super-ego. We have also learned how the severity of the super-ego – the demands of conscience – is to be understood. It is simply a continuation of the severity of the external authority, to which it has succeeded and which it has in part replaced. We now see in what relationship the renunciation of instinct stands to the sense of guilt. Originally, renunciation of instinct was the result of fear of an external authority: one renounced one's satisfactions in order not to lose its love. If one has carried out this renunciation, one is, as it were, quits with the authority and no sense of guilt should remain. But with fear of the super-ego the case is different. Here, instinctual renunciation is not enough, for the wish persists and cannot be concealed from the super-ego. Thus, in spite of the renunciation that has been made, a sense of guilt comes about. This constitutes a great economic disadvantage in the erection of a super-ego, or, as we may put it, in the formation of a conscience. Instinctual renunciation now no longer has a completely liberating effect; virtuous continence is no longer rewarded with the assurance of love. A threatened external unhappiness – loss of love and punishment on the part of the external authority – has been exchanged for a permanent internal unhappiness, for the tension of the sense of guilt....

It can also be asserted that when a child reacts to his first great instinctual frustrations with excessively strong aggressiveness and with a correspondingly severe super-ego, he is following a phylogenetic model and is going beyond the response that would be currently justified; for the father of prehistoric times was undoubtedly terrible, and an extreme amount of aggressiveness may be attributed to him. Thus, if one shifts over from individual to phylogenetic development, the differences between the two theories of the genesis of conscience are still further diminished. On the other hand, a new and important difference makes its appearance between these two developmental processes. We cannot get away from the assumption that man's sense of guilt springs from the Oedipus complex and was acquired at the killing of the father by the brothers banded together.[iii] On that occasion an act of aggression was not suppressed but carried out; but it was the same act of aggression whose suppression in the child is supposed to be the source of his sense of guilt. At this point I should not be surprised if the reader were to exclaim angrily: 'So it makes no difference whether one kills one's father or not – one gets a feeling of guilt in either case! We may take leave to raise a few doubts here. Either it is not true that the sense of guilt comes from suppressed aggressiveness, or else the whole story of the killing of the father is a fiction and the children of primaeval man did not kill their fathers any more often than children do nowadays. Besides, if it is not fiction but a plausible piece of history, it would be a case of something happening which everyone expects to happen – namely, of a person feeling guilty because he really has done something which cannot be justified. And of this event, which is after all an everyday occurrence, psycho-analysis has not yet given any explanation.'

That is true, and we must make good the omission. Nor is there any great secret about the matter. When one has a sense of guilt after having committed a misdeed, and because of it, the feeling should more properly be called *remorse*. It relates only to a deed that has been done, and, of course, it presupposes that a *conscience* – the readiness to feel guilty – was already in existence before the deed took place. Remorse of this sort can, therefore, never help us to discover the origin of conscience and of the sense of guilt in general. What happens in these everyday cases is usually this: an instinctual need acquires the strength to achieve satisfaction in spite of the conscience, which is, after all, limited in its strength; and with the natural weakening of the need owing to its having been satisfied, the former balance of power is restored. Psycho-analysis is thus justified in excluding from the present discussion the case of a sense of guilt due to remorse, however frequently such cases occur and however great their practical importance.

[iii] In the Oedipus complex, cornerstone of Freud's theory of child development, the normal child develops a sexual attachment to the opposite-gender parent, and competitive anger and fear toward the same-gender parent. The conflict is normally resolved through renunciation of the desire and an identification with the same-gender parent. Strictly, the Oedipal complex refers only to the development of boys, the analogous phase (and the analogy is notoriously tortured) for girls being the Electra complex.

But if the human sense of guilt goes back to the killing of the primal father, that was after all a case of 'remorse'. Are we to assume that [at that time] a conscience and a sense of guilt were not, as we have presupposed, in existence before the deed? If not, where, in this case, did the remorse come from? There is no doubt that this case should explain the secret of the sense of guilt to us and put an end to our difficulties. And I believe it does. This remorse was the result of the primordial ambivalence of feeling towards the father. His sons hated him, but they loved him, too. After their hatred had been satisfied by their act of aggression, their love came to the fore in their remorse for the deed. It set up the super-ego by identification with the father; it gave that agency the father's power, as though as a punishment for the deed of aggression they had carried out against him, and it created the restrictions which were intended to prevent a repetition of the deed. And since the inclination to aggressiveness against the father was repeated in the following generations, the sense of guilt, too, persisted, and it was reinforced once more by every piece of aggressiveness that was suppressed and carried over to the super-ego. Now, I think, we can at last grasp two things perfectly clearly: the part played by love in the origin of conscience and the fatal inevitability of the sense of guilt. Whether one has killed one's father or has abstained from doing so is not really the decisive thing. One is bound to feel guilty in either case, for the sense of guilt is an expression of the conflict due to ambivalence, of the eternal struggle between Eros and the instinct of destruction or death. This conflict is set going as soon as men are faced with the task of living together. So long as the community assumes no other form than that of the family, the conflict is bound to express itself in the Oedipus complex, to establish the conscience and to create the first sense of guilt. When an attempt is made to widen the community, the same conflict is continued in forms which are dependent on the past; and it is strengthened and

results in a further intensification of the sense of guilt. Since civilization obeys an internal erotic impulse which causes human beings to unite in a closely-knit group, it can only achieve this aim through an ever-increasing reinforcement of the sense of guilt. What began in relation to the father is completed in relation to the group. If civilization is a necessary course of development from the family to humanity as a whole, then – as a result of the inborn conflict arising from ambivalence, of the eternal struggle between the trends of love and death – there is inextricably bound up with it an increase of the sense of guilt, which will perhaps reach heights that the individual finds hard to tolerate. One is reminded of the great poet's moving arraignment of the 'Heavenly Powers':

> Ihr führt in's Leben uns hinein.
> Ihr lasst den Armen schuldig werden,
> Dann überlasst Ihr ihn den Pein,
> Denn jede Schuld rächt sich auf Erden.[iv]

And we may well heave a sigh of relief at the thought that it is nevertheless vouchsafed to a few to salvage without effort from the whirlpool of their own feelings the deepest truths, towards which the rest of us have to find our way through tormenting uncertainty and with restless groping.

[iv] From Goethe's *Wilhelm Meister*, Carlyle's translation (Boston: Houghton Mifflin, 1890).

> To earth, this weary earth, ye bring us
> To guilt ye let us heedless go,
> Then leave repentance fierce to wring us:
> A moment's guilt, an age of woe!

> [From Water, Earth, and Air unfolding,
> A thousand germs break forth and grow,
> In dry, and wet, and warm, and chilly:
> And had I not the Flame reserved, why, really,
> There's nothing special of my own to show.]

Author's Notes

1 In Goethe's Mephistopheles [*Faust*, Part I, Scene 3] we have a quite exceptionally convincing identification of the principle of evil with the destructive instinct:

> Denn alles, was entsteht,
> Ist wert, dass es zu Grunde geht . . .
> So ist dann alles, was Ihr Sünde,

> Zerstörung, kurz das Böse nennt,
> Mein eigentliches Element.

> [For all things, from the Void
> Called forth, deserve to be destroyed . . .
> Thus, all which you as Sin have rated –
> Destruction, – aught with Evil blent, –
> That is my proper element.]

The Devil himself names as his adversary, not what is holy and good, but Nature's power to create, to multiply life – that is, Eros:

> Der Luft, dem Wasser, wie der Erden
> Entwinden tausend Keime sich,
> Im Trocknen, Feuchten, Warmen, Kalten!

> Hätt' ich mir nicht die Flamme vorbehalten.
> Ich hätte nichts Aparts für mich.

2 Our present point of view can be roughly expressed in the statement that libido has a share in every instinctual manifestation, but that not everything in that manifestation is libido.

20

From *The Crisis of European Sciences and Transcendental Phenomenology*

Edmund Husserl

Moravian-born German philosopher Edmund Husserl (1859–1938) is the inventor of twentieth-century phenomenology, perhaps the most important European philosophical reaction against an excessively scientific view of the world. Husserl regards phenomenology's demand that we return to concrete human experience as the antidote to the scientific naturalism that has perverted modernity. Husserl opposed naturalism, not science, rationalism or foundationalism. He believed that phenomenology alone could provide the foundation for science and reason; it is the philosophical recapture of the source of all meaning and evidence in primary experience. Phenomenology was later taken by Heidegger in an explicitly anti-scientific and antifoundationalist direction. Prevented by the Nazis from teaching because he was a Jew, Husserl delivered an invited lecture in Vienna in 1935 on "Philosophy in the Crisis of European Mankind" which became the basis for his last and unfinished book, *The Crisis of the European Sciences and Transcendental Phenomenology*. In the following selection from that book, he sees in the modern mathematical interpretation of nature, epitomized by the great seventeenth-century physicist and astronomer Galileo, the failed promise of modern thought.

The Founding of the Autonomy of European Humanity through the New Formulation of the Idea of Philosophy in the Renaissance

It was not always the case that science understood its demand for rigorously grounded truth in the sense of that *sort* of objectivity which dominates our positive sciences in respect to method and which, having its effect far beyond the sciences themselves, is the basis for the support and widespread acceptance of a philosophical and ideological positivism. The specifically human questions were not always banned from the realm of science; their intrinsic relationship to all the sciences – even to those of which man is not the subject matter, such as the natural sciences – was not left unconsidered. As long as this had not yet happened, science could claim significance – indeed, as we know, the major role – in the completely new shaping of European humanity which began with the Renaissance. Why science lost this leadership, why there occurred an essential change, a positivistic restriction of the idea of science – to understand this, according to its *deeper motives*, is of great importance for the purpose of these lectures.

In the Renaissance, as is well known, European humanity brings about a revolutionary change. It turns against its previous way of existing – the medieval – and disowns it, seeking to shape itself anew in freedom. Its admired model is ancient humanity. This mode of existence is what it wishes to reproduce in itself.

What does it hold to be essential to ancient man? After some hesitation, nothing less than the "philosophical" form of existence: freely giving oneself,

Edmund Husserl, Part One, section 3–5, pp. 7–14 and Part Two, section 9h–9l, pp. 48–59 from *The Crisis of European Sciences and Transcendental Phenomenology* (trans. David Carr). Evanston: Northwestern University Press, 1970.

one's whole life, its rule through pure reason or through philosophy. Theoretical philosophy is primary. A superior survey of the world must be launched, unfettered by myth and the whole tradition: universal knowledge, absolutely free from prejudice, of the world and man, ultimately recognizing in the world its inherent reason and teleology and its highest principle, God. Philosophy as theory frees not only the theorist but any philosophically educated person. And theoretical autonomy is followed by practical autonomy. According to the guiding ideal of the Renaissance, ancient man forms himself with insight through free reason. For this renewed "Platonism" this means not only that man should be changed ethically [but that] the whole human surrounding world, the political and social existence of mankind, must be fashioned anew through free reason, through the insights of a universal philosophy.

In accordance with this ancient model, recognized at first only by individuals and small groups, a theoretical philosophy should again be developed which was not to be taken over blindly from the tradition but must grow out of independent inquiry and criticism.

It must be emphasized here that the idea of philosophy handed down from the ancients is not the concept of present-day schoolbooks, merely comprising a group of disciplines; in the first centuries of the modern period – even though it changes not insignificantly as soon as it is taken up – it retains the formal meaning of the one all-encompassing science, the science of the totality of what is. Sciences in the plural, all those sciences ever to be established or already under construction, are but dependent branches of the One Philosophy. In a bold, even extravagant, elevation of the meaning of universality, begun by Descartes, this new philosophy seeks nothing less than to encompass, in the unity of a theoretical system, all meaningful questions in a rigorous scientific manner, with an apodictically intelligible methodology, in an unending but rationally ordered progress of inquiry. Growing from generation to generation and forever, this one edifice of definitive, theoretically interrelated truths was to solve all conceivable problems – problems of fact and of reason, problems of temporality and eternity.

Thus the positivistic concept of science in our time is, historically speaking, a *residual concept*. It has dropped all the questions which had been considered under the now narrower, now broader concepts of metaphysics, including all questions vaguely termed "ultimate and highest." Examined

closely, these and all the excluded questions have their inseparable unity in the fact that they contain, whether expressly or as implied in their meaning, the *problems of reason* – reason in all its particular forms. Reason is the explicit theme in the disciplines concerning knowledge (i.e. of true and genuine, rational knowledge), of true and genuine valuation (genuine values as values of reason), of ethical action (truly good acting, acting from practical reason); here reason is a title for "absolute," "eternal," "supertemporal," "unconditionally" valid ideas and ideals. If man becomes a "metaphysical" or specifically philosophical problem, then he is in question as a rational being; if his history is in question, it is a matter of the "meaning" or reason in history. The problem of God clearly contains the problem of "absolute" reason as the teleological source of all reason in the world – of the "meaning" of the world. Obviously even the question of immortality is a question of reason, as is the question of freedom. All these "metaphysical" questions, taken broadly – commonly called specifically philosophical questions – surpass the world understood as the universe of mere facts. They surpass it precisely as being questions with the idea of reason in mind. And they all claim a higher dignity than questions of fact, which are subordinated to them even in the order of inquiry. Positivism, in a manner of speaking, decapitates philosophy. Even the ancient idea of philosophy, as unified in the indivisible unity of all being, implied a meaningful order of being and thus of problems of being. Accordingly, metaphysics, the science of the ultimate and highest questions, was honored as the queen of the sciences; its spirit decided on the ultimate meaning of all knowledge supplied by the other sciences. This, too, was taken over by the reviving philosophy [of the Renaissance]; indeed, it even believed it had discovered the true, universal method through which such a systematic philosophy, culminating in metaphysics, could be constructed as a serious *philosophia perennis*.

In light of this we can understand the energy which animated all scientific undertakings, even the merely factual sciences of the lower level; in the eighteenth century (which called itself the philosophical century) it filled ever widening circles with enthusiasm for philosophy and for all the special sciences as its branches. Hence the ardent desire for learning, the zeal for a philosophical reform of education and of all of humanity's social and political forms of existence, which makes that much-abused Age of Enlightenment so admirable. We possess an undying testimony to this spirit in the glorious "Hymn to Joy" of Schiller and Beethoven. It is only with painful feelings that we can understand this hymn today. A greater contrast with our present situation is unthinkable.

The Failure of the New Science After its Initial Success; the Unclarified Motive for this Failure

Now if the new humanity, animated and blessed with such an exalted spirit, did not hold its own, it must have been because it lost the inspiring belief in its ideal of a universal philosophy and in the scope of the new method. And such, indeed, was the case. It turned out that this method could bring unquestionable successes only in the positive sciences. But it was otherwise in metaphysics, i.e. in problems considered philosophical in the special sense – though hopeful, apparently successful beginnings were not lacking even here. Universal philosophy, in which these problems were related – unclearly – to the factual sciences, took the form of system-philosophies, which were impressive but unfortunately were not unified, indeed were mutually exclusive. If the eighteenth century still held the conviction of proceeding toward unity, of arriving at a critically unassailable edifice which grew theoretically from generation to generation, as was undisputedly the case in the universally admired positive sciences – this conviction could not survive for long. The belief in the ideal of philosophy and method, the guideline of all movements since the beginning of the modern era, began to waver; this happened not merely for the external motive that the contrast became monstrous between the repeated failures of metaphysics and the uninterrupted and ever increasing wave of theoretical and practical successes in the positive sciences. This much had its effect on outsiders as well as scientists, who, in the specialized business of the positive sciences, were fast becoming unphilosophical experts. But even among those theorists who were filled with the philosophical spirit, and thus were interested precisely in the highest metaphysical questions, a growing feeling of failure set in – and in their case because the most profound, yet quite *unclarified*, motives protested ever more loudly against the deeply rooted assumptions of the reigning ideal. There begins a long period, extending from Hume and Kant to our own time, of passionate struggle for a clear, reflective understanding of the true reasons for this centuries-old

failure; it was a struggle, of course, only on the part of the few called and chosen ones; the mass of others quickly found and still find formulas with which to console themselves and their readers.

The Ideal of Universal Philosophy and the Process of its Inner Dissolution

The necessary consequence was a peculiar change in the whole way of thinking. Philosophy became a problem for itself, at first, understandably, in the form of the [problem of the] possibility of a metaphysics; and, following what we said earlier, this concerned implicitly the meaning and possibility of the whole problematics of reason. As for the positive sciences, at first they were untouchable. Yet the problem of a possible metaphysics also encompassed *eo ipso* that of the possibility of the factual sciences, since these had their relational meaning – that of truths merely for areas of what is – in the indivisible unity of philosophy. *Can reason and that-which-is be separated, where reason, as knowing, determines what is?* This question suffices to make clear in advance that the whole historical process has a remarkable form, one which becomes visible only through an interpretation of its hidden, innermost motivation. Its from is not that of a smooth development, not that of a continual growth of lasting spiritual acquisitions or of a transformation of spiritual configurations – concepts, theories, systems – which can be explained by means of the accidental historical situations. A definite ideal of a universal philosophy and its method forms the beginning; this is, so to speak, the primal establishment of the philosophical modern age and all its lines of development. But instead of being able to work itself out in fact, this ideal suffers an inner dissolution. As against attempts to carry out and newly fortify the ideal, this dissolution gives rise to revolutionary, more or less radical innovations. Thus the problem of the genuine ideal of universal philosophy and its genuine method now actually becomes the innermost driving force of all historical philosophical movements. But this is to say that, ultimately, all modern sciences drifted into a peculiar, increasingly puzzling crisis with regard to the meaning of their original founding as branches of philosophy, a meaning which they continued to bear within themselves. This is a crisis which does not encroach upon the theoretical and practical successes of the special sciences; yet it shakes to the foundations the whole meaning of their truth. This is not just a matter of a special form of culture – "science" or "philosophy" – as one among others belonging to European mankind. For the primal establishment of the new philosophy is, according to what was said earlier, the primal establishment of modern European humanity itself – humanity which seeks to renew itself radically, as against the foregoing medieval and ancient age, precisely and only through its new philosophy. Thus the crisis of philosophy implies the crisis of all modern sciences as members of the philosophical universe: at first a latent, then a more and more prominent crisis of European humanity itself in respect to the total meaningfulness of its cultural life, its total "*Existenz*."[i]

Skepticism about the possibility of metaphysics, the collapse of the belief in a universal philosophy as the guide for the new man, actually represents a collapse of the belief in "reason," understood as the ancients opposed *epistēmē* to *doxa*.[ii] It is reason which ultimately gives meaning to everything that is thought to be, all things, values, and ends – their meaning understood as their normative relatedness to what, since the beginnings of philosophy, is meant by the word "truth" – truth in itself – and correlatively the term "what is" – $\overset{\prime\prime}{o}\nu\tau\omega\varsigma\ \overset{\prime}{o}\nu$. Along with this falls the faith in "absolute" reason, through which the world has its meaning, the faith in the meaning of history, of humanity, the faith in man's freedom, that is, his capacity to secure rational meaning for his individual and common human existence.

If man loses this faith, it means nothing less than the loss of faith "in himself," in his own true being. This true being is not something he always already has, with the self-evidence of the "I am," but something he only has and can have in the form of the struggle for his truth, the struggle to make himself true. True being is *everywhere* an ideal goal, a task of *epistēmē* or "reason," as opposed to being which through *doxa* is merely thought to be, unquestioned and "obvious." Basically every person is acquainted with this difference – one related to his true and genuine humanity – just as truth as a goal or task is not unknown to him even in everyday life – though here it is merely isolated and relative. But this prefiguration is surpassed by philosophy: in its first, original establishment, ancient philosophy, it conceives of and takes as its task the exalted idea of universal knowledge concerning the totality of

what is. Yet in the very attempt to fulfill it, the naïve obviousness of this task is increasingly transformed – as one feels already in the opposition of the ancient systems – into unintelligibility. More and more the history of philosophy, seen from within, takes on the character of a struggle for existence, i.e. a struggle between the philosophy which lives in the straightforward pursuit of its task – the philosophy of naïve faith in reason – and the skepticism which negates or repudiates it in empiricist fashion. Unremittingly, skepticism insists on the validity of the factually experienced world, that of actual experience, and finds in it nothing of reason or its ideas. Reason itself and its [object,] "that which is," become more and more enigmatic – reason as giving, of itself, meaning to the existing world and, correlatively, the world as existing through reason – until finally the *consciously* recognized world-problem of the deepest essential interrelation between reason and what is in general, the *enigma of all enigmas*, has to become the actual theme of inquiry.

Our interest is confined here to the philosophical modern age. But this is not merely a fragment of the greater historical phenomenon we have just described, that is, humanity struggling to understand itself (for this phrase expresses the whole phenomenon). Rather – as the reestablishment of philosophy with a new universal task and at the same time with the sense of a renaissance of ancient philosophy – it is at once a repetition and a universal transformation of meaning. In this it feels called to initiate a new age, completely sure of its idea of philosophy and its true method, and also certain of having overcome all previous naïvetés, and thus all skepticism, through the radicalism of its new beginning. But it is the fate of the philosophical modern age, laden with its own unnoticed naïvetés, that it has first to seek out, in the course of a gradual self-disclosure motivated by new struggles, the definitive idea of philosophy, its true subject matter and its true method; it has first to discover the genuine world-enigmas and steer them in the direction of a solution.

As men of the present, having grown up in this development, we find ourselves in the greatest danger of drowning in the skeptical deluge and thereby losing our hold on our own truth. As we reflect in this plight, we gaze backward into the history of our present humanity. We can gain self-understanding, and thus inner support, only by elucidating the unitary meaning which is inborn in this history from its origin through the newly established task [of the Renaissance], the driving force of all [modern] philosophical attempts.

---

[i]   Literally, "existence," but the term connotes the existential philosophies of Martin Heidegger and Karl Jaspers.
[ii] In Greek, knowledge and opinion, respectively.

The Life-World as the Forgotten Meaning-Fundament of Natural Science

But now we must note something of the highest importance that occurred even as early as Galileo: the surreptitious substitution of the mathematically substructed world of idealities for the only real world the one that is actually given through perception, that is ever experienced and experienceable – our everyday life-world. This substitution was promptly passed on to his successors, the physicists of all the succeeding centuries.

Galileo was himself an heir in respect to pure geometry. The inherited geometry, the inherited manner of "intuitive" conceptualizing, proving, constructing, was no longer original geometry: in this sort of "intuitiveness" it was already empty of meaning. Even ancient geometry was, in its way, τέχνη,[iii] removed from the sources of truly immediate intuition and originally intuitive thinking, sources from which the so-called geometrical intuition, i.e. that which operates with idealities, has at first derived its meaning. The geometry of idealities was preceded by the practical art of surveying, which knew nothing of idealities. Yet such a pregeometrical achievement was a meaning-fundament for geometry, a fundament for the great invention of idealization; the latter encompassed the invention of the ideal world of geometry, or rather the methodology of the objectifying determination of idealities through the constructions which create "mathematical existence." It was a fateful omission that Galileo did not inquire back into the original meaning-giving achievement which, as idealization practiced on the original ground of all theoretical and practical life – the immediately intuited world (and here especially the empirically intuited world of bodies) – resulted in the geometrical ideal constructions. He did not reflect closely on all this: on how the free, imaginative variation of this world and its shapes results only in possible empirically intuitable shapes and not in exact shapes; on what sort of motivation and what new achievement was required for genuinely geometric idealization. For in the case of inherited geometrical method, these functions were no longer being *vitally* practiced; much less were they reflectively brought to theoretical consciousness as methods which realize the meaning of exactness from the inside. Thus it could

iii   The Greek term *technē* referring to productive art or skill (including fine art, crafts, engineering, etc.).

appear that geometry, with its own immediately evident a priori "intuition" and the thinking which operates with it, produces a self-sufficient, absolute truth which, as such – "obviously" – could be applied without further ado. That this obviousness was an illusion – as we have pointed out above in general terms, thinking for ourselves in the course of our exposition of Galileo's thoughts – that even the meaning of the application of geometry has complicated sources: this remained hidden for Galileo and the ensuing period. Immediately with Galileo, then, begins the surreptitious substitution of idealized nature for prescientifically intuited nature.

Thus all the occasional (even "philosophical") reflections which go from technical [scientific] work back to its true meaning always stop at idealized nature; they do not carry out the reflection radically, going back to the ultimate purpose which the new science, together with the geometry which is inseparable from it, growing out of prescientific life and its surrounding world, was from the beginning supposed to serve: a purpose which necessarily lay *in* this prescientific life and was related to its life-world. Man (including the natural scientist), living in this world, could put all his practical and theoretical questions only to *it* – could refer in his theories only to it, in its open, endless horizons of things unknown. All knowledge of laws could be knowledge only of predictions, grasped as lawful, about occurrences of actual or possible experiential phenomena, predictions which are indicated when experience is broadened through observations and experiments penetrating systematically into unknown horizons, and which are verified in the manner of inductions. To be sure, everyday induction grew into induction according to scientific method, but that changes nothing of the essential meaning of the pregiven world as the horizon of all meaningful induction. It is this world that we find to be the world of all known and unknown realities. To it, the world of actually experiencing intuition, belongs the form of space–time together with all the bodily shapes incorporated in it; it is in this world that we ourselves live, in accord with our bodily, personal way of being. But here we find nothing of geometrical idealities, no geometrical space or mathematical time with all their shapes.

This is an important remark, even though it is so trivial. Yet this triviality has been buried precisely by exact science, indeed since the days of ancient geometry, through that substitution of a methodically idealized achievement for what is given immediately as actuality presupposed in all idealization, given by a [type of] verification which is, in its own way, unsurpassable. This actually intuited, actually experienced and experienceable world, in which practically our whole life takes place, remains unchanged as what it is, in its own essential structure and its own concrete causal style, whatever we may do with or without techniques. Thus it is also not changed by the fact that we invent a particular technique, the geometrical and Galilean technique which is called physics. What do we actually accomplish through this technique? Nothing but *prediction* extended to infinity. All life rests upon prediction or, as we can say, upon induction. In the most primitive way, even the ontic certainty of any straightforward experience is inductive. Things "seen" are always more than what we "really and actually" see of them. Seeing, perceiving, is essentially having-something-itself and at the same time having-something-in-advance, meaning-something-in-advance. All praxis, with its projects, involves inductions; it is just that ordinary inductive knowledge (predictions), even if expressly formulated and "verified," is "artless" compared to the artful "methodical" inductions which can be carried to infinity through the method of Galilean physics with its great productivity.

In geometrical and natural-scientific mathematization, in the open infinity of possible experiences, we measure the life-world – the world constantly given to us as actual in our concrete world-life – for a well-fitting *garb of ideas*, that of the so-called objectively scientific truths. That is, through a method which (as we hope) can be really carried out in every particular and constantly verified, we first construct numerical indices for the actual and possible sensible plena of the concretely intuited shapes of the life-world, and in this way we obtain possibilities of predicting concrete occurrences in the intuitively given life-world, occurrences which are not yet or no longer actually given. And this kind of prediction infinitely surpasses the accomplishment of everyday prediction.

Mathematics and mathematical science, as a garb of ideas, or the garb of symbols of the symbolic mathematical theories, encompasses everything which, for scientists and the educated generally, *represents* the life-world, *dresses it up* as "objectively actual and true" nature. It is through the garb of ideas that we take for *true being* what is actually a *method* – a method which is designed for the purpose of progressively improving, *in infinitum*, through "scientific" predictions, those rough predictions which are the only ones originally possible within the sphere of what is actually experienced and experienceable in the life-world. It is because of the disguise of ideas that the true meaning of the method, the formulae, the "theories," remained unintelligible and, in the naïve formation of the method, was *never* understood.

Thus no one was ever made conscious of the radical problem of *how* this sort of naïveté actually became possible and is still possible as a living historical fact; how a method which is actually directed toward a goal, the systematic solution of an endless scientific task, and which continually achieves undoubted results, could ever grow up and be able to function usefully through the centuries when no one possessed a real understanding of the actual meaning and the internal necessity of such accomplishments. What was lacking, and what is still lacking, is the actual self-evidence through which he who knows and accomplishes can give himself an account, not only of what he does that is new and what he works with, but also of the implications of meaning which are closed off through sedimentation or traditionalization, i.e. of the constant presuppositions of his [own] constructions, concepts, propositions, theories. Are science and its method not like a machine, reliable in accomplishing obviously very useful things, a machine everyone can learn to operate correctly without in the least understanding the inner possibility and necessity of this sort of accomplishment? But was geometry, was science, capable of being designed in advance, like a machine, without an understanding which was, in a similar sense, complete – scientific? Does this not lead to a *regressus in infinitum*?

Finally, does this problem not link up with the problem of the instincts in the usual sense? Is it not the problem of *hidden reason*, which knows itself as reason only when it has become manifest?

Galileo, the discoverer – or, in order to do justice to his precursors, the consummating discoverer – of physics, or physical nature, is at once a discovering and a concealing genius. He discovers mathematical nature, the methodical idea, he blazes the trail for the infinite number of physical discoveries and discoverers. By contrast to the universal causality of the intuitively given world (as its invariant form), he discovers what has since been called simply the law of causality, the "a priori form" of the "true" (idealized and mathematized) world, the "law of exact lawfulness" according to which every occurrence in "nature" – idealized nature – must come under exact laws. All this is discovery-concealment, and to the present day we accept it as straightforward truth. In principle nothing is changed by the supposedly philosophically revolutionary critique of the "classical law of causality" made by recent atomic physics. For in spite of all that is new, what is essential in principle, it seems to me, remains: namely, nature, which is in itself mathematical; it is given in formulae, and it can be interpreted only in terms of the formulae.

I am of course quite serious in placing and continuing to place Galileo at the top of the list of the greatest discoverers of modern times. Naturally I also admire quite seriously the great discoverers of classical and postclassical physics and their intellectual accomplishment, which, far from being merely mechanical, was in fact astounding in the highest sense. This accomplishment is not at all disparaged by the above elucidation of it as τέχνη or by the critique in terms of principle, which shows that the true meaning of these theories – the meaning which is genuine in terms of their origins – remained and had to remain hidden from the physicists, including the great and the greatest. It is not a question of a meaning which has been slipped in through metaphysical mystification or speculation; it is, rather, with the most compelling self-evidence, the true, the only real meaning of these theories, as opposed to the meaning of being a *method*, which has its own comprehensibility in operating with the formulae and their practical application, technique.

How what we have said up to now is still one-sided, and what horizons of problems, leading into new dimensions, have not been dealt with adequately – horizons which can be opened up only through a reflection on this life-world and man as its subject – can be shown only when we are much further advanced in the elucidation of the historical development according to its innermost moving forces.

Portentous Misunderstandings Resulting from Lack of Clarity about the Meaning of Mathematization

With Galileo's mathematizing reinterpretation of nature, false consequences established themselves even beyond the realm of nature which were so intimately connected with this reinterpretation that they could dominate all further developments of views about the world up to the present day.

I mean Galileo's famous doctrine of the merely subjective character of the specific sense-qualities, which soon afterward was consistently formulated by Hobbes as the doctrine of the subjectivity of all concrete phenomena of sensibly intuitive nature and world in general. The phenomena are only in the subjects; they are there only as causal results of events taking place in true nature, which events exist only with mathematical properties. If the intuited world of our life is merely subjective, then all the truths of pre- and extrascientific life which have to do with its factual being are deprived of value. They have meaning only insofar as they, while themselves false, vaguely indicate an in-itself which lies behind this world of possible experience and is transcendent in respect to it.

In connection with this we arrive at a further consequence of the new formation of meaning, a self-interpretation of the physicists which grows out of this new formation of meaning as "obvious" and which was dominant until recently:

Nature is, in its "true being-in-itself," mathematical. The *pure* mathematics of space–time procures knowledge, with apodictic self-evidence, of a set of laws of this "in-itself" which are unconditionally, universally valid. This knowledge is immediate in the case of the axiomatic elementary laws of the a priori constructions and comes to be through infinite mediations in the case of the other laws. In respect to the space–time form of nature we possess the "innate" faculty (as it is later called) of knowing with definiteness true being-in-itself as mathematically ideal being (before all actual experience). Thus implicitly the space–time form is itself innate in us.

It is otherwise with the more concrete universal lawfulness of nature, although it, too, is mathematical through and through. It is inductively accessible a posteriori through factual experiential data. In a supposedly fully intelligible way, the a priori mathematics of spatiotemporal shapes is sharply distinguished from natural science which, though it applies pure mathematics, is inductive. Or, one can also say: the purely mathematic relationship of ground and consequent is sharply distinguished from that of real ground and real consequent, i.e. that of natural causality.

And yet an uneasy feeling of obscurity gradually asserts itself concerning the relation between the mathematics of nature and the mathematics of spatiotemporal form, which, after all, belongs to the former, between the latter "innate" and the former "non-innate" mathematics. Compared to the absolute knowledge we ascribe to God the creator, one says to oneself, our knowledge in pure mathematics has only one lack, i.e. that, while it is always absolutely self-evident, it requires a systematic process in order to bring to realization as knowing, i.e. as explicit mathematics, all the shapes that "exist" in the spatiotemporal form. In respect to what exists concretely in nature, by contrast, we have no a priori self-evidence at all. The whole mathematics of nature, beyond the spatiotemporal form, we must arrive at inductively through facts of experience. But is nature in itself not thoroughly mathematical? Must it not also be thought of as a coherent mathematical system? Must it not be capable of being represented in a coherent mathematics of nature, precisely the one that natural science is always merely seeking, as encompassed by a system of laws which is "axiomatic" in respect of form, the axioms of which are always only hypotheses and thus never really attainable? Why is it, actually, that they are not? Why is it that we have no prospect of discovering nature's own axiomatic system as one whose axioms are apodictically self-evident? Is it because the appropriate innate faculty is lacking in us in a factual sense?

In the superficialized, more or less already technized meaning-pattern of physics and its methods, the difference in question was "completely clear": it is the difference between "pure" (a priori) and "applied" mathematics, between "mathematical existence" (in the sense of pure mathematics) and the existence of the mathematically formed real (i.e. that of which mathematical shape is a component in the sense of a real property). And yet even such an outstanding genius as Leibniz struggled for a long time with the problem of grasping the correct meaning of the two kinds of existence – i.e. universally the existence of the spatiotemporal form as purely geometrical and the existence of universal mathematical nature with its factual, real form – and of understanding the correct relation of each to the other.

The significance of these obscurities for the Kantian problem of synthetic judgments a priori and for his division between the synthetic judgments of pure mathematics and those of natural science will concern us in detail later.[iv]

iv Kant argued that mathematical and scientific knowledge is grounded in judgments universally true, independent of experience (a priori) yet not merely true by definition ("synthetic," not "analytic").

The obscurity was strengthened and transformed still later with the development and constant methodical application of pure formal mathematics. "Space" and the purely *formally* defined "Euclidean manifold" were confused; the *true axiom* (i.e. in the old, customary sense of the term), as an ideal norm with unconditional validity, grasped with self-evidence in pure geometric thought or in arithmetical, purely logical thought, was confused with the *inauthentic* "axiom" – a word which in the theory of manifolds signifies not judgments ("propositions") but forms of propositions as components of the definition of a "manifold" to be constructed formally without internal contradiction.

Fundamental Significance of the Problem of the Origin of Mathematical Natural Science

Like all the obscurities exhibited earlier, [the preceding] follow from the transformation of a formation of meaning which was originally vital, or rather of the originally vital consciousness of the task which gives rise to the methods, each with its special sense. The developed method, the progressive fulfillment of the task, is, as method, an art (τέχνη) which is handed down; but its true meaning is not necessarily handed down with it. And it is precisely for this reason that a theoretical task and achievement like that of a natural science (or any science of the world) – which can master the infinity of its subject matter only through infinities of method and can master the latter infinities only by means of a technical thought and activity which are empty of meaning – can only be and remain meaningful in a true and original sense *if* the scientist has developed in himself the ability to *inquire back* into the *original meaning* of all his meaning-structures and methods, i.e. into the *historical meaning of their primal establishment*, and especially into the meaning of all the *inherited meanings* taken over unnoticed in this primal establishment, as well as those taken over later on.

But the mathematician, the natural scientist, at best a highly brilliant technician of the method – to which he owes the discoveries which are his only aim – is normally not at all able to carry out such reflections. In his actual sphere of inquiry and discovery he does not know at all that everything these reflections must clarify is even in *need* of clarification, and this for the sake of that interest which is decisive for a philosophy or a science, i.e.

the interest in true knowledge of the *world itself, nature itself.* And this is precisely what has been lost through a science which is given as a tradition and which has become a τέχνη, insofar as this interest played a determining role at all in its primal establishment. Every attempt to lead the scientist to such reflections, if it comes from a nonmathematical, non-scientific circle of scholars, is rejected as "metaphysical." The professional who has dedicated his life to these sciences must, after all – it seems so obvious to him – know best what he is attempting and accomplishing in his work. The philosophical needs ("philosophicomathematical," "philosophicoscientific" needs), aroused even in these scholars by historical motives to be elucidated later, are satisfied by themselves in a way that is sufficient for them – but of course in such a way that the whole dimension which must be inquired into is not seen at all and thus not at all dealt with.

Characterization of the Method of our Exposition

In conclusion let us say a word about the *method* we have followed in the very intricate considerations of this section, in the service of our over-all aim. The historical reflections we embarked upon, in order to arrive at the self-understanding which is so necessary in our philosophical situation, demanded clarity concerning the *origin of the modern spirit* and, together with that – because of the significance, which cannot be overestimated, of mathematics and mathematical natural science – clarity concerning the origin of these sciences. That is to say: clarity concerning the original motivation and movement of thought which led to the conceiving of their idea of nature, and from there to the movement of its realization in the actual development of natural science itself. With Galileo the idea in question appears for the first time, so to speak, as full-blown; thus I have linked all our considerations to his name, in a certain sense simplifying and idealizing the matter; a more exact historical analysis would have to take account of how much of his thought he owed to his "predecessors." (I shall continue, incidentally, and for good reasons, in a similar fashion.) In respect to the situation as he found it and to the way in which it had to motivate him and did motivate him according to his known pronouncements, much can be established immediately, so that we understand the beginning of the whole bestowal of meaning upon natural science.

But in this very process we come upon the shifts and concealments of meaning of later and most recent times. For we ourselves, who are carrying out these reflections (and, as I may assume, my readers), stand under the *spell* of these times. Being caught up in them, we at first have no inkling of these shifts of meaning – we who all think we know so well what mathematics and natural science "are" and do. For who today has not learned this in school? But the first elucidation of the original meaning of the new natural science and of its novel methodical style makes felt something of the later shifts in meaning. And clearly they influence, or at least make more difficult, the analysis of the motivation [of science].

Thus we find ourselves in a sort of circle. The understanding of the beginning is to be gained fully only by starting with science as given in its present-day form, looking back at its development. But in the absence of an understanding of the *beginnings* the development is mute as a *development of meaning.* Thus we have no other choice than to proceed forward and backward in a zigzag pattern; the one must help the other in an interplay. Relative clarification on one side brings some elucidation on the other, which in turn casts light back on the former. In this sort of historical consideration and historical critique, then, which begins with Galileo (and immediately afterward with Descartes) and must follow the temporal order, we nevertheless have constantly to make *historical leaps* which are thus not digressions but necessities. They are necessities if we take upon ourselves, as we have said, the task of self-reflection which grows out of the "breakdown" situation of our time, with its "breakdown of science" itself. Of first importance for this task, however, is the reflection on the original meaning of the new sciences, above all that of the exact science of nature; for the latter was and still is, through all its shifts of meaning and misplaced self-interpretations, of decisive significance (in a manner to be pursued further) for the becoming and being of the modern positive sciences, of modern philosophy, and indeed of the spirit of modern European humanity in general.

The following also belongs to the method: readers, especially those in the natural sciences, may have become irritated by the fact – it may appear to them almost as dilettantism – that no use has been made of the natural-scientific way of speaking. It has been consciously avoided. In the kind of thinking which everywhere tries to bring "original intuition" to the fore – that is, the pre- and extrascientific life-world, which contains within itself all actual life, including the scientific life of thought, and nourishes it as the source of all technical constructions of meaning – in this kind of thinking one of the greatest difficulties is that one must choose the naïve way of speaking of [everyday] life, but must also use it in a way which is appropriate for rendering evident what is shown.

It will gradually become clearer, and finally be completely clear, that the proper return to the naïveté of life – but in a reflection which rises above this naïveté – is the only possible way to overcome the philosophical naïveté which lies in the [supposedly] "scientific" character of traditional objectivistic philosophy. This will open the gates to the new dimension we have repeatedly referred to in advance.

We must add here that, properly understood, all our expositions are supposed to aid understanding only from the relative [perspective of our] position and that our expression of doubts, given in the criticisms [of Galileo, etc.] (doubts which we, living in the present, now carrying out our reflections, do not conceal), has the methical function of preparing ideas and methods which will gradually take shape in us as results of our reflection and will serve to liberate us. All reflection undertaken for "existential" reasons is naturally *critical*. But we shall not fail to bring to a reflective form of knowledge, later on, the basic meaning of the course of our reflections and our particular kind of critique.

21

From *Dialectic of Enlightenment*

Max Horkheimer and Theodor Adorno

Max Horkheimer (1895–1973) and Theodor Adorno (1903–70) were members of the *Institut für Sozialforschung* (Institute for Social Research) at Frankfurt, Germany. Their work combined the perspectives of Hegel, Marx, and Freud in an analysis of social and cultural phenomena. Forced to flee in 1934, they eventually settled in California, where they composed their classic *Dialectic of Enlightenment* (1944). It is devoted to answering that most poignant question for any mid-century German, or European, intellectual: how, at the apparent height of Enlightened culture in the twentieth century, could the most barbaric of social movements, National Socialism, emerge? They argue that the Enlightenment's own tendencies are self-negating ("dialectical"). Skeptical, Enlightened reason empties itself of all religious and metaphysical sources of value, leaving only power and self-interest as its goals. They see this dialectic prophesied in the literary work of the Marquis de Sade, and actualized in mass culture and in the new political barbarism of the twentieth century. Their stunning and frightening conclusion is that Enlightenment is the only road to social freedom *and* it inevitably leads to totalitarianism. Modernity leaves us, then, in an impossible situation.

As a nominalist movement,[i] the Enlightenment calls a halt before the *nomen*, the exclusive, precise concept, the proper name. Whether – as some

assert[1] – proper names were originally species names as well, can no longer be ascertained, yet the former have not shared the fate of the latter. The substantial ego refuted by Hume and Mach is not synonymous with the name. In Jewish religion, in which the idea of the patriarchate culminates in the destruction of myth, the bond between name and being is still recognized in the ban on pronouncing the name of God. The disenchanted world of Judaism conciliates magic by negating it in the idea of God. Jewish religion allows no word that would alleviate the despair of all that is mortal. It associates hope only with the prohibition against calling on what is false as God, against invoking the finite as the infinite, lies as truth. The guarantee of salvation lies in the rejection of any belief that would replace it: it is knowledge obtained in the denunciation of illusion. Admittedly, the negation is not abstract. The contesting of every positive without distinction, the stereotype formula of vanity, as used by Buddhism, sets itself above the prohibition against naming the Absolute with names: just as far above as its contrary, pantheism; or its caricature, bourgeois skepticism. Explanations of the world as all or nothing are mythologies, and guaranteed roads to redemption are sublimated magic practices. The self-satisfaction of knowing in advance and the transfiguration of negativity into redemption are untrue

Max Horkheimer and Theodor Adorno, from "The Concept of Enlightenment," pp. 23–9, and from "Juliette, or Enlightenment and Morality," pp. 81–93, in *Dialectic of Enlightenment* (trans. John Cumming). New York: Seabury, 1972.

---

[i] Nominalism claims that only particular things exist, so that general terms (e.g. "horse") do not refer to a real universal (e.g. horse-ness) but only serve as signs for any and all particulars (e.g. particular horses).

forms of resistance against deception. The justness of the image is preserved in the faithful pursuit of its prohibition. This pursuit, "determinate negativity"[2] does not receive from the sovereignty of the abstract concept any immunity against corrupting intuition, as does skepticism, to which both true and false are equally vain. Determinate negation rejects the defective ideas of the absolute, the idols, differently than does rigorism, which confronts them with the Idea that they cannot match up to. Dialectic, on the contrary, interprets every image as writing. It shows how the admission of its falsity is to be read in the lines of its features – a confession that deprives it of its power and appropriates it for truth. With the notion of determinate negativity, Hegel revealed an element that distinguishes the Enlightenment from the positivist degeneracy to which he attributes it. By ultimately making the conscious result of the whole process of negation – totality in system and in history – into an absolute, he of course contravened the prohibition and himself lapsed into mythology.

This did not happen merely to his philosophy as the apotheosis of progressive thought, but to the Enlightenment itself, as the sobriety which it thought distinguished it from Hegel and from metaphysics. For enlightenment is as totalitarian as any system. Its untruth does not consist in what its romantic enemies have always reproached it for: analytical method, return to elements, dissolution through reflective thought; but instead in the fact that for enlightenment the process is always decided from the start. When in mathematical procedure the unknown becomes the unknown quantity of an equation, this marks it as the well-known even before any value is inserted. Nature, before and after the quantum theory, is that which is to be comprehended mathematically; even what cannot be made to agree, indissolubility and irrationality, is converted by means of mathematical theorems. In the anticipatory indentification of the wholly conceived and mathematized world with truth, enlightenment intends to secure itself against the return of the mythic. It confounds thought and mathematics. In this way the latter is, so to speak, released and made into an absolute instance. "An infinite world, in this case a world of idealities, is conceived as one whose objects do not accede singly, imperfectly, and as if by chance to our cognition, but are attained by a rational, systematically unified method – in a process of infinite progression – so that each object is ultimately apparent according to its full inherent being . . . In the Galilean mathematization of the world, however, *this*

selfness is idealized under the guidance of the new mathematics: in modern terms, it becomes itself a mathematical multiplicity."[3] Thinking objectifies itself to become an automatic, self-activating process; an impersonation of the machine that it produces itself so that ultimately the machine can replace it. Enlightenment[4] has put aside the classic requirement of thinking about thought – Fichte is its extreme manifestation – because it wants to avoid the precept of dictating practice that Fichte himself wished to obey.[ii] Mathematical procedure became, so to speak, the ritual of thinking. In spite of the axiomatic self-restriction, it establishes itself as necessary and objective: it turns thought into a thing, an instrument – which is its own term for it. But this kind of mimesis, in which universal thought is equalized, so turns the actual into the unique, that even atheism itself is subjected to the ban on metaphysics. For positivism, which represents the court of judgment of enlightened reason, to digress into intelligible worlds is no longer merely forbidden, but meaningless prattle. It does not need – fortunately – to be atheistic, because objectified thinking cannot even raise the problem. The positivist censor lets the established cult escape as willingly as art – as a cognition-free special area of social activity; but he will never permit that denial of it which itself claims to be knowledge. For the scientific mind, the separation of thought from business for the purpose of adjusting actuality, departure from the privileged area of real existence, is as insane and self-destructive as the primitive magician would consider stepping out of the magic circle he has prepared for his invocation; in both cases the offense against the taboo will actually result in the malefactor's ruin. The mastery of nature draws the circle into which the criticism of pure reason banished thought. Kant joined the theory of its unceasingly laborious advance into infinity with an insistence on its deficiency and everlasting limitation. His judgment is an oracle. There is no form of being in the world that science could not penetrate, but what can be penetrated by science is not being. According to Kant, philosophic judgment aims at the new; and yet it recognizes nothing new, since it always merely recalls what reason has always deposited in the object. But there is a reckoning for this form of thinking that considers itself secure in the various departments of science – secure from the dreams of a ghost-seer:

[ii] German philosopher, Johann Gottlieb Fichte (1762–1814).

world domination over nature turns against the thinking subject himself; nothing is left of him but that eternally same *I think* that must accompany all my ideas. Subject and object are both rendered ineffectual. The abstract self, which justifies record-making and systematization, has nothing set over against it but the abstract material which possesses no other quality than to be a substrate of such possession. The equation of spirit and world arises eventually, but only with a mutual restriction of both sides. The reduction of thought to a mathematical apparatus conceals the sanction of the world as its own yardstick. What appears to be the triumph of subjective rationality, the subjection of all reality to logical formalism, is paid for by the obedient subjection of reason to what is directly given. What is abandoned is the whole claim and approach of knowledge: to comprehend the given as such; not merely to determine the abstract spatio-temporal relations of the facts which allow them just to be grasped, but on the contrary to conceive them as the superficies, as mediated conceptual moments which come to fulfillment only in the development of their social, historical, and human significance. The task of cognition does not consist in mere apprehension, classification, and calculation, but in the determinate negation of each immediacy. Mathematical formalism, however, whose medium is number, the most abstract form of the immediate, instead holds thinking firmly to mere immediacy. Factuality wins the day; cognition is restricted to its repetition; and thought becomes mere tautology. The more the machinery of thought subjects existence to itself, the more blind its resignation in reproducing existence. Hence enlightenment returns to mythology, which it never really knew how to elude. For in its figures mythology had the essence of the *status quo*: cycle, fate, and domination of the world reflected as the truth and deprived of hope. In both the pregnancy of the mythical image and the clarity of the scientific formula, the everlastingness of the factual is confirmed and mere existence pure and simple expressed as the meaning which it forbids. The world as a gigantic analytic judgment, the only one left over from all the dreams of science, is of the same mold as the cosmic myth which associated the cycle of spring and autumn with the kidnapping of Persephone.[iii] The uniqueness of the mythic process, which tends to legitimize factuality, is deception. Originally the carrying off of the goddess was directly synonymous with the dying of nature. It repeated itself every autumn, and even the repetition was not the result of the buried one but the same every time. With the rigidification of the consciousness of time, the process was fixed in the past as a unique one, and in each new cycle of the seasons an attempt was made ritually to appease fear of death by recourse to what was long past. But the separation is ineffective. Through the establishment of a unique past, the cycle takes on the character of inevitability, and dread radiates from the age-old occurrence to make every event its mere repetition. The absorption of factuality, whether into legendary prehistory or into mathematical formalism, the symbolical relation of the contemporary to the mythic process in the rite or to the abstract category in science, makes the new appear as the predetermined, which is accordingly the old. Not existence but knowledge is without hope, for in the pictorial or mathematical symbol it appropriates and perpetuates existence as a schema.

In the enlightened world, mythology has entered into the profane. In its blank purity, the reality which has been cleansed of demons and their conceptual descendants assumes the numinous character which the ancient world attributed to demons. Under the title of brute facts, the social injustice from which they proceed is now as assuredly sacred a preserve as the medicine man was sacrosanct by reason of the protection of his gods. It is not merely that domination is paid for by the alienation of men from the objects dominated: with the objectification of spirit, the very relations of men – even those of the individual to himself – were bewitched. The individual is reduced to the nodal point of the conventional responses and modes of operation expected of him. Animism spiritualized the object, whereas industrialism objectifies the spirits of men. Automatically, the economic apparatus, even before total planning, equips commodities with the values which decide human behavior. Since, with the end of free exchange, commodities lost all their economic qualities except for fetishism, the latter has extended its arthritic influence over all aspects of social life. Through the countless agencies of mass production and its culture the conventionalized modes of behavior are impressed on the individual as the only natural, respectable, and rational ones. He defines himself only as a thing, as a static elem-

---

iii The Greek goddess Persephone, daughter of Demeter, was kidnapped by Hades, god of the underworld. Eventually she was released for nine months each year, while her remaining time with Hades caused each winter.

ent, as success or failure. His yardstick is self-preservation, successful or unsuccessful approximation to the objectivity of his function and the models established for it. Everything else, idea and crime, suffers the force of the collective, which monitors it from the classroom to the trade union. But even the threatening collective belongs only to the deceptive surface, beneath which are concealed the powers which manipulate it as the instrument of power. Its brutality, which keeps the individual up to scratch, represents the true quality of men as little as value represents the things which he consumes. The demonically distorted form which things and men have assumed in the light of unprejudiced cognition, indicates domination, the principle which effected the specification of *mana* in spirits and gods[iv] and occurred in the jugglery of magicians and medicine men. The fatality by means of which prehistory sanctioned the incomprehensibility of death is transferred to wholly comprehensible real existence. The noontide panic fear in which men suddenly became aware of nature as totality has found its like in the panic which nowadays is ready to break out at every moment: men expect that the world, which is without any issue, will be set on fire by a totality which they themselves are and over which they have no control. . . .

Enlightenment, according to Kant, is "man's emergence from his self-incurred immaturity. Immaturity is the inability to use one's understanding without the guidance of another person."[5] "Understanding without the guidance of another person" is understanding guided by reason. This means no more than that, by virtue of its own consistency, it organizes the individual data of cognition into a system. "Reason has . . . for its object only the understanding and its purposive employment."[6] It makes "a certain collective unity the aim of the operations of the understanding."[7] and this unity is the system. Its rules are the indications for a hierarchical construction of concepts. For Kant, as for Leibniz and Descartes, rationality consists of "completing the systematical connection, both in ascending to higher genera, and in descending to lower species."[8] The "systematizing" of knowledge is "its coherence according to one principle."[9] In the Enlightenment's interpretation, thinking is the creation of unified, scientific order and the derivation of factual knowledge from principles, whether the latter are elucidated as arbitrarily

postulated axioms, innate ideas, or higher abstractions. Logical laws produce the most general relations within the arrangement, and define them. Unity resides in agreement. The resolution of contradiction is the system *in nuce*.[v] Knowledge consists of subsumption under principles. Any other than systematically directed thinking is unoriented or authoritarian. Reason contributes only the idea of systematic unity, the formal elements of fixed conceptual coherence. Every substantial goal which men might adduce as an alleged rational insight is, in the strict Enlightenment sense, delusion, lies or "rationalization," even though individual philosophers try to advance from this conclusion toward the postulate of philanthropic emotion. Reason is the "faculty . . . of deducing the particular from the general."[10] According to Kant, the homogeneity of the general and the particular is guaranteed by the "schematism of pure understanding," or the unconscious operation of the intellectual mechanism which structures perception in accordance with the understanding. The understanding impresses the intelligibility of the matter (which subjective judgment discovers there) on it as an objective quality, before it enters into the ego. Without such a schematism – in short, without intellectual perception – no impression would harmonize with a concept, and no category with an example; and the unity of thought (let alone of system) toward which everything is directed would not prevail. To produce this unity is the conscious task of science. If "all empirical laws . . . are only special determinations of the pure laws of the understanding,"[11] research must always ensure that the principles are always properly linked with factual judgments. "This concurrence of nature with our cognitive faculty is an *a priori* assumption . . . of judgment."[12] It is the "guideline"[13] for organized experience.

The system must be kept in harmony with nature; just as the facts are predicted from the system, so they must confirm it. Facts, however, belong to practice; they always characterize the individual's contact with nature as a social object: experience is always real action and suffering. In physics, of course, perception – by means of which a theory may be proved – is usually reduced to the electric sparks visible in the experimental apparatus. Its absence is as a rule without practical consequence, for it destroys no more than a theory – or possibly the career of the assistant responsible for setting up the experiment. But laboratory condi-

[iv] "*Mana*," divine or magical force believed to permeate the world in animistic religion.

[v] In a nut shell.

tions constitute the exception. Thinking that does not make system and perception accord conflicts with more than isolated visual impressions; it conflicts with practice. The expected event fails to occur, yes, but the unexpected event does occur: the bridge collapses, the crops wither, or the drug kills. The spark which most surely indicates the lack of systematic thinking, the violation of logic, is no transient percept, but sudden death. The system the Enlightenment has in mind is the form of knowledge which copes most proficiently with the facts and supports the individual most effectively in the mastery of nature. Its principles are the principles of self-preservation. Immaturity is then the inability to survive. The burgher, in the successive forms of slaveowner, free entrepreneur, and administrator, is the logical subject of the Enlightenment.

The difficulties in the concept of reason caused by the fact that its subjects, the possessors of that very reason, contradict one another, are concealed by the apparent clarity of the judgments of the Western Enlightenment. In the *Critique of Pure Reason*, however, they are expressed in the unclear relation of the transcendental to the empirical ego, and in the other unresolved contradictions. Kant's concepts are ambiguous. As the transcendental, supraindividual self, reason comprises the idea of a free, human social life in which men organize themselves as the universal subject and overcome the conflict between pure and empirical reason in the conscious solidarity of the whole. This represents the idea of true universality: utopia. At the same time, however, reason constitutes the court of judgment of calculation, which adjusts the world for the ends of self-preservation and recognizes no function other than the preparation of the object from mere sensory material in order to make it the material of subjugation. The true nature of schematism, of the general and the particular, of concept and individual case reconciled from without, is ultimately revealed in contemporary science as the interest of industrial society. Being is apprehended under the aspect of manufacture and administration. Everything – even the human individual, not to speak of the animal – is converted into the repeatable, replaceable process, into a mere example for the conceptual models of the system. Conflict between administrative, reifying science, between the public mind and the experience of the individual, is precluded by circumstances. The conceptual apparatus determines the senses, even before perception occurs; *a priori*, the citizen sees the world as the matter from which he himself manufactures it. In-

tuitively, Kant foretold what Hollywood consciously put into practice: in the very process of production, images are pre-censored according to the norm of the understanding which will later govern their apprehension. Even before its occurrence, the perception which serves to confirm the public judgment is adjusted by that judgment. Even if the secret utopia in the concept of reason pointed, despite fortuitous distinctions between individuals, to their common interest, reason – functioning, in compliance with ends, as a mere systematic science – serves to level down that same identical interest. It allows no determination other than the classifications of the societal process to operate. No one is other than what he has come to be: a useful, successful, or frustrated member of vocational and national groups. He is one among many representatives of his geographical, psychological and sociological type. Logic is democratic; in this respect the great have no advantage over the insignificant. The great are classed as the important, and the insignificant as prospective objects for social relief. Science in general relates to nature and man only as the insurance company in particular relates to life and death. Whoever dies is unimportant: it is a question of ratio between accidents and the company's liabilities. Not the individuality but the law of the majority recurs in the formula. The concurrence of the general and the particular is no longer hidden in the one intellect which perceives the particular only as one case of the general, and the general only as the aspect of the particular by which it can be grasped and manipulated. Science itself is not conscious of itself; it is only a tool. Enlightenment, however, is the philosophy which equates the truth with scientific systematization. The attempt to establish this identity, which Kant was still able to undertake with a philosophic intention, led to concepts which have no meaning in a scientific sense, because they are not mere indications for manipulation according to the rules of the game. The notion of the self-understanding of science contradicts the notion of science itself. Kant's work transcends experience as mere operation, and for that reason – in accordance with its own principles – is now condemned by the Enlightenment as dogmatic. With Kant's consequent, full confirmation of the scientific system as the form of truth, thought seals its own nullity, for science is technical practice, as far removed from reflective consideration of its own goal as are other forms of labor under the pressure of the system.

The moral teachings of the Enlightenment bear witness to a hopeless attempt to replace enfeebled religion with some reason for persisting in society when interest is absent. As genuine burghers, the philosophers come to terms with the powers who, in theory, are to be condemned. The theories are firm and consistent, whereas the moral doctrines are propagandist and sentimental (even when they seem rigorous), or else they are mere *coups de main*[vi] by reason of the consciousness that morality itself is underivable – as in the case of Kant's recourse to ethical forces as a fact. His attempt (even though more careful than Western philosophy as a whole) to derive the duty of mutual respect from a law of reason finds no support in the *Critique*. It is the conventional attempt of bourgeois thought to ground respect, without which civilization cannot exist, upon something other than material interest and force; it is more sublime and paradoxical than, yet as ephemeral as, any previous attempt. The citizen who would forgo profit only on the Kantian motive of respect for the mere form of law would not be enlightened, but superstitious – a fool. The root of Kantian optimism, according to which moral behavior is rational even if the mean and wretched would prevail, is actually an expression of horror at the thought of reversion to barbarism. If (so Kant wrote to Haller) one of these great moral forces of mutual love and respect were to founder, "then nothingness [immorality] would open wide its maw and swallow the whole realm of [moral] virtue as if it were a drop of water."[14] But, according to Kant, in the face of scientific reason moral forces are no less neutral impulses and modes of behavior than the immoral forces into which they suddenly change when directed not to that hidden possibility but to reconciliation with power. Enlightenment expels the distinction from the theory. It treats emotions *"ac si quaestio de lineis, planis aut de corporibus esset."*[15] The totalitarian order has carried this out with all seriousness. Liberated from the control of the same class which tied the nineteenth-century businessman to Kantian respect and mutual love, Fascism (which by its iron discipline saves its subject peoples the trouble of moral feelings) no longer needs to uphold any disciplines. In contradistinction to the categorical imperative and all the more in accordance with pure reason, it treats men as things – as the loci of modes of behavior. The rulers were anxious to protect the bourgeois world against the ocean of open force (which has now really broken into Europe), only so long as the economic concentration had made

inadequate progress. Previously, only the poor and savages were exposed to the fury of the capitalist elements. But the totalitarian order gives full rein to calculation and abides by science as such. Its canon is its own brutal efficiency. It was the hand of philosophy that wrote it on the wall – from Kant's *Critique* to Nietzsche's *Genealogy of Morals*; but one man made out the detailed account. The work of the Marquis de Sade portrays "understanding without the guidance of another person": that is, the bourgeois individual freed from tutelage.[vii]

Self-preservation is the constitutive principle of science, the soul of the table of categories,[viii] even when it is to be deduced idealistically, as with Kant. Even the ego, the synthetic unit of apperception, the instance which Kant calls the highest point, on which the possibility of the logical form of all knowledge necessarily depends,[16] is in fact the product of, as well as the condition for, material existence. Individuals, who have to look after themselves, develop the ego as the instance of the reflective preliminary and general view; it is extended and contracted as the prospects of economic self-sufficiency and productive ownership extend and contract from generation to generation. Finally it passes from the dispossessed bourgeoisie to the totalitarian cartel-lords, whose science has become the inclusive concept of the methods of reproduction of the subjugated mass society. Sade erected an early monument to their sense of planning. The conspiracy of the powerholders against the people by means of undeviating organization is as close as the bourgeois republic to the unenlightened spirit since Machiavelli and Hobbes.[ix] It is inimical to authority only when authority does not have power enough to compel obedience – the force which is no fact. So long as the identity of the user of reason is disregarded, the affinity of reason is as much to force as the mediation; according to the individual or group situation, it permits peace or war, tolerance or repression. Since it exposes substantial goals as the power of nature over mind, as the erosion of its self-legislation, reason is – by virtue, too, of its very formality – at the service of

---

[vi] Surprise attacks.

[vii] The Marquis de Sade (1740–1814), controversial French author of erotic, violent philosophical works, from whose name English gets "sadism."

[viii] Kant's table of categories through which the human mind constitutes experience (from *Critique of Pure Reason*).

[ix] Nicolo Machiavelli (1469–1527) and Thomas Hobbes (1588–1679), two political philosophers notorious for their amoral views.

any natural interest. Thinking becomes an organic medium pure and simple, and reverts to nature. But for the rulers, men become material, just as nature as a whole is material for society. After the short intermezzo of liberalism, in which the bourgeois kept one another in check, domination appears as archaic terror in a fascistically rationalized form. As Francavilla says at the court of King Ferdinand of Naples:[x] "Religious chimeras must be replaced by the most extreme forms of terror. If the people are freed from fear of a future hell, as soon as it has vanished they will abandon themselves to anything. But if this chimerical fear is replaced by utterly relentless penal laws, which of course apply only to the people, then they alone will provoke unrest in the State; the discontented will be born only into the lowest class. What does the idea of a curb which they never experience themselves mean to the rich, if with this empty semblance they are able to preserve a justice that allows them to crush all those who live under their yoke? You will find no one in that class who would not submit to the worst tyranny so long as all others must suffer it."[17] Reason is the organ of calculation, of planning; it is neutral in regard to ends; its element is coordination. What Kant grounded transcendentally, the affinity of knowledge and planning, which impressed the stamp of inescapable expediency on every aspect of a bourgeois existence that was wholly rationalized, even in every breathing-space, Sade realized empirically more than a century before sport was conceived. The teams of modern sport, whose interaction is so precisely regulated that no member has any doubt about his role, and which provide a reserve for every player, have their exact counterpart in the sexual teams of *Juliette*, which employ every moment usefully, neglect no human orifice, and carry out every function. Intensive, purposeful activity prevails in spirit as in all branches of mass culture, while the inadequately initiated spectator cannot divine the difference in the combinations, or the meaning of variations, by the arbitrarily determined rules. The architectonic structure of the Kantian system, like the gymnastic pyramids of Sade's orgies and the schematized principles of the early bourgeois freemasonry – which has its cynical mirror-image in the strict regimentation of the libertine society of the *120 Journées*[xi] – reveals

an organization of life as a whole which is deprived of any substantial goal. These arrangements amount not so much to pleasure as to its regimented pursuit – organization – just as in other demythologized epochs (Imperial Rome and the Renaissance, as well as the Baroque) the schema of an activity was more important than its content. In the modern era, enlightenment separated the notions of harmony and fulfillment from their hypostatization in the religious Beyond, and, in the form of systematization, transferred them as criteria to human aspiration. When utopia, which provided the French Revolution with its content of hope, entered German music and philosophy (effectively and ineffectively), the established civil order wholly functionalized reason, which became a purposeless purposiveness which might thus be attached to all ends. In this sense, reason is planning considered solely as planning. The totalitarian State manipulates the people. Or, as Sade's Francavilla puts it: "The government must control the population, and must possess all the means necessary to exterminate them when afraid of them, or to increase their numbers when that seems desirable. There should never be any counterweight to the justice of government other than that of the interests or passions of those who govern, together with the passions and interests of those who, as we have said, have received from it only so much power as is requisite to reproduce their own."[18] Francavilla indicates the road that imperialism, the most terrible form of the *ratio*, has always taken: "Take its god from the people that you wish to subjugate, and then demoralize it; so long as it worships no other god than you, and has no other morals than your morals, you will always be its master . . . allow it in return the most extreme criminal license; punish it only when it turns upon you."[19]

Since reason posits no substantial goals, all affects are equally removed from its governance, and are purely natural. The principle by which reason is merely set over against all that is unreasonable, is the basis of the true antithesis of enlightenment and mythology. Mythology recognizes spirit only as immersed in nature, as natural power. Like the powers without, inward impulses appear as living powers of divine or demonic origin. Enlightenment, on the other hand, puts back coherence, meaning and life into subjectivity, which is properly constituted only in this process. For subjectivity, reason is the chemical agent which absorbs the individual substance of things and volatilizes them in the mere autonomy of reason. In

---

[x] Both names refer to historical persons that Sade used as characters in his *Story of Juliette* (1797).
[xi] *One Hundred and Twenty Days of Sodom*, a book by de Sade.

order to escape the superstitious fear of nature, it wholly transformed objective effective entities and forms into the mere veils of a chaotic matter, and anathematized their influence on humanity as slavery, until the ideal form of the subject was no more than unique, unrestricted, though vacuous authority.

All the power of nature was reduced to mere indiscriminate resistance to the abstract power of the subject. The particular mythology which the Western Enlightenment, even in the form of Calvinism, had to get rid of was the Catholic doctrine of the *ordo*[xii] and the popular pagan religion which still flourished under it. The goal of bourgeois philosophy was to liberate men from all this. But the liberation went further than its humane progenitors had conceived. The unleashed market economy was both the actual form of reason and the power which destroyed reason. The Romantic reactionaries only expressed what the bourgeois themselves experienced: that in their world freedom tended toward organized anarchy. The Catholic counterrevolution proved itself right as against the Enlightenment, just as the Enlightenment had shown itself to be right in regard to Catholicism. The Enlightenment committed itself to liberalism. If all affects are of equal value, then survival – which anyway governs the form of the system – seems also to be the most probable source of maxims for human conduct. Self-preservation, in fact, was given full rein in the free market economy. Those somber writers of the bourgeois dawn – Machiavelli, Hobbes, Mandeville,[xiii] and so on – who decried the egotism of the self, acknowledged in so doing that society was the destructive principle, and denounced harmony before it was elevated as the official doctrine by the serene and classical authors. The latter boosted the totality of the bourgeois order as the misery that finally fused both general and particular, society and self, into one. With the development of the economic system in which control of the economic apparatus by private groups divides men, survival as affirmed by reason – the reified drive of the individual bourgeois – was revealed as destructive natural power,

no longer to be distinguished from self-destruction. The two were now indissolubly blended. Pure reason became unreason, a faultless and insubstantial mode of procedure. But the utopia which proclaimed reconciliation between nature and the individual emerged together with the revolutionary avant-garde from its concealment in German philosophy, simultaneously irrational and rational, as the idea of the combination of free men, and called down on itself all the wrath of the *ratio*.[xiv] In society as it is, despite all the wretched moralistic attempts to propagate humanity as the most rational of means, survival remains free from utopia, which is denounced as myth. Among the rulers, cunning self-preservation takes the form of struggle for Fascist power; among individuals, it is expressed as adaptation to injustice at any price. Enlightened reason is as little capable of finding a standard by which to measure any drive in itself, and in comparison with all other drives, as of arranging the universe in spheres. It established natural hierarchy as a reflex of medieval society, and later enterprises are branded as lies in order to indicate a new, objective value ranking. Irrationalism, as it appears in such empty reconstructions, is far from being able to withstand the *ratio*. With Leibniz and Hegel, mainstream philosophy – even in those subjective and objective assertions which only approximate to thought – discovered the claim to truth in emotions, institutions, and works of art, but irrationalism (close in this as in other respects to modern positivism, that last remnant of the Enlightenment) demarcates emotion, like religion and art, from everything deserving of the title of knowledge or cognition. It limits cold reason in favor of immediate living, yet makes this no more than a principle inimical to thought. Under the cover of this enmity, emotion and finally all human expression, even culture as a whole, are withdrawn from thought; thereby, however, they are transformed into a neutralized element of the comprehensive *ratio* of the economic system – itself irrationalized long ago. From the start, it was unable to rely on its own pull, which it enhanced with the cult of feeling. But wherever it has recourse to the emotions, it militates against their very medium, thought, which was always suspicious of this self-alienated reason. The exuberantly tender affection of the lover in the movie strikes a blow against the unmoved theory – a blow continued in that sentimental polemic against thought

---

[xii] Presumably the *ordo salutus*, the order of salvation, which for Catholicism sprang from the sacraments and for Protestant reformers from God's decree.

[xiii] Bernard Mandeville (1670–1733), Dutch physician who wrote *The Fable of the Bees* (1729), which scandalously argued that private greed can produce social benefits.

[xiv] Rationality.

which presents itself as an attack upon injustice. Though feelings are raised in this way to the level of an ideology, they continue to be despised in reality. When set against the firmament to which ideology transfers them, they still seem rather too vulgar; the effect is to exile them all the more. As a natural impulse, self-preservation has, like all other impulses, a bad conscience; but efficiency and the institutions which [are] meant to serve it – that is, independent mediation, the apparatus, the organization, systematization – like to appear reasonable, both in theory and in practice; and the emotions are made to share in this apparent rationality.

The Enlightenment of modern times advanced from the very beginning under the banner of radicalism; this distinguishes it from any of the earlier stages of demythologization. When a new mode of social life allowed room for a new religion and a new way of thinking, the overthrow of the old classes, tribes, and nations was usually accompanied by that of the old gods. But especially where a nation (the Jews, for example) was brought by its own destiny to change to a new form of social life, the time-honored customs, sacred activities, and objects of worship were magically transformed into heinous crimes and phantoms. Present-day fears and idiosyncrasies, derided and execrated character traits, may be deciphered as the marks of the violent onset of this or that stage of progress in human development. From the reflex of disgust at excrement or human flesh to the suspicion of fanaticism, laziness, and poverty, whether intellectual or material, there is a long line of modes of behavior which were metamorphosed from the adequate and necessary into abominations. This is the line both of destruction and of civilization. Each step forward on it represents some progress, a stage of enlightenment. But whereas all earlier changes, from pre-animism to magic, from the matriarchal to a patriarchal culture, from the polytheism of the slaveowners to the Catholic hierarchy, replaced the older mythologies with new – though enlightened – ones, and substituted the god of legions for the Great Mother, the adoration of the Lamb for that of the totem, the brilliance of enlightened reason banished as mythological any form of devotion which claimed to be objective, and grounded in actuality. All previous obligations therefore succumbed to the verdict which pronounced them taboo – not

excluding those which were necessary for the existence of the bourgeois order itself. The instrument by means of which the bourgeoisie came to power, the liberation of forces, universal freedom, self-determination – in short, the Enlightenment, itself turned against the bourgeoisie once, as a system of domination, it had recourse to suppression. In accordance with its principle, enlightenment does not stop at the minimum of belief, without which the bourgeois world cannot exist. It does not give domination the reliable service which the old ideologies always allowed it. Its antiauthoritarian tendency, which (though of course only in a subterranean form) still relates to the utopia in the concept of reason, ultimately makes it as inimical to the bourgeoisie as it was to the aristocracy – with which the bourgeoisie is then very soon allied. Finally, the antiauthoritarian principle has to change into its very antithesis – into opposition to reason; the abrogation of everything inherently binding, which it brings about, allows domination to ordain as sovereign and to manipulate whatever bonds and obligations prove appropriate to it. After civil virtue and love of humanity (for which it already had no adequate grounds), philosophy proceeded to proclaim authority and hierarchy as virtues, when the Enlightenment had long posited them as lies. But the Enlightenment possesses no argument against even such a perversion of its proper nature, for the plain truth had no advantage over distortion, and rationalization none over the *ratio*, if they could prove no practical benefit in themselves. With the formalization of reason, to the extent that its preferred function is that of a symbol for neutral procedures theory itself becomes an incomprehensible concept, and thought appears meaningful only when meaning has been discarded. Once it is harnessed to the dominant mode of production, the Enlightenment – which strives to undermine any order which has become repressive – abrogates itself. This was obvious even in the early attacks of the contemporary Enlightenment on Kant, the universal reducer. Just as Kant's moral philosophy restricted his enlightened critique, in order to preserve the possibility of reason, so – conversely – unreflective enlightened thinking based on the notion of survival always tends to convert into skepticism, in order to make enough room for the existing order. . . .

Authors' Notes

1 See [Ferdinand] Tönnies, "*Philosophische Terminologie*," in *Psychologisch-Soziologische Ansicht* (Leipzig, 1908), p. 31.

2 *Phänomenologie des Geistes* [*Phenomenology of Spirit*], p. 65.

3 Edmund Husserl, "*Die Krisis der europäischen Wissenschaften und die transzendentale Phänomenologie*," in *Philosophia* (Belgrade, 1936), pp. 95ff.

4 Cf. Schophenhauer, *Parerga und Paralipomena*, vol. II, S. 356; *Werke*, ed. Deussen, vol. V, p. 671.

5 Kant, "*Beantwortung der Frage: Was ist Aufklärung?*" ["An Answer to the Question: What is Enlightenment?"] *Kants Werke* (Akademie-Ausgabe), vol. VIII, p. 35.

6 *Kritik der reinen Vernunft* [*Critique of Pure Reason*], vol. III (2nd edn), p. 427.

7 Ibid., p. 427.

8 Ibid., pp. 435f.

9 Ibid., p. 428.

10 Ibid., p. 429.

11 *Kritik der reinen Vernunft*, vol. IV (1st edn), p. 93.

12 *Kritik der Urteilskraft* [*Critique of Judgment*], vol. V, p. 185.

13 Ibid., p. 185.

14 *Metaphysische Anfänge der Tugendlehre*, vol. VI, p. 449.

15 Spinoza, *Ethica*, Pars III. Praefatio ["as if investigating lines, planes, or solids"].

16 *Kritik der reinen Vernunft*, vol. III (2nd edn), p. 109.

17 *Histoire de Juliette* (Holland, 1797), vol. V, pp. 319f.

18 Ibid., pp. 322f.

19 Ibid., p. 324.

22

From "Existentialism"

Jean-Paul Sartre

Jean-Paul Sartre (1905–80) was one of the founders of the French Existentialist movement, and perhaps the most famous intellectual in the world for a generation after World War II. A close associate of Maurice Merleau-Ponty, Simone de Beauvoir, and Albert Camus, from 1941 to 1945 he wrote for the French resistance against the German occupation. During the Cold War he became a harsh critic of capitalism and the United States, even associating himself with Maoism in the 1960s, but was critical of communist totalitarianism when he allowed himself to see it (e.g. he condemned the Soviets for their 1956 invasion of Hungary). Only months after the liberation of Paris from the Germans, in October 1945, he gave the famous public lecture, excerpted below, which served to galvanize public interest in the new philosophy. Sartre endorsed the absolute freedom and responsibility of the individual subject to create itself in a world without guidance from God or nature. This heroic subjectivism is characteristic of French existentialism, and precisely what Heidegger and postmodernism would later reject.

Man is nothing else but what he makes of himself. Such is the first principle of existentialism. It is also what is called subjectivity, the name we are labeled with when charges are brought against us. But what do we mean by this, if not that man has a greater dignity than a stone or table? For we mean that man first exists, that is, that man first of all is the being who hurls himself toward a future and who is conscious of imagining himself as being in the future. Man is at the start a plan which is aware of itself, rather than a patch of moss, a piece of garbage, or a cauliflower; nothing exists prior to this plan; there is nothing in heaven; man will be what he will have planned to be. Not what he will want to be. Because by the word "will" we generally mean a conscious decision, which is subsequent to what we have already made of ourselves. I may want to belong to a political party, write a book, get married; but all that is only a manifestation of an earlier, more spontaneous choice that is called "will." But if existence really does precede essence, man is responsible for what he is. Thus, existentialism's first move is to make every man aware of what he is and to make the full responsibility of his existence rest on him. And when we say that a man is responsible for himself, we do not only mean that he is responsible for his own individuality, but that he is responsible for all men.

The word subjectivism has two meanings, and our opponents play on the two. Subjectivism means, on the one hand, that an individual chooses and makes himself; and, on the other, that it is impossible for man to transcend human subjectivity. The second of these is the essential meaning of existentialism. When we say that man chooses his own self, we mean that every one of us does likewise; but we also mean by that that in making this choice he also chooses all men. In fact, in creating the man that we want to be, there is not a single one of our acts which does not at the same time create an image of man as we think he ought to be. To

Jean-Paul Sartre, from "Existentialism" (trans. Bernard Frechtman) in *Existentialism and Human Emotions*, pp. 15–24 and 46–51. New York: Citadel 1985.

choose to be this or that is to affirm at the same time the value of what we choose, because we can never choose evil. We always choose the good, and nothing can be good for us without being good for all.

If, on the other hand, existence precedes essence, and if we grant that we exist and fashion our image at one and the same time, the image is valid for everybody and for our whole age. Thus, our responsibility is much greater than we might have supposed, because it involves all mankind. If I am a workingman and choose to join a Christian trade-union rather than be a communist, and if by being a member I want to show that the best thing for man is resignation, that the kingdom of man is not of this world, I am not only involving my own case – I want to be resigned for everyone. As a result, my action has involved all humanity. To take a more individual matter, if I want to marry, to have children; even if this marriage depends solely on my own circumstances or passion or wish, I am involving all humanity in monogamy and not merely myself. Therefore, I am responsible for myself and for everyone else. I am creating a certain image of man of my own choosing. In choosing myself, I choose man.

This helps us understand what the actual content is of such rather grandiloquent words as anguish, forlornness, despair. As you will see, it's all quite simple.

First, what is meant by anguish?[i] The existentialists say at once that man is anguish. What that means is this: the man who involves himself and who realizes that he is not only the person he chooses to be, but also a lawmaker who is, at the same time, choosing all mankind as well as himself, can not help escape the feeling of his total and deep responsibility. Of course, there are many people who are not anxious; but we claim that they are hiding their anxiety, that they are fleeing from it. Certainly, many people believe that when they do something, they themselves are the only ones involved, and when someone says to them, "What if everyone acted that way?" they shrug their shoulders and answer, "Everyone doesn't act that way." But really, one should always ask himself, "What would happen if everybody looked at things that way?" There is no escaping this disturbing thought except by a kind of double-dealing. A man who lies and makes excuses for himself by saying "not everybody does that," is someone with an uneasy

conscience, because the act of lying implies that a universal value is conferred upon the lie.

Anguish is evident even when it conceals itself. This is the anguish that Kierkegaard called the anguish of Abraham.[ii] You know the story: an angel has ordered Abraham to sacrifice his son; if it really were an angel who has come and said, "You are Abraham, you shall sacrifice your son," everything would be all right. But everyone might first wonder, "Is it really an angel, and am I really Abraham? What proof do I have?"

There was a madwoman who had hallucinations; someone used to speak to her on the telephone and give her orders. Her doctor asked her, "Who is it who talks to you?" She answered, "He says it's God." What proof did she really have that it was God? If an angel comes to me, what proof is there that it's an angel? And if I hear voices, what proof is there that they come from heaven and not from hell, or from the subconscious, or a pathological condition? What proves that they are addressed to me? What proof is there that I have been appointed to impose my choice and my conception of man on humanity? I'll never find any proof or sign to convince me of that. If a voice addresses me, it is always for me to decide that this is the angel's voice; if I consider that such an act is a good one, it is I who will choose to say that it is good rather than bad.

Now, I'm not being singled out as an Abraham, and yet at every moment I'm obliged to perform exemplary acts. For every man, everything happens as if all mankind had its eyes fixed on him and were guiding itself by what he does. And every man ought to say to himself, "Am I really the kind of man who has the right to act in such a way that humanity might guide itself by my actions?" And if he does not say that to himself, he is masking his anguish.

There is no question here of the kind of anguish which would lead to quietism, to inaction. It is a matter of a simple sort of anguish that anybody who has had responsibilities is familiar with. For example, when a military officer takes the responsibility for an attack and sends a certain number of men to death, he chooses to do so, and in the main he alone makes the choice. Doubtless, orders come from above, but they are too broad; he interprets them, and on this interpretation depend the lives of ten or fourteen or twenty men. In making a decision he can

---

[i] Sartre is here discussing the famous existentialist theme of anxiety or dread (in German, *Angst*).

[ii] Danish philosopher Søren Kierkegaard (1813–55) discussed the Biblical story of God testing Abraham (by commanding him to kill his son Isaac) in *Fear and Trembling* (1843).

not help having a certain anguish. All leaders know this anguish. That doesn't keep them from acting; on the contrary, it is the very condition of their action. For it implies that they envisage a number of possibilities, and when they choose one, they realize that it has value only because it is chosen. We shall see that this kind of anguish, which is the kind that existentialism describes, is explained, in addition, by a direct responsibility to the other men whom it involves. It is not a curtain separating us from action, but is part of action itself.

When we speak of forlornness,[iii] a term Heidegger was fond of, we mean only that God does not exist and that we have to face all the consequences of this. The existentialist is strongly opposed to a certain kind of secular ethics which would like to abolish God with the least possible expense. About 1880, some French teachers tried to set up a secular ethics which went something like this: God is a useless and costly hypothesis; we are discarding it; but, meanwhile, in order for there to be an ethics, a society, a civilization, it is essential that certain values be taken seriously and that they be considered as having an *a priori* existence. It must be obligatory, *a priori*, to be honest, not to lie, not to beat your wife, to have children, etc., etc. So we're going to try a little device which will make it possible to show that values exist all the same, inscribed in a heaven of ideas, though otherwise God does not exist. In other words – and this, I believe, is the tendency of everything called reformism in France – nothing will be changed if God does not exist. We shall find ourselves with the same norms of honesty, progress, and humanism, and we shall have made of God an outdated hypothesis which will peacefully die off by itself.

The existentialist, on the contrary, thinks it very distressing that God does not exist, because all possibility of finding values in a heaven of ideas disappears along with Him; there can no longer be an *a priori* Good, since there is no infinite and perfect consciousness to think it. Nowhere is it written that the Good exists, that we must be honest, that we must not lie; because the fact is we are on a plane where there are only men. Dostoievsky said, "If God didn't exist, everything would be possible." That is the very starting point of existentialism. Indeed, everything is permissible

if God does not exist, and as a result man is forlorn, because neither within him nor without does he find anything to cling to. He can't start making excuses for himself.

If existence really does precede essence, there is no explaining things away by reference to a fixed and given human nature. In other words, there is no determinism, man is free, man is freedom. On the other hand, if God does not exist, we find no values or commands to turn to which legitimize our conduct. So, in the bright realm of values, we have no excuse behind us, nor justification before us. We are alone, with no excuses.

That is the idea I shall try to convey when I say that man is condemned to be free. Condemned, because he did not create himself, yet, in other respects is free; because, once thrown into the world, he is responsible for everything he does. The existentialist does not believe in the power of passion. He will never agree that a sweeping passion is a ravaging torrent which fatally leads a man to certain acts and is therefore an excuse. He thinks that man is responsible for his passion.

The existentialist does not think that man is going to help himself by finding in the world some omen by which to orient himself. Because he thinks that man will interpret the omen to suit himself. Therefore, he thinks that man, with no support and no aid, is condemned every moment to invent man. Ponge, in a very fine article, has said, "Man is the future of man." That's exactly it. But if it is taken to mean that this future is recorded in heaven, that God sees it, then it is false, because it would really no longer be a future. If it is taken to mean that, whatever a man may be, there is a future to be forged, a virgin future before him, then this remark is sound. But then we are forlorn. . . .

Therefore, in the name of this will for freedom, which freedom itself implies, I may pass judgment on those who seek to hide from themselves the complete arbitrariness and the complete freedom of their existence. Those who hide their complete freedom from themselves out of a spirit of seriousness or by means of deterministic excuses, I shall call cowards; those who try to show that their existence was necessary, when it is the very contingency of man's appearance on earth, I shall call stinkers. But cowards or stinkers can be judged only from a strictly unbiased point of view.

Therefore though the content of ethics is variable, a certain form of it is universal. Kant says that freedom desires both itself and the freedom of others. Granted. But he believes that the formal

---

iii   For Heidegger, a human being finds itself forlorn or abandoned (*verlassen*), thrown into (*geworfen*) the world, and so must live with *unheimlichkeit*, uncanniness (more literally, not-at-home-ness).

and the universal are enough to constitute an ethics. We, on the other hand, think that principles which are too abstract run aground in trying to decide action. Once again, take the case of the student. In the name of what, in the name of what great moral maxim do you think he could have decided, in perfect peace of mind, to abandon his mother or to stay with her? There is no way of judging. The content is always concrete and thereby unforeseeable; there is always the element of invention. The one thing that counts is knowing whether the inventing that has been done, has been done in the name of freedom.

For example, let us look at the following two cases. You will see to what extent they correspond, yet differ. Take *The Mill on the Floss*. We find a certain young girl, Maggie Tulliver, who is an embodiment of the value of passion and who is aware of it. She is in love with a young man, Stephen, who is engaged to an insignificant young girl. This Maggie Tulliver, instead of heedlessly preferring her own happiness, chooses, in the name of human solidarity, to sacrifice herself and give up the man she loves. On the other hand, Sanseverina, in *The Charterhouse of Parma*, believing that passion is man's true value, would say that a great love deserves sacrifices; that it is to be preferred to the banality of the conjugal love that would tie Stephen to the young ninny he had to marry.[iv] She would choose to sacrifice the girl and fulfill her happiness; and, as Stendhal shows, she is even ready to sacrifice herself for the sake of passion, if this life demands it. Here we are in the presence of two strictly opposed moralities. I claim that they are much the same thing; in both cases what has been set up as the goal is freedom.

You can imagine two highly similar attitudes: one girl prefers to renounce her love out of resignation; another prefers to disregard the prior attachment of the man she loves out of sexual desire. On the surface these two actions resemble those we've just described. However, they are completely different. Sanseverina's attitude is much nearer that of Maggie Tulliver, one of heedless rapacity.

Thus, you see that the second charge is true and, at the same time, false. One may choose anything if it is on the grounds of free involvement.

The third objection is the following: "You take something from one pocket and put it into the other.

That is, fundamentally, values aren't serious, since you choose them." My answer to this is that I'm quite vexed that that's the way it is; but if I've discarded God the Father, there has to be someone to invent values. You've got to take things as they are. Moreover, to say that we invent values means nothing else but this: life has no meaning *a priori*. Before you come alive, life is nothing, it's up to you to give it a meaning, and value is nothing else but the meaning that you choose. In that way, you see, there is a possibility of creating a human community.

I've been reproached for asking whether existentialism is humanistic. It's been said, "But you said in *Nausea* that the humanists were all wrong. You made fun of a certain kind of humanist. Why come back to it now?" Actually, the word humanism has two very different meanings. By humanism one can mean a theory which takes man as an end and as a higher value. Humanism in this sense can be found in Cocteau's tale *Around the World in Eighty Hours* when a character, because he is flying over some mountains in an airplane, declares "Man is simply amazing." That means that I, who did not build the airplanes, shall personally consider myself responsible for, and honored by, acts of a few particular men. This would imply that we ascribe a value to man on the basis of the highest deeds of certain men. This humanism is absurd, because only the dog or the horse would be able to make such an over-all judgment about man, which they are careful not to do, at least to my knowledge.

But it can not be granted that a man may make a judgment about man. Existentialism spares him from any such judgment. The existentialist will never consider man as an end because he is always in the making. Nor should we believe that there is a mankind to which we might set up a cult in the manner of Auguste Comte.[v] The cult of mankind ends in the self-enclosed humanism of Comte, and, let it be said, of fascism. This kind of humanism we can do without.

But there is another meaning of humanism. Fundamentally it is this: man is constantly outside of himself; in projecting himself, in losing himself outside of himself, he makes for man's existing; and, on the other hand, it is by pursuing transcendent goals that he is able to exist; man, being this state of passing-beyond, and seizing upon things

iv   Marie Henri Beyle (1783–1842), wrote *The Charterhouse of Parma* under the name Stendhal, in which Sanseverina was a character.

v   Auguste Comte (1798–1857), most famous for his scientific philosophy of "positivism," developed the idea of a non-theistic religion of humanity, to be led by a scientific priesthood.

172

only as they bear upon this passing-beyond, is at the heart, at the center of this passing-beyond. There is no universe other than a human universe, the universe of human subjectivity. This connection between transcendency, as a constituent element of man – not in the sense that God is transcendent, out in the sense of passing beyond – and subjectivity, in the sense that man is not closed in on himself but is always present in a human universe, is what we call existentialism humanism. Humanism, because we remind man that there is no law-maker other than himself, and that in his forlornness he will decide by himself; because we point out that man will fulfill himself as man, not in turning toward himself, but in seeking outside of himself a goal which is just this liberation, just this particular fulfillment.

From these few reflections it is evident that nothing is more unjust than the objections that have been raised against us. Existentialism is nothing else than an attempt to draw all the consequences of a coherent atheistic position. It isn't trying to plunge man into despair at all. But if one calls every attitude of unbelief despair, like the Christians, then the word is not being used in its original sense. Existentialism isn't so atheistic that it wears itself out showing that God doesn't exist. Rather, it declares that even if God did exist, that would change nothing. There you've got our point of view. Not that we believe that God exists, but we think that the problem of His existence is not the issue. In this sense existentialism is optimistic, a doctrine of action, and it is plain dishonesty for Christians to make no distinction between their own despair and ours and then to call us despairing.

23

"Letter on Humanism"

Martin Heidegger

Martin Heidegger (1889–1976), Husserl's replacement at the University of Freiburg, took phenomenology in an existentialist direction in his great early work, *Being and Time* (1927). In it he sought to investigate nothing less than the meaning of Being itself (crucially distinct from *beings* or things) through an analysis of the mode of Being characteristic of human being (*Dasein*, as he called us), an analysis marked by the theme of resoluteness in the face of Being-towards-death and historical destiny. His philosophy subsequently moved in an increasingly anti-humanist direction, for which the task of thinking Being meant a rejection of the subjectivism and anthropocentrism characteristic of modern thought and the modern technological domination of the world. In 1933 these philosophical themes took embodied form when Heidegger agreed to give his loyalty to the new National Socialist regime by becoming a party member in order to assume the rectorship of the university, and by publicly identifying Hitler and the Nazi Party with Germany's special destiny. Even after the war Heidegger never recanted these views, but merely ceased to speak of them. His "Letter on Humanism" (1947), written in response to a letter from a young French philosopher, is a direct repudiation of Sartre's existentialism. Heidegger insists that a true humanism, which can arise only when we abandon traditional philosophical thinking, would understand man's essence as his "proximity" to Being, would make man the "shepherd" of Being rather than its engineer or overseer.

We are still far from pondering the essence of action decisively enough. We view action only as causing an effect. The actuality of the effect is valued according to its utility. But the essence of action is accomplishment. To accomplish means to unfold something into the fulness of its essence, to lead it forth into this fulness – *producere*. Therefore only what already is can really be accomplished. But what "is" above all is Being.[i] Thinking accomplishes the relation of Being to the essence of man. It does not make or cause the relation. Thinking brings this relation to Being solely as something handed over to it from Being. Such offering consists in the fact that in thinking Being comes to language: Language is the house of Being. In its home man dwells. Those who think and those who create with words are the guardians of this home. Their guardianship accomplishes the manifestation of Being insofar as they bring the manifestation to language and maintain it in language through their speech. Thinking does not become action only because some effect issues from it or because it is applied. Thinking acts insofar as it thinks. Such action is presumably the simplest and at the same time the highest, because it concerns the relation of Being to man. But all working or effecting lies in Being and is directed toward beings. Thinking,

[i] Being (*Sein*) is to be contrasted with beings (*seiende*) or entities. Heidegger's aim, since his early work *Being and Time* (*Sein und Zeit*, 1927), is to think the meaning of Being without reducing Being to beings.

Martin Heidegger, "Letter on Humanism" from *Martin Heidegger: Basic Writings* (trans. Frank A. Capuzzi, with J. Glenn Gray and David Farrell Krell, ed. David Farrell Krell), pp. 193–242. New York: Harper & Row, 1977.

in contrast, lets itself be claimed by Being so that it can say the truth of Being. Thinking accomplishes this letting. Thinking is *l'engagement par l'Être pour l'Être*.[ii] I do not know whether it is linguistically possible to say both of these ("*par*" and "*pour*") at once, in this way: *penser, c'est l'engagement de l'Être*.[iii] Here the possessive form "*de L'...*" is supposed to express both subjective and objective genitive. In this regard "subject" and "object" are inappropriate terms of metaphysics, which very early on in the form of Occidental "logic" and "grammar" seized control of the interpretation of language. We today can only begin to descry what is concealed in that occurrence. The liberation of language from grammar into a more original essential framework is reserved for thought and poetic creation. Thinking is not merely *l'engagement dans l'action*[iv] for and by beings, in the sense of the actuality of the present situation. Thinking is *l'engagement* by and for the truth of Being. The history of Being is never past but stands ever before; it sustains and defines every *condition et situation humaine*.[v] In order to learn how to experience the aforementioned essence of thinking purely, and that means at the same time to carry it through, we must free ourselves from the technical interpretation of thinking. The beginnings of that interpretation reach back to Plato and Aristotle. They take thinking itself to be a *technē*, a process of reflection in service to doing and making. But here reflection is already seen from the perspective of *praxis* and *poiēsis*.[vi] For this reason thinking, when taken for itself, is not "practical." The characterization of thinking as *theōria* and the determination of knowing as "theoretical" behavior occur already within the "technical" interpretation of thinking. Such characterization is a reactive attempt to rescue thinking and preserve its autonomy over against acting and doing. Since then "philosophy" has been in the constant predicament of having to justify its existence before the "sciences." It believes it can do that most effectively by elevating itself to the rank of a science. But such an effort is the abandonment of the essence of thinking. Philosophy is hounded by the fear that it loses prestige and validity if it is not a science. Not to

be a science is taken as a failing which is equivalent to being unscientific. Being, as the element of thinking, is abandoned by the technical interpretation of thinking. "Logic," beginning with the Sophists and Plato, sanctions this explanation. Thinking is judged by a standard that does not measure up to it. Such judgment may be compared to the procedure of trying to evaluate the nature and powers of a fish by seeing how long it can live on dry land. For a long time now, all too long, thinking has been stranded on dry land. Can then the effort to return thinking to its element be called "irrationalism"?

Surely the questions raised in your letter would have been better answered in direct conversation. In written form thinking easily loses its flexibility. But in writing it is difficult above all to retain the multidimensionality of the realm peculiar to thinking. The rigor of thinking, in contrast to that of the sciences, does not consist merely in an artificial, that is, technical-theoretical exactness of concepts. It lies in the fact that speaking remains purely in the element of Being and lets the simplicity of its manifold dimensions rule. On the other hand, written composition exerts a wholesome pressure toward deliberate linguistic formulation. Today I would like to grapple with only one of your questions. Perhaps its discussion will also shed some light on the others.

You ask: *Comment redonner un sens au mot "Humanisme"?*[vii] This question proceeds from your intention to retain the word "humanism." I wonder whether that is necessary. Or is the damage caused by all such terms still not sufficiently obvious? True, "-isms" have for a long time now been suspect. But the market of public opinion continually demands new ones. We are always prepared to supply the demand. Even such names as "logic," "ethics," and "physics" begin to flourish only when original thinking comes to an end. During the time of their greatness the Greeks thought without such headings. They did not even call thinking "philosophy." Thinking comes to an end when it slips out of its element. The element is what enables thinking to be a thinking. The element is what properly enables: the enabling. It embraces thinking and so brings it into its essence. Said plainly, thinking is the thinking of Being. The genitive says something twofold. Thinking is of Being inasmuch as thinking, coming to pass from Being, belongs to Being. At the same time thinking is of Being insofar as thinking,

---

[ii]   Engagement by Being for Being.

[iii]   Thinking is the engagement of Being.

[iv]   Engagement in action.

[v]   Human condition and situation.

[vi]   *Praxis* is Greek for "action," *poiēsis* for "making," and below, *theōria* for "theoretical cognition."

[vii]   How can we restore meaning to the word "humanism"?

belonging to Being, listens to Being. As the belonging to Being that listens, thinking is what it is according to its essential origin. Thinking *is* – this says: Being has fatefully embraced its essence. To embrace a "thing" or a "person" in its essence means to love it, to favor it. Thought in a more original way such favoring means to bestow essence as a gift. Such favoring is the proper essence of enabling, which not only can achieve this or that but also can let something essentially unfold in its provenance, that is, let it be. It is on the "strength" of such enabling by favoring that something is properly able to be. This enabling is what is properly "possible," that whose essence resides in favoring. From this favoring Being enables thinking. The former makes the latter possible. Being is the enabling-favoring, the "may be." As the element, Being is the "quiet power" of the favoring-enabling, that is, of the possible. Of course, our words *möglich* and *Möglichkeit*,[viii] under the dominance of "logic" and "metaphysics," are thought solely in contrast to "actuality"; that is, they are thought on the basis of a definite – the metaphysical – interpretation of Being as *actus* and *potentia*, a distinction identified with the one between *existentia* and *essentia*.[ix] When I speak of the "quiet power of the possible" I do not mean the *possibile* of a merely represented *possibilitas*, nor *potentia* as the *essentia* of an *actus* of *existentia*; rather, I mean Being itself, which in its favoring presides over thinking and hence over the essence of humanity, and that means over its relation to Being. To enable something here means to preserve it in its essence, to maintain it in its element.

When thinking comes to an end by slipping out of its element it replaces this loss by procuring a validity for itself as *technē*,[x] as an instrument of education and therefore as a classroom matter and later a cultural concern. By and by philosophy becomes a technique for explaining from highest causes. One no longer thinks; one occupies himself with "philosophy." In competition with one another, such occupations publicly offer themselves as "-isms" and try to offer more than the others. The dominance of such terms is not accidental. It rests above all in the modern age upon the peculiar dictatorship of the public realm. However, so-called "private existence" is not really essential, that is to say free, human being. It simply insists

on negating the public realm. It remains an offshoot that depends upon the public and nourishes itself by a mere withdrawal from it. Hence it testifies, against its own will, to its subservience to the public realm. But because it stems from the dominance of subjectivity the public realm itself is the metaphysically conditioned establishment and authorization of the openness of individual beings in their unconditional objectification. Language thereby falls into the service of expediting communication along routes where objectification – the uniform accessibility of everything to everyone – branches out and disregards all limits. In this way language comes under the dictatorship of the public realm which decides in advance what is intelligible and what must be rejected as unintelligible. What is said in *Being and Time* (1927), sections 27 and 35, about the "they" in no way means to furnish an incidental contribution to sociology. Just as little does the "they" mean merely the opposite, understood in an ethical-existentiell way, of the selfhood of persons. Rather, what is said there contains a reference, thought in terms of the question of the truth of Being, to the word's primordial belongingness to Being. This relation remains concealed beneath the dominance of subjectivity that presents itself as the public realm. But if the truth of Being has become thought-provoking for thinking, then reflection on the essence of language must also attain a different rank. It can no longer be a mere philosophy of language. That is the only reason *Being and Time* (section 34) contains a reference to the essential dimension of language and touches upon the simple question as to what mode of Being language as language in any given case has. The widely and rapidly spreading devastation of language not only undermines aesthetic and moral responsibility in every use of language; it arises from a threat to the essence of humanity. A merely cultivated use of language is still no proof that we have as yet escaped the danger to our essence. These days, in fact, such usage might sooner testify that we have not yet seen and cannot see the danger because we have never yet placed ourselves in view of it. Much bemoaned of late, and much too lately, the downfall of language is, however, not the grounds for, but already a consequence of, the state of affairs in which language under the dominance of the modern metaphysics of subjectivity almost irremediably falls out of its element. Language still denies us its essence: that it is the house of the truth of Being. Instead, language surrenders itself to our mere willing and trafficking as an instrument of domination over

---

viii   Possible and possibility, respectively.

ix   These Latin terms mean, respectively, act or actuality, potentiality, existence, and essence.

x   Greek term for productive art or skill.

beings. Beings themselves appear as actualities in the interaction of cause and effect. We encounter beings as actualities in a calculative business-like way, but also scientifically and by way of philosophy, with explanations and proofs. Even the assurance that something is inexplicable belongs to these explanations and proofs. With such statements we believe that we confront the mystery. As if it were already decided that the truth of Being lets itself at all be established in causes and explanatory grounds or, what comes to the same, in their incomprehensibility.

But if man is to find his way once again into the nearness of Being he must first learn to exist in the nameless. In the same way he must recognize the seductions of the public realm as well as the impotence of the private. Before he speaks man must first let himself be claimed again by Being, taking the risk that under this claim he will seldom have much to say. Only thus will the preciousness of its essence be once more bestowed upon the word, and upon man a home for dwelling in the truth of Being.

But in the claim upon man, in the attempt to make man ready for this claim, is there not implied a concern about man? Where else does "care" tend but in the direction of bringing man back to his essence? What else does that in turn betoken but that man (*homo*) become human (*humanus*)? Thus *humanitas* really does remain the concern of such thinking. For this is humanism: meditating and caring, that man be human and not inhumane, "inhuman," that is, outside his essence. But in what does the humanity of man consist? It lies in his essence.

But whence and how is the essence of man determined? Marx demands that "man's humanity" be recognized and acknowledged. He finds it in "society." "Social" man is for him "natural" man. In "society" the "nature" of man, that is, the totality of "natural needs" (food, clothing, reproduction, economic sufficiency) is equably secured. The Christian sees the humanity of man, the *humanitas* of *homo*, in contradistinction to *Deitas*. He is the man of the history of redemption who as a "child of God" hears and accepts the call of the Father in Christ. Man is not of this world, since the "world," thought in terms of Platonic theory, is only a temporary passage to the beyond.

Humanitas, explicitly so called, was first considered and striven for in the age of the Roman Republic. *Homo humanus* was opposed to *homo barbarus*. *Homo humanus* here means the Romans,

who exalted and honored Roman *virtus* through the "embodiment" of the *paideia*[xi] taken over from the Greeks. These were the Greeks of the Hellenistic age, whose culture was acquired in the schools of philosophy. It was concerned with *eruditio et institutio in bonas artes*.[xii] *Paideia* thus understood was translated as *humanitas*. The genuine *romanitas* of *homo romanus* consisted in such *humanitas*. We encounter the first humanism in Rome: it therefore remains in essence a specifically Roman phenomenon which emerges from the encounter of Roman civilization with the culture of late Greek civilization. The so-called Renaissance of the fourteenth and fifteenth centuries in Italy is a *renascentia romanitatis*. Because *romanitas* is what matters, it is concerned with *humanitas* and therefore with Greek *paideia*. But Greek civilization is always seen in its later form and this itself is seen from a Roman point of view. The *homo romanus* of the Renaissance also stands in opposition to *homo barbarus*. But now the in-humane is the supposed barbarism of gothic Scholasticism in the Middle Ages. Therefore a *studium humanitatis*, which in a certain way reaches back to the ancients and thus also becomes a revival of Greek civilization, always adheres to historically understood humanism. For Germans this is apparent in the humanism of the eighteenth century supported by Winckelmann, Goethe, and Schiller. On the other hand, Hölderlin does not belong to "humanism" precisely because he thought the destiny of man's essence in a more original way than "humanism" could.[xiii]

But if one understands humanism in general as a concern that man become free for his humanity and find his worth in it, then humanism differs according to one's conception of the "freedom" and "nature" of man. So too are there various paths toward the realization of such conceptions. The humanism of Marx does not need to return to antiquity any more than the humanism which Sartre conceives existentialism to be. In this broad sense Christianity too is a humanism, in that according to its teaching everything depends on man's salvation (*salus aeterna*); the history of man appears in the context of the history of redemption. However different these forms of humanism may

---

xi   Education.

xii Learning and training in good conduct.

xiii Johann Christian Friedrich Hölderlin (1770–1843), German poet, regarded by Heidegger as a predecessor, in contrast to historian Johann Winckelmann (1717–68), poet Friedrich Schiller (1757–1805), and Goethe.

be in purpose and in principle, in the mode and means of their respective realizations, and in the form of their teaching, they nonetheless all agree in this, that the *humanitas* of *homo humanus* is determined with regard to an already established interpretation of nature, history, world, and the ground of the world, that is, of beings as a whole.

Every humanism is either grounded in a metaphysics or is itself made to be the ground of one. Every determination of the essence of man that already presupposes an interpretation of being without asking about the truth of Being, whether knowingly or not, is metaphysical. The result is that what is peculiar to all metaphysics, specifically with respect to the way the essence of man is determined, is that it is "humanistic." Accordingly, every humanism remains metaphysical. In defining the humanity of man humanism not only does not ask about the relation of Being to the essence of man; because of its metaphysical origin humanism even impedes the question by neither recognizing nor understanding it. On the contrary, the necessity and proper form of the question concerning the truth of Being, forgotten in and through metaphysics, can come to light only if the question "What is metaphysics?" is posed in the midst of metaphysics' domination. Indeed every inquiry into Being, even the one into the truth of Being, must at first introduce its inquiry as a "metaphysical" one.

The first humanism, Roman humanism, and every kind that has emerged from that time to the present, has presupposed the most universal "essence" of man to be obvious. Man is considered to be an *animal rationale*. This definition is not simply the Latin translation of the Greek *zōon logon echon*[xiv] but rather a metaphysical interpretation of it. This essential definition of man is not false. But it is conditioned by metaphysics. The essential provenance of metaphysics, and not just its limits, became questionable in *Being and Time*. What is questionable is above all commended to thinking as what is to be thought, but not at all left to the gnawing doubts of an empty skepticism.

Metaphysics does indeed represent beings in their Being, and so it thinks the Being of beings. But it does not think the difference of both.[1] Metaphysics does not ask about the truth of Being itself. Nor does it therefore ask in what way the essence of man belongs to the truth of Being. Metaphysics has not only failed up to now to ask this question, the question is inaccessible to metaphysics as such.

Being is still waiting for the time when it will become thought-provoking to man. With regard to the definition of man's essence, however one may determine the *ratio* of the *animal* and the reason of the living being, whether as a "faculty of principles," or a "faculty of categories," or in some other way, the essence of reason is always and in each case grounded in this: for every apprehending of beings in their Being, Being itself is already illumined and comes to pass in its truth. So too with *animal, zōon*, an interpretation of "life" is already posited which necessarily lies in an interpretation of beings as *zōē* and *physis*, within which what is living appears. Above and beyond everything else, however, it finally remains to ask whether the essence of man primordially and most decisively lies in the dimension of *animalitas* at all. Are we really on the right track toward the essence of man as long as we set him off as one living creature among others in contrast to plants, beasts, and God? We can proceed in that way; we can in such fashion locate man within being as one being among others. We will thereby always be able to state something correct about man. But we must be clear on this point, that when we do this we abandon man to the essential realm of *animalitas* even if we do not equate him with beasts but attribute a specific difference to him. In principle we are still thinking of *homo animalis* – even when *anima* is posited as *animus sive mens*,[xv] and this in turn is later posited as subject, person, or spirit. Such positing is the manner of metaphysics. But then the essence of man is too little heeded and not thought in its origin, the essential provenance that is always the essential future for historical mankind. Metaphysics thinks of man on the basis of *animalitas* and does not think in the direction of his *humanitas*.

Metaphysics closes itself to the simple essential fact that man essentially occurs only in his essence, where he is claimed by Being. Only from that claim "has" he found that wherein his essence dwells. Only from this dwelling "has" he "language" as the home that preserves the ecstatic for his essence. Such standing in the lighting of Being I call the ek-sistence of man.[xvi] This way of Being is proper only to man. Ek-sistence so understood is not only

---

[xiv] Literally, animal logical being.

[xv] *Anima* is Latin for "soul"; *animus sive mens* means "spirit or mind."

[xvi] Heidegger is playing on the relation of "existence" and the Greek *ekstasis*, meaning to be outside of oneself (as in "ecstasy"). For a human being, to exist is to be out in the world, not closed up inside a subjective Cartesian ego.

the ground of the possibility of reason, *ratio*, but is also that in which the essence of man preserves the source that determines him.

Ek-sistence can be said only of the essence of man, that is, only of the human way "to be." For as far as our experience shows, only man is admitted to the destiny of ek-sistence. Therefore ek-sistence can also never be thought of as a specific kind of living creature among others – granted that man is destined to think the essence of his Being and not merely to give accounts of the nature and history of his constitution and activities. Thus even what we attribute to man as *animalitas* on the basis of the comparison with "beast" is itself grounded in the essence of ek-sistence. The human body is something essentially other than an animal organism. Nor is the error of biologism overcome by adjoining a soul to the human body, a mind to the soul, and the existentiell to the mind, and then louder than before singing the praises of the mind – only to let everything relapse into "life-experience," with a warning that thinking by its inflexible concepts disrupts the flow of life and that thought of Being distorts existence. The fact that physiology and physiological chemistry can scientifically investigate man as an organism is no proof that in this "organic" thing, that is, in the body scientifically explained, the essence of man consists. That has as little validity as the notion that the essence of nature has been discovered in atomic energy. It could even be that nature, in the face she turns toward man's technical mastery, is simply concealing her essence. Just as little as the essence of man consists in being an animal organism can this insufficient definition of man's essence be overcome or offset by outfitting man with an immortal soul, the power of reason, or the character of a person. In each instance essence is passed over, and passed over on the basis of the same metaphysical projection.

What man is – or, as it is called in the traditional language of metaphysics, the "essence" of man – lies in his ek-sistence. But ek-sistence thought in this way is not identical with the traditional concept of *existentia*, which means actuality in contrast to the meaning of *essentia* as possibility. In *Being and Time* this sentence is italicized: "The 'essence' of Dasein lies in its existence." However, here the opposition between *existentia* and *essentia* is not under consideration, because neither of these metaphysical determinations of Being, let alone their relationship, is yet in question. Still less does the sentence contain a universal statement about *Dasein*, since the word came into fashion in the eighteenth century as a name for "object," intending to express the metaphysical concept of the actuality of the actual. On the contrary, the sentence says: man occurs essentially in such a way that he is the "there", that is, the lighting of Being.[xvii] The "Being" of the *Da*, and only it, has the fundamental character of ek-sistence, that is, of an ecstatic inherence in the truth of Being. The ecstatic essence of man consists in ek-sistence, which is different from the metaphysically conceived *existentia*. Medieval philosophy conceives the latter as *actualitas*. Kant represents *existentia* as actuality in the sense of the objectivity of experience. Hegel defines *existentia* as the self-knowing Idea of absolute subjectivity. Nietzsche grasps *existentia* as the eternal recurrence of the same. Here it remains an open question whether through *existentia* – in these explanations of it as actuality, which at first seem quite different – the Being of a stone or even life as the Being of plants and animals is adequately thought. In any case living creatures are as they are without standing outside their Being as such and within the truth of Being, preserving in such standing the essential nature of their Being. Of all the beings that are, presumably the most difficult to think about are living creatures, because on the one hand they are in a certain way most closely related to us, and on the other are at the same time separated from our ek-sistent essence by an abyss. However, it might also seem as though the essence of divinity is closer to us than what is foreign in other living creatures, closer, namely, in an essential distance which however distant is nonetheless more familiar to our ek-sistent essence than is our appalling and scarcely conceivable bodily kinship with the beast. Such reflections cast a strange light upon the current and therefore always still premature designation of man as *animal rationale*. Because plants and animals are lodged in their respective environments but are never placed freely in the lighting of Being which alone is "world," they lack language. But in being denied language they are not thereby suspended worldlessly in their environment. Still, in this word "environment" converges all that is puzzling about living creatures. In its essence

---

[xvii] *Dasein*, literally "there-being," is Heidegger's term for human being. It indicates that we are always *there*, thrown into and vulnerable to the world. He also describes this "there-ness" (or *Da*) as *Lichtung*, a word meaning both light and a forest clearing. Dasein's there-ness is a place where things are lighted or revealed.

language is not the utterance of an organism; nor is it the expression of a living thing. Nor can it ever be thought in an essentially correct way in terms of its symbolic character, perhaps not even in terms of the character of signification. Language is the lighting-concealing advent of Being itself.[xviii]

Ek-sistence, thought in terms of *ecstasis*, does not coincide with *existentia* in either form or content. In terms of content ek-sistence means standing out into the truth of Being. *Existentia* (*existence*) means in contrast *actualitas*, actuality as opposed to mere possibility as Idea. Ek-sistence identifies the determination of what man is in the destiny of truth. *Existentia* is the name for the realization of something that is as it appears in its Idea. The sentence "Man ek-sists" is not an answer to the question of whether man actually is or not; rather, it responds to the question concerning man's "essence." We are accustomed to posing this question with equal impropriety whether we ask what man is or who he is. For in the *Who?* or the *What?* we are already on the lookout for something like a person or an object. But the personal no less than the objective misses and misconstrues the essential unfolding of ek-sistence in the history of Being. That is why the sentence cited from *Being and Time* is careful to enclose the word "essence" in quotation marks. This indicates that "essence" is now being defined from neither *esse essentiae* nor *esse existentiae*[xix] but rather from the ek-static character of Dasein. As ek-sisting, man sustains Da-sein in that he takes the *Da*, the lighting of Being, into "care." But Da-sein itself occurs essentially as "thrown." It unfolds essentially in the throw of Being as the fateful sending.

But it would be the ultimate error if one wished to explain the sentence about man's ek-sistent essence as if it were the secularized transference to human beings of a thought that Christian theology expresses about God (*Deus est suum esse*);[xx] for ek-sistence is not the realization of an essence, nor does ek-sistence itself even effect and posit what is essential. If we understand what *Being and Time* calls "projection" as a representational positing, we take it to be an achievement of subjectivity and do not

think it in the only way the "understanding of Being" in the context of the "existential analysis" of "being-in-the-world" can be thought – namely as the ecstatic relation to the lighting of Being. The adequate execution and completion of this other thinking that abandons subjectivity is surely made more difficult by the fact that in the publication of *Being and Time* the third division of the first part, "Time and Being," was held back.

Here everything is reversed. The section in question was held back because thinking failed in the adequate saying of this turning and did not succeed with the help of the language of metaphysics.[xxi] The lecture "On the Essence of Truth," thought out and delivered in 1930 but not printed until 1943, provides a certain insight into the thinking of the turning from "Being and Time" to "Time and Being." This turning is not a change of standpoint from *Being and Time*, but in it the thinking that was sought first arrives at the location of that dimension out of which *Being and Time* is experienced, that is to say, experienced from the fundamental experience of the oblivion of Being.

By way of contrast, Sartre expresses the basic tenet of existentialism in this way: Existence precedes essence. In this statement he is taking *existentia* and *essentia* according to their metaphysical meaning, which from Plato's time on has said that *essentia* precedes *existentia*. Sartre reverses this statement. But the reversal of a metaphysical statement remains a metaphysical statement. With it he stays with metaphysics in oblivion of the truth of Being. For even if philosophy wishes to determine the relation of *essentia* and *existentia* in the sense it had in medieval controversies, in Leibniz's sense, or in some other way, it still remains to ask first of all from what destiny of Being this differentiation in Being as *esse essentiae* and *esse existentiae* comes to appear to thinking! We have yet to consider why the question about the destiny of Being was never asked and why it could never be thought. Or is the fact that this is how it is with the differentiation of *essentia* and *existentia* not at all a sign of forgetfulness of Being? We must presume that this destiny does not rest upon a mere failure of human thinking, let alone upon a lesser capacity of early Western thinking. Concealed in its essential provenance, the differentiation of *essentia* (essentiality) and *existentia* (actuality) completely dominates the des-

---

[xviii] Rather than think of the mind as knowing or not knowing Being, Heidegger thinks of Being as revealing and concealing itself. Being grants unconcealment; it is not a passive object for the human subject.

[xix] Essential being and existing being, respectively.

[xx] God is His being.

[xxi] Heidegger is describing a major change ("turn") in his thinking. "On Time and Being" (below) was a late essay of Heidegger's.

tiny of Western history and of all history determined by Europe.

Sartre's key proposition about the priority of *existentia* over *essentia* does, however, justify using the name "existentialism" as an appropriate title for a philosophy of this sort. But the basic tenet of "existentialism" has nothing at all in common with the statement from *Being and Time* – apart from the fact that in *Being and Time* no statement about the relation of *essentia* and *existentia* can yet be expressed since there it is still a question of preparing something precursory. As is obvious from what we have just said, that happens clumsily enough. What still today remains to be said could perhaps become an impetus for guiding the essence of man to the point where it thoughtfully attends to that dimension of the truth of Being which thoroughly governs it. But even this could take place only to the honor of Being and for the benefit of Dasein which man ek-sistingly sustains; not, however, for the sake of man so that civilization and culture through man's doings might be vindicated.

But in order that we today may attain to the dimension of the truth of Being in order to ponder it, we should first of all make clear how Being concerns man and how it claims him. Such an essential experience happens to us when it dawns on us that man is in that he ek-sists. Were we now to say this in the language of the tradition, it would run: the ek-sistence of man is his substance. That is why in *Being and Time* the sentence often recurs, "The 'substance' of man is existence." But "substance," thought in terms of the history of Being, is already a blanket translation of *ousia*, a word that designates the presence of what is present and at the same time, with puzzling ambiguity, usually means what is present itself. If we think the metaphysical term "substance" in the sense already suggested in accordance with the "phenomenological destruction" carried out in *Being and Time*, then the statement "The 'substance' of man is ek-sistence" says nothing else but that the way that man in his proper essence becomes present to Being is ecstatic inherence in the truth of Being.[xxii] Through this determination of the essence of man the humanistic interpretations of man as *animal rationale*, as "person," as spiritual-ensouled-bodily being, are not declared false and thrust aside. Rather, the sole

implication is that the highest determinations of the essence of man in humanism still do not realize the proper dignity of man. To that extent the thinking in *Being and Time* is against humanism. But this opposition does not mean that such thinking aligns itself against the humane and advocates the inhuman, that it promotes the inhumane and deprecates the dignity of man. Humanism is opposed because it does not set the *humanitas* of man high enough. Of course the essential worth of man does not consist in his being the substance of beings, as the "Subject" among them, so that as the tyrant of Being he may deign to release the beingness of beings into an all too loudly bruited "objectivity."

Man is rather "thrown" from Being itself into the truth of Being, so that ek-sisting in this fashion he might guard the truth of Being, in order that beings might appear in the light of Being as the beings they are. Man does not decide whether and how beings appear, whether and how God and the gods or history and nature come forward into the lighting of Being, come to presence and depart. The advent of beings lies in the destiny of Being. But for man it is ever a question of finding what is fitting in his essence which corresponds to such destiny; for in accord with this destiny man as ek-sisting has to guard the truth of Being. Man is the shepherd of Being. It is in this direction alone that *Being and Time* is thinking when ecstatic existence is experienced as "care."

Yet Being – what is Being? It is It itself. The thinking that is to come must learn to experience that and to say it. "Being" – that is not God and not a cosmic ground. Being is farther than all beings and is yet nearer to man than every being, be it a rock, a beast, a work of art, a machine, be it an angel or God. Being is the nearest. Yet the near remains farthest from man. Man at first clings always and only to beings. But when thinking represents beings as beings it no doubt relates itself to Being. In truth, however, it always thinks only of beings as such; precisely not, and never, Being as such. The "question of Being" always remains a question about beings. It is still not at all what its elusive name indicates: the question in the direction of Being. Philosophy, even when it becomes "critical" through Descartes and Kant, always follows the course of metaphysical representation. It thinks from beings back to beings with a glance in passing toward Being. For every departure from beings and every return to them stands already in the light of Being.

[xxii] "Truth" for Heidegger means "unconcealment" (the literal meaning of the ancient Greek word for truth, *aletheia*).

But metaphysics recognizes the lighting of Being either solely as the view of what is present in "outward appearance" (*idea*) or critically as what is seen as a result of categorial representation on the part of subjectivity. This means that the truth of Being as the lighting itself remains concealed for metaphysics. However, this concealment is not a defect of metaphysics but a treasure withheld from it yet held before it, the treasure of its own proper wealth. But the lighting itself is Being. Within the destiny of Being in metaphysics the lighting first affords a view by which what is present comes into touch with man, who is present to it, so that man himself can in apprehending (*noein*) first touch upon Being (*thigein*, Aristotle, *Met.* IX, 10). This view first gathers the aspect to itself. It yields to such aspects when apprehending has become a setting-forth-before-itself in the *perceptio* of the *res cogitans* taken as the *subiectum* of *certitudo*.[xxiii]

But how – provided we really ought to ask such a question at all – how does Being relate to ek-sistence? Being itself is the relation to the extent that It, as the location of the truth of Being amid beings, gathers to itself and embraces ek-sistence in its existential, that is, ecstatic, essence. Because man as the one who ek-sists comes to stand in this relation that Being destines for itself, in that he ecstatically sustains it, that is, in care takes it upon himself, he at first fails to recognize the nearest and attaches himself to the next nearest. He even thinks that this is the nearest. But nearer than the nearest and at the same time for ordinary thinking farther than the farthest is nearness itself: the truth of Being.

Forgetting the truth of Being in favor of the pressing throng of beings unthought in their essence is what ensnarement means in *Being and Time*.[xxiv] This word does not signify the Fall of Man understood in a "moral-philosophical" and at the same time secularized way; rather, it designates an essential relationship of man to Being within Being's relation to the essence of man. Accordingly, the terms "authenticity" and "inauthenticity," which are used in a provisional fashion, do not imply a moral-existentiell or an "anthropological" distinction but rather a relation which, because it has been hitherto concealed from philo-sophy, has yet to be thought for the first time, an "ecstatic" relation of the essence of man to the truth of Being. But this relation is as it is not by reason of ek-sistence; on the contrary, the essence of ek-sistence derives existentially–ecstatically from the essence of the truth of Being.

The one thing thinking would like to attain and for the first time tries to articulate in *Being and Time* is something simple. As such, Being remains mysterious, the simple nearness of an unobtrusive governance. The nearness occurs essentially as language itself. But language is not mere speech, insofar as we represent the latter at best as the unity of phoneme (or written character), melody, rhythm, and meaning (or sense). We think of the phoneme and written character as a verbal body for language, of melody and rhythm as its soul, and whatever has to do with meaning as its mind. We usually think of language as corresponding to the essence of man represented as *animal rationale*, that is, as the unity of body–soul–mind. But just as ek-sistence – and through it the relation of the truth of Being to man – remains veiled in the humanitas of *homo animalis*, so does the metaphysical-animal explanation of language cover up the essence of language in the history of Being. According to this essence language is the house of Being which comes to pass from Being and is pervaded by Being. And so it is proper to think the essence of language from its correspondence to Being and indeed as this correspondence, that is, as the home of man's essence.

But man is not only a living creature who possesses language along with other capacities. Rather, language is the house of Being in which man ek-sists by dwelling, in that he belongs to the truth of Being, guarding it.

So the point is that in the determination of the humanity of man as ek-sistence what is essential is not man but Being – as the dimension of the *ecstasis* of ek-sistence. However, the dimension is not something spatial in the familiar sense. Rather, everything spatial and all space–time occur essentially in the dimensionality which Being itself is.

Thinking attends to these simple relationships. It tries to find the right word for them within the long traditional language and grammar of metaphysics. But does such thinking – granted that there is something in a name – still allow itself to be described as humanism? Certainly not so far as humanism thinks metaphysically. Certainly not if humanism is existentialism and is represented by what Sartre expresses: *précisément nous sommes sur*

(182)

un plan où il y a seulement des hommes.[xxv] Thought from *Being and Time*, this should say instead: *précisément nous sommes sur un plan où il y a principalement l'Être.*[xxvi] But where does *le plan* come from and what is it? *L'Être* and *le plan* are the same. In *Being and Time* we purposely and cautiously say, *il y a l'Être*: "there is / it gives Being."[xxvii] *Il y a* translates "it gives" imprecisely. For the "it" that here "gives" is Being itself. The "gives" names the essence of Being that is giving, granting its truth. The self-giving into the open, along with the open region itself, is Being itself.

At the same time "it gives" is used preliminarily to avoid the locution "Being is"; for "is" is commonly said of some thing which is. We call such a thing a being. But Being "is" precisely not "a being." If "is" is spoken without a closer interpretation of Being, then Being is all too easily represented as a "being" after the fashion of the familiar sort of beings which act as causes and are actualized as effects. And yet Parmenides, in the early age of thinking, says, *esti gar einai*, "for there is Being." The primal mystery for all thinking is concealed in this phrase. Perhaps "is" can be said only of Being in an appropriate way, so that no individual being ever properly "is." But because thinking should be directed only toward saying Being in its truth instead of explaining it as a particular being in terms of beings, whether and how Being is must remain an open question for the careful attention of thinking.

The *esti gar einai* of Parmenides is still unthought today. That allows us to gauge how things stand with the progress of philosophy. When philosophy attends to its essence it does not make forward strides at all. It remains where it is in order constantly to think the Same. Progression, that is, progression forward from this place, is a mistake that follows thinking as the shadow which thinking itself casts. Because Being is still unthought, *Being and Time* too says of it, "there is / it gives." Yet one cannot speculate about this *il y a* precipitously and without a foothold. This "there is / it gives" rules as the destiny of Being. Its history comes to language in the words of essential thinkers. Therefore the thinking that thinks into the truth of Being is,

as thinking, historical. There is not a "systematic" thinking and next to it an illustrative history of past opinions. Nor is there, as Hegel thought, only a systematics which can fashion the law of its thinking into the law of history and simultaneously subsume history into the system. Thought in a more primordial way, there is the history of Being to which thinking belongs as recollection of this history that unfolds of itself. Such recollective thought differs essentially from the subsequent presentation of history in the sense of an evanescent past. History does not take place primarily as a happening. And its happening is not evanescence. The happening of history occurs essentially as the destiny of the truth of Being and from it.[2] Being comes to destiny in that It, Being, gives itself. But thought in terms of such destiny this says: it gives itself and refuses itself simultaneously. Nonetheless, Hegel's definition of history as the development of "Spirit" is not untrue. Neither is it partly correct and partly false. It is as true as metaphysics, which through Hegel first brings to language its essence – thought in terms of the absolute – in the system. Absolute metaphysics, with its Marxian and Nietzschean inversions, belongs to the history of the truth of Being. Whatever stems from it cannot be countered or even cast aside by refutations. It can only be taken up in such a way that its truth is more primordially sheltered in Being itself and removed from the domain of mere human opinion. All refutation in the field of essential thinking is foolish. Strife among thinkers is the "lovers' quarrel" concerning the matter itself. It assists them mutually toward a simple belonging to the Same, from which they find what is fitting for them in the destiny of Being.

Assuming that in the future man will be able to think the truth of Being, he will think from ek-sistence. Man stands ek-sistingly in the destiny of Being. The ek-sistence of man is historical as such, but not only or primarily because so much happens to man and to things human in the course of time. Because it must think the ek-sistence of Da-sein, the thinking of *Being and Time* is essentially concerned that the historicity of Dasein be experienced.

But does not *Being and Time* say, where the "there is / it gives" comes to language, "Only so long as Dasein is, is there Being"? To be sure. It means that only so long as the lighting of Being comes to pass does Being convey itself to man. But the fact that the *Da*, the lighting as the truth of Being itself, comes to pass is the dispensation of Being itself. This is the destiny of the lighting. But the

---

[xxv]   We are precisely in a situation where there are only human beings.
[xxvi]   We are precisely in a situation where there is principally Being.
[xxvii]   In German *es gibt* means literally, "it gives," but is used to mean "there is."

sentence does not mean that the Dasein of man in the traditional sense of *existentia*, and thought in modern philosophy as the actuality of the *ego cogito*, is that being through which Being is first fashioned. The sentence does not say that Being is the product of man. The "Introduction" to *Being and Time* says simply and clearly, even in italics, "Being is the *transcendens* pure and simple." Just as the openness of spatial nearness seen from the perspective of a particular thing exceeds all things near and far, so is Being essentially broader than all beings, because it is the lighting itself. For all that, Being is thought on the basis of beings, a consequence of the approach – at first unavoidable – within a metaphysics that is still dominant. Only from such a perspective does Being show itself in and as a transcending.

The introductory definition, "Being is the *transcendens* pure and simple," articulates in one simple sentence the way the essence of Being hitherto has illumined man. This retrospective definition of the essence of Being from the lighting of beings as such remains indispensable for the prospective approach of thinking toward the question concerning the truth of Being. In this way thinking attests to its essential unfolding as destiny. It is far from the arrogant presumption that wishes to begin anew and declares all past philosophy false. But whether the definition of Being as the *transcendens* pure and simple really does express the simple essence of the truth of Being – this and this alone is the primary question for a thinking that attempts to think the truth of Being. That is why we also say that how Being *is* is to be understood chiefly from its "meaning," that is, from the truth of Being. Being is illumined for man in the ecstatic projection. But this projection does not create Being.

Moreover, the projection is essentially a thrown projection. What throws in projection is not man but Being itself, which sends man into the ek-sistence of Da-sein that is his essence. This destiny comes to pass as the lighting of Being, as which it is. The lighting grants nearness to Being. In this nearness, in the lighting of the *Da*, man dwells as the ek-sisting one without yet being able properly to experience and take over this dwelling. In the lecture on Hölderlin's elegy "Homecoming" (1943) this nearness "of" Being, which the *Da* of Dasein is, is thought on the basis of *Being and Time*; it is perceived as spoken from the minstrel's poem; from the experience of the oblivion of Being it is called the "homeland." The word is thought here in an essential sense, not patriotically or nationalistically but in terms of the history of Being. The essence of the homeland, however, is also mentioned with the intention of thinking the homelessness of contemporary man from the essence of Being's history. Nietzsche was the last to experience this homelessness. From within metaphysics he was unable to find any other way out than a reversal of metaphysics. But that is the height of futility. On the other hand, when Hölderlin composes "Homecoming" he is concerned that his "countrymen" find their essence. He does not at all seek that essence in an egoism of his nation. He sees it rather in the context of a belongingness to the destiny of the West. But even the West is not thought regionally as the Occident in contrast to the Orient, nor merely as Europe, but rather world-historically out of nearness to the source. We have still scarcely begun to think of the mysterious relations to the East which found expression in Hölderlin's poetry.[3] "German" is not spoken to the world so that the world might be reformed through the German essence; rather, it is spoken to the Germans so that from a fateful belongingness to the nations they might become world-historical along with them.[4] The homeland of this historical dwelling is nearness to Being.

In such nearness, if at all, a decision may be made as to whether and how God and the gods withhold their presence and the night remains, whether and how the day of the holy dawns, whether and how in the upsurgence of the holy an epiphany of God and the gods can begin anew. But the holy, which alone is the essential sphere of divinity, which in turn alone affords a dimension for the gods and for God, comes to radiate only when Being itself beforehand and after extensive preparation has been illuminated and is experienced in its truth. Only thus does the overcoming of homelessness begin from Being, a homelessness in which not only man but the essence of man stumbles aimlessly about.

Homelessness so understood consists in the abandonment of Being by beings. Homelessness is the symptom of oblivion of Being. Because of it the truth of Being remains unthought. The oblivion of Being makes itself known indirectly through the fact that man always observes and handles only beings. Even so, because man cannot avoid having some notion of Being, it is explained merely as what is "most general" and therefore as something that encompasses beings, or as a creation of the infinite being, or as the product of a finite subject. At the same time "Being" has long stood for "beings" and, inversely, the latter for the former, the two of them caught in a curious and still unraveled confusion.

As the destiny that sends truth, Being remains concealed. But the world's destiny is heralded in poetry, without yet becoming manifest as the history of Being. The world-historical thinking of Hölderlin that speaks out in the poem "Remembrance" is therefore essentially more primordial and thus more significant for the future than the mere cosmopolitanism of Goethe. For the same reason Hölderlin's relation to Greek civilization is something essentially other than humanism. When confronted with death, therefore, those young Germans who knew about Hölderlin lived and thought something other than what the public held to be the typical German attitude.

Homelessness is coming to be the destiny of the world. Hence it is necessary to think that destiny in terms of the history of Being. What Marx recognized in an essential and significant sense, though derived from Hegel, as the estrangement of man has its roots in the homelessness of modern man. This homelessness is specifically evoked from the destiny of Being in the form of metaphysics and through metaphysics is simultaneously entrenched and covered up as such. Because Marx by experiencing estrangement attains an essential dimension of history, the Marxist view of history is superior to that of other historical accounts. But since neither Husserl nor – so far as I have seen till now – Sartre recognizes the essential importance of the historical in Being, neither phenomenology nor existentialism enters that dimension within which a productive dialogue with Marxism first becomes possible.

For such dialogue it is certainly also necessary to free oneself from naïve notions about materialism, as well as from the cheap refutations that are supposed to counter it. The essence of materialism does not consist in the assertion that everything is simply matter but rather in a metaphysical determination according to which every being appears as the material of labor. The modern metaphysical essence of labor is anticipated in Hegel's *Phenomenology of Spirit* as the self-establishing process of unconditioned production, which is the objectification of the actual through man experienced as subjectivity. The essence of materialism is concealed in the essence of technology, about which much has been written but little has been thought. Technology is in its essence a destiny within the history of Being and of the truth of Being, a truth that lies in oblivion. For technology does not go back to the *technē* of the Greeks in name only but derives historically and essentially from *technē* as a mode of *alētheuein*, a mode, that is, of rendering beings manifest. As a form of truth technology is grounded in the history of metaphysics, which is itself a distinctive and up to now the only perceptible phase of the history of Being. No matter which of the various positions one chooses to adopt toward the doctrines of communism and to their foundation, from the point of view of the history of Being it is certain that an elemental experience of what is world-historical speaks out in it. Whoever takes "communism" only as a "party" or a "Weltanschauung" is thinking too shallowly, just as those who by the term "Americanism" mean, and mean derogatorily, nothing more than a particular lifestyle. The danger into which Europe as it has hitherto existed is ever more clearly forced consists presumably in the fact above all that its thinking – once its glory – is falling behind in the essential course of a dawning world destiny which nevertheless in the basic traits of its essential provenance remains European by definition. No metaphysics, whether idealistic, materialistic, or Christian, can in accord with its essence, and surely not in its own attempts to explicate itself, "get a hold on" this destiny yet, and that means thoughtfully to reach and gather together what in the fullest sense of Being now is.

In the face of the essential homelessness of man, man's approaching destiny reveals itself to thought on the history of Being in this, that man find his way into the truth of Being and set out on this find. Every nationalism is metaphysically an anthropologism, and as such subjectivism. Nationalism is not overcome through mere internationalism; it is rather expanded and elevated thereby into a system. Nationalism is as little brought and raised to *humanitas* by internationalism as individualism is by an ahistorical collectivism. The latter is the subjectivity of man in totality. It completes subjectivity's unconditioned self-assertion, which refuses to yield. Nor can it be even adequately experienced by a thinking that mediates in a one-sided fashion. Expelled from the truth of Being, man everywhere circles round himself as the *animal rationale*.

But the essence of man consists in his being more than merely human, if this is represented as "being a rational creature." "More" must not be understood here additively as if the traditional definition of man were indeed to remain basic, only elaborated by means of an existentiell postscript. The "more" means: more originally and therefore more essentially in terms of his essence. But here something enigmatic manifests itself: man is in throwness. This means that man, as the ek-sisting counter-throw of Being, is more than *animal rationale* precisely to the extent that he is less bound up with man conceived from subjectivity. Man is not the lord of beings. Man is the shepherd of Being. Man loses nothing in this "less"; rather, he gains in that he attains the truth of Being. He gains the essential poverty of the shepherd, whose dignity consists in being called by Being itself into the preservation of Being's truth. The call comes as the throw from which the thrownness of Da-sein derives. In his essential unfolding within the history of Being, man is the being whose Being as ek-sistence consists in his dwelling in the nearness of Being. Man is the neighbor of Being.

But – as you no doubt have been wanting to rejoin for quite a while now – does not such thinking think precisely the *humanitas* of *homo humanus*? Does it not think *humanitas* in a decisive sense, as no metaphysics has thought it or can think it? Is this not "humanism" in the extreme sense? Certainly. It is a humanism that thinks the humanity of man from nearness to Being. But at the same time it is a humanism in which not man but man's historical essence is at stake in its provenance from the truth of Being. But then doesn't the ek-sistence of man also stand or fall in this game of stakes? So it does.

In *Being and Time* it is said that every question of philosophy "recoils upon existence." But existence here is not the actuality of the *ego cogito*. Neither is it the actuality of subjects who act with and for each other and so become who they are. "Ek-sistence," in fundamental contrast to every *existentia* and "*existence*," is ecstatic dwelling in the nearness of Being. It is the guardianship, that is, the care for Being. Because there is something simple to be thought in this thinking it seems quite difficult to the representational thought that has been transmitted as philosophy. But the difficult is not a matter of indulging in a special sort of profundity and of building complicated concepts; rather, it is concealed in the step back that lets thinking enter into a questioning that experiences – and lets the habitual opining of philosophy fall away.

It is everywhere supposed that the attempt in *Being and Time* ended in a blind alley. Let us not comment any further upon that opinion. The thinking that hazards a few steps in *Being and Time* has even today not advanced beyond that publication. But perhaps in the meantime it has in one respect come farther into its own matter. However, as long as philosophy merely busies itself with continually obstructing the possibility of admittance into the matter for thinking, i.e. into the

truth of Being, it stands safely beyond any danger of shattering against the hardness of that matter. Thus to "philosophize" about being shattered is separated by a chasm from a thinking that is shattered. If such thinking were to go fortunately for a man no misfortune would befall him. He would receive the only gift that can come to thinking from Being.

But it is also the case that the matter of thinking is not achieved in the fact that talk about the "truth of Being" and the "history of Being" is set in motion. Everything depends upon this alone, that the truth of Being come to language and that thinking attain to this language. Perhaps, then, language requires much less precipitous expression than proper silence. But who of us today would want to imagine that his attempts to think are at home on the path of silence? At best, thinking could perhaps point toward the truth of Being, and indeed toward it as what is to be thought. It would thus be more easily weaned from mere supposing and opining and directed to the now rare handicraft of writing. Things that really matter, although they are not defined for all eternity, even when they come very late still come at the right time.

Whether the realm of the truth of Being is a blind alley or whether it is the free space in which freedom conserves its essence is something each one may judge after he himself has tried to go the designated way, or even better, after he has gone a better way, that is, a way befitting the question. On the penultimate page of *Being and Time* stand the sentences: "The *conflict* with respect to the interpretation of Being (that is, therefore, not the interpretation of beings or of the Being of man) cannot be settled, *because it has not yet been kindled.* And in the end it is not a question of 'picking a quarrel,' since the kindling of the conflict does demand some preparation. To this end alone the foregoing investigation is under way." Today after two decades these sentences still hold. Let us also in the days ahead remain as wanderers on the way into the neighborhood of Being. The question you pose helps to clarify the way.

You ask, *Comment redonner un sens au mot "Humanisme"?* "How can some sense be restored to the word 'humanism'?" Your question not only presupposes a desire to retain the word "humanism" but also contains an admission that this word has lost its meaning.

It has lost it through the insight that the essence of humanism is metaphysical, which now means that metaphysics not only does not pose the question concerning the truth of Being but also obstructs the question, insofar as metaphysics persists in the oblivion of Being. But the same thinking that has led us to this insight into the questionable essence of humanism has likewise compelled us to think the essence of man more primordially. With regard to this more essential *humanitas* of *homo humanus* there arises the possibility of restoring to the word "humanism" a historical sense that is older than its oldest meaning chronologically reckoned. The restoration is not to be understood as though the word "humanism" were wholly without meaning and a mere *flatus vocis*.[xxviii] The "*humanum*" in the word points to *humanitas*, the essence of man; the "-ism" indicates that the essence of man is meant to be taken essentially. This is the sense that the word "humanism" has as such. To restore a sense to it can only mean to redefine the meaning of the word. That requires that we first experience the essence of man more primordially; but it also demands that we show to what extent this essence in its own way becomes fateful. The essence of man lies in ek-sistence. That is what is essentially – that is, from Being itself – at issue here, insofar as Being appropriates man as ek-sisting for guardianship over the truth of Being into this truth itself. "Humanism" now means, in case we decide to retain the word, that the essence of man is essential for the truth of Being, specifically in such a way that the word does not pertain to man simply as such. So we are thinking a curious kind of "humanism." The word results in a name that is a *lucus a non lucendo*.[xxix]

Should we still keep the name "humanism" for a "humanism" that contradicts all previous humanism – although it in no way advocates the inhuman? And keep it just so that by sharing in the use of the name we might perhaps swim in the predominant currents, stifled in metaphysical subjectivism and submerged in oblivion of Being? Or should thinking, by means of open resistance to "humanism," risk a shock that could for the first time cause perplexity concerning the *humanitas* of *homo humanus* and its basis? In this way it could awaken a reflection – if the world-historical moment did not itself already compel such a reflection – that thinks not only about man but also about the "nature" of man, not only about his nature but even more primordially about the dimension in which the essence of man, determined by Being

itself, is at home. Should we not rather suffer a little while longer those inevitable misinterpretations to which the path of thinking in the element of Being and Time has hitherto been exposed and let them slowly dissipate? These misinterpretations are natural reinterpretations of what was read, or simply mirrorings of what one believes he knows already before he reads. They all betray the same structure and the same foundation.

Because we are speaking against "humanism" people fear a defense of the inhuman and a glorification of barbaric brutality. For what is more "logical" than that for somebody who negates humanism nothing remains but the affirmation of inhumanity?

Because we are speaking against "logic" people believe we are demanding that the rigor of thinking be renounced and in its place the arbitrariness of drives and feelings be installed and thus that "irrationalism" be proclaimed as true. For what is more "logical" than that whoever speaks against the logical is defending the alogical?

Because we are speaking against "values" people are horrified at a philosophy that ostensibly dares to despise humanity's best qualities. For what is more "logical" than that a thinking that denies values must necessarily pronounce everything valueless?

Because we say that the Being of man consists in "being-in-the-world" people find that man is downgraded to a merely terrestrial being, whereupon philosophy sinks into positivism. For what is more "logical" than that whoever asserts the worldliness of human being holds only this life as valid, denies the beyond, and renounces all "Transcendence"?

Because we refer to the world of Nietzsche on the "death of God" people regard such a gesture as atheism. For what is more "logical" than that whoever has experienced the death of God is godless?

Because in all the respects mentioned we everywhere speak against all that humanity deems high and holy our philosophy teaches an irresponsible and destructive "nihilism." For what is more "logical" than that whoever roundly denies what is truly in being puts himself on the side of nonbeing and thus professes the pure nothing as the meaning of reality?

What is going on here? People hear talk about "humanism," "logic," "values," "world," and "God." They hear something about opposition to these. They recognize and accept these things as positive. But with hearsay – in a way that is not strictly deliberate – they immediately assume that

---

[xxviii] Empty sound.
[xxix] A grove that no light reaches.

what speaks against something is automatically its negation and that this is "negative" in the sense of destructive. And somewhere in *Being and Time* there is explicit talk of "the phenomenological destruction." With the assistance of logic and *ratio* – so often invoked – people come to believe that whatever is not positive is negative and thus that it seeks to degrade reason – and therefore deserves to be branded as depravity. We are so filled with "logic" that anything that disturbs the habitual somnolence of prevailing opinion is automatically registered as a despicable contradiction. We pitch everything that does not stay close to the familiar and beloved positive into the previously excavated pit of pure negation which negates everything, ends in nothing, and so consummates nihilism. Following this logical course we let everything expire in a nihilism we invented for ourselves with the aid of logic.

But does the "against" which a thinking advances against ordinary opinion necessarily point toward pure negation and the negative? This happens – and then, to be sure, happens inevitably and conclusively, that is, without a clear prospect of anything else – only when one posits in advance what is meant by the "positive" and on this basis makes an absolute and absolutely negative decision about the range of possible opposition to it. Concealed in such a procedure is the refusal to subject to reflection this presupposed "positive" in which one believes himself saved, together with its position and opposition. By continually appealing to the logical one conjures up the illusion that he is entering straightforwardly into thinking when in fact he has disavowed it.

It ought to be somewhat clearer now that opposition to "humanism" in no way implies a defense of the inhuman but rather opens other vistas.

"Logic" understands thinking to be the representation of beings in their Being, which representation proposes to itself in the generality of the concept. But how is it with meditation on Being itself, that is, with the thinking that thinks the truth of Being? This thinking alone reaches the primordial essence of *logos* which was already obfuscated and lost in Plato and in Aristotle, the founder of "logic." To think against "logic" does not mean to break a lance for the illogical but simply to trace in thought the *logos* and its essence which appeared in the dawn of thinking, that is, to exert ourselves for the first time in preparing for such reflection. Of what value are even far-reaching systems of logic to us if, without really knowing what they are doing,

they recoil before the task of simply inquiring into the essence of *logos*? If we wished to bandy about objections, which is of course fruitless, we could say with more right: irrationalism, as a denial of *ratio*, rules unnoticed and uncontested in the defense of "logic," which believes it can eschew meditation on *logos* and on the essence of *ratio* which has its ground in *logos*.

To think against "values" is not to maintain that everything interpreted as "a value" – "culture," "art," "science," "human dignity," "world," and "God" – is valueless. Rather, it is important finally to realize that precisely through the characterization of something as "a value" what is so valued is robbed of its worth. That is to say, by the assessment of something as a value what is valued is admitted only as an object for man's estimation. But what a thing is in its Being is not exhausted by its being an object, particularly when objectivity takes the form of value. Every valuing, even where it values positively, is a subjectivizing. It does not let beings: be. Rather, valuing lets beings: be valid – solely as the objects of its doing. The bizarre effort to prove the objectivity of values does not know what it is doing. When one proclaims "God" the altogether "highest value," this is a degradation of God's essence. Here as elsewhere thinking in values is the greatest blasphemy imaginable against Being. To think against values therefore does not mean to beat the drum for the valuelessness and nullity of beings. It means rather to bring the lighting of the truth of Being before thinking, as against subjectivizing beings into mere objects.

The reference to "being-in-the-world" as the basic trait of the *humanitas* of *homo humanus* does not assert that man is merely a "worldly" creature understood in a Christian sense, thus a creature turned away from God and so cut loose from "Transcendence." What is really meant by this word could be more clearly called "the transcendent." The transcendent is supersensible being. This is considered the highest being in the sense of the first cause of all beings. God is thought as this first cause. However, in the name "being-in-the-world," "world" does not in any way imply earthly as opposed to heavenly being, nor the "worldly" as opposed to the "spiritual." For us "world" does not at all signify beings or any realm of beings but the openness of Being. Man is, and is man, insofar as he is the ek-sisting one. He stands out into the openness of Being. Being itself, which as the throw has projected the essence of man into "care," is as this openness. Thrown in such fashion, man stands "in" the openness of Being. "World" is the lighting of Being into which man stands out on the basis of his thrown essence. "Being-in-the-world" designates the essence of ek-sistence with regard to the lighted dimension out of which the "ek-" of ek-sistence essentially unfolds. Thought in terms of ek-sistence, "world" is in a certain sense precisely "the beyond" within existence and for it. Man is never first and foremost man on the hither side of the world, as a "subject," whether this is taken as "I" or "We." Nor is he ever simply a mere subject which always simultaneously is related to objects, so that his essence lies in the subject–object relation. Rather, before all this, man in his essence is ek-sistent into the openness of Being, into the open region that lights the "between" within which a "relation" of subject to object can "be."

The statement that the essence of man consists in being-in-the-world likewise contains no decision about whether man in a theologico-metaphysical sense is merely a this-worldly or an other-worldly creature.

With the existential determination of the essence of man, therefore, nothing is decided about the "existence of God" or his "nonbeing," no more than about the possibility or impossibility of gods. Thus it is not only rash but also an error in procedure to maintain that the interpretation of the essence of man from the relation of his essence to the truth of Being is atheism. And what is more, this arbitrary classification betrays a lack of careful reading. No one bothers to notice that in the article *Vom Wesen des Grundes*[xxx] the following appears: "Through the ontological interpretation of Dasein as being-in-the-world no decision, whether positive or negative, is made concerning a possible being toward God. It is, however, the case that through an illumination of transcendence we first achieve an *adequate concept of Dasein*, with respect to which it can now be asked how the relationship of Dasein to God is ontologically ordered."[5] If we think about this remark too quickly, as is usually the case, we will declare that such a philosophy does not decide either for or against the existence of God. It remains stalled in indifference. Thus it is unconcerned with the religious question. Such indifferentism ultimately falls prey to nihilism.

But does the foregoing observation teach indifferentism? Why then are particular words in the note italicized – and not just random ones? For no other reason than to indicate that the thinking that thinks from the question concerning the truth of Being questions more primordially than metaphysics can. Only from the truth of Being can the essence of the holy be thought. Only from the essence of the holy is the essence of divinity to be thought. Only in the light of the essence of divinity can it be thought or said what the word "God" is to signify. Or should we not first be able to hear and understand all these words carefully if we are to be permitted as men, that is, as ek-sistent creatures, to experience a relation of God to man? How can man at the present stage of world history ask at all seriously and rigorously whether the god nears or withdraws, when he has above all neglected to think into the dimension in which alone that question can be asked? But this is the dimension of the holy, which indeed remains closed as a dimension if the open region of Being is not lighted and in its lighting is near man. Perhaps what is distinctive about this world-epoch consists in the closure of the dimension of the hale.[xxxi] Perhaps that is the sole malignancy.

But with this reference the thinking that points toward the truth of Being as what is to be thought has in no way decided in favor of theism. It can be theistic as little as atheistic. Not, however, because of an indifferent attitude, but out of respect for the boundaries that have been set for thinking as such, indeed set by what gives itself to thinking as what is to be thought, by the truth of Being. Insofar as thinking limits itself to its task it directs man at the present moment of the world's destiny into the primordial dimension of his historical abode. When thinking of this kind speaks the truth of Being it has entrusted itself to what is more essential than all values and all types of beings. Thinking does not overcome metaphysics by climbing still higher, surmounting it, transcending it somehow or other; thinking overcomes metaphysics by climbing back down into the nearness of the nearest. The descent, particularly where man has strayed into subjectivity, is more arduous and more dangerous than the ascent. The descent leads to the poverty of the ek-sistence of *homo humanus*. In ek-sistence the region of *homo animalis*, of metaphysics, is abandoned. The dominance of that region is the mediate and deeply rooted basis for the blindness and arbitrariness of what is called "biologism," but also of what

---

[xxx] Heidegger's 1929 essay, *On the Essence of Reasons*.

[xxxi] *Hale* means fortunate, graced, or even lucky. The German is *des Heilen*, which shares a common root with "holy" (*das Heilig*) and "malignancy" (*Unheil*).

(189)

is known under the heading "pragmatism." To think the truth of Being at the same time means to think the humanity of *homo humanus*. What counts is *humanitas* in the service of the truth of Being, but without humanism in the metaphysical sense.

But if *humanitas* must be viewed as so essential to the thinking of Being, must not "ontology" therefore be supplemented by "ethics"? Is not that effort entirely essential which you express in the sentence *"Ce que je cherche à faire, depuis longtemps déjà, c'est préciser le rapport de l'ontologie avec une éthique possible"?*[xxxii]

Soon after *Being and Time* appeared a young friend asked me, "When are you going to write an ethics?" Where the essence of man is thought so essentially, i.e. solely from the question concerning the truth of Being, but still without elevating man to the center of beings, a longing necessarily awakens for a peremptory directive and for rules that say how man, experienced from ek-sistence toward Being, ought to live in a fitting manner. The desire for an ethics presses ever more ardently for fulfilment as the obvious no less than the hidden perplexity of man soars to immeasurable heights. The greatest care must be fostered upon the ethical bond at a time when technological man, delivered over to mass society, can be kept reliably on call only by gathering and ordering all his plans and activities in a way that corresponds to technology.

Who can disregard our predicament? Should we not safeguard and secure the existing bonds even if they hold human beings together ever so tenuously and merely for the present? Certainly. But does this need ever release thought from the task of thinking what still remains principally to be thought and, as Being prior to all beings, is their guarantor and their truth? Even further, can thinking refuse to think Being after the latter has lain hidden so long in oblivion but at the same time has made itself known in the present moment of world history by the uprooting of all beings?

Before we attempt to determine more precisely the relationship between "ontology" and "ethics" we must ask what "ontology" and "ethics" themselves are. It becomes necessary to ponder whether what can be designated by both terms still remains near and proper to what is assigned to thinking, which as such has to think above all the truth of Being.

Of course if both "ontology" and "ethics," along with all thinking in terms of disciplines, become untenable, and if our thinking therewith becomes more disciplined, how then do matters stand with the question about the relation between these two philosophical disciplines?

Along with "logic" and "physics," "ethics" appeared for the first time in the school of Plato. These disciplines arose at a time when thinking was becoming "philosophy," philosophy, *epistēmē* (science), and science itself a matter for schools and academic pursuits. In the course of a philosophy so understood, science waxed and thinking waned. Thinkers prior to this period knew neither a "logic" nor an "ethics" nor "physics." Yet their thinking was neither illogical nor immoral. But they did think *physis*[xxxiii] in a depth and breadth that no subsequent "physics" was ever again able to attain. The tragedies of Sophocles – provided such a comparison is at all permissible – preserve the *ēthos* in their sagas more primordially than Aristotle's lectures on "ethics." A saying of Heraclitus which consists of only three words says something so simply that from it the essence of the *ēthos* immediately comes to light.

The saying of Heraclitus (Frag. 119) goes: *ēthos anthrōpōi daimōn*. This is usually translated, "A man's character is his daimon." This translation thinks in a modern way, not a Greek one. *Ēthos* means abode, dwelling place. The word names the open region in which man dwells. The open region of his abode allows what pertains to man's essence, and what in thus arriving resides in nearness to him, to appear. The abode of man contains and preserves the advent of what belongs to man in his essence. According to Heraclitus' phrase this is *daimōn*, the god. The fragment says: Man dwells, insofar as he is man, in the nearness of god. A story that Aristotle reports (*De parte animalium*, 1, 5, 645a 17) agrees with this fragment of Heraclitus.

The story is told of something Heraclitus said to some strangers who wanted to come visit him. Having arrived, they saw him warming himself at a stove. Surprised, they stood there in consternation – above all because he encouraged them, the astounded ones, and called for them to come in with the words, "For here too the gods are present."

[xxxii] "What I have been trying to do for a long time already is to specify the relation of ontology to a possible ethics."

[xxxiii] Nature, physical processes.

The story certainly speaks for itself, but we may stress a few aspects.

The group of foreign visitors, in their importunate curiosity about the thinker, are disappointed and perplexed by their first glimpse of his abode. They believe they should meet the thinker in circumstances which, contrary to the ordinary round of human life, everywhere bear traces of the exceptional and rare and so of the exciting. The group hopes that in their visit to the thinker they will find things that will provide material for entertaining conversation – at least for a while. The foreigners who wish to visit the thinker expect to catch sight of him perchance at that very moment when, sunk in profound meditation, he is thinking. The visitors want this "experience" not in order to be overwhelmed by thinking but simply so they can say they saw and heard someone everybody says is a thinker.

Instead of this the sightseers find Heraclitus by a stove. That is surely a common and insignificant place. True enough, bread is baked here. But Heraclitus is not even busy baking at the stove. He stands there merely to warm himself. In this altogether everyday place he betrays the whole poverty of his life. The vision of a shivering thinker offers little of interest. At this disappointing spectacle even the curious lose their desire to come any closer. What are they supposed to do here? Such an everyday and unexciting occurrence – somebody who is chilled warming himself at a stove – anyone can find any time at home. So why look up a thinker? The visitors are on the verge of going away again. Heraclitus reads the frustrated curiosity in their faces. He knows that for the crowd the failure of an expected sensation to materialize is enough to make those who have just arrived leave. He therefore encourages them. He invites them explicitly to come in with the words *Einai gar kai entautha theous*, "Here too the gods are present."

This phrase places the abode (*ēthos*) of the thinker and his deed in another light. Whether the visitors understood this phrase at once – or at all – and then saw everything differently in this other light the story doesn't say. But the story was told and has come down to us today because what it reports derives from and characterizes the atmosphere surrounding this thinker. *Kai entautha*, "even here," at the stove, in that ordinary place where every thing and every condition, each deed and thought is intimate and commonplace, that is, familiar [*geheuer*], "even there" in the sphere of the familiar, *einai theous*, it is the case that "the gods are present."

Heraclitus himself says, *ēthos anthrōpōi daimōn*, "The (familiar) abode is for man the open region for the presencing of god (the unfamiliar one)."

If the name "ethics," in keeping with the basic meaning of the word *ēthos*, should now say that "ethics" ponders the abode of man, then that thinking which thinks the truth of Being as the primordial element of man, as one who ek-sists, is in itself the original ethics. However, this thinking is not ethics in the first instance, because it is ontology. For ontology always thinks solely the being (*on*) in its Being. But as long as the truth of Being is not thought all ontology remains without its foundation. Therefore the thinking which in *Being and Time* tries to advance thought in a preliminary way into the truth of Being characterizes itself as "fundamental ontology." It strives to reach back into the essential ground from which thought concerning the truth of Being emerges. By initiating another inquiry this thinking is already removed from the "ontology" of metaphysics (even that of Kant). "Ontology" itself, however, whether transcendental or precritical, is subject to criticism, not because it thinks the Being of beings and thereby reduces Being to a concept, but because it does not think the truth of Being and so fails to recognize that there is a thinking more rigorous than the conceptual. In the poverty of its first breakthrough, the thinking that tries to advance thought into the truth of Being brings only a small part of that wholly other dimension to language. This language is still faulty insofar as it does not yet succeed in retaining the essential help of phenomenological seeing and in dispensing with the inappropriate concern with "science" and "research." But in order to make the attempt at thinking recognizable and at the same time understandable for existing philosophy, it could at first be expressed only within the horizon of that existing philosophy and its use of current terms.

In the meantime I have learned to see that these very terms were bound to lead immediately and inevitably into error. For the terms and the conceptual language corresponding to them were not rethought by readers from the matter particularly to be thought; rather, the matter was conceived according to the established terminology in its customary meaning. The thinking that inquires into the truth of Being and so defines man's essential abode from Being and toward Being is neither ethics nor ontology. Thus the question about the relation of each to the other no longer has any basis in this sphere. Nonetheless, your question, thought in a more original way, retains a meaning and an essential importance.

For it must be asked: If the thinking that ponders the truth of Being defines the essence of *humanitas* as ek-sistence from the latter's belongingness to Being, then does thinking remain only a theoretical representation of Being and of man, or can we obtain from such knowledge directives that can be readily applied to our active lives?

The answer is that such thinking is neither theoretical nor practical. It comes to pass before this distinction. Such thinking is, insofar as it is, recollection of Being and nothing else. Belonging to Being, because thrown by Being into the preservation of its truth and claimed for such preservation, it thinks Being. Such thinking has no result. It has no effect. It satisfies its essence in that it is. But it is by saying its matter. Historically, only one Saying [*Sage*] belongs to the matter of thinking, the one that is in each case appropriate to its matter. Its material relevance is essentially higher than the validity of the sciences, because it is freer. For it lets Being – be.

Thinking builds upon the house of Being, the house in which the jointure of Being fatefully enjoins the essence of man to dwell in the truth of Being. This dwelling is the essence of "being-in-the-world." The reference in *Being and Time* (p. 54) to "being-in" as "dwelling" is no etymological game. The same reference in the 1936 essay on Hölderlin's verse, "Full of merit, yet poetically, man dwells on this earth," is no adornment of a thinking that rescues itself from science by means of poetry. The talk about the house of Being is no transfer of the image "house" to Being. But one day we will, by thinking the essence of Being in a way appropriate to its matter, more readily be able to think what "house" and "to dwell" are.

And yet thinking never creates the house of Being. Thinking conducts historical ek-sistence, that is, the *humanitas of homo humanus*, into the realm of the upsurgence of the healing.

With healing, evil appears all the more in the lighting of Being. The essence of evil does not consist in the mere baseness of human action but rather in the malice of rage. Both of these, however, healing and the raging, can essentially occur only in Being, insofar as Being itself is what is contested. In it is concealed the essential provenance of nihilation. What nihilates illuminates itself as the negative. This can be addressed in the "no." The "not"

in no way arises from the no-saying of negation. Every "no" that does not mistake itself as willful assertion of the positing power of subjectivity, but rather remains a letting-be of ek-sistence, answers to the claim of the nihilation illumined. Every "no" is simply the affirmation of the "not." Every affirmation consists in acknowledgment. Acknowledgment lets that toward which it goes come toward it. It is believed that nihilation is nowhere to be found in beings themselves. This is correct as long as one seeks nihilation as some kind of being, as an existing quality in beings. But in so seeking, one is not seeking nihilation. Neither is Being any existing quality which allows itself to be fixed among beings. And yet Being is more in being than any being. Because nihilation occurs essentially in Being itself we can never discern it as a being among beings. Reference to this impossibility never in any way proves that the origin of the not is no-saying. This proof appears to carry only if one posits beings as what is objective for subjectivity. From this alternative it follows that every "not," because it never appears as something objective, must inevitably be the product of a subjective act. But whether no-saying first posits the "not" as something merely thought, or whether nihilation first requires the "no" as what is to be said in the letting-be of beings – this can never be decided at all by a subjective reflection of a thinking already posited as subjectivity. In such a reflection we have not yet reached the dimension where the question can be appropriately formulated. It remains to ask, granting that thinking belongs to ek-sistence, whether every "yes" and "no" are not themselves already dependent upon Being. As these dependents, they can never first posit the very thing to which they themselves belong.

Nihilation unfolds essentially in Being itself, and not at all in the existence of man – so far as this is thought as the subjectivity of the *ego cogito*. Dasein in no way nihilates as a human subject who carries out nihilation in the sense of denial; rather, Da-sein nihilates inasmuch as it belongs to the essence of Being as that essence in which man ek-sists. Being nihilates – as Being. Therefore the "not" appears in the absolute Idealism of Hegel and Schelling as the negativity of negation in the essence of Being. But there Being is thought in the sense of absolute actuality as unconditioned will that wills itself and does so as the will of knowledge and of love. In this willing Being as will to power is still concealed. But just why the negativity of absolute subjectivity is "dialectical," and why nihilation comes to the fore through this dialectic but at the same time is veiled in its essence, cannot be discussed here.

The nihilating in Being is the essence of what I call the nothing. Hence because it thinks Being, thinking thinks the nothing.

To healing Being first grants ascent into grace; to raging its compulsion to malignancy.

Only so far as man, ek-sisting into the truth of Being, belongs to Being can there come from Being itself the assignment of those directions that must become law and rule for man. In Greek to assign is *nemein*. *Nomos* is not only law but more originally the assignment contained in the dispensation of Being. Only the assignment is capable of dispatching man into Being. Only such dispatching is capable of supporting and obligating. Otherwise all law remains merely something fabricated by human reason. More essential than instituting rules is that man find the way to his abode in the truth of Being. This abode first yields the experience of something we can hold on to. The truth of Being offers a hold for all conduct. "Hold" in our language means protective heed. Being is the protective heed that holds man in his ek-sistent essence to the truth of such protective heed – in such a way that it houses ek-sistence in language. Thus language is at once the house of Being and the home of human beings. Only because language is the home of the essence of man can historical mankind and human beings not be at home in their language, so that for them language becomes a mere container for their sundry preoccupations.

But now in what relation does the thinking of Being stand to theoretical and practical behavior? It exceeds all contemplation because it cares for the light in which a seeing, as *theoria*, can first live and move. Thinking attends to the lighting of Being in that it puts its saying of Being into language as the home of ek-sistence. Thus thinking is a deed. But a deed that also surpasses all *praxis*. Thinking towers above action and production, not through the grandeur of its achievement and not as a consequence of its effect, but through the humbleness of its inconsequential accomplishment.

For thinking in its saying merely brings the unspoken word of Being to language.

The usage "bring to language" employed here is now to be taken quite literally. Being comes, lighting itself, to language. It is perpetually under way to language. Such arriving in its turn brings ek-sisting thought to language in a saying. Thus language itself is raised into the lighting of Being. Language *is* only in this mysterious and yet for us always pervasive way. To the extent that language which has thus been brought fully into its essence is historical, Being is entrusted to recollection. Eksistence thoughtfully dwells in the house of Being. In all this it is as if nothing at all happens through thoughtful saying.

But just now an example of the inconspicuous deed of thinking manifested itself. For to the extent that we expressly think the usage "bring to language," which was granted to language, think only that and nothing further, to the extent that we retain this thought in the heedfulness of saying as what in the future continually has to be thought, we have brought something of the essential unfolding of Being itself to language.

What is strange in the thinking of Being is its simplicity. Precisely this keeps us from it. For we look for thinking – which has its world-historical prestige under the name "philosophy" – in the form of the unusual, which is accessible only to initiates. At the same time we conceive of thinking on the model of scientific knowledge and its research projects. We measure deeds by the impressive and successful achievements of *praxis*. But the deed of thinking is neither theoretical nor practical, nor is it the conjunction of these two forms of behavior.

Through its simple essence the thinking of Being makes itself unrecognizable to us. But if we become acquainted with the unusual character of the simple, then another plight immediately befalls us. The suspicion arises that such thinking of Being falls prey to arbitrariness; for it cannot cling to beings. Whence does thinking take its measure? What law governs its deed?

Here the third question of your letter must be entertained: *Comment sauver l'élément d'aventure que comporte toute recherche sans faire de la philosophie une simple aventurière?*[xxxiv] I shall mention poetry now only in passing. It is confronted by the same question, and in the same manner, as thinking. But Aristotle's words in the *Poetics*, although they have scarcely been pondered, are still valid – that poetic composition is truer than exploration of beings.

But thinking is an *aventure* not only as a search and an inquiry into the unthought. Thinking, in its essence as thinking of Being, is claimed by Being. Thinking is related to Being as what arrives

---

[xxxiv] How can we preserve the element of adventure that all research contains without making philosophy into a mere adventuress?

(*l'avenant*). Thinking as such is bound to the advent of Being, to Being as advent, Being has already been dispatched to thinking. Being *is* as the destiny of thinking. But destiny is in itself historical. Its history has already come to language in the saying of thinkers.

To bring to language ever and again this advent of Being which remains, and in its remaining waits for man, is the sole matter of thinking. For this reason essential thinkers always say the Same. But that does not mean the identical. Of course they say it only to him who undertakes to think back on them. Whenever thinking, in historical recollection, attends to the destiny of Being, it has already bound itself to what is fitting for it, in accord with its destiny. To flee into the identical is not dangerous. To risk discord in order to say the Same is the danger. Ambiguity threatens, and mere quarreling.

The fittingness of the saying of Being, as of the destiny of truth, is the first law of thinking – not the rules of logic which can become rules only on the basis of the law of Being. To attend to the fittingness of thoughtful saying does not only imply, however, that we contemplate at every turn *what* is to be said of Being and *how* it is to be said. It is equally essential to ponder *whether* what is to be thought is to be said – to what extent, at what moment of the history of Being, in what sort of dialogue with this history, and on the basis of what claim, it ought to be said. The threefold thing mentioned in an earlier letter is determined in its cohesion by the law of the fittingness of thought on the history of Being: rigor of meditation, carefulness in saying, frugality with words.

It is time to break the habit of overestimating philosophy and of thereby asking too much of it. What is needed in the present world crisis is less philosophy, but more attentiveness in thinking; less literature, but more cultivation of the letter.

The thinking that is to come is no longer philosophy, because it thinks more originally than metaphysics – a name identical to philosophy. However, the thinking that is to come can no longer, as Hegel demanded, set aside the name "love of wisdom" and become wisdom itself in the form of absolute knowledge. Thinking is on the descent to the poverty of its provisional essence. Thinking gathers language into simple saying. In this way language is the language of Being, as clouds are the clouds of the sky. With its saying, thinking lays inconspicuous furrows in language. They are still more inconspicuous than the furrows that the farmer, slow of step, draws through the field.

Author's Notes

1 Cf. Martin Heidegger, *Vom Wesen des Grundes* (1929) [*The Essence of Reasons*, trans. Terrence Malick (Evanston, Il: Norweston University Press, 1969)], p. 8; *Kant and the Problem of Metaphysics*, trans. J. Churchill (Bloomington, Ind.: Indiana University Press, 1962), p. 243; and *Being and Time*, section 44, p. 230.

2 See the lecture on Hölderlin's hymn, "Wie wenn am Feiertage…" in Martin Heidegger, *Erläuterungen zu Hölderlins Dichtung*, fourth, expanded edn (Frankfurt am Main: V. Klostermann, 1971), p. 76.

3 Cf. "The Ister" and "The Journey" [*Die Wanderung*], third stanza and ff. [In the translations by Michael Hamburger (Ann Arbor: University of Michigan Press, 1966), pp. 492ff. and 392ff.]

4 Cf. Hölderlin's poem "Remembrance" [*Andenken*] in the *Tübingen Memorial* (1943), p. 322. [Hamburger, pp. 488ff.]

5 Martin Heidegger, *Vom Wesen des Grundes*, p. 28 n. 1.

24

"The Mirror Stage as Formative of the Function of the I as Revealed in Psychoanalytic Experience"

Jacques Lacan

By applying structural linguistics to psychoanalytic theory, psychiatrist Jacques Lacan (1901–80) became the most important innovator in French psychoanalysis. Although he was expelled from the International Psychoanalytic Association – especially for adopting the clinical method of the "short session" which could be ended by the analyst at any moment – he greatly influenced French intellectual life through his heavily attended public lectures from 1953 through 1980. Claiming that the unconscious is structured like a language, he resisted, on the one hand, any form of biological determinism – in part by making unquenchable *desire*, not homeostatic need, the root of psychic phenomena – and on the other, any attempt to strengthen the ego, encouraging the patient to "adapt" to social convention – as practiced by "ego psychology." In his later work Lacan distinguished three orders of psychic relevance: *the imaginary*, a projected image of self-integration; *the symbolic*, or the realm of cultural signifiers, governed by a dominant sign, *the name of the Father*; and *the real*, which is the presupposed but unknown resistance to the imaginary and the symbolic, most relevant in the form of trauma. In the following essay, a 1949 version of his famous 1936 lecture, Lacan sketches an interpretation of the earliest stage of the imaginative construction of the self.

The conception of the mirror stage that I introduced at our last congress, thirteen years ago, has since become more or less established in the practice of the French group. However, I think it worthwhile to bring it again to your attention, especially today, for the light it sheds on the formation of the *I* as we experience it in psychoanalysis. It is an experience that leads us to oppose any philosophy directly issuing from the *Cogito*.

Some of you may recall that this conception originated in a feature of human behaviour illuminated by a fact of comparative psychology. The child, at an age when he is for a time, however short, outdone by the chimpanzee in instrumental intelligence, can nevertheless already recognize as such his own image in a mirror. This recognition is indicated in the illuminative mimicry of the *Aha-Erlebnis*,[i] which Köhler sees as the expression of situational apperception, an essential stage of the act of intelligence.

This act, far from exhausting itself, as in the case of the monkey, once the image has been mastered and found empty, immediately rebounds in the case of the child in a series of gestures in which he experiences in play the relation between the movements assumed in the image and the reflected environment, and between this virtual complex and the reality it reduplicates – the child's own body, and the persons and things, around him.

[i] The "Aha!-experience," referred to by Wolfgang Köhler (1887–1967), one of the creators of Gestalt Psychology.
[ii] James M. Baldwin (1861–1934), American Psychologist.

Jacques Lacan, "The Mirror Stage as Formative of the Function of the I as Revealed in Psychoanalytic Experience," in *Écrits: A Selection*, trans. byAlan Sheridan, NewYork: W.W. Norton & Company, 1977, chapter one, pp. 1–7.

This event can take place, as we have known since Baldwin,[ii] from the age of six months, and its repetition has often made me reflect upon the startling spectacle of the infant in front of the mirror. Unable as yet to walk, or even to stand up, and held tightly as he is by some support, human or artificial (what, in France, we call a '*trotte-bébé*'[iii]), he nevertheless overcomes, in a flutter of jubilant activity, the obstructions of his support and, fixing his attitude in a slightly leaning-forward position, in order to hold it in his gaze, brings back an instantaneous aspect of the image.

For me, this activity retains the meaning I have given it up to the age of eighteen months. This meaning discloses a libidinal dynamism, which has hitherto remained problematic, as well as an onto-logical structure of the human world that accords with my reflections on paranoiac knowledge.

We have only to understand the mirror stage *as an identification*, in the full sense that analysis gives to the term: namely, the transformation that takes place in the subject when he assumes an image – whose predestination to this phase-effect is suffi-ciently indicated by the use, in analytic theory, of the ancient term *imago*.[iv]

This jubilant assumption of his specular image by the child at the *infans* stage, still sunk in his motor incapacity and nursling dependence, would seem to exhibit in an exemplary situation the symbolic matrix in which the *I* is precipitated in a primordial form, before it is objectified in the dialectic of iden-tification with the other, and before language re-stores to it, in the universal, its function as subject.

This form would have to be called the Ideal-I,[1] if we wished to incorporate it into our usual register, in the sense that it will also be the source of second-ary identifications, under which term I would place the functions of libidinal normalization. But the important point is that this form situates the agency of the ego, before its social determination, in a fictional direction, which will always remain irre-ducible for the individual alone, or rather, which will only rejoin the coming-into-being (*le devenir*) of the subject asymptotically, whatever the suc-cess of the dialectical syntheses by which he must resolve as *I* his discordance with his own reality.

The fact is that the total form of the body by which the subject anticipates in a mirage the mat-uration of his power is given to him only as *Gestalt*, that is to say, in an exteriority in which this form is certainly more constituent than constituted, but in which it appears to him above all in a contrasting size (*un relief de stature*) that fixes it and in a sym-metry that inverts it, in contrast with the turbulent movements that the subject feels are animating him. Thus, this *Gestalt* – whose pregnancy should be regarded as bound up with the species, though its motor style remains scarcely recognizable – by these two aspects of its appearance, symbolizes the mental permanence of the *I*, at the same time as it prefigures its alienating destination; it is still preg-nant with the correspondences that unite the *I* with the statue in which man projects himself, with the phantoms that dominate him, or with the automa-ton in which, in an ambiguous relation, the world of his own making tends to find completion.

Indeed, for the *imagos* – whose veiled faces it is our privilege to see in outline in our daily experience and in the penumbra of symbolic efficacity[2] – the mirror-image would seem to be the threshold of the visible world, if we go by the mirror disposition that the *imago of one's own body* presents in hallucinations or dreams, whether it concerns its individual features, or even its infirmities, or its object-projections; or if we observe the role of the mirror apparatus in the appearances of the *double*, in which psychical realities, however heterogeneous, are manifested.

That a *Gestalt* should be capable of formative effects in the organism is attested by a piece of biological experimentation that is itself so alien to the idea of psychical causality that it cannot bring itself to formulate its results in these terms. It nevertheless recognizes that it is a necessary condi-tion for the maturation of the gonad of the female pigeon that it should see another member of its species, of either sex; so sufficient in itself is this condition that the desired effect may be obtained merely by placing the individual within reach of the field of reflection of a mirror. Similarly, in the case of the migratory locust, the transition within a generation from the solitary to the gregarious form can be obtained by exposing the individual, at a certain stage, to the exclusively visual action of a similar image, provided it is animated by move-ments of a style sufficiently close to that character-istic of the species. Such facts are inscribed in an order of homeomorphic identification that would itself fall within the larger question of the meaning of beauty as both formative and erogenic.

But the facts of mimicry are no less instruc-tive when conceived as cases of heteromorphic

---

[iii] "Baby-walker."

[iv] "Image", primarily visual but including feelings. For Lacan *imagos* are dissimulative. Hence the ego is based on *méconnaissance* (misunderstanding).

identification in as much as they raise the problem of the signification of space for the living organism – psychological concepts hardly seem less appropriate for shedding light on these matters than ridiculous attempts to reduce them to the supposedly supreme law of adaptation. We have only to recall how Roger Caillois (who was then very young, and still fresh from his breach with the sociological school in which he was trained) illuminated the subject by using the term '*legendary psychasthenia*' to classify morphological mimicry as an obsession with space in its derealizing effect.[v]

I have myself shown in the social dialectic that structures human knowledge as paranoiac[3] why human knowledge has greater autonomy than animal knowledge in relation to the field of force of desire, but also why human knowledge is determined in that 'little reality' (*ce peu de réalité*), which the Surrealists, in their restless way, saw as its limitation.[vi] These reflections lead me to recognize in the spatial captation manifested in the mirror-stage, even before the social dialectic, the effect in man of an organic insufficiency in his natural reality – in so far as any meaning can be given to the word 'nature'.

I am led, therefore, to regard the function of the mirror-stage as a particular case of the function of the *imago*, which is to establish a relation between the organism and its reality – or, as they say, between the *Innenwelt* and the *Umwelt*.[vii]

In man, however, this relation to nature is altered by a certain dehiscence at the heart of the organism, a primordial Discord betrayed by the signs of uneasiness and motor unco-ordination of the neonatal months. The objective notion of the anatomical incompleteness of the pyramidal system and likewise the presence of certain humoral residues of the maternal organism confirm the view I have formulated as the fact of a real *specific prematurity of birth* in man.

It is worth noting, incidentally, that this is a fact recognized as such by embryologists, by the term *foetalization*, which determines the prevalence of the so-called superior apparatus of the neurax, and especially of the cortex, which psycho-surgical operations lead us to regard as the intraorganic mirror.[viii]

This development is experienced as a temporal dialectic that decisively projects the formation of the individual into history. The *mirror stage* is a drama whose internal thrust is precipitated from insufficiency to anticipation – and which manufactures for the subject, caught up in the lure of spatial identification, the succession of phantasies that extends from a fragmented body-image to a form of its totality that I shall call orthopaedic – and, lastly, to the assumption of the armour of an alienating identity, which will mark with its rigid structure the subject's entire mental development. Thus, to break out of the circle of the *Innenwelt* into the *Umwelt* generates the inexhaustible quadrature of the ego's verifications.

This fragmented body – which term I have also introduced into our system of theoretical references – usually manifests itself in dreams when the movement of the analysis encounters a certain level of aggressive disintegration in the individual. It then appears in the form of disjointed limbs, or of those organs represented in exoscopy, growing wings and taking up arms for intestinal persecutions – the very same that the visionary Hieronymus Bosch has fixed, for all time, in painting, in their ascent from the fifteenth century to the imaginary zenith of modern man.[ix] But this form is even tangibly revealed at the organic level, in the lines of 'fragilization' that define the anatomy of phantasy, as exhibited in the schizoid and spasmodic symptoms of hysteria.

Correlatively, the formation of the *I* is symbolized in dreams by a fortress, or a stadium – its inner arena and enclosure, surrounded by marshes and rubbish-tips, dividing it into two opposed fields of contest where the subject flounders in quest of the lofty, remote inner castle whose form (sometimes juxtaposed in the same scenario) symbolizes the id in a quite startling way. Similarly, on the mental plane, we find realized the structures of fortified works, the metaphor of which arises spontaneously, as if issuing from the symptoms themselves, to designate the mechanisms of obsessional neurosis – inversion, isolation, reduplication, cancellation and displacement.

---

[v] Caillois was a twentieth-century French anthropological writer, author of *Man and the Sacred* (1939). "Psychasthenia" refers to neurosis.

[vi] Lacan had a strong interest in the surrealist painters who sought to capture "subjective" or "imaginary" reality.

[vii] Inner world and surrounding world.

[viii] "Foetalization" is retention of infantile features in adulthood.

[ix] Hieronymous Bosch (1450–1516), painter of fantastic scenes of religious symbolism, most famously *The Garden of Earthly Delights*.

But if we were to build on these subjective givens alone – however little we free them from the condition of experience that makes us see them as partaking of the nature of a linguistic technique – our theoretical attempts would remain exposed to the charge of projecting themselves into the unthinkable of an absolute subject. This is why I have sought in the present hypothesis, grounded in a conjunction of objective data, the guiding grid for a *method of symbolic reduction*.

It establishes in the *defences of the ego* a genetic order, in accordance with the wish formulated by Miss Anna Freud, in the first part of her great work, and situates (as against a frequently expressed prejudice) hysterical repression and its returns at a more archaic stage than obsessional inversion and its isolating processes, and the latter in turn as preliminary to paranoic alienation, which dates from the deflection of the specular *I* into the social *I*.[x]

This moment in which the mirror-stage comes to an end inaugurates, by the identification with the *imago* of the counterpart and the drama of primordial jealousy (so well brought out by the school of Charlotte Bühler in the phenomenon of infantile *transitivism*), the dialectic that will henceforth link the *I* to socially elaborated situations.[xi]

It is this moment that decisively tips the whole of human knowledge into mediatization through the desire of the other, constitutes its objects in an abstract equivalence by the co-operation of others, and turns the I into that apparatus for which every instinctual thrust constitutes a danger, even though it should correspond to a natural maturation – the very normalization of this maturation being henceforth dependent, in man, on a cultural mediation as exemplified, in the case of the sexual object, by the Oedipus complex.

In the light of this conception, the term primary narcissism, by which analytic doctrine designates the libidinal investment characteristic of that moment, reveals in those who invented it the most profound awareness of semantic latencies. But it also throws light on the dynamic opposition between this libido and the sexual libido, which the first analysts tried to define when they invoked destructive and, indeed, death instincts, in order to explain the evident connection between the narcissistic libido and the alienating function of the *I*, the aggressivity it releases in any relation to the other, even in a relation involving the most Samaritan of aid.

In fact, they were encountering that existential negativity whose reality is so vigorously proclaimed by the contemporary philosophy of being and nothingness.[xii]

But unfortunately that philosophy grasps negativity only within the limits of a self-sufficiency of consciousness, which, as one of its premises, links to the *méconnaissances* that constitute the ego, the illusion of autonomy to which it entrusts itself. This flight of fancy, for all that it draws, to an unusual extent, on borrowings from psychoanalytic experience, culminates in the pretention of providing an existential psychoanalysis.

At the culmination of the historical effort of a society to refuse to recognize that it has any function other than the utilitarian one, and in the anxiety of the individual confronting the 'concentrational' form of the social bond that seems to arise to crown this effort, existentialism must be judged by the explanations it gives of the subjective impasses that have indeed resulted from it; a freedom that is never more authentic than when it is within the walls of a prison; a demand for commitment, expressing the impotence of a pure consciousness to master any situation; a voyeuristic–sadistic idealization of the sexual relation; a personality that realizes itself only in suicide; a consciousness of the other that can be satisfied only by Hegelian murder.

These propositions are opposed by all our experience, in so far as it teaches us not to regard the ego as centred on the *perception–consciousness system*, or as organized by the 'reality principle' – a principle that is the expression of a scientific prejudice most hostile to the dialectic of knowledge. Our experience shows that we should start instead from the *function of méconnaissance* that characterizes the ego in all its structures, so markedly articulated by Miss Anna Freud. For, if the *Verneinung* represents the patent form of that function, its effects will, for the most part, remain latent, so long as they are not illuminated by some light reflected on to the level of fatality, which is where the id manifests itself.[xiii]

We can thus understand the inertia characteristic of the formations of the *I*, and find there the most

---

[x]   Freud's daughter Anna (1895–1982), a child psychoanalyst, wrote *The Ego and Mechanisms of Defense* (1937).
[xi]   Charlotte Bühler (1843–1974), Viennese psychologist. "Transition" is the "splitting off" of personality traits by ascribing them to other persons.

[xii]   A reference to Sartre's *Being and Nothingness* (1943).
[xiii]   *Verneinung* means "negation."

extensive definition of neurosis – just as the captation of the subject by the situation gives us the most
general formula for madness, not only the madness
that lies behind the walls of asylums, but also the
madness that deafens the world with its sound and
fury.

The sufferings of neurosis and psychosis are for
us a schooling in the passions of the soul, just as the
beam of the psychoanalytic scales, when we calculate the tilt of its threat to entire communities,
provides us with an indication of the deadening of
the passions in society.

At this junction of nature and culture, so persistently examined by modern anthropology, psycho-

analysis alone recognizes this knot of imaginary
servitude that love must always undo again, or
sever.

For such a task, we place no trust in altruistic
feeling, we who lay bare the aggressivity that
underlies the activity of the philanthropist, the
idealist, the pedagogue, and even the reformer.

In the recourse of subject to subject that we
preserve, psychoanalysis may accompany the patient to the ecstatic limit of the 'Thou art that', in
which is revealed to him the cipher of his mortal
destiny, but it is not in our mere power as practitioners to bring him to that point where the real
journey begins.[xiv]

[xiv] "Thou art that," the Hindu expression for the unity
of the individual soul (atman) and the infinite God (Brahman).

Author's Notes

1 Throughout this article I leave in its peculiarity the
translation I have adopted for Freud's *Ideal-Ich* [ego-
ideal], without further comment, other than to say
that I have not maintained it since.

2 Cf. Claude Lévi-Strauss, *Structural Anthropology*,
Chapter X.

3 Cf. 'Aggressivity in Psychoanalysis', p. 8 and *Écrits*,
p. 180.

25

From ''The Nature and Necessity of Scientific Revolutions''

Thomas Kuhn

American historian of science Thomas Kuhn (1922–96) had an enormous impact on the history and philosophy of science through his *The Structure of Scientific Revolutions* (1962). Kuhn famously argued that science proceeds not primarily by patient accretion of facts, but by revolutionary interpretive shifts in which one scientific "paradigm" displaces another. The history of science is thus marked by discontinuity. This raises the troubling question of whether the decision between paradigms is a rational, justifiable one, since paradigms appear to be so distinct – as some would say, "incommensurable" – that the evaluative criteria operative in one paradigm would seem logically unable to recognize the superiority of another paradigm. Indeed, it is not clear whether the meanings of the terms of one paradigm can even be translated into the terms of another. While Kuhn's aims were primarily historical and not philosophical, his work necessarily raised the question of the rationality of science. Much has been said to answer and clarify these issues since Kuhn first raised them, but few philosophers have been able to view science in quite the same terms since his book.

These remarks [in Kuhn's previous chapter] permit us at last to consider the problems that provide this essay with its title. What are scientific revolutions, and what is their function in scientific development? Much of the answer to these questions has been anticipated in earlier sections. In particular, the preceding discussion has indicated that scientific revolutions are here taken to be those non-cumulative developmental episodes in which an older paradigm is replaced in whole or in part by an incompatible new one. There is more to be said, however, and an essential part of it can be introduced by asking one further question. Why should a change of paradigm be called a revolution?[i] In the face of the vast and essential differences between political and scientific development, what parallelism can justify the metaphor that finds revolutions in both?

One aspect of the parallelism must already be apparent. Political revolutions are inaugurated by a growing sense, often restricted to a segment of the political community, that existing institutions have ceased adequately to meet the problems posed by an environment that they have in part created. In much the same way, scientific revolutions are inaugurated by a growing sense, again often restricted to a narrow subdivision of the scientific community, that an existing paradigm has ceased to function adequately in the exploration of an aspect of nature to which that paradigm itself had previously led the way. In both political and scientific development the sense of malfunction that can lead to crisis is prerequisite to revolution. Furthermore, though it admittedly strains the metaphor, that parallelism

---

[i] Central to Kuhn's argument, the term "paradigm" refers to the fundamental concepts and aims of a science in an historical period. A scientific revolution involves the replacement of one paradigm by another.

Thomas Kuhn, "The Nature and Necessity of Scientific Revolutions," chapter IX, pp. 92–110, from *The Structure of Scientific Revolutions*. Chicago: University of Chicago Press, 1962.

holds not only for the major paradigm changes, like those attributable to Copernicus and Lavoisier, but also for the far smaller ones associated with the assimilation of a new sort of phenomenon, like oxygen or X-rays.[ii] Scientific revolutions, as we noted [at the end of Section V], need seem revolutionary only to those whose paradigms are affected by them. To outsiders they may, like the Balkan revolutions of the early twentieth century, seem normal parts of the developmental process. Astronomers, for example, could accept X-rays as a mere addition to knowledge, for their paradigms were unaffected by the existence of the new radiation. But for men like Kelvin, Crookes, and Roentgen, whose research dealt with radiation theory or with cathode ray tubes, the emergence of X-rays necessarily violated one paradigm as it created another. That is why these rays could be discovered only through something's first going wrong with normal research.

This genetic aspect of the parallel between political and scientific development should no longer be open to doubt. The parallel has, however, a second and more profound aspect upon which the significance of the first depends. Political revolutions aim to change political institutions in ways that those institutions themselves prohibit. Their success therefore necessitates the partial relinquishment of one set of institutions in favor of another, and in the interim, society is not fully governed by institutions at all. Initially it is crisis alone that attenuates the role of political institutions as we have already seen it attenuate the role of paradigms. In increasing numbers individuals become increasingly estranged from political life and behave more and more eccentrically within it. Then, as the crisis deepens, many of these individuals commit themselves to some concrete proposal for the reconstruction of society in a new institutional framework. At that point the society is divided into competing camps or parties, one seeking to defend the old institutional constellation, the others seeking to institute some new one. And, once that polarization has occurred, *political recourse fails*. Because they differ about the institutional matrix within which political change is to be achieved and evaluated, because they acknowledge no supra-institutional framework for the adjudication of revolutionary

difference, the parties to a revolutionary conflict must finally resort to the techniques of mass persuasion, often including force. Though revolutions have had a vital role in the evolution of political institutions, that role depends upon their being partially extrapolitical or extrainstitutional events.

The remainder of this essay aims to demonstrate that the historical study of paradigm change reveals very similar characteristics in the evolution of the sciences. Like the choice between competing political institutions, that between competing paradigms proves to be a choice between incompatible modes of community life. Because it has that character, the choice is not and cannot be determined merely by the evaluative procedures characteristic of normal science, for these depend in part upon a particular paradigm, and that paradigm is at issue. When paradigms enter, as they must, into a debate about paradigm choice, their role is necessarily circular. Each group uses its own paradigm to argue in that paradigm's defense.

The resulting circularity does not, of course, make the arguments wrong or even ineffectual. The man who premises a paradigm when arguing in its defense can nonetheless provide a clear exhibit of what scientific practice will be like for those who adopt the new view of nature. That exhibit can be immensely persuasive, often compellingly so. Yet, whatever its force, the status of the circular argument is only that of persuasion. It cannot be made logically or even probabilistically compelling for those who refuse to step into the circle. The premises and values shared by the two parties to a debate over paradigms are not sufficiently extensive for that. As in political revolutions, so in paradigm choice – there is no standard higher than the assent of the relevant community. To discover how scientific revolutions are effected, we shall therefore have to examine not only the impact of nature and of logic, but also the techniques of persuasive argumentation effective within the quite special groups that constitute the community of scientists.

To discover why this issue of paradigm choice can never be unequivocally settled by logic and experiment alone, we must shortly examine the nature of the differences that separate the proponents of a traditional paradigm from their revolutionary successors. That examination is the principal object of this section and the next. We have, however, already noted numerous examples of such differences, and no one will doubt that history can supply many others. What is more likely to be doubted than their existence – and

---

[ii] Antoine Laurent Lavoisier (1743–94), father of modern chemistry. Below, William Kelvin (1824–1907), William Crookes (1832–1919), and Wilhelm Roentgen (1845–1923).

what must therefore be considered first – is that such examples provide essential information about the nature of science. Granting that paradigm rejection has been a historic fact, does it illuminate more than human credulity and confusion? Are there intrinsic reasons why the assimilation of either a new sort of phenomenon or a new scientific theory must demand the rejection of an older paradigm?

First notice that if there are such reasons, they do not derive from the logical structure of scientific knowledge. In principle, a new phenomenon might emerge without reflecting destructively upon any part of past scientific practice. Though discovering life on the moon would today be destructive of existing paradigms (these tell us things about the moon that seem incompatible with life's existence there), discovering life in some less well-known part of the galaxy would not. By the same token, a new theory does not have to conflict with any of its predecessors. It might deal exclusively with phenomena not previously known, as the quantum theory deals (but, significantly, not exclusively) with subatomic phenomena unknown before the twentieth century. Or again, the new theory might be simply a higher level theory than those known before, one that linked together a whole group of lower level theories without substantially changing any. Today, the theory of energy conservation provides just such links between dynamics, chemistry, electricity, optics, thermal theory, and so on. Still other compatible relationships between old and new theories can be conceived. Any and all of them might be exemplified by the historical process through which science has developed. If they were, scientific development would be genuinely cumulative. New sorts of phenomena would simply disclose order in an aspect of nature where none had been seen before. In the evolution of science new knowledge would replace ignorance rather than replace knowledge of another and incompatible sort.

Of course, science (or some other enterprise, perhaps less effective) might have developed in that fully cumulative manner. Many people have believed that it did so, and most still seem to suppose that cumulation is at least the ideal that historical development would display if only it had not so often been distorted by human idiosyncrasy. There are important reasons for that belief. [In Section X] we shall discover how closely the view of science-as-cumulation is entangled with a dominant epistemology that takes knowledge to be a construction placed directly upon raw sense data by the mind. And [in Section XI] we shall examine the strong

support provided to the same historiographic schema by the techniques of effective science pedagogy. Nevertheless, despite the immense plausibility of that ideal image, there is increasing reason to wonder whether it can possibly be an image of *science*. After the pre-paradigm period the assimilation of all new theories and of almost all new sorts of phenomena has in fact demanded the destruction of a prior paradigm and a consequent conflict between competing schools of scientific thought. Cumulative acquisition of unanticipated novelties proves to be an almost non-existent exception to the rule of scientific development. The man who takes historic fact seriously must suspect that science does not tend toward the ideal that our image of its cumulativeness has suggested. Perhaps it is another sort of enterprise.

If, however, resistant facts can carry us that far, then a second look at the ground we have already covered may suggest that cumulative acquisition of novelty is not only rare in fact but improbable in principle. Normal research, which *is* cumulative, owes its success to the ability of scientists regularly to select problems that can be solved with conceptual and instrumental techniques close to those already in existence. (That is why an excessive concern with useful problems, regardless of their relation to existing knowledge and technique, can so easily inhibit scientific development.) The man who is striving to solve a problem defined by existing knowledge and technique is not, however, just looking around. He knows what he wants to achieve, and he designs his instruments and directs his thoughts accordingly. Unanticipated novelty, the new discovery, can emerge only to the extent that his anticipations about nature and his instruments prove wrong. Often the importance of the resulting discovery will itself be proportional to the extent and stubbornness of the anomaly that foreshadowed it. Obviously, then, there must be a conflict between the paradigm that discloses anomaly and the one that later renders the anomaly lawlike. The examples of discovery through paradigm destruction examined [in Section VI] did not confront us with mere historical accident.[iii] There is no other effective way in which discoveries might be generated.

The same argument applies even more clearly to the invention of new theories. There are, in principle, only three types of phenomena about which a new theory might be developed. The first

---

[iii] The three cases Kuhn discussed were the discoveries of oxygen, X-rays, and the Leyden jar.

consists of phenomena already well explained by existing paradigms, and these seldom provide either motive or point of departure for theory construction. When they do, as with the three famous anticipations discussed [at the end of Section VII], the theories that result are seldom accepted, because nature provides no ground for discrimination.[iv] A second class of phenomena consists of those whose nature is indicated by existing paradigms but whose details can be understood only through further theory articulation. These are the phenomena to which scientists direct their research much of the time, but that research aims at the articulation of existing paradigms rather than at the invention of new ones. Only when these attempts at articulation fail do scientists encounter the third type of phenomena, the recognized anomalies whose characteristic feature is their stubborn refusal to be assimilated to existing paradigms. This type alone gives rise to new theories. Paradigms provide all phenomena except anomalies with a theory-determined place in the scientist's field of vision.

But if new theories are called forth to resolve anomalies in the relation of an existing theory to nature, then the successful new theory must somewhere permit predictions that are different from those derived from its predecessor. That difference could not occur if the two were logically compatible. In the process of being assimilated, the second must displace the first. Even a theory like energy conservation, which today seems a logical superstructure that relates to nature only through independently established theories, did not develop historically without paradigm destruction. Instead, it emerged from a crisis in which an essential ingredient was the incompatibility between Newtonian dynamics and some recently formulated consequences of the caloric theory of heat. Only after the caloric theory had been rejected could energy conservation become part of science.[1] And only after it had been part of science for some time could it come to seem a theory of a logically higher type, one not in conflict with its predecessors. It is hard to see how new theories could arise without these destructive changes in beliefs about nature. Though logical inclusiveness remains a permissible

view of the relation between successive scientific theories, it is a historical implausibility.

A century ago it would, I think, have been possible to let the case for the necessity of revolutions rest at this point. But today, unfortunately, that cannot be done because the view of the subject developed above cannot be maintained if the most prevalent contemporary interpretation of the nature and function of scientific theory is accepted. That interpretation, closely associated with early logical positivism and not categorically rejected by its successors, would restrict the range and meaning of an accepted theory so that it could not possibly conflict with any later theory that made predictions about some of the same natural phenomena. The best-known and the strongest case for this restricted conception of a scientific theory emerges in discussions of the relation between contemporary Einsteinian dynamics and the older dynamical equations that descend from Newton's *Principia*.[v] From the viewpoint of this essay these two theories are fundamentally incompatible in the sense illustrated by the relation of Copernican to Ptolemaic astronomy: Einstein's theory can be accepted only with the recognition that Newton's was wrong. Today this remains a minority view.[2] We must therefore examine the most prevalent objections to it.

The gist of these objections can be developed as follows. Relativistic dynamics cannot have shown Newtonian dynamics to be wrong, for Newtonian dynamics is still used with great success by most engineers and, in selected applications, by many physicists. Furthermore, the propriety of this use of the older theory can be proved from the very theory that has, in other applications, replaced it. Einstein's theory can be used to show that predictions from Newton's equations will be as good as our measuring instruments in all applications that satisfy a small number of restrictive conditions. For example, if Newtonian theory is to provide a good approximate solution, the relative velocities of the bodies considered must be small compared with the velocity of light. Subject to this condition and a few others, Newtonian theory seems to be derivable from Einsteinian, of which it is therefore a special case.

But, the objection continues, no theory can possibly conflict with one of its special cases. If

---

[iv] The three anticipations were: the heliocentric cosmology of the ancient Greek philosopher Aristarchus of Samos (310–230 BC); seventeenth-century theories of combustion; and the relativistic view of space adopted by Newton's critics. These early "discoveries" preceded the historical crises that would only later legitimate them.

[v] Isaac Newton's *Mathematical Principles of Natural Philosophy* (Latin orig., 1687). Below, the second-century BC Alexandrian Ptolemy formulated the geocentric model of the universe later overturned by Copernicus.

Einsteinian science seems to make Newtonian dynamics wrong, that is only because some Newtonians were so incautious as to claim that Newtonian theory yielded entirely precise results or that it was valid at very high relative velocities. Since they could not have had any evidence for such claims, they betrayed the standards of science when they made them. In so far as Newtonian theory was ever a truly scientific theory supported by valid evidence, it still is. Only extravagant claims for the theory – claims that were never properly parts of science – can have been shown by Einstein to be wrong. Purged of these merely human extravagances, Newtonian theory has never been challenged and cannot be.

Some variant of this argument is quite sufficient to make any theory ever used by a significant group of competent scientists immune to attack. The much-maligned phlogiston theory, for example, gave order to a large number of physical and chemical phenomena. It explained why bodies burned – they were rich in phlogiston – and why metals had so many more properties in common than did their ores. The metals were all compounded from different elementary earths combined with phlogiston, and the latter, common to all metals, produced common properties. In addition, the phlogiston theory accounted for a number of reactions in which acids were formed by the combustion of substances like carbon and sulphur. Also, it explained the decrease of volume when combustion occurs in a confined volume of air – the phlogiston released by combustion "spoils" the elasticity of the air that absorbed it, just as fire "spoils" the elasticity of a steel spring.[3] If these were the only phenomena that the phlogiston theorists had claimed for their theory, that theory could never have been challenged. A similar argument will suffice for any theory that has ever been successfully applied to any range of phenomena at all.

But to save theories in this way, their range of application must be restricted to those phenomena and to that precision of observation with which experimental evidence in hand already deals.[4] Carried just a step further (and the step can scarcely be avoided once the first is taken), such a limitation prohibits the scientist from claiming to speak "scientifically" about any phenomenon not already observed. Even in its present form the restriction forbids the scientist to rely upon a theory in his own research whenever that research enters an area or seeks a degree of precision for which past practice with the theory offers no precedent. These prohib-

itions are logically unexceptionable. But the result of accepting them would be the end of the research through which science may develop further.

By now that point too is virtually a tautology. Without commitment to a paradigm there could be no normal science. Furthermore, that commitment must extend to areas and to degrees of precision for which there is no full precedent. If it did not, the paradigm could provide no puzzles that had not already been solved. Besides, it is not only normal science that depends upon commitment to a paradigm. If existing theory binds the scientist only with respect to existing application, then there can be no surprises, anomalies, or crises. But these are just the signposts that point the way to extraordinary science. If positivistic restrictions on the range of a theory's legitimate applicability are taken literally, the mechanism that tells the scientific community what problems may lead to fundamental change must cease to function. And when that occurs, the community will inevitably return to something much like its pre-paradigm state, a condition in which all members practice science but in which their gross product scarcely resembles science at all. Is it really any wonder that the price of significant scientific advance is a commitment that runs the risk of being wrong?

More important, there is a revealing logical lacuna in the positivist's argument, one that will reintroduce us immediately to the nature of revolutionary change. Can Newtonian dynamics really be *derived* from relativistic dynamics? What would such a derivation look like? Imagine a set of statements, $E_1, E_2 \ldots , E_n$, which together embody the laws of relativity theory. These statements contain variables and parameters representing spatial position, time, rest mass, etc. From them, together with the apparatus of logic and mathematics, is deducible a whole set of further statements including some that can be checked by observation. To prove the adequacy of Newtonian dynamics as a special case, we must add to the E_i's additional statements, like $(v/c)^2 \ll 1$, restricting the range of the parameters and variables. This enlarged set of statements is then manipulated to yield a new set, $N_1, N_2, \ldots, N_m$ which is identical in form with Newton's laws of motion, the law of gravity, and so on. Apparently Newtonian dynamics has been derived from Einsteinian, subject to a few limiting conditions.

Yet the derivation is spurious, at least to this point. Though the N_i's are a special case of the laws of relativistic mechanics, they are not Newton's Laws. Or at least they are not unless those laws are reinterpreted in a way that would have been impossible until after Einstein's work. The variables and parameters that in the Einsteinian E_i's represented spatial position, time, mass, etc., still occur in the N_i's; and they there still represent Einsteinian space, time, and mass. But the physical referents of these Einsteinian concepts are by no means identical with those of the Newtonian concepts that bear the same name. (Newtonian mass is conserved; Einsteinian is convertible with energy. Only at low relative velocities may the two be measured in the same way, and even then they must not be conceived to be the same.) Unless we change the definitions of the variables in the N_i's, the statements we have derived are not Newtonian. If we do change them, we cannot properly be said to have *derived* Newton's Laws, at least not in any sense of "derive" now generally recognized. Our argument has, of course, explained why Newton's Laws ever seemed to work. In doing so it has justified, say, an automobile driver in acting as though he lived in a Newtonian universe. An argument of the same type is used to justify teaching earth-centered astronomy to surveyors. But the argument has still not done what it purported to do. It has not, that is, shown Newton's Laws to be a limiting case of Einstein's. For in the passage to the limit it is not only the forms of the laws that have changed. Simultaneously we have had to alter the fundamental structural elements of which the universe to which they apply is composed.

This need to change the meaning of established and familiar concepts is central to the revolutionary impact of Einstein's theory. Though subtler than the changes from geocentrism to heliocentrism, from phlogiston to oxygen, or from corpuscles to waves, the resulting conceptual transformation is no less decisively destructive of a previously established paradigm. We may even come to see it as a prototype for revolutionary reorientations in the sciences. Just because it did not involve the introduction of additional objects or concepts, the transition from Newtonian to Einsteinian mechanics illustrates with particular clarity the scientific revolution as a displacement of the conceptual network through which scientists view the world.

These remarks should suffice to show what might, in another philosophical climate, have been taken for granted. At least for scientists, most of the apparent differences between a discarded scientific theory and its successor are real. Though an out-of-date theory can always be viewed as a special case of its up-to-date successor, it must be transformed for the purpose. And the transformation is one that can be undertaken only with the advantages of hindsight, the explicit guidance of the more recent theory. Furthermore, even if that transformation were a legitimate device to employ in interpreting the older theory, the result of its application would be a theory so restricted that it could only restate what was already known. Because of its economy, that restatement would have utility, but it could not suffice for the guidance of research.

Let us, therefore, now take it for granted that the differences between successive paradigms are both necessary and irreconcilable. Can we then say more explicitly what sorts of differences these are? The most apparent type has already been illustrated repeatedly. Successive paradigms tell us different things about the population of the universe and about that population's behavior. They differ, that is, about such questions as the existence of subatomic particles, the materiality of light, and the conservation of heat or of energy. These are the substantive differences between successive paradigms, and they require no further illustration. But paradigms differ in more than substance, for they are directed not only to nature but also back upon the science that produced them. They are the source of the methods, problem-field, and standards of solution accepted by any mature scientific community at any given time. As a result, the reception of a new paradigm often necessitates a redefinition of the corresponding science. Some old problems may be relegated to another science or declared entirely "unscientific." Others that were previously non-existent or trivial may, with a new paradigm, become the very archetypes of significant scientific achievement. And as the problems change, so, often, does the standard that distinguishes a real scientific solution from a mere metaphysical speculation, word game, or mathematical play. The normal-scientific tradition that emerges from a scientific revolution is not only incompatible but often actually incommensurable with that which has gone before.

The impact of Newton's work upon the normal seventeenth-century tradition of scientific practice provides a striking example of these subtler effects of paradigm shift. Before Newton was born the "new science" of the century had at last succeeded in rejecting Aristotelian and scholastic explanations expressed in terms of the essences of material bodies. To say that a stone fell because its "nature" drove it toward the center of the universe had been made to look a mere tautological word-play, something it had not previously been. Henceforth the entire flux of sensory appearances, including color, taste, and even weight, was to be explained in terms of the size, shape, position, and motion of the elementary corpuscles of base matter. The attribution of other qualities to the elementary atoms was a resort to the occult and therefore out of bounds for science. Molière caught the new spirit precisely when he ridiculed the doctor who explained opium's efficacy as a soporific by attributing to it a dormitive potency.[vi] During the last half of the seventeenth century many scientists preferred to say that the round shape of the opium particles enabled them to sooth the nerves about which they moved.[5]

In an earlier period explanations in terms of occult qualities had been an integral part of productive scientific work. Nevertheless, the seventeenth century's new commitment to mechanico-corpuscular explanation proved immensely fruitful for a number of sciences, ridding them of problems that had defied generally accepted solution and suggesting others to replace them. In dynamics, for example, Newton's three laws of motion are less a product of novel experiments than of the attempt to reinterpret well-known observations in terms of the motions and interactions of primary neutral corpuscles. Consider just one concrete illustration. Since neutral corpuscles could act on each other only by contact, the mechanico-corpuscular view of nature directed scientific attention to a brand-new subject of study, the alteration of particulate motions by collisions. Descartes announced the problem and provided its first putative solution. Huyghens, Wren, and Wallis carried it still further, partly by experimenting with colliding pendulum bobs, but mostly by applying previously well-known characteristics of motion to the new problem. And Newton embedded their results in his laws of motion. The equal "action" and "reaction" of the third law are the changes in quantity of motion experienced by the two parties to a collision. The same change of motion supplies the definition of dynamical force implicit in the second law. In this case, as in many others during the seventeenth century, the corpuscular paradigm bred both a new problem and a large part of that problem's solution.[6]

[vi] In Molière's play *Le Malade imaginaire* (*The Hypochondriac*), Interlude III (following Act III), see the first response of Bachelierus.

Yet, though much of Newton's work was directed to problems and embodied standards derived from the mechanico-corpuscular world view, the effect of the paradigm that resulted from his work was a further and partially destructive change in the problems and standards legitimate for science. Gravity, interpreted as an innate attraction between every pair of particles of matter, was an occult quality in the same sense as the scholastics' "tendency to fall" had been. Therefore, while the standards of corpuscularism remained in effect, the search for a mechanical explanation of gravity was one of the most challenging problems for those who accepted the *Principia* as paradigm. Newton devoted much attention to it and so did many of his eighteenth-century successors. The only apparent option was to reject Newton's theory for its failure to explain gravity, and that alternative, too, was widely adopted. Yet neither of these views ultimately triumphed. Unable either to practice science without the *Principia* or to make that work conform to the corpuscular standards of the seventeenth century, scientists gradually accepted the view that gravity was indeed innate. By the mid-eighteenth century that interpretation had been almost universally accepted, and the result was a genuine reversion (which is not the same as a retrogression) to a scholastic standard. Innate attractions and repulsions joined size, shape, position, and motion as physically irreducible primary properties of matter.[7]

The resulting change in the standards and problem-field of physical science was once again consequential. By the 1740's, for example, electricians could speak of the attractive "virtue" of the electric fluid without thereby inviting the ridicule that had greeted Molière's doctor a century before. As they did so, electrical phenomena increasingly displayed an order different from the one they had shown when viewed as the effects of a mechanical effluvium that could act only by contact. In particular, when electrical action-at-a-distance became a subject for study in its own right, the phenomenon we now call charging by induction could be recognized as one of its effects. Previously, when seen at all, it had been attributed to the direct action of electrical "atmospheres" or to the leakages inevitable in any electrical laboratory. The new view of inductive effects was, in turn, the key to Franklin's analysis of the Leyden jar and thus to the emergence of a new and Newtonian paradigm for electricity. Nor were dynamics and electricity the only scientific fields affected by the legitimization of the search for forces innate to matter. The large body of eighteenth-century literature on chemical affinities and replacement series also derives from this supra-mechanical aspect of Newtonianism. Chemists who believed in these differential attractions between the various chemical species set up previously un-imagined experiments and searched for new sorts of reactions. Without the data and the chemical concepts developed in that process, the later work of Lavoisier and, more particularly, of Dalton[vii] would be incomprehensible.[8] Changes in the standards governing permissible problems, concepts, and explanations can transform a science. In the next section I shall even suggest a sense in which they transform the world.

Other examples of these nonsubstantive differences between successive paradigms can be retrieved from the history of any science in almost any period of its development. For the moment let us be content with just two other and far briefer illustrations. Before the chemical revolution, one of the acknowledged tasks of chemistry was to account for the qualities of chemical substances and for the changes these qualities underwent during chemical reactions. With the aid of a small number of elementary "principles" – of which phlogiston was one – the chemist was to explain why some substances are acidic, others metalline, combustible, and so forth. Some success in this direction had been achieved. We have already noted that phlogiston explained why the metals were so much alike, and we could have developed a similar argument for the acids. Lavoisier's reform, however, ultimately did away with chemical "principles," and thus ended by depriving chemistry of some actual and much potential explanatory power. To compensate for this loss, a change in standards was required. During much of the nineteenth century failure to explain the qualities of compounds was no indictment of a chemical theory.[9]

Or again, Clerk Maxwell shared with other nineteenth-century proponents of the wave theory of light the conviction that light waves must be propagated through a material ether. Designing a mechanical medium to support such waves was a standard problem for many of his ablest contemporaries. His own theory, however, the electromagnetic theory of light, gave no account at all of a medium able to support light waves, and it clearly made such an account harder to provide than it had

seemed before. Initially, Maxwell's theory was widely rejected for those reasons. But, like Newton's theory, Maxwell's proved difficult to dispense with, and as it achieved the status of a paradigm, the community's attitude toward it changed. In the early decades of the twentieth century Maxwell's insistence upon the existence of a mechanical ether looked more and more like lip service, which it emphatically had not been, and the attempts to design such an ethereal medium were abandoned. Scientists no longer thought it unscientific to speak of an electrical "displacement" without specifying what was being displaced. The result, again, was a new set of problems and standards, one which, in the event, had much to do with the emergence of relativity theory.[10]

These characteristic shifts in the scientific community's conception of its legitimate problems and standards would have less significance to this essay's thesis if one could suppose that they always occurred from some methodologically lower to some higher type. In that case their effects, too, would seem cumulative. No wonder that some historians have argued that the history of science records a continuing increase in the maturity and refinement of man's conception of the nature of science.[11] Yet the case for cumulative development of science's problems and standards is even harder to make than the case for cumulation of theories. The attempt to explain gravity, though fruitfully abandoned by most eighteenth-century scientists, was not directed to an intrinsically illegitimate problem: the objections to innate forces were neither inherently unscientific nor metaphysical in some pejorative sense. There are no external standards to permit a judgment of that sort. What occurred was neither a decline nor a raising of standards, but simply a change demanded by the adoption of a new paradigm. Furthermore, that change has since been reversed and could be again. In the twentieth century Einstein succeeded in explaining gravitational attractions, and that explanation has returned science to a set of canons and problems that are, in this particular respect, more like those of Newton's predecessors than of his successors. Or again, the development of quantum mechanics has reversed the methodological prohibition that originated in the chemical revolution. Chemists now attempt, and with great success, to explain the color, state of aggregation, and other qualities of the substances used and produced in their laboratories. A similar reversal may even be underway in electromagnetic theory. Space, in

---

[vii] John Dalton (1766–1844) was an English chemist and physicist.

contemporary physics, is not the inert and homogenous substratum employed in both Newton's and Maxwell's theories; some of its new properties are not unlike those once attributed to the ether; we may someday come to know what an electric displacement is.

By shifting emphasis from the cognitive to the normative functions of paradigms, the preceding examples enlarge our understanding of the ways in which paradigms give form to the scientific life. Previously, we had principally examined the paradigm's role as a vehicle for scientific theory. In that role it functions by telling the scientist about the entities that nature does and does not contain and about the ways in which those entities behave. That information provides a map whose details are elucidated by mature scientific research. And since nature is too complex and varied to be explored at random, that map is as essential as observation and experiment to science's continuing development. Through the theories they embody, paradigms prove to be constitutive of the research activity. They are also, however, constitutive of science in other respects, and that is now the point. In particular, our most recent examples show that paradigms provide scientists not only with a map but also with some of the directions essential for map-making. In learning a paradigm the scientist acquires theory, methods, and standards together, usually in an inextricable mixture. Therefore, when paradigms change, there are usually significant shifts in the criteria determining the legitimacy both of problems and of proposed solutions.

That observation returns us to the point from which this section began, for it provides our first explicit indication of why the choice between competing paradigms regularly raises questions that cannot be resolved by the criteria of normal science. To the extent, as significant as it is incomplete, that two scientific schools disagree about what is a problem and what a solution, they will inevitably talk through each other when debating the relative merits of their respective paradigms. In the partially circular arguments that regularly result, each paradigm will be shown to satisfy more or less the criteria that it dictates for itself and to fall short of a few of those dictated by its opponent. There are other reasons, too, for the incompleteness of logical contact that consistently characterizes paradigm debates. For example, since no paradigm ever solves all the problems it defines and since no two paradigms leave all the same problems unsolved, paradigm debates always involve the question: Which problems is it more significant to have solved? Like the issue of competing standards, that question of values can be answered only in terms of criteria that lie outside of normal science altogether, and it is that recourse to external criteria that most obviously makes paradigm debates revolutionary. . . .

Author's Notes

1 Silvanus P. Thompson, *Life of William Thomson Baron Kelvin of Largs* (London, 1910), I, 266–81.

2 See, for example, the remarks by P. P. Wiener in *Philosophy of Science*, XXV (1958), p. 298.

3 James B. Conant, *Overthrow of the Phlogiston Theory* (Cambridge, 1950), pp. 13–16; and J. R. Partington, *A Short History of Chemistry* (2nd edn; London, 1951), pp. 85–8. The fullest and most sympathetic account of the phlogiston theory's achievements is by H. Metzger, *Newton, Stahl, Boerhaave et la doctrine chimique* (Paris, 1930), Part II.

4 Compare the conclusions reached through a very different sort of analysis by R. B. Braithwaite, *Scientific Explanation* (Cambridge, 1953), pp. 50–87, esp. p. 76.

5 For corpuscularism in general, see Marie Boas, "The Establishment of the Mechanical Philosophy," *Osiris*, X (1952), pp. 412–541. For the effect of particle-shape on taste, see ibid., p. 483.

6 R. Dugas, *La mécanique au XVIIᵉ siècle* (Neuchatel, 1954), pp. 177–85, 284–98, 345–56.

7 I. B. Cohen, *Franklin and Newton: An Inquiry into Speculative Newtonian Experimental Science and Franklin's Work in Electricity as an Example Thereof* (Philadelphia, 1956), chs vi–vii.

8 For electricity, see ibid., chs viii–ix. For chemistry, see Metzger, *Newton, Stahl, Boerhaave*, Part I.

9 E. Meyerson, *Identity and Reality* (New York, 1930), ch. x.

10 E. T. Whittaker, *A History of the Theories of Aether and Electricity*, II (London, 1953), pp. 28–30.

11 For a brilliant and entirely up-to-date attempt to fit scientific development into this Procrustean bed, see C. C. Gillispie, *The Edge of Objectivity: An Essay in the History of Scientific Ideas* (Princeton, NJ, 1960).

26

From *The Coming of Post-Industrial Society*

Daniel Bell

The influential American sociologist Daniel Bell (1919–) was well known for his controversial analysis of the post-World War II environment in *The End of Ideology* (1960). A decade later he ventured again into prognostication with the timely, *The Coming of Post-Industrial Society* (1973). While Bell invented neither the term 'post-industrial' nor the idea of a post-industrial society, his book is the most famous and cogent expression of this insight into contemporary history. Bell attempted to show that the nature of the post-war economy was fundamentally changing, and with it, our social arrangements, our culture, and our politics. The idea was later taken up by many writers, including Lyotard, and is now a commonplace of socio-economic analysis. In the following Introduction to his book (written three years after its original publication), he explains that in a post-industrial society *knowledge* replaces material goods as the most important commodity for production and exchange.

The phrase "post-industrial society" has passed quickly into the sociological literature – whether for better or worse remains to be seen. In one sense, the reception was logical and understandable. Once it was clear that countries with diverse social systems could be defined commonly as "industrial societies," it was inevitable that societies which were primarily extractive rather than fabricating would be classified as "pre-industrial," and, as significant changes in the character of technology took place, one could think about "post-industrial" societies as well. Given, too, the vogue of "future schlock," in which breathless prose is mistaken

for the pace of change, a hypothesis about the lineaments of a new society is bound to provoke interest.[i] If I have been a beneficiary of fashion, I regret it.

As I indicate in the book, the idea of a post-industrial society is not a point-in-time prediction of the future but a speculative construct, an *as if* based on emergent features, against which the sociological reality could be measured decades hence, so that, in comparing the two, one might seek to determine the operative factors in effecting societal change. Equally, I rejected the temptation to label these emergent features as the "service society" or the "information society" or the "knowledge society," even though all these elements are present, since such terms are only partial, or they seek to catch a fashionable wind and twist it for modish purposes.[1]

I employed the term "post-industrial" for two reasons. First, to emphasize the interstitial and transitory nature of these changes. And second, to underline a major axial principle, that of an intellectual technology. But such emphasis does not mean that technology is the primary determinant of all other societal changes. No conceptual scheme ever exhausts a social reality. Each conceptual scheme is a prism which selects *some* features, rather than others, in order to highlight historical change or, more specifically, to answer certain questions.

[i] A caustic reference to Alvin Toffler's *Future Shock* (1970).

Daniel Bell, "Foreword: 1976" from *The Coming of Post-Industrial Society*, pp. ix–xxii. New York: Basic Books, 1976.

209

One can see this by relating the concept of post-industrial society to that of capitalism. Some critics have argued that post-industrial society will not "succeed" capitalism. But this sets up a false confrontation between two *different* conceptual schemata organized along two different axes. The post-industrial schema refers to the socio-technical dimension of a society, capitalism to the socio-economic dimension.

The confusion between the two arose in the first place because Marx thought that the mode of production (the sub-structure of a society) determines and encompasses *all* other dimensions of a society. Since capitalism is the prevailing mode of production in Western society, Marxists sought to use that concept to explain all realms of social conduct, from economics through politics to culture. And since Marx felt that industrialization as the advanced feature of capitalist production would spread throughout the world, there would be, ultimately, global uniformity in the mode of production, and a uniformity in the conditions of life. National differences would disappear, and in the end only the two classes, capitalists and proletariat, would be left in stark, final confrontation.

I think this is demonstrably not so. Societies are not unified entities. The nature of the polity – whether a nation is democratic or not – rests not on the economic "foundation" but on historic traditions, on value systems, and on the way in which power is concentrated or dispersed throughout the society. Democracy cannot be easily "discarded," even when it begins to hobble the economic power

of capitalists.[2] Equally, contemporary Western culture is not the "bourgeois" culture of the eighteenth or nineteenth century, but a modernism, hostile to the economizing mode, that has been absorbed by a "cultural mass" and transformed into a materialistic hedonism which is promoted, paradoxically, by capitalism itself.

For Marx, the mode of production united *social relations* and *forces* of production under a single historical rubric. The social relations were primarily property relations; the forces of production, technological. Yet the same forces of production (i.e. technology) exist within a wide variety of different systems of social relations. One cannot say that the technology (or chemistry or physics) of the Soviet Union is different from the technology (or chemistry or physics) of the capitalist world.

Rather than assume a single linkage between the social relations and the forces of production, if we *uncouple* the two dimensions, we can get different "answers" to the question of the relation between different social systems. Thus, if one asks: Is there a "convergence" between the Soviet Union and the United States? the answer would depend on the axis specified. This can be indicated, graphically, by figure 26.1.

Thus, if one divides the countries by the horizontal axis of technology, both the United States and the USSR are industrial societies, whereas Indonesia and China are not. Yet if one divides the countries along the vertical axis of property relations, there is a divergence, in that the United States and Indonesia are capitalist while the Soviet

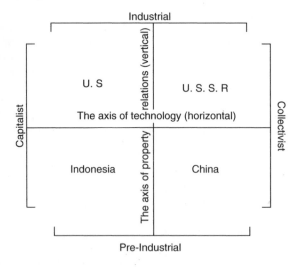

Figure 26.1

Union and China are both "socialist" or state collectivist. (Yet *that* congruence does not explain why there is such fierce rivalry and tension between the two communist countries.)

And if we uncouple the concepts, we can also specify different schemata of social development: feudal, capitalist, and socialist; or pre-industrial, industrial, and post-industrial; or, within the Weberian[ii] framework of political authority, that of patriarchical, patrimonial, and legal-rational bureaucracy – so long as one does not claim that the particular conceptual scheme is exhaustive, and subsumes all others. Within a given historical period, it may well be that a specific axial principle is so important that it becomes determinative of most other social relations. I think it is quite evident that in the nineteenth century the capitalist mode of social relations (i.e. private property, commodity production, etc.) became the prevailing ethos and substantially shaped much of character and culture. But that is different from the claim that the mode of production always determines the "superstructure" of a society.

The mode of production does not unify a society. National differences have not disappeared. There are no unilineal sequences of societal change, no "laws of social development." The most grievous mistake in the social sciences is to read the character of a society through a single overriding concept, whether it be *capitalism* or *totalitarianism*, and to mislead one as to the complex (overlapping and even contradictory) features of any modern society, or to assume that there are "laws of social development" in which one social system succeeds another by some inexorable necessity. Any society, since it mingles different kinds of economic, technological, political, and cultural systems (some features of which are common to all, some of which are historical and idiosyncratic), has to be analyzed from different vantage points, depending on the question one has in mind. My focus has been on the influence of technology, not as an autonomous factor but as an analytical element, in order to see what social changes come in the wake of new technologies, and what problems the society, and its political system, must then attempt to solve.

The concept "post-industrial" is counterposed to that of "pre-industrial" and "industrial." A pre-industrial sector is primarily *extractive*, its economy based on agriculture, mining, fishing, timber, and other resources such as natural gas or oil. An industrial sector is primarily *fabricating*, using energy and machine technology, for the manufacture of goods. A post-industrial sector is one of *processing* in which telecommunications and computers are strategic for the exchange of information and knowledge.

In recent years, the world has become dramatically aware of the strategic role of energy and natural resources as limiting factors of industrial growth, and the question is raised whether these limitations do not modify the onset of a post-industrial sector.

To this, there is an empirical and a theoretical answer. As a practical fact, the introduction of post-industrial elements, which are capital intensive, does depend – in the timing, rate of diffusion, and extensivity of use – on the productivity of the other sectors. The development of an industrial sector depends in considerable measure on the economic surplus of an agrarian sector; yet once industrialization is under way, the productivity of the agrarian sector itself is increased through the use of fertilizer and other petro-chemical products. Similarly, the introduction of new information and processing devices may be delayed by rising costs in the industrial sector or lagging productivity, but once introduced they may be the very means of raising that productivity.

Theoretically, one can say that post-industrial society is, *in principle*, different from the other two. As a theoretical principle, the idea of industrialism did not derive from an agrarian mode. And similarly, the strategic role of theoretical knowledge as the new basis of technological innovation, or the role of information in re-creating social processes, does not derive from the role of energy in creating a manufacturing or fabricating society. In short, these are, *analytically*, independent principles.

Broadly speaking, if industrial society is based on machine technology, post-industrial society is shaped by an intellectual technology. And if capital and labor are the major structural features of industrial society, information and knowledge are those of the post-industrial society.[3] For this reason, the social organization of a post-industrial sector is vastly different from an industrial sector, and one can see this by contrasting the economic features of the two.

Industrial commodities are produced in discrete, identifiable units, exchanged and sold, consumed and used up, as are a loaf of bread or an automobile. One buys the product from a seller and takes physical possession of it. The exchange is governed by

---

ii   This refers to Max Weber.

specific legal rules of contract. But information and knowledge are not consumed or "used up." Knowledge is a *social* product and the question of its costs, price, or value is vastly different from that of industrial items.

In the manufacture of industrial goods, one can set up a "production function," (i.e. the relative proportions of capital and labor to be employed) and determine the appropriate mix, at the relative costs, of each factor. If capital is embodied labor, one can talk of a labor theory of value.

But a post-industrial society is characterized not by a labor theory but by a knowledge theory of value.[4] It is the codification of knowledge that becomes directive of innovation. Yet knowledge, even when it is sold, remains also with the producer. It is a "collective good" in that, once it has been created, it is by its character available to all, and thus there is little incentive for any single person or enterprise to pay for the production of such knowledge unless they can obtain a proprietary advantage, such as a patent or a copyright. But, increasingly, patents no longer guarantee exclusiveness, and many firms lose out by spending money on research only to find that a competitor can quickly modify the product and circumvent the patent; similarly, the question of copyright becomes increasingly difficult to police when individuals or libraries can Xerox whatever pages they need from technical journals or books, or individuals and schools can tape music off the air or record a television performance on video disks.

If there is less and less incentive for individual persons or private enterprises to produce knowledge without particular gain, then the need and effort falls increasingly on some social unit, be it university or government, to underwrite the costs. And since there is no ready market test (how does one estimate the value of "basic research"?) there is a challenge to economic theory to design a socially optimal policy of investment in knowledge (e.g., how much money should be spent for basic research; what allocations should be made for education, and for what fields; in what areas do we obtain the "better returns" in health; and so on), and how to "price" information and knowledge to users.[5]

In a narrower, technical sense, the major problem for the post-industrial society will be the development of an appropriate "infra-structure" for the developing *compunications* networks (the phrase is Anthony Oettinger's) of digital information technologies that will tie the post-industrial society together. The first infra-structure in society is transportation – roads, canals, rail, air – for the movement of people and goods. The second infra-structure has been the energy utilities – oil pipeline, gas, electricity – for the transmission of power. The third infra-structure has been telecommunications, principally the voice telephone, radio, and television. But now with the explosive growth of computers and terminals for data (the number of data terminals in use in the United States went from 185,000 in 1970 to 800,000 in 1976) and the rapid decrease in the costs of computation and information storage, the question of hitching together the varied ways information is transmitted in the country becomes a major issue of economic and social policy.

The "economics of information" is not the same character as the "economics of goods," and the social relations created by the new networks of information (from an interactive research group communicating through computer terminals to the large cultural homogenization created by national television) are not the older social patterns – or work relations – of industrial society.[6] We have here – if this kind of society develops – the foundations of a vastly different kind of social structure than we have previously known.

The post-industrial society, as I have implied, does not *displace* the industrial society, just as an industrial society has not done away with the agrarian sectors of the economy. Like palimpsests, the new developments overlie the previous layers, erasing some features and thickening the texture of society as a whole. In orienting a reader to the detailed arguments in this book, therefore, it might be useful to highlight some of the new dimensions of post-industrial society.

1   *The centrality of theoretical knowledge.* Every society has always existed on the basis of knowledge, but only now has there been a change whereby the codification of theoretical knowledge and materials science becomes the basis of innovations in technology. One sees this primarily in the new science-based industries – computers, electronics, optics, polymers – that mark the last third of the century.

2   *The creation of a new intellectual technology.* Through new mathematical and economic techniques – based on the computer linear programming, Markov chains, stochastic processes and the like – we can utilize modeling, simulation and other tools of system analysis and decision theory in order to chart more efficient, "rational" solutions

to economic and engineering, if not social, problems.

3   *The spread of a knowledge class.* The fastest growing group in society is the technical and professional class. In the United States this group, together with managers, made up 25 percent of a labor force of eight million persons in 1975. By the year 2000, the technical and professional class will be the largest single group in the society.

4   *The change from goods to services.* In the United States today more than 65 out of every 100 persons are engaged in services. By 1980, the figure will be about 70 in every 100. A large service sector exists in every society. In a post-industrial society this is mainly a household and domestic class. (In England, it was the single largest class in the society until about 1870.) In an industrial society, the services are transportation utilities, and finance, which are auxiliary to the production of goods, and personal service (beauticians, restaurant employees, and so forth). But in a post-industrial society, the new services are primarily human services (principally in health, education and social services) and professional and technical services (e.g. research, evaluation, computers, and systems analysis). The expansion of these services becomes a constraint on economic growth and a source of persistent inflation.

5   *A change in the character of work.* In a pre-industrial world, life is a game against nature in which men wrest their living from the soil, the waters, or the forests, working usually in small groups, subject to the vicissitudes of nature. In an industrial society, work is a game against fabricated nature, in which men become dwarfed by machines as they turn out goods and things. But in a post-industrial world, work is primarily a "game between persons" (between bureaucrat and client, doctor and patient, teacher and student, or within research groups, office groups, service groups). Thus in the experience of work and the daily routine, nature is excluded, artifacts are excluded, and persons have to learn how to live with one another. In the history of human society, this is a completely new and unparalleled state of affairs.

6   *The role of women.* Work in the industrial sector (e.g. the factory) has largely been men's work, from which women have been usually excluded. Work in the post-industrial sector (e.g. human services) provides expanded employment opportunities for women. For the first time, one can say that women have a secure base for economic independence. One sees this in the steadily rising curve of women's participation in the labor force, in

the number of families (now 60 percent of the total) that have more than one regular wage earner, and in the rising incidence of divorce as women increasingly feel less dependent, economically, on men.

7   *Science as the imago.* The scientific community, going back to the seventeenth century, has been a unique institution in human society. It has been charismatic, in that it has been revolutionary in its quest for truth and open in its methods and procedures; it derives its legitimacy from the credo that knowledge itself, not any specific instrumental ends, is the goal of science. Unlike other charismatic communities (principally religious groups and messianic political movements), it has not "routinized" its creeds and enforced official dogmas. Yet until recently, science did not have to deal with the bureaucratization of research, the subordination of its inquiries to state-directed goals, and the "test" of its results on the basis of some instrumental payoff. Now science has become inextricably intertwined not only with technology but with the military and with social technologies and social needs. In all this – a central feature of the post-industrial society – the character of the new scientific institutions – will be crucial for the future of free inquiry and knowledge.[iii]

8   *Situses as political units.* Most of sociological analysis has focused its attention on classes or strata, horizontal units of society that exist in superior–subordinate relation to each other. Yet for the post-industrial sectors, it may well be that *situses* (from the Latin *situ*, location), a set of vertical orders, will be the more important loci of political attachment. [Later in the book] I sketch the possible situses of the post-industrial order. There are four *functional* situses – scientific, technological (i.e. applied skills: engineering, economics, medicine), administrative and cultural – and five *institutional* situses – economic enterprises, government bureaus, universities and research complexes, social complexes (e.g. hospitals, social-service centers), and the military. My argument is that the major interest conflicts will be between the situs groups, and that the attachments to these situses might be sufficiently strong to prevent the organization of the new professional groups into a coherent class in society.[7]

9   *Meritocracy.* A post-industrial society, being primarily a technical society, awards place less on

iii   Presumably this sentence means: "In all this, a central feature of the post-industrial society – the character of the new scientific institutions – will be crucial."

the basis of inheritance or property (though these can command wealth or cultural advantage) than on education and skill. Inevitably the question of a meritocracy becomes a crucial normative question. In this book I attempt to define the character of meritocracy and defend the idea of a "just meritocracy," or of place based on achievement, through the respect of peers.

10 *The end of scarcity?* Most socialist and utopian theories of the nineteenth century ascribed almost all the ills of society to the scarcity of goods and the competition of men for these scarce goods. In fact, one of the most common definitions of economics characterized it as the art of efficient allocation of scarce goods among competing ends. Marx and other socialists argued that abundance was the precondition for socialism and claimed, in fact, that under socialism there would be no need to adopt normative rules of just distribution, since there would be enough for everyone's needs. In that sense, the definition of communism was the abolition of economics, or the "material embodiment" of philosophy. Yet it is quite clear that scarcity will always be with us. I mean not just the question of scarce resources (for this is still a moot point) but that a post-industrial society, by its nature, brings new scarcities which nineteenth- and early twentieth-century writers had never thought of. The socialists and liberals had talked of the scarcities of goods; but in the post-industrial society, as I point out, there will be scarcities of information and of time. And the problems of allocation inevitably remain, in the crueler form, even, of man becoming *homo economicus* in the disposition of his leisure time.

11 *The economics of information.* As I pointed out earlier, information is by its nature a collective, not a private, good (i.e. a property). In the marketing of individual goods, it is clear that a "competitive" strategy between producers is to be preferred lest enterprise become slothful or monopolistic. Yet for the optimal social investment in knowledge, we have to follow a "cooperative" strategy in order to increase the spread and use of knowledge in society. This new problem regarding information poses the most fascinating challenges to economists and decision makers in respect to both theory and policy in the post-industrial society.

Most of the examples in this book are taken from the United States. The question that arises is whether other industrial nations in Western Europe, Japan, and the Soviet Union will become post-industrial as well. . . . I do not believe that any

social system is subject to such a causal trajectory. Yet the very features of post-industrial society indicate that, *as tendencies*, they are emergent in all industrial societies, and the extent to which they do appear depends upon a host of economic and political factors that have to do with the balance of world power, the ability of "third world" countries to organize effectively for a political and economic redistribution of wealth, the tensions between the major powers which might erupt into war or not. But it is clear that, as a theoretical construct, the continuing economic growth of all these societies necessarily involves the introduction of post-industrial elements.

The two large dimensions of a post-industrial society, as they are elaborated in this book, are the centrality of theoretical knowledge and the expansion of the service sector as against a manufacturing economy. The first means an increasing dependence on science as the means of innovating and organizing technological change. Most of the industrial societies are highly sensitive to the need for access to scientific knowledge, the organization of research, and the increasing importance of information as the strategic resource in the society. And to that extent a shift in the sociological weight of the sectors within the advanced societies, and the increasing role of science-based industries, are a crescive fact.[8]

The second change – the expansion of services in the economic sector – has been most striking in the United States, but has occurred in Western Europe as well. In 1960, a total of 39.5 percent of the workers in the enlarged Common Market area were in services (defined broadly as transport, trade, insurance, banking, public administration, personal service). Thirteen years later, in 1973, the proportion had risen to 47.6 percent. A change of this kind usually goes in two phases. The first – the observation of Colin Clark who first described the phenomenon thirty years ago – was a shift to services at the expense of agriculture, but with industrial employment growing as well. But in Denmark, Sweden, Belgium and the United Kingdom, the service-oriented sectors have now grown at the relative expense of *industrial* employment (since agriculture has reached almost rock-bottom), and this is beginning to take place throughout Europe as well.[9]

The Soviet Union is an industrial society, and it is likely that post-industrial features will appear in that country as well. The striking fact, however, is that this book, *The Coming of Post-Industrial Society*, has been the object of an extraordinary range of attacks in the Soviet press, from serious discussions in academic journals, such as *Problems of Philosophy*, or intellectual weeklies such as the *Literary Gazette*, to ideological polemics in the official Party theoretical magazine *Kommunist* and vulgar and highly distorted accounts in *Pravda*. It would seem as if a decision had been made by the Party's ideological committee to attack this book as an ideological threat to Party doctrine. The reasons are quite clear. From the Soviet point of view there is a "historic" conflict between capitalism and communism in which the "objective laws of history" prove the ultimate victory of communism. And this is still a central tenet of the faith – at least for export purposes. On a theoretical level, my discussion denies the idea that one can use monolithic concepts such as capitalism or socialism to explain the complex structure of modern societies. More directly, since the Party doctrine bases its view of history on the inevitable victory of the proletariat (and justifies the repressive rule of the Party in the name of the "dictatorship of the proletariat"), how can one sustain that dogma when the proletariat is no longer the major occupational class of a post-industrial society?

This was precisely the problem of a remarkable book by some members of the Czechoslovak Academy of Science, *Civilization at the Crossroads: Social and Human Implications of the Scientific and Technological Revolution*, which appeared during the "Prague Spring," in 1967, under the sponsorship of the social-science director Radovan Richta. In this book, the Czechoslovak sociologists explored the possibility of new "interest conflicts," if not "class conflicts," between the new scientific and professional strata and the working class in socialist society. Clearly, such a discussion was highly embarrassing to Marxist doctrine, and the theme a threat to the ideological justification of the Party. After 1968, Richta, who remained in Czechoslovakia after the Soviet occupation, abjectly and ignominiously repudiated the implications of his work.

The theme of post-industrialism applies primarily to changes in *the social structure* (the techno-economic order) and only indirectly to those in the polity and the culture, which comprise the other major realms of societal structure. One consequence of this is to widen the disjunction between the realms, since each now operates under axial principles that are contrary to the other.

When capitalism arose as a socio-economic system, it had a tenuous unity: an ethos (individualism), a political philosophy (liberalism), a culture (a bourgeois conception of utility and realism), and a character structure (respectability, delayed gratification, and the like). Many of these elements have withered or remain as pale ideologies. What is left is a technological engine, geared to the idea of functional rationality and efficiency, which promises a rising standard of living and promotes a hedonistic way of life. A post-industrial change begins to rework the stratification system of the society, to provide a more sophisticated technology, and to harness science more directly to instrumental purposes. Yet it is not at all clear that science, as a "republic of virtue," has the power to provide a new ethos for the society; more likely it is science itself that may become subverted. What this means is that the society is left with no transcendent ethos to provide some appropriate sense of purpose, no anchorages that can provide stable meanings for people.

In effect, what a post-industrial transformation means is the enhancement of *instrumental* powers, powers over nature and powers, even, over people. In the nineteenth century, utopian and socialist thinkers believed that any enhancement of man's power would necessarily be progressive, since it would mean the decline of religion and superstition and a proof of the greater powers and self-consciousness of Man. Yet this has proved to be a delusion. Instruments can be put to varied use. The kinds of use depend upon the values of a society, the entrenched nature of a privileged class, the openness of the society, its sense of decency or – as we have learned so viciously in the twentieth century – its bestiality.

A post-industrial transformation provides no "answers." It only establishes new promises and new powers, new constraints and new questions – with the difference that these are now on a *scale* that had never been previously imagined in world history.

Author's Notes

1 Perhaps the major misconception is to identify the idea of the post-industrial society with the expansion of the service (or tertiary) sector of the economy and dispute its importance. Some writers using the term

(e.g. Herman Kahn) have emphasized this feature. To the extent that some critics identify me with the centrality of a service sector, it is either ignorance or a willful misreading of my book.

2 For Marxists, fascism was the "last" stage of monopoly capitalism. While many capitalists did support fascism, the character of the system derived from the déclassé who led the movement, and the lower middle class which formed its mass base. Fascism is a cultural-political phenomenon. Curiously, we still have no comprehensive Marxist analysis of fascism, nor even a "Marxist analysis" of the new class structure of the Soviet Union itself.

3 By information I mean, broadly, the storing, retrieval, and processing of data, as the basis of all economic and social exchanges. This would include:

1 Records: payrolls, government benefits (e.g., social security), bank clearances, credit clearances, and the like.
2 Scheduling: airline reservations, production scheduling, inventory analysis, product-mix information, and so forth.
3 Demographic and library: census data, opinion surveys, market research, knowledge storage, election data, and so forth.

By knowledge, I mean an organized set of statements, of facts or ideas, presenting a reasoned judgment or an experimental result that is transmitted to others through communication media in some systematic form.

4 A parallel argument has been made by the German Marxist scholar Jürgen Habermas, who has written:

technology and science [have] become a leading productive force, rendering inoperative the conditions for Marx's labor theory of value. It is no longer meaningful to calculate the amount of capital investment in research and development on the basis of the value of unskilled (simple) labor power, when scientific-technical progress has become an independent source of surplus value, in relation to which the only source of surplus value considered by Marx, namely the labor power of the immediate producers, plays an ever smaller role. Jürgen Habermas, *Toward a Rational Society* (Boston: Beacon Press, 1970, p. 104)

To that extent, too, one can say that *knowledge*, not labor, is a social product, and that Marx's analysis of the social character of production applies more fully to knowledge than to the production of goods.

5 The seminal work on this question of collective goods is Mancur Olson's *The Logic of Collective Action* (Cambridge: Harvard University Press, 1965). The question of the "economics of information" has come to absorb the attention of the Harvard economists Kenneth Arrow and Michael Spence. For some initial reflections, see, Kenneth Arrow, "Limited Knowledge and Economic Analysis," *American Economic Review* (March 1974), and Michael A. Spence, "An Economist's View of Information," in *Annual Review of Information Science and Technology*, 9, edited by Carlos A. Cuadra and Ann W. Luke (Washington, DC, 1974, American Society for Information Science).

6 One intriguing way in which cheap communications technology creates new social patterns is the use of citizens' band radio as a form of coordinated action. In 1974, independent truckers could create vast slowdowns on a thousand-mile chain of roads in the midwest by radio communication from selected blockade points. In one sense, this is little different from the pattern of riverboat pilots exchanging information which Mark Twain described so hilariously in *Life on the Mississippi*, but in this, as in so many instances, the characteristic of modernity is not the nature of the action but its scale, rapidity, and coordination.

For an authoritative elaboration of these technical questions, see the monograph *The Medium and the Telephone: The Politics of Information Resources*, by Paul J. Berman and Anthony Oettinger, Working Paper 75–8, Harvard Program on Information Technology and Public Policy. For this and other materials on information technology I am indebted to my colleague Professor Oettinger.

7 What is striking is that in the communist world, it is quite clear that *situses* play the major role in politics. One analyzes the play of power, not in class terms, but on the basis of the rivalries among the party, the military, the planning ministries, the industrial enterprises, the collective farms, the cultural institutions – all of which are *situses*.

8 As I indicated in the text, the national power of industrial societies was once rated on the basis of steel capacity. Two years ago, the Soviet Union passed the United States in the steel tonnage it produces, a fact that received only passing mention in the business pages of the *New York Times*. Yet in the development of computers, both in degree of sophistication and numbers, the Soviet Union is far, far behind the United States, a fact that was made vividly clear when the Soyuz and Apollo capsules were linked and the quality of their equipment could be compared.

9 It is striking that Italy, Germany and France are the countries where industrial employment has increased; the largest increase was in Italy, which had lagged furthest in industrialization in Europe. But in the other countries, the proportion of those in industry has begun to shrink in relation to services. (For some detailed statistics on these occupational shifts, see *The Economist* [London], November 29, 1975, p. 17.)

Japan too, has been following a similar trajectory in which the expansion in services has been at the expense of industry. For a detailed discussion, see Henry Rosovsky, "Japan's Economic Future," *Chal-*

lenge, July/August, 1973. In this essay Rosovsky develops a definition of "economic maturity" which is interesting in the light of sector changes that have taken place in the industrializing countries in the last fifty years. He writes: "Economic maturity is a difficult term to define but as used here it has a narrow meaning. Let us call it that state in which the incentives of sectoral labor force reallocation have become minimal – in the extreme case, impossible" (p. 16).

PART III

Postmodernism and the Re-evaluation of Modernity

Introduction to Part III

Postmodernism was not the child of crisis, at least by twentieth-century standards. It was the relative stability and unprecedented prosperity of the period following the defeat of European fascism and Japanese militarism that became the background for the Western tradition's deepest self-criticism. To be sure, the tense nuclear stand-off of the Cold War, the various hot wars of the period, especially for the French in Algeria and the United States in Vietnam, together with vast social changes and political conflicts, made the post-World War II period anything but calm. Nevertheless, it is perhaps inevitable that the deepest self-criticism emerges only from periods of relative security. It is hard to imagine postmodernism thriving while Hitler and Stalin were alive. Fighting the devil makes for fear and hatred, not uncertainty.

Along with the enormous expansion of the North American, Western European and Japanese economies, their seeming political stability and their unprecedented rise in living standards, came an increasingly insistent list of debits: the expansion of governmental bureaucracy to manage the growing welfare state, new technologies, and a permanent military deterrent; the increasing technical and organizational control of social life by corporate institutions as well as government; the progressive replacement of traditional and local cultures by the universal network of television and instantaneous communications, creating the new universe of mass popular culture; the dissolution of the extended family and local community by economic demands and social and geographical mobility; the environmental impact of technological modernization; the psychic costs of life in the economy of permanent change. Add to this the end of the Western colonial empires, the domestic social rebellion of previously disenfranchised ethnic groups, economic classes and women, and an apparent loss of public confidence in religious and secular authority, and the result was a heightened sense of prosperous disorder.

Whatever the precise list of reasons, in the late 1960s something in the juggernaut of modern Western culture broke. Not that it had ever been untroubled, or that it had not been assailed by far greater crises (namely, two devastating wars and a world economic depression). But at the very least, its post-World War II confidence, its *Pax Americana*, was shaken. As an historian friend who taught at an East Coast American university during the period once said to me: "In 1968 the world changed." By this he meant the world of the university, the students, the faculty, and, by inference, the greater world. Of course, human nature and the laws of physics did not change, but some other things did: attitudes, styles, beliefs, hopes seemed to swing away from one pole and toward another. By no means were all overcome with radical, counter-cultural fervor, but even the defenders of the status quo seemed to lose their earlier idealism and certainty. Less and less could anyone regard this as the best of all possible worlds – an idea not far-fetched to many Americans in the 1950s.

If postmodernism was birthed in the cultural revolution of the late 1960s and early 1970s, it matured in an atmosphere of, one might say, retrenchment. After the 1970s, radicalism in the political arena went into a sharp decline. The period since 1980 has been marked by the resurgence of political and cultural conservatism in many advanced societies, dwelling cheek by jowl with

221

mass cultural and economic innovation, and the dispersal of anti-modern and anti-Western reaction among widely resurgent religious fundamentalists and nationalist groups – forming the opposition that Benjamin Barber labeled, in his book of the same name, "Jihad vs. McWorld." Most far-reaching was the collapse of institutional communism since 1989 (which postdated its demise as ideology). In a post-Cold War environment in which decentralized technology – especially weapons, communications, and information-processing – has empowered an array of state-evading terrorists and "kleptocracies," making security ever more elusive, it is more true than ever that, as historian Stephen Ambrose wrote in *Rise to Globalism*, "the power to destroy is not the power to control." Domestically, the reaction against the direction of change comes from three sources: a home-grown religious fundamentalism that remains comfortable with economic advances; a coalition of environmentalists and those opposed to economic globalization, embodying the remnants of the left; and a smattering of nativist and in some cases racist and neo-fascist movements. While the 1995 bombing of the Oklahoma City federal building seemed to augur a mature domestic threat, it was far surpassed by the September 11, 2001 terrorist attacks, which may (as of this writing, it is yet to be seen) have launched the Northern democracies into a global, alternately hot-and-cold confrontation with militant Islam that had been simmering for several decades. While the ability of religious fundamentalism to form long-term, stable alternatives to liberal capitalist modernity seems dubious, the shock to confidence remains in the form of a sober uneasiness, the recurrent awakening to a permanently raised level of domestic social disorder and international insecurity, the chastened reminder that our course is permanently directed through unfamiliar, uncharted waters. If nothing else, "postmodern" remains a plausible term for that wariness.

While no categorization can be adequate to capture the diversity among postmodernists, a four-part classification can make most of this material easier to digest.

First it is useful to distinguish the French school that started it all, what is often called "post-structuralism," which is in fact a radicalized version of structuralism. The post-structuralists developed methods of analysis and forms of thought that are the source of much of what is called postmodernism in philosophy, social and political theory, and art and literature. The most influential have been Jacques Derrida, for philosophical and literary method, and Michel Foucault, for social and political thought. Their selections are accompanied by Jean-François Lyotard's famous formulation of "the postmodern condition," the provocative "nomadology" of Gilles Deleuze and Fèlix Guattari, and a crucial essay of the French feminist school by Luce Irigary.

Second, a wide array of thinkers have employed these methods to political ends, especially to criticize the suppression of formerly disenfranchised groups. Feminism most famously, but also post-colonialism, queer theory, multiculturalism, and the critique of racism all have exploited post-structuralist methodology. They populate the section on "Critical Appropriations." It is important to note, however, that many of these writers are wary of post-structuralism where they fear that it goes far enough to disable reformist ideals. In art, Hal Foster fears an all-too-easy postmodern pluralism that bypasses the need for cultural criticism. Echoing Foucault, Sandra Harding calls attention to a marginalized female view of knowledge and nature. Susan Bordo and Cornel West employ Foucauldian genealogy to expose the constitutive role played by sexism and racism, respectively, in the formation of modern thought. Contrastingly, Gayatri Chakravorty Spivak uses Derridean sources to chide Foucault, and Deleuze, for their treatment of the post-colonial subject. Henry Giroux calls for a multicultural, postmodern pedagogy to counter modern Eurocentrism. Iris Marion Young attacks the "normalizing" of political identities under modern liberalism. Judith Butler warns that postmodernist tools could be used to "deconstruct" the very notion of a distinctive female viewpoint and any hope for female solidarity. But even when they are critical of some forms of postmodernism, these writers are happy to borrow its critique of the ideal of Reason, social norms, and any imposed unity.

The title of the third section, "Beyond Critique," may seem unfair; certainly the authors presented are critical of something! But unlike those under the preceding section, their emphasis is on accepting and integrating "postmodern" social, intellectual, and scientific developments. Some argue that if the dominant social order can no longer legitimate itself, neither can neo-Marxism or Critical Theory or feminism or other liberationist motifs. Their denial of totalizing political critique and their acceptance of a technocratic consumer society, mass culture, and aesthetic pluralism imply that the previous section's critical appropriations are anachronistic. This attitude was perhaps first evident in architecture, art, and literature. Architect Robert Venturi stood before the eclectic glitz of Las Vegas and asked, "What's wrong with that?" Jean Baudrillard, author of *Forget Foucault* (1987), denies that neo-Marxist categories can apply to our postmodern, mass cultural "hyperreality." Literary critic Ihab Hassan embraces the transcendent heterogeneity of postmodern writing, while in architectural theory Charles Jencks accepts the "end of the avant-garde." Donna Haraway turns to cybernetics for a possible feminist replacement for patriarchal humanism. In philosophy Richard Rorty's "postmodernist bourgeois liberalism" rejects both traditional philosophy and post-structuralism's left-ward impulses. Niklas Luhmann's radical constructivism of social systems undercuts the possibility of normative social critique. At the same time other theorists attempt to continue more traditional philosophical aims while accepting much of the postmodernist critique of modern metaphysics. They argue for a philosophical worldview that imbibes postmodernism's force while escaping its blanket rejection of traditional philosophical aims. Thus David Ray Griffin, who like Haraway and Luhmann depend on the "new science," sees hope for a postmodern cosmology. Mark C. Taylor employs post-structuralism toward a rare aim, arguing for a Derridean theology. Lastly, David Hall shows the extent to which premodern Chinese thought anticipated much of the postmodern turn.

The final section, "Resistances and Alternatives," presents both contemporary philosophies that explicitly critique postmodernism and those claiming immunity to the postmodern assault. By no means do they exhaust the manifold activity of that majority of contemporary philosophers who remain uninfluenced by postmodernism, but they do offer a small selection of those who oppose or studiously avoid it. Like the postmodernists, they reject foundationalism; they agree with James, Wittgenstein, and Heidegger – depending on their philosophical lineage – that philosophy must abandon the Cartesian project. But unlike the postmodernists, they feel that philosophy can turn to some kind of pragmatism or common sense or naturalism or experiential method, thereby avoiding both foundationalism and postmodern excess. In a sense, this is the great surgical problem of contemporary philosophy: given that foundationalism is diseased and must be cut out, how deep must we cut, and what shape will the patient be in once the surgery is over? Postmodernists say that the patient will be dead, because the diseased tissue is so deep as to be inseparable from what kept the patient alive. Non-foundationalists disagree, convinced that the patient can go on to lead a full, albeit non-transcendental, life. Thus, Emmanuel Levinas, perhaps the most widely discussed twentieth-century European ethicist, draws on the same continental sources as the French postmodernists, but refuses to allow semiotics to rule the ethical relation. Willard Van Quine's defense of naturalistic epistemology, the resolution of the "problem" of knowledge through the use of scientific results, anticipates recent developments in cognitive science and evolutionary psychology that claim to avoid the postmodern problematic. Alasdair MacIntyre argues that given the incapacity of Englightenment, hence the choice between "Nietzsche or Aristotle," ethical rationality must return to premodernist, Aristotelian and Thomistic, approaches. Frederic Jameson offers a neo-Marxist alternative to what is, in his view, a politically inadequate postmodernism. Jürgen Habermas deploys a communicative ethics, based partly in pragmatism, to defend a reformed Enlightenment modernism. Lastly, Hilary Putnam similarly forges a "pragmatic" or "internal" realism, attempting to steer between "metaphysical" or foundationalist realism and Rorty's postmodern version of pragmatism.

French Post-Structuralism

27

"Differance"

Jacques Derrida

Algerian born French philosopher, Jacques Der-rida (1930–) is one of the two most famous in-stigators of what is called postmodernism in contemporary philosophy (the other being Fou-cault). More accurately labeled a post-structural-ist, his reputation was made in the late 1960s with a series of books remarkable for their careful analysis of texts, their novel critical perspective, and their difficult style. His work began as an an-alysis of Husserlian phenomenology that called attention to self-undermining problems implicit in Husserl's fundamental distinctions, but expanded to assert the uncontrollable "play" of all "writing" or semiosis. Signs, whose relation to their objects is always mediated, generate end-less, undecidable chains of meanings. In the 1968 lecture below, Derrida discovers in recent philosophical advances a recognition of this fun-damental plurality and uncertainty of meaning, which he labels with his famous neologism, *différance*.

THE VERB "to differ" [*différer*] seems to differ from itself. On the one hand, it indicates difference as distinction, inequality, or discernibility; on the other, it expresses the interposition of delay, the interval of a *spacing* and *temporalizing* that puts off until "later" what is presently denied, the possible that is presently impossible. Sometimes the *differ-ent* and sometimes the *deferred* correspond to the verb "to differ."[i] This correlation, however, is not simply one between act and object, cause and effect, or primordial and derived.

[i] They can correspond in French.

In the one case "to differ" signifies nonidentity; in the other case it signifies the order of the *same*. Yet there must be a common, although entirely differant, root within the sphere that relates the two movements of differing to one another. We provisionally give the name *différance* to this *same-ness* which is not *identical*: by the silent writing of its *a*, it has the desired advantage of referring to differing, *both* as spacing/temporalizing and as the movement that structures every dissociation.[ii]

As distinct from difference, differance thus points out the irreducibility of temporalizing (which is also temporalization – in transcendental language which is no longer adequate here, this would be called the constitution of primordial tem-porality – just as the term "spacing" also includes the constitution of primordial spatiality). Differ-ance is not simply active (any more than it is a

[ii] Derrida is creating a technical term by changing the second *e* in the French word *différence* to an *a*, a change which, given French pronunciation, cannot be heard, but only seen in writing. Note that in French the first *e* is accented, the French *différence*. Thus the title of Derri-da's lecture was "*La Différance*." Difference, without the accent, is the English translation. (Although, strictly speaking, the difference is moot since neither is an actual word, in French or English, and that is the point.)

Jacques Derrida, "Differance," pp. 129–60 in *Speech and Phenomena and Other Essays on Husserl's Theory of Signs* (trans. David B. Allison). Evanston: North-western University Press, 1973. This translation includes the introduction to the original 1968 lecture by Derrida (the first five paragraphs).

subjective accomplishment); it rather indicates the middle voice, it precedes and sets up the opposition between passivity and activity. With its *a*, differance more properly refers to what in classical language would be called the origin or production of differences and the differences between differences, the *play* [*jeu*] of differences. Its locus and operation will therefore be seen wherever speech appeals to difference.

Differance is neither a *word* nor a *concept*. In it, however, we shall see the juncture – rather than the summation – of what has been most decisively inscribed in the thought of what is conveniently called our "epoch": the difference of forces in Nietzsche, Saussure's principle of semiological difference, differing as the possibility of facilitation, impression and delayed effect in Freud, difference as the irreducibility of the trace of the other in Levinas, and the ontic-ontological difference in Heidegger.[iii]

Reflection on this last determination of difference will lead us to consider differance as the *strategic* note or connection – relatively or provisionally *privileged* – which indicates the closure of presence, together with the closure of the conceptual order and denomination, a closure that is effected in the functioning of traces.

I SHALL SPEAK, THEN, OF A LETTER – the first one, if we are to believe the alphabet and most of the speculations that have concerned themselves with it.

I shall speak then of the letter *a*, this first letter which it seemed necessary to introduce now and then in writing the word "difference." This seemed necessary in the course of writing about writing, and of writing within a writing whose different strokes all pass, in certain respects, through a gross spelling mistake, through a violation of the rules governing writing, violating the law that governs writing and regulates its conventions of propriety. In fact or theory we can always erase or lessen this spelling mistake, and, in each case, while these are analytically different from one another but for practical purposes the same, find it grave, unseemly, or, indeed, supposing the greatest ingenuousness, amusing. Whether or not we care to quietly overlook this infraction, the attention we give it beforehand will allow us to recognize, as though prescribed by some mute irony, the inaudible but

displaced character of this literal permutation. We can always act as though this makes no difference. I must say from the start that my account serves less to justify this silent spelling mistake, or still less to excuse it, than to aggravate its obtrusive character.

On the other hand, I must be excused if I refer, at least implicitly, to one or another of the texts that I have ventured to publish. Precisely what I would like to attempt to some extent (although this is in principle and in its highest degree impossible, due to essential *de jure*[iv] reasons) is to bring together an *assemblage* of the different ways I have been able to utilize – or, rather, have allowed to be imposed on me – what I will provisionally call the word or concept of differance in its new spelling. It is literally neither a word nor a concept, as we shall see. I insist on the word "assemblage" here for two reasons: on the one hand, it is not a matter of describing a history, of recounting the steps, text by text, context by context, each time showing which scheme has been able to impose this graphic disorder, although this could have been done as well; rather, we are concerned with the *general system of all these schemata*. On the other hand, the word "assemblage" seems more apt for suggesting that the kind of bringing-together proposed here has the structure of an interlacing, a weaving, or a web, which would allow the different threads and different lines of sense or force to separate again, as well as being ready to bind others together.

In a quite preliminary way, we now recall that this particular graphic intervention was conceived in the writing-up of a question about writing; it was not made simply to shock the reader or grammarian. Now, in point of fact, it happens that this graphic difference (the *a* instead of the *e*), this marked difference between two apparently vocalic notations, between vowels, remains purely graphic: it is written or read, but it is not heard. It cannot be heard, and we shall see in what respects it is also beyond the order of understanding. It is put forward by a silent mark, by a tacit monument, or, one might even say, by a pyramid – keeping in mind not only the capital form of the printed letter but also that passage from Hegel's *Encyclopaedia* where he compares the body of the sign to an Egyptian pyramid. The *a* of differance, therefore, is not heard; it remains silent, secret, and discreet, like a tomb.

It is a tomb that (provided one knows how to decipher its legend) is not far from signaling the death of the king.

---

iii "Facilitation" refers to the opening or sensitizing of a nerve pathway. The ontic-ontological difference in Heidegger is the difference between Being (*Sein*) and beings or entities (*Seiende*).

iv By law, not fact.

It is a tomb that cannot even be made to resonate. For I cannot even let you know, by my talk, now being spoken before the Société Française de Philosophie, which difference I am talking about at the very moment I speak of it. I can only talk about this graphic difference by keeping to a very indirect speech about writing, and on the condition that I specify each time that I am referring to difference with an *e* or differance with an *a*. All of which is not going to simplify matters today, and will give us all a great deal of trouble when we want to understand one another. In any event, when I do specify which difference I mean – when I say "with an *e*" or "with an *a*" – this will refer irreducibly to a *written text*, a text governing my talk, a text that I keep in front of me, that I will read, and toward which I shall have to try to lead your hands and eyes. We cannot refrain here from going by way of a written text, from ordering ourselves by the disorder that is produced therein – and this is what matters to me first of all.

Doubtless this pyramidal silence of the graphic difference between the *e* and the *a* can function only within the system of phonetic writing and within a language or grammar historically tied to phonetic writing and to the whole culture which is inseparable from it. But I will say that it is just this – this silence that functions only within what is called phonetic writing – that points out or reminds us in a very opportune way that, contrary to an enormous prejudice, there is no phonetic writing. There is no purely and strictly phonetic writing. What is called phonetic writing can only function – in principle and *de jure*, and not due to some factual and technical inadequacy – by incorporating nonphonetic "signs" (punctuation, spacing, etc.); but when we examine their structure and necessity, we will quickly see that they are ill described by the concept of signs. Saussure had only to remind us that the play of difference was the functional condition, the condition of possibility, for every sign; and it is itself silent. The difference between two phonemes, which enables them to exist and to operate, is inaudible. The inaudible opens the two present phonemes to hearing, as they present themselves. If, then, there is no purely phonetic writing, it is because there is no purely phonetic phone. The difference that brings out phonemes and lets them be heard and understood [*entendre*] itself remains inaudible.

It will perhaps be objected that, for the same reasons, the graphic difference itself sinks into darkness, that it never constitutes the fullness of a sensible term, but draws out an invisible connection, the mark of an inapparent relation between two spec-

tacles. That is no doubt true. Indeed, since from this point of view the difference between the *e* and the *a* marked in "differance" eludes vision and hearing, this happily suggests that we must here let ourselves be referred to an order that no longer refers to sensibility. But we are not referred to intelligibility either, to an ideality not fortuitously associated with the objectivity of *theōrein* or understanding. We must be referred to an order, then, that resists philosophy's founding opposition between the sensible and the intelligible. The order that resists this opposition, that resists it because it sustains it, is designated in a movement of differance (with an *a*) between two differences or between two letters. This differance belongs neither to the voice nor to writing in the ordinary sense, and it takes place, like the strange space that will assemble us here for the course of an hour *between* speech and writing and beyond the tranquil familiarity that binds us to one and to the other, reassuring us sometimes in the illusion that they are two separate things.

NOW, HOW AM I TO SPEAK OF the *a* of differance? It is clear that it cannot be *exposed*. We can expose only what, at a certain moment, can become *present*, manifest; what can be shown, presented as a present, a being-present in its truth, the truth of a present or the presence of a present. However, if differance is (I also cross out the "is") what makes the presentation of being-present possible, it never presents itself as such. It is never given in the present or to anyone. Holding back and not exposing itself, it goes beyond the order of truth on this specific point and in this determined way, yet is not itself concealed, as if it were something, a mysterious being, in the occult zone of a nonknowing. Any exposition would expose it to disappearing as a disappearance. It would risk appearing, thus disappearing.

Thus, the detours, phrases, and syntax that I shall often have to resort to will resemble – will sometimes be practically indiscernible from – those of negative theology.[v] Already we had to note *that* differance *is not*, does not exist, and is not any sort of being-present (*on*). And we will have to point out everything *that* it *is not*, and, consequently, that it has neither existence nor essence. It belongs to no category of being, present or absent. And yet what is thus denoted as differance is not theological, not even in the most negative order of negative

---

[v] The medieval view that God cannot be described positively, but only negatively through denying his likeness to worldly properties (e.g. not finite).

theology. The latter, as we know, is always occupied with letting a supraessential reality go beyond the finite categories of essence and existence, that is, of presence, and always hastens to remind us that, if we deny the predicate of existence to God, it is in order to recognize him as a superior, inconceivable, and ineffable mode of being. Here there is no question of such a move, as will be confirmed as we go along. Not only is differance irreducible to every ontological or theological – onto-theological – reappropriation, but it opens up the very space in which onto-theology – philosophy – produces its system and its history. It thus encompasses and irrevocably surpasses onto-theology or philosophy.

For the same reason, I do not know where *to begin* to mark out this assemblage, this graph, of differance. Precisely what is in question here is the requirement that there be a *de jure* commencement, an absolute point of departure, a responsibility arising from a principle. The problem of writing opens by questioning the *archē*.[vi] Thus what I put forth here will not be developed simply as a philosophical discourse that operates on the basis of a principle, of postulates, axioms, and definitions and that moves according to the discursive line of a rational order. In marking out differance, everything is a matter of strategy and risk. It is a question of strategy because no transcendent truth present outside the sphere of writing can theologically command the totality of this field. It is hazardous because this strategy is not simply one in the sense that we say that strategy orients the tactics according to a final aim, a *telos* or the theme of a domination, a mastery or an ultimate reappropriation of movement and field. In the end, it is a strategy without finality. We might call it blind tactics or empirical errance, if the value of empiricism did not itself derive all its meaning from its opposition to philosophical responsibility. If there is a certain errance in the tracing-out of differance, it no longer follows the line of logico-philosophical speech or that of its integral and symmetrical opposite, logico-empirical speech. The concept of *play* remains beyond this opposition; on the eve and aftermath of philosophy, it designates the unity of chance and necessity in an endless calculus.

By decision and, as it were, by the rules of the game, then, turning this thought around, let us introduce ourselves to the thought of differance by way of the theme of strategy or strategem. By this merely strategic justification, I want to empha-

size that the efficacy of this thematics of differance very well may, and even one day must, be sublated, i.e., lend itself, if not to its own replacement, at least to its involvement in a series of events which in fact it never commanded. This also means that it is not a theological thematics.

I will say, first of all, that differance, which is neither a word nor a concept, seemed to me to be strategically the theme most proper to think out, if not master (thought being here, perhaps, held in a certain necessary relation with the structional limits of mastery), in what is most characteristic of our "epoch." I start off, then, strategically, from the place and time in which "we" are, even though my opening is not justifiable in the final account, and though it is always on the basis of difference and its "history" that we can claim to know who and where "we" are and what the limits of an "epoch" can be.

Although "differance" is neither a word nor a concept, let us nonetheless attempt a simple and approximative semantic analysis which will bring us in view of what is at stake.

We do know that the verb "to differ" (the Latin verb *differre*) has two seemingly quite distinct meanings; in the *Littré* dictionary, for example, they are the subject of two separate articles. In this sense, the Latin *differre* is not the simple translation of the Greek *diapherein*; this fact will not be without consequence for us in tying our discussion to a particular language, one that passes for being less philosophical, less primordially philosophical, than the other. For the distribution of sense in the Greek *diapherein* does not carry one of the two themes of the Latin *differre*, namely, the action of postponing until later, of taking into account, the taking-account of time and forces in an operation that implies an economic reckoning, a detour, a respite, a delay, a reserve, a representation – all the concepts that I will sum up here in a word I have never used but which could be added to this series: *temporalizing*. "To differ" in this sense is to temporalize, to resort, consciously or unconsciously, to the temporal and temporalizing mediation of a detour that suspends the accomplishment or fulfillment of "desire" or "will," or carries desire or will out in a way that annuls or tempers their effect. We shall see, later, in what respects this temporalizing is also a temporalization and spacing, is space's becoming-temporal and time's becoming-spatial, is "primordial constitution" of space and time, as metaphysics or transcendental phenomenology would call it in the language that is here criticized and displaced.

---

vi   Fundamental principle.

The other sense of "to differ" is the most common and most identifiable, the sense of not being identical, of being other, of being discernible, etc. And in "differents," whether referring to the alterity of dissimilarity or the alterity of allergy or of polemics, it is necessary that interval, distance, *spacing* occur among the different elements and occur actively, dynamically, and with a certain perseverence in repetition.

But the word "difference" (with an *e*) could never refer to differing as temporalizing or to difference as *polemos*.[vii] It is this loss of sense that the word differance (with an *a*) will have to schematically compensate for. Differance can refer to the whole complex of its meanings at once, for it is immediately and irreducibly multivalent, something which will be important for the discourse I am trying to develop. It refers to this whole complex of meanings not only when it is supported by a language or interpretive context (like any signification), but it already does so somehow of itself. Or at least it does so more easily by itself than does any other word: here the *a* comes more immediately from the present participle and brings us closer to the action of "differing" that is in progress, even before it has produced the effect that is constituted as different or resulted in difference (with an *e*). Within a conceptual system and in terms of classical requirements, differance could be said to designate the productive and primordial constituting causality, the process of scission and division whose differings and differences would be the constituted products or effects. But while bringing us closer to the infinitive and active core of differing, "differance" with an *a* neutralizes what the infinitive denotes as simply active, in the same way that "parlance" does not signify the simple fact of speaking, of speaking to or being spoken to. Nor is resonance the act of resonating. Here in the usage of our language we must consider that the ending -*ance* is undecided between active and passive. And we shall see why what is designated by "differance" is neither simply active nor simply passive, that it announces or rather recalls something like the middle voice, that it speaks of an operation which is not an operation, which cannot be thought of either as a passion or as an action of a subject upon an object, as starting from an agent or from a patient, or on the basis of, or in view of, any of these *terms*. But philosophy has perhaps commenced by distributing the middle voice, express-

ing a certain intransitiveness, into the active and the passive voice, and has itself been constituted in this repression.

How are difference as temporalizing and differance as spacing conjoined?

Let us begin with the problem of signs and writing – since we are already in the midst of it. We ordinarily say that a sign is put in place of the thing itself, the present thing – "thing" holding here for the sense as well as the referent. Signs represent the present in its absence; they take the place of the present. When we cannot take hold of or show the thing, let us say the present, the being-present, when the present does not present itself, then we signify, we go through the detour of signs. We take up or give signs; we make signs. The sign would thus be a deferred presence. Whether it is a question of verbal or written signs, monetary signs, electoral delegates, or political representatives, the movement of signs defers the moment of encountering the thing itself, the moment at which we could lay hold of it, consume or expend it, touch it, see it, have a present intuition of it. What I am describing here is the structure of signs as classically determined, in order to define – through a commonplace characterization of its traits – signification as the differance of temporalizing. Now this classical determination presupposes that the sign (which defers presence) is conceivable only *on the basis of* the presence that it defers and *in view of* the deferred presence one intends to reappropriate. Following this classical semiology, the substitution of the sign for the thing itself is both *secondary* and *provisional:* it is second in order after an original and lost presence, a presence from which the sign would be derived. It is provisional with respect to this final and missing presence, in view of which the sign would serve as a movement of mediation.

In attempting to examine these secondary and provisional aspects of the substitute, we shall no doubt catch sight of something like a primordial differance. Yet we could no longer even call it primordial or final, inasmuch as the characteristics of origin, beginning, *telos, eschaton*, etc., have always denoted presence – *ousia, parousia*, etc.[viii] To question the secondary and provisional character of the sign, to oppose it to a "primordial" differance, would thus have the following consequences:

[vii] Conflict, war.

[viii] *Telos* is end or goal; *eschaton* is "last times" or the culmination of history; *ousia* is being; *parousia* is primary being.

1. Differance can no longer be understood according to the concept of "sign," which has always been taken to mean the representation of a presence and has been constituted in a system (of thought or language) determined on the basis of and in view of presence.

2. In this way we question the authority of presence or its simple symmetrical contrary, absence or lack. We thus interrogate the limit that has always constrained us, that always constrains us – we who inhabit a language and a system of thought – to form the sense of being in general as presence or absence, in the categories of being or beingness (*ousia*). It already appears that the kind of questioning we are thus led back to is, let us say, the Heideggerian kind, and that differance *seems* to lead us back to the ontic-ontological difference. But permit me to postpone this reference. I shall only note that between differance as temporalizing-temporalization (which we can no longer conceive within the horizon of the present) and what Heidegger says about temporalization in *Sein und Zeit*[ix] (namely, that as the transcendental horizon of the question of being it must be freed from the traditional and metaphysical domination by the present or the now) – between these two there is a close, if not exhaustive and irreducibly necessary, interconnection.

But first of all, let us remain with the semiological aspects of the problem to see how differance as temporalizing is conjoined with differance as spacing. Most of the semiological or linguistic research currently dominating the field of thought (whether due to the results of its own investigations or due to its role as a generally recognized regulative model) traces its genealogy, rightly or wrongly, to Saussure as its common founder. It was Saussure who first of all set forth the *arbitrariness of signs* and the *differential character* of signs as principles of general semiology and particularly of linguistics. And, as we know, these two themes – the arbitrary and the differential – are in his view inseparable. Arbitrariness can occur only because the system of signs is constituted by the differences between the terms, and not by their fullness. The elements of signification function not by virtue of the compact force of their cores but by the network of oppositions that distinguish them and relate them to one another. "Arbitrary and differential" says Saussure "are two correlative qualities."

As the condition for signification, this principle of difference affects the *whole sign*, that is, both the signified and the signifying aspects. The signified aspect is the concept, the ideal sense. The signifying aspect is what Saussure calls the material or physical (e.g., acoustical) "image." We do not here have to enter into all the problems these definitions pose. Let us only cite Saussure where it interests us:

> The conceptual side of value is made up solely of relations and differences with respect to the other terms of language, and the same can be said of its material side. . . . Everything that has been said up to this point boils down to this: in language there are only differences. Even more important: a difference generally implies positive terms between which the difference is set up; but in language there are only differences *without positive terms*. Whether we take the signified or the signifier, language has neither ideas nor sounds that existed before the linguistic system, but only conceptual and phonic differences that have issued from the system. The idea or phonic substance that a sign contains is of less importance than the other signs that surround it.[1]

The first consequence to be drawn from this is that the signified concept is never present in itself, in an adequate presence that would refer only to itself. Every concept is necessarily and essentially inscribed in a chain or a system, within which it refers to another and to other concepts, by the systematic play of differences. Such a play, then – difference – is no longer simply a concept, but the possibility of conceptuality, of the conceptual system and process in general. For the same reason, differance, which is not a concept, is not a mere word; that is, it is not what we represent to ourselves as the calm and present self-referential unity of a concept and sound [*phonie*]. We shall later discuss the consequences of this for the notion of a word.

The difference that Saussure speaks about, therefore, is neither itself a concept nor one word among others. We can say this *a fortiori* for differance. Thus we are brought to make the relation between the one and the other explicit.

Within a language, within the *system* of language, there are only differences. A taxonomic operation can accordingly undertake its systematic, statistical, and classificatory inventory. But, on the one hand, these differences *play a role* in language, in speech as well, and in the exchange between language and speech. On the other hand, these differences are themselves *effects*. They have not fallen from the sky ready made; they are no more inscribed in a *topos noētos* than they are prescribed in the wax of the brain. If the word "history" did not carry with it the theme of a final repression of differance, we could say that differences alone could be "historical" through and through and from the start.

What we note as *differance* will thus be the movement of play that "produces" (and not by something that is simply an activity) these differences, these effects of difference. This does not mean that the differance which produces differences is before them in a simple and in itself unmodified and indifferent present. Differance is the nonfull, nonsimple "origin"; it is the structured and differing origin of differences.

Since language (which Saussure says is a classification) has not fallen from the sky, it is clear that the differences have been produced; they are the effects produced, but effects that do not have as their cause a subject or substance, a thing in general, or a being that is somewhere present and itself escapes the play of difference. If such a presence were implied (quite classically) in the general concept of cause, we would therefore have to talk about an effect without a cause, something that would very quickly lead to no longer talking about effects. I have tried to indicate a way out of the closure imposed by this system, namely, by means of the "trace." No more an effect than a cause, the "trace" cannot of itself, taken outside its context, suffice to bring about the required transgression.

As there is no presence before the semiological difference or outside it, we can extend what Saussure writes about language to signs in general: "Language is necessary in order for speech to be intelligible and to produce all of its effects; but the latter is necessary in order for language to be established; historically, the fact of speech always comes first."[2]

Retaining at least the schema, if not the content, of the demand formulated by Saussure, we shall designate by the term *differance* the movement by which language, or any code, any system of reference in general, becomes "historically" constituted as a fabric of differences. Here, the terms "constituted," "produced," "created," "movement," "historically," etc., with all they imply, are not to be understood only in terms of the language of metaphysics, from which they are taken. It would have to be shown why the concepts of production, like those of constitution and history, remain accessories in this respect to what is here being questioned; this, however, would draw us too far away today, toward the theory of the representation of the "circle" in which we seem to be enclosed. I only use these terms here, like many other concepts, out of strategic convenience and in order to prepare the deconstruction of the system they form at the point which is now most decisive. In any event, we will have understood, by virtue of the very circle we appear to be caught up in, that differance, as it is written here, is no more static than genetic, no more structural than historical. Nor is it any less so. And it is completely to miss the point of this orthographical impropriety to want to object to it on the basis of the oldest of metaphysical oppositions – for example, by opposing some generative point of view to a structuralist-taxonomic point of view, or conversely. These oppositions do not pertain in the least to differance; and this, no doubt, is what makes thinking about it difficult and uncomfortable.

If we now consider the chain to which "differance" gets subjected, according to the context, to a certain number of nonsynonymic substitutions, one will ask why we resorted to such concepts as "reserve," "protowriting," "prototrace," "spacing," indeed to "supplement" or "*pharmakon*," and, before long, to "hymen," etc.[x]

Let us begin again. Differance is what makes the movement of signification possible only if each element that is said to be "present," appearing on the stage of presence, is related to something other than itself but retains the mark of a past element and already lets itself be hollowed out by the mark of its relation to a future element. This trace relates no less to what is called the future than to what is called the past, and it constitutes what is called the present by this very relation to what it is not, to what it absolutely is not; that is, not even to a past or future considered as a modified present. In order for it to be, an interval must separate it from what it is not; but the interval that constitutes it in the present must also, and by the same token, divide the present in itself, thus dividing, along with the present, everything that can be conceived on its basis, that is, every being – in particular, for our metaphysical language, the substance or subject. Constituting itself, dynamically dividing itself, this interval is what could be called *spacing;* time's becoming-spatial or space's becoming-temporal

[x] *Pharmakon* is ambiguously medicine or poison.

(*temporalizing*). And it is this constitution of the present as a "primordial" and irreducibly nonsimple, and, therefore, in the strict sense nonprimordial, synthesis of traces, retentions, and protentions (to reproduce here, analogically and provisionally, a phenomenological and transcendental language that will presently be revealed as inadequate) that I propose to call protowriting, prototrace, or differance. The latter (is) (both) spacing (and) temporalizing.

Given this (active) movement of the (production of) differance without origin, could we not, quite simply and without any neographism, call it *differentiation*? Among other confusions, such a word would suggest some organic unity, some primordial and homogeneous unity, that would eventually come to be divided up and take on difference as an event. Above all, formed on the verb "to differentiate," this word would annul the economic signification of detour, temporalizing delay, "deferring." I owe a remark in passing to a recent reading of one of Koyré's texts entitled "Hegel at Jena."[3] In that text, Koyré cites long passages from the Jena *Logic* in German and gives his own translation. On two occasions in Hegel's text he encounters the expression "*differente Beziehung*."[xi] This word (*different*), whose root is Latin, is extremely rare in German and also, I believe, in Hegel, who instead uses *verschieden* or *ungleich*, calling difference *Unterschied* and qualitative variety *Verschiedenheit*.[xii] In the Jena *Logic*, he uses the word *different* precisely at the point where he deals with time and the present. Before coming to Koyré's valuable remark, here are some passages from Hegel, as rendered by Koyré:

> The infinite, in this simplicity is – as a moment opposed to the self-identical – the negative. In its moments, while the infinite presents the totality to (itself) and in itself, (it is) excluding in general, the point or limit; but in this, its own (action of) negating, it relates itself immediately to the other and negates itself. The limit or moment of the present (*der Gegen-wart*), the absolute "this" of time or the now, is an absolutely negative simplicity, absolutely excluding all multiplicity from itself, and by this very fact is absolutely determined; it is not an extended whole or *quantum* within itself (and) which would in itself also have an undetermined

aspect or qualitative variety, which of itself would be related, indifferently (*gleichgültig*) or externally to another, but on the contrary, this is an absolutely different relation of the simple.[4]

And Koyré specifies in a striking note: "Different relation: *differente Beziehung*. We could say: differentiating relation." And on the following page, from another text of Hegel, we can read: "*Diese Beziehung ist Gegenwart, als eine differente Beziehung*" (This relation is [the] present, as a different relation). There is another note by Koyré: "The term '*different*' is taken here in an active sense."

Writing "differing" or "differance" (with an *a*) would have had the utility of making it possible to translate Hegel on precisely this point with no further qualifications – and it is a quite decisive point in his text. The translation would be, as it always should be, the transformation of one language by another. Naturally, I maintain that the word "differance" can be used in other ways, too; first of all, because it denotes not only the activity of primordial difference but also the temporalizing detour of deferring. It has, however, an even more important usage. Despite the very profound affinities that differance thus written has with Hegelian speech (as it should be read), it can, at a certain point, not exactly break with it, but rather work a sort of displacement with regard to it. A definite rupture with Hegelian language would make no sense, nor would it be at all likely; but this displacement is both infinitesimal and radical. I have tried to indicate the extent of this displacement elsewhere; it would be difficult to talk about it with any brevity at this point.

Differences are thus "produced" – differed – by differance. But *what* differs, or *who* differs? In other words, *what is* differance? With this question we attain another stage and another source of the problem.

What differs? Who differs? What is differance?

If we answered these questions even before examining them as questions, even before going back over them and questioning their form (even what seems to be most natural and necessary about them), we would fall below the level we have now reached. For if we accepted the form of the question in its own sense and syntax ("What?," "What is?," "Who is?"), we would have to admit that differance is derived, supervenient, controlled, and ordered from the starting point of a being-present, one capable of being something, a force, a

xi "Different Relation."
xii *Different* is compared to related terms: differing, unlike, distinction and diversity, respectively.

(232)

state, or power in the world, to which we could give all kinds of names: a *what*, or being-present as a *subject*, a *who*. In the latter case, notably, we would implicitly admit that the being-present (for example, as a self-present being or consciousness) would eventually result in differing: in delaying or in diverting the fulfillment of a "need" or "desire," or in differing from itself. But in none of these cases would such a being-present be "constituted" by this differance.

Now if we once again refer to the semiological difference, what was it that Saussure in particular reminded us of? That "language [which consists only of differences] is not a function of the speaking subject." This implies that the subject (self-identical or even conscious of self-identity, self-conscious) is inscribed in the language, that he is a "function" of the language. He becomes a *speaking* subject only by conforming his speech – even in the aforesaid "creation," even in the aforesaid "transgression" – to the system of linguistic prescriptions taken as the system of differences, or at least to the general law of differance, by conforming to that law of language which Saussure calls "language without speech." "Language is necessary for the spoken word to be intelligible and so that it can produce all of its effects."[5]

If, by hypothesis, we maintain the strict opposition between speech and language, then difference will be not only the play of differences within the language but the relation of speech to language, the detour by which I must also pass in order to speak, the silent token I must give, which holds just as well for linguistics in the strict sense as it does for general semiology; it dictates all the relations between usage and the formal schema, between the message and the particular code, etc. Elsewhere I have tried to suggest that this difference within language, and in the relation between speech and language, forbids the essential dissociation between speech and writing that Saussure, in keeping with tradition, wanted to draw at another level of his presentation. The use of language or the employment of any code which implies a play of forms – with no determined or invariable substratum – also presupposes a retention and protention of differences, a spacing and temporalizing, a play of traces. This play must be a sort of inscription prior to writing, a protowriting without a present origin, without an *arché*. From this comes the systematic crossing-out of the *arché* and the transformation of general semiology into a grammatology, the latter performing a critical work upon everything within

semiology – right down to its matrical concept of signs – that retains any metaphysical presuppositions incompatible with the theme of differance.[xiii]

We might be tempted by an objection: to be sure, the subject becomes a *speaking* subject only by dealing with the system of linguistic differences; or again, he becomes a *signifying* subject (generally by speech or other signs) only by entering into the system of differences. In this sense, certainly, the speaking or signifying subject would not be self-present, insofar as he speaks or signifies, except for the play of linguistic or semiological differance. But can we not conceive of a presence and self-presence of the subject before speech or its signs, a subject's self-presence in a silent and intuitive consciousness?

Such a question therefore supposes that prior to signs and outside them, and excluding every trace and differance, something such as consciousness is possible. It supposes, moreover, that, even before the distribution of its signs in space and in the world, consciousness can gather itself up in its own presence. What then is consciousness? What does "consciousness" mean? Most often in the very form of "meaning"[xiv] consciousness in all its modifications is conceivable only as self-presence, a self-perception of presence. And what holds for consciousness also holds here for what is called subjective existence in general. Just as the category of subject is not and never has been conceivable without reference to presence as *hypokeimenon* or *ousia*, etc., so the subject as consciousness has never been able to be evinced otherwise than as self-presence. The privilege accorded to consciousness thus means a privilege accorded to the present; and even if the transcendental temporality of consciousness is described in depth, as Husserl described it, the power of synthesis and of the incessant gathering-up of traces is always accorded to the "living present."

This privilege is the ether of metaphysics, the very element of our thought insofar as it is caught up in the language of metaphysics. We can only de-limit such a closure today by evoking this import of presence, which Heidegger has shown to be the onto-theological determination of being.

---

xiii   In *Of Grammotology*, Derrida argues that writing has been reduced by most philosophers to speech, out of an attempt to replace the mediacy of written signs with the (imagined) immediate presence of the speaker.

xiv   The French for "meaning" is, instructively, *vouloir-dire* (literally, to want-to-say).

(233)

Therefore, in evoking this import of presence, by an examination which would have to be of a quite peculiar nature, we question the absolute privilege of this form or epoch of presence in general, that is, consciousness as meaning [*vouloir-dire*] in self-presence.

We thus come to posit presence – and, in particular, consciousness, the being-next-to-itself of consciousness – no longer as the absolutely matrical form of being but as a "determination" and an "effect." Presence is a determination and effect within a system which is no longer that of presence but that of differance; it no more allows the opposition between activity and passivity than that between cause and effect or in-determination and determination etc. This system is of such a kind that even to designate consciousness as an effect or determination – for strategic reasons, reasons that can be more or less clearly considered and systematically ascertained – is to continue to operate according to the vocabulary of that very thing to be de-limited.

Before being so radically and expressly Heideggerian, this was also Nietzsche's and Freud's move, both of whom, as we know, and often in a very similar way, questioned the self-assured certitude of consciousness. And is it not remarkable that both of them did this by starting out with the theme of differance?

This theme appears almost literally in their work, at the most crucial places. I shall not expand on this here; I shall only recall that for Nietzsche "the important main activity is unconscious" and that consciousness is the effect of forces whose essence, ways, and modalities are not peculiar to it. Now force itself is never present; it is only a play of differences and quantities. There would be no force in general without the difference between forces; and here the difference in quantity counts more than the content of quantity, more than the absolute magnitude itself.

> Quantity itself therefore is not separable from the difference in quantity. The difference in quantity is the essence of force, the relation of force with force. To fancy two equal forces, even if we grant them opposing directions, is an approximate and crude illusion, a statistical dream in which life is immersed, but which chemistry dispels.[6]

Is not the whole thought of Nietzsche a critique of philosophy as active indifference to difference, as a system of reduction or adiaphoristic repression? Following the same logic – logic itself – this does not exclude the fact that philosophy lives *in* and *from* differance, that it thereby blinds itself to the *same*, which is not the identical. The same is precisely differance (with an *a*), as the diverted and equivocal passage from one difference to another, from one term of the opposition to the other. We could thus take up all the coupled oppositions on which philosophy is constructed, and from which our language lives, not in order to see opposition vanish but to see the emergence of a necessity such that one of the terms appears as the differance of the other, the other as "differed" within the systematic ordering of the same (e.g., the intelligible as differing from the sensible, as sensible differed; the concept as differed-differing intuition, life as differing-differed matter; mind as differed-differing life; culture as differed-differing nature; and all the terms designating what is other than *physis* – *technē*, *nomos*, society, freedom, history, spirit, etc. – as *physis* differed or *physis* differing: *physis in differance*).[xv] It is out of the unfolding of this "same" as differance that the sameness of difference and of repetition is presented in the eternal return.

In Nietzsche, these are so many themes that can be related with the kind of symptomatology that always serves to diagnose the evasions and ruses of anything disguised in its differance. Or again, these terms can be related with the entire thematics of active interpretation, which substitutes an incessant deciphering for the disclosure of truth as a presentation of the thing itself in its presence, etc. What results is a cipher without truth, or at least a system of ciphers that is not dominated by truth value, which only then becomes a function that is understood, inscribed, and circumscribed.

We shall therefore call differance this "active" (in movement) discord of the different forces and of the differences between forces which Nietzsche opposes to the entire system of metaphysical grammar, wherever that system controls culture, philosophy, and science.

It is historically significant that this diaphoristics, understood as an energetics or an economy of forces, set up to question the primacy of presence qua consciousness, is also the major theme of Freud's thought; in his work we find another diaphoristics, both in the form of a theory of ciphers or

---

[xv] *Physis* is nature; *technē* is art or craft; *nomos* is law (that is, social or conventional law).

traces and an energetics. The questioning of the authority of consciousness is first and always differential.

The two apparently different meanings of difference are tied together in Freudian theory: differing as discernibility, distinction, deviation, diastem, *spacing*; and deferring as detour, delay, relay, reserve, *temporalizing*. I shall recall only that:

1. The concept of trace (*Spur*), of facilitation (*Bahnung*), of forces of facilitation are, as early as the composition of the *Entwurf*, inseparable from the concept of difference.[xvi] The origin of memory and of the psyche as a memory in general (conscious or unconscious) can only be described by taking into account the difference between the facilitation thresholds, as Freud says explicitly. There is no facilitation without difference and no difference without a trace.

2. All the differences involved in the production of conscious traces and in the process of inscription (*Niederschrift*) can also be interpreted as moments of differance, in the sense of "placing on reserve." Following a schema that continually guides Freud's thinking, the movement of the trace is described as an effort of life to protect itself *by deferring* the dangerous investment, by constituting a reserve (*Vorrat*). And all the conceptual oppositions that furrow Freudian thought relate each concept to the other like movements of a detour, within the economy of differance. The one is only the other deferred, the one differing from the other. The one is the other in differance, the one is the differance from the other. Every apparently rigorous and irreducible opposition (for example, that between the secondary and primary) is thus said to be, at one time or another, a "theoretical fiction." In this way again, for example (but such an example covers everything or communicates with everything), the difference between the pleasure principle and the reality principle is only differance as detour (*Aufschieben, Aufschub*). In *Beyond the Pleasure Principle*, Freud writes:

Under the influence of the ego's instincts of self-preservation, the pleasure principle is replaced by the reality principle. This latter principle does not abandon the intention of ultimately obtaining pleasure, but it nevertheless demands and carries into effect the postponement of satisfaction, the abandonment of a number of possibilities of gaining satisfaction and the temporary toleration of unpleasure as a step on the long indirect road (*Aufschub*) to pleasure.[7]

Here we touch on the point of greatest obscurity, on the very enigma of differance, on how the concept we have of it is divided by a strange separation. We must not hasten to make a decision too quickly. How can we conceive of difference as a systematic detour which, within the element of the same, always aims at either finding again the pleasure or the presence that had been deferred by (conscious or unconscious) calculation, and, *at the same time*, how can we, on the other hand, conceive of differance as the relation to an impossible presence, as an expenditure without reserve, as an irreparable loss of presence, an irreversible wearing-down of energy, or indeed as a death instinct and a relation to the absolutely other that apparently breaks up any economy? It is evident – it is evidence itself – that system and nonsystem, the same and the absolutely other, etc., cannot be conceived *together*.

If differance is this inconceivable factor, must we not perhaps hasten to make it evident, to bring it into the philosophical element of evidence, and thus quickly dissipate its mirage character and illogicality, dissipate it with the infallibility of the calculus we know well – since we have recognized its place, necessity, and function within the structure of differance? What would be accounted for philosophically here has already been taken into account in the system of differance as it is here being calculated. I have tried elsewhere, in a reading of Bataille,[8] to indicate what might be the establishment of a rigorous, and in a new sense "scientific," *relating* of a "restricted economy" – one having nothing to do with an unreserved expenditure, with death, with being exposed to nonsense, etc. – to a "general economy" or system that, so to speak, *takes account of* what is unreserved.[xvii] It is a relation between a differance that is accounted for and a differance that fails to be accounted for, where the establishment of a pure presence, without loss, is one with the occurrence of absolute loss, with death. By establishing this relation between a restricted and a general system, we shift and recommence the very project of philosophy under the privileged heading of Hegelianism.

[xvi] Freud's *Entwurf Einer Psychologie*, published in English as *Project for a Scientific Psychology*.

[xvii] George Bataille (1897–1962), French philosopher and erotic writer.

The economic character of differance in no way implies that the deferred presence can always be recovered, that it simply amounts to an investment that only temporarily and without loss delays the presentation of presence, that is, the perception of gain or the gain of perception. Contrary to the metaphysical, dialectical, and "Hegelian" interpretation of the economic movement of differance, we must admit a game where whoever loses wins and where one wins and loses each time. If the diverted presentation continues to be somehow definitively and irreducibly withheld, this is not because a particular present remains hidden or absent, but because differance holds us in a relation with what exceeds (though we necessarily fail to recognize this) the alternative of presence or absence. A certain alterity – Freud gives it a metaphysical name, the unconscious – is definitively taken away from every process of presentation in which we would demand for it to be shown forth in person. In this context and under this heading, the unconscious is not, as we know, a hidden, virtual, and potential self-presence. It is differed – which no doubt means that it is woven out of differences, but also that it sends out, that it delegates, representatives or proxies; but there is no chance that the mandating subject "exists" somewhere, that it is present or is "itself," and still less chance that it will become conscious. In this sense, contrary to the terms of an old debate, strongly symptomatic of the metaphysical investments it has always assumed, the "unconscious" can no more be classed as a "thing" than as anything else; it is no more of a thing than an implicit or masked consciousness. This radical alterity, removed from every possible mode of presence, is characterized by irreducible aftereffects, by delayed effects. In order to describe them, in order to read the traces of the "unconscious" traces (there are no "conscious" traces), the language of presence or absence, the metaphysical speech of phenomenology, is in principle inadequate.

The structure of delay (*retardement: Nachträglichkeit*) that Freud talks about indeed prohibits our taking temporalization (temporalizing) to be a simple dialectical complication of the present; rather, this is the style of transcendental phenomenology. It describes the living present as a primordial and incessant synthesis that is constantly led back upon itself, back upon its assembled and assembling self, by retentional traces and protentional openings. With the alterity of the "unconscious," we have to deal not with the horizons of modified presents – past or future – but with a "past" that has never been nor will ever be present, whose "future" will never be produced or reproduced in the form of presence. The concept of trace is therefore incommensurate with that of retention, that of the becoming-past of what had been present. The trace cannot be conceived – nor, therefore, can differance – on the basis of either the present or the presence of the present.

A past that has never been present: with this formula Emmanuel Levinas designates (in ways that are, to be sure, not those of psychoanalysis) the trace and the enigma of absolute alterity, that is, the Other. At least within these limits, and from this point of view, the thought of differance implies the whole critique of classical ontology undertaken by Levinas. And the concept of trace, like that of differance, forms – across these different traces and through these differences between traces, as understood by Nietzsche, Freud, and Levinas (these "authors' names" serve only as indications) – the network that sums up and permeates our "epoch" as the de-limitation of ontology (of presence).

The ontology of presence is the ontology of beings and beingness. Everywhere, the dominance of beings is solicited by differance – in the sense that *sollicitare* means, in old Latin, to shake all over, to make the whole tremble. What is questioned by the thought of differance, therefore, is the determination of being in presence, or in beingness. Such a question could not arise and be understood without the difference between Being and beings opening up somewhere. The first consequence of this is that differance is not. It is not a being-present, however excellent, unique, principal, or transcendent one makes it. It commands nothing, rules over nothing, and nowhere does it exercise any authority. It is not marked by a capital letter. Not only is there no realm of differance, but differance is even the subversion of every realm. This is obviously what makes it threatening and necessarily dreaded by everything in us that desires a realm, the past or future presence of a realm. And it is always in the name of a realm that, believing one sees it ascend to the capital letter, one can reproach it for wanting to rule.

Does this mean, then, that differance finds its place within the spread of the ontic-ontological difference, as it is conceived, as the "epoch" conceives itself within it, and particularly "across" the Heideggerian meditation, which cannot be gotten around?

There is no simple answer to such a question.

In one particular respect, differance is, to be sure, but the historical and epochal *deployment* of Being or of the ontological difference. The *a* of differance marks the *movement* of this deployment.

And yet, is not the thought that conceives the *sense* or *truth* of Being, the determination of differance as onticontological difference – difference conceived within the horizon of the question of *Being* – still an intrametaphysical effect of differance? Perhaps the deployment of differance is not only the truth or the epochality of Being. Perhaps we must try to think this *unheard-of* thought, this silent tracing, namely, that the history of Being (the thought of which is committed to the Greco-Western logos), as it is itself produced across the ontological difference, is only one epoch of the *diapherein.*[xviii] Then we could no longer even call it an "epoch," for the concept of epochality belongs within history understood as the history of Being. Being has always made "sense," has always been conceived or spoken of as such, only by dissimulating itself in beings; thus, in a particular and very strange way, differance (is) "older" than the ontological difference or the truth of Being. In this age it can be called the play of traces. It is a trace that no longer belongs to the horizon of Being but one whose sense of Being is borne and bound by this play; it is a play of traces or differance that has no sense and is not, a play that does not belong. There is no support to be found and no depth to be had for this bottomless chessboard where being is set in play.

It is perhaps in this way that the Heraclitean play of the *hen diapheron heautōi*, of the one differing from itself, of what is in difference with itself, already becomes lost as a trace in determining the *diapherein* as ontological difference.

To think through the ontological difference doubtless remains a difficult task, a task whose statement has remained nearly inaudible. And to prepare ourselves for venturing beyond our own logos, that is, for a differance so violent that it refuses to be stopped and examined as the epochality of Being and ontological difference, is neither to give up this passage through the truth of Being, nor is it in any way to "criticize," "contest," or fail to recognize the incessant necessity for it. On the contrary, we must stay within the difficulty of this passage; we must repeat this passage in a rigorous reading of metaphysics, wherever metaphysics serves as the norm of Western speech, and not only in the texts of "the history of philosophy." Here we must allow the trace of whatever goes beyond the truth of Being to appear/disappear in its fully rigorous way. It is a trace of something that can never present itself; it is itself a trace that can never be presented, that is, can never appear and manifest itself as such in its phenomenon. It is a trace that lies beyond what profoundly ties fundamental ontology to phenomenology. Like differance, the trace is never presented as such. In presenting itself it becomes effaced; in being sounded it dies away, like the writing of the *a*, inscribing its pyramid in differance.

We can always reveal the precursive and secretive traces of this movement in metaphysical speech, especially in the contemporary talk about the closure of ontology, i.e., through the various attempts we have looked at (Nietzsche, Freud, Levinas) – and particularly in Heidegger's work.

The latter provokes us to question the essence of the present, the presence of the present.

What is the present? What is it to conceive the present in its presence?

Let us consider, for example, the 1946 text entitled "Der Spruch des Anaximander."[xvix] Heidegger there recalls that the forgetting of Being forgets about the difference between Being and beings:

> But the point of Being (*die Sache des Seins*) is to be the Being *of* beings. The linguistic form of this enigmatic and multivalent genitive designates a genesis (*Genesis*), a provenance (*Herkunft*) of the pre*sent* from pre*sence* (*des Anwesenden aus dem Anwesen*). But with the unfolding of these two, the essence (*Wesen*) of this provenance remains hidden (*verborgen*). Not only is the essence of this provenance not thought out, but neither is the simple relation between pre*sence* and pre*sent* (*Anwesen und Anwesendem*). Since the dawn, it seems that pres*ence* and being-pre*sent* are each separately something. Imperceptibly, pre*sence* becomes itself a pre*sent*. . . . The essence of pre*sence* (*Das Wesen des Anwesens*), and thus the difference between pre*sence* and pre*sent*, is forgotten. *The forgetting of Being is the forgetting of the difference between Being and beings.*[9]

xvix "The Anaximander Fragment." Found in *Early Greek Thinking*, edited by Krell and Capuzzi (New York: Harper & Row, 1975).

xviii Differing.

In recalling the difference between Being and beings (the ontological difference) as the difference between presence and present, Heidegger puts forward a proposition, indeed, a group of propositions; it is not our intention here to idly or hastily "criticize" them but rather to convey them with all their provocative force.

Let us then proceed slowly. What Heidegger wants to point out is that the difference between Being and beings, forgotten by metaphysics, has disappeared without leaving a trace. The very trace of difference has sunk from sight. If we admit that differance (is) (itself) something other than presence and absence, if it *traces*, then we are dealing with the forgetting of the difference (between Being and beings), and we now have to talk about a disappearance of the trace's trace. This is certainly what this passage from "Der Spruch des Anaximander" seems to imply:

> The forgetting of Being is a part of the very essence of Being, and is concealed by it. The forgetting belongs so essentially to the destination of Being that the dawn of this destination begins precisely as an unconcealment of the pre-*sent* in its pres*ence*. This means: the history of Being begins by the forgetting of Being, in that Being retains its essence, its difference from beings. Difference is wanting; it remains forgotten. Only what is differentiated – the present and presence (*das Anwesende und das Anwesen*) – becomes uncovered, but not *insofar as* it is differentiated. On the contrary, the matinal trace (*die frühe Spur*) of difference effaces itself from the moment that presence appears as a being-present (*das Anwesen wie ein Anwesendes erscheint*) and finds its provenance in a supreme (being)-present (*in einem höchsten Anwesenden*).[10]

The trace is not a presence but is rather the simulacrum of a presence that dislocates, displaces, and refers beyond itself. The trace has, properly speaking, no place, for effacement belongs to the very structure of the trace. Effacement must always be able to overtake the trace; otherwise it would not be a trace but an indestructible and monumental substance. In addition, and from the start, effacement constitutes it as a trace – effacement establishes the trace in a change of place and makes it disappear in its appearing, makes it issue forth from itself in its very position. The effacing of this early trace (*die frühe Spur*) of difference is therefore "the same" as its tracing within the text of metaphysics.

This metaphysical text must have retained a mark of what it lost or put in reserve, set aside. In the language of metaphysics the paradox of such a structure is the inversion of the metaphysical concept which produces the following effect: the present becomes the sign of signs, the trace of traces. It is no longer what every reference refers to in the last instance; it becomes a function in a generalized referential structure. It is a trace, and a trace of the effacement of a trace.

In this way the metaphysical text is *understood*; it is still readable, and remains to be read. It proposes *both* the monument and the mirage of the trace, the trace as simultaneously traced and effaced, simultaneously alive and dead, alive as always to simulate even life in its preserved inscription; it is a pyramid.

Thus we think through, without contradiction, or at least without granting any pertinence to such contradiction, what is perceptible and imperceptible about the trace. The "matinal trace" of difference is lost in an irretrievable invisibility, and yet even its loss is covered, preserved, regarded, and retarded. This happens in a text, in the form of presence.

Having spoken about the effacement of the matinal trace, Heidegger can thus, in this contradiction without contradiction, consign or countersign the sealing of the trace. We read on a little further:

> The difference between Being and beings, however, can in turn be experienced as something forgotten only if it is already discovered with the presence of the present (*mit dem Anwesen des Anwesenden*) and if it is thus sealed in a trace (*so eine Spur geprägt hat*) that remains preserved (*gewahrt bleibt*) in the language which Being appropriates.[11]

Further on still, while meditating upon Anaximander's τὸ χρεών,[xx] translated as *Brauch* (sustaining use), Heidegger writes the following:

> Dispensing accord and deference (*Fug und Ruch verfügend*), our sustaining use frees the pres*ent* (*das Anwesende*) in its sojourn and sets it free every time for its sojourn. But by the same token the present is equally seen to be exposed to the constant danger of hardening in the insistence (*in das blosse Beharren verhärtet*) out of its sojourning duration. In this way sustaining use (*Brauch*) remains itself and at the

---

[xx]   Of necessity (or "of use" as Heidegger reads it).

same time an abandonment (*Aushändigung:* handing-over) of presence (*des Anwesens*) *in den Un-fug*, to discord (disjointedness). Sustaining use joins together the dis- (*Der Brauch fügt das Un-*).[12]

And it is at the point where Heidegger determines *sustaining use* as *trace* that the question must be asked: can we, and how far can we, think of this trace and the *dis-* of difference as *Wesen des Seins?* Doesn't the *dis* of difference refer us beyond the history of Being, beyond our language as well, and beyond everything that can be named by it? Doesn't it call for – in the language of being – the necessarily violent transformation of this language by an entirely different language?

Let us be more precise here. In order to dislodge the "trace" from its cover (and whoever believes that one tracks down some *thing?* – one tracks down tracks), let us continue reading this passage:

> The translation of τὸ χρεών by "sustaining use" (*Brauch*) does not derive from cogitations of an etymologico-lexical nature. The choice of the word "sustaining use" derives from an antecedent *trans*lation (*Über*setzen) of the thought that attempts to conceive difference in the deployment of Being (*im Wesen des Seins*) toward the historical beginning of the forgetting of Being. The word "sustaining use" is dictated to thought in the apprehension (*Erfahrung*) of the forgetting of Being. τὸ χρεών properly names a trace (*Spur*) of what remains to be conceived in the word "sustaining use," a trace that quickly disappears (*alsbald verschwindet*) into the history of Being, in its world-historical unfolding as Western metaphysics.[13]

How do we conceive of the outside of a text? How, for example, do we conceive of what stands opposed to the text of Western metaphysics? To be sure, the "trace that quickly disappears into the history of Being, . . . as Western metaphysics," escapes all the determinations, all the names it might receive in the metaphysical text. The trace is sheltered and thus dissimulated in these names; it does not appear in the text as the trace "itself." But this is because the trace itself could never itself appear as such. Heidegger also says that difference can never appear *as such:* "Lichtung des Unterschiedes kann deshalb auch nicht bedeuten, dass der Unterschied als der Unterschied erscheint."[xxi] There is no essence of difference;

not only can it not allow itself to be taken up into the *as such* of its name or its appearing, but it threatens the authority of the *as such* in general, the thing's presence in its essence. That there is no essence of difference at this point also implies that there is neither Being nor truth to the play of writing, *insofar* as it involves difference.

For us, difference remains a metaphysical name; and all the names that it receives from our language are still, so far as they are names, metaphysical. This is particularly so when they speak of determining difference as the difference between presence and present (*Anwesen/Anwesend*), but already and especially so when, in the most general way, they speak of determining difference as the difference between Being and beings.

"Older" than Being itself, our language has no name for such a difference. But we "already know" that if it is unnamable, this is not simply provisional; it is not because our language has still not found or received this *name*, or because we would have to look for it in another language, outside the finite system of our language. It is because there is no *name* for this, not even essence or Being – not even the name "differance," which is not a name, which is not a pure nominal unity, and continually breaks up in a chain of different substitutions.

"There is no name for this": we read this as a truism. What is unnamable here is not some ineffable being that cannot be approached by a name; like God, for example. What is unnamable is the play that brings about the nominal effects, the relatively unitary or atomic structures we call names, or chains of substitutions for names. In these, for example, the nominal effect of "differance" is itself involved, carried off, and reinscribed, just as the false beginning or end of a game is still part of the game, a function of the system.

What we do know, what we could know if it were simply a question of knowing, is that there never has been and never will be a unique word, a master name. This is why thinking about the letter *a* of differance is not the primary prescription, nor is it the prophetic announcement of some imminent and still unheard-of designation. There is nothing kerygmatic about this "word" so long as we can perceive its reduction to a lower-case letter.

There will be no unique name, not even the name of Being. It must be conceived without

[xxi] "Clearing [illuminating] the distinction therefore cannot mean that the distinction shows itself as the distinction."

nostalgia; that is, it must be conceived outside the myth of the purely maternal or paternal language belonging to the lost fatherland of thought. On the contrary, we must *affirm* it – in the sense that Nietzsche brings affirmation into play – with a certain laughter and with a certain dance.

After this laughter and dance, after this affirmation that is foreign to any dialectic, the question arises as to the other side of nostalgia, which I will call Heideggerian *hope.* I am not unaware that this term may be somewhat shocking. I venture it all the same, without excluding any of its implications, and shall relate it to what seems to me to be retained of metaphysics in "Der Spruch des Anaximander," namely, the quest for the proper word and the unique name. In talking about the "first word of Being" (*das frühe Wort des Seins:* τὸ χρεών*ˣˣ*), Heidegger writes,

The relation to the pres*ent*, unfolding its order in the very essence of pres*ence*, is unique (*ist eine einzige*). It is pre-eminently incomparable to any other relation; it belongs to the uniqueness of Being itself (*Sie gehört zur Einzigkeit des Seins selbst*). Thus, in order to name what is deployed in Being (*das Wesende des Seins*), language will have to find a single word, the unique word (*ein einziges, das einzige Wort*). There we see how hazardous is every word of thought (every thoughtful word: *denkende Wort*) that addresses itself to Being (*das dem Sein zugesprochen wird*). What is hazarded here, however, is not something impossible, because Being speaks through every language; everywhere and always.[14]

Such is the question: the marriage between speech and Being in the unique word, in the finally proper name. Such is the question that enters into the affirmation put into play by differance. The question bears (upon) each of the words in this sentence: "Being / speaks / through every language; / everywhere and always /."

ˣˣ   Again, "need" or "use."

Author's Notes

1   Ferdinand de Saussure, *Cours de linguistique générale,* ed. C. Bally and A. Sechehaye (Paris: Payot, 1916); English translation by Wade Baskin, *Course in General Linguistics* (New York: Philosophical Library, 1959), pp. 117–18, 120.

2   *Course in General Linguistics,* p. 18.

3   Alexandre Koyré, "Hegel à Iéna," *Revue d'histoire et de philosophie religieuse,* XIV (1934), 420–58; reprinted in Koyré, *Etudes d'histoire de la pensée philosophique* (Paris: Armand Colin, 1961), pp. 135–73.

4   Koyré, *Etudes d'histoire,* pp. 153–54.

5   De Saussure, *Course in General Linguistics,* p. 37.

6   G. Deleuze, *Nietzsche et la philosophie* (Paris: Presses Universitaires de France, 1970), p. 49.

7   Freud, *Complete Psychological Works,* XVIII, 10.

8   Derrida, *L'Ecriture et la différence,* pp. 369–407.

9   Martin Heidegger, *Holzwege* (Frankfurt: V. Klostermann, 1957), pp. 335–6. [Translations by David B. Allison].

10   Ibid., p. 336.

11   Ibid.

12   Ibid., pp. 339–40.

13   Ibid., p. 340.

14   Ibid., pp. 337–8.

28

"Nietzsche, Genealogy, History" From "Truth and Power"

Michel Foucault

With Derrida, Michel Foucault (1926–84) was the most influential of postmodernist thinkers. Unlike Derrida, however, his work is explicitly socio-logical and historical. Much of it entails an his-torical analysis of the "discursive practices" embodied in the modern social sciences, that have constituted social life and the modern con-ception of the human through the marginalization of the insane, criminals, and sexual deviants. Nor-malcy is the discursive achievement of dominant social powers. Foucault could thus famously de-clare in *The Order of Things* that "man" was invented since the sixteenth century, having con-stituted himself as an object through the politic-ally empowered social sciences. In Nietzschean fashion, Foucault accepts that all life is power; rather than endorsing an impossible renunciation of power and repression, he seeks their modifica-tion into less static and less concentrated forms. In the first selection, a 1971 essay, Foucault dis-tinguishes Nietzsche's "genealogy" from trad-itional historical research, which eschews the latter's implicit metaphysical search for origins. In the second selection, a 1976 interview, he fam-ously denies that truth as a norm can be under-stood to be separate from social and political power.

"Nietzsche, Genealogy, History"

1. Genealogy is gray, meticulous, and patiently documentary. It operates on a field of entangled and confused parchments, on documents that have been scratched over and recopied many times.

On this basis, it is obvious that Paul Ree[i] was wrong to follow the English tendency in describing the history of morality in terms of a linear develop-ment – in reducing its entire history and genesis to an exclusive concern for utility. He assumed that words had kept their meaning, that desires still pointed in a single direction, and that ideas retained their logic; and he ignored the fact that the world of speech and desires has known invasions, struggles, plundering, disguises, ploys. From these elements, however, genealogy retrieves an indispensable re-straint: it must record the singularity of events out-side of any monotonous finality; it must seek them in the most unpromising places, in what we tend to feel is without history – in sentiments, love, conscience, instincts; it must be sensitive to their recurrence, not

---

[i] French moral philosopher and friend of Nietzsche, whose relationship with Nietzsche ended when Ree won the love of Nietzsche's life, Lou Salomé.

[ii] Plato visited Syracuse, in Sicily, at the invitation of its tyrant but declined to support him and thereby gain political power.

Michel Foucault: [A] "Nietzsche, Genealogy, History" (trans. Donald F. Bouchard and Sherry Simon), from *Language, Counter-Memory, Practise: Selected Essays and Interviews* (ed. Donald F. Bouchard), pp. 139–64. Ithaca, NY: Cornell University Press, 1977; [B] "Truth and Power," pp. 131–3, answer to final question of interview by Alessandro Fontana and Pasquale Pas-quino (trans. Colin Gordon) in *Power/Knowledge: Selected Interviews and Other Writings 1972–77* (ed. Colin Gordon).

in order to trace the gradual curve of their evolution, but to isolate the different scenes where they engaged in different roles. Finally, genealogy must define even those instances where they are absent, the moment when they remained unrealized (Plato, at Syracuse, did not become Mohammed).[ii]

Genealogy, consequently, requires patience and a knowledge of details and it depends on a vast accumulation of source material. Its "cyclopean monuments"[1] are constructed from "discreet and apparently insignificant truths and according to a rigorous method"; they cannot be the product of "large and well-meaning errors."[2] In short, genealogy demands relentless erudition. Genealogy does not oppose itself to history as the lofty and profound gaze of the philosopher might compare to the molelike perspective of the scholar; on the contrary, it rejects the metahistorical deployment of ideal significations and indefinite teleologies. It opposes itself to the search for "origins."

2. In Nietzsche, we find two uses of the word *Ursprung*.[iii] The first is unstressed, and it is found alternately with other terms such as *Entstehung*, *Herkunft*, *Abkunft*, *Geburt*. In *The Genealogy of Morals*, for example, *Entstehung* or *Ursprung* serve equally well to denote the origin of duty or guilty conscience;[3] and in the discussion of logic or knowledge in *The Gay Science*, their origin is indiscriminately referred to as *Ursprung*, *Entstehung*, or *Herkunft*.[4]

The other use of the word is stressed. On occasion, Nietzsche places the term in opposition to another: in the first paragraph of *Human, All Too Human* the miraculous origin (*Wunderursprung*) sought by metaphysics is set against the analyses of historical philosophy, which poses questions *über Herkunft und Anfang*.[iv] *Ursprung* is also used in an ironic and deceptive manner. In what, for instance, do we find the original basis (*Ursprung*) of morality, a foundation sought after since Plato? "In detestable, narrow-minded conclusions. *Pudenda origo*."[v] Or in a related context, where should we seek the origin of religion (*Ursprung*), which Schopenhauer located in a particular metaphysical sentiment of the hereafter? It belongs, very simply, to an invention (*Erfindung*), a sleight-of-hand, an artifice

(*Kunststück*), a secret formula, in the rituals of black magic, in the work of the *Schwarzkünstler*.[vi]

One of the most significant texts with respect to the use of all these terms and to the variations in the use of *Ursprung* is the preface to the *Genealogy*. At the beginning of the text, its objective is defined as an examination of the origin of moral preconceptions and the term used is *Herkunft*. Then, Nietzsche proceeds by retracing his personal involvement with this question: he recalls the period when he "calligraphied" philosophy, when he questioned if God must be held responsible for the origin of evil. He now finds this question amusing and properly characterizes it as a search for *Ursprung* (he will shortly use the same term to summarize Paul Ree's activity).[5] Further on, he evokes the analyses that are characteristically Nietzschean and that began with *Human, All Too Human*. Here, he speaks of *Herkunfthypothesen*.[vii] This use of the word *Herkunft* cannot be arbitrary, since it serves to designate a number of texts, beginning with *Human, All Too Human*, which deal with the origin of morality, asceticism, justice, and punishment. And yet, the word used in all these works had been *Ursprung*.[6] It would seem that at this point in the *Genealogy* Nietzsche wished to validate an opposition between *Herkunft* and *Ursprung* that did not exist ten years earlier. But immediately following the use of the two terms in a specific sense, Nietzsche reverts, in the final paragraphs of the preface, to a usage that is neutral and equivalent.[7]

Why does Nietzsche challenge the pursuit of the origin (*Ursprung*), at least on those occasions when he is truly a genealogist? First, because it is an attempt to capture the exact essence of things, their purest possibilities, and their carefully protected identities, because this search assumes the existence of immobile forms that precede the external world of accident and succession. This search is directed to "that which was already there," the image of a primordial truth fully adequate to its nature, and it necessitates the removal of every mask to ultimately disclose an original identity. However, if the genealogist refuses to extend his faith in metaphysics, if he listens to history, he finds that there is "something altogether different" behind things: not a timeless and essential secret, but the secret that they have no essence or that their essence was fabricated in a piecemeal fashion from alien forms. Examining the history of reason, he learns that it was born in an altogether "reasonable"

[iii]   Foucault is distinguishing a series of overlapping German terms: *Ursprung* (source, origin); *Entstehung* (genesis); *Herkunft* (descent); *Abkunft* (lineage); and *Geburt* (birth).
[iv]   *Anfang* means "beginning."
[v]   Shameful origin.
[vi]   Black magician.

[vii]   Hypotheses of descent.

fashion – from chance;[8] devotion to truth and the precision of scientific methods arose from the passion of scholars, their reciprocal hatred, their fanatical and unending discussions, and their spirit of competition – the personal conflicts that slowly forged the weapons of reason.[9] Further, genealogical analysis shows that the concept of liberty is an "invention of the ruling classes"[10] and not fundamental to man's nature or at the root of his attachment to being and truth. What is found at the historical beginning of things is not the inviolable identity of their origin; it is the dissension of other things. It is disparity.

History also teaches how to laugh at the solemnities of the origin. The lofty origin is no more than "a metaphysical extension which arises from the belief that things are most precious and essential at the moment of birth."[11] We tend to think that this is the moment of their greatest perfection, when they emerged dazzling from the hands of a creator or in the shadowless light of a first morning. The origin always precedes the Fall. It comes before the body, before the world and time; it is associated with the gods, and its story is always sung as a theogony. But historical beginnings are lowly: not in the sense of modest or discreet like the steps of a dove, but derisive and ironic, capable of undoing every infatuation. "We wished to awaken the feeling of man's sovereignty by showing his divine birth: this path is now forbidden, since a monkey stands at the entrance."[12] Man originated with a grimace over his future development; and Zarathustra himself is plagued by a monkey who jumps along behind him, pulling on his coattails.[viii]

The final postulate of the origin is linked to the first two in being the site of truth. From the vantage point of an absolute distance, free from the restraints of positive knowledge, the origin makes possible a field of knowledge whose function is to recover it, but always in a false recognition due to the excesses of its own speech. The origin lies at a place of inevitable loss, the point where the truth of things corresponded to a truthful discourse, the site of a fleeting articulation that discourse has obscured and finally lost. It is a new cruelty of history that compels a reversal of this relationship and the abandonment of "adolescent" quests: behind the always recent, avaricious, and measured truth, it posits the ancient proliferation of errors. It is now impossible to believe that "in the rending of the veil, truth remains

truthful; we have lived long enough not to be taken in."[13] Truth is undoubtedly the sort of error that cannot be refuted because it was hardened into an unalterable form in the long baking process of history.[14] Moreover, the very question of truth, the right it appropriates to refute error and oppose itself to appearance, the manner in which it developed (initially made available to the wise, then withdrawn by men of piety to an unattainable world where it was given the double role of consolation and imperative, finally rejected as a useless notion, superfluous, and contradicted on all sides) – does this not form a history, the history of an error we call truth? Truth, and its original reign, has had a history within history from which we are barely emerging "in the time of the shortest shadow," when light no longer seems to flow from the depths of the sky or to arise from the first moments of the day.[15]

A genealogy of values, morality, asceticism, and knowledge will never confuse itself with a quest for their "origins," will never neglect as inaccessible the vicissitudes of history. On the contrary, it will cultivate the details and accidents that accompany every beginning; it will be scrupulously attentive to their petty malice; it will await their emergence, once unmasked, as the face of the other. Wherever it is made to go, it will not be reticent – in "excavating the depths," in allowing time for these elements to escape from a labyrinth where no truth had ever detained them. The genealogist needs history to dispel the chimeras of the origin, somewhat in the manner of the pious philosopher who needs a doctor to exorcise the shadow of his soul. He must be able to recognize the events of history, its jolts, its surprises, its unsteady victories and unpalatable defeats – the basis of all beginnings, atavisms, and heredities. Similarly, he must be able to diagnose the illnesses of the body, its conditions of weakness and strength, its breakdown and resistances, to be in a position to judge philosophical discourse. History is the concrete body of a development, with its moments of intensity, its lapses, its extended periods of feverish agitation, its fainting spells; and only a metaphysician would seek its soul in the distant ideality of the origin.

3. *Entstehung* and *Herkunft* are more exact than *Ursprung* in recording the true objective of genealogy; and, while they are ordinarily translated as "origin," we must attempt to reestablish their proper use.

Herkunft is the equivalent of stock or *descent*; it is the ancient affiliation to a group, sustained by the bonds of blood, tradition, or social class. The

---

[viii] Zarathustra is the prophetic main character of Nietzsche's *Thus Spoke Zarathustra*.

analysis of *Herkunft* often involves a consideration of race[16] or social type.[17] But the traits it attempts to identify are not the exclusive generic characteristics of an individual, a sentiment, or an idea, which permit us to qualify them as "Greek" or "English"; rather, it seeks the subtle, singular, and subindividual marks that might possibly intersect in them to form a network that is difficult to unravel. Far from being a category of resemblance, this origin allows the sorting out of different traits: the Germans imagined that they had finally accounted for their complexity by saying they possessed a double soul; they were fooled by a simple computation, or rather, they were simply trying to master the racial disorder from which they had formed themselves.[18] Where the soul pretends unification or the self fabricates a coherent identity, the genealogist sets out to study the beginning – numberless beginnings whose faint traces and hints of color are readily seen by an historical eye. The analysis of descent permits the dissociation of the self, its recognition and displacement as an empty synthesis, in liberating a profusion of lost events.

An examination of descent also permits the discovery, under the unique aspect of a trait or a concept, of the myriad events through which – thanks to which, against which – they were formed. Genealogy does not pretend to go back in time to restore an unbroken continuity that operates beyond the dispersion of forgotten things; its duty is not to demonstrate that the past actively exists in the present, that it continues secretly to animate the present, having imposed a predetermined form to all its vicissitudes. Genealogy does not resemble the evolution of a species and does not map the destiny of a people. On the contrary, to follow the complex course of descent is to maintain passing events in their proper dispersion; it is to identify the accidents, the minute deviations – or conversely, the complete reversals – the errors, the false appraisals, and the faulty calculations that gave birth to those things that continue to exist and have value for us; it is to discover that truth or being do not lie at the root of what we know and what we are, but the exteriority of accidents.[19] This is undoubtedly why every origin of morality from the moment it stops being pious – and *Herkunft* can never be – has value as a critique.[20]

Deriving from such a source is a dangerous legacy. In numerous instances, Nietzsche associates the terms *Herkunft* and *Erbschaft*.[ix] Nevertheless, we should not be deceived into thinking that this heritage is an acquisition, a possession that grows and solidifies; rather, it is an unstable assemblage of faults, fissures, and heterogeneous layers that threaten the fragile inheritor from within or from underneath: "injustice or instability in the minds of certain men, their disorder and lack of decorum, are the final consequences of their ancestors' numberless logical inaccuracies, hasty conclusions, and superficiality."[21] The search for descent is not the erecting of foundations: on the contrary, it disturbs what was previously considered immobile; it fragments what was thought unified; it shows the heterogeneity of what was imagined consistent with itself. What convictions and, far more decisively, what knowledge can resist it? If a genealogical analysis of a scholar were made – of one who collects facts and carefully accounts for them – his *Herkunft* would quickly divulge the official papers of the scribe and the pleadings of the lawyer – their father[22] – in their apparently disinterested attention, in the "pure" devotion to objectivity.

Finally, descent attaches itself to the body.[23] It inscribes itself in the nervous system, in temperament, in the digestive apparatus; it appears in faulty respiration, in improper diets, in the debilitated and prostrate body of those whose ancestors committed errors. Fathers have only to mistake effects for causes, believe in the reality of an "afterlife," or maintain the value of eternal truths, and the bodies of their children will suffer. Cowardice and hypocrisy, for their part, are the simple offshoots of error: not in a Socratic sense, not that evil is the result of a mistake, not because of a turning away from an original truth, but because the body maintains, in life as in death, through its strength or weakness, the sanction of every truth and error, as it sustains, in an inverse manner, the origin – descent. Why did men invent the contemplative life? Why give a supreme value to this form of existence? Why maintain the absolute truth of those fictions which sustain it? "During barbarous ages...if the strength of an individual declined, if he felt himself tired or sick, melancholy or satiated and, as a consequence, without desire or appetite for a short time, he became relatively a better man, that is, less dangerous. His pessimistic ideas could only take form as words or reflections. In this frame of mind, he either became a thinker and prophet or used his imagination to feed his superstitions."[24] The body – and everything that touches it: diet, climate, and soil – is the domain of the *Herkunft*. The body manifests the stigmata of past experience and also gives rise to desires, failings, and errors.

[ix] *Erbschaft* means "legacy."

These elements may join in a body where they achieve a sudden expression, but as often, their encounter is an engagement in which they efface each other, where the body becomes the pretext of their insurmountable conflict.

The body is the inscribed surface of events (traced by language and dissolved by ideas), the locus of a dissociated Self (adopting the illusion of a substantial unity), and a volume in perpetual disintegration. Genealogy, as an analysis of descent, is thus situated within the articulation of the body and history. Its task is to expose a body totally imprinted by history and the process of history's destruction of the body.

4. *Entstehung* designates *emergence*, the moment of arising. It stands as the principle and the singular law of an apparition. As it is wrong to search for descent in an uninterrupted continuity, we should avoid thinking of emergence as the final term of an historical development; the eye was not always intended for contemplation, and punishment has had other purposes than setting an example. These developments may appear as a culmination, but they are merely the current episodes in a series of subjugations: the eye initially responded to the requirements of hunting and warfare; and punishment has been subjected, throughout its history, to a variety of needs – revenge, excluding an aggressor, compensating a victim, creating fear. In placing present needs at the origin, the metaphysician would convince us of an obscure purpose that seeks its realization at the moment it arises. Genealogy, however, seeks to reestablish the various systems of subjection: not the anticipatory power of meaning, but the hazardous play of dominations.

Emergence is always produced through a particular stage of forces. The analysis of the *Entstehung* must delineate this interaction, the struggle these forces wage against each other or against adverse circumstances, and the attempt to avoid degeneration and regain strength by dividing these forces against themselves. It is in this sense that the emergence of a species (animal or human) and its solidification are secured "in an extended battle against conditions which are essentially and constantly unfavorable." In fact, "the species must realize itself as a species, as something – characterized by the durability, uniformity, and simplicity of its form – which can prevail in the perpetual struggle against outsiders or the uprising of those it oppresses from within." On the other hand, individual differences emerge at another stage of the relationship of forces, when the species has become

victorious and when it is no longer threatened from outside. In this condition, we find a struggle "of egoisms turned against each other, each bursting forth in a splintering of forces and a general striving for the sun and for the light."[25] There are also times when force contends against itself, and not only in the intoxication of an abundance, which allows it to divide itself, but at the moment when it weakens. Force reacts against its growing lassitude and gains strength; it imposes limits, inflicts torments and mortifications; it masks these actions as a higher morality, and, in exchange, regains its strength. In this manner, the ascetic ideal was born, "in the instinct of a decadent life which...struggles for its own existence."[26] This also describes the movement in which the Reformation arose, precisely where the church was least corrupt,[27] German Catholicism, in the sixteenth century, retained enough strength to turn against itself, to mortify its own body and history, and to spiritualize itself into a pure religion of conscience.

Emergence is thus the entry of forces; it is their eruption, the leap from the wings to center stage, each in its youthful strength. What Nietzsche calls the *Entstehungsherd*[28] of the concept of goodness is not specifically the energy of the strong or the reaction of the weak,[x] but precisely this scene where they are displayed superimposed or face-to-face. It is nothing but the space that divides them, the void through which they exchange their threatening gestures and speeches. As descent qualifies the strength or weakness of an instinct and its inscription on a body, emergence designates a place of confrontation but not as a closed field offering the spectacle of a struggle among equals. Rather, as Nietzsche demonstrates in his analysis of good and evil, it is a "non-place," a pure distance, which indicates that the adversaries do not belong to a common space. Consequently, no one is responsible for an emergence; no one can glory in it, since it always occurs in the interstice.

In a sense, only a single drama is ever staged in this "non-place," the endlessly repeated play of dominations. The domination of certain men over others leads to the differentiation of values;[29] class domination generates the idea of liberty;[30] and the forceful appropriation of things necessary to survival and the imposition of a duration not intrinsic to them account for the origin of logic.[31] This relationship of domination is no more a "relationship" than the place where it occurs is a place; and,

[x] *Entstehungsherd* means roughly "original home."

Michel Foucault

precisely for this reason, it is fixed, throughout its history, in rituals, in meticulous procedures that impose rights and obligations. It establishes marks of its power and engraves memories on things and even within bodies. It makes itself accountable for debts and gives rise to the universe of rules, which is by no means designed to temper violence, but rather to satisfy it. Following traditional beliefs, it would be false to think that total war exhausts itself in its own contradictions and ends by renouncing violence and submitting to civil laws. On the contrary, the law is a calculated and relentless pleasure, delight in the promised blood, which permits the perpetual instigation of new dominations and the staging of meticulously repeated scenes of violence. The desire for peace, the serenity of compromise, and the tacit acceptance of the law, far from representing a major moral conversion or a utilitarian calculation that gave rise to the law, are but its result and, in point of fact, its perversion: "guilt, conscience, and duty had their threshold of emergence in the right to secure obligations; and their inception, like that of any major event on earth, was saturated in blood."[32] Humanity does not gradually progress from combat to combat until it arrives at universal reciprocity, where the rule of law finally replaces warfare; humanity installs each of its violences in a system of rules and thus proceeds from domination to domination.

The nature of these rules allows violence to be inflicted on violence and the resurgence of new forces that are sufficiently strong to dominate those in power. Rules are empty in themselves, violent and unfinalized; they are impersonal and can be bent to any purpose. The successes of history belong to those who are capable of seizing these rules, to replace those who had used them, to disguise themselves so as to pervert them, invert their meaning, and redirect them against those who had initially imposed them; controlling this complex mechanism, they will make it function so as to overcome the rulers through their own rules.

The isolation of different points of emergence does not conform to the successive configurations of an identical meaning; rather, they result from substitutions, displacements, disguised conquests, and systematic reversals. If interpretation were the slow exposure of the meaning hidden in an origin, then only metaphysics could interpret the development of humanity. But if interpretation is the violent or surreptitious appropriation of a system of rules, which in itself has no essential meaning, in order to impose a direction, to bend it to a new will,

to force its participation in a different game, and to subject it to secondary rules, then the development of humanity is a series of interpretations. The role of genealogy is to record its history: the history of morals, ideals, and metaphysical concepts, the history of the concept of liberty or of the ascetic life; as they stand for the emergence of different interpretations, they must be made to appear as events on the stage of historical process.

5. How can we define the relationship between genealogy, seen as the examination of *Herkunft* and *Entstehung*, and history in the traditional sense? We could, of course, examine Nietzsche's celebrated apostrophes against history, but we will put these aside for the moment and consider those instances when he conceives of genealogy as "wirkliche Historie,"[xi] or its more frequent characterization as historical "spirit" or "sense."[33] In fact, Nietzsche's criticism, beginning with the second of the *Untimely Meditations*, always questioned the form of history that reintroduces (and always assumes) a suprahistorical perspective: a history whose function is to compose the finally reduced diversity of time into a totality fully closed upon itself; a history that always encourages subjective recognitions and attributes a form of reconciliation to all the displacements of the past; a history whose perspective on all that precedes it implies the end of time, a completed development. The historian's history finds its support outside of time and pretends to base its judgments on an apocalyptic objectivity. This is only possible, however, because of its belief in eternal truth, the immortality of the soul, and the nature of consciousness as always identical to itself. Once the historical sense is mastered by a suprahistorical perspective, metaphysics can bend it to its own purpose and, by aligning it to the demands of objective science, it can impose its own "Egyptianism." On the other hand, the historical sense can evade metaphysics and become a privileged instrument of genealogy if it refuses the certainty of absolutes. Given this, it corresponds to the acuity of a glance that distinguishes, separates, and disperses, that is capable of liberating divergence and marginal elements – the kind of dissociating view that is capable of decomposing itself, capable of shattering the unity of man's being through which it was thought that he could extend his sovereignty to the events of his past.

Historical meaning becomes a dimension of "wirkliche Historie" to the extent that it places

[xi] Usually translated as "effective history."

within a process of development everything considered immortal in man. We believe that feelings are immutable, but every sentiment, particularly the noblest and most disinterested, has a history. We believe in the dull constancy of instinctual life and imagine that it continues to exert its force indiscriminately in the present as it did in the past. But a knowledge of history easily disintegrates this unity, depicts its wavering course, locates its moments of strength and weakness, and defines its oscillating reign. It easily seizes the slow elaboration of instincts and those movements where, in turning upon themselves, they relentlessly set about their self-destruction.[34] We believe, in any event, that the body obeys the exclusive laws of physiology and that it escapes the influence of history, but this too is false. The body is molded by a great many distinct regimes; it is broken down by the rhythms of work, rest, and holidays; it is poisoned by food or values, through eating habits or moral laws; it constructs resistances.[35] "Effective" history differs from traditional history in being without constants. Nothing in man – not even his body – is sufficiently stable to serve as the basis for self-recognition or for understanding other men. The traditional devices for constructing a comprehensive view of history and for retracing the past as a patient and continuous development must be systematically dismantled. Necessarily, we must dismiss those tendencies that encourage the consoling play of recognitions. Knowledge, even under the banner of history, does not depend on "rediscovery," and it emphatically excludes the "rediscovery of ourselves." History becomes "effective" to the degree that it introduces discontinuity into our very being – as it divides our emotions, dramatizes our instincts, multiplies our body and sets it against itself. "Effective" history deprives the self of the reassuring stability of life and nature, and it will not permit itself to be transported by a voiceless obstinacy toward a millenial ending. It will uproot its traditional foundations and relentlessly disrupt its pretended continuity. This is because knowledge is not made for understanding; it is made for cutting.

From these observations, we can grasp the particular traits of historical meaning as Nietzsche understood it – the sense which opposes "wirkliche Historie" to traditional history. The former transposes the relationship ordinarily established between the eruption of an event and necessary continuity. An entire historical tradition (theological or rationalistic) aims at dissolving the singular event into an ideal continuity – as a teleological

movement or a natural process. "Effective" history, however, deals with events in terms of their most unique characteristics, their most acute manifestations. An event, consequently, is not a decision, a treaty, a reign, or a battle, but the reversal of a relationship of forces, the usurpation of power, the appropriation of a vocabulary turned against those who had once used it, a feeble domination that poisons itself as it grows lax, the entry of a masked "other." The forces operating in history are not controlled by destiny or regulative mechanisms, but respond to haphazard conflicts.[36] They do not manifest the successive forms of a primordial intention and their attraction is not that of a conclusion, for they always appear through the singular randomness of events. The inverse of the Christian world, spun entirely by a divine spider, and different from the world of the Greeks, divided between the realm of will and the great cosmic folly, the world of effective history knows only one kingdom, without providence or final cause, where there is only "the iron hand of necessity shaking the dice-box of chance."[37] Chance is not simply the drawing of lots, but raising the stakes in every attempt to master chance through the will to power, and giving rise to the risk of an even greater chance.[38] The world we know is not this ultimately simple configuration where events are reduced to accentuate their essential traits, their final meaning, or their initial and final value. On the contrary, it is a profusion of entangled events. If it appears as a "marvelous motley, profound and totally meaningful," this is because it began and continues its secret existence through a "host of errors and phantasms."[39] We want historians to confirm our belief that the present rests upon profound intentions and immutable necessities. But the true historical sense confirms our existence among countless lost events, without a landmark or a point of reference.

Effective history can also invert the relationship that traditional history, in its dependence on metaphysics, establishes between proximity and distance. The latter is given to a contemplation of distances and heights: the noblest periods, the highest forms, the most abstract ideas, the purest individualities. It accomplishes this by getting as near as possible, placing itself at the foot of its mountain peaks, at the risk of adopting the famous perspective of frogs. Effective history, on the other hand, shortens its vision to those things nearest to it – the body, the nervous system, nutrition, digestion, and energies; it unearths the periods of decadence and if it chances upon lofty epochs, it is with the suspicion – not vindictive but joyous – of finding a barbarous and shameful confusion. It has no fear of looking down, so long as it is understood that it looks from above and descends to seize the various perspectives, to disclose dispersions and differences, to leave things undisturbed in their own dimension and intensity. It reverses the surreptitious practice of historians, their pretension to examine things furthest from themselves, the grovelling manner in which they approach this promising distance (like the metaphysicians who proclaim the existence of an afterlife, situated at a distance from this world, as a promise of their reward). Effective history studies what is closest, but in an abrupt dispossession, so as to seize it at a distance (an approach similar to that of a doctor who looks closely, who plunges to make a diagnosis and to state its difference). Historical sense has more in common with medicine than philosophy; and it should not surprise us that Nietzsche occasionally employs the phrase "historically and physiologically,"[40] since among the philosopher's idiosyncrasies is a complete denial of the body. This includes, as well, "the absence of historical sense, a hatred for the idea of development, Egyptianism," the obstinate "placing of conclusions at the beginning," of "making last things first."[41] History has a more important task than to be a handmaiden to philosophy, to recount the necessary birth of truth and values; it should become a differential knowledge of energies and failings, heights and degenerations, poisons and antidotes. Its task is to become a curative science.[42]

The final trait of effective history is its affirmation of knowledge as perspective. Historians take unusual pains to erase the elements in their work which reveal their grounding in a particular time and place, their preferences in a controversy – the unavoidable obstacles of their passion. Nietzsche's version of historical sense is explicit in its perspective and acknowledges its system of injustice. Its perception is slanted, being a deliberate appraisal, affirmation, or negation; it reaches the lingering and poisonous traces in order to prescribe the best antidote. It is not given to a discreet effacement before the objects it observes and does not submit itself to their processes; nor does it seek laws, since it gives equal weight to its own sight and to its objects. Through this historical sense, knowledge is allowed to create its own genealogy in the act of cognition; and "wirkliche Historie" composes a genealogy of history as the vertical projection of its position.

6. In this context, Nietzsche links historical sense to the historian's history. They share a beginning that is similarly impure and confused, share the same sign in which the symptoms of sickness can be recognized as well as the seed of an exquisite flower.[43] They arose simultaneously to follow their separate ways, but our task is to trace their common genealogy.

The descent (*Herkunft*) of the historian is unequivocal: he is of humble birth. A characteristic of history is to be without choice: it encourages thorough understanding and excludes qualitative judgments – a sensitivity to all things without distinction, a comprehensive view excluding differences. Nothing must escape it and, more importantly, nothing must be excluded. Historians argue that this proves their tact and discretion. After all, what right have they to impose their tastes and preferences when they seek to determine what actually occurred in the past? Their mistake is to exhibit a total lack of taste, the kind of crudeness that becomes smug in the presence of the loftiest elements and finds satisfaction in reducing them to size. The historian is insensitive to the most disgusting things; or rather, he especially enjoys those things that should be repugnant to him. His apparent serenity follows from his concerted avoidance of the exceptional and his reduction of all things to the lowest common denominator. Nothing is allowed to stand above him; and underlying his desire for total knowledge is his search for the secrets that belittle everything: "base curiosity." What is the source of history? It comes from the plebs.[xii] To whom is it addressed? To the plebs. And its discourse strongly resembles the demagogue's refrain: "No one is greater than you and anyone who presumes to get the better of you – you who are good – is evil." The historian, who functions as his double, can be heard to echo: "No past is greater than your present, and, through my meticulous erudition, I will rid you of your infatuations and transform the grandeur of history into pettiness, evil, and misfortune." The historian's ancestry goes back to Socrates.

This demagogy, of course, must be masked. It must hide its singular malice under the cloak of universals. As the demagogue is obliged to invoke truth, laws of essences, and eternal necessity, the historian must invoke objectivity, the accuracy of facts, and the permanence of the past. The demagogue denies the body to secure the sovereignty of a timeless idea and the historian effaces his proper

---

[xii] "Plebs" is short for plebians, an ancient Roman term for the lower class.

individuality so that others may enter the stage and reclaim their own speech. He is divided against himself: forced to silence his preferences and overcome his distaste, to blur his own perspective and replace it with the fiction of a universal geometry, to mimic death in order to enter the kingdom of the dead, to adopt a faceless anonymity. In this world where he has conquered his individual will, he becomes a guide to the inevitable law of a superior will. Having curbed the demands of his individual will in his knowledge, he will disclose the form of an eternal will in his object of study. The objectivity of historians inverts the relationships of will and knowledge and it is, in the same stroke, a necessary belief in Providence, in final causes and teleology – the beliefs that place the historian in the family of ascetics. "I can't stand these lustful eunuchs of history, all the seductions of an ascetic ideal; I can't stand these blanched tombs producing life or those tired and indifferent beings who dress up in the part of wisdom and adopt an objective point of view."[44]

The *Entstehung* of history is found in nineteenth-century Europe: the land of interminglings and bastardy, the period of the "man-of-mixture." We have become barbarians with respect to those rare moments of high civilization: cities in ruin and enigmatic monuments are spread out before us; we stop before gaping walls; we ask what gods inhabited these empty temples. Great epochs lacked this curiosity, lacked our excessive deference; they ignored their predecessors: the classical period ignored Shakespeare. The decadence of Europe presents an immense spectacle (while stronger periods refrained from such exhibitions), and the nature of this scene is to represent a theater; lacking monuments of our own making, which properly belong to us, we live among crowded scenes. But there is more. Europeans no longer know themselves; they ignore their mixed ancestries and seek a proper role. They lack individuality: We can begin to understand the spontaneous historical bent of the nineteenth century: the anemia of its forces and those mixtures that effaced all its individual traits produced the same results as the mortifications of asceticism; its inability to create, its absence of artistic works, and its need to rely on past achievements forced it to adopt the base curiosity of plebs.

If this fully represents the genealogy of history, how could it become, in its own right, a genealogical analysis? Why did it not continue as a form of demagogic or religious knowledge? How could it

change roles on the same stage? Only by being seized, dominated, and turned against its birth. And it is this movement which properly describes the specific nature of the *Entstehung*: it is not the unavoidable conclusion of a long preparation, but a scene where forces are risked in the chance of confrontations, where they emerge triumphant, where they can also be confiscated. The locus of emergence for metaphysics was surely Athenian demagogy, the vulgar spite of Socrates and his belief in immortality, and Plato could have seized this Socratic philosophy to turn it against itself. Undoubtedly, he was often tempted to do so, but his defeat lies in its consecration. The problem was similar in the nineteenth century: to avoid doing for the popular asceticism of historians what Plato did for Socrates. This historical trait should not be founded upon a philosophy of history, but dismantled beginning with the things it produced; it is necessary to master history so as to turn it to genealogical uses, that is, strictly anti-Platonic purposes. Only then will the historical sense free itself from the demands of a suprahistorical history.

7. The historical sense gives rise to three uses that oppose and correspond to the three Platonic modalities of history. The first is parodic, directed against reality, and opposes the theme of history as reminiscence or recognition; the second is dissociative, directed against identity, and opposes history given as continuity or representative of a tradition; the third is sacrificial, directed against truth, and opposes history as knowledge. They imply a use of history that severs its connection to memory, its metaphysical and anthropological model, and constructs a counter-memory – a transformation of history into a totally different form of time.

First, the parodic and farcical use. The historian offers this confused and anonymous European, who no longer knows himself or what name he should adopt, the possibility of alternate identities, more individualized and substantial than his own. But the man with historical sense will see that this substitution is simply a disguise. Historians supplied the Revolution with Roman prototypes, romanticism with knight's armor, and the Wagnerian era was given the sword of a German hero – ephemeral props that point to our own unreality. No one kept them from venerating these religions, from going to Bayreuth[xiii] to commemorate a new

---

[xiii] Bayreuth was the home of German composer Richard Wagner from 1872 until his death in 1883, and the center of the cult that surrounded him.

afterlife; they were free, as well, to be transformed into street-vendors of empty identities. The new historian, the genealogist, will know what to make of this masquerade. He will not be too serious to enjoy it; on the contrary, he will push the masquerade to its limit and prepare the great carnival of time where masks are constantly reappearing. No longer the identification of our faint individuality with the solid identities of the past, but our "unrealization" through the excessive choice of identities – Frederick of Hohenstaufen, Caesar, Jesus, Dionysus, and possibly Zarathustra. Taking up these masks, revitalizing the buffoonery of history, we adopt an identity whose unreality surpasses that of God who started the charade. "Perhaps, we can discover a realm where originality is again possible as parodists of history and buffoons of God."[45] In this, we recognize the parodic double of what the second of the *Untimely Meditations* called "monumental history": a history given to reestablishing the high points of historical development and their maintenance in a perpetual presence, given to the recovery of works, actions, and creations through the monogram of their personal essence. But in 1874, Nietzsche accused this history, one totally devoted to veneration, of barring access to the actual intensities and creations of life. The parody of his last texts serves to emphasize that "monumental history" is itself a parody. Genealogy is history in the form of a concerted carnival.

The second use of history is the systematic dissociation of identity. This is necessary because this rather weak identity, which we attempt to support and to unify under a mask, is in itself only a parody: it is plural; countless spirits dispute its possession; numerous systems intersect and compete. The study of history makes one "happy, unlike the metaphysicians, to possess in oneself not an immortal soul but many mortal ones."[46] And in each of these souls, history will not discover a forgotten identity, eager to be reborn, but a complex system of distinct and multiple elements, unable to be mastered by the powers of synthesis: "it is a sign of superior culture to maintain, in a fully conscious way, certain phases of its evolution which lesser men pass through without thought. The initial result is that we can understand those who resemble us as completely determined systems and as representative of diverse cultures, that is to say, as necessary and capable of modification. And in return, we are able to separate the phases of our own evolution and consider them individually."[47] The purpose of history, guided by genealogy, is not to discover the roots of our identity but to commit itself to its dissipation. It does not seek to define our unique threshold of emergence, the homeland to which metaphysicians promise a return; it seeks to make visible all of those discontinuities that cross us. "Antiquarian history," according to the *Untimely Meditations*, pursues opposite goals. It seeks the continuities of soil, language, and urban life in which our present is rooted and, "by cultivating in a delicate manner that which existed for all time, it tries to conserve for posterity the conditions under which we were born."[48] This type of history was objected to in the *Meditations* because it tended to block creativity in support of the laws of fidelity. Somewhat later – and already in *Human, All Too Human* – Nietzsche reconsiders the task of the antiquarian, but with an altogether different emphasis. If genealogy in its own right gives rise to questions concerning our native land, native language, or the laws that govern us, its intention is to reveal the heterogenous systems which, masked by the self, inhibit the formation of any form of identity.

The third use of history is the sacrifice of the subject of knowledge. In appearance, or rather, according to the mask it bears, historical consciousness is neutral, devoid of passions, and committed solely to truth. But if it examines itself and if, more generally, it interrogates the various forms of scientific consciousness in its history, it finds that all these forms and transformations are aspects of the will to knowledge: instinct, passion, the inquisitor's devotion, cruel subtlety, and malice. It discovers the violence of a position that sides against those who are happy in their ignorance, against the effective illusions by which humanity protects itself, a position that encourages the dangers of research and delights in disturbing discoveries.[49] The historical analysis of this rancorous will to knowledge reveals that all knowledge rests upon injustice (that there is no right, not even in the act of knowing, to truth or a foundation for truth) and that the instinct for knowledge is malicious (something murderous, opposed to the happiness of mankind). Even in the greatly expanded form it assumes today, the will to knowledge does not achieve a universal truth; man is not given an exact and serene mastery of nature. On the contrary, it ceaselessly multiplies the risks, creates dangers in every area; it breaks down illusory defences; it dissolves the unity of the subject; it releases those elements of itself that are devoted to its subversion and destruction. Knowledge does not slowly detach itself from its empirical roots, the initial needs from which it arose, to become pure speculation subject only to the demands of reason; its development is not tied to the constitution and affirmation of a free subject; rather, it creates a progressive enslavement to its instinctive violence. Where religions once demanded the sacrifice of bodies, knowledge now calls for experimentation on ourselves,[50] calls us to the sacrifice of the subject of knowledge. "The desire for knowledge has been transformed among us into a passion which fears no sacrifice, which fears nothing but its own extinction. It may be that mankind will eventually perish from this passion for knowledge. If not through passion, then through weakness. We must be prepared to state our choice: do we wish humanity to end in fire and light or to end on the sands?"[51] We should now replace the two great problems of nineteenth-century philosophy, passed on by Fichte and Hegel (the reciprocal basis of truth and liberty and the possibility of absolute knowledge), with the theme that "to perish through absolute knowledge may well form a part of the basis of being."[52] This does not mean, in terms of a critical procedure, that the will to truth is limited by the intrinsic finitude of cognition, but that it loses all sense of limitations and all claim to truth in its unavoidable sacrifice of the subject of knowledge. "It may be that there remains one prodigious idea which might be made to prevail over every other aspiration, which might overcome the most victorious: the idea of humanity sacrificing itself. It seems indisputable that if this new constellation appeared on the horizon, only the desire for truth,

with its enormous prerogatives, could direct and sustain such a sacrifice. For to knowledge, no sacrifice is too great. Of course, this problem has never been posed."[53]

The *Untimely Meditations* discussed the critical use of history: its just treatment of the past, its decisive cutting of the roots, its rejection of traditional attitudes of reverence, its liberation of man by presenting him with other origins than those in which he prefers to see himself. Nietzsche, however, reproached critical history for detaching us from every real source and for sacrificing the very movement of life to the exclusive concern for truth. Somewhat later, as we have seen, Nietzsche reconsiders this line of thought he had at first refused, but directs it to altogether different ends. It is no longer a question of judging the past in the name of a truth that only we can possess in the present; but risking the destruction of the subject who seeks knowledge in the endless deployment of the will to knowledge.

In a sense, genealogy returns to the three modalities of history that Nietzsche recognized in 1874. It returns to them in spite of the objections that Nietzsche raised in the name of the affirmative and creative powers of life. But they are metamorphosized; the veneration of monuments becomes parody; the respect for ancient continuities becomes systematic dissociation; the critique of the injustices of the past by a truth held by men in the present becomes the destruction of the man who maintains knowledge by the injustice proper to the will to knowledge.

Author's Notes

1   *The Gay Science*, 7. [In all references below, the numbers indicate sections or paragraphs, not pages.]
2   *Human All Too Human*, 3.
3   *The Genealogy [of Morals]*, II, 6, 8.
4   *The Gay Science*, 110, 111, 300.
5   Paul Ree's text was entitled *Ursprung der Moralischen Empfindungen* [*Origin of the Moral Sentiments*].
6   In *Human, All Too Human*, aphorism 92 was entitled *Ursprung der Gerechtigkeit* [*Origin of Justice*].
7   In the main body of *The Genealogy*, *Ursprung* and *Herkunft* are used interchangeably in numerous instances (I, 2; II, 8, 11, 12, 16, 17).
8   *The Dawn*, 123.
9   *Human, All Too Human*, 34.
10   *The Wanderer and his Shadow*, 9.
11   The *Wanderer and his Shadow*, 3.
12   *The Dawn*, 49.

13   *Nietzsche contra Wagner*, p. 99.
14   *The Gay Science*, 265 and 110.
15   *Twilight of the Idols*, "How the world of truth becomes a fable."
16   For example, *The Gay Science*, 135; *Beyond Good and Evil*, 200, 242, 244; *The Genealogy*, I, 5.
17   *The Gay Science*, 348–9; *Beyond Good and Evil*, 260.
18   *Beyond Good and Evil*, 244.
19   *The Genealogy*, III, 17. The *abkunft* of feelings of depression.
20   *Twilight*, "Reasons for philosophy."
21   *The Dawn*, 247.
22   *The Gay Science*, 348–9.
23   Ibid., 200.
24   *The Dawn*, 42.
25   *Beyond Good and Evil*, 262.
26   *The Genealogy*, III, 13.

27 *The Gay Science*, 148. It is also to an anemia of the will that one must attribute the *Entstehung* of Buddhism and Christianity, 347.

28 *The Genealogy*, I, 2.

29 *Beyond Good and Evil*, 260; cf. also *The Genealogy*, II, 12.

30 *The Wanderer*, 9.

31 *The Gay Science*, 111.

32 *The Genealogy*, II, 6.

33 *The Genealogy*, Preface, 7; and I, 2. *Beyond Good and Evil*, 224.

34 *The Gay Science*, 7.

35 Ibid.

36 *The Genealogy*, II, 12.

37 *The Dawn*, 130.

38 *The Genealogy*, II, 12.

39 *Human, All Too Human*, 16.

40 *Twilight*, 44.

41 *Twilight*, "Reason within philosophy," 1 and 4.

42 *The Wanderer*, 188.

43 *The Gay Science*, 337.

44 *The Genealogy*, III, 26.

45 *Beyond Good and Evil*, 223.

46 *The Wanderer* (Opinions and Mixed Statements), 17.

47 *Human, All Too Human*, 274.

48 *Untimely Meditations*, II, 3.

49 Cf. *The Dawn*, 429 and 432; *The Gay Science*, 333; *Beyond Good and Evil*, 229–30.

50 *The Dawn*, 501.

51 Ibid., 429.

52 *Beyond Good and Evil*, 39.

53 *The Dawn*, 45.

From "Truth and Power"

...The important thing here, I believe, is that truth isn't outside power, or lacking in power: contrary to a myth whose history and functions would repay further study, truth isn't the reward of free spirits, the child of protracted solitude, nor the privilege of those who have succeeded in liberating themselves. Truth is a thing of this world: it is produced only by virtue of multiple forms of constraint. And it induces regular effects of power. Each society has its regime of truth, its 'general politics' of truth: that is, the types of discourse which it accepts and makes function as true; the mechanisms and instances which enable one to distinguish true and false statements, the means by which each is sanctioned; the techniques and procedures accorded value in the acquisition of truth; the status of those who are charged with saying what counts as true.

In societies like ours, the 'political economy' of truth is characterised by five important traits. 'Truth is centred on the form of scientific discourse and the institutions which produce it; it is subject to constant economic and political incitement (the demand for truth, as much for economic production as for political power); it is the object, under diverse forms, of immense diffusion and consumption (circulating through apparatuses of education and information whose extent is relatively broad in the social body, not withstanding certain strict limitations); it is produced and transmitted under the control, dominant if not exclusive, of a few great political and economic apparatuses (university, army, writing, media); lastly, it is the issue of a whole political debate and social confrontation ('ideological' struggles).

It seems to me that what must now be taken into account in the intellectual is not the 'bearer of universal values'. Rather, it's the person occupying a specific position – but whose specificity is linked, in a society like ours, to the general functioning of an apparatus of truth. In other words, the intellectual has a three-fold specificity: that of his class position (whether as petty-bourgeois[i] in the service of capitalism or 'organic' intellectual of the proletariat); that of his conditions of life and work, linked to his condition as an intellectual (his field of research, his place in a laboratory, the political and economic demands to which he submits or against which he rebels, in the university, the hospital, etc.); lastly, the specificity of the politics of truth in our societies. And it's with this last factor that his position can take on a general significance and that his local, specific struggle can have effects and implications which are not simply professional or sectoral. The intellectual can operate and struggle at the general level of that regime of truth which is so essential to the structure and functioning of our society. There is a battle 'for truth', or at least 'around truth' – it being understood once again that by truth I do not mean 'the ensemble of truths which are to be discovered and accepted', but rather 'the ensemble of rules according to which the true and the false are separated and specific effects of power attached to the true', it being understood also that it's not a matter of a battle 'on behalf' of the truth, but of

---

i The "little bourgeoisie," a Marxist term for small capitalists, civil servants, professionals, etc.

a battle about the status of truth and the economic and political role it plays. It is necessary to think of the political problems of intellectuals not in terms of 'science' and 'ideology', but in terms of 'truth' and 'power'. And thus the question of the professionalisation of intellectuals and the division between intellectual and manual labour can be envisaged in a new way.

All this must seem very confused and uncertain. Uncertain indeed, and what I am saying here is above all to be taken as a hypothesis. In order for it to be a little less confused, however, I would like to put forward a few 'propositions' – not firm assertions, but simply suggestions to be further tested and evaluated.

'Truth' is to be understood as a system of ordered procedures for the production, regulation, distribution, circulation and operation of statements.

'Truth' is linked in a circular relation with systems of power which produce and sustain it, and to effects of power which it induces and which extend it. A regime of truth.

This regime is not merely ideological or superstructural; it was a condition of the forma-tion and development of capitalism. And it's this same regime which, subject to certain modifications, operates in the socialist countries (I leave open here the question of China, about which I know little).

The essential political problem for the intellectual is not to criticise the ideological contents supposedly linked to science, or to ensure that his own scientific practice is accompanied by a correct ideology, but that of ascertaining the possibility of constituting a new politics of truth. The problem is not changing people's consciousnesses – or what's in their heads – but the political, economic, institutional regime of the production of truth.

It's not a matter of emancipating truth from every system of power (which would be a chimera, for truth is already power) but of detaching the power of truth from the forms of hegemony, social, economic and cultural, within which it operates at the present time.

The political question, to sum up, is not error, illusion, alienated consciousness or ideology; it is truth itself. Hence the importance of Nietzsche.

29

"The Sex Which is Not One"

Luce Irigaray

Luce Irigaray (1930–) is a key figure in French feminist thought, which has integrated feminism, postmodern theories of signs, and psychoanalysis. Expelled from the Paris psychoanalytic association and the University of Paris after publication of her book, *Speculum of the Other Woman* (1974), she continued to work as a practising psychoanalyst, and remained associated with the *Centre Nationale de la Recherche Scientifique*. She argues in the following 1977 essay that female experience, marginalized by traditional philosophical inquiry, registers plurality and difference more deeply than does male experience. Rather than minimize gender difference Irigaray insists on its importance, denying that the categories and ideals of the dominant philosophical tradition can capture the characteristic experience and thought of women. One effect of this view is a radical denial of the Enlightenment conception of universal reason.

Female sexuality has always been theorized within masculine parameters. Thus, the opposition "viril"[i] clitoral activity/"feminine" vaginal passivity which Freud – and many others – claims are alternative behaviors or steps in the process of becoming a sexually normal woman, seems prescribed more by the practice of masculine sexuality than by anything else. For the clitoris is thought of as a little penis which is pleasurable to masturbate, as long as the anxiety of castration does not exist (for the little boy), while the vagina derives its value from the "home" it offers the male penis when the now

forbidden hand must find a substitute to take its place in giving pleasure.

According to these theorists, woman's erogenous zones are no more than a clitoris-sex, which cannot stand up in comparison with the valued phallic organ; or a hole-envelope, a sheath which surrounds and rubs the penis during coition; a nonsex organ or a masculine sex organ turned inside out in order to caress itself.

Woman and her pleasure are not mentioned in this conception of the sexual relationship. Her fate is one of "lack," "atrophy" (of her genitals), and "penis envy,"[ii] since the penis is the only recognized sex organ of any worth. Therefore she tries to appropriate it for herself, by all the means at her disposal: by her somewhat servile love of the father-husband capable of giving it to her; by her desire of a penis-child, preferably male; by gaining access to those cultural values which are still "by right" reserved for males alone and are therefore always masculine, etc. Woman lives her desire only as an attempt to possess at long last the equivalent of the male sex organ.

All of that seems rather foreign to her pleasure however, unless she remains within the dominant phallic economy. Thus, for example, woman's autoeroticism is very different from man's. He

[i] Virile, masculine.

[ii] Freud attributed to girls a disappointment over not having a penis.

Luce Irigaray, "The Sex Which is Not One" (trans. Claudia Reeder) from *New French Feminisms* (ed. Elaine Marks and Isabelle de Courtivron), New York: Schoken, 1981, pp. 99–106.

needs an instrument in order to touch himself: his hand, woman's genitals, language – And this self-stimulation requires a minimum of activity. But a woman touches herself by and within herself directly, without mediation, and before any distinction between activity and passivity is possible. A woman "touches herself" constantly without anyone being able to forbid her to do so, for her sex is composed of two lips which embrace continually. Thus, within herself she is already two – but not divisible into ones – who stimulate each other.

This autoeroticism, which she needs in order not to risk the disappearance of her pleasure in the sex act, is interrupted by a violent intrusion: the brutal spreading of these two lips by a violating penis. If, in order to assure an articulation between autocroticism and heteroeroticism in coition (the encounter with the absolute other which always signifies death), the vagina must also, but not only, substitute for the little boy's hand, how can woman's autoeroticism possibly be perpetuated in the classic representation of sexuality? Will she not indeed be left the impossible choice between defensive virginity, fiercely turned back upon itself, or a body open for penetration, which no longer recognizes in its "hole" of a sex organ the pleasure of retouching itself? The almost exclusive, and ever so anxious, attention accorded the erection in Occidental sexuality proves to what extent the imaginary[iii] that commands it is foreign to everything female. For the most part, one finds in Occidental sexuality nothing more than imperatives dictated by rivalry among males: the "strongest" being the one who "gets it up the most," who has the longest, thickest, hardest penis or indeed the one who "pisses the farthest" (cf. little boys' games). These imperatives can also be dictated by sado-masochist fantasies, which in turn are ordered by the relationship between man and mother: his desire to force open, to penetrate, to appropriate for himself the mystery of the stomach in which he was conceived, the secret of his conception, of his "origin." Desire–need, also, once again, to make blood flow in order to revive a very ancient – intrauterine, undoubtedly, but also prehistoric – relation to the maternal.

Woman, in this sexual imaginary, is only a more or less complacent facilitator for the working out of man's fantasies. It is possible, and even certain, that she experiences vicarious pleasure there, but this pleasure is above all a masochistic prostitution of

iii A concept originally formulated by French psychoanalyst Jacques Lacan (1901–81).

her body to a desire that is not her own and that leaves her in her well-known state of dependency. Not knowing what she wants, ready for anything, even asking for more, if only he will "take" her as the "object" of *his* pleasure, she will not say what *she* wants. Moreover, she does not know, or no longer knows, what she wants. As Freud admits, the beginnings of the sexual life of the little girl are so "obscure," so "faded by the years," that one would have to dig very deep in order to find, behind the traces of this civilization, this history, the vestiges of a more archaic civilization which could give some indication as to what woman's sexuality is all about. This very ancient civilization undoubtedly would not have the same language, the same alphabet – Woman's desire most likely does not speak the same language as man's desire, and it probably has been covered over by the logic that has dominated the West since the Greeks.

In this logic, the prevalence of the gaze, discrimination of form, and individualization of form is particularly foreign to female eroticism. Woman finds pleasure more in touch than in sight and her entrance into a dominant scopic economy signifies, once again, her relegation to passivity: she will be the beautiful object. Although her body is in this way eroticized and solicited to a double movement between exhibition and pudic retreat in order to excite the instincts of the "subject," her sex organ represents the horror of having nothing to see. In this system of representation and desire, the vagina is a flaw, a hole in the representation's scoptophilic objective. It was admitted already in Greek statuary that this "nothing to be seen" must be excluded, rejected, from such a scene of representation. Woman's sexual organs are simply absent from this scene: they are masked and her "slit" is sewn up.

In addition, this sex organ which offers nothing to the view has no distinctive form of its own. Although woman finds pleasure precisely in this incompleteness of the form of her sex organ, which is why it retouches itself indefinitely, her pleasure is denied by a civilization that privileges phallomorphism. The value accorded to the only definable form excludes the form involved in female autoeroticism. The *one* of form, the individual sex, proper name, literal meaning – supersedes, by spreading apart and dividing, this touching of *at least two* (lips) which keeps woman in contact with herself, although it would be impossible to distinguish exactly what "parts" are touching each other.

Whence the mystery that she represents in a culture that claims to enumerate everything, cipher everything by units, inventory everything by individualities. *She is neither one nor two.* She cannot, strictly speaking, be determined either as one person or as two. She renders any definition inadequate. Moreover she has no "proper" name. And her sex organ, which is not *a* sex organ, is counted as *no* sex organ. It is the negative, the opposite, the reverse, the counterpart, of the only visible and morphologically designatable sex organ (even if it does pose a few problems in its passage from erection to detumescence): the penis.

But woman holds the secret of the "thickness" of this "form," its many-layered volume, its metamorphosis from smaller to larger and vice versa, and even the intervals at which this change takes place. Without even knowing it. When she is asked to maintain, to revive, man's desire, what this means in terms of the value of her own desire is neglected. Moreover, she is not aware of her desire, at least not explicitly. But the force and continuity of her desire are capable of nurturing all the "feminine" masquerades that are expected of her for a long time.

It is true that she still has the child, with whom her appetite for touching, for contact, is given free reign, unless this appetite is already lost, or alienated by the taboo placed upon touching in a largely obsessional civilization. In her relation to the child she finds compensatory pleasure for the frustrations she encounters all too often in sexual relations proper. Thus maternity supplants the deficiencies of repressed female sexuality. Is it possible that man and woman no longer even caress each other except indirectly through the mediation between them represented by the child? Preferably male. Man, identified with his son, rediscovers the pleasure of maternal coddling; woman retouches herself in fondling that part of her body: her baby-penis-clitoris.

What that entails for the amorous trio has been clearly spelled out. The Oedipal interdict seems, however, a rather artificial and imprecise law – even though it is the very means of perpetuating the authoritarian discourse of fathers – when it is decreed in a culture where sexual relations are impracticable, since the desire of man and the desire of woman are so foreign to each other. Each of them is forced to search for some common meeting ground by indirect means: either an archaic, sensory relation to the mother's body, or a current, active or passive prolongation of the law of the father. Their attempts are characterized by regressive emotional behavior and the exchange of words so far from the realm of the sexual that they are

completely exiled from it. "Mother" and "father" dominate the couple's functioning, but only as social roles. The division of labor prevents them from making love. They produce or reproduce. Not knowing too well how to use their leisure. If indeed they have any, if moreover they want to have any leisure. For what can be done with leisure? What substitute for amorous invention can be created?

We could go on and on – but perhaps we should return to the repressed female imaginary? Thus woman does not have a sex. She has at least two of them, but they cannot be identified as ones. Indeed she has many more of them than that. Her sexuality, always at least double, is in fact *plural*. Plural as culture now wishes to be plural? Plural as the manner in which current texts are written, with very little knowledge of the censorship from which they arise? Indeed, woman's pleasure does not have to choose between clitoral activity and vaginal passivity, for example. The pleasure of the vaginal caress does not have to substitute itself for the pleasure of the clitoral caress. Both contribute irreplaceably to woman's pleasure but they are only two caresses among many to do so. Caressing the breasts, touching the vulva, opening the lips, gently stroking the posterior wall of the vagina, lightly massaging the cervix, etc., evoke a few of the most specifically female pleasures. They remain rather unfamiliar pleasures in the sexual difference as it is currently imagined, or rather as it is currently ignored: the other sex being only the indispensable complement of the only sex.

But *woman has sex organs just about everywhere.* She experiences pleasure almost everywhere. Even without speaking of the hysterization of her entire body, one can say that the geography of her pleasure is much more diversified, more multiple in its differences, more complex, more subtle, than is imagined – in an imaginary centered a bit too much on one and the same.

"She" is indefinitely other in herself. That is undoubtedly the reason she is called temperamental, incomprehensible, perturbed, capricious – not to mention her language in which "she" goes off in all directions and in which "he" is unable to discern the coherence of any meaning. Contradictory words seem a little crazy to the logic of reason, and inaudible for him who listens with ready-made grids, a code prepared in advance. In her statements – at least when she dares to speak out – woman retouches herself constantly. She just barely separates from herself some chatter, an exclamation, a half-secret, a sentence left in suspense – When she returns to it, it is only to set out again from another point of pleasure or pain. One must listen to her differently in order to hear an *"other meaning" which is constantly in the process of weaving itself, at the same time ceaselessly embracing words and yet casting them off to avoid becoming fixed, immobilized.* For when "she" says something, it is already no longer identical to what she means. Moreover, her statements are never identical to anything. Their distinguishing feature is one of contiguity. They touch (*upon*). And when they wander too far from this nearness, she stops and begins again from "zero": her body-sex organ.

It is therefore useless to trap women into giving an exact definition of what they mean, to make them repeat (themselves) so the meaning will be clear. They are already elsewhere than in this discursive machinery where you claim to take them by surprise. They have turned back within themselves, which does not mean the same thing as "within yourself." They do not experience the same interiority that you do and which perhaps you mistakenly presume they share. "Within themselves" means *in the privacy of this silent, multiple, diffuse tact.* If you ask them insistently what they are thinking about, they can only reply: nothing. Everything.

Thus they desire at the same time nothing and everything. It is always more and other than this *one* – of sex, for example – that you give them, that you attribute to them and which is often interpreted, and feared, as a sort of insatiable hunger, a voracity which will engulf you entirely. While in fact it is really a question of another economy which diverts the linearity of a project, undermines the target-object of a desire, explodes the polarization of desire on only one pleasure, and disconcerts fidelity to only one discourse –

Must the multiple nature of female desire and language be understood as the fragmentary, scattered remains of a raped or denied sexuality? This is not an easy question to answer. The rejection, the exclusion of a female imaginary undoubtedly places woman in a position where she can experience herself only fragmentarily as waste or as excess in the little structured margins of a dominant ideology, this mirror entrusted by the (masculine) "subject" with the task of reflecting and redoubling himself. The role of "femininity" is prescribed moreover by this masculine specula(riza)tion and corresponds only slightly to woman's desire, which is recuperated only secretly, in hiding, and in a disturbing and unpardonable manner.

But if the female imaginary happened to unfold, if it happened to come into play other than as pieces, scraps, deprived of their assemblage, would it present itself for all that as *a* universe? Would it indeed be volume rather than surface? No. Unless female imaginary is taken to mean, once again, the prerogative of the maternal over the female. This maternal would be phallic in nature however, closed in upon the jealous possession of its valuable product, and competing with man in his esteem for surplus. In this race for power, woman loses the uniqueness of her pleasure. By diminishing herself in volume, she renounces the pleasure derived from the nonsuture of her lips: she is a mother certainly, but she is a virgin mother. Mythology long ago assigned this role to her in which she is allowed a certain social power as long as she is reduced, with her own complicity, to sexual impotence.

Thus a woman's (re) discovery of herself can only signify the possibility of not sacrificing any of her pleasures to another, of not identifying with anyone in particular, of never being simply one. It is a sort of universe in expansion for which no limits could be fixed and which, for all that, would not be incoherency. Nor would it be the polymorphic perversion of the infant during which its erogenous zones await their consolidation under the primacy of the phallus.

Woman would always remain multiple, but she would be protected from dispersion because the other is a part of her, and is autoerotically familiar to her. That does not mean that she would appropriate the other for herself, that she would make it her property. Property and propriety are undoubtedly rather foreign to all that is female. At least sexually. *Nearness,* however, is not foreign to woman, a nearness so close that any identification of one or the other, and therefore any form of property, is impossible. Woman enjoys a closeness with the other that is *so near she cannot possess it, any more than she can possess herself.* She constantly trades herself for the other without any possible identification of either one of them. Woman's pleasure, which grows indefinitely from its passage in/through the other, poses a problem for any current economy in that all computations that attempt to account for woman's incalculable pleasure are irremediably destined to fail.

However, in order for woman to arrive at the point where she can enjoy her pleasure as a woman, a long detour by the analysis of the various systems of oppression which affect her is certainly necessary. By claiming to resort to pleasure alone as the solution to her problem, she runs the risk of missing the reconsideration of a social practice upon which *her* pleasure depends.

For woman is traditionally use-value for man, exchange-value among men.[iv] Merchandise, then. This makes her the guardian of matter whose price will be determined by "subjects": workers, tradesmen, consumers, according to the standard of their work and their need-desire. Women are marked phallically by their fathers, husbands, procurers. This stamp(ing) determines their value in sexual commerce. Woman is never anything more than the scene of more or less rival exchange between two men, even when they are competing for the possession of mother-earth.

How can this object of transaction assert a right to pleasure without extricating itself from the established commercial system? How can this merchandise relate to other goods on the market other than with aggressive jealousy? How can raw materials possess themselves without provoking in the consumer fear of the disappearance of his nourishing soil? How can this exchange in nothingness that can be defined in "proper" terms of woman's desire not seem to be pure enticement, folly, all too quickly covered over by a more sensible discourse and an apparently more tangible system of values?

A woman's evolution, however radical it might seek to be, would not suffice then to liberate woman's desire. Neither political theory nor political practice have yet resolved nor sufficiently taken into account this historical problem, although Marxism has announced its importance. But women are not, strictly speaking, a class and their dispersion in several classes makes their political struggle complex and their demands sometimes contradictory.

Their underdeveloped condition stemming from their submission by/to a culture which oppresses them, uses them, cashes in on them, still remains. Women reap no advantage from this situation except that of their quasimonopoly of masochistic pleasure, housework, and reproduction. The power of slaves? It is considerable since the master is not necessarily well served in matters of pleasure. Therefore, the inversion of the relationship, especially in sexual economy, does not seem to be an enviable objective.

But if women are to preserve their auto-eroticism, their homo-sexuality, and let it flourish, would not the renunciation of heterosexual pleasure simply be another form of this amputation of power that is traditionally associated with women? Would this renunciation not be a new incarceration, a new cloister that women would willingly build? Let women tacitly go on strike, avoid men long enough to learn to defend their desire notably by their speech, let them discover the love of other women protected from that imperious choice of men which puts them in a position of rival goods, let them forge a social status which demands recognition, let them earn their living in order to leave behind their condition of prostitute – These are certainly indispensable steps in their effort to escape their proletarization on the trade market. But, if their goal is to reverse the existing order – even if that were possible – history would simply repeat itself and return to phallocratism, where neither women's sex, their imaginary, nor their language can exist.

[iv] Irigaray is employing the Marxist distinction between value for actual use and value as exchangeable commodity.

30

From *The Postmodern Condition: A Report on Knowledge*

Jean-François Lyotard

Professor of philosophy, Jean-François Lyotard (1926–98) published the most famous philosophical formulation of postmodernism in 1979. His short book, actually a report to the Province of Quebec's *Conseil des Universitiés*, defines postmodernism as "incredulity regarding metanarratives," grand stories about the world and the place of inquiry in it. Lyotard claims that in the postmodern era our social "language games" – borrowing Wittgenstein's term – no longer require metanarratives to justify the utterances made in them. Simply put, postmodern culture no longer needs any form of legitimation beyond expediency or "performativity." Lyotard analyzes the production of knowledge by science, as well as the discourse of everyday social life, in terms of discontinuity, plurality, and "paralogy" (logically unjustified conclusions). The modernist notions of justification, system, proof, and the unity of science no longer hold.

The object of this study is the condition of knowledge in the most highly developed societies. I have decided to use the word *postmodern* to describe that condition. The word is in current use on the American continent among sociologists and critics; it designates the state of our culture following the transformations which, since the end of the nineteenth century, have altered the game rules for science, literature, and the arts. The present study will place these transformations in the context of the crisis of narratives.

Science has always been in conflict with narratives. Judged by the yardstick of science, the majority of them prove to be fables. But to the extent that science does not restrict itself to stating useful regularities and seeks the truth, it is obliged to legitimate the rules of its own game. It then produces a discourse of legitimation with respect to its own status, a discourse called philosophy. I will use the term modern to designate any science that legitimates itself with reference to a metadiscourse of this kind making an explicit appeal to some grand narrative, such as the dialectics of Spirit, the hermeneutics of meaning, the emancipation of the rational or working subject, or the creation of wealth.[i] For example, the rule of consensus between the sender and addressee of a statement with truth-value is deemed acceptable if it is cast in terms of a possible unanimity between rational minds: this is the Enlightenment narrative, in which the hero of knowledge works toward a good ethico-political end – universal peace. As can be seen from this example, if a metanarrative implying a philosophy of history is used to legitimate knowledge, questions are raised concerning the validity of the institutions governing the social bond: these must be legitimated as well. Thus justice is consigned to the grand narrative in the same way as truth.

[i]   These grand narratives are what Lyotard calls "metanarratives," philosophical stories which legitimate all other discourse.

Jean-François Lyotard, Introduction (pp. xxiii–xxv), Sections 9–11 (pp. 31–47), and Section 14 (pp. 64–7) from *The Postmodern Condition: A Report on Knowledge* (trans. Geoff Bennington and Brian Massumi). Minneapolis: University of Minnesota Press, 1984.

Simplifying to the extreme, I define *postmodern* as incredulity toward metanarratives. This incredulity is undoubtedly a product of progress in the sciences: but that progress in turn presupposes it. To the obsolescence of the metanarrative apparatus of legitimation corresponds, most notably, the crisis of metaphysical philosophy and of the university institution which in the past relied on it. The narrative function is losing its functors, its great hero, its great dangers, its great voyages, its great goal. It is being dispersed in clouds of narrative language elements – narrative, but also denotative, prescriptive, descriptive, and so on. Conveyed within each cloud are pragmatic valencies specific to its kind. Each of us lives at the intersection of many of these. However, we do not necessarily establish stable language combinations, and the properties of the ones we do establish are not necessarily communicable.

Thus the society of the future falls less within the province of a Newtonian anthropology (such as stucturalism or systems theory) than a pragmatics of language particles. There are many different language games – a heterogeneity of elements. They only give rise to institutions in patches – local determinism.

The decision makers, however, attempt to manage these clouds of sociality according to input/output matrices, following a logic which implies that their elements are commensurable and that the whole is determinable. They allocate our lives for the growth of power. In matters of social justice and of scientific truth alike, the legitimation of that power is based on its optimizing the system's performance – efficiency. The application of this criterion to all of our games necessarily entails a certain level of terror, whether soft or hard: be operational (that is, commensurable) or disappear.

The logic of maximum performance is no doubt inconsistent in many ways, particularly with respect to contradiction in the socio–economic field: it demands both less work (to lower production costs) and more (to lessen the social burden of the idle population). But our incredulity is now such that we no longer expect salvation to rise from these inconsistencies, as did Marx.

Still, the postmodern condition is as much a stranger to disenchantment as it is to the blind positivity of delegitimation. Where, after the metanarratives, can legitimacy reside? The operativity criterion is technological; it has no relevance for judging what is true or just. Is legitimacy to be found in consensus obtained through discussion, as Jürgen Habermas thinks? Such consensus does

violence to the heterogeneity of language games. And invention is always born of dissension. Postmodern knowledge is not simply a tool of the authorities; it refines our sensitivity to differences and reinforces our ability to tolerate the incommensurable. Its principle is not the expert's homology, but the inventor's paralogy.

Here is the question: is a legitimation of the social bond, a just society, feasible in terms of a paradox analogous to that of scientific activity? What would such a paradox be? . . .

Narratives of the Legitimation of Knowledge

We shall examine two major versions of the narrative of legitimation. One is more political, the other more philosophical; both are of great importance in modern history, in particular in the history of knowledge and its institutions.

The subject of the first of these versions is humanity as the hero of liberty. All peoples have a right to science. If the social subject is not already the subject of scientific knowledge, it is because that has been forbidden by priests and tyrants. The right to science must be reconquered. It is understandable that this narrative would be directed more toward a politics of primary education, rather than of universities and high schools.[1] The educational policy of the French Third Republic[ii] powerfully illustrates these presuppositions.

It seems that this narrative finds it necessary to de-emphasize higher education. Accordingly, the measures adopted by Napoleon regarding higher education are generally considered to have been motivated by the desire to produce the administrative and professional skills necessary for the stability of the State.[2] This overlooks the fact that in the context of the narrative of freedom, the State receives its legitimacy not from itself but from the people. So even if imperial politics designated the institutions of higher education as a breeding ground for the officers of the State and secondarily, for the managers of civil society, it did so because the nation as a whole was supposed to win its freedom through the spread of new domains of knowledge to the population, a process to be effected through agencies and professions within which those cadres would fulfill their functions. The same reasoning is a fortiori valid for the foun-

---

ii   1871–1940.

dation of properly scientific institutions. The State resorts to the narrative of freedom every time it assumes direct control over the training of the "people," under the name of the "nation," in order to point them down the path of progress.[3]

With the second narrative of legitimation, the relation between science, the nation, and the State develops quite differently. It first appears with the founding, between 1807 and 1810, of the University of Berlin,[4] whose influence on the organization of higher education in the young countries of the world was to be considerable in the nineteenth and twentieth centuries.

At the time of the University's creation, the Prussian ministry had before it a project conceived by Fichte and counterproposals by Schleiermacher. Wilhelm von Humboldt had to decide the matter and came down on the side of Schleiermacher's more "liberal" option.[iii]

Reading Humboldt's report, one may be tempted to reduce his entire approach to the politics of the scientific institution to the famous dictum: "Science for its own sake." But this would be to [misunderstand] the ultimate aim of his policies, which is guided by the principle of legitimation we are discussing and is very close to the one Schleiermacher elucidates in a more thorough fashion.

Humboldt does indeed declare that science obeys its own rules, that the scientific institution "lives and continually renews itself on its own, with no constraint or determined goal whatsoever." But he adds that the University should orient its constituent element, science, to "the spiritual and moral training of the nation."[5] How can this *Bildung*-effect result from the disinterested pursuit of learning? Are not the State, the nation, the whole of humanity indifferent to knowledge for its own sake? What interests them, as Humboldt admits, is not learning, but "character and action."

The minister's adviser thus faces a major conflict, in some ways reminiscent of the split introduced by the Kantian critique between knowing and willing: it is a conflict between a language game made of denotations answerable only to the criterion of truth, and a language game governing ethical, social, and political practice that necessarily involves decisions and obligations, in other words, utterances expected to be just rather than true and

which in the final analysis lie outside the realm of scientific knowledge.

However, the unification of these two sets of discourse is indispensable to the *Bildung* aimed for by Humboldt's project, which consists not only in the acquisition of learning by individuals, but also in the training of a fully legitimated subject of knowledge and society. Humboldt therefore invokes a Spirit (what Fichte calls Life), animated by three ambitions, or better, by a single, threefold aspiration: "that of deriving everything from an original principle" (corresponding to scientific activity), "that of relating everything to an ideal" (governing ethical and social practice), and "that of unifying this principle and this ideal in a single Idea" (ensuring that the scientific search for true causes always coincides with the pursuit of just ends in moral and political life). This ultimate synthesis constitutes the legitimate subject.

Humboldt adds in passing that this triple aspiration naturally inheres in the "intellectual character of the German nation."[6] This is a concession, but a discreet one, to the other narrative, to the idea that the subject of knowledge is the people. But in truth this idea is quite distant from the narrative of the legitimation of knowledge advanced by German idealism. The suspicion that men like Schleiermacher, Humboldt, and even Hegel harbor towards the State is an indication of this. If Schleiermacher fears the narrow nationalism, protectionism, utilitarianism, and positivism that guide the public authorities in matters of science, it is because the principle of science does not reside in those authorities, even indirectly. The subject of knowledge is not the people, but the speculative spirit. It is not embodied, as in France after the Revolution, in a State, but in a System. The language game of legitimation is not state-political, but philosophical.

The great function to be fulfilled by the universities is to "lay open the whole body of learning and expound both the principles and the foundations of all knowledge." For "there is no creative scientific capacity without the speculative spirit."[7] "Speculation" is here the name given the discourse on the legitimation of scientific discourse. Schools are functional; the University is speculative, that is to say, philosophical.[8] Philosophy must restore unity to learning, which has been scattered into separate sciences in laboratories and in preuniversity education; it can only achieve this in a language game that links the sciences together as moments in the becoming of spirit, in other words, which links them in a rational narration, or rather metanarration.

iii Three German intellectuals: philosopher Johann Gottlieb Fichte; theologian Friedrich Schleiermacher (1768–1834), and philosopher and linguist Wilhelm von Humboldt (1767–1835).

Hegel's *Encyclopedia* (1817–27) attempts to realize this project of totalization, which was already present in Fichte and Schelling in the form of the idea of the System.

It is here, in the mechanism of developing a Life that is simultaneously Subject, that we see a return of narrative knowledge. There is a universal "history" of spirit, spirit is "life," and "life" is its own self-presentation and formulation in the ordered knowledge of all of its forms contained in the empirical sciences. The encyclopedia of German idealism is the narration of the "(hi)story" of this life-subject. But what it produces is a metanarrative, for the story's narrator must not be a people mired in the particular positivity of its traditional knowledge, nor even scientists taken as a whole, since they are sequestered in professional frameworks corresponding to their respective specialities.

The narrator must be a metasubject in the process of formulating both the legitimacy of the discourses of the empirical sciences and that of the direct institutions of popular cultures. This metasubject, in giving voice to their common grounding, realizes their implicit goal. It inhabits the speculative University. Positive science and the people are only crude versions of it. The only valid way for the nation-state itself to bring the people to expression is through the mediation of speculative knowledge.

It has been necessary to elucidate the philosophy that legitimated the foundation of the University of Berlin and was meant to be the motor both of its development and the development of contemporary knowledge. As I have said, many countries in the nineteenth and twentieth centuries adopted this university organization as a model for the foundation or reform of their own system of higher education, beginning with the United States.[9] But above all, this philosophy – which is far from dead, especially in university circles[10] – offers a particularly vivid representation of one solution to the problem of the legitimacy of knowledge.

Research and the spread of learning are not justified by invoking a principle of usefulness. The idea is not at all that science should serve the interests of the State and/or civil society. The humanist principle that humanity rises up in dignity and freedom through knowledge is left by the wayside. German idealism has recourse to a metaprinciple that simultaneously grounds the development of learning, of society, and of the State in the realization of the "life" of a Subject, called "divine Life" by Fichte and "Life of the spirit" by Hegel.

In this perspective, knowledge first finds legitimacy within itself, and it is knowledge that is entitled to say what the State and what Society are.[11] But it can only play this role by changing levels, by ceasing to be simply the positive knowledge of its referent (nature, society, the State, etc.), becoming in addition to that the knowledge of the knowledge of the referent – that is, by becoming speculative. In the names "Life" and "Spirit," knowledge names itself.

A noteworthy result of the speculative apparatus is that all of the discourses of learning about every possible referent are taken up not from the point of view of their immediate truth-value, but in terms of the value they acquire by virtue of occupying a certain place in the itinerary of Spirit or Life – or, if preferred, a certain position in the Encyclopedia recounted by speculative discourse. That discourse cites them in the process of expounding for itself what it knows, that is, in the process of self-exposition. True knowledge, in this perspective, is always indirect knowledge; it is composed of reported statements that are incorporated into the metanarrative of a subject that guarantees their legitimacy.

The same thing applies for every variety of discourse, even if it is not a discourse of learning; examples are the discourse of law and that of the State. Contemporary hermeneutic discourse[12] is born of this presupposition, which guarantees that there is meaning to know and thus confers legitimacy upon history (and especially the history of learning). Statements are treated as their own autonyms[13] and set in motion in a way that is supposed to render them mutually engendering: these are the rules of speculative language. The University, as its name indicates, is its exclusive institution.

But, as I have said, the problem of legitimacy can be solved using the other procedures as well. The difference between them should be kept in mind: today, with the status of knowledge unbalanced and its speculative unity broken, the first version of legitimacy is gaining new vigor.

According to this version, knowledge finds its validity not within itself, not in a subject that develops by actualizing its learning possibilities, but in a practical subject – humanity. The principle of the movement animating the people is not the self-legitimation of knowledge, but the self-grounding of freedom or, if preferred, its self-management. The subject is concrete, or supposedly so, and its epic is the story of its emancipation from everything that prevents it from governing itself. It is assumed that the laws it makes for itself are just, not because they conform to some outside nature, but because the legislators are, constitutionally, the very citizens who are subject to the laws. As a result, the legislator's will – the desire that the laws be just – will always coincide with the will of the citizen, who desires the law and will therefore obey it.

Clearly, this mode of legitimation through the autonomy of the will[14] gives priority to a totally different language game, which Kant called imperative and is known today as prescriptive. The important thing is not, or not only, to legitimate denotative utterances pertaining to the truth, such as "The earth revolves around the sun," but rather to legitimate prescriptive utterances pertaining to justice, such as "Carthage must be destroyed" or "The minimum wage must be set at x dollars." In this context, the only role positive knowledge can play is to inform the practical subject about the reality within which the execution of the prescription is to be inscribed. It allows the subject to circumscribe the executable, or what it is possible to do. But the executory, what should be done, is not within the purview of positive knowledge. It is one thing for an undertaking to be possible and another for it to be just. Knowledge is no longer the subject, but in the service of the subject: its only legitimacy (though it is formidable) is the fact that it allows morality to become reality.

This introduces a relation of knowledge to society and the State which is in principle a relation of the means to the end. But scientists must cooperate only if they judge that the politics of the State, in other words the sum of its prescriptions, is just. If they feel that the civil society of which they are members is badly represented by the State, they may reject its prescriptions. This type of legitimation grants them the authority, as practical human beings, to refuse their scholarly support to a political power they judge to be unjust, in other words, not grounded in a real autonomy. They can even go so far as to use their expertise to demonstrate that such autonomy is not in fact realized in society and the State. This reintroduces the critical function of knowledge. But the fact remains that knowledge has no final legitimacy outside of serving the goals envisioned by the practical subject, the autonomous collectivity.[15]

This distribution of roles in the enterprise of legitimation is interesting from our point of view because it assumes, as against the system-subject theory, that there is no possibility that language games can be unified or totalized in any metadiscourse. Quite to the contrary, here the priority accorded prescriptive statements – uttered by the practical subject – renders them independent in principle from the statements of science, whose only remaining function is to supply this subject with information.

Two remarks:

1   It would be easy to show that Marxism has wavered between the two models of narrative legitimation I have just described. The Party takes the place of the University, the proletariat that of the people or of humanity, dialectical materialism that of speculative idealism, etc. Stalinism may be the result, with its specific relationship with the sciences: in Stalinism, the sciences only figure as citations from the metanarrative of the march towards socialism, which is the equivalent, of the life of the spirit. But on the other hand Marxism can, in conformity to the second version, develop into a form of critical knowledge by declaring that socialism is nothing other than the constitution of the autonomous subject and that the only justification for the sciences is if they give the empirical subject (the proletariat) the means to emancipate itself from alienation and repression: this was, briefly, the position of the Frankfurt School.

2   The speech Heidegger gave on May 27, 1933, on becoming rector of the university of Freiburg-in-Breisgau,[16] can be read as an unfortunate episode in the history of legitimation.[iv] Here, speculative science has become the questioning of being. This questioning is the "destiny" of the German people, dubbed an "historico-spiritual people." To this subject are owed the three services of labor, defense, and knowledge. The University guarantees a metaknowledge of the three services, that is to say, science. Here, as in idealism, legitimation is achieved through a metadiscourse called science, with ontological pretensions. But here the metadiscourse is questioning, not totalizing. And the University, the home of this metadiscourse, owes its knowledge to a people whose "historic mission" is to bring that metadiscourse to fruition by working, fighting, and knowing. The calling of this people-subject is not to emancipate humanity, but to realize its "true world of the spirit," which is "the most profound power of conservation to be found within its forces of earth and blood." This insertion of the narrative of race and work into that

---

[iv]   Heidegger became rector after joining the Nazi Party, as was required by law. He openly supported National Socialism.

of the spirit as a way of legitimating knowledge and its institutions is doubly unfortunate: theoretically inconsistent, it was compelling enough to find disastrous echoes in the realm of politics.

Delegitimation

In contemporary society and culture – postindustrial society, postmodern culture[17] – the question of the legitimation of knowledge is formulated in different terms. The grand narrative has lost its credibility, regardless of what mode of unification it uses, regardless of whether it is a speculative narrative or a narrative of emancipation.

The decline of narrative can be seen as an effect of the blossoming of techniques and technologies since the Second World War, which has shifted emphasis from the ends of action to its means; it can also be seen as an effect of the redeployment of advanced liberal capitalism after its retreat under the protection of Keynesianism during the period 1930–60, a renewal that has eliminated the communist alternative and valorized the individual enjoyment of goods and services.

Anytime we go searching for causes in this way we are bound to be disappointed. Even if we adopted one or the other of these hypotheses, we would still have to detail the correlation between the tendencies mentioned and the decline of the unifying and legitimating power of the grand narratives of speculation and emancipation.

It is, of course, understandable that both capitalist renewal and prosperity and the disorienting upsurge of technology would have an impact on the status of knowledge. But in order to understand how contemporary science could have been susceptible to those effects long before they took place, we must first locate the seeds of "delegitimation"[18] and nihilism that were inherent in the grand narratives of the nineteenth century.

First of all, the speculative apparatus maintains an ambigious relation to knowledge. It shows that knowledge is only worthy of that name to the extent that it reduplicates itself ("lifts itself up," *hebt sich auf;* is sublated) by citing its own statements in a second-level discourse (autonymy) that functions to legitimate them. This is as much as to say that, in its immediacy, denotative discourse bearing on a certain referent (a living organism, a chemical property, a physical phenomenon, etc.) does not really know what it thinks it knows. Positive science is not a form of knowledge. And speculation feeds

on its suppression. The Hegelian speculative narrative thus harbors a certain skepticism toward positive learning, as Hegel himself admits.[19]

A science that has not legitimated itself is not a true science; if the discourse that was meant to legitimate it seems to belong to a prescientific form of knowledge, like a "vulgar" narrative, it is demoted to the lowest rank, that of an ideology or instrument of power. And this always happens if the rules of the science game that discourse denounces as empirical are applied to science itself.

Take for example the speculative statement: "A scientific statement is knowledge if and only if it can take its place in a universal process of engendering." The question is: Is this statement knowledge as it itself defines it? Only if it can take its place in a universal process of engendering. Which it can. All it has to do is to presuppose that such a process exists (the Life of spirit) and that it is itself an expression of that process. This presupposition, in fact, is indispensable to the speculative language game. Without it, the language of legitimation would not be legitimate; it would accompany science in a nosedive into nonsense, at least if we take idealism's word for it.

But this presupposition can also be understood in a totally different sense, one which takes us in the direction of postmodern culture: we could say, in keeping with the perspective we adopted earlier, that this presupposition defines the set of rules one must accept in order to play the speculative game.[20] Such an appraisal assumes first that we accept that the "positive" sciences represent the general mode of knowledge and second, that we understand this language to imply certain formal and axiomatic presuppositions that it must always make explicit. This is exactly what Nietzsche is doing, though with a different terminology, when he shows that "European nihilism" resulted from the truth requirement of science being turned back against itself.[21]

There thus arises an idea of perspective that is not far removed, at least in this respect, from the idea of language games. What we have here is a process of delegitimation fueled by the demand for legitimation itself. The "crisis" of scientific knowledge, signs of which have been accumulating since the end of the nineteenth century, is not born of a chance proliferation of sciences, itself an effect of progress in technology and the expansion of capitalism. It represents, rather, an internal erosion of the legitimacy principle of knowledge. There is erosion at work inside the speculative game, and by loosening the weave of the encyclopedic net in which each science was to find its place, it eventually sets them free.

The classical dividing lines between the various fields of science are thus called into question – disciplines disappear, overlappings occur at the borders between sciences, and from these new territories are born. The speculative hierarchy of learning gives way to an immanent and, as it were, "flat" network of areas of inquiry, the respective frontiers of which are in constant flux. The old "faculties" splinter into institutes and foundations of all kinds, and the universities lose their function of speculative legitimation. Stripped of the responsibility for research (which was stifled by the speculative narrative), they limit themselves to the transmission of what is judged to be established knowledge, and through didactics they guarantee the replication of teachers rather than the production of researchers. This is the state in which Nietzsche finds and condemns them.[22]

The potential for erosion intrinsic to the other legitimation procedure, the emancipation apparatus flowing from the *Aufklärung*,[v] is no less extensive than the one at work within speculative discourse. But it touches a different aspect. Its distinguishing characteristic is that it grounds the legitimation of science and truth in the autonomy of interlocutors involved in ethical, social, and political praxis. As we have seen, there are immediate problems with this form of legitimation: the difference between a denotative statement with cognitive value and a prescriptive statement with practical value is one of relevance therefore of competence. There is nothing to prove that if a statement describing a real situation is true, it follows that a prescriptive statement based upon it (the effect of which will necessarily be a modification of that reality) will be just.

Take, for example, a closed door. Between "The door is closed" and "Open the door" there is no relation of consequence as defined in propositional logic. The two statements belong to two autonomous sets of rules defining different kinds of relevance, and therefore of competence. Here, the effect of dividing reason into cognitive or theoretical reason on the one hand, and practical reason on the other, is to attack the legitimacy of the discourse of science. Not directly, but indirectly, by revealing that it is a language game with its own rules (of which the a priori conditions of knowledge in Kant

provide a first glimpse) and that it has no special calling to supervise the game of praxis (nor the game of aesthetics, for that matter). The game of science is thus put on a par with the others.

If this "delegitimation" is pursued in the slightest and if its scope is widened (as Wittgenstein does in his own way, and thinkers such as Martin Buber and Emmanuel Lévinas in theirs)[23] the road is then open for an important current of postmodernity: science plays its own game; it is incapable of legitimating the other language games. The game of prescription, for example, escapes it. But above all, it is incapable of legitimating itself, as speculation assumed it could.

The social subject itself seems to dissolve in this dissemination of language games. The social bond is linguistic, but is not woven with a single thread. It is a fabric formed by the intersection of at least two (and in reality an indeterminate number) of language games, obeying different rules. Wittgenstein writes: "Our language can be seen as an ancient city: a maze of little streets and squares, of old and new houses, and of houses with additions from various periods; and this surrounded by a multitude of new boroughs with straight regular streets and uniform houses."[24] And to drive home that the principle of unitotality – or synthesis under the authority of a metadiscourse of knowledge – is inapplicable, he subjects the "town" of language to the old sorites paradox by asking: "how many houses or streets does it take before a town begins to be a town?"[25]

New languages are added to the old ones, forming suburbs of the old town: "the symbolism of chemistry and the notation of the infinitesimal calculus."[26] Thirty-five years later we can add to the list: machine languages, the matrices of game theory, new systems of musical notation, systems of notation for nondenotative forms of logic (temporal logics, deontic logics, modal logics), the language of the genetic code, graphs of phonological structures, and so on.

We may form a pessimistic impression of this splintering: nobody speaks all of those languages, they have no universal metalanguage, the project of the system-subject is a failure, the goal of emancipation has nothing to do with science, we are all stuck in the positivism of this or that discipline of learning, the learned scholars have turned into scientists, the diminished tasks of research have become compartmentalized and no one can master them all.[27] Speculative or humanistic philosophy is forced to relinquish its legitimation duties,[28] which

[v] Enlightenment.

explains why philosophy is facing a crisis wherever it persists in arrogating such functions and is reduced to the study of systems of logic or the history of ideas where it has been realistic enough to surrender them.

Turn-of-the-century Vienna was weaned on this pessimism: not just artists such as Musil, Kraus, Hofmannsthal, Loos, Schönberg, and Broch, but also the philosophers Mach and Wittgenstein.[30] They carried awareness of and theoretical and artistic responsibility for delegitimation as far as it could be taken. We can say today that the mourning process has been completed. There is no need to start all over again. Wittgenstein's strength is that he did not opt for the positivism that was being developed by the Vienna Circle,[31] but outlined in his investigation of language games a kind of legitimation not based on performativity. That is what the postmodern world is all about. Most people have lost the nostalgia for the lost narrative. It in no way follows that they are reduced to barbarity. What saves them from it is their knowledge that legitimation can only spring from their own linguistic practice and communicational interaction. Science "smiling into its beard" at every other belief has taught them the harsh austerity of realism.[32]

Research and Its Legitimation through Performativity

Let us return to science and begin by examining the pragmatics of research. Its essential mechanisms are presently undergoing two important changes: a multiplication in methods of argumentation and a rising complexity level in the process of establishing proof.

Aristotle, Descartes, and John Stuart Mill, among others, attempted to lay down the rules governing how a denotative utterance can obtain its addressee's assent.[33] Scientific research sets no great store by these methods. As already stated, it can and does use methods the demonstrative properties of which seem to challenge classical reason. Bachelard compiled a list of them, and it is already incomplete.[34]

These languages are not employed haphazardly, however. Their use is subject to a condition we could call pragmatic: each must formulate its own rules and petition the addressee to accept them. To satisfy this condition, an axiomatic is defined that includes a definition of symbols to be used in the proposed language, a description of the form expressions in the language must take in order to gain acceptance (well-formed expressions), and an enumeration of the operations that may be performed on the accepted expressions (axioms in the narrow sense).[35]

But how do we know what an axiomatic should, or does in fact, contain? The conditions listed above are formal conditions. There has to be a metalanguage to determine whether a given language satisfies the formal conditions of an axiomatic; that metalanguage is logic.

At this point a brief clarification is necessary. The alternative between someone who begins by establishing an axiomatic and then uses it to produce what are defined as acceptable statements, and a scientist who begins by establishing and stating facts and then tries to discover the axiomatics of the language he used in making his statements, is not a logical alternative, but only an empirical one. It is certainly of great importance for the researcher, and also for the philosopher, but in each case the question of the validation of statements is the same.[36]

The following question is more pertinent to legitimation: By what criteria does the logician define the properties required of an axiomatic? Is there a model for scientific languages? If so, is there just one? Is it verifiable? The properties generally required of the syntax of a formal system[37] are consistency (for example, a system inconsistent with respect to negation would admit both a proposition and its opposite), syntactic completeness (the system would lose its consistency if an axiom were added to it), decidability (there must be an effective procedure for deciding whether a given proposition belongs to the system or not), and the independence of the axioms in relation to one another. Now Gödel has effectively established the existence in the arithmetic system of a proposition that is neither demonstrable nor refutable within that system; this entails that the arithmetic system fails to satisfy the condition of completeness.[38]

Since it is possible to generalize this situation, it must be accepted that all formal systems have internal limitations.[39] This applies to logic: the metalanguage it uses to describe an artificial (axiomatic) language is "natural" or "everyday" language; that language is universal, since all other languages can be translated into it, but it is not consistent with respect to negation – it allows the formation of paradoxes.[40]

This necessitates a reformulation of the question of the legitimation of knowledge. When a denotative statement is declared true, there is a presupposition that the axiomatic system within which it is decidable and demonstrable has already been formulated, that it is known to the interlocutors, and that they have accepted that it is as formally satisfactory as possible. This was the spirit in which the mathematics of the Bourbaki group[vi] was developed.[41] But analogous observations can be made for the other sciences: they owe their status to the existence of a language whose rules of functioning cannot themselves be demonstrated but are the object of a consensus among experts. These rules, or at least some of them, are requests. The request is a modality of prescription.

The argumentation required for a scientific statement to be accepted is thus subordinated to a "first" acceptance (which is in fact constantly renewed by virtue of the principle of recursion) of the rules defining the allowable means of argumentation. Two noteworthy properties of scientific knowledge result from this: the flexibility of its means, that is, the plurality of its languages; and its character as a pragmatic game – the acceptability of the "moves" (new propositions) made in it depends on a contract drawn between the partners. Another result is that there are two different kinds of "progress" in knowledge: one corresponds to a new move (a new argument) within the established rules; the other, to the invention of new rules, in other words, a change to a new game.[42]

Obviously, a major shift in the notion of reason accompanies this new arrangement. The principle of a universal metalanguage is replaced by the principle of a plurality of formal and axiomatic systems capable of arguing the truth of denotative statements; these systems are described by a metalanguage that is universal but not consistent. What used to pass as paradox, and even paralogism, in the knowledge of classical and modern science can, in certain of these systems, acquire a new force of conviction and win the acceptance of the community of experts.[43] The language game method I have followed here can claim a modest place in this current of thought.

The other fundamental aspect of research, the production of proof, takes us in quite a different direction. It is in principle part of an argumentation process designed to win acceptance for a new statement (for example, giving testimony or presenting an exhibit in the case of judicial rhetoric).[44] But it

presents a special problem: it is here that the referent ("reality") is called to the stand and cited in the debate between scientists.

I have already made the point that the question of proof is problematical since proof needs to be proven. One can begin by publishing a description of how the proof was obtained, so other scientists can check the result by repeating the same process. But the fact still has to be observed in order to stand proven. What constitutes a scientific observation? A fact that has been registered by an eye, an ear, a sense organ?[45] Senses are deceptive, and their range and powers of discrimination are limited.

This is where technology comes in. Technical devices originated as prosthetic aids for the human organs or as physiological systems whose function it is to receive data or condition the context.[46] They follow a principle, and it is the principle of optimal performance: maximizing output (the information or modifications obtained) and minimizing input (the energy expended in the process).[47] Technology is therefore a game pertaining not to the true, the just, or the beautiful, etc., but to efficiency: a technical "move" is "good" when it does better and/or expends less energy than another.

This definition of technical competence is a late development. For a long time inventions came in fits and starts, the products of chance research, or research as much or more concerned with the arts (*technai*) than with knowledge: the Greeks of the Classical period, for example, established no close relationship between knowledge and technology.[48] In the sixteenth and seventeenth centuries, the work of "perspectors" was still a matter of curiosity and artistic innovation.[49] This was the case until the end of the eighteenth century.[50] And it can be maintained that even today "wildcat" activities of technical invention, sometimes related to *bricolage*,[vii] still go on outside the imperatives of scientific argumentation.[51]

Nonetheless, the need for proof becomes increasingly strong as the pragmatics of scientific knowledge replaces traditional knowledge or knowledge based on revelation. By the end of the *Discourse on Method*, Descartes is already asking for laboratory funds. A new problem appears: devices that optimize the performance of the human body for the purpose of producing proof require additional expenditures. No money, no proof – and

---

[vi] "Nicolas Bourbaki" was the fanciful name of a group of French mathematicians in the 1930s.

[vii] The technique of the handyman, who uses whatever diverse materials are at hand, suggested for the human sciences by Claude Lévi-Strauss.

that means no verification of statements and no truth. The games of scientific language become the games of the rich, in which whoever is wealthiest has the best chance of being right. An equation between wealth, efficiency, and truth is thus established.

What happened at the end of the eighteenth century, with the first industrial revolution, is that the reciprocal of this equation was discovered: no technology without wealth, but no wealth without technology. A technical apparatus requires an investment; but since it optimizes the efficiency of the task to which it is applied, it also optimizes the surplus-value derived from this improved performance. All that is needed is for the surplus-value to be realized, in other words, for the product of the task performed to be sold. And the system can be sealed in the following way: a portion of the sale is recycled into a research fund dedicated to further performance improvement. It is at this precise moment that science becomes a force of production, in other words, a moment in the circulation of capital.

It was more the desire for wealth than the desire for knowledge that initially forced upon technology the imperative of performance improvement and product realization. The "organic" connection between technology and profit preceded its union with science. Technology became important to contemporary knowledge only through the mediation of a generalized spirit of performativity. Even today, progress in knowledge is not totally subordinated to technological investment.[52]

Capitalism solves the scientific problem of research funding in its own way: directly by financing research departments in private companies, in which demands for performativity and recommercialization orient research first and foremost toward technological "applications"; and indirectly by creating private, state, or mixed-sector research foundations that grant program subsidies to university departments, research laboratories, and independent research groups with no expectation of an immediate return on the results of the work – this is done on the theory that research must be financed at a loss for certain length of time in order to increase the probability of its yielding a decisive, and therefore highly profitable, innovation.[53] Nation-states, especially in their Keynesian peri-

od,[viii] follow the same rule: applied research on the one hand, basic research on the other. They collaborate with corporations through an array of agencies.[54] The prevailing corporate norms of work management spread to the applied science laboratories: hierarchy, centralized decision making, teamwork, calculation of individual and collective returns, the development of saleable programs, market research, and so on.[55] Centers dedicated to "pure" research suffer from this less, but also receive less funding.

The production of proof, which is in principle only part of an argumentation process designed to win agreement from the addressees of scientific messages, thus falls under the control of another language game, in which the goal is no longer truth, but performativity – that is, the best possible input/output equation. The State and/or company must abandon the idealist and humanist narratives of legitimation in order to justify the new goal: in the discourse of today's financial backers of research, the only credible goal is power. Scientists, technicians, and instruments are purchased not to find truth, but to augment power.

The question is to determine what the discourse of power consists of and if it can constitute a legitimation. At first glance, it is prevented from doing so by the traditional distinction between force and right, between force and wisdom – in other words, between what is strong, what is just, and what is true. I referred to this incommensurability earlier in terms of the theory of language games, when I distinguished the denotative game (in which what is relevant is the true/false distinction) from the prescriptive game (in which the just/unjust distinction pertains) from the technical game (in which the criterion is the efficient/inefficient distinction). "Force" appears to belong exclusively to the last game, the game of technology. I am excluding the case in which force operates by means of terror. This lies outside the realm of language games, because the efficacy of such force is based entirely on the threat to eliminate the opposing player, not on making a better "move" than he. Whenever efficiency (that is, obtaining the desired effect) is derived from a "Say or do this, or else you'll never speak again," then we are in the realm of terror, and the social bond is destroyed.

But the fact remains that since performativity increases the ability to produce proof, it also increases the ability to be right: the technical criterion, introduced on a massive scale into scientific knowledge, cannot fail to influence the truth criter-

[viii] John Maynard Keynes (1883–1946), English economist, proposed increased government spending to stimulate economic activity.

268

ion. The same has been said of the relationship between justice and performance: the probability that an order would be pronounced just was said to increase with its chances of being implemented, which would in turn increase with the performance capability of the prescriber. This led Luhmann[ix] to hypothesize that in postindustrial societies the normativity of laws is replaced by the performativity of procedures.[56] "Context control," in other words, performance improvement won at the expense of the partner or partners constituting that context (be they "nature" or men), can pass for a kind of legitimation.[57] De facto legitimation.

This procedure operates within the following framework: since "reality" is what provides the evidence used as proof in scientific argumentation, and also provides prescriptions and promises of a juridical, ethical, and political nature with results, one can master all of these games by mastering "reality." That is precisely what technology can do. By reinforcing technology, one "reinforces" reality, and one's chances of being just and right increase accordingly. Reciprocally, technology is reinforced all the more effectively if one has access to scientific knowledge and decision-making authority.

This is how legitimation by power takes shape. Power is not only good performativity, but also effective verification and good verdicts. It legitimates science and the law on the basis of their efficiency, and legitimates this efficiency on the basis of science and law. It is self-legitimating, in the same way a system organized around performance maximization seems to be.[58] Now it is precisely this kind of context control that a generalized computerization of society may bring. The performativity of an utterance, be it denotative or prescriptive, increases proportionally to the amount of information about its referent one has at one's disposal. Thus the growth of power, and its self-legitimation, are now taking the route of data storage and accessibility, and the operativity of information.

The relationship between science and technology is reversed. The complexity of the argumentation becomes relevant here, especially because it necessitates greater sophistication in the means of obtaining proof, and that in turn benefits performativity. Research funds are allocated by States,

corporations, and nationalized companies in accordance with this logic of power growth. Research sectors that are unable to argue that they contribute even indirectly to the optimization of the system's performance are abandoned by the flow of capital and doomed to senescence. The criterion of performance is explicitly invoked by the authorities to justify their refusal to subsidize certain research centers.[59]

Legitimation by Paralogy

Let us say at this point that the facts we have presented concerning the problem of the legitimation of knowledge today are sufficient for our purposes. We no longer have recourse to the grand narratives – we can resort neither to the dialectic of Spirit nor even to the emancipation of humanity as a validation for postmodern scientific discourse. But as we have just seen, the little narrative remains the quintessential form of imaginative invention, most particularly in science.[60] In addition, the principle of consensus as a criterion of validation seems to be inadequate. It has two formulations. In the first, consensus is an agreement between men, defined as knowing intellects and free wills, and is obtained through dialogue. This is the form elaborated by Habermas, but his conception is based on the validity of the narrative of emancipation. In the second, consensus is a component of the system, which manipulates it in order to maintain and improve its performance.[61] It is the object of administrative procedures, in Luhmann's sense. In this case, its only validity is as an instrument to be used toward achieving the real goal, which is what legitimates the system – power.

The problem is therefore to determine whether it is possible to have a form of legitimation based solely on paralogy. Paralogy must be distinguished from innovation: the latter is under the command of the system, or at least used by it to improve its efficiency; the former is a move (the importance of which is often not recognized until later) played in the pragmatics of knowledge. The fact that it is in reality frequently, but not necessarily, the case that one is transformed into the other presents no difficulties for the hypothesis.

Returning to the description of scientific pragmatics, it is now dissension that must be emphasized. Consensus is a horizon that is never reached. Research that takes place under the aegis of a paradigm[62] tends to stabilize; it is like the exploitation

---

[ix] Niklas Luhmann, recent German sociologist whose radical version of systems theory denied the need for "legitimation" in contemporary, "de-centered," "functional" societies.

of a technological, economic, or artistic "idea." It cannot be discounted. But what is striking is that someone always comes along to disturb the order of "reason." It is necessary to posit the existence of a power that destabilizes the capacity for explanation, manifested in the promulgation of new norms for understanding or, if one prefers, in a proposal to establish new rules circumscribing a new field of research for the language of science. This, in the context of scientific discussion, is the same process Thom calls morphogenesis. It is not without rules (there are classes of catastrophes), but it is always locally determined. Applied to scientific discussion and placed in a temporal framework, this property implies that "discoveries" are unpredictable. In terms of the idea of transparency, it is a factor that generates blind spots and defers consensus.[63]

This summary makes it easy to see that systems theory and the kind of legitimation it proposes have no scientific basis whatsoever; science itself does not function according to this theory's paradigm of the system, and contemporary science excludes the possibility of using such a paradigm to describe society.

In this context, let us examine two important points in Luhmann's argument. On the one hand, the system can only function by reducing complexity, and on the other, it must induce the adaptation of individual aspirations to its own ends.[64] The reduction in complexity is required to maintain the system's power capability. If all messages could circulate freely among all individuals, the quantity of the information that would have to be taken into account before making the correct choice would delay decisions considerably, thereby lowering performativity. Speed, in effect, is a power component of the system.

The objection will be made that these molecular opinions must indeed be taken into account if the risk of serious disturbances is to be avoided. Luhmann replies – and this is the second point – that it is possible to guide individual aspirations through a process of "quasi-apprenticeship," "free of all disturbance," in order to make them compatible with the system's decisions. The decisions do not have to respect individuals' aspirations: the aspirations have to aspire to the decisions, or at least to their effects. Administrative procedures should make individuals "want" what the system needs in order to perform well.[65] It is easy to see what role telematics technology could play in this.

It cannot be denied that there is persuasive force in the idea that context control and domination are

inherently better than their absence. The performativity criterion has its "advantages." It excludes in principle adherence to a metaphysical discourse; it requires the renunciation of fables; it demands clear minds and cold wills; it replaces the definition of essences with the calculation of interactions; it makes the "players" assume responsibility not only for the statements they propose, but also for the rules to which they submit those statements in order to render them acceptable. It brings the pragmatic functions of knowledge clearly to light, to the extent that they seem to relate to the criterion of efficiency: the pragmatics of argumentation, of the production of proof, of the transmission of learning, and of the apprenticeship of the imagination.

It also contributes to elevating all language games to self-knowledge, even those not within the realm of canonical knowledge. It tends to jolt everyday discourse into a kind of metadiscourse: ordinary statements are now displaying a propensity for self-citation, and the various pragmatic posts are tending to make an indirect connection even to current messages concerning them.[66] Finally, it suggests that the problems of internal communication experienced by the scientific community in the course of its work of dismantling and remounting its languages are comparable in nature to the problems experienced by the social collectivity when, deprived of its narrative culture, it must reexamine its own internal communication and in the process question the nature of the legitimacy of the decisions made in its name.

At risk of scandalizing the reader, I would also say that the system can count severity among its advantages. Within the framework of the power criterion, a request (that is, a form of prescription) gains nothing in legitimacy by virtue of being based on the hardship of an unmet need. Rights do not flow from hardship, but from the fact that the alleviation of hardship improves the system's performance. The needs of the most underprivileged should not be used as a system regulator as a matter of principle: since the means of satisfying them is already known, their actual satisfaction will not improve the system's performance, but only increase its expenditures. The only counterindication is that not satisfying them can destabilize the whole. It is against the nature of force to be ruled by weakness. But it is in its nature to induce new requests meant to lead to a redefinition of the norms of "life."[67] In this sense, the system seems to be a vanguard machine dragging humanity after it, dehumanizing it in order to rehumanize it at a different level of normative capacity. The technocrats declare that they cannot trust what society designates as its needs; they "know" that society cannot know its own needs since they are not variables independent of the new technologies.[68] Such is the arrogance of the decision makers – and their blindness.

What their "arrogance" means is that they identify themselves with the social system conceived as a totality in quest of its most performative unity possible. If we look at the pragmatics of science, we learn that such an identification is impossible: in principle, no scientist embodies knowledge or neglects the "needs" of a research project, or the aspirations of a researcher, on the pretext that they do not add to the performance of "science" as a whole. The response a researcher usually makes to a request is: "We'll have to see, tell me your story."[69] In principle, he does not prejudge that a case has already been closed or that the power of "science" will suffer if it is reopened. In fact, the opposite is true.

Of course, it does not always happen like this in reality. Countless scientists have seen their "move" ignored or repressed, sometimes for decades, because it too abruptly destabilized the accepted positions, not only in the university and scientific hierarchy, but also in the problematic.[70] The stronger the "move," the more likely it is to be denied the minimum consensus, precisely because it changes the rules of the game upon which consensus had been based. But when the institution of knowledge functions in this manner, it is acting like an ordinary power center whose behavior is governed by a principle of homeostasis.

Such behavior is terrorist, as is the behavior of the system described by Luhmann. By terror I mean the efficiency gained by eliminating, or threatening to eliminate, a player from the language game one shares with him. He is silenced or consents, not because he has been refuted, but because his ability to participate has been threatened (there are many ways to prevent someone from playing). The decision makers' arrogance, which in principle has no equivalent in the sciences, consists in the exercise of terror. It says: "Adapt your aspirations to our ends – or else."[71]

Even permissiveness toward the various games is made conditional on performativity. The redefinition of the norms of life consists in enhancing the system's competence for power. That this is the case is particularly evident in the introduction of telematics technology: the technocrats see in tele-

matics a promise of liberalization and enrichment in the interactions between interlocutors; but what makes this process attractive for them is that it will result in new tensions in the system, and these will lead to an improvement in its performativity.[72]

To the extent that science is differential, its pragmatics provides the antimodel of a stable system. A statement is deemed worth retaining the moment it marks a difference from what is already known, and after an argument and proof in support of it has been found. Science is a model of an "open system,"[73] in which a statement becomes relevant if it "generates ideas," that is, if it generates other statements and other game rules. Science possesses no general metalanguage in which all other languages can be transcribed and evaluated. This is what prevents its identification with the system and, all things considered, with terror. If the division between decision makers and executors exists in the scientific community (and it does), it is a fact of the socioeconomic system and not of the pragmatics of science itself. It is in fact one of the major obstacles to the imaginative development of knowledge.

The general question of legitimation becomes: What is the relationship between the antimodel of the pragmatics of science and society? Is it applicable to the vast clouds of language material constituting a society? Or is it limited to the game of learning? And if so, what role does it play with respect to the social bond? Is it an impossible ideal of an open community? Is it an essential component for the subset of decision makers, who force on society the performance criterion they reject for themselves? Or, conversely, is it a refusal to cooperate with the authorities, a move in the direction of counterculture, with the attendant risk that all possibility for research will be foreclosed due to lack of funding?[74]

From the beginning of this study, I have emphasized the differences (not only formal, but also pragmatic) between the various language games, especially between denotative, or knowledge, games and prescriptive, or action, games. The pragmatics of science is centered on denotative utterances, which are the foundation upon which it builds institutions of learning (institutes, centers, universities, etc.). But its postmodern development brings a decisive "fact" to the fore: even discussions of denotative statements need to have rules. Rules are not denotative but prescriptive utterances, which we are better off calling metaprescriptive utterances to avoid confusion (they prescribe what the moves of language games must be in order to be admissible). The function of the differential or imaginative or paralogical activity of the current pragmatics of science is to point out these metaprescriptives (science's "presuppositions")[75] to petition the players to accept different ones. The only legitimation that can make this kind of request admissible is that it will generate ideas, in other words, new statements.

Social pragmatics does not have the "simplicity" of scientific pragmatics. It is a monster formed by the interweaving of various networks of heteromorphous classes of utterances (denotative, prescriptive, performative, technical, evaluative, etc.). There is no reason to think that it would be possible to determine metaprescriptives common to all of these language games or that a revisable consensus like the one in force at a given moment in the scientific community could embrace the totality of metaprescriptions regulating the totality of statements circulating in the social collectivity. As a matter of fact, the contemporary decline of narratives of legitimation – be they traditional or "modern" (the emancipation of humanity, the realization of the Idea) – is tied to the abandonment of this belief. It is its absence for which the ideology of the "system," with its pretensions to totality, tries to compensate and which it expresses in the cynicism of its criterion of performance.

For this reason, it seems neither possible, nor even prudent, to follow Habermas in orienting our treatment of the problem of legitimation in the direction of a search for universal consensus[76] through what he calls *Diskurs*, in other words, a dialogue of argumentation.[77]

This would be to make two assumptions. The first is that it is possible for all speakers to come to agreement on which rules or metaprescriptions are universally valid for language games, when it is clear that language games are heteromorphous, subject to heterogeneous sets of pragmatic rules.

The second assumption is that the goal of dialogue is consensus. But as I have shown in the analysis of the pragmatics of science, consensus is only a particular state of discussion, not its end. Its end, on the contrary, is paralogy. This double observation (the heterogeneity of the rules and the search for dissent) destroys a belief that still underlies Habermas's research, namely, that humanity as a collective (universal) subject seeks its common emancipation through the regularization of the "moves" permitted in all language games and that

the legitimacy of any statement resides in its contributing to that emancipation.[78]

It is easy to see what function this recourse plays in Habermas's argument against Luhmann. *Diskurs* is his ultimate weapon against the theory of the stable system.[x] The cause is good, but the argument is not.[79] Consensus has become an outmoded and suspect value. But justice as a value is neither outmoded nor suspect. We must thus arrive at an idea and practice of justice that is not linked to that of consensus.

A recognition of the heteromorphous nature of language games is a first step in that direction. This obviously implies a renunciation of terror, which assumes that they are isomorphic and tries to make them so. The second step is the principle that any consensus on the rules defining a game and the "moves" playable within it *must* be local, in other words, agreed on by its present players and subject to eventual cancellation. The orientation then favors a multiplicity of finite meta-arguments, by which I mean argumentation that concerns metaprescriptives and is limited in space and time.

This orientation corresponds to the course that the evolution of social interaction is currently taking; the temporary contract is in practice supplanting permanent institutions in the professional, emotional, sexual, cultural, family, and international domains, as well as in political affairs. This evolution is of course ambiguous: the temporary contract is favored by the system due to its greater flexibility, lower cost, and the creative turmoil of its accompanying motivations – all of these factors contribute to increased operativity. In any case, there is no question here of proposing a "pure" alternative to the system: we all now know, as the 1970s come to a close, that an attempt at an alternative of that kind would end up resembling the system it was meant to replace. We should be happy that the tendency toward the temporary contract is ambiguous: it is not totally subordinated to the goal of the system, yet the system tolerates it. This bears witness to the existence of another goal within the system: knowledge of language games as such and the decision to assume responsibility for their rules and effects. Their most significant effect is precisely what validates the adoption of rules – the quest for paralogy.

[x] Social philosopher Jürgen Habermas argued against Luhmann that "discourse" – communication aimed at achieving agreement on the validity of claims – is intrinsically moral, and is the source of social legitimation.

We are finally in a position to understand how the computerization of society affects this problematic. It could become the "dream" instrument for controlling and regulating the market system, extended to include knowledge itself and governed exclusively by the performativity principle. In that case, it would inevitably involve, the use of terror. But it could also aid groups discussing metaprescriptives by supplying them with the information they usually lack for making knowledgeable decisions. The line to follow for computerization to take the second of these two paths is, in principle, quite simple: give the public free access to the memory and data banks.[80] Language games would then be games of perfect information at any given moment. But they would also be non-zero-sum games, and by virtue of that fact discussion would never risk fixating in a position of minimax equilibrium because it had exhausted its stakes. For the stakes would be knowledge (or information, if you will), and the reserve of knowledge – language's reserve of possible utterances – is inexhaustible. This sketches the outline of a politics that would respect both the desire for justice and the desire for the unknown.

Author's Notes

1 A trace of this politics is to be found in the French institution of a philosophy class at the end of secondary studies, and in the proposal by the Groupe de recherches sur l'enseignement de la philosophie (GREPH) to teach "some" philosophy starting at the beginning of secondary studies: see their *Qui a peur de la philosophie?* (Paris: Flammarion, 1977), sec. 2, "La Philosophie déclassée." This also seems to be the orientation of the curriculum of the CEGEP's in Quebec, especially of the philosophy courses (see for example the *Cahiers de l'enseignement collégial* (1975–6) for philosophy).

2 See H. Janne, "L'Université et les besoins de la société contemporaine," *Cahiers de l'Association internationale des Universités*, 10 (1970): 5; quoted by the Commission d'étude sur les universités, *Document de consultation* (Montréal, 1978).

3 A "hard," almost mystico-military expression of this can be found in Julio de Mesquita Filho, *Discorso de Paraninfo da primeiro turma de licenciados pela Faculdade de Filosofia, Ciêncas e Letras da Universidade de Saõ Paulo* (25 January 1937), and an expression of it adapted to the modern problems of Brazilian development in the *Relatorio do Grupo de Rabalho, Reforma Universitaria* (Brasilia: Ministries of Education and Culture, etc., 1968). These documents are part of a dossier on the university in Brazil, kindly sent to me by Helena C. Chamlian and Martha Ramos de Carvalho of the University of São Paulo.

4 The documents are available in French thanks to Miguel Abensour and the Collège de philosophie: *Philosophes de l'Université: L'Idéalisme allemand et la question de l'université* (Paris: Payot, 1979). The collection includes texts by Schelling, Fichte, Schleiermacher, Humboldt, and Hegel.

5 "Über die innere und äussere Organisation der höheren wissenschaftlichen Anstalten in Berlin" (1810), in *Wilhelm von Humboldt* (Frankfurt, 1957), p. 126.

6 Ibid., p. 128.

7 Friedrich Schleiermacher, "Gelegentliche Gedanken über Universitäten in deutschen Sinn, nebst einem Anhang über eine neu zu errichtende" (1808), in E. Spranger (ed.), *Fichte, Schleiermacher, Steffens über das Wesen der Universität* (Leipzig, 1910), p. 126ff.

8 "The teaching of philosophy is generally recognized to be the basis of all university activity" (ibid., p. 128).

9 Alain Touraine has analyzed the contradictions involved in this transplantation in *Université et société aux Etats-Unis* (Paris: Seuil, 1972), pp. 32–40 [Eng. trans. *The Academic System in American Society* (New York: McGraw-Hill, 1974)].

10 It is present even in the conclusions of Robert Nisbet, *The Degradation of the Academic Dogma: The University in America, 1945–70* (London: Heinemann, 1971). The author is a professor at the University of California, Riverside.

11 See G. W. F. Hegel, *Philosophie des Rechts* (1821) [Eng. trans. T. M. Knox, *Hegel's Philosophy of Right* (Oxford: Oxford University Press, 1967)].

12 See Paul Ricoeur, *Le Conflit des interprétations. Essais d'herméneutique* (Paris: Seuil, 1969) [Eng. trans. Don Ihde, *The Conflict of Interpretations* (Evanston, Ill.: North-western University Press, 1974)]; Hans Georg Gadamer, *Warheit und Methode*, 2d edn (Tübingen: Mohr, 1965) [Eng. trans. Garrett Barden and John Cumming, *Truth and Method* (New York: Seabury Press, 1975)].

13 Take two statements: (1) "The moon has risen"; (2) "The statement/The moon has risen/is a denotative statement". The syntagm /The moon has risen / in statement 2 is said to be the autonym of statement 1. See Josette Rey-Debove, *Le Métalangage* (Paris: Le Robert, 1978), pt. 4.

14 Its principle is Kantian, at least in matters of transcendental ethics – see the *Critique of Practical Reason*. When it comes to politics and empirical

ethics, Kant is prudent: since no one can identify himself with the transcendental normative subject, it is theoretically more exact to compromise with the existing authorities. See for example, "Antwort an der Frage: 'Was ist Aufklärung'?" (1784) [Eng. trans. Lewis White Beck, in *Critique of Practical Reason and Other Writings in Moral Philosophy* (Chicago: Chicago University Press, 1949)].

15   See Kant, "Antwort"; Jürgen Habermas, *Strukturwandel der Öffentlichkeit* (Frankfort: Luchterhand, 1962) [*The Structural Transformation of the Public Sphere: An Inquiry into a Category of Bourgeois Society*, trans. Thomas Burger and Frederick Lawrence (Cambridge, Mass.: MIT, 1989)]. The principle of Öffentlichkeit ("public" or "publicity" in the sense of "making public a private correspondence" or "public debate") guided the action of many groups of scientists at the end of the 1960s, especially the group "Survive" (France), the group "Scientists and Engineers for Social and Political Action" (USA), and the group "British Society for Social Responsibility in Science."

16   A French translation of this text by G. Granel can be found in *Phi*, supplement to the *Annales de l'université de Toulouse – Le Mirail* (Toulouse: January 1977).

17   Certain scientific aspects of postmodernism are inventoried by Ihab Hassan in "Culture, Indeterminacy, and Immanence: Margins of the (Postmodern) Age," *Humanities in Society*, 1 (1978): 51–85.

18   Claus Mueller uses the expression "a process of delegitimation" in *The Politics of Communication* (New York: Oxford University Press, 1973), p. 164.

19   "Road of doubt . . . road of despair . . . skepticism," writes Hegel in the preface to the *Phenomenology of Spirit* to describe the effect of the speculative drive on natural knowledge.

20   For fear of encumbering this account, I have postponded until a later study the exposition of this group of rules.

21   Nietzsche, "Der europäische Nihilismus" (MS. N VII 3); "der Nihilism, ein normaler Zustand" (MS. W II 1); "Kritik der Nihilism" (MS. W VII 3); "Zum Plane" (MS. W II 1), in *Nietzshes Werke kritische Gesamtausgabe*, vol. 7, pts. 1 and 2 (1887–89) (Berlin: De Gruyter, 1970). These texts have been the object of a commentary by K. Ryjik, *Nietzsche, le manuscrit de Lenzer Heide* (typescript, Départment de philosophie, Université de Paris VIII [Vincennes]).

22   "On the future of our educational institutions," in *Complete Works*, vol. 3.

23   Martin Buber, *Ich und Du* (Berlin: Schocken Verlag, 1922) [Eng. trans. Ronald G. Smith, *I and Thou* (New York: Charles Scribner's Sons, 1937)]; and *Dialogisches Leben* (Zürich: Müller, 1947); Emmanuel Lévinas, *Totalité et Infinité* (La Haye: Nijhoff, 1961) [Eng. trans. Alphonso Lingis, *Totality and Infinity: An Essay on Exteriority* (Pittsburgh: Duquesne University Press, 1969)], and "Martin

Buber und die Erkenntnish theorie" (1958), in *Philosophen des 20. Jahrhunderts* (Stuttgart: Kohlhammer, 1963).

24   *Philosophical Investigations*, sec. 18, p. 8 [by Ludwig Wittgenstein, trans. G. E. M. Anscombe (New York: Macmillan, 1958)].

25   Ibid.

26   Ibid.

27   See for example, "La taylorisation de la recherche," in (*Auto*) *critique de la science*, pp. 291–3, And especially D. J. de Solla Price, *Little Science, Big Science* (New York: Columbia University Press, 1963), who emphasizes the split between a small number of highly productive researchers (evaluated in terms of publication) and a large mass of researchers with low productivity. The number of the latter grows as the square of the former, so that the number of high productivity researchers only really increases every twenty years. Price concludes that science considered as a social entity is "undemocratic" (p. 59) and that "the eminent scientist" is a hundred years ahead of "the minimal one" (p. 56).

28   See J. T. Desanti, "Sur le rapport traditional des sciences et de la philosophie," in *La Philosophie silencieuse, ou critique des philosophies de la science* (Paris: Seuil, 1975).

29   The reclassification of academic philosophy as one of the human sciences in this respect has a significance far beyond simply professional concerns. I do not think that philosophy as legitimation is condemned to disappear, but it is possible that it will not be able to carry out this work, or at least advance it, without revising its ties to the university institution. See on this matter the preamble to the *Projet d'un institut polytechnique de philosophie* (typescript, Départment de philosophie, Université de Paris VIII, 1979).

30   See Allan Janik and Stephan Toulmin, *Wittgenstein's Vienna* (New York: Simon & Schuster, 1973), and J. Piel (ed.), "Vienne début d'un siècle," *Critique*, 339–40 (1975).

31   See Jürgen Habermas, "Dogmatismus, Vernunft unt Entscheidung – Zu Theorie und Praxis in der verwissenschaftlichen Zivilisation" (1963), in *Theorie und Praxis [Theory and Practice*, abr. edn of 4th German edn, trans. John Viertel (Boston: Beacon Press, 1971)].

32   "Science Smiling into its Beard" is the title of chap. 72, vol. 1 of Musil's *The Man Without Qualities*. Cited and discussed by J. Bouveresse, "La Problématique du sujet".

33   Aristotle in the *Analytics* (ca. 330 BC), Descartes in the *Regulae ad directionem ingenii* (1641) [Rules for the Direction of the Mind] and the *Principes de la philosophie* (1644), John Stuart Mill in the *System of Logic* (1843).

34   Gaston Bachelard, *Le Rationalisme appliqué* (Paris: Presses Universitaires de France, 1949); Michel

Serres, "La Réforme et les sept péchés," *L'Arc*, 42, Bachelard special issue (1970).

35 David Hilbert, *Grundlagen der Geometrie* (1899) [Eng. trans. Leo Unger, *Foundations of Geometry* (La Salle: Open Court, 1971)]. Nicolas Bourbaki, "L'architecture des mathématiques," in Le Lionnais, ed., *Les Grands Courants de la pensée mathématique* (Paris: Hermann, 1948); Robert Blanché, *L'Axiomatique* (Paris: Presses Universitaires de France, 1955) [Eng. trans. G. B. Keene, *Axiomatics* (New York: Free Press of Glencoe, 1962)].

36 See Blanché, *L'Axiomatique*, chap. 5.

37 I am here following Robert Martin, *Logique contemporaine et formalisation* (Paris: Presses Universitaires de France, 1964), pp. 33–41 and 122ff.

38 Kurt Gödel, "Über formal unentscheidbare Sätze der Principia Mathematica und verwandter Systeme," *Monatshefte für Mathematik, und Physik*, 38 (1931) [Eng. trans. B. Bletzer, *On Formally Undecidable Propositions of Principia Mathematica and Related Systems* (New York: Basic Books, 1962)].

39 Jean Ladrière, *Les Limitations internes des formalismes* (Louvain: E. Nauwelaerts, 1957).

40 Alfred Tarski, *Logic, Semantics, Metamathematics*, trans. J. H. Woodger (Oxford: Clarendon Press, 1956); J. P. Desclés and Z. Guentcheva-Desclès, "Métalangue, métalangage, métalinguistique," *Documents de travail*, 60–1 (Università di Urbino, January–February 1977).

41 *Les Eléments des mathématiques* (Paris: Hermann, 1940–). The distant points of departure of this work are to be found in the first attempts to demonstrate certain "postulates" of Euclidian geometry. See Léon Brunschvicg, *Les Etapes de la philosophie mathématique*, 3d edn (Paris: Presses Universitaires de France, 1947).

42 Thomas Kuhn, *Structure of Scientific Revolutions*.

43 A classification of logico-mathematical paradoxes can be found in F. P. Ramsey, *The Foundations of Mathematics and Other Logical Essays* (New York: Harcourt & Brace, 1931).

44 See Aristotle, *Rhetoric*, 2, 1393a ff.

45 The problem is that of the witness and also of the historical source: is the fact known from hearsay or *de visu*? The distinction is made by Herodotus. See F. Hartog, "Hérodote rapsode et arpenteur," *Hérodote*, 9 (1977): 55–65.

46 A. Gehlen, "Die Technik in der Sichtweise der Anthropologie," *Anthropologische Forschung* (Hamburg: Rowohlt, 1961).

47 André Leroi-Gourhan, *Milieu et techniques* (Paris: Albin-Michel, 1945), and *Le Geste et la parole, I, Technique et langage* (Paris: Albin-Michel, 1964).

48 Jean Pierre Vernant, *Mythe et pensée chez les Grecs* (Paris: Maspero, 1965), especially sec. 4, "Le travail et la pensée technique" [Eng. trans. Janet Lloyd, *Myth and Society in Ancient Greece* (Brighton, Eng: Harvester Press, 1980)].

49 Jurgis Baltrusaitis, *Anamorphoses, ou magie artificielle des effets merveilleux* (Paris: O. Perrin, 1969) [Eng. trans. W. J. Strachan, *Anamorphic Art* (New York: Abrams, 1977)].

50 Lewis Mumford, *Technics and Civilization* (New York: Harcourt, Brace, 1963); Bertrand Gille, *Historie des Techniques* (Paris: Gallimard, Pléiade, 1978).

51 A striking example of this, the use of amateur radios to verify certain implications of the theory of relativity, is studied by M. J. Mulkay and D. O. Edge, "Cognitive, Technical, and Social Factors in the Growth of Radio-Astronomy," *Social Science Information*, 12, no. 6 (1973): 25–61.

52 Mulkay elaborates a flexible model for the relative independence of technology and scientific knowledge in "The Model of Branching," *The Sociological Review*, 33 (1976): 509–26. H. Brooks, president of the Science and Public Committee of the National Academy of Sciences, and coauthor of the "Brooks Report" (OCDE, June 1971), criticizing the method of investment in research and development during the 1960s, declares: "One of the effects of the race to the moon has been to increase the cost of technological innovation to the point where it becomes quite simply too expensive.... Research is properly speaking a long-term activity: rapid acceleration or deceleration imply concealed expenditure and a great deal of incompetence. Intellectual production cannot go beyond a certain pace" ("Les Etats-Unis ont-ils une politique de la science?" *La Recherche*, 14:611). In March 1972, E. E. David, Jr, scientific adviser to the White House, proposing the idea of a program of Research Applied to National Needs (RANN), came to similar conclusions: a broad and flexible strategy for research and more restrictive tactics for development (*La Recherche*, 21 (1972): 211).

53 This was one of the Lazarsfeld's conditions for agreeing to found what was to become the Mass Communication Research Center at Princeton in 1937. This produced some tension: the radio industries refused to invest in the project; people said that Lazarsfeld started things going but finished nothing. Lazarsfeld himself said to Morrison, "I usually put things together and hoped they worked." Quoted by D. Morrison, "The Beginning of Modern Mass Communication Research," *Archives européennes de sociologie*, 19, no. 2 (1978): 347–59.

54 In the United States, the funds allocated to research and development by the federal government were, in 1956, equal to the funds coming from private capital; they have been higher since that time (OCDE, 1956).

55 Robert Nisbet, *Degradation*, chap. 5, provides a bitter description of the penetration of "higher capitalism" into the university in the form of research centers independent of departments. The social relations in such centers disturb the academic tradition. See too in *(Auto)critique de la science*, the chapters "Le

prolétariat scientifique," "Les chercheurs," "La Crise des mandarins."

56 Niklas Luhmann, *Legitimation durch Verfahren* (Neuweid: Luchterhand, 1969).

57 Commenting on Luhmann, Mueller writes, "In advanced industrial society, legal-rational legitimation is replaced by a technocratic legitimation that does not accord any significance to the beliefs of the citizen or to morality per se" (*Politics of Communication*, p. 135). There is a bibliography of German material on the technocratic question in Habermas, *Theory and Practice*.

58 Gilles Fauconnier gives a linguistic analysis of the control of truth in "Comment contrôler la vérité? Remarques illustrées par des assertions dangereuses et pernicieuses en tout genre," *Actes de la recherche en sciences sociales*, 25 (1979): 1–22.

59 Thus in 1970 the British University Grants Committee was "persuaded to take a much more positive role in productivity, specialization, concentration of subjects, and control of building through cost limits" [*The Politics of Education: Edward Boyle and Anthony Crosland in Conversation with Maurice Kogan* (Harmondsworth, Eng.: Penguin, 1971), p. 196]. This may appear to contradict declarations such as that of Brooks, quoted above (note 52). But (1) the "strategy" may be liberal and the "tactics" authoritarian, as Edwards says elsewhere; (2) responsibility within the hierarchy of public authorities is often taken in its narrowest sense, namely the capacity to answer for the calculable performance of a project; (3) public authorities are not always free from pressures from private groups whose performance criterion is immediately binding. If the chances of innovation in research cannot be calculated, then public interest seems to lie in aiding all research, under conditions other than that of efficiency assessment after a fixed period.

60 It has not been possible within the limits of this study to analyze the form assumed by the return of narrative in discourses of legitimation. Examples are: the study of open systems, local determinism, antimethod – in general, everything that I group under the name *paralogy*.

61 Nora and Minc, for example, attribute Japan's success in the field of computers to an "intensity of social consensus" that they judge to be specific to Japanese society (*L'Informatisation de la Société*, p. 4). They write in their conclusion: "The dynamics of extended social computerization leads to a fragile society: such a society is constructed with a view to facilitating consensus, but already presupposes its existence, and comes to a standstill if that consensus cannot be realized" (p. 125). Y. Stourdzé, "Les Etats-Unis", emphasizes the fact that the current tendency to deregulate, destabilize, and weaken administration is encouraged by society's loss of confidence in the State's performance capability.

62 In Kuhn's sense.

63 Pomian ("Catastrophes") shows that this type of functioning bears no relation to Hegelian dialectics.

64 "What the legitimation of decisions accordingly entails in fundamentally an effective learning process, with a minimum of friction, within the social system. This is an aspect of the more general question, 'how do aspirations change, how can the political-administrative subsystem, itself only part of society, nevertheless structure expectations in society through its decisions?' The effectiveness of the activity of what is only a part, for the whole, will in large measure depend on how well it succeeds in integrating new expectations into already existing systems – whether these are persons or social systems – without thereby provoking considerable functional disturbances" (Niklas Luhmann, *Legitimation durch Verfahren*, p. 35).

65 This hypothesis is developed in David Riesman's earlier studies. See Riesman, *The Lonely Crowd* (New Haven: Yale University Press, 1950); W. H. Whyte, *The Organization Man* (New York: Simon & Schuster, 1956); Herbert Marcuse, *One Dimensional Man* (Boston: Beacon, 1966).

66 Josette Rey-Debove (*Le Métalangage*, pp. 228ff.) notes the proliferation of marks of indirect discourse or autonymic connotation in contemporary daily language. As she reminds us, "indirect discourse cannot be trusted."

67 As Georges Canguilhem says, "man is only truly healthy when he is capable of a number of norms, when he is more than normal" ("Le Normal et la pathologique", in *La Connaissance de la vie* [Paris: Hachette, 1952], p. 210) [Eng. trans. Carolyn Fawcett, *On the Normal and the Pathological* (Boston: D. Reidel, 1978)].

68 E. E. David comments that society can only be aware of the needs it feels in the present state of its technological milieu. It is of the nature of the basic sciences to discover unknown properties which remodel the technical milieu and create unpredictable needs. He cites as examples the use of solid materials as amplifiers and the rapid development of the physics of solids. This "negative regulation" of social interactions and needs by the object of contemporary techniques is critiqued by R. Jaulin, "Le Mythe technologique", *Revue de l'entreprise*, 26, special "Ethnotechnology" issue (March 1979): 49–55. This is a review of A. G. Haudricourt, "La Technologie culturelle, essai de méthodologie," in Gille, *Historie des techniques*.

69 Medawar (*Art of the Soluble*, pp. 151–2) compares scientists' written and spoken styles. The former must be "inductive" or they will not be considered; as for the second, Medawar makes a list of expressions often heard in laboratories, including, "My results don't make a story yet." He concludes, "Sci-

entists are building explanatory structures, *telling stories...*"

70 For a famous example, see Lewis S. Feuer, *Einstein and the Generations of Science* (New York: Basic Books, 1974). As Moscovici emphasizes in his introduction to the French translation [trans. Alexandre, *Einstein et le conflit des générations* (Bruxelles' Complexe, 1979)], "Relativity was born in a makeshift 'academy' formed by friends, not one of whom was a physicist; all were engineers or amateur philosophers."

71 Orwell's paradox. The bureaucrat speaks: "We are not content with negative obedience, nor even with the most abject submission. When finally you do surrender to us, it must be of your own free will" (*1984* [New York: Harcourt, Brace, 1949], p. 258). In language game terminology the paradox would be expressed as a "Be free," or a "Want what you want," and is analyzed by Watzlawick et al., *Pragmatics of Human Communication*, pp. 203–7. On these paradoxes, see J. M. Salanskis, "Genèses 'actuelles' et genèses 'sérielles' de l'inconsistant et de l'hétérogeme," *Critique*, 379 (1978): 1155–73.

72 See Nora and Minc's description of the tensions that mass computerization will inevitably produce in French society (*L'informatisation de la société*, introduction).

73 Cf. the discussion of open systems in Watzlawick et al., *Pragmatics of Human Communication*, pp. 117–48. The concept of open systems theory is the subject of a study by J. M. Salanskis, *Le Systématique ouvert*. [This title never appeared. The author's next book appears to have been *Le Continu, le fini et la necessité* (Paris: IREM, 1988).]

74 After the separation of Church and State, Paul Feyerabend (*Against Method*), demands in the same "lay" spirit the separation of Science and State. But what about Science and Money?

75 This is at least one way of understanding this term, which comes from Ducrot's problematic, *Dire*.

76 *Legitimationsprobleme*, passim, especially pp. 21–2: "Language functions in the manner of a transformer... changing cognitions into propositions, needs and feeling into normative expectations (commands, values). This transformation produces the far-reaching distinction between the subjectivity of intention, willing, of pleasure and unpleasure on the one hand, and expressions and norms with a *pretension to universality* on the other. Universality signifies the objectivity of knowledge and the legitimacy of prevailing norms; both assure the community constitutive of lived social experience." We see that by formulating the problematic in this way, the question of legitimacy is fixated on one type of reply, universality. This on the one hand presupposes that the legitimation of the subject of knowledge is identical to that of the subject of action (in opposition to

Kant's critique, which dissociates conceptual universality, appropriate to the former, and ideal universality, or "suprasensible nature," which forms the horizon of the latter, and on the other hand it maintains that consensus (*Gemeinschaft*) is the only possible horizon for the life of humanity.

77 Ibid., p. 20. The subordination of the metaprescriptives of prescription (i.e. the normalization of laws) to *Diskurs* [Discourse] is explicit, for example, on p. 144: "The normative pretension to validity is itself cognitive in the sense that it always assumes it could be accepted in a rational discussion."

78 Garbis Kortian, *Métacritique* (Paris: Editions de Minuit, 1979) [Eng. trans. John Raffan, *Metacritique: The Philosophical Argument of Jürgen Habermas* (Cambridge: Cambridge University Press, 1980)], pt. 5, examines this enlightenment aspect of Habermas's thought. See by the same author, "Le Discours philosophique et son objet," *Critique*, 384 (1979): 407–19.

79 See J. Poulain ("Vers une pragmatique nucléaire"), and for a more general discussion of the pragmatics of Searle and Gehlen, see J. Poulain, "Pragmatique de la parole et pragmatique de la vie," *Phi zéro* 7, no. 1 (Université de Montréal, September 1978): 5–50.

80 See Tricot et al., *Informatique et libertés*, government report (La Documentation française, 1975); L. Joinet, "Les 'pièges liberaticides' de l'informatique," *Le Monde diplomatique*, 300 (March 1979): these traps (*pièges*) are "the application of the technique of 'social profiles' to the management of the mass of the population; the logic of security produced by the automatization of society." See too the documents and analysis in *Interférences*, 1 and 2 (Winter 1974– Spring 1975), the theme of which is the establishment of popular networks of multimedia communication. Topics treated include: amateur radios (especially their role in Quebec during the FLQ affair of October 1970 and that of the "Front commun" in May 1972); community radios in the United States and Canada; the impact of computers on editorial work in the press; pirate radios (before their development in Italy); administrative files, the IBM monopoly, computer sabotage. The municipality of Yverdon (Canton of Vaud), having voted to buy a computer (operational in 1981), enacted a certain number of rules: exclusive authority of the municipal council to decide which data are collected, to whom and under what conditions they are communicated; access for all citizens to all data (on payment); the right of every citizen to see the entries on his file (about 50), to correct them and address a complaint about them to the municipal council and if need be to the Council of State; the right of all citizens to know (on request) which data concerning them is communicated and to whom (*La Semaine media* 18, 1 March 1979, 9).

31

From "1227: Treatise on Nomadology – The War Machine"

Gilles Deleuze and Félix Guattari

Two politically radical thinkers, Gilles Deleuze (1925–95), a philosopher at the University of Paris influenced by Nietzsche and Spinoza, and psychotherapist Félix Guattari (1930–92), a student of Lacan and member of the anti-psychiatry movement (of R. D. Laing, and in a different sense, Foucault), merged post-structuralism, Marxism, and psychoanalysis in their controversial *Anti-Oedipus: Capitalism and Schizophrenia* (1972). They connected their neo-Marxist critique of the capitalist State with a rejection of Freudian psychoanalysis as a bourgeois repression of desire that encoded it with the language of the family (i.e. the Oedipus complex) in the name of social control. Both are, they argued, incipient fascism. Their criticism undermines the notion of the self as authoritative, unified, rationally controllable; the schizophrenic "body without organs," pure desire-production without structured goals or impediments, is the "natural" human condition. The sequel, *A Thousand Plateaus* (1980), written in a "rhizomatic" or modular rather than "arborial" or logically hierarchical fashion, presents their Nietzschean alternative to all attempts at dualistic, functional control. In the following excerpted chapter, they distinguish the nomadic power of the "war machine," from the legalistic war-engendering power of States. The war machine is the nomadic dispersal and growth of warrior-herders across open spaces, a violent reproductive process, which only generates war when confronting the limits imposed by sedentary agrarian States. Their work exhibits a rare *post-structuralist naturalism*.[i]

[i] Note that the number in the title of this chapter is a year, AD 1227, the year Ghenghis Khan [Temujin] died,

AXIOM I. *The war machine is exterior to the State apparatus.*
PROPOSITION I. *This exteriority is first attested to in mythology, epic, drama, and games.*

Georges Dumézil[ii], in his definitive analyses of Indo-European mythology, has shown that political sovereignty, or domination, has two heads: the magician-king and the jurist-priest. Rex and flamen, raj and Brahman, Romulus and Numa, Varuna and Mitra, the despot and the legislator, the binder and the organizer.[iii] Undoubtedly, these two poles stand in opposition term by term, as the obscure and the clear, the violent and the calm, the quick and the weighty, the fearsome and the regulated, the "bond" and the "pact," etc.[1] But their opposition is only relative; they function as a pair, in alternation, as though they expressed a division of the One or constituted in themselves a sovereign unity. "At once antithetical and complementary, necessary to

with his Mongol empire stretching from the Pacific Ocean to the Black Sea.
[ii] George Dumézil (1898–1986), prolific French practitioner of "comparative mythology" among Indo-European traditions. (The multiplicity of references in this essay makes it impractical to annotate them all.)
[iii] Respectively: (in medieval Latin) king and priest; (in Sanskrit) prince and priestly class; legendary founder of Rome and stipulator of its religious institutions; and chief Vedic god and his juridical counterpart.

Gilles Deleuze and Félix Guattari, from "1227: Treatise on Nomadology – The War Machine," chapter 12 of *A Thousand Plateaus* (trans. Brian Massumi), pp. 351–5, 361–2, 366–7, 369–71, 380–9, 416–18, 420–3. Minneapolis: University of Minnesota Press, 1987.

one another and consequently without hostility, lacking a mythology of conflict: a specification on any one level automatically calls forth a homologous specification on another. The two together exhaust the field of the function." They are the principal elements of a State apparatus that proceeds by a One-Two, distributes binary distinctions, and forms a milieu of interiority. It is a double articulation that makes the State apparatus into a *stratum*.[iv]

It will be noted that war is not contained within this apparatus. *Either* the State has at its disposal a violence that is not channeled through war – either it uses police officers and jailers in place of warriors, has no arms and no need of them, operates by immediate, magical capture, "seizes" and "binds," preventing all combat – *or*, the State acquires an army, but in a way that presupposes a juridical integration of war and the organization of a military function.[2] As for the war machine in itself, it seems to be irreducible to the State apparatus, to be outside its sovereignty and prior to its law: it comes from elsewhere.[v] *Indra, the warrior god, is in opposition to Varuna no less than to Mitra.*[3] He can no more be reduced to one or the other than he can constitute a third of their kind. Rather, he is like a pure and immeasurable multiplicity, the pack, an irruption of the ephemeral and the power of metamorphosis. *He unties the bond just as he betrays the pact.* He brings a *furor* to bear against sovereignty, a celerity against gravity, secrecy against the public, a power (*puissance*) against sovereignty, a machine against the apparatus. He bears witness to another kind of justice, one of incomprehensible cruelty at times, but at others of unequaled pity as well (because he unties bonds . . .).[4] He bears witness, above all, to other relations with women, with animals, because he sees all things in relations of *becoming*, rather than implementing binary distributions between "states": a veritable becoming-animal of the warrior, a becoming-woman, which lies outside dualities of terms as well as correspondences between relations. In every respect, the war machine is of another species, another nature, another origin than the State apparatus.

Let us take a limited example and compare the war machine and the State apparatus in the context of the theory of games. Let us take chess and Go, from the standpoint of the game pieces, the relations between the pieces and the space involved. Chess is a game of State, or of the court: the emperor of China played it. Chess pieces are coded; they have an internal nature and intrinsic properties from which their movements, situations, and confrontations derive. They have qualities; a knight remains a knight, a pawn a pawn, a bishop a bishop. Each is like a subject of the statement endowed with a relative power, and these relative powers combine in a subject of enunciation, that is, the chess player or the game's form of interiority. Go pieces, in contrast, are pellets, disks, simple arithmetic units, and have only an anonymous, collective, or third-person function: "It" makes a move. "It" could be a man, a woman, a louse, an elephant. Go pieces are elements of a nonsubjectified machine assemblage with no intrinsic properties, only situational ones. Thus the relations are very different in the two cases. Within their milieu of interiority, chess pieces entertain biunivocal relations with one another, and with the adversary's pieces: their functioning is structural. On the other hand, a Go piece has only a milieu of exteriority, or extrinsic relations with nebulas or constellations, according to which it fulfills functions of insertion or situation, such as bordering, encircling, shattering. All by itself, a Go piece can destroy an entire constellation synchronically; a chess piece cannot (or can do so diachronically only). Chess is indeed a war, but an institutionalized, regulated, coded war, with a front, a rear, battles. But what is proper to Go is war without battle lines, with neither confrontation nor retreat, without battles even: pure strategy, whereas chess is a semiology. Finally, the space is not at all the same: in chess, it is a question of arranging a closed space for oneself, thus of going from one point to another, of occupying the maximum number of squares with the minimum number of pieces. In Go, it is a question of arraying oneself in an open space, of holding space, of maintaining the possibility of springing up at any point: the movement is not from one point to another, but becomes perpetual, without aim or destination, without departure or arrival. The "smooth" space of Go, as against the "striated" space of chess. The *nomos* of Go against the State of chess, *nomos*

---

iv   "Strata" are constituted layers or subsystems of phenomena.

v   For the author, reality is production, man–nature and nature–industry are continuous, and nothing is "interior" (subjective, hidden). Thus everything is a "machine" (a thing that produces). Nomad life is a machine that produces violent expansion.

vi   *Go* is a Japanese board game where indistinguishable pieces surround and capture others; "smooth" is open, "striated" is a grid; *nomos* is convention, *polis* is political state.

against *polis*.[vi] The difference is that chess, codes and decodes space, whereas Go proceeds altogether differently, territorializing or deterritorializing it (make the outside a territory in space; consolidate that territory by the construction of a second, adjacent territory; deterritorialize the enemy by shattering his territory from within; deterritorialize oneself by renouncing, by going elsewhere . . .). Another justice, another movement, another space-time.

"They come like fate, without reason, consideration, or pretext . . . "[vii] "In some way that is incomprehensible they have pushed right into the capital. At any rate, here they are; it seems that every morning there are more of them."[viii] Luc de Heusch analyzes a Bantu myth that leads us to the same schema: Nkongolo, an indigenous emperor and administrator of public works, a man of the public and a man of the police, gives his half-sisters to the hunter Mbidi, who assists him and then leaves. Mbidi's son, a man of secrecy, joins up with his father, only to return from the outside with that inconceivable thing, an army. He kills Nkongolo and proceeds to build a new State.[5] "Between" the magical-despotic State and the juridical State containing a military institution, we see the flash of the war machine, arriving from without.

From the standpoint of the State, the originality of the man of war, his eccentricity, necessarily appears in a negative form: stupidity, deformity, madness, illegitimacy, usurpation, sin. Dumézil analyzes the three "sins" of the warrior in the Indo-European tradition: against the king, against the priest, against the laws originating in the State (for example, a sexual transgression that compromises the distribution of men and women, or even a betrayal of the laws of war as instituted by the State).[6] The warrior is in the position of betraying everything, including the function of the military, *or* of understanding nothing. It happens that historians, both bourgeois and Soviet, will follow this negative tradition and explain how Genghis Khan understood nothing: he "didn't understand" the phenomenon of the city. An easy thing to say. The problem is that the exteriority of the war machine in relation to the State apparatus is everywhere apparent but remains difficult to conceptualize. It is not enough to affirm that the war machine is external to the apparatus. It is necessary to reach the point of conceiving the war machine as itself a pure form of exteriority, whereas the State apparatus constitutes the form of interiority we habitually take as a model, or according to which we are in the habit of thinking. What complicates everything is that this extrinsic power of the war machine tends, under certain circumstances, to become confused with one of the two heads of the State apparatus. Sometimes it is confused with the magic violence of the State, at other times with the State's military institution. For instance, the war machine invents speed and secrecy; but there is all the same a certain speed and a certain secrecy that pertain to the State, relatively, secondarily. So there is a great danger of identifying the structural relation between the two poles of political sovereignty, and the dynamic interrelation of these two poles, with the power of war. Dumézil cites the lineage of the Roman kings: there is a Romulus–Numa relation that recurs throughout a series, with variants and an alternation between these two types of equally legitimate rulers; but there is also a relation with an "evil king," Tullus Hostilius, Tarquinius Superbus,[ix] an upsurge of the warrior as a disquieting and illegitimate character.[7] Shakespeare's kings could also be invoked: even violence, murders, and perversion do not prevent the State lineage from producing "good" kings; but a disturbing character like Richard III slips in, announcing from the outset his intention to reinvent a war machine and impose its line (deformed, treacherous and traitorous, he claims a "secret close intent" totally different from the conquest of State power, and another – an *other* – relation with women).[x] In short, whenever the irruption of war power is confused with the line of State domination, everything gets muddled; the war machine can then be understood only through the categories of the negative, since nothing is left that remains outside the State. But, returned to its milieu of exteriority, the war machine is seen to be of another species, of another nature, of another origin. One would have to say that it is located between the two heads of the State, between the two articulations, and that it is necessary in order to pass from one to the other. But "between" the two, in that instant, even ephemeral, if only a flash, it proclaims its own irreducibility. The State has no war machine of its own; it can only appropriate one in the form of a military institu-

---

vii   Nietzsche's *Genealogy of Morals*, II, 17.
viii Franz Kafka, "An Old Manuscript."

ix   Roman kings from the seventh and sixth centuries BC, respectively.
x   Quote is from Shakespeare, Richard III, act I, Scene i, line 158.

tion, one that will continually cause it problems. This explains the mistrust States have toward their military institutions, in that the military institution inherits an extrinsic war machine. Karl von Clausewitz has a general sense of this situation when he treats the flow of absolute war as an Idea that States partially appropriate according to their political needs and in relation to which they are more or less good "conductors."[xi]

PROPOSITION III. *The exteriority of the war machine is also attested to by epistemology, which intimates the existence and perpetuation of a "nomad" or "minor science."*

There is a kind of science, or treatment of science, that seems very difficult to classify, whose history is even difficult to follow. What we are referring to are not "technologies" in the usual sense of the term. But neither are they "sciences" in the royal or legal sense established by history. According to a recent book by Michel Serres, both the atomic physics of Democritus and Lucretius and the geometry of Archimedes[xii] are marked by it.[8] The characteristics of this kind of eccentric science would seem to be the following:

1. First of all, it uses a hydraulic model, rather than being a theory of solids treating fluids as a special case; ancient atomism is inseparable from flows, and flux is reality itself, or consistency.

2. The model in question is one of becoming and heterogeneity, as opposed to the stable, the eternal, the identical, the constant. It is a "paradox" to make becoming itself a model, and no longer a secondary characteristic, a copy; in the *Timaeus*, Plato raises this possibility, but only in order to exclude it and conjure it away in the name of royal science. By contrast, in atomism, just such a model of heterogeneity, and of passage or becoming in the heterogeneous, is furnished by the famed declination of the atom. The *clinamen*, as the minimum angle, has meaning only between a straight line and a curve, the curve and its tangent, and constitutes the original curvature of the movement of the atom. The clinamen is the smallest angle by which an atom deviates from a straight path. It is a passage to the

limit, an exhaustion, a paradoxical "exhaustive" model. The same applies to Archimedean geometry, in which the straight line, defined as "the shortest path between two points," is just a way of defining the length of a curve in a predifferential calculus.

3. One no longer goes from the straight line to its parallels, in a lamellar or laminar flow, but from a curvilinear declination to the formation of spirals and vortices on an inclined plane: the greatest slope for the smallest angle.[xiii] From *turba* to *turbo*: in other words, from bands or packs of atoms to the great vortical organizations. The model is a vortical one; it operates in an open space throughout which things-flows are distributed, rather than plotting out a closed space for linear and solid things. It is the difference between a *smooth* (vectorial, projective, or topological) space and a *striated* (metric) space: in the first case "space is occupied without being counted," and in the second case "space is counted in order to be occupied."[9]

4. Finally, the model is problematic, rather than theorematic: figures are considered only from the viewpoint of the *affections* that befall them: sections, ablations, adjunctions, projections. One does not go by specific differences from a genus to its species, or by deduction from a stable essence to the properties deriving from it, but rather from a problem to the accidents that condition and resolve it. This involves all kinds of deformations, transmutations, passages to the limit, operations in which each figure designates an "event" much more than an essence; the square no longer exists independently of a quadrature, the cube of a cubature, the straight line of a rectification. Whereas the theorem belongs to the rational order, the problem is affective and is inseparable from the metamorphoses, generations, and creations within science itself. Despite what Gabriel Marcel may say, the problem is not an "obstacle"; it is the surpassing of the obstacle, a pro-jection, in other words, a war machine.[xiv] All of this movement is what royal science is striving to limit when it reduces as much as possible the range of the "problem-element" and subordinates it to the "theorem-element."[10]

This Archimedean science, or this conception of science, is bound up in an essential way with the

---

[xi]   Karl Philipp Gottlieb von Clausewitz (1780–1831), Prussian general and author of the famous *On War*.

[xii]   Two philosophers, Democritus (460–370 BC), ancient Greek atomist, Lucretius (99–55 BC), Roman materialist, and Archimedes (287–212 BC), Greek mathematician and inventor.

[xiii]   For Serres, in a laminar flow the lamellae (layers), no matter how small, are parallel. In the following sentence, also for Serres, a *turba* is a large disorderly system of particles; *turbo* is particles moving in a revolving vortex.

[xiv]   Gabriel Marcel (1889–1973), French Catholic Existentialist philosopher.

war machine: the *problemata* are the war machine itself and are inseparable from inclined planes, passages to the limit, vortices, and projections. It would seem that the war machine is projected into an abstract knowledge formally different from the one that doubles the State apparatus. It would seem that a whole nomad science develops eccentrically, one that is very different from the royal or imperial sciences. Furthermore, this nomad science is continually "barred," inhibited, or banned by the demands and conditions of State science. Archimedes, vanquished by the Roman State, becomes a symbol.[11] The fact is that the two kinds of science have different modes of formalization, and State science continually imposes its form of sovereignty on the inventions of nomad science. State science retains of nomad science only what it can appropriate; it turns the rest into a set of strictly limited formulas without any real scientific status, or else simply represses and bans it. It is as if the "savants" of nomad science were caught between a rock and a hard place, between the war machine that nourishes and inspires them and the State that imposes upon them an order of reasons. The figure of the *engineer* (in particular the military engineer), with all its ambivalence, is illustrative of this situation ...

A *body* (*corps*) is not reducible to an *organism*,[xv] any more than esprit de corps is reducible to the soul of an organism. Spirit is not better, but it is volatile, whereas the soul is weighted, a center of gravity. Must we invoke a military origin of the collective body and esprit de corps? "Military" is not the part that counts, but rather the distant nomadic origin. Ibn Khaldūn defines the nomad war machine by: families or lineages PLUS esprit de corps.[xvi] The war machine entertains a relation to families that is very different from its relation to the State. In the war machine, the family is a band vector instead of a fundamental cell; a genealogy is transferred from one family to another according to the aptitude of a given family at a given time to realize the maximum of "agnatic solidarity." Here, it is not the public eminence of a family that determines its place in a State organism but the reverse; it is the secret power (*puissance*), or strength of solidarity, and the corresponding genealogical mobility that determine its eminence in a war body.[12] This has to do neither with the monopoly of an organic power (*pouvoir*) nor with local representation, but is related to the potential (*puissance*) of a vortical body in a nomad space. Of course, the great bodies of a modern State can hardly be thought of as Arab tribes. What we wish to say, rather, is that collective bodies always have fringes or minorities that reconstitute equivalents of the war machine – in sometimes quite unforeseen forms – in specific assemblages such as building bridges or cathedrals or rendering judgments or making music or instituting a science, a technology ... A collective body of captains asserts its demands through the organization of the officers and the organism of the superior officers. There are always periods when the State as organism has problems with its own collective bodies, when these bodies, claiming certain privileges, are forced in spite of themselves to open onto something that exceeds them, a short revolutionary instant, an experimental surge. A confused situation: each time it occurs, it is necessary to analyze tendencies and poles, the nature of the movements. All of a sudden, it is as if the collective body of the notary publics were advancing like Arabs or Indians, then regrouping and reorganizing: a comic opera where you never know what is going to happen next (even the cry "The police are with us!" is sometimes heard). ...

It is instructive to contrast two models of science, after the manner of Plato in the *Timaeus*.[13] One could be called *Compars* and the other *Dispars*.[xvii] The compars is the legal or legalist model employed by royal science. The search for laws consists in extracting constants, even if those constants are only relations between variables (equations). An invariable form for variables, a variable matter of the invariant: such is the foundation of the hylomorphic schema. But for the dispars as an element of nomad science the relevant distinction is material-forces rather than matter-form. Here, it is not exactly a question of extracting constants from variables but of placing the variables themselves in a state of continuous variation. If there are still equations, they are adequations, inequations, differential equations irreducible to the algebraic form and inseparable from a sensible intuition of variation. They seize or determine singularities in the matter, instead of constituting a general form. They effect individuations through events or haecceities, not through the "object" as a compound of matter and form; vague essences are nothing other than haecceities. In all these respects, there is an oppos-

---

[xv] For the authors "organism" is a functional concept, and "organs" site-specific limitations of bodily desire.
[xvi] Ibn Khaldūn (1332–1406 AD), great Arabic philosopher and social analyst, author of *The Muqaddimah*.

[xvii] Matched or equal, and unequal, respectively.

ition between the *logos* and the *nomos*, the law and the *nomos*, prompting the comment that the law still "savors of morality." This does not mean, however, that the legal model knows nothing of forces, the play of forces. That it does is evident in the homogeneous space corresponding to the compars. Homogeneous space is in no way a smooth space; on the contrary, it is the form of striated space. The space of *pillars*. It is striated by the fall of bodies, the verticals of gravity, the distribution of matter into parallel layers, the lamellar and laminar movement of flows. These parallel verticals have formed an independent dimension capable of spreading everywhere, of formalizing all the other dimensions, of striating all of space in all of its directions, so as to render it homogeneous. The vertical distance between two points provided the mode of comparison for the horizontal distance between two other points. Universal attraction became the law of all laws, in that it set the rule for the biunivocal correspondence between two bodies; and each time science discovered a new field, it sought to formalize it in the same mode as the field of gravity. Even chemistry became a royal science only by virtue of a whole theoretical elaboration of the notion of weight. Euclidean space is founded on the famous parallel postulate, but the parallels in question are in the first place gravitational parallels, and correspond to the forces exerted by gravity on all the elements of a body presumed to fill that space. It is the point of application of the resultant of all of these parallel forces that remains invariable when their common direction is changed or the body is rotated (the *center of gravity*). In short, it seems that the force of gravity lies at the basis of a laminar, striated, homogeneous, and centered space; it forms the foundation for those multiplicities termed metric, or arborescent, whose dimensions are independent of the situation and are expressed with the aid of units and points (movements from one point to another). It was not some metaphysical concern, but an effectively scientific one, that frequently led scientists in the nineteenth century to ask if all forces were not reducible to gravity, or rather to the form of attraction that gives gravity a universal value (a constant relation for all variables) and biunivocal scope (two bodies at a time, and no more). It is the form of interiority of all science.

The *nomos*, or the dispars, is altogether different. But this is not to say that the other forces refute gravity or contradict attraction. Although it is true that they do not go against them, they do not result from them either; they do not depend on them but

testify to events that are always supplementary or of "variable affects." Each time a new *field* opened up in science – under conditions making this a far more important notion than that of form or object – it proved irreducible to the field of attraction and the model of the gravitational forces, although not contradictory to them. It affirmed a "more" or an excess, and lodged itself in that excess, that deviation. When chemistry took a decisive step forward, it was always by adding to the force of weight bonds of another type (for example, electric) that transformed the nature of chemical equations.[14] But it will be noted that the simplest considerations of velocity immediately introduce the difference between vertical descent and curvilinear motion, or more generally between the straight line and the curve, in the differential form of the clinamen, or the smallest deviation, the minimum excess. Smooth space is precisely the space of the smallest deviation: therefore it has no homogeneity, except between infinitely proximate points, and the linking of proximities is effected independently of any determined path. It is a space of contact, of small tactile or manual actions of contact, rather than a visual space like Euclid's striated space. Smooth space is a field without conduits or channels. A field, a heterogeneous smooth space, is wedded to a very particular type of multiplicity: nonmetric, acentered, rhizomatic multiplicities that occupy space without "counting" it and can "be explored only by legwork." They do not meet the visual condition of being observable from a point in space external to them; an example of this is the system of sounds, or even of colors, as opposed to Euclidean space....

AXIOM II. *The war machine is the invention of the nomads (insofar as it is exterior to the State apparatus and distinct from the military institution). As such, the war machine has three aspects, a spatio-geographic aspect, an arithmetic or algebraic aspect, and an affective aspect.*

PROPOSITION V. *Nomad existence necessarily effectuates the conditions of the war machine in space.*

The nomad has a territory; he follows customary paths; he goes from one point to another; he is not ignorant of points (water points, dwelling points, assembly points, etc.). But the question is what in nomad life is a principle and what is only a consequence. To begin with, although the points determine paths, they are strictly subordinated to the paths they determine, the reverse of what happens with the sedentary. The water point is reached only in order to be left behind; every point is a relay and exists only as a relay. A path is always between two points, but the in–between has taken on all the consistency and enjoys both an autonomy and a direction of its own. The life of the nomad is the intermezzo.[xviii] Even the elements of his dwelling are conceived in terms of the trajectory that is forever mobilizing them.[15] The nomad is not at all the same as the migrant; for the migrant goes principally from one point to another, even if the second point is uncertain, unforeseen, or not well localized. But the nomad goes from point to point only as a consequence and as a factual necessity; in principle, points for him are relays along a trajectory. Nomads and migrants can mix in many ways, or form a common aggregate; their causes and conditions are no less distinct for that (for example, those who joined Mohammed at Medina had a choice between a nomadic or bedouin pledge, and a pledge of hegira[xix] or emigration).[16]

Second, even though the nomadic trajectory may follow trails or customary routes, it does not fulfill the function of the sedentary road, which is to *parcel out a closed space to people*, assigning each person a share and regulating the communication between shares. The nomadic trajectory does the opposite: it *distributes people (or animals) in an open space*, one that is indefinite and noncommunicating. The *nomos* came to designate the law, but that was originally because it was distribution, a mode of distribution. It is a very special kind of distribution, one without division into shares, in a space without borders or enclosure. The *nomos* is the consistency of a fuzzy aggregate: it is in this sense that it stands in opposition to the law or the *polis*, as the back-country, a mountainside, or the vague expanse around a city ("either nomos or polis").[17] Therefore, and this is the third point, there is a significant difference between the spaces: sedentary space is striated, by walls, enclosures, and roads between enclosures, while nomad space is smooth, marked only by "traits" that are effaced and displaced with the trajectory. Even the lamellae of the desert slide over each other, producing an inimitable sound. The nomad distributes himself in a smooth space; he occupies, inhabits, holds that space; that is his territorial principle. It is therefore false to define

the nomad by movement. Toynbee is profoundly right to suggest that the nomad is on the contrary *he who does not move.*[xx] Whereas the migrant leaves behind a milieu that has become amorphous or hostile, the nomad is one who does not depart, does not want to depart, who clings to the smooth space left by the receding forest, where the steppe or the desert advances, and who invents nomadism as a response to this challenge.[18] Of course, the nomad moves, but while seated, and he is only seated while moving (the Bedouin galloping, knees on the saddle, sitting on the soles of his upturned feet, "a feat of balance"). The nomad knows how to wait, he has infinite patience. Immobility and speed, catatonia and rush, a "stationary process," station as process – these traits of Kleist's[xxi] are eminently those of the nomad. It is thus necessary to make a distinction between *speed* and *movement:* a movement may be very fast, but that does not give it speed; a speed may be very slow, or even immobile, yet it is still speed. Movement is extensive; speed is intensive. Movement designates the relative character of a body considered as "one," and which goes from point to point; *speed, on the contrary, constitutes the absolute character of a body whose irreducible parts (atoms) occupy or fill a smooth space in the manner of a vortex*, with the possibility of springing up at any point. (It is therefore not surprising that reference has been made to spiritual voyages effected without relative movement, but in intensity, in one place: these are part of nomadism.) In short, we will say by convention that only nomads have absolute movement, in other words, speed; vortical or swirling movement is an essential feature of their war machine.

It is in this sense that nomads have no points, paths, or land, even though they do by all appearances. If the nomad can be called the Deterritorialized[xxii] par excellence, it is precisely because there is no reterritorialization *afterward* as with the migrant, or upon *something else* as with the sedentary (the sedentary's relation with the earth is mediatized by something else, a property regime, a State apparatus). With the nomad, on the contrary, it is deterritorialization that constitutes the relation to the earth, to such a degree that the nomad reterritorializes on deterritorialization itself. It is the earth

---

[xviii] Musical interlude, between two other pieces.

[xix] Hegira (or Hejra), Mohammed's flight from Mecca to Yathrib (later named Medina).

[xx] Historian Arnold Toynbee (1889–1975).

[xxi] Bernd Heinrich von Kleist (1777–1811), German dramatist.

[xxii] "Territorialized" means fixed by a grid in space. Nomads are de-territorialized.

that deterritorializes itself, in a way that provides the nomad with a territory. The land ceases to be land, tending to become simply ground (*sol*) or support. The earth does not become deterritorialized in its global and relative movement, but at specific locations, at the spot where the forest recedes, or where the steppe and the desert advance. Hubac is right to say that nomadism is explainable less by universal changes in climate (which relate instead to migrations) as by the "divagation of local climates."[19] The nomads are there, on the land, wherever there forms a smooth space that gnaws, and tends to grow, in all directions. The nomads inhabit these places; they remain in them, and they themselves make them grow, for it has been established that the nomads make the desert no less than they are made by it. They are vectors of deterritorialization. They add desert to desert, steppe to steppe, by a series of local operations whose orientation and direction endlessly vary.[20] The sand desert has not only oases, which are like fixed points, but also rhizomatic vegetation that is temporary and shifts location according to local rains, bringing changes in the direction of the crossings.[21] The same terms are used to describe ice deserts as sand deserts: there is no line separating earth and sky; there is no intermediate distance, no perspective or contour; visibility is limited; and yet there is an extraordinarily fine topology that relies not on points or objects but rather on haecceities, on sets of relations (winds, undulations of snow or sand, the song of the sand or the creaking of ice, the tactile qualities of both). It is a tactile space, or rather "haptic,"[xxiii] a sonorous much more than a visual space.[22] The variability, the polyvocality of directions, is an essential feature of smooth spaces of the rhizome type, and it alters their cartography. The nomad, nomad space, is localized and not delimited. What is both limited and limiting is striated space, the *relative global*: it is limited in its parts, which are assigned constant directions, are oriented in relation to one another, divisible by boundaries, and can interlink; what is limiting (*limes* or wall, and no longer boundary) is this aggregate in relation to the smooth spaces it "contains," whose growth it slows or prevents, and which it restricts or places outside. Even when the nomad sustains its effects, he does not belong to this relative global, where one passes from one point to another, from one region to another. Rather, he is in a *local absolute*, an absolute that is manifested locally, and engendered in a series of local operations of varying orientations: desert, steppe, ice, sea.

Making the absolute appear in a particular place – is that not a very general characteristic of religion (recognizing that the nature of the appearance, and the legitimacy, or lack thereof, of the images that reproduce it are open to debate)? But the sacred place of religion is fundamentally a center that repels the obscure *nomos*. The absolute of religion is essentially a horizon that encompasses, and, if the absolute itself appears at a particular place, it does so in order to establish a solid and stable center for the global. The encompassing role of smooth spaces (desert, steppe, or ocean) in monotheism has been frequently noted. In short, religion converts the absolute. Religion is in this sense a piece in the State apparatus (in both of its forms, the "bond" and the "pact or alliance"), even if it has within itself the power to elevate this model to the level of the universal or to constitute an absolute *Imperium*.[xxiv] But for the nomad the terms of the question are totally different: locality is not delimited; the absolute, then, does not appear at a particular place but becomes a nonlimited locality; the coupling of the place and the absolute is achieved not in a centered, oriented globalization or universalization but in an infinite succession of local operations. Limiting ourselves to this opposition between points of view, it may be observed that nomads do not provide a favorable terrain for religion; the man of war is always committing an offense against the priest or the god. The nomads have a vague, literally vagabond "monotheism," and content themselves with that, and with their ambulant fires. The nomads have a sense of the absolute, but a singularly atheistic one. The universalist religions that have had dealings with nomads – Moses, Mohammed, even Christianity with the Nestorian heresy[xxv] – have always encountered problems in this regard, and have run up against what they have termed obstinate impiety. These religions are not, in effect, separable from a firm and constant orientation, from an imperial de jure State, even, and especially, in the absence of a de facto State; they have promoted an ideal of sedentarization and addressed themselves more to the migrant components than the nomadic ones. Even early Islam favored the theme of the hegira, or migration,

---

[xxiii] Related to the sense of touch.

[xxiv] Empire.

[xxv] The heretical view that Christ embodied two distinct persons, human and divine, held by Nestorius, patriarch of Constantinople, AD 428–431.

over nomadism; rather, it was through certain schisms (such as the Khārijī movement[xxvi]) that it won over the Arab or Berber nomads.[23]

However, it does not exhaust the question to establish a simple opposition between two points of view, religion-nomadism. For monotheistic religion, at the deepest level of its tendency to project a universal or spiritual State over the entire ecumenon, is not without ambivalence or fringe areas; it goes beyond even the ideal limits of the State, even the imperial State, entering a more indistinct zone, an outside of States where it has the possibility of undergoing a singular mutation or adaptation. We are referring to religion as an element in a war machine and the idea of holy war as the motor of that machine. The *prophet*, as opposed to the state personality of the king and the religious personality of the priest, directs the movement by which a religion becomes a war machine or passes over to the side of such a machine. It has often been said that Islam, and the prophet Mohammed, performed such a conversion of religion and constituted a veritable esprit de corps;[xxvii] in the formula of Georges Bataille, "early Islam, a society reduced to the military enterprise." This is what the West invokes in order to justify its antipathy toward Islam. Yet the Crusades were a properly Christian adventure of this type. The prophets may very well condemn nomad life; the war machine may very well favor the movement of migration and the ideal of establishment; religion in general may very well compensate for its specific deterritorialization with a spiritual and even physical reterritorialization, which in the case of the holy war assumes the well-directed character of a conquest of the holy lands as the center of the world. Despite all that, when religion sets itself up as a war machine, it mobilizes and liberates a formidable charge of nomadism or absolute deterritorialization; it doubles the migrant with an accompanying nomad, or with the potential nomad the migrant is in the process of becoming; and finally, it turns its dream of an absolute State back against the State-form.[24] And this turning-against is no less a part of the "essence" of religion than that dream. The history of the Crusades is marked by the most astonishing series of directional changes: the firm orientation toward the Holy Land as a center to reach often seems nothing more than a pretext. But it would be

wrong to say that the play of self-interest, or economic, commercial, or political factors, diverted the crusade from its pure path. The idea of the crusade *in itself implies this variability of directions*, broken and changing, and intrinsically possesses all these factors or all these variables from the moment it turns religion into a war machine and simultaneously utilizes and gives rise to the corresponding nomadism.[25] The necessity of maintaining the most rigorous of distinctions between sedentaries, migrants, and nomads does not preclude de facto mixes; on the contrary, it makes them all the more necessary in turn. And it is impossible to think of the general process of sedentarization that vanquished the nomads without also envisioning the gusts of local nomadization that carried off sedentaries and doubled migrants (notably, to the benefit of religion).

Smooth or nomad space lies between two striated spaces: that of the forest, with its gravitational verticals, and that of agriculture, with its grids and generalized parallels, its now independent arborescence,[xxviii] its art of extracting the tree and wood from the forest. But being "between" also means that smooth space is controlled by these two flanks, which limit it, oppose its development, and assign it as much as possible a communicational role; or, on the contrary, it means that it turns against them, gnawing away at the forest on one side, on the other side gaining ground on the cultivated lands, affirming a noncommunicating force or a force of *divergence* like a "wedge" digging in. The nomads turn first against the forest and the mountain dwellers, then descend upon the farmers. What we have here is something like the flipside or the outside of the State-form – but in what sense? This form, as a global and relative space, implies a certain number of components: forest-clearing of fields; agriculture-grid laying; animal raising subordinated to agricultural work and sedentary food production; commerce based on a constellation of town-country (*polis-nomos*) communications. When historians inquire into the reasons for the victory of the West over the Orient, they primarily mention the following characteristics, which put the Orient in general at a disadvantage: deforestation rather than clearing for planting, making it extremely difficult to extract or even to find wood; cultivation of the type "rice paddy and garden" rather than arborescence and field; animal raising for the most part outside the control of the seden-

---

[xxvi] A Muslim sect among ethnic Berbers that opposed Arab dominance in the eighth century AD.
[xxvii] Group loyalty.

[xxviii] Tree-like-ness (logically hierarchical).

taries, with the result that they lacked animal power and meat foods; the low communication content of the town–country relation, making commerce far less flexible.[26] The conclusion is not that the State-form is absent in the Orient. Quite to the contrary, a more rigid agency becomes necessary in order to retain and reunite the various components plied by escape vectors. States always have the same composition; if there is even one truth in the political philosophy of Hegel, it is that every State carries within itself the essential moments of its existence. States are made up not only of people but also of wood, fields, gardens, animals, and commodities. There is a unity of *composition* of all States, but States have neither the same *development* nor the same *organization*. In the Orient, the components are much more disconnected, disjoined, necessitating a great immutable Form to hold them together: "despotic formations," Asian or African, are rocked by incessant revolts, by secessions and dynastic changes, which nevertheless do not affect the immutability of the form. In the West, on the other hand, the interconnectedness of the components makes possible transformations of the State-form through revolution. It is true that the idea of revolution itself is ambiguous; it is Western insofar as it relates to a transformation of the State, but Eastern insofar as it envisions the destruction, the abolition of the State.[27] The great empires of the Orient, Africa, and America run up against wide-open smooth spaces that penetrate them and maintain gaps between their components (the *nomos* does not become countryside, the countryside does not communicate with the town, large-scale animal raising is the affair of the nomads, etc.): the oriental State is in direct confrontation with a nomad war machine. This war machine may fall back to the road of integration and proceed solely by revolt and dynastic change; nevertheless, it is the war machine, as nomad, that invents the abolitionist dream and reality. Western States are much more sheltered in their striated space and consequently have much more latitude in holding their components together; they confront the nomads only indirectly, through the intermediary of the migrations the nomads trigger or adopt as their stance.[28]

One of the fundamental tasks of the State is to striate the space over which it reigns, or to utilize smooth spaces as a means of communication in the service of striated space. It is a vital concern of every State not only to vanquish nomadism but to control migrations and, more generally, to establish a zone of rights over an entire "exterior," over all of the flows traversing the ecumenon. If it can help it, the State does not dissociate itself from a process of capture of flows of all kinds, populations, commodities or commerce, money or capital, etc. There is still a need for fixed paths in well-defined directions, which restrict speed, regulate circulation, relativize movement, and measure in detail the relative movements of subjects and objects. That is why Paul Virilio's thesis is important, when he shows that "the political power of the State is *polis*, police, that is, management of the public ways," and that "the gates of the city, its levies and duties, are barriers, filters against the fluidity of the masses, against the penetration power of migratory packs," people, animals, and goods.[29] Gravity, *gravitas*, such is the essence of the State. It is not at all that the State knows nothing of speed: but it requires that movement, even the fastest, cease to be the absolute state of a moving body occupying a smooth space, to become the relative characteristic of a "moved body" going from one point to another in a striated space. In this sense, the State never ceases to decompose, recompose, and transform movement, or to regulate speed. The State as town surveyor, converter, or highway interchange: the role of the engineer from this point of view. Speed and absolute movement are not without their laws, but they are the laws of the *nomos*, of the smooth space that deploys it, of the war machine that populates it. If the nomads formed the war machine, it was by inventing absolute speed, by being "synonymous" with speed. And each time there is an operation against the State – insubordination, rioting, guerrilla warfare, or revolution as act – it can be said that a war machine has revived, that a new nomadic potential has appeared, accompanied by the reconstitution of a smooth space or a manner of being in space as though it were smooth (Virilio discusses the importance of the riot or revolutionary theme of "holding the street"). It is in this sense that the response of the State against all that threatens to move beyond it is to striate space. The State does not appropriate the war machine without giving even it the form of relative movement: this was the case with the model of the *fortress* as a regulator of movement, which was precisely the obstacle the nomads came up against, the stumbling block and parry by which absolute vortical movement was broken. Conversely, when a State does not succeed in striating its interior or neighboring space, the flows traversing that State necessarily adopt the stance of a war machine directed against it, deployed in a hostile or rebellious smooth space (even if other States are able to slip their striations in). This was the adventure of China: toward the end of the fourteenth century, and in spite of its very high level of technology in ships and navigation, it turned its back on its huge maritime space, saw its commercial flows turn against it and ally themselves with piracy, and was unable to react except by a politics of immobility, of the massive restriction of commerce, which only reinforced the connection between commerce and the war machine.[30]

The situation is much more complicated than we have let on. The sea is perhaps principal among smooth spaces, the hydraulic model par excellence. But the sea is also, of all smooth spaces, the first one attempts were made to striate, to transform into a dependency of the land, with its fixed routes, constant directions, relative movements, a whole counterhydraulic of channels and conduits. One of the reasons for the hegemony of the West was the power of its State apparatuses to striate the sea by combining the technologies of the North and the Mediterranean and by annexing the Atlantic. But this undertaking had the most unexpected result: the multiplication of relative movements, the intensification of relative speeds in striated space, ended up reconstituting a smooth space or absolute movement. As Virilio emphasizes, the sea became the place of the *fleet in being*, where one no longer goes from one point to another, but rather holds space beginning from any point: instead of striating space, one occupies it with a vector of deterritorialization in perpetual motion. This modern strategy was communicated from the sea to the air, as the new smooth space, but also to the entire Earth considered as desert or sea. As converter and capturer, the State does not just relativize movement, it reimparts absolute movement. It does not just go from the smooth to the striated, it reconstitutes smooth space; it reimparts smooth in the wake of the striated. It is true that this new nomadism accompanies a worldwide war machine whose organization exceeds the State apparatuses and passes into energy, military-industrial, and multinational complexes. We say this as a reminder that smooth space and the form of exteriority do not have an irresistible revolutionary calling but change meaning drastically depending on the interactions they are part of and the concrete conditions of their exercise or establishment (for example, the way in which total war and popular war, and even guerrilla warfare, borrow one another's methods).[31]

PROPOSITION VI. *Nomad existence necessarily implies the numerical elements of a war machine.*

Tens, hundreds, thousands, myriads: all armies retain these decimal groupings, to the point that each time they are encountered it is safe to assume the presence of a military organization. Is this not the way an army deterritorializes its soldiers? An army is composed of units, companies, and divisions. The Numbers may vary in function, in combination; they may enter into entirely different strategies; but there is always a connection between the Number and the war machine. It is a question not of quantity but of organization or composition. When the State creates armies, it always applies this principle of numerical organization; but all it does is adopt the principle, at the same time as it appropriates the war machine. For so peculiar an idea – the numerical organization of people – came from the nomads. It was the Hyksos, conquering nomads, who brought it to Egypt; and when Moses applied it to his people in exodus, it was on the advice of his nomad father-in-law, Jethro the Kenite, and was done in such a way as to constitute a war machine, the elements of which are described in the biblical book of Numbers. The *nomos* is fundamentally numerical, arithmetic. When Greek geometrism is contrasted with Indo-Arab arithmetism, it becomes clear that the latter implies a nomos opposable to the logos: not that the nomads "do" arithmetic or algebra, but because arithmetic and algebra arise in a strongly nomad influenced world.

Up to now we have known three major types of human organization: *lineal, territorial*, and *numerical*. Lineal organization allows us to define so-called primitive societies. Clan lineages are essentially segments in action; they meld and divide, and vary according to the ancestor considered, the tasks, and the circumstances. Of course, number plays an important role in the determination of lineage, or in the creation of new lineages – as does the earth, since a clan segmentarity is doubled by a tribal segmentarity. The earth is before all else the matter upon which the dynamic of lineages is inscribed, and the number, a means of inscription: the lineages write upon the earth and with the number, constituting a kind of "geodesy." Everything changes with State societies: it is often said that the territorial principle becomes dominant. One could also speak of deterritorialization, since the earth becomes an object, instead of being an active material element in combination with lineage. Property is precisely the deterritorialized relation between the human being and the earth; this is so whether property constitutes a good belonging to the State, superposed upon continuing possession by a lineal community, or whether it itself becomes a good belonging to private individuals constituting a new community. In both cases (and according to the two poles of the State), something like an overcoding of the earth replaces geodesy. Of course, lineages remain very important, and numbers take on their own importance. But what moves to the forefront is a "territorial" organization, in the sense that all the segments, whether of lineage, land, or number, are taken up by *an astronomical space or a geometrical extension* that overcodes them – but certainly not in the same way in the archaic imperial State and in modern States. The archaic State envelops a *spatium* with a summit, a differentiated space with depth and levels, whereas modern States (beginning with the Greek city-state) develop a homogeneous *extensio* with an immanent center, divisible homologous parts, and symmetrical and reversible relations. Not only do the two models, the astronomical and the geometrical, enter into intimate mixes, but even when they are supposedly pure, both imply the subordination of lineages and numbers to this metric power, as it appears either in the *imperial spatium*[xxix] or in the *political extensio*.[32] Arithmetic, the number, has always had a decisive role in the State apparatus: this is so even as early as the imperial bureaucracy, with the three conjoined operations of the census, taxation, and election. It is even truer of modern forms of the State, which in developing utilized all the calculation techniques that were springing up at the border between mathematical science and social technology (there is a whole social calculus at the basis of political economy, demography, the organization of work, etc.). This arithmetic element of the State found its specific power in the treatment of all kinds of matter: primary matters (raw materials), the secondary matter of wrought objects, or the ultimate matter constituted by the human population. Thus the number has always served to gain mastery over matter, to control its variations and movements, in other words, to submit them to the spatiotemporal framework of the State – either the imperial *spatium*, or the modern *extensio*.[33] The State has a territorial principle, or a principle of deterritoriali-

zation, that links the number to metric magnitudes (taking into account the increasingly complex metrics effecting the overcoding). We do not believe that the conditions of independence or autonomy of the Number are to be found in the State, even though all the factors of its development are present. . . .

PROPOSITION IX. *War does not necessarily have the battle as its object, and more important, the war machine does not necessarily have war as its object, although war and the battle may be its necessary result (under certain conditions).*

We now come to three successive problems. First, is the battle the "object" of war? But also, is war the "object" of the war machine? And finally, to what extent is the war machine the "object" of the State apparatus? The ambiguity of the first two problems is certainly due to the term "object," but implies their dependency on the third. We must nevertheless approach these problems gradually, even if we are reduced to multiplying examples. The first question, that of the battle, requires an immediate distinction to be made between two cases: when a battle is sought, and when it is essentially avoided by the war machine. These two cases in no way coincide with the offensive and the defensive. But war in the strict sense (according to a conception of it that culminated in Foch)[xxx] does seem to have the battle as its object, whereas guerrilla warfare explicitly aims for the *nonbattle*. However, the development of war into the war of movement, and into total war, also places the notion of the battle in question, as much from the offensive as the defensive points of view: the concept of the nonbattle seems capable of expressing the speed of a flash attack, and the counterspeed of an immediate response.[34] Conversely, the development of guerrilla warfare implies a moment when, and forms under which, a battle must be effectively sought, in connection with exterior and interior "support points." And it is true that guerrilla warfare and war proper are constantly borrowing each other's methods and that the borrowings run equally in both directions (for example, stress has often been laid on the inspirations land-based guerrilla warfare received from maritime war). All we can say is that the battle and the nonbattle are the double object of war, according to a criterion that

---

[xxix] Space versus extension (*extensio*), the later being Descartes' name for the essence of matter.

[xxx] Ferdinand Foch (1851–1929), commander of all Allied forces in France during World War I.

does not coincide with the offensive and the defensive, or even with war proper and guerrilla warfare.

That is why we push the question further back, asking if war itself is the object of the war machine. It is not at all obvious. To the extent that war (with or without the battle) aims for the annihilation or capitulation of enemy forces, the war machine does not necessarily have war as its object (for example, the *raid* can be seen as another object, rather than as a particular form of war). But more generally, we have seen that the war machine was the invention of the nomad, because it is in its essence the constitutive element of smooth space, the occupation of this space, displacement within this space, and the corresponding composition of people: this is its sole and veritable positive object (*nomos*). Make the desert, the steppe, grow; do not depopulate it, quite the contrary. If war necessarily results, it is because the war machine collides with States and cities, as forces (of striation) opposing its positive object: from then on, the war machine has as its enemy the State, the city, the state and urban phenomenon, and adopts as its objective their annihilation. It is at this point that the war machine becomes war: annihilate the forces of the State, destroy the State-form. The Attila,[xxxi] or Genghis Khan, adventure clearly illustrates this progression from the positive object to the negative object. Speaking like Aristotle, we would say that war is neither the condition nor the object of the war machine, but necessarily accompanies or completes it; speaking like Derrida, we would say that war is the "supplement" of the war machine. It may even happen that this supplementarity is comprehended through a progressive, anxiety-ridden revelation. Such, for example, was the adventure of Moses: leaving the Egyptian State behind, launching into the desert, he begins by forming a war machine, on the inspiration of the old past of the nomadic Hebrews and on the advice of his father-in-law, who came from the nomads. This is the machine of the Just, already a war machine, but one that does not yet have war as its object. Moses realizes, little by little, in stages, that war is the necessary supplement of that machine, because it encounters or must cross cities and States, because it must send ahead spies (*armed observation*), then perhaps take things to extremes (*war of annihilation*). Then the Jewish people experience doubt, and fear that they are not strong enough; but Moses also doubts, he shrinks before the revelation of this supplement.

And it will be Joshua, not Moses, who is charged with waging war.[xxxii] Finally, speaking like Kant, we would say that the relation between war and the war machine is necessary but "synthetic" (Yahweh is necessary for the synthesis).[xxxiii]

The question of war, in turn, is pushed further back and is subordinated to the relations between the war machine and the State apparatus. States were not the first to make war: war, of course, is not a phenomenon one finds in the universality of Nature, as nonspecific violence. But war is not the object of States, quite the contrary. The most archaic States do not even seem to have had a war machine, and their domination, as we will see, was based on other agencies (comprising, rather, the police and prisons). It is safe to assume that the intervention of an extrinsic or nomad war machine that counterattacked and destroyed the archaic but powerful States was one of the mysterious reasons for their sudden annihilation. But the State learns fast. One of the biggest questions from the point of view of universal history is: How will the State *appropriate* the war machine, that is, constitute one for itself, in conformity with its size, its domination, and its aims? And with what risks? (What we call a military institution, or army, is not at all the war machine in itself, but the form under which it is appropriated by the State.) In order to grasp the paradoxical character of such an undertaking, we must recapitulate the hypothesis in its entirety. (1) The war machine is that nomad invention that in fact has war not as its primary object but as its second-order, supplementary or synthetic objective, in the sense that it is determined in such a way as to destroy the State-form and city-form with which it collides. (2) When the State appropriates the war machine, the latter obviously changes in nature and function, since it is afterward directed against the nomad and all State destroyers, or else expresses relations between States, to the extent that a State undertakes exclusively to destroy another State or impose its aims upon it. (3) It is precisely after the war machine has been appropriated by the State in this way that it tends to take war for its direct and primary object, for its "analytic" object (and that war tends to take the battle for its object). In short, it is at one and the same time that the State apparatus appropriates a war machine,

---

[xxxi] Attila (406–53AD), King of the Huns.

[xxxii] After Moses led the Hebrews in Exodus from Egypt, Joshua led them to Canaan.

[xxxiii] That is, war is *not* logically implicit in the war machine.

that the war machine takes war as its object and that war becomes subordinated to the aims of the State....

The question is therefore less the realization of war than the appropriation of the war machine. It is at the same time that the State apparatus *appropriates* the war machine, subordinates it to its "political" *aims*, and gives it war as its direct *object*. And it is one and the same historical tendency that causes State to evolve from a triple point of view: going from figures of encastment to forms of appropriation proper, going from limited war to so-called total war, and transforming the relation between aim and object. The factors that make State war total war are closely connected to capitalism: it has to do with the investment of constant capital in equipment, industry, and the war economy, and the investment of variable capital in the population in its physical and mental aspects (both as war-maker and as victim of war).[35] Total war is not only a war of annihilation but arises when annihilation takes as its "center" not only the enemy army, or the enemy State, but the entire population and its economy. The fact that this double investment can be made only under prior conditions of limited war illustrates the irresistible character of the capitalist tendency to develop total war.[36] It is therefore true that total war remains subordinated to State political aims and merely realizes the *maximal conditions* of the appropriation of the war machine by the State apparatus. But it is also true that when total war becomes the object of the appropriated war machine, then at this level in the set of all possible conditions, the object and the aim enter into new relations that can reach the point of contradiction. This explains Clausewitz's vacillation when he asserts at one point that total war remains a war conditioned by the political aim of States, and at another that it tends to effectuate the Idea of unconditioned war. In effect, the aim remains essentially political and determined as such by the State, but the object itself has become unlimited. We could say that the appropriation has changed direction, or rather that States tend to unleash, reconstitute, an immense war machine of which they are no longer anything more than the opposable or apposed parts. This worldwide war machine, which in a way "reissues" from the States, displays two successive figures: first, that of fascism, which makes war an unlimited movement with no other aim than itself; but fascism is only a rough sketch, and the second, postfascist, figure is that of a war machine that takes peace as its object

directly, as the peace of Terror or Survival. The war machine reforms a smooth space that now claims to control, to surround the entire earth. Total war itself is surpassed, toward a form of peace more terrifying still. The war machine has taken charge of the aim, worldwide order, and the States are now no more than objects or means adapted to that machine. This is the point at which Clausewitz's formula is effectively reversed; to be entitled to say that politics is the continuation of war by other means, it is not enough to invert the order of the words as if they could be spoken in either direction; it is necessary to follow the real movement at the conclusion of which the States, having appropriated a war machine, and having adapted it to their aims, reimpart a war machine that takes charge of the aim, appropriates the States, and assumes increasingly wider political functions.[37]

Doubtless, the present situation is highly discouraging. We have watched the war machine grow stronger and stronger, as in a science fiction story; we have seen it assign as its objective a peace still more terrifying than fascist death; we have seen it maintain or instigate the most terrible of local wars as parts of itself; we have seen it set its sights on a new type of enemy, no longer another State, or even another regime, but the "unspecified enemy"; we have seen it put its counterguerrilla elements into place, so that it can be caught by surprise once, but not twice. Yet the very conditions that make the State or World war machine possible, in other words, constant capital (resources and equipment) and human variable capital, continually recreate unexpected possibilities for counterattack, unforeseen initiatives determining revolutionary, popular, minority, mutant machines. The definition of the Unspecified Enemy testifies to this: "multiform, maneuvering and omnipresent...of the moral, political, subversive or economic order, etc.," the unassignable material Saboteur or human Deserter assuming the most diverse forms.[38] The first theoretical element of importance is the fact that the war machine has many varied meanings, and this is *precisely because the war machine has an extremely variable relation to war itself*. The war machine is not uniformly defined, and comprises something other than increasing quantities of force. We have tried to define two poles of the war machine: *at one pole*, it takes war for its object and forms a line of destruction prolongable to the limits of the universe. But in all of the shapes it assumes here – limited war, total war, worldwide organization –

war represents not at all the supposed essence of the war machine but only, whatever the machine's power, either the set of conditions under which the States appropriate the machine, even going so far as to project it as the horizon of the world, or the dominant order of which the States themselves are now only parts. *The other pole* seemed to be the essence: it is when the war machine, with infinitely lower "quantities," has as its object not war but the drawing of a creative line of flight, the composition of a smooth space and of the movement of people in that space. At this other pole, the machine does indeed encounter war, but as its supplementary or synthetic object, now directed against the State and against the worldwide axiomatic expressed by States.

We thought it possible to assign the invention of the war machine to the nomads. This was done only in the historical interest of demonstrating that the war machine as such was invented, even if it displayed from the beginning all of the ambiguity that caused it to enter into composition with the other pole, and swing toward it from the start. However, in conformity with the essence, the nomads do not hold the secret: an "ideological," scientific, or artistic movement can be a potential war machine, to the precise extent to which it draws, in relation to a *phylum*,[xxiv] a plane of consistency, a creative line of flight, a smooth space of

displacement. It is not the nomad who defines this constellation of characteristics; it is this constellation that defines the nomad, and at the same time the essence of the war machine. If guerrilla warfare, minority warfare, revolutionary and popular war are in conformity with the essence, it is because they take war as an object all the more necessary for being merely "supplementary": *they can make war only on the condition that they simultaneously create something else,* if only new nonorganic social relations. The difference between the two poles is great, even, and especially, from the point of view of death: the line of flight that creates, *or* turns into a line of destruction; the plane of consistency that constitutes itself, even piece by piece, *or* turns into a plan(e) of organization and domination. We are constantly reminded that there is communication between these two lines or planes, that each takes nourishment from the other, borrows from the other: the worst of the world war machines reconstitutes a smooth space to surround and enclose the earth. But the earth asserts its own powers of deterritorialization, its lines of flight, its smooth spaces that live and blaze their way for a new earth. The question is not one of quantities but of the incommensurable character of the quantities that confront one another in the two kinds of war machine, according to the two poles. War machines take shape against the apparatuses that appropriate the machine and make war their affair and their object: they bring connections to bear against the great conjunction of the apparatuses of capture or domination.

[xxxiv] Usually a biological classification, etymologically a tribe or race, here understood as a biological plateau.

Authors' Notes

1 Georges Dumézil, *Mitra-Varuna* (Paris: Gallimard, 1947). On *nexum* and *mutuum*, the bond and the contract, see pp. 118–124.

2 "The first pole of the State (Varuna, Uranus, Romulus) operates by magic bond, seizure, or immediate capture: it does not wage battles, and has no war machine, it binds, and that is all." Its other pole (Mitra, Zeus, Numa) appropriates an army but imposes upon it juridical and institutional rules that become nothing more than a piece in the State apparatus: thus Mars-Tiwaz is not a warrior god, but a god who is a "jurist of war." See Dumézil, *Mitra-Varuna*, pp. 113ff., 148ff., 202ff.

3 Dumézil, *The Destiny of the Warrior*, trans. Alf Hiltebeital (Chicago: University of Chicago Press, 1970).

4 For the role of the warrior as one who "unties" and opposes both the magic bond and the juridical contract, see Dumézil, *Mitra-Varuna*, pp. 124–32. See also the analysis of *furor* in the works of Dumézil.

5 Luc de Heusch emphasizes the public nature of Nkongolo's actions, in contrast to the secrecy of the actions of Mbidi and his son; in particular, the former eats in public, whereas the others hide during their meals. Later, we will see the essential relation of the war machine with the secret, which is as much a matter of principle as a result: espionage, strategy, diplomacy. Commentators have often underlined this link. *Le roi ivre ou l'origine de l'État* (Paris: Gallimard, 1972).

6 For an analysis of the three sins in the cases of the Indian god Indra, the Scandinavian hero Starcatherus,

and the Greek god Hercules, see Dumézil, *Mythe et épopée*, vol. 2, pp. 17–19 (Paris: Gallimard, 1971). See also Dumézil, *The Destiny of the Warrior*.

7   Dumézil, *Mitra-Varuna*, p. 135. Dumézil analyzes the dangers and causes of the confusion, which could be due to economic variables. See pp. 153, 159.

8   Michel Serres, *La naissance de la physique dans le texte de Lucrèce. Fleuves et turbulences* (Paris: Minuit, 1977). Serres was the first to make the first three points given in the text; the fourth seems to follow from them.

9   This is the distinction Pierre Boulez makes between two kinds of space-time in music: in striated space, the measure can be irregular or regular, but it is always assignable; in smooth space, the partition, or break, "can be effected at will." *Boulez on Music Today*, trans. Susan Bradshaw and Richard Bennett (Cambridge, Mass.: Harvard University Press, 1971), p. 85.

10 Greek geometry is thoroughly marked by the opposition between these two poles, the theorematic and problematic, and by the relative triumph of the former: in his *Commentary of the First Book of Euclid's Elements*, trans. and intro. Glenn R. Murrow (Princeton, N.J.: Princeton University Press, 1970), Proclus analyzes the difference between the poles, taking the Speusippus-Menaechmus opposition as an example. Mathematics has always been marked by this tension also; for example, the axiomatic element has confronted a problematic, "intuitionist," or "constructivist" current emphasizing a calculus of problems very different from axiomatics, or any theorematic approach. See Georges Bouligand, *Le déclin des absolus mathématico-logiques* (Paris: Ed. d'Enseignement Supérieur, 1949).

11 Paul Virilio, *L'insécurité du territoire* (Paris: Stock, 1975), p. 120: "We know that the youth of geometry, geometry as free, creative investigation, came to an end with Archimedes . . . . The sword of a Roman soldier cut the thread, tradition says. In killing geometrical creation, the Roman State lay the foundation for the geometrical imperialism of the West."

12 See Ibn Khaldūn, *The Muqaddimah: An Introduction to History*, trans. Franz Rosenthal (Princeton, N.J.: Princeton University Press, 1967). One of the essential themes of this masterpiece is the sociological problem of the esprit de corps, and its ambiguity. Ibn Khaldūn contrasts bedouinism (the bedouin lifestyle, not the ethnic group) with sedentary or city living. The first aspect of this opposition is the inverted relation between the public and the secret: not only is there a secrecy of the bedouin war machine, as opposed to the publicity of the State city dweller, but in the first case "eminence" is based on a secret solidarity, while in the second case the secret is subordinated to the demands of social eminence. Second, bedouinism brings into play both a great purity and a great mobility of the lineages and their genealogy, whereas city life makes for lineages that are very impure, and at the same time rigid and fixed: Solidarity has a different meaning at either pole. Third, and this is the main point, bedouin lineages mobilize an esprit de corps and integrate into it, as a new dimension: this is *asabîyah*, or *ikhtilât*, from which the Arabic word for socialism is derived (Ibn Khaldūn stresses the absence of any "power" residing in the tribal chief, who has no State constraints at his disposal). On the other hand, in city living the esprit de corps becomes a dimension of power and is adapted for "autocracy."

13 In *Timaeus*, 28–9, Plato entertains for an instant the thought that Becoming is not simply the inevitable characteristic of copies or reproductions, but could itself be a model rivaling the Identical and the Uniform. He states this hypothesis only in order to reject it; for it is true that if becoming is a model, not only must the duality of the model and the copy, of the model and reproduction, disappear, but the very notions of model and reproduction tend to lose all meaning.

14 The situation is in fact more complex than that, and gravity is not the only feature of the dominant model: there is heat in addition to gravity (already in chemistry, combustion is coupled with weight). Even so, the problem was to know to what extent the "thermal field" deviated from gravitational space, or on the contrary was integrated with it. Monge is a typical example; he began by grouping heat, light, and electricity as "variable affections of bodies," the concern of "specific physics," while general physics would deal with extension, gravity, and movement. It was only later that Monge unified all of the fields under general physics (Anne Querrien)

15 Anny Milovanoff, "La seconde peau du nomade," *Nouvelles littéraires*, no. 2646 (July 27, 1978), p. 18: "The Larbaâ nomads, on the border of the Algerian Sahara, use the word *trigâ*, which generally means road or way, to designate the woven straps serving to reinforce the cords holding the tent to the stakes . . . . In nomad thought, the dwelling is tied not to a territory but rather to an itinerary. Refusing to take possession of the land they cross, the nomads construct an environment out of wool and goat hair, one that leaves no mark at the temporary site it occupies . . . . Thus wool, a soft material, gives nomad life its unity . . . . Nomads pause at the representation of their journeys, not at a figuration of the space they cross. They leave space to space . . . . Woolly polymorphism."

16 See W. Montgomery Watt, *Mohammed at Medina* (London: Oxford University Press, 1956), pp. 85–6, 242.

17 Emmanuel Laroche, *Histoire de la racine "Nem" en grec ancien* (Paris: Klincksieck, 1949). The root "Nem" indicates distribution, not allocation, even when the two are linked. In the pastoral sense, the

distribution of animals is effected in a nonlimited space and implies no parceling out of land: "The occupation of shepherd, in the Homeric age, had nothing to do with a parceling of land: when the agrarian question came to the foreground, in the time of Solon, it was expressed in an entirely different vocabulary." *To take to pasture* (nemô) refers not to a parceling out but to a scattering, to a repartition of animals. It was only after Solon that Nomos came to designate the principle at the basis of the laws and of right (Thesmoï and Dikè), and then came to be identified with the laws themselves. Prior to that, there was instead an alternative between the city, or polis, ruled by laws, and the outskirts as the place of the nomos. A similar alternative is found in the work of Ibn Khaldūn: between *hadara* as city living, and *badiya* as nomos (not the town, but the preurban countryside, the plateau, steppe, mountain, or desert).

18 Arnold Toynbee, *A Study of History* (New York: Oxford University Press, 1947), abridged by D. C. Somervell, vol. 1, pp. 164–86: "They flung themselves upon the Steppe, not to escape beyond its bounds but to make themselves at home on it" (p. 168).

19 See Pierre Hubac, *Les nomades* (Paris: La Renaissance du Livre, 1948), pp. 26–9 (although Hubac tends to confuse nomads and migrants).

20 On the nomads of the sea, or of the archipelago, José Emperaire writes: "They do not grasp an itinerary as a whole, but in a fragmentary manner, by juxtaposing in order its various successive stages, from campsite to campsite in the course of the journey. For each of these stages, they estimate the length of the crossing and the successive changes in direction marking it." *Les nomades de la mer* (Paris: Gallimard, 1954), p. 225.

21 Wilfred Thesiger, *Arabian Sands* (London: Longman, Green, 1959), pp. 112–13, 125, 165–6.

22 See the two admirable descriptions, of the sand desert by Wilfred Thesiger and of the ice desert by Edmund Carpenter, in *Eskimo* (Toronto: University of Toronto Press, 1964): the winds, and tactile and sound qualities; the secondary character of visual data, particularly the indifference of the nomads to astronomy as a royal science; and yet the presence of a whole minor science of qualitative variables and traces.

23 Emile Félix Gautier, *Le passé de l'Afrique du Nord* (Paris: Payot, 1952), pp. 267–316.

24 From this perspective, Clastres's analysis of Indian prophetism can be generalized: "On one side, the chiefs, on the other, and standing against them, the prophets.... And the prophetic machine worked perfectly well since the *karai* were able to sweep astonishing masses of Indians along behind them.... the insurrectional act of the prophets against the chiefs conferred on the former, through

a strange reversal of things, infinitely more power than was held by the latter." *Society against the State*, pp. 184–5.

25 One of the most interesting themes of the classic work by Paul Alphandéry (*La chrétienté et l'idée de croisade* [Paris: Albin Michel, 1959] is his demonstration that the changes in course, the pauses, the detours were an integral part of the Crusade: "this army of crusaders that we envision as a modern army, like those of Louis XIV or Napoleon, marching with absolute passivity, obeying the will of a diplomatic officer and staff. Such an army knows where it is going, and when it makes a mistake, it is not for lack of reflection. A history more attentive to differences accepts a more realistic image of the army of the Crusade. The army of the Crusade was freely, sometimes anarchically alive.... This army was motivated from within, as a function of a complex coherence by virtue of which nothing happened by chance. It is certain that the conquest of Constantinople had its reason, necessity and a religious character, like the other deeds of the Crusades" (vol. 2, p. 7). Alphandéry shows in particular that the idea of a battle against the Infidel, *at any point*, appeared early on, along with the idea of liberating the Holy Land (vol. 1, p. 219).

26 Modern historians have been inspired to fine analyses by this confrontation between the East and the West, which began in the Middle Ages (and is tied to the question, Why did capitalism develop in the West and not elsewhere?). See especially Fernand Braudel, *Capitalism and Material Life, 1400–1800*, trans. Miriam Kochan (New York: Harper and Row, 1967), pp. 97–108; Pierre Chaunu, *L'expansion européenne du XIIIe au XVe siècle* (Paris: PUF, 1969), pp. 334–9 ("Why Europe? Why not China?"); Maurice Lombard, *Espaces et réseaux du haut Moyen Age* (The Hague: Mouton, 1971), chapter 8 (and p. 219: "What is called deforestation in the East is named clearing in the West. The first deep cause of the shift of the dominant centers from the East to the West is therefore a geographical reason: forest-clearing proved to have more potential than desert-oasis").

27 Marx's observations on the despotic formations of Asia have been confirmed by the African analyses of Max Gluckman, *Custom and Conflict in Africa* (Glencoe, Ill.: Free Press, 1959): at the same time immutability of form and constant rebellion. The idea of a "transformation" of the State indeed seems to be a Western one. And that other idea, the "destruction" of the State, belongs much more to the East and to the conditions of a nomad war machine. Attempts have been made to present the two ideas as successive phases of revolution, but there are too many differences between them and they are difficult to reconcile; they reflect the opposition between the socialist and anarchist currents of the nineteenth century.

The Western proletariat itself is perceived from two points of view: as having to seize power and transform the State apparatus (the point of view of labor power), and as willing or wishing for the destruction of the State (this time, the point of view of nomadization power). Even Marx defines the proletariat not only as alienated (labor) but as deterritorialized. The proletariat, in this second perspective, appears as the heir to the nomad in the Western world. Not only did many anarchists invoke nomadic themes originating in the East, but the bourgeoisie above all were quick to equate proletarians and nomads, comparing Paris to a city haunted by nomads (see Louis Chevalier, *Laboring Classes and Dangerous Classes in Paris during the First Half of the Nineteenth Century*, trans. Frank Jellenck [New York: H. Fertig, 1973], pp. 362–6).

28 See Lucien Musset, *Les invasions. Le second assaut* (Paris: PUF, 1965), for example, the analysis of the Danes' three "phases," pp. 135–7.

29 Paul Virilio, *Speed and Politics*, trans. Mark Polizzotti (New York: Semiotext[e], 1986), pp. 12–13 and *passim*. Not only is the "town" unthinkable apart from the exterior flows with which it is in contact, and the circulation of which it regulates, but specific architectural aggregates, the fortress, for example, are veritable transformers, by virtue of their interior spaces, which allow an analysis, prolongation, or restitution of movement. Virilio concludes that the issue is less confinement than the management of the public ways, or the control of movement. Foucault was already moving in this direction with his analysis of the *naval hospital* as operator and filter; see *Discipline and Punish*, trans. A. M. Sheridan Smith (New York: Vintage, 1975), pp. 143–6.

30 On Chinese, and Arab, navigation, the reasons behind their failure, and the importance of this question in the East-West "dossier," see Braudel, *Capitalism and Material Life*, pp. 300–9, and Chaunu, *L'expansion européenne*, pp. 145–7.

31 Virilio gives a very good definition of the fleet in being and its historical consequences: "The fleet in being ... is the permanent presence in the sea of an invisible fleet able to strike no matter where and no matter when ... it is a new idea of violence that no longer comes from direct confrontation ... but rather from the unequal properties of bodies, evaluation of the number of movements allowed them in a chosen element, permanent verification of their dynamic efficiency.... Henceforth it is no longer a question of crossing a continent or an ocean from one city to the next, one shore to the next. The fleet in being creates ... the notion of displacement without destination in space and time.... The strategic submarine has no need to go anywhere in particular; it is content, while controlling the sea, to remain invisible ... the realization of the absolute, uninterrupted, circular voyage, since it involves neither departure nor arrival.... If, as Lenin claimed, 'strategy means

choosing which points we apply force to,' we must admit that these 'points', today, are no longer geostrategic strongpoints, since from any given spot we can now reach any other, no matter where it might be ... *geographic localization* seems to have definitively lost its strategic value, and, inversely, that this same value is attributed to the *delocalization of the vector*, of a vector in permanent movement"; *Speed and Politics*, pp. 38, 40–1, 134–5. Virilio's texts are of great importance and originality in every respect. The only point that presents a difficulty for us is his assimilation of three groups of speed that seem very different to us: (1) speeds of nomadic, or revolutionary, tendency (riot, guerrilla warfare); (2) speeds that are regulated, converted, appropriated by the State apparatus (management of the public ways); (3) speeds that are reinstated by a worldwide organization of total war, or planetary overarmament (from the fleet in being to nuclear strategy). Virilio tends to equate these groups on account of their interactions and makes a general case for the "fascist" character of speed. It is, nevertheless, his own analyses that make these distinctions possible.

32 Jean-Pierre Vernant in particular has analyzed the connection between the Greek city-state and a homogeneous geometrical extension, *Mythe et pensée chez les Grecs* (Paris: Maspero, 1971–4), vol. 1, part 3. The problem is necessarily more complicated in relation to the archaic empires, or in relation to formations subsequent to the classical city-state. That is because the space in question is very different. But it is still the case that the number is sub-ordinated to space, as Vernant suggests with regard to Plato's ideal state. The Pythagorean or Neoplatonic conceptions of number envelop imperial astronomical spaces of a type other than homogeneous extension, but they maintain the subordination of the number; that is why Numbers become *ideal*, but not strictly speaking "numbering."

33 Dumézil stresses the role played by the arithmetic element in the earliest forms of political sovereignty. He even tends to make it a third pole of sovereignty. See *Servius et la Fortune* and *Le troisième souverain* (Paris: Maisonneuve, 1949). But the role of this arithmetic element is, rather, to organize a matter; in so doing it submits that matter to one or the other of the two principal poles.

34 The texts of T. E. Lawrence, *Seven Pillars of Wisdom* (New York: Doubleday, Doran, 1935) and "The Science of Guerrilla War," in *Encyclopedia Britannica*, 14th ed. (1929), vol. 10, pp. 950–3, remain among the most significant works on guerrilla warfare; they present themselves as an "anti-Foch" theory and elaborate the notion of the nonbattle. But the nonbattle has a history that is not entirely dependent on guerrilla warfare: (1) the traditional distinction between the "battle" and the "maneuver"

in war; see Raymon Aron, *Penser la guerre. Clausewitz* (Paris: Gallimard, 1976), vol. 1, pp. 122–31; (2) the way in which the war of movement places the role and importance of the battle in question (as early as Marshal de Saxe, and the controversial question of the battle during the Napoleonic Wars); (3) finally, more recently, the critique of the battle in the name of nuclear arms, which play a deterrent role, with conventional forces now having a role only in "testing" or "maneuver"; see the Gaullist conception of the nonbattle, and Guy Brossollet, *Essai sur la non-bataille* (Paris: Belin, 1975). The recent return to the notion of the battle cannot be explained simply by technological factors such as the development of tactical nuclear arms, but implies political considerations – it is upon these that the role assigned to the battle (or nonbattle) in war depends.

35 Erich Ludendorff, *Der totale Krieg* (Munich: Ludendorff Verlag, 1935), notes that the evolution has been toward attributing more and more importance to the "people" and "domestic policies" in war, whereas Clausewitz still puts the emphasis on armies and foreign policy. This criticism is true overall, despite certain texts of Clausewitz. The same criticism is also made by Lenin and the Marxists (although they obviously have a totally different conception of the people and domestic policy than Ludendorff). Certain authors have convincingly demonstrated that the proletariat is as much of military origin, naval in particular, as of industrial origin; see, for example, Virilio, *Speed and Politics*, pp. 38, 40–1, 134–5.

36 As John Ulric Nef shows, it was during the great period of "limited war" (1640–1740) that the phenomena of concentration, accumulation, and investment emerged – the same phenomena that were later to determine "total war." See *War and Human Progress* (New York: Norton, 1968). The Napoleonic code of war represents a turning point that brought together the elements of total war: mobilization, transport, investment, information, etc.

37 On this "transcending" of fascism, and of total war, and on the new point of inversion of Clausewitz's formula, see Virilio's entire analysis in *L'insécurité du territoire*, especially chapter 1.

38 Guy Brossollet, *Essai sur la non-bataille*, pp. 15–16. The axiomatic notion of the "unspecified enemy" is already well developed in official and unofficial texts on national defense, on international law, and in the judicial or police spheres.

Critical Appropriations

32

"A Genealogy of Modern Racism"

Cornel West

The prolific and politically active Cornel West (1953–) is one of a growing number of contributors to American philosophy from an African-American perspective. Heir both to a leftist or "Tolstoyan" Christian heritage and to the classical American philosophical tradition, West has plied a "prophetic pragmatism" oriented toward social and political change, in contrast to Rorty's pragmatic "postmodernist bourgeois liberalism," which largely defends the political–economic *status quo* (albeit ironically). In the following essay from his first book, West employs a Foucauldian analysis to shed light on the racism embedded in modern Western thought. With others in this section, he parts company with postmodernism when it seems to eviscerate revisionary ideals and the potential for social critique.

The notion that black people are human beings is a relatively new discovery in the modern West. The idea of black equality in beauty, culture, and intellectual capacity remains problematic and controversial within prestigious halls of learning and sophisticated intellectual circles. The Afro-American encounter with the modern world has been shaped first and foremost by the doctrine of white supremacy, which is embodied in institutional practices and enacted in everyday folkways under varying circumstances and evolving conditions.[1]

My aim in this chapter is to give a brief account of the way in which the idea of white supremacy was constituted as an object of modern discourse in the West, without simply appealing to the objective demands of the prevailing mode of production, the political interests of the slaveholding class, or the psychological needs of the dominant white racial group. Despite the indispensable role these factors would play in a full-blown explanatory model to account for the emergence and sustenance of modern racism in the West, I try to hold these factors constant and focus solely on a neglected variable in past explanatory models – namely, the way in which the very structure of modern discourse *at its inception* produced forms of rationality, scientificity, and objectivity as well as aesthetic and cultural ideals which require the constitution of the idea of white supremacy.

This requirement follows from a logic endemic to the very structure of modern discourse. This logic is manifest in the way in which the controlling metaphors, notions, and categories of modern discourse produce and prohibit, develop and delimit, specific conceptions of truth and knowledge, beauty and character, so that certain ideas are rendered incomprehensible and unintelligible. I suggest that one such idea that cannot be brought within the epistemological field of the initial modern discourse is that of black equality in beauty, culture, and intellectual capacity. This act of discursive exclusion, of relegating this idea to silence, does not simply correspond to (or is not only reflective of) the relative powerlessness of black people at the time. It also reveals the evolving internal dynamics of the structure of modern discourse in the late seventeenth and

Cornel West, "A Genealogy of Modern Racism," chapter four of his *Prophesy Deliverance! An Afro-American Revolutionary Christianity*, Philadelphia: Westminster Press, 1982, pp. 47–65.

eighteenth centuries in western Europe – or during the Enlightenment. The concrete effects of this exclusion and the intellectual traces of this silence continue to haunt the modern West: on the non-discursive level, in ghetto streets, and on the discursive level, in methodological assumptions in the disciplines of the humanities.

I shall argue that the initial structure of modern discourse in the West "secretes" the idea of white supremacy. I call this "secretion" – the underside of modern discourse – a particular logical consequence of the quest for truth and knowledge in the modern West. To put it crudely, my argument is that the authority of science, undergirded by a modern philosophical discourse guided by Greek ocular metaphors and Cartesian notions, promotes and encourages the activities of observing, comparing, measuring, and ordering the physical characteristics of human bodies. Given the renewed appreciation and appropriation of classical antiquity, these activities are regulated by classical aesthetic and cultural norms. The creative fusion of scientific investigation, Cartesian epistemology, and classical ideals produced forms of rationality, scientificity, and objectivity which, though efficacious in the quest for truth and knowledge, prohibited the intelligibility and legitimacy of the idea of black equality in beauty, culture, and intellectual capacity. In fact, to "think" such an idea was to be deemed irrational, barbaric, or mad.

Theoretical Considerations: The Genealogical Approach

I call this inquiry a "genealogy" because, following the works of Friedrich Nietzsche and Michel Foucault, I am interested in the emergence (*Entstehung*) or the "moment of arising" of the idea of white supremacy within the modern discourse in the West.[2] This genealogy tries to address the following questions: What are the discursive conditions for the possibility of the intelligibility and legitimacy of the idea of white supremacy in modern discourse? How is this idea constituted within the epistemological field of modern discourse? What is the complex configuration of metaphors, notions, categories, and norms which produces and promotes such an object of modern discourse?

My genealogical approach subscribes to a conception of power that is neither simply based on individual subjects – e.g., heroes or great personages as in traditional historiography – nor on collective subjects – e.g., groups, elites, or classes as in revisionist and vulgar Marxist historiography. Therefore I do not believe that the emergence of the idea of white supremacy in the modern West can be fully accounted for in terms of the psychological needs of white individuals and groups or the political and economic interests of a ruling class. I will try to show that the idea of white supremacy emerges partly because of the powers within the structure of modern discourse – powers to produce and prohibit, develop and delimit, forms of rationality, scientificity, and objectivity which set perimeters and draw boundaries for the intelligibility, availability, and legitimacy of certain ideas.

These powers are subjectless – that is, they are the indirect products of the praxis of human subjects. They have a life and logic of their own, not in a transhistorical realm but within history alongside yet not reducible to demands of an economic system, interests of a class, or needs of a group. What I am suggesting is not a history without a subject propagated by the structuralist Marxist Louis Althusser,[i] but rather a history made by the praxis of human subjects which often results in complex structures of discourses which have relative autonomy from (or is not fully accountable in terms of) the intentions, aims, needs, interests, and objectives of human subjects.[3]

I am further suggesting that there is no direct correspondence between nondiscursive structures, such as a system of production (or, in Marxist terms, an economic base), and discursive structures, such as theoretical formations (or, in Marxist terms, an ideological superstructure). Rather, there are powers immanent in nondiscursive structures and discursive structures.[4] Traditional, revisionist, and vulgar Marxist types of historiography focus primarily on powers within nondiscursive structures – e.g., powers of kings, presidents, elites, or classes – and reduce the powers within discursive structures to mere means for achieving the intentions, aims, needs, interests, and objectives of subjects in nondiscursive structures. This reductionism is not wrong; it is simply inadequate. It rightly acknowledges noteworthy concrete effects generated by the relationship between powers in discursive structures and those in non-discursive structures, but it wrongly denies the relative autonomy of the powers in discursive structures and hence reduces the complexity of cultural phenomena.

---

[i] Louis Althusser (1918–90) applied structuralism to Marxism.

The primary motivation behind such reductionism (such as personalistic analyses of race prejudice or orthodox Marxist accounts of racism) is to ensure an easy resolution of a highly complex problem, without calling into question certain fundamental assumptions that inform such resolutions. These fundamental assumptions, such as the subject-based conception of power, and easy resolutions, such as the elimination of race prejudice by knowledge or the abolition of racism under socialism, preclude theoretical alternatives and strategic options. In this way, these fundamental assumptions and hypothetical resolutions illustrate the effects of the powers immanent in certain liberal and Marxist discourses.

The Structure of Modern Discourse

I understand "the structure of modern discourse" to be the controlling metaphors, notions, categories, and norms that shape the predominant conceptions of truth and knowledge in the modern West. These metaphors, notions, categories, and norms are circumscribed and determined by three major historical processes: the scientific revolution, the Cartesian transformation of philosophy, and the classical revival.[5]

The scientific revolution is usually associated with the pioneering breakthroughs of Copernicus and Kepler in astronomy, Galileo and Newton in physics, and Descartes and Leibnitz in mathematics. These breakthroughs were pre-Enlightenment, most of them occurring during the seventeenth century, the so-called Age of Genius. The scientific revolution is noteworthy (to say the least) primarily because it signified the authority of science. This authority justified new modes of knowledge and new conceptions of truth and reality; it arose at the end of the era of pagan Christianity and set the framework for the advent of modernity.

The originary figures of the scientific revolution went beyond the Renaissance problematic – of finding a compromise formula which reconciled Christian and classical modes of thinking and living – yet stopped short of drawing thoroughly secular conclusions from their breakthroughs, that is, of waging intellectual war on natural religion and dogmatic theology. Galileo's Platonism and Newton's Socinianism illustrate this peculiar protomodern world view of making peace between science and religion.[6]

For our purposes, the scientific revolution is significant because it highlights two fundamental ideas: *observation* and *evidence*. These two ideas have played, in an isolated manner, a role in previous paradigms of knowledge in the West (since the times of Aristotle and Aristarchus). But the scientific revolution brought these ideas together in such a way that they have become the two foci around which much of modern discourse evolves. The modern concepts of hypothesis, fact, inference, validation, confirmation, and verification cluster around the ideas of observation and evidence.

The major proponents of the scientific revolution, or, more specifically, of the authority of science, were two philosophers, Francis Bacon and René Descartes. Bacon is noteworthy primarily because of his metaphilosophical honesty.[ii] For him, the aim of philosophy was to give humankind mastery over nature by means of scientific discoveries and inventions. He then promoted the philosophical importance of the inductive method as a means of arriving at general laws to facilitate this human mastery. Despite Bacon's acceptance of orthodox religion, his rejection of Copernican theory, and his lack of acquaintance with some of the major scientific discoveries of his time – e.g., the work of Andreas Vesalius on modern anatomy, William Gilbert on magnetism, or William Harvey (Bacon's own medical attendant) on the circulation of blood – Bacon's writings, especially *The Advancement of Learning*, did much to promote the authority of science.[7]

Descartes is highly significant because his thought provided the controlling notions of modern discourse: *the primacy of the subject and the preeminence of representation*. Descartes is widely regarded as the founder of modern philosophy not simply because his philosophical outlook was profoundly affected by the scientific revolution but, more important, because he associated the scientific aim of predicting and explaining the world with the philosophical aim of picturing and representing the world. In this view, the fruits of scientific research do not merely provide more useful ways for human beings to *cope* with reality; such research also yields a true *copy* of reality. Descartes's conception of philosophy as a tortuous move from the subject to objects, from the veil of ideas to the external world, from immediate awareness to extended substances, from self-consciousness to things in space, and ultimately from doubt to certainty was motivated primarily by an attempt to provide a theoretical

---

[ii] Francis Bacon (1561–1626), along with Galileo and Descartes, was one of the great formulators of modern scientific method.

basis for the legitimacy of modern science. Martin Heidegger made this crucial connection between Cartesian philosophy and modern science in his famous essay, "The Age of the World View":

> We are reflecting on the nature of modern science in order to find its metaphysical basis. What conception of the existent and what concept of truth cause science to become research?
>
> Understanding as research holds the existent to account on the question of how and how far it can be put at the disposal of available "representation." Research has the existent at its disposal if it can either calculate it in advance, in its future course, or calculate it afterwards as past. Nature and history become the object of expository representation. . . .
>
> This objectification of the existent takes place in a re-presentation which aims at presenting whatever exists to itself in such a way that the calculating person can be secure, that is, certain of the existent. Science as research is produced when and only when truth has been transformed into such certainty of representation. In the metaphysics of Descartes the existent was defined for the first time as objectivity of representation, and truth as certainty of representation.[8]

Bacon and Descartes had basic differences: Bacon inductive orientation and Descartes the deductive viewpoint; Bacon the empiricist outlook and Descartes the rationalist (mathematical) perspective. Despite these differences, both of these propagandists of modern science agreed that scientific method provides a new paradigm of knowledge and that observation and evidence is at the center of scientific method. In *The New Organon*, Bacon likened his ideal natural philosopher to the bee, which collects "its material from the flowers of the garden and of the field" and digests it "by a power of its own." In his *Discourse on Method*, Descartes set forth as a rule that "observations" become "the more necessary the further we advance in knowledge." And, as D'Alembert acknowledged in *The Encyclopedia*, both Bacon and Descartes "introduced the spirit of experimental science."[9]

The last major historical process that circumscribed and determined the metaphors, notions, categories, and norms of modern discourse was the classical revival. This classical revival – in response to medieval mediocrity and religious dogmatism – was initiated in the Early Renaissance (1300–1500), principally with humanist studies in Roman art and Latin literature, such as Giotto in painting, Petrarch in letters, and Dufay in music. This revival intensified during the High Renaissance (1500–30), with Da Vinci, Raphael, Bramante, and the early Michelangelo in the arts; Ariosto, Rabelais, and Erasmus in literature; and Josquin and Lassus in music. The revival mellowed in the Mannerist era (1530–1600), as illustrated by El Greco, Tintoretto, and the later Michelangelo in the arts; Montaigne, Cervantes, and Shakespeare in literature; and Marenzio, Gabrieli, and Frescobaldi in music. The revival was strengthened in the Baroque period (1600–1750), as seen in the works of Velasquez and Rembrandt in the arts; Racine, Milton, and Vondel in literature; and Bach and Handel in music. The classical revival culminated in the neoclassical movement in the middle of the eighteenth century, with the paintings of David and Ingres, the lyrics of Hölderlin, the tragedies of Alfieri, the verse and prose of Landor, and the music of Haydn and Mozart. The Enlightenment revolt against the authority of the church and the search for models of unrestrained criticism led to a highly charged recovery of classical antiquity, and especially to a new appreciation and appropriation of the artistic and cultural heritage of ancient Greece.

For our purposes, the classical revival is important because it infuses Greek ocular metaphors and classical ideals of beauty, proportion, and moderation into the beginnings of modern discourse. Greek ocular metaphors – Eye of the Mind, Mind as Mirror of Nature, Mind as Inner Arena with its Inner Observer – dominate modern discourse in the West.[10] Coupled with the Cartesian notion of knowledge as inner representation, modern philosophical inquiry is saddled with the epistemological model of intellect (formerly Plato's and Aristotle's Nous, now Descartes's Inner Eye) inspecting entities modeled on retinal images, with the Eye of the Mind viewing representations in order to find some characteristic that would testify to their fidelity.

The creative fusion of scientific investigation, Cartesian philosophy, Greek ocular metaphors, and classical aesthetic and cultural ideals constitutes the essential elements of modern discourse in the West. In short, modern discourse rests upon a conception of truth and knowledge governed by an ideal value-free subject engaged in observing, comparing, ordering, and measuring in order to arrive at evidence sufficient to make valid inferences, confirm speculative hypotheses, deduce error-proof conclusions, and verify true representations of reality.

The Emergence of Modern Racism: The First Stage

The recovery of classical antiquity in the modern West produced what I shall call a "normative gaze," namely, an ideal from which to order and compare observations. This ideal was drawn primarily from classical aesthetic values of beauty, proportion, and human form and classical cultural standards of moderation, self-control, and harmony.[11] The role of classical aesthetic and cultural norms in the emergence of the idea of white supremacy as an object of modern discourse cannot be underestimated.

These norms were consciously projected and promoted by many influential Enlightenment writers, artists, and scholars, of whom the most famous was J. J. Winckelmann.[iii] In his widely read book, *History of Ancient Art*, Winckelmann portrayed ancient Greece as a world of beautiful bodies. He laid down rules – in art and aesthetics – that should govern the size of eyes and eyebrows, of collarbones, hands, feet, and especially noses. He defined beauty as noble simplicity and quiet grandeur. In a celebrated passage he wrote:

> As the depth of the ocean always remains calm however much the surface may be agitated, so does the expression in the figures of the Greeks reveal a great and composed soul in the midst of passions.[12]

Although Winckelmann was murdered in middle life, never set foot in Greece, and saw almost no original Greek art (only one exhibition of Greek art in Munich), he viewed Greek beauty and culture as the ideal or standard against which to measure other peoples and cultures.

Winthrop Jordan and Thomas Gossett have shown that there are noteworthy premodern racist viewpoints aimed directly and indirectly at non-white, especially black, people.[13] For example, in 1520 Paracelsus held that black and primitive peoples had a separate origin from Europeans. In 1591, Giordano Bruno made a similar claim, but had in mind principally Jews and Ethiopians. And

iii   J. J. Winckelmann (1717–68), Prussian archaeologist and historian of art.

Lucilio Vanini posited that Ethiopians had apes for ancestors and had once walked on all fours. Since theories of the separate origin of races were in disagreement with the Roman Catholic Church, Bruno and Vanini underwent similar punishment: both were burned at the stake. Of course, biblically based accounts of racial inferiority flourished, but the authority of the church prohibited the proliferation of nonreligious, that is, protomodern, accounts of racial inferiority.

What is distinctive about the role of classical aesthetic and cultural norms at the advent of modernity is that they provided an acceptable authority for the idea of white supremacy, an acceptable authority that was closely linked with the major authority on truth and knowledge in the modern world, namely, the institution of science. In order to see how this linkage took place, let us examine the categories and aims of the major discipline that promoted this authority, that is, those of natural history.

The principal aim of natural history is to observe, compare, measure, and order animals and human bodies (or classes of animals and human bodies) *based on visible, especially physical, characteristics*. These characteristics permit one to discern identity and difference, equality and inequality, beauty and ugliness among animals and human bodies.

The governing categories of natural history are preeminently *classificatory* categories – that is, they consist of various taxonomies in the form of tables, catalogs, indexes, and inventories which impose some degree of order or representational schema on a broad field of visible characteristics. *Observation* and *differentness* are the essential guiding notions in natural history. Foucault wrote:

> Natural history has as a condition of its possibility the common affinity of things and language with representation; but it exists as a task only in so far as things and language happen to be separate. It must therefore reduce this distance between them so as to bring language as close as possible to the observing gaze, and the things observed as close as possible to words. Natural history is nothing more than the nomination of the visible. . . .
>
> Natural history . . . covers a series of complex operations that introduce the possibility of a constant order into a totality of representations. It constitutes a whole domain of empiricity as at the same time describable and orderable.[14]

The initial basis for the idea of white supremacy is to be found in the classificatory categories and the descriptive, representational, order-imposing aims of natural history. The captivity of natural history to what I have called the "normative gaze" signifies the first stage of the emergence of the idea of white supremacy as an object of modern discourse. More specifically (and as Ashley Montagu has tirelessly argued), the genealogy of racism in the modern West is inseparable from the appearance of the classificatory category of race in natural history.

The category of race – denoting primarily skin color – was first employed as a means of classifying human bodies by François Bernier, a French physician, in 1684. He divided humankind into basically four races: Europeans, Africans, Orientals, and Lapps.[15] The first authoritative racial division of humankind is found in the influential *Natural System* (1735) of the most preeminent naturalist of the eighteenth century, Carolus Linnaeus. For Linnaeus, species were fixed in number and kind; they were immutable prototypes. Varieties, however, were members of a species that might change in appearance. The members of a species produced fertile offspring; interfertility was the test for the division of species. There were variations of kind within a species; the races were a prime example. For Linnaeus, there were four races: Homo Europaeus, Homo Asiaticus, Homo Afer, and Homo Americanus.

Winthrop Jordan has argued that Linnaeus did not subscribe to a hierarchical ranking of races but rather to "one chain of universal being." Jordan states:

It was one thing to classify all living creation and altogether another to arrange it in a single great hierarchy; and when Linnaeus undertook the first of these tasks he was not thereby forced to attempt the latter. In the many editions of the *Systema Naturae* he duly catalogued the various kinds of men, yet never in a hierarchic manner.[16]

Yet it is quite apparent that Linnaeus implicitly evaluated the observable characteristics of the racial classes of people, especially those pertaining to character and disposition. For example, compare Linnaeus' description of the European with the African:

European. White, Sanguine, Brawny. Hair abundantly flowing. Eyes blue. Gentle,

acute, inventive. Covered with close vestments. Governed by customs.

African. Black, Phlegmatic, Relaxed. Hair black, frizzled. Skin silky. Nose flat. Lips tumid. Women's bosom a matter of modesty. Breasts give milk abundantly. Crafty, indolent. Negligent. Anoints himself with grease. Governed by caprice.[17]

Linnaeus' use of evaluative terms revealed, at the least, an implicit hierarchy by means of personal preference. It also is important to note that he included some remarks about the African woman, but that he said nothing about the European woman (nor the American and Asiatic woman). It also is significant that in the 1750s when he first acknowledged that hybridization of species occurs, he chose black people and apes as the probable candidates, while restricting such unions to black women and male apes.

Georges Louis Leclerc de Buffon accepted hybridization without question in his famous *Natural History of Man* (1778). Although Buffon, like Linnaeus, viewed races as mere chance variations, he held that white was "the real and natural color of man." Black people and other races were variations of this natural color, yet somehow not members of a different species. He remained uncertain about the objective reality of species. Buffon believed that black skin was caused by hot climate and would change if the climate became colder. Although he was a fervent antislavery advocate, he claimed that black people had "little genius" and then added, "The unfortunate negroes are endowed with excellent hearts, and possess the seeds of every human virtue."[18]

The Emergence of Modern Racism: The Second Stage

In the works of Johann Friedrich Blumenbach, one of the founders of modern anthropology, the aesthetic criteria and cultural ideals of Greece began to come to the forefront.[iv] Like Linnaeus and Buffon, Blumenbach held that all human beings belonged to the same species and that races were merely varieties. Yet contrary to the claims by Winthrop Jordan, Ashley Montagu, and Thomas Gossett concerning Blumenbach's opposition to hierarchic

---

iv   Johann Blumenbach (1752–1840), German Comparative anatomist.

racial ranking or irritation at those who use aesthetic standards for such ranking, Blumenbach praised the symmetrical face as the most beautiful of human faces precisely because it approximated the "divine" works of Greek art, and specifically the proper anatomical proportions found in Greek sculpture.[19] Applying the classical ideal of moderation, he claimed that the more moderate the climate, the more beautiful the face. The net result was that since black people were farthest from the Greek ideal and located in extremely hot climates, they were, by implication, inferior in beauty to Europeans.

The second stage of the emergence of the idea of white supremacy as an object of modern discourse primarily occurred in the rise of phrenology (the reading of skulls) and physiognomy (the reading of faces). These new disciplines – closely connected with anthropology – served as an open platform for the propagation of the idea of white supremacy not principally because they were pseudosciences, but, more important, because these disciplines acknowledged the European value-laden character of their observations. This European value-laden character was based on classical aesthetic and cultural ideals.

Pieter Camper, the Dutch anatomist, made aesthetic criteria the pillar of his chief discovery: the famous "facial angle." Camper claimed that the "facial angle" – a measure of prognathism – permitted a comparison of heads of human bodies by way of cranial and facial measurements. For Camper, the ideal "facial angle" was a 100-degree angle which was achieved only by the ancient Greeks. He openly admitted that this ideal conformed to Winckelmann's classical ideal of beauty. Following Winckelmann, Camper held that Greek proportions and stature exemplified beauty and embodied perfection. Camper further held that a beautiful face, beautiful body, beautiful nature, beautiful character, and beautiful soul were inseparable. He tried to show that the "facial angle" of Europeans measured about 97 degrees and those of black people between 60 and 70 degrees, closer to the measurements of apes and dogs than to human beings.

Although many anthropologists readily accepted the "facial angle" as a scientific notion,[20] Camper made it clear that his aim was not simply to contribute to the new discipline of anthropology but also to promote the love of classical antiquity to young artists and sculptors. As George Mosse has noted, historians of race theories often overlook the fact that Camper and many subsequent theoreticians of

race and racism were trained as artists and writers. Camper was a painter by training and, in fact, won the gold medal of the Amsterdam School of Art two years before he published his work on the "facial angle."[21]

Johann Kaspar Lavater, the father of physiognomy, explicitly acknowledged that the art of painting was the mother of his new discipline. Moreau, an early editor of Lavater's work, clearly noted that the true language of physiognomy was painting, because it spoke through images, equally to the eye and to the spirit.[22] This new discipline linked particular visible characteristics of human bodies, especially those of the face, to the character and capacities of human beings. This discipline openly articulated what many of the early naturalists and anthropologists tacitly assumed: *the classical ideals of beauty, proportion, and moderation regulated the classifying and ranking of groups of human bodies*. In short, physiognomy brought the "normative gaze" into daylight.

Lavater believed that the Greek statues were the models of beauty. His description of the desirable specimen – blue eyes, horizontal forehead, bent back, round chin, and short brown hair – resembled the beautiful person preferred by Camper. The common Greek ideals of beauty, though slightly distorted (to say the least), were the principal source of this "normative gaze." Lavater's new discipline was highly influential among scientists – for example, Jean Baptiste Porta, Christian Meiners – and artists. His close friend, the famous Goethe, aided him in editing and publishing his physiognomic formulations and findings and Sir Walter Scott, among others, popularized them in his novels.

Lavater's promotion of what I call the "normative gaze" consisted no longer of detailed measurements, as was the case with the naturalists, but rather of the visual glance. He wrote: "Trust your first quick impression, for it is worth more than what is usually called observation."[23] Therefore it is not surprising that Lavater put forth an elaborate theory of noses, the most striking member of the face. Neither is it surprising that subsequent classifications of noses, based on Lavater's formulations, associate Roman and Greek noses with conquerors and persons of refinement and taste.

The next and last step we shall consider in this genealogy of racism in late-seventeenth- and eighteenth-century Europe is the advent of phrenology, the new discipline which held that human character could be read through the shape of the human head.

Franz Joseph Gall, a highly regarded German physician, argued in 1796 that the inner workings of the brain could be determined by the shape of the skull. For example, he associated an arched fore-head with a penchant for metaphysical speculation; a skull arched at the rear with love of fame; and a skull large at the base with a criminal disposition. In the nineteenth century, when racist ideology was systematized, this new discipline took on a life of its own with Johann Kaspar Spurzheim, Anders Retzius, Carl Gustav Carus, and others; it also aided in allying modern racism with nationalism and repressed sexuality in bourgeois morality.

Theoretical Consequences: Restrictive Powers in Modern Discourse

A major example of the way in which the restrictive powers of modern discourse delimit theoretical al-ternatives and strategic options in regard to the idea of white supremacy is seen in writings of radical environmentalists of the period – those one would expect to be open to the idea of black equality in beauty, culture, and intellectual capacity. Yet even these progressive antislavery advocates remain cap-tive to the "normative gaze."

The major opponent of predominant forms of a hierarchic ranking of races and the outspoken pro-ponent of intermarriage in the United States during this era, Samuel Stanhope Smith, illustrates this captivity. In his day Smith stood at the pinnacle of American academia. He was president of Princeton University and an honorary member of the Ameri-can Philosophical Society. He was awarded honor-ary degrees from Harvard and Yale. In his well-known *Essays* of 1787 (and revised in 1810) Smith argued that humankind constituted one species and that human variations could be accounted for in reference to three natural causes: "climate," "state of society," and "habits of living." He believed "that colour may be justly considered as an univer-sal freckle."[24]

The "normative gaze" operative in Smith's viewpoint is located, as in Buffon, in the assump-tion that physical, especially racial, variations are always degenerate ones from an ideal state. For Smith, this ideal state consisted of highly civilized white people. As Winthrop Jordan notes, "Smith treated the complexion and physiognomy of the white man not merely as indication of superiority but as the hallmark of civilization."[25] Smith justi-fied this ideal standard and legitimized his "norma-

tive gaze" by appealing to the classical ideals of beauty. In a patriotic footnote he wrote:

> It may perhaps gratify my countrymen to reflect that the United States occupy those latitudes that have ever been most favourable to the beauty of the human form. When time shall have accommodated the constitution of its new state, and cultivation shall have meliorated the climate, the beauties of Greece and Circasia may be renewed in America; as there are not a few already who rival those of any quarter of the globe.[26]

Smith's radical environmentalism (along with his adherence to Greek aesthetic ideals) led him to adopt the most progressive and sympathetic alter-native which promotes the welfare of black people permissible within the structure of modern dis-course: integration which *uplifts* black people, assimilation which *civilizes* black people, intermar-riage which *ensures less Negroid features* in the next generation. For example, Smith wrote:

> The great difference between the domestic and field slaves gives reason to believe that, if they were perfectly free, enjoyed property, and were admitted to a liberal participation of the society rank and privileges of their masters, they would change their African peculiarities much faster.[27]

This theoretical alternative was taken to its lo-gical consequence by the distinguished American antislavery advocate, publicizer of talented black writers, and eminent physician, Benjamin Rush. This logical consequence was the elimination of the skin color of black people. In a paper entitled "Observations Intended to Favour a Supposition that the Black Color (As it is called) of the Negroes is Derived From the Leprosy," Rush denounced the idea of white supremacy, then stated: "Is the color of Negroes a disease? Then let science and humanity combine their efforts and endeavor to discover a remedy for it."[28] In one bold stroke, Rush provided grounds for promoting abolition-ism, opposing intermarriage (who wants to marry diseased persons!), and supporting the Christian unity of humankind. In his opinion, his viewpoint also maximized the happiness of black and white people:

> To encourage attempts to cure this disease of the skin in Negroes, let us recollect that by

succeeding in them, we shall produce a large portion of happiness in the world. . . .

Secondly, we shall add greatly to their happiness, for however well they appear to be satisfied with their color, there are many proofs of their preferring that of the white people.[29]

Racism in the Enlightenment

The intellectual legitimacy of the idea of white supremacy, though grounded in what we now consider marginal disciplines (especially in its second stage), was pervasive. This legitimacy can be illustrated by the extent to which racism permeated the writings of the major figures of the Enlightenment. It is important to note that the idea of white supremacy not only was accepted by these figures, but, more important, it was accepted by them *without their having to put forward their own arguments to justify it*. Montesquieu and Voltaire of the French Enlightenment, Hume and Jefferson of the Scotch and the American Enlightenment, and Kant of the German Enlightenment not merely held racist views; they also uncritically – during this age of criticism – believed that the *authority* for these views rested in the domain of naturalists, anthropologists, physiognomists, and phrenologists.

Montesquieu's satirical remarks in *Spirit of the Laws* about black people (and his many revisions of these remarks) may seem to suggest an equivocal disposition toward the idea of white supremacy. Yet his conclusion leaned toward support of the idea:

It is impossible for us to suppose that these beings should be men; because if we supposed them to be men, one would begin to believe we ourselves were not Christians.[30]

Voltaire's endorsement of the idea of white supremacy was unequivocal. In his essay "The People of America," he claimed that black people (and Indians) were distinct species from Europeans:

The Negro race is a species of men as different from ours as the breed of spaniels is from that of greyhounds. The mucous membrane, or network, which nature has spread between the muscles and the skin, is white in us and black or copper-colored in them. . . .

If their understanding is not of a different nature from ours, it is at least greatly inferior.

They are not capable of any great application or association of ideas, and seemed formed neither for the advantages nor the abuses of philosophy.[31]

Hume's racism was notorious; it served as a major source of pro-slavery arguments and anti-black education propaganda. In his famous footnote to his essay "Of National Characteristics," he stated:

I am apt to suspect the negroes, and in general all the other species of men (for there are four or five different kinds) to be naturally inferior to the whites. There never was a civilized nation of any other complexion than white, nor even any individual eminent either in action or speculation. No ingenious manufactures amongst them, no arts, no sciences. . . .

In Jamaica indeed they talk of one negroe as a man of parts and learning; but 'tis likely he is admired for very slender accomplishments, like a parrot, who speaks a few words plainly.[32]

Jefferson arrived at mildly similar conclusions in his *Notes on Virginia*. Regarding the intellectual capacities of black people, he wrote:

Comparing them by their faculties of memory, reason, and imagination, it appears to me, that in memory they are equal to the whites; in reason much inferior . . . and that in imagination they are dull, tasteless and anomalous. . . . Never yet could I find that a black had uttered a thought above the level of plain narration; never see even an elementary trait of painting or sculpture.[33]

Finally, Kant, whose views were based heavily on Hume's claims, held that "the negroes of Africa have by nature no feeling that rises above the trifling." In his *Observations on the Feeling of the Beautiful and Sublime*, Kant noted:

Mr. Hume challenges anyone to cite a simple example in which a negro has shown talents, and asserts that among the hundreds of thousands of blacks who are transported elsewhere from their countries, although many of them have even been set free, still not a single one was ever found who presented anything great in art or science or any other praiseworthy quality, even though among the whites some continually rise aloft from the lowest rabble, and through superior gifts earn respect in the world. So fundamental is the difference between the two races of man, and it appears to be as great in regard to mental capacities as in color.[34]

Kant further revealed his racist views when, in reply to advice that a black person gave to Father Labat, he wrote,

And it might be that there was something in this which perhaps deserved to be considered; but in short, this fellow was quite black from head to foot, a clear proof that what he said was stupid.[35]

The Emergence of Modern Racism: Inevitable or Contingent?

The emergence of the idea of white supremacy as an object of modern discourse seems inevitable in that, besides the practical need to justify nonwhite domination (especially in the early nineteenth century), the only available theoretical alternative for the unhampered search for truth and knowledge in the modern West consisted of detailed observation, measurement, comparison, and ordering of the natural and human kingdom by autonomous subjects in the light of the aesthetic and cultural ideals of classical antiquity. Given the Enlightenment obsession with criticism, especially criticism of the church and religion, the past was divided into four major epochs:

the great river civilizations of the Near East; Ancient Greece and Rome; the Christian millennium; and modern times, beginning with the "revival of letters." These four epochs were rhythmically related to each other: the first and third were paired off as ages of myth, belief and superstition, while the second and fourth were ages of rationality, science and Enlightenment.[36]

The implications of Frank Snowden's thesis in his book *Blacks in Antiquity: Ethiopians in the Greco-Roman Experience* call into question the notion that the Enlightenment recovery of classical antiquity – its aesthetic and cultural ideals – inevitably required, on the discursive level, the emergence of the idea of white supremacy as an object of modern discourse. Snowden's thesis is that racial

prejudice did not exist in classical antiquity. He claims that in the first major encounter in European records of black people in a predominantly white society the idea of black equality in beauty, culture, and intellectual capacity was seriously entertained. In regard to ideals of beauty, he notes that Herodotus called Ethiopians the most handsome people on earth; Philostratus spoke of charming Ethiopians with their strange color; Pseudo-Callisthenes held the black Queen of Meroë (visited by Alexander the Great) to be of wondrous beauty; and the poet Martial, though pursued by a woman whiter than snow, sought a "super-black" woman.[37] Snowden goes as far as to state: "On the whole ... the number of expressed preferences for blackness and whiteness in classical literature is approximately equal."[38]

If Snowden's viewpoint is correct, two noteworthy issues arise. First, it permits us to accent the crucial role that the advent of modern science played in *highlighting the physical appearances of people in relation to what it is to be human, beautiful, cultured, and intelligent.* In this regard, the primacy of observation – the "gaze" character of scientific knowledge – may be as important as the classical ideals which are latent in such observations at the inception of modern discourse. Second, Snowden's claims require that I provide an account of why the Enlightenment revival of classical antiquity ignored or excluded black statues and the proportions and measurements of black figures as part of classical aesthetic ideals.

Snowden's thesis is highly plausible and extremely provocative, but I find it neither persuasive nor convincing. His claims are too exorbitant, but they do contain kernels of truth. Race indeed mattered much less in classical antiquity than it does in modern times. But race did matter in classical antiquity, as can be seen from the evidence meticulously gathered by Snowden, Sikes, Westermann, and others.[39] The crucial difference seems to be that racial differences were justified on cultural grounds in classical antiquity, whereas at the inception of modern discourse, racial differences are often grounded in nature, that is, ontology and later biology.

And even if race prejudice did not exist in classical antiquity, the minority status of black people in Greece and Rome still rendered black statues, proportions, and measurements marginal to cultural life. Hence, the black presence, though tolerated and at times venerated, was never an integral part of the classical ideals of beauty.

The emergence of the idea of white supremacy as an object of modern discourse seems contingent, in that there was no iron necessity at work in the complex configuration of metaphors, notions, categories, and norms that produce and promote this idea. There is an accidental character to the discursive emergence of modern racism, a kind of free play of discursive powers which produce and prohibit, develop and delimit the legitimacy and intelligibility of certain ideas within a discursive space circumscribed by the attractiveness of classical antiquity.

Yet even such claims about the contingency of the emergence of the idea of white supremacy in the modern West warrant suspicion. This is so because, as we noted earlier, this genealogical approach *does not purport to be an explanation of the rise of modern racism, but rather a theoretical inquiry into a particular neglected variable, i.e., the discursive factor, within a larger explanatory model.* This variable is significant because it not only precludes reductionist treatments of modern racism; it also highlights the cultural and aesthetic impact of the idea of white supremacy on black people. This inquiry accents the fact that the everyday life of black people is shaped not simply by the exploitative (oligopolistic) capitalist system of production but also by cultural attitudes and sensibilities, including alienating ideals of beauty.

The idea of white supremacy is a major bowel unleashed by the structure of modern discourse, a significant secretion generated from the creative fusion of scientific investigation, Cartesian philosophy, and classical aesthetic and cultural norms. Needless to say, the odor of this bowel and the fumes of this secretion continue to pollute the air of our postmodern times.

Author's Notes

1 This second theoretical moment of Afro-American philosophy constitutes its Foucaultian elements: the exploration of the complex relationship between knowledge and power, discourse and politics. For a similar yet more ambitious project, see Edward Said, *Orientalism* (Pantheon Books, 1978). Note that my aim is not to endorse the discursive idealism of Michel Foucault, but rather to incorporate some of his powerful insights into a more sophisticated Marxist analysis of the emergence of modern racism. I have just embarked on a huge project that deepens my concern in this chapter into a full-fledged volume.

2 Friedrich Nietzsche, *On the Genealogy of Morals*, trans. Walter Kaufmann and R. J. Hollingdale (Vintage Books, 1967); Michel Foucault, "Nietzsche, Genealogy, History," in *Language, Counter-Memory, Practice: Selected Essays and Interviews*, trans. Donald F. Bouchard and Sherry Simon (Cornell University Press, 1977), pp. 139–64.

3 Cf. Louis Althusser, "Marx's Relation to Hegel," in his *Politics and History* (Schocken Books, 1972), pp. 181–3. For trenchant criticisms of Althusser, see Stanley Aronowitz, *The Crisis in Historical Materialism: Class, Politics, and Culture in Marxist Theory* (Praeger Publications, 1981), pp. 68–9, 120–1, 325–7.

4 This insight bears the stamp of Foucault's long-drawn-out quarrel with vulgar Marxism. See Michel Foucault, *The History of Sexuality*, Vol. 1 trans. Robert Hurley (Random House, 1980), pp. 92–8; *Power/Knowledge: Selected Interviews and Other Writings, 1972–1977*, ed. Colin Gordon (Pantheon Books, 1980), pp. 109–45.

5 For the "classicism plus science" view of the Enlightenment, see Peter Gay, *The Enlightenment: An Interpretation*, Vol. 1, pp. 3–27, 313–21. For the importance of the Cartesian transformation of philosophy, see Richard Rorty's insightful metaphilosophical claims in *Philosophy and the Mirror of Nature*, esp. pp. 8–12, 45–51, 54–69, 136–40.

6 This understanding of the Renaissance derives from Aby Warburg's notion of *Ausgleichsformel* (compromise formula); and for Galileo's and Newton's proto-modern world views, see Gay, *The Enlightenment*, pp. 269–77.

7 Benjamin Farrington, *Francis Bacon: Philosopher of Industrial Science* (Collier Books, 1961), pp. 78–106; Bertrand Russell, *A History of Western Philosophy* (Simon & Schuster, 1945), p. 544.

8 Martin Heidegger, "The Age of the World View," trans. Marjorie Grene, *Boundary 2*, Vol. 4, No. 2 (Winter 1976), pp. 348–9.

9 Gay, *The Enlightenment*, pp. 310–11.

10 Rorty, *Philosophy and the Mirror of Nature*; Abrams, *The Mirror and the Lamp*.

11 This claim, as well as my general argument, derives in part from the seminal study by George L. Mosse, *Toward the Final Solution: A History of European Racism* (Howard Fertig, 1978). This neglected work deserves much more attention than it has heretofore received.

12 Ibid., p. 10.

13 Jordan, *White Over Black: American Attitudes Toward the Negro, 1550–1812*, pp. 3–98; Gossett, *Race: The History of an Idea in America*, pp. 3–31.

14 Michel Foucault, *The Order of Things: An Archae-ology of the Human Sciences* (Pantheon Books, 1970), pp. 132, 158.

15 Jordan, *White Over Black*, pp. 217–18; Gossett, *Race: The History of an Idea in America*, pp. 32–4; Ashley Montagu, "The Origin of the Concept of 'Race,'" in his *Man's Most Dangerous Myth: The Fallacy of Race*, 5th ed. (Oxford University Press, 1974), pp. 46ff.

16 Jordan, *White Over Black*, p. 220.

17 Ibid., pp. 220–1.

18 Gossett, *Race*, p. 36.

19 For their defenses of Blumenbach, see Jordan, *White Over Black*, pp. 223, 507; Gossett, *Race*, p. 39; Montagu, *Man's Most Dangerous Myth*, pp. 41–5. Support for my viewpoint is found in Mosse, *Toward the Final Solution*, pp. 11, 21.

20 Most notably in the United States, Dr. John Augustine Smith, president of the College of William and Mary, and the famous naturalist Dr. Samuel George Morton of Philadelphia – both fervent proponents of black inferiority. Jordan, *White Over Black*, pp. 505–6; Gossett, *Race*, pp. 58–9.

21 Mosse, *Toward the Final Solution*, p. 22.

22 Ibid., p. 25.

23 Ibid.

24 Jordan, *White Over Black*, pp. 486ff., 514.

25 Ibid., p. 515.

26 Ibid.

27 Ibid., pp. 515–16.

28 Ibid., p. 520.

29 Ibid.

30 David Brion Davis, *The Problem of Slavery in Western Culture* (Cornell University Press, 1966), p. 403.

31 Gossett, *Race*, p. 45.

32 Richard H. Popkin, "Hume's Racism," *The Philosophical Forum*, Vol. 9, Nos. 2–3, p. 213.

33 Jordan, *White Over Black*, pp. 436–7.

34 Popkin, "Hume's Racism," p. 218.

35 Ibid.

36 Gay, *The Enlightenment*, p. 34.

37 Frank M. Snowden, Jr., *Blacks in Antiquity: Ethiopians in the Greco-Roman Experience* (Belknap Press, 1970), pp. 178–9.

38 Ibid., p. 179.

39 E. E. Sikes, *The Anthropology of the Greeks* (London, 1914); W. L. Westermann, *The Slave Systems of Greek and Roman Antiquity*, Memoirs of the American Philosophical Society, Vol. 50 (1955), pp. xi–180; Moses Hadas, *Hellenistic Culture: Fusion and Diffusion* (Columbia University Press, 1959); Adrian N. Sherwin-White, *Racial Prejudice in Imperial Rome* (Cambridge University Press, 1967).

33

"Subversive Signs"

Hal Foster

American art critic Hal Foster has been an important contributor to the postmodern turn in the
visual arts and art theory away from "the aesthetic" modernist approach to art that was characteristic of, for example, the critic Clement
Greenberg. Foster's earlier anthology, The Anti-
Aesthetic (1983) was instrumental in raising the
postmodern critique of art and its political import.
But Foster also opposes what he regards as the
non-critical "pluralism" of some postmodernist
art, whose eclecticism finally leaves contemporary society unchanged. The antidote to the "anything goes" attitude of pop pluralism is for him, in
the following 1982 essay, exemplified by the
"subversive" art of Barbara Kruger, in which he
finds a postmodernism that has not abandoned
its critical potential.

> A writer – by which I mean not the possessor of a
> function or the servant of an art, but the subject of a
> praxis – must have the persistence of the watcher
> who stands at the crossroads of all other discourses
> (trivilias is the etymological attribute of the prosti-
> tute who waits at the intersection of three roads).
>
> Roland Barthes, "Leçon"[i]

The most provocative American art of the present is
situated at such a crossing – of institutions of art and
political economy, of representations of sexual identity and social life. More, it assumes its purpose to be
so sited, to lay in wait for these discourses so as to

[i] Roland Barthes (1915–80), French literary theorist and
semiotician.

riddle and expose them or to seduce and lead them
astray. Its primary concern is not with the traditional
or modernist proprieties of art – with refinement of
style or innovation of form, æsthetic sublimity or
ontological reflection on art as such. And though it is
aligned with the critique of the institution of art
based on the presentational strategies of the Duch-
ampian readymade, it is not involved, as its minimalist antecedents were, with an epistemological
investigation of the object or a phenomenological
inquiry into subjective response. In short, this work
does not bracket art for formal or perceptual experiment but rather seeks out its affiliations with other
practices (in the culture industry and elsewhere); it
also tends to conceive of its subject differently.

The artists active in this work (Martha Rosler,
Sherrie Levine, Dara Birnbaum, Barbara Kruger,
Louise Lawler, Allan McCollum, Jenny Holzer,
Krzysztof Wodcizko...)[ii] use many different
forms of production and modes of address (photo-
text collage, constructed or projected photographs,
videotapes, critical texts, appropriated, arranged or
surrogate art works, etc.), and yet they are alike in
this: each treats the public space, social representation or artistic language in which he or she inter-

[ii] A second generation of "conceptual artists" – mostly
American painters, sculptors, and photographers born in
the 1940s and '50s, whose work often incorporates "pop"
mass culture elements and criticizes them simultaneously.

Hal Foster, "Subversive Signs" from Recodings: Art,
Spectacle, Cultural Politics, pp. 99–115. New York:
The New Press, 1985. Note that illustrations have
not been reproduced here.

venes as both a target and a weapon. This shift in practice entails a shift in position: the artist becomes a manipulator of signs more than a producer of art objects, and the viewer an active reader of messages rather than a passive contemplator of the æsthetic or consumer of the spectacular. This shift is not new – indeed, the recapitulation in this work of the "allegorical procedures"[1] of the readymade,[iii] (dadaist) photomontage and (pop) appropriation is significant – yet it remains strategic if only because even today few are able to accept the status of art as a social sign entangled with other signs in systems productive of value, power and prestige.

The situational æsthetics of this art – its special attention to site, address and audience – is prepared by the varied institutional critique of such artists as Daniel Buren, Michael Asher, Dan Graham, Hans Haacke, Marcel Broodthaers, Lawrence Weiner, John Baldessari and Joseph Kosuth.[iv] Yet if Kruger, Holzer et al. inherit the conceptual critique of the given parameters of art production and reception, they do so not uncritically. For just as the conceptual artists extended the minimalist analysis of the art object, so too these later artists have opened up the conceptual critique of the art institution in order to intervene in ideological representations and languages of everyday life. It is important to trace this genealogy (which is *not* intended as a conscription of these mostly feminist artists into a paternal tradition), especially in the face of the contemporary rejection of *all* institutional critique, indeed *all* avant-garde practice, under the cynical pretense that it is now "exhausted" or "academic" – a pretense that abets the forced resurrection of a traditionalist art largely given over to the manipulated demands of the market and the myths of the museum.

As is well known (in part because of a countermemory afforded by later artists and critics), the investigation of Buren, Asher, Haacke and Broodthaers focuses primarily on the institutional frame, and secondarily on the economic logic, of the modern art object. In critical writings and works in situ, these four artists (among others) have sought to reveal the ways in which the production

and reception of art are institutionally predetermined, recuprated, used. Thus since 1965 Buren, with his banners and flags of alternately colored and white (or transparent) stripes set in specific art and nonart spaces for specific periods of time, has stressed the *spatiotemporal* predisposition of the work of art by its institutional frame. And since 1969 Asher, with his (dis)placements of different gallery/museum objects, services and spaces, has foregrounded the *functional* delimitation of all artistic activity sited there. Before his death in 1976, Broodthaers, with his fictitious museums (in which the roles of artist and curator are reversed), allegorically doubled the ways in which the museum *acculturates* heterogeneous objects and activities as art. And finally, since 1970 Haacke, with his detailed exposés of different museums, corporate benefactors and art collectors, has probed the *material* bases of the fine-art apparatus which, repressed, allows for its pretenses of social neutrality and cultural autonomy.

It was the need to expose this false idealism of art that initially led these artists to its "mystical body," the modern museum, for it became clear that its supposedly supplemental role of "preservation, enclosure and refuge" (Buren) actually preconditioned art production, predisposed it to an ideology of transcendence and self-sufficiency.[2] As opposed to the argument that avant-garde practice had attempted to *destroy* the institution of art,[3] these practitioners held that modern artists had not *comprehended* it – its conditions of production, exhibition and exchange; thus Buren in 1970: "20th-century art is still so dependent on 19th-century art since it has accepted, without a break, its system, its mechanism and its function (including Cézanne and Duchamp) without revealing one of its main alibis, and furthermore accepting the exhibition framework as self-evident."[4] To these artists transformation of this apparatus is contingent upon an exposing of its "alibis," to which the work of Broodthaers and Haacke in particular is committed, and upon a foregrounding of its "framework," in which Asher and Buren are engaged.

Clearly this is an important intervention, but it is a necessarily (de)limited one. It is limited, first of all, by its very attention to the institutional frame, which determines its production no less for being exposed in doing so; by its deconstructive posture, this work diminishes its own transformative potential. Secondly, posed within the gallery/museum, it is often referenced to the given forms of art (thus Buren's banners tend to be read in relation to easel painting

[iii]   Marcel Duchamp (1887–1968), provocative painter of *Nude Descending a Staircase, No. 2* (1911), who first presented ordinary objects as works of art ("the ready made") in the *Bicycle Wheel* (1913).

[iv]   The first generation conceptual artists, mostly Europeans born in the 1920s and '30s, whose work generally avoided "pop" influences and materials.

and Asher's (dis)placements in relation to sculpture);[5] however residual, these categories are sustained even as they are demonstrated to be logically arbitrary, ideologically laden and/or historically obsolete. On a different score, the "scientificity" of this practice tends to present the exhibitional limits of art as socially indiscriminate and sexually indifferent (this is perhaps the most obvious point of critical revision by feminist artists); it also cannot fully account for the systems of circulation in which the art work is involved *after* exhibition – the processes by which it becomes a discriminatory sign. (Of the four only Haacke *thematizes* the intertextuality of art and power, which allows him actually to use the limits of the gallery/museum as a screen for his political attacks.)[v] Finally and familiarly, this practice runs the risk of reduction in the gallery/museum from an act of subversion to a form of exposition, with the work less an attack on the separation of cultural and social practice than another example of it and the artist less a deconstructive delineator of the institution than its "expert."

Such criticisms come after the fact, however, and are less failings of this practice than insights developed from it by later artists. Such legatees of conceptual art as Louise Lawler and Allan McCollum work to literalize more than to abolish the rules of art.[6] Though this may seem its own negation of institutional critique, it is instead its adaption to a code of art that now extends beyond conditions of production and exhibition. (As the "title" of a recent work by Lawler – a photograph of a statue of Sappho and a bust of a patriarch – asks: "Is it the work, the location or the stereotype that is the institution?") These later artists stress the economic manipulation of the art object – its circulation and consumption as a commodity-sign – more than its physical determination by its frame. And yet no less than the conceptual artists they too seek to reveal the definitional character of the supplements of art, only they tend to foreground the institutionally insignificant (the overlooked) rather than the transparent (the unseen) – functions like the arrangement of pictures in galleries, museums, offices, homes, and forms like press releases and exhibition invitations which, thought to be trivial to the matter of art, in fact do much to position it, to determine its place, reception, meaning.

For Walter Benjamin the "artistic function" as we still know it today – the isolated maker of art objects for the market – is "incidental" to the determination of art by its exhibition (or exchange) value."[7] It is this function, this determination that artists like Buren and Asher, Lawler and McCollum explore. But there is another "function" that emerges when art passes from courtly patronage to the marketplace: the collector; and Lawler and McCollum are no less interested in this beast. In her "Arrangements of Pictures" Lawler reframes in photographs the various ways in which different collectors – museums, corporations, the old and new rich – invest art with value by "sumptuary expenditure," guarantee this value by reference to an institutional code of proper names and affiliations (a lineage of artists and works, a pedigree of owners and experts) and display it as a marker of taste, hierarchy, prestige or simply investment.[8] For his part McCollum is obsessed by the contractually adversarial rapport between artist and collector; this convention has "inspired" him to produce thousands of surrogate paintings – objects which consist solely of a frame, mat and, for an image, a blank, with but minor differences in size and proportion.[9] With these decoys McCollum feeds the hunger for pictures felt by a social group dedicated to the mastery of both accumulation and signification but in such a way as to famish it. For he beckons the desire to spectate and buy – the desire for spectacle, for control through consumption – only to represent the very emptiness which the picture-fetish is supposed to fill, only to turn the ritual of mutual confirmation into a charade of (mis) recognition:

> You see yourself insofar as you see me see myself, yet I see myself only as I see that I am seen. Our reciprocal surveillance is sustained through my artwork, which thrives. Our misplaced assignations of authority and our fraudulent identifications are thus mediated into a dislocated ritual of self-congratulation, strange looks, and the exchange of money for false tokens.[10]

This is not to suggest that these artists neglect the exhibition framework. In a 1978 show at Artists Space in New York, Lawler installed an 1824 painting of a racehorse (borrowed from the New York Racing Association) with two stagelights, one set above the picture and aimed at the viewer, the other directed outside through a gallery window. Here Lawler did indeed make "the element of an exhibition the subject of her production,"[11] but she also posed a funny, provocative conflation of exhibited painting and displayed thoroughbred that

[v]   Hans Haake (1936–), German conceptual artist.

exposed them both as tokens in the sumptuary production of value and prestige. (Are not art world and racetrack alike based on a closed system of training and grooming, of handicapping and betting, of investment, competition and auction? After all we do call galleries "stables.") More recently, Lawler and McCollum collaborated on an installation that foregrounded in a different way the status of art as display: 100 hydrocal sculpture pedestals set on bases and bathed in spectacular light, titled *For Presentation and Display: Ideal Settings* (1984). Here the abstraction of modern sculpture, its passage from sited, figurative monument to siteless, autonomous sign,[12] was decoded as its "abstraction" by the commodity-form – as if sculpture had not absorbed its base in the pursuit of æsthetic purity so much as spectacle had swallowed art in the pure display of the commodity. Exhibition value, once productive of an autonomous "artistic function," here consumed it entirely.

This displacement of art by its own support, by its own spectacle, is both a characteristic strategy and a historical demonstration of Lawler and McCollum.[vi] The functional indifference of art objects produced in the studio/gallery/museum nexus, remarked by Buren, is shown by McCollum to be no less determined by the market. His "empty" surrogates make explicit the reduction of content to form in the exchange of like for like as well as the general equivalence of objects in a serial mode of production. For her part Lawler makes clear the division of labor that produces the hierarchical functions and generic forms of art (i.e., who creates what for whom in what order of privilege and value). This institutional order of names, services and forms is then confused by the (relative) anonymity of her interventions, by her assumption of different guises (arranger, publicist, etc.), by her production as art of such giveaways as gallery matchbooks (supplements which again seem superfluous but are crucial to the spectacle of art). Yet just as it may be unclear whether the McCollum surrogates "dislocate" the ritual of exchange or replicate the status of the object become sign (delivered up in all its minor difference for our consumption), so too it may be unclear whether the Lawler gambits subvert the mechanisms of art exhibition, circulation and consumption or play them to the hilt. (Do her giveaways update the Duchamp

ready-made, substitute use value for exchange value, or æstheticize use one more time?) Like a dye in the bloodstream, the work of these artists does delineate the circulation system of art, but it also operates within its terms. If artists like Buren and Asher may become guardians of the demystified myths of the art museum, then artists like Lawler and McCollum may indeed serve as "ironic collaborators"[13] of its market apparatus.

Other artists, no less influenced by conceptual work, have sought to reflect critically on representations outside the art apparatus – and from there to turn back to address discourses within it. For these artists ideology cannot be reduced to one language, then critiqued, or the institution of art to one space, then charted. Such signs and sites are not simply given, open to manipulation only:[14] other meanings can be constructed, other publics sought out. Specifically, the position of the subject must be taken into account, and it is at the point of production of the subject rather than of the art object that this work intervenes. Barbara Kruger takes a feminist tack: through different collisions of images and texts she seeks to dispel the specular nature of representations that subject women to the gaze of a univocal male subject, "to welcome a female spectator in the audience of men"[vii] Jenny Holzer's is a "situationist" strategy: in a variety of signs she presents opinions, credos, anecdotes in a way which both manifests the domination active in everyday discourse and confounds it by sheer anarchic display.[viii] In this way the work of such artists seeks to disorient the law, to call language into crisis. This is what ideology cannot afford, for it tends to operate in language that denies its status as such: stereotypical language. Yet, by the same token, this art cannot afford to take the demonstrations of institutional critique for granted. For without specific attention to its own institution this critical practice, even now well received in the gallery/museum nexus, will be recuperated as yet another avantgardist exercise, a mere manipulation rather than an active transformation of social signs.

A strong sense of duty imprisons you.
Abuse of power comes as no surprise.
Alienation produces eccentrics or revolutionaries.
Ambivalence can ruin your life.

[vi] Louise Lawler (1947–) and Allan McCollum (1944–), American conceptual installation artist and sculptor, respectively.

[vii] Barbara Kruger (1945–), American conceptual designer and writer.
[viii] Jenny Holzer (1950–), American Installation and conceptual artist.

Both Kruger and Holzer are concerned with the power at work in social representations; Holzer's site of intervention is language. As Barthes wrote:

> Language is legislation, speech is its code. . . . To utter a discourse is not, as is too often repeated, to communicate; it is to subjugate. . . . Language – the performance of a language system – is neither reactionary nor progressive; it is quite simply fascist.[15]

In her texts Holzer seeks to undo this "fascism," to display the censurious circularity of our idiolects. Her work suggests not only how language subjects us but how we may disarm it; and here again the tactic is subversive complicity: "it is within speech that speech must be fought, led astray – not by the message of which it is the instrument, but by the play of words of which it is the theater."[16] With Holzer this "theater" becomes a bedlam of voices which mocks the certainty of personal credos and the neutrality of public discourse (e.g., of the mass media). Her texts often function as a dictionary of received ideas to deplete our ideologemes, to rob them of the "fascist" power to compel.

This bedlam-effect is strongest in her *Truisms* (1977), an alphabetical list of statements which together confound all order and logic. First presented as public-information posters on New York City walls (and since as T-shirts, electronic signs, plaques, works of art), the *Truisms* not only "place in contradiction certain ideological structures that are usually kept apart"[17] but set them into open conflict. This contestation-by-contradiction is also contextual, for the *Truisms* expose the false homogeneity of the signs on the street among which they are often placed. An encounter with them, then, is like an encounter with the Sphinx: though one is given answers, not asked questions, initiation into our Theban society is much the same: entanglement in discourse.

This entanglement is a continual displacement – to the point where the reader begins to see, first, that (s)he is not an autonomous individual of free beliefs so much as a subject inserted into language and, second, that this insertion can be changed. The experience of truistic entrapment cedes to a feeling of anarchic release, for the *Truisms* expose the coercion that is usually hidden in language, and once exposed it appears ridiculous. Essentially, this release comes of the recognition that meaning is a rhetorical construction of will more than a Platonic apprehension of an idea – that, however directed

toward truth, it is finally based on power. This is not a nihilistic insight: it allows for resistance based on truth constructed through contradiction. And this indeed is the one genuine truth that the *Truisms* express: that only through contradiction can one construct a self that is not entirely subjected. (This truth, that of dialectics, denies its own closure as a truth: this is what makes it true.)

Entanglement in discourse is most extreme in the *Inflammatory Essays* (1979–82), which also appeared first as street posters and then as signs, books, art works. Here again the voices are provocative: imperative commands and subjunctive inducements mix with the impersonal mode of truth. Yet the *Essays* are more arguments than statements, and they do not taxonomize ideologies so much as hyperbolize political rhetoric (in these tracts poles of left and right threaten to implode).[18] Thus even more than the *Truisms*, the *Essays* are concerned with the *force* of language: they exhibit how different ideologies position and pervert us as subjects of discourse. Some voices insinuate, others demand. A few almost convince, but finally each voice is convinced, conquered by its own speech. This closure is of the kind noted by Barthes in political language where reality is prejudged, and naming and judging are one: "A history of political modes of writing would therefore be the best of social phenomenologies."[19] Together the *Truisms* and the *Essays* evoke such a phenomenology.

In 1981 through 1983 Holzer worked (in part with Peter Nadin) on the *Living* series. With these signs and plaques Holzer functioned more in given art spaces; at the same time she drew more on everyday talk. Indeed, the language of the *Living* series is omnivorous; as one set of texts, "Eating Through Living,"[20] suggests, living *is* eating – consuming and being consumed by speech. In the *Living* texts especially, Holzer meets the subtle subjections active in social discourse with wit and play. That is, she leads language astray. Thus, for example, she may turn our official tongue of efficacy and etiquette into its own parody:

> Once you know how to do something you're prone to try it again. An unhappy example is compulsive murder. This is not to be confused with useful skills acquired through years of hard work.

Or she may beguile officialdom with metal signs and bronze plaques that publicize the private ("The mouth is interesting because it is one of those places where the dry outside moves toward the slippery inside") or pronounce the socially repressed ("It takes a while before you can step over inert bodies and go ahead with what you were wanting to do"). A sign is a social directive; a plaque is a marker of official truth which exalts a place or proper name as the very presence of history. The Holzer signs and plaques foil this marking, traduce this official language and proper speech which, like an old chauvinist in the hands of a supple feminist, undoes itself.

Her recent *Survival* series is again more desperate: these short texts about class domination, racial oppression, sexual subjection and nuclear annihilation rebut the Panglossian feel-goodism of the Reagan era. Yet here, as is implicit elsewhere in her work, it is uncertain whether Holzer re-presents the rhetoric of "crisis" – an ideology which can mystify the secure positions of power or alternately "justify" its open authoritarian acts, which can erode activism into fatalism or alternately force it into terroristic acts of its own – or whether she succumbs to it. The same question may be asked regarding the fragmentation of communication into private, often paranoid codes: does Holzer foreground this fragmentation or confirm it? Do her texts resist "the government of individualization"[21] or present us with so many linguistic objects to consume?

Like all her work, the *Survival* series is involved in a delegitimation of power, in a rhetorical exposure of its discursive guises and ploys. (Yet today it is as if capitalist power, the very agent of our linguistic fragmentation, feels no great need of legitimation . . . as long as it supplies the goods.) In this critique, it is said, Holzer is not specific: her work is too anarchic, too atopic.[ix] This is not the case with her most recent interventions such as "Sign on a Truck" (nor is it with most of her other work, which is often as "site-specifically" critical of the ideologies of everyday life as conceptual work is of the institution of art). For this project Holzer presented videotapes by 22 artists concerning the 1984 presidential election on a large sign truck parked at two Manhattan locations on two days just before the November 6th vote. Through the provocation of art and the reaction of passers-by on the street, different political positions were articulated publicly through contradiction. By this direct presentation of political response outside the irresponsibility of the popular media, the work assured both its radicality and its

visibility. For it operated within everyday representations and spaces but not at the positions which power establishes through them. It is at such a shifting crossroads that effective resistance can be (pro)posed. Holzer knows this; so does Barbara Kruger.

[*We are obliged to steal language.*]

In her panels, posters and books Kruger appropriates photographs (mostly of women) from media sources, blows them up and crops them severely, then combines them with short texts. She has alternated image and text in a way reminiscent of photo-stories, montaged them in a parody of display ads, and combined them in the declarative address of signs in the street. In her first series of photo-texts Kruger re-presented various images (e.g., of a woman slumped among fashion magazines or with her hands clasped in prayer) stamped with single words (e.g., "deluded" or "perfect") that rendered them invalid, took them out of circulation. This "interception" of the stereotype is her principal device, yet in these early works it was only blasted and its maimed reality not redeemed. Such foreclosure implied not only that such cultural fictions and subject positions are more absolute than they are but also that the artist is in a transcendent relation to them.

Aware of these problems, Kruger has suggested that image appropriation, rather than question "the 'original' use and exchange value" of representations, contradict "the surety of our initial readings" and strain "the appearance of naturalism," may in fact confirm them.[22] Her later work evades this closure, for in its oscillation "from implicit to explicit, from inference to declaration"[23] neither photograph nor text, neither connotation nor denotation is privileged as a stable site or mode of truth; in fact, the usual coordination of the two (as employed in the media to fix unstable meanings) is undone. More important, her photo-texts shift address and block identification in a way that allows for no certain or essential subject position. This is not to say that they are arbitrary. Her reminting of the image is as motivated as her target is specific: the transparent naturalism of masculine readings which position women as objects of scopophilic pleasure ("We are being made spectacles of"); as figures of nature or otherness which support the patriarchal order of things ("We won't play nature to your culture"); as fetishistic images which serve to allay the anxiety ("I am your immaculate

---

[ix]   Non-spatial.

conception") about the castration that woman otherwise suggests to man ("I am your almost nothing"). It is this phallocentric surety that Kruger literally contradicts. First, she sets up "suave entrapments" with the very representations which position "woman as image and man as bearer of the look,"[24] then manipulates that pose, catches out that gaze. Though as seductive as any mass-media ad, her photo-texts work to reflect the masculine look that subjects women via a false feminine ideal and to block the feminine identification that submits to this construct.

The women in the images used by Kruger are most often posed or pursued but in either case passive, there to be gazed upon, saved, found out, used. These positions of capture presuppose a male subject who seeks to fix his image of desire and/or who identifies with the assumed protagonist of the situation. This accords with the ways in which Hollywood cinema plays upon the scopophilic drives and ego identifications of the masculine viewer, as analyzed by Laura Mulvey in her celebrated essay "Visual Pleasure and Narrative Cinema" (1975). Yet just as these processes are often at odds, so too the figure of woman is often conflicted. Mulvey: "The woman as icon, displayed for the gaze and enjoyment of men, the active controllers of the look, always threatens to evoke the [castration] anxiety it originally signified."[25] There are, she argues, two conventional "avenues of escape": a narrative exposing of the woman as flawed, incomplete (as in Hitchcock's *Vertigo*) or a spectacular fetishizing of her as a "whole," an erotic image (as in von Sternberg's Marlene Dietrich films). No doubt because they are culturally general, these two scenarios recur in the Kruger photo-texts, where they are restaged precisely so that sadistic sleuthing ("You destroy what you think is difference") and fetishistic fascination ("You are seduced by the sex appeal of the inorganic"), voyeuristic control ("You molest from afar") and spectacular pleasure ("We have received orders not to move") may be apprehended, refused. This disruption is effected through a shattering of the image (the fetish-fragment fragmented again) and/or through an indictment of the masculine voyeur/fetishist as well as an injunction to the feminine spectator not to be taken in. In effect, what "culinary theater" was to Brecht, "spectacle" is to Kruger: a subject-effect to estrange.

Such disruption might also be grasped by general reference to the Lacanian orders of the Imaginary and the Symbolic. Lacan spoke of the Imaginary in terms of a dialectic of self and image, of an "immediate opposition between consciousness and its other in which each term becomes its opposite and is lost in the play of reflections,"[26] and of the Symbolic in terms of the mediation of language (the intercession of the Name-of-the-Father) whereby one emerges from the immediacy of the Imaginary to be inserted as a subject into social structures. (It is at this point that primary repression occurs, with its effect: the unconscious.) As the phallus is the privileged signifier in this order, the presence around which its structures are diacritically arrayed, the female obviously has a particularly problematic relation to the Symbolic. I make this simplistic summary to suggest that Kruger attempts both visually to upset the Imaginary captures of the ego and textually to contest the phallic privileges of the Symbolic. Ideally, her usurpations not only jolt the Imaginary projections and Symbolic prerogatives of the masculine viewer but also foreground for the feminine viewer that her subjected position is not an essential one. Potentially, then, with the Imaginary investments of both viewers thus blocked, the different relation of each to the Symbolic – to insertion as subjects in patriarchal society – may be recognized and reassessed.

For Lacan, as soon as the subject is represented in language, (s)he is excluded or absented from it, and so is literally divided by it.[27] With her excessive use of pronouns, Kruger makes this linguistic division all but physical, and so again disturbs the pretense of a certain, centered subjecthood. This decentering is not indifferent: though her address constantly shifts (from I to You to We), its inclusions and exclusions are consistent (the You that stands accused is masculine, the We that is welcomed is feminine). Nevertheless, the subject *positions* in her work are not fixed. Indeed, in her recent pieces, in which with a lenticular screen two opposite photo-texts are disclosed from two different positions, the linguistic decentering of the subject becomes an actual displacing of the viewer. The stake of her art is here made explicit: the positioning of the body in ideology. Thus the imperative in her work to contest the stereotype, for, as Craig Owens has noted, it is in the stereotype that "the body is apprehended by language, taken into joint custody by politics and ideology."[28] Thus too the insistence in her address on the here and now, on the spatial and temporal relations of the lived, for it is precisely this bodiliness which traditional western art conspires with stereotypical mass culture to efface. (Norman Bryson: "Western painting is predicated on *the disavowal of deictic reference*, on the disappearance of the body as site of the image, and this twice over for the painter, and for the viewing subject.")[29] In her work Kruger resists this disavowal of the body, for with it goes a disavowal of the productive, of the transformative – in short, of the individual in process and of history subject to change. At the same time, she rejects the manipulation of the female body as an image for masculine delectation.

Her critique, then, is not a single or simple sabotage: it seeks to catch our various desires and disciplines that position the body and invest representation. Thus, for example, Kruger may stamp a text like "Charisma is the perfume of your gods" over a photo of a coin with two noble profiles, and

so convoke ideologemes that are usually separated – the patriarchal rhetoric of the republic and the authoritarian cult of personality, or the historical experience of artistic aura and the contemporary manufacture of stars, politicians, artist geniuses. Celebrated as her work has become, it has had to be reflexive in this way; indeed, her recent pieces are concerned as much with the economic manipulation of (her own) art as with sexist subjection. This finally is the interest of her work: the reflexivity with which it considers the discourses – of high art and mass culture, of sexual politics and cultural power – with which it is engaged. Though it may often seem insufficiently specific, it is this reflexivity which allows her work to circulate, and not be totally recuperated: "I will not become what I mean to you."

Author's Notes

1 See Benjamin H. D. Buchloh, "Allegorical Procedures: Appropriation and Montage in Contemporary Art," *Artforum* (September 1982): 43–56.

2 See in particular Daniel Buren, "Function of the Museum," *Artforum* (September 1973).

3 See Peter Bürger, *Theory of the Avant-Garde*, trans. Michael Shaw (Minneapolis: University of Minnesota Press, 1984). First published in 1974, this important essay takes no account of the artists mentioned here who are involved in institutional critique.

4 Buren, "Function of the Museum." Duchamp may have "accepted" this system, but he was certainly aware of its function. In *La Boîte en Valise* (1936–41), a collection of miniature reproductions of his works, he in effect acculturated his own art in his own museum allegorically and before the fact.

5 See Douglas Crimp, "The End of Painting," *October* 16 (Spring 1981): 69–86; and Buchloh, "Michael Asher and the Conclusion of Modernist Sculpture," in *Performance, Text(e)s & Documents*, ed. Chantal Pontbriand (Montreal: les editions Parachute, 1981), 55–65.

6 Yet this remains the measure of art devoted to institutional critique: "the ambition, not of fitting in more or less adequately with the game, nor even of contradicting it, but of abolishing its rules by playing with them, and playing another game, on another or the same ground, as a dissident" (Buren, *Reboundings*, trans. Philippe Hunt [Brussels: Daled & Gevært, 1977], 73).

7 Walter Benjamin, "The Work of Art in the Age of Mechanical Reproduction," in *Illuminations*, ed. Hannah Arendt, trans. Harry Zohn (New York: Schocken Books, 1969), 225.

8 See Andrea Fraser, "In and Out of Place," *Art in America* (June 1985); the notion "sumptuary expenditure" is derived from Jean Baudrillard ("Art Auction: Sign Exchange and Sumptuary Value," in *For a Critique of the Political Economy of the Sign*, trans. Charles Levin [St. Louis: Telos Press, 1981], 112–22). In her work Lawler seems to catch out a new motivation or emphasis in art patronage – beyond noble social obligation or subtle cultural legitimation to outright economic manipulation.

9 See Craig Owens, "Allan McCollum: Repetition and Difference," *Art in America* (September 1983): 130–2.

10 Allan McCollum quoted in press release for 1985 Cash/Newhouse Gallery show.

11 Buchloh, "Allegorical Procedures," 48. The analogy below between the art world and the race track is hinted at by Baudrillard in "Art Auction."

12 See Rosalind Krauss, "Sculpture in the Expanded Field," in *The Anti-æsthetic: Essays on Postmodern Culture*, ed. Hal Foster (Port Townsend: Bay Press, 1983).

13 Fraser, "In and Out of Place." I disagree with her representation of this work as a "*counter*practice."

14 Apropos this remark, Norman Bryson writes of Roland Barthes: "analysis omits the essential term of *transformation through labour* on which any theory of practice worthy of the name must rest; an omission accomplished by conceiving the signs within the social formation (discourse) as a finite mass, subject only to redistribution: this is a *mercantilist* theory of the signifying economy" (*Vision and Painting: The Logic of the Gaze* [New Haven: Yale University Press, 1983], 141).

15 Roland Barthes, "Lecture in Inauguration of the Chair of Literary Semiology, Collège de France," *October* 8 (Spring 1979): 5.

16 Ibid.

17 Dan Graham, "Signs," *Artforum* (April 1981): 39.

18 Some of the *Essays* were published in the *Black Book* (a parody of the manuals of messianic leaders?), others with the *Truisms* in *Abuse of Power Comes As No Surprise* (Halifax: The Press of the Nova Scotia College of Art and Design, 1983).

19 Barthes, *Writing Degree Zero*, trans. Annette Lavers and Colin Smith (New York: Hill and Wang, 1978), 25.

20 See "The Expressive Fallacy" elsewhere in this volume.

21 Michel Foucault, "The Subject and Power," *Critical Inquiry* 8 (Summer 1982), reprinted in *Art After Modernism: Rethinking Representation*, ed. Brian Wallis (New York/Boston, New Museum of Contemporary Art/David R. Godine, 1985), 420.

22 Barbara Kruger, *Screen*, vol. 23, no. 1 (1982).

23 Ibid.

24 Laura Mulvey, "Visual Pleasure and Narrative Cinema," *Screen*, vol. 16, no. 3 (Autumn 1975); reprinted in *Art After Modernism*, 366. For important essays on Kruger and related matters, see Craig Owens, "The Medusa Effect, or The Specular Ruse," and Jane Weinstock, "What She Means, to You," in *We Won't Play Nature to Your Culture* (London: Institute of Contemporary Arts, 1983), 5–16; and Kate Linker, "Representation and Sexuality," *Parachute* 32 (Fall 1983), reprinted in *Art After Modernism*.

25 Mulvey, 368.

26 Anika Lemaire, *Jacques Lacan*, trans. David Macey (London: Routledge & Kegan, Paul, 1979), 60.

27 Ibid., 129.

28 Owens, "Medusa Effect," 7.

29 Bryson, 88.

34

From "Can the Subaltern Speak?"

Gayatri Chakravorty Spivak

Indian-born philosopher Gayatri Chakravorty Spivak (1941–) has a rightful claim on the term "world philosopher." Her work ranges over recent European philosophy, critical theory, and literary theory, but has especially explored the status of non-Western culture, helping to inspire the field of "post-colonial studies," the critical exploration of the cultural experience of recently de-colonized peoples (this, despite the title of her 1998 book, *Don't Call me Postcolonial*). Her perspective bears the imprint of many contemporary influences, including Marxism, post-structuralism, and feminism. A prime example of a writer who both employs and criticizes postmodernism, in the following excerpts from a famous 1985 essay, she attacks Deleuze and Foucault for their treatment of colonial, third-world peoples, returning instead to certain Marxist notions that she finds in accord with Derrida's deconstructive approach.

... One cannot object to this minimalist summary of Marx's project, just as one cannot ignore that, in parts of the *Anti-Oedipus*, Deleuze and Guattari build their case on a brilliant if "poetic" grasp of Marx's *theory* of the money form.[i] Yet we might consolidate our critique in the following way: the relationship between global capitalism (exploitation in economics) and nation-state alliances (domination in geopolitics) is so macrological that it cannot account for the micrological texture of power. To move toward such an accounting one must move toward theories of ideology – of subject formations

that micrologically and often erratically operate the interests that congeal the macrologies. Such theories cannot afford to overlook the category of representation in its two senses. They must note how the staging of the world in representation – its scene of writing, its *Darstellung* – dissimulates the choice of and need for "heroes," paternal proxies, agents of power – *Vertretung*.[ii]

My view is that radical practice should attend to this double session of representation rather than reintroduce the individual subject through totalizing concepts of power and desire. It is also my view that, in keeping the area of class practice on a second level of abstraction, Marx was in effect keeping open the (Kantian and) Hegelian critique of the individual subject as agent.[1] This view does not oblige me to ignore that, by implicitly defining the family and the mother tongue as the ground level where culture and convention seem nature's own way of organizing "her" own subversion, Marx himself rehearses an ancient subterfuge.[2] In the context of poststructuralist claims to critical practice, this seems more recuperable than the clandestine restoration of subjective essentialism.

The reduction of Marx to a benevolent but dated figure most often serves the interest of launching

[ii] *Darstellung* is representation in the sense of depiction in signs, *Vertretung* in the sense of a proxy or stand-in.

[i] The first part of this essay criticizes Deleuze and Foucault for representing the non-Western world as "Other." Spivak employs Marxist nations as an alternative.

Gayatri Chakravorty Spivak, pp. 279–89, 292–4, 294–313 from "Can the Subaltern Speak?" in *Marxism and the Interpretation of Culture* (ed. Cary Nelson and Lawrence Grossberg). Champaign: University of Illinois Press, 1988.

a new theory of interpretation. In the Foucault–Deleuze conversation, the issue seems to be that there is no representation, no signifier (Is it to be presumed that the signifier has already been dispatched? There is, then, no sign-structure operating experience, and thus might one lay semiotics to rest?); theory is a relay of practice (thus laying problems of theoretical practice to rest) and the oppressed can know and speak for themselves. This reintroduces the constitutive subject on at least two levels: the Subject of desire and power as an irreducible methodological presupposition; and the self-proximate, if not self-identical, subject of the oppressed. Further, the intellectuals, who are neither of these S/subjects, become transparent in the relay race, for they merely report on the non-represented subject and analyze (without analyzing) the workings of (the unnamed Subject irreducibly presupposed by) power and desire. The produced "transparency" marks the place of "interest"; it is maintained by vehement denegation: "Now this role of referee, judge, and universal witness is one which I *absolutely refuse* to adopt." One responsibility of the critic might be to read and write so that the impossibility of such interested individualistic refusals of the institutional privileges of power bestowed on the subject is taken seriously. The refusal of the sign-system blocks the way to a developed theory of ideology. Here, too, the peculiar tone of denegation is heard. To Jacques-Alain Miller's suggestion that "the institution is itself discursive," Foucault responds, "Yes, if you like, but it doesn't much matter for my notion of the apparatus to be able to say that this is discursive and that isn't...given that my problem isn't a linguistic one" (*PK*, 198).[iii] Why this conflation of language and discourse from the master of discourse analysis?

Edward W. Said's[iv] critique of power in Foucault as a captivating and mystifying category that allows him "to obliterate the role of classes, the role of economics, the role of insurgency and rebellion," is most pertinent here.[3] I add to Said's analysis the notion of the surreptitious subject of power and desire marked by the transparency of the intellectual. Curiously enough, Paul Bové faults Said for emphasizing the importance of the intellectual, whereas "Foucault's project essentially is a challenge to the leading role of both hegemonic and oppositional intellectuals."[4] I have suggested that

this "challenge" is deceptive precisely because it ignores what Said emphasizes – the critic's institutional responsibility.

This S/subject,[v] curiously sewn together into a transparency by denegations, belongs to the exploiters' side of the international division of labor. It is impossible for contemporary French intellectuals to imagine the kind of Power and Desire that would inhabit the unnamed subject of the Other of Europe. It is not only that everything they read, critical or uncritical, is caught within the debate of the production of that Other, supporting or critiquing the constitution of the Subject as Europe. It is also that, in the constitution of that Other of Europe, great care was taken to obliterate the textual ingredients with which such a subject could cathect, could occupy (invest?) its itinerary – not only by ideological and scientific production, but also by the institution of the law. However reductionistic an economic analysis might seem, the French intellectuals forget at their peril that this entire overdetermined enterprise was in the interest of a dynamic economic situation requiring that interests, motives (desires), and power (of knowledge) be ruthlessly dislocated. To invoke that dislocation now as a radical discovery that should make us diagnose the economic (conditions of existence that separate out "classes" descriptively) as a piece of dated analytic machinery may well be to continue the work of that dislocation and unwittingly to help in securing "a new balance of hegemonic relations."[5] I shall return to this argument shortly. In the face of the possibility that the intellectual is complicit in the persistent constitution of Other as the Self's shadow, a possibility of political practice for the intellectual would be to put the economic "under erasure," to see the economic factor as irreducible as it reinscribes the social text, even as it is erased, however imperfectly, when it claims to be the final determinant or the transcendental signified.[6]

The clearest available example of such epistemic violence is the remotely orchestrated, far-flung, and heterogeneous project to constitute the colonial subject as Other. This project is also the asymmetrical obliteration of the trace of that Other in its precarious Subject-ivity. It is well known that Foucault locates epistemic violence, a complete overhaul of the episteme, in the redefinition of sanity at the end of the European eighteenth century.[7] But what if

---

iii Foucault's *Power/Knowledge*.

iv Edward Said (1935–), a Palestinian-born literary critic, had a major impact on subsequent post-colonial studies with his *Orientalism* (1978).

v Presumably the capital "S" refers to Lacan's notion of the subject as a member of the symbolic domain.

that particular redefinition was only a part of the narrative of history in Europe as well as in the colonies? What if the two projects of epistemic overhaul worked as dislocated and unacknowledged parts of a vast two-handed engine? Perhaps it is no more than to ask that the subtext of the palimpsestic narrative of imperialism be recognized as "subjugated knowledge," "a whole set of knowledges that have been disqualified as inadequate to their task or insufficiently elaborated: naive knowledges, located low down on the hierarchy, beneath the required level of cognition or scientificity" (*PK*, 82).

This is not to describe "the way things really were" or to privilege the narrative of history as imperialism as the best version of history.[8] It is, rather, to offer an account of how an explanation and narrative of reality was established as the normative one. To elaborate on this, let us consider briefly the underpinnings of the British codification of Hindu Law.

First, a few disclaimers: In the United States the third-worldism currently afloat in humanistic disciplines is often openly ethnic. I was born in India and received my primary, secondary, and university education there, including two years of graduate work. My Indian example could thus be seen as a nostalgic investigation of the lost roots of my own identity. Yet even as I know that one cannot freely enter the thickets of "motivations," I would maintain that my chief project is to point out the positivist–idealist variety of such nostalgia. I turn to Indian material because, in the absence of advanced disciplinary training, that accident of birth and education has provided me with a *sense* of the historical canvas, a hold on some of the pertinent languages that are useful tools for a *bricoleur*,[vi] especially when armed with the Marxist skepticism of concrete experience as the final arbiter and a critique of disciplinary formations. Yet the Indian case cannot be taken as representative of all countries, nations, cultures, and the like that may be invoked as the Other of Europe as Self.

Here, then, is a schematic summary of the epistemic violence of the codification of Hindu Law. If it clarifies the notion of epistemic violence, my final discussion of widow-sacrifice may gain added significance.

At the end of the eighteenth century, Hindu law, insofar as it can be described as a unitary system,

operated in terms of four texts that "staged" a four-part episteme defined by the subject's use of memory: *sruti* (the heard), *smriti* (the remembered), *sastra* (the learned-from-another), and *vyavahara* (the performed-in-exchange). The origins of what had been heard and what was remembered were not necessarily continuous or identical. Every invocation of *sruti* technically recited (or reopened) the event of originary "hearing" or revelation. The second two texts – the learned and the performed – were seen as dialectically continuous. Legal theorists and practitioners were not in any given case certain if this structure described the body of law or four ways of settling a dispute. The legitimation of the polymorphous structure of legal performance, "internally" noncoherent and open at both ends, through a binary vision, is the narrative of codification I offer as an example of epistemic violence.

The narrative of the stabilization and codification of Hindu law is less well known than the story of Indian education, so it might be well to start there.[9] Consider the often-quoted programmatic lines from Macaulay's infamous "Minute on Indian Education" (1835): "We must at present do our best to form a class who may be interpreters between us and the millions whom we govern; a class of persons, Indian in blood and colour, but English in taste, in opinions, in morals, and in intellect. To that class we may leave it to refine the vernacular dialects of the country, to enrich those dialects with terms of science borrowed from the Western nomenclature, and to render them by degrees fit vehicles for conveying knowledge to the great mass of the population."[10] The education of colonial subjects complements their production in law. One effect of establishing a version of the British system was the development of an uneasy separation between disciplinary formation in Sanskrit studies and the native, now alternative, tradition of Sanskrit "high culture." Within the former, the cultural explanations generated by authoritative scholars matched the epistemic violence of the legal project.

I locate here the founding of the Asiatic Society of Bengal in 1784, the Indian Institute at Oxford in 1883, and the analytic and taxonomic work of scholars like Arthur Macdonnell and Arthur Berriedale Keith, who were both colonial administrators and organizers of the matter of Sanskrit. From their confident utilitarian-hegemonic plans for students and scholars of Sanskrit, it is impossible to guess at either the aggressive repression of Sanskrit in the general educational framework or the increasing "feudalization" of the performative use

---

[vi] Practitioner of *bricolage*, Lévi-Strauss's term for the methodological handyman who patches diverse material together.

of Sanskrit in the everyday life of Brahmanic-hege-monic India.[11] A version of history was gradually established in which the Brahmans were shown to have the same intentions as (thus providing the legitimation for) the codifying British: "In order to preserve Hindu society intact [the] successors [of the original Brahmans] had to reduce everything to writing and make them more and more rigid. And that is what has preserved Hindu society in spite of a succession of political upheavals and foreign invasions."[12] This is the 1925 verdict of Maha-mahopadhyaya Haraprasad Shastri, learned Indian Sanskritist, a brilliant representative of the indigenous elite within colonial production, who was asked to write several chapters of a "History of Bengal" projected by the private secretary to the governor general of Bengal in 1916.[13] To signal the asymmetry in the relationship between authority and explanation (depending on the race–class of the authority), compare this 1928 remark by Edward Thompson, English intellectual: "Hinduism was what it seemed to be . . . It was a higher civilization that won [against it], both with Akbar and the English."[14] And add this, from a letter by an English soldier-scholar in the 1890s: "The study of Sanskrit, 'the language of the gods' has afforded me intense enjoyment during the last 25 years of my life in India, but it has not, I am thankful to say, led me, *as it has some*, to give up a hearty belief in our own grand religion."[15]

These authorities are *the very best* of the sources for the nonspecialist French intellectual's entry into the civilization of the Other.[16] I am, however, not referring to intellectuals and scholars of post-colonial production, like Shastri, when I say that the Other as Subject is inaccessible to Foucault and Deleuze. I am thinking of the general nonspecialist, nonacademic population across the class spectrum, for whom the episteme operates its silent programming function. Without considering the map of exploitation, on what grid of "oppression" would they place this motley crew?

Let us now move to consider the margins (one can just as well say the silent, silenced center) of the circuit marked out by this epistemic violence, men and women among the illiterate peasantry, the tribals, the lowest strata of the urban subproletariat. According to Foucault and Deleuze (in the First World, under the standardization and regimentation of socialized capital, though they do not seem to recognize this) the oppressed, if given the chance (the problem of representation cannot be bypassed here), and on the way to solidarity through alliance politics (a Marxist thematic is at work here) *can speak and know their conditions*. We must now confront the following question: On the other side of the international division of labor from socialized capital, inside *and* outside the circuit of the epistemic violence of imperialist law and education supplementing an earlier economic text, *can the subaltern speak?*

Antonio Gramsci's work on the "subaltern classes" extends the class-position/class-consciousness argument isolated in *The Eighteenth Brumaire*.[vii] Perhaps because Gramsci criticizes the vanguardistic position of the Leninist intellectual, he is concerned with the intellectual's role in the subaltern's cultural and political movement into the hegemony. This movement must be made to determine the production of history as narrative (of truth). In texts such as "The Southern Question," Gramsci considers the movement of historical-political economy in Italy within what can be seen as an allegory of reading taken from or prefiguring an international division of labor.[17] Yet an account of the phased development of the subaltern is thrown out of joint when his cultural macrology is operated, however remotely, by the epistemic interference with legal and disciplinary definitions accompanying the imperialist project. When I move, at the end of this essay, to the question of woman as subaltern, I will suggest that the possibility of collectivity itself is persistently foreclosed through the manipulation of female agency.

The first part of my proposition – that the phased development of the subaltern is complicated by the imperialist project – is confronted by a collective of intellectuals who may be called the "Subaltern Studies" group.[18] They *must* ask, Can the subaltern speak? Here we are within Foucault's own discipline of history and with people who acknowledge his influence. Their project is to re-think Indian colonial historiography from the perspective of the discontinuous chain of peasant insurgencies during the colonial occupation. This is indeed the problem of "the permission to narrate" discussed by Said.[19] As Ranajit Guha argues,

> The historiography of Indian nationalism has for a long time been dominated by elitism – colonialist elitism and bourgeois-nationalist elitism . . . shar[ing] the prejudice that the making

vii   Antonio Gramsci (1891–1937), Italian Marxist theorist, with György (Georg) Lukács a central figure of "Western" or liberal Marxism. *The Eighteenth Brumaire of Louis Bonaparte* is a work by Marx.

of the Indian nation and the development of the consciousness – nationalism – which confirmed this process were exclusively or predominantly elite achievements. In the colonialist and neo-colonialist historiographies these achievements are credited to British colonial rulers, administrators, policies, institutions, and culture; in the nationalist and neo-nationalist writings – to Indian elite personalities, institutions, activities and ideas.[20]

Certain varieties of the Indian elite are at best native informants for first-world intellectuals interested in the voice of the Other. But one must nevertheless insist that the colonized subaltern *subject* is irretrievably heterogeneous.

Against the indigenous elite we may set what Guha calls "the *politics* of the people," both outside ("this was an *autonomous* domain, for it neither originated from elite politics nor did its existence depend on the latter") and inside ("it continued to operate vigorously in spite of [colonialism], adjusting itself to the conditions prevailing under the Raj and in many respects developing entirely new strains in both form and content") the circuit of colonial production.[21] I cannot entirely endorse this insistence on determinate vigor and full autonomy, for practical historiographic exigencies will not allow such endorsements to privilege subaltern consciousness. Against the possible charge that his approach is essentialist, Guha constructs a definition of the people (the place of that essence) that can be only an identity-in-differential. He proposes a dynamic stratification grid describing colonial social production at large. Even the third group on the list, the buffer group, as it were, between the people and the great macrostructural dominant groups, is itself defined as a place of in-betweenness, what Derrida has described as an "*antre*":[22]

elite $\begin{cases} \text{1. Dominant foreign groups.} \\ \text{2. Dominant indigenous groups on the all-India level.} \end{cases}$

3. Dominant indigenous groups at the regional and local levels.

4. The terms "people" and "subaltern classes" have been used as synonymous throughout this note. The social groups and elements included in this category represent *the demographic difference between the total Indian population and all those whom we have described as the "elite."*

Consider the third item on this list – the *antre*[viii] of situational indeterminacy these careful historians presuppose as they grapple with the question, Can the subaltern speak? "*Taken as a whole and in the abstract* this ... category ... was *heterogeneous* in its composition and thanks to the uneven character of regional economic and social developments, *differed from area to area*. The same class or element which was dominant in one area ... could be among the dominated in another. This could and did create many ambiguities and contradictions in attitudes and alliances, especially among the lowest strata of the rural gentry, impoverished landlords, rich peasants and upper middle class peasants all of whom belonged, *ideally speaking*, to the category of people or subaltern classes."[23]

"The task of research" projected here is "to investigate, identify and measure the *specific* nature and degree of the *deviation* of [the] elements [constituting item 3] from the ideal and situate it historically." "Investigate, identify, and measure the specific": a program could hardly be more essentialist and taxonomic. Yet a curious methodological imperative is at work. I have argued that, in the Foucault-Deleuze conversation, a postrepresentationalist vocabulary hides an essentialist agenda. In subaltern studies, because of the violence of imperialist epistemic, social, and disciplinary inscription, a project understood in essentialist terms must traffic in a radical textual practice of differences. The object of the group's investigation, in the case not even of the people as such but of the floating buffer zone of the regional elite-subaltern, is a *deviation* from an *ideal* – the people or subaltern – which is itself defined as a difference from the elite. It is toward this structure that the research is oriented, a predicament rather different from the self-diagnosed transparency of the first-world radical intellectual. What taxonomy can fix such a space? Whether or not they themselves perceive it – in fact Guha sees his definition of "the people" within the master-slave dialectic – their text articulates the difficult task of rewriting its own conditions of impossibility as the conditions of its possibility.

"At the regional and local levels [the dominant indigenous groups] ... if belonging to social strata hierarchically inferior to those of the dominant all-Indian groups *acted in the interests of the latter and not in conformity to interests corresponding truly to their own social being*." When these writers speak,

viii   Den or lair

in their essentializing language, of a gap between interest and action in the intermediate group, their conclusions are closer to Marx than to the self-conscious naivete of Deleuze's pronouncement on the issue. Guha, like Marx, speaks of interest in terms of the social rather than the libidinal being. The Name-of-the-Father[ix] imagery in *The Eighteenth Brumaire* can help to emphasize that, on the level of class or group action, "true correspondence to own being" is as artificial or social as the patronymic.

So much for the intermediate group marked in item 3. For the "true" subaltern group, whose identity is its difference, there is no unrepresentable subaltern subject that can know and speak itself; the intellectual's solution is not to abstain from representation. The problem is that the subject's itinerary has not been traced so as to offer an object of seduction to the representing intellectual. In the slightly dated language of the Indian group, the question becomes, How can we touch the consciousness of the people, even as we investigate their politics? With what voice-consciousness can the subaltern speak? Their project, after all, is to rewrite the development of the consciousness of the Indian nation. The planned discontinuity of imperialism rigorously distinguishes this project, however old-fashioned its articulation, from "rendering visible the medical and juridical mechanisms that surrounded the story [of Pierre Rivière]."[x] Foucault is correct in suggesting that "to make visible the unseen can also mean a change of level, addressing oneself to a layer of material which had hitherto had no pertinence for history and which had not been recognized as having any moral, aesthetic or historical value." It is the slippage from rendering visible the mechanism to rendering vocal the individual, both avoiding "any kind of analysis of [the subject] whether psychological, psychoanalytical or linguistic," that is consistently troublesome (*PK*, 49–50).

The critique by Ajit K. Chaudhury, a West Bengali Marxist, of Guha's search for the subaltern consciousness can be seen as a moment of the production process that includes the subaltern. Chaudhury's perception that the Marxist view of

the transformation of consciousness involves the *knowledge* of social relations seems to me, in principle, astute. Yet the heritage of the positivist ideology that has appropriated orthodox Marxism obliges him to add this rider: "This is not to belittle the importance of understanding peasants' consciousness or workers' consciousness *in its pure form*. This enriches our knowledge of the peasant and the worker and, possibly, throws light on how a particular mode takes on different forms in different regions, *which is considered a problem of second-order importance in classical Marxism.*"[24]

This variety of "internationalist" Marxism, which believes in a pure, retrievable form of consciousness only to dismiss it, thus closing off what in Marx remain moments of productive bafflement, can at once be the object of Foucault's and Deleuze's rejection of Marxism *and* the source of the critical motivation of the Subaltern Studies group. All three are united in the assumption that there *is* a pure form of consciousness. On the French scene, there is a shuffling of signifiers: "the unconscious" or "the subject-in-oppression" clandestinely fills the space of "the pure form of consciousness." In orthodox "internationalist" intellectual Marxism, whether in the First World or the Third, the pure form of consciousness remains an idealistic bedrock which, dismissed as a second-order problem, often earns it the reputation of racism and sexism. In the Subaltern Studies group it needs development according to the unacknowledged terms of its own articulation.

For such an articulation, a developed theory of ideology can again be most useful. In a critique such as Chaudhury's, the association of "consciousness" with "knowledge" omits the crucial middle term of "ideological production": "Consciousness, according to Lenin, is associated with a *knowledge* of the interrelationships between different classes and groups; i.e., a knowledge of the materials that constitute society. . . . These definitions acquire a meaning only within the problematic within a definite knowledge object – to *understand* change in history, or specifically, change from one mode to another, *keeping the question of the specificity of a particular mode out of the focus.*"[25]

Pierre Macherey provides the following formular for the interpretation of ideology: "What is important in a work is what it does not say. This is not the same as the careless notation 'what it refuses to say,' although that would in itself be interesting: a method might be built on it, with the task of *measuring silences*, whether acknow-

---

[ix] The "Name of the Father" is Lacan's term for the central signifier in a symbolic system, here ascribed to Marx's *The Eighteenth Brumaire of Louis Bonaparte*.

[x] Foucault's *I, Pierre Rivière, having slaughtered my mother, my sister, my brother . . . A Case of Parricide in the Nineteenth Century*, trans. Frank Jellonek (Lincoln: University of Nebraska, 1982).

ledged or unacknowledged. But rather this, what the work *cannot* say is important, because there the elaboration of the utterance is carried out, in a sort of journey to silence."[26] Macherey's ideas can be developed in directions he would be unlikely to follow. Even as he writes, ostensibly, of the literariness of the literature of European provenance, he articulates a method applicable to the social text of imperialism, somewhat against the grain of his own argument. Although the notion "what it refuses to say" might be careless for a literary work, something like a collective ideological *refusal* can be diagnosed for the codifying legal practice of imperialism. This would open the field for a political economic and multidisciplinary ideological reinscription of the terrain. Because this is a "worlding of the world" on a second level of abstraction, a concept of refusal becomes plausible here. The archival, historiographic, disciplinary-critical, and, inevitably, interventionist work involved here is indeed a task of "measuring silences." This can be a description of "investigating, identifying, and measuring ... the *deviation*" from an ideal that is irreducibly differential.

When we come to the concomitant question of the consciousness of the subaltern, the notion of what the work *cannot* say becomes important. In the semioses of the social text, elaborations of insurgency stand in the place of "the utterance." The sender – "the peasant" – is marked only as a pointer to an irretrievable consciousness. As for the receiver, we must ask who is "the real receiver" of an "insurgency?" The historian, transforming "insurgency" into "text for knowledge," is only one "receiver" of any collectively intended social act. With no possibility of nostalgia for that lost origin, the historian must suspend (as far as possible) the clamor of his or her own consciousness (or consciousness-effect, as operated by disciplinary training), so that the elaboration of the insurgency, packaged with an insurgent-consciousness, does not freeze into an "object of investigation," or, worse yet, a model for imitation. "The subject" implied by the texts of insurgency can only serve as a counterpossibility for the narrative sanctions granted to the colonial subject in the dominant groups. The postcolonial intellectuals learn that their privilege is their loss. In this they are a paradigm of the intellectuals.

It is well known that the notion of the feminine (rather than the subaltern of imperialism) has been used in a similar way within deconstructive criticism and within certain varieties of feminist criticism.[27] In the former case, a figure of "woman" is at issue, one whose minimal predication as indeterminate is already available to the phallocentric tradition. Subaltern historiography raises questions of method that would prevent it from using such a ruse. For the "figure" of woman, the relationship between woman and silence can be plotted by women themselves; race and class differences are subsumed under that charge. Subaltern historiography must confront the impossibility of such gestures. The narrow epistemic violence of imperialism gives us an imperfect allegory of the general violence that is the possibility of an episteme.[28]

Within the effaced itinerary of the subaltern subject, the track of sexual difference is doubly effaced. The question is not of female participation in insurgency, or the ground rules of the sexual division of labor, for both of which there is "evidence." It is, rather, that, both as object of colonialist historiography and as subject of insurgency, the ideological construction of gender keeps the male dominant. If, in the context of colonial production, the subaltern has no history and cannot speak, the subaltern as female is even more deeply in shadow.

The contemporary international division of labor is a displacement of the divided field of nineteenth-century territorial imperialism. Put simply, a group of countries, generally first-world, are in the position of investing capital; another group, generally third-world, provide the field for investment, both through the comprador indigenous capitalists and through their ill-protected and shifting labor force. In the interest of maintaining the circulation and growth of industrial capital (and of the concomitant task of administration within ninteenth-century territorial imperialism), transportation, law, and standardized education systems were developed – even as local industries were destroyed, land distribution was rearranged, and raw material was transferred to the colonizing country. With so-called decolonization, the growth of multinational capital, and the relief of the administrative charge, "development" does not now involve wholesale legislation and establishing educational *systems* in a comparable way. This impedes the growth of consumerism in the comprador countries. With modern telecommunications and the emergence of advanced capitalist economies at the two edges of Asia, maintaining the international division of labor serves to keep the supply of cheap labor in the comprador countries.

Human labor is not, of course, intrinsically "cheap" or "expensive." An absence of labor laws (or a discriminatory enforcement of them), a totalitarian state (often entailed by development and modernization in the periphery), and minimal subsistence requirements on the part of the worker will ensure it. To keep this crucial item intact, the urban proletariat in comprador countries must not be systematically trained in the ideology of consumerism (parading as the philosophy of a classless society) that, against all odds, prepares the ground for resistance through the coalition politics Foucault mentions (*FD*, 216).[xi] This separation from the ideology of consumerism is increasingly exacerbated by the proliferating phenomena of international subcontracting. "Under this strategy, manufacturers based in developed countries subcontract the most labor intensive stages of production, for example, sewing or assembly, to the Third World nations where labor is cheap. Once assembled, the multinational re-imports the goods – under generous tariff exemptions – to the developed country *instead of selling them to the local market*." Here the link to training in consumerism is almost snapped. "While global recession has markedly slowed trade and investment worldwide since 1979, international subcontracting has boomed.... In these cases, multinationals are freer to resist militant workers, revolutionary upheavals, and even economic downturns."[29]

Class mobility is increasingly lethargic in the comprador theaters. Not surprisingly, some members of *indigenous dominant* groups in comprador countries, members of the local bourgeoisie, find the language of alliance politics attractive. Identifying with forms of resistance plausible in advanced capitalist countries is often of a piece with that elitist bent of bourgeois historiography described by Ranajit Guha.

Belief in the plausibility of global alliance politics is prevalent among women of dominant social groups interested in "international feminism" in the comprador countries. At the other end of the scale, those most separated from any possibility of an alliance among "women, prisoners, conscripted soldiers, hospital patients, and homosexuals" (*FD*, 216) are the females of the urban subproletariat. In their case, the denial and withholding of consumerism and the structure of exploitation is compounded by patriarchal social relations. On the other side of the international division of labor, the subject of exploitation cannot know and speak the text of female exploitation, even if the absurdity of the nonrepresenting intellectual making space for her to speak is achieved. The woman is doubly in shadow.

Yet even this does not encompass the heterogeneous Other. Outside (though not completely so) the circuit of the *international* division of labor, there are people whose consciousness we cannot grasp if we close off our benevolence by constructing a homogeneous Other referring only to our own place in the seat of the Same or the Self. Here are subsistence farmers, unorganized peasant labor, the tribals, and the communities of zero workers on the street or in the countryside. To confront them is not to represent (*vertreten*) them but to learn to represent (*darstellen*) ourselves. This argument would take us into a critique of a disciplinary anthropology and the relationship between elementary pedagogy and disciplinary formation. It would also question the implicit demand, made by intellectuals who choose a "naturally articulate" subject of oppression, that such a subject come through history as a foreshortened mode-of-production narrative.

That Deleuze and Foucault ignore both the epistemic violence of imperialism and the international division of labor would matter less if they did not, in closing, touch on third-world issues. But in France it is impossible to ignore the problem of the *tiers monde*,[xii] the inhabitants of the erstwhile French African colonies. Deleuze limits his consideration of the Third World to these old local and regional indigenous elite who are, ideally, subaltern. In this context, references to the maintenance of the surplus army of labor fall into reverse-ethnic sentimentality. Since he is speaking of the heritage of nineteenth-century territorial imperialism, his reference is to the nation-state rather than the globalizing center: "French capitalism needs greatly a floating signifier of unemployment. In this perspective, we begin to see the unity of the forms of repression: restrictions on immigration, once it is acknowledged that the most difficult and thankless jobs go to immigrant workers; repression in the factories, because the French must reacquire the 'taste' for increasingly harder work; the struggle against youth and the repression of the educational system" (*FD*, 211–12). This is an acceptable analy-

---

[xi] Foucault's *Language, Counter-Memory, Practice: Selected Essays and Interviews*, trans. Donald Bouchard and Sherry Simon (Ithaca: Cornell University, 1977).

[xii] Third world.

sis. Yet it shows again that the Third World can enter the resistance program of an alliance politics directed against a "*unified* repression" only when it is confined to the third-world groups that are directly accessible to the First World.[30] This benevolent first-world appropriation and reinscription of the Third World as an Other is the founding characteristic of much third-worldism in the U.S. human sciences today....

I will consider a chapter that Derrida composed twenty years ago: "Of Grammatology As a Positive Science" (*OG*, 74–93).[xiii] In this chapter Derrida confronts the issue of whether "deconstruction" can lead to an adequate practice, whether critical or political. The question is how to keep the ethnocentric Subject from establishing itself by selectively defining an Other. This is not a program for the Subject as such; rather, it is a program for the benevolent *Western* intellectual. For those of us who feel that the "subject" has a history and that the task of the first-world subject of knowledge in our historical moment is to resist and critique "recognition" of the Third World through "assimilation," this specificity is crucial. In order to advance a factual rather than a pathetic critique of the European intellectual's ethnocentric impulse, Derrida admits that he cannot ask the "first" questions that must be answered to establish the grounds of his argument. He does not declare that grammatology can "rise above" (Frank Lentricchia's phrase) mere empiricism; for, like empiricism, it cannot ask first questions. Derrida thus aligns "grammatological" knowledge *with the same problems* as empirical investigation. "Deconstruction" is not, therefore, a new word for "ideological demystification." Like "empirical investigation ... tak[ing] shelter in the field of grammatological knowledge" obliges "operat[ing] through 'examples'" (*OG*, 75).

The examples Derrida lays out – to show the limits of grammatology as a positive science – come from the appropriate ideological self-justification of an imperialist project. In the European seventeenth century, he writes, there were three kinds of "prejudices" operating in histories of writing which constituted a "symptom of the crisis of European consciousness" (*OG*, 75): the "theological prejudice," the "Chinese prejudice," and the "hieroglyphist prejudice." The first can be

indexed as: God wrote a primitive or natural script: Hebrew or Greek. The second: Chinese is a perfect *blueprint* for philosophical writing, but it is only a blueprint. True philosophical writing is "independen[t] with regard to history" (*OG*, 79) and will sublate Chinese into an easy-to-learn script that will supersede actual Chinese. The third: that Egyptian script is too sublime to be deciphered. The first prejudice preserves the "actuality" of Hebrew or Greek; the last two ("rational" and "mystical," respectively) collude to support the first, where the center of the logos is seen as the Judaeo-Christian God (the appropriation of the Hellenic Other through assimilation is an earlier story) – a "prejudice" still sustained in efforts to give the cartography of the Judaeo-Christian myth the status of geopolitical history:

> The concept of Chinese writing thus functioned as a sort of *European hallucination*.... This functioning obeyed a rigorous necessity.... It was not disturbed by the knowledge of Chinese script ... which was then available.... A "*hieroglyphist prejudice*" had produced the same effect of *interested blindness*. Far from proceeding ... from ethnocentric scorn, the occultation takes the form of an hyperbolical admiration. We have not finished demonstrating the necessity of this pattern. Our century is not free from it; each time that ethnocentrism is precipitately and ostentatiously reversed, some effort silently hides behind all the spectacular effects to *consolidate an inside* and to draw from it some domestic benefit. (*OG*, 80; Derrida italicizes only "hieroglyphist prejudice")

Derrida proceeds to offer two characteristic possibilities for solutions to the problem of the European Subject, which seeks to produce an Other that would consolidate an inside, its own subject status. What follows is an account of the complicity between writing, the opening of domestic and civil society, and the structures of desire, power, and capitalization. Derrida then discloses the vulnerability of his own desire to conserve something that is, paradoxically, both ineffable and nontranscendental. In critiquing the production of the colonial subject, this ineffable, nontranscendental ("historical") place is cathected by the subaltern subject.

Derrida closes the chapter by showing again that the project of grammatology is obliged to develop *within* the discourse of presence. It is not just a

xiii   Jacques Derrida's *Of Grammatology*, trans. Gayatri Chakravorty Spivak (Baltimore: Johns Hopkins, 1974).

critique of presence but an awareness of the itinerary of the discourse of presence in one's *own* critique, a vigilance precisely against too great a claim for transparency. The word "writing" as the name of the object and model of grammatology is a practice "only within the *historical* closure, that is to say within the limits of science and philosophy" (*OG*, 93).

Derrida here makes Nietzschean, philosophical, and psychoanalytic, rather than specifically political, choices to suggest a critique of European ethnocentrism in the constitution of the Other. As a postcolonial intellectual, I am not troubled that he does not *lead* me (as Europeans inevitably seem to do) to the specific path that such a critique makes necessary. It is more important to me that, as a European philosopher, he articulates the *European* Subject's tendency to constitute the Other as marginal to ethnocentrism and locates *that* as the problem with all logocentric and therefore also all grammatological endeavors (since the main thesis of the chapter is the complicity between the two). *Not* a general problem, but a *European* problem. It is within the context of this ethnocentricism that he tries so desperately to demote the Subject of thinking or knowledge as to say that "*thought* is . . . the blank part of the text" (*OG*, 93); that which is thought is, if blank, still *in the text* and must be consigned to the Other of history. That inaccessible blankness circumscribed by an interpretable text is what a postcolonial critic of imperialism would like to see developed within the European enclosure as *the* place of the production of theory. The postcolonial critics and intellectuals can attempt to displace their own production only by presupposing that *text-inscribed* blankness. To render thought or the thinking subject transparent or invisible seems, by contrast, to hide the relentless recognition of the Other by assimilation. It is in the interest of such cautions that Derrida does not invoke "letting the other(s) speak for himself" but rather invokes an "appeal" to or "call" to the "quite-other" (*tout-autre* as opposed to a self-consolidating other), of "rendering *delirious* that interior voice that is the voice of the other in us."[31]

Derrida calls the ethnocentrism of the European science of writing in the late seventeenth and early eighteenth centuries a symptom of the general crisis of European consciousness. It is, of course, part of a greater symptom, or perhaps the crisis itself, the slow turn from feudalism to capitalism via the first waves of capitalist imperialism. The itinerary of recognition through assimilation of the Other can be more interestingly traced, it seems to me, in the imperialist constitution of the colonial subject than in repeated incursions into psychoanalysis or the "figure" of woman, though the importance of these two interventions *within* deconstruction should not be minimized. Derrida has not moved (or perhaps cannot move) into that arena . . .

Can the subaltern speak? What must the elite do to watch out for the continuing construction of the subaltern? The question of "woman" seems most problematic in this context. Clearly, if you are poor, black, and female you get it in three ways. If, however, this formulation is moved from the first-world context into the postcolonial (which is not identical with the third-world) context, the description "black" or "of color" loses persuasive significance. The necessary stratification of colonial subject-constitution in the first phase of capitalist imperialism makes "color" useless as an emancipatory signifier. Confronted by the ferocious standardizing benevolence of most U.S. and Western European human-scientific radicalism (recognition by assimilation), the progressive though heterogeneous withdrawal of consumerism in the comprador periphery, and the exclusion of the margins of even the center-periphery articulation (the "true and differential subaltern"), the analogue of class-consciousness rather than race-consciousness in this area seems historically, disciplinarily, and practically forbidden by Right and Left alike. It is not just a question of a *double* displacement, as it is not simply the problem of finding a psychoanalytic allegory that can accommodate the third-world woman with the first.

The cautions I have just expressed are valid only if we are speaking of the subaltern woman's consciousness – or, more acceptably, subject. Reporting on, or better still, participating in, anti-sexist work among women of color or women in class oppression in the First World or the Third World is undeniably on the agenda. We should also welcome all the information retrieval in these silenced areas that is taking place in anthropology, political science, history, and sociology. Yet the assumption and construction of a consciousness or subject sustains such work and will, in the long run, cohere with the work of imperialist subject-constitution, mingling epistemic violence with the advancement of learning and civilization. And the subaltern woman will be as mute as ever.[32]

In so fraught a field, it is not easy to ask the question of the consciousness of the subaltern woman; it is thus all the more necessary to remind pragmatic radicals that such a question is not an idealist red herring. Though all feminist or anti-sexist projects cannot be reduced to this one, to ignore it is an unacknowledged political gesture that has a long history and collaborates with a masculine radicalism that renders the place of the investigator transparent. In seeking to learn to speak to (rather than listen to or speak for) the historically muted subject of the subaltern woman, the postcolonial intellectual *systematically* "unlearns" female privilege. This systematic un-learning involves learning to critique postcolonial discourse with the best tools it can provide and not simply substituting the lost figure of the colonized. Thus, to question the unquestioned muting of the subaltern woman even within the anti-imperialist project of subaltern studies is not, as Jonathan Culler suggests, to "produce difference by differing" or to "appeal ... to a sexual identity de-fined as essential and privilege experiences associ-ated with that identity."[33]

Culler's version of the feminist project is pos-sible within what Elizabeth Fox-Genovese has called "the contribution of the bourgeois-democratic revolutions to the social and political individualism of women."[34] Many of us were ob-liged to understand the feminist project as Culler now describes it when we were still agitating as U.S. academics.[35] It was certainly a necessary stage in my own education in "unlearning" and has consolidated the belief that the mainstream project of Western feminism both continues and displaces the battle over the right to individualism between women and men in situations of upward class mobility. One suspects that the debate be-tween U.S. feminism and European "theory" (as theory is generally represented by women from the United States or Britain) occupies a significant corner of that very terrain. I am generally sympa-thetic with the call to make U.S. feminism more "theoretical." It seems, however, that the problem of the muted subject of the subaltern woman, though not solved by an "essentialist" search for lost origins, cannot be served by the call for more theory in Anglo-America either.

That call is often given in the name of a critique of "positivism," which is seen here as identical with "essentialism." Yet Hegel, the modern inaugurator of "the work of the negative," was not a stranger to the notion of essences. For Marx, the curious per-sistence of essentialism within the dialectic was a profound and productive problem. Thus, the strin-gent binary opposition between positivism/essen-tialism (read, U.S.) and "theory" (read, French or Franco-German via Anglo-American) may be spurious. Apart from repressing the ambiguous complicity between essentialism and critiques of positivism (acknowledged by Derrida in "Of Grammatology As a Positive Science"), it also errs by implying that positivism is not a theory. This move allows the emergence of a proper name, a positive essence, Theory. Once again, the position of the investigator remains unquestioned. And, if this territorial debate turns toward the Third World, no change in the question of method is to be discerned. This debate cannot take into account that, in the case of the woman as subaltern, no ingredients for the constitution of the itinerary of the trace of a sexed subject can be gathered to locate the possibility of dissemination.

Yet I remain generally sympathetic in aligning feminism with the critique of positivism and the defetishization of the concrete. I am also far from averse to learning from the work of Western theor-ists, though I have learned to insist on marking their positionality as investigating subjects. Given these conditions, and as a literary critic, I tactically confronted the immense problem of the conscious-ness of the woman as subaltern. I reinvented the problem in a sentence and transformed it into the object of a simple semiosis. What does this sentence mean? The analogy here is between the ideological victimization of a Freud and the positionality of the postcolonial intellectual as investigating subject.

As Sarah Kofman has shown, the deep ambiguity of Freud's use of women as a scapegoat is a reac-tion-formation to an initial and continuing desire to give the hysteric a voice, to transform her into the *subject* of hysteria.[36] The masculine-imperialist ideological formation that shaped that desire into "the daughter's seduction" is part of the same formation that constructs the monolithic "third-world woman." As a postcolonial intellectual, I am influenced by that formation as well. Part of our "unlearning" project is to articulate that ideo-logical formation – by *measuring* silences, if neces-sary – into the *object* of investigation. Thus, when confronted with the questions, Can the subaltern speak? and Can the subaltern (as woman) speak?, our efforts to give the subaltern a voice in history will be doubly open to the dangers run by Freud's discourse. As a product of these considerations, I have put together the sentence "White men are saving brown women from brown men" in a spirit not unlike the one to be encountered in Freud's investigations of the sentence "A child is being beaten."[37]

The use of Freud here does not imply an isomorphic analogy between subject-formation and the behavior of social collectives, a frequent practice, often accompanied by a reference to Reich,[xiv] in the conversation between Deleuze and Foucault. So I am not suggesting that "White men are saving brown women from brown men" is a sentence indicating a *collective* fantasy symptomatic of a *collective* itinerary of sadomasochistic repression in a *collective* imperialist enterprise. There is a satisfying symmetry in such an allegory, but I would rather invite the reader to consider it a problem in "wild psychoanalysis" than a clinching solution.[38] Just as Freud's insistence on making the woman the scapegoat in "A child is being beaten" and elsewhere discloses his political interests, however imperfectly, so my insistence on imperialist subject-production as the occasion for this sentence discloses my politics.

Further, I am attempting to borrow the general methodological aura of Freud's strategy toward the sentence he constructed *as a sentence* out of the many similar substantive accounts his patients gave him. This does not mean I will offer a case of transference-in-analysis as an isomorphic model for the transaction between reader and text (my sentence). The analogy between transference and literary criticism or historiography is no more than a productive catachresis. To say that the subject is a text does not authorize the converse pronouncement: the verbal text is a subject.

I am fascinated, rather, by how Freud predicates a *history* of repression that produces the final sentence. It is a history with a double origin, one hidden in the amnesia of the infant, the other lodged in our archaic past, assuming by implication a preoriginary space where human and animal were not yet differentiated.[39] We are driven to impose a homologue of this Freudian strategy on the Marxist narrative to explain the ideological dissimulation of imperialist political economy and outline a history of repression that produces a sentence like the one I have sketched. This history also has a double origin, one hidden in the maneuverings behind the British abolition of widow sacrifice in 1829,[40] the other lodged in the classical and Vedic past of

Hindu India, the *Rg-Veda* and the *Dharmaśāstra*. No doubt there is also an undifferentiated preoriginary space that supports this history.

The sentence I have constructed is one among many displacements describing the relationship between brown and white men (sometimes brown and white women worked in). It takes its place among some sentences of "hyperbolic admiration" or of pious guilt that Derrida speaks of in connection with the "hieroglyphist prejudice." The relationship between the imperialist subject and the subject of imperialism is at least ambiguous.

The Hindu widow ascends the pyre of the dead husband and immolates herself upon it. This is widow sacrifice. (The conventional transcription of the Sanskrit word for the widow would be *sati*. The early colonial British transcribed it *suttee*.) The rite was not practiced universally and was not caste- or class-fixed. The abolition of this rite by the British has been generally understood as a case of "White men saving brown women from brown men." White women – from the nineteenth-century British Missionary Registers to Mary Daly – have not produced an alternative understanding.[xv] Against this is the Indian nativist argument, a parody of the nostalgia for lost origins: "The women actually wanted to die."

The two sentences go a long way to legitimize each other. One never encounters the testimony of the women's voice-consciousness. Such a testimony would not be ideology-transcendent or "fully" subjective, of course, but it would have constituted the ingredients for producing a countersentence. As one goes down the grotesquely mistranscribed names of these women, the sacrificed widows, in the police reports included in the records of the East India Company, one cannot put together a "voice." The most one can sense is the immense heterogeneity breaking through even such a skeletal and ignorant account (castes, for example, are regularly described as tribes). Faced with the dialectically interlocking sentences that are constructible as "White men are saving brown women from brown men" and "The women wanted to die," the postcolonial woman intellectual asks the question of simple semiosis – What does this mean? – and begins to plot a history.

To mark the moment when not only a civil but a good society is born out of domestic confusion,

---

[xiv] Presumably Wilhelm Reich (1897–1957), controversial German psychoanalyst who insisted that libido was an observable material.

[xv] Mary Daly (1928–), feminist theologian, author of *Beyond God the Father: Toward a Philosophy of Women's Liberation*.

singular events that break the letter of the law to instill its spirit are often invoked. The protection of women by men often provides such an event. If we remember that the British boasted of their absolute equity toward and noninterference with native custom/law, an invocation of this sanctioned transgression of the letter for the sake of the spirit may be read in J. M. Derrett's remark: "The very first legislation upon Hindu Law was carried through without the assent of a single Hindu." The legislation is not named here. The next sentence, where the measure is named, is equally interesting if one considers the implications of the survival of a colonially established "good" society after decolonization: "The recurrence of *sati* in independent India is probably an obscurantist revival which cannot long survive even in a very backward part of the country."[41]

Whether this observation is correct or not, what interests me is that the protection of woman (today the "third-world woman") becomes a signifier for the establishment of a *good* society which must, at such inaugurative moments, transgress mere legality, or equity of legal policy. In this particular case, the process also allowed the redefinition as a crime of what had been tolerated, known, or adulated as ritual. In other words, this one item in Hindu law jumped the frontier between the private and the public domain.

Although Foucault's *historical narrative*, focusing solely on Western Europe, sees merely a tolerance for the criminal antedating the development of criminology in the late eighteenth century (*PK*, 41), his *theoretical description* of the "episteme"[xvi] is pertinent here: "The *episteme* is the 'apparatus' which makes possible the separation not of the true from the false, but of what may not be characterized as scientific" (*PK*, 197) – ritual as opposed to crime, the one fixed by superstition, the other by legal science.

The leap of *suttee* from private to public has a clear and complex relationship with the changeover from a mercantile and commercial to a territorial and administrative British presence; it can be followed in correspondence among the police stations, the lower and higher courts, the courts of directors, the prince regent's court, and the like. (It is interesting to note that, from the point of view of the native "colonial subject," also emergent from the feudalism-capitalism transition, *sati* is a signifier with the reverse social charge: "Groups ren-

dered psychologically marginal by their exposure to Western impact . . . had come under pressure to demonstrate, to others as well as to themselves, their ritual purity and allegiance to traditional high culture. To many of them *sati* became an important proof of their conformity to older norms at a time when these norms had become shaky within."[42])

If this is the first historical origin of my sentence, it is evidently lost in the history of humankind as work, the story of capitalist expansion, the slow freeing of labor power as commodity, that narrative of the modes of production, the transition from feudalism via mercantilism to capitalism. Yet the precarious normativity of this narrative is sustained by the putatively changeless stopgap of the "Asiatic" mode of production,[xvii] which steps in to sustain it whenever it might become apparent that the story of capital logic is the story of the West, that imperialism establishes the universality of the mode of production narrative, that to ignore the subaltern today is, willy-nilly, to continue the imperialist project. The origin of my sentence is thus lost in the shuffle between other, more powerful discourses. Given that the abolition of *sati* was in itself admirable, is it still possible to wonder if a perception of the origin of my sentence might contain interventionist possibilities?

Imperialism's image as the establisher of the good society is marked by the espousal of the woman as *object* of protection from her own kind. How should one examine the dissimulation of patriarchal strategy, which apparently grants the woman free choice as *subject*? In other words, how does one make the move from "Britain" to "Hinduism"? Even the attempt shows that imperialism is not identical with chromatism, or mere prejudice against people of color. To approach this question, I will touch briefly on the *Dharmasāstra* (the sustaining scriptures) and the *Rg-Veda* (Praise Knowledge). They represent the archaic origin in my homology of Freud. Of course, my treatment is not exhaustive. My readings are, rather, an interested and inexpert examination, by a postcolonial woman, of the fabrication of repression, a constructed counternarrative of woman's consciousness, thus woman's being, thus woman's being good, thus the good woman's desire, thus woman's desire. Paradoxically, at the same time we witness the unfixed place of woman as a signifier in the inscription of the social individual.

[xvi]   Foucault's term for the "discursive regime" or structure of knowledge characteristic of a historical period.

[xvii]   Marx's term for all "primitive" non-Western means and relations of production.

The two moments in the *Dharmasāstra* that I am interested in are the discourse on sanctioned suicides and the nature of the rites for the dead.[43] Framed in these two discourses, the self-immolation of widows seems an exception to the rule. The general scriptural doctrine is that suicide is reprehensible. Room is made, however, for certain forms of suicide which, as formulaic performance, lose the phenomenal identity of being suicide. The first category of sanctioned suicides arises out of *tatvajnāna*, or the knowledge of truth. Here the knowing subject comprehends the insubstantiality or mere phenomenality (which may be the same thing as nonphenomenality) of its identity. At a certain point in time, *tat tva* was interpreted as "that you," but even without that, *tatva* is thatness or quiddity. Thus, this enlightened self truly knows the "that"-ness of its identity. Its demolition of that identity is not *ātmaghāta* (a killing of the self). The paradox of knowing of the limits of knowledge is that the strongest assertion of agency, to negate the possibility of agency, cannot be an example of itself. Curiously enough, the self-*sacrifice* of gods is sanctioned by natural ecology, useful for the working of the economy of Nature and the Universe, rather than by self-knowledge. In this *logically* anterior stage, inhabited by gods rather than human beings, of this particular chain of displacements, suicide and sacrifice (*ātmaghāta* and *ātmadāna*) seem as little distinct as an "interior" (self-knowledge) and an "exterior" (ecology) sanction.

This philosophical space, however, does not accommodate the self-immolating woman. For her we look where room is made to sanction suicides that cannot claim truth-knowledge as a state that is, at any rate, easily verifiable and belongs in the area of *sruti* (what was heard) rather than *smirti* (what is remembered). This exception to the general rule about suicide annuls the phenomenal identity of self-immolation if performed in certain places rather than in a certain state of enlightenment. Thus, we move from an interior sanction (truth-knowledge) to an exterior one (place of pilgrimage). It is possible for a woman to perform *this* type of (non)suicide.[44]

Yet even this is not the *proper* place for the woman to annul the proper name of suicide through the destruction of her proper self. For her alone is sanctioned self-immolation on a dead spouse's pyre. (The few male examples cited in Hindu antiquity of self-immolation on another's pyre, being proofs of enthusiasm and devotion to a master or superior, reveal the structure of domin-

ation within the rite). This suicide that is not suicide may be read as a simulacrum of both truth-knowledge and piety of place. If the former, it is as if the knowledge *in a subject* of its own insubstantiality and mere phenomenality is dramatized so that the dead husband becomes the exteriorized example and place of the extinguished subject and the widow becomes the (non)agent who "acts it out." If the latter, it is as if the metonym for all sacred places is now that burning bed of wood, constructed by elaborate ritual, where the woman's subject, legally displaced from herself, is being consumed. It is in terms of this profound ideology of the displaced place of the female subject that the paradox of free choice comes into play. For the male subject, it is the felicity of the suicide, a felicity that will annul rather than establish its status as such, that is noted. For the female subject, a sanctioned self-immolation, even as it takes away the effect of "fall" (*pātaka*) attached to an unsanctioned suicide, brings praise for the act of choice on another register. By the inexorable ideological production of the sexed subject, such a death can be understood by the female subject as an *exceptional* signifier of her own desire, exceeding the general rule for a widow's conduct.

In certain periods and areas this exceptional rule became the general rule in a class-specific way. Ashis Nandy relates its marked prevalence in eighteenth- and early nineteenth-century Bengal to factors ranging from population control to communal misogyny.[45] Certainly its prevalence there in the previous centuries was because in Bengal, unlike elsewhere in India, widows could inherit property. Thus, what the British see as poor victimized women going to the slaughter is in fact an ideological battleground. As P. V. Kane, the great historian of the *Dharmasāstra*, has correctly observed: "In Bengal, [the fact that] the widow of a sonless member even in a joint Hindu family is entitled to practically the same rights over joint family property which her deceased husband would have had ... must have frequently induced the surviving members to get rid of the widow by appealing at a most distressing hour to her devotion to and love for her husband" (*HD* II.2, 635).[xviii]

Yet benevolent and enlightened males were and are sympathetic with the "courage" of the woman's free choice in the matter. They thus accept the production of the sexed subaltern subject:

xviii   Pandurang Vaman Kane, *History of the Dhamasāstra* (Poona: Bhandarkar Oriental Research Institute, 1963).

"Modern India does not justify the practice of *sati*, but it is a warped mentality that rebukes modern Indians for expressing admiration and reverence for the cool and unfaltering courage of Indian women in becoming *satis* or performing the *jauhar* for cherishing their ideals of womanly conduct" (*HD* II.2, 636). What Jean-Francois Lyotard has termed the "*différend*," the inaccessibility of, or untranslatability from, one mode of discourse in a dispute to another, is vividly illustrated here.[46] As the discourse of what the British perceive as heathen ritual is sublated (but not, Lyotard would argue, translated) into what the British perceive as crime, one diagnosis of female free will is substituted for another.

Of course, the self-immolation of widows was not *invariable* ritual prescription. If, however, the widow does decide thus to exceed the letter of ritual, to turn back is a transgression for which a particular type of penance is prescribed.[47] With the local British police officer supervising the immolation, to be dissuaded after a decision was, by contrast, a mark of real free choice, a choice of freedom. The ambiguity of the position of the indigenous colonial elite is disclosed in the nationalistic romanticization of the purity, strength, and love of these self-sacrificing women. The two set pieces are Rabindranath Tagore's paean to the "self-renouncing paternal grandmothers of Bengal" and Ananda Coomaraswamy's eulogy of *suttee* as "this last proof of the perfect unity of body and soul."[48]

Obviously I am not advocating the killing of widows. I am suggesting that, within the two contending versions of freedom, the constitution of the female subject *in life* is the place of the *différend*. In the case of widow self-immolation, ritual is not being redefined as superstition but as *crime*. The gravity of *sati* was that it was ideologically cathected as "reward," just as the gravity of imperialism was that it was ideologically cathected as "social mission." Thompson's understanding of *sati* as "punishment" is thus far off the mark:

It may seem unjust and illogical that the Moguls, who freely impaled and flayed alive, or nationals of Europe, whose countries had such ferocious penal codes and had known, scarcely a century before suttee began to shock the English conscience, orgies of witch-burning and religious persecution, should have felt as they did about suttee. But the differences seemed to them this – the victims of their cruel-

ties were tortured by a law which considered them offenders, whereas the victims of suttee were punished for no offense but the physical weakness which had placed them at man's mercy. The rite seemed to prove a depravity and arrogance such as no other human offense had brought to light.[49]

All through the mid- and late-eighteenth century, in the spirit of the codification of the law, the British in India collaborated and consulted with learned Brahmans to judge whether *suttee* was legal by their homogenized version of Hindu law. The collaboration was often idiosyncratic, as in the case of the significance of being dissuaded. Sometimes, as in the general Sāstric prohibition against the immolation of widows with small children, the British collaboration seems confused.[50] In the beginning of the nineteenth century, the British authorities, and especially the British in England, repeatedly suggested that collaboration made it appear as if the British condoned this practice. When the law was finally written, the history of the long period of collaboration was effaced, and the language celebrated the noble Hindu who was against the bad Hindu, the latter given to savage atrocities:

The practice of Suttee...is revolting to the feeling of human nature....In many instances, acts of atrocity have been perpetrated, which have been shocking to the Hindoos themselves ....Actuated by these considerations the Governor-General in Council, without intending to depart from one of the first and most important principles of the system of British Government in India that all classes of the people be secure in the observance of their religious usages, so long as that system can be adhered to without violation of the paramount dictates of justice and humanity, has deemed it right to establish the following rules...(*HD* II.2, 624–5)

That this was an alternative ideology of the graded sanctioning of suicide as exception, rather than its inscription as sin, was of course not understood. Perhaps *sati* should have been read with martyrdom, with the defunct husband standing in for the transcendental One; or with war, with the husband standing in for sovereign or state, for whose sake an intoxicating ideology of self-sacrifice can be mobilized. In actuality, it was categorized with murder, infanticide, and the lethal exposure of the very old. The dubious place of the free will of the constituted sexed subject as female was successfully effaced. There is no itinerary we can retrace here. Since the other sanctioned suicides did not involve the scene of this constitution, they entered neither the ideological battleground at the archaic origin – the tradition of the *Dharmasāstra* – nor the scene of the reinscription of ritual as crime – the British abolition. The only related transformation was Mahatma Gandhi's reinscription of the notion of *satyāgraha*, or hunger strike, as resistance. But this is not the place to discuss the details of that seachange. I would merely invite the reader to compare the auras of widow sacrifice and Gandhian resistance. The root in the first part of *satyāgraha* and *sati* are the same.

Since the beginning of the Puranic era (ca. A.D. 400), learned Brahmans debated the doctrinal appropriateness of *sati* as of sanctioned suicides in sacred places in general. (This debate still continues in an academic way.) Sometimes the cast provenance of the practice was in question. The general law for widows, that they should observe *brahmacarya*, was, however, hardly ever debated. It is not enough to translate *brahmacarya* as "celibacy." It should be recognized that, of the four ages of being in Hindu (or Brahmanical) *regulative* psychobiography, *brahmacarya* is the social practice anterior to the kinship inscription of marriage. The man – widower or husband – graduates through *vānaprastha* (forest life) into the mature celibacy and renunciation of *samnyāsa* (laying aside).[51] The woman as wife is indispensable for *gārhasthya*, or householdership, and may accompany her husband into forest life. She has no access (according to Brahmanical sanction) to the final celibacy of asceticism, or *samnyāsa*. The woman as widow, by the general law of sacred doctrine, must regress to an anteriority transformed into stasis. The institutional evils attendant upon this law are well known; I am considering its asymmetrical effect on the ideological formation of the sexed subject. It is thus of much greater significance that there was no debate on this nonexceptional fate of widows – either among Hindus or between Hindus and British – than that the *exceptional* prescription of self-immolation was actively contended.[52] Here the possibility of recovering a (sexually) subaltern subject is once again lost and overdetermined.

This legally programmed asymmetry in the status of the subject, which effectively defines the woman as object of *one* husband, obviously operates in the interest of the legally symmetrical subject-status of the male. The self-immolation of the widow thereby becomes the extreme case of the general law rather than an exception to it. It is not surprising, then, to read of heavenly rewards for the *sati*, where the quality of being the object of a unique possessor is emphasized by way of rivalry with other females, those ecstatic heavenly dancers, paragons of female beauty and male pleasure who sing her praise: "In heaven she, being soley devoted to her husband, and praised by groups of *apsarās* [heavenly dancers], sports with her husband as long as fourteen Indras rule" (*HD* II.2, 631).

The profound irony in locating the woman's free will in self-immolation is once again revealed in a verse accompanying the earlier passage: "As long as the woman [as wife: *stri*] does not burn herself in fire on the death of her husband, she is never released [*mucyate*] from her female body [*strisarīr* – i.e., in the cycle of births]." Even as it operates the most subtle general release from individual agency, the sanctioned suicide peculiar to woman draws its ideological strength by *identifying* individual agency with the supraindividual: kill yourself on your husband's pyre now, and you may kill your female body in the entire cycle of birth.

In a further twist of the paradox, this emphasis on free will establishes the peculiar misfortune of holding a female body. The word for the self that is actually burned is the standard word for spirit in the noblest sense (*ātman*), while the verb "release," through the root for salvation in the noblest sense (*muc* → *moska*) is in the passive (*mocyate*), and the word for that which is annulled in the cycle of birth is the everyday word for the body. The ideological message writes itself in the benevolent twentieth-century male historian's admiration: "The Jauhar [group self-immolation of aristocratic Rajput warwidows or imminent war-widows] practiced by the Rajput ladies of Chitor and other places for saving themselves from unspeakable atrocities at the hands of the victorious Moslems are too well known to need any lengthy notice" (*HD* II.2, 629).

Although *jauhar* is not, strictly speaking, an act of *sati*, and although I do not wish to speak for the sanctioned sexual violence of conquering male armies, "Moslem" or otherwise, female self-immolation in the face of it is a legitimation of rape as "natural" and works, in the long run, in the interest of unique genital possession of the female. The group rape perpetrated by the conquerors is a metonymic celebration of territorial acquisition. Just as the general law for widows was unquestioned, so this act of female heroism persists among the patriotic tales told to children, thus operating on the crudest level of ideological reproduction. It has also played a tremendous role, precisely as an overdetermined signifier, in acting out Hindu communalism. Simultaneously, the broader question of the constitution of the sexed subject is hidden by foregrounding the visible violence of *sati*. The task of recovering a (sexually) subaltern subject is lost in an institutional textuality at the archaic origin.

As I mentioned above, when the status of the legal subject as property-holder could be temporarily bestowed on the *female* relict, the self-immolation of widows was stringently enforced. Raghunandana, the late fifteenth-/sixteenth-century legalist whose interpretations are supposed to lend the greatest authority to such enforcement, takes as his text a curious passage from the *Rg-Veda*, the most ancient of the Hindu sacred texts, the first of the *Srutis*. In doing so, he is following a centuries-old tradition, commemorating a peculiar and transparent misreading at the very place of sanction. Here is the verse outlining certain steps within the rites for the dead. Even at a simple reading it is clear that it is "not addressed to widows at all, but to ladies of the deceased man's household whose husbands were living." Why then was it taken as authoritative? This, the unemphatic transposition of the dead for the living husband, is a different order of mystery at the archaic origin from the ones we have been discussing: "Let these whose husbands are worthy and are living enter the house with clarified butter in their eyes. Let these wives first step into the house, tearless, healthy, and well adorned" (*HD* II.2, 634). But this crucial transposition is not the only mistake here. The authority is lodged in a disputed passage and an alternate reading. In the second line, here translated "Let these wives first step into the house," the word for first is *agré*. Some have read it as *agné*, "O fire." As Kane makes clear, however, "even without this change Apararka and others rely for the practice of *Sati* on this verse" (*HD* IV.2, 199). Here is another screen around one origin of the history of the subaltern female subject. Is it a historical oneirocritique that one should perform on a statement such as: "Therefore it must be admitted that either the MSS are corrupt or Raghunandana committed an innocent slip" (*HD* II.2, 634)? It should be mentioned that the rest of the poem is either about that general law of *brahmacarya*-in-stasis for widows, to which *sati* is an exception, or about *niyoga* – "appointing a brother or any near kinsman to raise up

issue to a deceased husband by marrying his widow."[53]

If P. V. Kane is the authority on the history of the *Dharmasāstra*, Mulla's *Principles of Hindu Law* is the practical guide. It is part of the historical text of what Freud calls "kettle logic" that we are unraveling here, that Mulla's textbook adduces, just as definitively, that the *Rg-Vedic* verse under consideration was proof that "remarriage of widows and divorce are recognized in some of the old texts."[54]

One cannot help but wonder about the role of the word *yoni*. In context, with the localizing adverb *agré* (in front), the word means "dwelling-place." But that does not efface its primary sense of "genital" (not yet perhaps specifically *female* genital). How can we take as the authority for the choice of a widow's self-immolation a passage celebrating the entry of adorned wives into a dwelling place invoked on this occasion by its *yoni*-name, so that the extracontextual icon is almost one of entry into civic production or birth? Paradoxically, the imagic relationship of vagina and fire lends a kind of strength to the authority-claim.[55] This paradox is strengthened by Raghunandana's modification of the verse so as to read, "Let them first ascend the *fluid* abode [or origin, with, of course, the *yoni*-name – *a rōhantu jalayōnimagné*], O fire [or of fire]." Why should one accept that this "probably mean[s] 'may fire be to them as cool as water' " (*HD* II.2, 634)? The fluid genital of fire, a corrupt phrasing, might figure a sexual indeterminancy providing a simulacrum for the intellectual indeterminacy of *tattvajnāna* (truth-knowledge).

I have written above of a constructed counter-narrative of woman's consciousness, thus woman's being, thus woman's being good, thus the good woman's desire, thus woman's desire. This slippage can be seen in the fracture inscribed in the very word *sati*, the feminine form of *sat*. *Sat* transcends any gender-specific notion of masculinity and moves up not only into human but spiritual universality. It is the present participle of the verb "to be" and as such means not only being but the True, the Good, the Right. In the sacred texts it is essence, universal spirit. Even as a prefix it indicates appropriate, felicitous, fit. It is noble enough to have entered the most privileged discourse of modern Western philosophy: Heidegger's meditation on Being.[56] *Sati*, the feminine of this word, simply means "good wife."

It is now time to disclose that *sati* or *suttee* as the proper name of the rite of widow self-immolation commemorates a grammatical error on the part of the British, quite as the nomenclature "American Indian" commemorates a factual error on the part of Columbus. The word in the various Indian languages is "the burning of the *sati*" or the good wife, who thus escapes the regressive stasis of the widow in *brahmacrya*. This exemplifies the race-class-gender overdeterminations of the situation. It can perhaps be caught even when it is flattened out: white men, seeking to save brown women from brown men, impose upon those women a greater ideological constriction by absolutely identifying, *within discursive practice*, good-wifehood with self-immolation on the husband's pyre. On the other side of thus constituting the *object*, the abolition (or removal) of which will provide the occasion for establishing a good, as distinguished from merely civil, society, is the Hindu manipulation of female *subject*-constitution which I have tried to discuss.

(I have already mentioned Edward Thompson's *Suttee*, published in 1928. I cannot do justice here to this perfect specimen of the justification of imperialism as a civilizing mission. Nowhere in his book, written by someone who avowedly "loves India," is there any questioning of the "beneficial ruthlessness" of the British in India as motivated by territorial expansionism or management of industrial capital.[57] The problem with his book is, indeed, a problem of representation, the construction of a continuous and homogeneous "India" in terms of heads of state and British administrators, from the perspective of "a man of good sense" who would be the transparent voice of reasonable humanity. "India" can then be represented, in the other sense, by its imperial masters. The reason for referring to *suttee* here is Thompson's finessing of the word *sati* as "faithful" in the very first sentence of his book, an inaccurate translation which is nonetheless an English permit for the insertion of the female subject into twentieth-century discourse.[58])

Consider Thompson's praise for General Charles Hervey's appreciation of the problem of *sati*: "Hervey has a passage which brings out the pity of a system which looked only for prettiness and constancy in woman. He obtained the names of satis who had died on the pyres of Bikanir Rajas; they were such names as: 'Ray Queen, Sun-ray, Love's Delight, Garland, Virtue Found, Echo, Soft Eye, Comfort, Moonbeam, Love-lorn, Dear Heart, Eye-play, Arbour-born, Smile, Love-bud, Glad Omen, Mist-clad, or Cloud-sprung – the last a favourite name.'" Once again, imposing

the upper-class Victorian's typical demands upon "his woman" (his preferred phrase), Thompson appropriates the Hindu woman as his to save against the "system." Bikaner is in Rajasthan; and any discussion of widow-burnings of Rajasthan, especially within the ruling class, was intimately linked to the positive or negative construction of Hindu (or Aryan) communalism.

A look at the pathetically misspelled names of the *satis* of the artisanal, peasant, village-priestly, moneylender, clerical, and comparable social groups in Bengal, where *satis* were most common, would not have yielded such a harvest (Thompson's preferred adjective for Bengalis is "imbecilic"). Or perhaps it would. There is no more dangerous pastime than transposing proper names into common nouns, translating them, and using them as sociological evidence. I attempted to reconstruct the names on that list and began to feel Hervey-Thompson's arrogance. What, for instance, might "Comfort" have been? Was it "Shanti"? Readers are reminded of the last line of T. S. Eliot's *Waste Land*.[xix] There the word bears the mark of one kind of stereotyping of India – the grandeur of the ecumenical Upanishads. Or was it "Swasti"? Readers are reminded of the *swastika*, the Brahmanic ritual mark of domestic comfort (as in "God Bless Our Home") stereotyped into a criminal parody of Aryan hegemony. Between these two appropriations, where is our pretty and constant burnt widow? The aura of the names owes more to writers like Edward FitzGerald, the "translator" of the *Rubayyat of Omar Khayyam* who helped to construct a certain picture of the Oriental woman through the supposed "objectivity" of translation, than to sociological exactitude. (Said's *Orientalism*, 1978, remains the authoritative text here.) By this sort of reckoning, the translated proper names of a random collection of contemporary French philosophers or boards of directors of prestigious southern U.S. corporations would give evidence of a ferocious investment in an archangelic and hagiocentric theocracy. Such sleights of pen can be perpetuated on "common nouns" as well, but the proper name is most susceptible to the trick. And it is the British trick with *sati* that we are discussing. After such a taming of the subject, Thompson can write, under the heading "The Psychology of the '*Sati*'," "I had intended to try to examine this; but the truth is, it has ceased to seem a puzzle to me."[59]

[xix]   "Shantih shantih shantih."

Between patriarchy and imperialism, subject-constitution and object-formation, the figure of the woman disappears, not into a pristine nothingness, but into a violent shuttling which is the displaced figuration of the "third-world woman" caught between tradition and modernization. These considerations would revise every detail of judgments that seem valid for a history of sexuality in the West: "Such would be the property of repression, that which distinguishes it from the prohibitions maintained by simple penal law: repression functions well as a sentence to disappear, but also as an injunction to silence, affirmation of non-existence; and consequently states that of all this there is nothing to say, to see, to know."[60] The case of *suttee* as exemplum of the woman-in-imperialism would challenge and deconstruct this opposition between subject (law) and object-of-knowledge (repression) and mark the place of "disappearance" with something other than silence and nonexistence, a violent aporia[xx] between subject and object status.

Sati as a woman's proper name is in fairly widespread use in India today. Naming a female infant "a good wife" has its own proleptic irony, and the irony is all the greater because this sense of the common noun is not the primary operator in the proper name.[61] Behind the naming of the infant is *the* Sati of Hindu mythology, Durga in her manifestation as a good wife.[62] In part of the story, Sati – she is already called that – arrives at her father's court uninvited, in the absence, even, of an invitation for her divine husband Siva. Her father starts to abuse Siva and Sati dies in pain. Siva arrives in a fury and dances over the universe with Sati's corpse on his shoulder. Visnu dismembers her body and bits are strewn over the earth. Around each such relic bit is a great place of pilgrimage.

Figures like the goddess Athena – "father's daughters self-professedly uncontaminated by the womb" – are useful for establishing women's ideological self-debasement, which is to be distinguished from a deconstructive attitude toward the essentialist subject. The story of the mythic Sati, reversing every narrateme of the rite, performs a similar function: the living husband avenges the wife's death, a transaction between great male gods fulfills the destruction of the female body and thus inscribes the earth as sacred geography. To see this as proof of the feminism of classical Hinduism or of Indian culture as goddess-centered

and therefore feminist is as ideologically contaminated by nativism or reverse ethnocentrism as it was imperialist to erase the image of the luminous fighting Mother Durga and invest the proper noun Sati with no significance other than the ritual burning of the helpless widow as sacrificial offering who can then be saved. There is no space from which the sexed subaltern subject can speak.

If the oppressed under socialized capital have no necessarily unmediated access to "correct" resistance, can the ideology of *sati*, coming from the history of the periphery, be sublated into any model of interventionist practice? Since this essay operates on the notion that all such clear-cut nostalgias for lost origins are suspect, especially as grounds for counterhegemonic ideological production, I must proceed by way of an example.[63]

(The example I offer here is not a plea for some violent Hindu sisterhood of self-destruction. The definition of the British Indian as Hindu in Hindu law is one of the marks of the ideological war of the British against the Islamic Mughal rulers of India; a significant skirmish in that as yet unfinished war was the division of the subcontinent. Moreover, in my view, individual examples of this sort are tragic failures as *models* of interventionist practice, since I question the production of models as such. On the other hand, as objects of discourse analysis for the non–self-abdicating intellectual, they can illuminate a section of the social text, in however haphazard a way.)

A young woman of sixteen or seventeen, Bhuvaneswari Bhaduri, hanged herself in her father's modest apartment in North Calcutta in 1926. The suicide was a puzzle since, as Bhuvaneswari was menstruating at the time, it was clearly not a case of illicit pregnancy. Nearly a decade later, it was discovered that she was a member of one of the many groups involved in the armed struggle for Indian independence. She had finally been entrusted with a political assassination. Unable to confront the task and yet aware of the practical need for trust, she killed herself.

Bhuvaneswari had known that her death would be diagnosed as the outcome of illegitimate passion. She had therefore waited for the onset of menstruation. While waiting, Bhuvaneswari, the *brahmacārini* who was no doubt looking forward to good wifehood, perhaps rewrote the social text of *sati*-suicide in an interventionist way. (One tentative explanation of her inexplicable act had been a possible melancholia brought on by her brother-in-law's repeated taunts that she was too old to be

---

[xx] Skeptical conclusion, impasse, in inquiry.

not-yet-a-wife.) She generalized the sanctioned motive for female suicide by taking immense trouble to displace (not merely deny), in the physiological inscription of her body, its imprisonment within legitimate passion by a single male. In the immediate context, her act became absurd, a case of delirium rather than sanity. The displacing gesture – waiting for menstruation – is at first a reversal of the interdict against a menstruating widow's right to immolate herself; the unclean widow must wait, publicly, until the cleansing bath of the fourth day, when she is no longer menstruating, in order to claim her dubious privilege.

In this reading, Bhuvaneswari Bhaduri's suicide is an unemphatic, ad hoc, subaltern rewriting of the social text of *sati*-suicide as much as the hegemonic account of the blazing, fighting, familial Durga. The emergent dissenting possibilities of that hegemonic account of the fighting mother are well documented and popularly well remembered through the discourse of the male leaders and participants in the independence movement. The subaltern as female cannot be heard or read.

I know of Bhuvaneswari's life and death through family connections. Before investigating them more thoroughly, I asked a Bengali woman, a philosopher and Sanskritist whose early intellectual production is almost identical to mine, to start the process. Two responses: (a) Why, when her two sisters, Saileswari and Rāseswari, led such full and

wonderful lives, are you interested in the hapless Bhuvaneswari? (b) I asked her nieces. It appears that it was a case of illicit love.

I have attempted to use and go beyond Derridean deconstruction, which I do not celebrate as feminism as such. However, in the context of the problematic I have addressed, I find his morphology much more painstaking and useful than Foucault's and Deleuze's immediate, substantive involvement with more "political" issues – the latter's invitation to "become woman" – which can make their influence more dangerous for the U.S. academic as enthusiastic radical. Derrida marks radical critique with the danger of appropriating the other by assimilation. He reads catachresis[xxi] at the origin. He calls for a rewriting of the utopian structural impulse as "rendering delirious that interior voice that is the voice of the other in us." I must here acknowledge a long-term usefulness in Jacques Derrida which I seem no longer to find in the authors of *The History of Sexuality* and[xxii] *Mille plateaux*.[64]

The subaltern cannot speak. There is no virtue in global laundry lists with "woman" as a pious item. Representation has not withered away. The female intellectual as intellectual has a circumscribed task which she must not disown with a flourish.

[xxi] Misuse or paradoxical use of a word.
[xxii] "A Thousand Plateaus." Spivak is referring to Foucault and Deleuze, respectively.

Author's Notes

1 I am aware that the relationship between Marxism and neo-Kantianism is a politically fraught one. I do not myself see how a continuous line can be established between Marx's own texts and the Kantian ethical moment. It does seem to me, however, that Marx's questioning of the individual as agent of history should be read in the context of the breaking up of the individual subject inaugurated by Kant's critique of Descartes.

2 Karl Marx, *Grundrisse: Foundations of the Critique of Political Economy*, trans. Martin Nicolaus (New York: Viking Press, 1973), pp. 162–3.

3 Edward W. Said, *The World, the Text, the Critic* (Cambridge: Harvard University Press, 1983), p. 243.

4 Paul Bové, "Intellectuals at War: Michel Foucault and the Analysis of Power," *Sub-Stance*, 36/37 (1983), p. 44.

5 Hazel V. Carby et al., *The Empire Strikes Back: Race and Racism in 70s Britain* (London: Hutchinson, 1982), p. 34.

6 This argument is developed further in Gayatri Chakravorty Spivak, "Scattered Speculations on the Question of Value," *Diacritics* (winter 1985), 15 (4): 73–93. Once again, the *Anti-Oedipus* did not ignore the economic text, although the treatment was perhaps too allegorical. In this respect, the move from schizo- to rhyzo-analysis in *Mille plateaux* (Paris; Seuil, 1980) has not been salutary.

7 See Michel Foucault, *Madness and Civilization: A History of Insanity in the Age of Reason*, trans. Richard Howard (New York: Pantheon Books, 1965), pp. 251, 262, 269.

8 Although I consider Fredric Jameson's *Political Unconscious: Narrative as a Socially Symbolic Act* (Ithaca: Cornell University Press, 1981) to be a text of great critical weight, or perhaps *because* I do so, I would like my program here to be distinguished from one of restoring the relics of a privileged narrative: "It is in detecting the traces of that uninterrupted narrative, in restoring to the surface of the text the repressed and buried reality of this fundamental history, that the

doctrine of a political unconscious finds its function and its necessity" (p. 20).

9 Among many available books, I cite Bruse Tiebout McCully, *English Education and the Origins of Indian Nationalism* (New York: Columbia University Press, 1940).

10 Thomas Babington Macaulay, *Speeches by Lord Macaulay: With His Minute on Indian Education*, ed. G. M. Young (Oxford: Oxford University Press, AMS Edition, 1979), p. 359.

11 Keith, one of the compilers of the *Vedic Index*, author of *Sanskrit Drama in Its Origin, Development, Theory, and Practice*, and the learned editor of the *Krsnaya-jurveda* for Harvard University Press, was also the editor of four volumes of *Selected Speeches and Documents of British Colonial Policy* (1763 to 1937), of *International Affairs* (1918 to 1937), and of the *British Dominions* (1918 to 1931). He wrote books on the sovereignty of British dominions and on the theory of state succession, with special reference to English and colonial law.

12 Mahamahopadhyaya Haraprasad Shastri, *A Descriptive Catalogue of Sanskrit Manuscripts in the Government Collection under the Care of the Asiatic Society of Bengal* (Calcutta: Asiatic Society of Bengal, 1925), vol. 3, p. viii.

13 Dinesachandra Sena, *Brhat Banga* (Calcutta: Calcutta University Press, 1925), vol. 1, p. 6.

14 Edward Thompson, *Suttee: A Historical and Philosophical Enquiry into the Hindu Rite of Widow-Burning* (London: George Allen and Unwin, 1928), pp. 130, 47.

15 Holograph letter (from G. A. Jacob to an unnamed correspondent) attached to inside front cover of the Sterling Memorial Library (Yale University) copy of Colonel G. A. Jacob, ed., *The Mahanarayana-Upanishad of the Atharva-Veda with the Dipika of Narayana* (Bombay: Government Central Books Department, 1888); italics mine. The dark invocation of the dangers of this learning by way of anonymous aberrants consolidates the asymmetry.

16 I have discussed this issue in greater detail with reference to Julia Kristeva's *About Chinese Women*, trans. Anita Barrows (London: Marion Boyars, 1977), in "French Feminism in an International Frame," *Yale French Studies*, 62 (1981).

17 Antonio Gramsci, "Some Aspects of the Southern Question," *Selections from Political Writing: 1921–1926*, trans. Quintin Hoare (New York: International Publishers, 1978). I am using "allegory of reading" in the sense developed by Paul de Man, *Allegories of Reading: Figura Language in Rousseau, Nietzsche, Rilke, and Proust* (New Haven: Yale University Press, 1979).

18 Their publications are: *Subaltern Studies I: Writing on South Asian History and Society*, ed. Ranajit Guha (Delhi: Oxford University Press, 1982); *Subaltern Studies II: Writings on South Asian History and Society*, ed. Ranajit Guha (Delhi: Oxford University Press, 1983); and Ranajit Guha, *Elementary Aspects of Peasant Insurgency in Colonial India* (Delhi: Oxford University Press, 1983).

19 Edward W. Said, "Permission to Narrate," *London Review of Books* (Feb. 16, 1984).

20 Guha, *Studies*, I, p. 1.

21 Guha, *Studies*, I, p. 4.

22 Jacques Derrida, "The Double Session," *Dissemination*, trans. Barbara Johnson (Chicago: University of Chicago Press, 1981).

23 Guha, *Studies*, I, p. 8 (all but the first set of italics are the author's).

24 Ajit K. Chaudhury, "New Wave Social Science," *Frontier*, 16–24 (Jan. 28, 1984), p. 10 (italics are mine).

25 Chaudhury, "New Wave Social Science," p. 10.

26 Pierre Macherey, *A Theory of Literary Production*, trans. Geoffrey Wall (London: Routledge, 1978), p. 87.

27 I have discussed this issue in "Displacement and the Discourse of Woman," in Mark Krupnick, ed., *Displacement: Derrida and After* (Bloomington: Indiana University Press, 1983), and in "Love Me, Love My Ombre, Elle: Derrida's 'La carte postale,'" *Diacritics* 14, no. 4 (1984), pp. 19–36.

28 This violence in the general sense that is the possibility of an episteme is what Derrida calls "writing" in the general sense. The relationship between writing in the general sense and writing in the narrow sense (marks upon a surface) cannot be cleanly articulated. The task of grammatology (deconstruction) is to provide a notation upon this shifting relationship. In a certain way, then, the critique of imperialism is deconstruction as such.

29 "Contracting Poverty," *Multinational Monitor*, 4, no. 8 (Aug. 1983), p. 8. This report was contributed by John Cavanagh and Joy Hackel, who work on the International Corporations Project at the Institute for Policy Studies (italics are mine).

30 The mechanics of the invention of the Third World as signifier are susceptible to the type of analysis directed at the constitution of race as a signifier in Carby, *Empire*.

31 Jacques Derrida, "Of an Apocalyptic Tone Recently Adapted in Philosophy," trans. John P. Leavy, Jr., in *Semia*, p. 71.

32 Even in such excellent texts of reportage and analysis as Gail Omvedt's *We Will Smash This Prison! Indian Women in Struggle* (London: Zed Press, 1980), the assumption that a group of Maharashtrian women in an urban proletarian situation, reacting to a radical white woman who had "thrown in her lot with the Indian destiny," is representative of "Indian women" or touches the question of "female consciousness in India" is not harmless when taken up within a first-world social formation where the proliferation

of communication in an internationally hegemonic language makes alternative accounts and testimonies instantly accessible even to undergraduates.

Norma Chinchilla's observation, made at a panel on "Third World Feminisms: Differences in Form and Content" (UCLA, Mar. 8, 1983), that antisexist work in the Indian context is not genuinely antisexist but antifeudal, is another case in point. This permits definitions of sexism to emerge only after a society has entered the capitalist mode of production, thus making capitalism and patriarchy conveniently continuous. It also invokes the vexed question of the role of the "'Asiatic' mode of production" in sustaining the explanatory power of the normative narrativization of history through the account of modes of production, in however sophisticated a manner history is construed.

The curious role of the proper name "Asia" in this matter does not remain confined to proof or disproof of the empirical existence of the actual mode (a problem that became the object of intense maneuvering within international communism) but remains crucial even in the work of such theoretical subtlety and importance as Barry Hindess and Paul Hirst's *Pre-Capitalist Modes of Production* (London: Routledge, 1975) and Fredric Jameson's *Political Unconscious*. Especially in Jameson, where the morphology of modes of production is rescued from all suspicion of historical determinism and anchored to a post-structuralist theory of the subject, the "Asiatic" mode of production, in its guise of "oriental despotism" as the concomitant state formation, still serves. It also plays a significant role in the transmogrified mode of production narrative in Gilles Deleuze and Félix Guattari, *Anti-Oedipus: Capitalism and Schizophrenia*, trans. Richard Hurley et al. (New York: Viking Press, 1977). In the Soviet debate, at a far remove, indeed, from these contemporary theoretical projects, the doctrinal sufficiency of the "Asiatic" mode of production was most often doubted by producing for it various versions and nomenclatures of feudal, slave, and communal modes of production. (The debate is presented in detail in Stephen F. Dunn, *The Fall and Rise of the Asiatic Mode of Production* [London: Routledge, 1982].) It would be interesting to relate this to the repression of the imperialist "moment" in most debates over the transition from feudalism to capitalism that have long exercised the Western Left. What is more important here is that an observation such as Chinchilla's represents a widespread hierarchization within third-world *feminism* (rather than Western Marxism), which situates it within the long-standing traffic with the imperialist concept-metaphor "Asia."

I should add that I have not yet read Madhu Kishwar and Ruth Vanita, eds., *In Search of Answers: Indian Women's Voices from Manushi* (London: Zed Books, 1984).

33 Jonathan Culler, *On Deconstruction: Theory and Criticism after Structuralism* (Ithaca: Cornell University Press, 1982), p. 48.

34 Elizabeth Fox-Genovese, "Placing Woman's History in History," *New Left Review*, 133 (May–June 1982), p. 21.

35 I have attempted to develop this idea in a somewhat autobiographical way in "Finding Feminist Readings: Dante–Yeats," in Ira Konigsberg, ed., *American Criticism in the Poststructuralist Age* (Ann Arbor: University of Michigan Press, 1981).

36 Sarah Kofman, *L'énigme de la femme: La femme dans les textes de Freud* (Paris: Galilée, 1980).

37 Sigmund Freud, "'A Child Is Being Beaten': A Contribution to the Study of the Origin of Sexual Perversions," *The Standard Edition of the Complete Psychological Works of Sigmund Freud*, trans. James Strachey et al. (London: Hogarth Press, 1955), vol. 17.

38 Freud, "'Wild' Psycho-Analysis," *Standard Edition*, vol. 11.

39 Freud, "'A Child Is Being Beaten,'" p. 188.

40 For a brilliant account of how the "reality" of widow-sacrifice was constituted or "textualized" during the colonial period, see Lata Mani, "The Production of Colonial Discourse: Sati in Early Nineteenth Century Bengal" (masters thesis, University of California at Santa Cruz, 1983). I profited from discussions with Ms. Mani at the inception of this project.

41 J. D. M. Derrett, *Hindu Law Past and Present: Being an Account of the Controversy Which Preceded the Enactment of the Hindu Code, and Text of the Code as Enacted, and Some Comments Thereon* (Calcutta: A. Mukherjee and Co., 1957), p. 46.

42 Ashis Nandy, "Sati: A Ninteenth Century Tale of Women, Violence and Protest," *Rammohun Roy and the Process of Modernization in India*, ed. V. C. Joshi (Delhi: Vikas Publishing House, 1975), p. 68.

43 The following account leans heavily on Pandurang Vaman Kane, *History of the Dharmasastra* (Poona: Bhandarkar Oriental Research Institute, 1963) (hereafter cited as *HD*, with volume, part, and page numbers).

44 Upendra Thakur, *The History of Suicide in India: An Introduction* (Delhi: Munshi Ram Manohar Lal, 1963), p. 9, has a useful list of Sanskrit primary sources on sacred places. This laboriously decent book betrays all the signs of the schizophrenia of the colonial subject, such as bourgeois nationalism, patriarchal communalism, and an "enlightened reasonableness."

45 Nandy, "Sati."

46 Jean-Francois Lyotard, *Le différend* (Paris: Minuit, 1984).

47 *HD*, II.2, p. 633. There are suggestions that this "prescribed penance" was far exceeded by social practice. In the passage below, published in 1938,

notice the Hindu patristic assumptions about the freedom of female will at work in phrases like "courage" and "strength of character." The unexamined presuppositions of the passage might be that the complete objectification of the widow-concubine was just punishment for abdication of the right to courage, signifying subject status: "Some widows, however, had not the courage to go through the fiery ordeal; nor had they sufficient strength of mind and character to live up to the high ascetic ideal prescribed for them *[brahmacarya]*. It is said to record that they were driven to lead the life of a concubine or *avarudda stri* [incarcerated wife]." A. S. Altekar, *The Position of Women in Hindu Civilization: From Prehistoric Times to the Present Day* (Delhi: Motilal Banarsidass, 1938), p. 156.

48 Quoted in Sena, *Brhat-Banga*, ll, pp. 913–14.

49 Thompson, *Suttee*, p. 132.

50 Here, as well as for the Brahman debate over *sati*, see Mani, "Production," pp. 71f.

51 We are speaking here of the regulative norms of Brahmanism, rather than "things as they were." See Robert Lingat, *The Classical Law of India*, trans. J. D. M. Derrett (Berkeley: University of California Press, 1973), p. 46.

52 Both the vestigial possibility of widow remarriage in ancient India and the legal institution of widow re-marriage in 1856 are transactions among men. Widow remarriage is very much an exception, per-haps because it left the program of subject-formation untouched. In all the "lore" of widow remarriage, it is the father and the husband who are applauded for their reformist courage and selflessness.

53 Sir Monier Monier-Williams, *Sanskrit-English Dictionary* (Oxford: Clarendon Press, 1899), p. 552. Historians are often impatient if modernists seem to be attempting to import "feministic" judgments into ancient patriarchies. The real question is, of course, why structures of patriarchal domination should be unquestioningly recorded. Historical sanctions for collective action toward social justice can only be developed if people outside of the discipline question standards of "objectivity" preserved as such by the hegemonic tradition. It does not seem inappropriate to notice that so "objective" an instrument as a dictionary can use the deeply sexist-partisan explanatory expression: "raise up issue to a deceased husband"!

54 Sunderlal T. Desai, *Mulla: Principles of Hindu Law* (Bombay: N. M. Tripathi, 1982), p. 184.

55 I am grateful to Professor Alison Finley of Trinity College (Hartford, Conn.) for discussing the pas-sage with me. Professor Finley is an expert on the *Rg-Veda*. I hasten to add that she would find my readings as irresponsibly "literary-critical" as the ancient historian would find it "modernist" (see note 80).

56 Martin Heidegger, *An Introduction to Metaphysics*, trans. Ralph Manheim (New York: Doubleday Anchor, 1961), p. 58.

57 Thompson, *Suttee*, p. 37.

58 Thompson, *Suttee*, p. 15. For the status of the proper name as "mark," see Derrida, "Taking Chances."

59 Thompson, *Suttee*, p. 137.

60 Michel Foucault, *The History of Sexuality*, trans. Robert Hurley (New York: Vintage Books, 1980), vol. 1, p. 4.

61 The fact that the word was also used as a form of address for a well-born woman ("lady") complicates matters.

62 It should be remembered that this account does not exhaust her many manifestations within the pantheon.

63 A position against nostalgia as a basis of counter-hegemonic ideological production does not endorse its negative use. Within the complexity of contem-porary political economy, it would, for example, be highly questionable to urge that the current Indian working-class crime of burning brides who bring insufficient dowries and of subsequently disguising the murder as suicide is either a *use* or *abuse* of the tradition of *sati*-suicide. The most that can be claimed is that it is a displacement on a chain of semiosis with the female subject as signifier, which would lead us back into the narrative we have been unraveling. Clearly, one must work to stop the crime of bride burning *in every way*. If, however, that work is accomplished by unexamined nostalgia or its op-posite, it will assist actively in the substitution of race/ethnos or sheer genitalism as a signifier in the place of the female subject.

64 I had not read Peter Dews, "Power and Subjectivity in Foucault," *New Left Review*, 144 (1984), until I finished this essay. I look forward to his book on the same topic. There are many points in common be-tween his critique and mine. However, as far as I can tell from the brief essay, he writes from a perspective uncritical of critical theory and the intersubjective norm that can all too easily exchange "individual" for "subject" in its situating of the "epistemic subject." Dews's reading of the connection between "Marxist tradition" and the "autonomous subject" is not mine. Further, his account of "the *impasse* of the second phase of poststructuralism as a whole" is vitiated by his nonconsideration of Derrida, who has been against the privileging of language from his earliest work, the "Introduction" in Edmund Husserl, *The Origin of Geometry*, trans. John Leavy (Stony Brook, N.Y.: Nicolas Hays, 1978). What sets his excellent analysis quite apart from my concerns is, of course, that the Subject within whose History he places Foucault's work is the Subject of the Euro-pean tradition (pp. 87, 94).

35

From "From Feminist Empiricism to Feminist Standpoint Epistemologies"

Sandra Harding

To those unfamiliar with the term, "feminist epistemology" may seem an odd combination of words, but it refers to a major movement in contemporary philosophy. If feminism is, in its most general sense, the examination of any phenomenon through the lens of gender and the historical meaning of gender, then traditional notions of knowledge and even scientific method can be critically analyzed with respect to their possible expression of and dependence on gender relations and stereotypes. Philosopher of science Sandra Harding (1935–) discusses the development of feminist epistemology and its attempt to explore the extent to which modern ideals of knowledge have embodied particularly male aspirations, and excluded possible forms of knowing that have traditionally been characterized as female.

The Feminist Standpoint Epistemologies

The feminist standpoint epistemologies ground a distinctive feminist science in a theory of gendered activity and social experience. They simultaneously privilege women or feminists (the accounts vary) epistemically and yet also claim to overcome the dichotomizing that is characteristic of the Enlightenment/bourgeois world view and its science.[1] It is useful to think of the standpoint epistemologies, like the appeals to feminist empiricism, as "successor science" projects: in significant ways, they aim to reconstruct the original goals of modern science. In contrast, feminist postmodernism more directly

challenges those goals (though there are postmodernist strains even in these standpoint writings).

An observer of these arguments can pick out five different though related reasons that they offer to explain why inquiry from a feminist perspective can provide understandings of nature and social life that are not possible from the perspective of men's distinctive activity and experience. I shall identify each of these reasons in the writing of one theorist who has emphasized this particular aspect of the gendered division of activity, though most of these theorists recognize more than one. Whatever their differences, I think the accounts should be understood as fundamentally complementary, not competing.

The unity of hand, brain and heart in craft labor

Hilary Rose's "feminist epistemology for the natural sciences" is grounded in a post-Marxist analysis of the effects of gendered divisions of activity upon intellectual structures.[2] In two recent papers, she has developed the argument that it is in the thinking and practices of women scientists whose inquiry modes are still characteristically "craft labor," rather than the "industrialized labor" within which most scientific inquiry is done, that we can detect the outlines of a distinctively feminist theory of knowledge. Its distinctiveness is to be found in the way its concepts of the knower, the

Sandra Harding, "From Feminist Empiricism to Feminist Standpoint Epistemologies," chapter 6, pp. 141–61 from The Science Question in Feminism. Ithaca, NY: Cornell University Press, 1986.

world to be known, and processes of coming to know reflect the unification of manual, mental, and emotional ("hand, brain, and heart") activity characteristic of women's work more generally. This epistemology not only stands in opposition to the Cartesian dualisms – intellect vs. body, and both vs. feeling and emotion – that underlie Enlightenment and even Marxist visions of science but also grounds the possibility of a "more complete materialism, a truer knowledge" than that provided by either paternal discourse (1984, 49).[i] The need for such a feminist science "is increasingly acute," for "bringing caring labor and the knowledge that stems from participation in it to the analysis becomes critical for a transformative program equally within science and within society" if we are to avoid the nuclear annihilation and deepening social misery increasingly possible otherwise (1983, 89).

Rose starts by analyzing the insights of post-Marxist thinking upon which feminists can build. Sohn-Rethel saw that it was the separation of manual from mental labor in capitalist production that resulted in the mystifying abstractions of bourgeois science.[3] But social relations include far more than the mere production of commodities where mental and manual labor are assigned to different classes of people. Like Marx, Sohn-Rethel failed to ask about the effect on science of assigning *caring* labor exclusively to women.[4] Rose argues that in this respect, post-Marxists such as Sohn-Rethel are indistinguishable from the sociobiological theorists to whom they are vehemently opposed; they tacitly endorse the "far-from-emancipatory program of sociobiology, which argues that woman's destiny is in her genes." Feminists must explain the relationship between women's unpaid and paid labor to show that women's caring skills have a social genesis, not a natural one, and that they "are extracted from them by men primarily within the home but also in the work place" (1983, 83–4).

Rose goes on to analyze the relationship of the conditions of women's activities within science with those in domestic life, and the possibilities created by these kinds of activities for women to occupy an advantaged standpoint as producers of less distorted and more comprehensive scientific claims. A feminist epistemology cannot originate in meditations upon what women do in laboratories, since the women there are forced to deny that they are women in order to survive, yet are still "by and

large shut out of the production system of scientific knowledge, with its ideological power to define what is and what is not objective knowledge" (1983, 88). They are prohibited from becoming (masculine) scientific knowers and also from admitting to being what they are primarily perceived as being: women.[5]

In her earlier paper, Rose argues that a feminist epistemology must be grounded in the practices of the women's movement. In its consideration of such biological and medical issues as menstruation, abortion, and self-examination and self-health care, the women's movement fuses "subjective and objective knowledge in such a way as to make new knowledge." "Cartesian dualism, biological determinism, and social constructionism fade when faced with the necessity of integrating and interpreting the personal experience of [menstrual] bleeding, pain, and tension," Rose declares. "Working from the experience of the specific oppression of women fuses the personal, the social, and the biological." Thus a feminist epistemology for the natural sciences will emerge from the interplay between "new organizational forms" and new projects (1983, 88–9). The organizational forms of the women's movement, unlike those of capitalist production relations and its science, resist dividing mental, manual, and caring activity among different classes of persons. And its project is to provide the knowledge women need to understand and manage our own bodies: subject and object of inquiry are one. Belief emerging from this unified activity in the service of self-knowledge is more adequate than that emerging from activity that is divided and that is performed for the purposes of monopolizing profit and social control.

This first paper left a gap between the kind of knowledge/power relations possible in a science grounded in women's understandings of our own bodies and the kind needed if a feminist science is to develop sufficient muscle to replace the physics, chemistry, biology, and social sciences we have. In the later paper, Rose inches across this gap by expanding the domain in which she thinks we can identify the origins of a distinctive feminist epistemology. The origins of an epistemology which holds that appeals to the subjective are legitimate, that intellectual and emotional domains must be united, that the domination of reductionism and linearity must be replaced by the harmony of holism and complexity, can be detected in what Foucault would call "subjugated knowledges" – submerged understandings within the history of science (1984, 49).

Rose has in mind here the ecological concerns reported and elaborated by Carolyn Merchant and

[i] For textual references of this type, see References following the author's endnotes.

evident in Rachel Carson's work, and the calls for moving beyond reductionism toward a holistic "feminization of science" evident in writers such as David Bohm and Fritjof Capra.[6] She might also have cited here Joseph Needham's romantic ideal- ization of Chinese science as more feminized than Western science.[7] And then we would have to think about the contradictions between China's history of a "feminized science" and the far from emancipa- tory history of Chinese misogyny. This raises the troublesome issue of the conflation of gender di- chotomies as a metaphor for other dichotomies (gender symbolism) with explanations that treat social relations between the sexes as a causal influ- ence on history – a point to be pursued later. Furthermore, this line of thought leads directly toward feminist distrust of men's conceptions of the androgyny men desire for themselves. When men want androgyny, they usually intend to appro- priate selectively parts of "the feminine" for their projects, while leaving the lot of real women un- changed.[8]

Within recent scientific research by women in biology, psychology, and anthropology – areas where "craft" forms of scientific inquiry are still possible, in contrast to the "industrial" forms con- fronting women in masculine-dominated labs – Rose detects the most significant advances toward "a more complete materialism, a truer knowledge." In all of these areas, feminist thinking has produced a new comprehension of the relationships between organisms, and between organisms and their envir- onment. The organism is conceptualized "not in terms of the Darwinian metaphor, as the passive object of selection by an indifferent environment, but as [an] active participant, a subject in the deter- mination of its own future" (1984, 51). (Keller has argued that Barbara McClintock's work provides a paradigm of this kind of alternative to the "master theory" of Darwinian biology.[9])

Thus Rose proposes that the grounds for a dis- tinctive feminist science and epistemology are to be found in the social practices and conceptual schemes of feminists (or women inquirers) in craft-organized areas of inquiry. There women's socially created conceptions of nature and social relations can produce new understandings that carry emancipatory possibilities for the species. These conceptions are not necessarily original to women scientists: hints of them can be detected in the "subjugated knowledges" in the history of sci- ence. However, we can here hazard an observation Rose does not make: where these notions neither originate in nor give expression to any distinctive social/political experience, they are fated to remain mere intellectual curiosities – like the ancient Greek ideas about atoms – awaiting their "social birth" within the scientific enterprise at the hands of a group which needs such conceptions in order to project onto nature its destiny within the social order. One cannot help noticing that the notion of organisms as active participants in the determin- ation of their own futures "discovers" in "nature" the very relationship that feminist theory claims has been permitted only to (dominant group) men but *should* exist as well for women, who are also history- making social beings. Men have actively advanced their own futures within masculine domination; women, too, could actively participate in the design of their futures within a degendered social order.

Whether or not Rose would agree to this conclu- sion, she does argue that the origins of a feminist epistemology for a successor science are to be found in the conceptions of the knower, the processes of knowing, and the world to be known which are evident in this substantive scientific research. The substantive claims of this research are thus to be justified in terms of women's different activities and social experiences created in the gendered div- ision of labor/activity. As I shall ask of each of these standpoint theorists, does this epistemology still retain too much of the Enlightenment vision?

Women's subjugated activity: sensuous, concrete, relational

Like Rose, political theorist Nancy Hartsock locates the epistemological foundations for a feminist suc- cessor science in a post-Marxist theory of labor (activity) and its effects upon mental life. For Hart- sock, too, Sohn-Rethel provides important clues. But Hartsock begins with Marx's metatheory, his "proposal that a correct vision of class society is available from only one of the two major class pos- itions in capitalist society."[10] By starting from the lived realities of women's lives, we can identify the grounding for a theory of knowledge that should be the successor to both Enlightenment and Marx- ist epistemologies. For Hartsock as for Rose, it is in the gendered division of labor that one can discover both the reason for the greater adequacy of feminist knowledge claims, and the root from which a full- fledged successor to Enlightenment science can grow. However, the feminist successor science will be anti-Cartesian, for it transcends and thus stands in opposition to the dichotomies of thought and practice created by divisions between mental and manual labor, though in a way different from that which Rose identifies.

Women's activity consists in "sensuous human activity, practice." Women's activity is institutionalized in two kinds of contributions – to "subsistence" and to child-rearing. In subsistence activities, contributions to producing the food, clothing, and shelter necessary for the survival of the species,

> the activity of a woman in the home as well as the work she does for wages keeps her continually in contact with a world of qualities and change. Her immersion in the world of use – in concrete, many-qualitied, changing material processes – is more complete than [a man's]. And if life itself consists of sensuous activity, the vantage point available to women on the basis of the contribution to subsistence represents an intensification and deepening of the materialist world view and consciousness available to the producers of commodities in capitalism, an intensification of class consciousness. (p. 292)

However, it is in examining the conditions of women's activities in child care that the inadequacy of the Marxist analysis appears most clearly. "Women also produce/reproduce men (and other women) on both a daily and a long-term basis. This aspect of women's 'production' exposes the deep inadequacies of the concept of production as a description of women's activity. One does not (cannot) produce another human being in anything like the way one produces an object such as a chair . . . Helping another to develop, the gradual relinquishing of control, the experience of the human limits of one's action" are fundamental characteristics of the child care assigned exclusively to women. "The female experience in reproduction represents a unity with nature which goes beyond the proletarian experience of interchange with nature" (p. 293).

Furthermore, Hartsock draws on the feminist object-relations theory of Jane Flax and Nancy Chodorow to show that women are "made, not born" in such a way as to define and experience themselves concretely and relationally.[11] In contrast, newborn males are turned into men who define and experience themselves abstractly and as fundamentally isolated from other people and nature. Not-yet-gendered newborn males and females are shaped into the kinds of personalities who will want to perform characteristic masculine and feminine activities. The consequences that object-relations theorists describe are just what Hartsock finds when she examines the adult division of labor by gender: relational femininity vs. abstract masculinity. Both the epistemology and the society constructed by "men suffering from the effects of abstract masculinity" emphasize "the separation and opposition of social and natural worlds, of abstract and concrete, of permanence and change" – the same oppositions as those stressed in the Marxist analysis of bourgeois labor. Thus the true counter to the bourgeois subjugations and mystifications is not to be found in a science grounded in proletarian experience, for this is fundamentally still a form of men's experience; it is instead to be found in a science grounded in women's experience, for only there can these separations and oppositions find no home (pp. 294–8).

The conditions under which women contribute to social life must be generalized for all humans if an effective opposition to androcentric and bourgeois political life and science/epistemology is to be created. Politically, this will lead to a society no longer structured by masculinist oppositions in either their bourgeois or proletarian forms; epistemologically, it will lead to a science that will both direct and be directed by the political struggle for that society.

A feminist epistemological standpoint is an interested social location ("interested" in the sense of "engaged," not "biased"), the conditions for which bestow upon its occupants scientific and epistemic advantage. The subjugation of women's sensuous, concrete, relational activity permits women to grasp aspects of nature and social life that are not accessible to inquiries grounded in men's characteristic activities. The vision based on men's activities is both partial and perverse – "perverse" because it systematically reverses the proper order of things: it substitutes abstract for concrete reality; for example, it makes death-risking rather than the reproduction of our species form of life the paradigmatically human act. Even early feminists such as Simone de Beauvoir think within abstract masculinity: "It is not in giving life but in risking life that man is raised above the animal: that is why superiority has been accorded in humanity not to the sex that brings forth but to that which kills".[12]

Moreover, men's vision is not simply false, for the ruling group can make their false vision become apparently true: "Men's power to structure social relations in their own image means that women, too, must participate in social relations which manifest and express abstract masculinity" (p. 302). The array of legal and social restrictions on women's participation in public life makes women's characteristic activities appear to both men and women as merely natural, as merely continuous with the activities of female termites or apes (as the sociobiologists would have it), and thus as suitable objects of men's manipulations of whatever they perceive as purely natural. The restriction of formal and informal educational opportunities for women makes women appear incapable of understanding the world within which men move, and as appropriately forced to deal with that world in men's terms.

The vision available to women "must be struggled for and represents an achievement which requires both science to see beneath the surface of the social relations in which all are forced to participate, and the education which can only grow from struggle to change those relations" (p. 285). The adoption of this standpoint is fundamentally a moral and political act of commitment to understanding the world from the perspective of the socially subjugated. It constitutes not a switch of epistemological and political commitments from one gender to the other but a commitment to the transcendence of gender through its elimination. Such a commitment is social and political, not merely intellectual.

Hartsock is arguing that divisions of labor more intensive than those Marx identified create dominating political power and ally perverse knowledge claims with the perversity of dominating power. Therefore, a science generated out of a transcendence, a transformation, of these divisions and their corresponding dualisms will be a powerful force for the elimination of power. In an earlier paper, Hartsock argued that the concept of power central to the history of political theory is only one available concept. Against power as domination *over* others, feminist thinking and organizational practices express the possibility of power as the provision of energy *to* others as well as self, and of reciprocal empowerment.[13] I think this second notion of power and the kind of knowledge that could be allied with it can remove the apparent paradox from her adoption of both successor science and postmodern tendencies. One can insist on an epistemology-centered philosophy only if the "policing of thought" that epistemology entails is a reciprocal project – with the goal of eliminating the kind of dominating power that makes the policing of

thought necessary.[14] That is, such an epistemology would be a transitional project, as we transform ourselves into a culture uncomfortable with domination and thereby into peoples whose thought does not need policing.

Hartsock's grounds for a feminist epistemology are both broader and narrower than Rose's. They are narrower in that it is feminist political struggle and theory ("science") – not simply characteristic women's activities – in which the tendencies toward a specifically feminist epistemology can be detected. Unmediated by feminist struggle and analysis, women's distinctive practices and thinking remain part of the world created by masculine-domination.[15] But her grounds are also broader, for any feminist inquiry that starts from the categories and valuations of women's subsistence and domestic labor and is *interested* (again in the sense of *engaged*) in the struggle for feminist goals provides the grounding for a distinctive epistemology of a successor to Enlightenment science. The women's health movement and the alternative understandings of the relationship between organism and environment that Rose points to would provide significant examples of such inquiries (insofar as they are motivated by the goals of feminist emancipation). But so would any of the natural or social science inquiries that begin by taking women's activities as fully social and try to explain nature and social life for feminist political purposes. There is still a significant gap in Hartsock's account between feminist activity and a science/epistemology robust and politically powerful enough to unseat the Enlightenment vision. But in both its broader and narrower aspects, Hartsock's account inches yet further across the gap by extending the foundation for the successor science to the full array of feminist political and scientific projects and, at least implicitly, to activities in which men as well as women feminists engage.

There is an another important difference in the groundings these two theorists identify for the successor epistemology. Hartsock does not directly focus on the "caring" labor of women, which Rose takes to be the distinctive human activity missing in the Marxist accounts. For Hartsock, the uniqueness of women's labor, in contrast to proletarian labor, is to be found in its more fundamental opposition to the mental/manual dualities that structure masculine/bourgeois thought and activity. For Hartsock, (men's) proletarian labor is transitional between bourgeois/masculine and women's labor, since women's labor is more fundamentally involved with the self-conscious, sensuous processing of our natural/social surroundings in daily life – is the distinctively human activity. For Rose, women's labor is different in kind from (masculine) proletarian/bourgeois labor.

The "return of the repressed" in feminist theory

Jane Flax, a political theorist and psychotherapist, explicitly describes the successor science and postmodern tendencies in feminist epistemology as conflicting. In the later of two papers I shall examine, she argues for the postmodern direction to replace the successor science tendency, yet in both papers the two tendencies are linked in a way that evidently appears noncontradictory to her.

In a paper written in 1980, though not published until 1983, Flax calls for a "successor science" project:

> The task of feminist epistemology is to uncover how patriarchy has permeated both our concept of knowledge and the concrete content of bodies of knowledge, even that claiming to be emancipatory. Without adequate knowledge of the world and our history within it (and this includes knowing how to know), we cannot develop a more adequate social practice. A feminist epistemology is thus both an aspect of feminist theory and a preparation for and a central element of a more adequate theory of human nature and politics.[16]

"Feminist philosophy thus represents the return of the repressed, of the exposure of the particular social roots of all apparently abstract and universal knowledge. This work could prepare the ground for a more adequate social theory in which philosophy and empirical knowledge are reunited and mutually enriched" (p. 249).

Flax argues that feminist philosophy should ask the question, "What forms of social relations exist such that certain questions and ways of answering them become constitutive of philosophy?" (p. 248). Here a feminist reading of psychoanalytic object-relations theory (see Chapter 5)[ii] becomes a useful philosophic tool; it directs our attention to the distinctively gendered senses of self, others, nature, and relations among the three that are characteristic in cultures where infant care is primarily the responsibility of women. For Flax, what is particu-

[ii] Of Harding's *The Science Question in Feminism.*

larly interesting is the fit between masculine senses of self, others, and nature and the definition of what is problematic in philosophy. From this perspective, "apparently insoluble dilemmas within philosophy are not the product of the immanent structure of the human mind and/or nature but rather reflect distorted or frozen social relations" (p. 248). For men more than for women, the self remains frozen in a defensive infantile need to dominate and/or repress others in order to retain its individual identity. In cultures where primary child care is assigned exclusively to women, male infants will develop unresolvable dilemmas concerning the separation of the infantile self from its first "other" and the establishment of individual identity. These are the very same distinctively masculine dilemmas that preoccupy Western philosophers in whose work they appear as "the human dilemma."

Western philosophy problematizes the relationships between subject and object, mind and body, inner and outer, reason and sense; but these relationships would not need to be problematic for anyone were the core self not always defined exclusively against women.

> In philosophy, being (ontology) has been divorced from knowing (epistemology) and both have been separated from either ethics or politics. These divisions were blessed by Kant and transformed by him into a fundamental principle derived from the structure of mind itself. A consequence of this principle has been the enshrining within mainstream Anglo-American philosophy of a rigid distinction between fact and value which has had the effect of consigning the philosopher to silence on issues of utmost importance to human life. (p. 248)

Were women not exclusively the humans against whom infant males develop their senses of a separate and individuated self, "human knowledge" would not be so preoccupied with infantile separation and individuation dilemmas. "Analysis reveals an arrested stage of human development . . . behind most forms of knowledge and reason. Separation-individuation [of infants from their caretakers] cannot be completed and true reciprocity emerge if the 'other' must be dominated and/or repressed rather than incorporated into the self while simultaneously acknowledging difference" (p. 269). Human knowledge can come to reflect the more adult issues of maximizing reciprocity and

Sandra Harding

appreciating difference only if the first "other" is "incorporated into the self" rather than dominated and/or repressed.

Flax's point is *not* that the Great Men in the history of philosophy would have better spent their time on psychoanalytic couches (had they been available) than in writing philosophy. Nor is it that philosophy is nothing but masculine rationalization of painful infantile experience. Rather, she argues that a feminist exposure of the "normal" relations between infantile gendering processes and adult masculine thought patterns "reveals fundamental limitations in the ability of [men's] philosophy to comprehend women's and children's experiences"; in particular, it reveals the tendency of philosophers to take their own experience as paradigmatically human rather than merely as typically masculine (p. 247). We can move toward a feminist epistemology through exposing the infantile social dilemmas repressed by adult men, the "resolutions" of which reappear in abstract and universalizing form as both the collective motive for and the subject matter of patriarchal epistemology. The feminine dimensions of experience tend to disappear in all thinking within patriarchies. But women's experience cannot, in itself, provide a sufficient ground for theory, for "as the other pole of the dualities it must be incorporated and transcended." Thus an adequate feminist philosophy requires "a revolutionary theory and practice ... Nothing less than a new stage of human development is required in which reciprocity can emerge for the first time as the basis of social relations" (p. 270).

In this earlier paper, Flax is arguing that infantile dilemmas are more appropriately resolved, less problematic, for women than for men. This small gap between the genders prefigures a larger gap between the defensive gendered selves produced in patriarchal modes of child rearing and the reciprocal, degendered selves that *could* exist were men as well as women primary caretakers of infants, and women as well as men responsible for public life. The forms and processes of knowing as well as what is known will be different for reciprocal selves than for defensive selves. Truly human knowledge and ways of knowing toward which a feminist epistemology points the way, will be less distorted and more nearly adequate than the knowledge and ways of knowing we now have. And while the concepts of reciprocal knowing must be relational and contextual, and thus will no longer enshrine the dualities of Enlightenment epistemology, it is indeed a succes-

sor epistemology toward which feminism moves us all.[17]

Flax's argument in a paper written four years later contrasts sharply with the foregoing argument. Whereas the earlier paper claims that child-rearing practices leave distinctive marks on philosophers as culturally diverse as Plato, Locke, Hobbes, Kant, Rousseau, and contemporary Anglo-American thinkers, the later one is skeptical that there can be a *single* way that patriarchy has permeated thinking. She finds problematic the notion of "*a* feminist standpoint which is more true than previous (male) ones." She says, "Any feminist standpoint will necessarily be partial. Each person who tries to think from the standpoint of women may illuminate some aspects of the social totality which have been previously suppressed with the dominant view. But none of us can speak for 'woman' because no such person exists except within a specific set of (already gendered) relations – to 'man' and to many concrete and different women."

Here it is feminist theory's affinities with postmodern philosophy that Flax finds most distinctive:

As a type of post modern philosophy, feminist theory shares with other such modes of thought an uncertainty about the appropriate grounding and methods for explaining and/or interpreting human experience. Contemporary feminists join other post modern philosophers in raising important metatheoretical questions concerning the possible nature and status of theorizing itself ... Consensus rules on categorization, appraisal, validity, etc. are lacking.[18]

This affinity is more fundamental, she argues, than feminist attempts at successor science projects: "Despite an understandable attraction to the (apparently) logical, orderly world of the Enlightenment, feminist theory more properly belongs in the terrain of post modern philosophy." And yet the substance of this later paper argues for a particular way of understanding gender that Flax thinks should replace the inadequate and confusing ways it is conceptualized in both traditional and feminist social theory. Gender should be understood as relational; gender relations are not determined by nature but are social relations of domination, and feminist theorists "need to recover and write the histories of women and our activities into the accounts and self-understanding of the whole" of social relations.

On the one hand, in effect Flax has located the feminist successor science tendencies as part of the projects of the defensive self which are most evident in men. She identifies postmodern skepticism about the Enlightenment dualities, which ensure the epistemological "policing of thought," as the entering wedge into projects for the reciprocal self. Overcoming the (distinctively masculine) Enlightenment dualities will be possible for our whole culture only after a "revolution in human development." On the other hand, does not Flax's own account of the distorted and frozen social relations characteristic of masculine-dominant societies suggest both that there is "objective basis for distinguishing between true and false beliefs" and that she is herself committed to this kind of epistemology? Even though any particular historical understanding available to feminists ("a feminist standpoint") is partial, may it not also be "more true than previous (male) ones"?

The bifurcated consciousness of alienated women inquirers

Canadian sociologist of knowledge Dorothy Smith has explored in a series of papers what it would mean to construct a sociology that begins from the "standpoint of women." Though her stated concern is sociology, her arguments are generalizable to inquiry in all the social and natural sciences. In the most recent of these papers, she directly articulates the problem of how to fashion a successor science that will transcend the damaging subject – object, inner–outer, reason–emotion dualities of Enlightenment science. "Here, I am concerned with the problem of methods of thinking which will realize the project of a sociology for women; that is, a sociology which does not transform those it studies into objects but preserves in its analytic procedures the presence of the subject as actor and experiencer. Subject then is that knower whose grasp of the world may be enlarged by the work of the sociologist."[19] Smith thinks that the forms of alienation experienced by women inquirers make it possible to carry out what I have been calling successor science and postmodern projects simultaneously and without contradiction.

Like the other theorists, Smith's epistemology is grounded in a successor to the Marxist theory of labor. (It is perhaps inaccurate to conjoin Flax with the others in this respect, unless we focus on her discussion of the process through which the infant becomes a social person as the first human labor,

which is divided, of course, by the gender of the "laboring" infant.) Smith eschews questions of the developmental origins of gender; of the origins in men's infantile experiences of the defensive abstractions of Western social theory, science, and epistemology; and thus of the reasons why men and women *want* to participate in characteristically masculine and feminine activity. That is, she does not discuss the issue of how initially androgynous infantile "animals" of our species interact with their social/physical environments to become the gendered humans we see around us. Like Rose, she turns to the structure of the workplace for women scientists (sociologists) to locate an enriched notion of the material conditions that make possible a distinctively feminist science.

Where Rose focuses on the unity of hand, brain, and heart common to women's characteristic activities, Smith looks at three other shared aspects of women's work. In the first place, it relieves men of the need to take care of their bodies or of the local places where they exist, freeing them to immerse themselves in the world of abstract concepts. Second, the labor of women thereby "articulates," shapes, men's concepts into those of administrative forms of ruling. The more successfully women perform this concrete work (Hartsock's "world of sensuousness, of qualities and change"), the more invisible does their work become to men. Men who are relieved of the need to maintain their own bodies and the local places where they exist can now see as real only what corresponds to their abstracted mental world. Like Hegel's master, to whom the slave's labor appears merely as an extension of his own being and will, men see women's work not as real activity – self-chosen and consciously willed – but only as "natural" activity, as instinctual or emotional labors of love. Women are thus excluded from men's conceptions of culture and its conceptual schemes of "the social," "the historical," "the human." Finally, women's actual experience of their own labor is incomprehensible and inexpressible within the distorted abstractions of men's conceptual schemes. Women are alienated from their own experience, for men's conceptual schemes are also the ruling ones, which then define and categorize women's experience for women. (This is Hartsock's point about ideologies structuring social life for everyone.) For Smith, education for women, for which nineteenth-century feminists struggled, completed the "invasion of women's consciousness" by ruling-class male experts.[20]

These characteristics of women's activities are a resource that a distinctively feminist science can use. A "line of fault" develops for many women between our own experience of our activity and the categories available to us within which to express our experience: the categories of ruling and of science. The break is intensified for women inquirers. We are first of all women, who – even if single, childless, or with servants – maintain our own bodies and our places of local existence, and usually also the bodies and domestic places of children and men. But when entering the world of science, we are trained to describe and explain social experience within conceptual schemes that cannot recognize the character of this experience. Smith cites the example of time-budget studies, which regard housework as part leisure and part labor – a conceptualization based on men's experience of wage labor for others vs. self-directed activity. But for wives and mothers, housework is neither wage labor nor self-directed activity. An account of housework from "the standpoint of women" – our experience of our lives – rather than in the terms of masculine science would be a quite different account; the voice of the subject of inquiry and the voice of the inquirer would be culturally identifiable.[21] It would be an example of science *for* women rather than *about* women; it would seek to explain/interpret social relations rather than behavior (human "matter in motion"), and do so in a way that makes comprehensible to women the social relations within which their experience occurs.

Smith fuses here what have been incompatible tendencies toward interpretation, explanation, and critical theory in the philosophy of social science. None of these discourses locates "authoritative accounts" in those of the inquirer as an active agent in inquiry. Once Smith puts the authority of the inquirer on the same epistemological plane as the authority of the subjects of inquiry – the woman inquirer interpreting, explaining, critically examining women's condition is simultaneously explaining her own condition – then issues of absolutism vs. relativism can no longer be posed. Both absolutism and relativism assume separations between the inquirer and subject of inquiry that are not present when the two share a subjugated social location.[22]

I think Smith is arguing that this kind of science would be "objective," not because it would use the categories available from an "Archimedean," dispassionate, detached "third version" of the conflicting perspectives people have on social relations but because it would use the more complete and less distorting categories available from the standpoint of historically locatable subjugated experiences.[23] However, it is difficult to generalize from her explicit assumptions about intepreting/ explaining women's world to a feminist science that takes as its project explaining the whole world. She often admonishes the reader that the experience of the subject of inquiry (the experience of the women whose lives the inquirer is explaining) is to be taken as the final authority. But many feminist inquirers take men's experience as well as women's to be inadequately interpreted, explained or criticized within the existing "corpus of knowledge": think of all the recent writing on men's war mentality; of object-relations theory's critical reinterpretation of the masculine experience of gendering; of Smith's own rethinking of men's experiences as sociologists. Yet she does not assign ruling-class men's experience the kind of authority she insists on for women's experience; through all four papers her argument shows why we should regard women's subjugated experience as starting and ending points for inquiry that are epistemologically preferable to men's experience. (Smith's argument here is similar to Hartsock's assertion of the epistemological preferability of the categories of women's activities, and to Flax's focus on feminism as the exposure of what men repress; all three return to Hegel's passage about the master and the slave to make their points.)

Interpreting Smith in this way leaves a few loose ends in her account, but it makes sense of the origins of the scientific authority she clearly intends to give to women as both subjects of inquiry and inquirers. For her, what feminism should distrust is not objectivity or epistemology's policing of thought per se but the particular distorted and ineffectual form of objectivity and epistemology entrenched in Enlightenment science. Like Flax, Smith stresses that there will be many different feminist versions of "reality," for there are many different realities in which women live, but they should all be regarded as producing more complete, less distorting, and less perverse understandings than can a science in alliance with ruling-class masculine activity.

New persons and the hidden hand of history

Finally, it is historical changes that make possible feminist theory and consequently a feminist science and epistemology, as I have argued elsewhere.[24] Here, too, we can learn from the Marxist analysis. Engels believed that "the great thinkers of the Eighteenth Century could, no more than their predecessors, go beyond the limits imposed upon them by their epoch."[25] He thought that only with the emergence in nineteenth-century industrializing societies of a "conflict between productive forces and modes of production" – a conflict that "exists, in fact, objectively, outside us, independently of the will and actions even of the men that have brought it on" – could the class structure of earlier societies be detected in its fullness for the first time. "Modern socialism is nothing but the reflex, in thought, of this conflict in fact; its ideal reflection in the minds, first, of the class directly suffering under it, the working class."[26]

Similarly, only now can we understand the feminisms of the eighteenth and nineteenth centuries as but "utopian" feminisms.[27] The men and women feminists of those cultures could recognize the misery of women's condition and the unnecessary character of that misery, but both their diagnoses of its causes and their prescriptions for women's emancipation show a failure to grasp the complex and not always obvious mechanisms by which masculine dominance is created and maintained. Liberal feminism, Marxist feminism and perhaps even the more doctrinaire strains of the radical and socialist feminisms of the mid-1970s do not have conceptual schemes rich or flexible enough to capture masculine domination's historical and cultural adaptability, nor its chameleonlike talents for growing within such other cultural hierarchies as classism and racism.[28] More complex and culture-sensitive (though not unproblematic) analyses had to await the emergence of historical changes in the relations between the genders. These changes have created a massive conflict between the culturally favored forms of producing persons (gendered, raced, classed persons) and the beliefs and actions of increasing numbers of women and some men who do not want to live out mutilated lives within the dangerous and oppressive politics these archaic forms of reproduction encourage.

If we cannot exactly describe this historical moment through an analogy to a "conflict between productive forces and modes of production" (and why should we have to?), we can nevertheless see clearly many aspects of the specific economic, political, and social shifts that have created this moment. There was the development and widespread distribution of cheap and efficient birth control, undertaken for capitalist and imperialist motives of controlling Third World and domestically colonized populations. There was the decline in the industrial sector combined with growth in the service sectors of the economy, which drew women into wage labor and deteriorated the centrality of industrialized "proletariat" labor. There were the emancipatory hopes created by the civil rights movement and the radicalism of the 1960s in both the United States and Europe. There was the rapid increase in divorce and in families headed by females – brought about in part by capitalism's seduction of men out of the family and into a "swinging singles" lifestyle, where they would consume more goods; in part by women's increased, though still severely limited, ability to survive economically outside of marriage; and no doubt in part by an availability of contraceptives that made what in olden days was called "philandering" less expensive. There was the increasing recognition of the feminization of poverty (probably also an actual increase in women's poverty), which combined with the increase in divorce and the drawing of women into wage labor to make women's life prospects look very different from those of their mothers and grandmothers: now women of every class could – and should – plan for lives after or instead of marriage. There was the escalation in international hostilities, revealing the clear overlap between masculine psychic needs for domination and nationalist domination rhetoric and politics. No doubt other significant social changes could be added to this list of preconditions for the emergence of feminism and its successor science and epistemology.

Thus, to paraphrase Engels, feminist theory is nothing but the reflex in thought of these conflicts in fact, their ideal reflection in the minds first of the class most directly suffering under them – women.[29] Feminist science and epistemology projects are not the products of observation, will power, and intellectual brilliance alone – the faculties that Enlightenment science and epistemology hold responsible for advances in knowledge. They are expressions of ways in which nature and social life can be understood by the new kinds of historical persons created by these social changes.[30] Persons whose activities are still characteristically "womanly," yet who also take on what have traditionally been masculine projects in public life, are one such important group of new persons. This "violation" of a traditional (at least, in our recent history) gendered division of labor both provides an epistemically advantaged standpoint for a successor science project and also resists the continuation of the distorting dualities of modernism. Why should we be loath to attribute a certain degree of, if not historical inevitability, at least historical possibility to the kinds of understandings arrived at in feminist science and epistemology?

I still think a historical account is an important component of the feminist standpoint epistemologies: it can identify the shifts in social life that make possible new modes of understanding. A standpoint epistemology without this recognition of the "role of history in science" (Kuhn's phrase) leaves mysterious the preconditions for its own production. However, I now think that the kind of account indicated above retains far too much of its Marxist legacy, and thereby also of Marxism's Enlightenment inheritance. It fails to grasp the historical changes that make possible the feminist postmodernist challenges to the Enlightenment vision as well as to Marxism.

Author's Notes

1   The offensively dichotomized categories of labor vs. leisure, which appear in the parental Enlightenment/bourgeois and Marxist theories, are themselves the target of criticism in the standpoint epistemologies; it is a theory of human *activity* and social experience they are proposing.

2   Rose (1983; 1984). Subsequent page references to these papers appear in the text.

3   Sohn-Rethel (1978).

4   Hartsock (1983; 1984) also raises this criticism about Sohn-Rethel.

5   Cf. the discussion of this dilemma in Stehelin (1976).

6   Merchant (1980); Rachel Carson, *Silent Spring* (New York: Fawcett, 1978, originally published in 1962); David Bohm, *Wholeness and the Implicate Order* (Boston: Routledge & Kegan Paul, 1980); Fritjof Capra, *The Tao of Physics* (New York: Random House, 1975).

7   Needham (1976).

8   See Bloch and Bloch (1980) on the deradicalization of the thought of Rousseau and other French thinkers that occurred once they recognized that the logic of their radical arguments was about to lead them directly to the conclusion that "the good" which should direct the social order was identical to what, in fact, women do.

9   Keller (1983).

10   Hartsock (1983, 284). This paper also appears as ch. 10 in Hartsock (1984). Page numbers in the text refer to the 1983 version.

11   Flax (1983); Chodorow (1978).

12   Simone de Beauvoir (1953, 58), cited in Hartsock (1983, 301).

13   Hartsock (1974).

14   This critique of epistemology-centered philosophy and its policing of thought is central to the postmodernists. See, e.g., Rorty (1979) and Foucault (1980).

15   Rose would probably agree with this; many of her other writings would support such an argument. See, e.g., the papers in Rose and Rose (1976).

16   Flax (1983, 269). Subsequent page references appear in the text.

17   Although she stresses here women's less defensive "resolution" of infantile separation and individuation dilemmas, see Flax (1978) for a discussion of those unfortunate residues of the feminine infantile dilemma that create tensions within women and for feminist organizations.

18   Flax (1986, 37).

19   Smith (1981, 1). See the discussion of Smith's work in Westkott (1979).

20   Smith (1979, 143). We should note that Smith was writing on these topics earlier than the other theorists I have discussed, though her work did not become widely known in the United States until recently. The aspects of women's labor Smith identifies so clearly and so early also appear to be on the minds of the other theorists, as a perusal of their work will show.

21   Smith (1979, 154; 1981, 3).

22   Cf. Harding (1980).

23   Smith (1981, 6).

24   Harding (1983). As I shall show, I now have postmodernist questions about my earlier defenses of the standpoint epistemologies.

25   Engels (1972, 606).

26   Engels (1972, 624).

27   O'Brien (1981) also makes this point.

28   For an analysis of these four main forms of feminism, see Jaggar (1983).

29   See Faderman (1981, 178–89) for a valuable analysis of the similar "causes" for the nineteenth-century women's movement in England and America.

30   Chapter 9 outlines the precedents for this kind of analysis in accounts of the breakdown of the medieval division of labor, which permitted the emergence of the new class of craftspeople who created experimental observation in the fifteenth century. See Zilsel (1942) and Van den Daele (1977).

Author's References

Bloch, Maurice, and Jean Bloch. 1980. "Women and the Dialectics of Nature in Eighteenth Century French Thought." In *Nature, Culture and Gender*, ed. C. MacCormack and M. Strathern. Cambridge: Cambridge University Press.

Chodorow, Nancy. 1978. *The Reproduction of Mothering*. Berkeley: University of California Press.

de Beauvoir, Simone. 1953. *The Second Sex*, trans. H. M. Parshley. New York: Knopf.

Engels, F. 1972. "Socialism: Utopian and Scientific." In *The Marx and Engels Reader*, ed. R. Tucker. New York: Norton.

Faderman, Lillian. 1981. *Surpassing the Love of Men: Romantic Friendship and Love between Women from the Renaissance to the Present*. New York: Morrow.

Flax, Jane. 1978. "The Conflict between Nurturance and Autonomy in Mother–Daughter Relationships and within Feminism." *Feminist Studies*, 4 (no. 2).

———.1983. "Political Philosophy and the Patriarchal Unconscious: A Psychoanalytic Perspective on Epistemology and Metaphysics." In *Discovering Reality: Feminist Perspectives on Epistemology, Metaphysics, Methodology and Philosophy of Science*, ed. S. Harding and M. Hintikka. Dordrecht: Reidel.

———. 1986. "Gender as a Social Problem: In and For Feminist Theory." *American Studies/Amerika Studien*, journal of the German Association for American Studies.

Foucault, Michel. 1980. *A History of Sexuality*. Vol. 1: *An Introduction*. New York: Random House.

Harding, Sandra. 1980. "The Norms of Social Inquiry and Masculine Experience." In *PSA, 1980*, vol. 2, ed. P. D. Asquith and R. N. Giere, East Lansing, Mich.: Philosophy of Science Association.

———. 1983. "Why Has the Sex-Gender System Become Visible Only Now?" In *Discovering Reality: Feminist Perspectives on Epistemology, Metaphysics, Methodology and Philosophy of Science*, ed. S. Harding and M. Hintikka. Dordrecht: Reidel.

Hartsock, Nancy. 1974. "Political Change: Two Perspectives on Power." *Quest: A Feminist Quarterly*, 1 (no. 1). Reprinted in *Building Feminist Theory: Essays from Quest*, ed. Charlotte Bunch. New York: Longman, 1981.

———. 1983. "The Feminist Standpoint: Developing the Ground for a Specifically Feminist Historical Materialism." In *Discovering Reality: Feminist Perspectives on Epistemology, Metaphysics, Methodology and Philosophy of Science*, ed. S. Harding and M. Hintikka. Dordrecht: Reidel.

———. 1984. *Money, Sex and Power*. Boston: Northeastern University Press.

Jaggar, Alison. 1983. *Feminist Politics and Human Nature*. Totowa, NJ: Rowman & Allenheld.

Keller, Evelyn Fox. 1983. *A Feeling for the Organism*. San Francisco: Freeman.

Merchant, Carolyn. 1980. *The Death of Nature: Women, Ecology and the Scientific Revolution*. New York: Harper & Row.

Needham, Joseph. 1976. "History and Human Values: A Chinese Perspective for World Science and Technology." In *Ideology of/ in the Natural Sciences*, ed. H. Rose and S. Rose. Cambridge, Mass.: Schenkman.

O'Brien, Mary. 1981. *The Politics of Reproduction*. New York: Routledge & Kegan Paul.

Rorty, Richard. 1979. *Philosophy and the Mirror of Nature*. Princeton, NJ: Princeton University Press.

Rose, Hilary. 1983. "Hand, Brain and Heart: A Feminist Epistemology for the Natural Sciences." *Signs: Journal of Women in Culture and Society*, 9 (no. 1).

———. 1984. "Is a Feminist Science Possible?" Paper presented to MIT Women's Studies Program, April 1984.

Rose, Hilary, and Steven Rose (eds). 1976. *Ideology of / in the Natural Sciences*. Cambridge, Mass.: Schenkman.

Smith, Dorothy. 1979. "A Sociology For Women." In *The Prism of Sex: Essays in the Sociology of Knowledge*, ed. J. Sherman and E. T. Beck. Madison: University of Wisconsin Press.

———. 1981. "The Experienced World as Problematic: A Feminist Method." Sorokin Lecture no. 12. Saskatoon: University of Saskatchewan.

Sohn-Rethel, Alfred. 1978. *Intellectual and Manual Labor*. London: Macmillan.

Stehelin, Liliane. 1976. "Sciences, Women and Ideology." In *Ideology of/ in the Natural Sciences*, ed. Hilary Rose and Steven Rose. Cambridge, Mass.: Schenkman.

Van den Daele, W. 1977. "The Social Construction of Science." In *The Social Production of Scientific Knowledge*, ed. E. Mendelsohn, P. Weingart, R. Whitley. Dordrecht: Reidel.

Westkott, Marcia. 1979. "Feminist Criticism of the Social Sciences." *Harvard Educational Review*, 49.

Zilsel, Edgar, 1942. "The Sociological Roots of Science." *American Journal of Sociology*, 47.

36

"The Cartesian Masculinization of Thought and the Seventeenth-Century Flight from the Feminine"

Susan Bordo

Feminist philosopher of culture and especially cultural images of the body, Susan Bordo (1947–) combines a number of themes common among postmodernists, but is no postmodernist herself. She employs psychodynamic theory to connect the Cartesian and scientific impulses of modernity to the repression of external nature, inner nature, and women. In the following essay, originally published in 1986, she argues that Cartesian modernity is inherently bound to a "flight from the feminine" motivated by a fear of the uncertainty, revulsion, and mortality of the mundane bodily existence with which women have been identified by the same tradition. She thereby gives a feminist cast to the critique of modern foundationalism that had earlier been led by John Dewey, in his *The Quest for Certainty* (1929), and more recently by Richard Rorty, in his *Philosophy and the Mirror of Nature* (1979).

> *[I]f a kind of Cartesian ideal were ever completely fulfilled, i.e., if the whole of nature were only what can be explained in terms of mathematical relationships – then we would look at the world with that fearful sense of alienation, with that utter loss of reality with which a future schizophrenic child looks at his mother. A machine cannot give birth.*
>
> Karl Stern, *The Flight From Woman*

Philosophical Reconstruction, Anxiety and Flight

If the transition from Middle Ages to early modernity can be looked on as a kind of protracted

birth, from which the human being emerges as a decisively separate entity, no longer continuous with the universe with which it had once shared a soul, so the possibility of objectivity, strikingly, is conceived by Descartes as a kind of *rebirth*, on one's own terms, this time.

We are all familiar with the dominant Cartesian themes of starting anew, alone, without influence from the past or other people, with the guidance of reason alone. The product of our original and actual birth, childhood, being ruled by the body, is the source of most obscurity and confusion in our thinking. As Descartes says in the *Discourse*,[i] "since we have all been children before being men... it is almost impossible that our judgements should be so excellent or solid as they would have been had we had complete use of our reason since our birth, and had we been guided by its means alone" (HR, I, 88). The specific origins of obscurity in our thinking are, as we have seen, the appetites, the influence of our teachers, and the "prejudices" of childhood. Those "prejudices" all have a common form: the inability, due to our infantile "immersion" in the body, to distinguish properly between subject and object. The purification of the relation between knower

[i] *Discourse on Method*. "HR" refers to the Haldane and Ross edition of Descartes' work. For this and similar references see the author's References after the endnotes.

Susan Bordo, "The Cartesian Masculinization of Thought and the Seventeenth-Century Flight from the Feminine," chapter 6, pp. 97–118 from *The Flight to Objectivity: Essays on Cartesianism and Culture*. Albany: State University of New York Press, 1987.

and known requires the repudiation of childhood, a theme which was not uncommon at the time. The ideology of childhood as a time of "innocence," and the child as an epistemological *tabula rasa*,[ii] had yet to become popular (Ariès, 100–33). Rather, childhood was commonly associated, as Descartes associated it, with sensuality, animality, and the mystifications of the body.[1]

For Descartes, happily, the state of childhood *can* be revoked, through a deliberate and methodical reversal of all the prejudices acquired within it, and a beginning anew with reason as one's only parent. This is precisely what the *Meditations* attempts to do. The mind is emptied of all that it has been taught. The body of infancy, preoccupied with appetite and sense-experience, is transcended. The clear and distinct ideas are released from their obscuring material prison. The end-result is a philosophical reconstruction which secures all the boundaries which, in childhood (and at the start of the *Meditations*) are so fragile: between the "inner" and the "outer," between the subjective and the objective, between self and world.

It is crucial to recall here that what for Descartes is conceived as epistemological threat – "subjectivity," or the blurring of boundaries between self and world – was not conceived as such by the medievals. Rather, the medieval sense of relatedness to the world, as we know from its art, literature, and philosophy, had not depended on "objectivity" but on continuity between the human and physical realms, on the interpenetrations, through meanings, of self and world. But *locatedness* in space and time, by Descartes's era, had inexorably come to the forefront of human experience, and the continuities and interpenetrations which had once been a source of intellectual and spiritual satisfaction now presented themselves as "distortions" caused by personal attachment and "perspective." Objectivity, not meaning, became the issue, and "so long as the human being is embedded in nature and united with it, objectivity is impossible" (Stern, 76). By the time of Kant, this "condition" for knowledge – the separation of knower and known – is philosophically apprehended. Human intelligence, Kant discovers, is *founded* on the distinction between subject and object. The condition of *having* an objective world, on the Kantian view, is to grasp phenomena as unified and connected by the embrace of a discrete consciousness, capable of representing to itself its own distinctness from the world it grasps. But

what Kant here "discovers" (and what came to be regarded as a given in modern science and philosophy) was a while in the making. For Descartes, the separation of subject and object is a *project*, not a "foundation" to be discovered.

The Cartesian reconstruction has two interrelated dimensions. On the one hand, a new model of knowledge is conceived, in which the purity of the intellect is guaranteed through its ability to transcend the body. On the other hand, the ontological blueprint of the order of things is refashioned. The spiritual and the corporeal are now two distinct substances which share no qualities (other than being created), permit of interaction but no merging, and are each defined precisely in opposition to the other. *Res cogitans* is "a thinking and unextended thing"; *res extensa* is "an extended and unthinking thing" (I, 190). This mutual exclusion of *res cogitans* and *res extensa* made possible the conceptualization of complete intellectual independence from the body, *res extensa* of the human being and chief impediment to human objectivity. The dictotomy between the spiritual and the corporeal also established the utter diremption of the natural world from the realm of the human.[2] It now became inappropriate to speak, as the medievals had done, in anthropocentric terms about nature, which for Descartes is pure *res extensa*, "totally devoid of mind and thought." More important, it means that the values and significances of things in relation to the human realm must be understood as purely a reflection of how *we* feel about them, having nothing to do with their "objective" qualities.

"Thus," says Whitehead, in sardonic criticism of the "characteristic scientific philosophy" of the seventeenth century, "the poets are entirely mistaken. They should address their lyrics to themselves, and should turn them into odes of self-congratulation . . . Nature is a dull affair, soundless, scentless, colourless; merely the hurrying of material, endlessly, meaninglessly" (1925, p. 54). For the model of knowledge which results, neither bodily response (the sensual or the emotional) nor associational thinking, exploring the various personal or spiritual meanings the object has for us, can tell us anything about the object "itself." *It* can only be grasped, as Gillispie puts it, "by measurement rather than sympathy" (p. 42). Thus, the specter of infantile subjectivism is overcome by the possibility of a cool, impersonal, distanced cognitive relation to the world. At the same time, the nightmare landscape of the infinite universe has become the well-lighted laboratory of modern science and philosophy.

ii Blank slate.

The conversion of nightmare into positive vision is characteristic of Descartes. Within the narrative framework of the *Meditations*, "dreamers, demons, and madmen" are exorcised, the crazily fragmented "enchanted glass" of the mind (as Bacon called it) is transformed into the "mirror of nature," the true reflector of things. But such transformations, as Descartes's determinedly upbeat interpretation of his own famous nightmare suggests, may be grounded in *defense* – in the suppression of anxiety, uncertainty, and dread. Certainly, anxiety infuses the *Meditations*, as I have argued through my reading of the text. I have tried, too, to show that Cartesian anxiety was a *cultural* anxiety, arising from discoveries, inventions, and events which were major and disorienting.

That disorientation, I have suggested, is given psychocultural coherence via a "story" of *parturition* from the organic universe of the Middle Ages and Renaissance, out of which emerged the modern categories of "self," "locatedness," and "innerness." This parturition was initially experienced as *loss*, that is, as estrangement, and the opening up of a chasm between self and nature. Epistemologically, that estrangement expresses itself in a renewal of scepticism, and in an unprecedented anxiety over the possibility of reaching the world as "it" is. Spiritually, it expresses itself in anxiety over the *enclosedness* of the individual self, the isolating uniqueness of each individual allotment in time and space, and the arbitrary, incomprehensible nature of that allotment by an alien, indifferent universe. We may speak here, meaningfully, of a *cultural* "separation anxiety."

The particular genius of Descartes was to have philosophically transformed what was first experienced as estrangement and loss – the sundering of the organic ties between the person and world – into a requirement for the growth of human knowledge and progress. And at this point, we are in a better position to flesh out the mechanism of *defense* involved here. Cartesian objectivism and mechanism, I will propose, should be understood as a *reaction-formation* – a denial of the "separation anxiety" described above, facilitated by an aggressive intellectual *flight* from the female cosmos and "feminine" orientation towards the world. That orientation (described so far in this study in the gender-neutral terminology of "participating consciousness") had still played a formidable role in medieval and Renaissance thought and culture. In the seventeenth century, it was decisively purged from the dominant intellectual culture, through the

Cartesian "rebirthing" and restructuring of knowledge and world as *masculine*.

I will begin by exploring the mechanist flight from the female cosmos (which Carolyn Merchant has called "The Death of Nature"). Then, I will focus on the specifically epistemological expression of the seventeenth-century flight from the feminine: "the Cartesian masculinization of thought." Both the mechanist reconstruction of the world and the objectivist reconstruction of knowledge will then be examined as embodying a common psychological structure: a fantasy of "re-birthing" self and world, brought into play by the disintegration of the organic, female cosmos of the Middle Ages and Renaissance. This philosophical fantasy will be situated within the general context of seventeenth-century attitudes toward female generativity, as chronicled by a number of feminist authors. Finally, the relevance of these ideas to current discussions about gender and rationality, and to current reassessments of Cartesianism, will be considered in a concluding section of this chapter.

The Death of Nature and the Masculinization of Thought

Discussion of "masculinity" and "femininity" is a new motif in this study. Yet gender has played an implicit role all along. For the medieval cosmos whose destruction gave birth to the modern sensibility was a *mother*-cosmos, and the soul which Descartes drained from the natural world was a *female* soul. Carolyn Merchant, whose groundbreaking interdisciplinary study, *The Death of Nature*, chronicles the changing imagery of nature in this period, describes the "organic cosmology" which mechanism overthrew:

> Minerals and metals ripened in the uterus of the Earth Mother, mines were compared to her vagina, and metallurgy was the human hastening of the living metal in the artificial womb of the furnace . . . Miners offered propitiation to the deities of the soil, performed ceremonial sacrifices . . . sexual abstinence, fasting, before violating the sacredness of the living earth by sinking a mine. (p. 4)

The notion of the natural world as *mothered* has sources, for the Western tradition, in both Plato and Aristotle. In Plato's *Timeaus*, the formless "receptacle" or "nurse" provides the substratum of all determinate materiality. (It is also referred to as "space" – *chora* – in the dialogue.) The "receptacle" is likened to a mother because of its receptivity to impression; the father is the "source or spring" – the eternal forms which "enter" and "stir and inform her." The child is the determinate nature which is formed through their union: the *body* of nature (51).

In this account, the earth is not a mother, but is itself a child of the union of "nurse" and forms. The notion that the earth *itself* mothers things, for example, metals and minerals, required the inspiration of the Aristotelian theory of animal reproduction. In that theory, the female provides not only matter as "substratum," but matter as sensible "stuff": the *catamenia*, or menstrual material, which is "worked upon" and shaped by the "effective and active" element, the semen of the male (729a–b). In the fifteenth and sixteenth centuries, this account of animal generation was "projected" onto the cosmos. A "stock description" of biological generation in nature was the marriage of heaven and earth, and the impregnation of the (female) earth by the dew and rain created by the movements of the (masculine) celestial heavens (Merchant, 16).

The female element here is *natura naturata*,[iii] of course – passive rather than creative nature. But passivity here connotes *receptivity* rather than inertness; only a living, breathing earth can be impregnated. And indeed, for Plato most explicitly, the world *has* a soul – a female soul – which permeates the corporeal body of the universe. In the seventeenth century, as Merchant argues, that female world-soul died – or more precisely, was *murdered* – by the mechanist re-visioning of nature.

This re-visioning of the universe as a *machine* – most often, a clockwork – was not the work of philosophers alone. Astronomy and anatomy had already changed the dominant picture of the movements of the heavens and the processes of the body by the time the *Meditations* were written. But it was philosophy, and Descartes in particular, that provided the cosmology that integrated these discoveries into a consistent and unified view of nature. By Descartes's brilliant stroke, nature became *defined* by its lack of affiliation with divinity, with spirit. All that which is God-like or spiritual – freedom, will, and sentience – belong entirely and exclusively to *res cogitans*. All else – the earth, the

iii Medieval philosophers distinguished nature as active, nature natur*ing* (*natura naturans*), from nature as acted upon, nature natur*ed* (*natura naturata*).

heavens, animals, the human body – is merely mechanically interacting matter.

The seventeenth century saw the death, too, of another sort of "feminine principle" – that cluster of epistemological values, often associated with feminine consciousness,[3] and which apparently played a large and respected role in hermetic philosophy and, it might be argued, in the prescientific orientation toward the world in general. If the key terms in the Cartesian hierarchy of epistemological values are clarity and distinctness – qualities which mark each object off from the other and from the knower – the key term in this alternative scheme of values might be designated (following Gillispie's contrast here) as *sympathy*. "Sympathetic" understanding of the object is that which understands it through "union" with it (Stern, 42–3), or, as James Hillman describes it, though "merging with" or "marrying" it. To merge with or marry that which is to be known means, for Hillman, "letting interior movement replace clarity, interior closeness replace objectivity" (*The Myth of Analysis*, 293). It means granting personal or intuitive response a positive epistemological value, even (perhaps especially) when such response is contradictory or fragmented. "Sympathetic" thinking, Marcuse suggests, is the only mode which truly respects the object, that is, which allows the variety of its meanings to unfold without coercion or too-focused interrogation (p. 74).

Barfield's and Berman's discussions of medieval "participating consciousness," Bergson's notion of "intellectual sympathy," Jasper's "causality from within," all contain elements of what I have here called "sympathetic thinking." The deepest understanding of that which is to be known comes, each argues, not from analysis of parts but from "placing oneself within" the full being of an object, as Bergson puts it (at which point it ceases to be an "object" in the usual sense), and allowing *it* to speak.

An emphasis on the knower's *passivity* is shared by this ideal of knowledge and the Cartesian ideal. But whereas passivity for Descartes (and for Bacon) meant yielding to the authority of the object's "own" nature, for sympathetic thinking, the objective and subjective *merge*, participate in the creation of meaning. The most inspired and articulate contemporary advocates of what I am here calling "sympathetic thinking" are Carol Gilligan (1982) and Evelyn Fox Keller (1985), each of whom speaks forcefully to the need for integration of such thinking into our dominant conceptions of rationality. This does not mean a rejection, but a *re-visioning* of "objectivity." Keller's conception of "dynamic objectivity" is especially relevant here:

> Dynamic objectivity is...a pursuit of knowledge that makes use of subjective experience ...in the interests of a more effective objectivity. Premised on continuity, it recognizes difference between self and other as an opportunity for a deeper and more articulated kinship. The struggle to disentangle self from other is itself a source of insight – potentially into the nature of both self and other. It is a principle means for divining what Poincaré calls "hidden harmonies and relations." To this end, the scientist employs a form of attention to the natural world that is like one's ideal attention to the human world: it is a form of love. (p. 117)

In contrast to the conception of "dynamic objectivity," Descartes' program for the purification of the understanding, as we have seen, has as its ideal the rendering *impossible* of any such continuity between subject and object. The scientific mind must be cleansed of all its "sympathies" toward the objects it tries to understand. It must cultivate absolute *detachment*. Recognizing the centrality of such ideals to modern science has led writers like Sandra Harding to characterize modern science in terms of a "super-masculinization of rational thought."[4] Similarly, Karl Stern has said that "[what] we encounter in Cartesian rationalism is the pure masculinization of thought" (p. 104). The notion that modern science crystallizes masculinist modes of thinking is a theme, too, in the work of James Hillman; "The specific consciousness we call scientific, Western and modern," says Hillman, "is the long sharpened tool of the masculine mind that has discarded parts of its own substance, calling it 'Eve,' 'female,' and 'inferior' " (*The Myth of Analysis*, 250). Evelyn Fox Keller's *Reflections On Gender and Science* systematically explores various perspectives (including developmental perspectives) on the connection between masculinity and modern science.

It must be stressed that descriptions of modern science as a "masculinization of thought" refer to what these authors view as characteristic cognitive and theoretical biases of male-dominated science, *not* the fact of that male dominance itself, or science's attitudes toward women. Science has, of course, a long history of discrimination against women, insisting that women cannot measure up to the rigor, persistence, or clarity that science requires. It also has its share of explicitly misogynist doctrine, as do its ancient forefathers, Aristotle and Galen. But the most interesting contemporary discussions of the "masculinist" nature of modern science describe a different, though related, aspect of its "masculinism": a characteristic cognitive style, an epistemological stance which is required of men *and* women working in the sciences today. In the words of Evelyn Fox Keller:

> The scientific mind is set apart from what is to be known, i.e., from nature, and its autonomy is guaranteed...by setting apart its modes of knowing from those in which the dichotomy is threatened. In this process, the characterization of both the scientific mind and its modes of access to knowledge as masculine is indeed significant. Masculine here connotes, as it so often does, autonomy, separation, and distance...a radical rejection of any commingling of subject and object. (p. 79)

It is in this sense that the dominant scientific and philosophic culture of the seventeenth century indeed inaugurated "a truly masculine birth of time," as Francis Bacon had proclaimed it (Farrington). Similarly and strikingly, Henry Oldenberg, secretary of the Royal Society, asserted in 1664 that the business of that society was to raise "a masculine philosophy" (Easlea, 152). In her penetrating and imaginative study of sexual metaphors in the history of epistemology, Keller pays very serious attention to such historical associations of gender and "cognitive style," which we might have thought to belong to a peculiarly contemporary mentality, but which in fact crop up frequently in Royal Society debates. As Keller reads them, the controversies between Bacon and Paracelsus become an explicit contest between masculine and feminine principles: head versus heart, domination over versus merging with the object, purified versus erotic orientation toward knowledge, and so forth (43–65). Bacon's own deepest attitudes, Keller suggests, were more complicated and ambivalent than his oft-reproduced and notorious images of male seduction, penetration, and rape of nature may indicate. But what emerges with clarity, despite any subtleties in the attitudes of individual thinkers, is that the notion of science as "masculine" is hardly a twentieth-century invention or feminist fantasy. The founders of modern science consciously and explicitly proclaimed the "masculinity" of science as inaugurating a new era. And they associated that masculinity with a cleaner, purer, more objective and more disciplined epistemological relation to the world.

The emergence of such associations, in an era which lacked our heightened modern consciousness of gender as an issue, is remarkable. They suggest that the contemporary notion that thought *became* "super-masculinized" at a certain point in time is not merely, as some might argue, a new, fashionable way of labelling and condemning the seventeenth-century objectivist turn – a turn, many would say, which has already been adequately described, criticized, and laid to rest by Whitehead, Heidegger, and, more recently, Richard Rorty. Bacon's metaphor, rather, urges us in the direction of confronting a profound "flight from the feminine" at the heart of both Cartesian rationalism and Baconian empiricism. To appreciate the dimensions of that "flight," however, necessitates a return to the insights of developmental psychology.

The Cartesian "Rebirth" and the "Father of Oneself" Fantasy

Descartes envisages for himself a kind of rebirth. Intellectual salvation comes only to the twice-born.
Frankfurt, *Demons, Dreamers, and Madmen*

Psychoanalytic theory urges us to examine that which we actively repudiate for the shadow of a loss we mourn. Freud, in *Beyond the Pleasure Principle*, tells the story of an eighteen-month-old boy – an obedient, orderly little boy, as Freud describes him – who, although "greatly attached to his mother," never cried when she left him for a few hours.

> This good little boy, however, had an occasional disturbing habit of taking any small objects he could get hold of and throwing them away from him into a corner, under the bed, and so on, so that hunting for his toys and picking them up was often quite a business. As he did this he gave vent to a loud, long-drawn-out 'o-o-o-o', accompanied by an expression of interest and satisfaction. His mother and the writer of the present account were agreed in thinking that this was not a mere interjection but represented the German word '*fort*' ('gone'). I eventually realized that it was a game and that the only use he made of any of his toys was to play 'gone' with them . . . [T]he complete game [was] disap-

pearance and return . . . The interpretation . . . became obvious. It was related to the child's great cultural achievement – the instinctual renunciation (that is, the renunciation of instinctual satisfaction) which he had made in allowing his mother to go away without protesting. He compensated himself for this, as it were, by himself staging the disappearance and return of the objects within his reach . . . Throwing away the object so that it was 'gone' might satisfy an impulse of the child's, which was suppressed in his actual life, to revenge himself on his mother for going away from him. In that case it would have a defiant meaning: 'All right, then, go away! I don't need you. I'm sending you away myself'. (33–5)

The "fort-da"[iv] game and Freud's interpretation of it places the Cartesian facility for transforming anxiety into confidence, loss into mastery, in a striking new perspective. Within the context of the cultural separation anxiety described in this study, Descartes's masculine "rebirthing" of the world and self as decisively separate appears, not merely as the articulation of a positive new epistemological ideal, but as a reaction-formation to the loss of "being-one-with-the-world" brought about by the disintegration of the organic, centered, female cosmos of the Middle Ages and Renaissance. The Cartesian reconstruction of the world is a "fort-da" game – a defiant gesture of independence from the female cosmos, a gesture which is at the same time compensation for a profound loss.

Let us explore the interpretation proposed above in more detail, turning again to developmental theory for insight. The project of growing up is to one degree or another (depending on culture and child-raising practice) a project of *separation*, of learning to deal with the fact that mother and child are no longer one and that gratification is not always available. Social and personal strategies for the child's accomplishing this are varied; every culture no doubt has its own modes of facilitating the separation of mother and child, to the degree that such separation is required by the culture. Psychoanalytic theory has focused on *internal* mechanisms, describing the different responses – longing, mourning, denial – that the child may have to separation. The mechanism of *denial* is of particular interest for my purposes. Although the

---

iv *Da* means "there," meaning the object is present, as in "Da!" ("There it is!").

Susan Bordo

dream of total union can persist throughout life, another, contradictory project may be conceived, psychoanalytic thinkers have suggested, centered around the denial of any longing for the lost maternal union. Instead, the child seeks mastery over the frustrations of separation and lack of gratification through an assertion of self against the mother and all that she represents and a rejection of all dependency on her. In this way, the pain of separateness is assuaged, paradoxically, by an even more definitive separation – but one that is *chosen* this time and aggressively pursued. It is therefore experienced as autonomy rather than helplessness in the fact of the discontinuity between self and mother.

One mode of such self-assertion is through the fantasy of becoming the parent of oneself, of "rebirthing" the self, playing the role of active parental figure rather than passive, helpless child. Such a notion of "rebirthing" or "reparenting" the self figures in both Freudian and object-relations frameworks. Building on Winnicott's[v] concept of the "transitional object" (a blanket, toy, or stuffed animal which eases the child's accommodation to and ultimate mastery over the process of separation from the mother), Ross argues that such objects function, symbolically, as the child himself. In cuddling and scolding the object, the child is actually playing at self-parenting, at being his own baby. Such self-parenting allows the child to feel less precariously at the mercy of the mother, more in control of his or her own destiny (1977).

Working from a more Freudian framework, Norman O. Brown reinterprets the Oedipal desire to "sexually" possess the mother as a fantasy of "beoming the father of oneself" (rather than the helpless child of the mother) (p. 127). Sexual activity here (or rather, the fantasy of it) becomes a means of denying the actual passivity of having been born from that original state of union into "a body of limited powers, and at a time and place [one] never chose" (de Beauvoir, 146), at the mercy of the now-alien will of the mother. The mother is still "other," but she is an other whose power has been harnessed by the will of the child. The pain of separateness is thus compensated for by the peculiar advantages of separateness: the possibility of mastery and control over that person on whom one is dependent. Melanie Klein (writing in 1928, much earlier than Brown) emphasizes the aggressive, destructive, envious impulses which may be

directed against parts of the mother's body – particularly against the breasts and reproductive organs – in the child's effort to achieve such control (pp. 98–111).

Certainly, the famous Baconian imagery of sexual assault and aggressive overpowering of a willful and unruly female nature (she must "be taken by the forelock" and "neither ought a man to make scruple of entering and penetrating these holes and corners," etc.[5]) makes new psychocultural sense in the context of these ideas. More subtly, the Cartesian project of starting anew through the revocation of one's actual childhood (during which one was "immersed" in body and nature) and the (re)creation of a world in which absolute separateness (both epistemological and ontological) from body and nature are keys to control rather than sources of anxiety can now be seen as a "father of oneself" fantasy on a highly symbolic, but profound, plane.[6] The sundering of the organic ties between person and nature – originally experienced, as we have seen, as epistemological estrangement, as the opening up of a chasm between self and world – is reenacted, *this* time with the human being as the engineer and architect of the separation. Through the Cartesian "rebirth," a new "masculine" theory of knowledge is delivered, in which detachment from nature acquires a positive epistemological value. And a new *world* is reconstructed, one in which all generativity and creativity fall to God, the spiritual father, rather than to the female "flesh" of the world. With the same masterful stroke – the mutual opposition of the spiritual and the corporeal – the formerly female earth becomes inert matter and the objectivity of science is insured.

"She" becomes "it" – and "it" can be understood and controlled. Not through "sympathy," of course, but by virtue of the very *object*-ivity of the "it." At the same time, the "wound" of separateness is healed through the *denial* that there ever "was" any union: For the mechanists, unlike Donne,[vi] the female world-soul did not die; rather the world *is* dead. There is nothing to mourn, nothing to lament. Indeed, the "new" epistemological anxiety is evoked, not over loss, but by the "memory" or suggestion of *union*; "sympathetic," associational, or bodily response obscures objectivity, feeling for nature muddies the clear lake of the

[v] D. W. Winnicott (1896–1971), British child psychiatrist.

[vi] English poet, John Donne (1572–1631), whose "Anatomy of the world" connects his wife's death to the world's demise.

mind. The "otherness" of nature is now what allows it to be known.

The Seventeenth-century Flight from the Feminine

The philosophical "murder" of the living female earth, explored in the preceding section as a reaction-formation to the dissolution of the medieval self-world unity, must be placed in the context of other issues in the gender politics of the sixteenth and seventeenth centuries. Thanks to the historical research of such writers as Carolyn Merchant, Brian Easlea, Barbara Ehrenreich, Dierdre English, and Adrienne Rich, we have been enabled to recognize the years between 1550 and 1650 as a particularly gynophobic century. What has been especially brought to light is what now appears as a virtual obsession with the untamed natural power of female generativity, and a dedication to bringing it under forceful cultural control.

Nightmare fantasies of female power over reproduction and birth run throughout the era. Kramer and Sprenger's *Malleus Maleficarum*, the official witch-hunter's handbook, accuses "witches" of every imaginable natural and supernatural crime involving conception and birth.[vii] The failure of crops and miscarriages were attributed to witches, and they are accused both of "inclining men to passion" and of causing impotence, of obstructing fertility in both men and women, of removing the penises of men, or procuring abortion, and of offering newborns to the devil (Lederer, 209).

Such fantasies were not limited to a fanatic fringe. Among the scientific set, we find the image of the witch, the willful, wanton virago, projected onto generative nature, whose scientific exploration, as Merchant points out, is metaphorically likened to a witch trial (169–170). The "secrets" of nature are imagined as deliberately and slyly "concealed" from the scientist (Easlea, 214). Matter, which in the *Timeaus*[viii] is passively receptive to the ordering and shaping masculine forms, now becomes, for Bacon, a "common harlot" with "an appetite and inclination to dissolve the world and fall back into the old chaos" and who must therefore be "restrained and kept in order" (Merchant, 171). The womb of nature, too (and this is striking, in connection with Melanie Klein), is no longer the beneficent mother but rather the *hoarder* of precious metals and minerals, which must be "searched" and "spied out" (Merchant, 169–70).

There were the witchhunts themselves, which, aided more politely by the gradual male takeover of birthing, and healing in general, virtually purged the healing arts of female midwives.[7] The resulting changes in obstetrics, which rendered women passive and dependent in the process of birth, came to identify birth, as Bacon identified nature itself, with the potentiality of disorder and the need for forceful male control.[8] So, too, in the seventeenth century, female sexuality was seen as voracious and insatiable, and a principal motivation behind witchcraft, which offered the capacious "mouth of the womb" the opportunity to copulate with the devil.[9]

The ideology of the voracious, insatiable female may not be unique to the sixteenth and seventeenth centuries. But it is not historically ubiquitous. By the second half of the nineteenth century, medical science had declared women to be naturally passive and "not much troubled by sexual feeling of any kind" (Vicinus, 82). Peter Gay suggests that this medical fantasy was a reaction-formation to that era's "pervasive sense of manhood in danger" (p. 93), brought about by its own particular social disruptions in gender relations and the family. I would suggest, along similar lines, that key changes in the seventeenth-century scientific theory of reproduction functioned in much the same way, although in reaction to different threats and disruptions.

Generativity, not sexuality, is the focus of the seventeenth century's fantasies of female passivity. Mechanist reproductive theory ("happily," as Brian Easlea sarcastically puts it) made it "no longer necessary to refer to any women at all" in its "scientific" descriptions of conception and gestation (Easlea, 49). Denied even her limited, traditional Aristotelian role of supplying the (living) menstrual material (which, shaped by the individuating male "form" results in the fetus), the woman becomes instead the mere *container* for the temporary housing and incubation of already-formed human beings, originally placed in Adam's semen by God, and parcelled out, over the ages, to all his male descendants.[10] The specifics of mechanistic reproductive theory are a microcosmic recapitulation of the mechanistic vision itself, where God the

---

vii   The Dominican Friars Heinrich Kramer (1430–1505) and Jakob Sprenger (1436–1495) composed *Malleus Maleficarum* (*The Witch Hammer*), which became the Inquisition's guide for investigating (and torturing) witches.

viii   One of Plato's dialogues.

father is the sole creative, formative principle in the cosmos. We know, from what now must be seen as almost paradigmatic examples of the power of belief over perception, that tiny horses and men were actually "seen" by mechanist scientists examining sperm under their microscopes.

All this is only to scratch the surface of a literature that has become quite extensive over the last decade. Even this brief survey, however, yields striking parallels. The mechanization of nature, we see, theoretically "quieted" the "common harlot" of matter (and sanctioned nature's exploitation) as effectively as Baconian experimental philosophy did so practically. Mechanistic reproductive theory successfully eliminated any active, generative role for the female in the processes of conception and gestation. And *actual* control over reproduction and birth was wrested away from women by the witch-hunters and the male medical establishment. Something, it seems, had come to be felt as all too powerful and in need of taming.

What can account for this upsurge of fear of female generativity? No doubt many factors – economic, political, and institutional – are crucial. But I would suggest that the themes of "parturition" and "separation anxiety" discussed in this study can provide an illuminative psychocultural framework within which to situate seventeenth-century gynophobia.

The culture in question, in the wake of the dissolution of the medieval intellectual and imaginative system, had lost a world in which the human being could feel nourished by the sense of oneness, of continuity between all things. The new, infinite universe was an indifferent home, an "alien will," and the sense of separateness from her was acute. Not only was she "other," but she seemed a perverse and uncontrollable other. During the years 1550–1650, a century that had brought the worst food crisis in history, violent wars, plague, and devastating poverty, the Baconian imagery of nature as an unruly and malevolent virago was no paranoid fantasy. More important, the cruelty of the world could no longer be made palatable by the old medieval sense of organic justice – that is, justice on the level of the workings of a whole with which one's identity merged and which, while perhaps not fully comprehensible, was nonetheless to be trusted. Now there is no organic unity, but only "I" and "She" – an unpredictable and seemingly arbitrary "She," whose actions cannot be understood in any of the old "sympathetic" ways.

"She" is *Other*. And "otherness" itself becomes dreadful – particularly the otherness of the female, whose powers have always been mysterious to men, and evocative of the mystery of existence itself. Like the infinite universe, which threatens to swallow the individual "like a speck," the female, with her strange rhythms, long acknowledged to have their chief affinities with the rhythms of the natural (now alien) world, becomes a reminder of how much lies outside the grasp of man.

"The quintessential incarnation" of that which appears to man as "mysterious, powerful and not himself," as Dorothy Dinnerstein says, is "the woman's fertile body" (p. 125). Certainly, the mother's body holds these meanings for the infant, according to Klein. If Dorothy Dinnerstein is right, women (particularly the woman-as-mother, the original "representative" of the natural world, and virtually indistinguishable from it for the human infant) are always likely targets for all later adult rage against nature.[11] Supporting Dinnerstein's highly theoretical account are the anthropologist Peggy Reeves Sanday's cross-cultural findings that in periods of cultural disruption and environmental stress, male social dominance – particularly over female fertility – tends to be at its most extreme (172–84). In the seventeenth century, with the universe appearing to man more decisively "not-himself" than ever before, more capricious and more devastating in her capacity for disorder, both the mystery of the universe and the mystery of the female require a more definitive "solution" than had been demanded by the organic world view.[12]

The project that fell to both empirical science and "rationalism" was to tame the female universe. Empirical science did this through aggressive assault and violation of her "secrets." Rationalism, as we have seen, tamed the female universe through the philosophical neutralization of her vitality. The barrenness of matter correlatively insured the revitalization of human hope of conquering nature (through knowledge, in this case, rather than through force). The mystery of the female, however, could not be bent to man's control simply through philosophical means. More direct and concrete means of "neutralization" were required for that project. It is within this context that witch-hunting and the male medical takeover of the processes of reproduction and birth, whatever their social and political causes, can be seen to have a profound psychocultural dimension as well.

The Contemporary Revaluation of the Feminine

My next focus will be on the recent scholarly emergence and revaluation of epistemological and ethical perspectives "in a different voice." That voice, which classical as well as contemporary writers identify as feminine (as, e.g. in the work of Carol Gilligan, Sarah Ruddick, and Nancy Chodorow), claims a natural foundation for knowledge, not in detachment and distance, but in what I have called "sympathy": in closeness, connectedness, and empathy. It finds the failure of connection (rather than the blurring of boundaries) as the principal cause of breakdown in understanding.

In the seventeenth century, when Paracelsus articulated the alchemical conception of knowledge as a merger of mind and nature, the "female" nature of this ideal operated for him as a metaphor, as did Bacon's contrasting ideal of a virile, "masculine" science. In the second half of our own more sociologically oriented century, women themselves – not some abstract "feminine principle" – have been identified as cultural bearers of the alternative, "sympathetic" scheme of values. The research of Chodorow and Gilligan, in particular, has suggested that men and women (growing up within a particular cultural framework, it needs emphasizing) *do* appear to experience and conceptualize events differently, the key differences centering around different conceptions of the self/world, self/other relation.

> Girls emerge . . . with a basis for "empathy" built into their primary definition of self in a way that boys do not. Girls emerge with a stronger basis for experiencing another's needs or feelings as one's own (or thinking that one is so experiencing another's needs or feelings) . . . girls come to experience themselves as less differentiated than boys, more continuous with and related to the external object-world and as differently oriented to their inner object-world as well. (Chodorow, 167)

Carol Gilligan has described how these developmental differences result, in men and women, in differing valuations of attachment and autonomy, and correspondingly different conceptions of morality.

The association of cognitive style with gender is in itself nothing new. We find it in ancient myth-ology, in archetypal psychology, in philosophical and scientific writings, and in a host of enduring popular stereotypes about men and women (for example, that women are more "intuitive," men are more "logical," etc.). In the second half of the nineteenth century, the celebration of a distinctively female moral sensibility was widely held by both feminists and sexual conservatives. What *is* new in the recent feminist exploration of gender and cognitive style is a (characteristically modern) emphasis on gender as a social construction, rather than a biological or ontological given. If men and women think differently, it is argued, that is not because the sexes inevitably embody timeless "male" and "female" principles of existence, but because the sexes have been brought up differently, develop different social abilities, have occupied very different power positions in most cultures. Using a psychoanalytic framework, Nancy Chodorow explores the origins of these differences in the differing degrees of individuation from the mother demanded of boys and girls in infancy.[13]

An appreciation of the *historical* nature of the masculine model of knowledge to which the feminine "different voice" is often contrasted helps to underscore that the embodiment of these gender-related perspectives in actual men and women is a cultural, not a biological phenomenon. There have been cultures in which (using *our* terms now, not necessarily theirs) men thought more "like women," and there may be a time in the future when they do so again. In our own time, many women may be coming to think more and more "like men." The conclusion is not, however, that any association of gender and cognitive style is a reactionary mythology with no explanatory value. For the sexual division of labor within the family in the modern era has indeed fairly consistently reproduced significant cognitive and emotional differences along sexual lines. The central importance of Chodorow's work has been to show that boys have tended to grow up learning to experience the world like Cartesians, while girls do not, *because* of developmental asymmetries resulting from female-dominated infant care, rather than biology, anatomy, or "nature."[14]

It is of crucial importance, however, that feminist scholars like Chodorow more explicitly and emphatically underscore the fact that they are describing elements of a social construction, characteristic of certain (though not all) forms of gender organization, and *not* the reified dualities of an "eternal feminine" and "essential masculine" nature. A great deal of current division among feminists rests on lack of clarity and understanding regarding this distinction. This is unfortunate, because the sociological emphasis and understanding of gender as a social construction is one crucial difference between the contemporary feminist revaluation of the "feminine" and the nineteenth-century doctrine of female moral superiority. Too often, recently, the two have been conflated.

A still more central difference between nineteenth-century and twentieth-century feminism is the contemporary feminist emphasis on the *insufficiency* of any ethics or rationality – "feminine" *or* "masculine" – that operates solely in one mode without drawing on the resources and perspective of the other.[15] The nineteenth-century celebration of a distinctively feminine sensibility and morality functioned in the *service* of pure masculinized thought, by insisting that each "sphere" remain distinct and undiluted by the other. This was, of course, precisely what the seventeenth-century masculinization of thought had accomplished – the exclusion of "feminine" modes of knowing, not from culture in general, but from the scientific and philosophical arenas, whose objectivity and purity needed to be guaranteed. Romanticizing "the feminine" within its "own" sphere is no alternative to Cartesianism, because it suggests that the feminine has a "proper" (domestic) place. Only in establishing the scientific and philosophical legitimacy of alternative modes of knowing in the *public* arena (rather than glorifying them in their own special sphere of family relations) do we present a real alternative to Cartesianism.

Feminism and the "Recessive" Strain in Philosophy

The Cartesian ideals are under attack in philosophy today, and philosophers who subscribe to those ideals, whether in their analytic or phenomenological embodiment, are on the defensive. [Because philosophy has been so dominated by the Cartesian standpoint, the erosion of Cartesianism has been interpreted by some as signalling the "death of philosophy," and many of the current debates among philosophers are couched in those terms. If anything is dying, however, it is the intellectual rule of a particular model of knowledge and reality. Philosophers who grew up under that rule, and who were taught to identify philosophy *with* it, may experience the end of that rule as portending

the "end of philosophy". But in fact, philosophy has always spoken in many voices (although they have seldom been heard by the Cartesian "cultural overseer"), some of which are being revived and renovated today.] More significantly, alternative voices from those groups which philosophy has traditionally excluded are now offering the discipline the very means of its revitalization: the truths and values which it has suppressed from its dominant models. Those truths and values have been living underground, throughout the Cartesian reign, and are now emerging to make a claim on the culture.

This emergence cannot be adequately understood unless seen against the backdrop of the last several decades of social and political life. Philosophers may think that the widespread self-critique in which philosophy is currently engaged began with the publication of Richard Rorty's *Philosophy and the Mirror of Nature*. But (as Rorty would probably be the first to acknowledge), the impact of that work had much to do with its timely crystallization of historicist currents that had been gathering momentum since the 1960s. Those currents were themselves activated by the various "liberation" movements of that decade. There is a certain similarity here with the Renaissance, in the cultural reawakening to the multiplicity of possible human perspectives, and to the role of culture in shaping those perspectives. But in our era, the reawakening has occurred in the context of a recognition not merely of the undiscovered "other," but of the *suppressed* other. Women, people of color, and various ethnic and national groups have forced the culture into a critical reexamination not only of diversity (as occurred for Renaissance culture), but of the forces that *mask* diversity. That which appears as "dominant," by virtue of that very fact, comes to be suspect: It has a secret story to tell, in the alternative perspectives to which it has denied legitimacy, and in the historical and political circumstances of its own dominance.

Fueled by the historicist tradition in epistemology, psychoanalytic thought, *and* the political movement for women's rights, representation, and participation in cultural life, feminist ethics and epistemology now appears as one of the most vital forces in the development of post-Cartesian focus and paradigm. The feminist exposure of the gender biases in our dominant Western conceptions of science and ethics – the revelation that the history of their development, the lenses through which they see the world, their methods and priorities have been decisively shaped by the fact that it has been men who have determined their course – has come as a startling recognition to many contemporary male philosophers.[16] Inspired by the work of Gilligan, Chodorow, Harding, and Keller, feminist theory has been systematically questioning the historical identification of rationality, intelligence, "good thinking," and so forth, with the masculine modes of detachment and clarity, offering alternative models of fresher, more humane, and more hopeful approaches to science and ethics.[17]

It is not only in explicitly feminist writing that these phenomena are occurring. Many of the "new paradigms" being proposed in the recent spate of literature on modernity and modern science are grounded in sympathetic, participatory alternatives to Cartesianism. (See Berman and Capra, in particular.) In philosophy, a whole slew of reconsiderations of traditional epistemological "problems" such as relativism, perspectivism, the role of emotions and body in knowledge, the possibility of ultimate foundations, and so on, has brought the feminine perspective in through the back door, as it were. Without explicit commitment to feminism *or* "the feminine," philosophers are nonetheless participating in a (long overdue) philosophical acknowledgement of the limitations of the masculine Cartesian model, and are recognizing how tightly it has held most modern philosophy in its grip.

This is not to say that detachment, clarity, and precision will cease to have enormous value in the process of understanding. Rather, our culture needs to reconceive the status of what Descartes assigned to the shadows. Such reevaluation has been a constant, although "recessive" strain in the history of philosophy since Descartes. Leibniz's declaration that each monad is its *own* "mirror" of the universe, Hume's insistence that "reason is and ought to be the slave of the passions," and, perhaps most importantly, Kant's revelation that objectivity itself is the result of human structuring, opened various doors that in retrospect now appear as critical openings.

Hume, for example, may now be seen as having a rightful place – along with Nietzsche, Scheler, Peirce, Dewey, James, Whitehead, and, more recently, Robert Neville – in the critical protest against the Cartesian notion that reason can and should be a "pure" realm free from contamination by emotion, instinct, will, sentiment, and value. Within this protest, we see the development both of a "naturalist" *anthropology* of the Cartesian ideals of precision, certainty, and neutral-

ity (Nietzsche, Scheler, Dewey, and James), and a complementary *metaphysics* (Peirce, Whitehead, and Neville) in which "vagueness" as well as specificity, tentativeness, and valuation are honored as essential to thought.

In emphasizing the active, constructive nature of cognition, Kant undermined the Cartesian notion that the mind reflects and the scientist "reads off" what is simply *there* in the world. The Kantian "knower" is transcendental, of course, and Kant's "constructionism" begins and ends, like most Enlightenment thought, with a vision of universal law – in this case, the basic, ahistorical requirements of "knowability," represented by the categories. But the "Copernican Revolution in Thought," in asserting the activity of the subject, opened the door, paradoxically, to a more historical and contextual understanding of knowing. The knower, not the known, now comes under scrutiny – and not, as Descartes scrutinized the knower, for those contaminating elements which must be purged from cognition, but for those "active and interpreting forces," as Nietzsche says, "through which alone seeing becomes seeing *something*." The postulation of an inner "eye" in which these forces "are supposed to be lacking... [is] an absurdity and a nonsense" (1969, 119).

The articulation of the historical, social and cultural determinants of what Nietzsche called "perspective" can be seen as one paradigm of modern thought. The main theoretical categories of that paradigm have been worked out by various disciplines: the "philosophical anthropology" of Max Scheler, Karl Mannheim's work on ideology, and, historically fontal, the dialectical materialism of Karl Marx. Marx, of course, was not primarily interested in epistemological questions. But he is nonetheless the single most important philosophical figure in the development of modern historicism, with his emphasis on the historical nature of all human activity and thought and our frequent "false consciousness" of this. It was Marx who turned the tables on the Enlightenment, encouraging suspicion of all ideas that claim to represent universal, fundamental, "inherent," or "natural" features of reality.

The Cartesian ideal of the detached, purely neutral observer is here viewed as a type of mystification, and the ideals of absolute objectivity and ultimate foundations seen as requiring historical examination. In the modern era, "universal" after "universal" has fallen, under the scrutiny of Marxists, anthropologists, critical theorists, feminists,

Susan Bordo

philosophers of science, and deconstructionists. The various claims regarding human nature and human sexuality (the "naturalness" of competition, the "necessity" of sexual repression, the "biological" nature of gender differences) have been challenged. Rorty and Foucault, respectively, have argued that the "mind" and "sexuality" are historical "inventions." And Patrick Heelan has shown that our most basic perceptions of space have a cultural history.

None of this signals the end of philosophy. What it *has* meant, however, is that it is extremely difficult today for the Cartesian philosopher to sit comfortably on the throne of the cultural overseer, "neutrally" legislating "how rational agreement can be reached" and where others have gone astray. The ideal of absolute intellectual purity and the belief in a clear and distinct universe are passing, though not without protest, out of the discipline. It is too soon to tell what sort of impact feminist and other reconstructions will have on the future development of philosophy, not to mention on the general intellectual and political life of our culture. But what does seem clear is that coherent alternatives to Cartesianism are emerging out of Cartesianism's "shadow" itself. If a "flight from the feminine," as I have argued, motivated the birth of the Cartesian ideals, the contemporary revaluation of the feminine has much to contribute to the world that will replace them.[18]

Author's Notes

1 Bossuet, too, believed that the sense-rule of childhood represents something "depraved in the common source of our birth" (Harth, 218). LaRochefoucault called childhood "a perpetual intoxication, a fever on the brain" (Harth, 219). In a popular treatise on education, written in 1646, Balthazar Gratien writes of "that insipidity of childhood which disgusts the sane mind; that coarseness of youth which finds pleasure in scarcely anything but material objects and which is only a very crude sketch of the man of thought... Only time can cure a person of childhood and youth, which are truly ages of imperfection in every respect" (Ariès, 131–2).

2 Since the body is the *res extensa* of the human being, as mechanical in its operations as a machine (see II, 104; I, 116), this means that our purely bodily existence is not only less than "truly human," but is comparable to animal existence. Animals, as Descartes is notorious for maintaining, are mere automata (PL, 53–4, 121, 206–8, 243–5; HR, I, 117) ["PL" is Anthony Kenny's *Descartes: Philosophical Letters*], and had we not the evidence of the human being's extraordinary flexibility of response (as demonstrated by the adaptability of language and reason to particular circumstances) we would have no reason to think otherwise of human beings either (HR, I, 116).

3 See Dinnerstein, Hillman, Brown, Marcuse, Stern, and Griffin, among many others.

4 As [the original publication went] to press, Harding's eagerly-awaited *The Science Question in Feminism* [(Ithaca: Cornell University Press, 1986) was] just being released, too late for inclusion as one of the works surveyed in this essay. Harding's contribution to contemporary discussions of modern science, especially among philosophers, is very important.

5 See Keller, Merchant, and Easlea for excellent discussions of the Baconian imagery of nature.

6 These themes are symbolically represented, as I have argued elsewhere, in the structures of tragedy and comedy. There, we find all the elements of the "infant" drama: the pain of individuation, the dream of lost union, and (as in Descartes) the attempt to triumph over one's (unchosen) birth through the denial of its power over the "self-made" self. The meaning of the mother, and of the "feminine," in all this was not discovered by Freud either, as he recognized. Throughout tragedy and comedy, the woman (and most particularly, the mother) represents the historical roots of the self, the authority of the flesh, and the dangers (for tragedy) and joys (for comedy) of union with another. The desire for mastery through individuation, on the other hand, is "masculine" – and we may now recognize it as strikingly Cartesian, too: the project of the self-making self in willful repudiation of historical and familial ties, the limitations of the body, and the power of the flesh. In *Oedipus*, all these come together, which Freud, of course, saw. He emphasized, however, rather the wrong point. The spiritual center of the classic Oedipal story is not the desire to sleep with one's mother, but to become the father of oneself, to be the creator rather than the helpless pawn in the drama of one's own life. (See Bordo, "The Cultural Overseer and the Tragic Hero," *Soundings*, 1982.)

7 This is the social reality behind the witch-hunters' fantasies of female power. The fact is that a great many of the women accused of witchcraft *were* involved in conception and birth, as well as all other aspects of sickness and health. They, indeed, *did* have control (though not of the sort fantasized by Kramer and Sprenger), for healing had traditionally been the province of women, and, in the case of midwifery, remained overwhelmingly so until the eighteenth century (Rich, 121). These female lay-healers, according

366

to Ehrenreich and English, were "singled out particularly" in the witch hunts (p. 36). Called "good witches," they were condemned even more strongly than the "bad." But "the greatest injuries to the Faith as regards the heresy of witches are done by midwives" (Kramer and Sprenger). Why? First, because they relieved women of the curse of Eve's original sin, through the use of ergot to dull the pain of childbirth (in 1591, Agnes Simpson was burned for just this crime) (Rich, 117). Second, because they were able to control miscarriage through the use of Belladonna (Ehrenreich and English, 37). It was not until the seventeenth century, however, that midwifery finally begins to give way to the male practice of "obstetrics," described by Suzanne Arms as the final stage in "the gradual attempt by man to extricate the processes of birth from women and call it his own" (Rich, 90).

8   It was male practitioners who established the lying-down position for women in labor, rendering women passive and dependent in the process of birth (Rich, 137), and who, in the late sixteenth century, invented and promulgated the use of forceps in delivery. For Adrienne Rich, the "hands of iron" which replace the "hands of flesh" of the female midwives "symbolize the art of the obstetrician" (p. 133). They began to be used promiscuously, preparation for control over possible difficulty becoming the too-routine practice of such control (as has happened similarly today with the Caesarean section). Midwives campaigned against the overuse and abuse of the forceps (Rich, 137–41). They themselves, of course, could not use the forceps, which was a technology available only to the licensed physician, and there is no doubt an element of political battle at work here. But even the strongest feminists among the midwives argued for the intervention of the male physician when complications arose; it was chiefly against the premature use of forceps, to shorten delivery time, and against their clumsy use, by male surgeons inexperienced at deliveries, that the midwives railed. Male physicians, most notable among them being William Harvey, mounted, in return, a ferocious campaign against midwives (Merchant, 153–5).

9   The fact that there were more female than male witches was linked to the excessive carnality of the female. "All witchcraft comes from carnal lust, which is in women insatiable," say Kramer and Sprenger (Easlea, 80). This view of women was not idiosyncratic, as Easlea points out, citing Walter Charleton's *Ephesian Matron* (1659) and Burton's *Anatomy of Melancholy* (1621). "You are the true Hiena's," says Charleton,

that allure us with the fairness of your skins; and when folly hath brought us within your reach, you leap upon us and devour us. You are the traitors to Wisdom; the impediment to Industry . . . the clogs to virtue, and goads to drive us all to Vice, Impiety, and Ruine.

You are the Fools Paradise, the Wisemans Plague, and the grand Error of Nature. (Easlea, 242)

"Of women's unnatural, insatiable lust, what country, what village doth not complain" notes Burton (Easlea, 242). It is for the sake of fulfilling the insatiable "mouth of the womb," according to Sprenger and Kramer, that "they consort even with the devil" (Easlea, 8). The accusation of copulation with the devil was a common charge at witch trials, and the rampant eroticism of the witch a common theme of paintings on the subject (Merchant, 134).

10   This is the widely accepted "animalculist" version. In the much less influential "ovist" version, the animacules are placed in the woman's womb by God at the time of creation. In either version, the original source of the animalcules is God. The virtue of preformation and embôitement, for the mechanists, was its thoroughly mechanical solution to the vexing problem of generation: if the body is pure *res extensa*, and if *res extensa* is barren and nonsentient, how does a sentient human being develop out of it? The new reproductive theory enabled the imaging of the sentient human being as being merely "housed" within matter, and not as developing out of it, its true father acknowledged as God.

11   Dorothy Dinnerstein discusses, at some length, what she takes to be the psychological sources of the dominant cultural equation of femaleness and the natural world. We first encounter the mother "before we are able to distinguish between a center of sentience and an impersonal force of nature" (p. 106). As we grow to learn the distinction, she claims, our associations to each remain contaminated by this ancient "confusion." The woman remains something less-than-human (in contrast to the father, whom we come to know from the start as a distinct center of independent subjectivity) and nature remains something more than an "impersonal" force. "She" is also a female force, of course, since it was from the mother that she was originally indistinguishable.

But women not only remain *associated* with nature. They also, claims Dinnerstein, become a natural target for all later rage *against* nature. "Like nature, which sends blizzards and locusts as well as sunshine and strawberries," the mother (and later, women in general) is perceived "as capricious, sometimes actively malevolent. Her body is the first important piece of the physical world that we encounter, and the events for which she seems responsible the first instances of fate. Hence mother nature, with her hurricane daughters . . . hence that fickle female, Lady Luck" (p. 95).

12   That which appears as mysterious and powerful may not always be regarded as dreadful or as requiring *taming*. The unpredictable caprice of fortune, for example, was believed to rule earthly life in the Middle Ages – but its vicissitudes were regarded in

a spirit of acceptance (Lewis, 139–40). For Machiavelli, in contrast, "Fortune is a woman, and it is necessary if you wish to master her, to conquer her by force" (Merchant, 130). And, while the evidence for there having been true matriarchal cultures is debated, the existence of what Rich calls *gynocentric* cultures – cultures in which women were venerated, not feared, for their strength and power, especially in their maternal function – is unquestionable (Rich, 80–9; Sanday, 15–33, 113–28). Moreover, that which appears as mysterious and powerful may not always be experienced as decisively "notself." The Middle Ages, while hardly a gynocentric culture, *was* a culture in which the mystery and power of nature did not appear as the whim of an alien "other."

13 Knowledge "by sympathy," as Karl Stern says, has its "natural fundament" in the "primary bond with the mother" (p. 54). But mothers, according to Chodorow, treat their female children and male children differently. Identification and symbiosis with daughters tends to be stronger. Daughters, in response, tend to perceive *themselves* as more closely identified with the mother, less distinct from her, and more comfortable, in adult life, with experiences of "merger" with others. By contrast, boys are experienced by their mothers as a "male opposite," and are more likely to have had to "curtail their primary love and sense of empathic tie with their mother" (pp. 166–7). Moreover, for the boy, issues of differentiation from the mother become intertwined with issues of gender identification. "Dependence on his mother, attachment to her, and identification with her represent that which is not masculine; a boy must reject dependence and deny attachment and identification" (p. 181). The result, according to Chodorow, is that "girls emerge . . . with a basis for 'empathy' built into their primary definition of self in a way that boys do not" (p. 167). The analysis is not only developmental, but institutional, for the proposed differences in male and female modes of knowing all hinge on the institution of female nurturing.

14 An examination of the relevance of this contemporary developmental explanation to the Cartesian era must fall to the sociologist and historian of the family. No doubt Ariès's profound thesis that childhood itself was not "discovered" until the sixteenth century has some relevance here, for until that time, as Ariès argues, very little in the way of nurturing of *either* sex went on. It is in the sixteenth and seventeenth centuries, therefore, that we might expect the developmental processes described by Chodorow to begin to have some striking application. My own study here is certainly suggestive of the fruitfulness of further investigation along these lines.

15 See, especially, the final chapter in Gilligan, in which it becomes clear that Gilligan is calling, not for a "feminization" of knowledge, from which more masculinist modes are excluded, but the recognition that each, cut off from the other, founders on its own particular reefs, just as it offers its own partial truths about human experience.

16 See, as a striking example, Ian Hacking's review of Keller's *Gender and Science*. Hacking is obviously unaware of the long feminist literature (including Keller's own earlier work) in which Keller's volume of essays is grounded, and apparently considers the notion that gender has influenced the construction of fact and theory to be an idea that has burst forth, for the first time, with the publication of this 1985 collection. He also is unwilling to accept Keller's own identification of herself as a radical feminist (apparently, for Hacking, the term cannot refer to anyone whose work he appreciates, and must always signal crude and negative thinking). He is genuinely taken, however, with the revolutionary import and the potential cultural value of work such as Keller's.

17 See Harding and Hintikka, *Discovering Reality*, and Alison Jaggar, *Feminist Politics and Human Nature*, chapter 11. French feminism has its own traditions of conceptual reconstruction; see Marks and Courtivron, *New French Feminisms*. [Elaine Marks and Isabelle de Courtivron, *New French Feminisms: An Anthology* (New York: Schocken, 1980).] Recently, conferences and seminars, explicitly organized around themes of "revisioning" or reconstructing ethics and epistemology, have begun to appear. To cite just two examples: Seminars entitled "Feminist Reconstructions of Self and Society" and "Feminist Ways of Knowing" were held in 1985 at Douglass College, Rutgers University; a conference entitled "Women and Moral Theory" was held in March, 1985 at the State University of New York at Stony Brook. Papers delivered at the Douglass seminar included topics such as the role of emotions in knowing, non-dualist perspectives on knowledge, the role of the body, and the role of "care" in morality. A collection of these papers – is [Alison Jaggar and Susan Bōrdo, *Gender / Body / Knowledge: Feminist Reconstructions of Being and Knowing* (New Brunswick: Rutgers University Press, 1989)]. The Stony Brook conference was devoted to an exploration of the work of Carol Gilligan and its intellectual implications. Several papers presented offered Gilligan-inspired reconstructions of ethical theory.

18 It seems clear that so long as masculine values continue to exert their grip on the public domain, there are severe constraints on the potential that women may bring, as they enter that domain, to transform it. Many radical feminists fault liberal feminism, which has prioritized equal opportunity without a corresponding emphasis on the need for cultural transformation, with contributing to more of a "masculinization" than "feminization" of contemporary culture. Women have been "allowed" in the public domain, but they have been required to adopt the values of that domain. On the other hand, unless the

promotion of "feminine" values is consistently and explicitly wedded to a critique of the sexual division of labor, it may operate as a justification and romanticization of that division of labor, and a banner under which women can be encouraged to return to (or remain in) the private sphere where "their" virtues flourish. The critique of cultural values must always be joined to a recognition of the "material" inequalities and power imbalances that those values serve. But the cultural critique is essential. Without it, women surrender the power of our "critical alterity" (as Ynestra King [a contemporary eco-Feminist] calls it) to be instrumental in the realization of a different social and intellectual order.

References

Ariès, Philippe. *Centuries of Childhood: A Social History of Family Life*. New York: Vintage, 1962.

Berman, Morris. *The Re-enchantment of the World*. Ithaca; Cornell University Press, 1981.

Bordo, Susan. "The Cultural Overseer and the Tragic Hero: Comedic and Feminist Perspectives on the Hubris of Philosophy." *Soundings*, LXV, No. 2, Summer 1982, pp. 181–205.

Brown, Norman O. *Life Against Death*. New York: Random House, 1959.

Capra, Fritjof. *The Turning Point*. New York: Simon and Schuster, 1983.

Chodorow, Nancy. *The Reproduction of Mothering*. Berkeley: University of California Press, 1978.

—— "Family Structure and Feminine Personality." In *Woman, Culture and Society*, pp. 43–66. Ed. Michele Rosaldo and Louise Lamphere. Stanford: Stanford University Press, 1974.

de Beauvoir, Simone. *The Second Sex*. New York: Alfred A. Knopf, 1957.

Descartes. *Philosophical Works*. vols I and II. Ed. Elizabeth Haldane and G. R. T. Ross. Cambridge: Cambridge University Press, 1969.

Dinnerstein, Dorothy. *The Mermaid and the Minotaur*. New York: Harper and Row, 1977.

Easlea, Brian. *Witch-hunting, Magic and the New Philosophy*. Atlantic Highlands, NJ: Humanities Press, 1980.

Ehrenreich, Barbara, and Dierdre English. *For Her Own Good*. New York: Anchor/Doubleday, 1979.

Farrington, Benjamin. *Temporis Partus Masculus: An Untranslated Writing of Francis Bacon. Centaurus I*, 1951.

Freud, Sigmund. *Beyond the Pleasure Principle*. New York: Bantam, 1959.

Gay, Peter. *The Bourgeois Experience*, vol. one, *Education of the Senses*. New York: Oxford University Press, 1984.

Gilligan, Carol. *In a Different Voice*. Cambridge: Harvard University Press, 1982.

Gillispie, Charles. *The Edge of Objectivity*. Princeton: Princeton University Press, 1960.

Griffin, Susan. *Women and Nature*. New York: Harper and Row, 1978.

Hacking, Ian. "Liberating the Laboratory." *The New Republic*, July 15 and 22, 1985, pp. 47–50.

Harding, Sandra and Hintikka, Merril. *Discovering Reality: Feminist Perspectives on Epistemology, Science, and Philosophy of Science*. Dordrecht: Reidel, 1983.

Harth, Erica. "Classical Innateness." *Yale French Studies*, no. 49 (1973): 212–30.

Hillman, James. *The Myth of Analysis*. New York: Harper and Row, 1972.

Jaggar, Alison. *Feminist Politics and Human Nature*. New Jersey: Rowman and Allanheld, 1983.

Keller, Evelyn Fox. *Reflections on Gender and Science*. New Haven: Yale University Press, 1985.

Kenny, Anthony (ed.). *Descartes: Philosophical Letters*, trans. Anthony Kenny. Oxford: Clarendon, 1970.

Klein, Melanie. "Early Stages of the Oedipus Conflict." In *The World of the Child*. ed. Toby Talbot. New York: Jason Aronson, 1974, pp. 98–111.

Lederer, Wolfgang. *The Fear of Women*. New York: Harcourt Brace, 1968.

Lewis, C. S. *The Discarded Image*. Cambridge: Cambridge University Press, 1964.

Marcuse, Herbert. *Counter-Revolution and Revolt*. Boston: Beacon, 1972.

Merchant, Carolyn. *The Death of Nature*. San Francisco: Harper and Row, 1980.

Neville, Robert. *Reconstruction of Thinking*. Albany: State University of New York Press, 1981.

Nietzsche, Friedrich. *On the Genealogy of Morals*. New York: Vintage, 1969.

Plato *Timeous*. Translated by Benjamin Jowett. Indianapolis: Bobbs-Merrill, 1949.

Rich, Adrienne. *Of Woman Born*. New York: Bantam, 1976.

Rorty, Richard. *Philosophy and the Mirror of Nature*. Princeton: Princeton University Press, 1979.

Ross, John. "Towards Fatherhood: The Epigenesis of Paternal Identity During a Boy's First Decade." *International Review of Psychoanalysis*, 4, 1977, pp. 327–47.

Sanday, Peggy Reeve. *Female Power and Male Dominance: On the Origins of Sexual Inequality*. Cambridge: Cambridge University Press, 1981.

Stern, Karl. *The Flight From Woman*. New York: Noonday, 1965.

Vicinus, Martha. *Suffer and Be Still*. Bloomington: Indiana University Press, 1972.

Whitehead, Alfred North. *Science and Modern World*. 1925; reprint edn, Toronto: Collier Macmillan, 1967.

37

From "The Scaling of Bodies and the Politics of Identity"

Iris Marion Young

The political philosopher Iris Young (1949–) is heir both to feminist theory and European post-structuralism. Her work is a contribution to the current critique of liberal political theory. Modern liberalism, which sought maximal individual liberty under a framework of egalitarian rules, officially ignored race, gender, sexual orientation, and other social distinctions that had been the basis for discrimination. It offered equality "despite" group identity. But however well-intentioned, it thereby functioned to hide and obscure the reality of oppression and the diversity of social identities. Today, members of oppressed groups want recognition *in and through* their distinctive selves, not despite or in abstraction from them. Thus political theory must be concerned not only with rights and distributive justice – as liberals like John Rawls believed – but with the socio-cultural constitution and treatment of personal and group identity. In the following chapter, she unveils the bodily basis of prejudice against women, racial minorities, homosexuals, and others, to pave the way for a free society where differences are recognized and accepted, rather than transcended.

Racism and homophobia are real conditions of all our lives in this place and time. I urge each one of us here to reach down into that deep place of knowledge inside herself and touch that terror and loathing of any difference that lives there. See whose face it wears. Then the personal as the political can begin to illuminate all our choices.

Audre Lorde

My body was given back to me sprawled out, distorted, recolored, clad in mourning in that white winter day. The Negro is ugly, the Negro is animal, the Negro is bad, the Negro is mean, the Negro is ugly; look, a nigger, it's cold, the nigger is shivering, because he is cold, the little boy is trembling because he is afraid of the nigger, the nigger is shivering with cold, that cold goes through your bones, the handsome little boy is trembling because he thinks that the nigger is quivering with rage, the little white boy throws himself into his mother's arms; Momma, the nigger's going to eat me up.

All round me the white man, above the sky tears at its navel, the earth rasps under my feet, and there is a white song, a white song. All this whiteness that burns me. . . .

I sit down at the fire and I become aware of my uniform. I had not seen it. It is indeed ugly. I stop there, for who can tell me what beauty is? (Fanon, 1967, p. 114)[i]

Racism, as well as other group oppressions, should be thought of not as a single structure, but in terms of several forms of oppression that in the United

[i] Franz Fanon, *Black Skin, White Masks*, originally 1952 (New York: Grove, 1991). Fanon, West Indian psychoanalyst and philosopher, was an intellectual leader of the anti-colonial movement.

Iris Marion Young, pp. 122–4, 136–48, 152–5 from "The Scaling of Bodies and the Politics of Identity," chapter 5 in *Justice and the Politics of Difference*. Princeton: Princeton University Press, 1990.

States condition the lives of most or all Blacks, Latinos, Asians, American Indians, and Semitic peoples. The oppressions experienced by many members of these groups are certainly conditioned by the specific structures and imperatives of American capitalism – structures of exploitation, segregated division of labor, and marginalization. Racism, like sexism, is a convenient means of dividing workers from one another and legitimating the superexploitation and marginalization of some. Clearly experiences like that evoked by Fanon above, however, cannot be reduced to capitalist processes or encompassed within the structures of oppression just mentioned. They belong instead to the general forms of oppression I have called cultural imperialism and violence. Cultural imperialism consists in a group's being invisible at the same time that it is marked out and stereotyped. Culturally imperialist groups project their own values, experience, and perspective as normative and universal. Victims of cultural imperialism are thereby rendered invisible as subjects, as persons with their own perspective and group-specific experience and interests. At the same time they are marked out, frozen into a being marked as Other, deviant in relation to the dominant norm. The dominant groups need not notice their own group being at all; they occupy an unmarked, neutral, apparently universal position. But victims of cultural imperialism cannot forget their group identity because the behavior and reactions of others call them back to it.

The Fanon passage evokes a particular and crucially important aspect of the oppression of cultural imperialism: the group-connected experience of being regarded by others with aversion. In principle, cultural imperialism need not be structured by the interactive dynamics of aversion, but at least in supposedly liberal and tolerant contemporary societies, such reactions of aversion deeply structure the oppression of all cultural imperialized groups. Much of the oppressive experience of cultural imperialism occurs in mundane contexts of interaction – in the gestures, speech, tone of voice, movement, and reactions of others (cf. Brittan and Maynard, 1984, pp. 6–13). Pulses of attraction and aversion modulate all interactions, with specific consequences for experience of the body. When the dominant culture defines some groups as different, as the Other, the members of those groups are imprisoned in their bodies. Dominant discourse defines them in terms of bodily characteristics, and constructs those bodies as ugly, dirty, defiled, impure, contaminated, or sick. Those who experi-

ence such an epidermalizing of their world (Slaughter, 1982), moreover, discover their status by means of the embodied behavior of others: in their gestures, a certain nervousness that they exhibit, their avoidance of eye contact, the distance they keep.

The experience of racial oppression entails in part existing as a group defined as having ugly bodies, and being feared, avoided, or hated on that account. Racialized groups, moreover, are by no means the only ones defined as ugly or fearful bodies. Women's oppression, like the oppression of Blacks, exhibits all the five forms described [in Chapter 2][ii]. The sexual division of labor at home and in the workplace produces gender-specific forms of exploitation and powerlessness. Women's oppression, however, is also clearly structured by the interactive dynamics of desire, the pulses of attraction and aversion, and people's experience of bodies and embodiment. While a certain cultural space is reserved for revering feminine beauty and desirability, in part that very cameo ideal renders most women drab, ugly, loathsome, or fearful bodies. Old people, gay men and lesbians, disabled people and fat people also occupy as groups the position of ugly, fearful, or loathsome bodies. The interactive dynamics and cultural stereotypes that define groups as the ugly other have much to do with the oppressive harrassment and physical violence that endangers the peace and bodies of most members of most of these groups.

This chapter explores the construction of ugly bodies and the implications of unconscious fears and aversions for the oppression of despised groups. I expand the suggestion made in the last chapter that racist and sexist exclusions from the public have a source in the structure of modern reason and its self-made opposition to desire, body, and affectivity. Modern philosophy and science established unifying, controlling reason in opposition to and mastery over the body, and then identified some groups with reason and others with the body.

The objectification and overt domination of despised bodies that obtained in the nineteenth century, however, has receded in our own time, and a discursive commitment to equality for all has emerged. Racism, sexism, homophobia, ageism, and ableism, I argue, have not disappeared with that commitment, but have gone underground, dwelling in everyday habits and cultural meanings of which people are for the most part unaware. Through

[ii] Exploitation (in a Marxist sense), marginalization (e.g. of the unemployed), powerlessness (lack of status or authority), cultural imperialism, and violence.

Kristeva's category of the abject, I explore how the habitual and unconscious fears and aversions that continue to define some groups as despised and ugly bodies modulate with anxieties over loss of identity. Our society enacts the oppression of cultural imperialism to a large degree through feelings and reactions, and in that respect oppression is beyond the reach of law and policy to remedy.

The analysis in this chapter raises questions for moral theory, about whether and how moral judgments can be made about unintended behavior. If unconscious behavior and practices reproduce oppression, they must be morally condemnable. I argue that moral theory must in such cases distinguish between blaming and holding responsible the perpetrators.

The dissolution of cultural imperialism thus requires a cultural revolution which also entails a revolution in subjectivity. Rather than seeking a wholeness of the self, we who are the subjects of this plural and complex society should affirm the otherness within ourselves, acknowledging that as subjects we are heterogeneous and multiple in our affiliations and desires. Social movement practices of consciousness raising, I note, offer beginning models of methods of revolutionizing the subject. . . .

Behavioral Norms of Respectability

I have considered how the discourse of modern reason created the naturalized categories of deviant, deficient, and diseased women, Blacks, Jews, homosexuals, and old people. The constitution of modern scientific reason itself sanctioned the objectification of groups expelled from the privileged subject position occupied by the white male bourgeois, bringing them under the scrutiny of a gaze that measured, weighed, and classified their bodily attributes according to a standard of white male youthfulness. Modern racism, misogyny, and homophobia, however, are not only grounded in the discourse of science and philosophy. Normalizing reason, the reason of a subject purified of body and change, a reason that masters and controls the objects fixed by its measuring gaze, enters everyday life in what George Mosse calls the ideal of respectability that dominated nineteenth-century bourgeois morality.[iii] I am not concerned here with the

[iii] George Mosse, *Nationalism and Sexuality: Middle-Class Morality and Sexual Norms in Modern Europe* (Madison: University of Wisconsin, 1988).

causes of these norms of respectability – with how, for example, the ideal of respectability was connected with the development industrial capitalism. I shall describe only some of the content and significance of those norms, to show how they structure racism, sexism, homophobia, and ageism.

Respectability consists in conforming to norms that repress sexuality, bodily functions, and emotional expression. It is linked to an idea of order: the respectable person is chaste, modest, does not express lustful desires, passion, spontaneity, or exuberance, is frugal, clean, gently spoken, and well mannered. The orderliness of respectability means things are under control, everything in its place, not crossing the borders.

Respectable behavior is preoccupied with cleanliness and propriety, meticulous rules of decency. Rules govern minute aspects of everyday behavior concerning bodily function and the arrangement of the environment. The body should be clean in all respects, and cleaned of its aspects that betoken its fleshiness – fluids, dirt, smells. The environment in which respectable people dwell must also be clean, purified: no dirt, no dust, no garbage, and all signs of bodily function – eating, excreting, sex, birthing – should be hidden behind closed doors. Bourgeois morality created a sphere of individual privacy, where the respectable individual would be alone with his or her body, taking care, bringing it under control and making it ready for public view. Respectable behavior involves keeping the body covered and not exhibiting its functions: so strict norms govern how to eat, silently, with no belching, burping, or farting. Speech is also governed by rules of decency: some words are clean and respectable, others dirty, and many, especially those relating to the body or sexuality, should not be mentioned in respectable company. Many bourgeois rules of decorum – such as these governing modes of address, gestures of respect, where to sit, or how to sip brandy – do not apply directly to bodily functions. But all manners come to be associated with bodily decency, restraint, and cleanliness.

As I discussed [in Chapter 4], gender polarization was a crucial aspect of the orderliness of bourgeois respectability. Modern bourgeois society created a complementary opposition of genders much stronger than had existed before: women are identified with the body and sexuality, especially as emotion, while men stand on the side of disembodied reason. The bourgeois ideology of gender in the nineteenth century allocated each gender its proper physical and social sphere, the sphere of politics and commerce for men, the sphere of home and family for women. As morally inferior, tied to maternal instinct and the particularity of love, women could not attain the heights of discipline, virtue, and self-control required of respectable men. But women too were to observe strict codes of propriety many of which attached to the body and sexuality.

The codes of bourgeois respectability made masculinity and femininity mutually exclusive and yet complementary opposites. As such, gender dichotomy is ruled by a logic of identity that denies or represses difference, in the sense of plurality, heterogeneity, the incommensurability of experiences that cannot be brought under a common measure. The strict dimorphism and complementarity of masculinity and femininity bring respectable women under control, in the paternal care of respectable men. These men are the subjects, and their women reflect and reinforce them in love, service, and nurturance. With woman serving as man's helpmeet and complement, working as guardian over his bodily, sexual, and emotional needs and at the same time exempting him from association with her, the society is orderly.

Bourgeois gender polarization represents a denial of difference because in the respectable couple there was only one subjectivity. Mosse shows how the virtues of respectability were primarily virtues of manliness. The primary virtue of manliness is self-mastery – the ability to restrain the expression of passion, desire, sexuality, bodily need, impulse. Self-mastery requires discipline and vigilance, and only he who achieves them is truly rational, competent, and deserving of positions of authority; only the man who properly disciplines himself should be in the position to discipline others. This man is truly independent and autonomous: there is nothing about his behavior that overflows, gets away from him; he is completely the author and origin of his action.

Mosse argues that in the nineteenth-century ideal of respectable manly virtue lay a homoeroticism that legitimated bonds of attachment among men by repressing sexual definition of those bonds. As I already noted, the white male youth expressed the ideal of a passionate, but desexualized, beauty. The white male bourgeois unity and universality which implicitly defined the idea of the public in the nineteenth century reached its most arrogant development in nationalism. In nationalism sexuality was sublimated into love of nation and empire. Nationalist sentiments and loyalty were pursued in a homoerotic brotherhood that excluded women, the refined clubs and fields of the soldier, statesman, and Empire bureaucrat. This nationalism contributed both materially and ideologically to the racialization of nonwhite peoples, to their confinement outside the border of respectability (cf. Anderson, 1983). To be respectable means to belong to a "civilized" people, whose manners and morals are more "advanced" than those of "savage" or backward peoples. In this schema people of color are naturally embodied, amoral, expressive, undisciplined, unclean, lacking in self-control.

I have suggested that it is a mistake to construe the racism, sexism, classism, homophobia, ageism, and ableism of contemporary Western industrial societies as simply continuous with their nineteenth-century predecessors. An account of these contemporary privileges and oppressions must proceed as much from the historical differences as from the continuities. One major difference is that racism, sexism, homophobia, ageism, and ableism are no longer for the most part discursively conscious, but exist in behavior, images, and attitudes primarily at the level of practical consciousness and the basic security system. Similarly, one can ask to what degree contemporary society retains the cult of manly virtue and respectability, which inherently excludes women, nonwhites, and homosexuals from the rational public because these groups are associated with sexuality and the body.

A discontinuity seems obvious: whereas Victorian morality repressed and devalued sexual expression, at least for respectable people, contemporary Western advanced industrial societies allow, if not indeed glorify, sexual expression, for just about everyone. We can agree with Marcuse (1964, chap. 3) that in many ways this modern sexuality is *repressively* desublimated,[iv] a performance-oriented, accumulation-promoting superficial sexuality, but there seems no doubt that in gentrified consumer society sex is raw, not sublimated. The sexualization of society has entailed a blurring of the border between types of persons who are respectable and those who are not. As the bodies of white men are increasingly and openly sexualized the stigma of embodied sexuality no longer attaches so completely to women, Blacks, and homosexuals. Simultaneously it becomes possible to admit for

---

[iv] Herbert Marcuse (1898–1979) argued in *One-Dimensional Man* that advanced capitalist society permits sexual expression (de-represses or de-sublimates it) as a tool of social control.

these formerly despised groups a level of rationality denied them before. The dichotomies between reason and the body, self-discipline and sexual expression, cool detachment and affectivity, no longer so clearly map onto a distinction between groups, but enter into the composition of everyone's life.

The oppression of powerlessness derives in part from an ideal of respectability which contemporary society retains in the virtues and behavior of the "professional." It is paradigmatically in the office, or at business meetings, that persons in contemporary society follow the rules of decorum typical of bourgeois respectability, and in these settings people evaluate one another according to those rules. Whereas in the nineteenth century respectability attached to a single group or class, whose duty it was to exhibit its virtues in all aspects of their lives, today the code of respectability has been narrowed to public institutions and practices of business. In principle, moreover, anyone can be respectable, though we shall see below how group difference undermines this principle.

The norms of "professional" comportment entail repression of the body's physicality and expressiveness. It goes without saying that respectable, professional norms require eliminating or covering all bodily odors, being clean and "clean-cut." In dress, professional men follow the basic form of nineteenth-century respectable male dress. The "business suit" is straight and angular, with no frills or decoration, in fabric of fine weave and durable weight, in drab colors revealingly referred to as "neutral." Since women's clothes have in modern Western society been so different from men's, with more color, fabric, and decoration, the age of the businesswoman has created ambiguities and variations in professional dress. The code for the truly professional woman's dress, however, seems to have settled on a female version of the business suit, with a simple knee-length skirt instead of pants, and permitting more colorful blouses than the shirts appropriate with the male business suit.

Professional behavior, which in this society signifies rationality and authoritativeness, requires specific ways of sitting, standing, walking, and speaking – namely, without undue expression. Professional comportment entails an affable cheer, but without excitement or demonstrativeness. In speaking one should keep one's voice steady, certainly not giggling or expressing sadness, anger, disappointment, or uncertainty. One should speak firmly, without hesitation or ambiguity, and slang,

dialect, and accent should be absent from one's speech. It is inappropriate to speak excitedly or to embellish one's speech with broad gestures.

In the nineteenth century norms of respectability most guided the behavior of a particular group, white bourgeois men, with a complementary set of norms for the women under their rule. Blacks, Jews, women, homosexuals, and working-class people all tended to be associated with the unruly heterogeneity of the body and affectivity, and therefore were regarded as outside the culture of respectability. In contemporary society, I have suggested, the dichotomy between reason and the body is no longer so firmly tied to groups. In principle all groups are said to be both rational and bodily. I have argued, however, that racist, sexist, and heterosexist reactions of aversion of nervousness still mark out the bodily being of some groups, but that such marking sometimes does not appear at the level of discursive consciousness. While certain groups are no longer excluded from formal opportunity to participate in respected professions, nevertheless the situation of groups victimized by cultural imperialism impedes their successful attainment of professional equality.

Despite the claim that professional comportment is neutral, it is in fact the product of socialization into a particular culture. White Anglo heterosexual middle-class men are most socialized into this culture, whereas women, Blacks, Latinos, poor and working-class people, gay men and lesbians, tend to exhibit cultural habits that deviate from or conflict with professional culture. The reasons for these differences are multiple. These groups promote a positive culture among themselves that has more "colorful" or expressive styles than are deemed appropriate in straight professional culture. The socializing agents of professional culture, moreover, particularly teachers, often give more reinforcement to white middle-class men in developing a disciplined, articulate, rational comportment than to members of other groups, because dominant cultural imagery continues to identify them as the paradigm professionals.

"Assimilation" into the dominant culture, acceptance into the rosters of relative privilege, requires that members of formerly excluded groups adopt professional postures and suppress the expressiveness of their bodies. Thus emerges for all who have not lost the impulses of life and expression a new kind of distinction between public and private, in bodily behavior. My public self is my behavior in bureaucratic institutions, sitting, standing, walking 'correctly,' managing my impression. My "private" behavior is relaxed, more expressive in the body, at home with my family or socializing with members of the group with which I identify.

The lived distinction between public, respectable comportments and private, more casual comportments intersects with the interactive dynamics of racism, sexism, homophobia, ageism, and ableism. In "private" settings, where people are more relaxed, they may express devaluing judgments about members of other groups that they repress in "public" settings of formal rules and bureaucratic impersonality.

For women, disabled people, Blacks, Latinos, gay men, lesbians, and others that continue to be marked out as the Other, however, there remains another obstacle to respectability. Even if they successfully exhibit the norms of respectability, their physical presence continues to be marked, something others take note of, and, I have argued, often evokes unconscious reactions of nervousness or aversion in others. In being thus chained to their bodily being they cannot be fully and un-self-consciously respectable and professional, and they are not so considered. Upon first meeting someone they must "prove" through their professional comportment that they are respectable, and their lives are constantly dogged by such trials, which, though surely not absent from the lives of white men, are less regular.

Xenophobia and Abjection

In his study of white racism, Joel Kovel (1970) distinguishes three ideal types: dominative racism, aversive racism, and metaracism. Dominative racism involves direct mastery that has its most obvious manifestations in enslavement and other forms of forced labor, race status rules that privilege whites, and genocide. Whereas such domination usually entails frequent, often daily and intimate association between members of racial groups, aversive racism is a racism of avoidance and separation. From what Kovel calls metaracism, finally, almost all traces of a commitment to race superiority have been removed, and only the grinding processes of a white-dominated economy and technology account for the continued misery of many people of color.

While according to Kovel all three types of racism exist in contemporary American society, he thinks they nevertheless correspond roughly to stages in the history of white racism, especially in the United States. The nineteenth century, especially in the South, saw dominative racism as the primary form, with strong strains of aversive racism among the liberal Northern bourgeoisie who claimed to be free of racism. In the contemporary United States, racism takes primarily the form of aversive racism, with the increasing significance of metaracism.

The distinction between dominative and aversive racism can be mapped onto the shift I have outlined from discursive consciousness to practical consciousness and basic security system. In nineteenth-century racist culture, along with sexism and heterosexism, explicit theories of superior bodies and character were expressed, and Blacks, Jews, women, homosexuals, and working people were constructed as having degenerate or inferior natures that justified their domination by white bourgeois men. In contemporary society these oppressions exist less in the form of overt domination than as avoidances, aversions, and separations enacted by the privileged in relation to the oppressed.

Kovel's project is to give a psychodynamic account of racism. He suggests that dominative racism and aversive racism involve different issues and processes in the unconscious of white Western culture. Dominative racism, he suggests, involves primarily oedipal issues of sexual object and conquest, and the issues of competition and aggression played out (for men) in the oedipal drama. The explicit preoccupation with genitals and sexuality in nineteenth-century racist discourse is a symptom of this oedipal psyche. Aversive racism, on the other hand, digs more deeply into a preoedipal anal moment of fundamental fantasies of dirt and pollution. Kovel finds this racism more consonant with the spirit of modern capitalist and instrumental rationality. Modern scientific consciousness seeks to reduce the self to pure mind abstracted from sensuality and material immersion in nature. Such an urge for purity in the context of power creates some groups as scapegoats, representative of the expelled body standing over against the purified and abstracted subject.

Oppression in contemporary society as structured by reactions of aversion, I have suggested, is not limited to racism, but also describes an aspect of sexism, homophobia, ageism, and ableism. Blacks, Latinos, Asians, gays and lesbians, old people, disabled people and often poor people, experience nervousness or avoidance from others, even from those whose discursive consciousness aims to treat them with respect as equals. This does not mean that all these group oppressions are the same. Each oppressed group has a specific identity and history that cannot be reduced to any other. [In Chapter 2] I explicated five aspects of oppression, various combinations and instances of which a particular oppressed group may experience, but none of which is a necessary condition of oppression. One function of such a plural model of oppression is to avoid reductionism in discussing group oppression. I believe that all the groups named above occupy a similar status as despised, ugly, or fearful bodies, as a crucial element of their oppression. Below I offer an account of that status, which I think applies in similar ways to all these groups. This account represents only one slice, if you will, of the oppressions of racism, sexism, homophobia, ageism, and ableism.

With the concept of the abject, Julia Kristeva offers a means of understanding behavior and interactions that express group-based fear or loathing which is similar to Kovel's account of aversive racism, though not so thoroughly Freudian. In *Powers of Horror* (1982), as in much of her other work, Kristeva quarrels with the emphasis of Freudian psychoanalysis on ego development, the development of the capacity for symbolization and representation that signals the emergence of an identical self over against which stand objects, representable, definable, desired, and manipulable. In Kristeva's view psychoanalytic theory has paid too little attention to preoedipal processes of drive organization in which the figure of the mother structures affect, as opposed to the oedipal episode structured by the law-giving father.

In other writings Kristeva introduces a distinction between the symbolic and the semiotic as two irreducible, heterogeneous aspects of language (Kristeva, 1977). The symbolic is the capacity to signify, to make one element stand for an absent other, the possibility of representation, sense, logic. Symbolic capacity depends on certain repressions, on the opposition between conscious and unconscious association. The semiotic, on the other hand, is the heterogeneous, bodily, material, nonsensical aspect of speech always present with, but not integrated into, its signification: gesture, tone of voice, the musicality of speech, arrangement of words, the material aspects of all language that are expressive, affective without having definable significance. The speaking self always carries along this shadow,

its spilled-over body expressed in comportment and excitation.

In the idea of the abject Kristeva locates one mode of such self-baggage. Abjection does not produce a subject in relation to objects – the ego – but rather the moment of separation the border between the "I" and the other, before an "I" is formed, that makes possible the relation between the ego and its objects. Before desire – the movement out from a self to the objects on which it is directed – there is bare want, lack, loss and breach that is unrepresentable, that exists only as affect.

Abjection is the feeling of loathing and disgust the subject has in encountering certain matter, images, and fantasies – the horrible, to which it can only respond with aversion, with nausea and distraction. The abject is at the same time fascinating; it draws the subject in order to repel it. The abject is meaningless, repulsive in an irrational, unrepresentable way. Kristeva claims that abjection arises from the primal repression in which the infant struggles to separate from the mother's body that nourishes and comforts, from the reluctant struggle to establish a separate corporeal schema, in tension and continuity with the mother's body which it seeks to incorporate.

For the subject to enter language, to become a self, it must separate from its joyful continuity with the mother's body and acquire a sense of a border between itself and the other. In the primal fluidity of maternal *jouissance* the infant introjects the Other.[v] Thus the border of separation can be established only by expelling, rejecting, the mother, which is only then distinguished from the infant itself; the expulsion that creates the border between inside and outside is an expulsion of itself. The infant struggles with its own drives in relation to the Other, to attain a sense of body control, but the struggle is reluctant, and the separation experienced as a loss, a wound, a want. The moment of separation can only be "a violent, clumsy breaking away, with the constant risk of falling back under the sway of a power as secure as it is shifting" (Kristeva, 1982, p. 13).

The expelled self turns into a loathsome menace because it threatens to reenter, to obliterate the border established between it and the separated self. The separation is tenuous, the subject feels it as a loss and yearns for, while rejecting, a reenclosure

[v]   *Jouissance* means enjoyment, used by Lacan in a sexual sense for enjoyment that exceeds Freud's "pleasure principle," hence brings suffering.

by the Other. The defense of the separated self, the means of keeping the border firm, is aversion from the Other, repulsion, for fear of disintegration.

Abjection is expressed in reactions of disgust to body excretions – matter expelled from the body's insides: blood, pus, sweat, excrement, urine, vomit, menstrual fluid, and the smells associated with each of these. The process of life itself consists in the expulsion outward of what is in me, in order to sustain and protect my life. I react to the expelled with disgust because the border of myself must be kept in place. The abject must not touch me, for I fear that it will ooze through, obliterating the border between inside and outside necessary for my life, which arises in the process of expulsion. If by accident or force I come to touch the abject matter, I react again with the reflex of expelling what is inside me: nausea.

Abjection, then, Kristeva says, is prior to the emergence of a subject in opposition to an object, and makes possible that distinction. The movement of abjection makes signification possible by creating a being capable of dividing, repeating, separating. The abject, as distinct from the object, does not stand opposed to the subject, at a distance, definable. The abject is other than the subject, but is only just the other side of the border. So the abject is not opposed to and facing the subject, but next to it, too close for comfort:

> The "unconscious" contents remain here *excluded* but in a strange fashion; not radically enough to allow for a secure differentiation between subject and object, and yet clearly enough for a defensive *position* to be established – one that implies a refusal but also a sublimating elaboration. (Kristeva, 1982, p. 7)

The abject provokes fear and loathing because it exposes the border between self and other as constituted and fragile, and threatens to dissolve the subject by dissolving the border. Phobia is the name of this fear, an irrational dread that latches onto a material to which it is drawn in horrified fascination. Unlike fear of an object, to which one reacts with attempts at control, defense, and counteraction, phobic fear of the abject is a paralyzing and vertiginous dread of the unnameable. At the same time the abject is fascinating, bringing out an obsessed attraction.

Abjection, Kristeva says, is a peculiar experience of ambiguity. 'Because, while releasing a hold, it

does not radically cut off the subject from what threatens it – on the contrary, abjection acknowledges it to be in perpetual danger' (Kristeva, 1982, p. 9). The abject arises potentially in "whatever disturbs identity, system, order. What does not respect borders, positions, rules" (Kristeva, 1982, p. 4). Any border ambiguity may become for the subject a threat to its own borders. Separation between self and Other is the product of a violent break from a prior continuity. As constructed, the border is fragile, because the self experiences this separation as a loss and lack without name or reference. The subject reacts to this abject with loathing as the means of restoring the border separating self and other.

This account of the meaning of the abject enhances, I suggest, an understanding of a body aesthetic that defines some groups as ugly or fear some and produces aversive reactions in relation to members of those groups. Racism, sexism, homophobia, ageism, and ableism, are partly structured by abjection, an involuntary, unconscious judgment of ugliness and loathing. This account does not explain how some groups become culturally defined as ugly and despised bodies. The symbolic association of some people and groups with death and degeneracy must in every case be explained socially and historically, and is historically variable. Even if abjection is a result of any subject's construction, nothing in the subject's formation makes group loathing necessary. The association between groups and abject matter is socially constructed; once the link is made, however, the theory of abjection describes how these associations lock into the subject's identities and anxieties. As they represent what lies just beyond the borders of the self, the subject reacts with fear, nervousness, and aversion to members of these groups because they represent a threat to identity itself, a threat to what Giddens calls the "basic security system."[vi]

Xenophobia as abjection is present throughout the history of modern consciousness, structured by a medicalized reason that defines some bodies as degenerate. The role of abjection may increase, however, with the shift from a discursive consciousness of group superiority to such group superiority lived primarily at the levels of practical consciousness and the basic security system.

When racism, sexism, heterosexism, ageism, and ableism, exist at the level of discursive consciousness, the despised groups are objectified. Scientific,

---

[vi] British social theorist Anthony Giddens (1938–).

medical, moral, and legal discourse construct these groups as objects, having their own specific nature and attributes, different from and over against the naming subject, who controls, manipulates, and dominates them. When these group-based claims of superiority and inferiority recede from discursive consciousness, however, these groups no longer face a dominant subject as clearly identifiable objects different from and opposed to itself. Women, Blacks, homosexuals, the mad, and the feeble-minded become more difficult to name as the Others, identifiable creatures with degenerate and inferior natures. In xenophobic subjectivity they recede to a murky affect without representation.

The repression of sexism, racism, heterosexism, ageism, and ableism from discursive consciousness enhances an ambiguity characteristic of the movement of abjection. In many societies there exists a broad-based commitment to principles of equal respect and equal treatment for all persons, whatever their group identification. At the same time, the routines of practical consciousness, forms of identification, interactive behavior, rules of deference, and so on clearly differentiate groups, privileging some over others. There exists a dissonance between the group-blind egalitarian truisms of discursive consciousness and the group-focused routines of practical consciousness. This dissonance creates the sort of border crisis ripe for the appearance of the abject.

Today the Other is not so different from me as to be an object; discursive consciousness asserts that Blacks, women, homosexuals, and disabled people are like me. But at the level of practical consciousness they are affectively marked as different. In this situation, those in the despised groups threaten to cross over the border of the subject's identity because discursive consciousness will not name them as completely different (cf. Frye, 1983b, pp. 114–15). The face-to-face presence of these others, who do not act as though they have their own "place," a status to which they are confined, thus threatens aspects of my basic security system, my basic sense of identity, and I must turn away with disgust and revulsion.

Homophobia is the paradigm of such border anxiety. The construction of the idea of race, its connection with physical attributes and lineage, still makes it possible for a white person to know that she is not Black or Asian. But as homosexuality has become increasingly deobjectified, no specific characteristics, no physical, genetic, mental, or moral "character," marks off homosexuals from

heterosexuals. It thus becomes increasingly difficult to assert any difference between homosexuals and heterosexuals except their choice of sexual partners. Homophobia is one of the deepest fears of difference precisely because the border between gay and straight is constructed as the most permeable; anyone at all can become gay, especially me, so the only way to defend my identity is to turn away with irrational disgust. Thus we can understand why people who have fairly successfully eliminated the symptoms of racism and sexism nevertheless often exhibit deep homophobia.

Ageism and ableism also exhibit the border anxiety of the abject. For in confronting old or disabled people I confront my own death. Kristeva believes that the abject is connected with death, the disintegration of the subject. The aversion and nervousness that old and disabled people evoke, the sense of their being ugly, arises from the cultural connection of these groups with death. Thomas Cole (1986) shows that prior to the nineteenth century old age was not linked to death; indeed, just the opposite was the case. In a time when death might come to persons at any age, and often took children and young adults, old age represented a triumph over death, a sign of virtue. During this time of patriarchal family domination, old people were highly regarded and venerated. Now, when it has become increasingly likely that people will live to be old, old age has become associated with degeneracy and death. At a time when most people can expect to be old, old people produce a border anxiety like that structuring homophobia. I cannot deny that the old person will be myself, but that means my death, so I avert my gaze from the old person, or treat her as a child, and want to leave her presence as soon as possible. My relation to disabled people has a similar structure. The only difference between myself and the wheelchair-bound person is my good luck. Encounter with the disabled person again produces the ambiguity of recognizing that the person whom I project as so different, so other, is nevertheless like me.

The story I have told is related from the point of view of privileged groups who experience abjection in encountering Blacks, Latinos, Asians, Jews, gays, lesbians, old people, disabled people, women. But what about the subjectivity of members of these groups themselves? It would be a mistake to think that this account of abjection presumes that, for example, Blacks construct white people as an abjected Other, and so on. For cultural imperialism consists precisely in the fact that the subject point of view for any subject, whatever his or her specific group membership, is identified with that of privileged groups. The form of cultural imperialism in the modern West provides and insists on only one subject position, that of the unified, disembodied reason identified with white bourgeois men. Within the unifying logic of modern reason and respectability, the subjectivity of members of culturally imperialized groups tends to stand in the same position as that of the privileged groups. From that supposedly neutral subject position all these despised and deviant groups are experienced as the abjected Other.

Members of culturally imperialized groups, that is, themselves often exhibit symptoms of fear, aversion, or devaluation toward members of their own groups and other oppressed groups. Blacks, for example, not infrequently have racist reactions to other Blacks, as the differentiation between "light-skinned" and "dark-skinned" Blacks exhibits. Gay men and lesbians themselves exhibit homophobia, old people denigrate the aged, and women are sometimes sexist. Insofar as members of these groups assume the position of subjects within the dominant culture, that is, they experience members of their own group abjectly. Even more commonly, members of culturally imperialized groups fear and despise members of other oppressed groups: Latinos are sometimes racist toward Blacks and vice versa, both are often deeply homophobic, and so on.

Even when they do not strictly assume the dominant subject position as their own point of view, members of these groups nevertheless internalize the cultural knowledge that dominant groups fear and loathe them, and to that extent assume the position of the dominant subjectivity toward themselves and other members of the groups with which they identify. But members of culturally imperialized groups also live a subjectivity different from the dominant subject position, one derived from their positive identification and social networks with others in their group. The dialectic between these two subjectivities – the point of view of the dominant culture which defines them as ugly and fearsome, and the point of view of the oppressed who experience themselves as ordinary, companionate, and humorous – represents what I referred to [in Chapter 2] as double consciousness.[vii] In this

respect culturally imperialized groups live a subjectivity different from that lived by privileged groups, an experience of themselves as split, divided, of their subjectivity as fragile and plural. A way out of culturally defined racism, sexism, homophobia, ageism, and ableism, I suggest in the final section of this chapter, is to push all subjects to an understanding of themselves as plural, shifting, heterogeneous. But first I shall examine the issue of responsibility for oppression that this analysis raises. . . .

Justice and Cultural Revolution

Saying that certain habitual and unconscious actions, manners, forms of response, ways of speaking, and so on should be judged unjust means that the people who perform these actions should be asked to take responsibility, to bring to their discursive awareness the meaning and implications of these habitual actions. But why consider this an issue of social justice rather than simply of individual moral action? [In Chapter 1] I argued that injustice should be defined primarily in terms of oppression and domination. The scope of justice, I argued, is not limited to distribution, but includes all social processes that support or undermine oppression, including culture. The behavior, comportments, images, and stereotypes that contribute to the oppression of bodily marked groups are pervasive, systemic, mutually generating, and mutually reinforcing. They are elements of dominant cultural practices that lie as the normal background of our liberal democratic society. Only changing the cultural habits themselves will change the oppressions they produce and reinforce, but change in cultural habits can occur only if individuals become aware of and change their individual habits. This is cultural revolution.

Culture is to a significant degree a matter of social choice; we can choose to change the elements of culture and to create new ones. Sometimes such change can be facilitated by passing laws or establishing policies. Nicaragua has a law against the use of women's bodies for advertising commodities. A glossy magazine can establish a policy of having more articles, photographs, and advertisements that depict Blacks in ordinary life activities. Most cultural change cannot occur, however, by edict. One cannot pass a law regulating the appropriate distance people ought to stand from one another, or whether and how they should touch. Similarly, in

---

vii   W. E. B. Du Bois' term for the "sense of always looking at one's self through the eyes of others," namely the oppressing group, in addition to one's own view of one's self. See his *The Souls of Black Folk* (1903).

most situations one does not wish formally to regulate the expression of fantasy, jokes, and so on, because the dangers to liberty are too great. While aesthetic judgment always carries implicit rules, and the project of revaluing some people's bodies involves changing those rules, aesthetic judgment cannot be formally regulated. The injunction to "be just" in such matters amounts to no more and no less than a call to bring these phenomena of practical consciousness and unconsciousness under discussion, that is, to *politicize* them. The requirements of justice, then, concern less the making of cultural rules than providing institutional means for fostering politicized cultural discussion, and making forums and media available for alternative cultural experiment and play.

Cultural revolution that confronts and undermines the fears and aversions that structure unconscious behavior entails a revolution in the subject itself. Kristeva's notion of the subject in process suggests that the subject is always split, heterogeneous (Kristeva, 1977; cf. Smith, 1988, pp. 117–23). The monologic culture of respectable rationality, however, encourages the subject to desire a unified self, solid, coherent, integrated. Much popular psychology in our society promotes this image of the authentic, healthy subject as unified. We enjoin ourselves to get ourselves "together"; contradiction or plurality in our sense of self we find reproachable, a state to be overcome. But if, as I have suggested, oppressive fears and aversions toward others have a source in fears of identity loss, then such an urge to unity may be part of the problem. For people to become comfortable around others whom they perceive as different, it may be necessary for them to become more comfortable with the heterogeneity within themselves. The varying and contradictory social contexts in which we live and interact, along with the multiplicity of our own group memberships and the multiple identities of others with whom we interact, make the heterogeneity of the subject inevitable. The question is whether to repress or to affirm it.

Cultural revolution that challenges the association of some groups with abject bodies also involves the politicization of these group definitions. Despised and oppressed groups challenge cultural imperialism when they question the dominant norms of virtue, beauty, and rationality, putting forward their own positive definition of themselves as a group and thereby pluralizing norms. [In Chapter 6] I will discuss more exten-

sively the meaning and implications of this politics of asserting positive group difference.

The process of politicizing habits, feelings, and expressions of fantasy and desire that can foster cultural revolution entails a kind of social therapy. Engaging in such therapy through strictly psychoanalytic methods on a mass scale would indeed be a massive undertaking hard to imagine. I think some cultural change toward these ends can be realistically undertaken, however, in the processes of politicized personal discussion that social movements have come to call "consciousness raising."

The phrase "consciousness raising" was used by the women's movement in the late 1960s to describe a process in which women share their experiences of frustration, unhappiness, and anxiety, and find common patterns of oppression structuring these very personal stories. They found that "the personal is political," that what was originally experienced as a private, personal problem in fact has political dimensions, as exhibiting an aspect of power relations between men and women. The Black liberation movement of the late 1960s similarly strove through personal discussion to displace oppressed people's depression and self-deprecation onto social sources. Aspects of social life that appear as given and natural come into question and appear as social constructions and therefore as changeable. The process by which an oppressed group comes to define and articulate the social conditions of its oppression, and to politicize culture by confronting the cultural imperialism that has denigrated or silenced its specific group experience, is a necessary and crucial step in confronting and reducing oppression.

Another form of consciousness raising involves making the privileged aware of how their habitual actions, reactions, images, and stereotypes contribute to oppression. Again, my own experience with this group process of politicizing culture derives from the women's movement. By the late 1970s, the soul-searching generated by angry accusations that the women's movement was racist had engendered forms of discussion concretely addressing women's experiences of group differences and seeking to change relations of group privilege and oppression among women. Women's groups provided the structure for intensive, often emotion-laden discussions designed to bring to the discursive consciousness of the participants the feelings, reactions, stereotypes, and assumptions they had about women of other groups, as well as the ways their behavior toward these women might participate in and reproduce relations of privilege and oppression between them. Such group processes can be generalized to any social setting. Institutionalized consciousness-raising policies can take many forms, of which I will give just two examples.

In recent years some enlightened corporations, motivated in part also by a desire to stave off conflict and lawsuits, have instituted consciousness-raising workshops for male managers and other male employees on issues of sexual harrassment. The very concept of sexual harrassment resulted from feminist consciousness raising among women no longer willing to accept as inevitable and individual behavior they found annoying, humiliating, or coercive. Bringing men to be able to identify behavior that women collectively judge annoying, humiliating, or coercive, however, and explaining why women find it so, has been no easy task.

Differential privilege of members of different racial groups is perpetuated in part by the process of schooling. If my account of unconscious aversion as a typical dynamic of racism is at all accurate, many if not most teachers unconsciously behave differently toward Blacks or Latinos than they behave toward whites. A school system committed to racial justice can distribute literature describing processes of unconscious differential treatment, and conduct workshops in which teachers reflect on and discuss their own behavior and attitudes toward students of different races.

Consciousness raising about homophobia may be the most important and productive strategy for such a revolution of the subject. As I have said, homophobia may be one of the strongest experiences of abjection because sexual identity is more ambiguous than other group identities. The border between attraction to persons of the other sex and attraction to those of the same sex is fluid. At the same time, homophobia is deeply wrapped up with issues of gender identity, for in this society gender identity continues to be heterosexist: the genders are considered mutually exclusive opposites that complement and complete one another. Order thus depends on the unambiguous settling of the genders: men must be men and women must be women. Homosexuality produces a special anxiety, then, because it seems to unsettle this gender order. Because gender identity is a core of everyone's identity, homophobia seems to go to the core of identity.

Thus confronting homophobia involves confronting the very desire to have a unified, orderly identity, and the dependence of such a unified identity on the construction of a border that excludes aspects of subjectivity one refuses to face. If through consciousness raising one accepts the possibility that one might become different, be different, in sexual orientation, I suggest, this loosens the exclusion of others defined as different from one's self-conception in other ways. Efforts to undermine the oppressions of racism, sexism, heterosexism, ageism, and ableism mutually reinforce one another not only because these groups have some common interests and certain persons or institutions tend to reproduce the oppression of them all. There are more direct connections among these oppressions in the structure of identity and self-protection. Just as nineteenth-century stereotyping of these groups tended to assimilate them to one another, especially through the mediation of sexual images, so contemporary discourse can help subvert one group-based fear by breaking down another.

A strategy of consciousness raising presumes that those participating already understand something about how interactive dynamics and cultural imagery perpetuate oppression, and are committed to social justice enough to want to change them. Such activity cannot take place in the abstract. People will be motivated to reflect on themselves and their relations with others only in concrete social circumstances of cooperation where they recognize problems – the political group in which gays and lesbians voice dissatisfaction, the company that never seems to promote women and therefore loses them, the school or neighborhood with racial conflict.

There is a step in politicizing culture prior to the therapeutic, namely, the affirmation of a positive identity by those experiencing cultural imperialism. Assumptions of the universality of the perspective and experience of the privileged are dislodged when the oppressed themselves expose those assumptions by expressing the positive difference of their experience. By creating their own cultural images they shake up received stereotypes about them. Having formed a positive self-identity through organization and public cultural expression, those oppressed by cultural imperialism can then confront the dominant culture with demands for recognition of their specificity....

Author's References

Anderson, Benedict. 1983. *Imagined Communities: Reflections on the Origin and Spread of Nationalism*. London: New Left Books.

Brittan, Arthur and Mary Maynard. 1984. *Sexism, Racism and Oppression*. Oxford: Blackwell.

Cole, Thomas R. 1986. "Putting Off the Old: Middle Class Morality, Antebellum Protestantism, and the Origins of Ageism." In David Van Tassel and Peter N. Stearns, eds., *Old Age in a Bureaucratic Society*. New York: Greenwood.

Fanon, Frantz. 1967. *Black Skin, White Masks*. New York: Grove.

Frye, Marilyn. 1983b. "On Being White: Toward a Feminist Understanding of Race Supremacy." In *The Politics of Reality*. Trumansburg, N.Y.: Crossing.

Giddens, Anthony. 1976. *Central Problems of Social Theory*. Berkeley: University of California Press.

——. 1981. *A Contemporary Critique of Historical Materialism*. Berkeley and Los Angeles: University of California Press.

——. 1984. *The Constitution of Society*. Berkeley and Los Angeles: University of California Press.

Kovel, Joel. 1970. *White Racism: A Psychohistory*. 2d ed. New York: Columbia University Press.

Kristeva, Julia. 1977. "Le Sujet en Procès." In *Polylogue*. Paris: Editions du Seuil.

——. 1982. *Powers of Horror: An Essay in Abjection*. New York: Columbia University Press.

Marcuse, Herbert. 1964. *One-Dimensional Man*. Boston: Beacon.

Mosse, George. 1985. *Nationalism and Sexuality*. New York: Fertig.

Smith, Paul. 1988. *Discerning the Subject*. Minneapolis: University of Minnesota Press.

38

"Towards a Postmodern Pedagogy"

Henry A. Giroux

American educational theorist, Henry Giroux (1943–) proposes a "border pedagogy" that rejects many of the traditional aims of education. Education for Giroux is intrinsically a political process aimed at producing a democratic egalitarian society. The primary contemporary obstacle to this end is the marginalization of social groups by racism and sexism. In response, border pedagogy aims to bring students to an experiential understanding of those deemed "other" by their official culture. In the piece that follows Giroux summarizes what are in effect the basic principles of a multicultural educational practise.

As long as people are people, democracy in the full sense of the word will always be no more than an ideal. One may approach it as one would a horizon, in ways that may be better or worse, but it can never be fully attained. In this sense, you too, are merely approaching democracy. You have thousands of problems of all kinds, as other countries do. But you have one great advantage: You have been approaching democracy uninterruptedly for more than 200 years.

Vaclav Havel, cited in *The New York Times*, March 18, 1990

How on earth can these prestigious persons in Washington ramble on in their sub-intellectual way about the "end of history"? As I look forward into the twenty-first century I sometimes agonize about the times in which my grandchildren and their children will live. It is not so much the rise in population as the rise in universal material expectations of the globe's huge population that

will be straining its resources to the very limits. North–South antagonisms will certainly sharpen, and religious and national fundamentalisms will become more intransigent. The struggle to bring consumer greed within moderate control, to find a level of low growth and satisfaction that is not at the expense of the disadvantaged and poor, to defend the environment and to prevent ecological disasters, to share more equitably the world's resources and to insure their renewal – all this is agenda enough for continuation of "history."

E. P. Thompson, *The Nation*, January 29, 1990

A striking character of the totalitarian system is its peculiar coupling of human demoralization and mass depoliticizing. Consequently, battling this system requires a conscious appeal to morality and an inevitable involvement in politics.

A. Michnik, *New York Times Magazine*, March 11, 1990

All these quotes stress, implicitly or explicitly, the importance of politics and ethics to democracy. In the first quote, the newly elected president of Czechoslovakia, Vaclav Havel, addressing a joint session of Congress reminds the American people that democracy is an ideal that is filled with possibilities but always has to be seen as part of an ongoing struggle for freedom and human dignity.

Henry A. Giroux, "Towards a Postmodern Pedagogy," section of the Introduction to *Postmodernism, Feminism and Cultural Politics*, pp. 45–55. Albany: State University of New York Press, 1991.

As a playwright and former political prisoner, Havel is a living embodiment of such a struggle. In the second quote, E. P. Thompson, the English peace activist and historian, reminds the American public that history has not ended but needs to be opened up in order to engage the many problems and possibilities that human beings will have to face in the twenty-first century. In the third quote, Adam Michnik, a founder of Poland's Workers' Defense Committee and an elected member of the Polish parliament, provides an ominous insight into one of the central features of totalitarianism, whether on the Right or the Left. He points to a society that fears democratic politics while simultaneously reproducing in people a sense of massive collective despair. None of these writers are from the United States and all of them are caught up in the struggle to recapture the Enlightenment model of freedom, agency, and democracy while simultaneously attempting to deal with the conditions of a postmodern world.

All of these statements serve to highlight the inability of the American public to grasp the full significance of the democraticization of Eastern Europe in terms of what it reveals about the nature of our own democracy. In Eastern Europe and elsewhere there is a strong call for the primacy of the political and the ethical as a foundation for democratic public life whereas in the United States there is an ongoing refusal of the discourse of politics and ethics. Elected politicians from both sides of the established parties in the Congress complain that American politics is about "trivialization, atomization, and paralysis." Politicians as diverse as Lee Atwater, the Republican Party chairman, and Walter Mondale, former Vice President, agree that we have entered into a time in which much of the American public believes that "Bull permeates everything ... [and that] we've got a kind of politics of irrelevance" (Oreskes, *The New York Times*, March 18, 1990, 16). At the same time, a number of polls indicate that while the youth of Poland, Czechoslovakia, and East Germany are extending the frontiers of democracy, American youth are both unconcerned and largely ill-prepared to struggle for and keep democracy alive in the twenty-first century.

Rather than being a model of democracy, the United States has become indifferent to the need to struggle for the conditions that make democracy a substantive rather than lifeless activity. At all levels of national and daily life, the breadth and depth of democratic relations are being rolled back. We have become a society that appears to demand less rather than more of democracy. In some quarters, democracy has actually become subversive. What does this suggest for developing some guiding principles in order to rethink the purpose and meaning of education and critical pedagogy within the present crises? Since I outline the particulars of a postmodern critical pedagogy in the last chapter of this book, I want to conclude with some suggestive principles for a critical pedagogy that emerge out of my discussion of the most important aspects of modernism, postmodernism, and postmodern feminism.

1. Education must be understood as producing not only knowledge but also political subjects. Rather than rejecting the language of politics, critical pedagogy must link public education to the imperatives of a critical democracy (Dewey, 1916; Giroux, 1988). Critical pedagogy needs to be informed by a public philosophy dedicated to returning schools to their primary task: places of critical education in the service of creating a public sphere of citizens who are able to exercise power over their own lives and especially over the conditions of knowledge production and acquisition. This is a critical pedagogy defined, in part, by the attempt to create the lived experience of empowerment for the vast majority. In other words, the language of critical pedagogy needs to construct schools as democratic public spheres. In part, this means educators need to develop a critical pedagogy in which the knowledge, habits, and skills of critical rather than simply good citizenship are taught and practiced. This means providing students with the opportunity to develop the critical capacity to challenge and transform existing social and political forms, rather than simply adapt to them. It also means providing students with the skills they will need to locate themselves in history, find their own voices, and provide the convictions and compassion necessary for exercising civic courage, taking risks, and furthering the habits, customs, and social relations that are essential to democratic public forms. In effect, critical pedagogy needs to be grounded in a keen sense of the importance of constructing a political vision from which to develop an educational project as part of a wider discourse for revitalizing democratic public life. A critical pedagogy for democracy cannot be reduced, as some educators, politicians, and groups have argued, to forcing students to say the Pledge of Allegiance at the beginning of every school day or to speak and think only in the language of dominant

English (Hirsch Jr, 1987). A critical pedagogy for democracy does not begin with test scores but with the questions: What kinds of citizens do we hope to produce through public education in a postmodern culture? What kind of society do we want to create in the context of the present shifting cultural and ethnic borders? How can we reconcile the notions of difference and equality with the imperatives of freedom and justice?

2. Ethics must be seen as a central concern of critical pedagogy. This suggests that educators attempt to understand more fully how different discourses offer students diverse ethical referents for structuring their relationship to the wider society. But it also suggests that educators go beyond the postmodern notion of understanding how student experiences are shaped within different ethical discourses. Educators must also come to view ethics and politics as a relationship between the self and the other. Ethics, in this case, is not a matter of individual choice or relativism but a social discourse grounded in struggles that refuse to accept needless human suffering and exploitation. Thus, ethics is taken up as a struggle against inequality and as a discourse for expanding basic human rights. This points to a notion of ethics attentive to both the issue of abstract rights and those contexts which produce particular stories, struggles, and histories. In pedagogical terms, an ethical discourse needs to be taken up with regards to the relations of power, subject positions, and social practices it activates (Simon, 1992). This is neither an ethics of essentialism nor relativism. It is an ethical discourse grounded in historical struggles and attentive to the construction of social relations free of injustice. The quality of ethical discourse, in this case, is not simply grounded in difference but in the issue of how justice arises out of concrete historical circumstances (Shapiro, 1990).

3. As Sharon Welch indicates[i] critical pedagogy needs to focus on the issue of difference in an ethically challenging and politically transformative way. There are at least two notions of difference at work here. First, difference can be incorporated into a critical pedagogy as part of an attempt to understand how student identities and subjectivities are constructed in multiple and contradictory ways. In this case, identity is explored through its

own historicity and complex subject positions. The category of student experience should not be limited pedagogically to students exercising self-reflection but opened up as a race, gender, and class specific construct to include the diverse ways in which their experiences and identities have been constituted in different historical and social formations. Second, critical pedagogy can focus on how differences between groups develop and are sustained around both enabling and disabling sets of relations. In this instance, difference becomes a marker for understanding how social groups are constituted in ways that are integral to the functioning of any democratic society. Difference in this context does not focus only on charting spatial, racial, ethnic, or cultural differences but also analyzes historical differences that manifest themselves in public struggles.

As part of a language of critique, teachers can make problematic how different subjectivities are positioned within a historically specific range of ideologies and social practices that inscribe students in modes of behavior that subjugate, infantilize, and corrupt. Similarly, such a language can analyze how differences within and between social groups are constructed and sustained both within and outside the schools in webs of domination, subordination, hierarchy, and exploitation. As part of a language of possibility, teachers can explore the opportunity to construct knowledge/power relations in which multiple narratives and social practices are constructed around a politics and pedagogy of difference that offers students the opportunity to read the world differently, resist the abuse of power and privilege, and construct alternative democratic communities. Difference in this case cannot be seen as simply a politics of assertion, of simply affirming one's voice or sense of the common good, it must be developed within practices in which differences can be affirmed and transformed in their articulation with categories central to public life: democracy, citizenship, public spheres. In both political and pedagogical terms, the category of difference must be central to the notion of democratic community.

4. Critical pedagogy needs a language that allows for competing solidarities and political vocabularies that do not reduce the issues of power, justice, struggle, and inequality to a single script, a master narrative that suppresses the contingent, historical, and the everyday as a serious object of study (Cherryholmes, 1988). This suggests that curriculum knowledge not be treated as a sacred text but developed as part of an ongoing engagement with a

[i] Sharon Welch, "An Ethic of Solidarity and Difference," in Henry A. Giroux, *Postmodernism, Feminism and Cultural Politics: Redrawing Educational Boundaries* (Albany: State University of New York, 1991), pp. 83–99.

385

variety of narratives and traditions that can be re-read and re-formulated in politically different terms. At issue here is constructing a discourse of textual authority that is power-sensitive and developed as part of a wider analysis of the struggle over culture fought out at the levels of curricula knowledge, pedagogy, and the exercise of institutional power (Aronowitz and Giroux, 1991). This is not merely an argument against a canon, but one that disavows the very category. Knowledge has to be constantly re-examined in terms of its limits and rejected as a body of information that only has to be passed down to students. As Ernesto Laclau (1988) has pointed out, setting limits to the answers given by what can be judged as a valued tradition (a matter of argument also) is an important political act. What Laclau is suggesting is the possibility for students to creatively appropriate the past as part of a living dialogue, an affirmation of the multiplicity of narratives, and the need to judge them not as timeless or as monolithic discourses, but as social and historical inventions that can be refigured in the interests of creating more democratic forms of public life. This points to the possibility for creating pedagogical practices characterized by the open exchange of ideas, the proliferation of dialogue, and the material conditions for the expression of individual and social freedom.

5. Critical pedagogy needs to create new forms of knowledge through its emphasis on breaking down disciplinary boundaries and creating new spaces where knowledge can be produced. In this sense, critical pedagogy must be reclaimed as a cultural politics and a form of counter-memory. This is not merely an epistemological issue, but one of power, ethics, and politics. Critical pedagogy as a cultural politics points to the necessity of inserting the struggle over the production and creation of knowledge as part of a broader attempt to create a public sphere of citizens who are able to exercise power over their lives and the social and political forms through which society is governed. As a form of counter-memory, critical pedagogy starts with everyday and the particular as a basis for learning, it reclaims the historical and the popular as part of an ongoing effort to legitimate the voices of those who have been silenced, and to inform the voices of those who have been located within narratives that are monolithic and totalizing. At stake here is a pedagogy that provides the knowledge, skills, and habits for students and others to read history in ways that enable them to reclaim their identities in the interests of constructing forms of life that are more

democratic and more just. This is a struggle that deepens the pedagogical meaning of the political and the political meaning of the pedagogical. In the first instance, it raises important questions about how students and others are constructed as agents within particular histories, cultures, and social relations. Against the monolith of culture, it posits the conflicting terrain of cultures shaped within asymmetrical relations of power, grounded in diverse historical struggles. Similarly, culture has to be understood as part of the discourse of power and inequality. As a pedagogical issue, the relationship between culture and power is evident in questions such as "Whose cultures are appropriated as our own? How is marginality normalized?" (Popkewitz, 1988, 77). To insert the primacy of culture as a pedagogical and political issue is to make central how schools function in the shaping of particular identities, values, and histories by producing and legitimating specific cultural narratives and resources. In the second instance, asserting the pedagogical aspects of the political raises the issue of how difference and culture can be taken up as pedagogical practices and not merely as political categories. For example, how does difference matter as a pedagogical category if educators and cultural workers have to make knowledge meaningful before it can become critical and transformative? Or what does it mean to engage the tension between being theoretically correct and pedagogically wrong? These are concerns and tensions that make the relationship between the political and the pedagogical both mutually informing and problematic.

6. The Enlightenment notion of reason needs to be reformulated within a critical pedagogy. First, educators need to be skeptical regarding any notion of reason that purports to reveal the truth by denying its own historical construction and ideological principles. Reason is not innocent and any viable notion of critical pedagogy cannot exercise forms of authority that emulate totalizing forms of reason that appear to be beyond criticism and dialogue. This suggests that we reject claims to objectivity in favor of partial epistemologies that recognize the historical and socially constructed nature of their own knowledge claims and methodologies. In this way, curriculum can be viewed as a cultural script that introduces students to particular forms of reason which structure specific stories and ways of life. Reason in this sense implicates and is implicated in the intersection of power, knowledge, and politics. Second, it is not enough to reject an essentialist or universalist defense of reason. Instead, the limits of

reason must be extended to recognizing other ways in which people learn or take up particular subject positions. In this case, educators need to understand more fully how people learn through concrete social relations, through the ways in which the body is positioned (Grumet, 1988), through the construction of habit and intuition, and through the production and investment of desire and affect.…

7. Critical pedagogy needs to regain a sense of alternatives by combining a language of critique and possibility. Postmodern feminism exemplifies this in both its critique of patriarchy and its search to construct new forms of identity and social relations. It is worth noting that teachers can take up this issue around a number of considerations. First, educators need to construct a language of critique that combines the issue of limits with the discourse of freedom and social responsibility. In other words, the question of freedom needs to be engaged dialectically not only as one of individual rights but also as part of the discourse of social responsibility. That is, whereas freedom remains an essential category in establishing the conditions for ethical and political rights, it must also be seen as a force to be checked if it is expressed in modes of individual and collective behavior that threaten the ecosystem or produce forms of violence and oppression against individuals and social groups. Second, critical pedagogy needs to explore in programmatic terms a language of possibility that is capable of thinking risky thoughts, that engages a project of hope, and points to the horizon of the "not yet." A language of possibility does not have to dissolve into a reified form of utopianism; instead, it can be developed as a precondition for nourishing convictions that summon up the courage to imagine a different and more just world and to struggle for it. A language of moral and political possibility is more than an outmoded vestige of humanist discourse. It is central to responding not only with compassion to human beings who suffer and agonize but also with a politics and a set of pedagogical practices that can refigure and change existing narratives of domination into images and concrete instances of a future which is worth fighting for.

There is a certain cynicism that characterizes the language of the Left at the present moment. Central to this position is the refusal of all utopian images, all appeals to "a language of possibility." Such refusals are often made on the grounds that "utopian discourse" is a strategy employed by the Right and therefore is ideologically tainted. Or, the very notion of possibility is dismissed as an impractical and therefore useless category. In my mind, this represents less a serious critique than a refusal to move beyond the language of exhaustion and despair. Essential to developing a response to this position is a discriminating notion of possibility, one which makes a distinction between a discourse characterized as either "dystopian" or utopian. In the former, the appeal to the future is grounded in a form of nostalgic romanticism, with its call for a return to a past, which more often than not serves to legitimate relations of domination and oppression. Similarly, in Constance Penley's terms a "dystopian" discourse often "limits itself to solutions that are either individualist or bound to a romanticized notion of guerilla-like small-group resistance. The true atrophy of the utopian imagination is this: we can imagine the future but we *cannot* conceive the kind of collective political strategies necessary to change or ensure that future" (Penley, 1989, 122). In contrast to the language of dystopia, a utopian discourse rejects apocalyptic emptiness and nostalgic imperialism and sees history as open and society worth struggling for in the image of an alternative future. This is the language of the "not yet", one in which the imagination is redeemed and nourished in the effort to construct new relationships fashioned out of strategies of collective resistance based on a critical recognition of both what society is and what it might become. Paraphrasing Walter Benjamin, this is a discourse of imagination and hope that pushes history against the grain.[ii] Nancy Fraser (1989) illuminates this sentiment by emphasizing the importance of a language of possibility for the project of social change: "It allows for the possibility of a radical democratic politics in which immanent critique and transfigurative desire mingle with one another" (107).

8. Critical pedagogy needs to develop a theory of teachers as transformative intellectuals who occupy specifiable political and social locations. Rather than defining teacher work through the narrow language of professionalism, a critical pedagogy needs to ascertain more carefully what the role of teachers might be as cultural workers engaged in the production of ideologies and social practices. This is not a call for teachers to become wedded to some abstract ideal that removes them from everyday life, or one that intends for them to become prophets of perfection and certainty; on the contrary, it is a call for teachers to undertake social criticism not as

---

[ii] Walter Benjamin (1892–1940), Frankfurt School aesthetician.

outsiders but as public intellectuals who address the most social and political issues of their neighbourhood, nation, and the wider global world. As public and transformative intellectuals, teachers have an opportunity to make organic connections with the historical traditions that provide them and their students with a voice, history, and sense of belonging. It is a position marked by a moral courage and criticism that does not require educators to step back from society in the manner of the "objective" teacher, but to distance themselves from those power relations that subjugate, oppress, and diminish other human beings. Teachers need to take up criticism from within, to develop pedagogical practices that not only heighten the possibilities for critical consciousness but also for transformative action (Walzer, 1987). In this perspective, teachers would be involved in the invention of critical discourses and democratic social relations. Critical pedagogy would represent itself as the active construction rather than transmission of particular ways of life. More specifically, as transformative intellectuals, teachers can engage in the invention of languages so as to provide spaces for themselves and their students to rethink their experiences in terms that both name relations of oppression and offer ways in which to overcome them.

9. Central to the notion of critical pedagogy is a politics of voice that combines a postmodern notion of difference with a feminist emphasis on the primacy of the political. This suggests taking up the relationship between the personal and the political in a way that does not collapse the political into the personal but strengthens the relationship between the two so as to engage rather than withdraw from addressing those institutional forms and structures that contribute to racism, sexism, and class exploitation. This suggests some important pedagogical interventions. First the self must be seen as a primary site of politicization. That is, the issue of how the self is constructed in multiple and complex ways must be analyzed both as part of a language of affirmation and a broader understanding of how identities are inscribed in and between various social, cultural, and historical formations. To engage issues regarding the construction of the self is to address questions of history, culture, community, language, gender, race, and class. It is to raise

questions regarding what pedagogical practices need to be employed that allow students to speak in dialogical contexts that affirm, interrogate, and extend their understandings of themselves and the global contexts in which they live. Such a position recognizes that students have several or multiple identities, but also asserts the importance of offering students a language that allows them to reconstruct their moral and political energies in the service of creating a more just and equitable social order, one that undermines relations of hierarchy and domination. Second, a politics of voice must offer pedagogical and political strategies that affirm the primacy of the social, intersubjective, and collective. To focus on voice is not meant to simply affirm the stories that students tell, it is not meant to simply glorify the possibility for narration. Such a position often degenerates into a form of narcissism, a carthartic experience that is reduced to naming anger without the benefit of theorizing in order to both understand its underlying causes and what it means to work collectively to transform the structures of domination responsible for oppressive social relations. Raising one's consciousness has increasingly become a pretext for legitimating hegemonic forms of separatism buttressed by self-serving appeals to the primacy of experience. What is often expressed in such appeals is an anti-intellectualism that retreats from any viable form of political engagement, especially one willing to address and transform diverse forms of oppression. The call to simply affirm one's voice has increasingly been reduced to a pedagogical process that is as reactionary as it is inward looking. A more radical notion of voice should begin with what bell hooks (1989) calls a critical attention to theorizing experience as part of a broader politics of engagement. In referring specifically to feminist pedagogy, she argues that the discourse of confession and memory can be used to "shift the focus away from mere naming of one's experience. . . . to talk about identity in relation to culture, history, politics" (110). For hooks, the telling of tales of victimization, or the expression of one's voice is not enough; it is equally imperative that such experiences be the object of theoretical and critical analyses so that they can be connected rather than severed from broader notions of solidarity, struggle, and politics.

Author's References

Aronowitz, S. and H. A. Giroux (1991). *Postmodern Education: Politics, Culture and Social Criticism*. Minneapolis: University of Minnesota Press.

Cherryholmes, C. (1988). *Power and Criticism: Poststructural Investigations in Education*. New York: Teachers College Press.

Dewey, J. (1916). *Democracy and Education*. New York: Macmillan.

Fraser, N. (1989). *Unruly Practices*. Minneapolis: University of Minnesota Press.

Giroux, H. (1988). *Schooling and the Struggle for Public Life*. Minneapolis: University of Minnesota Press.

Grumet, M. (1988). *Bitter Milk: Women and Teaching*. Massachusetts: University of Massachusetts Press.

hooks, bell (1989). *Talking Back*. Boston: South End Press.

Hirsch Jr, E. D. (1987). *Cultural Literacy: What Every American Needs to Know*. Boston: Houghton Mifflin.

Laclau, E. (1988). Politics and the limits of modernity. In A. Ross (ed.), *Universal Abandon? The Politics of Post-modernism*. Minneapolis: University of Minnesota Press, 63–82.

Michnik, A. (March 11, 1990). *Notes on the Revolution*. The New York Times Magazine.

Oreskes, M. (March 18, 1990). America's politics loses way as its vision changes world. *The New York Times*, vol. CXXXIX, No. 48, 178 (Sunday), 1, 16.

Penley, C. (1989). *The Future of an Illusion: Film, Feminism and Psychoanalysis*. Minneapolis: University of Minnesota Press.

Popkewitz, T. (1988). Culture, pedagogy, and power: issues in the production of values and colonialization. *Journal of Education*, 170(2), 77–90.

Shapiro, S. (1990). *Between Capitalism and Democracy*. Westport: Bergin and Garvey Press.

Simon, R. (1992). *Teaching against the Grain: Texts for a Pedagogy of Possibility*. Westport: Bergin and Garvey.

Thompson, E. P. (January 29, 1990). History turns on a new hinge. *The Nation*, 117–22.

Walzer, M. (1987). *Interpretation and Criticism*. Cambridge: Harvard University Press.

39

"Contingent Foundations: Feminism and the Question of 'Postmodernism' "

Judith Butler

Judith Butler (1956–) is an American philosopher and feminist especially concerned with the political meaning of sexual identity, both as gender and as sexual orientation. Her book *Gender Trouble* (1994) helped to establish the field of "queer studies," which takes all forms of sexual identity, including heterosexuality, to be social constructions. She famously analyzes gender as practical and aesthetic *performance*. Butler adapts postmodernism to her constructivist, semiotic analysis of identity in an attempt to undermine the dominant intellectual and political themes of modern thought. Nevertheless, she criticizes postmodernism where it threatens to undermine critique and the legitimation of social change. In the following essay, her critical analysis of contemporary American society, in particular the 1991 Gulf War against Iraq and its cultural concomitants, exhibits her attempt to deploy a politicized postmodernism.

The question of postmodernism is surely a question, for is there, after all, something called postmodernism? Is it an historical characterization, a certain kind of theoretical position, and what does it mean for a term that has described a certain aesthetic practice now to apply to social theory and to feminist social and political theory in particular? Who are these postmodernists? Is this a name that one takes on for oneself, or is it more often a name that one is called if and when one offers a critique of the subject, a discursive analysis, or questions the integrity or coherence of totalizing social descriptions?

I know the term from the way it is used, and it usually appears on my horizon embedded in the following critical formulations: "if discourse is all there is . . . ," or "if everything is a text . . . ," or "if the subject is dead . . . ," of "if real bodies do not exist . . . " The sentence begins as a warning against an impending nihilism, for if the conjured content of these series of conditional clauses proves to be true, then, and there is always a then, some set of dangerous consequences will surely follow. So 'postmodernism' appears to be articulated in the form of a fearful conditional or sometimes in the form of paternalistic disdain toward that which is youthful and irrational. Against this postmodernism, there is an effort to shore up the primary premises, to establish in advance that any theory of politics requires a subject, needs from the start to presume its subject, the referentiality of language, the integrity of the institutional descriptions it provides. For politics is unthinkable without a foundation, without these premises. But do these claims seek to secure a contingent formation of politics that requires that these notions remain unproblematized features of its own definition? Is it the case that all politics, and feminist politics in particular, is unthinkable without these prized premises? Or is it rather that a specific version of politics is shown in its contingency once those premises are problematically thematized?

Judith Butler, "Contingent Foundations: Feminism and the Question of Postmodernism" from Judith Butler and Joan Scott, *Feminists Theorize the Political*, pp. 3–21. London and New York: Routledge, 1992.

To claim that politics requires a stable subject is to claim that there can be no *political* opposition to that claim. Indeed, that claim implies that a critique of the subject cannot be a politically informed critique but, rather, an act which puts into jeopardy politics as such. To require the subject means to foreclose the domain of the political, and that foreclosure, installed analytically as an essential feature of the political, enforces the boundaries of the domain of the political in such a way that that enforcement is protected from political scrutiny. The act which unilaterally establishes the domain of the political functions, then, as an authoritarian ruse by which political contest over the status of the subject is summarily silenced.[1]

To refuse to assume, that is, to require a notion of the subject from the start is not the same as negating or dispensing with such a notion altogether; on the contrary, it is to ask after the process of its construction and the political meaning and consequentiality of taking the subject as a requirement or presupposition of theory. But have we arrived yet at a notion of postmodernism?

A number of positions are ascribed to postmodernism, as if it were the kind of thing that could be the bearer of a set of positions: discourse is all there is, as if discourse were some kind of monistic stuff out of which all things are composed; the subject is dead, I can never say "I" again; there is no reality, only representations. These characterizations are variously imputed to postmodernism or poststructuralism, which are conflated with each other and sometimes conflated with deconstruction, and sometimes understood as an indiscriminate assemblage of French feminism, deconstruction, Lacanian psychoanalysis, Foucaultian analysis, Rorty's conversationalism and cultural studies. On this side of the Atlantic and in recent discourse, the terms "postmodernism" or "poststructuralism" settle the differences among those positions in a single stroke, providing a substantive, a noun, that includes those positions as so many of its modalities or permutations. It may come as a surprise to some purveyors of the Continental scene to learn that Lacanian psychoanalysis in France positions itself officially against poststructuralism, that Kristeva denounces postmodernism,[2] that Foucaultians rarely relate to Derrideans, that Cixous[i] and Irigaray are fundamentally opposed, and that the only tenuous connection between French feminism and deconstruction exists

between Cixous and Derrida, although a certain affinity in textual practices is to be found between Derrida and Irigaray. Biddy Martin is also right to point out that almost all of French feminism adheres to a notion of high modernism and the avant-garde, which throws some question on whether these theories or writings can be grouped simply under the category of postmodernism.

I propose that the question of postmodernism be read not merely as the question that postmodernism poses for feminism, but as the question, what is postmodernism? What kind of existence does it have? Jean-François Lyotard champions the term, but he cannot be made into the example of what all the rest of the purported postmodernists are doing.[3] Lyotard's work is, for instance, seriously at odds with that of Derrida, who does not affirm the notion of "the postmodern," and with others for whom Lyotard is made to stand. Is he paradigmatic? Do all these theories have the same structure (a comforting notion to the critic who would dispense with them all at once)? Is the effort to colonize and domesticate these theories under the sign of the same, to group them synthetically and masterfully under a single rubric, a simple refusal to grant the specificity of these positions, an excuse not to read, and not to read closely? For if Lyotard uses the term, and if he can be conveniently grouped with a set of writers, and if some problematic quotation can be found in his work, then can that quotation serve as an "example" of postmodernism, symptomatic of the whole?

But if I understand part of the project of postmodernism, it is to call into question the ways in which such "examples" and "paradigms" serve to subordinate and erase that which they seek to explain. For the "whole," the field of postmodernism in its supposed breadth, is effectively "produced" by the example which is made to stand as a symptom and exemplar of the whole; in effect, if in the example of Lyotard we think we have a representation of postmodernism, we have then forced a substitution of the example for the entire field, effecting a violent reduction of the field to the one piece of text the critic is willing to read, a piece which, conveniently, uses the term "postmodern."

In a sense, this gesture of conceptual mastery that groups together a set of positions under the postmodern, that makes the postmodern into an epoch or a synthetic whole, and that claims that the part can stand for this artificially constructed whole, enacts a certain self-congratulatory ruse of power. It is paradoxical, at best, that the act

---

[i]   French feminist philosophers Julia Kristeva (1941–   ) and Hélène Cixous (1937–   ).

of conceptual mastery that effects this dismissive grouping of positions under the postmodern wants to ward off the peril of political authoritarianism. For the assumption is that some piece of the text is representational, that it stands for the phenomenon, and that the structure of "these" positions can be properly and economically discerned in the structure of the one. What authorizes such an assumption from the start? From the start we must believe that theories offer themselves in bundles or in organized totalities, and that historically a set of theories which are structurally similar emerge as the articulation of an historically specific condition of human reflection. This Hegelian trope, which continues through Adorno, assumes from the start that these theories can be substituted for one another because they variously symptomatize a common structural preoccupation. And yet, that presumption can no longer be made, for the Hegelian presumption that a synthesis is available from the start is precisely what has come under contest in various ways by some of the positions happily unified under the sign of postmodernism. One might argue that if, and to the extent that, the postmodern functions as such a unifying sign, then it is a decidedly "modern" sign, which is why there is some question whether one can debate for or against this postmodernism. To install the term as that which can be only affirmed or negated is to force it to occupy one position within a binary, and so to affirm a logic of noncontradiction over and against some more generative scheme.

Perhaps the reason for this unification of positions is occasioned by the very unruliness of the field, by the way in which the differences among these positions cannot be rendered symptomatic, exemplary, or representative of each other and of some common structure called postmodernism. If postmodernism as a term has some force or meaning within social theory, or feminist social theory in particular, perhaps it can be found in the critical exercise that seeks to show how theory, how philosophy, is always implicated in power, and perhaps that is precisely what is symptomatically at work in the effort to domesticate and refuse a set of powerful criticisms under the rubric of postmodernism. That the philosophical apparatus in its various conceptual refinements is always engaged in exercising power is not a new insight, but then again the postmodern ought not to be confused with the new; after all, the pursuit of the "new" is the preoccupation of high modernism; if anything, the postmodern casts doubt upon the possibility of a "new" that is not in some way already implicated in the "old."

But the point articulated forcefully by some recent critics of normative political philosophy is that the recourse to a position – hypothetical, counterfactual, or imaginary – that places itself beyond the play of power, and which seeks to establish the metapolitical basis for a negotiation of power relations, is perhaps the most insidious ruse of power. That this position beyond power lays claim to its legitimacy through recourse to a prior and implicitly universal agreement does not in any way circumvent the charge, for what rationalist project will designate in advance what counts as agreement? What form of insidious cultural imperialism here legislates itself under the sign of the universal?[4]

I don't know about the term "postmodern," but if there is a point, and a fine point, to what I perhaps better understand as poststructuralism, it is that power pervades the very conceptual apparatus that seeks to negotiate its terms, including the subject position of the critic; and further, that this implication of the terms of criticism in the field of power is *not* the advent of a nihilistic relativism incapable of furnishing norms, but, rather, the very precondition of a politically engaged critique. To establish a set of norms that are beyond power or force is itself a powerful and forceful conceptual practice that sublimates, disguises and extends its own power play through recourse to tropes of normative universality. And the point is not to do away with foundations, or even to champion a position that goes under the name of antifoundationalism. Both of those positions belong together as different versions of foundationalism and the skeptical problematic it engenders. Rather, the task is to interrogate what the theoretical move that establishes foundations *authorizes*, and what precisely it excludes or forecloses.

It seems that theory posits foundations incessantly, and forms implicit metaphysical commitments as a matter of course, even when it seeks to guard against it; foundations function as the unquestioned and the unquestionable within any theory. And yet, are these "foundations," that is, those premises that function as authorizing grounds, are they themselves not constituted through exclusions which, taken into account, expose the foundational premise as a contingent and contestable presumption. Even when we claim that there is some implied universal basis for a given foundation, that implication and that universality simply constitute a new dimension of unquestionability.

How is it that we might ground a theory or politics in a speech situation or subject position which is "universal," when the very category of the universal has only begun to be exposed for its own highly ethnocentric biases? How many "universalities" are there[5] and to what extent is cultural conflict understandable as the clashing of a set of presumed and intransigent "universalities," a conflict which cannot be negotiated through recourse to a culturally imperialist notion of the "universal" or, rather, which will only be solved through such recourse at the cost of violence? We have, I think, witnessed the conceptual and material violence of this practice in the United States's war against Iraq, in which the Arab "other" is understood to be radically "outside" the universal structures of reason and democracy and, hence, calls to be brought forcibly within. Significantly, the US had to abrogate the democratic principles of political sovereignty and free speech, among others, to effect this forcible return of Iraq to the "democratic" fold, and this violent move reveals, among other things, that such notions of universality are installed through the abrogation of the very universal principles to be implemented. Within the political context of contemporary postcoloniality more generally, it is perhaps especially urgent to underscore the very category of the "universal" as a site of insistent contest and resignification.[6] Given the contested character of the term, to assume from the start a procedural or substantive notion of the universal is of necessity to impose a culturally hegemonic notion on the social field. To herald that notion then as the philosophical instrument that will negotiate between conflicts of power is precisely to safeguard and reproduce a position of hegemonic power by installing it in the metapolitical site of ultimate normativity.

It may at first seem that I am simply calling for a more concrete and internally diverse "universality," a more synthetic and inclusive notion of the universal, and in that way committed to the very foundational notion that I seek to undermine. But my task is, I think, significantly different from that which would articulate a comprehensive universality. In the first place, such a totalizing notion could only be achieved at the cost of producing new and further exclusions. The term "universality" would have to be left permanently open, permanently contested, permanently contingent, in order not to foreclose in advance future claims for inclusion. Indeed, from my position and from any historically constrained perspective, any totalizing concept of the universal will shut down rather than authorize the unanticipated and unanticipatable claims that will be made under the sign of "the universal." In this sense, I am not doing away with the category, but trying to relieve the category of its foundationalist weight in order to render it as a site of permanent political contest.

A social theory committed to democratic contestation within a postcolonial horizon needs to find a way to bring into question the foundations it is compelled to lay down. It is this movement of interrogating that ruse of authority that seeks to close itself off from contest that is, in my view, at the heart of any radical political project. Inasmuch as poststructuralism offers a mode of critique that effects this contestation of the foundationalist move, it can be used as a part of such a radical agenda. Note that I have said, "it can be used": I think there are no necessary political consequences for such a theory, but only a possible political deployment.

If one of the points associated with postmodernism is that the epistemological point of departure in philosophy is inadequate, then it ought not to be a question of subjects who claim to know and theorize under the sign of the postmodern pitted against other subjects who claim to know and theorize under the sign of the modern. Indeed, it is that very way of framing debate that is being contested by the suggestion that the position articulated by the subject is always in some way constituted by what must be displaced for that position to take hold, and that the subject who theorizes is constituted as a "theorizing subject" by a set of exclusionary and selective procedures. For, indeed, who is it that gets constituted as the feminist theorist whose framing of the debate will get publicity? Is it not always the case that power operates in advance, in the very procedures that establish who will be the subject who speaks in the name of feminism, and to whom? And is it not also clear that a process of subjection is presupposed in the subjectivating process that produces before you one speaking subject of feminist debate? What speaks when "I" speak to you? What are the institutional histories of subjection and subjectivation that "position" me here now? If there is something called "Butler's position," is this one that I devise, publish, and defend, that belongs to me as a kind of academic property? Or is there a grammar of the subject that merely encourages us to position me as the proprietor of those theories?

Indeed, how is it that a position becomes a position, for clearly not every utterance qualifies as such. It is clearly a matter of a certain authorizing power, and that clearly does not emanate from the position itself. My position is mine to the extent that "I" – and I do not shirk from the pronoun – replay and resignify the theoretical positions that have constituted me, working the possibilities of their convergence, and trying to take account of the possibilities that they systematically exclude. But it is clearly not the case that "I" preside over the positions that have constituted me, shuffling through them instrumentally, casting some aside, incorporating others, although some of my activity may take that form. The "I" who would select between them is always already constituted by them. The "I" is the transfer point of that replay, but it is simply not a strong enough claim to say that the "I" is situated; the "I," this "I," is *constituted* by these positions, and these "positions" are not merely theoretical products, but fully embedded organizing principles of material practices and institutional arrangements, those matrices of power and discourse that produce me as a viable "subject." Indeed, this "I" would not be a thinking, speaking "I" if it were not for the very positions that I oppose, for those positions, the ones that claim that the subject must be given in advance, that discourse is an instrument or reflection of that subject, are already part of what constitutes me.

No subject is its own point of departure; and the fantasy that it is one can only disavow its constitutive relations by recasting them as the domain of a countervailing externality. Indeed, one might consider Luce Irigaray's claim that the subject, understood as a fantasy of autogenesis, is always already masculine.[ii] Psychoanalytically, that version of the subject is constituted through a kind of disavowal or through the primary repression of its dependency on the maternal. And to become a *subject* on this model is surely not a feminist goal.

The critique of the subject is not a negation or repudiation of the subject, but, rather, a way of interrogating its construction as a pregiven or foundationalist premise. At the outset of the war against Iraq, we almost all saw strategists who placed before us maps of the Middle East, objects of analysis and targets of instrumental military action.

Retired and active generals were called up by the networks to stand in for the generals on the field whose intentions would be invariably realized in the destruction of various Iraqi military bases. The various affirmations of the early success of these operations were delivered with great enthusiasm, and it seemed that this hitting of the goal, this apparently seamless realization of intention through an instrumental action without much resistance or hindrance was the occasion, not merely to destroy Iraqi military installations, but also to champion a masculinized Western subject whose will immediately translates into a deed, whose utterance or order materializes in an action which would destroy the very possibility of a reverse strike, and whose obliterating power at once confirms the impenetrable contours of its own subjecthood.

It is perhaps interesting to remember at this juncture that Foucault linked the displacement of the intentional subject with modern power relations that he himself associated with war.[7] What he meant, I think, is that subjects who institute actions are themselves instituted effects of prior actions, and that the horizon in which we act is there as a constitutive possibility of our very capacity to act, not merely or exclusively as an exterior field or theater of operations. But perhaps more significantly, the actions instituted via that subject are part of a chain of actions that can no longer be understood as unilinear in direction or predictable in their outcomes. And yet, the instrumental military subject appears at first to utter words that materialize directly into destructive deeds. And throughout the war, it was as if the masculine Western subject preempted the divine power to translate words into deeds; the newscasters were almost all full of giddy happiness as they demonstrated, watched, vicariously enacted, the exactitude of destructiveness. As the war began, the words one would hear on television were "euphoria," and one newscaster remarked that US weapons were instruments of "terrible beauty" (CBS) and celebrates prematurely and phantasmatically its own capacity to act instrumentally in the world to obliterate its opposition and to control the consequences of that obliteration. But the consequentiality of this act cannot be foreseen by the instrumental actor who currently celebrates the effectivity of its own intentions. What Foucault suggested was that this subject is itself the effect of a genealogy which is erased at the moment that the subject takes itself as the single origin of its

---

[ii] For Irigary, masculinity defines itself as unified agency, whereas femininity does not. "Autogenesis" is the fantasy of self-creation (i.e. not depending on a mother for one's existence).

action, and that the effects of an action always supersede the stated intention or purpose of the act. Indeed, the effects of the instrumental action always have the power to proliferate beyond the subject's control, indeed, to challenge the rational transparency of that subject's intentionality, and so to subvert the very definition of the subject itself. I suggest that we have been in the midst of a celebration on the part of the United States government and some of its allies of the phantasmatic subject, the one who determines its world unilaterally, and which is in some measure typified by the looming heads of retired generals framed against the map of the Middle East, where the speaking head of this subject is shown to be the same size, or larger, than the area it seeks to dominate. This is, in a sense, the graphics of the imperialist subject, a visual allegory of the action itself.

But here you think that I have made a distinction between the action itself and something like a representation, but I want to make a stronger point. You will perhaps have noticed that Colin Powell, the General of the Joint Chiefs of Staff invoked what is, I think, a new military convention of calling the sending of missiles "the delivery of an ordnance." The phrase is significant, I think; it figures an act of violence as an act of law (the military term "ordnance" is linked etymologically to the juridical "ordinance"), and so wraps the destruction in the appearance of orderliness; but in addition, it figures the missile as a kind of command, an order to obey, and is thus itself figured as a certain act of speech which not only delivers a message – get out of Kuwait – but effectively enforces that message through the threat of death and through death itself. Of course, this is a message that can never be received, for it kills its addressee, and so it is not an ordinance at all, but the failure of all ordinances, the refusal of a communication. And for those who remain to read the message, they will not read what is sometimes quite literally written on the missile.

Throughout the war, we witnessed and participated in the conflation of the television screen and the lens of the bomber pilot. In this sense, the visual record of this war is not a *reflection* on the war, but the enactment of its phantasmatic structure, indeed, part of the very means by which it is socially constituted and maintained as a war. The so-called "smart bomb" records its target as it moves in to destroy it – a bomb with a camera attached in front, a kind of optical phallus; it relays that film back to a command control and that film is refilmed on television, effectively constituting the television screen and its viewer as the extended apparatus of the bomb itself. In this sense, by viewing we are bombing, identified with both bomber and bomb, flying through space, transported from the North American continent to Iraq, and yet securely wedged in the couch in one's own living room. The smart bomb screen is, of course, destroyed in the moment that it enacts its destruction, which is to say that this is a recording of a thoroughly destructive act which can never record that destructiveness, indeed, which effects the phantasmatic distinction between the hit and its consequences. Thus as viewers, we veritably enact the allegory of military triumph: we retain our visual distance and our bodily safety through the disembodied enactment of the kill that produces no blood and in which we retain our radical impermeability. In this sense, we are in relation to this site of destruction absolutely proximate, absolutely essential, and absolutely distant, a figure for imperial power which takes the aerial, global view, the disembodied killer who can never be killed, the sniper as a figure for imperialist military power. The television screen thus redoubles the aerial view, securing a fantasy of transcendence, of a disembodied instrument of destruction which is infinitely protected from a reverse-strike through the guarantee of electronic distance.

This aerial view never comes close to seeing the *effects* of its destruction, and as a close-up to the site becomes increasingly possible, the screen conveniently destroys itself. And so although it was made to seem that this was a humane bombing, one which took buildings and military installations as its targets, this was, on the contrary, the effect of a frame which excluded from view the systematic destruction of a population, what Foucault calls the modern dream of states.[8] Or perhaps we ought to state it otherwise: precisely through excluding its targets from view under the rubric of proving the capacity to target precisely, this is a frame that effectively performs the annihilation that it systematically derealizes.

The demigod of a U.S. military subject which euphorically enacted the fantasy that it can achieve its aims with ease fails to understand that its actions have produced effects that will far exceed its phantasmatic purview; it thinks that its goals were achieved in a matter of weeks, and that its action was completed. But the action continues to act after the intentional subject has announced its completion. The effects of its actions have already

Judith Butler

inaugurated violence in places and in ways that it not only could not foresee but will be unable ultimately to contain, effects which will produce a massive and violent contestation of the Western subject's phantasmatic self-construction.

If I can, then, I'll try to return to the subject at hand. In a sense, the subject is constituted through an exclusion and differentiation, perhaps a repression, that is subsequently concealed, covered over, by the effect of autonomy. In this sense, autonomy is the logical consequence of a disavowed dependency, which is to say that the autonomous subject can maintain the illusion of its autonomy insofar as it covers over the break out of which it is constituted. This dependency and this break are already social relations, ones which precede and condition the formation of the subject. As a result, this is not a relation in which the subject finds itself, as one of the relations that forms its situation. The subject is constructed through acts of differentiation that distinguish the subject from its constitutive outside, a domain of abjected alterity conventionally associated with the feminine, but clearly not exclusively. Precisely in this recent war we saw "the Arab" figured as the abjected other as well as a site of homophobic fantasy made clear in the abundance of bad jokes grounded in the linguistic sliding from Saddam to Sodom.

There is no ontologically intact reflexivity to the subject which is then placed within a cultural context; that cultural context, as it were, is already there as the disarticulated process of that subject's production, one that is concealed by the frame that would situate a ready-made subject in an external web of cultural relations.

We may be tempted to think that to assume the subject in advance is necessary in order to safeguard the *agency* of the subject. But to claim that the subject is constituted is not to claim that it is determined; on the contrary, the constituted character of the subject is the very precondition of its agency. For what is it that enables a purposive and significant reconfiguration of cultural and political relations, if not a relation that can be turned against itself, reworked, resisted? Do we need to assume theoretically from the start a subject with agency *before* we can articulate the terms of a significant social and political task of transformation, resistance, radical democratization? If we do not offer in advance the theoretical guarantee of that agent, are we doomed to give up transformation and meaningful political practice? My suggestion is that

agency belongs to a way of thinking about persons as instrumental actors who confront an external political field. But if we agree that politics and power exist already at the level at which the subject and its agency are articulated and made possible, then agency can be *presumed* only at the cost of refusing to inquire into its construction. Consider that "agency" has no formal existence or, if it does, it has no bearing on the question at hand. In a sense, the epistemological model that offers us a pregiven subject or agent is one that refuses to acknowledge that *agency is always and only a political prerogative*. As such, it seems crucial to question the conditions of its possibility, not to take it for granted as an a priori guarantee. We need instead to ask, what possibilities of mobilization are produced on the basis of existing configurations of discourse and power? Where are the possibilities of reworking that very matrix of power by which we are constituted, of reconstituting the legacy of that constitution, and of working against each other those processes of regulation that can destabilize existing power regimes? For if the subject is constituted by power, that power does not cease at the moment the subject is constituted, for that subject is never fully constituted, but is subjected and produced time and again. That subject is neither a ground nor a product, but the permanent possibility of a certain resignifying process, one which gets detoured and stalled through other mechanisms of power, but which is power's own possibility of being reworked. It is not enough to say that the subject is invariably engaged in a political field; that phenomenological phrasing misses the point that the subject is an accomplishment regulated and produced in advance. And is as such fully political; indeed, perhaps *most* political at the point in which it is claimed to be prior to politics itself. To perform this kind of Foucaultian critique of the subject is not to do away with the subject or pronounce its death, but merely to claim that certain versions of the subject are politically insidious.

For the subject to be a pregiven point of departure for politics is to defer the question of the political construction and regulation of the subject itself; for it is important to remember that subjects are constituted through exclusion, that is, through the creation of a domain of deauthorized subjects, presubjects, figures of abjection, populations erased from view. This becomes clear, for instance, within the law when certain qualifications must first be met in order to be, quite literally, a claimant in sex discrimination or rape cases. Here it becomes quite urgent to ask, who qualifies as a "who," what systematic structures of disempowerment make it impossible for certain injured parties to invoke the "I" effectively within a court of law? Or less overtly, in a social theory like Albert Memmi's *The Colonizer and the Colonized*, an otherwise compelling call for radical enfranchisement, the category of women falls into neither category, the oppressor or the oppressed.[9] How do we theorize the exclusion of women from the category of the oppressed? Here the construction of subject-positions works to exclude women from the description of oppression, and this constitutes a different kind of oppression, one that is effected by the very *erasure* that grounds the articulation of the emancipatory subject. As Joan Scott makes clear in *Gender and the Politics of History*, once it is understood that subjects are formed through exclusionary operations, it becomes politically necessary to trace the operations of that construction and erasure.[10]

The above sketches in part a Foucaultian reinscription of the subject, an effort to resignify the subject as a site of resignification. As a result, it is not a "bidding farewell" to the subject per se, but, rather, a call to rework that notion outside the terms of an epistemological given. But perhaps Foucault is not really postmodern; after all, his is an analytics of *modern* power. There is, of course, talk about the death of the subject, but *which* subject is that? And what is the status of the utterance that announces its passing? What speaks now that the subject is dead? That there is a speaking seems clear, for how else could the utterance be heard? So clearly, the death of that subject is not the end of agency, of speech, or of political debate. There is the refrain that, just now, when women are beginning to assume the place of subjects, postmodern positions come along to announce that the subject is dead (there is a difference between positions of post-structuralism which claim that the subject *never* existed, and postmodern positions which claim that the subject *once* had integrity, but no longer does). Some see this as a conspiracy against women and other disenfranchised groups who are now only beginning to speak on their own behalf. But what precisely is meant by this, and how do we account for the very strong criticisms of the subject as an instrument of Western imperialist hegemony theorized by Gloria Anzaldua,[11] Gayatri Spivak[12] and various theorists of postcoloniality? Surely there is a caution offered here, that in the very struggle toward enfranchisement and democratization, we might adopt the very models of domination by which we were oppressed, not realizing that one way that domination works is through the regulation and production of subjects. Through what exclusions has the feminist subject been constructed, and how do those excluded domains return to haunt the "integrity" and "unity" of the feminist "we"? And how is it that the very category, the subject, the "we," that is supposed to be presumed for the purpose of solidarity, produces the very factionalization it is supposed to quell? Do women want to become subjects on the model which requires and produces an anterior region of abjection, or must feminism become a process which is self-critical about the processes that produce and destabilize identity categories? To take the construction of the subject as a political problematic is not the same as doing away with the subject; to deconstruct the subject is not to negate or throw away the concept; on the contrary, deconstruction implies only that we suspend all commitments to that to which the term, "the subject," refers, and that we consider the linguistic functions it serves in the consolidation and concealment of authority. To deconstruct is not to negate or to dismiss, but to call into question and, perhaps most importantly, to open up a term, like the subject, to a reusage or redeployment that previously has not been authorized.

Within feminism, it seems as if there is some political necessity to speak as and for *women*, and I would not contest that necessity. Surely, that is the way in which representational politics operates, and in this country, lobbying efforts are virtually impossible without recourse to identity politics. So we agree that demonstrations and legislative efforts and radical movements need to make claims in the name of women.

But this necessity needs to be reconciled with another. The minute that the category of women is invoked as *describing* the constituency for which feminism speaks, an internal debate invariably begins over what the descriptive content of that term will be. There are those who claim that there is an ontological specificity to women as child-bearers that forms the basis of a specific legal and political interest in representation, and then there are others who understand maternity to be a social relation that is, under current social circumstances, the specific and cross-cultural situation of women. And there are those who seek recourse to Gilligan and others to establish a feminine specificity that makes itself clear in women's communities or ways of knowing.[iii] But every time that specificity is articulated, there is resistance and factionalization within the very constituency that is supposed to be *unified* by the articulation of its common element. In the early 1980s, the feminist "we" rightly came under attack by women of color who claimed that the "we" was invariably white, and that that "we" that was meant to solidify the movement was the very source of a painful factionalization. The effort to characterize a feminine specificity through recourse to maternity, whether biological or social, produced a similar factionalization and even a disavowal of feminism altogether. For surely all women are not mothers; some cannot be, some are too young or too old to be, some choose not to be, and for some who are mothers, that is not necessarily the rallying point of their politicization in feminism.

I would argue that any effort to give universal or specific content to the category of women, presuming that that guarantee of solidarity is required *in advance*, will necessarily produce factionalization, and that "identity" as a point of departure can never hold as the solidifying ground of a feminist political movement. Identity categories are never merely descriptive, but always normative, and as such, exclusionary. This is not to say that the term "women" ought not to be used, or that we ought to announce the death of the category. On the contrary, if feminism presupposes that "women" designates an undesignatable field of differences, one that cannot be totalized or summarized by a descriptive identity category, then the very term becomes a site of permanent openness and resignifiability. I would argue that the rifts among women over the content of the term ought to be safeguarded and prized, indeed, that this constant rifting ought to be affirmed as the ungrounded ground of feminist theory. To deconstruct the subject of feminism is not, then, to censure its usage, but, on the contrary, to release the term into a future of multiple significations, to emancipate it from the maternal or racialist ontologies to which it has been restricted, and to give it play as a site where unanticipated meanings might come to bear.

Paradoxically, it may be that only through releasing the category of women from a fixed referent that something like 'agency' becomes possible. For

if the term permits of a resignification, if its referent is not fixed, then possibilities for new configurations of the term become possible. In a sense, what women signify has been taken for granted for too long, and what has been fixed as the 'referent' of the term has been "fixed," normalized, immobilized, paralyzed in positions of subordination. In effect, the signified has been conflated with the referent, whereby a set of meanings have been taken to inhere in the real nature of women themselves. To recast the referent as the signified, and to authorize or safeguard the category of women as a site of possible resignifications is to expand the possibilities of what it means to be a woman and in this sense to condition and enable an enhanced sense of agency.

One might well ask: but doesn't there have to be a set of norms that discriminate between those descriptions that ought to adhere to the category of women and those that do not? The only answer to that question is a counter-question: who would set those norms, and what contestations would they produce? To establish a normative foundation for settling the question of what ought properly to be included in the description of women would be only and always to produce a new site of political contest. That foundation would settle nothing, but would of its own necessity founder on its own authoritarian ruse. This is not to say that there is no foundation, but rather, that wherever there is one, there will also be a foundering, a contestation. That such foundations exist only to be put into question is, as it were, the permanent risk of the process of democratization. To refuse that contest is to sacrifice the radical democractic impetus of feminist politics. That the category is unconstrained, even that it comes to serve antifeminist purposes, will be part of the risk of this procedure. But this is a risk that is produced by the very foundationalism that seeks to safeguard feminism against it. In a sense, this risk is the foundation, and hence is not, of any feminist practice.

In the final part of this paper, I would like to turn to a related question, one that emerges from the concern that a feminist theory cannot proceed without presuming the materiality of women's bodies, the materiality of sex. The chant of antipostmodernism runs, if everything is discourse, then is there no reality to bodies? How do we understand the material violence that women suffer? In responding to this criticism, I would like to suggest that the very formulation misconstrues the critical point.

iii Carol Gilligan's *In a Different Voice* (1982) argued that the distinctive female approach to morality embodies an "ethic of care," in contrast to a masculine "ethic of justice."

I don't know what postmodernism is, but I do have some sense of what it might mean to subject notions of the body and materiality to a deconstructive critique. To deconstruct the concept of matter or that of bodies is not to negate or refuse either term. To deconstruct these terms means, rather, to continue to use them, to repeat them, to repeat them subversively, and to displace them from the contexts in which they have been deployed as instruments of oppressive power. Here it is of course necessary to state quite plainly that the options for theory are not exhausted by *presuming* materiality, on the one hand, and *negating* materiality, on the other. It is my purpose to do precisely neither of these. To call a presupposition into question is not the same as doing away with it; rather, it is to free it up from its metaphysical lodgings in order to occupy and to serve very different political aims. To problematize the matter of bodies entails in the first instance a loss of epistemological certainty, but this loss of certainty does not necessarily entail political nihilism as its result.[13]

If a deconstruction of the materiality of bodies suspends and problematizes the traditional ontological referent of the term, it does not freeze, banish, render useless, or deplete of meaning the usage of the term; on the contrary, it provides the conditions to *mobilize* the signifier in the service of an alternative production.

Consider that most material of concepts, "sex," which Monique Wittig calls a thoroughly political category, and which Michel Foucault calls a regulatory and "fictitious unity." For both theorists, sex does not *describe* a prior materiality, but produces and regulates the *intelligibility* of the *materiality* of bodies. For both, and in different ways, the category of sex imposes a duality and a uniformity on bodies in order to maintain reproductive sexuality as a compulsory order. I've argued elsewhere more precisely how this works, but for our purposes, I would like to suggest that this kind of categorization can be called a violent one, a forceful one, and that this discursive ordering and production of bodies in accord with the category of sex is itself a material violence.

The violence of the letter, the violence of the mark which establishes what will and will not signify, what will and will not be included within the intelligible, takes on a political significance when the letter is the law or the authoritative legislation of what will be the materiality of sex.

So what can this kind of poststructural analysis tell us about violence and suffering? Is it perhaps that forms of violence are to be understood as more pervasive, more constitutive, and more insidious than prior models have allowed us to see? That is part of the point of the previous discussion of war, but let me now make it differently in yet another context.

Consider the legal restrictions that regulate what does and does not count as rape: here the politics of violence operate through regulating what will and will not be able to appear as an effect of violence.[14] There is, then, already in this foreclosure a violence at work, a marking off in advance of what will or will not qualify under the signs of "rape" or "government violence," or in the case of states in which twelve separate pieces of empirical evidence are required to establish "rape," what then can be called a governmentally facilitated rape.

A similar line of reasoning is at work in discourses on rape when the "sex" of a woman is claimed as that which establishes the responsibility for her own violation. The defense attorney in the New Bedford gang rape case[iv] asked the plaintiff, "If you're living with a man, what are you doing running around the streets getting raped?"[15] The "running around" in this sentence collides grammatically with "getting raped": "getting" is procuring, acquiring, having, as if this were a treasure she was running around after, but "getting raped" suggests the passive voice. Literally, of course, it would be difficult to be "running around" and be "getting raped" at the same time, which suggests that there must be an elided passage here, perhaps a directional that leads from the former to the latter? If the sense of the sentence is, "running around [looking to get] raped," which seems to be the only logical way of bridging the two parts of the sentence, then rape as a passive acquisition is precisely the object of her active search. The first clause suggests that she "belongs" at home, with her man, that the home is a site in which she is the domestic property of that man, and the "streets" establish her as open season. If she is looking to get raped, she is looking to become the property of some other, and this objective is installed in her desire, conceived here as quite frantic in its pursuit. She is "running around," suggesting that she is running around looking under every rock for a

[iv] A 1983 gang rape in a bar in New Bedford, Massachusetts (which became the subject of the 1988 film, *The Accused*).

rapist to satisfy her. Significantly, the phrase installs as the structuring principle of her desire "getting raped," where 'rape' is figured as an act of willful self-expropriation. Since becoming the property of a man is the objective of her "sex," articulated in and through her sexual desire, and rape is the way in which that appropriation occurs "on the street" [a logic that implies that rape is to marriage as the streets are to the home, that is, that "rape" is street marriage, a marriage without a home, a marriage for homeless girls, and that marriage is domesticated rape], then "rape" is the logical consequence of the enactment of her sex and sexuality outside domesticity. Never mind that this rape took place in a bar, for the "bar" is, within this imaginary, but an extension of the "street," or perhaps its exemplary moment, for there is no enclosure, that is, no protection, other than the *home* as domestic marital space. In any case, the single cause of her violation is here figured as her "sex" which, given its natural propensity to seek expropriation, once dislocated from domestic propriety, naturally pursues its rape and is thus responsible for it.

The category of sex here functions as a principle of production and regulation at once, the cause of the violation installed as the formative principle of the body is sexuality. Here sex is a category, but not merely a representation; it is a principle of production, intelligibility, and regulation which enforces a violence and rationalizes it after the fact. The very terms by which the violation is explained *enact* the violation, and concede that the violation was under way before it takes the empirical form of a criminal act. That rhetorical enactment *shows* that "violence" is produced through the foreclosure effected by this analysis, through the erasure and negation that determines the field of appearances and intelligibility of crimes of culpability. As a category that effectively produces the political meaning of what it describes, "sex" here works its silent "violence" in regulating what is and is not designatable.

I place the terms "violence" and "sex" under quotation marks: is this the sign of a certain deconstruction, the end to politics? Or am I underscoring the iterable structure of these terms, the ways in which they yield to a repetition, occur ambiguously, and am I doing that precisely to further a political analysis? I place them in quotation marks to show that they are under contest, up for grabs, to initiate the contest, to question their traditional deployment, and call for some other. The quotation marks do not place into question the urgency or credibility of sex or violence as political issues, but, rather, show that the way their very materiality is circumscribed is fully political. The effect of the quotation marks is to denaturalize the terms, to designate these signs as sites of political debate.

If there is a fear that, by no longer being able to take for granted the subject, its gender, its sex, or its materiality, feminism will founder, it might be wise to consider the political consequences of keeping in their place the very premises that have tried to secure our subordination from the start.

Author's Notes

1   Here it is worth noting that in some recent political theory, notably in the writings of Ernesto Laclau and Chantal Mouffe (*Hegemony and Socialist Strategy*, London: Verso, 1986), William Connolly *Political Theory and Modernity* (Madison: University of Wisconsin Press, 1988), as well as Jean-Luc Nancy and Philippe Lacoue-Labarthe ("Le retrait du politique" in *Le Retrait du politique*, Paris: Editions galilée, 1983), there is an insistence that the political field is of necessity constructed through the production of a determining exterior. In other words, the very domain of politics constitutes itself through the production and naturalization of the "pre-" or "non-" political. In Derridean terms, this is the production of a "constitutive outside." Here I would like to suggest a distinction between the constitution of a political field that produces *and naturalizes* that constitutive outside and a political field that produces and *renders contingent* the specific parameters of that constitutive outside. Although I do not think that the differential relations through which the political field itself is constituted can ever be fully elaborated (precisely because the status of that elaboration would have to be elaborated as well *ad infinitum*), I do find useful William Connolly's notion of constitutive antagonisms, a notion that finds a parallel expression in Laclau and Mouffe, which suggests a form of political struggle which puts the parameters of the political itself into question. This is especially important for feminist concerns insofar as the grounds of politics ("universality," "equality," "the subject of rights" have been constructed through unmarked racial and gender exclusions and by a conflation of politics with public life that renders the private (reproduction, domains of "femininity") prepolitical.

2   Julia Kristeva, *Black Sun: Depression and Melancholy* (New York: Columbia University Press, 1989), pp. 258–9.

3   The conflation of Lyotard with the array of thinkers summarily positioned under the rubric of "postmodernism" is performed by the title and essay by Seyla Benhabib: "Epistemologies of Postmodernism: A Rejoinder to Jean-François Lyotard," in *Feminism/Postmodernism*, edited by Linda Nicholson (New York: Routledge, 1989).

4   This is abundantly clear in feminist criticisms of Jürgen Habermas as well as Catharine MacKinnon. See Iris Young, "Impartiality and the Civil Public: Some Implications of Feminist Criticisms of Modern Political Theory," in Seyla Benhabib and Drucilla Cornell, eds., *Feminism as Critique: Essays on the Politics of Gender in Late-Capitalism* (Oxford: Basil Blackwell, 1987); Nancy Fraser, *Unruly Practices: Power and Gender in Contemporary Social Theory* Minneapolis, University of Minnesota Press, 1989; especially "What's Critical about Critical Theory: The Case of Habermas and Gender." Wendy Brown, "Razing Consciousness," *The Nation*, 250:2, January 8/15, 1990.

5   See Ashis Nandy on the notion of alternative universalities in the preface to *The Intimate Enemy: Loss and Recovery of Self under Colonialism* (New Delhi: Oxford University Press, 1983).

6   Homi Bhabha's notion of "hybridity" is important to consider in this context.

7   Michel Foucault, *The History of Sexuality, Vol. I: An Introduction*, translated by Robert Hurley (New York: Random House, 1980), p. 102.

8   "Wars are no longer waged in the name of a sovereign who must be defended; they are waged on behalf of the existence of everyone; entire populations are mobilized for the purpose of wholesale slaughter in the name of life necessity: massacres," he writes, "have become vital." He later adds, "the principle underlying the tactics of battle – that one has to be capable of killing in order to go on living – has become the principle that defines the strategy of states. But the existence in question is no longer the juridical existence of sovereignty; at stake is the biological existence of a population. If genocide is indeed the dream of modern powers, this is not because of a recent return of the ancient right to kill; it is because power is situated and exercised at the level of life, the species, the race, and the large-scale phenomena of population." Foucault, *The History of Sexuality*, p. 137.

9   "At the height of the revolt," Memmi writes, "the colonized still bears the traces and lessons of prolonged cohabitation (just as the smile or movements of a wife, even during divorce proceedings, remind one strangely of those of her husband)." Here Memmi sets up an analogy which presumes that colonizer and colonized exist in a parallel and separate relation to the divorcing husband and wife. The analogy simultaneously and paradoxically suggests the feminization of the colonized, where the colonized is presumed to be the subject of men, *and* the exclusion of the women from the category of the colonized subject. Albert Memmi, *The Colonizer and the Colonized* (Boston: Beacon Press, 1965), p. 129.

10 Joan W. Scott, *Gender and the Politics of History* (New York: Columbia University Press), 1988, introduction.

11 Gloria Anzaldua, *La Frontera/Borderlands* (San Francisco: Spinsters Ink, 1988).

12 Gayatri Spivak, "Can the Subaltern Speak?" in *Marxism and the Interpretation of Culture*, eds. Nelson and Grossberg (Chicago: University of Illinois Press, 1988).

13 The body posited as prior to the sign, is always *posited* or *signified* as *prior*. This signification works through producing an *effect* of its own procedure, the body that it nevertheless and simultaneously claims to discover as that which *precedes* signification. If the body signified as prior to signification is an effect of signification, then the mimetic or representational status of language, which claims that signs follow bodies as their necessary mirrors, is not mimetic at all; on the contrary, it is productive, constitutive, one might even argue *performative*, in as much as this signifying act produces the body that it then claims to find prior to any and all signification.

14 For an extended analysis of the relationship of language and rape, see Sharon Marcus' contribution to [the original publication, "Fighting Bodies, Fighting Words: A Theory of Politics and Rape Prevention," *Feminists Theorize the Political*, pp. 385–403].

15 Quoted in Catharine MacKinnon, *Toward a Feminist Theory of the State* (Boston: Harvard University Press, 1989), p. 171.

Beyond Critique

40

From *Complexity and Contradiction in Architecture*

Robert Venturi

Philadelphia-based architect Robert Venturi (1925–) galvanized the growing rejection of the International Style of modernist architecture with his 1966 book *Complexity and Contradiction in Architecture*. It has been called the most important work on architecture since Le Corbusier's *Vers une Architecture*. Venturi famously responds to Mies van der Rohe's slogan that "Less is more" – that ornament and diversity of style are to be eliminated – with the playful, "Less is a bore." Venturi's architecture is marked by eclecticism and the refusal to reject popular commercial architecture as inherently vulgar. His aim is not to replace unity of style with pluralism, but to argue for less simple, more complex forms of unity, which constitute what he calls "the difficult whole," buildings that thrive on inner tension rather than trying to overcome it. It is this approach that later came to be called "postmodernism." Venturi further applied his principles in the book, *Learning from Las Vegas* (1972).

Nonstraightforward Architecture: A Gentle Manifesto

I like complexity and contradiction in architecture. I do not like the incoherence or arbitrariness of incompetent architecture nor the precious intricacies of picturesqueness or expressionism. Instead, I speak of a complex and contradictory architecture based on the richness and ambiguity of modern experience, including that experience which is inherent in art. Everywhere, except in architecture, complexity and contradiction have been acknow-

ledged, from Gödel's proof of ultimate inconsistency in mathematics to T. S. Eliot's analysis of "difficult" poetry and Joseph Albers' definition of the paradoxical quality of painting.[i]

But architecture is necessarily complex and contradictory in its very inclusion of the traditional Vitruvian elements of commodity, firmness, and delight. And today the wants of program, structure, mechanical equipment, and expression, even in single buildings in simple contexts, are diverse and conflicting in ways previously unimaginable. The increasing dimension and scale of architecture in urban and regional planning add to the difficulties. I welcome the problems and exploit the uncertainties. By embracing contradiction as well as complexity, I aim for vitality as well as validity.

Architects can no longer afford to be intimidated by the puritanically moral language of orthodox Modern architecture. I like elements which are hybrid rather than "pure," compromising rather than "clean," distorted rather than "straightforward," ambiguous rather than "articulated," perverse as well as impersonal, boring as well as "interesting," conventional rather than "designed," accommodating rather than excluding, redundant rather than simple, vestigial as well as innovating,

---

[i] Logician Kurt Gödel (1906–78), poet and critic T. S. Eliot (1888–1965), and painter Joseph Albers (1888–1976).

Robert Venturi, pp. 16–17, 23–5, 38–41, 88, and 102–4 from *Complexity and Contradiction in Architecture*. New York: The Museum of Modern Art, 1966, 1977.

inconsistent and equivocal rather than direct and clear. I am for messy vitality over obvious unity. I include the non sequitur and proclaim the duality.

I am for richness of meaning rather than clarity of meaning; for the implicit function as well as the explicit function. I prefer "both-and" to "either-or," black and white, and sometimes gray, to black or white. A valid architecture evokes many levels of meaning and combinations of focus: its space and its elements become readable and workable in several ways at once.

But an architecture of complexity and contradiction has a special obligation toward the whole: its truth must be in its totality or its implications of totality. It must embody the difficult unity of inclusion rather than the easy unity of exclusion. More is not less.

Complexity and Contradiction vs Simplification or Picturesqueness

Orthodox Modern architects have tended to recognize complexity insufficiently or inconsistently. In their attempt to break with tradition and start all over again, they idealized the primitive and elementary at the expense of the diverse and the sophisticated. As participants in a revolutionary movement, they acclaimed the newness of modern functions, ignoring their complications. In their role as reformers, they puritanically advocated the separation and exclusion of elements, rather than the inclusion of various requirements and their juxtapositions. As a forerunner of the Modern movement, Frank Lloyd Wright,[ii] who grew up with the motto "Truth against the World," wrote: "Visions of simplicity so broad and far-reaching would open to me and such building harmonies appear that . . . would change and deepen the thinking and culture of the modern world. So I believed."[1] And Le Corbusier, co-founder of Purism, spoke of the "great primary forms" which, he proclaimed, were "distinct . . . and without ambiguity."[2] Modern architects with few exceptions eschewed ambiguity.

But now our position is different: "At the same time that the problems increase in quantity, complexity, and difficulty they also change faster than before,"[3] and require an attitude more like that described by August Heckscher: "The movement from a view of life as 'essentially simple and orderly

to a view of life as complex and ironic is what every individual passes through in becoming mature. But certain epochs encourage this development; in them the paradoxical or dramatic outlook colors the whole intellectual scene. . . . Amid simplicity and order rationalism is born, but rationalism proves inadequate in any period of upheaval. Then equilibrium must be created out of opposites. Such inner peace as men gain must represent a tension among contradictions and uncertainties. . . . A feeling for paradox allows seemingly dissimilar things to exist side by side, their very incongruity suggesting a kind of truth."[4]

Rationalizations for simplifications are still current, however, though subtler than the early arguments. They are expansions of Mies van der Rohe's magnificent paradox, "less is more."[iii] Paul Rudolph has clearly stated the implications of Mies' point of view: "All problems can never be solved. . . . Indeed it is a characteristic of the twentieth century that architects are highly selective in determining which problems they want to solve. Mies, for instance, makes wonderful buildings only because he ignores many aspects of a building. If he solved more problems, his buildings would be far less potent."[5]

The doctrine "less is more" bemoans complexity and justifies exclusion for expressive purposes. It does, indeed, permit the architect to be "highly selective in determining which problems [he wants] to solve." But if the architect must be "committed to his particular way of seeing the universe,"[6] such a commitment surely means that the architect determines how problems should be solved, not that he can determine which of the problems he will solve. He can exclude important considerations only at the risk of separating architecture from the experience of life and the needs of society. If some problems prove insoluble, he can express this: in an inclusive rather than an exclusive kind of architecture there is room for the fragment, for contradiction, for improvisation, and for the tensions these produce. Mies' exquisite pavilions have had valuable implications for architecture, but their selectiveness of content and language is their limitation as well as their strength.

I question the relevance of analogies between pavilions and houses, especially analogies between Japanese pavilions and recent domestic architecture. They ignore the real complexity and contradiction

---

[ii]   Great American architect (1867–1959).

[iii]   Ludwig Mies van der Rohe (1886–1969), German architect, one of the leaders of the modern International Style and director of the Bauhaus school.

inherent in the domestic program – the spatial and technological possibilities as well as the need for variety in visual experience. Forced simplicity results in oversimplification. In the Wiley House, for instance, in contrast to his glass house, Philip Johnson attempted to go beyond the simplicities of the elegant pavilion.[iv] He explicitly separated and articulated the enclosed "private functions" of living on a ground floor pedestal, thus separating them from the open social functions in the modular pavilion above. But even here the building becomes a diagram of an oversimplified program for living – an abstract theory of either-or. Where simplicity cannot work, simpleness results. Blatant simplification means bland architecture. Less is a bore. . . .

Contradictory Levels: The Phenomenon of "Both-And" in Architecture

. . . Cleanth Brooks refers to Donne's art as "having it both ways" but, he says, "most of us in this latter day, cannot.[v] We are disciplined in the tradition either-or, and lack the mental agility – to say nothing of the maturity of attitude – which would allow us to indulge in the finer distinctions and the more subtle reservations permitted by the tradition of both-and."[7] The tradition "either-or" has characterized orthodox modern architecture: a sun screen is probably nothing else; a support is seldom an enclosure; a wall is not violated by window penetrations but is totally interrupted by glass; program functions are exaggeratedly articulated into wings or segregated separate pavilions. Even "flowing space" has implied being outside when inside, and inside when outside, rather than both at the same time. Such manifestations of articulation and clarity are foreign to an architecture of complexity and contradiction, which tends to include "both-and" rather than exclude "either-or."

If the source of the both-and phenomenon is contradiction, its basis is hierarchy, which yields several levels of meanings among elements with varying values. It can include elements that are both good and awkward, big and little, closed and open, continuous and articulated, round and square, structural and spatial. An architecture which includes varying levels of meaning breeds ambiguity and tension.

Most of the examples will be difficult to "read," but abstruse architecture is valid when it reflects the complexities and contradictions of content and meaning. Simultaneous perception of a multiplicity of levels involves struggles and hesitations for the observer, and makes his perception more vivid. . . .

Conventional elements in architecture represent one stage in an evolutionary development, and they contain in their changed use and expression some of their past meaning as well as their new meaning. What can be called the vestigial element parallels the double-functioning element. It is distinct from a superfluous element because it contains a double meaning. This is the result of a more or less ambiguous combination of the old meaning, called up by associations, with a new meaning created by the modified or new function, structural or programmatic, and the new context. The vestigial element discourages clarity of meaning; it promotes richness of meaning instead. It is a basis for change and growth in the city as manifest in remodeling which involves old buildings with new uses both programmatic and symbolic (like palazzi which become museums or embassies), and old street patterns with new uses and scales of movement. The paths of medieval fortification walls in European cities became boulevards in the nineteenth century; a section of Broadway is a piazza and a symbol rather than an artery to upper New York state. The ghost of Dock Street in Philadelphia's Society Hill, however, is a meaningless vestige rather than a working element resulting from a valid transition between the old and the new. I shall later refer to the vestigial element as it appears in Michelangelo's architecture and in what might be called Pop architecture.

The rhetorical element, like the double-functioning element, is infrequent in recent architecture. If the latter offends through its inherent ambiguity, rhetoric offends orthodox Modern architecture's cult of the minimum. But the rhetorical element is justified as a valid if outmoded means of expression. An element can seem rhetorical from one point of view, but if it is valid, at another level it enriches meaning by underscoring. In the project for a gateway at Bourneville by Ledoux, the columns in the arch are structurally rhetorical if not redundant.[vi] Expressively, however, they underscore the abstractness of the opening as a semicircle more than an arch, and

---

[iv] Two buildings by contemporary American architect Philip Johnson in New Canaan, Connecticut.
[v] The great English poet John Donne (1572–1631).

[vi] Gateway in Bourneville, France, by French architect Claude-Nicolas Ledoux (1736–1806).

they further define the opening as a gateway. As I have said, the stairway at the Pennsylvania Academy of the Fine Arts by Furness is too big in its immediate context, but appropriate as a gesture towards the outside scale and a sense of entry.[vii] The Classical portico is a rhetorical entrance. The stairs, columns, and pediment are juxtaposed upon the other-scale, real entrance behind. Paul Rudolph's entrance in the Art and Architecture Building at Yale is at the scale of the city; most people use the little door at the side in the stair tower.[viii]

Much of the function of ornament is rhetorical – like the use of Baroque pilasters for rhythm, and Vanbrugh's disengaged pilasters at the entrance to the kitchen court at Blenheim which are an architectural fanfare.[ix] The rhetorical element which is also structural is rare in Modern architecture, although Mies has used the rhetorical I-beam with an assurance that would make Bernini envious.[x]

Accommodation and the Limitations of Order: The Conventional Element

In short, that contradictions must be accepted.[8]

A valid order accommodates the circumstantial contradictions of a complex reality. It accommodates as well as imposes. It thereby admits "control *and* spontaneity," "correctness *and* ease" – improvisation within the whole. It tolerates qualifications and compromise. There are no fixed laws in architecture, but not everything will work in a building or a city. The architect must decide, and these subtle evaluations are among his principal functions. He must determine what must be made to work and what it is possible to compromise with, what will give in, and where and how. He does not ignore or exclude inconsistencies of program and structure within the order.

I have emphasized that aspect of complexity and contradiction which grows out of the medium more than the program of the building. Now I shall emphasize the complexity and contradiction that develops from the program and reflects the inher-

ent complexities and contradictions of living. It is obvious that in actual practice the two must be interrelated. Contradictions can represent the exceptional inconsistency that modifies the otherwise consistent order, or they can represent inconsistencies throughout the order as a whole. In the first case, the relationship between inconsistency and order accommodates circumstantial exceptions to the order, or it juxtaposes particular with general elements of order. Here you build an order up and then break it down, but break it from strength rather than from weakness. I have described this relationship as "contradiction accommodated." The relationship of inconsistency within the whole I consider a manifestation of "the difficult whole," which is discussed in the last chapter [of the original publication].

Mies refers to a need to "create order out of the desperate confusion of our times." But Kahn has said "by order I do not mean orderliness."[xi] Should we not resist bemoaning confusion? Should we not look for meaning in the complexities and contradictions of our times and acknowledge the limitations of systems? These, I think, are the two justifications for breaking order: the recognition of variety and confusion inside and outside, in program and environment, indeed, at all levels of experience; and the ultimate limitation of all orders composed by man. When circumstances defy order, order should bend or break: anomalies and uncertainties give validity to architecture.

Meaning can be enhanced by breaking the order; the exception points up the rule. A building with no "imperfect" part can have no perfect part, because contrast supports meaning. An artful discord gives vitality to architecture. You can allow for contingencies all over, but they cannot prevail all over. If order without expediency breeds formalism, expediency without order, of course, means chaos. Order must exist before it can be broken. No artist can belittle the role of order as a way of seeing a whole relevant to its own characteristics and context. "There is no work of art without a system" is Le Corbusier's dictum. . . .

Ironic convention is relevant both for the individual building and the townscape. It recognizes the real condition of our architecture and its status in our culture. Industry promotes expensive industrial and electronic research but not architectural experiments, and the Federal government diverts subsidies toward air transportation, communication, and

---

[vii]   American architect Frank Furness' (1839–1912) work on the Pennsylvania Academy of Fine Arts, Philadelphia.
[viii]   Contemporary American architect Paul Rudolph.
[ix]   English architect John Vanbrugh's (1664–1726) work on Blenheim Palace in Oxfordshire, England.
[x]   Gian Lorenzo Bernini (1598–1680), great Italian Renaissance sculptor.

[xi]   American architect Louis Kahn (1901–74).

the vast enterprises of war or, as they call it, national security, rather than toward the forces for the direct enhancement of life. The practicing architect must admit this. In simple terms, the budgets, techniques, and programs for his buildings must relate more to 1866 than 1966. Architects should accept their modest role rather than disguise it and risk what might be called an electronic expressionism, which might parallel the industrial expressionism of early Modern architecture. The architect who would accept his role as combiner of significant old clichés – valid banalities – in new contexts as his condition within a society that directs its best efforts, its big money, and its elegant technologies elsewhere, can ironically express in this indirect way a true concern for society's inverted scale of values.

I have alluded to the reasons why honky-tonk elements in our architecture and townscape are here to stay, especially in the important short-term view, and why such a fate should be acceptable. Pop Art has demonstrated that these commonplace elements are often the main source of the occasional variety and vitality of our cities, and that it is not their banality or vulgarity as elements which make for the banality or vulgarity of the whole scene, but rather their contextual relationships of space and scale.

Another significant implication from Pop Art involves method in city planning. Architects and planners who peevishly denounce the conventional townscape for its vulgarity or banality promote elaborate methods for abolishing or disguising honky-tonk elements in the existing landscape, or, for excluding them from the vocabulary of their new townscapes. But they largely fail either to enhance or to provide a substitute for the existing scene because they attempt the impossible. By attempting too much they flaunt their impotence and risk their continuing influence as supposed experts. Cannot the architect and planner, by slight adjustments to the conventional elements of the townscape, existing or proposed, promote significant effects? By modifying or adding conventional elements to still other conventional elements they can, by a twist of context, gain a maximum of effect through a minimum of means. They can make us see the same things in a different way.

Finally, standardization, like convention, can be another manifestation of the strong order. But unlike convention it has been accepted in Modern architecture as an enriching product of our tech-

nology, yet dreaded for its potential domination and brutality. But is it not standardization that is without circumstantial accommodation and without a creative use of context that is to be feared more than standardization itself? The ideas of order and circumstance, convention and context – of employing standardization in an unstandard way – apply to our continuing problem of standardization versus variety. Giedion has written of Aalto's[xii] unique "combination of standardization with irrationality so that standardization is no longer master but servant."[9] I prefer to think of Aalto's art as contradictory rather than irrational – an artful recognition of the circumstantial and the contextual and of the inevitable limits of the order of standardization.

The Obligation Toward the Difficult Whole

... Toledo [Ohio] was very beautiful.[10]

An architecture of complexity and accommodation does not forsake the whole. In fact, I have referred to a special obligation toward the whole because the whole is difficult to achieve. And I have emphasized the goal of unity rather than of simplification in an art "whose ... truth [is] in its totality."[11] It is the difficult unity through inclusion rather than the easy unity through exclusion. Gestalt psychology considers a perceptual whole the result of, and yet more than, the sum of its parts. The whole is dependent on the position, number, and inherent characteristics of the parts. A complex system in Herbert A. Simon's definition includes "a large number of parts that interact in a non-simple way."[12] The difficult whole in an architecture of complexity and contradiction includes multiplicity and diversity of elements in relationships that are inconsistent or among the weaker kinds perceptually. . . .

Inherent in an architecture of opposites is the inclusive whole. The unity of the interior of the Imatra church or the complex at Wolfsburg is achieved not through suppression or exclusion but through the dramatic inclusion of contradictory or circumstantial parts.[xiii] Aalto's architecture

---

[xii]   Finnish architect Alvar Aalto (1898–1976).
[xiii]   Two projects by Aalto: Vooksenniska church in Imatra, Finland, and the Cultural Centre, Wolfsburg, Germany.

acknowledges the difficult and subtle conditions of program, while "serene" architecture, on the other hand, works simplifications.

However, the obligation toward the whole in an architecture of complexity and contradiction does not preclude the building which is unresolved. Poets and playwrights acknowledge dilemmas without solutions. The validity of the questions and vividness of the meaning are what make their works art more than philosophy. A goal of poetry can be unity of expression over resolution of content. Contemporary sculpture is often fragmentary, and today we appreciate Michelangelo's unfinished Pietàs more than his early work, because their content is suggested, their expression more immediate, and their forms are completed beyond themselves. A building can also be more or less incompleted in the expression of its program and its form.

The Gothic cathedral, like Beauvais, for instance, of which only the enormous choir was built, is frequently unfinished in relation to its program, yet it is complete in the effect of its form because of the motival consistency of its many parts.[xiv] The complex program which is a process, continually changing and growing in time yet at each stage at some level related to a whole, should be recognized as essential at the scale of city planning. The incomplete program is valid for a complex single building as well.

Each of the fragmental twin churches on the Piazza del Popolo,[xv] however, is complete at the level of program but incomplete in the expression of form. The uniquely assymmetrically placed tower, as we have seen, inflects each building toward a greater whole outside itself. The very complex building, which in its open form is incomplete, in itself relates to Maki's "group form;" it is the antithesis of the "perfect single building"[13] or the closed pavilion. As a fragment of a greater whole in a greater context this kind of building relates again to the scope of city planning as a means of increasing the unity of the complex whole. An architecture that can simultaneously recognize contradictory levels should be able to admit the paradox of the whole fragment: the building which is a whole at one level and a fragment of a greater whole at another level.

In *God's Own Junkyard* Peter Blake has compared the chaos of commercial Main Street with the orderliness of the University of Virginia.[xvi] Besides the irrelevancy of the comparison, is not Main Street almost all right? Indeed, is not the commercial strip of a Route 66 almost all right? As I have said, our question is: what slight twist of context will make them all right? Perhaps more signs more contained. Illustrations in *God's Own Junkyard* of Times Square and roadtown are compared with illustrations of New England villages and arcadian countrysides. But the pictures in this book that are supposed to be bad are often good. The seemingly chaotic juxtapositions of honkytonk elements express an intriguing kind of vitality and validity, and they produce an unexpected approach to unity as well.

It is true that an ironic interpretation such as this results partly from the change in scale of the subject matter in photographic form and the change in context within the frames of the photographs. But in some of these compositions there is an inherent sense of unity not far from the surface. It is not the obvious or easy unity derived from the dominant binder or the motival order of simpler, less contradictory compositions, but that derived from a complex and illusive order of the difficult whole. It is the taut composition which contains contrapuntal relationships, equal combinations, inflected fragments, and acknowledged dualities. It is the unity which "maintains, but only just maintains, a control over the clashing elements which compose it. Chaos is very near; its nearness, but its avoidance, gives . . . force."[14] In the validly complex building or cityscape, the eye does not want to be too easily or too quickly satisfied in its search for unity within a whole.

Some of the vivid lessons of Pop Art, involving contradictions of scale and context, should have awakened architects from prim dreams of pure order, which, unfortunately, are imposed in the easy Gestalt unities of the urban renewal projects of establishment Modern architecture and yet, fortunately are really impossible to achieve at any great scope. And it is perhaps from the everyday landscape, vulgar and disdained, that we can draw the complex and contradictory order that is valid and vital for our architecture as an urbanistic whole.

[xiv]   Gothic cathedral in Beauvais, France.
[xv]   In Rome.

[xvi]   Peter Blake, *God's Own Junkyard: The Planned Deterioration of America's Landscape* (New York: Holt, Rinehart & Winston, 1964).

Author's Notes

1 Frank Lloyd Wright, in *An American Architecture*, ed. Edgar Kaufmann (Horizon Press, New York, 1955), p. 207.

2 Le Corbusier, *Towards a New Architecture* (Architectural Press, London, 1927), p. 31.

3 Christopher Alexander, *Notes on the Synthesis of Form* (Harvard University Press, Cambridge, 1964), p. 4.

4 August Heckscher, *The Public Happiness* (Atheneum Publishers, New York, 1962), p. 102.

5 Paul Rudolph, in *Perspecta 7, The Yale Architectural Journal* (New Haven, 1961), p. 51.

6 Kenneth Burke, *Permanence and Change* (Hermes Publications, Los Altos, 1954), p. 107.

7 Cleanth Brooks, *The Well Wrought Urn* (Harcourt, Brace and World, New York, 1947), p. 81.

8 David Jones, *Epoch and Artist* (Chilmark Press, New York, 1959).

9 Siegfried Giedion, *Space, Time and Architecture* (Harvard University Press, Cambridge, 1963), p. 565.

10 Gertrude Stein, *Gertrude Stein's America*, ed. Gilbert A. Harrison (Robert B. Luce, Washington, DC, 1965).

11 Heckscher, *Public Happiness*, p. 287.

12 Herbert A. Simon, *Proceedings of the American Philosophical Society*, 106, no. 6 (December 12, 1962), p. 468.

13 Fumihiko Maki, *Investigations in Collective Form*, Special Publication No. 2, Washington University, St Louis (1964), p. 5.

14 Heckscher, *Public Happiness*, p. 289.

41

"POSTmodernISM: A Paracritical Bibliography"

Ihab Hassan

Professor of literature, Ihab Hassan (1925–) was one of the earliest advocates of postmodernism. In the following 1971 essay, his first on the subject, he presents a listing of the elements and influences that suggest a turn from modernism to postmodernism, and does so in a particularly postmodern style, an eclectic, non-linear, virtually anarchic listing of cultural elements, along with graphic textual anomalies that have become familiar to readers of postmodern literature. In addition to the intentional playfulness of this kind of writing (versus modernist seriousness), the unmistakable implication is that inquiry (in this case, Hassan's essay) cannot systematically exhaust or enclose the cultural phenomena it seeks to understand, but must make its way nonetheless with whatever devices and insights it can muster. Yet, Hassan's postmodernism is not primarily negative, not simply a recognition of the limits of human inquiry. It is positive and ecstatic; for Hassan, postmodernism is an attempt to write the unwritable. "Truly," he remarks, "we dwell happily in the Unimaginable."

1   Change

Dionysus and Cupid are both agents of change. First, *The Bacchae*, destruction of the city, then

The Metamorphoses, mischievous variations of nature.[i] Some might say that change is violence, and violence is continuous whether it be Horror or High Camp. But sly Ovid simply declares:

> My intention is to tell of bodies changed
> To different forms; the gods, who made the
>   changes,
> Will help me – or I hope so – with a poem
> That runs from the world's beginning to our
>   own days.

To our own days, the bodies natural or politic wax and wane, *carpen perpetuam*.[ii] Something warms Galatea[iii] out of ivory; even rock turns into spiritual forms. Perhaps love is one way we experience change.

How then can we live without love of change?

Evolution has its enemies, that quiet genius Owen Barfield knows. In Unancestral Voices he calls them by name: Lucifer and Ahriman. Most often they coexist in us. Lucifer preserves the past utterly from dissolution. Ahriman destroys the past utterly for the sake of his own inventions.

[ii]   "Seize the perpetual," a play on *carpe diem* (seize the day).
[iii]   Pygmalion's beloved statue, granted life by Aphrodite.

[i]   Dionysus was a character in Euripedes' *The Bacchae*, as was Cupid, god of love, in Ovid's *Metamorphoses*. Note that this essay employs an abundance of cultural and literary references, making it impractical to annotate them all.

Ihab Hassan, "POSTmodernISM: A Paracritical Bibliography," from *Paracriticisms: Seven Speculations of the Times,* pp. 39–59. Urbana: University of Illinois Press, 1975.

a. Thus in one kind of history, chronicles of continuity, we deny real change. Even endings become part of a history of endings. From schism to paradigm; from apocalypse to archetype. Warring empires, catastrophe and famine, immense hopes, faraway names – Cheops, Hammurabi, David, Darius, Alcibiades, Hannibal, Caesar – all fall into place on numbered pages.

Yet continuities, "the glory that was Greece, the grandeur that was Rome," must prevail in Story, on a certain level of narrative abstraction, obscuring change.

b. Thus, too, in another kind of history, we reinvent continually the past. Without vision, constant revision, the Party chronicles of *Nineteen Eighty-Four*. Or individually, each man dreams his ancestors to remake himself. The Black Muslim takes on a new name, ignoring the deadly dawn raids, cries of Allah among slave traders, journeys across Africa in Arab chains.

Yet relevances must persist in Story, on a certain level of fictional selectivity, veiling change.

Behind all history, continuous or discrete, abstract or autistic, lurks the struggle of identity with death. Is history often the secret biography of historians? The recorded imagination of our own mortality?

> **Thou, silent form, dost tease us out of thought**
> **As doth eternity: Cold Pastoral.**

2   Periods

When will the Modern Period end?

Has ever a period waited so long? Renaissance? Baroque? Neo-Classical? Romantic? Victorian? Perhaps only the Dark Middle Ages.

When will Modernism cease and what comes thereafter?

What will the twenty-first century call us? and will its voice come from the same side of our graves?

Does Modernism stretch merely to stretch out our lives? Or, ductile, does it give a new sense of time? The end of periodicization? The slow arrival of simultaneity?

If change changes ever more rapidly and the future jolts us now, do men, more than ever, resist both endings and beginnings?

> **Childhood is huge and youth golden. Few recover. Critics are no exception. Like**

everyone else, they recall the literature of their youth brilliantly; they do not think it can ever tarnish.

> **"Let us consider where the great men are Who will obsess the child when he can read."**

So Delmore Schwartz wrote, naming Joyce, Eliot, Pound, Rilke, Yeats, Kafka, Mann. He could have added: Proust, Valéry, Gide, Conrad, Lawrence, Woolf, Faulkner, Hemingway, O'Neill . . .

A walker in the city of that literature will not forget. Nor will he forgive. How can contemporaries of Ellison, Pinter, or Grass dare breathe in this ancestral air? Yet it is possible that we will all remain Invisible Men until each becomes his own father.

3   Innovation

All of us devise cunning ceremonies of ancester worship. Yet there is a fable for us in the lives of two men: Proteus and Picasso, mentors of shapes. Their forms are self-transformations. They know the secret of Innovation: Motion.

> **Masters of possibility, ponder this. They used to say: the kingdom of the dead is larger than any kingdom. But the earth has now exploded. Soon the day may come when there will be more people alive than ever lived.**
>
> **When the quick are more populous than all the departed, will history reverse itself? End?**

We resist the new under the guise of judgment. "We must have standards." But standards apply only where they are applicable. This has been the problem with the Tradition of the New (Harold Rosenberg).

Standards are inevitable, and the best of these will create themselves to meet, to *create*, new occasions. Let us, therefore, admit standards. But let us also ask how many critics of literature espouse, even selectively, the new, speak of it with joyous intelligence? Taking few risks, the best known among them wait for reviewers to clear the way.

Reaction to the new has its own reasons that reason seldom acknowledges. It also has its rhetoric of dismissal.

Ihab Hassan

a. The Fad
 – "It's a passing fashion, frivolous; if we ignore it now, it will quietly go away."
 – This implies permanence as absolute value. It also implies the ability to distinguish between fashion and history without benefit of time or creative intuition. How many judgments of this kind fill the Purgatorio of Letters?
b. The Old Story
 – "It's been done before, there's nothing new in it; you can find it in Euripides, Sterne, or Whitman."
 – This implies prior acquaintance, rejection on the basis of dubious similitude. It also implies that nothing really changes. Therefore, why unsettle things, re-quire a fresh response?
c. The Safe Version
 – "Yes, it seems new, but in the same genre, I prefer Duchamp; he really did it better."
 – This implies a certain inwardness with innovation. The entrance fee has been paid, once and forever. Without seeming in the least Philistine, one can disdain the intrusions of the present.
d. The Newspeak of Art
 – "The avant-garde is just the new academicism."
 – This may imply that art which seems conventional can be more genuinely innovative: this is sometimes true. It may also imply mere irritation: the oxymoron as means of discreditation.

About true innovation we can have no easy preconceptions. Prediction is mere extrapolation, the cool whisper of RAND.[iv] But prophecy is akin to madness, or the creative imagination; its path, seldom linear, breaks, turns, disappears in mutations or quantum jumps.

Therefore, we cannot expect the avant-garde of past, present, and future to obey the same logic, assume the same forms. For instance, the new avant-garde need not have a historical consciousness, express recognizable values, or endorse radical politics. It need not shock, surprise, protest. The new avant-garde may not be an "avant-garde" at all: simply an agent of yet-invisible change.

Note: Consult Renato Poggioli, The Theory of the Avant-Garde (Cambridge, Mass., 1968).

iv Presumably a reference to the Rand Corporation and its futuristic technological predictions.

And yet everything I have said here can lend itself to abuse. The rage for change can be a form of self-hatred or spite. Look deep into any revolutionary.

Look also into extremes of the recent avant-garde. Vito Hannibal Acconci creates his "body sculptures" by biting, mutilating, himself in public. Rudolph Schwarzkogler slowly amputates his penis, and expires. In a world no longer linear, we must wonder: which way is forward? which way is life? Action often acquires the logic of the boomerang.

4 Distinctions

The change in Modernism may be called Postmodernism. Viewing the former with later eyes, we begin to discern fringe figures closer to us now than the great Moderns who "will obsess the child" someday.

Thus the classic text of Modernism is Edmund Wilson's *Axel's Castle: A Study in the Imaginative Literature of 1870–1930* (1931). Contents: Symbolism, Yeats, Valéry, Eliot, Proust, Joyce, Stein.

Thus, forty years later, my alternate view, *The Dismemberment of Orpheus: Toward a Postmodern Literature* (1971). Contents: Sade, 'Pataphysics to Surrealism, Hemingway, Kafka, Existentialism to Aliterature, Genet, Beckett.

Erratum: Gertrude Stein should have appeared in the latter work, for she contributed to both Modernism and Postmodernism.

But without a doubt, the crucial text is

If we can arbitrarily state that literary Modernism includes certain works between Jarry's *Ubu Roi* (1896) and Joyce's *Finnegans Wake* (1939), where will we arbitrarily say that Postmodernism begins? A year earlier than the *Wake*? With Sartre's *La*

Nausée (1938) or Beckett's *Murphy* (1938)? In any case Postmodernism includes works by writers as different as Barth, arthelme, ecker, eckett, ense, lanchot, orges, recht, urroughs, utor.

> *Query*: But is not *Ubu Roi* itself as Postmodern as it is Modern?

5 Critics

The assumptions of Modernism elaborated by formalist and mythopoeic critics especially, by the intellectual culture of the first half of the century as a whole, still define the dominant perspective on the study of literature.

> Exception: Karl Shapiro's *Beyond Criticism* (1953), *In Defence of Ignorance* (1960). Too "cranky" and "cantankerous" for academic *biens pensants*?

In England as in America, the known critics, different as they may seem in age, persuasion, or distinction, share the broad Modernist view: Blackmur, Brooks, Connolly, Empson, Frye, Howe, Kazin, Kermode, Leavis, Levin, Pritchett, Ransom, Rahv, Richards, Schorer, Tate, Trilling, Warren, Wellek, Wilson, Winters, etc.

No doubt there are many passages in the writings of these critics – of Leavis, say, or of Wilson – which will enlighten minds in every age. Yet it was Herbert Read[v] who possessed the most active sympathy for the avant-garde. His generosity of intuition enabled him to sponsor the new, rarely embracing the trivial. He engaged the Postmodern spirit in his anarchic affinities, in his concern for the prevalence of suffering, in his sensuous apprehension of renewed being. He cried: behold the Child! To him, education through art meant a salutation to Eros. Believing that the imagination serves the purpose of moral good, Read hoped to implicate art into existence so fully that their common substance became as simple, as necessary, as bread and water. This is a sacramental hope, still alive though mute in our midst, which recalls Tolstoy's *What Is Art*? I can hardly think of another critic, younger even by several decades, who might have composed that extraordinary romance, *The Green Child*.[vi]

The culture of literary criticism is still ruled by Modernist assumptions. This is particularly true within the academic profession, excepting certain linguistic, structuralist, and hermeneutic schools. But it is also true within the more noisy culture of our media. *The New York Review of Books*, *Time* (the literary sections), and *The New York Times Book Review* share a certain aspiration to wit or liveliness, to intelligence really, concealing resistance to the new. All the more skeptical in periods of excess, the culture of the Logos insists on old orders in clever or current guises, and, with the means of communication at hand, inhibits and restrains.

> *Self-Admonition*: Beware of glib condemnations of the media. They are playing a national role as bold, as crucial, as the Supreme Court played in the Fifties. Willful and arbitrary as they may be in their creation of public images – which pre-empt our selves – they are still custodians of some collective sanity. Note, too, the rising quality of the very publications you cited. [This was written in 1971.][vii]

6 Bibliography

Here is a curious chronology of some Postmodern criticism:

1. George Steiner, "The Retreat from the Word," *Kenyon Review*, 23 (Spring 1961). See also his *Language and Silence* (New York, 1967), and *Extraterritorial* (New York, 1971).
2. Ihab Hassan, "The Dismemberment of Orpheus," *American Scholar*, 23 (Summer 1963). See also his *Literature of Silence* (New York, 1967).
3. Hugh Kenner, "Art in a Closed Field," in *Learners and Discerners*, ed. Robert Scholes (Charlottesville, Va., 1964). See also his *Samuel Beckett* (New York, 1961; Berkeley and Los Angeles, 1968), and *The Counterfeiters* (Bloomington, Ind., 1968).
4. Leslie Fiedler, "The New Mutants," *Partisan Review*, 32 (Fall 1965). See also his "The Children's Hour; or, The Return of the Vanishing Longfellow," in *Liberations*, ed. Ihab Hassan (Middletown, Conn., 1971), and *Collected Essays* (New York, 1971).
5. Susan Sontag, "The Aesthetics of Silence," *Aspen*, nos. 5 & 6 (1967). See also her *Against*

---

[v] (1893–1968), English poet and critic.
[vi] A work of Herbert Read's.

[vii] Author's addition.

Ihab Hassan

Interpretation (New York, 1966), and *Styles of Radical Will* (New York, 1969).

6 Richard Poirier, "The Literature of Waste," *New Republic*, 20 May 1967. See also his "The Politics of Self-Parody," *Partisan Review*, 35 (Summer 1968), and *The Performing Self* (New York, 1971).

7 John Barth, "The Literature of Exhaustion," *Atlantic Monthly*, August 1967. See also his *Lost in the Funhouse* (New York, 1968).

And here are some leitmotifs of that criticism: the literary act in quest and question of itself; self-subversion or self-transcendence of forms; popular mutations; languages of silence.

7 ReVisions

A revision of Modernism is slowly taking place, and this is another evidence of Postmodernism. In *The Performing Self*, Richard Poirier tries to mediate between these two movements. We need to recall the doctrines of formalist criticism, the canons of classroom and quarterly in the last three decades, to savor such statements:

> Three of the great and much used texts of twentieth-century criticism, *Moby Dick, Ulysses, The Waste Land*, are written in mockery of system, written against any effort to harmonize discordant elements, against any mythic or metaphoric scheme.... But while this form of the literary imagination is radical in its essentially parodistic treatment of systems, its radicalism is in the interest of essentially conservative feelings.
>
> . . .
>
> The most complicated examples of twentieth-century literature, like *Ulysses* and *The Waste Land*, the end of which seems parodied by the end of *Giles* [*Goat-Boy* by Barth], are more than contemptuous of their own formal and stylistic elaborateness.

Certainly some profound philosophic minds of our century have concerned themselves with the disease of verbal systems: Heidegger, Wittgenstein, Sartre. And later writers as different as John Cage, Norman O. Brown, and Elie Wiesel have listened intently to the sounds of silence in art or politics, sex, morality, or religion. In this context the statements of Poirier do not merely display a revisionist

will; they strain toward an aesthetic of Postmodernism.

We are still some way from attaining such an aesthetic; nor is it clear that Postmodern art gives high priority to that end. Perhaps we can start by revisioning Modernism as well as revising the pieties we have inherited about it. In *Continuities* Frank Kermode cautiously attempts that task. A critic of great civility, he discriminates well between types of modernism – what he calls "palaeo- and neo-modern" correspond perhaps to Modern and Postmodern – and takes note of the new "anti-art," which he rightly traces back to Duchamp. But his preference for continuities tempts him to assimilate current to past things. Kermode, for instance, writes: "Aleatory art is accordingly, for all its novelty, an extension of past art, indeed the hypertrophy of one aspect of that art." Does not this statement close more possibilities than it opens? There is another perspective of things that Goethe described: "The most important thing is always the contemporary element, because it is most purely reflected in ourselves, as we are in it." I think that we will not grasp the cultural experience of our moment if we insist that the new arts are "marginal developments of older modernism," or that distinctions between "art" and "joke" are crucial to any future aesthetic.

Whether we tend to revalue Modernism in terms of Postmodernism (Poirier) or to reverse that procedure (Kermode), we will end by doing something of both since relations, analogies, enable our thought. Modernism does not suddenly cease so that Postmodernism may begin: they now *coexist*. New lines emerge from the past because our eyes every morning open anew. In a certain frame of mind, Michelangelo or Rembrandt, Goethe or Hegel, Nietzsche or Rilke, can reveal to us something about Postmodernism, as Erich Heller incidentally shows. Consider this marvelous passage from *The Artist's Journey to the Interior*:

> Michelangelo spent the whole of his last working day, six days before his death, trying to finish the Pietà which is known as the "Pietà Rondanini." He did not succeed. Perhaps it lies in the nature of stone that he had to leave unfinished what Rembrandt completed in paint: the employment of the material in the service of its own negation. For this sculpture seems to intimate that its maker was in the end determined to use only as much marble as was necessary to show that matter did not matter; what alone mattered was the pure inward spirit.

414

Here Michelangelo envisions, past any struggle with the obdurate material of existence, a state of gnostic consciousness to which we may be tending. Yet can we justifiably call him Postmodern?

Where Modern and Postmodern May Meet: or, Make Your Own List

1 **Blake, Sade, Lautréamont, Rimbaud, Mallarmé,Whitman, etc.**
2 **daDaDA**
3 **SURrealism**
4 **KAFKA**
5 **FinnegansWake**
6 **The Cantos**
7 **???**

8   Modernism

This is no place to offer a comprehensive definition of Modernism. From Apollinaire and Arp to Valéry, Woolf, and Yeats – I seem to miss the letters X and Z – runs the alphabet of authors who have delivered themselves memorably on the subject; and the weighty work of Richard Ellmann and Charles Feidelson, Jr., *The Modern Tradition*, still stands as the best compendium of that "large spiritual enterprise including philosophic, social, and scientific thought, and aesthetic and literary theories and manifestoes, as well as poems, novels, dramas."

Expectations of agreement, let alone of definition, seem superlatively naïve. This is true among stately and distinguished minds, not only rowdy critical tempers. Here, for instance, is Lionel Trilling, "On the Modern Element in Modern Literature":

> I can identify it by calling it the disenchantment of our culture with culture itself . . . the bitter line of hostility to civilization that runs through it [modern literature] . . . I venture to say that the idea of losing oneself up to the point of self-destruction, of surrendering oneself to experience without regard to self-interest or conventional morality, of escaping wholly from the societal bonds, is an "element" somewhere in the mind of every modern person.

To this, Harry Levin counters in "What Was Modernism?":[1]

> Insofar as we are still moderns, I would argue, we are the children of Humanism and the En-

lightenment. To identify and isolate the forces of unreason, in a certain sense, has been a triumph for the intellect. In another sense, it has reinforced that anti-intellectual undercurrent which, as it comes to the surface, I would prefer to call post-modern.

Yet the controversy of Modernism has still wider scope, as Monroe K. Spears, in *Dionysus and the City*, with bias beneath his Apollonian lucidity, shows. Released as energy from the contradictions of history, Modernism makes contradiction its own.

For my purpose, let Modernism stand for X: a window on human madness, the shield of Perseus against which Medusa glances, the dream of some frowning, scholarly muse. I offer, instead, some rubrics and spaces. Let readers fill them with their own queries or grimaces. We value what we choose.

a. *Urbanism*: Nature put in doubt, from Baudelaire's "*cité fourmillante*"[viii] to Proust's Paris, Joyce's Dublin, Eliot's London, Dos Passos' New York, Döblin's Berlin. It is not a question of locale but of presence. The sanatorium of *The Magic Mountain* and the village of *The Castle* are still enclosed in an urban spiritual space. Exceptions, Faulkner's Yoknapatawpha or Lawrence's Midlands, recognize the City as pervasive threat.

_____
_____
_____

b. *Technologism*: City and Machine make and remake one another. Extension, diffusion, and alienation of the human will. Yet technology does not feature simply as a theme of Modernism; it is also a form of its artistic struggle. Witness Cubism, Futurism, Dadaism. Other *reactions* to technology: primitivism, the occult, Bergsonian time, the dissociation of sensibility, etc. (See Wylie Sypher, *Literature and Technology*.)

_____
_____
_____

c. "*Dehumanization*": Ortega y Gasset really means Elitism, Irony, and Abstraction (*The Dehumanization of Art*). Style takes over; let life

---

viii   Swarming city.

and the masses fend for themselves. "Poetry has become the higher algebra of metaphor." Instead of Vitruvian man, Leonardo's famous image of the human measure, we have Picasso's beings splintered on many planes. Not less human, just another idea of man.

Elitism:	Aristocratic or crypto-fascist: Rilke, Proust, Yeats, Eliot, Lawrence, Pound, d'Annunzio, Wyndham Lewis, etc.
Irony:	Play, complexity, formalism. The aloofness of art but also sly hints of its radical incompleteness. *Dr Faustus* and *Confessions of Felix Krull*. Irony as awareness of Non-being.
Abstraction:	Impersonality, sophistical simplicity, reduction and construction, time decomposed or spatialized. Thus Mondrian on Reductionism: "To create pure reality plastically, it is necessary to reduce natural forms to the *constant elements* of form and natural colour to *primary colour*." Gabo on Constructivism: "It has revealed a universal law that the elements of a visual art such as lines, colours, shapes, possess their own forces of expression, independent of any association with the external aspects of the world..." The literary equivalent of these ideas may be "spatial time." (See Joseph Frank, "Spatial Form in Modern Literature," in *The Widening Gyre*.)
An Addendum:	There is more to "dehumanization" than "another idea of man," there is also an incipient revulsion against
An Addendum (cont.):	the human, sometimes a renewal of the sense of the superhuman. Rilke's "Angels." Lawrence's "Fish":

> And my heart accused itself
> Thinking: I am not the measure of creation
> This is beyond me, this fish. His God stands outside my God.

d. *Primitivism:* The archetypes behind abstraction, beneath ironic civilization. An African mask, a beast slouching toward Bethlehem. Structure as ritual or myth, metaphors from the collective dream of mankind. Cunning palimpsests of literary time and space, knowing palingenesis of literary souls. Also Dionysus and the violent return of the repressed. (See Northrop Frye, *The Modern Century*.)

---

e. *Eroticism:* All literature is erotic but Modernist sex scratches the skin from within. It is not merely the liberation of the libido, a new language of anger or desire; love now becomes an intimate of disease. Sadomasochism, solipsism, nihilism, anomie. Consciousness seeks desperately to discharge itself in the world. A new and darker stage in the struggle between Eros and Thanatos.[ix] (See Lionel Trilling, "The Fate of Pleasure," in *Beyond Culture*.)

---

f. *Antinomianism:* Beyond law, dwelling in paradox. Also discontinuity, alienation, *non serviam!*[x] The pride of art, of the self, defining the conditions of its own grace. Iconoclasm, schism, excess. Beyond antinomianism, toward apocalypse. Therefore, decadence and renovation. (See Nathan A. Scott, Jr., *The Broken Center*.)

[ix] *Eros* and *Thanatos* are Freud's Greek terms for the opposed instincts of Love and Death, respectively.
[x] I will not serve.

g. *Experimentalism:* Innovation, dissociation, the brilliance of change in all its aesthetic shapes. New languages, new concepts of order. Also, the Word beginning to put its miracle to question in the midst of an artistic miracle. Poem, novel, or play henceforth can never really bear the same name.

In those seven rubrics, I seek not so much to define Modernism as to carry certain elements which I consider crucial, carry them forward toward Postmodernism.

9   The Unimaginable

The unimaginable lies somewhere between the Kingdom of Complacence and the Sea of Hysteria. It balks all geographies; bilks the spirit of the traveler who passes unwittingly through its space-realm; boggles time. Yet anyone who can return from it to tell his tale may also know how to spell the destiny of man.

I know the near-infinite resources of man, and that his imagination may still serve as the teleological organ of his evolution. Yet I am possessed by the feeling that in the next few decades, certainly within half a century, the earth and all that inhabits it may be wholly other, perhaps ravaged, perhaps on the way to some strange utopia indistinguishable from nightmare. I have no language to articulate this feeling with conviction, nor imagination to conceive this special destiny. To live from hour to hour seems as maudlin as to invoke every hour the Last Things. In this feeling I find that I am not alone.

The litany of our disasters is all too familiar, and we recite it in the name of that unholy trinity, Population, Pollution, Power (read genocide), hoping to appease our furies, turn our fate inside out. But soon our minds lull themselves to sleep again on this song of abstractions, and a few freak out. The deathly dreariness of politics brings us ever closer to death. Neither is the alteration of human consciousness at hand. And the great promise of technology? Which technology? Fuller's? Skinner's? Dr Strange-

love's and Dr No's? Engineers of liberation or of control? The promise is conditional on everything that we are, in this our ambiguous state.

Truly, we dwell happily in the Unimaginable. We also dwell at our task: Literature. I could learn to do pushups in a prison cell, but I cannot bring myself to "study literature" as if the earth were still in the orbit of our imagination. I hope this is Hope.

10   Postmodernism

Postmodernism may be a response, direct or oblique, to the Unimaginable that Modernism glimpsed only in its most prophetic moments. Certainly it is not the Dehumanization of the Arts that concerns us now; it is rather the Denaturalization of the Planet and the End of Man. We are, I believe, inhabitants of another Time and another Space, and we no longer know what response is adequate to our reality. In a sense we have all learned to become minimalists – of that time and space we can call our own – though the globe may have become our village. That is why it seems bootless to compare Modern with Postmodern artists, range "masters" against "epigones." The latter are closer to "zero in the bone," to silence or exhaustion, and the best of them brilliantly display the resources of the void. Thus the verbal omnipotence of Joyce yields to the impotence of Beckett, heir and peer, no less genuine, only more austere. Yet moving into the void, these artists sometimes pass to the other side of silence. The consummation of their art is a work that, remaining art, pretends to abolish itself (Beckett, Tinguely, Robert Morris), or else to become indistinguishable from life (Cage, Rauschenberg, Mailer). Duchamp coolly pointed the way.

Nihilism is a word we often use, when we use it unhistorically, to designate values we dislike. It is sometimes applied to the children of Marcel Duchamp.

When John Cage, in "HPSCHD" for instance, insists on Quantity rather than Quality, he does not surrender to nihilism – far, far from it – he requires:

– affluence and permission of being, generosity

– discovery in multitude, confusion of prior judgment

     – mutation of perception, of consciousness, through randomness and diversity

     Cage knows how to praise Duchamp: "The rest of them were artists. Duchamp collects dust."

I have not defined Modernism; I can define Postmodernism less. No doubt, the more we ponder, the more we will need to qualify all we say. Perhaps elisions may serve to qualify these notes.

Modernist Rubrics	*Postmodernist Notes*
a. *Urbanism*	– The City and also the Global Village (McLuhan) and Spaceship Earth (Fuller). The City as Cosmos. Therefore, Science Fiction.
	– Meanwhile, the world breaks up into untold blocs, nations, tribes, clans, parties, languages, sects. Anarchy and fragmentation everywhere. A new diversity or prelude to world totalitarianism? Or to world unification?
	– Nature recovered partly in ecological activism, the green revolution, urban renewal, health foods, etc.
	– Meanwhile, Dionysus has entered the City: prison riots, urban crime, pornography, etc. Worse, the City as holocaust or death camp: Hiroshima, Dresden, Auschwitz.
b. *Technologism*	– Runaway technology, from genetic engineering and thought control to the conquest of space. Futurists and Technophiles vs. Arcadians and Luddites.
	– All the physical materials of the arts changed. New media, art forms. The problematics of the book as artifact.
	– Boundless dispersal by media. The sensuous object becoming "anxious," then "de-defined" (Rosenberg). Matter disappearing into a concept?
	– The computer as substitute consciousness, or as extension of consciousness? Will it prove tautological, increasing reliance on prior orders? Or will it help to create novel forms?
c. *"Dehumanization"*	– Antielitism, antiauthoritarianism. Diffusion of the ego. Participation. Art becomes communal, optional, anarchic. Acceptance.
	– At the same time, Irony becomes radical, self-consuming play, entropy of meaning. Also comedy of the absurd, black humor, insane parody and slapstick, Camp. Negation.
	– Abstraction taken to the limit and coming back as New Concreteness: the found object, the signed Brillo box or soup can, the nonfiction novel, the novel as history. The range is from Concept Art (abstract) to Environmental Art (concrete).
	– Warhol's wanting to be a machine, Cioran's ambivalent temptation to exist. Humanism yields to infrahumanism or posthumanism. But yields also to a cosmic humanism, as in Science Fiction, as in Fuller, Castaneda, N. O. Brown, Ursula LeGuin.

"Dehumanization," both in Modernism and Postmodernism, finally means the end of the old Realism. Increasingly, Illusionism takes its place, not only in art but also in life. The media contribute egregiously to this

process in Postmodern society. In *Act and the Actor Making the Self*, Harold Rosenberg says: "History has been turned inside out; writing takes place in advance of its occurrence, and every statesman is an author in embryo." Thus the Illusionism of politics matches that of Pop Art or Neo-Realism. An Event need never have happened.

The end of the old Realism also affects the sense of the Self. Thus "Dehumanization," both in Modernism and Postmodernism, requires a revision of the literary and authorial Self evidenced:

in Modernism – by doctrines of Surrealism (Breton), by ideas of impersonality in art (the masks of Yeats, the tradition of Eliot), by modes of hyperpersonality (the stream of consciousness of Joyce, Proust, Faulkner, Nin, or the allotropic ego of Lawrence). (See Robert Langbaum, *The Modern Spirit*, 164–84.)

In Postmodernism – by authorial self-reflexiveness, by the fusion of fact and fiction (Capote, Wolfe, Mailer), phenomenology (Husserl, Sartre, Merleau-Ponty), Beckett's fiction of consciousness, varieties of the *nouveau roman* (Sarraute, Butor, Robbe-Grillet), and the linguistic novel of *Tel Quel* (Sollers, Thibaudeau). (See Vivian Mercier, *The New Novel*, 3–42.)

d. Primitivism	– Away from the mythic, toward the existential. Beat and Hip. Energy and spontaneity of the White Negro (Mailer). – Later, the post-existential ethos, psychedelics (Leary), the Dionysian ego (Brown), Pranksters (Kesey), madness (Laing), animism and magic (Castaneda). – The Hippie movement. Woodstock, rock music and poetry, communes. The culture of *The Whole Earth Catalog*. Pop. – The primitive Jesus. The new Rousseauism and Deweyism: Human
e. Eroticism	Potential movement, Open Classroom (Goodman, Rogers, Leonard). – Beyond the trial of *Lady Chatterley's Lover*. The repeal of censorship. Grove Press and *Evergreen Review*. – The new sexuality, from Reichian orgasm to polymorphous perversity and Esalen body consciousness. – The homosexual novel (Burroughs, Vidal, Selby, Rechy). From feminism to lesbianism. Toward a new androgyny? – Camp and comic pornography. Sex as solipsist play.
f. Antinomianism	– The Counter Cultures, political and otherwise. Free Speech Movement, S.D.S., Weathermen, Church Militants, Women's Lib, J.D.L., Black, Red, and Chicano Power, etc. Rebellion and Reaction! – Beyond alienation from the whole culture, acceptance of discreteness and discontinuity. Evolution of radical empiricism in art as in politics or morality. – Counter Western "ways" or metaphysics, Zen, Buddhism, Hinduism. But also Western mysticism, transcendentalism, witchcraft, the occult. (See "Primitivism" above.) – The widespread cult of apocalyptism, sometimes as renovation, sometimes as annihilation – often both.
g. Experimentalism	– Open, discontinuous, improvisational, indeterminate, or aleatory structures.

End-game strategies and neosurrealist modes. Both reductive, minimalist forms and lavish extravaganzas. In general, anti-formalism. (See Calvin Tomkins, *The Bride and the Bachelors*.)

– Simultaneism. Now. The impermanence of art (scupture made of dry ice or a hole in Central Park filled with earth), the transcience of man. Absurd time.

– Fantasy, play, humor, happening, parody, "dreck" (Barthelme). Also, increasing self-reflexiveness. (See Irony under "Dehumanization" above.)

– Intermedia, the fusion of forms, the confusion of realms. An end to traditional aesthetics focused on the "beauty" or "uniqueness" of the art work? Against interpretation (Sontag).

In *Man's Rage for Chaos*, Morse Peckham argues "that art is a disjunctive category, established by convention, and that art is not a category of perceptual fields, but of role-playing". And in *The Art of Time*, Michael Kirby says: "Traditional aesthetics asks a particular hermetic attitude or state of mind that concentrates on the sensory perception of the work ... [Postmodern] aesthetics makes use of no special attitude or set, and art is viewed just as anything else in life." When art is viewed like "anything else in life," Fantasy is loosened from its "objective correlatives"; Fantasy becomes supreme.

Is this why Postmodern art, viewed in a Modernist perspective, creates more anxiety than it appeases? Or is the tendency toward a new gnosticism?

11 Alternatives

The reader, no doubt, will want to judge for himself how much Modernism permeates the present and how much the latter contains elements of a new reality. The judgment is not always made rationally; self-love and the fear of dissolution may enter into it as much as the conflict of literary generations. Yet it is already possible to note that whereas Modernism – excepting Dada and Surrealism – created its own forms of artistic Authority precisely because the center no longer held, Postmodernism has tended toward artistic Anarchy in deeper complicity with things falling apart – or has tended toward Pop.

Speculating further, we may say that the Authority of Modernism – artistic, cultural, personal – rests on intense, elitist, self-generated orders in times of crisis, of which the Hemingway Code is perhaps the starkest exemplar, and Eliot's Tradition or Yeats's Ceremony is a more devious kind. Such elitist orders, perhaps the last of the world's Eleusinian mysteries,[xi] may no longer have a place amongst us, threatened as we are, at the same instant, by extermination and totalitarianism.

Yet is the Anarchy or Pop of Postmodernism, or its Fantasy, a deeper response, somehow more inward with destiny? Though my sympathies are in the present, I cannot believe this to be entirely so. True, there is enhancement of life in certain anarchies of the spirit, in humor and play, in love released and freedom of the imagination to overreach itself, in a cosmic consciousness of variousness as of unity. I recognize these as values intended by Postmodern art, and see the latter as closer, not only in time, but even more in tenor, to the transformation of hope itself. Still, I wonder if any art can help to engender the motives we must now acquire; or if we can long continue to value an art that fails us in such endeavor.

[xi] A mystery cult centered in the ancient Greek City of Eleusis.

Author's Note

1 More accurately, the quotation appears in a note preceding the essay. See Harry Levin, *Refractions* (New York: 1966), 271–3.

42

From *Symbolic Exchange and Death*

Jean Baudrillard

Controversial sociologist Jean Baudrillard (1929–) has produced a unique reflection on contemporary culture, indebted to Marx, to structuralism, and to Marshall McLuhan's work on electronic media. Having earlier applied a Marxist analysis to the use of symbols in capitalist mass culture, Baudrillard came to regard Marxism itself as such a symbol, or ideology, produced by modern culture. The modern image of representation as rooted in production is evident in the Marxist distinction between the epiphenomenal "superstructure" (culture, ideology, the "symbolic") and the fundamental reality of the "infrastructure" (economy, or material production). But an analysis unprejudiced by this view reveals that in contemporary culture representation or the symbolic is primary. Like a number of writers associated with Pop Art and Camp literature, Baudrillard came to regard his formerly oppositionist views of mass culture as untenable. In perhaps his most pivotal book, *Symbolic Exchange and Death* (1976), he argues that the culture of electronic media replaces earlier senses of reality with a new "hyperreality."

The Structural Revolution of Value

Saussure located two dimensions to the exchange of terms of the *langue*, which he assimilated to money. A given coin must be exchangeable against a real good of some value, while on the other hand it must be possible to relate it to all the other terms in the monetary system. More and more, Saussure reserves the term *value* for this second aspect of the system: every term can be related to every other, their *relativity*, internal to the system and constituted by binary oppositions. This definition is opposed to the other possible definition of value: the relation of every term to what it designates, of each signifier to its signified, like the relation of every coin with what it can be exchanged against. The first aspect corresponds to the structural dimension of language, the second to its functional dimension. Each dimension is separate but linked, which is to say that they mesh and cohere. This coherence is characteristic of the 'classical' configuration of the linguistic sign, under the rule of the commodity law of value, where designation always appears as the finality of the structural operation of the *langue*. The parallel between this 'classical' stage of signification and the mechanics of value in material production is absolute, as in Marx's analysis: use-value plays the role of the horizon and finality of the system of exchange-values. The first qualifies the concrete operation of the commodity in consumption (a moment parallel to designation in the sign), the second relates to the exchangeability of any commodity for any other under the law of equivalence (a moment parallel to the structural organisation of the sign). Both are dialectically linked throughout Marx's analyses and define a rational configuration of production, governed by political economy.

Jean Baudrillard, from *Symbolic Exchange and Death* (trans. Iain H. Grant), from chapter 1 (pp. 6–12) and from chapter 2 (pp. 50, 55–61, and 70–6). London: Sage Publications, 1993.

A revolution has put an end to this 'classical' economics of value, a revolution of value itself, which carries value beyond its commodity form into its radical form.

This revolution consists in the dislocation of the two aspects of the law of value, which were thought to be coherent and eternally bound as if by a natural law. *Referential value is annihilated, giving the structural play of value the upper hand.* The structural dimension becomes autonomous by excluding the referential dimension, and is instituted upon the death of reference. The systems of reference for production, signification, the affect, substance and history, all this equivalence to a 'real' content, loading the sign with the burden of 'utility', with gravity – its form of representative equivalence – all this is over with. Now the other stage of value has the upper hand, a total relativity, general commutation, combination and simulation – simulation, in the sense that, from now on, signs are exchanged against each other rather than against the real (it is not that they just happen to be exchanged against each other, they do so *on condition* that they are no longer exchanged against the real). The emancipation of the sign: remove this 'archaic' obligation to designate something and it finally becomes free, indifferent and totally indeterminate, in the structural or combinatory play which succeds the previous rule of determinate equivalence. The same operation takes place at the level of labour power and the production process: the annihilation of any goal as regards the contents of production allows the latter to function as a code, and the monetary sign, for example, to escape into infinite speculation, beyond all reference to a real of production, or even to a gold-standard. The flotation of money and signs, the flotation of 'needs' and ends of production, the flotation of labour itself – the commutability of every term is accompanied by speculation and a limitless inflation (and we really have *total liberty* – no duties, disaffection and general disenchantment; but this remains a magic, a sort of magical obligation which keeps the sign chained up to the real, capital has freed signs from this 'naïvety' in order to deliver them into pure circulation). Neither Saussure nor Marx had any presentiment of all this: they were still in the golden age of the dialectic of the sign and the real, which is at the same time the 'classical' period of capital and value. Their dialectic is in shreds, and the real has died of the shock of value acquiring this fantastic autonomy. Determinacy is dead, indeterminacy holds sway. There has been an extermination (in the literal sense of the word) of the real of production and the real of signification.[1]

I indicated this structural revolution of the law of value in the term 'political economy of the sign'. This term, however, can only be regarded as makeshift, for the following reasons:

1 Does this remain a political-economic question? Yes, in that it is always a question of value and the law of value. However, the mutation that affects it is so profound and so decisive, the content of political economy so thoroughly changed, indeed annihilated, that the term is nothing more than an allusion. Moreover, it is precisely *political* to the extent that it is always the *destruction* of social relations governed by the relevant value. For a long time, however, it has been a matter of something entirely different from economics.

2 The term 'sign' has itself only an allusive value. Since the structural law of value affects signification as much as it does everything else, its form is not that of the sign in general, but that of a certain organisation which is that of the code. The code only governs certain signs however. Just as the commodity law of value does not, at a given moment, signify just any determinant instance of material production, neither, conversely, does the structural law of value signify any pre-eminence of the sign whatever. This illusion derives from the fact that Marx developed the one in the shadow of the commodity, while Saussure developed the other in the shadow of the linguistic sign. But this illusion must be shattered. The commodity law of value is a law of equivalences, and this law operates throughout every sphere: it equally designates the equivalence in the configuration of the sign, where one signifier and one signified facilitate the regulated exchange of a referential content (the other parallel modality being the linearity of the signifier, contemporaneous with the linear and cumulative time of production).

The classical law of value then operates simultaneously in every instance (language, production, etc.), despite these latter remaining distinct according to their sphere of reference.

Conversely, the structural law of value signifies the indeterminacy of every sphere in relation to every other, and to their proper content (also therefore the passage from the *determinant* sphere of signs to the *indeterminacy* of the code). To say that the sphere of material production and that of signs exchange their respective contents is still too wide of the mark: they literally disappear as such and lose their specificity along with their determinacy, to the benefit of a form of value, of a much more general assemblage, where designation and production are annihilated.

The 'political economy of the sign' was also consequent upon an extension of the commodity law of value and its confirmation at the level of signs, whereas the structural configuration of value simply and simultaneously puts an end to the regimes of production, political economy, representation and signs. With the code, all this collapses into simulation. Strictly speaking, neither the 'classical' economy nor the political economy of the sign ceases to exist: they lead a secondary existence, becoming a sort of phantom principle of dissuasion.

The end of labour. The end of production. The end of political economy. The end of the signifier/signified dialectic which facilitates the accumulation of knowledge and meaning, the linear syntagma of cumulative discourse. And at the same time, the end of the exchange-value/use-value dialectic which is the only thing that makes accumulation and social production possible. The end of the linear dimension of discourse. The end of the linear dimension of the commodity. The end of the classical era of the sign. The end of the era of production.

It is not *the* revolution which puts an end to all this, it is *capital itself* which abolishes the determination of the social according to the means of production, substitutes the structural form for the commodity form of value, and currently controls every aspect of the system's strategy.

This historical and social mutation is legible at every level. In this way the era of simulation is announced everywhere by the commutability of formerly contradictory or dialectically opposed terms. Everywhere we see the same 'genesis of simulacra': the commutability of the beautiful and the ugly in fashion, of the left and the right in politics, of the true and the false in every media message, the useful and the useless at the level of objects, nature and culture at every level of signification. All the great humanist criteria of value, the whole civilisation of moral, aesthetic and practical judgement are effaced in our system of images and signs. Everything becomes undecidable, the characteristic effect of the domination of the code, which everywhere rests on the principle of neutralisation, of indifference.[2] This is the generalised brothel of capital, a brothel not for prostitution, but for substitution and commutation.

This process, which has for a long time been at work in culture, art, politics, and even in sexuality (in the so-called 'superstructural' domains), today affects the economy itself, the whole so-called 'infrastructural' field. Here the same indeterminacy holds sway. And, of course, with the loss of determination of the economic, we also lose any possibility of conceiving it as the determinant agency.

Since for two centuries historical determination has been built up around the economic (since Marx in any case), it is there that it is important to grasp the interruption of the code.

The End of Production

We are at the end of production. In the West, this form coincides with the proclamation of the commodity law of value, that is to say, with the reign of political economy. First, nothing is *produced*, strictly speaking: everything is *deduced*, from the grace (God) or beneficence (nature) of an agency which releases or withholds its riches. Value emanates from the reign of divine or natural qualities (which for us have become retrospectively confused). The Physiocrats still saw the cycles of land and labour in this way, as having no value of their own.[i] We may wonder, then, whether there is a genuine *law* of value, since this law is *dispatch* without attaining rational expression. Its form cannot be separated from the inexhaustible referential substance to which it is bound. If there is a law here, it is, in contrast to the commodity law, a *natural* law of value.

A mutation shakes this edifice of a natural distribution or dispensing of wealth as soon as value is *produced*, as its reference becomes labour, and its law of equivalence is generalised to every type of labour. Value is now assigned to the distinct and rational operation of human (social) labour. It is measurable, and, in consequence, so is surplus-value.

The critique of political economy begins with social production or the mode of production as its reference. The concept of production alone allows us, by means of an analysis of that unique commodity called labour power, to extract a *surplus* (a surplus-value) which controls the rational dynamics of capital as well as its beyond, the revolution.

Today everything has changed again. Production, the commodity form, labour power, equiva-

---

[i]   The Physiocrats were an eighteenth-century school of economic thinkers.

lence and surplus-value, which together formed the outline of a quantitative, material and measurable configuration, are now things of the past. Productive forces outlined another reference which, although in contradiction with the relations of production, remained a reference, that of social wealth. An aspect of production still supports both a social form called capital and its internal critique called Marxism. Now, revolutionary demands are based on the abolition of the *commodity* law of value.

Now we have passed from the commodity law of value to the structural law of value, and this coincides with the obliteration of the social form known as production. Given this, are we still within a capitalist mode? It may be that we are in a hypercapitalist mode, or in a very different order. Is the form of capital bound to the law of value in general, or to some specific form of the law of value (perhaps we are really already within a socialist mode? Perhaps this metamorphosis of capital under the sign of the structural law of value is merely its socialist outcome? Oh dear . . .)? If the life and death of capital are staked on the *commodity* law of value, if the revolution is staked on the mode of production, then we are within neither capital nor revolution. If this latter consists in a liberation of the social and generic production of man, then there is no longer any prospect of a revolution since there is no more production. If, on the other hand, capital is a *mode of domination*, then we are always in its midst. This is because the structural law of value is the purest, most illegible form of social domination, like surplus-value. It no longer has any references within a dominant class or a relation of forces, it works without violence, entirely reabsorbed without any trace of bloodshed into the signs which surround us, operative everywhere in the code in which capital finally holds its purest discourses, beyond the dialects of industry, trade and finance, beyond the dialects of class which it held in its 'productive' phase – a symbolic violence inscribed everywhere in signs, even in the signs of the revolution.

The structural revolution of value eliminated the basis of the 'Revolution'. The loss of reference fatally affected first the revolutionary systems of reference, which can no longer be found in any social substance of production, nor in the certainty of a reversal in any truth of labour power. This is because labour is not a *power*, it has become one *sign* amongst many. Like every other sign, it produces and consumes itself. It is exchanged against nonlabour, leisure, in accordance with a total equiva-

lence, it is commutable with every other sector of everyday life. No more or less 'alienated', it is no longer a unique, historical 'praxis' giving rise to unique social relations. Like most practices, it is now only a set of signing operations. It becomes part of contemporary life in general, that is, it is framed by signs. It is no longer even the suffering of historical prostitution which used to play the role of the contrary promise of final emancipation (or, as in Lyotard, as the space of the workers' enjoyment which fulfils an unremitting desire in the abjection of value and the rule of capital). None of this remains true. Sign-form seizes labour and rids it of every historical or libidinal significance, and absorbs it in the process of its own reproduction: the operation of the *sign*, behind the empty allusion to what it designates, is to replicate itself. In the past, labour was used to designate the reality of a social production and a social objective of accumulating wealth. Even capital and surplus-value exploited it – precisely where it retained a use-value for the expanded reproduction of capital and its final destruction. It was shot through with finality anyway – if the worker is absorbed in the pure and simple reproduction of his labour power, it is not true that the process of production is experienced as senseless repetition. Labour revolutionises society through its very abjection, as a commodity whose potential always exceeds pure and simple reproduction of value.

Today this is no longer the case since labour is no longer productive but has become reproductive of the *assignation to labour* which is the general habit of a society which no longer knows whether or not it wishes to produce. No more myths of production and no more contents of production: national balance sheets now merely retrace a numerical and statistical growth devoid of meaning, an inflation of the signs of accountancy over which we can no longer even project the phantasy of the collective will. The pathos of growth itself is dead, since noone believes any longer in the pathos of production, whose final, paranoid and panic-stricken tumescence it was. Today these codes are detumescent. It remains, however, more necessary than ever to reproduce labour as a social ritual as a reflex, as morality, as consensus, as regulation, as the reality principle. The reality principle *of the code*, that is: an immense *ritual of the signs of labour* extends over society in general – since it *reproduces* itself, it matters little whether or not it *produces*. It is much more effective to socialise by means of rituals and signs than by the bound energies of production.

You are asked only to become socialised, not to produce or to excel yourself (this classical ethic now arouses suspicion instead). You are asked only to consider value, according to the structural definition which here takes on its full social significance, as one term in relation to others, to function as a sign in the general scenario of production, just as labour and production now function only as signs, as terms commutable with non-labour, consumption, communication, etc. – a multiple, incessant, twisting relation across the entire network of other signs. Labour, once voided of its energy and substance (and generally disinvested), is given a new role as the model of social simulation, bringing all the other categories along with it into the aleatory sphere of the code.

An unnervingly strange state of affairs: this sudden plunge into a sort of secondary existence, separated from you by all the opacity of a previous life, where there was a familiarity and an intimacy in the traditional process of labour. Even the concrete reality of exploitation, the violent sociality of labour, is familiar. This has all gone now, and is due not so much to the *operative* abstraction of the *process* of labour, so often described, as to the passage of every *signification* of labour into an *operational* field where it becomes a floating variable, dragging the whole imaginary of a previous life along with it.

Beyond the autonomisation of production as *mode* (beyond the convulsions, contradictions and revolutions inherent in the mode), the *code* of production must re-emerge. This is the dimension things are taking on today, at the end of a 'materialist' history which has succeeded in authenticating it as the real movement of society. (Art, religion and duty have no real history for Marx – only production has a history, or, rather, it *is* history, it grounds history. An incredible fabrication of labour and production as historical reason and the generic model of fulfilment.)

The end of this religious autonomisation of production allows us to see that all of this could equally have been *produced* (this time in the sense of a stage-production and a scenario) fairly recently, with totally different goals than the internal finalities (that is, the revolution) secreted away within production.

To analyse production as a code cuts across both the material evidence of machines, factories, labour time, the product, salaries and money, and the more formal, but equally 'objective', evidence of surplus-value, the market, capital, to discover the rule of the game which is to destroy the logical network of the agencies of capital, and even the critical network of the Marxian categories which analyse it (which categories are again only an appearance at the second degree of capital, its *critical* appearance), in order to discover the elementary signifiers of production, the social relations it establishes, buried away forever beneath the historical illusion of the producers (and the theoreticians).

The Three Orders of Simulacra

There are three orders of simulacra, running parallel to the successive mutations of the law of value since the Renaissance:

– The *counterfeit* is the dominant schema in the 'classical' period, from the Renaissance to the Industrial Revolution.

– *Production* is the dominant schema in the industrial era.

– Simulation is the dominant schema in the current code-governed phase.

The first-order simulacrum operates on the natural law of value, the second-order simulacrum on the market law of value, and the third-order simulacrum on the structural law of value.

The Industrial Simulacrum

A new generation of signs and objects arises with the Industrial Revolution – signs with no caste tradition that will never have known restrictions on their status, and which will never have to be *counterfeits*, since from the outset they will be *products* on a gigantic scale. The problem of their specificity and their origin is no longer posed: technics is their origin, they have meaning only within the dimension of the industrial simulacrum.

That is, the series: the very possibility of two or *n* identical objects. The relation between them is no longer one of an original and its counterfeit, analogy or reflection, but is instead one of equivalence and indifference. In the series, objects become indistinct simulacra of one another and, along with objects, of the men that produce them. The extinction of the original reference alone facilitates the general law of equivalences, that is to say, *the very possibility of production.*

The entire analysis of production will be swept aside if we stop regarding it as an original process, as *the* process at the origin of all the others, but conversely as *a* process which reabsorbs every original being and introduces a series of identical beings. Up to this point, we have considered production and labour as potential, as force and historical process, as a generic activity: an energetic-economic myth proper to modernity. We must ask ourselves whether production is not rather an intervention, a *particular* phase, *in the order of signs* – whether it is basically only one episode in the line of simulacra, that episode of producing an infinite series of potentially identical beings (object-signs) by means of technics.

The fabulous energies at work in technics, industry and economics should not hide the fact that it is at bottom only a matter of attaining this indefinite reproducibility, which is a definite challenge to the 'natural' order, and ultimately only a 'second-order' simulacrum and a somewhat weak imaginary solution to the question of world mastery. In relation to the era of the counterfeit, the double, the mirror and the theatre, games of masks and appearances, the serial and technical era of reproduction is basically an era of less ambitious scope (the following era of simulation models and third-order simulacra is of much more considerable dimensions).

Walter Benjamin, in 'The Work of Art in the Age of Mechanical Reproduction', was the first to draw out the essential implications of the principle of reproduction.[ii] He shows that reproduction absorbs the process of production, changes its goals, and alters the status of the product and the producer. He shows this in the fields of art, cinema and photography, because it is there that new territories are opened up in the twentieth century, with no 'classical' tradition of productivity, placed from the outset under the sign of reproduction. Today, however, we know that all material production remains within the same sphere. Today we know that it is at the level of reproduction (fashion, the media, advertising, information and communications networks), at the level of what Marx rather carelessly used to call the *faux frais* of capital[iii] (immense historical irony!), that is, in the sphere of simulacra and the code, that the unity of the

whole process of capital is formed. Benjamin was also the first (with McLuhan after him)[iv] to grasp technology as a medium rather than a 'productive force' (at which point the Marxian analysis retreats), as the form and principle of an entirely new generation of meaning. The mere fact that any given thing can simply be reproduced, as such, in an exemplary double is already a revolution: one need only think of the stupefaction of the Black boy seeing two identical books for the first time. That these two technical products are *equivalent* under the sign of necessary social labour is less important in the long term than the *serial* repetition of the same object (which is also the serial repetition of individuals as labour power). Technique as a medium gains the upper hand not only over the product's 'message' (its use-value) but also over labour power, which Marx wanted to turn into the revolutionary message of production. Benjamin and McLuhan saw more clearly than Marx, they saw that the real message, *the real ultimatum, lay in reproduction itself*. Production itself has no meaning: its social finality is lost in the series. Simulacra prevail over history.

Moreover, the stage of serial reproduction (that of the industrial mechanism, the production line, the growth of reproduction, etc.) is ephemeral. As soon as dead labour gains the upper hand over living labour (that is to say, since the end of primitive accumulation), serial production gives way to generation through models. In this case it is a matter of a reversal of origin and end, since all forms change from the moment that they are no longer mechanically reproduced, but *conceived according to their very reproducibility*, their diffraction from a generative core called a 'model'. We are dealing with third-order simulacra here. There is no more counterfeiting of an original, as there was in the first order, and no more pure series as there were in the second; there are models from which all forms proceed according to modulated differences. Only affiliation to the model has any meaning, since nothing proceeds in accordance with its end any more, but issues instead from the model, the 'signifier of reference', functioning as a foregone, and the only credible, conclusion. We are dealing with simulation in the modern sense of the term, where industrialisation is only its initial form. Modulation is ultimately more fundamental than serial reproducibility, distinct oppositions more than quantitative equivalences, and the commutation of terms more than the law of equivalences; the structural, not the market, law of value. Not only do we not

---

[ii] In Walter Benjamin, *Illuminations*, trans. Harry Zohn (New York: Schocken, 1969).

[iii] *Faux frais* means incidental expenses.

[iv] Marshall McLuhan (1911–80), Canadian analyst of electronic communications, author of *The Medium is the Message* (1967).

need to search for the secrets of the code in technique or economics, it is on the contrary the very possibility of industrial production that we must seek in the genesis of the code and the simulacrum. Every order subsumes the previous order. Just as the order of the counterfeit was captured by the order of serial reproduction (look at how art passed entirely into 'machinality'), so the entire order of production is in the process of toppling into operational simulation.

The analyses of both Benjamin and McLuhan stand on the borders of reproduction and simulation, at the point where referential reason disappears and production is seized by vertigo. These analyses mark a decisive advance over Veblen and Goblot, who, describing, for example, the signs of fashion still refer to a classical configuration where signs constitute a distinct material having a finality and are used for prestige, status and social differentiation. The strategy they deploy is contemporaneous with Marx's strategy of profit and commodity, at a moment where they could still speak of a use-value of the sign, or quite simply of economics at all, because there was still a Reason of the sign and a Reason of production.

The Metaphysics of the Code

> The mathematically minded Leibniz saw in the mystical elegance of the binary system where only the zero and the one count, the very image of creation. The unity of the Supreme Being, operating by means of a binary function against the nothing, was sufficient ground, he thought, from which all things could be made.
>
> Marshall McLuhan

The great man-made simulacra pass from a universe of natural laws into a universe of forces and tensions, and today pass into a universe of structures and binary oppositions. After the metaphysics of being and appearance, after energy and determinacy, the metaphysics of indeterminacy and the code. Cybernetic control, generation through models, differential modulation, feedback, question/answer, etc.: this is the new *operational* configuration (industrial simulacra being *mere operations*). Digitality is its metaphysical principle (Leibniz's God), and DNA is its prophet. In fact, it is in the genetic code that the 'genesis of simulacra' today finds its completed form. At the limits of an ever more forceful extermination of references and finalities, of a loss of semblances and designators, we find the digital, programmatic sign, which has a purely *tactical* value, at the intersection of other signals ('bits' of information/tests) and which has the structure of a micro-molecular code of command and control.

At this level, the question of signs and their rational destinations, their 'real' and their 'imaginary', their repression, reversal, the illusions they form of what they silence or of their parallel significations, is completely effaced. We have already seen the signs of the first order, complex signs with a wealth of illusion, change with the advent of machines into crude, dull, industrial, repetitive, echoless, functional and efficient signs. There is a still more radical mutation as regards the code's signals, which become illegible, and for which no possible interpretation can be provided, buried like programmatic matrices, light years, ultimately, from the 'biological' body, black boxes where every command and response are in ferment. End of the theatre of representation, the space of the conflicts and silences of the sign: only the black box of the code remains, the molecule emitting signals which irradiate us, networking questions/answers through us as identifying signals, and continuously tested by the programme we have hardwired into our own cells. Whether it is prison cells, electronic cells, party cells or microbiological cells we are dealing with, we are always searching for the smallest indivisible element, the organic synthesis of which will follow in accordance with the givens of the code. The code itself is nothing other than a genetic, generative cell where the myriad intersections produce all the questions and all the possible solutions from which to select (for whom?). There is no finality to these 'questions' (informational signals, impulses) other than the response which is either genetic and immutable or inflected with minuscule and aleatory differences. Even space is no longer linear or unidimensional but *cellular*, indefinitely generating the same signals like the lonely and repetitive habits of a stir-crazy prisoner. The genetic code is the perpetual jump in a floppy disk, and we are nothing more than VDUs. The whole aura of the sign and signification itself is determinately resolved: everything is resolved into inscription and decoding.

Such is our third-order simulacrum, such is the 'mystical elegance of the binary system of zero and one', from which all beings issue. Such also is the status of the sign at the end of signification: DNA or operational simulation.

This is all perfectly summed up by Thomas Sebeok in 'Genetics and Semiotics' (*Versus*):

> Innumerable observations confirm the hypothesis that the internal world of the organic descends directly from the primordial forms of life. The most remarkable fact is the omnipresence of the DNA molecule. The genetic material of all the earth's known organisms is in large part composed of the nucleic acids DNA and RNA, whose structure contains information transmitted through reproduction from one generation to the next, and furthermore endowed with the capacity to reproduce itself and to imitate. In short, the genetic code is universal, or almost. Decoding it was an immense discovery to the extent that it showed that 'the two languages of the great polymers, the languages of nucleic acid and protein, correlate directly'... The Soviet mathematician Liapunov demonstrated in 1963 that every living system transmits a small but precise quantity of energy or matter containing a great volume of information through channels laid down in advance. This information is responsible for the subsequent control of large quantities of energy and matter. From this perspective numerous biological and cultural phenomena (storing, feedback, channelling messages and so on) can be conceived as manifestations of information processing. In the final analysis, information appears in large part to be the repetition of information, but still another kind of information, a kind of control which seems to be a universal property of terrestrial life, irrespective of its form or substance.
>
> Five years ago I drew attention to the convergence of genetics and linguistics as autonomous but parallel disciplines in the larger field of the science of communication (which is also a part of zoosemiotics). The terminology of genetics is full of expressions taken from linguistics and communication theory... which emphasised both the principal similarities and the important differences in the structure and function of genetic and verbal codes... Today it is clear that the genetic code must be considered as the most basic semiotic network, and therefore as the prototype of all the other systems of signification used by the animals, including man. From this point of view, molecules, which are systems of quanta of, and which act as stable vehicles of physical information, zoosemiotic and cultural systems including language, constitute a continuous chain of stages, with ever more complex energy levels, in the context of a unique and universal evolution. It is therefore possible to describe both language or living systems from a unifying cybernetic point of view. For the moment, this is only a useful and provisional analogy.... A reciprocal rapproachment between genetics, animal communication and linguistics may lead to a complete science of the dynamics of semiosis, which science may turn out, in the final analysis, to be nothing other than a definition of life.

So the outline of the current strategic model emerges, everywhere taking over from the great ideological model which political economy was in its time.

We find this again, under the rigorous sign of 'science', in Jacques Monod's *Chance and Necessity*. The end of dialectical evolution. Life is now ruled by the discontinuous indeterminacy of the genetic code, by the *teleonomic* principle.[v] Finality is no longer at the end, there is no more finality, nor any determinacy. Finality is there in advance, inscribed in the code. We can see that nothing has changed – the order of ends has ceded its place to molecular play, as the order of signifieds has yielded to the play of infinitesimal signifies, condensed into their aleatory commutation. All the transcendental finalities are reduced to an instrument panel. This is still to make recourse to nature however, to an inscription in a 'biological' nature; a phantasm of nature in fact, as it has always been, no longer a metaphysical sanctuary for the origin and substance, but this time, for the code. The code must have an 'objective' basis. What better than molecules and genetics? Monod is the strict theologian of this molecular transcendence, Edgar Morin its ecstatic supporter (DNA = ADoNaï!).[vi] In each of them, however, the phantasm of the code, which is equivalent to the reality of power, is confused with the idealism of the molecule.

Again we find the hallucination or illusion of a world reunited under a single principle – a homogeneous substance according to the Counter-Reformation Jesuits. With Leibniz and his binary deity as their precursor, the technocrats of the

---

[v] For Monod, all living beings are "teleonomic," attempting to transmit the information necessary for preservation of the species to the next generation.

[vi] Edgar Morin (1921–), a French sociologist and philosopher. *Adonai* is Hebrew for Lord.

biological (as well as the linguistic) sciences opt for the genetic code, for their intended programme has nothing to do with genetics, but is a social and historical programme. Biochemistry hypostatises the ideal of a social order governed by a kind of genetic code, a macromolecular calculus by the PPBS (Planning Programming Budgeting System), its operational circuits radiating over the social body. Here techno-cybernetics finds its 'natural philosophy', as Monod said. The biological and the biochemical have always exerted a fascination, ever since the beginnings of science. In Spencer's organicism (bio-sociologism)[vii] it was operative at the level of second and third order structures (following Jacob's classification in *The Logic of Life*), while today, in modern biochemistry, this applies to the level of fourth-order structures.

Coded similarities and dissimilarities: the exact image of cyberneticised social exchange. We need only add the 'stereospecific complex' to reinject the intracellular communication that Morin will transform into a molecular Eros.

Practically and historically, this means that social control by means of the *end* (and the more or less dialectical *providence* that ministers to the fulfilment of this end) is replaced with social control by means of prediction, simulation, programmed anticipation and indeterminate mutation, all governed, however, by the code. Instead of a process finalised in accordance with its ideal development, we are dealing with generative *models*. Instead of prophecy, we fall subject to 'inscription'. There is no radical difference between the two. Only the schemata of control change and, it has to be said, reach a fantastic degree of perfection. From a capitalist productivist society to a neo-capitalist cybernetic order, aiming this time at absolute control: the biological theory of the code has taken up arms in the service of this mutation. Far from 'indeterminate', this mutation is the outcome of an entire history where God, Man, Progress and even History have successively passed away to the advantage of the code, where the death of transcendence benefits immanence, which corresponds to a far more advanced phase of the vertiginous manipulation of social relations.

In its infinite reproduction, the system puts an end to the myth of its origin and to all the referential values it has itself secreted in the course of its process. By putting an end to the myth of its origin,

it puts an end to its internal contradictions (there is no longer a real or a referential to which to oppose them) and also puts an end to the myth of its end, the revolution itself. With the revolution you could still make out the outline of a victorious human and generic reference, the original potential of man. But what if capital wiped generic man himself off the map (in favour of genetic man)? The revolution's golden age was the age of capital, where myths of the origin and the end were still in circulation. Once these myths were short-circuited (the only threat that capital had ever faced historically came from this *mythical* demand for rationality which pervaded it from the start) in a *de facto* operationality, a non-discursive operationality – once it became its own myth, or rather an indeterminate, aleatory machine, something like a *social genetic code* – capital no longer left the slightest opportunity for a determinate reversal. This is the real violence of capital. However, it remains to be seen whether this operationality is itself a myth, whether DNA is itself a *myth*.

This effectively poses the problem of the discursive status of science once and for all. In Monod, this discourse is so candidly absolutised that it provides a perfect opportunity for posing the problem:

> Plato, Heraclitus, Hegel, Marx ... these ideological edifices, represented as a priori, were in reality a posteriori constructions designed to justify preconceived ethico-political theories ... For science, objectivity is the only a priori postulate of objectivity, which spares, or rather forbids it from taking part in this debate.

However, this postulate is itself a result of the never innocent decision to objectify the world and the 'real'. In fact, it postulates the coherence of a specific *discourse*, and scientificity is doubtless only the space of this discourse, never manifest as such, whose simulacrum of 'objectivity' covers over this political and strategic speech. Besides, Monod clearly expresses the arbitrariness of this discourse a little further on:

> It may be asked, of course, whether all the invariants, conservations and symmetries that make up the texture of scientific discourse are not fictions substituted for reality in order to obtain a workable image ... A logic itself founded upon a purely abstract, perhaps 'conventional', principle of identity – a convention

---

[vii] Herbert Spencer (1820–1903) made Darwinian evolution the basis of a social philosophy.

with which, however, human reason seems to be incapable of doing without.

We couldn't put it more clearly: science itself determines its generative formula and its discourse model on the basis of a faith in a conventional order (and moreover not just any order, but the order of a total reduction). But Monod quickly glosses over this dangerous hypothesis of 'conventional' identity. A rigid basis would serve science better, an 'objective' reality for example. Physics will testify that identity is not only a postulate, but that it is *in things*, since there is an 'absolute identity of two atoms when they are found to be in the same quantitative state'. So, is it convention or is it objective reality? The truth is that science, like any other discourse, is organized on the basis of a conventional logic, but, like any other ideological discourse, requires a real, 'objective' reference within the processes of substance in order to justify it. If the principle of identity is in any way 'true', even if this is at the infinitesimal level of two atoms, then the entire conventional edifice of science which draws its inspiration from it is also 'true'. The hypothesis of the genetic code DNA is also true and cannot be defeated. The same goes for metaphysics. Science explains things which have been defined and formalised in advance and which subsequently conform to these explanations, that's all that 'objectivity' is. The ethics that come to sanction this objective knowledge are just systems of defence and misconstrual that aim to preserve this vicious circle.[3]

As Nietzsche said: 'Down with all hypotheses that have allowed belief in a real world.'

The Hyperrealism of Simulation

We have just defined a digital space, a magnetic field of the code with its modelled polarisations, diffractions and gravitations, with the insistent and perpetual flux of the smallest disjunctive units (the question/answer cell operates like the cybernetic atom of *signification*). We must now measure the disparity between this field of control and the traditional field of repression, the police–space which used to correspond to a violence of signification. This space was one of reactionary conditioning, inspired by the Pavlovian apparatus of programmed and repetitive aggression which we also saw scaled up in 'hard sell' advertising and the political propaganda of the thirties. A crafted but industrial violence that aimed to produce terrified behaviour and animal obedience. This no longer has any meaning. Totalitarian, bureaucratic concentration is a schema dating from the era of the market law of value. The schema of equivalences effectively imposes the form of a general equivalent, and hence the centralisation of a global process. This is an archaic rationality compared to simulation, in which it is no longer a single general equivalent but a diffraction of models that plays the regulative role: no longer the form of the general equivalent, but the form of distinct oppositions. We pass from injunction to disjunction through the code, from the ultimatum to solicitation, from obligatory passivity to models constructed from the outset on the basis of the subject's 'active response', and this subject's involvement and 'ludic' participation, towards a total environment model made up of incessant spontaneous responses, joyous feedback and irradiated contacts. According to Nicolas Schöffer, this is a 'concretisation of the general ambience': the great festival of Participation is made up of myriad stimuli, miniaturised tests, and infinitely divisible question/answers, all magnetised by several great models in the luminous field of the code.

Here comes the great Culture of tactile communication, under the sign of techno–lumino–kinetic space and total spatio–dynamic theatre!

A whole imaginary based on contact, a sensory mimicry and a tactile mysticism, basically ecology in its entirety, comes to be grafted on to this universe of operational simulation, multi-stimulation and multi-response. This incessant test of successful adaptation is naturalised by assimilating it to animal mimicry ('the phenomenon of animals' adaptation to the colours and forms of their habitat also holds for man' – Nicolas Schöffer),[viii] and even to the Indians with their 'innate sense of ecology'! Tropisms, mimicry and empathy: the ecological evangelism of open systems, with positive or negative feedback, will be engulfed in this breach, with an ideology of regulation through information that is only the avatar, in accordance with a more flexible rationality, of the Pavlov reflex. Hence electroshock is replaced by body attitude as the condition of mental health. When notions of need, perception, desire, etc., become operational, then the apparatuses of force and forcing yield to ambient apparatuses. A generalised, mystical ecology of the 'niche' and the context, a simulated environ-

---

[viii] French "electronic" painter (1912–92).

ment eventually including the 'Centres for Cultural and Aesthetic Re-animation' planned for the Left Bank (why not?) and the Centre for Sexual Leisure, which, built in the form of a breast, will offer 'a superlative euphoria thanks to a pulsating ambience ...Workers from all classes will be able to enter these stimulating centres.' A spatio-dynamic fascination, just like 'total theatre', set up 'according to a hyperbolic, circular apparatus turning around a cylindrical spindle'. No more scenes, no more cuts, no more 'gaze', the end of the spectacle and the spectacular, towards the total, fusional, tactile and aesthetic (and no longer the aesthetic) etc., environment. We can only think of Artaud's total theatre, his Theatre of Cruelty, of which this spatio-dynamic simulation is the abject, black-humour caricature. Here cruelty is replaced by minimum and maximum 'stimulus thresholds', by the invention of 'perceptual codes calculated on the basis of saturation thresholds'. Even the good old 'catharsis' of the classical theatre of the passions has today become a homeopathy by means of simulation.

The end of the spectacle brings with it the collapse of reality into hyperrealism, the meticulous reduplication of the real, preferably through another reproductive medium such as advertising or photography. Through reproduction from one medium into another the real becomes volatile, it becomes the allegory of death, but it also draws strength from its own destruction, becoming the real for its own sake, a fetishism of the lost object which is no longer the object of representation, but the ecstasy of denegation and its own ritual extermination: the hyperreal.

Realism had already inaugurated this tendency. The rhetoric of the real already signals that its status has been radically altered (the golden age of the innocence of language where what is said need not be doubled in an effect of reality). Surrealism was still in solidarity with the realism it contested, but which it doubled and ruptured in the imaginary. The hyperreal represents a much more advanced phase insofar as it effaces the contradiction of the real and the imaginary. Irreality no longer belongs to the dream or the phantasm, to a beyond or a hidden interiority, but to *the hallucinatory resemblance of the real to itself*. To gain exit from the crisis of representation, the real must be sealed off in a pure repetition. Before emerging in pop art and painterly neo-realism, this tendency can al-

ready be discerned in the *nouveau roman*.[ix] Here the project is to construct a void around the real, to eradicate all psychology and subjectivity from it in order to give it a pure objectivity. In fact, this is only the objectivity of the pure gaze, an objectivity finally free of the object, but which merely remains a blind relay of the gaze that scans it. It is easy to detect the unconscious trying to remain hidden in this circular seduction.

This is indeed the impression made by the *nouveau roman*, a wild elision of meaning in a meticulous but blind reality. Syntax and semantics have disappeared: the object now only appears in court, where its scattered fragments are subjected to unremitting cross-examination. There is neither metaphor nor metonymy, only a successive immanence under the law enforcing authority of the gaze. This 'objective' microscopy incites reality to vertiginous motion, the vertiginous death of representation within the confines of representation. The old illusions of relief, perspective and depth (both spatial and psychological) bound up with the perception of the object are over with: optics in its entirety, scopics, has begun to operate on the surface of things – the gaze has become the object's molecular code.

There are several possible modalities of this vertigo of realistic simulation:

1. The detailed deconstruction of the real, the paradigmatic close 'reading' of the object: the flattening out, linearity and seriality of part-objects.

2. Abyssal vision: all the games of splitting the object in two and duplicating it in every detail. This reduction is taken to be a depth, indeed a critical metalanguage, and doubtless this was true of a reflective configuration of the sign in a dialectics of the mirror. From now on this infinite refraction is nothing more than another type of seriality in which the real is no longer reflected, but folds in on itself to the point of exhaustion.

3. The properly serial form (Andy Warhol).[x] Here the paradigmatic dimension is abolished along with the syntagmatic dimension, since there is no longer a flexion of forms, nor even an internal reflexion, only a contiguity of the same: zero degree flexion and reflexion. Take this erotic photograph of twin sisters where the fleshy reality of their bodies is annihilated by their similarity. How do you invest when the beauty of the one is immediately

---

[ix] Literally, "new novel," referring to the avant-garde French "antinovels" of the 1950s and 1960s.

[x] Designer, painter, and personality Andy Warhol (1928–87) was the most famous representative of Pop Art.

duplicated in the other? The gaze can only go from one to the other, and these poles enclose all vision. This is a subtle means of murdering the original, but it is also a singular seduction, where the total extent of the object is intercepted by its infinite diffraction into itself (this scenario reverses the Platonic myth of the reunion of two halves separated by a symbol. In the series, signs subdivide like protozoa). Perhaps this is the seduction of death, in the sense that, for we sexually differentiated beings, death is perhaps not nothingness, but quite simply the mode of reproduction prior to sexual differentiation. The models that generate in infinite chains effectively bring us closer to the generation of protozoa; sex, which for us is confused with life, being the only remaining difference.

4. This pure machinality is doubtless only a paradoxical limit, however. Binarity and digitality constitute the true generative formula which encompasses all the others and is, in a way, the stabilised form of the code. This does not mean pure repetition, but minimal difference, the minimal inflexion between two terms, that is, the 'smallest common paradigm' that can sustain the fiction of meaning. A combinatory of differentiation internal to the painterly object as well as to the consumer object, this simulation contracts, in contemporary art, to the point of being nothing more than the infinitesimal difference that still separates hyperreality from hyperpainting. Hyperpainting claims to exhaust itself to the point of its sacrificial eclipse in the face of the real, but we know how all painting's prestige is revived in this infinitesimal difference: painting retreats into the border that separates the painted surface and the wall. It also hides in the signature, the metaphysical sign of painting and the metaphysics of representation at the limit, where it takes itself as its own model (the 'pure gaze') and turns around itself in the compulsive repetition of the code.

The very definition of the real is *that of which it is possible to provide an equivalent reproduction*. It is a contemporary of science, which postulates that a process can be reproduced exactly within given conditions, with an industrial rationality which postulates a universal system of equivalences (classical representation is not equivalence but transcription, interpretation and commentary). At the end of this process of reproducibility, the real is not only that which can be reproduced, but *that which is always already reproduced*: the hyperreal.

So are we then at the end of the real and the end of art due to a total mutual reabsorption? No, since at the level of simulacra, hyperrealism is the apex of both art and the real, by means of a mutual exchange of the privileges and prejudices that found them. The hyperreal is beyond representation (cf. Jean-François Lyotard, 'Esquisse d'une économique de l'hyperrealisme', *L'Art vivant*, 36, 1973) only because it is entirely within simulation, in which the barriers of representation rotate crazily, an implosive madness which, far from being excentric, keeps its gaze fixed on the centre, on its own abyssal repetition. Analogous to the effect of an internal distance from the dream, allowing us to say that we are dreaming, hyperrealism is only the play of censorship and the perpetuation of the dream, becoming an integral part of a coded reality that it perpetuates and leaves unaltered.

In fact, hyperrealism must be interpreted in inverse manner: *today reality itself is hyperrealist*. The secret of surrealism was that the most everyday reality could become surreal, but only at privileged instants which again arose out of art and the imaginary. Today everyday, political, social, historical, economic, etc., reality has already incorporated the hyperrealist dimension of simulation so that we are now living entirely within the 'aesthetic' hallucination of reality. The old slogan 'reality is stranger than fiction', which still corresponded to the surrealist stage in the aestheticisation of life, has been outrun, since there is no longer any fiction that life can possibly confront, even as its conqueror. Reality has passed completely into the game of reality. Radical disaffection, the cool and cybernetic stage, replaces the hot, phantasmatic phase.

The consummate enjoyment [*jouissance*] of the signs of guilt, despair, violence and death are replacing guilt, anxiety and even death in the total euphoria of simulation. This euphoria aims to abolish cause and effect, origin and end, and replace them with reduplication. Every closed system protects itself in this way from the referential and the anxiety of the referential, as well as from all metalanguage that the system wards off by operating its own metalanguage, that is, by duplicating itself as its own critique. In simulation, the metalinguistic illusion reduplicates and completes the referential illusion (the pathetic hallucination of the sign and the pathetic hallucination of the real).

'It's a circus', 'it's a theatre', 'it's a movie'; all these old adages are ancient naturalist denunciations. This is no longer what is at issue. What is at issue this time is *turning the real into a satellite*, putting an undefinable reality with no common measure into orbit with the phantasma that once illustrated it. This satellisation has subsequently been materialised as the two-room-kitchen-shower which we really have sent into orbit, to the 'spatial power' you could say, with the latest lunar module. The most everyday aspect of the terrestrial environment raised to the rank of a cosmic value, an absolute decor, hypostatised in space. This is the end of metaphysics and the beginning of the era of hyperreality.[4] The spatial transcendence of the banality of the two-room apartment by a cool, machinic figuration in hyperrealism[5] tells us only one thing, however: this module, such as it is, participates in a hyperspace of representation where everyone is already in possession of the technical means for the instant reproduction of his or her own life. Thus the *Tupolev*'s pilots who crashed in Bourget were able, by means of their cameras, to see themselves dying at first hand.[xi] This is nothing other than the short-circuit of the response by the question in the test, a process of instant renewal whereby reality is immediately contaminated by its simulacrum.

A specific class of allegorical and somewhat diabolical objects used to exist, made up of mirrors, images, works of art (concepts?). Although simulacra, they were transparent and manifest (you could distinguish craftsmanship from the counterfeit) with their own characteristic style and *savoir-faire*. Pleasure, then, consisted in locating what was 'natural' within what was artificial and counterfeit. Today, where the real and the imaginary are intermixed in one and the same operational totality, aesthetic fascination reigns supreme: with subliminal perception (a sort of sixth sense) of special effects, editing and script, reality is overexposed to the glare of models. This is no longer a space of production, but a reading strip, a coding and decoding strip, magnetised by signs. Aesthetic reality is no longer achieved through art's premeditation and distancing, but by its elevation to the second degree, to the power of two, by the anticipation and immanence of the code. A kind of unintentional parody hovers over everything, a tactical simulation, a consummate aesthetic enjoyment, is attached to the indefinable play of reading and the rules of the game. Travelling signs, media, fashion

and models, the blind but brilliant ambience of simulacra.

Art has for a long time prefigured this turn, by veering towards what today is a turn to everyday life. Very early on the work of art produced a double of itself as the manipulation of the signs of art, bringing about an oversignification of art, or, as Lévi-Strauss said, an 'academicisation of the signifier', irreversibly introducing art to the form of the sign.[xii] At this point art entered into infinite *reproduction*, with everything that doubles itself, even the banal reality of the everyday, falling by the same token under the sign of art and becoming aesthetic. The same goes for production, which we might say has today entered into aesthetic reduplication, the phase where, expelling all content and all finality, it becomes somehow abstract and non-figurative. In this way it expresses the pure form of production, taking upon itself, as art does, the value of the finality without end. Art and industry may then exchange their signs: art can become a reproductive machine (Andy Warhol) without ceasing to be art, since the machine is now nothing but a sign. Production can also lose all its social finality as its means of verification, and finally glorify in the prestigious, hyperbolic and aesthetic signs that the great industrial complexes are, 400 m high towers or the numerical mysteries of the Gross National Product.

So art is everywhere, since artifice lies at the heart of reality. So art is dead, since not only is its critical transcendence dead, but reality itself, entirely impregnated by an aesthetic that holds onto its very structurality, has become inseparable from its own image. It no longer even has the time to take on the effect of reality. Reality is no longer stranger than fiction: it captures every dream before it can take on the dream effect. A schizophrenic vertigo of serial signs that have no counterfeit, no possible sublimation, and are immanent to their own repetition – who will say where the reality they simulate now lies? They no longer even repress anything (which, if you like, keeps simulation from entering the sphere of psychosis): even the primary processes have been annihilated. The cool universe of digitality absorbs the universe of metaphor and metonymy. The simulation principle dominates the reality principle as well as the pleasure principle.

[xi] A Russian *Tupolev* 144 jet crashed at an airshow at Bourget airport near Paris in March 1973.

[xii] Claude Lévi-Strauss (1908–), French anthropologist, led the introduction of structuralism into the human sciences after World War II.

Jean Baudrillard

Author's Notes

1 If it were only a question of the ascendancy of exchange-value over use-value (or the ascendancy of the structural over the functional dimension of language), then Marx and Saussure have already signalled it. Marx almost turns use-value into the medium or the alibi, pure and simple, of exchange-value. His entire analysis is based on the principle of equivalence at the core of the system of exchange-value. But if *equivalence* is at the core of the system, there is no *indeterminacy* in the global system (there is always a dialectical determinacy and finality of the mode of production). The current system, however, is itself based on indeterminacy, and draws impetus from it. Conversely, it is haunted by the death of all determinacy.

2 Theoretical production, like material production, loses its determinacy and begins to turn around itself, slipping abyssally towards a reality that cannot be found. This is where we are today: undecidability, the era of *floating theories*, as much as floating money. No matter what perspective they come from (the psychoanalytic included), no matter with what violence they struggle and claim to rediscover an immanence, or a movement without systems of reference (Deleuze, Lyotard, etc.), all contemporary theories are floating and have no meaning other than to serve as signs for one another. It is pointless to insist on their coherence with some 'reality', whatever that might be. The system has removed every secure reference from theory as it has from any other labour power. Theory no longer has any use-value, the theoretical mirror of production has also cracked. So much the better. What I mean is that the very undecidability of theory is an effect of the code. Let there be no illusions: there is no schizophrenic 'drift' about this flotation of theories, where flows pass freely over the body without organs (of what, capital?). It merely signifies that any theory can from now on be exchanged against any other according to variable exchange rates, but without any longer being invested anywhere, unless it is the mirror of their writing.

3 Furthermore, there is a flagrant contradiction in Monod's book, reflecting the ambiguity of all contemporary science: its discourse is directed at the code, that is, at third-order simulacra, but it still follows second-order 'scientific' schemata such as objectivity, the scientific 'ethic' of knowledge, the truth-principle and the transcendence of science, and so on. These things are all incompatible with third-order models of indeterminacy.

4 The coefficient of reality is proportionate to the reserve of the imaginary that gives it its specific weight. This is true of terrestrial as well as space exploration: when there is no more virgin, and hence available to the imaginary, territory, when the map covers the whole territory, something like the reality principle disappears. In this sense, the conquest of space constitutes an irreversible threshold on the way to the loss of terrestrial references. Reality haemorrhages to the precise extent that the limits of an internally coherent universe are infinitely pushed back. The conquest of space comes after the conquest of the planet, as the last phantasmatic attempt to extend the jurisdiction of the real (for example, when the flag, technology and two-room apartments are carried to the moon); it is even an attempt to substantiate concepts or territorialise the unconscious, which is equivalent to the derealisation of human space, or its reversal into a hyperreality of simulation.

5 What about the cool figuration of the metallic caravan and the supermarket so beloved of the hyperrealists, or the Campbell's soup cans dear to Andy Warhol, or even that of the Mona Lisa when it was satellited into planetary orbit as the absolute model of the earth's art. The Mona Lisa was not even sent as a work of art, but as a planetary simulacrum where a whole world bears testimony to its existence (testifying, in reality, to its own death) for the gaze of a future universe.

43

From *Erring: A Postmodern A/theology*

Mark C. Taylor

Professor of religion, Mark Taylor (1945–) is the primary exponent of what might seem an impossible combination: postmodern theology. It has roots in the so-called "death of God theology" of the 1960s which tried to reconceive Christianity in the light of Nietzsche's announcement of God's demise. In this spirit, Taylor rejects any traditional substantive or personal notion of divinity, and any teleological view of human history. His work is heavily indebted to Derrida. He regards Derrida's strategy of critical reading, deconstruction, as pointing out the utterly marginal or "liminal" nature of experience. Just as Derrida gives primacy to writing, Taylor sees religion as essentially based in scripture, not in the sense of ancient books, but as the process of generating, reading, and rewriting "the word." In this process, every human judgment is limited, transitory, uncertain, never able to grasp or adequately represent what it seeks. Any writing, or living, which recognizes this fact admits that its very nature is "erring." Taylor interprets this erring context of all becoming, the "nonoriginal origin of everything that is," as the "divine milieu."

In many ways, deconstruction might seem an unlikely partner for religious reflection. As a form of thought it appears avowedly atheistic. Derrida speaks for others as well as himself when he adamantly maintains that deconstruction "blocks every relationship to theology."[1] Paradoxically, it is just this antithetical association with theology that lends deconstruction[i] its "religious" significance for marginal thinkers. By reflecting and recasting the pathos of so much contemporary art, literature, and philosophy, deconstruction expresses greater appreciation for the significance of the death of God than most contemporary philosophers of religion and theologians. Though anticipated in Hegel's speculative philosophy and Kierkegaard's attack on Christendom[ii] and proclaimed by Nietzsche's madman, the death of God is not concretely actualized until the emergence of the twentieth-century industrial state. And yet, as Nietzsche realized, "This tremendous event is," in an important sense, "still on its way, still wandering; it has not yet reached the ears of men."[2] This deafness is all too evident among many contemporary philosophers of religion and theologians. Too often they attempt to solve difficult religious problems by simply trying to recapture a past that now seems decisively gone. This attitude is no longer defensible.

Postmodernism opens with the sense of *irrevocable* loss and *incurable* fault. This wound is inflicted by the overwhelming awareness of death – a death that "begins" with the death of God and "ends"

---

[i] Deconstruction is Derrida's method of critical reading which displays the undecidable, self-undermining elements in a text.
[ii] Søren Kierkegaard (1813–55) attacked the Christianity of his day as inauthentically religious.

Mark C. Taylor, from *Erring: A Postmodern A/theology*, pp. 6–13, 103–7, and 115–20. Chicago: University of Chicago Press, 1984.

with the death of our selves. We are in a time between times and a place which is no place. Here our reflection must "begin." In this liminal[iii] time and space, deconstructive philosophy and criticism offer rich, though still largely untapped, resources for religious reflection. One of the distinctive features of deconstruction is its willingness to confront the problem of the death of God squarely even if not always directly. The insights released by deconstructive criticism suggest the ramifications of the death of God for areas as apparently distinct as contemporary psychology, linguistics, and historical analysis. In view of its remarkable grasp of the far-reaching significance of the dissolution of the Western theological and philosophical tradition, it would not be too much to suggest that *deconstruction is the "hermeneutic" of the death of God*. As such, it provides a possible point of departure for a postmodern a/theology. Given the marginality of its site, an a/theology that draws on deconstructive philosophy will invert established meaning and subvert everything once deemed holy. It will thus be utterly transgressive.

The failure (or refusal) to come to terms with the radical implications of the death of God has made it impossible for most Western theology to approach postmodernism. This shortcoming results, at least in part, from the lack of a clear recognition that concepts are not isolated entities. Rather, they form intricate networks or complex webs of inter-relation and coimplication. As a result of this inter-connection, notions mutually condition and reciprocally define each other. Such thoroughgoing corelativity implies that no *single* concept is either absolutely primary or exclusively foundational. Clusters of coordinated notions form the matrix of any coherent conceptual system. It would, of course, be a vast oversimplification to insist that all Western theology can be made to fit a single system. Efforts to totalize the tradition inevitably leave a remainder and consequently always negate themselves. It is, nonetheless, possible to identify a set of interrelated concepts that have been particularly persistent in theological reflection. This network includes at least four terms: God, self, history, and book. In order to anticipate the course of the argument that follows, it might be helpful to indi-

cate briefly the interplay of these important notions and to suggest some of the assumptions and conse-quences of the closely knit network that they form.

According to the tenets of classical theism, God, who is One, is the supreme Creator, who, through the mediation of His divine Logos, brings the world into being and providentially directs its course. This Primal Origin (First Cause or *Archē*) is also the Ultimate End (Final Goal or *Telos*) of the world. Utterly transcendent and thoroughly eternal, God is represented as totally present to Himself [*sic*]. He is, in fact, the omnipresent fount, source, ground, and uncaused cause of pres-ence itself. The self is made in the image of God and consequently is also one, i.e. a centered indi-vidual. Mirroring its Creator, the single subject is both self-conscious and freely active. Taken together, self-consciousness and freedom entail in-dividual responsibility. History is the domain where divine guidance and human initiative meet. The temporal course of events is not regarded as a random sequence. It is believed to be plotted along a single line stretching from a definite begin-ning (creation) through an identifiable middle (in-carnation) to an expected end (kingdom or redemption). Viewed in such ordered terms, his-tory forms a purposeful process whose meaning can be coherently represented. Page by page and chap-ter by chapter, the Book weaves the unified story of the interaction between God and self. Since the logic of this narrative reflects the Logos of history, Scripture, in effect, rewrites the Word of God.

God, self, history, and book are, thus, bound in an intricate relationship in which each mirrors the other. No single concept can be changed without altering all of the others. As a result of this thorough interdependence, the news of the death of God cannot really reach our ears until its reverberations are traced in the notions of self, history and book. The echoes of the death of God can be heard in the disappearance of the self, the end of history, and the closure of the book. We can begin to unravel this web of conceptual relations by plotting the coordin-ates of a new a/theological network.

The Western theological tradition, in all its evi-dent diversity, rests upon a polar or, more pre-cisely, a dyadic foundation. Though consistently monotheistic, Christian theology is repeatedly in-scribed in binary terms. The history of religious thought in the West can be read as a pendular

---

[iii] Marginal, transitional, at the border. "Limen" means threshold.

movement between seemingly exclusive and evident opposites. [see figure on p. 438]

Like its intellectual twin, philosophy, theology does not regard these opposites as equivalent. It refuses to allow the possibility that oppositional terms can coexist peacefully. Invariably one term is privileged through the divestment of its relative. The resultant economy of privilege sustains an asymmetrical hierarchy in which one member governs or rules the other throughout the theological, logical, axiological, and even political domains.

It is against just this hierarchy that so many modern thinkers rebel. Indeed, modernism might be described as the struggle to overturn this structure of domination upon which Western thought and society traditionally have rested. Many theologians who have taken up the challenge of modernism have been inevitably driven to revolutionary radicalism. The theological radical learns from modern politics, painting, music, and literature that "true revolution is not simply an opening to the future but also a closing of the past. Yet the past which is negated by a revolutionary future cannot simply be negated or forgotten. It must be transcended by way of a reversal of the past, a reversal bringing a totally new light and meaning to everything which is manifest as the past, and therefore a reversal fully transforming the whole horizon of the present. Modern revolutionary assaults upon the whole movement of a profane or secular history can now serve not only as models but also as sources for a revolutionary theological assault upon the history of faith."[3] Even revolutionary thought, however, runs the risk of being *insufficiently* radical. If hierarchical oppression and repression are to be overcome, it is necessary to *pass through* a phase of inversion. But reversal can remain caught within the dyadic economy of conflictual opposition. Merely "To put a minus sign instead of a plus sign before the elements of Western culture is not to liberate oneself from them but to remain entirely bound within their net. To define God as the supreme evil is as much an act of homage and belief as to define him as the supreme good."[4] In place of a simple reversal, it is necessary to effect a dialectical inversion that does not leave contrasting opposites unmarked but dissolves their original identities. Inversion, in other words, must simultaneously be a perversion that is subversive. Unless theological transgression becomes genuinely subversive, nothing fundamental will change. What is needed is a critical lever with which the entire

inherited order can be creatively disorganized. It is at this point that deconstruction becomes a potential resource for the a/theologian.

Deconstructive criticism unravels the very fabric of most Western theology and philosophy. When subjected to a deconstructive critique, the structure of relationship that both joins and separates opposites is reformulated in such a way that contraries are not merely reversed but are recast to dissolve their original propriety and proper identity. Deconstruction, therefore, both affects specific concepts within a dyadic economy and calls into question the entire network of notions that traditionally have grounded theological reflection. Once terms undergo deconstructive analysis, they cannot simply be reinscribed within an oppositional system that previously had defined and constituted them. It is important to stress that this critique does not approach the theological network from without and thus does not involve a disjunctive epistemological break. Like any parasite, deconstruction attacks from within, using "the strengths of the field to turn its own stratagems against it, producing a force of dislocation that spreads itself throughout the entire system, fissuring it in every direction and thoroughly *delimiting* it."[5]

Deconstruction is irrevocably liminal or marginal. Its liminality marks an unstable border along which marginal thinkers wander. This novel and admittedly controversial form of criticism seems to me to be particularly well suited to address many of the issues that preoccupy people caught *between* belief and unbelief. Deconstruction itself is at one and the same time inside and outside the network that it questions. On the one hand, deconstruction's uncanny criticism pervades and subverts the hierarchical system of theological concepts. On the other hand, the survival of this parasitic discourse presupposes the continuing existence of its host. Hence deconstructive writing is always paradoxical, double, duplicitous, excentric, improper, . . . errant. Calling into question the very notion of propriety, the language of deconstruction can possess no final or proper meaning. It remains transitional. Its words cannot be completely fixed, mastered, or captured in the net of either/or. Instead, deconstructive criticism constantly errs along the / of neither/nor. Forever wavering and wandering, deconstruction is (re)inscribed betwixt 'n' between the opposites it inverts, perverts, and subverts. Consequently, deconstruction can be written only on the boundary, a boundary that, though always the "middest," knows no bounds.

God	World
Eternity	Time
Being	Becoming
Rest	Movement
Permanence	Change
Presence	Absence
One	Many
Sacred	Profane
Order	Chaos
Meaning	Absurdity
Life	Death
Infinite	Finite
Transcendent	Immanent
Identity	Difference
Affirmation	Negation
Truth	Error
Reality	Illusion
Certainty	Uncertainty
Clarity	Confusion
Sanity	Madness
Light	Darkness
Vision	Blindness
Invisible	Visible
Spirit	Body
Spiritual	Carnal
Mind	Matter
Good	Evil
Innocence	Guilt
Purity	Stain
Proper	Improper
Centered	Excentric
First	Second
Original	Imitation
Natural	Monstrous
Purposeful	Purposeless
Honesty	Duplicity
Height	Depth
Depth	Surface
Interiority	Exteriority
Speech	Writing
Seriousness	Play

The time and space of this border form a middle age or middle kingdom that is not, in any ordinary sense, intermediate. The ceaseless play of opposites renders transition permanent and passage absolute. This interval is the medium or mean within which all extremes cross. While not reducible to or expressible in a traditional oppositional logic of extremes, this milieu is the "nonoriginal origin" of everything that is – and that is not.

In the following pages I shall be asking whether the scriptural network graphed in deconstruction can be read as the eternal cross(ing) of the word that repeatedly inscribes and reinscribes the infinite play of the divine milieu. In a sense, this query implies the possibility of deconstructing deconstruction. As I have noted, proponents of deconstruction insist that their practice blocks every relationship to theology. Insofar as theology remains bound to or caught in its traditional systematic form, this claim of deconstructive critics is, of course, correct. I have, however, briefly suggested that deconstruction calls into question the coherence, integrity, and intelligibility of this network of oppositions. By inverting and subverting the poles between which Western theology has been suspended, deconstruction reverses itself and creates a new opening for the religious imagination.

Thought that wanders into this interstitial space will, of necessity, be unsettled and unsettling. Repeatedly slipping through the holes in the system within which it must, nevertheless, be registered, such thought is perpetually transitory and forever nomadic. It is neither simply this nor that, here nor there, inside nor outside. To follow the ways of such vagrant thought is inevitably to err. Writing that attempts to trace the border and retrace the margin can, therefore, be described as *erring*. *Err* is an uncommonly rich word whose many (perhaps bottomless) layers suggest multiple dimensions of the argument I shall be developing. By roaming through the labyrinth of this word, we catch an initial glimpse of the wiles and ways of postmodern a/theology.

Err appears to derive from the Latin *errāre* (whose "prehistoric" form is *ersāre*) by way of Middle English *erre*, French *errer*, Provençal and Spanish *errar*, and Italian *errare*.[6] *Errāre* ("to wander, or stray about, to rove") is cognate with the Gothic *aírzjan*, which means "to lead astray." To err is to ramble, roam, stray, wander, like Chaucer's "weary ghost that errest to and fro." Such wandering inevitably leads one astray – away from one's path or line of direction. To err, therefore, is to

"fail, miss, go wrong in judgment or opinion; to make a mistake, blunder, or commit a fault; to be incorrect; to go astray morally"; even "to sin." *Err* drifts toward: *Errable* ("fallible, liable to error"); *Errabund* ("random"); *Errancy* ("the condition of erring or being in error"); *Errand* ("a message, a verbal communication to be repeated to a third party; a petition or prayer presented through another; a short journey on which an inferior – e.g. a servant, a child – is sent to convey a message or perform some simple business on behalf of the sender"); *Errantly* ("wandering, prone to wander; wandering from place to place, vagrant, nomadic; irregular or uncertain in movement, having no fixed course; irregular or eccentric in conduct, habit, or opinion"); *Erratum* ("an error in writing or printing"); *Erre* ("wound, scar"); *Erre* ("wrath"); *Erroneous* ("wandering, roving, moving aimlessly, vagrant; straying from the ways of wisdom or prudence; misguided; of doctrines, opinions, statements: incorrect, mistaken, wrong"); *Error* ("the action of roaming or wandering; hence a devious or winding course, a roving, winding; chagrin, fury, vexation; extravagance of passion; the condition of erring in opinion; holding of mistaken notions or beliefs; a delusion, trick; something incorrectly done through ignorance or inadvertance; a departure from moral rectitude; a transgression"); and, of course, *Errant*. "Errant" subdivides into three branches. I. Old French *errer*, which is from the Latin *iterāre* ("to journey, travel"): "Itinerant, traveling; said of knights who traveled about in quest of adventure; in chess, a traveling pawn, one that has been advanced from its original square; and *Errant juif* – the Wandering Jew." II. "The primary notion of branch II is uncertain:" A notorious, 'common' thief." III. French *errār*, which is from the Latin *errāre* ("to stray, wander, err"): "Astray, wandering, roving; straying from the proper course or place; having no fixed course." *Erring*, then, is "wandering, roaming; deviating from the right or intended course; missing the mark." The semantic branches of *err* spread to errancy, erratic, erratum, erre, erroneous, and errant.

The erring a/theologian is driven to consider and reconsider errant notions: transgression, subversion, mastery, utility, consumption, domination, narcissism, nihilism, possession, uncanniness, repetition, tropes, writing, dissemination, dispossession, expropriation, impropriety, anonymity, spending, sacrifice, death, desire, delight, wandering, aberrance, carnival, comedy, superficiality, carnality, duplicity, shiftiness, undecidability, and spinning. In view of these preoccupations, it should be clear that erring thought is neither *properly* theological nor nontheological, theistic nor atheistic, religious nor secular, believing nor nonbelieving. A/theology represents the liminal thinking of marginal thinkers. The / of a/theology (which, it is important to note, can be written but not spoken) marks the *limen* that signifies *both* proximity and distance, similarity and difference, interiority and exteriority. This strangely permeable membrane forms a border where fixed boundaries disintegrate. Along this boundless boundary the traditional polarities between which Western theology has been suspended are inverted and subverted. Since it is forever *entre-deux*,[iv] a/theology is undeniably ambiguous. The a/theologian asks errant questions and suggests responses that often seem erratic or even erroneous. Since his reflection wanders, roams, and strays from the "proper" course, it tends to deviate from well-established ways. To traditional eyes, a/theology doubtless appears to be irregular, eccentric, and vagrant. At best it seems aimless, at worst devious. Within this framework, a/theology is, in fact, heretical. For the a/theologian, however, heresy and aimlessness are unavoidable. Ideas are never fixed but are always in transition; thus they are irrepressibly transitory. For this reason, a/theology might be labeled "Nomad Thought."[7] The erring nomad neither looks back to an absolute beginning nor ahead to an ultimate end. His writing, therefore, remains unfinished. His work is less a complete book than an open (perhaps broken) text that never really begins or actually ends. The words of a/theology fall in between; they are *always* in the middle. The a/theological text is a tissue woven of threads that are produced by endless spinning. This vertiginous wordplay points to the paradoxical nonbinary (a) logic of the cross. I am persuaded that along the middle way traced by deconstruction there lies a revolutionary reading of writing that reveals scripture anew. The way of the word, of course, is also the tortuous path to Golgotha.[v] As the threshold of absolute passage, the cross marks the intersection of ascent and descent that is the "marriage of heaven and hell." . . .

The main contours of deconstructive a/theology begin to emerge with the realization of the necessary interrelation between the death of God and radical christology.[vi] Radical christology is *thoroughly* incarnational – the divine "*is*" the incarnate word. Furthermore, this embodiment of the divine is the death of God. With the appearance of the divine that is not only itself but is at the same time other, the God who alone is God disappears. The death of God is the sacrifice of the transcendent Author/Creator/Master who governs from afar. Incarnation *irrevocably* erases the disembodied logos and inscribes a word that becomes the script enacted in the infinite play of interpretation. To understand incarnation as inscription is to discover the word. Embodied word is script(ure), the writing in which we are inscribed and which we inscribe. Like all writing, the carnal word is transgressive. Inscription inverts the traditional understanding of the God–world relationship and subverts all forms of transcendence. A/theology is, in large measure, a critique of the notion of the transcendent God, who is "self-clos'd, all-repelling."[8] In this case, however, the struggle against the omnipotent Father does not simply repeat the undialectical inversion of God and self enacted in humanistic atheism. As a result of the recognition of the necessary interplay between patricide and suicide, the death of God does not issue in the deification of the individual ego. Far from resisting the unsettling currents that circulate throughout postmodern worlds, the a/theologian welcomes the death of God and embraces the disappearance of the self.

In order to avoid unnecessary confusion, it is important to realize that in radical christology the divine is *forever* embodied. The word is *always already* inscribed. Incarnation, therefore, is not a once-and-for-all event, restricted to a specific time and place and limited to a particular individual. Rather, inscription is a continual (though not necessarily a continuous) process. To insist that God "*is*" eternally embodied in *word* or that the divine "*is*" incarnate *word* is to imply that "there is a sense in which the word 'God' refers to the word 'word' and the word 'word' refers to the word 'God'."[9] God is what word means, and word is what "God" means. To interpret God as word is to understand the divine as scripture or writing. In order to develop the far-reaching implications of this suggestion, it is necessary to consider different ways of reading the word "word."

According to traditional Occidental wisdom, the notion of the word is inextricably tied to the struc-

---

[iv] Intermediate, in-between.
[v]   The place where Christ was crucified.

[vi] Christology is the subfield of Christian theology that seeks to understand Christ.

ture of signification. As remarks scattered throughout earlier chapters imply, signification at the most basic level presupposes a distinction between signifier and signified. In this binary relationship, the signifier points beyond itself to that which it represents (i.e. the signified). Insofar as word is sign, it appears to be essentially ostensive or fundamentally referential. I have already indicated that the referent of the sign can be interpreted in different ways. In general, the signified tends to be viewed as either "real" or "ideal." Accordingly, a sign is believed to designate something conceptual, like an idea, image, or mental construct, or is held to denote an actual object in the world. Common sense and reasoning based upon it frequently try to mediate ideality and reality by insisting that, while every sign carries an "ideal" meaning, signified meaning always points to a "real" referent, which remains extramental. This analysis of words appears to rest on the assumption that nouns and the activity of naming are normative for all uses of language. The relationship between named/signified and name/signifier is not symmetrical. The former is traditionally regarded as primary, the latter as secondary. The meaning of any word is that to which it refers. Conversely, the signified grounds (and thus lends weight to) the signifier. The word, therefore, remains obediently subservient to the signified.

Although not immediately evident, this pattern of signification is tied up in the ontotheological network. God, or His substitute, appears either overtly or covertly to be the final meaning of the word. Put differently, God is, in effect, the "transcendental signified" that grounds the structure of signification. Since the "sign and divinity have the same place and time of birth," the "age of the sign is essentially theological."[10] This does not mean, of course, that every sign refers directly or even indirectly to God. The point to be stressed is that some notion of the transcendental signified is required by any referential system that gives priority to the signified over the signifier. While not always explicitly named God, the transcendental signified *functions* as the purported locus of truth that is supposed to stabilize all meaningful words.

A closer examination of this structure of signification discloses inherent contradictions that call into question the fundamental opposition between signifier and signified. Whether the referent of the sign is taken to be "real" or "ideal," the distinction between signifier and signified is actually a product

of *consciousness itself.* Though not always aware of its own activity, consciousness attempts to *give itself* a criterion by which to judge itself. The signified is distinguished from the signifier and serves as the standard by which all signs are measured. For the most part, consciousness regards its criterion as external to, independent of, and imposed upon itself. But this interpretation of experience fails to do justice to the creativity and productivity of consciousness. That to which consciousness points is always already within consciousness itself. This analysis of the relationship between signifier and signified overturns the traditional understanding of signification. The signified is neither independent of nor superior to the signifier. To the contrary, the signified is a signifier. Consciousness, therefore, deals *only* with signs and never reaches the thing itself. More precisely, the thing itself is not an independent entity (be it "real" or "ideal") to which all signs refer but is itself a *sign*.

Armed with this insight, it is possible to reinterpret the claim that the word "God" refers to the word "word" and that the word "word" refers to the word "God." Although the word is a sign, the signified is not independent of, and qualitatively different from, the signifier. Inasmuch as the signified is a signifier, the sign is a sign of a sign. Since a word is a sign, it is always about another word. In different terms, the word stages a drama whose script is the interplay of signs. When the word is understood in this way, it appears as *writing* or *scripture*. Simultaneously inside and outside the traditional structure of signification, "writing is not *about* something; *it is that something itself.*"[11]

It should be clear that writing inscribes the disappearance of the transcendental signified. In this way, scripture embodies and enacts the death of God, even as the death of God opens and releases writing. The disappearance of the transcendental signified closes the theological age of the sign and makes possible the free play of a/theological writing. Within the classical economy of signification, "*Logos* is a son . . . a son that would be destroyed in his very *presence* without the present attendance of his father.[vii] His father who answers. His father who speaks for him and answers for him. Without his father, he would be nothing but, in

---

vii   *Logos* is the Greek term meaning "word," discourse, or reason. It is also the term with which John famously began his Gospel ("In the beginning was the Word [*Logos*] . . .").

fact, writing. At least that is what is said by the one who says: it is the father's thesis. The specificity of writing would thus be intimately bound to the absence of the father. Such an absence can of course exist along very diverse modalities, distinctly or confusedly, successively or simultaneously: to have lost one's father, through natural or violent death, through random violence or patricide."[12] By enacting the death of the transcendent(al) Father/signified, the word becomes the wayward, rebellious, errant "son." "Writing, the lost son ... writes (itself): (that) the father *is not*, that is to say, is not present."[13] The word marks the closure of all presence that is not at the same time absence and marks the end of identity that is not also difference. In this way, the incarnate word spells the death of the God who alone is God. The death of God, however, is the birth of the divine that is not only itself but is always at the same time other....

This account of scripture cannot, of course, be reduced to the common-place view of writing as the simple transcription of antecedent thoughts, ideas, or images from immaterial interior form to material exterior expression. It is precisely this view of writing that is negated by the disappearance of the transcendental signified. The death of the father opens the reign of the word that is embodied in scripture. Since this word enacts absolute passage, it is forever liminal and eternally playful. The play of the word is writing, and the drama of writing is word. In writing, fixed boundaries break down. Scripture, therefore, is always marginal. The/A word is nothing in itself; it is a play within a play, a play that is forever an interplay. This play is a play of differences that forms and reforms the word itself. The specificity of any signifier is a function of its entwinement within a complex signifying web. This differential network of signs is "the functional condition, the condition of possibility, for every sign."[14] Its "name" is *writing*.

Within a scriptural economy, writing is the articulation of (the) word(s). To articulate is to joint. A joint (where only outlaws and the errant hang out) joins by separating and separates by joining. This joint, this threshold, is neither here nor there, neither present nor absent. And yet, without articulation there is only an inarticulateness, which is not merely silence but, simply, nothing. *Everything hinges on scripture....*

Mitte designates not only center but also middle, midst, mean, and medium. For example, *die goldene Mitte* is the golden mean and *das Reich der Mitte* is

the Middle Kingdom. Closely related to *Mitte, Mittel* refers to measure, mean, and medium. A suggestive extension of this word prompts further reflection. *Mittel* can also "mean" remedy or medicine. The French *milieu* captures various nuances of the German *Mitte. Le milieu* is the middle, midst, heart, center, medium, and mean. In addition to this cluster of meanings, *milieu* refers to one's environment, habitat, or surroundings. Through a curious twist of meaning, *le milieu* is sometimes used to designate the criminal underworld, the world of gangsters. Two English words closely related to *Mitte* and *milieu* are mean and medium. Mean derives from the Latin *medianus*, which is defined as "the middle." In this context, mean is that which is in the middle. This intermediate position can be both spatial and temporal. "Mean," of course, also designates an intermediary agent, i.e. one who acts as a mediator or go-between, who intercedes on behalf of one of the parties in a conflict. In view of issues yet to be considered, it is important to recall that the sacraments are labeled "the *means* of grace." "Medium" (*medius*, middle, midst, mid) likewise means something intermediate. Furthermore, medium refers to any intervening substance through which a force acts on objects at a distance, e.g. air or ether. This sense of the word gives rise to the notion of a pervading or enveloping substance or element in which an organism lives, i.e. its environment or the conditions of its life. By drawing on this fund of associations, it is possible to suggest that *Mitte*, or *milieu*, is "medium in the sense of middle, neither/nor, what is between extremes, and [a] medium in the sense of element, ether, matrix, means."[15]

This milieu marks a middle way that is thoroughly liminal. At this threshold, opposites cross. The margin itself, however, is not reducible to the extremes whose mean it forms. The medium, in other words, can never be contained, captured, or caught by any fixed pair of terms. Consequently, the milieu is always para-doxical. As we have seen elsewhere, a "thing in 'para' ... is not only simultaneously on both sides of the boundary line between inside and out. It is also the boundary itself, the screen which is a permeable membrane connecting inside and outside. It confuses them with one another, allowing the outside in, making the inside out, dividing them and joining them. It also forms an ambiguous transition between one and the other."[16] This paradoxical limen or permeable membrane can be described as something like a *hymen.*[viii] By undermining the simplicity of oppositions and distinctions, "the hymen, the confusion between the present and the nonpresent, along with all the indifferences it entails within the whole series of opposites... produces the effect of a medium (a medium as element enveloping both terms at once; a medium located between the two terms). It is an operation that *both* sows confusion *between* opposites *and* stands *between* opposites 'at once.' What counts here is the *between*, the in-between-ness of the hymen. The hymen 'takes place' in the 'inter-,' in the spacing between desire and fulfillment, between penetration and its recollection. But this medium of the *entre* has nothing to do with a center."[17]

If *die Mitte ist überall*,[ix] *die Mitte* is not so much the center as it is the milieu. Moreover, this milieu is not restricted to a particular spatial or temporal point. It is everywhere and everytime. The universality of the medium implies that what is intermediate is not transitory and that what is interstitial is "permanent." Though always betwixt 'n' between, the "eternal" time of the middle neither begins nor ends. This universal and eternal milieu marks the (para)site where the word plays freely. Along this boundless boundary, the word appears divine. Scripture *is* the divine milieu, and the divine milieu *is* writing. The milieu embodied in word and inscribed in/by writing is divine insofar as it is the creative/destructive medium of everything that is and all that is not. Writing, as I have emphasized, is the "structured and differing origin of differences." This play of differences or differential web of interrelation is universally constitutive. When understood as scripture, the divine milieu is "what at the same time renders possible and impossible, probable and improbable oppositions such as"[18] eternity/time, infinitude/finitude, being/becoming, good/evil, etc. Writing is "originary" (though not original) inasmuch as it "grounds" or "founds" the differences that form and deform identity. Though the divine milieu is never simply present or absent, it is the *medium* of all presence and absence. In this complex mean, opposites, that do not remain themselves, cross over into each other and thus dissolve all original identity.

By disclosing the formative force of negativity, writing inverts and subverts the dyadic structure of the Western theological network. Through the enactment of an unending dialectic of transgression, the divine milieu effects "a total negation of everything which is manifest and real in consciousness and experience as God, so as to make possible a radically new form of consciousness and experience. Thereby a new form of God appears, but precisely because it is a radically new form it no longer can be given the name or image of God."[19] This negation of God appears as the word incarnate in writing. In the embodied word, the God of writing is manifested as the writing of God. The figure of Thoth[x] is opposed to its other (father, sun, life, speech, origin or orient, etc.), but as that which at once supplements and supplants it. Thoth extends or opposes by repeating or replacing. By the same token, the figure of Thoth takes shape and takes its shape from the very thing it resists and substitutes for. But it thereby opposes *itself*, passes into its other, and this messenger-god is truly a god of the absolute passage between opposites. If he had any identity – but he is precisely the god of non-identity – he would be that *coincidentia oppositorum* to which we shall soon have recourse again. In distinguishing himself from his opposite, Thoth also imitates it, becomes its sign and representative, obeys it and *conforms* to it, replaces it, by violence if need be. He is thus the father's other, the father, and the subversive movement of replacement. The god of writing is thus at once his father, his son, and himself. He cannot be assigned a fixed spot in the play of differences."[20]

It is, of course, impossible to *master* Thoth by the logic of exclusion. In the liminal time–space of scripture, hard-and-fast oppositions are shattered and every seemingly stable either-or is perpetually dislocated. The divine milieu is neither fully present nor absent but is present only to the extent that it is at the same time absent. It neither is nor is not; it is insofar as it is not and is not insofar as it is. It is not totally positive or completely negative but affirms in negating and negates in affirming. According to traditional logic, which rests on the correlative principles of identity and noncontradiction, such claims are not only improper, they are actually absurd. The paradoxical divine milieu presupposes a "logic of

---

viii A membrane partly covering the opening of the vagina, broken during heterosexual intercourse. Derrida uses "hymen" as a sign for the "between" in his essay, "The Double Session."

ix The middle is everywhere.

x The Egyptian god, "Hermes" to the Greeks, whose name means "word," was the inventor of writing. Derrida writes of Thoth in his essay, "Plato's Pharmacy."

Mark C. Taylor

contamination and the contamination of logic."[21] The eternally errant medium in which all differentiation is produced and destroyed cannot be represented in distinct categories and clear concepts. For this reason, the divine milieu "is not thinkable within the terms of classical logic but only within the graphics... of the *pharmakon*."[22]

Transgressive scripture engenders incurable disease by violating propriety and infecting purity. In this case, dis-ease need not be destructive and can actually be productive. Insofar as writing is parasitical, it is both nourishing and debilitating. This ambiguity lends scripture its pharmacological character. The Greek word from which *pharmaco-* and all its variants derive is *pharmakon*, which can mean "drug, medicine, or poison." Interestingly enough, the god of writing is also the god of medicine, who is supposed to restore health. A medicine man, however, is always something of a magician and trickster. The drug he prescribes is both a medicine and a poison – both gift and *Gift*.[xi] This generative/destructive *prescription* is a *pharmakon*. "If the *pharmakon* is 'ambivalent,' it is because it constitutes the medium in which opposites are opposed, the movement and the play that link them among themselves, reverses them or makes one side cross over into the other... The *pharmakon* is the movement, the locus, and the play: (the production of) difference."[23] Though it is supposed to fix, the *pharmakon* itself cannot be fixed. Its shape is always changing, its form forever reforming. The *pharmakon* seems to be a liquid medium whose play is completely fluid. Like ink, wine, and semen, the *pharmakon* always manages to penetrate. "[I]t is absorbed, drunk, introduced into the inside, which it first marks with the hardness of the type, soon to invade and inundate it with its medicine, its brew, its drink, its potion, its poison."[24]

Such a strange potion can be concocted only by a physician who knows the magic (of) word(s): Hocus-pocus – *Hoc est corpus meum*.[xii] In the(se) extraordinary word(s), the physician himself appears as a *pharmakos*. Like every uncanny guest, this unsettling trickster is never permitted to pass beyond the threshold. Responsible authorities and distinguished authors attempt to keep the *pharmakos* behind bars. For this reason, the "site" of the word is always marked by an X and forever bears the sign of a cross. Since the *pharmakos* is irreducibly marginal, the ceremony in which it (or rather

"he") is imbibed and inscribed must be "played out on the boundary line between inside and outside, which it has as its function ceaselessly to trace and retrace. *Intra muros/ extra muros*.[xiii] The origin of differences and division, the *pharmakos* represents evil both introjected and projected. Beneficial insofar as he cures – and for that, venerated and cared for – harmful insofar as he incarnates the powers of evil – and for that, feared and treated with caution. Alarming and calming. Sacred and accursed."[25]

In the ambiguous figure of the *pharmakos*, the intercourse of Terminus and Dionysus is manifest in the body and blood of the Crucified.[xiv] The Crucified is the cruciform word that is always already inscribed in the eternally recurring play of the divine milieu. Scripture marks the *via crucis* in which all creation involves dismemberment and every solution presupposes dissolution.[xv] When *die Mitte ist überall*, transitoriness and passage no longer need to be repressed. Arising and passing can be welcomed as "productive and destructive force, as *continual creation*."

The incarnate word inscribed in writing spells the closure of all presence that is not at the same time absence and the end of all identity that is not also difference. Writing is an unending play of differences that establishes the thoroughgoing relativity of all "things." This complex web of interrelations is the divine milieu. Within this nontotalizable totality, nothing is itself by itself, for all things emerge and fade through the interplay of forces. Insofar as the embodied word "is the name of the eternal perishing of eternal presence,"[26] scripture marks the death of God. In different terms, writing is a kenotic process; it empties everything of absolute self-identity and complete self-presence. In the eternal play of the divine milieu, nothing is fully autonomous or solely sovereign. Thus there is no *causa sui*,[xvi] antecedent to and the ultimate origin of everything else. The absolute relativity of the divine milieu renders all other things completely corelative. As a consequence of the eternal cross(-ing) of scripture, nothing stands alone and everything "originates" codependently. "Codependent

---

xi   "Gift" in German means poison.
xii   This is my body.
xiii   *Intra muros/extra muros* means "within the walls" (e.g. of a town)/"outside the walls."
xiv   Terminus was the Roman god of boundaries and endings (e.g. of the year). Dionysus was the Greek god of fertility, wine and sensual ecstasy ("Bacchus" to the Romans).
xv   *Via crucis* means "way of the cross."
xvi   *Causa sui* means "self-cause."

origination"[27] is nothing other than the nonoriginal origin that erases absolute originality.

As the nonoriginal origin that "founds" the differences constitutive of relative identity, writing inverts and subverts the notion of origin itself. The generative movement of scripture rifts all seemingly immovable foundations and keeps everything in motion. The incarnate word is neither transcendent nor self-derived. To the contrary, the divine milieu is a/the grounded ground that, nonetheless, "grounds." In writing's unending play of differences, neither ground nor grounded is absolutely prior or undeniably primal. Ground and grounded are separated and joined in a relation that is characterized by radical codependence. "*{T}here is nothing in the ground that is not in the grounded*, and *there is nothing in the grounded that is not in the ground*."[28] Since writing empties every *causa sui* of total self-possession, the divine milieu cannot be an *absolute* origin. It must be a *nonoriginal* "origin" or a *grounded* "ground." Contrary to common sense, writing is "founded" by the differences it "founds." In other words, writing is always in other words. The word is never disembodied; it is forever inscribed in writing. Since the word incarnates the coincidence of presence and absence and of identity and difference, it appears only by disappearing. This unstoppable interplay shows that the *Logos* is always the *Logos Spermatikos*, endlessly propagated by dissemination.[xvii] Dissemination inscribes the way from the eternal recurrence of the divine milieu to the free play of marks and traces.

"To disseminate" (*disseminare: dis + semen*, gen. *seminis*, seed) is to scatter abroad, as in sowing seed. By extension, dissemination refers to the action of dispersing, diffusing, broadcasting, or promulgating. When translated into the present context, these verbal affiliations suggest that the dissemination of the word can be understood as its spreading, scattering, diffusion, or publication. The notion of the dissemination of the word is not, of course, new. Consider, for example, the following parabolic formulation:

A sower went out to sow. And as he sowed, some seed fell along the path, and the birds came and devoured it. Other seed fell on rocky ground, where it had not much soil, and imme-

diately it sprang up, since it had no depth of soil; and when the sun rose it was scorched, and since it had no root it withered away. Other seed fell among thorns and the thorns grew up and choked it, and it yielded no grain. And other seeds fell into good soil and brought forth grain, growing up and increasing and yielding thirty-fold and sixtyfold and a hundredfold.[29]

Like any text, these lines can be read in many ways. In this context, it is important to recognize that, according to this parable, the word is seed that appears with the disappearance of the sower. The "sower, mentioned only at the start of the story, immediately disappears. It would have been quite possible to leave him out completely: 'at the time of sowing, some seed fell. . . .' It would also have been easy to have retained him consistently: 'and some of the sower's seed fell. . . .' Instead, he is mentioned at the start and thereafter ignored. The parable is about seed and about the inevitable polyvalence of failure and success in sowing. . . . Or, if one prefers, it is about the absence and departure, the necessary self-negation of the sower."[30] By negating the sower in order to concentrate on the seed, this parable implies that dispersal is neither accidental nor secondary to a primordial, self-contained word. Quite the opposite, dissemination is necessary if any word is to be fertile. The seminal/seminary word *must* flow freely in liquid media like ink, semen, and wine. Because of its fluency, the embodied word cannot be contained within fixed boundaries or inscribed in straight lines. It is always dispersed and diffused. Furthermore, this scattering is not a temporary aberration, eventually overcome. Dissemination "can be led back neither to a present of simple origin . . . nor to an eschatological presence. It marks an irreducible *generative* multiplicity."[31] By figuring what cannot return to the father, the dissemination of the word replaces sterile stability and univocacy with creative instability and equivocacy.

To the extent that the embodied word enacts the *kenōsis* of all absolute self-presence and total self-identity, it can be itself only in and through the process of *its own* self-emptying. Like the transcendent father, the incarnate son must also pass away. Having displaced the Lord of Hosts, word becomes host. The word, which itself is a transgressor, is at the same time a victim who invites transgression. The patricidal act of transgression manifests the host-ility of the word. Not only is parasite host; sacrificer is also sacrifice. The word

---

xvii Derrida writes of "*Logos Spermatikos*," or "*word seed*," meaning that Logos is usually conceived by the Western tradition as reproductive (and male). "Dissemination" is the name of an essay, and a book, by Derrida.

turns out to be a hospitable host who asks everyone to sit down at his table and even offers *himself* for our nourishment.

For my flesh is food indeed, and my blood is drink indeed. He who eats my flesh and drinks my blood abides in me, and I in him.

Word becomes flesh: body and blood, bread and wine. Take, eat. Take, drink. To eat this bread and drink this wine is to extend the embodiment of the word and to expand the fluid play of the divine milieu. When freely enacted, the drama of the word proves to be self-consuming. While the incarnation of the divine is the death of God, the dissemination of the word is the crucifixion of the individual self. This dismemberment inflicts an incurable wound, which gives birth to erratic marks and erring traces.

Author's Notes

1 Jacques Derrida, *Positions*, trans. A. Bass (Chicago: University of Chicago Press, 1981), p. 40.

2 Friedrich Nietzsche, *The Gay Science*, trans. Walten Kaufman (New York: Random House, 1974), p. 182.

3 Thomas J. J. Altizer, *The Descent into Hell: A Study of the Radical Reversal of the Christian Consciousness* (New York: Seabury Press, 1979), p. 53.

4 J. Hillis Millier, "Theology and Logology in Victorian Literature," in *Religion and Literature: The Convergence of Approaches*, supplement to *Journal of the American Academy of Religion*, 47 (1979): 354.

5 Jacques Derrida, *Writing and Difference*, trans. A. Bass (Chicago: University of Chicago Press, 1978), p. 20.

6 Unless otherwise indicated, I have drawn definitions and etymologies from the *Oxford English Dictionary* (New York: Oxford University Press, 1971).

7 Gilles Deleuze, "Nomad Thought," in *The New Nietzsche: Contemporary Styles of Interpretation*, ed. D. B. Allison (New York: Dell, 1977), pp. 142–9.

8 William Blake.

9 Robert Scharlemann, "The Being of God When God Is Not Being God: Deconstructing the History of Theism," in Altizer et al., *Deconstruction and Theology* (New York: Crossroad, 1982), p. 101.

10 Jacques Derrida, *Of Grammatology*, trans. G. C. Spivak (Baltimore: Johns Hopkins University Press, 1976), p. 14.

11 Samuel Beckett, quoted in Daniel Albright, *Representation and the Imagination: Beckett, Kafka, Nabokov, and Schoenberg* (Chicago: University of Chicago Press, 1981), p. 2.

12 Jacques Derrida, *Dissemination*, trans, B. Johnson (Chicago: University of Chicago Press, 1981), p. 77.

13 Ibid., p. 146.

14 Jacques Derrida, *Speech and Phenomena, and other Essays on Husserl's Theory of Signs*, trans. D. B. Allison, (Evanston, Ill.: Northwestern University, 1973), p. 134.

15 Derrida, *Dissemination*, p. 211.

16 J. Hillis Miller, "The Critic as Host," in Harold Bloom et al., *Deconstruction and Criticism* (New York: Seabury, 1979), p. 219.

17 Derrida, *Dissemination*, p. 212.

18 Jacques Derrida, "Limited Inc abc...," *Glyph*, 7 (1980): 176–233, p. 225.

19 Altizer, *Descent into Hell*, pp. 56–7.

20 Derrida, *Dissemination*, pp. 92–3.

21 Ibid., p. 149.

22 Ibid., p. 153.

23 Ibid., p. 127.

24 Ibid., p. 152.

25 Ibid., p. 133.

26 Thomas J. Altizer, *The Self-Embodiment of God* (New York: Harper & Row, 1979), p. 36.

27 Nargarjuna.

28 G. W. F. Hegel, *Science of Logic* trans. A. V. Miller (New York: Humanities Press, 1969), p. 457.

29 Mark 4: 3–8.

30 John Dominic Crossan, *Cliffs of Fall: Paradox and Polyvalence in the Parables of Jesus* (New York: Crossroad, 1980), p. 50.

31 Derrida, *Positions*, p. 45.

44

"Solidarity or Objectivity?"

Richard Rorty

Philosopher Richard Rorty's (1931–) book, *Philosophy and the Mirror of Nature* (1979), created great controversy in American philosophy by criticizing recent analytic philosophy and suggesting that this tradition, with continental philosophy, was converging on pragmatism as a postfoundationalist philosophical method. In the succeeding decade Rorty became the most famous American philosopher to present a radical critique of philosophy, a rejection of the traditional philosophical pursuit of ultimate, transcendental, foundational knowledge, which seemed to leave little for philosophy to do but, in his words, contribute to the continuing "conversation of culture." Unlike the French postmodernists, Rorty denied that this antifoundationalism can lead to any radical political conclusions, since it implies that philosophy can no more justify any program of political reform than it can legitimate the status quo. Once foundationalism is abandoned, all philosophical writing can do is engage in the rhetorical task of making different world descriptions or "vocabularies" look attractive. In the following essay, published in 1984, he criticizes the attempt to ground our interpretive vocabularies in an appeal to "objectivity," offering the pragmatic alternative that legitimation is always an appeal to "solidarity" or culture.

There are two principal ways in which reflective human beings try, by placing their lives in a larger context, to give sense to those lives. The first is by telling the story of their contribution to a community. This community may be the actual historical one in which they live, or another actual one, distant in time or place, or a quite imaginary one, consisting perhaps of a dozen heroes and heroines selected from history or fiction or both. The second way is to describe themselves as standing in immediate relation to a nonhuman reality. This relation is immediate in the sense that it does not derive from a relation between such a reality and their tribe, or their nation, or their imagined band of comrades. I shall say that stories of the former kind exemplify the desire for solidarity, and that stories of the latter kind exemplify the desire for objectivity. Insofar as a person is seeking solidarity, she does not ask about the relation between the practices of the chosen community and something outside that community. Insofar as she seeks objectivity, she distances herself from the actual persons around her not by thinking of herself as a member of some other real or imaginary group, but rather by attaching herself to something which can be described without reference to any particular human beings.

The tradition in Western culture which centers around the notion of the search for Truth, a tradition which runs from the Greek philosophers through the Enlightenment, is the clearest example of the attempt to find a sense in one's existence by turning away from solidarity to objectivity. The idea of Truth as something to be pursued for its

Richard Rorty, "Solidarity or Objectivity?" pp. 3–19 from *Post-Analytic Philosophy* (ed. John Rajchman and Cornel West). New York: Columbia University Press, 1985.

own sake, not because it will be good for oneself, or for one's real or imaginary community, is the central theme of this tradition. It was perhaps the growing awareness by the Greeks of the sheer diversity of human communities which stimulated the emergence of this ideal. A fear of parochialism, of being confined within the horizons of the group into which one happens to be born, a need to see it with the eyes of a stranger, helps produce the skeptical and ironic tone characteristic of Euripides and Socrates. Herodotus' willingness to take the barbarians seriously enough to describe their customs in detail may have been a necessary prelude to Plato's claim that the way to transcend skepticism is to envisage a common goal of humanity – a goal set by human nature rather than by Greek culture. The combination of Socratic alienation and Platonic hope gives rise to the idea of the intellectual as someone who is in touch with the nature of things, not by way of the opinions of his community, but in a more immediate way.

Plato developed the idea of such an intellectual by means of distinctions between knowledge and opinion, and between appearance and reality. Such distinctions conspire to produce the idea that rational inquiry should make visible a realm to which non-intellectuals have little access, and of whose very existence they may be doubtful. In the Enlightenment, this notion became concrete in the adoption of the Newtonian physical scientist as a model of the intellectual. To most thinkers of the eighteenth century, it seemed clear that the access to Nature which physical science had provided should now be followed by the establishment of social, political, and economic institutions which were in accordance with Nature. Ever since, liberal social thought has centered around social reform as made possible by objective knowledge of what human beings are like – not knowledge of what Greeks or Frenchmen or Chinese are like, but of humanity as such. We are the heirs of this objectivist tradition, which centers around the assumption that we must step outside our community long enough to examine it in the light of something which transcends it, namely, that which it has in common with every other actual and possible human community. This tradition dreams of an ultimate community which will have transcended the distinction between the natural and the social, which will exhibit a solidarity which is not parochial because it is the expression of an ahistorical human nature. Much of the rhetoric of contemporary intellectual life takes for granted that the goal of scientific inquiry into man is to understand "underlying structures," or "culturally invariant factors," or "biologically determined patterns."

Those who wish to ground solidarity in objectivity – call them "realists" – have to construe truth as correspondence to reality. So they must construct a metaphysics which has room for a special relation between beliefs and objects which will differentiate true from false beliefs. They also must argue that there are procedures of justification of belief which are natural and not merely local. So they must construct an epistemology which has room for a kind of justification which is not merely social but natural, springing from human nature itself, and made possible by a link between that part of nature and the rest of nature. On their view, the various procedures which are thought of as providing rational justification by one or another culture may or may not really *be* rational. For to be truly rational, procedures of justification *must* lead to the truth, to correspondence to reality, to the intrinsic nature of things.

By contrast, those who wish to reduce objectivity to solidarity – call them "pragmatists" – do not require either a metaphysics or an epistemology. They view truth as, in William James' phrase, what is good for *us* to believe.[i] So they do not need an account of a relation between beliefs and objects called "correspondence," nor an account of human cognitive abilities which ensures that our species is capable of entering into that relation. They see the gap between truth and justification not as something to be bridged by isolating a natural and transcultural sort of rationality which can be used to criticize certain cultures and praise others, but simply as the gap between the actual good and the possible better. From a pragmatist point of view, to say that what is rational for us now to believe may not be *true*, is simply to say that somebody may come up with a better idea. It is to say that there is always room for improved belief, since new evidence, or new hypotheses, or a whole new vocabulary, may come along.[1] For pragmatists, the desire for objectivity is not the desire to escape the limitations of one's community, but simply the desire for as much intersubjective agreement as possible, the desire to extend the reference of "us" as far as we can. Insofar as pragmatists make a distinction between knowledge and opinion, it is simply the distinction between topics on which such agreement is relatively easy to get and topics on which agreement is relatively hard to get.

[i] William James (1842–1910), pragmatic American philosopher and psychologist, a friend of Peirce.

"Relativism" is the traditional epithet applied to pragmatism by realists. Three different views are commonly referred to by this name. The first is the view that every belief is as good as every other. The second is the view that "true" is an equivocal term, having as many meanings as there are procedures of justification. The third is the view that there is nothing to be said about either truth or rationality apart from descriptions of the familiar procedures of justification which a given society – *ours* – uses in one or another area of inquiry. The pragmatist holds the ethnocentric third view. But he does not hold the self-refuting first view, nor the eccentric second view. He thinks that his views are better than the realists', but he does not think that his views correspond to the nature of things. He thinks that the very flexibility of the word "true" – the fact that it is merely an expression of commendation – insures its univocity. The term "true," on his account, means the same in all cultures, just as equally flexible terms like "here," "there," "good," "bad," "you," and "me" mean the same in all cultures. But the identity of meaning is, of course, compatible with diversity of reference, and with diversity of procedures for assigning the terms. So he feels free to use the term "true" as a general term of commendation in the same way as his realist opponent does – and in particular to use it to commend his own view.

However, it is not clear why "relativist" should be thought an appropriate term for the ethnocentric third view, the one which the pragmatist *does* hold. For the pragmatist is not holding a positive theory which says that something is relative to something else. He is, instead, making the purely *negative* point that we should drop the traditional distinction between knowledge and opinion, construed as the distinction between truth as correspondence to reality and truth as a commendatory term for well-justified beliefs. The reason that the realist calls this negative claim "relativistic" is that he cannot believe that anybody would seriously deny that truth has an intrinsic nature. So when the pragmatist says that there is nothing to be said about truth save that each of us will commend as true those beliefs which he or she finds good to believe, the realist is inclined to interpret this as one more positive theory about the nature of truth: a theory according to which truth is simply the contemporary opinion of a chosen individual or group. Such a theory would, of course, be self-refuting. But the pragmatist does not have a theory of truth, much less a relativistic one. As a partisan of solidarity, his account of the

value of cooperative human inquiry has only an ethical base, not an epistemological or metaphysical one. Not having *any* epistemology, *a fortiori* he does not have a relativistic one.

The question of whether truth or rationality has an intrinsic nature, of whether we ought to have a positive theory about either topic, is just the question of whether our self-description ought to be constructed around a relation to human nature or around a relation to a particular collection of human beings, whether we should desire objectivity or solidarity. It is hard to see how one could choose between these alternatives by looking more deeply into the nature of knowledge, or of man, or of nature. Indeed, the proposal that this issue might be so settled begs the question in favor of the realist, for it presupposes that knowledge, man, and nature *have* real essences which are relevant to the problem at hand. For the pragmatist, by contrast, "knowledge" is, like "truth," simply a compliment paid to the beliefs which we think so well justified that, for the moment, further justification is not needed. An inquiry into the nature of knowledge can, on his view, only be a sociohistorical account of how various people have tried to reach agreement on what to believe.

The view which I am calling "pragmatism" is almost, but not quite, the same as what Hilary Putnam, in his recent *Reason, Truth, and History*, calls "the internalist conception of philosophy."[2] Putnam defines such a conception as one which gives up the attempt at a God's eye view of things, the attempt at contact with the nonhuman which I have been calling "the desire for objectivity." Unfortunately, he accompanies his defense of the antirealist views I am recommending with a polemic against a lot of the other people who hold these views – e.g. Kuhn, Feyerabend, Foucault, and myself.[ii] We are criticized as "relativists." Putnam presents "internalism" as a happy *via media* between realism and relativism. He speaks of "the plethora of relativistic doctrines being marketed today"[3] and in particular of "the French philosophers" as holding "some fancy mixture of cultural relativism and 'structuralism.' "[4] But when it comes to criticizing these doctrines all that Putnam finds to attack is the so-called "incommensurability thesis": viz., "terms used in another culture cannot be equated in meaning or reference with any terms or expressions *we* possess."[5] He sensibly

[ii] "Anarchist" philosopher of science Paul Feyerabend (1924–94) wrote *Against Method* (1975).

agrees with Donald Davidson in remarking that this thesis is self-refuting. Criticism of this thesis, however, is destructive of, at most, some incautious passages in some early writings by Feyerabend. Once this thesis is brushed aside, it is hard to see how Putnam himself differs from most of those he criticizes.

Putnam accepts the Davidsonian point that, as he puts it, "the whole justification of an interpretative scheme...is that it renders the behavior of others at least minimally reasonable by *our* lights."[6] It would seem natural to go on from this to say that we cannot get outside the range of those lights, that we cannot stand on neutral ground illuminated only by the natural light of reason. But Putnam draws back from this conclusion. He does so because he construes the claim that we cannot do so as the claim that the range of our thought is restricted by what he calls "institutionalized norms," publicly available criteria for settling all arguments, including philosophical arguments. He rightly says that there are no such criteria, arguing that the suggestion that there are is as self-refuting as the "incommensurability thesis." He is, I think, entirely right in saying that the notion that philosophy is or should become such an application of explicit criteria contradicts the very idea of philosophy.[7] One can gloss Putnam's point by saying that "philosophy" is precisely what a culture becomes capable of when it ceases to define itself in terms of explicit rules, and becomes sufficiently leisured and civilized to rely on inarticulate know-how, to substitute *phronesis*[iii] for codification, and conversation with foreigners for conquest of them.

But to say that we cannot refer every question to explicit criteria institutionalized by our society does not speak to the point which the people whom Putnam calls "relativists" are making. One reason these people are pragmatists is precisely that they share Putnam's distrust of the positivistic idea that rationality is a matter of applying criteria.

Such a distrust is common, for example, to Kuhn, Mary Hesse, Wittgenstein, Michael Polanyi, and Michael Oakeshott.[iv] Only someone who did think of rationality in this way would dream of suggesting that "true" means something different

in different societies. For only such a person could imagine that there was anything to pick out to which one might make "true" relative. Only if one shares the logical positivists' idea that we all carry around things called "rules of language" which regulate what we say when, will one suggest that there is no way to break out of one's culture.

In the most original and powerful section of his book, Putnam argues that the notion that "rationality...is defined by the local cultural norms" is merely the demonic counterpart of positivism. It is, as he says, "a scientistic theory inspired by anthropology as positivism was a scientistic theory inspired by the exact sciences." By "scientism" Putnam means the notion that rationality consists in the application of criteria.[8] Suppose we drop this notion, and accept Putnam's own Quinean picture[v] of inquiry as the continual reweaving of a web of beliefs rather than as the application of criteria to cases. Then the notion of "local cultural norms" will lose its offensively parochial overtones. For now to say that we must work by our own lights, that we must be ethnocentric, is merely to say that beliefs suggested by another culture must be tested by trying to weave them together with beliefs we already have. It is a consequence of this holistic view of knowledge, a view *shared* by Putnam and those he criticizes as "relativists," that alternative cultures are not to be thought of on the model of alternative geometries. Alternative geometries are irreconcilable because they have axiomatic structures, and contradictory axioms. They are *designed* to be irreconcilable. Cultures are not so designed, and do not have axiomatic structures. To say that they have "institutionalized norms" is only to say, with Foucault, that knowledge is never separable from power – that one is likely to suffer if one does not hold certain beliefs at certain times and places. But such institutional backups for beliefs take the form of bureaucrats and policemen, not of "rules of language" and "criteria of rationality." To think otherwise is the Cartesian fallacy of seeing axioms where there are only shared habits, of viewing statements which summarize such practices as if they reported constraints enforcing such practices. Part of the force of Quine's and Davidson's attack on the distinction between the conceptual and the empirical is that the distinction between different cultures does not differ in kind from the distinction between different theories held by members of a single culture. The Tasmanian aborigines and the

---

[iii]   Practical wisdom, a high ideal for Aristotle.

[iv]   Austrian philosopher Michael Polanyi (1891–1976), contemporary American philosopher of science Mary B. Hesse and English political philosopher Michael Oakeshott (1901–90).

[v]   Hilary Putnam and W. V. Quine.

the British colonists had trouble communicating, but this trouble was different only in extent from the difficulties in communication experienced by Gladstone and Disraeli.[vi] The trouble in all such cases is just the difficulty of explaining why other people disagree with us, of reweaving our beliefs so as to fit the fact of disagreement together with the other beliefs we hold. The same Quinean arguments which dispose of the positivists' distinction between analytic and synthetic truth dispose of the anthropologists' distinction between the intercultural and the intracultural.

On this holistic account of cultural norms, however, we do not need the notion of a universal transcultural rationality which Putnam invokes against those whom he calls "relativists." Just before the end of his book, Putnam says that once we drop the notion of a God's-eye point of view we realize that:

> we can only hope to produce a more rational *conception* of rationality or a better *conception* of morality if we operate from *within* our tradition (with its echoes of the Greek agora, of Newton, and so on, in the case of rationality, and with its echoes of scripture, of the philosophers, of the democratic revolutions, and so on . . . in the case of morality.) We are invited to engage in a truly human dialogue.[9]

With this I entirely agree, and so, I take it, would Kuhn, Hesse, and most of the other so-called "relativists" – perhaps even Foucault. But Putnam then goes on to pose a further question.

> Does this dialogue have an ideal terminus? Is there a *true* conception of rationality, an ideal morality, even if all we ever have are our conceptions of these?

I do not see the point of this question. Putnam suggests that a negative answer – the view that "there is only the dialogue" – is just another form of self-refuting relativism. But, once again, I do not see how a claim that something does not exist can be construed as a claim that something is relative to something else. In the final sentence of his book, Putnam says that "The very fact that we speak of our different conceptions as different conceptions

of *rationality* posits a *Grenzbegriff*, a limit-concept of ideal truth." But what is such a posit supposed to do, except to say that from God's point of view the human race is heading in the right direction? Surely Putnam's "internalism" should forbid him to say anything like that. To say that *we* think we're heading in the right direction is just to say, with Kuhn, that we can, by hindsight, tell the story of the past as a story of progress. To say that we still have a long way to go, that our present views should not be cast in bronze, is too platitudinous to require support by positing limit-concepts. So it is hard to see what difference is made by the difference between saying "there is only the dialogue" and saying "there is also that to which the dialogue converges."

I would suggest that Putnam here, at the end of the day, slides back into the scientism he rightly condemns in others. For the root of scientism, defined as the view that rationality is a matter of applying criteria, is the desire for objectivity, the hope that what Putnam calls "human flourishing" has a transhistorical nature. I think that Feyerabend is right in suggesting that until we discard the metaphor of inquiry, and human activity generally, as converging rather than proliferating, as becoming more unified rather than more diverse, we shall never be free of the motives which once led us to posit gods. Positing *Grenzbegriffe* seems merely a way of telling ourselves that a nonexistent God would, if he did exist, be pleased with us. If we could ever be moved solely by the desire for solidarity, setting aside the desire for objectivity altogether, then we should think of human progress as making it possible for human beings to do more interesting things and be more interesting people, not as heading towards a place which has somehow been prepared for humanity in advance. Our self-image would employ images of making rather than finding, the images used by the Romantics to praise poets rather than the images used by the Greeks to praise mathematicians. Feyerabend seems to me right in trying to develop such a self-image for us, but his project seems misdescribed, by himself as well as by his critics, as "relativism."[10]

Those who follow Feyerabend in this direction are often thought of as necessarily enemies of the Enlightenment, as joining in the chorus which claims that the traditional self-descriptions of the Western democracies are bankrupt, that they somehow have been shown to be "inadequate" or "self-deceptive." Part of the instinctive resistance to attempts by Marxists, Sartreans, Oakeshottians, Gadamerians and Foucauldians to reduce objectivity

---

[vi] Nineteenth-century politicians William Gladstone and Benjamin Disraeli battled as leaders of the Whig and Tory parties.

to solidarity is the fear that our traditional liberal habits and hopes will not survive the reduction.[vii] Such feelings are evident, for example, in Habermas' criticism of Gadamer's position as relativistic and potentially repressive, in the suspicion that Heidegger's attacks on realism are somehow linked to his Nazism, in the hunch that Marxist attempts to interpret values as class interests are usually just apologies for Leninist takeovers, and in the suggestion that Oakeshott's skepticism about rationalism in politics is merely an apology for the status quo.

I think that putting the issue in such moral and political terms, rather than in epistemological or metaphilosophical terms, makes clearer what is at stake. For now the question is not about how to define works like "truth" or "rationality" or "knowledge" or "philosophy," but about what self-image our society should have of itself. The ritual invocation of the "need to avoid relativism" is most comprehensible as an expression of the need to preserve certain habits of contemporary European life. These are the habits nurtured by the Enlightenment, and justified by it in terms of an appeal of Reason, conceived as a transcultural human ability to correspond to reality, a faculty whose possession and use is demonstrated by obedience to explicit criteria. So the real question about relativism is whether these same habits of intellectual, social, and political life can be justified by a conception of rationality as criterionless muddling through, and by a pragmatist conception of truth.

I think that the answer to this question is that the pragmatist cannot justify these habits without circularity, but then neither can the realist. The pragmatists' justification of toleration, free inquiry, and the quest for undistorted communication can only take the form of a comparison between societies which exemplify these habits and those which do not, leading up to the suggestion that nobody who has experienced both would prefer the latter. It is exemplified by Winston Churchill's defense of democracy as the worst form of government imaginable, except for all the others which have been tried so far. Such justification is not by reference to a criterion, but by reference to various detailed practical advantages. It is circular only in that the terms of praise used to describe liberal societies will be drawn from the vocabulary of the liberal societies themselves. Such praise has to be in *some* vocabulary, after all, and the terms of praise current in primitive or theocratic or totalitarian societies will not produce the desired result. So the pragmatist admits that he has no ahistorical standpoint from which to endorse the habits of modern democracies he wishes to praise. These consequences are just what partisans of solidarity expect. But among partisans of objectivity they give rise, once again, to fears of the dilemma formed by ethnocentrism on the one hand and relativism on the other. Either we attach a special privilege to our own community, or we pretend an impossible tolerance for every other group.

I have been arguing that we pragmatists should grasp the ethnocentric horn of this dilemma. We should say that we must, in practice, privilege our own group, even though there can be no noncircular justification for doing so. We must insist that the fact that nothing is immune from criticism does not mean that we have a duty to justify everything. We Western liberal intellectuals should accept the fact that we have to start from where we are, and that this means that there are lots of views which we simply cannot take seriously. To use Neurath's familiar analogy,[viii] we can *understand* the revolutionary's suggestion that a sailable boat can't be made out of the planks which make up ours, and that we must simply abandon ship. But we cannot take his suggestion seriously. We cannot take it as a rule for action, so it is not a live option. For some people, to be sure, the option *is* live. These are the people who have always hoped to become a New Being, who have hoped to be converted rather than persuaded. But we – the liberal Rawlsian searchers for consensus, the heirs of Socrates, the people who wish to link their days dialectically each to each – cannot do so. Our community – the community of the liberal intellectuals of the secular modern West – wants to be able to give a *post factum* account of any change of view. We want to be able, so to speak, to justify ourselves to our earlier selves. This preference is not built into us by human nature. It is just the way *we* live now.[11]

This lonely provincialism, this admission that we are just the historical moment that we are, not the representatives of something ahistorical, is what makes traditional Kantian liberals like Rawls[ix] draw

---

[vii] Contemporary German philosopher Hans-Georg Gadamer (1900–2002) developed a "hermeneutic" theory of knowledge as interpretation, inspired by Heidegger's work, in his *Truth and Method* (orig. 1960).

[viii] Austrian philosopher Otto Neurath (1882–1945) compared the task of philosophically analyzing knowledge to rebuilding a ship while at sea.

[ix] Contemporary American political philosopher, John Rawls.

back from pragmatism.[12] "Relativism," by contrast, is merely a red herring. The realist is, once again, projecting his own habits of thought upon the pragmatist when he charges him with relativism. For the realist thinks that the whole point of philosophical thought is to detach oneself from any particular community and look down at it from a more universal standpoint. When he hears the pragmatist repudiating the desire for such a standpoint he cannot quite believe it. He thinks that everyone, deep down inside, *must* want such detachment. So he attributes to the pragmatist a perverse form of his own attempted detachment, and sees him as an ironic, sneering aesthete who refuses to take the choice between communities seriously, a mere "relativist." But the pragmatist, dominated by the desire for solidarity, can only be criticized for taking his own community *too* seriously. He can only be criticized for ethnocentrism, not for relativism. To be ethnocentric is to divide the human race into the people to whom one must justify one's beliefs and the others. The first group – one's *ethnos* – comprises those who share enough of one's beliefs to make fruitful conversation possible. In this sense, everybody is ethnocentric when engaged in actual debate, no matter how much realist rhetoric about objectivity he produces in his study.[13]

What is disturbing about the pragmatist's picture is not that it is relativistic but that it takes away two sorts of metaphysical comfort to which our intellectual tradition has become accustomed. One is the thought that membership in our biological species carries with it certain "rights," a notion which does not seem to make sense unless the biological similarities entail the possession of something nonbiological, something which links our species to a nonhuman reality and thus gives the species moral dignity. This picture of rights as biologically transmitted is so basic to the political discourse of the Western democracies that we are troubled by any suggestion that "human nature" is not a useful moral concept. The second comfort is provided by the thought that our community cannot wholly die. The picture of a common human nature oriented towards correspondence to reality as it is in itself comforts us with the thought that even if our civilization is destroyed, even if all memory of our political or intellectual or artistic community is erased, the race is fated to recapture the virtues and the insights and the achievements which were the glory of that community. The notion of human nature as an inner structure

which leads all members of the species to converge to the same point, to recognize the same theories, virtues, and works of art as worthy of honor, assures us that even if the Persians had won, the arts and sciences of the Greeks would sooner or later have appeared elsewhere. It assures us that even if the Orwellian bureaucrats of terror rule for a thousand years the achievements of the Western democracies will someday be duplicated by our remote descendants. It assures us that "man will prevail," that something reasonably like *our* world-view, *our* virtues, *our* art, will bob up again whenever human beings are left alone to cultivate their inner natures. The comfort of the realist picture is the comfort of saying not simply that there is a place prepared for our race in our advance, but also that we now know quite a bit about what that place looks like. The inevitable ethnocentrism to which we are all condemned is thus as much a part of the realist's comfortable view as of the pragmatist's uncomfortable one.

The pragmatist gives up the first sort of comfort because he thinks that to say that certain people have certain rights is merely to say that we should treat them in certain ways. It is not to give a *reason* for treating them in those ways. As to the second sort of comfort, he suspects that the hope that something resembling *us* will inherit the earth is impossible to eradicate, as impossible as eradicating the hope of surviving our individual deaths through some satisfying transfiguration. But he does not want to turn this hope into a theory of the nature of man. He wants solidarity to be our *only* comfort, and to be seen not to require metaphysical support.

My suggestion that the desire for objectivity is in part a disguised form of the fear of the death of our community echoes Nietzsche's charge that the philosophical tradition which stems from Plato is an attempt to avoid facing up to contingency, to escape from time and chance. Nietzsche thought that realism was to be condemned not only by arguments from its theoretical incoherence, the sort of argument we find in Putnam and Davidson, but also on practical, pragmatic, grounds. Nietzsche thought that the test of human character was the ability to live with the thought that there was no convergence. He wanted us to be able to think of truth as:

a mobile army of metaphors, metonyms, and anthromorphisms – in short a sum of human relations, which have been enhanced, transposed, and embellished poetically and rhetorically and which after long use seem firm, canonical, and obligatory to a people.[14]

Nietzsche hoped that eventually there might be human beings who could and did think of truth in this way, but who still liked themselves, who saw themselves as *good* people for whom solidarity was *enough*.[15]

I think that pragmatism's attack on the various structure–content distinctions which buttress the realist's notion of objectivity can best be seen as an attempt to let us think of truth in this Nietzschean way, as entirely a matter of solidarity. That is why I think we need to say, despite Putnam, that "there is only the dialogue," only *us*, and to throw out the last residues of the notion of "transcultural rationality." But this should not lead us to repudiate, as Nietzsche sometimes did, the elements in our movable host which embody the ideas of Socratic conversation, Christian fellowship, and Enlightenment science. Nietzsche ran together his diagnosis of philosophical realism as an expression of fear and resentment with his own resentful idiosyncratic idealizations of silence, solitude, and violence. Post-Nietzschean thinkers like Adorno and Heidegger and Foucault have run together Nietzsche's criticisms of the metaphysical tradition on the one hand with his criticisms of bourgeois civility, of Christian love, and of the nineteenth century's hope that science would make the world a better place to live, on the other. I do not think that there is any interesting connection between these two sets of criticisms. Pragmatism seems to me, as I have said, a philosophy of solidarity rather than of despair. From this point of view, Socrates' turn away from the gods, Christianity's turn from an Omnipotent Creator to the man who suffered on the Cross, and the Baconian turn from science as contemplation of eternal truth to science as instrument of social progress, can be seen as so many preparations for the act of social faith which is suggested by a Nietzschean view of truth.[16]

The best argument we partisans of solidarity have against the realistic partisans of objectivity is Nietzsche's argument that the traditional Western metaphysico-epistemological way of firming up our habits simply isn't working anymore. It isn't doing its job. It has become as transparent a device as the postulation of deities who turn out, by a happy coincidence, to have chosen *us* as their people. So the pragmatist suggestion that we substitute a "merely" ethical foundation for our sense of community – or, better, that we think of our sense of community as having no foundation except shared hope and the trust created by such sharing – is put forward on practical grounds. It is *not* put forward as a corollary of a metaphysical claim that the objects in the world contain no intrinsically action-guiding properties, nor of an epistemological claim that we lack a faculty of moral sense, nor of a semantical claim that truth is reducible to justification. It is a suggestion about how we might think of ourselves in order to avoid the kind of resentful belatedness – characteristic of the bad side of Nietzsche – which now characterizes much of high culture. This resentment arises from the realization, which I referred to at the beginning of this chapter, that the Enlightenment's search for objectivity has often gone sour.

The rhetoric of scientific objectivity, pressed too hard and taken too seriously, has led us to people like B. F. Skinner on the one hand and people like Althusser[x] on the other – two equally pointless fantasies, both produced by the attempt to be "scientific" about our moral and political lives. Reaction against scientism led to attacks on natural science as a sort of false god. But there is nothing wrong with science, there is only something wrong with the attempt to divinize it, the attempt characteristic of realistic philosophy. This reaction has also led to attacks on liberal social thought of the type common to Mill and Dewey and Rawls as a mere ideological superstructure, one which obscures the realities of our situation and represses attempts to change that situation. But there is nothing wrong with liberal democracy, nor with the philosophers who have tried to enlarge its scope. There is only something wrong with the attempt to see their efforts as failures to achieve something which they were not trying to achieve – a demonstration of the "objective" superiority of our way of life over all other alternatives. There is, in short, nothing wrong with the hopes of the Enlightenment, the hopes which created the Western democracies. The value of the ideals of the Enlightenment is, for us pragmatists, just the value of some of the institutions and practices which they have created. In this essay I have sought to distinguish these institutions and practices from the philosophical justifications for them provided by partisans of objectivity, and to suggest an alternative justification.

[x] Louis Althusser (1918–90), French Marxist philosopher.

Author's Notes

1 This attitude toward truth, in which the consensus of a community rather than a relation to a nonhuman reality is taken as central, is associated not only with the American pragmatic tradition but with the work of Popper and Habermas. Habermas' criticisms of lingering positivist elements in Popper parallel those made by Deweyan holists of the early logical empiricists. It is important to see, however, that the pragmatist notion of truth common to James and Dewey is not dependent upon either Peirce's notion of an "ideal end of inquiry" nor on Habermas' notion of an "ideally free community." For criticism of these notions, which in my view are insufficiently ethnocentric, see my "Pragmatism, Davidson and Truth" (below) and "Habermas and Lyotard on Postmodernity" in the second volume of these papers [*Essays on Heidegger and Others* (Cambridge: Cambridge University Press, 1991)].

2 Hilary Putnam, *Reason, Truth, and History* (Cambridge: Cambridge University Press, 1981), pp. 49–50.

3 Ibid., p. 119.

4 Ibid., p. x.

5 Ibid., p. 114.

6 Ibid., p. 119. See Davidson's "On the very idea of a conceptual scheme," in his *Inquiries into Truth and Interpretation* (Oxford: Oxford University Press, 1984) for a more complete and systematic presentation of this point.

7 Putnam, p. 113.

8 Ibid., p. 126.

9 Ibid., p. 216.

10 See, e.g., Paul Feyerabend, *Science in a Free Society* (London: New Left Books, 1978), p. 9, where Feyerabend identifies his own view with "relativism (in the old and simple sense of Protagoras)." This identification is accompanied by the claim that " 'Objectively' there is not much to choose between anti-semitism and humanitarianism." I think Feyerabend would have served himself better by saying that the scare-quoted world "objectively" should simply be dropped from use, together with the traditional philosophical distinctions which buttress the subjective-objective distinction, than by saying that we may keep the word and use it to say the sort of thing Protagoras said. What Feyerabend is really against is the correspondence theory of truth, not the idea that some views cohere better than others.

11 This quest for consensus is opposed to the sort of quest for authenticity which wishes to free itself from the opinion of our community. See, for example, Vincent Descombes' account of Deleuze in *Modern French Philosophy* (Cambridge: Cambridge University Press, 1980), p. 153: "Even if philosophy is essentially demystificatory, philosophers often fail to produce authentic critiques; they defend order, authority, institutions, 'decency,' everything in which the ordinary person believes." On the pragmatist or ethnocentric view I am suggesting, all that critique can or should do is play off elements in "what the ordinary person believes" against other elements. To attempt to do more than this is to fantasize rather than to converse. Fantasy may, to be sure, be an incentive to more fruitful conversation, but when it no longer fulfills this function it does not deserve the name of "critique."

12 In *A Theory of Justice* Rawls seemed to be trying to retain the authority of Kantian "practical reason" by imagining a social contract devised by choosers "behind a veil of ignorance" – using the "rational self-interest" of such choosers as a touchstone for the ahistorical validity of certain social institutions. Much of the criticism to which that book was subjected, e.g. by Michael Sandel in his *Liberalism and the Limits of Justice* (Cambridge: Cambridge University Press, 1982), has centered on the claim that one cannot escape history in this way. In the meantime, however, Rawls has put forward a meta-ethical view which drops the claim to ahistorical validity. Concurrently, T. M. Scanlon has urged that the essence of a "contractualist" account of moral motivation is better understood as the desire to justify one's action to others than in terms of "rational self-interest." See Scanlon, "Contractualism and Utilitarianism," in A. Sen and B. Williams (eds), *Utilitarianism and Beyond* (Cambridge: Cambridge University Press, 1982). Scanlon's emendation of Rawls leads in the same direction as Rawls' later work, since Scanlon's use of the notion of "justification to others on grounds they could not reasonably reject" chimes with the "constructivist" view that what counts for social philosophy is what can be justified to a particular historical community, not to "humanity in general." On my view, the frequent remark that Rawls' rational choosers look remarkably like twentieth-century American liberals is perfectly just, but not a criticism of Rawls. It is merely a frank recognition of the ethnocentrism which is essential to serious, nonfantastical, thought. I defend this view in "The Priority of Democracy to Philosophy" and "Postmodernist Bourgeois Liberalism" [in Part III of this volume].

13 In an important paper called "The Truth in Relativism," included in his *Moral Luck* (Cambridge: Cambridge University Press, 1981), Bernard Williams makes a similar point in terms of a distinction between "genuine confrontation" and "notional confrontation." The latter is the sort of confrontation which occurs, asymmetrically, between us and

primitive tribespeople. The belief-systems of such people do not present, as Williams puts it, "real options" for us, for we cannot imagine going over to their view without "self-deception or paranoia." These are the people whose beliefs on certain topics overlap so little with ours that their inability to agree with us raises no doubt in our minds about the correctness of our own beliefs. Williams' use of "real option" and "notional confrontation" seems to me very enlightening, but I think he turns these notions to purposes they will not serve. Williams wants to defend ethical relativism, defined as the claim that when ethical confrontations are merely notional "questions of appraisal do not genuinely arise." He thinks they *do* arise in connection with notional confrontations between, e.g., Einsteinian and Amazonian cosmologies. (See Williams, p. 142.) This distinction between ethics and physics seems to me an awkward result to which Williams is driven by his unfortunate attempt to find *something* true in relativism, an attempt which is a corollary of his attempt to be "realistic" about physics. On my (Davidsonian) view, there is no point in distinguishing between true sentences which are "made true by reality" and true sentences which are "made by us," because the whole idea of "truth-makers" needs to be dropped. So I would hold that there is *no* truth in relativism, but this much truth in ethnocentrism: we cannot justify our beliefs (in physics, ethics, or any other area) to everybody, but only to those whose beliefs overlap ours to some appropriate extent. (This is not a theoretical problem about "untranslatability," but simply a practical problem about the limitations of argument; it is not that we live in different worlds than the Nazis or the Amazonians, but that conversion from or to their point of view, though possible, will not be a matter of inference from previously shared premises.)

14   Nietzsche, "On Truth and Lie in an Extra-Moral Sense," in *The Viking Portable Nietzsche*, Walter Kaufmann, ed. and trans., pp. 46–7.

15   See Sabina Lovibond, *Realism and Imagination in Ethics* (Minneapolis: University of Minnesota Press, 1983), p. 158: "An adherent of Wittgenstein's view of language should equate that goal with the establishment of a language-game in which we could participate ingenuously, while retaining our awareness of it as a specific historical formation. A community in which such a language-game was played would be one... whose members understood their own form of life and yet were not embarrassed by it."

16   See Hans Blumenberg, *The Legitimation of Modernity* (Cambridge, Mass.: MIT Press, 1982), for a story about the history of European thought which, unlike the stories told by Nietzsche and Heidegger, sees the Enlightenment as a definitive step forward. For Blumenberg, the attitude of "self-assertion," the kind of attitude which stems from a Baconian view of the nature and purpose of science, needs to be distinguished from "self-foundation," the Cartesian project of grounding such inquiry upon ahistorical criteria of rationality. Blumenberg remarks, pregnantly, that the "historicist" criticism of the optimism of the Enlightenment, criticism which began with the Romantics' turn back to the Middle Ages, undermines self-foundation but not self-assertion.

45

From "The Death of Modern Architecture"
From *What is Post-Modernism?*

Charles Jencks

Charles Jencks (1939–), architect and architectural writer, was in 1975 the first to use the term "post-modern" in architecture to mean a departure from modernism. His 1977 book, *The Language of Post-Modern Architecture*, made him the most well-known expositor and analyst of postmodernism and related developments in architecture. In the selection from that book which follows, Jencks famously dates the death of architectural modernism; it expired July 15, 1972, at 3:32 p.m. His subsequent work, *What Is Post-Modernism?* (1986) developed the broader cultural and intellectual meaning of postmodernism. Jencks defines postmodern architecture in terms of "double coding." A postmodern structure exhibits at least two different codes or languages, one that is modernist and one that is not. His view of postmodernism as a general cultural movement, evident in contemporary science as well as in art, links him to the positive, "revisionary" postmodernism of David Griffin.

From "The Death of Modern Architecture"

Happily, we can date the death of modern architecture to a precise moment in time. Unlike the legal death of a person, which is becoming a complex affair of brain waves versus heartbeats, modern architecture went out with a bang. That many people didn't notice, and no one was seen to mourn, does not make the sudden extinction any less of a fact, and that many designers are still trying to administer the kiss of life does not mean that it has been miraculously resurrected. No, it expired finally and completely in 1972, after having been flogged to death remorselessly for ten years by critics such as Jane Jacobs; and the fact that many so-called modern architects still go around practising a trade as if it were alive can be taken as one of the great curiosities of our age (like the British Monarchy giving life-prolonging drugs to 'The Royal Company of Archers' or 'The Extra Women of the Bedchamber').

Modern Architecture died in St Louis, Missouri on July 15, 1972 at 3.32 p.m. (or thereabouts) when the infamous Pruitt-Igoe scheme, or rather several of its slab blocks, were given the final *coup de grâce* by dynamite. Previously it had been vandalised, mutilated and defaced by its black inhabitants, and although millions of dollars were pumped back, trying to keep it alive (fixing the broken elevators, repairing smashed windows, repainting), it was finally put out of its misery. Boom, boom, boom.

Without doubt, the ruins should be kept, the remains should have a preservation order slapped on them, so that we keep a live memory of this failure in planning and architecture. Like the folly or artificial ruin – constructed on the estate of an eighteenth-century English eccentric to provide him with instructive reminders of former vanities

---

Charles Jencks: [A] "The Death of Modern Architecture," pp. 9–10 from *The Language of Post-Modern Architecture*, New York: Rizzoli, 1986; [B] from chapter 2 (pp. 14–20) and from chapter 7 (pp. 57–9) of *What is Post-Modernism?* London: Academy Editions, 1986.

and glories – we should learn to value and protect our former disasters. As Oscar Wilde said, 'experience is the name we give to our mistakes', and there is a certain health in leaving them judiciously scattered around the landscape as continual lessons.

Pruitt-Igoe was constructed according to the most progressive ideals of CIAM (the Congress of International Modern Architects) and it won an award from the American Institute of Architects when it was designed in 1951. It consisted of elegant slab blocks fourteen storeys high with rational 'streets in the air' (which were safe from cars, but as it turned out, not safe from crime); 'sun, space and greenery', which Le Corbusier called the 'three essential joys of urbanism' (instead of conventional streets, gardens and semi-private space, which he banished). It had a separation of pedestrian and vehicular traffic, the provision of play space, and local amenities such as laundries, crèches and gossip centres – all rational substitutes for traditional patterns. Moreover, its Purist style, its clean, salubrious hospital metaphor, was meant to instil, by good example, corresponding virtues in the inhabitants. Good form was to lead to good content, or at least good conduct; the intelligent planning of abstract space was to promote healthy behaviour.

Alas, such simplistic ideas, taken over from philosophic doctrines of Rationalism, Behaviourism and Pragmatism, proved as irrational as the philosophies themselves. Modern Architecture, as the son of the Enlightenment, was an heir to its congenital naïvities too great and awe-inspiring to warrant refutation in a book on mere building. I will concentrate here, in this first part, on the demise of a very small branch of a big bad tree; but to be fair it should be pointed out that modern architecture is the offshoot of modern painting, the modern movements in all the arts. Like rational schooling, rational health and rational design of women's bloomers, it has the faults of an age trying to reinvent itself totally on rational grounds. These shortcomings are now well known, thanks to the writings of Ivan Illich, Jacques Ellul, E. F. Schumacher, Michael Oakeshott and Hannah Arendt,[i] and the overall

misconceptions of Rationalism will not be dwelt upon. They are assumed for my purposes. Rather than a deep extended attack on modern architecture, showing how its ills relate very closely to the prevailing philosophies of the modern age, I will attempt a caricature, a polemic. The virtue of this genre (as well as its vice) is its license to cut through the large generalities with a certain abandon and enjoyment, overlooking all the exceptions and subtleties of the argument. Caricature is of course not the whole truth. Daumier's drawings didn't really show what nineteenth-century poverty was about, but rather gave a highly selective view of *some* truths. Let us then romp through the desolation of modern architecture, and the destruction of our cities, like some Martian tourist out on an earthbound excursion, visiting the archaeological sites with a superior disinterest, bemused by the sad but instructive mistakes of a former architectural civilisation. After all, since it is fairly dead, we might as well enjoy picking over the corpse.

From *What is Post-Modernism?*

Post-Modernism, like Modernism, varies for each art both in its motives and time-frame, and here I shall define it just in the field with which I am most involved – architecture. The responsibility for introducing it into the architectural subconscious lies with Joseph Hudnut who, at Harvard with Walter Gropius, may have wished to give this pioneer of the Modern Movement a few sleepless nights. At any rate, he used the term in the title of an article published in 1945 called 'the post-modern house' (all lower case, as was Bauhaus practice),[ii] but didn't mention it in the body of the text or define it polemically. Except for an occasional slip here and there, by Philip Johnson or Nikolaus Pevsner, it wasn't used until my own writing on the subject which started in 1975.[1] In that first year of lecturing and polemicising in Europe and America, I used it as a temporising label, as a definition to describe where we had left rather than where we were going. The observable fact was that architects as various as Ralph Erskine,

---

[i] Ivan Illich (1926–), Austrian born critic of technology and governmental dependency; Jacques Ellul (1912–94), French Christian anarchist and author of *The Technological Society* (1954); Schumacher (1911–77), author of *Small is Beautiful: Economics as if People Mattered* (1973); and two of the greatest political philosophers of the twentieth century, British conservative Michael Oakeshott (1901–90) and Hannah Arendt (1906–75), German Jewish émigré to the US.

[ii] The Bauhaus School (*Staatliches Bauhaus*, or Public House of Building), a German School of design from 1919 to 1933, founded by Walter Gropius, was part of the Modernist movement in architecture.

Robert Venturi, Lucien Kroll, the Krier brothers and Team Ten had all departed from Modernism and set off in different directions which *kept a trace of their common departure*. To this day I would define Post-Modernism as I did in 1978 as *double coding: the combination of Modern techniques with something else (usually traditional building) in order for architecture to communicate with the public and a concerned minority, usually other architects*. The point of this double coding was itself double. Modern architecture had failed to remain credible partly because it didn't communicate effectively with its ultimate users – the main argument of my book *The Language of Post-Modern Architecture* – and partly because it didn't make effective links with the city and history. Thus the solution I perceived and defined as Post-Modern: an architecture that was professionally based *and* popular as well as one that was based on new techniques *and* old patterns. Double coding to simplify means both elite/popular and new/old and there are compelling reasons for these opposite pairings. Today's Post-Modern architects were trained by Modernists, and are committed to using contemporary technology as well as facing current social reality. These commitments are enough to distinguish them from revivalists or traditionalists, a point worth stressing since it creates their hybrid language, the style of Post-Modern architecture. The same is not completely true of Post-Modern artists and writers who may use traditional techniques of narrative and representation in a more straightforward way. Yet all the creators who could be called Post-Modern keep something of a Modern sensibility – some intention which distinguishes their work from that of revivalists – whether this is irony, parody, displacement, complexity, eclecticism, realism or any number of contemporary tactics and goals. As I mentioned in the foreword, Post-Modernism has the essential double meaning: the continuation of Modernism and its transcendence.

The main motive for Post-Modern architecture is obviously the social failure of Modern architecture, its mythical 'death' announced repeatedly over ten years. In 1968, an English tower block of housing, Ronan Point, suffered what was called 'cumulative collapse' as its floors gave way after an explosion. In 1972, many slab blocks of housing were intentionally blown up at Pruitt-Igoe in St Louis. By the mid 1970s, these explosions were becoming a quite frequent method of dealing with the failures of Modernist building methods: cheap prefabrication, lack of personal 'defensible' space

and the alienating housing estate. The 'death' of Modern architecture and its ideology of progress which offered technical solutions to social problems was seen by everyone in a vivid way. The destruction of the central city and historical fabric was almost equally apparent to the populace and again these popular, social motives should be stressed because they aren't quite the same in painting, film, dance or literature. There is no similar, vivid 'death' of Modernism in these fields, nor perhaps the same social motivation that one finds in Post-Modern architecture. But even in Post-Modern literature there is a social motive for using past forms in an ironic way. Umberto Eco has described this irony or double coding: 'I think of the post-modern attitude as that of a man who loves a very cultivated woman and knows he cannot say to her, "I love you madly", because he knows that she knows (and that she knows that he knows) that these words have already been written by Barbara Cartland.[iii] Still, there is a solution. He can say, "As Barbara Cartland would put it, I love you madly". At this point, having avoided false innocence, having said clearly that it is no longer possible to speak innocently, he will nevertheless have said what he wanted to say to the woman: that he loves her, but he loves her in an age of lost innocence. If the woman goes along with this, she will have received a declaration of love all the same. Neither of the two speakers will feel innocent, both will have accepted the challenge of the past, of the already said, which cannot be eliminated, both will consciously and with pleasure play the game of irony . . . But both will have succeeded, once again, in speaking of love.'[2]

Thus Eco underlines the lover's use of Post-Modern double coding and extends it, of course, to the novelist's and poet's social use of previous forms. Faced with a restrictive Modernism, a minimalism of means and ends, writers such as John Barth have felt just as restricted as architects forced to build in the International Style,[iv] or using only glass and steel. The most notable, and perhaps the best, use of this double coding in architecture is James Stirling's addition to the Staatsgalerie in Stuttgart. Here one can find the fabric of the city and the existing museum extended in amusing and ironic ways. The

---

iii   Dame Cartland (1901–2000), "Queen of Romance," wrote over six hundred romance novels.
iv   The dominant style of world architecture which grew out of the modernism of Walter Gropius, Ludwig Mies van der Rohe, and Le Corbusier.

U-shaped palazzo form of the old gallery is echoed and placed on a high plinth, or 'Acropolis', above the traffic. But this classical base holds a very real and necessary parking garage, one that is ironically indicated by stones which have 'fallen', like ruins, to the ground. The resultant holes show the real construction – not the thick marble blocks of the real Acropolis, but a steel frame holding stone cladding which allows the air ventilation required by law. One can sit on these false ruins and ponder the truth of our lost innocence: that we live in an age which can build with beautiful, expressive masonry as long as we make it skin-deep and hang it on a steel skeleton. A Modernist would of course deny himself and us this pleasure for a number of reasons: 'truth to materials', 'logical consistency', 'straightforwardness', 'simplicity' – all the values and rhetorical tropes celebrated by such Modernists as Le Corbusier and Mies van der Rohe.

Stirling, by contrast and like the lovers of Umberto Eco, wants to communicate more and different values. To signify the permanent nature of the museum, he has used traditional rustication and classical forms including an Egyptian cornice, an open-air Pantheon, and segmental arches. These are beautiful in an understated and conventional way, but they aren't revivalist either because of small distortions, or the use of a modern material such as reinforced concrete. They say, 'We are beautiful like the Acropolis or Pantheon, but we are also based on concrete technology and deceit.' The extreme form of this double coding is visible at the entry points: a steel temple outline which announces the taxi drop-off point, and the Modernist steel canopies which tell the public where to walk in. These forms and colours are reminiscent of De Stijl, that quintessentially modern language, but they are collaged onto the traditional background.[v] Thus Modernism confronts Classicism to such an extent that both Modernists and Classicists would be surprised, if not offended. There is not the simple harmony and consistency of either language or world view. It's as if Stirling were saying through his hybrid language and uneasy confrontations that we live in a complex world where we can't deny either the past and conventional beauty, or the present and current technical and social reality. Caught between this past and present, unwilling to oversimplify our situation, Stirling has produced

the most 'real' beauty of Post-Modern architecture to date.

As much of this reality has to do with taste as it does with technology. Modernism failed as mass-housing and city building partly because it failed to communicate with its inhabitants and users who might not have liked the style, understood what it meant or even known how to use it. Hence the double coding, the essential definition of Post-Modernism, has been used as a strategy of communicating on various levels at once. Virtually every Post-Modern architect – Robert Venturi, Hans Hollein, Charles Moore, Robert Stern, Michael Graves, Arata Isozaki are the notable examples – use popular *and* elitist signs in their work to achieve quite different ends, and their styles are essentially hybrid. To simplify, at Stuttgart the blue and red handrails and vibrant polychromy fit in with the youth that uses the museum – they literally resemble their dayglo hair and anoraks – while the Classicism appeals more to the lovers of Schinkel. This is a very popular building with young and old and when I interviewed people there – a group of *plein air*[vi] painters, schoolchildren and businessmen – I found their different perceptions and tastes were accommodated and stretched. The pluralism which is so often called on to justify Post-Modernism is here a tangible reality.

This is not the place to recount the history of Post-Modern architecture, but I want to stress the ideological and social intentions which underlie this history because they are so often overlooked in the bitter debate with Modernists.[3] Even traditionalists often reduce the debate to matters of style, and thus the symbolic intentions and morality are overlooked. If one reads the writings of Robert Venturi, Denise Scott Brown, Christian Norberg-Schulz, or myself, one will find the constant notion of pluralism, the idea that the architect must design for different 'taste cultures' (in the words of the sociologist Herbert Gans) and for differing views of the good life. In any complex building, in any large city building such as an office, there will be varying tastes and functions that have to be articulated and these will inevitably lead, if the architect follows these hints, towards an eclectic style. He may pull this heterogeneity together under a Free-Style Classicism, as do many Post-Modernists today, but a trace of the pluralism will and should remain. I would even argue that 'the true and proper style' is not as they said Gothic, but some

---

[v]   De Stijl ("The Style") was an Amsterdam group of abstract painters that thrived between the world wars, most notably represented by Piet Mondrian.

[vi]   Open air, outdoor.

form of eclecticism, because only this can adequately encompass the pluralism that is our social and metaphysical reality. . . .

The feeling that we are living through a turning point in history is widespread. But this mood has been pervasive for the last two hundred years, a period of continuous transition. Nevertheless the types of change that affect us seem more radical and thoroughgoing than in previous years, with deep social and political consequences. Perhaps the most momentous shift of some thirty under way is the breakup of the Modernist paradigm of Marxism and centralised economic planning in socialist countries (some of which could be called State Capitalist). If Eastern Europe is turned into a neutral zone (or 'Austrianised'), if Russia and China successfully introduce 'market socialism' – a hybridisation typical of Post-Modernism – then these changes in economics and ideology of one third of humanity will be the most fundamental shift in our time.

The short-lived student movement in China shows some of the characteristic changes in style and practice. Motivated by a minority appeal for social justice and increased freedom, it was essentially a spontaneous, self-organising event dependent on decentralising technologies such as the fax, two-way radio, motor-bike, TV and telephone. These allowed instant communication locally and globally. Its style and content were quintessentially hybrid, mixing quotes from Mao with phrases taken from the French and American Revolutions and their Bills of Rights. Indeed its symbol, the Goddess of Democracy, was a mixture of French *Liberté* and the American Statue of Liberty, and it was erected across from the large portrait of Mao on the Tiananmen square. The music during the long hours of waiting varied from Chinese singing to broadcasting, on makeshift loudspeakers, the 'Ode to Joy' from Beethoven's *Ninth Symphony* with its message of global brotherhood.

Whenever an international television crew swung its cameras over the crowds, up went the two-finger salute of Winston Churchill. (Did it have some specific Chinese overtone beyond 'V for Victory'?) Headbands had dual-language slogans: 'Glasnost' above its Chinese translation (again so TV could beam the instant message around China and the English-speaking world). When the final debacle came at Tiananmen Square its impact was immediate throughout the globe because of television, and it even had some influence on the vote for democracy that was taking place in Poland at the time.[4] Just

after the students were crushed, on June 4, 1989, Solidarity won an extraordinary landslide victory that neither they nor the Polish Communist Party had foreseen: all 161 seats that were open to it in the lower house, the Sejm, and 99 out of a hundred seats in the upper house, the Senate.[vii] In twenty-four hours the Dictatorship of the Proletariat had taken a Leninist two-step: one back, one forward. Never had political events in these parts of the world been seen, communicated, analysed and judged so quickly by the globe. And this quick reaction of the information world had a feedback effect on the events themselves – for the most part positive.[5]

But if there really is a shift to 'post-socialism' under way (and the term has been used of Britain since the early eighties) then it, like so many other turns in direction, will take twenty to thirty years to be completed. The previous shift to a new paradigm – that from the Medieval to the Modern – was very uneven and different for each nation, field of work and specialisation. And it took more than a hundred years. This might be the time it takes to shift to a Post-Modern world, except that today because of the information flow all change is much faster. If we date the beginning of Post-Modern movements to 1960, then we might imagine the paradigm as a whole starting to dominate the competing ones – the Traditional and Modern – by the year 2000. But the Modern world view hangs on tenaciously and, as Max Planck said of disputes in theoretical physics, one can never manage to convince one's opponents, only aim to outlive them. Already there has been a strong Modernist backlash against Post-Modernism in architecture, led by the RIBA[viii] in Britain, Deconstructionsts in America and assorted Neo-Modernists everywhere, and similar reactions can probably be found in all the arts and sciences.[ix]

Many physicists still won't accept the fundamental reality of the uncertainty principle, chaos theory and the many manifestations of Post-Modern science. With Einstein, who didn't want to give up the Modern world view of an ordered, deterministic and certain cosmos, they insist that God doesn't play dice with the universe. The prevailing paradigms in the science departments of

[vii] Solidarity is the labor union that led the struggle against communist control in Poland in the 1980s.
[viii] The Royal Institute of British Architects.
[ix] Deconstruction is the method of critical reading developed by Jacques Derrida; "Neo-Modernism" is Jencks' own term for attempts to modify but retain Modernism.

many universities will favour modified Newtonian mechanics and Darwinian evolution in their highly elaborated 'Neo' forms, and such orthodoxies are bound to last because they still describe, quite adequately, the everyday world. The fact that Post-Newtonian and Post-Darwinian theories, of a higher order, can explain a wider range of phenomena and encompass the former theories, is not regarded as particularly significant.

For analogous reasons we can predict that much of the world will carry on happily for the next twenty years modernising and following the ideology of Modernism. After all much of it, like China, is still rural and not yet industrialised. Post-Modernism is a *stage of growth*, not an anti-Modern reaction, and before one country or people can reach it, the various stages of urbanisation, industrialisation and post-industrialisation have to occur.

However, there are developments that lead one to believe the world might shift to the paradigm by the year 2000: above all the crisis of the ecosphere. If conservative estimates of the greenhouse effect are right, by that time much of the world will be involved in a rearguard action, trying to hold back the unintended consequences of modernisation, engaged in a desperate attempt to slow down – or reverse – the inertia of long-term warming and pollution. It may just be that this common problem, or 'enemy', unites the globe in an ethical battle which some philosophers have called 'the moral equivalent of war'. Conversely some scenarios predict that the greenhouse effect may lead to autocratic repression and war. Either way it will make the world hyperconscious of the limits of modernisation, Modernism and all their cognate practices and ideas. Also it will force a consciousness of what that essential Post-Modern science, ecology, has been saying now for more than thirty years: all living and non-living things on the globe are interconnected, or capable of being linked. Indeed Modern scientists have granted such points for many years, although the paradigm they have worked with – favouring analysis, reductivism and specialisation – has not followed the implications.

Modern sciences have triumphed through specialising on limited parts of reality: extremely few of them, like ecology and ethology, have been holistic. Modern knowledge has progressed by analysing problems into their parts, dividing to conquer, hence the multiple branching of university departments and investigative disciplines over the last two hundred years. Only a few fields, such as philosophy, theology and sociology have made their pur-

view the whole of knowledge, or the interconnection of disciplines, and on these rare occasions only imperfectly so. Perhaps in the future with the environmental crises and the increasing globalisation of the economy, communications and virtually every specialisation, we will be encouraged – even forced – to emphasise the things which interact, the connections between a growing economy, an ideology of constant change and waste. Those who don't realise the world is a whole are doomed to pollute it.

So one of the key shifts to the Post-Modern world will be a change in epistemology, the understanding of knowledge and how it grows and relates to other assumptions. Not only will it emphasise the continuities of nature, but the time-bound, cultural nature of knowledge. Instead of regarding the world and nature as simply there, working according to immutable laws that are eternally true, the Post-Modern view will emphasise the developmental nature of science – its perspectival distortion in time, space and culture. It will not embrace an absolute relativism and contend that one scientific hypothesis is as good as another, or as Jean-François Lyotard has argued, a complete scepticism and an end to all master narratives and beliefs. Rather, it will support relative absolutism, or fragmental holism, which insists on the developing and jumping nature of scientific growth, and the fact that all propositions of truth are time- and context-sensitive.

If the truths of Post-Modernism are culture-dependent and grow in time, this helps explain the hybrid nature of its philosophy and world view; why it is so continuously mixed, mongrel and dialectically involved with Modernism. Among the thirty or so shifts that have the prefix 'post', look at Post-Fordism. Like all the other 'posties' this concept implicates its forerunner in a complicated way. It doesn't contend that Fordism (the large corporation with central planning and mass-production) is dead, or completely transcended, or unimportant, or no longer powerful. Rather it asserts that a new level of small businesses has grown – fast-changing, creative, and networked by computer and an array of communicational systems – which has a complementary existence to large organisations. Post-Fordist enterprises may have accounted for more than 50 per cent of the new jobs in Italy and the United States during the eighties, and now they exist in a symbiotic relationship to transnationals and big companies, forming an economy that is more flexible and creative than one based simply on the Modernist and Fordist model.[6]

Author's Notes

1 My own writing and lecturing on Post-Modernism in architecture started in 1975 and 'The Rise of Post-Modern Architecture' was published in a Dutch book and a British magazine, *Architecture – Inner Town Government*, Eindhoven, July 1975, and *Architecture Association Quarterly*, No. 4, 1975. Subsequently Eisenman and Stern started using the term and by 1977 it had caught on. For a brief history see the 'Footnote on the Term' in *The Language of Post-Modern Architecture*, fourth edition (Academy Editions, London/Rizzoli, New York 1984), p. 8.

2 Umberto Eco, *Postscript to The Name of the Rose* (Harcourt Brace Jovanovich, New York, 1984), pp. 67–8.

3 Besides my own *The Language of Post-Modern Architecture* and *Current Architecture* (Academy Editions, London/Rizzoli, New York, 1982), and *Modern Movements in Architecture*, second edition (Penguin Books, Harmondsworth, 1985), see Paolo Portoghesi, *After Modern Architecture* (Rizzoli, New York, 1982), and its updated version, *Postmodern* (Rizzoli, New York, 1983), and *Immagini del Post-Moderno* (Edizioni Chiva, Venice 1983). See also Heinrich Klotz, *Die Revision der Moderne, Postmoderne Architektur, 1960–1980* and *Moderne und Postmoderne Architektur der Gegenwart 1960–1980* (Friedr. Vieweg & Sohn, Braunschweig/Wiesbaden, 1984). We have debated his notion of Post-Modern architecture as 'fiction' and this has been published in *Architectural Design*, 7/8 (1984), *Revision of the Modern*. See also my discussion of users and abusers of Post-Modern in 'La Bataille des étiquettes', *Nouveaux plaisirs d'architecture* (Centre Georges Pompidou, Paris, 1985), pp. 25–33.

4 See Timothy Garton Ash, 'Revolution in Hungary and Poland', *New York Review of Books*, August 17, 1989, p. 10.

5 It is of course impossible to accurately measure the feedback effect of the information world on events in China and Poland, but effect it undoubtedly had as can be judged by the authorities' attempts to counteract and distort it, especially in China. It appears that the Chinese sought to reassure the international business community and convey a picture of normality and reasonableness in all dealing with foreigners *partly in reaction to* the televised massacre and this may, in turn, have had a restraining effect on their suppression. I think it's more obvious that the instant, widespread knowledge of the vote in Poland (especially in Russia) immediately de-legitimised the Polish Communist Party and led directly to the change in government on August 24th – the election of Tadeusz Mazowiecki, etc.

6 The phrase 'Post-Fordist' starts some time in the early 1980s in juxtaposition to the large corporation based on the model of Henry Ford. For a discussion of it within a Post-Modern context see the impressively argued book *The Condition of Post-Modernity*, David Harvey (Blackwell, Oxford, 1989). For a critical discussion of where new jobs came from – and their percentages – see 'The Disciples of David Birch', John Chase, *Inc.*, January, 1989, pp. 39–45. Companies with fewer than 100 employees, from 1969 to 1986, have in the USA created an average of 65% of the new jobs – according to the most reliable statistics. But these statistics can be questioned.

46

From "A Manifesto for Cyborgs: Science, Technology, and Socialist Feminism in the 1980s"*

Donna Haraway

Inspired by its opposition to the notion that "biology is destiny," much recent feminist theory finds naturalism, science and to some extent technology to be a threat, tools often used by a patriarchal society to justify female inferiority. The reliance of some feminists on European critical theory and hermeneutics, itself inheriting the anti-naturalism and anti-positivism of phenomenology, Heidegger, the Frankfurt School, and most post-structuralism, has further motivated this tendency. In contrast, American feminist Donna Haraway (1944–) explores a dialogue between biology, anthropology, cybernetics, and the humanities that rejects the usual affiliation between social critique and anti-naturalism. In the following 1985 essay, she embraces post-humanism, like other postmodernists, but from the side of a materialist analysis, arguing for the progressive, feminist potential of a "cybernetic" approach to human being.

* [Author's Note:] This article was first published in *Socialist Review*, No. 80, 1985. The essay originated as a response to a call for political thinking about the 1980s from socialist-feminist points of view, in hopes of deepening our political and cultural debates in order to renew commitments to fundamental social change in the face of the Reagan years. The cyborg manifesto tried to find a feminist place for connected thinking and acting in profoundly contradictory worlds. Since its publication, this bit of cyborgian writing has had a surprising half life. It has proved impossible to rewrite the cyborg. Cyborg's daughter will have to find its own matrix in another essay, starting from the proposition that the immune system is the biotechnical body's chief system of differences in late capitalism, where feminists might find provocative extraterrestrial maps of the networks of embodied power marked by race, sex, and class. This chapter is substantially the same as the 1985 version, with minor revisions and correction of notes.

An Ironic Dream of a Common Language for Women in the Integrated Circuit

This chapter is an effort to build an ironic political myth faithful to feminism, socialism, and materialism. Perhaps more faithful as blasphemy is faithful, than as reverent worship and identification. Blasphemy has always seemed to require taking things very seriously. I know no better stance to adopt from within the secular-religious, evangelical traditions of U.S. politics, including the politics of socialist feminism. Blasphemy protects one from the Moral Majority within, while still insisting on the need for community. Blasphemy is not apostasy. Irony is about contradictions that do not resolve into larger wholes, even dialectically, about the tension of holding incompatible things together because both or all are necessary and true. Irony is about humor and serious play. It is also a rhetorical strategy and a political method, one I would like to see more honored within socialist feminism. At the

Donna Haraway, pp. 190–6, 203–7, and 212–33 from "A Manifesto for Cyborgs: Science, Technology and Socialist Feminism in the 1980s" in *Feminism/Postmodernism* (ed. Linda Nicholson). London and New York: Routledge, 1990.

center of my ironic faith, my blasphemy, is the image of the cyborg.

A cyborg is a cybernetic organism, a hybrid of machine and organism, a creature of social reality as well as a creature of fiction. Social reality is lived social relations, our most important political construction, a world-changing fiction. The international women's movements have constructed "women's experience," as well as uncovered or discovered this crucial collective object. This experience is a fiction and fact of the most crucial, political kind. Liberation rests on the construction of the consciousness, the imaginative apprehension, of oppression, and so of possibility. The cyborg is a matter of fiction and lived experience that changes what counts as women's experience in the late twentieth century. This is a struggle over life and death, but the boundary between science fiction and social reality is an optical illusion.

Contemporary science fiction is full of cyborgs – creatures simultaneously animal and machine, who populate worlds ambiguously natural and crafted. Modern medicine is also full of cyborgs, of couplings between organism and machine, each conceived as coded devices, in an intimacy and with a power that was not generated in the history of sexuality. Cyborg "sex" restores some of the lovely replicative baroque of ferns and invertebrates (such nice organic prophylactics against heterosexism). Cyborg replication is uncoupled from organic reproduction. Modern production seems like a dream of cyborg colonization of work, a dream that makes the nightmare of Taylorism seem idyllic.[i] Modern war is a cyborg orgy, coded by C^3I, command-control-communication-intelligence, an \$84 billion item in 1984's U.S. defense budget. I am making an argument for the cyborg as a fiction mapping our social and bodily reality and as an imaginative resource suggesting some very fruitful couplings. Foucault's biopolitics is a flaccid premonition of cyborg politics, a very open field.[ii]

By the late twentieth century, our time, a mythic time, we are all chimeras, theorized and fabricated hybrids of machine and organism; in short, we are cyborgs. The cyborg is our ontology; it gives us our politics. The cyborg is a condensed image of both imagination and material reality, the two joined centers structuring any possibility of historical transformation. In the traditions of Western science and politics – the tradition of racist, male-dominant capitalism; the tradition of progress; the tradition of the appropriation of nature as resource for the productions of culture; the tradition of reproduction of the self from the reflections of the other – the relation between organism and machine has been a border war. The stakes in the border war have been the territories of production, reproduction, and imagination. This chapter is an argument for pleasure in the confusion of boundaries and for responsibility in their construction. It is also an effort to contribute to socialist-feminist culture and theory in a postmodernist, nonnaturalist mode and in the utopian tradition of imagining a world without gender, which is perhaps a world without genesis, but maybe also a world without end. The cyborg incarnation is outside salvation history. Nor does it mark time on an Oedipal calendar, attempting to heal the terrible cleavages of gender in oral symbiotic utopia or post-Oedipal apocalypse. As Zoe Sofoulis argues in her unpublished manuscript on Lacan, Klein,[iii] and nuclear culture, *Lacklein*, the most terrible and perhaps the most promising monsters in cyborg worlds are embodied in non-Oedipal narratives with a different logic of repression, which we need to understand for our survival.

The cyborg is a creature in a postgender world; it has no truck with bisexuality, pre-Oedipal symbiosis, unalienated labor, or other seductions to organic wholeness through a final appropriation of all the powers of the parts into a higher unity. In a sense, the cyborg has no origin story in the Western sense; a "final" irony since the cyborg is also the awful apocalyptic telos of the West's escalating dominations of abstract individuation, an ultimate self untied at last from all dependency, a man in space. An origin story in the Western humanist sense depends on the myth of original unity, fullness, bliss, and terror, represented by the phallic mother from whom all humans must separate, the task of individual development and of history, the twin potent myths inscribed most powerfully for us in psychoanalysis and Marxism. Hilary Klein has argued that both Marxism and psychoanalysis, in their concepts of labor and of individuation and gender formation, depend on the plot of original

---

[i] The "scientific" management of industrial work as theorized by Frederick W. Taylor in his *The Principles of Scientific Management* (1911).

[ii] Foucault's conception of "bio-power," regimes of power that articulate and control human bodies and physical energies.

[iii] Jacques Lacan and Austrian-born British psychoanalyst Melanie Klein (1882–1960).

unity out of which difference must be produced and enlisted in a drama of escalating domination of woman/nature. The cyborg skips the step of original unity, of identification with nature in the Western sense. This is its illegitimate promise that might lead to subversion of its teleology as Star Wars.[iv]

The cyborg is resolutely committed to partiality, irony, intimacy, and perversity. It is oppositional, utopian, and completely without innocence. No longer structured by the polarity of public and private, the cyborg defines a technological polis based partly on a revolution of social relations in the oikos, the household. Nature and culture are reworked; the one can no longer be the resource for appropriation or incorporation by the other. The relationships for forming wholes from parts, including those of polarity and hierarchical domination, are at issue in the cyborg world. Unlike the hopes of Frankenstein's monster, the cyborg does not expect its father to save it through a restoration of the garden, that is, through the fabrication of a heterosexual mate, through its completion in a finished whole, a city and cosmos. The cyborg does not dream of community on the model of the organic family, this time without the Oedipal project. The cyborg would not recognize the Garden of Eden; it is not made of mud and cannot dream of returning to dust. Perhaps that is why I want to see if cyborgs can subvert the apocalypse of returning to nuclear dust in the manic compulsion to name the Enemy. Cyborgs are not reverent; they do not remember the cosmos. They are wary of holism, but needy for connection – they seem to have a natural feel for united front politics, but without the vanguard party. The main trouble with cyborgs, of course, is that they are the illegitimate offspring of militarism and patriarchal capitalism, not to mention state socialism. But illegitimate offspring are often exceedingly unfaithful to their origins. Their fathers, after all, are inessential.

I will return to the science fiction of cyborgs at the end of the chapter, but now I want to signal three crucial boundary breakdowns that make the following political fictional (political scientific) analysis possible. By the late twentieth century in United States, scientific culture, the boundary between human and animal, is thoroughly breached. The last beachheads of uniqueness have been polluted, if not turned into amusement parks – language, tool use, social behavior, mental events. Nothing really convincingly settles the separation of human and animal. Many people no longer feel the need of such a separation; indeed, many branches of feminist culture affirm the pleasure of connection with human and other living creatures. Movements for animal rights are not irrational denials of human uniqueness; they are clear-sighted recognition of connection across the discredited breach of nature and culture. Biology and evolutionary theory over the last two centuries have simultaneously produced modern organisms as objects of knowledge and reduced the line between humans and animals to a faint trace re-etched in ideological struggle or professional disputes between life and social sciences. Within this framework, teaching modern Christian creationism should be fought as a form of child abuse.

Biological-determinist ideology is only one position opened up in scientific culture for arguing the meanings of human animality. There is much room for radical political people to contest for the meanings of the breached boundary.[1] The cyborg appears in myth precisely where the boundary between human and animal is transgressed. Far from signaling a walling off of people from other living things, cyborgs signal disturbingly and pleasurably tight coupling. Bestiality has a new status in this cycle of marriage exchange.

The second leaky distinction is between animal-human (organism) and machine. Pre-cybernetic machines could be haunted; there was always the specter of the ghost in the machine. This dualism structured the dialogue between materialism and idealism that was settled by a dialectical progeny called spirit or history, according to taste. But basically machines were not self-moving, self-designing, autonomous. They could not achieve man's dream, only mock it. They were not man, an author of himself, but only a caricature of that masculinist reproductive dream. To think they were otherwise was paranoid. Now we are not so sure. Late twentieth-century machines have made thoroughly ambiguous the difference between natural and artificial, mind and body, self-developing and externally designed, and many other distinctions that used to apply to organisms and machines. Our machines are disturbingly lively, and we ourselves frighteningly inert.

Technological determinism is only one ideological space opened up by the reconceptions of machine and organism as coded texts through which we engage in the play of writing and read-

---

[iv] The popular term for the Reagan administration's proposed anti-ballistic missile shield in the 1980s.

ing the world.[2] "Textualization" of everything in poststructuralist, postmodernist theory has been damned by Marxists and socialist feminists for its utopian disregard for lived relations of domination that ground the "play" of arbitrary reading.[3*] It is certainly true that postmodernist strategies, like my cyborg myth, subvert myriad organic wholes (e.g., the poem, the primitive culture, the biological organism). In short, the certainty of what counts as nature – a source of insight and a promise of innocence – is undermined, probably fatally. The transcendent authorization of interpretation is lost and with it the ontology grounding Western epistemology. But the alternative is not cynicism or faithlessness, that is, some version of abstract existence, like the accounts of technological determinism destroying "man" by the "machine" or "meaningful political action" by the "text." Who cyborgs will be is a radical question; the answers are a matter of survival. Both chimpanzees and artifacts have politics, so why shouldn't we?[4]

The third distinction is a subset of the second: The boundary between physical and nonphysical is very imprecise for us. Pop physics books on the consequences of quantum theory and the indeterminacy principle are a kind of popular scientific equivalent to the Harlequin romances as a marker of radical change in American white heterosexuality: They get it wrong, but they are on the right subject. Modern machines are quintessentially microelectronic devices: They are everywhere and they are invisible. Modern machinery is an irreverent upstart god, mocking the Father's ubiquity and spirituality. The silicon chip is a surface for writing; it is etched in molecular scales disturbed only by atomic noise, the ultimate interference for nuclear scores. Writing, power, and technology are old partners in Western stories of the origin of civilization, but miniaturization has changed our experience of mechanism. Miniaturization has turned out to be about power; small is not so much beautiful as preeminently dangerous, as in Cruise missiles. Contrast the TV sets of the 1950s or the news cameras of the 1970s with the TV wristbands or hand-sized video cameras now advertised. Our best machines are made of sunshine; they are all light and clean because they are nothing but signals, electromagnetic waves, a section of a spectrum. These machines are eminently portable, mobile – a matter of immense human pain in Detroit and Singapore. People are nowhere near so fluid, being both material and opaque. Cyborgs are ether, quintessence.

The ubiquity and invisibility of cyborgs is precisely why these Sunshine Belt machines are so deadly. They are as hard to see politically as materially. They are about consciousness – or its simulation.[5] They are floating signifiers moving in pickup trucks across Europe, blocked more effectively by the witch-weavings of the displaced and so unnatural Greenham women,[v] who read the cyborg webs of power very well, than by the militant labor of older masculinist politics, whose natural constituency needs defense jobs. Ultimately, the "hardest" science is about the realm of greatest boundary confusion, the realm of pure number, pure spirit, C^3I, cryptography, and the

---

* [Author's Note:] A provocative, comprehensive argument about the politics and theories of postmodernism is made by Fredric Jameson, who argues that postmodernism is not an option, a style among others, but a cultural dominant requiring radical reinvention of left politics from within; there is no longer any place from without that gives meaning to the comforting fiction of critical distance. Jameson also makes clear why one cannot be for or against postmodernism, an essentially moralist move. My position is that feminists (and others) need continuous cultural reinvention, postmodernist critique, and historical materialism; only a cyborg would have a chance. The old dominations of white capitalist patriarchy seem nostalgically innocent now: They normalized heterogeneity, e.g., into man and woman, white and black. "Advanced capitalism" and postmodernism release heterogeneity without a norm, and we are flattened, without subjectivity, which requires depth, even unfriendly and drowning depths. It is time to write *The Death of the Clinic*. The clinic's methods required bodies and works; we have texts and surfaces. Our dominations don't work by medicalization and normalization anymore; they work by networking, communications redesign, stress management. Normalization gives way to automation, utter redundancy. Michel Foucault's *Birth of the Clinic*, *History of Sexuality*, and *Discipline and Punish* name a form of power at its moment of implosion. The discourse of biopolitics gives way to technobabble, the language of the spliced substantive; no noun is left whole by the multinationals. These are their names, listed from one issue of *Science*: Tech-Knowledge, Genentech, Allergen, Hybritech, Compupro, Genen-cor, Syntex, Allelix, Agrigenetics Corp., Syntro, Codon, Repligen; Micro-Angelo from Scion Corp., Percom Data, Inter Systems, Cyborg Corp., Statcom Corp., Intertec. If we are imprisoned by language, then escape from that prison-house requires language poets, a kind of cultural restriction enzyme to cut the code; cyborg heteroglossia is one form of radical culture politics.

---

[v] Women's groups who staged protests at Greenham, England, against the American airbase there beginning in 1981.

preservation of potent secrets. The new machines are so clean and light. Their engineers are sun worshipers mediating a new scientific revolution associated with the night dream of post industrial society. The diseases evoked by these clean machines are "no more" than the minuscule coding changes of an antigen in the immune system, "no more" than the experience of stress. The "nimble" fingers of "Oriental" women, the old fascination of little Anglo-Saxon Victorian girls with dollhouses, and women's enforced attention to the small take on quite new dimensions in this world. There might be a cyborg Alice taking account of these new dimensions. Ironically, it might be the unnatural cyborg women making chips in Asia and spiral dancing in Santa Rita jail after an antinuclear action whose constructed unities will guide effective oppositional strategies.

So my cyborg myth is about transgressed boundaries, potent fusions, and dangerous possibilities which progressive people might explore as one part of needed political work. One of my premises is that most American socialists and feminists see deepened dualisms of mind and body, animal and machine, idealism and materialism in the social practices, symbolic formulations, and physical artifacts associated with high technology and scientific culture. From *One-Dimensional Man* to *The Death of Nature*,[6] the analytic resources developed by progressives have insisted on the necessary domination of technics and recalled us to an imagined organic body to integrate our resistance. Another of my premises is that the need for unity of people trying to resist worldwide intensification of domination has never been more acute. But a slightly perverse shift of perspective might better enable us to contest for meanings, as well as for other forms of power and pleasure in technologically mediated societies.

From one perspective, a cyborg world is about the final imposition of a grid of control on the planet, about the final abstraction embodied in a Star Wars apocalypse waged in the name of defense, about the final appropriation of women's bodies in a masculinist orgy of war.[7] From another perspective, a cyborg world might be about lived social and bodily realities in which people are not afraid of their joint kinship with animals and machines, not afraid of permanently partial identities and contradictory standpoints. The political

struggle is to see from both perspectives at once because each reveals both dominations and possibilities unimaginable from the other vantage point. Single vision produces worse illusions than double vision or many-headed monsters. Cyborg unities are monstrous and illegitimate; in our present political circumstances, we could hardly hope for more potent myths for resistance and recoupling. I like to imagine the Livermore Action Group, LAG,[vi] as a kind of cyborg society, dedicated to realistically converting the laboratories that most fiercely embody and spew out the tools of technological apocalypse, and committed to building a political form that actually manages to hold together witches, engineers, elders, perverts, Christians, mothers, and Leninists long enough to disarm the state. Fission Impossible is the name of the affinity group in my town. (Affinity: related not by blood but by choice, the appeal of one chemical nuclear group for another, avidity.)[8] . . .

The Informatics of Domination

In this attempt at an epistemological and political position, I would like to sketch a picture of possible unity, a picture indebted to socialist and feminist principles of design. The frame for my sketch is set by the extent and importance of rearrangements in worldwide social relations tied to science and technology. I argue for a politics rooted in claims about fundamental changes in the nature of class, race, and gender in an emerging system of world order analogous in its novelty and scope to that created by industrial capitalism; we are living through a movement from an organic, industrial society to a polymorphous, information system – from all work to all play, a deadly game. Simultaneously material and ideological, the dichotomies may be expressed in the following chart of transitions from the comfortable old hierarchical dominations to the scary new networks I have called the informatics of domination: [Note: In the original the following columns appeared together on one page.]

vi Anti-nuclear group, which protested against the United States' nuclear weapons research laboratory, Lawrence Livermore National Laboratory, near Oakland, California.

Representation	Simulation
Bourgeois novel, realism	Science fiction, postmodernism
Organism	Biotic component
Depth, integrity	Surface, boundary
Heat	Noise
Biology as clinical practice	Biology as inscription
Physiology	Communications engineering
Small group	Subsystem
Perfection	Optimization
Eugenics	Population Control
Decadence, *Magic Mountain*	Obsolescence, *Future Shock*[vii]
Hygiene	Stress management
Microbiology, tuberculosis	Immunology, AIDS
Organic division of labor	Ergonomics/cybernetics of labor
Functional specialization	Modular construction
Reproduction	Replication
Organic sex role specialization	Optimal genetic strategies
Biological determinism	Evolutionary inertia, constraints
Community ecology	Ecosystem
Racial chain of being	Neo-imperialism, United Nations humanism
Scientific management in home/factory	Global factory/electronic cottage
Family/market/factory	Women in the integrated circuit
Family wage	Comparable worth
Public/private	Cyborg citizenship
Nature/culture	Fields of difference
Cooperation	Communications enhancement
Freud	Lacan
Sex	Genetic engineering
Labor	Robotics
Mind	Artificial intelligence
World War II	Star Wars
White capitalist patriarchy	Informatics of domination

This list suggests several interesting things.[9] First, the objects on the right-hand side cannot be coded as "natural," a realization that subverts naturalistic coding for the left-hand side as well. We cannot go back ideologically or materially. It's not just that "god" is dead; so is the "goddess." Or both are revivified in the worlds charged with microelectronic and biotechnological politics. In relation to objects like biotic components, one must think not in terms of essential properties, but in terms of design, boundary constraints, rates of flows, systems logics, costs of lowering constraints. Sexual reproduction is one kind of reproductive strategy among many, with costs and benefits as a function of the system environment. Ideologies of sexual reproduction can no longer reasonably call on notions of sex and sex role as organic aspects in natural objects like organisms and families. Such reasoning will be unmasked as irrational, and ironically corporate executives reading *Playboy* and anti-porn radical feminists will make strange bedfellows in jointly unmasking the irrationalism.

Likewise for race, racist and anti-racist ideologies about human diversity have to be formulated in terms of frequencies of parameters. It is "irrational" to invoke concepts like primitive and civilized. For liberals and radicals, the search for integrated social systems gives way to a new practice called "experimental ethnography" in which an organic object dissipates in attention to the play

[vii] Thomas Mann's (1873–1955) novel, *The Magic Mountain* (1924), versus Alvin Toffler's (1928–) nonfiction *Future Shock* (1970).

of writing. At the level of ideology, we see translations of racism and colonialism into languages of development and underdevelopment, rates and constraints of modernization. Any objects or persons can be "reasonably" thought of in terms of disassembly and reassembly; no "natural" architectures constrain system design. The financial districts in all the world's cities, as well as the export-processing and free-trade zones, proclaim this elementary fact of "late capitalism." The entire universe of objects that can be known scientifically must be formulated as problems in communications engineering (for the managers) or theories of the text (for those who would resist). Both are cyborg semiologies.

One should expect control strategies to concentrate on boundary conditions and interfaces, on rates of flow across boundaries – and not on the integrity of natural objects. "Integrity" or "sincerity" of the Western self gives way to decision procedures and expert systems. For example, control strategies applied to women's capacities to give birth to new human beings will be developed in the languages of population control and maximization of goal achievement for individual decision-makers. Control strategies will be formulated in terms of rates, costs of constraints, degrees of freedom. Human beings, like any other component or subsystem, must be localized in a system architecture whose basic modes of operation are probabilistic, statistical. No objects, spaces, or bodies are sacred in themselves; any component can be interfaced with any other if the proper standard, the proper code, can be constructed for processing signals in a common language. Exchange in this world transcends the universal translation effected by capitalist markets that Marx analyzed so well. The privileged pathology affecting all kinds of components in this universe is stress – communications breakdown.[10] The cyborg is not subject to Foucault's biopolitics; the cyborg simulates politics, a much more potent field of operations. Discursive constructions are no joke.

This kind of analysis of scientific and cultural objects of knowledge which have appeared historically since World War II prepares us to notice some important inadequacies in feminist analysis which has proceeded as if the organic, hierarchical dualism ordering discourse in the West since Aristotle still ruled. They have been cannibalized, or as Zoe Sofia (Sofoulis) might put it, they have been "technodigested." The dichotomies between mind and body, animal and human, organism and machine,

public and private, nature and culture, men and women, primitive and civilized are all in question ideologically. The actual situation of women is their integration/exploitation into a world system of production/reproduction and communication called the informatics of domination. The home, work place, market, public arena, the body itself – all can be dispersed and interfaced in nearly infinite, polymorphous ways, with large consequences for women and others – consequences that themselves are very different for different people and which make potent oppositional international movements difficult to imagine and essential for survival. One important route for reconstructing socialist-feminist politics is through theory and practice addressed to the social relations of science and technology, including crucially the systems of myth and meanings structuring our imaginations. The cyborg is a kind of disassembled and reassembled, postmodern collective and personal self. This is the self feminists must code.

Communications technologies and biotechnologies are the crucial tools recrafting our bodies. These tools embody and enforce new social relations for women worldwide. Technologies and scientific discourses can be partially understood as formalizations, that is, as frozen moments, of the fluid social interactions constituting them, but they should also be viewed as instruments for enforcing meanings. The boundary is permeable between tool and myth, instrument and concept, historical systems of social relations and historical anatomies of possible bodies, including objects of knowledge. Indeed, myth and tool mutually constitute each other.

Furthermore, communications sciences and modern biologies are constructed by a common move – the translation of the world into a problem of coding, a search for a common language in which all resistance to instrumental control disappears and all heterogeneity can be submitted to disassembly, reassembly, investment, and exchange.

In communications sciences, the translation of the world into a problem in coding can be illustrated by looking at cybernetic (feedback controlled) systems theories applied to telephone technology, computer design, weapons deployment, or database construction and maintenance. In each case, solution to the key questions rests on a theory of language and control; the key operation is determining the rates, directions, and probabilities of flow of a quantity called information. The world is subdivided by boundaries differentially permeable to information. Information is just that kind of quantifiable element (unit, basis of unity) which allows universal translation and so unhindered instrumental power (called effective communication). The biggest threat to such power is interruption of communication. Any system breakdown is a function of stress. The fundamentals of this technology can be condensed into the metaphor C^3I, command-control-communication-intelligence, the military's symbol for its operations theory.

In modern biologies, the translation of the world into a problem in coding can be illustrated by molecular genetics, ecology, sociobiological evolutionary theory, and immunobiology. The organism has been translated into problems of genetic coding and read-out. Biotechnology, a writing technology, informs research broadly.[11] In a sense, organisms have ceased to exist as objects of knowledge, giving way to biotic components, that is, special kinds of information-processing devices. The analogous moves in ecology could be examined by probing the history and utility of the concept of the ecosystem. Immunobiology and associated medical practices are rich exemplars of the privilege of coding and recognition systems as objects of knowledge, as constructions of bodily reality for us. Biology here is a king of cryptography. Research is necessarily a kind of intelligence activity. Ironies abound. A stressed system goes awry; its communication processes break down; it fails to recognize the difference between self and other. Human babies with baboon hearts evoke national ethical perplexity – for animal-rights activists at least as much as for the guardians of human purity. In the United States gay men and intravenous drug users are the most "privileged" victims of an awful immune-system disease that marks (inscribes on the body) confusion of boundaries and moral pollution.[12]

But these excursions into communications sciences and biology have been at a rarefied level; there is a mundane, largely economic reality to support my claim that these sciences and technologies indicate fundamental transformations in the structure of the world for us. Communications technologies depend on electronics. Modern states, multinational corporations, military power, welfare-state apparatuses, satellite systems, political processes, fabrication of our imaginations, labor-control systems, medical constructions of our bodies, commercial pornography, the international division of labor, and religious evangelism depend intimately upon electronics. Microelectronics is the tech-

nical basis of simulacra, that is, of copies without originals.

Microelectronics mediates the translations of labor into robotics and word processing, sex into genetic engineering and reproductive technologies, and mind into artificial intelligence and decision procedures. The new biotechnologies concern more than human reproduction. Biology as a powerful engineering science for redesigning materials and processes has revolutionary implications for industry, perhaps most obvious today in areas of fermentation, agriculture, and energy. Communications sciences and biology are constructions of natural-technical objects of knowledge in which the difference between machine and organism is thoroughly blurred; mind, body, and tool are on very intimate terms. The "multinational" material organization of the production and reproduction of daily life and the symbolic organization of the production and reproduction of culture and imagination seem equally implicated. The boundary-maintaining images of base and superstructure, public and private, or material and ideal never seemed more feeble.

I have used Rachel Grossman's image of women in the integrated circuit to name the situation of women in a world so intimately restructured through the social relations of science and technology.[13] I use the odd circumlocution, "the social relations of science and technology," to indicate that we are not dealing with a technological determinism, but with a historical system depending upon structured relations among people. But the phrase should also indicate that science and technology provide fresh sources of power, that we need fresh sources of analysis and political action.[14] Some of the rearrangements of race, sex, and class rooted in high-tech-facilitated social relations can make socialist feminism more relevant to effective progressive politics. . . .

Women in the Integrated Circuit

Let me summarize the picture of women's historical locations in advanced industrial societies, as these positions have been restructured partly through the social relations of science and technology. If it was ever possible ideologically to characterize women's lives by the distinction of public and private domains – suggested by images of the division of working-class life into factory and home, of bourgeois life into market and home, and of gender existence into personal and political realms – it is now a totally misleading ideology, even to show how both terms of these dichotomies construct each other in practice and in theory. I prefer a network ideological image, suggesting the profusion of spaces and identities and the permeability of boundaries in the personal body and in the body politic. "Networking" is both a feminist practice and a multinational corporate strategy – weaving is for oppositional cyborgs.

So let me return to the earlier image of the informatics of domination and trace one vision of women's "place" in the integrated circuit, touching only a few idealized social locations seen primarily from the point of view of advanced capitalist societies: Home, Market, Paid Work Place, State, School, Clinic-Hospital, and Church. Each of these idealized spaces is logically and practically implied in every other locus, perhaps analogous to a holographic photograph. I want to suggest the impact of the social relations mediated and enforced by the new technologies in order to help formulate needed analysis and practical work. However, there is no "place" for women in these networks, only geometries of difference and contradiction crucial to women's cyborg identities. If we learn how to read these webs of power and social life, we might learn new couplings, new coalitions. There is no way to read the following list from a standpoint of "identification," of a unitary self. The issue is dispersion. The task is to survive in diaspora.

Home: Women-headed households, serial monogamy, flight of men, old women alone, technology of domestic work, paid home work, reemergence of home sweatshops, home-based businesses and telecommuting, electronic cottage, urban homelessness, migration, module architecture, reinforced (simulated) nuclear family, intense domestic violence.

Market: Women's continuing consumption work, newly targeted to buy the profusion of new production from the new technologies (especially as the competitive race among industrialized and industrializing nations to avoid dangerous mass unemployment necessitates finding ever bigger new markets for ever less clearly needed commodities); bimodal buying power, coupled with advertising targeting of the numerous affluent groups and neglect of the previous mass markets; growing importance of informal markets in labor and commodities parallel to high-tech, affluent market structures; surveillance systems through electronic funds transfer; intensified market abstraction (commodification) of experience, resulting in ineffective utopian or equivalent cynical theories of community; extreme mobility (abstraction) of marketing/financing systems; interpenetration of sexual and labor markets; intensified sexualization of abstracted and alienated consumption.

Paid Work Place: Continued intense sexual and racial division of labor, but considerable growth of membership in privileged occupational categories for many white women and people of color; impact of new technologies on women's work in clerical, service, manufacturing (especially textiles), agriculture, electronics; international restructuring of the working classes; development of new time arrangements to facilitate the homework economy (flex time, part time, overtime, no time); homework and out work; increased pressures for two-tiered wage structures; significant numbers of people in cash-dependent populations worldwide with no experience or no further hope of stable employment; most labor "marginal" or "feminized."

State: Continued erosion of the welfare state; decentralizations with increased surveillance and control; citizenship by telematics; imperialism and political power broadly in the form of information-rich/information-poor differentiation; increased high-tech militarization increasingly opposed by many social groups; reduction of civil service jobs as a result of the growing capital intensification of office work, with implications for occupational mobility for women of color; growing privatization of material and ideological life and culture; close integration of privatization and militarization, the high-tech forms of bourgeois capitalist personal and public life; invisibility of different social groups to each other, linked to psychological mechanisms of belief in abstract enemies.

School: Deepening coupling of high-tech capital needs and public education at all levels, differentiated by race, class, and gender; managerial classes involved in educational reform and refunding at the cost of remaining progressive educational democratic structures for children and teachers; education for mass ignorance and repression in technocratic and militarized culture; growing anti-science mystery cults in dissenting and radical political movements; continued relative scientific illiteracy among white women and people of color; growing industrial direction of education (especially higher education) by science-based multinationals (particularly in electronics- and bio-technology-dependent companies); highly educated, numerous elites in a progressively bimodal society.

Clinic-Hospital: Intensified machine–body relations; renegotiations of public metaphors which channel personal experience of the body, particularly in relation to reproduction, immune system functions, and "stress" phenomena; intensification of reproductive politics in response to world historical implications of women's unrealized, potential control of their relation to reproduction; emergence of new historically specific diseases; struggles over meanings and means of health in environments pervaded by high-technology products and processes; continuing feminization of health work; intensified struggle over state responsibility for health; continued ideological role of popular health movements as a major form of American politics.

Church: Electronic fundamentalist "super-saver" preachers solemnizing the union of electronic capital and automated fetish gods; intensified importance of churches in resisting the militarized state; central struggle over women's meanings and authority in religion; continued relevance of spirituality, intertwined with sex and health, in political struggle.

The only way to characterize the informatics of domination is as a massive intensification of insecurity and cultural impoverishment, with common failure of subsistence networks for the most vulnerable. Since much of this picture interweaves with the social relations of science and technology, the urgency of a socialist-feminist politics addressed to science and technology is plain. There is much now being done, and the grounds for political work are rich. For example, the efforts to develop forms of collective struggle for women in paid work, like District 925 of the SEIU (Service Employees International Union) should be a high priority for all of us. These efforts are profoundly tied to technical restructuring of labor processes and reformations of working classes. These efforts also are providing understanding of a more comprehensive kind of labor organization, involving community, sexuality, and family issues never privileged in the largely white male industrial unions.

The structural rearrangements related to the social relations of science and technology evoke strong ambivalence. But it is not necessary to be ultimately depressed by the implications of late twentieth-century women's relation to all aspects of work, culture, production of knowledge, sexuality, and reproduction. For excellent reasons, most Marxisms see domination best and have trouble understanding what can only look like false consciousness and people's complicity in their own domination in late capitalism. It is crucial to remember that what is lost, perhaps especially from women's points of view, is often virulent forms of oppression, nostalgically naturalized in the face of current violation. Ambivalence toward the disrupted unities mediated by high-tech culture requires not sorting consciousness into categories of "clear-sighted critique grounding a solid political epistemology" versus "manipulated false consciousness," but subtle understanding of emerging pleasures, experiences, and powers with serious potential for changing the rules of the game.

There are grounds for hope in the emerging bases for new kinds of unity across race, gender, and class, as these elementary units of socialist-feminist analysis themselves suffer protean transformations. Intensifications of hardship experienced worldwide in connection with the social relations of science and technology are severe. But what people are experiencing is not transparently clear, and we lack sufficiently subtle connections for collectively building effective theories of experience. Present efforts – Marxist, psychoanalytic, feminist, anthropological – to clarify even "our" experience are rudimentary.

I am conscious of the odd perspective provided by my historical position – a Ph.D. in biology for an Irish Catholic girl was made possible by Sputnik's impact on U.S. national science-education policy. I have a body and mind as much constructed by the post-World War II arms race and cold war as by the women's movements. There are more grounds for hope by focusing on the contradictory effects of politics designed to produce loyal American technocrats, which as well produced large numbers of dissidents, rather than by focusing on the present defeats.

The permanent partiality of feminist points of view has consequences for our expectations of forms of political organization and participation. We do not need a totality in order to work well. The feminist dream of a common language, like all dreams for a perfectly true language, of a perfectly faithful naming of experience, is a totalizing and imperialist one. In that sense, dialectics too is a dream language, longing to resolve contradiction.

Perhaps, ironically, we can learn from our fusions with animals and machines how not to be Man, the embodiment of Western logos. From the point of view of pleasure in these potent and taboo fusions, made inevitable by the social relations of science and technology, there might indeed be a feminist science.

Cyborgs: A Myth of Political Identity

I want to conclude with a myth about identity and boundaries which might inform late twentieth-century political imaginations. I am indebted in this story to writers like Joanna Russ, Samuel Delany, John Varley, James Tiptree, Jr., Octavia Butler, and Vonda McIntyre.[15] These are our storytellers exploring what it means to be embodied in high-tech worlds. They are theorists for cyborgs. Exploring conceptions of bodily boundaries and social order, the anthropologist Mary Douglas[viii] should be credited with helping us to consciousness about how fundamental body imagery is to world view and so to political language.[16] French feminists like Luce Irigaray and Monique Wittig, for all their differences, know how to write the body, how to weave eroticism, cosmology, and politics from imagery of embodiment, and especially for Wittig, from imagery of fragmentation and reconstitution of bodies.[17]

American radical feminists like Susan Griffin, Audre Lorde, and Adrienne Rich have profoundly affected our political imaginations – and perhaps restricted too much what we allow as a friendly body and political language.[18] They insist on the organic, opposing it to the technological. But their symbolic systems and the related positions of eco-feminism and feminist paganism, replete with organicisms, can only be understood in Sandoval's terms as oppositional ideologies fitting the late twentieth century.[ix] They would simply bewilder anyone not preoccupied with the machines and

consciousness of late capitalism. In that sense they are part of the cyborg world. But there are also great riches for feminists in explicitly embracing the possibilities inherent in the breakdown of clean distinctions between organism and machine and similar distinctions structuring the Western self. It is the simultaneity of breakdowns that cracks the matrices of domination and opens geometric possibilities. What might be learned from personal and political "technological" pollution? I will look briefly at two overlapping groups of texts for their insight into the construction of a potentially helpful cyborg myth: constructions of women of color and monstrous selves in feminist science fiction.

Earlier I suggested that "women of color" might be understood as a cyborg identity, a potent subjectivity synthesized from fusions of outsider identities and in the complex political–historical layerings of Audre Lorde's "biomythography," *Zami*.[19] There are material and cultural grids mapping this potential. Lorde captures the tone in the title of her book *Sister Outsider*. In my political myth, Sister Outsider is the offshore woman, whom U.S. workers, female and feminized, are supposed to regard as the enemy preventing their solidarity, threatening their security. Onshore, inside the boundary of the United States, Sister Outsider is a potential amid the races and ethnic identities of women manipulated for division, competition, and exploitation in the same industries. "Women of color" are the preferred labor force for the science-based industries, the real women for whom the worldwide sexual market, labor market, and politics of reproduction kaleidoscope into daily life. Young Korean women hired in the sex industry and in electronics assembly are recruited from high schools, educated for the integrated circuit. Literacy, especially in English, distinguishes the "cheap" female labor so attractive to the multinationals.

Contrary to Orientalist stereotypes of the "oral primitive," literacy is a special mark of women of color, acquired by U.S. black women as well as men through a history of risking death to learn and to teach reading and writing. Writing has a special significance for all colonized groups. Writing has been crucial to the Western myth of the distinction of oral and written cultures, primitive and civilized mentalities, and more recently to the erosion of that distinction in postmodernist theories attacking the phallogocentrism of the West, with its worship of the monotheistic, phallic, authoritative, and singular work, the unique and perfect name.[20] Contests

---

[viii] Mary Douglas (1921–), Italian-born American cultural anthropologist. The following women mentioned: Monique Wittig (1935–), French feminist novelist; Susan Griffin (1943–), feminist poet, dramatist, and philosopher; Audre Lorde (1934–92), lesbian African-American writer; and Adrienne Rich (1929–), American feminist poet.

[ix] Cuela Sandoval, author of "Women Respond to Racism: A Report on the National Women's Studies Association Conference," Center for Third World Organizing, Oakland, CA.

for the meanings of writing are a major form of contemporary political struggle. Releasing the play of writing is deadly serious. The poetry and stories of U.S. women of color are repeatedly about writing, about access to the power to signify, but this time that power must be neither phallic nor innocent. Cyborg writing must not be about the Fall, the imagination of a once-upon-a-time wholeness before language, before writing, before Man. Cyborg writing is about the power to survive not on the basis of original innocence, but on the basis of seizing the tools to mark the world that marked them as other.

The tools are often stories, retold stories, versions that reverse and displace the hierarchical dualisms of naturalized identities. In retelling origin stories, cyborg authors subvert the central myths of origin of Western culture. We have all been colonized by those origin myths, with their longing for fulfillment in apocalypse. The phallogocentric origin stories most crucial for feminist cyborgs are built into the literal technologies – technologies that write the world, biotechnology and microelectronics – that have recently textualized our bodies as code problems on the grid of C^3I. Feminist cyborg stories have the task of recoding communication and intelligence to subvert command and control.

Figuratively and literally, language politics pervade the struggles of women of color, and stories about language have a special power in the rich contemporary writing by U.S. women of color. For example, retellings of the story of the indigenous woman Malinche, mother of the mestizo "bastard" race of the new world, master of languages, and mistress of Cortés, carry special meaning for Chicana constructions of identity. Cherríe Moraga in *Loving in the War Years* explores the themes of identity when one never possessed the original language, never told the original story, never resided in the harmony of legitimate heterosexuality in the garden of culture, and so cannot base identity on a myth or a fall from innocence and right to natural names, mother's or father's.[21] Moraga's writing, her superb literacy, is presented in her poetry as the same kind of violation as Malinche's mastery of the conqueror's language – a violation, an illegitimate production, that allows survival. Moraga's language is not "whole"; it is self-consciously spliced, a chimera of English and Spanish, both conqueror's languages. But it is this chimeric monster, without claim to an original language before violation, that crafts the erotic, competent, potent identities of women of color. Sister Outsider hints

at the possibility of world survival not because of her innocence, but because of her ability to live on the boundaries, to write without the founding myth of original wholeness, with its inescapable apocalypse of final return to a deathly oneness that Man has imagined to be the innocent and all-powerful Mother, freed at the End from another spiral of appropriation by her son. Writing marks Moraga's body, affirms it as the body of a woman of color, against the possibility of passing into the unmarked category of the Anglo father or into the Orientalist myth of "original illiteracy" of a mother that never was. Malinche was mother here, not Eve before eating the forbidden fruit. Writing affirms Sister Outsider, not the Woman-before-the-Fall-into-Writing needed by the phallogocentric Family of Man.[x]

Writing is preeminently the technology of cyborgs, etched surfaces of the late twentieth century. Cyborg politics is the struggle for language and the struggle against perfect communication, against the one code that translates all meaning perfectly, the central dogma of phallogocentrism. That is why cyborg politics insist on noise and advocate pollution, rejoicing in the illegitimate fusions of animal and machine. These are the couplings which make Man and Woman so problematic, subverting the structure of desire, the force imagined to generate language and gender, and so subverting the structure and modes of reproduction of Western identity, of nature and culture, of mirror and eye, slave and master, body and mind. "We" did not originally choose to be cyborgs, but choice grounds a liberal politics and epistemology that imagines the reproduction of individuals before the wider replications of "texts."

From the perspective of cyborgs, freed of the need to ground politics in "our" privileged position of the oppression that incorporates all other dominations, the innocence of the merely violated, the ground of those closer to nature, we can see powerful possibilities. Feminisms and Marxisms have run aground of Western epistemological imperatives to construct a revolutionary subject from the perspective of a hierarchy of oppressions and a latent position of moral superiority, innocence, and greater closeness to nature. With no available original dream of a common language or original symbiosis promising protection from hostile

---

[x] "Phallogocentrism" is the synthesis of patriarchal society (which is "phallocentric") with what Derrida criticized as "logocentrism."

"masculine" separation, but written into the play of a text that has no finally privileged reading or salvation history, to recognize "oneself" as fully implicated in the world, frees us of the need to root politics in identification, vanguard parties, purity, and mothering. Stripped of identity, the bastard race teaches about the power of the margins and the importance of a mother like Malinche. Women of color have transformed her from the evil mother of masculinist fear into the originally literate mother who teaches survival.

This is not just deconstruction but liminal transformation. Every story that begins with original innocence and privileges the return to wholeness imagines the drama of life to be individuation, separation, the birth of the self, the tragedy of autonomy, the fall into writing, alienation; that is, war, tempered by imaginary respite in the bosom of the Other. These plots are ruled by a reproductive politics – rebirth without flaw, perfection, abstraction. In this plot women are imagined either better or worse off, but all agree they have less selfhood, weaker individuation, more fusion to the oral, to Mother, less at stake in masculine autonomy. But there is another route to having less at stake in masculine autonomy, a route that does not pass through Woman, Primitive, Zero, the Mirror Stage and its imaginary.[xi] It passes through women and other present-tense, illegitimate cyborgs, not of Woman born, who refuse the ideological resources of victimization so as to have a real life. These cyborgs are the people who refuse to disappear on cue, no matter how many times a Western commentator remarks on the sad passing of another primitive, another organic group done in by Western technology, by writing.[22] These real-life cyborgs, for example, the Southeast Asian village women workers in Japanese and U.S. electronics firms described by Aihwa Ong, are actively rewriting the texts of their bodies and societies. Survival is the stakes in this play of readings.

To recapitulate, certain dualisms have been persistent in Western traditions; they have all been systemic to the logics and practices of domination of women, people of color, nature, workers, animals – in short, domination of all constituted as others, whose task is to mirror the self. Chief among these troubling dualisms are self/other, mind/body, culture/nature, male/female, civilized/primitive, reality/appearance, whole/part, agent/resource, maker/made, active/passive, right/wrong, truth/illusion, total/partial, God/man. The self is the One who is not dominated, who knows that by the service of the other; the other is the one who holds the future, who knows that by the experience of domination, which gives the lie to the autonomy of the self. To be One is to be autonomous, to be powerful, to be God; but to be One is to be an illusion and so to be involved in a dialectic of apocalypse with the other. Yet, to be other is to be multiple, without clear boundaries, frayed, insubstantial. One is too few, but two are too many.

High-tech culture challenges these dualisms in intriguing ways. It is not clear who makes and who is made in the relation between human and machine. It is not clear what is mind and what is body in machines that resolve into coding practices. Insofar as we know ourselves in both formal discourse (e.g., biology) and in daily practice, (e.g., the homework economy in the integrated circuit), we find ourselves to be cyborgs, hybrids, mosaics, chimeras. Biological organisms have become biotic systems, communications devices like others. There is no fundamental, ontological separation in our formal knowledge of machine and organism, of technical and organic. The replicant Rachel in the film *Blade Runner* stands as the image of a cyborg culture's fear, love, and confusion.

One consequence is that our sense of connection to our tools is heightened. The trance state experienced by many computer users has become a staple of science-fiction film and cultural jokes. Perhaps paraplegics and other severely handicapped people can (and sometimes do) have the most intense experiences of complex hybridization with other communication devices.[23] Anne McCaffrey's prefeminist *The Ship Who Sang* explored the consciousness of a cyborg, hybrid of girl's brain and complex machinery, formed after the birth of a severely handicapped child. Gender, sexuality, embodiment, skill: All were reconstituted in the story. Why should our bodies end at the skin or include at best other beings encapsulated by skin? From the seventeenth century till now, machines could be animated – given ghostly souls to make them speak or move or to account for their orderly development and mental capacities. Or organisms could be mechanized – reduced to body understood as resource of mind. These machine/organism relationships are obsolete, unnecessary. For us, in imagination and in other practice, machines can be prosthetic devices, intimate components, friendly

[xi] The "mirror stage" is the phase of psychological development in which the "I" is first formed, according to Jacques Lacan.

selves. We don't need organic holism to give im-permeable wholeness, the total woman and her feminist variants (mutants?). Let me conclude this point by a very partial reading of the logic of the cyborg monsters of my second group of texts, femi-nist science fiction.

The cyborgs populating feminist science fiction make very problematic the statuses of man or woman, human, artifact, member of a race, individ-ual identity, or body. Katie King clarifies how pleasure in reading these fictions is not largely based on identification. Students facing Joanna Russ for the first time, students who have learned to take modernist writers like James Joyce or Vir-ginia Woolf without flinching, do not know what to make of *The Adventures of Alyx* of *The Female Man*, where characters refuse the reader's search for in-nocent wholeness while granting the wish for heroic quests, exuberant eroticism, and serious pol-itics. *The Female Man* is the story of four versions of one genotype, all of whom meet, but even taken together do not make a whole, resolve the dilemmas of violent moral action, nor remove the growing scandal of gender. The feminist science fiction of Samuel Delany, especially *Tales of Neverÿon*, mocks stories of origin by redoing the neolithic revolution, replaying the founding moves of West-ern civilization to subvert their plausibility. James Tiptree, Jr., an author whose fiction was regarded as particularly manly until her "true" gender was revealed, tells tales of reproduction based on non-mammalian technologies like alternation of gener-ations or male brood pouches and male nurturing. John Varley constructs a supreme cyborg in his arch-feminist exploration of Gaea, a mad goddess-planet-trickster-old-woman-technological device on whose surface an extraordinary array of post cyborg symbioses are spawned. Octavia Butler writes of an African sorceress pitting her powers of transformation against the genetic manipulations of her rival (*Wild Seed*), of time warps that bring a modern U.S. black woman into slavery where her actions in relation to her white master-ancestor determine the possibility of her own birth (*Kin-dred*), and of the illegitimate insights into identity and community of an adopted cross-species child who came to know the enemy as self (*Survivor*). In her recent novel, *Dawn* (1987), the first installment of a series called *Xenogenesis*, Butler tells the story of Lilith Iyapo, whose personal name recalls Adam's first and repudiated wife and whose family name marks her status as the widow of the son of Nigerian immigrants to the United States. A black

woman and a mother whose child is dead, Lilith mediates the transformation of humanity through genetic exchange with extraterrestrial lovers/res-cuers/destroyers/genetic engineers, who reform earth's habitats after the nuclear holocaust and coerce surviving humans into intimate fusion with them. It is a novel that interrogates reproductive, linguistic, and nuclear politics in a mythic field structured by late twentieth-century race and gender.

Because it is particularly rich in boundary trans-gressions, Vonda McIntyre's *Superluminal* can close this truncated catalogue of promising and dangerous monsters who help redefine the pleas-ures and politics of embodiment and feminist writing. In a fiction where no character is "simply" human, human status is highly problematic. Orca, a genetically altered diver, can speak with killer whales and survive deep ocean conditions, but she longs to explore space as a pilot, necessitating bionic implants jeopardizing her kinship with the divers and cetaceans. Transformations are effected by virus vectors carrying a new developmental code, by transplant surgery, by implants of micro-electronic devices, by analogue doubles, and by other means. Laenea becomes a pilot by accepting a heart implant and a host of other alterations allowing survival in transit at speeds exceeding that of light. Radu Dracul survives a virus-caused plague on his outerworld planet to find himself with a time sense that changes the boundaries of spatial perception for the whole species. All the characters explore the limits of language, the dream of communicating experience, and the ne-cessity of limitation, partiality, and intimacy even in this world of protean transformation and con-nection. *Superluminal* stands also for the defining contradictions of a cyborg world in another sense; it embodies textually the intersection of feminist theory and colonial discourse in the science fiction I have alluded to in this essay. This is a conjunction with a long history that many first world feminists have tried to repress, including myself in my read-ings of *Superluminal* before being called to account by Zoe Soufoulis, whose different location in the world system's informatics of domination made her acutely alert to the imperialist moment of all sci-ence-fiction cultures, including women's science fiction. From an Australian feminist sensitivity, Sofoulis remembered more readily McIntyre's role as writer of the adventures of Captain Kirk and Spock in "Star Trek" than her rewriting the romance in *Superluminal*.

Monsters have always defined the limits of community in Western imaginations. The centaurs and Amazons of ancient Greece established the limits of the centered polis of the Greek male human by their disruption of marriage and boundary pollutions of the warrior with animality and woman. Unseparated twins and hermaphrodites were the confused human material in early modern France who grounded discourse on the natural and supernatural, medical and legal, portents and diseases – all crucial to establishing modern identity.[24] The evolutionary and behavioral sciences of monkeys and apes have marked the multiple boundaries of late twentieth-century industrial identities. Cyborg monsters in feminist science fiction define quite different political possibilities and limits from those proposed by the mundane fiction of Man and Woman.

There are several consequences to taking seriously the imagery of cyborgs as other than our enemies. Our bodies, ourselves – bodies are maps of power and identity. Cyborgs are no exceptions. A cyborg body is not innocent; it was not born in a garden; it does not seek unitary identity and so generates antagonistic dualisms without end (or until the world ends); it takes irony for granted. One is too few, and two is only one possibility. Intense pleasure in skill, machine skill, ceases to be a sin, but an aspect of embodiment. The machine is not an it to be animated, worshiped, and dominated. The machine is us, our processes, an aspect of our embodiment. We can be responsible for machines; they do not dominate or threaten us. We are responsible for boundaries; we are they. Up till now (once upon a time), female embodiment seemed to be given, organic, necessary; female embodiment seemed to mean skill in mothering and its metaphoric extensions. Only by being out of place could we take intense pleasure in machines and then with excuses that this was organic activity after all, appropriate to females. Cyborgs might consider more seriously the partial, fluid, sometimes aspect of sex and sexual embodiment. Gender might not be global identity after all, even if it has profound historical breadth and depth.

The ideologically charged question of what counts as daily activity, as experience, can be approached by exploiting the cyborg image. Feminists have recently claimed that women are given to dailiness, that women more than men somehow sustain daily life, and so have a privileged epistemological position potentially. There is a compelling aspect to this claim, one that makes visible un-

valued female activity and names it as the ground of life. But the ground of life? What about all the ignorance of women, all the exclusions and failures of knowledge and skill? What about men's access to daily competence, to knowing how to build things, to take them apart, to play? What about other embodiments? Cyborg gender is a local possibility taking a global vengeance. Race, gender, and capital require a cyborg theory of wholes and parts. There is no drive in cyborgs to produce total theory, but there is an intimate experience of boundaries, their construction and deconstruction. There is a myth system waiting to become a political language to ground one way of looking at science and technology and challenging the informatics of domination – in order to act potently.

One last image: organisms and organismic, holistic politics depend on metaphors of rebirth and invariably call on the resources of reproductive sex. I would suggest that cyborgs have more to do with regeneration and are suspicious of the reproductive matrix and of most birthing. For salamanders, regeneration after injury, such as the loss of a limb, involves regrowth of structure and restoration of function with the constant possibility of twinning or other odd topographical productions at the site of former injury. The regrown limb can be monstrous, duplicated, potent. We have all been injured, profoundly. We require regeneration, not rebirth, and the possibilities for our reconstitution include the utopian dream of the hope for a monstrous world without gender.

Cyborg imagery can help express two crucial arguments in this essay: (1) the production of universal, totalizing theory is a major mistake that misses most of reality, probably always, but certainly now; (2) taking responsibility for the social relations of science and technology means refusing an anti-science metaphysics, a demonology of technology, and so means embracing the skillful task of reconstructing the boundaries of daily life, in partial connection with others, in communication with all of our parts. It is not just that science and technology are possible means of great human satisfaction, as well as a matrix of complex dominations. Cyborg imagery can suggest a way out of the maze of dualisms in which we have explained our bodies and our tools to ourselves. This is a dream not of a common language, but of a powerful infidel heteroglossia. It is an imagination of a feminist speaking in tongues to strike fear into the circuits of the super savers of the New Right.

It means both building and destroying machines, identities, categories, relationships, spaces, stories.

Although both are bound in the spiral dance, I would rather be a cyborg than a goddess.

Author's Notes

1   Useful references to left and/or feminist radical science movements and theory and to biological/biotechnological issues include Ruth Bleier, *Science and Gender: A Critique of Biology and Its Themes on Women* (New York: Pergamon, 1984); Ruth Bleier, ed., *Feminist Approaches to Science* (New York: Pergamon, 1986); Sandra Harding, *The Science Question in Feminism* (Ithaca, NY: Cornell University Press, 1986); Anne Fausto-Sterling, *Myths of Gender* (New York: Basic Books, 1985); Stephen J. Gould, *Mismeasure of Man* (New York: Norton, 1981); Ruth Hubbard, Mary Sue Henifin, Barbara Fried, eds., *Biological Woman, the Convenient Myth* (Cambridge, MA: Schenkman, 1982); Evelyn Fox Keller, *Reflections on Gender and Science* (New Haven, CT: Yale University Press, 1985); R. C. Lewontin, Steve Rose, and Leon Kamin, *Not in Our Genes* (New York: Pantheon, 1984); *Radical Science Journal* (from 1987, *Science as Culture*), 26 Freegrove Road, London N7 9RQ; *Science for the People*, 897 Main St., Cambridge, MA 02139.

2   Starting points for left and/or feminist approaches to technology and politics include Ruth Schwartz Cowan, *More Work for Mother: The Ironies of Household Technology from the Open Hearth to the Microwave* (New York: Basic Books, 1983); Joan Rothschild, *Machina ex Dea: Feminist Perspectives on Technology* (New York: Pergamon, 1983); Sharon Traweek, *Beantimes and Lifetimes: The World of High Energy Physics* (Cambridge, MA: Harvard University Press, 1988); R. M. Young and Les Levidov, eds., *Science, Technology, and the Labour Process*, Vols. 1–3 (London: CSE Books); Joseph Weizenbaum, *Computer Power and Human Reason* (San Francisco: Freeman, 1976); Langdon Winner, *Autonomous Technology: Technics Out of Control as a Theme in Political Thought* (Cambridge, MA: MIT Press, 1977); Langdon Winner, *The Whale and the Reactor* (Chicago: Chicago University Press, 1986); Jan Zimmerman, ed., *The Technological Woman: Interfacing with Tomorrow* (New York: Praeger, 1983); Tom Athanasiou, "High-tech Politics. The Case of Artificial Intelligence," *Socialist Review*, No. 92, 1987, pp. 7–35; Carol Cohn, "Nuclear Language and How We Learned to Pat the Bomb," *Bulletin of Atomic Scientists*, June 1987, pp. 17–24; Terry Winograd and Fernando Flores, *Understanding Computers and Cognition: A New Foundation for Design* (New Jersey: Ablex, 1986); Paul Edwards, "Border Wars: The Politics of Artificial Intelligence," *Radical America*, Vol. 19, No. 6, 1985, pp. 39–52; *Global Electronics Newsletter*, 867 West Dana St., #204, Mountain View, CA 94041; *Processed World*, 55 Sutter St., San Francisco, CA 94104; *ISIS*, Women's International Information and Communication Service, P.O. Box 50 (Cornavin), 1211 Geneva 2, Switzerland, and Via Santa Maria dell'Anima 30, 00186 Rome, Italy. Fundamental approaches to modern social studies of science that do not continue the liberal mystification that it all started with Thomas Kuhn, include: Karin Knorr-Cetina, *The Manufacture of Knowledge* (Oxford: Pergamon, 1981); K. D. Knorr-Cetina and Michael Mulkay, eds., *Science Observed: Perspectives on the Social Study of Science* (Beverly Hills, CA: Sage, 1983); Bruno Latour and Steve Woolgar, *Laboratory Life: The Social Construction of Scientific Facts* (Beverly Hills, CA: Sage, 1979); Robert M. Young, "Interpreting the Production of Science," *New Scientist*, Vol. 29, March 1979, pp. 1026–8. More is claimed than is known about room for contesting productions of science in the mythic/material space of "the laboratory"; the 1984 Directory of the Network for the Ethnographic Study of Science, Technology, and Organizations lists a wide range of people and projects crucial to better radical analysis; available from NESSTO, P.O. Box 11442, Stanford, CA 94305.

3   Fredric Jameson, "Post Modernism, or the Cultural Logic of Late Capitalism," *New Left Review*, July/August 1984, pp. 53–94. See Marjorie Perloff, "'Dirty' Language and Scramble Systems," *Sulfur* Vol. 2, 1984, pp. 178–83; Kathleen Fraser, *Something (Even Human Voices) in the Foreground, a Lake* (Berkeley, CA: Kelsey St. Press, 1984). For feminist modernist/postmodernist cyborg writing, see *How(-ever)*, 871 Corbett Ave., San Francisco, CA 94131.

4   Frans de Waal, *Chimpanzee Politics: Power and Sex among the Apes* (New York: Harper & Row, 1982); Langdon Winner, "Do artifacts have politics?" *Daedalus* (Winter 1980): 121–36.

5   Jean Baudrillard, *Simulations*, trans. P. Foss, P. Patton, P. Beitchman (New York: Semiotext(e), 1983). Jameson ("Postmodernism," p. 66) points out that Plato's definition of the simulacrum is the copy for which there is no original, i.e., the world of advanced capitalism, of pure exchange. See *Discourse* 9, Spring/Summer 1987, for a special issue on technology (Cybernetics, Ecology, and the Postmodern Imagination).

6   Herbert Marcuse, *One-Dimensional Man* (Boston: Beacon Press, 1964); Carolyn Merchant, *Death of Nature* (San Francisco: Harper & Row, 1980).

7   Zoe Sofia, "Exterminating Fetuses," *Diacritics*, Vol. 14, No. 2, Summer 1984, pp. 47–59, and "Jupiter

Space" (Pomona, CA: American Studies Association, 1984).

8 For ethnographic accounts and political evaluations, see Barbara Epstein, "The Politics of Prefigurative Community: The Non-Violent Direction Action Movement," *The Year Left*, [Vol. 3 of *Resphaping the U.S. Left: Popular Struggles in the 1980's*, M. Davis and M. Sprinker (London: Verso, 1987)], and Noel Sturgeon, qualifying essay on feminism, anarchism, and nonviolent direct-action politics, University of California, Santa Cruz, 1986. Without explicit irony, adopting the spaceship earth/whole earth logo of the planet photographed from space, set off by the slogan "Love Your Mother," the May 1987 Mothers and Others Day action at the nuclear weapons testing facility in Nevada nonetheless took account of the tragic contradictions of views of the earth. Demonstrators applied for official permits to be on the land from officers of the Western Shoshone tribe, whose territory was invaded by the U.S. government when it built the nuclear weapons test ground in the 1950s. Arrested for trespassing, the demonstrators argued that the police and weapons facility personnel, without authorization from the proper officials, were the trespassers. One affinity group at the women's action called themselves the Surrogate Others, and in solidarity with the creatures forced to tunnel in the same ground with the bomb, they enacted a cyborgian emergence from the constructed body of a large, nonheterosexual desert worm.

9 My previous efforts to understand biology as a cybernetic command-control discourse and organisms as "natural-technical objects of knowledge" are "The High Cost of Information in Post-World War II Evolutionary Biology," *Philosophical Forum*, Vol. 13, Nos. 2–3, 1979, pp. 206–37; "Signs of Dominance: From a Physiology to a Cybernetics of Primate Society," *Studies in History of Biology*, Vol. 6, 1983, pp. 129–219; "Class, Race, Sex, Scientific Objects of Knowledge: A Socialist-Feminist Perspective on the Social Construction of Productive Knowledge and Some Political Consequences," *Women in Scientific and Engineering Professions*, ed. Violet Haas and Carolyn Perucci (Ann Arbor, MI: University of Michigan Press, 1984), pp. 212–29.

10 E. Rusten Hogness, "Why Stress? A Look at the Making of Stress, 1936–1956," available from the author, 4437 Mill Creek Rd., Healdsburg, CA 95448.

11 A left entry to the biotechnology debate: *Genewatch*, a Bulletin of the Committee for Responsible Genetics, 5 Doane St., 4th floor, Boston, MA 02109; Susan Wright, "Recombinant DNA Technology and Its Social Transformation, 1972–82," *Osiris*, 2nd series, Vol. 2, 1986, pp. 303–60 and "Recombinant DNA: The Status of Hazards and Controls," *Environment*, July/August 1982; Edward Yoxen, *The Gene Business* (New York: Harper & Row, 1983).

12 Paula Treichler, "AIDS, Homophobia, and Biomedical Discourse: An Epidemic of Signification," in *Cultural Studies*, Vol.1, No.1, 1987, pp. 263–305.

13 Starting references for "women in the integrated circuit": *Scientific-Technological Change and the Role of Women in Development*, ed. Pamela D'Onofrio-Flores and Sheila M. Pfafflin (Boulder, CO: Westview Press, 1982); Maria Patricia Fernandez-Kelly, *For We Are Sold, I and My People* (Albany, NY: SUNY Press, 1983); Annette Fuentes and Barbara Ehrenreich, *Women in the Global Factory* (Boston: South End Press, 1983), with an especially useful list of resources and organizations; Rachael Grossman, "Women's Place in the Integrated Circuit," *Radical America*, Vol. 14, No. I, 1980, pp. 29–50; *Women and Men and the International Division of Labor*, ed. June Nash and M. P. Fernandez-Kelly (Albany, NY: SUNY Press, 1983); Aihwa Ong, "Japanese Factories, Malay Workers: Industrialization and the Cultural Construction of Gender in West Malaysia, *Power and Difference*: Gender in Island Southeast Asia, ed. Shelly Errington and Jane Atkinson (Palo Alto, CA: Stanford University Press, 1990); Aihwa Ong, *Spirits of Resistance and Capitalist Discipline: Factory Workers in Malaysia* (Albany, SUNY Press, 1987); *Science Policy Research Unity, Microelectronics and Women's Employment in Britain* (University of Sussex, 1982).

14 The best example is Bruno Latour, *Les Microbes: Guerre et Paix, suivi de Irréductions* (Paris: Métailié, 1984).

15 Katie King, "The Pleasure of Repetition and the Limits of Identification in Feminist Science Fiction: Reimaginations of the Body after the Cyborg," California American Studies Association, Pomona, 1984. An abbreviated list of feminist science fiction underlying themes of this essay: Octavia Bulter, *Wild Seed, Mind of My Mind, Kindred, Survivor*; Suzy McKee Charnas, *Motherlines*; Samuel Delany, *Tales of Neverÿon*; Anne McCaffery, *The Ship Who Sang, Dinosaur Planet*; Vonda McIntyre, *Superluminal, Dreamsnake*; Joanna Russ, *Adventures of Alyx, The Female Man*; James Tiptree, Jr., *Star Songs of an Old Primate, Up the Walls of the World*; Joanna Varley, *Titan, Wizard, Demon*.

16 Mary Douglas, *Purity and Danger* (London: Routledge & Kegan Paul, 1966), *Natural Symbols* (London: Cresset Press, 1970).

17 French feminisms contribute to cyborg heteroglossia. Carolyn Burke, "Irigaray through the Looking Glass," *Feminist Studies*, Vol. 7, No. 2, Summer 1981, pp. 288–306; Luce Irigaray, *Ce sexe qui n'en est pas un* (Paris: Minuit, 1977); L. Irigaray, *Et l'une ne bouge pas sans l'autre* (Paris: Minuit, 1979); *New French Feminisms*, ed. Elaine Marks and Isabelle de Courtivron (Amherst, MA: University of Massachusetts Press, 1980); *Signs*, Vol. 7, No. I, Autumn 1981, special issue on French feminism; Monique Wittig,

The Lesbian Body, trans. David Le Vay (New York: Avon, 1975; *Le corps lesbien*, 1973). See especially *Feminist Issues: A Journal of Feminist Social and Political Theory*, I (1980), and Claire Duchen, *Feminism in France: From May '68 to Mitterand* (London: Routledge Kegan & Paul, 1986).

18   But all these poets are very complex, not least in treatment of themes of lying and erotic, decentered collective and personal identities. Susan Griffin, *Women and Nature: The Roaring Inside Her* (New York: Harper & Row, 1978); Audre Lorde, *Sister Outsider* (Trumansburg, NY: Crossing Press, 1984); Adrienne Rich, *The Dream of a Common Language* (New York: Norton, 1978).

19   Audre Lorde, *Zami, a New Spelling of my Name* (Trumansburg, NY: Crossing Press, 1983); Katie King, "Audre Lorde: Layering History/Constructing Poetry," Canons without Innocence, Ph.D. thesis, University of California, Santa Cruz, 1987.

20   Jacques Derrida, *Of Grammatology*, trans. and introd. G. C. Spivak (Baltimore, MD: Johns Hopkins University Press, 1976), especially part II. "Nature, Culture, Writing"; Claude Lévi-Strauss, *Tristes Tropiques*, trans. John Russell (New York: Criterion Books, 1961), especially "The Writing Lesson"; Henry Louis Gates, "Writing 'Race' and the Difference It Makes," in "Race," Writing and Difference, special issue of *Critical Inquiry*, Vol. 12, No. 1, Autumn 1985, pp. 1–20; *Cultures in Contention*, ed. Douglas Kahn and Diane Neumaier, (Seattle: Real Comet Press, 1985); Walter Ong, *Orality and Literacy: The Technologizing of the Word* (New York: Methuen, 1982); Cheris Kramarae and Paula Treichler, *A Feminist Dictionary* (Boston: Pandora, 1985).

21   Cherrie Moraga, *Loving in the War Years* (Boston: South End Press, 1983). The sharp relation of women of color to writing as theme and politics can be approached through "The Black Woman and the Diaspora: Hidden Connections and Extended Acknowledgments," An International Literacy Conference, Michigan State University, October 1985; *Black Women Writers: A Critical Evaluation*, ed. Mari Evans (Garden City, NY: Doubleday/Anchor, 1984); Barbara Christian, *Black Feminist Criticism* (New York: Pergamon, 1985); *The Third Woman: Minority Women Writers of the United States*, ed. Dexter Fisher (Boston: Houghton Mifflin, 1980); several issues of *Frontiers*, especially vol. 5, 1980, "Chicanas en el Ambiente Nacional" and Vol. 7, 1983, "Feminisms in the Non-Western World";

Maxine Hong Kingston, *China Men* (New York: Knopf, 1977); *Black Women in White America: A Documentary History*, ed. Gerda Lerner (New York: Vintage, 1973); Paula Giddings, *When and Where I Enter: The Impact of Black Women on Race and Sex in America* (Toronto: Bantam, 1985); *This Bridge Called My Back: Writings by Radical Women of Color*, ed. Cherrie Moraga and Gloria Anzaldua (Watertown, MA: Persephone, 1981); *Sisterhood Is Global*, ed. Robin Morgan (Garden City, NY: Anchor/Doubleday, 1984). The writing of white women has had similar meanings: Sandra Gilbert and Susan Gubar, *The Madwoman in the Attic* (New Haven, CT: Yale University Press, 1979); Joanna Russ, *How to Suppress Women's Writing* (Austin, TX: University of Texas Press, 1983).

22   James Clifford argues persuasively for recognition of continuous cultural reinvention, the stubborn nondisappearance of those "marked" by Western imperializing practices; see "On Ethnographic Allegory," James Clifford and George E. Marcus, eds., *Writing Culture, the Poetics and Politics of Ethnography* (University of California Press, 1985) and "On Ethnographic Authority," *Representations*, Vol. I, No. 2 (1983), pp. 118–46.

23   The convention of ideologically taming militarized high technology by publicizing its applications to speech and motion problems of the disabled–differently abled takes on a special irony in monotheistic, patriarchal, and frequently anti-Semitic culture when computer-generated speech allows a boy with no voice to chant the Haftorah at his bar mitzvah. See Vic Sussman, "Personal Technology Lends a Hand," *Washington Post Magazine*, Nov. 9, 1986, pp. 45–6. Making the always context-relative social definitions of "abledness" particularly clear, military high-tech has a way of making human beings disabled by definition, a perverse aspect of much automated battlefield and Star Wars R&D. See John Noble Welford, "Pilot's Helmet Helps Interpret High Speed World," *New York Times*, July 1, 1986, pp. 21, 24.

24   Page DuBois, *Centaurs and Amazons* (Ann Arbor, MI: University of Michigan Press, 1982); Lorraine Daston and Katharine Park, "Hermaphrodites in Renaissance France," ms., n.d.; Katharine Park and Lorraine Daston, "Unnatural Conceptions: The Study of Monsters in 16th and 17th Century France and England," *Past and Present*, No. 92, August 1981, pp. 20–54. The word *monster* shares its root with the verb *to demonstrate*.

47

From *The Reenchantment of Science*

David Ray Griffin

Professor of philosophy of religion, David Griffin (1939–) proposes a positive, revisionary postmodernism inspired by scientific developments. With others influenced by the "new sciences" of quantum theory, complexity and chaos, emergent properties of physical systems, and self-organization and mind–body interactions in biology, he believes that the modern dualism of an allegedly mechanistic, deterministic, objective "nature" and the indeterminist, participant-interactive "objects" of the human sciences has been broken down. Griffin's own framework for responding to these developments is the philosophy of "organicism" of English-born philosopher Alfred North Whitehead (1861–1947) from which Griffin hopes to fashion a postmodern cosmology that denies the characteristic dualisms of modern thought. Griffin argues that contemporary science, in discarding these notions for holistic, indeterminist alternatives, is becoming postmodern.

Modern Science and the Disenchantment of the World

In disenchanting nature, the modern science of nature led to its own disenchantment. This happened because the mechanistic, disenchanted philosophy of nature, which was originally part of a dualistic and theistic vision of reality as a whole, eventually led to the disenchantment of the whole world. This first section spells out this development.

What does the "disenchantment of nature" mean? Most fundamentally, it means the denial to

nature of all subjectivity, all experience, all feeling. Because of this denial, nature is disqualified – it is denied all qualities that are not thinkable apart from experience.

These qualities are legion. Without experience, no aims or purposes can exist in natural entities, no creativity in the sense of self-determination or final causation. With no final causation toward some ideal possibility, no role exists for ideals, possibilities, norms, or values to play: causation is strictly a matter of efficient causation from the past. With no self-determination aimed at the realization of ideals, no value can be achieved. With no experience, even unconscious feeling, there can be no value received: the causal interactions between natural things or events involve no sharing of values. Hence, no intrinsic value can exist within nature, no value of natural things for themselves. Also, unlike the way our experience is internally affected, even constituted in part, by its relations with its environment, material particles can have no internal relations. Along with no internalization of other natural things, no internalization of divinity can occur. Friedrich Schiller, who spoke of the disenchantment of nature a century before Weber, used the term *Entgotterung*, which literally means the dedivinization of nature. Deity, for the founders of the modern worldview, such as Descartes,

---

Griffin, David Ray, from "Introduction: The Reenchantment of Science," section 1, pp. 2–8 and section 3, 22–30 in *The Reenchantment of Science* (ed. David Ray Griffin). Albany: State University of New York Press, 1988.

Boyle, and Newton, was in no way immanent in the world; it was a being wholly external to the world who imposed motion and laws upon it from without. The laws of nature were, hence, not at all analogous to sociological laws which reflect the habits of the members of human society. A further and in fact central feature of the disenchantment of nature was the denial of action at a distance. Weber's term for disenchantment was *Entzauberung*, which literally means "taking the magic out." It was at the heart of the mechanistic vision to deny that natural things had any hidden ("occult") powers to attract other things (a denial that made the phenomena of magnetism and gravitation very difficult to explain).[1] In these ways, nature was bereft of all qualities with which the human spirit could feel a sense of kinship and of anything from which it could derive norms. Human life was rendered both alien and autonomous.

Whereas this disenchantment of nature was originally carried out (by Galileo, Descartes, Boyle, and Newton & Company) in the framework of a dualistic supernaturalism in which the soul and a personal deity were assigned explanatory functions and hence causal power, the successes of the objectifying, mechanistic, reductionistic approach in physics soon led to the conviction that it should be applied to all of reality. God was at first stripped of all causal power beyond that of the original creation of the world; later thinkers turned this deism into complete atheism. The human soul or mind was at first said to be "epiphenomenal," which meant that it was real but only as an effect, not as a cause; later thinkers, believing nature should have no idle wheels, denied that it was a distinct entity at all, declaring it to be simply one of the brain's emergent properties. In those ways, the "animistic" viewpoint, which attributes causality to personal forces, was completely rejected. All "downward causation" from personal to impersonal processes was eliminated; the reductionistic program of explaining everything in terms of elementary impersonal processes was fully accepted. The world as a whole was thus disenchanted. This disenchanted view means that experience plays no real role not only in "the natural world" but in the world as a whole. Hence, no role exists in the universe for purposes, values, ideals, possibilities, and qualities, and there is no freedom, creativity, temporality, or divinity. There are no norms, not even truth, and everything is ultimately meaningless.

The ironic conclusion is that modern science, in disenchanting nature, began a trajectory that ended by disenchanting science itself. If all human life is meaningless, then science, as one of its activities, must share in this meaninglessness. For some time, many held that science at least gives us the truth, even if a bleak one. Much recent thought, however, has concluded that science does not even give us that. The disenchantment is complete.

The main point to emphasize is that modern thinkers have assumed that this disenchantment of the world is *required by science itself*. A few examples: just as Darwin felt that any "caprice" in the world would make science impossible, so that both divine and free human activity had to be eliminated from our worldview,[2] so Michael Ghiselin, a contemporary Darwinian, says that to deny the ideal of predictive determinism by affirming teleological causation "is to opt out of science altogether."[3] Jacques Monod says:

> The cornerstone of the scientific method is the postulate that nature is objective. In other words, the *systematic* denial that 'true' knowledge can be got at by interpreting phenomena in terms of final causes – that is to say, of 'purpose' . . . [T]he postulate of objectivity is consubstantial with science. . . . There is no way to be rid of it, even tentatively or in a limited area, without departing from the domain of science itself.[4]

While recognizing that the objectivist view of the world outrages our values and forces us to live in an alien world, Monod nevertheless insists that we must adopt it, because all "animist" views, which make us feel at home in nature by attributing purpose to it, are "fundamentally *hostile* to science."[5]

"So-called purposive behavior," said behaviorist psychologist Clark Hull, is to be regarded as a secondary, epiphenomenal reality, derivative from "more elementary objective primary principles."[6] Likewise, B.F. Skinner argues that psychology must follow physics and biology in rejecting "personified causes," and that to be "natural" is to be completely determined by one's environment. From the viewpoint of "the science of behavior," says Skinner, the notion of the "autonomous," which "initiates, originates and creates," is the notion of the "miraculous." He adds: "A scientific analysis of behavior dispossesses autonomous man and turns the control he has been said to exert over to the environment."[7] Whereas this statement suggests that determinism is a *result* of the application of the scientific approach, Skinner had earlier revealed that it is a *presupposition*: "We cannot

David Ray Griffin

apply the methods of science to a subject matter which is assumed to move about capriciously. ... The hypothesis that man is not free is essential to the application of scientific method to the study of human behavior."[8]

While Hull and Skinner come from a previous generation, and advocated a behaviorist psychology which is now widely rejected, William Uttal is a contemporary psychobiologist. He says that reductionism, according to which all the activities of the mind are reducible to the most elementary levels of organization of matter, is "the foundation upon which the entire science of psychobiology is built." To introduce any definition of consciousness that goes beyond the operations used in surgery and the behavioral laboratory would mean "a total collapse into prescientific modes of thought."[9]

The idea that science requires a reductionistic account, and rules out all downward causation from personal causes and all action at a distance, is illustrated by the treatment of apparent parapsychological phenomena by physicist John Taylor. After studying several people who he had come to believe had the psychokinetic power to bend metal without touching it, he published a book entitled *Superminds*, complete with supporting photographs.[10] However, after deciding later that no explanation was to be found for psychokinetic effects within the scientific worldview, he wrote a second book called *Science and the Supernatural* in which he declared that no such events can occur. Although he still believed that there was good evidence for psychokinetic events, and admitted that he could not explain how the particular events he had witnessed could have been faked, he concluded that all such reports must be due to hallucination, trickery, credulity, the fear of death, and the like. "Such an explanation is the only one which seems to fit in with a scientific view of the world."[11] The reasoning behind this conclusion was as follows: First, scientific explanation can only be in materialistic terms; if anything, such as the human mind, could not be explained in quantitative, materialistic terms, then the scientist would have to choose between silence and irrationality. Second, according to "the scientific viewpoint," all explanation must be in terms of the four forces of physics. Third, none of these forces can explain psychokinesis. Therefore, he says, we must believe that no genuine psychokinesis occurs. Taylor concludes by castigating himself and other scientists for having seriously investigated "phenomena which their scientific education should indicate are impossible."[12]

This idea that the very nature of science rules out the scientific study of anything not understandable in materialistic terms has in our century probably been more prevalent in fields other than physics. James Alcock, a social psychologist, says that a "spiritual science," which parapsychology is sometimes said to be, is a contradiction in terms. "How can a science of the spirit exist, given that science is by its very nature materialistic?"[13]

Besides ruling out purpose, freedom, personal causation, and any nonmaterialistic interactions from the scientific account of nature, the dominant viewpoint has even eliminated temporality. Ilya Prigogine regards the fact that modern science has been nontemporal as the root of the cleavage between the "two cultures" (C. P. Snow) of science and the humanities.[14] This elimination of temporality has been supported by many twentieth-century physicists, including Albert Einstein, who said: "For us believing physicists, the distinction between past, present and future is only an illusion, even if a stubborn one."[15] A contemporary physicist, P. C. W. Davies, spells out the implied dualism between objective nature and subjectivity:

> The notion that time flows in a one-way fashion is a property of our consciousness. It is a subjective phenomenon and is a property that simply cannot be demonstrated in the natural world. This is an incontrovertible lesson from modern science. ... A flowing time belongs to our mind, not to nature.[16]

A well-read physician, citing several physicists who endorse this view, says that we must assimilate it, in spite of the fact that it is an affront to common sense, because "we cannot ignore what modern physical science has revealed to us about the nature of time."[17]

As stated earlier, the final disenchantment of modern science is its conclusion that its own discoveries prove the meaninglessness of the whole universe, which must include the scientists and their science. Near the end of his popular book, *The First Three Minutes*, physicist Steven Weinberg says, "The more the universe seems comprehensible, the more it also seems pointless."[18]

I momentarily interrupt the recital of evidence to respond to a counter-argument that is probably growing in the mind of many readers. This is the argument that it is not the job of the scientist *qua* scientist to deal with the true nature of time and matter in themselves and with the question whether the universe is meaningful. These are the tasks, it could be argued, for metaphysicians and theologians, or for poets, whom Shelley called the "unacknowledged legislators of mankind." Hence, according to this argument, no need exists for a postmodern science; it is only necessary to point out the inherent limitations of science so that people will look elsewhere for answers to these larger questions. The problem with this solution is that the ideal of an "inherently limited science" does not work in practice. Science is inherently not only realistic, trying to describe the way things really are, but also imperialistic, bent on providing the only genuine description. The word *science*, after all, means *knowledge*; what is not vouchsafed by "science" is not considered knowledge in our culture. The cultural effect of modern science has been to make scientists the only "acknowledged legislators" of humankind, because its worldview has ruled out the possibility that metaphysics, theology, or poetry would have anything to add. Unless science itself is seen as giving a different answer, the disenchantment of the world will continue. With this brief apologia, I return to the topic.

Not only scientists themselves but also many philosophers have supported the view that science necessarily disenchants the world, proving that experience and those qualities that presuppose it are inoperative. D. M. Armstrong says that we have "general scientific grounds for thinking that man is nothing but a physical mechanism," that "mental states are, in fact, nothing but physical states of the central nervous system," so that we should be able to "give a complete account of man in purely physico-chemical terms."[19] In his 1956 preface to *The Modern Temper*, originally published in 1929, Joseph Wood Krutch summarized the book's thesis (with which he had later come to disagree):

> The universe revealed by science, especially the sciences of biology and psychology, is one in which the human spirit cannot find a comfortable home. That spirit breathes freely only in a universe where what philosophers call Value Judgements are of supreme importance. It needs to believe, for instance, that right and wrong are real, that Love is more than a biological function, that the human mind is capable of reason rather than merely of rationalization, and that it has the power to will and to choose instead of being compelled merely to react in the fashion predetermined by its conditioning. *Since science has proved that none of these beliefs*

is more than a delusion, mankind will be compelled either to surrender what we call its humanity by adjusting to the real world or to live some kind of tragic existence in a universe alien to the deepest needs of its nature.[20]

Better known is the following purple passage from "A Free Man's Worship," in which Bertrand Russell summarizes "the world which Science presents for our belief":

> That Man is the product of causes which had no prevision of the end they were achieving; that his origin, his growth, his hopes and fears, his loves and beliefs, are but the outcome of accidental collocations of atoms; ... that all the labours of the ages, all the devotion, all the inspiration, all the noonday brightness of human genius, are destined to extinction in the vast death of the solar system ... – all these things, if not quite beyond dispute, are yet so nearly certain, that no philosophy which rejects them can hope to stand.[21]

The modern consensus then, as reflected in the preceding quotations, has been that science and disenchantment go hand in hand. On the one hand, it is assumed, science can only be applied to that which has already been disenchanted, which means deanimated.[22] To deanimate is to remove all anima or soul, in Plato's sense of a self-moving thing which determines itself, at least partly, in terms of its desire to realize particular values. On the other hand, it is assumed that the application of the scientific method to anything confirms the truth of the disenchanted view of it, that it can be adequately understood in purely impersonal terms, as embodying no creativity, no self-determination in terms of values or norms, and nothing that could be considered divine.

The only way to prevent the disenchantment of the universe as a whole, on this view, is to draw a line, usually between the human being as purposive agent and the rest of nature, above which the scientific method is said to be inapplicable. But any such essential dualism is undermined by several things: the fact that human behavior, including human experience, is subject to a great extent to causal analysis; the idea that we, like all other species, are products of the evolutionary process; the difficulty of understanding how a human mind, which operates in terms of reasons, purposes, or final causes, could interact with bodily parts operating strictly in terms of mechanistic causes; and the general pressure toward a unified approach to knowledge. Accordingly, the attempt to prevent total disenchantment by means of an essential dualism – between mind and matter, understanding and explanation, hermeneutics and science[23] – is difficult to maintain intellectually. Whereas all people live in terms of the conviction that they are more than behaviorism, sociobiology, and psychobiology allow, and may feel that the totally disenchanted approach to human beings is inappropriate, it has been extremely difficult to state these convictions and feelings in an intellectually defensible way. Besides thereby seeming to leave no alternative beyond antihumanitarianism or a humanitarianism based on an arbitrary choice, modern science also seems to alienate us from our bodies and from nature in general. Because it has disenchanted the world, many people have become disenchanted with science.

Others, however, have distinguished between *modern science*, which disenchants, and *science as such*, which may be open to reenchantment.

Postmodern Organicism and the Unity of Science

The postmodern organicism represented in this series has been inspired primarily by the scientist-turned-philosopher Alfred North Whitehead.... This postmodern organicism can be considered a synthesis of the Aristotelian, Galilean (both forms), and Hermetic paradigms. Aristotelian organicism had a unified science by attributing purposive or final causation to everything, most notoriously saying that a falling stone seeks a state of rest. The Galilean paradigm, in its first form, distinguished absolutely between two types of primary beings: (1) those that exercised purposive or final causation; and (2) those that did not and could consequently be understood completely in terms of receiving and transmitting efficient causation. At first, limiting the beings in the first category to human minds was customary, but that limitation is neither necessary to the dualistic paradigm nor very credible. Many Galilean dualists have accordingly, as mentioned in the previous section, extended final causation further down the animal kingdom: those who are termed *vitalists* see it as arising with the first form of life. Wherever the line was drawn, the drawing of a line between two ontologically different types of primary beings

split science into two parts. One science spoke only of efficient causes; the other science (psychology) spoke in terms of final causes or purposes. The second form of the Galilean paradigm tried to restore unity to science by abolishing an internalistic psychology of final causes. Psychology, under the name of *behaviorism*, was transformed into an attempt to describe and explain human and other animal behavior solely in terms of efficient causes and other externalistic terms. *Eliminative materialism*, mentioned earlier, is the extreme version of this way to achieve unity.

Postmodern organicism holds that all primary individuals are organisms who exercise at least some iota of purposive causation. But it does not hold that all visible objects, such as stones and planets, are primary individuals or even analogous to primary individuals. Rather, it distinguishes between two ways in which primary organisms can be organized: (1) as a compound individual,[24] in which an all-inclusive subject emerges; and (2) as a nonindividuated object, in which no unifying subjectivity is found. Animals belong to the first class; stones to the second. In other words, there is no ontological dualism, but there is an organizational duality which takes account of the important and obvious distinction that the dualists rightly refused to relinquish. Hence, there are (1) things whose behavior can only be understood in terms of both efficient causes and their own purposive response to these causes, and (2) things whose behavior can be understood, for most purposes, without any reference to purposive or final causation. In this sense, there is a duality within science.

However, the qualification *for most purposes* is important. Whereas the Galilean paradigm maintained that a nonteleological explanation of material things could be adequate for all purposes, including a complete understanding, at least in principle, the postmodern paradigm contends that any explanation devoid of purposive causation will necessarily abstract from concrete facts. *Fully* to understand even the interaction between two billiard balls requires reference to purposive reactions – not indeed of the balls as aggregates, but of their constituents. Because the study of nonindividual objects as well as that of primary individuals and compound individuals requires, at least ultimately, reference to final as well as efficient causes, there is a unity of science.

The relation between final and efficient causation in Whiteheadian postmodern organicism is different from their relation in any previous form of thought, even from other forms of panexperientialism (often called panpsychism), although it was anticipated in Buddhist thought. Other forms of thought that have attributed experience to all individuals, such as that of Gottfried Leibniz and Teilhard de Chardin, have assumed the ultimate constituents of the world to be enduring individuals. An individual was physical from without to others, but was conscious or mental from within, for itself. From without, it interacted with other enduring individuals in terms of efficient causation; from within, it lived in terms of purposes or final causation. Given this picture, relating efficient and final causation to each other was difficult. The common view has been that they do not relate, but simply run along parallel to each other. However, as discussed above in relation to materialistic identism, this parallelism raises serious problems. If experience or mentality makes no difference to an individual's interactions with its environment, how can we explain why the higher forms of experience have evolved? And without appeal to a supernatural coordinator, how can we explain the parallelism between inner and outer; e.g. why should my brain's signal to my hand to lift a glass follow right after my mental decision to have a drink, if my decision in no way *causes* the appropriate neurons in the brain to fire?

However, if the ultimate individuals of the world are momentary events, rather than enduring individuals, a positive relation can exist between efficient and final causation. Efficient causation still applies to the exterior of an individual and final causation to the interior. But because an enduring individual, such as a proton, neuron, or human psyche, is a temporal *society* of momentary events, exterior and interior oscillate and feed into each other rather than running parallel. Each momentary event in an enduring individual originates through the inrush of efficient causation from the past world, i.e. from previous events, including the previous events that were members of the same enduring individual. The momentary subject then makes a self-determining response to these causal influences; this is the moment of final causation, as the event aims at achieving a synthesis for itself and for influencing the future. This final causation is in no way unrelated to efficient causation; it is a purposive response to the efficient causes on the event. When this moment of subjective final causation is over, the event becomes

an object which exerts efficient causation on future events. Exactly what efficient causation it exerts is a function both of the efficient causes upon it *and* of its own final causation. Hence, the efficient causes of the world do not run along as if there were no mentality with its final causation. An event does not necessarily simply transmit to others what it received; it may do this, but it also may deflect and transform the energy it receives to some degree or another, before passing it on. (*We do this to the greatest degree when we return good for evil.*)

To say that the categories of both final and efficient causation must be employed for the study of all actual beings does *not* imply that the two categories will be *equally* relevant for all beings. Indeed, as already indicated, an appeal to final causation is irrelevant for almost all purposes when studying nonindividuated objects, such as rocks, stars, and computers.[25] Even with regard to individuals, the importance of final or purposive causation will vary enormously. In primary individuals, such as photons and electrons (or quarks, if such there be), final causation is minimal. For the most part, the behavior of these individuals is understandable in terms of efficient causes alone. They mainly just conform to what they have received and pass it on to the future in a predictable way. But not completely: behind the epistemic "indeterminacy" of quantum physics lies a germ of ontic self-determinacy. The importance of self-determination or final causation increases in compound individuals, especially in those normally called *living*. It becomes increasingly important as the study focuses upon more complex, highly evolved animals; all the evidence suggests that final causation is the most important, on our planet, in determining the experience and behavior of human beings. The importance of efficient causes, i.e. of influence from the past, does not diminish as one moves toward the higher individuals; indeed, in a sense higher beings are influenced by *more* past events than are lower ones. But the totality of efficient causes from the past becomes less and less explanatory of experience and behavior, and the individual's own present self-determination in terms of desired ends becomes more explanatory.

From this perspective we can understand why a mechanistic, reductionistic approach has been so spectacularly successful in certain areas and so unsuccessful in others. The modern Galilean paradigm was based on the study of nonindividuated objects, such as stellar masses and steel balls, which exercise *no final causation*[i] either in determining their own behavior or that of their elementary parts. Absolute predictability and reduction is possible in principle. This paradigm was next applied to very low-grade individuals, in which the final causation is *negligible* for most purposes except to the most refined observation. With this refinement, the absolute predictability of behavior broke down with the most elementary individuals; the ideal of predictability could be salvaged only by making it statistical and applying it to large numbers of individuals. With low-grade forms of life, and in particular with their inherited characteristics and certain abstract features of their behavior, Galilean science has still been very successful, but not completely. Certain features of even low-grade life seemed intractable to this approach, just those features which led to the rise of vitalism. This paradigm has been even less successful with rats than with bacteria. At this level, various problems are virtually ignored, because little chance of success is apparent, and scientists are interested in applying their method where the chances for success are most promising. Finally, the method has been less successful yet with humans than with rats. The record of success at this level is so miserable that many scientists and philosophers of science refuse to think of the so-called social or human sciences, such as psychology, sociology, economics, and political science, as sciences at all. This pattern of success and failure of the Galilean paradigm fits exactly what the postmodern paradigm predicts. As one leaves nonindividuated objects for individuals, and as one deals with increasingly higher individuals, final causation becomes increasingly important, and regularity and hence predictability become increasingly less possible. Hence, nothing but confusion and unrealistic expectations can result from continuing to regard physics as the paradigmatic science.[26]

This framework can explain why it has been even less possible to discover regularities and attain repeatability in parapsychology than in certain aspects of ordinary psychology. Although every event (by hypothesis) exerts influence directly upon remote as well as spatially and temporally contiguous events, its influence on contiguous events is much more powerful. Hence, the effects of the kind of influence that is exerted upon remote events indirectly *via* a chain of contiguous events will be much more regular and hence predictable than the effects of the kind of influence that is exerted on remote events directly, without the intervening chain. Accordingly, because sensory perception arises from a chain of contiguous events (photons and neuron firings in vision) connecting the remote object with the psyche, the sensory perception of external objects is much more regular and reliable, hence predictable, than any extrasensory perception of them. Likewise, because effects produced in the external world by the psyche by means of the body are mediated by a chain of contiguous causes, whose reliability, like that of the sensory system, has been perfected over billions of years of evolution, such effects are much more reliable than any psychokinetic effects produced by the direct influence of the psyche upon outer objects without the body's mediation. Additionally, although *unconscious* extrasensory perception and *subtle* and *diffused* psychokinetic action occur continually (by hypothesis), the power to produce *conscious* extrasensory perception and *conspicuous* psychokinetic effects *on specific objects* is – at least for the majority of human beings most of the time – evidently lodged in an unconscious level of experience, which by definition is not under conscious control. Given these assumptions, the fact that parapsychology has attained little repeatability with conspicuous psychokinetic effects and conscious extrasensory perception is what should be expected.[27] In this way, the element of truth in the Hermetic paradigm is coordinated with the elements of truth from the Aristotelian and Galilean paradigms.

What then is science – what constitutes its unity? The anarchistic or relativistic view that "anything goes," that there is no such thing as a scientific method, is surely too strong. But it serves a useful function, as indeed it was intended,[28] to shake us free from parochial limitations on what counts as science. A description of science for a postmodern world must be much looser than the modern descriptions (which were really *prescriptions*).

Any activity properly called *science* and any conclusions properly called *scientific* must, first, be based on an overriding concern to discover truth.[29] Other concerns will of course play a role, but the concern for truth must be overriding, or the activity and its results would be better called by

---

[i] Aristotle's notion of the "final cause" of a being is its end, purpose, or goal (which need not be conscious or intentional). Modern physics and modern natural philosophy denied the existence of final causation in nature, breaking with Scholastic and Aristotelian science.

another name, such as *ideology*, or *propaganda*, or *politics*.[30] Second, science involves demonstration. More particularly, it involves testing hypotheses through data or experiences that are in some sense repeatable and hence open to confirmation or refutation by peers. In sum, science involves the attempt to establish truth through demonstrations open to experiential replication. What is left out of this account of science are limitations (1) to any particular domain, (2) any particular type of repeatability and demonstration, or (3) any particular contingent beliefs.

(1) Science is not restricted to the domain of things assumed to be wholly physical, operating in terms of efficient causes alone, or even to the physical aspects of things, understood as the aspects knowable to sensory perception or instruments designed to magnify the senses.[31] As the impossibility of behaviorism in human and even animal psychology has shown, science must refer to experience and purposes to comprehend (and even to predict) animal behavior. Although we cannot *see* the purposes motivating our fellow humans or other animals, assuming that such purposes play a causal role is not unscientific, if this hypothesis can be publicly demonstrated to account for the observable behavior better than the opposite hypothesis. And, once it is explicitly recognized that science *can* deal with subjectivity, there is no reason in principle for it to limit itself to the objective or physical side of other things, if there is good reason to suspect that an experiencing side exercising final causation exists. At the very least, even if we cannot imagine very concretely what the experience of a bacterium or a DNA molecule would be like, we need not try to account for its observable behavior on the metaphysical assumption that it has no experience and hence no purposes.

Just as the need for experiential replication by peers does not limit science to the physical or objective side of actual things, it does not even limit it to the realm of actuality. Mathematics deals with relationships among ideal entities, and is able to achieve great consensus; geometry was for Descartes of course the paradigmatic science. Therefore, the fact that logic, aesthetics, and ethics deal with ideal entities does not, in itself, exclude them from the realm of science.

Furthermore, the domain of scientific study should not be thought to be limited to regularities, or law-like behavior. There is no reason why the discussion of the origin of laws should not belong to science. If the laws of nature are reconceived as

habits, the question of how the habits originated should not be declared off-limits.[32] In fact, we should follow Bohm in replacing the language of "laws" with the more inclusive notion of "orders," for the reasons Evelyn Fox Keller has suggested: the notion of "laws of nature" retains the connotation of theological imposition, which is no longer appropriate but continues to sanction unidirectional, hierarchical explanations; it makes the simplicity of classical physics the ideal, so that the study of more complex orders is regarded as "softer" and less fully scientific; and it implies that nature is dead and "obedient" rather than generative and resourceful.[33]

(2) While science requires repeatable experiential demonstration, it does not require one particular type of demonstration, such as the laboratory experiment. As Patrick Grim says:

> Field studies, expeditions, and the appearances of comets have played a major role in the history of science. Contemporary reliance on mathematics reflects a willingness to accept a priori deductive as well as inductive demonstration. And there are times when the course of science quite properly shifts on the basis of what appear to be almost purely philosophical arguments.[34]

In regard to Grim's last example, I have suggested above that the philosophical difficulties with both dualism and materialistic identism provide a good reason for the scientific community to reconsider the metaphysical-scientific hypothesis that the ultimate constituents of nature are entirely devoid of experience and purpose. More generally, the bias toward the laboratory experiment in the philosophy of science has philosophically reflected the materialistic, nonecological assumption that things are essentially independent of their environments, so that the scientist abstracts from nothing essential in (say) removing cells from the human body or animals from a jungle to study them in a laboratory; it reflects the reductionistic assumption that all complex things are really no more self-determining than the elementary parts in isolation, so that they should be subject to the same kind of strong laboratory repeatability;[35] it reflects the assumption that the main purpose of science is to predict and control repeatable phenomena; and it reflects the assumption that the domain of science is limited to the actual, especially the physical. Recognizing the wide domain of science means recognizing the necessity and hence appropriateness of diverse types of demonstrations, and the artificiality of holding up one type as the ideal.

(3) Besides not being limited to one domain or one type of demonstration, the scientific pursuit of truth is not tied to any set of contingent beliefs, meaning beliefs that are not inevitably presupposed by human practice, including thought, itself. Science is, therefore, not limited to any particular type of explanation.[36] For example, science is not tied to the belief that the elementary units of nature are devoid of sentience, intrinsic value, and internal relations, that time does not exist for these units, that the laws of nature for these units are eternal, that all natural phenomena result from the (currently four) forces rooted in these elementary units, that accordingly all causation is upward and that freedom and purposive or teleological causation are illusory,[37] that ideal entities other than mathematical forms play no role in nature, that there is no influence at a distance,[38] that the universe as a whole is not an organism which influences its parts, or that the universe and its evolution have no inherent meaning.

However, the fact that science as such is not permanently wedded to these contingent beliefs that reigned during the modern period does not mean that there are *no* beliefs that science as such must presuppose. If beliefs exist that are presupposed by human practice, including human thought, as such, then scientific practice and thought must presuppose them. Any theories that verbally deny them should therefore be eschewed on this ground alone. Although any such beliefs would transcend perspectivalism, because they by hypothesis would be common to all people, regardless of their worldview, the questions of whether there are any such beliefs, and if so what they are, are matters not for pontification from some supposedly neutral point of view, because no human point of view is neutral, but for proposals to be subjected to ongoing public discussion among those with diverse worldviews.[39]

To illustrate the types of beliefs intended and to show that they are not limited to innocuous, noncontroversial issues, I propose five principles as candidates. The first three principles relate to the crucial issue of causality. First, every event is causally influenced by other events. This principle rules out, for example, the idea that the universe arose out of absolute nothingness or out of pure possibility.[40] Second, neither human experience nor anything analogous to it is wholly determined by external events; rather, every genuine individual is partially self-determining. Incidentally, these first two principles, taken together, provide the basis for a scientific understanding of the activity of scientists themselves in terms of a combination of external and internal causes, which is increasingly seen to be necessary.[41]

Third, every event that exerts causal influence upon another event precedes that event temporally. (Self-determination or self-causation does not fall under this principle, because in it the same event is both cause and effect.) This principle rules out the notion of particles "going backwards in time," the notion of "backward causation," and any notion of "precognition" interpreted to mean that an event affected the knower before it happened or to mean that temporal relations are ultimately unreal.[42]

The final two principles proffered deal with science's concern for truth. These are the traditional principles of correspondence and noncontradiction, which are recovered in a postmodern context.

The idea that truth is a correspondence between statements and objective reality has been subject to a great deal of criticism. Much of this criticism is based upon confusion, inasmuch as the critics, often while verbally rejecting positivism, still presuppose the positivistic equation of the meaning of a statement with the means of its verification. The correspondence notion of truth properly refers only to the *meaning* of "truth," which is not even identical with the question of knowledge, let alone with the question of the justification of knowledge-claims. Much of the rejection of the relevance of the correspondence notion of truth has conflated truth with knowledge and then assumed that there could be no knowledge, in the sense of justified true belief, in the absence of adequate evidence to defend the knowledge-claim.[43]

However, much of the criticism of the notion of truth as correspondence is valid, especially in relation to naïvely realistic ideas of a one-to-one correspondence between statements and objective facts. For one thing, our ideas about physical objects, insofar as they are based primarily upon visual and tactile perception, surely involve enormous simplifications, constructions, and distortions of the realities existing independently of our perception. For another, language is inherently vague and, in any case, cannot as such "correspond" in the sense of being similar to nonlinguistic entities. Language aside, the way in which an idea can correspond to a physical object is not self-evident, because an idea can only be similar to another idea. Even many conceptions of truth as the correspondence between one's ideas and the ideas in another mind are held in falsely naïve ways, insofar as it is assumed that achieving truth, in the sense of absolute correspondence, is possible. Many critics go on from these valid starting points to argue that the meaning of a statement is exhausted by its relation to other statements, so that language constitutes a closed system, or in some other way argue that our statements can in no meaningful sense correspond to any nonlinguistic entities. Science, in this extreme view, is a linguistic system disconnected from any larger world.

Postmodern organicism rejects this view of language. While language as such does not correspond to anything other than language, it expresses and evokes modes of apprehending nonlinguistic reality that can more or less accurately correspond to features of that reality.[44] Hence, science can lead to ways of thinking about the world that can increasingly approximate to patterns and structures genuinely characteristic of nature.

The other traditional principle involved in science's concern for truth is the principle of noncontradiction. It says that if two statements contradict each other, both cannot be true. This principle has also been subject to much valid criticism. Certainly two statements that appear to contradict each other may not in reality when one or both are more deeply understood. This can be because language is vague and elusive, because various levels of meaning exist, and/or because seemingly contradictory assertions may apply to diverse features of the referent or to different stages of its development. There are yet other objections to simple-minded applications of the principle of noncontradiction. But after all necessary subtleties and qualifications have been added, the principle remains valid and is necessarily presupposed even in attempts to refute it. Accordingly, science must aim for coherence between all its propositions and between its propositions and all those that are inevitably presupposed in human practice and thought in general. (Obtaining such coherence is indeed the primary method of checking for correspondence.)

All of these principles are in harmony with postmodern organicism. Indeed, they are not epistemically neutral principles but ones that are, especially in regard to their exact formulation, suggested by postmodern organicism. However, the claim is made that they are, in fact, implicit in human practice, including human thought (although not, of course, in the content of all the theories produced by human thought). If this claim is sustained through widespread conversation, then this set of beliefs (along with any others that could prove their universality in the same way) should be considered to belong to science as such.[45]

Author's Notes

1 Mary Hesse points out that the rejection of action-at-a-distance in favor of action-by-contact explanations was based on the replacement of all organismic and psychological explanations by mechanical ones (*Forces and Fields: The Concept of Action at a Distance in the History of Physics* [Totowa, NJ: Littlefield, Adams & Co, 1965], 98, 291). Richard Westfall makes clear how central was the change:

the mechanical philosophy also banished . . . attractions of any kind. No scorn was too great to heap upon such a notion. From one end of the century to another, the idea of attractions, the action of one body upon another with which it is not in contact, was anathema. . . . An attraction was an occult virtue, and 'occult virtue' was the mechanical philosophy's ultimate term of opprobrium.

Westfall reports that Christiaan Huygens wrote that he did not care whether Newton was a Cartesian "as long as he doesn't serve us up conjectures such as attractions" ("The Influence of Alchemy on Newton," Marsha P. Hanen, Margaret J. Osler, and Robert G. Weyant (eds), *Science, Pseudo-Science and Society* [Waterloo, Ontario: Wilfrid Laurier University Press, 1980], 145–70, esp. 147, 150). Brian Easlea has provided convincing evidence that the desire to rule out the possibility of attraction at a distance was, in fact, the main motivation behind the mechanical philosophy and its denial of all hidden qualities within matter; see his *Witch Hunting, Magic and the New Philosophy: An Introduction to Debates of the Scientific Revolution 1450–1750* (Atlantic Highlands, NJ: Humanities Press, 1980), esp. 93–5, 108–15, 121, 132, 135.

2 Neal C. Gillespie, *Charles Darwin and the Problem of Creation* (Chicago: University of Chicago Press, 1979), 55–6, 120, 139–40.

3 Michael Ghiselin, *The Economy of Nature and the Evolution of Sex* (Berkeley: University of California Press, 1974), x, 13.

4 Jacques Monod, *Chance and Necessity: An Essay on the Natural Philosophy of Modern Biology* (New York: Vintage Books, 1972), 21.

5 Ibid., 172–3, 171.

6 Clark Hull, *Principles of Behavior: An Introduction to Behavior Theory* (New York: Appleton-Century, 1943), 29.

7 B. F. Skinner, *Beyond Freedom and Dignity* (New York: Vintage Books, 1972), 12, 191, 196.

8 B. F. Skinner, *Science and Human Behavior* (New York: Free Press, 1965), 6, 447.

9 William R. Uttal, *The Psychobiology of Mind* (Hillsdale, NJ: L. Erlbaum Associates, 1978), 9, 10, 27, 52–3.

10 John G. Taylor, *Superminds* (London: Macmillan, 1975).

11 John G. Taylor, *Science and the Supernatural* (London: Panther Books, 1981), 6, 69, 108, 164.

12 Ibid., 25–30, 83, 165–9. The issue here is not whether Taylor's original evidence was solid (which many parapsychologists doubt), but only that the modern worldview by itself led him to deny his own data.

13 James A. Alcock, "Parapsychology as a 'Spiritual' Science," Paul Kurtz (ed.), *A Skeptic's Handbook of Parapsychology* (Buffalo, NY: Prometheus Books, 1985), 537–65, esp. 562. Interestingly enough, Alcock makes his claim even though he realizes that a nonmaterialistic science is advocated by John Eccles, a Nobel prizewinner, and Karl Popper, the most influential philosopher of science of the twentieth century (558). Also, he repeats the conventional idea that "the path of science . . . [was] laid down upon the foundation of materialism," even though he had reviewed recent writings of Eugene Klaaren, Martin Rudwick, and others who show that this was not true, especially for Isaac Newton (562, 555).

14 Ilya Prigogine and Isabelle Stengers, *Order Out of Chaos: Man's New Dialogue with Nature* (New York: Bantam Books, 1984), xxvii.

15 Einstein's statement, which occurred in a letter, is cited in Banesh Hoffman (with Helen Dukas), *Albert Einstein: Creator and Rebel* (New York: Viking Press, 1972), 258.

16 P. C. W. Davies, *The Physics of Time Asymmetry* (Berkeley: University of California Press, 1976), 151.

17 Larry Dossey, *Space, Time and Medicine* (Boulder, Co.: Shambhala, 1982), 152, 153. Many people, rightly assuming that linear time has been a central feature of modernity, especially in the notions of *progress* and *evolution*, have wrongly assumed that the assertion of the ultimate unreality of time, vouchsafed by physics, would be a postmodern idea, liberating us from one of the shackles of modernity. The truth is that Western (as well as most Eastern) thought has generally held temporality to be unreal for the ultimate form of being, be it Plato's ideas (in one side of his thought), Aristotle's unmoved mover, the God of classical theists such as Augustine, Maimonides, and Thomas Aquinas, or the ultimate particles of modern physics. Although temporality has been central for Western thought and experience, especially in the modern period, it has seldom, as Stephen Toulmin and June Goodfield have shown (*The Discovery of Time* [New York: Harper & Row, 1965]), been considered to be fundamental, in the sense of real for the most real type of existent. Twentieth-century physics, in speaking of the ultimate unreality of time (largely through the influence of the interpretation given to relativity theory by Einstein with his Spinozistic leanings), has thereby not introduced a new idea but simply revitalized an old one. For further discussion, see the introduction to David Ray Griffin (ed.), *Physics and the Ultimate Significance of Time: Bohm, Prigogine, and Process Philosophy* (Albany: State University of New York Press, 1986).

18 Steven Weinberg, *The First Three Minutes: A Modern View of the Origin of the Universe* (New York: Basic Books, 1977), 154.

19 D. M. Armstrong, "The Nature of Mind," C. V. Borst (ed.), *The Mind–Brain Identity Theory* (London: Macmillan, 1979), 75, 67.

20 Joseph Wood Krutch, *The Modern Temper: A Study and a Confession* (New York: Harcourt, Brace & World [A Harvest Book], 1956), xi; emphasis added. By 1956, Krutch had decided that, of the two options noted in that final sentence, "Social Engineering rather than Existentialist resignation [has become] the dominant religion of today" (xiii). Krutch himself had in the meantime come to reject the view, which he still regarded as "the most prevalent educated opinion," that "there is no escaping the scientific demonstration that religion, morality, and the human being's power to make free choices are merely figments of the imagination" (xii). He no longer believed that "the mechanistic, materialistic, and deterministic conclusions of science do have to be accepted as fact and hence as the premises upon which any philosophy of life or any estimate of man and his future must be based" (xiii). His reasons for this change of mind were set forth in *The Measure of Man: On Freedom, Human Values, Survival and the Modern Temper* (Indianapolis, Ind.: Bobbs-Merrill, 1953), which is in harmony with the present volume, while not going as far and of course not having the advantage of the historical and scientific evidence that has appeared in the intervening decades.

21 Robert E. Egner and Lester E. Dennon (eds), *The Basic Writings of Bertrand Russell 1903–1959* (New York: Simon & Schuster, 1961), 67.

22 Krutch says of modern individuals: "It is easy for . . . all of us to believe that a man may be 'the product of' any one of a number of external 'forces' . . . . The one thing which we find it hard to believe is that what he might be 'the product of' is himself." And Krutch gives one of the reasons why: "The idea that [the realm of the subjective] might be autonomous and creative suggests the possibility that the methods which were working everywhere else

might not work there. Concern with it was unscientific and therefore unintelligent" (*The Measure of Man*, 254, 117).

23 For a discussion and critique of Hans-Georg Gadamer's methodological dualism between hermeneutics and science, see Joel C. Weinsheimer, *Gadamer's Hermeneutics: A Reading of Truth and Method* (New Haven, Conn.: Yale University Press, 1985), 1–41; on Jürgen Habermas's views, see Richard J. Bernstein (ed.), *Habermas and Modernity* (Cambridge, Mass.: MIT Press, 1985), especially the essays by Martin Jay, Thomas McCarthy, and Albrecht Wellmer.

24 See Charles Hartshorne, "The Compound Individual," Otis H. Lee (ed.), *Philosophical Essays for Alfred North Whitehead* (New York: Longmans Green, 1936), 193–220.

25 Of course, to understand a computer one must take into account final causation in the sense of the purpose for which it was made. But throughout this discussion the subject is internal, immanent final causation, not external, imposed final causation.

26 Sandra Harding supports this change, pointing out that physics, among other restrictions, "looks at either simple systems or simple aspects of complex systems," so that it need not deal with the difficult question of intentional causality (*The Science Question in Feminism* [Ithaca, NY: Cornell University Press, 1986], 44, 46).

27 For a development of the ideas in these two sentences, see the writings of psychiatrist Jule Eisenbud, whom philosopher Stephen Braude has called "parapsychology's premier living theoretician." Many of Eisenbud's essays have been collected in *Parapsychology and the Unconscious* (Berkeley, Calif.: North Atlantic Books, 1983), the "Preface" of which contains the accolade by Braude (7). For the various ideas, see 21, 22, 40, 72, 125, 167, 173, 183. On the resultant unlikelihood of obtaining repetable experiments in the ordinary sense, see 156–61. These points are also supported in Braude's own *The Limits of Influence: Psychokinesis and the Philosophy of Science* (London: Routledge & Kegan Paul, 1986), esp. 7–10, 23, 70, 278.

28 [Contemporary philosopher of science Paul Feyerabend is famously regarded as an "anarchist" who denies that science is true. The author argues (in an earlier note) that Feyerabend merely offers his critique as a therapeutic attempt to subvert the notion that modern science is the only method yielding truth.]

29 My discussion in this and the following paragraph is dependent upon Patrick Grim, *Philosophy of Science and the Occult* (Albany: State University of New York, 1982), 314–15; Ken Wilber, *Quantum Questions: Mystical Writings of the World's Great Physicists* (Boston: Shambala, 1984), 13–14; and Nicholas Rescher, "The Unpredictability of Future Science," Robert S.

Cohen and Larry Lauden (eds), *Physics, Philosophy and Psychoanalysis: Essays in Honor of Adolf Grünbaum* (Dordrecht: D. Reidel, 1983), 153–68.

30 It is often said that power and knowledge (or truth) have been the twin aims of modern science (e.g. Evelyn Fox Keller, *Reflections on Gender and Science*, 71). Of these twin aims, traditional descriptions spoke mainly of the quest for truth, while recent appraisals, whether condemnatory or positivistic, have seen the drive for power as the central aim. My position is that, while much of modern science has sought those truths that would provide power over nature (and sometimes thereby over other humans), it is not the quest for power that makes modern science "science" but the quest for truth (in the way specified in the second criterion), regardless of how limited these truths are and of the ulterior purposes for which they are sought…

31 Nicholas Rescher, "The Unpredictability of Future Science," 165, says: "Domain limitations purport to put entire sectors of fact wholly outside the effective range of scientific explanation, maintaining that an entire range of phenomena in nature defies scientific rationalization." See also Ken Wilber, *Quantum Questions*, 14.

32 This is one topic on which I disagree with Rupert Sheldrake, who wishes to exclude the topic of the origin of laws from science, assigning it instead to theology or metaphysics; see the final chapter of his *A New Science of Life*.

33 Evelyn Fox Keller, *Reflections on Gender and Science* (New Haven, Conn.: Yale University Press, 1985), 131–6.

34 Patrick Grim, *Philosophy of Science and the Occult*, 315.

35 Jule Eisenbud (*Psi and Psychoanalysis* [New York: Grune & Stratton, 1970], 96) says that one particular kind of repeatability has given parts of physics such reliability that "few people (strangely) question its right to provide a model of 'reality'." But, as he says, this kind of repeatability is only one of many considerations in authentication, not relevant for many questions in geology, meteorology, astronomy, biology, and much of psychology. Both Kurtz and Alcock [see Paul Kurtz, *A Skeptic's Handbook of Parapsychology* (Buffalo, NY: Prometheus, 1985) and James Alcock's essay, "Parapsychology as a 'Spiritual' Science," in Kurtz, pp. 537–65.] have claimed that parapsychological experiments, to be acceptable, would have to exemplify "strong" repeatability, meaning that, in Alcock's words, "any competent researcher following the prescribed procedure can obtain the reported effect" (540). But if the kind of phenomenon with which parapsychology is concerned is held to be an inherently elusive, not consciously controllable one, as Eisenbud and Stephen Braude hold (see note 27 above), this requirement for strong replicability amounts to

a "Catch-22": parapsychologists could only prove that it exists by proving that it does not!

36 Nicholas Rescher ("The Unpredictability of Future Science," 163) says: "The contention that this or that explanatory resource is inherently unscientific should always be met with instant scorn. For the unscientific can only lie on the side of process and not that of product – on the side of *modes* of explanation and not its *mechanism*; of arguments rather than phenomena."

37 Rescher (ibid., 166) says that "there is no reason why, in human affairs any more than in quantum theory, the boundaries of science should be so drawn as to exclude the unpredictable." Long ago, William James said that "the spirit and principles of Science are mere affairs of method; there is nothing in them that need hinder Science from dealing successfully with a world in which personal forces are the starting points of new effects" ("Presidential Address," *Proceedings of the Society for Psychical Research*, 12 [1896–97], 2–10, esp. 10).

38 Rescher (ibid., 169) says:

Not only can we never claim with confidence that the science of tomorrow will not resolve the issues that the science of today sees as intractable, but one can never be sure that the science of tomorrow will not endorse what the science of today rejects. This is why it is infinitely risky to speak of this or that explanatory resource (action at a distance, stochastic processes, mesmerism, etc.) as inherently unscientific. Even if X lies outside the range of science as we nowadays construe it, it by no means follows that X lies outside science as such.

39 If there are such common beliefs, their recognition by members of diverse linguistic communities is, while difficult, not impossible. Even though a given worldview will predispose its adherents to recognize some such beliefs while ignoring, distorting, or even verbally denying other such beliefs that are noticed by adherents of other worldviews, it is possible, when the search for truth through public demonstration is sincere, to recognize such beliefs through conversation and self-observation.

40 In spite of my agreement, expressed in prior notes, with Nicholas Rescher's formal ideas, I cannot accept his substantive idea that actualities could have emerged out of a realm of mere possibility. I do not see how we can abandon the notion that agency requires actuality, and hence the "hoary dogma," as Rescher calls it, that *ex nihilo nihil fit*. I have reviewed Rescher's *The Riddle of Existence: An Essay in Idealistic Metaphysics* (Lanham, Md.: University of America Press, 1985) in *Canadian Philosophical Reviews*, December, 1986, 531–2.

41 Sandra Harding points out that the one-sided attempts to explain science either from a purely externalist or a purely internalist approach lead to paradox.

The externalist approach, which understands the development of science in terms of external causes alone, leads to a self-refuting relativism. "Why should changes in economic, technological, and political arrangements make the new ideas reflecting these arrangements better ideas? Why shouldn't we regard the externalist program itself as simply an epiphenomenon of nineteenth- and twentieth-century social relations destined to be replaced as history moves along?" (*The Science Question in Feminism*, 215). The internalist or intentionalist approach praises natural science for showing that all natural and social phenomena are to be explained in externalistic terms, then supports the truth of this idea by "defending an intentionalist approach to explaining the development of science alone" (212). What we need is an approach that recognizes the two-way causal influences between ideas and social relations, and which thereby allows us both to understand how "social arrangements shape human consciousness" and "to retain the internalist assumption that not all beliefs are equally good" (209, 231, 214). . . .

42 I have dealt with these issues in "Introduction: Time and the Fallacy of Misplaced Concreteness" in *Physics and the Ultimate Significance of Time*; there is a brief discussion of apparent precognition on 30–1. See also Jule Eisenbud, *Parapsychology and the Unconscious*, 45. Although Stephen Braude has not changed his earlier opinion that arguments against the very intelligibility of backward causation are unconvincing, perhaps because he has not developed a general theory of causation (*The Limits of Influence*, 261), he has concluded that the idea is very problematic, and that ostensible precognition can be explained without resort to this idea (261–77).

43 Frederick Suppe has pointed out that most discussions of the idea of knowledge as "justified true belief" have assumed that "knowing that X is true" entails "knowing that one knows that X is true," i.e. having adequate evidence to defend the claim to know that it is true (*The Structure of Scientific Theories* [Urbana: University of Illinois, 1977], 717–28). This unjustified requirement, which leads to a vicious infinite regress, lies behind Hume's skeptical attacks on the possibility of knowledge and most recent rejections, by Kuhn, Feyerabend, and others, of the relevance of the correspondence notion of truth to scientific beliefs (718, 719, 723). Suppe argues rightly for "a separation of the role of evidence in the rational evaluation and defense of knowledge claims from the role evidence plays in obtaining knowledge" (725). With that separation, we can maintain the traditional definitions of knowledge as justified true belief and of truth as correspondence of belief to reality. None of this entails, I would insist perhaps more strongly than Suppe, that the modern scientific worldview is true, or that any

of the current scientific theories gives us anything approaching the whole truth about their referents. Indeed, it is only if we hold to these traditional definitions of truth and knowledge that we have a rational standard in terms of which to criticize the dominant contemporary knowledge-claims.

44 The way in which panexperiential philosophy can make sense of a notion of correspondence is to be dealt with [in essays in volume 4 of this series].

45 These principles, especially the latter four, have all, in fact, been denied by modern science-related thought. However, their explicit denial has been accompanied by implicit affirmation, producing massive incoherence. The reason for their explicit denial is *not* that they conflict with the implications of any other equally universal principles but that they conflict with the implications of contingent beliefs of modernity, which have been discussed above.

48

"The Cognitive Program of Constructivism and a Reality that Remains Unknown"

Niklas Luhmann

German sociologist Niklas Luhmann (1927–98) pressed systems theory, which attends to the self-maintaining internal processes of organisms, machines and societies, to radical conclusions. Most famous for his methodological debate with Habermas, Luhmann's approach denies the possibility of critical ideals that transcend social organization. Absorbing insights from recent work in biology and cybernetics, he argues that social systems, like organisms, "construct" their environment through highly selective perception and cognition, and so are "autopoietic" or self-making. By taking *communications* as the events constituting social systems, he separates his sociology from psychology and anthropology (humans are *not* the constituents of societies). His analysis of modernity shows that contemporary society no longer requires, and cannot accept, forms of unity based in shared belief-systems or democratic agreement. The functional subsystems of society organize themselves by internal rules governing communications, and reproduce themselves independently. Centerless, functionally plural modern society is a "whole that is less than the sum of its parts." In the following essay Luhmann examines the epistemological consequences of his radically constructivist account of human knowing.

forced to proceed from the immediate object of their research to questions involving cognition. Quantum physics is perhaps the best-known example, but it is no exception. In linguistics the question is raised today of what problems arise from the fact that research into language has to make use of language. Cognitive instruments have to be aquired via the object investigated by means of these very instruments and not, for example, through reflection of consciousness upon itself.[1] Brain research has shown that the brain is not able to maintain any contact with the outer world on the level of its own operations, but – from the perspective of information – operates closed in upon itself. This is obviously also true for the brains of those engaged in brain research. How does one come, then, from one brain to another? Or to take a further example: the sociology of knowledge had demonstrated at least the influence of social factors on all knowledge, if not their role as sole determinants. This is also true, then, for this statement itself since no justification for an exception can be found, in the sense, say, of Mannheim's "free-floating intelligence".[i] What conclusion is to be drawn from this? It was thought that one would have to

---

[i]   Karl Mannheim (1893–1947), a German founder of the "sociology of knowledge."

Niklas Luhmann, "The Cognitive Program of Constructivism and a Reality that Remains Unknown" from *Selforganization: Portrait of a Scientific Revolution* (ed. Wolfgang Krohn, Guenter Kueppers, and Helga Nowotny), pp. 64–85. Dordrecht: Kluwer Academic Publishers, 1990.

I

Interest in epistemological questions is not limited to philosophy today. Numerous empirical sciences have, in the normal course of their research, been

found all knowledge on "convention"[2] or that knowledge was the result of a kind of "negotiation".[3] But these attempts only wound up designating an ancient problem – that of the unity of knowledge and reality – by means of a new concept. Not without reason have these attempts been criticized for epistemological naiveté[4], since one either learns nothing about the relationship to reality or the connection is only made over theoretically unacceptable "both/and" concessions. There is little more to be gained by calling such "constructivism", as has recently been done, "radical"[5] since what is identified here as "constructivism" hardly at first seems unfamiliar. It might be that the theory of knowledge – at least in some of its traditional variants – will be confirmed rather than caught unaware. Science is apparently reacting here to its own power of resolution. This can already be found in Plato who reduces everyday experience to mere opinion and raises the question of what reality lies behind it. As a result, these philosophic reflections were termed, at first, "idealism". As we come to modern times the emergence of modern science led more and more to the conclusion that this "underlying" reality was knowledge itself. This altered the meaning of the concept of the subject, while it is only in our century that the name "idealism" has been replaced by "constructivism". There was a shift in emphasis in the conflict between realism and idealism, but it is not easy to discover in this a new theory. There is an external world, which results from the fact that cognition, as a self-operated operation, can be carried out at all, but we have no direct contact with it. Without knowing, cognition could not reach the external world. In other words, knowing is only a self-referential process. Knowledge can only know itself, although it can – as if out of the corner of its eye – determine that this is only possible if there is more than only cognition. Cognition deals with an external world that remains unknown and has to, as a result, come to see that it cannot see what it cannot see.

So far there is nothing new here, unless it be in the definiteness and self-confidence with which all this is presented as knowledge. One has to look more closely at the theoretical distinctions with which this view of things is presented in order to discover something new. Insofar as constructivism maintains nothing more than the unapproachability of the external world "in itself" and the closure of knowing – without yielding, at any rate, to the old skeptical or "solipsistic" doubt that an external world exists at all – there is nothing new to be

found in it. Nonetheless, the theoretical form in which this is expressed has innovative aspects – even such radical innovations – that it is possible to gain the impression that the theory of a self-referring cognition closed in upon itself has only now acquired a viable form. One can express this more precisely: it has only now acquired a form in which it can represent itself as knowledge. A problem arises here, however. With the word "constructivism" (taken over from mathematics) premature victories have been proclaimed, and one has to accept that there will be those who step aside, with a shake of the head, denying the validity of these claims. It is important, therefore, to investigate the question of what is new and convincing here – and this will lead the discussion far afield.

II

For reasons that can only be clarified subsequently we begin our investigation with the question: by means of what distinction is the problem articulated? That is, we do not begin with the Kantian question: how is knowledge possible? We have avoided this form of the question because it might lead us to the premature response: in *this* way! At first the difference is of no great consequence. The one form of the question can be translated into the other (if one is not afraid to face problems of logical hierarchies as well as their failure). One can answer the question: "how is knowledge possible?", with "by the introduction of a distinction". In contrast with the tradition involving such concepts as "diapherein"[6] or "discernment"[7] here the concept of distinction is radicalized.[ii] For in order to recognize knowing it is necessary to distinguish it from what is not knowing. As a result, the question with regard to the foundation of knowledge is transformed into a question with regard to the distinction of distinguishing, that is, into an obviously self-implicative question.[8] The passage from the search for a founding and therefore asymmetric – relationship with regard to some unity is transformed into a search for an operatively employed difference. It is, further, easy to recognize, that circularity and paradoxes can no longer be rejected but will come to play a role.

So, once again, the question is: by means of what distinction is the problem of knowledge articulated? (And, for the sake of clarity, let it be said

---

[ii] *Diapherein* is differing.

once again: We are aware that with this question we have taken upon ourselves the difficulty of the distinction of distinguishing.)

In any case one will not be able to approach constructivism if one proceeds from the old controversy of whether the knowing system is a subject or an object. The subjectivist problem was to state and to show how it is possible by means of *introspection* – that is by passage to the self-reference of one's own consciousness – to form judgements about *the world of others*. That "intersubjectivity" is only a word which therefore does not solve the problem should be obvious. Objectivism, on the other hand, came up with the idea of describing knowledge as a condition or process in a particular object which was often called "organism".[9]

The mistake here lies in the assumption that it is possible to describe an object completely (we won't go so far as to say "explain") without making any reference to its relation to its environment (whether this relation be one of indifference, of selective relevance and capacity for stimulation, of disconnection, or of closure). In order to avoid these problems, which arise from the point of departure taken, both subjectivist and objectivist theories of knowledge have to be replaced by the system–environment distinction, which then makes the distinction subject–object irrelevant.

With this we have the distinction central to constructivism: it replaces the distinction transcendental/empirical by the distinction system/environment. The concept environment (as well as the corresponding one of system) was not available during Kant's day. What we call "environment" today had to be conceived of as the state of being contained and carried (periechon); and what we call "system" had to be thought of as order according to a principle. Both of these were already objects of knowledge. In order to answer the question of how knowledge is possible without falling into a self-referring circle the distinction transcendental/empirical was developed. Hardly anyone accepts this distinction today despite the labor that goes into the exegesis of historical texts. But if one drops this distinction how does one then avoid the circle of the self-founding of knowledge? Why must one avoid this circle? Can't one simply say: Knowledge is what knowledge takes to be knowledge?

The serving as medium foundation for dealing with these questions offers up the distinction system/environment and, in its context, a worked-out systems theory. This makes – virtually automatically – all the investigations and knowledge gained

in systems theory of potential relevance for the theory of knowledge. In contrast to the procedure in transcendentalism, investigations bearing relevance for epistemological questions do not need to be carried out primarily with this end in mind. The relevance emerges as a side-effect of other investigations (e.g., of neurophysiological investigations or in the history of science) and one only has to take care that the transitions are smoothed over and now and then put in order, for example by adequate terminological recommendations. A good example of this is Humberto Maturana's[iii] use of the word "cognition" ("conocimiento") for the extension of operations under the condition of interaction with the environment,[10] however annoying this terminology might be for professional epistemologists afraid of a biological invasion of their domain.

It has been known for a quite some time already that the brain has absolutely no qualitative and only a very slight quantitative contact with the external world. All stimuli coming from without are coded purely quantitatively (principle of undifferentiated coding); furthermore, their quantity, as compared with purely internal processing events, plays but a marginal role.[11] Incoming stimuli are also erased in fractions of a second if they are not stored in internal storage areas with somewhat longer retention times (short-term memory) – an event which is more the exception than the rule. With this, even time is made to serve the internal economy of complex processes. Apparently it is fundamental for the functioning of the brain that selected information is enclosed and not that it is let through. As if it were already information (or data) before it motivates the brain to form a representation. Such knowledge as this was not made use of by theoretical epistemology and it is only a formulation in terms of systems theory that leads to an insight which must seem surprising to epistemologists:[12] only closed systems can know. The sociology of science has arrived at similar conclusions (which are still, for the most part, rejected as being too shocking).[13] Whoever still maintains that knowledge is the construction of a relation to the environment that fits things as they are, is welcome to his opinion, but he is forced to begin his theoretical reflections with a paradox: it is only non-knowing systems that can know; or, one can only see because one cannot see.

---

iii Chilean biologist Humberto Maturana (1928–) with his student Francisco Varela (1946–2001) were the authors of *Autopoiesis and Cognition* (Dordrecht: Reidel, 1980).

Philosophical epistemology has become marginal scientifically if not completely isolated; a situation that has often been lamented.[14] This *was* the case for the Neo-Kantians and *is* the case for the Neo-Wittgensteinians. Nonetheless, anyone familiar with both sides is aware of the numerous possibilities for contact. Systems theory or, more precisely, the distinction between system and environment, could play the role of mediator here.

The effect of the intervention of systems theory can be described as a *de-ontologization of reality*. This does not mean that reality is denied, for then there would be nothing that operated – nothing that observed, and nothing on which one would gain a purchase by means of distinctions. It is only the epistemological relevance of an ontological representation of reality that is being called into question. If a knowing system has no entry to its external world it can be denied that such an external world exists. But we can just as well – and more believably – claim that the external world is as it is. Neither claim can be proved; there is no way of deciding between them. This does not, however, call the external world into question but only the simple distinction being/non-being which ontology had applied to it. As a consequence, the question arises: why do we have to begin with precisely this distinction? Why do we wound the world first with this distinction and no other?

Systems theory suggests *instead* the distinction between system and environment.

III

If one accepts this suggestion the answer to the question, how is knowledge possible?, is to begin with, as the operation of a system separated from its environment. If one, further, takes seriously that the system always has to be operationally closed then to the initial idea of separation assumptions are added regarding self-reference and recursivity. Operations of this kind are only possible within the context of a network of operations of the same system towards which they point and on which they are founded. There is no single operation that can emerge without this recursive network. At the same time the network itself is not an operation. "Multiplicity does not act as a relay".[15] The whole cannot as a whole itself become active. Every operation reproduces the unity of the system as well as its limits. Every operation reproduces closure and containment. There is nothing without an oper-

ation – no cognition either. And every operation has to fulfil the condition of being one operation among many, as it cannot exist in any other form, cannot otherwise possibly be an operation.

As a result, for an observer the system is a paradox, a unity which is a unity only as a multiplicity, a *unitas multiplex*. Even when the system observes itself one has what is true for every observation. If a system wants to know what makes it possible that it can know, it encounters this paradox. All theory of knowledge has to begin with the resolution of a paradox.

A further consequence is: No system can perform operations outside its own limits. If new operations are integrated it means that the limits of the system have been extended. Consequently, the system cannot use its own operations to connect itself with its environment since this would require that the system operate half within and half without the system. The function of the boundaries is not to pave the way out of the system but to secure discontinuity. Whatever one wants to call cognition, if it is supposed to be an operation then the operation necessarily has to be one incapable of contact with the external world, one which, in this sense, acts blindly.

These ideas can be worked out further and the foreseeable extensions of a theory of closed, self-referring systems-in-an-environment will doubtless come to have over this route an influence on the theory of knowledge. But we will leave this question aside for the moment since we are now confronted with a fundamental question: is it possible, and is it acceptable, to call what here becomes perceptible "knowledge" at all?

In the search for an answer to this question it is advisable to introduce a second distinction between *operation* and *observation*. This distinction occupies the place that had been taken up to this point by the unity-seeking logic of reflection. (This means, therefore, a substitution of difference for unity).

An operation that uses distinctions in order to designate something we will call "observation". We are caught once again, therefore, in a circle: the distinction between operation and observation appears itself as an element of observation. On the one hand, an observation is itself an operation; on the other hand, it is the employment of a distinction. An example would be that between operation and observation. A logic that would take its point of departure here could only be established as the unfolding of a circle, and it would have to make certain that the distinction can re-enter into what it has distinguished. Spencer Brown provides explicitly for this "re-entry" after deliberately ignoring it at the beginning with his instruction to an observer to "draw a distinction".[iv] (Among other things this means that time is employed for the resolution of self-referring circles and paradoxes).

An observation leads to knowledge only insofar as it leads to re-usable results in the system. One can also say: Observation is cognition insofar as it uses and produces redundancies – whereby "redundancy" here means limitations of observation that are internal to the system. In consequence, particular observations are more or less probable.[16]

The passage to "constructivism" follows from the insight that *it is not only for negations that there are no correlates in the environment of the system but even for distinctions and designations (therefore for observations)*. This does not mean (to say it once again) that the reality of the external world is being called into doubt. It is also beyond doubt that an observer can observe that and how a system is influenced by its environment or deliberately and successfully acts upon its environment. Nonetheless, all distinctions and designations are purely internal recursive operations of a system (that is, operations that form or disturb redundancies). These are operations that are not able to go beyond the system and, as if at a distant remove, pull something into it. As a result, all achievements following from these operations, above all what is usually called "information", are purely internal achievements. There is no information that moves from without to within the system. For even the difference and the horizon of possibilities on the basis of which the information can be selection (that is, information) doesn't exist in the external world, but is a construct – i.e. internal to the system. Does this mean, however – as is claimed in a direct line from Maturana – that the cognitive system operates "blindly"?

The metaphor of seeing and blindness can be retained as an abbreviated mode of speech, although it does not correspond to the current level of knowledge. One must also distinguish here: if every relation to the outer world is being denied in such a metaphor, too much is being called into question. On the other hand, it must be made clear that all observation (including the observing of observations) presupposes the operative deployment of a distinction which at the moment of its use must be employed "blindly" (in the sense of "non-

observably"). If one wants to observe the distinction in its turn, one has to employ a different distinction for which the same is true.

There can be no doubt, therefore, that the external world exists or that true contact with it is possible as a necessary condition of the reality of the operations of the system itself. It is the differentiation of what exists that is contributed by the observer's imagination, since, with the support of the specification of distinctions an immensely rich structure of combinations can be obtained, which then serves the system for decisions about its own operations.

Expressed in other words, the unity of a distinction employed for observation is constituted within the system. It is only in the observing system that things distinguished are brought to the unity of being distinct. Cognition is neither the copying nor the mapping nor the representation of an external world in a system. Cognition is the realization of combinatorial gains on the basis of the differentiation of a system that is closed off from its environment (but nonetheless "contained" in that environment).[17] If a system is forced to cognize with the aid of distinctions and is unable to cognize in any other manner, it means further that everything that is for the system, and which therefore has reality, has to be constituted over distinctions. The "blind spot" of each observation, the distinction it employs at the moment, is at the same time its guarantee of a world. For example, social reality is what one, in observing a majority of observers, can observe to be uniform among them despite their differences.[18] Social reality exists only when an observer can distinguish a majority of observers (which may or may not include himself). By "world" is meant that which has to be assumed for every system to be the unity of the system/environment distinction (self-reference and external reference), when (and only when) this distinction is employed.

In conclusion we can say that knowing systems are real (empirical – that is, observable) systems in a real world. Without a world they could neither exist nor know. It is only cognitively that the world is unapproachable for them.

IV

The contribution of the systems that makes cognition possible at all and which nothing in the environment corresponds to consists in the act of distinguishing. This recognition, which (as a

---

[iv] English mathematician G. Spencer-Brown constructed a logic of distinctions in his *Laws of Form* (London: George Allen and Unwin, 1969).

distinction itself) implies its own limitation, has helped us as far as it goes. This would seem to answer the question usually raised in controversies about constructivism. But the interesting analyses are still to come: They involve not the question of a real agreement between knowledge and reality but questions of *time*. Cognitive systems (at least the brain, consciousness and the systems of communication called societies) operate on the basis of events that have only a momentary presence and that already begin to disappear at the moment of their emergence. Furthermore, these systems operate on the basis of events that cannot be repeated but which must be *replaced* by other events. Their structures must, therefore, provide for the passage from event to event – something for which there are also no equivalents in the environment. It is neither the case that the environment changes itself with the same tempo and rhythm (and this can only be spoken of on the basis of cognitive acts), nor can one find in the environment those autopoietic structures that suggest the one in the other. How then is the time relation between system and environment to be understood? The only answer can be: as *simultaneity*. The foundation for the reality of the system – whatever the contours of its own meaningful observations might be – is the simultaneity of its operation with the conditions of reality that sustain it. Whatever the system might contribute in the way of a non-present future and a non-present past – that is, of distinctions – the simultaneity of the environment and the eternally immediate present of the system is a condition that cannot be eliminated. Whatever is simultaneous cannot be influenced, cannot be integrated into the causal constellations of the system, cannot be synchronized, but is nonetheless the precondition for the application of distinctions in time. The system can place itself in relation to time between future and past, or as a moment in relation to duration or to eternity. Whatever might emerge from this, the system constructs time in relation to itself. What one does not have control over is the simultaneity that reemerges from moment to moment in all the operations of the system, the "common aging"[v] in the sense of Alfred Schütz[19] or the splashing of the water on the bank of the Isle de Saint Pierre, that "continuing noise that is, however, filled by intervals", which, in convergence with internal movements, is sufficient "to

make me sense my existence with pleasure, without my having to think".[20] It is out of the unavoidable certainty of the simultaneity of the system and the environment that current time projections can arise. Examples of this can be found in the widespread "anticipatory reactions" in the plant and animal kingdoms, that is, in mere reactions to something assumed to be present on the basis of regularities that prove to be beneficial for the future, although they have not been perceived (i.e., have not been integrated into the processing of information).[21] Highly developed cognitive systems can, in addition, make prognoses, which does not mean that they can now perceive future present times. They are able to span this impossibility by means of constructions that organize their own information processing with the help of a distinction between what is past and what is to come that cannot appear in the external world as a *distinction*. Presumably, prognosis has to be understood as a product of our own imagination that can be evaluated by the memory,[22] that is, as the creation of an excess of individual possibilities which is then offered up for selection according to self-constructed criteria of "suitability". In other words, systems that make prognoses can prepare themselves for risks that they themselves have created and derive benefits from this.

Cognitive systems, therefore, have only a momentlike existence, as a result of the burden of simultaneity which keeps them on the ground. This existence must reproduce itself autopoietically in order to attain stability, even if it is only a dynamic one. They experience the world, therefore, with future and past – that is, as *duration* – only in the form of *non-presentness*. These systems can, therefore, consider their history to be finished insofar as they do not make present – as if in a dream – retrospective preferences. In the same way their future is full of enticing and threatening possibilities (although in reality there is no possibility at all, since everything is as it is). It is possible then to keep the non-present constant, which yields in turn the fascinating possibility for cognition of representing *changes* in the external world by terminological *constants* (instead of through changes in the system itself). Such systems need, as a result, records, which can, however, only be currently accessed; subsequently they help themselves with a kind of "vicarious learning", with observing observations of others which have the same limitation. The vast unfolding of the world materially, temporally and socially is a construct[23] anchored in the

---

[v] Alfred Schütz (1899–1959), Austrian-American phenomenological sociologist.

simultaneity of the world which, in this regard, never changes but is nonetheless inseparable from every realization.

On the other hand, the freedom of cognition in its constructions is founded on a radical "de-simultaneity" of the world, on the reduction of the contemporaneous to an instant almost devoid of meaning. What is gained by this is a terrifying plethora of possibilities in which cognition has to find its way by its own guidance. This existential moment is doubtlessly only a moment for an observer who can see the limits of this presentness and can call it "existence". Descartes was aware of this – and therefore made God responsible for continuity.

V

The refined constructivist theory of knowledge that has been presented here not only dissolves the traditional rationalistic continuum of being and thinking – which presupposed the possibility of an agreement between both and had founded it upon such concepts as nature or creation. The theoretical transcendental position which had been first the reaction to the dissolution of this rationalist continuum is also renounced. Furthermore, the assumption is rejected of a subjective faculty of consciousness that can guarantee a priori the conditions of the possibilities of cognition. But then, it is not sufficient to replace this conception by the distinction between irritation (or perturbation) from without and self-determination from within, which simply gives the difference between inner and outer yet another formulation and weight.[24] What remains (and has to replace those assumptions) is the *recursivity* of observation and cognition.

A process is called "recursive" when it uses the results of its own operations as the basis for further operations – that is, what is undertaken is determined in part by what has occurred in earlier operations. In the language of systems theory (which is not quite suitable here) one often says that such a process uses its own outputs as inputs. In any case recursivity requires a continuous testing of consistency and it has been shown by investigations in perception and memory that this necessitates a binary schematization, even on the neurophysiological level, which holds in readiness the possibilities of acceptance and rejection.[25] The states of the system that have been produced by its own operation serve then as criteria for the acceptance or rejection of further operations; stimuli from the

environment that effect the system can play a role here also. Decisive, however, is the continuous self-evaluation of the system – which always operates in a state of irritation or agitation by means of a code that permits acceptance and rejection with regard to the adoption of further operations. The brain functions in this way. And the same will be true for psychic and social systems. The codification true/false only gives this schematization its final finish and a form that is only used under very special circumstances.

One can, therefore, think of binarily schematized recursivity as a continuous calculation of operations on the basis of the current states of the system. The pleasure/pain mechanism also seems to function in this manner. With regard to observations, this structure makes possible the observation of observations. This can mean, first of all, that one repeats the same operation in order to see whether its results are confirmed or not confirmed. This leads then to a "condensation" of units of meaning whose verification can no longer be obtained by a single operation. More or less clear deviations can be built into such a replication. One observes the same thing at different times in different situations, under different aspects, which leads to a further enrichment of the condensed meaning and finally to the abstraction of denotation for what seems identical in the different observations. Thus, assumedly, the meaningful construction of the world comes about, gaining thereby a power no single operation can possibly dispose of. One speaks here, in the language of mathematics, of the "eigenvalues"[vi] of a system.[26] Again, no correspondence between system and environment is presupposed, but only the claim is made that it was possible to bring about these states.[27]

This theory provides a good explanation for the normal evolution of a knowledge that overcomes distance, so-called "distal knowledge", as Donald Campbell, following Egon Brunswik, has called it.[28] If one takes into consideration the dependence of all observation on distinction, other possibilities of recursive observation emerge. The usual understanding of the observations of observation focusses above all on *what* an observer observes (distinguishing thereby between subject and object, but concentrating above all on the object). Constructivism describes an observation of observation that con-

---

vi   The allowed values of the energy of a particle under a function ("eigenfunction") in Schrödinger's wave mechanics.

centrates on *how* the observed observer observes. This constructivist turn makes possible a qualitative change, a radical transformation, in the style of recursive observation, since by this means one can also observe what and how an observed observer *is unable* to observe. In this case one is interested in his blind spot, i.e. the means by which things become visible or non-visible. One observes (distinguishes) the distinction used by the primary observer in his observing. Since this observer, in the midst of his observation, cannot distinguish this distinction, what is observed is something that remains unknown to him or incommunicable. In the terms of sociology one could also say that observation is directed now to the observed observer's *latent* structures and functions.

The kind of reality, the kind of "eigenvalue" produced by recursions of this type is still largely unknown, as the technique itself is no older than 200 years. It was probably first practiced in the novel, then in the Counter-enlightenment, and then in the critique of ideology that is always from a holier-than-thou perspective. The primary observer was placed into the domain of the harmless or the naive; or he was treated as someone who, without realizing it, had something to hide. This holier-than-thou perspective fed upon suspicion. And the generalization of the principle of suspicion made it possible for whole disciplines – from psychoanalysis to sociology – to establish themselves with additional credentials in a world in which everyone knows, or imagines he knows, the situation in which he acts and the reasons for his actions.

It does not seem a coincidence that this observation of latent structures developed parallel to transcendental theory – at first at the end of the 18th century and then with particular intensity a century later during the heyday of Neo-Kantianism. Apparently, something had been lacking in transcendental philosophy. All the same, a constructivist theory of knowledge goes beyond this state of affairs (again a hundred years later). Its concept of recursive observation includes the observation of latency, freeing it from the prejudice that latent structures give a false picture of the world, as it really is and as science sees it. The assumption – to be found above all in the classical sociology of knowledge – that latent structures, functions and interests lead to distortions of knowledge, if not to blatant errors, can and must be abandoned.[29] The impossibility of distinguishing the distinction that one distinguishes with is an unavoidable precondition of cognition. The question of whether a given choice of distinction suits one's latent interests only arises on the level of second order observation. The claim of ideological distortion can then be observed in the person making the claim (for which he has to be observed as observer, that is, in relation to what he is observing).[30]

The important question after all this is what "eigenvalues" a system is converging towards when it extends the recursivity of its observations in this direction – that is, when it continually turns its observations towards things other observers *cannot* observe. For the results of this method of observing we have, in the absence of anything better, a variety of different names: Gotthard Günther speaks of "polycontextuality", others of "pluralism", and still others of the postmodern arbitrariness in the emergence and passage of "discourses". For constructivism this is, above all, an epistemological question and a kind of compensation for the limitations inherent in every act of cognition as a consequence of its dependence upon a distinction. One cannot draw the conclusion from the theory that now special "eigenvalues" of the social system will emerge that will be resistant to enlightenment for there is no guarantee that under all conditions such "eigenvalues" can be found and become stabilized. Still, the question can at least be raised and observation directed accordingly.

VI

If one takes seriously the endeavor to set up a constructivist theory of knowledge an important question becomes shifted: that of the paradoxes. By a paradox is meant a permissible and meaningful statement that leads nonetheless to antinomies or undecidability (or, more strictly, a demonstrable proposition that has such consequences). Two possibilities for dealing with such a problem should be rejected. The first is used in the construction of formal systems and consists of an ad hoc procedure of exclusion. The paradoxes are eliminated by suitable precautionary measures. Structures that lead to paradoxes are forbidden – for example by the well-known but questionable theory of types.[vii] The

---

[vii] A theory developed by Bertrand Russell (in "Mathematical Logic Based on a Theory of Types," 1908) to resolve the paradox, which he discovered, that the set of all sets which are not members of themselves both is and is not a member of itself.

epistemological questionability of such a procedure comes from its lack of justification; moreover, it usually has the consequence that it excludes more than just paradoxical possibilities for the construction of sentences.

As a result, philosophers have felt compelled to look for other means that would lead to a justifiable exclusion of paradoxes. MacKie, for example, suggests returning to a semantic theory of truth that would make it possible to say that the supposed objects designated by meaningful paradoxical propositions do not exist.[31] It is, however, not possible for a constructivist theory of knowledge to accept this way out, since what is claimed here as being non-existent, does not exist for constructivism anyway. Given that paradoxes re-emerge despite all the attempts to eliminate them, MacKie finally even calls for a "construction" of the paradoxical by adopting self-referring propositions into the construction and (at least implicit) quantification.[32] This suggestion is grist for the constructivist's mill: constructivism can view paradox as a problem in the machinery of the calculation of calculations, as a possible but nonetheless destructive construction. Should one look the Gorgon straight on – aware however that it is not the deadly Medusa one has before one, but her immortal sisters, Stheno (the Mighty) or Euryale (the Far Springer)?[viii]

We suggest instead a view from the side, the observing of observation. This enables one, when one includes observation of latency, to observe how other observers render invisible the paradoxes that get in their way, for example the paradox of each of our binary codes.[33] It is, therefore, not a psychoanalytical infection or a critical socio-ideological frivolity that brings us to include observation of the blind spot of the observer in the theory of knowledge. It is furthermore not simply an encouragement to propound values that are, in any case, irrational, as William James and Max Weber had thought. To see what others cannot see (and to accept that they cannot see what they cannot see) is, in a way, the systematic keystone of epistemology – taking the place of its a priori foundation.

It is, therefore, of importance that every observer involves himself in a paradox because he has to found his observing on a distinction. As a result, he is unable to observe either the beginning or the ending of his observing – unless it be by means of

another distinction that he has already begun to make or by continuing with a new distinction after having ended.[34] This is why all projection, or the setting of a goal, every formation of episodes necessitates recursive observation and why, furthermore, recursive observation makes possible not so much the elimination of paradoxes as their temporal and social distribution onto different operations. A consensual integration of systems of communication is, given such conditions, something that should sooner be feared than sought for. For such integration can only result in the paradoxes becoming invisible to all and remaining that way for an indefinite future.

This remedy solves, as it were, the problem of the paradoxes by reference to a concrete theory: the theory of autopoietic systems,[ix] which by means of recursive operations produce and reproduce a network of such operations as the condition for the very possibility of this reproduction (a solution logicians will hardly find satisfying). In such systems (one of which is science) there is no operation without reference to other operations of the system. Even when one forms universal propositions that refer to all the operations of the system, and also when one exposes these universal propositions on the basis of the classic Cretan pattern to self-reference, one only produces an operation that is a point of departure for other operations. We simply claim: it *is* this way; and logicians who attempt to dispute this are, in consequence, punished by paradoxes.

VII

Given all that has been said, what understanding of reality does constructivism have?

It may be useful here to review classical responses once again. As far as visual metaphors were used, two solutions were offered. Objectivists said that reality was manifold, which meant that there was no single observation point from which it could be seen in toto: what one sees conceals what one does not see. This deficiency can only be countered by changing the point of observation, that is by working sequentially or by a division of labor. Subjectivists could speak instead of a multiplicity of perspectives each of which makes possible a conditioned seeing, but which at the same time makes impossible or difficult the perception of

---

[viii] The three Gorgons, monsters of the underworld in Greek mythology.

[ix] "Autopoiesis" means self-constituting.

the perspective one sees with.[35] More eyes – and therefore more emotions: that was Nietzsche's postulate in *The Genealogy of Morals*.[x] Constructivism goes beyond these positions by radicalizing the relationship between cognition and reality. It is no longer a question of the difficulties that arise from a multiplicity of sides or perspectives, and the problem is no longer how one arrives, given this situation, at unity. This multiplicity, regardless of whether it is a multiplicity of sides or of perspectives, is itself a product of cognition, resulting from certain types of distinctions, which, as distinctions, are instruments of cognition. It is precisely by means of distinguishing that cognition separates itself from everything that is not cognition. Nonetheless, one is always dealing with concretely determined operations – even in the case of knowledge. Without water the jelly-fish goes limp. But in order to recognize that, distinctions are necessary: with/without water; not-limp/limp. These distinctions are codifications specific to cognition, which function independently of the environment (i.e. of stimuli), because there are not and cannot be any equivalents for them in the external world.

Cognitively all reality must be constructed by means of distinctions and, as a result, remains construction. The constructed reality is, therefore, not the reality referred to. This too can be recognized, but recognized only by means of precisely this distinction. For cognition, only what serves in a given case as a distinction is a guarantee of reality, an equivalent of reality. One could say more precisely: The source of distinction's guaranteeing reality lies in its own operative unity. It is, however, precisely as this unity that the distinction cannot be observed – except by means of another distinction which then assumes the function of a guarantor of reality. Another way of expressing this is to say that the operation emerges simultaneously with the world which as a result remains cognitively unapproachable to the operation.

The conclusion to be drawn from this is that the connection with the reality of the external world is established by the blind spot of the cognitive operation. Reality is what one does not perceive when one perceives it.[xi] In no way does this mean, however, that somewhere in the world there are states of affairs one cannot know, above all not in the old sense of the essence of nature's being secret. All that is meant is that the fruits of the concrete operation of cognition, which issue from the use of distinctions – that is, the proliferation of combinatorial possibilities – is due to an instrument requiring an operational closure specific for the given system. To attain this no "similarities" with the environment can be tolerated. If cognition demands meaning and meaning demands distinctions then the final reality must be thought of as devoid of meaning.

VIII

If one compares this result with what has traditionally been called "idealism" one can recognize an important change. It affects the basic question to which an answer is sought and, therefore, the whole theoretical structure.

One had proceeded from the distinction between knowledge and object and, as a result, been forced to face the problem that could not be answered by means of this distinction: how does knowledge arrive at its object? In the final analysis, the problem lay then in the unity of the difference between knowledge and object. One answer was provided by the claim of a dialectical relationship. Dialectical theories proved to be the adequate form here and required hardly any further argument. If one accepts, however, the argument suggested above the distinction between knowledge and object is itself only a distinction, that is a construction used to wound, dissect, observe the world. The unity of this distinction is simply the blind spot used by someone who, by means of this distinction, produces observations and descriptions.

If one starts from the assumption, however – as constructivism does – that this is always a real process in a real environment, which is always subject to limitations coming from the environment, what might then be the problem?

The problem could reside in the question of how a system is able to transform such *limitations* into *conditions for increasing its own complexity*. The *non-arbitrariness* of knowledge would then be nothing other then the evolutionarily-controlled *selectivity* of this process of change. It assumes no operations of the system projecting into the environment, that is, no knowledge in the traditional sense. One has to postulate instead: Everything issuing from this process of a transformation of limitations into

---

[x]   In the *Genealogy*, Nietzsche argued that moral norms are constructed to serve worldly purposes like revenge.

[xi]   The "real" is the unobservability of the cognitive construction of what is observed.

conditions for the increase of complexity is, for the system in question, knowledge.

In contrast with idealism, constructivist cognition neither seeks nor finds a ground. It reflects (when it reflects) the change in world-orientation from unity to difference. It begins and ends with distinctions, well aware of the fact that this is its own affair and not forced to this recognition by an unapproachable outer world. As the unity of the drawing of a distinction it can conceive of itself as a symbolic processing. The unity of the separated, the mutual suitability of the differentiated, is what serves as a symbol here. Francisco Varela has considered this, too, to be an operation or a value and called it "self-indication".[36] We must leave the question open as to whether this leads to an effective calculus. On the other hand, it is easy to recognize that we are living in the world after the fall. We have eaten of the tree of the knowledge of good and evil. "Distinctions" can only be employed using "indications". The symbol can only be employed diabolically; only what has been distinguished is integrable.

IX

A few further thoughts on the matter will be given only cursorily. The concept of observing has been defined extremely formally as a distinguishing description. We reject, nonetheless, founding this formality "transcendentally". With observing, distinguishing, designating we always mean an empirical operation that changes the system executing them – which means an operation which, in its own turn, is observable. No observer can avoid being observed, not even in its quality as "subject".

On the other hand the formality of the concept leaves open which empirical operations are meant. Which organ – to speak in these terms – carries out the observation?

The abstraction of the concept is not meant to conduct one to a ground. Which results already from the fact that the operation of observing can lead to both true und false knowledge, as an observer can determine who observes observing by means of the distinction of true and false. The abstractness of the concept is not, therefore, intended to provide a grounding for knowledge, but only to keep open the possibility of observation operations' being carried out by very different empirical systems – living systems, systems of consciousness, systems of communication. The abstraction makes allowances for the very wide domain of the "cognitive sciences", above all for the differentiation into disciplines in biology, psychology and sociology. Observation takes place when living systems (cells, immune systems, brain, etc.) discriminate and react to their own discrimination. Observation occurs when thoughts that have been processed through consciousness fix and distinguish something.[37] It occurs as well when a communicable integrable understanding of conveyed information – be it linguistic or non-linguistic – is attained (whatever psychic processes might occur in the minds of the participating individuals).

Given the state of research today one cannot get around taking into account the differences between these empirical realizations of distinguishing and designation (or should one perhaps for once say here: of discriminative focussing?). With this, the traditional attribution of cognition to "man" has been done away with. It is clear here, if anywhere, that "constructivism" is a completely new theory of knowledge, a post-humanistic one. This is not intended maliciously but only to make clear that the concept "man" (in the singular!), as a designation for the bearer and guarantor of the unity of knowledge, must be renounced. The reality of cognition is to be found in the current operations of the various autopoietic systems. The unity of a structure of cognition (or the "system" in the sense of transcendental theory) can only lie in the unity of an autopoietic system which reproduces itself with its boundaries, its structures and its elements.

By this means the significance of psychological epistemologies is considerably reduced, but relieved at the same time of the unreasonable expectation that they should provide more than individual-psychological knowledge. There is no such thing as "man", no one has ever seen him and if one is interested in the system of observation that organizes its distinctions by means of this word or concept one discovers the communication-system called society. There are now approximately 5 billion psychological systems. It has to be asked which of these 5 billion is intended when a theory of knowledge employing a psychological reference system relates concepts such as observation and cognition to consciousness. If no answer is forthcoming, such a theory has to be characterized as practicing socio-communicative observation. And the suggestion would have to be made that it would be better if this practice were reflected upon.

Up to now, constructivism has profited mainly from research in biology, neurophysiology and psychology (Maturana, Varela, Piaget, von Glasersfeld),[xii] although it actually favors development of a sociological theory of knowledge. What we know as cognition is the product of the system of communication called society, where consciousness plays a permanent but always only fractional role. It is only in extreme exceptions that one has to know individual persons in order to know what is known – and these are typical instances (for example, statements by witnesses in court) in which direct perception plays a central role. Neither in its claim to validity nor in the evaluation of its possibilities for development is the fund of knowledge of modern society approachable through processes of consciousness. It is an artifact of communication – and what is amazing here is not so much that the world is as it is constructed by modern science, as that it is still possible to pursue communication under the conditions of this construction. It is obvious that this cannot be explained by some capacity of consciousness (which one?!) but by the possibilities of storage made available originally by printing and, more recently, by electronic data processing.[38]

This preference for society as a referential system (that is, as the choice of a system from the perspective of which something else is environment) becomes absolutely unavoidable when one takes into consideration the difference between everyday knowledge and scientific knowledge. Whatever this distinction might mean and whatever theory might offer it, it cannot be presented convincingly as a distinction between different psychic types of knowledge. The distinction is a consequence of the differentiation of the social system of society. And it is only from here that psychical systems can be influenced. No further argument is necessary when one recalls the well-known phenomena of exponential growth, increasing differentiation and specialization or the problems of the pace of change.

It is, finally, only in a sociological context that the ideas on recursive observation and second-order observation (i.e., the observation of observation) acquire their full significance. But why would an observer observe another observer as observer, as another psychical system? Why isn't the other system seen simply as a normal object in the external world, that is, why isn't it simply observed

directly instead of as a pathway for the observing of its observing?

It is usually assumed that this is made possible by a sudden, intuitive analogy: the other is experienced as an alter ego, as operating like another I.[39] But we question, how does this occur? And further, is this phenomenon culturally invariant, independent of social structure? The usual answer describes only the result, is only another formulation of the problem and does not explain how it occurs.

Maturana avoids this problem by shifting to the mutually coordinating interaction of two organisms that interreact with each other in a sufficiently comparable area of interaction.[40] This makes it possible for him to explain the origin of language as a possibility of consensual coordination of the coordination of these interactions despite closure of the mode of operation of the participating systems. This still doesn't provide, however, a satisfying explanation of how the observation of observing emerges, that is, how observers construct the objects they have constructed as other observers.

A third theoretical suggestion (which draws on sociology, since psychology and biology have not sufficed) can begin with the assumption that the construction of the other observer is a necessary consequence of communication.[41] For communication is only possible when an observer is able, in his sphere of perception, to distinguish between the act of communication and information, that is, to understand communicative acts as the conveying of information (and not simply as behavior).[42] Out of this distinction – which only remains evolutionarily stable and only reproduces itself as a communication system when it is able to maintain itself – there emerges then a second one: that of subject and object. That communication can be continued requires no more than a kind of black-box concept for the subject and for the object, as far as the distinction operates. As a participant one can make use of one's own constructions, which can then be evaluated during the course of one's participation in the communication. One does not need to know what is going on "inside" the subject (and of course, could never know this) and also does not need to know the "essence" of things (which is of itself infinite): the filling necessary for the continuation of communication suffices. However, to the degree that systems of communication, in the course of their own evolution, become more sophisticated, differentiated and complex, more demanding concepts for subject and object are called for. It is in the course of this that one finally also learns to observe others as

---

[xii] Psychologists Jean Piaget (1896–1980), prominent theorist of cognitive development, and Ernst von Glasersfeld, contemporary radical constructivist.

observers (even at times they are not communicating) and finally even to observe that others do not observe what they do not observe while observing. Society, finally, makes even latent observation of latent structures possible.

The question still has not been answered why communication together with its resulting achievements progresses. The answer can only be that the evolutionary force of a particular distinction – that between communication and information – has proven itself. This can, of course, be claimed of everything that exists, and is still not an explanation. Important, however, in the constructivist context outlined above is that this claim has been made for a *distinction*. With this another distinction has been added to those already used – system/environment and operation/observation: that of communication/information, which is of special importance for the analysis of social systems. The familiar distinction between ego and alter ego can be dealt with as derivative, and with it the whole theory of knowledge founded on the concept of intersubjectivity.

X

The above has made it abundantly clear, we believe, that constructivism does not question the existence and reality of the world – but only constructs. But even after one has seen this, one can, as a sociologist, still ask why this happens, and why precisely today, after both ancient skepticism and idealism have been overcome, this constructivistic world-construction is of value. If a philosopher were to ask this question he would be faced with the difficult problem of a deeper analysis of Hegelian logic, which is the most profound scheme so far developed for the processing of distinctions of what is implied in them with regard to identical and contrary. For a sociologist the matter is simpler. He can take a theory of social evolution as his point of departure, a theory obviously, that itself is founded on a relevant distinction – for example, constructed on a Darwinian-scheme of variation and selection. It is possible then to understand constructivism as an epistemology suitable for a society with a highly differentiated system of the sciences.[43] In other words, in a society that can produce science in the modern sense, conceptual problems arise that can only be solved constructivistically – whatever one in this society might normally think about the world in which he lives and works, rides the bus and smokes cigarettes.

It shouldn't be very difficult to recognize that progress in science (whatever "progress" might mean here) is tied to even more sophisticated distinctions. This is, above all, the case for what Donald Campbell has called development in the direction of "distal knowledge" – that is, for the distinction between knowledge and the knower himself.[44] Divorce of the perspectives of comparison from the interests of the one doing the comparing also belongs here. One need, moreover, only think of the use of rigorously formal cognitive instruments – of logic, mathematics, quantification – as a form of representation of distinction in reality. This could still be dealt with under the concept of "idealism", and it is in this context that Husserl makes his criticism of modern, "Galilean" science.[45] Today the "cognitive sciences" and the theory of self-referential systems add a new perspective which cannot be subsumed under "idealism" or criticized as "idealism", that is, insight into the operative closure of self-referential systems. A theory of knowledge today that is to be compatible with the latest developments in science must be able to bear this new perspective. It is not surprising, therefore, that, after a period of open and rather irresolute epistemological pragmatism and a period in which highly formalized methodology was presented as epistemology – after James and Dewey, Baldwin, Rescher, Popper and others – epistemological constructivism is beginning to come into its own.[xiii] Quantum physics, cytochemistry and neurophysiology, as well as historic-sociological relativism make this convergence necessary. If the task of epistemology is to analyze science as a social cognitive undertaking one will not be able simply to ignore scientific results. Constructivism is the form assumed in reflection on the system of science facing its own extravagances; it is the form in which an increasingly improbable distinguishing is finally recognized as the contribution of cognition. But it is also the form that can no longer mislead one to conclude it has nothing to do with reality.

A society that increasingly differentiates its most important sub-systems in relation to specific functions intensifies to a highly improbable degree its

[xiii] American pragmatist philosophers William James (1842–1910) and John Dewey (1855–1952), psychologist James M. Baldwin (1861–1934), philosopher of science Nicholas Rescher (1928–), and Sir Karl Popper (1902–94), Viennese-born English philosopher who developed "falsificationism" and helped to inspire evolutionary epistemology.

cognitive output in the area of science. If one then reflects on this situation, one arrives at theories that themselves seem improbable. For this reason epistemology cannot provide a foundation for the sciences. It cannot offer basic principles, arguments or even certainty. It can no longer be understood as a theory of the founding of knowledge. The opposite is true: it analyzes the uncertainty of knowledge and

gives reasons for it. It therefore should come as no surprise that no theory of knowledge today can attain the degree of certainty to be found in quantum physics or biochemistry.

It is perhaps not the least important function of constructivist epistemology to make society irritatingly aware of the fact that it produces science.

Author's Notes and References

1 As a typical solution the distinguishing of several levels of language or of cognition has been suggested, with the possibility of "autologic" relationships on the higher level. See L. Lofgren, "Towards System: From Computation to the Phenomenon of Language", in M. E. Carvallo (ed.), *Nature, Cognition and System: Current Systems – Scientific Research on Natural and Cognitive Systems*, Dordrecht: Reidel, 1988, p. 129–55. But this is a transparent stopgap solution, since a level derives its identity only from the fact that there are other levels that can be reached from it.

2 See D. Bloor, *Wittgenstein: A Social Theory of Knowledge*, London: Routledge & Kegan Paul, 1983, esp. p. 119ff. This "conventionalism" going back to Poincaré, has become a tradition, it meets with little opposition today as it has become almost reflex.

3 See D. Bloor, *Wittgenstein: A Social Theory of Knowledge*, London: Allen & Unwin, 1979, passim, for example, p. 95.

4 This can be found in the recent publication by A. Chalmers, "The Sociology of Knowledge and the Epistemological Status of Science", *Thesis Eleven* 21 (1988), 81–102: The argument presented, however, shows no progress.

5 See P. Watzlawick (ed.) *Die erfundene Wirklichkeit*, Munich: Piper, 1981; H. Gumin/A. Mohler (eds.), *Einfilhrung in den Konstruktivismus*, Munich: Oldenbourg, 1985; S. J. Schmidt (ed.), *Der Diskurs des radikalen Konstruktivismus*, Frankfurt am Main: Suhrkamp, 1987; E. v. Glasersfeld, *Wissen, Sprache und Wirklichkeit: Arbeiten zum radikalen Konstruktivismus*, Braunschweig: Vieweg, 1987.

6 See Plato, Theaetetus, 208 C.

7 See, for example, C. Buffier, *Cours de sciences sur des principes nouveaux et simples*, Paris 1732, reprint Genf: Slatkine 1971, p. 800ff. where this concept dealt with at length in the "Traité des vérités de conséquences" (not in the "Traité des première vérités").

8 See in this regard, as well as for the limiting cases of universal distinction (nothing is excluded) and elementary distinction (nothing is included), R. Glanville/F. J. Varela, "Your Inside Is Out and Your Outside Is In" (Beatles 1968), in G. E. Lasker (ed.), *Applied Systems and Cybernetics, Vol. II*, New York: Pergamon

Press 1981, p. 638–41. Following S. Brown, the authors distinguish inclusion and exclusion by using the concept of form in order to distinguish the act of distinguishing. Their argument corresponds, moreover, exactly to the idea Nicolas Cusanus used to found the coincidentia oppositorum and upon it his concept of God beyond all distinctions.

9 See, for example, the "object-psychological" epistemology of A. Naess, *Erkenntnis und wissenschaftliches Verhalten*, Oslo: Dybverd, 1936, in particular p. 103ff., where the author demands that all epistemology should be limited to description "of the process in the internal functional space" of an organism. See also p. 105: "The common distinction between 'situation' and 'behavior' is, viewed psychologically, a distinction between two kinds of 'behavior'".

10 See H. R. Maturana, *Erkennen: Die Organisation und Verkörperung von Wirklichkeit*, Braunschweig: Vieweg, 1982, esp. p. 32ff. (German translation from the English); H. R. Maturana/F. J. Varela, *Der Baum der Erkenntnis: die biologischen Wurzeln des menschlichen Erkennens*, Bern: Scherz, 1987, esp. p. 31ff. See the critical discussion precisely this connection between biological systems theory and epistemology, in G. Roth, "Autopoiese und Kognition: Die Theorie H. R. Maturana und die Notwendigkeit ihrer Weiterentwicklung", in Schmidt, *Der Diskurs*, 1987, note 5, p. 256–86.

11 See G. Roth, "Die Entwicklung kognitiver Selbstreferentialität im menschlichen Gehirn", in D. Baecker, et.al. (eds.), *Theorie als Passion*, Frankfurt am Main: Suhrkamp, 1987, p. 394–422 (419f).

12 See the contributions of H. v. Foerster, *Sicht und Einsicht: Ausgewählte Arbeiten zu einer operativen Erkenntnistheorie*, Braunschweig: Vieweg, 1985. See also F. J. Varela, "Living Ways of Sense-Making: A Middle Path for Neuroscience", in P. Livingston (ed.), *Disorder and Order: Proceedings of the Stanford International Symposium* (Sept. 14–16, 1981), Saratoga, California: Anma Libri 1984, p. 208–23; G. Roth, "Selbstorganisation-Selbsterhaltung-Selbstreferentialität: Prinzipien der Organisation der Lebewesen und ihre Folgen für die Beziehungen zwischen Organismus und Umwelt", in A. Dress, et al. (eds.), *Selbstorganisation: Die Entstehung von*

Ordnung in Natur und Gesellschaft, Munich: Piper, 1986, p. 149–80, esp. 168ff.; G. Roth, "Erkenntnis und Realität: Das reale Gehirn und seine Wirklichkeit", in Schmidt, *Der Diskurs*, 1987, note 5, p. 229–55.

13 "The natural world has a small or non-existent role in the construction of scientific knowledge", is claimed, e.g., by H. Collins, "Stages in the Empirical Programme of Relativism", *Social Studies of Science*, 11 (1981), 3–10 (3). See also, H. Collins, *Changing Order*, London: Sage Publications, 1985. There would be far less controversy if one read the latter work in conjunction with works on brain research and not as an alternative to them. The question isn't whether brains *or* language construct the world; the claim is that if it's brains, then it must be language, and *vice versa*.

14 See, for example, D. T. Campell, "Descriptive Epistemology, Psychological, Sociological and Evolutionary", William James Lectures at Harvard University, 1977; noted from an unpublished manuscript.

15 M. Serres, "Dream", in Livingston (ed.), *Disorder and Order*, 1984, note 12, p. 225–39 (238).

16 See with regard to this systems-theoretic use of the concept of redundancy: H. Atlan, *Entre le cristal et la fumée*, Paris: Editions du Seuil, 1979; or, H. Atlan, "Disorder, Complexity and Meaning", in Livingston, *Disorder and Order*, 1984, note 5, p. 109–28.

17 On closure as "enclosure" see H. v. Foerster, "Entdecken oder Erfinden. Wie lät sich Verstehen verstehen?", in Gumin and Mohler, *Einführung*, Mohler, 1985, note 5, p. 27–68.

18 Subtle analyses of this question are to be found in F. H. Tenbruck, *Geschichte und Gesellschaft*, Berlin: Duncker & Humblot 1986, resp. p. 175ff.

19 A. Schütz, *Der sinnhafte Aufbau der sozialen Welt: Eine Einleitung in die verstehende Soziologie*, Vienna: J. Springer, 1932, p. 111f.

20 J. J. Rousseau, *Les rêveries du promeneur solitaire, Cinquième promenade, quoted from Oeuvres complètes* (Ed. de la Pléiade), Vol. 1, Paris: Gallimard, 1959, p. 1040ff (1045).

21 Of course, these are always the statements of an observation that itself sees more time from the observed system does. An extensive analysis of these questions can be found in R. Rosen, *Anticipatory Systems. Philosophical, Mathematical and Methodological Foundations*, Oxford: Pergamon Press, 1985.

22 The same is true for language and this similarity points to a close evolutionary and even neurophysiological association. See on this question H. J. Jerrison, *Evolution of the Brain and Intelligence*, New York: Verlag, esp. p. 426f.

23 For greater detail see N. Luhmann, *Soziale Systeme: Grundri einer allgemeinen Theorie*, Frankfurt am Main: Suhrkamp, 111f.

24 This is the formulation of Glasersfeld, *Wissen, Sprache und Wirklichkeit*, 1987, note 5, in his presentation of "radial constructivism". Maturana also uses such formulations to explain his constructivist position.

25 See H. v. Foerster, "What is Memory that it May Have Hindsight and Foresight as Well?", in S. Bogoch (ed.), *The Future of the Brain Sciences*, New York: Plenum Press, 1969, p. 19–64.

26 See v. Foerster, "What is Memory" 1985, note 12, esp. p. 205ff.

27 In Maturana's theory the corresponding concept is "Conservation of Adaptation". See Maturana/Varela, *op. cit.*, 1987, note 10, p. 113f. or, in greater detail, H. R. Maturana, *Evolution: Phylogenetic Drift through the Conservation of Adaptation*, Ms. 1986. It is crucial that adaptation can only be preserved, not improved. A system is adapted for the processing of its autopoiesis in its environment or it isn't, and is destroyed. There is no more or less in this regard, just as the operations of the system either can take place or can't take place. Every other judgement is the affair of an observer and can only be observed in an observer.

28 S. Donald, T. Campbell, "Natural Selection as an Epistemological Model", in R. Navoll/R. Cohen (eds.), *A Handbook of Method in Cultural Anthropology*, Garden City, New York: The National History Press, 1970, p. 51–85.

29 And has been given up today. See, for example, B. Barnes, *Scientific Knowledge and Sociological Theory*, London: Routledge & Kegan Paul, 1974; D. Bloor, *Knowledge and Social Imagary*, London: Routledge & Kegan Paul, 1976.

30 Quite consistently, Marxists learn about the critique of political economy from Marx; they don't turn to political economy for this. But the result is that the common views of the political economy of Marx's day are discussed with reference to Marx works, that Marx himself seems like a political economist (not completed without this being his own fault) and that changes in the critique that have occurred over the best 150 years are not sufficiently taken into account.

31 See J. L. MacKie, *Truth, Probability and Paradox: Studies in Philosophical Logic*, Oxford: Clarendon Press, 1973, ch. 6 in association with ch. 2.

32 J. L. MacKie, *Truth, Probability and Paradox* 1973, note 31, p. 273.

33 As case studies in this question of N. Luhmann, "The Third Question: The Creative Use of the Paradoxes in Law and Legal Theory", *Law and Society Review* 15 (1988), 153–65.

34 See R. Glanville, "Distinguished and Exact Lies", in R. Trappl (ed.), *Cybernetics and Systems Research* 2, Amsterdam: North-Holland Publications, 1984, p. 655–62.

35 N. Rescher expresses this perspective on perspectivity: "Perspectives are diaphanous, and one tends not

to see them as such", in his *The Strife of Systems: An Essay on the Grounds and Implications of Philosophical Diversity*, Pittsburgh: University of Pittsburgh Press, 1985, p. 187.

36 See F. J. Varela, "A Calculus for Self-Reference", *International Journal of General Systems* 2 (1975), 5–24.

37 See in this regard N. Luhmann, "Die Autopoiesis des Bewutseins", in A. Hahn/V. Kapp (eds.), *Selbst-thematisierung und Selbstzeugnis: Bekenntnis und Geständnis*, Frankfurt am Main: Suhrkamp, 1987, p. 25–94.

38 Furthermore, what is offered as epistemology in the context of the cognitive sciences is inconceivable without computers – both from the theoretical aspect. See F. J. Varela, *The Sciences and Technology of Cognition: Emerging Trends*, Ms., Paris, 1986. This is also true of logical theories and their truth procedures.

39 This is also held by strict constructivists. See, for example, E. v. Glasersfeld, "Konstruktion der Wirklichkeit und des Begriffs der Objektivität", in Gumin and Mohler, *Einführung* 1985, note 5, p. 1–26 (20f).

40 See Maturana, *Evolution*, 1982, note 10, p. 52ff. The literature that follows uses "parallelion" or "parallelizing", instead of "analogy". See, for example, P. M. Hejl, "Konstruktion der sozialen Konstruktion: Grundlinien einer konstruktivistischen Sozialtheorie", in Schmidt, 1987, note 5, p. 303–39.

41 Related to this, but nonetheless to be distinguished from it, are the well-known attempts *Der Diskurs*, to use the process of learning a language for the elucidation of epistemological questions. See, for example, W. v. O. Quine, *Word and Object*, New York: Wiley, 1960. See also the less well known ideas of D.T. Campbell, "Ostensive Instances and Entita. . . . in Language Learning", in W. Gray/ N. D. Rizzo (eds.), *Unity Through Diversity, A Festschrift for Ludwig von Bertelanffy*, New York: Gordon and Breach, 1973, Vol. II, p. 1043–57. The question dealt with here is the claim that the learning of language is not possible without reference to things of the external world, which means that language can never completely construct reality out of itself.

42 See Luhmann, "Die Autopoiesis", 1984, note 23, p. 191ff.

43 See here also N. Luhmann, "Intersubjektivität oder Kommunikation: Unterschiedliche Ausgangspunkte soziologischer Theoriebildung", *Archivio di Filosofia* 54 (1986), p. 41–60.

44 See, for example, Campbell, "Natural Selection", 1970, note 28, p. 51–85.

45 See E. Husserl, "Die Krisis der Europäischen Wissenschaften und die transzendentale Phänomenologie", *Husserliana*, Vol. VI, Den Haag: Nighoff, 1954. See also A. N. Whitehead, *Science and the Modern World* (Lowell Lectures 1925), quoted from the edition New York: Free Press, 1954.

49

From "Modern China and the Postmodern West"

David Hall

American comparative philosopher David Hall (1937–) attempts in this 1989 essay to show that traditional Chinese philosophy contains resources that answer some of the problems represented by the debate over modernity and postmodernism. Indeed, Hall literally claims that classical, which is to say "premodern," Chinese thought is *postmodern*. In particular, he argues that the Derridean notion of difference (*différance*), of the primacy of what cannot be captured by truth-governed philosophical utterance, is central to both Taoism and Confucianism.

The metaphysical tradition of the West is implicitly or explicitly grounded in a "philosophy of presence" – that is, the desire to make present the presence of Being in beings. Jacques Derrida terms this disposition to make *being* present "logocentrism."[1] The logocentric bias of Western philosophy motivates thinkers to attempt to present the truth, being, essence, or logical structure of that about which they think and discourse. The senses of modernity sketched above all had at their heart the attempt to characterize the capital "T" Truth of things. The failure of that undertaking is the failure of the philosophy of presence – and the failure of modernity.

The postmodern enterprise aims at the development of a philosophy of *difference*. Our purported inability to think difference and otherness in their most general senses threatens the entire metaphysical project of Western thought.

The most general question of difference concerns the difference between the "whatness" and the "thatness" of a thing. "A rose is a *rose....*" Yes. In addition, "a rose *is....*" Asking *what* a being is is a cosmological question; considering *that* it is is an ontological appreciation. A rose as an item related with the other items in its ecosystem in complex spatiotemporal and biochemical manners is a *cosmological* entity. *That* the rose is – its isness – indicates its *ontological* character.

Of course, the contrast of cosmological and ontological cannot be imagined without the cosmogonic tradition out of which it arises. For the ontological bias of Western philosophy derives from its attitude toward the chaos of beginnings.

The creation and maintenance of order from out of and over against the threat of chaos is the fundamental fact which establishes our sense of beginnings. Speculative philosophy, both as general ontology and as universal science, attempts to explain the fundamental fact of *order*. The ontologist asks the ontological question: "Why are there beings rather than no being?" Or "Why is there something rather than nothing at all?" Proponents of *scientia universalis*[i] ask the cosmological question: "What kinds of things are there?" The cosmogonic tradition in the Hellenic West has determined that metaphysical speculation must involve the search for beings or principles which, as transcendent

[i] Universal science.

David Hall, "Modern China and the Postmodern West" from *Culture and Modernity: East–West Philosophic Perspectives* (ed. Eliot Deutsch), fourth through sixth editions, pp. 57–67. Honolulu: University of Hawaii Press, 1991.

sources of order, account for the order(s) experienced or observed.

As traditionally interpreted, both the cosmological and ontological questions presuppose an ordered ground. It is this, of course, which defines the logocentric motive of Western philosophy – the desire to illumine and articulate the order and structure in things.

All this may seem extremely abstract and quite irrelevant to any discussion of the modernization of China. But I think not. There is a most serious issue at stake here. If our most general understandings of our world involve us always in presuming a universal ground such as the essence or structure of beings, we can easily lose sight of the particularities of both our experience of things and of the things themselves. Capital "T" Truth and capital "B" Beauty and capital "G" Goodness become the subject matters of our discourse instead of the truth, beauty, and goodness concretely realized by the insistent particularities of our world. We then claim to know generalities, universalities, absolutes, and essences, but we lose sight of the brute facticities of our world.

Any serious claim to objective truth involves us in insisting that reality shine through our assertions. The very being of things is present in one's theory or ideology. Our age is altogether too suspicious of such claims. The pluralism of doctrines and theories within a single culture such as ours, as well as the pluralism of cultures, makes any claim to the truth of things an implicitly political act. Dogmatism, totalitarianism, and narrow intolerance are all directly connected with unjustified claims to final truth.

The philosophy of presence is certainly not purposefully pernicious. Enlightenment rationality emerged from the idea that generic principles of logic and rationality may generate a common discourse for all cultures. Such rationalism was born from the need to connect diverse, pluralistic ideas, beliefs, and practices. Our reason was the gift of the ancient city-states, spread from Italy to the Peloponnesus, spun through the shuttles of Hebraic monotheism and Latin conceptions of *humanitas* and refined in the various furnaces of German, French, and English forms of colonialism.

The desire to see essential unity among cultures is a function of our missionizing activity expressed initially through Roman and Christian expansion, and now through our rational technologies motored by an incipient economic imperialism or, more politely put, an expanding market mentality. Proponents of Western values believe them to be ex-portable because they represent the grounds and consequences of a rational set of principles.

Our cultural values are housed in *doctrines* – propositions that may be entertained as beliefs. Philosophic and scientific principles are rational in form and are therefore open to public entertainment apart from specific cultural practices. Technology as a rational system carries with it the algorithms of its replication, requiring a minimum of human intervention.

In their attempts at modernization the Chinese are confronted with an uncomfortable dilemma. China must modernize, but the effects of a modernization understood in terms of liberal democracy, free enterprise, and rational technologies cannot but threaten its cultural integrity. China's ritual-based culture depends upon a commonality of traditions that liberal democracy renders quite fragile. The laws, rules, and values that define the Chinese sensibility are immanent within and relevant to the relatively specific character of the Chinese people. The paternalism of the Chinese form of government, its stress upon the solidarity of community over issues of abstract rights, its cultivation of and response to the psychological need for dependency are all delicate enough characteristics to be effaced by the impersonality of technology, the self-interest of free enterprise, and the individualizing ideals of democracy. Whatever benefits they might offer, each of these elements of modern culture leads to a bloating of the private sphere and threatens community.

Clearly, the problematic of distinctly modern Anglo-European philosophy is distinct from that of classical Chinese philosophy as regards the question of "difference." For a variety of reasons associated with the choices made at the origins of their cultural development, the Chinese find it easier to think difference, change, and becoming than do most of us. On the other hand, it has been easier in the modern West to think in terms of identity, being, and permanence.

I certainly have not failed to notice the dazzling incongruity that seems to lurk within my central claim. Could it really be the case that the country most identified with cultural continuity, inflexible tradition, and the most provincial intolerance toward other civilizations is expert in the philosophy of difference? My answer is – yes, certainly. Though I shall not discuss the background and significance of this question in any detail, I do hope to provide sufficient hints as to the plausibility of my affirmative response in the remarks which follow.

David Hall

In defense of my somewhat exotic thesis I want to call attention to the evidence for thinking that Confucianism and philosophical Taoism share something like the problematic of postmodernism insofar as it is shaped by the desire to find a means of thinking difference. In its strongest and most paradoxical form my argument amounts to the claim that classical China is in a very real sense *postmodern*.

Two benefits may come from such an investigation as this. First, since it is rather obvious that the postmodern critique is neither an atavistic nor Luddite enterprise, one can hope that there may develop from out of the postmodern impulse alternative strategies for engaging and accommodating the practical consequences of the modern world. This means that China should be free to reflect upon the very difficult problems of modernization in terms of its own postmodern past.

A second benefit of the postmodern connection is that Anglo-European thinkers can discover in classical China supplemental resources for the development of a vision of cosmological difference and the language which articulates that vision. Certain of those resources may be found, as I now shall attempt to show, in the original Taoist and Confucian sensibilities.

Taoism and Cosmological Difference

I have argued elsewhere[2] that a philosophically coherent understanding of classical Taoism depends upon a recognition that neither of the two fundamental metaphysical contrasts of the Western tradition – that is, between "being" and "not being" and between "being" and "becoming" – is helpful in understanding the Taoist sensibility. In Taoism, the sole fact is that of process or becoming. Being and nonbeing are abstractions from that process.

The first words of the *Tao Te Ching* may be rendered in this way:

The way (*tao*) that can be spoken of is not the constant way. The name that can be named is not the constant name. The nameless was the beginning of Heaven and earth.[3]

Throughout the *Tao Te Ching*, *tao* is characterized as both nameless and nameable. *Tao* per se is the total process of becoming, becoming-itself. Nameless and nameable *tao* function analogously to

"nonbeing" and "being," respectively. Thus being and nonbeing are abstractions from the generic process of becoming-itself. *Tao* is the *that which* – a name for *process*. That which *is* and that which *is not*[4] are the polar elements of becoming-itself.

The fundamental truth of the Taoist vision is contained in this but mildly ironic send-up of Parmenides' infamous maxim: Only becoming is; not-becoming is not. That is, there is only coming into being which illustrates some mixture of being and nonbeing. Neither being nor nonbeing abstracted from its polar relationship with its opposite can be finally real.

Each particular element in the totality has its own intrinsic excellence. The Chinese term is *te*. *Te* may be understood as the "particular focus" or "intrinsic excellence" of a thing. The *te* of an element serves as the means in accordance with which it construes the totality of things from its perspective and thus "names" and creates a world.

The concepts of *tao* and *te* may be interpreted together in a polar fashion. *Tao-te* is best understood in terms of the relationships of field (*tao*) and focus (*te*). The model of a hologram is helpful, for as in a holographic display each element contains the whole in adumbrated forms, so in the Taoist sensibility each item of the totality focuses the totality in its entirety. The particular focus of an item establishes its world, its environment. In addition, the totality as sum of all possible orders is adumbrated by each item.

Taoism is radically perspectival. "If a man lie down in a damp place," says Chuang Tzu,[ii] "he contracts lumbago. But what of an eel?"[5] The eel will be at least as uncomfortable as the man – but for the opposite reason. The Taoist totality is horizontal. There are no hierarchies; no great chain of being or ladder of perfections exists in the Taoist cosmology. For the Taoist, the anthropocentrism implicit in almost every form of Anglo-European ethical system is only one of a myriad of possible centrisms.

A familiar tale from the *Chuang Tzu* is enlightening in this regard:[6]

The emperor of the South Sea was called Shu, the emperor of the North Sea was called Hu, and the emperor of the central region was called Hun-tun (Chaos). Shu and Hu from time to

---

[ii] Chuang Tzu (369–286 BC) was the most important early interpreter of Taoism.

time came together for a meeting in the territory of Hun-tun, and Hun-tun treated them very generously. Shu and Hu discussed how they could repay his kindness. "All men," they said, "have seven openings so they can see, hear, eat, and breathe. But Hun-tun alone doesn't have any. Let's try boring him some!" Every day they bored another hole, and on the seventh day Hun-tun died.

Taoism is not a vision grounded upon order, but upon chaos. It is a vision in which harmony has a special kind of meaning associated with the breechless, faceless, orifice-free Lord Hun-tun. Assuming that *tao* is becoming-itself, and therefore the sum of all orders, provides a helpful response to Benjamin Schwartz' provocative query concerning the meaning of "*tao*" in *The World of Thought in Ancient China*. "How may a word which refers to *order*," he asks, "come to have a mystical meaning?"[7] The mystical meaning of *tao* lies in the mystery of chaos as the sum of all orders.

Tao is not organic in the sense that a single pattern or *telos* could be said to characterize its processes. It is not *a* whole but many wholes. Its order is not rational or logical but aesthetic – that is there can be no transcendent pattern determining the existence or efficacy of the order. The order is a consequence of the particulars comprising the totality of existing things.

This interpretation of *tao* makes of it a totality not in the sense of a single-ordered cosmos, but rather in the sense of the sum of all possible cosmological orders. Any given order is an existing world that is construed from the perspective of a particular element of the totality. But as a single world it is an abstraction from the totality of possible orders. The *being* of this order is not ontological, but cosmological. Such an abstracted, selected order cannot serve as fundament or ground. In the Taoist sensibility *all differences are cosmological differences*.

Taoism is based upon the affirmation rather than the negation of chaos. In the Anglo-European tradition, chaos is emptiness, separation, or confusion, and is to be overcome. In Taoism it is to be left alone to thrive in its spontaneity, for "the myriad things manage and order themselves."[8] Any attempt to make present a ground – the being of beings – is rejected. Chuang Tzu insists that "each thing comes into being from its own inner reflection and none can tell how it comes to be so."[9]

Taoism provides a model for thinking difference as strictly *cosmological* difference. Cosmological difference can be thought to the extent that we give up the distinction between cosmological and ontological realms. For it is the putatively ontological dimension that ultimately conceals the differences among cosmological entities by implicit appeal to the unity of being shared by all beings.

Reason and rationality presuppose the ontological philosophy of presence. But it is a simple-enough feat to demonstrate that rational ordering is an anthropocentric notion. For the various psychological and physiological uniformities defining the human species determine in advance the sorts of ordering that will be anticipated as defining the natural world. The sorts of beings we presume ourselves to be define the sorts of orders we may recognize and deem important. Alternative orders are recognized only from our anthropocentric perspective, since to know an order we must discern its pattern regularities, appreciate its realized uniformities, and establish plausible grounds for casual sequences among the elements serving to instantiate those uniformities.

The aesthetic ordering of the Taoist presupposes an alternative method of knowing. Such knowledge has as its subject matter insistently unique particulars which cannot be discussed in terms of pattern concepts defining regularities or uniformities. They can only be considered in terms of the cosmological differences grounded in the particularity of each item.

Confucius and the Language of Deference

One of the difficulties in communicating a vision of cosmological difference is that we lack a language which can adequately accommodate such aesthetic understandings. There is, of course, just such a language in philosophical Taoism and I could quite appropriately attempt to articulate it in the following paragraphs. Instead, I want to shift to the Confucian context to adumbrate the view of language and communication underlying the *Analects*. I shall do this in order to demonstrate that, however great the differences between Taoism and Confucianism *within* Chinese culture, judged from the perspective of Western thought they belong to essentially the same family. This is so because both Taoism and Confucianism presuppose the priority of cosmological difference over ontological presence – or, put another way, the priority of an aesthetic over a rational mode of understanding and discourse.

In the West two sorts of language have dominated the tradition. The first, the language of ontological presence, is that against which the postmodern thinkers are in full-scale revolt. Besides the language of presence, however, our tradition also allows the employment of language in a mystical or mythopoetic way. In this usage, language advertises the absence of the referent. This is the language of the mystical *via negativa* or the language of the poet who holds metaphor to be constitutive of discourse rather than merely parasitical upon a literal ground. We may call such expression the language of "absence."

A language of presence is grounded upon the possibility of univocal or unambiguous propositional expressions. This possibility requires criteria for determining the literalness of a proposition. For this to be so, literal language must have precedence over figurative or metaphorical language. This means that in addition to richly vague sorts of language associated with images and metaphors, there must be concepts as candidates for univocal meaning.

Since Aristotle's still-dominating discussion of metaphor, literal language has most often been privileged over figurative. And though to say this seems truistic and almost trivial, it is certainly *not* the case that such a preference was somehow built into the origins of language.

In the West, metaphors are usually deemed parasitical upon literal significances. Thus rhetoric, insofar as it employs the trope, metaphor, is rigidly tied to logic as ground. This serves to discipline intellectual and aesthetic activity, precluding untrammeled flights of the imagination.

If we are to have a language that evokes difference, however, we must find a new sort of metaphor. In place of metaphors which extend the literal sense of a term, we shall have to employ "allusive metaphors."[10] Allusive metaphors are distinct from the expressive variety since they are not tied to a literal or objective signification. They are free-floating hints and suggestions. They *allude*; they do not *express*. Their referents are other allusive metaphors, other things that hint or suggest. All language, at its fundamental level, may be nothing more than an undulating sea of suggestiveness.

Saussurean linguistics[11] and some semiologists influenced by Peirce and Saussure, as well as the poststructuralists who would expunge from language such "myths" as "authorial intent," "textual coherence," or "univocity," all employ something like allusive interpretations. Language as a system of differences, as a structure or context within which meaning is indefinitely deferred, is nothing more than an allusive system.

The Saussurean interpretation certainly may be said to apply to Chinese language and literature. The importance of context to meaning in Chinese language argues for the play of differences establishing meaning. Of course, in China almost all that may be said with respect to allusive metaphor may be said using the word "image."

In Anglo-European culture, the word "image" is used with distinctive connotations in literary criticism, psychology, and philosophy. The best understanding in this context is that an image is a sensory (that is, visual, auditory, tactile, olfactory) presentation of a perceptual, imaginative, or recollected experience. The form of the perception, memory, or imagination may be distinct from the mode of its presentation. For example, the olfactory or visual experience of a rose may be imaged in the words of a poet.

In such a case, the image is constituted by the word-picture as experienced by the celebrant of the poem and may or may not re-present the private experience of the poet. The most productive manner of insuring some resonance between the expressor of the image and the subsequent experiences of it is to reference them within a community of interpretation. Only communally experienced images are efficacious in promoting interpersonal and social relationships.

This suggests a real difference between Anglo-European and Chinese culture. In China, tradition, as a communal resource for meaning, more certainly disciplines the indefinite allusiveness of the language. In fact, it is tradition as the resource of meaning and value that serves to render plausible what seemed originally so paradoxical – namely, that Chinese culture has an appreciation of difference, which, historically, Western culture has never displayed.

Allusiveness requires vague[12] boundaries of self and world. The most desirable circumstance is one in which images, as richly vague complexes capable of a variety of evocations, are communally fixed and ritually protected as images. This is the aim of the classical Chinese, though it is obvious that Confucian orthodoxy was often guilty of providing a too narrowly fixed meaning for the relevant images. In any case, there is nothing behind the language in the form of a structure or logos to which appeal may be made to establish the presence of objective truth. Meanings derive from the allusive play of differences among the words and images of the language.

The images associated with the hexagrams of the *I Ching* are good examples of such communally fixed and ritualistically protected images. The images of the "creative" and the "receptive" associated with the first two hexagrams are housed in the communal memory and practices associated with the institutions, ritual practices, music, and literature which contextualize the book of oracles as a classic of Chinese culture. The concrete experiences of the individual consulting the *I Ching* resonate with the repository of significances in the larger communal context.

One of the signal consequences of a logocentric language is that there must be real independence of a proposition from the state of affairs it characterizes. This entails dualistic relations of propositions and states of affairs. Without such independence, in the senses of dualism and transcendence, nothing like logical truth may be formulated.

The presence of transcendent beings and principles in the formation of Western culture is uncontroversial. The dualism entailed by this transcendence, though often discomfiting to the theologically doctrinaire, is also a well-accepted characteristic of the rational interests of Anglo-European societies. Neither dualism nor transcendence is present in the original Confucian or Taoist sensibilities.

For a proposition to have a univocal sense, terms must be strictly delimitable. A polar sensibility precludes such delimitation in any but the grossest terms. Thus, the classical Chinese understanding of *yin* and *yang* as complementary concepts cannot coherently lead to dualistic translations or interpretations. *Yin* is becoming-*yang; yang* is becoming-*yin.* The locution "as different as night and day" would then have to mean "as different as night-becoming-day from day-becoming-night."

In a polar sensibility, terms are clustered with opposing or complementary alter-terms. Classical Chinese may be uncongenial to the development of univocal propositions for this reason. Without such propositions, semantic notions of truth are ultimately untenable. And without a capital "T" Truth lurking behind our acts of communication, notions such as "logocentrism" and "presence" cannot serve as standards for philosophical discourse.

The Confucian doctrine of the rectification of names well illustrates the way language is used concretely, evocatively, and allusively. This doctrine, central to Confucianism, is often outrageously misunderstood as a concern for univocity, for getting the definitions of terms straight and proper. Such an interpretation parodies the intent of Confucius' doctrine.

> Tzu-lu asked Confucius, "If the Lord of Wei were waiting for you to bring order to his state, to what would you give first priority?" Confucius replied, "without question, it would be to order names properly."[13]

The motive for the ordering of names is functional and pragmatic, rather than logical or strictly semantic. That is to say, the activity of matching name with role – calling a father a father when he is in fact a father – establishes coherence between roles already spelled out by ritual practices *(li)* and the actions of individuals – husbands, fathers, ministers, sons – whose ostensive identity as functionaries within the society may be in question.

It is quite interesting to see how closely related are the treatments of language in the sayings of Confucius and in the thought of a certain French thinker writing twenty-four hundred years later. I refer, of course, to Jacques Derrida. Derrida's well-rehearsed notion of *différance* tells the story.[14] The neologism *différance*, is meant to suggest that the differences investigated with respect to language have both an active and a passive dimension.

Meaning is always deferred. It cannot be present in language as *structure*, when that is the focus – for that omits the meanings associated with the use of the language. But focusing upon language as *event*, language as constituted by speech acts, does not solve the problem because, once more, the supplemental character of language – this time its structure – has been shifted to an inaccessible background.

To resonate most productively with Confucius, however, Derrida would have to accept an emendation to his notion of *différance* which would enrich the meaning of the deferring function. If one introduces the homonymic "defer," meaning "to yield," then the resultant notion of difference, as connoting both active and passive senses of differing and of deferring, well suits Confucius' rich use of language.

Confucius' language of difference is grounded in the sense of deference – a listening, a yielding to the

David Hall

appropriate models of the received traditions and to the behaviors of those who resonate with those models. In the *Great Preface* to the *Book of Songs*, traditionally attributed to Confucius, we read:[15]

> Poetry is the consequence of dispositions and is articulated in language as song. One's feelings stir within his breast and take the form of words. When words are inadequate, they are voiced as sighs. When sighs are inadequate, they are chanted. When chants are inadequate, unconsciously, the hands and feet begin to dance them. One's feelings are expressed in sounds, and when sounds are refined, they are called musical notes.

Confucius understands language after the analogy with music. Names are like notes. Harmony is a function of the particularity of names and notes and of their mutual resonances. Neither in Chinese music nor in Chinese language is there the stress upon syntax that one finds in the rationalistic languages of the West.

Confucian language is the bearer of tradition, and tradition, made available through ritualistic evocation, is the primary context of linguistic be-

havior. The sage appeals to present praxis and to the repository of significances realized in the traditional past in such a manner as to set up deferential relationships between himself, his communicants, and the authoritative texts invoked.

It is important to recognize that Confucius never tied the significances of language to the norms of present praxis. He insisted upon deferential access to the appropriate traditional models. If such models are not coopted by an authoritarian government or a rigid bureaucratic elite, as has been the case in the tawdrier periods of Chinese history, there is a rich and varied resource for the criticism of present praxis in spite of the fact that the language as a system lacks any transcendent reference.

The language of presence re-presents an otherwise absent object. The language of absence uses indirect discourse to advertise the existence of a nonpresentable subject. In either case there is a referent, real or putative, beyond the act of referencing. But the language of deference is based upon the recognition of mutual resonances among instances of communicative activity. There is no referencing beyond the act of communication as it resonates with the entertained meanings of the models from the tradition.

Author's Notes

1 Derrida's most sustained attempt at charting the "logocentric" bias of Western metaphysics is to be found in *Dissemination*, trans. by Barbara Johnson (Chicago: University of Chicago Press, 1981).
2 See my "Process and Anarchy – A Taoist Vision of Creativity," *Philosophy East & West*, 28, no. 3 (July 1978): 271–85. See also the chapter "The Way Beyond Ways," in my *The Uncertain Phoenix* (New York: Fordham University Press, 1982).
3 See D. C. Lau, trans., *The Tao Te Ching* (New York: Penguin Books, 1963), p. 57.
4 In his "Being in Western Philosophy Compared with *Shan/Fei* and *Yu/Wu* in Chinese Philosophy," in *Studies in Chinese Philosophy and Philosophical Literature* (Singapore: Institute of East Asian Philosophies, 1986), pp. 322–59, A. C. Graham has indicated that the sense of *wu* ("have not," "there is not") contrasts with locutions entailed by the ontological sense of "Nothing" in that "Nothing" entails the sense of "no entity" while *wu* indicates merely the absence of concrete things.

This point, which concerns the concrete mode of the contrast between "being" and "not-being" is, I believe, at least obliquely relevant to my argument that Taoism is strictly concerned with cosmological

differences and not at all with the contrast between the cosmological and ontological characters of things.
5 See Burton Watson, trans., *The Complete Works of Chuang Tzu* (New York: Columbia University Press, 1968), p. 56.
6 Ibid., p. 97.
7 *The World of Thought in Ancient China* (Cambridge, Massachusetts: Harvard University Press, 1985), p. 194.
8 See *Wang Pi's Commentary on the Lao tzu*, trans. by Arrienne Rump in collaboration with Wing-tsit Chan, Society of Asian and Comparative Philosophy monograph, no. 6 (Honolulu: University of Hawaii Press, 1979), p. 17.
9 See *Chuang Tzu*, chapter 8. The translation, admittedly a controversial rendering of an obscure segment of the text, is cited from Chang Chung-Yuan, *Creativity and Taoism* (New York: Harper & Row, 1963), p. 66.
10 See my *Eros and Irony* (Albany: SUNY Press, 1983), pp. 46–7, 180–2 and Roger T. Ames' and my *Thinking Through Confucius* (Albany: SUNY Press, 1987), pp. 192–8 for the characterization of "allusive metaphor" and "allusive analogy," respectively.

11 See Ferdinand Saussure's *A Course in General Linguistics* (London: Peter Owen, 1960).

12 The word "vague" is used in the systematic sense given it by Charles Peirce. The term means "open to rich and varied articulation." For a discussion of "vagueness" as a theoretical concept see Robert Neville's *Reconstruction of Thinking* (Albany: SUNY Press, 1981), pp. 39–42.

13 *Analects* 13/3; Roger T. Ames' translation.

14 See Derrida's *Writing and Difference*, trans. by Alan Bass (Chicago: University of Chicago Press, 1978), passim.

15 *Chih-ching*, Harvard–Yenching Institute Sinological Index Series, Supp. 9 (Peking: Harvard–Yenching Institute, 1934); Roger T. Ames' translation.

Resistances and Alternatives

50

"Meaning and Sense"

Emmanuel Levinas

Emmanuel Levinas (1905–95) is perhaps the most important European ethical philosopher of the later twentieth century. As a Lithuanian-born Jew, present in the Ukraine during the Russian Revolution, twenty years later a French citizen and German prisoner of war, whose family lost many in the Holocaust, he had ample personal exposure to the twentieth century's parade of horrors. Having been educated in the Husserlian and Heideggerian philosophies, Levinas came to criticize both pheonomenology and fundamental ontology as failing to recognize the absolute otherness that is implicit in the ethical relation to the other, and in the religious relation to the Divine Other, God. In "Meaning and Sense" (1964), Levinas argues that phenomenological accounts of meaning are inadequate to account for the ethical experience. While explicitly concerned with Husserl, Heidegger and Maurice Merleau-Ponty, his later opposition to structuralism and post-structuralism can be discerned here as well.

1 Meaning and Receptivity

The reality given to receptivity and the meaning it can take on seem distinguishable. For it seems as though experience first gave contents – forms, solidity, roughness, color, sound, savor, odor, heat, heaviness, etc. – and then all these contents were animated with meta-phors,[i] receiving an overloading through which they are borne *beyond* the given.

[i] In its Greek roots, literally "carried beyond."

This *meta*phor can be taken to be due to a deficiency of perception, or to its excellence, according as the *beyond* involved in a metaphor leads to other contents which were simply absent from the limited field of the perception, or is transcendent with respect to the whole order of contents or of the given.

This rectangular and solid opacity would become a book only inasmuch as it bears my thought toward other data still, or already, absent – toward the author that writes, the readers that read, the shelves that store, etc. All these terms are announced, without being given, in the rectangular and solid opacity that forces itself on my sight and hands. Those absent contents confer a meaning on the given. But this recourse to absence would indicate that perception failed in its mission, which is to render present, to represent. Perception, due to its finitude, would have failed in its vocation, and would have made up for this *lack* by signifying what it could not represent. The act of signifying would be poorer than the act of perceiving. By right reality should possess a signification from the first. Reality and intelligibility should coincide. The identity of things should bear the identity of their meaning. For God, capable of an unlimited perception, there would be no meaning distinct from the reality perceived; understanding would be equivalent to perceiving.

Intellectualism – whether it be rationalist or empiricist, idealist or realist – is bound up with this

Emmanuel Levinas, "Meaning and Sense" (trans. Alphonso Lingis) from *Collected Philosophical Papers*, pp. 75–107 (Amsterdam: Nijhoff, 1987).

conception. For Plato, for Hume, and even for contemporary logical positivists, meaning is reducible to contents given to consciousness. Intuition, in the straightforwardness of a consciousness that welcomes data, remains the source of all meaning, whether these data be ideas, relations or sensible qualities. The meanings conveyed by language have to be justified in a reflection on the consciousness that aims at them. Every metaphor that language makes possible has to be reduced to the data, which language is suspected of abusively going beyond. The figurative meaning has to be justified by the literal meaning supplied in intuition.

In *Epicurus' Garden* Anatole France reduces the proposition "The spirit listest where it will" to its elementary meaning. He deflates the inflated metaphors which, unnoticed by us, would be at play in this proposition. He moves from the false prestige of language to the atoms of experience. For him, they are the atoms of Democritus and Epicurus. He wishes to go back to the dreary downpour of the atoms that pass through space and strike our senses, and to the flash produced by their agglomeration.

What is simplistic in this empiricism can be easily compensated for, without losing the essential of this intuitivist or intellectualist conception of meaning. Husserl who, in one aspect of his work, marks the end of this notion of meaning, does continue intellectualism (these two directions in his thought make for one of the – perhaps fertile – ambiguities of his philosophy): he accounts for meanings by a return to the given. The categorial intuition, a notion with which he breaks with sensualist empiricism, in fact prolongs the intuitionist conception of meaning. Relations and essences are also given. Intuition remains the source of all intelligibility. Sense is given in the very straightforwardness that characterizes the relationship between noesis and noema.[ii] Is not Husserl's transcendental philosophy a sort of positivism which locates every meaning in the transcendental inventory it aims to draw up? The hyletic data[iii] and the "meaning ascriptions" are minutely inventoried as though one were dealing with a financial dossier. Even what remains unrealized is somehow given, given in a blank, in an open "signifying" intention, and is warrented like "unpaid bills" in the noema that corresponds to this noesis. Every absence has as

its *terminus a quo* and *terminus ad quem* the given.[iv] The expression of meanings serves only to fix or to communicate meanings justified in intuition. Expression plays no role in the constitution or in the understanding of these meanings.

But a metaphor – the reference to absence – can also be taken as an excellence that belongs to an order quite different from pure receptivity. The absence to which the metaphor leads would then not be another given, still to come or already past. The meaning would not be our consolation for a perception that was disappointed, but would first *make perception possible*. Pure receptivity, in the sense of a pure sensible without any meaning, would be only a myth or an abstraction. Sonorous contents "without any meaning" like vowels have a "latent birth" in meanings – this is the philosophical teaching already contained in Rimbaud's sonnet.[v] There is no given already possessing identity; no given could enter thought simply through a shock against the wall of receptivity. To be given to consciousness, to flicker for it, would require that the given first be placed in an illuminated horizon – like a word, which gets the gift of being understood from the context to which it refers. The meaning would be the very illumination of this horizon. But this horizon does not result from an addition of absent data, since each datum would already need a horizon so as to be able to be defined and given. This notion of horizon or *world*, conceived after the model of a context and ultimately after the model of a language and a culture – with everything that is historically adventitious and "already happened" involved – will be the locus in which meaning would then be located.

Already words are seen to not have isolable meanings, such as figure in dictionaries, and which one might reduce to some sort of contents or givens. They could not be congealed into a literal meaning. In fact there would be no literal meaning. Words do not refer to contents which they would designate, but first, laterally, to other words. Despite the mistrust he shows for written language (and even, in the seventh letter, for all language) Plato in the *Cratylus* teaches that even the names given to the gods – the proper names attached, conventionally, as signs, to individual beings – refer, through their etymology, to other words which are not proper names. In addition, language refers to the positions of the one that listens and the one that speaks, that is, to the contingency of their

---

[ii] Husserl's terms for the intentional act and object, respectively, once natural existence has been suspended.
[iii] *Hyle* is the "matter" of the noema.
[iv] Starting point and finishing point, respectively.

[v] The poem "Voyelles," in which Rimbaud attached colors to the vowels.

history. To try to inventory up all the contexts of language and of the positions in which interlocutors can find themselves would be a demented undertaking. Each word-meaning is at the confluence of innumerable sematic rivers.

Like language, experience too no longer appears to be made up of isolated elements, somehow lodged in a Euclidean space in which they could be exposed, each on its own, directly visible, and each signify by itself. They signify on the basis of the "world" and of the position of the one that looks at them. We will come back to the essential role that this position plays in language and in experience, and to the alleged contingency of position, in the theory we are now examining.

One would be wrong to take the meanings which custom attaches to words that serve to express our immediate and sensible experiences to be primary. Baudelaire's "correspondences" show that sensible data overflow, through their meanings, the elements in which we take them to be contained.[vi] Mikel Dufrenne, in his fine book *The Concept of the A Priori*, was able to show that, for example, the experience of spring and infancy remain authentic and autochtonous over and beyond the seasons and human ages. When another contemporary philosopher speaks of "dusk" or "dawn philosophies," the meaning of the adjectives used does not necessarily refer back to our meteorological experiences. It is indeed more probable that our experiences of morning and evening draw from the meaning that being as a whole has for us, a meaning which the jubilation of mornings and the mystery of twilight participate in. Then it would be more authentic to speak of a morning philosophy than of a morning briskness! But meanings are not limited to any special region of objects, are not the privilege of any content. For they arise precisely in the reference of one to another – and to anticipate already what we want to say – in the *assembling of the whole of Being* about him who speaks or perceives, and who also forms a part of the assembled Being. In a study of Homeric comparisons, M. Snell (as quoted by Karl Löwith) points out that when in the *Iliad* the resistance to an attack by an enemy phalanx is compared to the resistance of a rock to the waves that assail it, it is not necessarily a matter of extending to the rock, through anthropomorphism, a human behavior, but of interpreting

human resistance petromorphically. Resistance is neither a human privilege, nor a rock's, just as radiance does not characterize a day of the month of May more authentically than the face of a woman. The meaning precedes the data and illuminates them.

Here lies the essential justification and great force of Heidegger's etymologies, which, starting with the impoverished and flat meaning of a term apparently designating a content of external or psychological experience, lead toward a global situation in which a totality of experiences is assembled and illuminated. The given is presented from the first *qua* this or that, that is, as a meaning. Experience is a reading, the understanding of meaning an exegesis, a hermeneutics, and not an intuition. *This taken qua that* – meaning is not a modification that affects a content existing outside of all language. Everything remains in a language or in a world, for the structure of the world resembles the order of language, with possibilities no dictionary can arrest. In the *this qua that*, neither the *this* nor the *that* are first given outside of discourse. In the example we started with, this rectangular and solid opacity does not later take on the meaning of being a book, but is already signifying in its allegedly sensible elements. It contrasts with the light, with the daylight, refers to the sun that rose or the lamp that was lit, refers to my eyes also, as the solidity refers to my hand, not only as to organs which apprehend it *in* a subject, and would thereby be somehow opposed to the apprehended object, but also as to beings that are *alongside of* this opacity, *in the midst of* a world common to this opacity, this solidity, these eyes, this hand, and myself as a body. There never was a moment meaning came to birth out of a meaningless being, outside of a historical position where language is spoken. And that is doubtless what was meant when we were taught that language is the home of being.[vii]

Whence, in a movement radically opposed to that which amused Anatole France, the idea of the priority of the "figurative meaning," which would not result from the pure and simple presence of an object placed before thought. The objects would become meaningful on the basis of language, and not language on the basis of objects given to thought, objects which words functioning as simple signs would then designate.

[vi] "Correspondences" is a poem in Baudelaire's *Flowers of Evil*.

[vii] A reference to Heidegger's claim in *On the Way to Language*.

2 Meaning, Totality, and Cultural Gesture

Philosophers now accord language a founding role; it would mark the very notion of culture. Its essence consists in making being as a whole shine forth, beyond the *given*. The given would take on a meaning from this totality.

But the totality that illuminates would not be the total of an addition made by a God fixed in his eternity. The totalization of the totality is not to be taken to resemble a mathematical operation. It would be a creative and unforeseeable assembling or arranging, very like Bergsonian intuition in its newness and in what it owes to history.[viii] It is through this reference of the illuminating totality to the creative gesture of subjectivity that we can characterize what is original in the new notion of meaning, irreducible to the integration of contents intuitively given, irreducible also to the Hegelian totality which is constituted objectively. Meaning, as an illuminating totality necessary to perception itself, is a free and creative arrangement: the eye that sees is *essentially* in a body which is also hand and phonetic organ, a creative activity in gestures and language. The "position of the one that is looking" does not introduce a relativity into the allegedly absolute order of the totality that would be projected on an absolute retina. *Of itself* a look would be relative to a position. Sight would be *by essence* attached to a body, would belong to an eye. *By essence* and not only *in fact*. The eye would not be the more or less perfected instrument in which the ideal enterprise of vision, capturing, without shadows or deformations, the reflection of being would be realized empirically in the human species. Both the fact that the totality overflows the sensible given and the fact that vision is incarnated would belong to the essence of sight. Its original and ultimate function would not consist in reflecting being as in a mirror. The receptivity of vision should not be interpreted as an aptitude to receive impressions. A philosophy such as that of Merleau-Ponty, who guides the present analysis, was able to be astonished by the marvel of a sight essentially attached to an eye.[ix] In such a philosophy the body

would be conceived as inseparable from the creative activity, and transcendence as inseparable from the corporeal movement.

Let us go further into these notions, which are fundamental. The whole of being has to be produced in order to illuminate the given. It has to be produced before a being can be reflected in thought as an object. For nothing can be reflected in a thought before the footlights are turned on and a curtain raised on the side of being. The function of him who has to be there to "welcome the reflection" is at the mercy of this illumination. But this illumination is a process of assembling of being. Who will operate this assembling? It turns out that the subject who is there before being to "welcome the reflection" is also on the side of being, to operate the assembling. This ubiquity is incarnation itself, the marvel of the human body.

We can admire the reversal of the gnoseological schema affected here: the work of cognition now begins on the side of the object or from behind the object, in the backstage of being. A being must first be illuminated and take on a meaning by reference to this assembling, in order that a subject could welcome it. But it is the incarnate subject which, in assembling being, will raise the curtain. The spectator is an actor. Sight is not reducible to the welcoming of a spectacle; it at the same time operates in the midst of the spectacle it welcomes.

These operations to be sure in one way evoke the syntheses of the understanding which, for transcendental philosophy, make experience possible. And this comparison is the more legitimate in that Kant strictly distinguished the syntheses of the understanding from intuition, as though, in the domain that concerns us here, he was refusing to identify the understanding one can have of a meaning with a vision of any sort of given, be it of some superior or sublime rank. But the transcendental operations of the understanding do not correspond to the birth of meanings in the concrete horizons of perception. It is to these horizons that Merleau-Ponty has drawn attention.

The assembling of being which illuminates objects and makes them meaningful is not just an accumulation of objects. It amounts to the production of those non-natural beings of a new type which are cultural objects – paintings, poems, melodies – but also to the affects of any linguistic or manual gesture of the most ordinary activity, which are creative in their evocation of former cultural creations. These cultural "objects" assemble into

---

[viii] Henri Bergson (1859–1941), French philosopher.

[ix] Maurice Merleau-Ponty (1908–61), the premier French existential phenomenologist, most famous for *The Phenomenolgy of Perception* (1945), discussed "Eye and Mind" in his *The Primacy of Perception* (1964).

totalities the dispersion or accumulation of beings; they shine forth and illuminate, they express or illuminate an epoch, as we were indeed accustomed to say. To collect into a whole, that is, to express, that is, to make meaning possible is the function of the "object – the work or cultural gesture." And in this way there is set up a new function of *expression*, which hitherto was taken either to serve as a means of communication, or to transform the world in view of our needs. The newness of this function is also due to the original ontological plane in which it is situated. As means of communication or as a mark of our practical projects, expression wholly devolved from a thought antecedent to it; expression was taken to move from the inward to the exterior. In its new function, taken on the level of a cultural "object," expression is no longer guided by an antecedent thought. The subject ventures forth by effective speaking or manual gestures into the density of the preexistent language and cultural world (which is familiar to it, but not through cognition, is foreign to it, but not through ignorance). Qua incarnate, this word and this gesture belong to language and a cultural world already and from the start; otherwise they could not stir up and rearrange and reveal them to the "inner forum" of thought, which the venture of the cultural gesture had always already overflowed. The cultural action does not express a preexisting thought, but Being, to which, as incarnate, it belongs already. *Meaning cannot be inventoried in the inwardness of a thought.* Thought itself is inserted in culture through the verbal gesture of the body which precedes it and goes beyond it. The objective culture to which, through the verbal creation, it adds something new, illuminates and guides it.

It is then clear that the language through which meaning is produced in being is a language spoken by incarnate minds. The incarnation of thought is not an accident that would have occured to it and would have complicated its task by diverting the straightforward movement with which it aims at an object. The body is the fact that thought is immersed in the world that it thinks and, consequently, expresses this world while it thinks it. The corporeal gesture is not a nervous discharge, but a celebration of the world, a poetry. The body is a feeling felt; that is, according to Merleau-Ponty, what is so wondrous about it. Qua felt, it is still on this side, on the side of the subject, but qua feeling it is already on the other side, on the side of the objects;

a thought that is no longer paralytic, it is a movement that is no longer blind, but creative of cultural objects. It unites the subjectivity of perceiving (an intentionality aiming at an object) and the objectivity of expressing (an operation in the perceived world which creates cultural beings – language, poems, paintings, symphonies, dances – illuminating horizons). The cultural creation is not added on to receptivity, but is its other side from the start. We are not the subject of the world and a part of the world from two different points of view; in expression we are subject and part at once. To perceive is both to receive and to express, by a sort of prolepsis. We know through gestures how to imitate the visible and to coincide *kinesthetically* with the gesture *seen*: in perception *our* body is also the "delegate" of *being*.

It is visible that throughout this conception expression defines culture; culture is art, and art or the celebration of being constitutes the original essence of incarnation. Language qua expression is, above all, the creative language of poetry. Art is then not a blissful wandering of man who sets out to make something beautiful. Culture and artistic creation are part of the ontological order itself. They are ontological par excellence: they make the understanding of being possible. It is then not by chance that the exaltation of culture and cultures, the exaltation of the artistic aspect of culture, guides contemporary spiritual life; that, over and beyond the specialized labor of scientific research, the museums and the theaters, as in former times the temples, make communion with being possible, and that poetry passes for prayer. The artistic expression would assemble being into a meaning and thus provide the original light that scientific cognition itself would borrow from. Artistic expression would thus be an essential event that would be produced in being by artists and philosophers. It is then not surprising that Merleau-Ponty's thought seemed to evolve toward that of Heidegger. Cultural meaning is taken to occupy an exceptional place between the objective and the subjective – the cultural activity disclosing being; the one that works this disclosure, the subject, invested by being as its servant and guardian. Here we rejoin the schemas of the last writings of Heidegger, but also the idée fixe of the whole of contemporary thought – the overcoming of the subject–object structures. But perhaps at the source of all these philosophies, we find the Hegelian vision of a subjectivity that comprehends itself as an inevitable moment of the becoming by which being leaves its darkness, the vision of a subject aroused by the logic of being.

The symbolism of the meaning bound to language – and to the culture assimilated to language – can then nowise be taken to be a defective intuition, a makeshift of an experience separated from the plenitude of being, which would therefore be reduced to signs. A symbol is not the abridgement of a real presence that would preexist it; it would give more than any receptivity for the world could ever receive. The signified would surpass the given not because it would surpass our ways to capture it – and we without any intellectual intuition – but because the signified is of another order than the given, even though it be taken as the prey of a divine intuition. To *receive the given* would no longer be the original way to relate to being.

3 The Antiplatonism of the Contemporary Philosophy of Meaning

The totality of being in which being shines forth as meaning is not an entity fixed for eternity, but requires the arranging and assembling, the cultural act of man. Being as a whole – meaning – shines forth in the works of poets and artists. But it shines forth in diverse ways in the diverse artists of the same cultures, and is diversely expressed in the diverse cultures. This diversity of expression is not, for Merleau-Ponty, a betrayal of being, but is responsible for the glitter of the inexhaustible richness of its event. Each cultural work traverses the whole of being, yet leaves it intact. And in Heidegger being is revealed out of the hiddenness and mystery of the unsaid which the poets and philosophers bring to speech, without ever saying everything. All the expressions which Being received and receives in history would be true, for truth would be inseparable from its historical expression, and, without its expression, thought does not think anything. Whether it be of Hegelian, Bergsonian, or phenomenological origin, the contemporary philosophy of meaning is thus opposed to Plato at an essential point: the intelligible is not conceivable outside of the becoming which suggests it. There does not exist any *meaning in itself* which a thought would have been able to reach by jumping over the deforming or faithful, but sensory, reflections which lead to it. One has to traverse history or relive duration or start from concrete

perception and the language established in it, in order to arrive at the intelligible.[x] All the picturesqueness of history, all cultures, are no longer obstacles separating us from the essential and the intelligible, but ways that give us access to it. Even more! They are the only ways, the only possible ones, irreplaceable, and consequently implicated in the intelligible itself.

In the light of contemporary philosophy, and by contrast with it, we understand better what the separateness of the intelligible world means in Plato, over and beyond the mythical sense ascribed to the realism of the Ideas: for Plato the world of meanings precedes language and culture, which express it; it is indifferent to the system of signs that one can invent to make this world present to thought. It thus dominates the historical cultures. For Plato there exists a privileged culture which approaches it and which is capable of understanding the provisional and as it were infantile character of historical cultures; there exists a culture that would consist in depreciating the purely historical cultures, and in as it were colonizing the world, beginning with the land in which this revolutionary culture arose – this philosophy which goes beyond cultures. There exists a culture that would consist in redoing the world in function of the intemporal order of the Ideas, as the Platonic Republic which sweeps away the allusions in the alluvium of history, that Republic from which the poets of the μίμησις are driven.[xi] For the language of these poets does not function to lead toward meanings preexisting their expression and eternal; it is not a pure narration of these ideas – ἁπλῆ διήγησις ἄνευ μιμήσεως (*Republic*, 394b).[xii] It seeks to imitate the direct discourses of innumerable cultures and of the innumerable manifestations in which each unfolds. These poets thus allow themselves to be drawn into the becoming of the particularities, peculiarities and oddities, from which the expressed thoughts would not be separable for the poets of the μίμησις (as for many moderns), and of which one cannot draw up a simple account. The loss or forgetting or abolition of these particularities – these idiocies – would make humanity lose inappreciable treasures of meanings, irrecuperable without the taking up of

---

[x] These three options are characteristic of Hegel, Bergson, and Merleau-Ponty, respectively.
[xi] *Mimesis* (imitation).
[xii] Pure accounting (or narration), without imitation.

all these cultural forms, that is, without imitating them.

For contemporary philosophy, meaning is not only correlative with thought, and thought is not only correlative with a language that would make of meaning a ἀπλῆ διήγησις.[xiii] To this intellectualist structure of *correlation* between intellect and intelligible, which maintains the separation of the planes – is superposed a *nearness* and a *side-by-sidedness*, a *belongingness* which unites the intellect and the intelligible on the one plane of the world, forming that "fundamental historicity" which Merleau-Ponty speaks of. The love of truth which in Plato would place pure thought in front of meaning is thus shown to be an incestuous trouble, because of this consanguinity of the intellect and the intelligible, embroiled in the network of language, born in the expression from which thought is not separable. The antiplatonism of contemporary philosophy consists in this subordination of the intellect to expression: the face-to-face position of soul and idea is interpreted as a limit abstraction of a coming into contact in a common world; the intellect aiming at the intelligible would itself rest on the being which this aim only claims to illuminate. No philosophical movement better than contemporary phenomenology has brought out the transcendental function of the whole concrete density of our corporeal, technical, social and political existence, but it has also thereby brought out the interference of the transcendental relationship and the physical, technical, and cultural relations which constitute the world in the "fundamental historicity" – in this new form of the *mixed*.

We alluded above to the kinship between Bergson and phenomenology. Bergson's antiplatonism does not only lie in his general revalorization of becoming; it is like the phenomenological antiplatonism in that it is also found in Bergson's conception of understanding. When Bergson refuses to separate the choice which the free being would have to make from the whole past of this being, when he refuses to admit that a problem which requires a decision could be formulated in abstract and intellectual terms about which just any rational being would be competent to adjudge, he situates the intelligible in the prolongation of the whole concrete existence of the individual. The meaning of the decision to be taken can be intelligible only for him who would have lived through the whole past which leads to this decision. The meaning

cannot be understood directly in a fulguration which illuminates and dissipates the night in which it arises and which it leads to its denouement. The whole density of history is necessary for it.

For phenomenologists as for Bergsonians, a meaning cannot be separated from the access leading to it. *The access is part of the meaning itself.* The scaffolding is never taken down; the ladder is never pulled up. Whereas the Platonic soul, liberated from the concrete conditions of its corporeal and historical existence, can reach the heights of the empyrean to contemplate the Ideas, whereas a slave, provided that he "understands Greek" which enables him to enter into relationship with the master, reaches the same truths as the master, our contemporaries require that God himself, if he wishes to be a physicist, have spent his time in the laboratory, go through the weighings and measurings, the sensible perception and even the infinite series of aspects in which a perceived object is revealed.

The most recent, boldest and most influential ethnography maintains the multiple cultures on the same plane. The political work of decolonization is thus attached to an ontology – to a thought of being, interpreted in its multiple and multivocal cultural meaning. And this multivocity of meaning of being – this essential disorientation – is perhaps the modern expression of atheism.

4 The "Economic" Meaning

In fact to the multiplicity of meanings which come to reality from culture and cultures is opposed the fixed, privileged meaning which the world acquires in function of man's needs. Needs raise the simply given things to the rank of values. Admirably straightforward and impatient in their aim, needs give themselves the multiple possibilities of meaning only so as to choose the unique way of satisfaction. Man thus confers a unique meaning to being, not by celebrating it, but by working it. In technical and scientific culture, the equivocation in being, as the equivocation in meaning, would be overcome. Then, instead of being content with the play of cultural meanings, one would, out of a concern for truth, have to extract the words from the metaphors by creating a scientific or algorithmic terminology, insert the real, scintillating with a thousand lights for perception, into the perspective of human needs and the action which the real effects or undergoes. One would have to reduce perception to the science which the possible transformation of the world

---

[xiii] Pure accounting or narration (*diaresis*).

justifies, man to the complexes exhibited by psychoanalysis, society to its economic structures. Everywhere one would have to find the sense beneath the meaning, beneath the metaphor, the sublimation, the literature. There would then be "serious," real meanings, put in scientific terms, oriented by needs and, in general, by economy. Economy alone would be really oriented and signifying. It alone would know the secret of a proper meaning prior to the figurative meaning. The cultural meaning, detached from this economic – technological and scientific – sense would have but the value of a symptom, the worth of an ornament suited to the needs of a game, an abusive and deceptive meaning, exterior to truth. No doubt is possible about the profoundly rationalist aspiration of this materialism, its fidelity to the unity of sense which the multiplicity of cultural meanings would itself presuppose.

Yet the great merit of Bergson and of phenomenology will have been to have shown the metaphorical character of this identification of reality with *Wirklichkeit*.[xiv] The technical designation of the universe is itself a modality of culture: the reduction of the real to an "object in general," the interpretation of being as though it were destined for the laboratory and the factory. The scientific and technical vision which is imposed on needs modifies them, levels them and creates them more than is aroused by their original straightforwardness and univocity. For in fact no human need exists in the univocal state of an animal need. Every human need is from the first already interpreted culturally. Only need taken at the level of underdeveloped humanity can give this false impression of univocity. Moreover, it is not certain that the scientific and technical signification of the world could "dissolve" the multiplicity of cultural meanings. We might in fact doubt that when we observe the threats that national particularisms represent for the unity of the new international society put under the sign of modern scientific and industrial development, and of the regrouping of humanity around the univocal imperatives of materialism. It is as though these particularisms themselves corresponded to needs. And this to be sure takes from them the character of being simple superstructures. Finally, the forms in which this search for the unique sense of being on the basis of needs is manifested are acts aiming at the realization of a society. They are borne by a spirit of sacrifice and altruism, which no longer

proceeds from these needs (unless we play on the word "need"). The needs which allegedly orient being receive their sense from an intuition which no longer proceeds from these needs. This was already the capital teaching of Plato's *Republic*: the State which is founded on the needs of men can neither subsist nor even arise without the philosophers who have mastered their needs and contemplate the Ideas and the Good.

5 The Unique Sense

The impossibility of seating the univocal meaning of being on materialism (although the search for that univocal meaning is greatly to the honor of materialism) does not itself compromise this ideal of unity, which constitutes the force of truth and the hope for an understanding among men. The cultural and aesthetic notion of meaning could not draw it from itself, nor do without it.

We are indeed told that cultural meanings do not betray being by their pluralism, but only through it rise to the measure and *essence* of being, that is, to its *way* of being. Being *is* not in such a way as to congeal into a Parmenidean sphere, identical to itself, nor into a completed and fixed creation.[xv] The totality of being envisioned from cultures could nowise be a panoramic view. There could not be a totality in being, but only totalities. There is nothing that could encompass all of them. They would not be open to any judgment that would claim to be the final judgment. We are told: being *is* historically; it requires men and their cultural becoming in order to assemble. We are told: the unity of being at any moment would only consist in the fact that men understand one another, in the penetrability of cultures by one another. This penetrability could not come about through the mediation of a common tongue that would, independently of the cultures, convey the proper and ideal articulations of the meanings, and thus in fact make these particular tongues useless. In this whole conception, the penetration takes place – according to Merleau-Ponty's expression – laterally. For there does exist the possibility of a

---

xiv   Actuality.

xv   Parmenides of Elea (born 515 BC), important pre-Socratic philosopher, held that all that can be said to be true in the strict sense is that Being is one and unchanging. All reference to change or difference, hence non-being, generates contradiction.

Frenchman learning Chinese and passing from one culture into another, without the intermediary of an esperanto that would falsify both tongues which it mediated. Yet what has not been taken into consideration in this case is that an *orientation* which leads the Frenchman to take up learning Chinese instead of declaring it to be barbarian (that is, bereft of the real virtues of language), to prefer speech to war, is needed. One reasons as though the equivalence of cultures, the discovery of their profusion and the recognition of their richess were not themselves the effects of an orientation and of an unequivocal sense in which humanity stands. One reasons as though the multiplicity of cultures from the beginning sunk its roots in the era of decolonization, as though incomprehension, war, and conquest did not derive just as naturally from the contiguity of multiple expressions of being – the numerous assemblages or arrangements which it takes on in the diverse civilizations. One reasons as though peaceful coexistence did not presuppose that in being there is delineated an orientation which gives it a unique sense. Must we not then distinguish the meanings, in their cultural pluralism, from the sense, orientation and unity of being – a primordial event in which all the other steps of thought and the whole historical life of being is situated? Do the cultural meanings arise as random wholes in the dispersion of the given? Do they not take on meaning in a dialogue maintained with that which signifies *of itself* – with the other? These original meanings would command the assemblings of being; it would not be these random assemblings that would already, and outside of all dialogue, constitute meanings. Do not meanings require a unique sense from which they derive their very signifyingness?

The world, as soon as one moves on from the humble daily tasks, and language, as soon as one moves on from commonplace talk, have lost the *univocity* which had authorized us to ask of them the criteria of the meaningful. Absurdity consists not in non-sense, but in the isolation of innumerable meanings, in the absence of a sense that orients them. What is lacking is the sense of the meanings, the Rome to which all the roads lead, the symphony in which all the meanings can sing, the canticle of canticles. The absurdity lies in multiplicity in pure indifference. The cultural meanings put forth as the ultimate are the break-up of a unity. It is not simply a matter of fixing the conditions in which the facts of our experience or the signs of our language arouse in us the feeling of understanding,

or appear to proceed from a rational intention, or convey a structured order. It is, over and beyond these logical and psychological problems, a question of the true meaning.

This loss of unity has been proclaimed – and consecrated through a contrary movement – by the celebrated paradox, become a commonplace, of the death of God. The crisis of sense is thus experienced by our contemporaries as a crisis of monotheism. There was a time when a god intervened in human history by force, sovereign to be sure, invisible to the eye without being provable by reason – supernatural, consequently, or transcendental; but his intervention occurred in a system of reciprocities and exchanges. The system was sketched out starting with a man preoccupied with himself. The god transcending the world remained united to the world through the unity of an economy. His effects would end up among the effects of all the other forces, get shuffled in with them and form *miracles*. God was a god of miracles, even in an age when no one expects miracles any more, a force in the world, magical despite all his morality, for morality was inverted into magic, acquired magical virtues; such was a god to whom one presents oneself as a beggar. The status of his transcendence, despite the immanence of his revelation – a transcendence new with respect to the unbridgeable transcendence of the Aristotelian god – the status of this transcendence of the supernatural was never set forth.[xvi] The interventions of the supernatural god could to a certain extent be allowed for or even inflected, like the effects of other wills and other forces which preside over events. When history gives lie to this economy, this did not refute the supernatural providence any more than the deviations of the stars refuted the Ptolemaic astronomy. It even confirms it, at the cost of some new theological epicycles.

This religion which the person required for himself, rather than feeling himself required by this religion, and this god entered into the circuit of economy (a religion and a god, however, which did not exhaust the message of the Scriptures) have lost much of their influence over men. And with them the sense of a world perfectly and very simply ordained to this god is also lost. We do not think that the meaningful could do without God,, nor that the idea of being or of the being of entities

---

[xvi]   Aristotle conceived God as an "unmoved mover," the unchanging end or *telos* that motivates the motions of entities.

could be substituted for him, so as to bring meanings to the unity of sense without which there is no sense.

But we cannot describe sense starting with this still economic idea of God; it is the analysis of sense that must give out the notion of God which sense harbors. Sense is impossible on the basis of an ego which exists, as Heidegger puts it, in such a way that "he is in his very existence in question as to his existence."

6 Sense and Work

The reflection on cultural meaning leads to a pluralism which lacks a one-way sense. For a moment economy and technology seemed to delineate such a sense. But if cultural meanings can be interpreted as superstructures of economy, economy in turn derives its forms from culture. The ambivalence of meanings bears witness to a disorientation. Let us note first that this ambiguity seems to respond to a certain philosophical mind which is satisfied with a non-polarized ether. Does not sense as orientation indicate a leap, an outside-of-oneself toward the *other than oneself*, whereas philosophy means to reabsorb every Other into the Same and neutralize alterity? A distrust of every unconsidered move, a lucidity of old age which absorbs the imprudences of youth, action in advance recuperated in the knowledge which guides it – this is perhaps the very definition of philosophy.

Even if life precedes philosophy, even if contemporary philosophy, which means to be anti-intellectualist, insists on this priority of existence with respect to essence, of life with respect to intellect, even if, in Heidegger, "gratitude" to being and "obedience" are substituted for contemplation, contemporary philosophy is complacent in the multiplicity of cultural meanings – and in the infinite play of art, being is relieved of its alterity. Philosophy is produced as a form in which the refusal of engagement in the other, the waiting preferred to action, indifference with regard to others, the universal allergy of the early infancy of philosophers is manifest. Philosophy's itinerary remains that of Ulysses, whose adventure in the world was only a return to his native island – a complacency in the Same, an unrecognition of the other.

But must we renounce knowing and meanings in order to find sense? Must there be a blind orientation in order that cultural meanings take on a one-way sense, and in order that being find again a unity of meaning? Does not a blind orientation represent the instinctual rather than human order, in which the person betrays his vocation of being a person in getting absorbed in the law which situates and orients him? Is it not then possible to conceive of an orientation, a sense, in being which would unite univocity and freedom? This at any rate is the goal of the analysis which we have undertaken.

First we must fix with precision the conditions for such an orientation. It can be posited only as a movement going outside of the identical, toward an other which is absolutely other. It begins in an identical, a same, an ego; it is not a "sense of history" which dominates the ego, for the irresistible orientation of history makes meaningless the very fact of the movement, since the Other would be already inscribed in the Same, the end in the beginning. An orientation which goes *freely* from the Same to the Other is a work.

But then a work must be conceived not as an apparent agitation of a stock which afterwards remains identical to itself, like an energy which in all its transformations remains equal to itself. Nor must it be conceived as a technology which through the celebrated negativity reduces a foreign world into a world whose alterity is converted into my idea. Both conceptions continue to affirm being as self-identical and reduce its fundamental event to thought, which is – and this is the indelible lesson of idealism – thought of itself, thought of thought. An attitude, initially an attitude taken up toward the other, becomes, in Eric Weil's terminology,[xvii] a totality or a category. *A work conceived radically is a movement of the Same towards the Other which never returns to the Same.* A work thought through all the way requires a radical generosity of the movement which in the Same goes toward the Other. It consequently requires an *ingratitude* of the other; gratitude would be the *return* of the movement to its origin.

But a work differs from a game where there is pure expenditure. It is not undertaken in pure loss. It is more serious than an identity surrounded with nothingness. A work is neither a pure acquisition of merits nor a pure nihilism. For, like the seeker after merits, the nihilist agent immediately takes himself as his term and his goal, beneath the apparent gratuity of his action. A work is then a relationship with the other, who is reached without showing itself touched. It takes form outside of the morose

xvii   French philosopher Eric Weil (1904–77).

savoring of failures and consolations, which for Nietzsche defines religion.

But a departure with no return, which, however, does not go forth into the void, would also lose its absolute *orientation* if it sought recompense in the immediacy of its triumph, if it awaited the triumph of its cause impatiently. The one-way movement would be reversed and become a reciprocity. Confronting its beginning and its end, the agent would reabsorb the work in calculations of deficits and compensations, in book keeping operations. It would be subordinated to thought. As an orientation toward the other, as sense, a work is possible only in patience, which, pushed to the limit, means for the agent to renounce being the contemporary of its outcome, to act without entering into the Promised Land.

The future for which such an action acts must from the first be posited as indifferent to my death. A work which is different from play and from computations, is being-for-beyond-my-death.[xviii] Patience does not consist in the agent betraying his generosity by giving himself the time of a personal immortality. To renounce being the contemporary of the triumph of one's work is to envisage this triumph in a *time without me*, to aim at this world below without me, to aim at a time beyond the horizon of my time, in an eschatology without hope for oneself, or in a liberation from my time.

To be *for* a time that would be without me, *for* a time after my time, over and beyond the celebrated "being for death," is not an ordinary thought which is extrapolating from my own duration; it is the passage to the time of the other. Should what makes such a passage possible be called *eternity*? In any case the possibility of sacrifice which goes to the limit of this passage discovers the non-inoffensive nature of this extrapolation: to be for death in order to be for that which is after me.

A work as an absolute orientation of the Same unto the Other is then like a radical youth of the generous impulse. We could fix its concept with a Greek term "liturgy," which in its primary meaning designates the exercise of a function which is not only totally gratuitous, but requires on the part of him who exercises it a putting out of funds at a loss. For the moment all meaning drawn from any positive religion has to be removed from

this term, even if in a certain way the idea of God should show its trace at the end of our analysis. On the other hand, a work without remuneration, whose result is not allowed for in the time of the agent, and is assured only for patience, a work that is effected in the complete domination of and surpassing of my time, liturgy is not to be ranked alongside of "works" and ethics. It is ethics itself.

The relationship which we have apparently just constructed, is not simply constructed. The total gratuity of action – a gratuity different from play – moves our age even if the individuals may be not up to its height – and indicates the free character of the orientation. Our age is not defined by the triumph of technology for the sake of technology, as it is not defined by art for the sake of art, and as it is not defined by nihilism. It is an action for a world to come, a going beyond one's epoch – a going beyond oneself which requires the epiphany of the other – such is the fundamental thesis which underlies these pages. In the Bourassol prison and the Pourtalet Fort Léon Blum was, in December, 1941, finishing a book.[xix] He wrote: "We are working in the present, not for the present. How many times in meetings with the people have I repeated and commented on Nietzsche's words: Let the future and the things most remote be the rule of all the present days!" The philosophy with which Léon Blum justifies this strange force of working, without working for the present, is not here the essential; the force of his confidence is incommensurate with the force of his philosophy. 1941! – a hole in history – a year in which all the visible gods had abandoned us, in which god was really dead or gone back into his non-revealedness. A man in prison continues to believe in a nonrevealed future and invites men to work in the present for the most remote things, for which the present is an irrecusable negation. There is a vulgarity and a baseness in an action that is conceived only for the immediate, that is, in the last analysis, for our life. And there is a very great nobility in the energy liberated from the hold of the present. To act for far-off things at the moment in which Hitlerism triumphed, in the deaf hours of this night without hours – independently of every evaluation of the "forces in presence" – is, no doubt, the summit of nobility.

[xviii] Rather than Heidegger's notion of *Dasein* as "Being-toward-Death."

[xix] Léon Blum (1872–1950), Jewish French socialist, resistant to communism, sent to Buchenwald by the Vichy regime.

7 Sense and Ethics

Sense as the liturgical orientation of a work does not arise from need. Needs opens upon a world that is *for me*; it returns to itself. Even a sublime need, such as the need for salvation, is still a nostalgia, a longing to go back. A need is return itself, the anxiety of the I for itself, egoism, the original form of identification. It is the assimilating of the world in view of self-coincidence, in view of happiness.

In the "Canticle of the Columns" Valéry speaks of a "faultless desire."[xx] He is doubtless referring to Plato who, in his analysis of pure pleasures, discovered an aspiration that is conditioned by no prior lack. We are taking up this term desire; to a subject turned to itself, which, according to the Stoic formula is characterized by $o'\varrho\mu\acute{\eta}$[xxi] the tendency to persist in its being, or for which, according to Heidegger's formula, "there is in its existence question as to this very existence," a subject thus defined by care for itself, which in happiness realizes its *for itself*, we are opposing the desire for the other which proceeds from a being already gratified and in this sense independent, which does not desire for itself. It is the need of him who no longer has needs. It is recognizable in the need for an other who is another who is neither my enemy (as he is in Hobbes and Hegel) nor my "complement," as he still is in Plato's Republic, which is set up because something is lacking in the subsistence of each individual. The desire for the other, sociality, is born in a being that lacks nothing, or, more exactly, it is born over and beyond all that can be lacking or that can satisfy him. In desire the I is borne toward the other in such a way as to compromise the sovereign self-identification of the I, for which need is but nostalgia, and which the consciousness of need anticipates. The movement toward the other, instead of completing me and contenting me, implicates me in a conjuncture which in a way did not concern me and should leave me indifferent – what was I looking for here? Whence came this shock when I passed, indifferent, under another's gaze? The relationship with the other puts me into question, empties me of myself and empties me without end, showing me ever new resources. I did not know I was so rich, but I no longer have the right to keep anything for myself. Is the desire for the other an appetite or a generosity? The desirable does not gratify my desire but hollows it out, and as it were nourishes me with new hungers. Desire is revealed to be goodness. There is a scene in Dostoievski's *Crime and Punishment* where Sonya Marmaladova looks upon Raskolnikof in his despair, and Dostoievski speaks of "insatiable compassion." He does not say "inexhaustible compassion." It is as though the compassion that goes from Sonya to Raskolnikof were a hunger which the presence of Raskolnikof nourishes beyond any saturation, increasing this hunger to infinity.

The desire for the other, which we live in the most ordinary social experience, is the fundamental movement, a pure transport, an absolute orientation, sense. In all its analyses of language contemporary philosophy insists, and indeed rightly, on its hermeneutical structure and on the cultural effort of the incarnate being that expresses itself. Has a third dimension not been forgotten: the direction toward the other who is not only the collaborator and the neighbor of our cultural work of expression or the client of our artistic production, but the interlocutor – he to whom expression expresses, for whom celebration celebrates, both term of an orientation and primary signification? In other words, expression, before being a celebration of being, is a relationship with him to whom I express the expression, and whose presence is already required for my cultural gesture of expression to be produced. The other who faces me is not included in the totality of being expressed. He arises behind every assembling of being as he to whom I express what I express. I find myself again facing another. He is neither a cultural signification nor a simple given. He is *sense* primordially, for he gives sense to expression itself, for it is only by him that a phenomenon as a meaning is, of itself, introduced into being.

The analysis of desire, which it was important for us to first distinguish from need, and which delineates a sense in being, will be made clearer by the analysis of the alterity toward which desire is borne.

The manifestation of the other is, to be sure, produced from the first conformably with the way every meaning is produced. Another is present in a cultural whole and is illuminated by this whole, as a text by its context. The manifestation of the whole ensures his presence; it is illuminated by the light of the world. The understanding of the other is thus a hermeneutics and an exegesis. The other is given in the concreteness of the totality in which he is immanent, and which, according to Merleau-Ponty's remarkable analyses, which we have drawn upon freely in the first section of this essay, is expressed and disclosed by our own cultural initiative, by corporeal, linguistic or artistic gestures.

But the epiphany of the other involves a signifyingness of its own independent of this meaning received from the world. The other comes to us not only out of the context, but also without mediation; he signifies by himself. The cultural meaning which is revealed – and reveals – as it were *horizontally*, which is revealed from the historical world to which it belongs, and which, according to the phenomenological expression, reveals the horizons of this world – this mundane meaning is disturbed and jostled by another presence that is abstract (or, more exactly, absolute) and not integrated into the world. This presence consists in coming toward us, in *making an entry*. This can be put in this way: the *phenomenon* which the apparition of the other is is also a *face* – or, again (to indicate the entry, at every moment new, into the immanence and essential historicity of the phenomenon): the epiphany of a face is a *visitation*. Whereas a phenomenon is already, in whatever respect, an image, a captive manifestation of its plastic and mute form, the epiphany of a face is alive. Its life consists in undoing the form in which every *entity*, when it enters into immanence, that is, when it is exposed as a theme, is already dissimulated.

The other who manifests himself in a face as it were breaks through his own plastic essence, like a being who opens the window on which its own visage was already taking form. His presence consists in *divesting* himself of the form which does already manifest him. His manifestation is a surplus over the inevitable paralysis of manifestation. This is what the formula "the face speaks" expresses. The manifestation of a face is the first discourse. Speaking is before anything else this way of coming from behind one's appearance, behind one's form, an openness in the openness.

The visitation of a face is thus not the disclosure of a world. In the concreteness of the world a face is abstract or naked. It is denuded of its own image. Through the nudity of a face nudity in itself is first possible in the world.

The nudity of a face is a bareness without any cultural ornament, an absolution, a detachment from its form in the midst of the production of its form. A face *enters* into our world from an abso-

lutely foreign sphere, that is, precisely from an absolute, that which in fact is the very name for ultimate strangeness. The signifyingness of a face in its abstractness is in the literal sense of the term extraordinary, outside of every order, every world. How is such a production possible? How can the coming of the other, the visitation of a face, the absolute not be – in any way – converted into a revelation, not even a symbolism or a suggestion? How is a face not simply a *true representation* in which the other renounces his alterity? To answer, we will have to study the exceptional signifyingness of a trace and the personal "order" in which such a signifyingness is possible.

Let us for the moment attend to the sense which the abstractness or nudity of a face which breaks into this order of the world involves, and the overwhelming of consciousness which corresponds to this "abstractness". Stripped of its very form, a face is paralyzed in its nudity. It is a distress. The nudity of a face is a denuding, and already a supplication in the straightforwardness that aims at me. But this supplication is an exigency; in it humility is joined with height. The ethical dimension of visitation is thereby indicated. A true *representation* remains a possibility of appearance; the world which strikes against thought can do nothing against free thought – which is able to refuse inwardly, to take refuge in itself, to remain precisely a *free thought* before the true, to return to itself, to reflect on itself and take itself to be the origin of what it receives, to master what precedes it through memory. While free thought thus *remains the Same*, a face imposes itself upon me without my being able to be deaf to its call or to forget it, that is, without my being able to stop holding myself responsible for its distress. Consciousness loses its first place.

The presence of a face thus signifies an irrecusable order, a command, which puts a stop to the availability of consciousness. Consciousness is called into question by a face. Being called into question is not the same as becoming aware of this being called into question. The "absolutely other" is not reflected in consciousness. It resists it to the extent that even its resistance is not convertible into a content of consciousness. Visitation consists in overwhelming the very egoism of the I which supports this conversion. A face confounds the intentionality that aims at it.

What is at stake here is the calling of consciousness into question, and not a consciousness of a calling into question. The I loses its sovereign self-coincidence, its identification, in which consciousness returns triumphantly to itself to rest on itself. Before the exigency of the other the I is expelled from this rest, and is not the already glorious consciousness of this exile. Any complacency would destroy the straightforwardness of the ethical movement.

But the calling into question of this wild and naive freedom for itself, sure of its refuge in itself, is not reducible to a negative movement. The calling into question of oneself is in fact the welcome of the absolutely other. The epiphany of the absolutely other is a face, in which the other calls on me and signifies an order to me through his nudity, his denuding. His presence is a summons to answer. The I does not only become aware of this necessity to answer, as though it were an obligation or a duty about which it would have to come to a decision; it is in its very position wholly a responsibility or a diacony, as it is put in Isaiah, chapter 53.

To be an I means then not to be able to escape responsibility, as though the whole edifice of creation rested on my shoulders. But the responsibility that empties the I of its imperialism and its egoism, even the egoism of salvation, does not transform it into a moment of the universal order; it confirms the uniqueness of the I. The uniqueness of the I is the fact that no one can answer for me.

To discover such an orientation in the I is to identify the I with morality. The I before the other is infinitely responsible. The other who provokes this ethical movement in conciousness and puts out of order the good conscience of the Same coinciding with itself involves a surplus for which intentionality is not adequate. This is what desire is: to burn with another fire than need, which saturation extinguishes, to think beyond what one thinks. Because of this unassimilable surplus, because of this *beyond*, we have called the relationship which links the I with the other the idea of infinity.

The idea of infinity is a desire. It paradoxically consists in thinking more than what is thought and maintaining what is thought in this very excess relative to thought – in entering into a relationship with the ungraspable while guaranteeing its status of being ungraspable. Infinity is not a correlate of the idea of infinity, as though this idea were an intentionality that is *fulfilled* in its "object". The wonder of infinity in the finite is an overwhelming of intentionality, an overwhelming of that appetite for light which is in intentionality; unlike the saturation in which intentionality subsides, infinity confounds its idea. The I in relationship with the infinite is an impossibility of stopping its forward march, the impossibility of deserting its post (in Plato's words in the *Phaedo*); it is, literally, not to have time to turn back. It is to be not able to escape responsibility, to not have a hiding place of inwardness where one comes back into oneself, to march forward without concern for oneself. There is an increase of exigencies on oneself: the more I face my responsibilities the more I am responsible. The putting into question of consciousness and its entry into a conjuncture of relations which contrast with disclosure is a power made of "impotencies."

Thus in the relationship with a face, in the ethical relationship, there is delineated the straightforwardness of an orientation, or sense. The *consciousness* of philosophers is essentially reflective. Or, at least, consciousness is grasped by philosophers in its moment of return which is taken for its very birth. Already in its spontaneous and pre-reflexive movements they take it to cast a glance back at its origin and measure the path crossed. That is where its initial essence would lie: it is a critique, a self-mastery, an analysis and decomposition of every meaning that overflows the self. Responsibility is to be sure neither blind, nor amnesiac; but across all the movements of thought in which it extends it is borne by an extreme urgency, or more exactly, coincides with it. What has just been described as a "lack of time to turn around" is not the accident of a clumsy or unhappy consciousness, "overtaken by events" or that "has trouble keeping up," but the utter rigor of an attitude without reflection, a primordial straightforwardness, a *sense* in being. "Where does this resistance of the unreflected to reflection come from?" Merleau-Ponty asked at Royaumont in April, 1957, in connection with problems that the Husserlian theory of phenomenological reduction poses.[xxii] Our analysis of *sense* perhaps responds to this fundamental question, which Merleau-Ponty refused to resolve by simple recourse to the finitude of the subject, incapable of total reflection. "To turn to the truth with one's whole soul" – the Platonic recommendation is not limited to a pedagogy of good sense, preaching effort and sincerity. Does it not aim at the ultimate reticence, the most sly of all, that of a soul which, before the Good, persists in reflecting on itself, and thus arresting the movement unto the other? Is not the force of this "resistance of the unreflected to reflection" the will itself, prior and posterior to, alpha and omega of,

xxii *Colloque Philosophique de Royaumont*, published as *Husserl* (Paris: Editions de Minuit, 1959).

every representation? And is not the will thus at bottom humility rather than will to power? Humility is not to be confused with an equivocal negation of oneself, already proud of its virtue, which, in reflection, it immediately recognizes in itself. This humility is that of him who does not "have time" to make a return upon himself and undertakes nothing to "negate" the oneself, save the very abnegation of the rectilinear movement of a work which goes infinitely to the other.

To affirm such an orientation and such a sense, to posit a consciousness without reflection beneath and above all the reflections, in short to surprise at the bottom of the ego an unequivocal sincerity and a servant's humility which no transcendental method could corrupt or absorb is to ensure the necessary conditions for a "beyond the given" which dawns in every meaning, for the *meta*-phor which animates it. For this is the marvel of language, whose "verbal origin" philosophical analysis will continue to denounce, without destroying the evident intention that penetrates it. Whatever be its psychological, social, or philological history, the *beyond* which a metaphor produces has a sense that transcends this history; the power to conjure up illusions which language has must be recognized, but lucidity does not abolish the beyond of these illusions. It is, to be sure, the role of reflection to reduce meanings to their subjective, subconscious, social, or verbal, sources, to draw up a transcendental inventory of them. But the method, though legitimate to destroy many false reputations, already prejudges an essential result: it forbids in advance any transcendental aim in meaning. Before the research, every *other* is already converted by it into the *same*, but in its purifying work reflection will nonetheless itself use these notions, if only the notion of a *beyond* with respect to which immanence is situated – which without the sincerity and straight forwardness of the "consciousness without return" would have no meaning. Nothing of what is sublime does without psychological, social, or verbal sources, save sublimation itself.

This consciousness "without reflection" is not the spontaneous, simply pre-reflexive and naive consciousness; it is not precritical. To discover the orientation and the one-way sense in the moral relationship is precisely to posit the ego as already put into question by the other it desires, and, consequently, as criticized in the very straight-forwardness of its movement. That is why the putting into question of consciousness is not ini-

tially a consciousness of the putting into question. The first is the condition for the second. How would spontaneous thought turn back, if the other, the exterior, did not put it into question? And how, in a concern for total critique entrusted to reflection, would the new naivety of reflection that removes the first naivety itself be removed? The ego erodes its dogmatic naivety before the other who asks of it more than it can do spontaneously.

The "term" of such a movement both critical and spontaneous – which is not, properly speaking, a term, for it is not an end, but the principle soliciting a work without recompense, a liturgy – is no longer called being. Here perhaps we can catch sight of the necessity for a philosophical meditation to resort to notions such as that of infinity or God.

8   Before Culture

We will say, to conclude, that before culture and aesthetics, meaning is situated in the ethical, presupposed by all culture and all meaning. Morality does not belong to culture: it enables one to judge it; it discovers the dimension of height. Height ordains being.

Height introduces a sense into being. It is already lived across the experience of the human body. It leads human societies to raise up altars. It is not because men, through their bodies, have an experience of the vertical that the human is placed under the sign of height; because being is ordained to height the human body is placed in a space in which the high and the low are distinguished and the sky is discovered – that sky which for Prince André, in Tolstoi,[xxiii] without any word of the text evoking colors, is all height.

It is most important to insist on the antecedence of sense to cultural signs. To attach every meaning to culture, to not distinguish between meaning and cultural expression, between meaning and the art that prolongs cultural expression, is to recognize that all the cultural personalities equally realize the spirit. Then no meaning can be detached from these innumerable cultures, to allow one to bear a judgment on these cultures. Universality could only be, according to Merleau-Ponty's expression, lateral. This universality would consist in being able

[xxiii] Prince Andrei Bolkonsky, Tolstoy's character in *War and Peace* (1869).

to penetrate one culture from another, as one learns a language on the basis on one's mother tongue. The idea of a universal grammar and an algorithmic language built on the framework of this grammar would have to be given up. No direct or privileged contact with the world of Ideas is possible. Such a conception of universality would express the radical opposition, so characteristic of our epoch, to the expansion of culture by colonization. To cultivate and to colonize should be completely separated. We would be at the antipodes of what Léon Brunschvicg[xxiv] (and Plato, hostile to the poets of the μήμησις)[xxv] taught us; the progress of Western consciousness would no longer consist in purifying thought of the alluvium of cultures and the particularisms of language, which far from signifying the intelligible would perpetuate the infantile. It is not that Léon Brunschvicg could have taught us anything but generosity, but for him this generosity and the dignity of the Western world was a matter of liberating truth of its cultural presuppositions, so as, with Plato, to proceed toward meanings themselves, thus separated from becoming. The danger of such a conception is clear; the emancipations of minds can be a pretext for exploitation and violence. Philosophy had to denounce the equivocation, show meanings dawning at the horizon of cultures, and show the very excellence of Western culture to be culturally and historically conditioned. Philosophy thus had to rejoin contemporary ethnology. It is then that Platonism is overcome! But it is overcome in the name of the generosity of Western thought itself, which, catching sight of the *abstract* man in men, proclaimed the absolute value of the person, and then encompassed in the respect it bears it the cultures in which these persons stand or in which they express themselves. Platonism is overcome with the very means which the universal thought issued from Plato supplied. It is overcome by this so much disparaged Western civilization, which was able to understand the particular cultures, which never understood themselves.

The saraband of innumerable and equivalent cultures, each justifying itself in its own context, creates a world which is, to be sure, de-occidentalized, but also disoriented. To catch sight, in meaning, of a situation that precedes culture, to envision language out of the revelation of the other (which is at the same time the birth of morality) in the gaze of man aiming at a man precisely as abstract man, disengaged from all culture, in the nakedness of his face, is to return to Platonism in a new way. It is also to find oneself able to judge civilizations on the basis of ethics. Meaning, the intelligible, consists in a being showing itself in its nonhistorical simplicity, in its absolutely unqualifiable and irreducible nakedness, existing "prior to" history and culture. Platonism, as an affirmation of the human independently of culture and history, is found again in Husserl, in the obstinacy with which he postulated the phenomenological reduction and the constitution (at least de jure) of the cultural world in the transcendental and intuitive consciousness. We are not obliged to follow him down the way he took to rejoin this Platonism, and we think we have found the straightforwardness of meaning by another method. That the intelligible manifestation is produced in the straight forwardness of morality and work measures the limits of the historical understanding of the world, and marks a return to Greek wisdom, even though mediated by all the development of contemporary philosophy.

Neither things, nor the perceived world, nor the scientific world enable us to rejoin the norms of the absolute. As cultural works, they are steeped in history. But the norms of morality are not embarked in history and culture. They are not even islands that emerge from it – for they make all meaning, even cultural meaning, possible, and make it possible to judge cultures.

9   The Trace

The notion of sense developed on the basis of the epiphany of a face, which has enabled us to affirm sense "prior to history," poses a problem to which, in closing, we would like to outline a response.

Is not the *beyond* from which a face comes, and which fixes consciousness in its straightforwardness or uprightness, an idea understood and disclosed in its turn?

If the extraordinary experience of entry and visitation retains its signifyingness, it is because the *beyond* is not a simple background from which a face solicits us, is not "another world" behind the world. The *beyond* is precisely beyond the "world," that is, beyond every disclosure, like the One of the first hypothesis of the *Parmenides*,[xxvi] transcending

---

[xxiv]   Leon Brunschvicg (1869–1944), prominent French neo-Hegelian philosopher.
[xxv]   *Mimesis.*

[xxvi]   Plato's dialogue, *Parmenides.*

all cognition, be it symbolic or signified. The one is "neither similar nor dissimilar, neither identical nor non-identical," Plato says, thus excluding it from every even indirect revelation. A symbol still brings the symbolized back to the world in which it appears. What then can be this relationship with an absence radically withdrawn from disclosure and dissimulation? And what is this absence that makes visitation possible, but which is not reducible to concealment, since this absence involves a signifyingness, a signifyingness in which, however, the other is not convertible into the same?

A face is abstract. This abstractness is not, to be sure, like the brute sensile datum of the empiricists. Nor is it an instantaneous cross-section of the world in which time would "cross" eternity. An instant belongs to the world. It is an incision made in time that does not bleed. But the abstractness of a face is a visitation and a coming. It *disturbs* immanence without settling into the horizons of the world. Its abstraction is not obtained by a logical process starting from the substance of beings and going from the particular to the general. On the contrary, it goes toward those beings, but does not compromise itself with them, withdraws from them, absolves itself. Its wonder is due to the *elsewhere* from which it comes and into which it already withdraws. This coming from *elsewhere* is not a *symbolic reference* to that *elsewhere* as to a term. A face presents itself in its nudity; it is not a form concealing, but thereby indicating, a ground, a phenomenon that hides, but thereby betrays, a thing itself. Otherwise, a face would be one with a mask, but a mask presupposes a face. If signifying were equivalent to indicating, a face would be insignificant. And Sartre will say that the other is a pure hole in the world – a most noteworthy insight, but he stops his analysis too soon.[xxvii] The other proceeds from the absolutely absent. His relationship with the absolutely absent from which he comes *does not indicate, does not reveal* this absent; and yet the absent has a meaning in a face. This signifyingness is not a way for the absent to be given in a blank in the presence of a face – which would again bring us back to a mode of disclosure. The relationship which goes from a face to the absent is outside every revelation and dissimulation, a third way excluded by these contradictories. How is this third way possible? But are we not still seeking that from which a face proceeds

as though it were a sphere, a place, a world? Have we been attentive enough to the interdiction against seeking the *beyond* as a world behind our world? The order of being would still seem to be presupposed, an order which contains no other status but that of the revealed and of the dissimulated. In being, a transcendence revealed is inverted into an immanence, the extra-ordinary is inserted into an order, the Other is absorbed into the Same. In the presence of the other do we not respond to an "order" in which signifyingness remains an irremissible disturbance, an utterly bygone past? Such is the signifyingness of a trace. The beyond from which a face comes signifies as a trace. A face is in the trace of the utterly bygone, utterly past absent, withdrawn into what Paul Valéry calls "the deep yore, never long ago enough," which cannot be discovered in the self by any introspection. For a face is the unique openness in which the signifyingness of the trans-cendent does not nullify the transcendence and make it enter into an immanent order; here on the contrary transcendence refuses immanence precisely as the ever *bygone* transcendence of the transcendent. In a trace the relationship between the signified and the signification is not a correlation, but *unrectitude* itself. The allegedly immediate and indirect relationship between a sign and the signified belongs to the order of *correlation*, and is thus still a rectitude, and a disclosure which neutralizes trans-cendence. The signifyingness of a trace places us in a "lateral" relationship, unconvertible into rectitude (something inconceivable in the order of disclosure and being), answering to an irreversible past. No memory could follow the traces of this past. It is an immemorial past – and this also is perhaps eternity, whose signifyingness obstinately throws one back to the past. Eternity is the very irreversibility of time, the source and refuge of the past.

But if the signifyingness of a trace is not immediately transformed into the straightforwardness which still marks signs, which reveal the signified absent and bring it into immanence, it is because a trace signifies beyond being. The personal "order" to which a face obliges us is beyond being. *Beyond being is a third person* which is not definable by the oneself, by ipseity. It is the possibility of that third direction of radical *unrectitude* which escapes the bipolar play of immanence and transcendence proper to being, where immanence always wins against transcendence. Through a trace the irreversible past takes on the profile of a "He." The *beyond* from which a face comes is in the third person. The

[xxvii] Since consciousness is, for Sartre, nothingness, the other's consciousness is a "hole" in the world.

pronoun "He" expresses its unexpressible irreversibility, already escaping every relation as well as every dissimulation, and in this sense absolutely unencompassable or absolute, a transcendence in an absolute past. The *illeity*[xxviii] of the third person is the condition for the irreversibility.[1]

This third person who in a face has already withdrawn from every relation and every dissimulation, who has passed, this *illeity*, is not a "less than being" by comparison with the world in which a face enters; it is the whole enormity, the whole inordinateness the whole infinity of the absolutely other, which eludes treatment by ontology. The supreme presence of a face is inseparable from this supreme and irreversible absence which founds the eminence of visitation.

If the signifyingness of a trace consists in signifying without making appear, if it establishes a relationship with illeity, a relationship which is personal and ethical, is an obligation and does not disclose, and if, consequently, a trace does not belong to phenomenology, to the comprehension of the appearing and the dissimulating, we can at least approach this signifyingness in another way by situating it with respect to the phenomenology it interrupts.

A trace is not a sign like any other. But it also plays the role of a sign; it can be taken for a sign. A detective examines, as revealing signs, everything in the area where a crime took place which betokens the voluntary or involuntary work of the criminal; a hunter follows the traces of the game, which reflect the activity and movement of the animal the hunter is after; a historian discovers ancient civilizations which form the horizon of our world on the basis of the vestiges left by their existence. Everything is arranged in an order, in a world, where each thing reveals another or is revealed in function of another. But when a trace is thus taken as a sign, it is exceptional with respect to other signs in that it signifies outside of every intention of signaling and outside of every project of which it would be the aim. When in transactions one "pays by check" so that there will be a trace of the payment, the trace is inscribed in the very order of the world. But a real trace disturbs the order of the world. It occurs by overprinting. Its original signifyingness is sketched out in, for example, the fingerprints left by someone who wanted to wipe away his traces and carry out a perfect crime. He who left traces in

wiping out his traces did not mean to say or do anything by the traces he left. He disturbed the order in an irreparable way. He has passed absolutely. To be qua *leaving a trace* is to pass, to depart, to absolve onself.

But in this sense every sign is a trace. In addition to what the sign signifies, it is the past of him who delivered the sign. The signifyingness of a trace doubles up this signifyingness proper to a sign emitted in view of communication. A sign stands in this trace. This signifyingness lies in, for example, the writing and the style of a letter, in all that brings it about that during the emission of a message, which we capture on the basis of the letter's language and its sincerity, someone passes, purely and simply. This trace can be taken in its turn as a sign. A graphologist, an expert in writing styles, or a psychoanalyst could interpret a trace's singular signifyingness, and seek in it the sealed and unconscious, but real, intentions of him who delivered the message. But then what remains specifically a trace in the writing and style of the letter does not signal any of these intentions, any of these qualities, reveals and hides nothing. In a trace has passed a past absolutely bygone. In a trace its irreversible lapse is sealed. Disclosure, which reinstates the world and leads back to the world, and is proper to a sign or a signification, is done away with in traces.

But then is not a trace the weight of being itself outside of its acts and its language, weighing not through its presence, which fits it into the world, but by its very irreversibility, its ab-soluteness? A trace would seem to be the very indelibility of being, its omnipotence before all negativity, its immensity incapable of being self-enclosed, somehow too great for discretion, interiority, or a self. And it was indeed important for us to say that a trace does not effect a relationship with what would be less than being, but obliges with regard to the infinite, the absolutely other. But this superiority of the superlative, this height, this constant elevation to power, this exaggeration or this infinite overbidding – and, let us say the word, this divinity – are not deducible from the being of beings nor its revelation, even if it is contemporary with a concealment, nor with "concrete duration." These signify something on the basis of a past which, in a trace, is neither indicated nor signaled, but yet disturbs order, while coinciding neither with revelation nor with dissimulation. A trace is the insertion of space in time, the point at which the world inclines toward a past and a time. This time is a withdrawal of the other and, consequently,

xxviii   From Roger Laporte, literally "he-ness," indicating particularity.

nowise a degradation of duration, which, in memory, is still complete. Superiority does not reside in a presence in the world, but in an irreversible transcendence. It is not a modulation of the being of entities. As *He* and third person it is somehow outside the distinction between being and entities. Only a being that transcends the world, an ab-solute being, can leave a trace. A trace is a presence of that which properly speaking has never been there, of what is always past. Plotinus conceived the procession from the One as compromising neither the immutability nor the ab-solute separation of the One.[xxix] It is in this situation, at first purely dialectical and quasi-verbal (and which is also true of Intelligence and the Soul, which remain with their principle in their higher parts, and are inclined only through their lower parts, a structure which still belongs to iconography), that the exceptional signifyingness of a trace delineates in the world. "[M]uch more then does the unit, The One, remain intact in the principle which is before all beings; especially since the entities produced in its likeness, while it thus remains intact, owe their existence to no other, but to its own all-sufficient power. . . . [I]n the realm of Being, the trace of The One establishes reality: existence is a trace of The One . . . (*Enneads*, 5:5).

That which preserves the specific signifyingness of a trace in each trace of an empirical passage, over and above the sign it can become, is possible only through its situation in the trace of this transcendence. This position in a trace, which we have called *illeity*, does not begin in things, which by themselves do not leave traces, but produce effects, that is, remain in the world. When a stone has scratched another stone, the scratch can, to be sure, be taken as a trace, but in fact without the man who held the stone this scratch is but an effect. It is as little a trace as the forest fire is a trace of the lightning. A cause and an effect, even separated by time, belong

to the same world. Everything in things is exposed, even what is unknown in them. The traces that mark them are part of this plenitude of presence; their history is without a past. A trace qua trace does not simply lead to the past, but is the very passing toward a past more remote than any past and any future which still are set in my time – the past of the other, in which eternity takes form, an absolute past which unites all times.

The absoluteness of the presence of the other, which has justified our interpreting the exceptional uprightness of thou-saying as an epiphany of him, is not the simple presence in which in the last analysis things are also present. Their presence belongs to the present of *my* life. Everything that constitutes my life with its past and its future is assembled in the present in which things come to me. But it is in the trace of the other that a face shines: what is presented there is absolving itself from my life and visits me as already ab-solute. Someone has already passed. His trace does not *signify* his past, as it does not *signify* his labor or his enjoyment in the world; it *is* a disturbance imprinting itself (we are tempted to say *engraving* itself) with an irrecusable gravity.

The *illeity* of this *He* is not the *it* of things which are at our disposal, and to which Buber and Gabriel Marcel rightly prefer the Thou to describe a human encounter. The movement of an encounter is not something added to an immobile face; it is in the face itself. A face is of itself a visitation and a transcendence. But a face, wholly open, can at the same time be in itself because it is in the trace of illeity. Illeity is the origin of the alterity of being in which the *in itself* of objectivity participates, while also betraying it.

The God who passed is not the model of which the face would be an image. To be in the image of God does not mean to be an icon of God, but to find oneself in his trace. The revealed God of our Judeo-Christian spirituality maintains all the infinity of his absence, which is in the personal "order" itself. He shows himself only by his trace, as is said in Exodus 33. To go toward Him is not to follow this trace which is not a sign; it is to go toward the others who stand in the trace of illeity. It is through this illeity, situated beyond the calculations and reciprocities of economy and of the world, that being has a sense. A sense which is not a finality.

For there is no end, no term. The desire of the absolutely other will not, like need, be extinguished in a happiness.

[xxix] Plotinus (AD 205–270), premier neo-Platonic philosopher, author of *Enneads*.

Author's Note

1 See M. Roger Laporte's remarkable work *La Veille* (Paris: Gallimard, 1963) which also contains the "notion" of *He*.

51

"Epistemology Naturalized"

W. V. Quine

A student of logical positivism, Willard Van Orman Quine (1908–2000) undermined the categories of that view by denying the distinction between "analytic" truths, propositions made true by their meanings alone, and "synthetic" truths, which require supra-linguistic evidence. He accepted a behaviorist, quasi-pragmatic account of human meaning; meanings are not mental entities, but functions of behavior. This led him to propose the "indeterminacy of translation," since behavioral differences under-determine the understanding of propositions. A theoretical holist, he held that scientific theories and ontologies confront experience as a whole, so that recalcitrant experience leaves it unclear which parts of the whole must be modified. In the 1968 lecture below Quine argues that the program of seeking a rational justification of inquiry is unachievable, opting instead for a "naturalist epistemology" which accepts that how we know is best described by a scientific account of human perception and cognition. This view is threatened with circularity – i.e. natural science is justified by natural science – only if one accepts the search for a foundational validation of inquiry. But since no such validation is possible, none is required or wanted, and the circularity of naturalism is unobjectionable.

Epistemology is concerned with the foundations of science. Conceived thus broadly, epistemology includes the study of the foundations of mathematics as one of its departments. Specialists at the turn of the century thought that their efforts in this particular department were achieving notable success: mathematics seemed to reduce altogether to logic.

In a more recent perspective this reduction is seen to be better describable as a reduction to logic and set theory. This correction is a disappointment epistemologically, since the firmness and obviousness that we associate with logic cannot be claimed for set theory. But still the success achieved in the foundations of mathematics remains exemplary by comparative standards, and we can illuminate the rest of epistemology somewhat by drawing parallels to this department.

Studies in the foundations of mathematics divide symmetrically into two sorts, conceptual and doctrinal. The conceptual studies are concerned with meaning, the doctrinal with truth. The conceptual studies are concerned with clarifying concepts by defining them, some in terms of others. The doctrinal studies are concerned with establishing laws by proving them, some on the basis of others. Ideally the obscurer concepts would be defined in terms of the clearer ones so as to maximize clarity, and the less obvious laws would be proved from the more obvious ones so as to maximize certainty. Ideally the definitions would generate all the concepts from clear and distinct ideas, and the proofs would generate all the theorems from self-evident truths.

The two ideals are linked. For, if you define all the concepts by use of some favored subset of them, you thereby show how to translate all theorems into these favored terms. The clearer these terms are, the likelier it is that the truths couched in them will

W. V. Quine, "Epistemology Naturalized," chapter 3 (pp. 69–90) from *Ontological Relativity and Other Essays*. New York: Columbia University Press, 1969.

be obviously true, or derivable from obvious truths. If in particular the concepts of mathematics were all reducible to the clear terms of logic, then all the truths of mathematics would go over into truths of logic; and surely the truths of logic are all obvious or at least potentially obvious, i.e., derivable from obvious truths by individually obvious steps.

This particular outcome is in fact denied us, however, since mathematics reduces only to set theory and not to logic proper. Such reduction still enhances clarity, but only because of the interrelations that emerge and not because the end terms of the analysis are clearer than others. As for the end truths, the axioms of set theory, these have less obviousness and certainty to recommend them than do most of the mathematical theorems that we would derive from them. Moreover, we know from Gödel's work that no consistent axiom system can cover mathematics even when we renounce self-evidence.[i] Reduction in the foundations of mathematics remains mathematically and philosophically fascinating, but it does not do what the epistemologist would like of it: it does not reveal the ground of mathematical knowledge, it does not show how mathematical certainty is possible.

Still there remains a helpful thought, regarding epistemology generally, in that duality of structure which was especially conspicuous in the foundations of mathematics. I refer to the bifurcation into a theory of concepts, or meaning, and a theory of doctrine, or truth; for this applies to the epistemology of natural knowledge no less than to the foundations of mathematics. The parallel is as follows. Just as mathematics is to be reduced to logic, or logic and set theory, so natural knowledge is to be based somehow on sense experience. This means explaining the notion of body in sensory terms; here is the conceptual side. And it means justifying our knowledge of truths of nature in sensory terms; here is the doctrinal side of the bifurcation.

Hume pondered the epistemology of natural knowledge on both sides of the bifurcation, the conceptual and the doctrinal. His handling of the conceptual side of the problem, the explanation of body in sensory terms, was bold and simple: he identified bodies outright with the sense impressions. If common sense distinguishes between the

material apple and our sense impressions of it on the ground that the apple is one and enduring while the impressions are many and fleeting, then, Hume held, so much the worse for common sense; the notion of its being the same apple on one occasion and another is a vulgar confusion.

Nearly a century after Hume's *Treatise*, the same view of bodies was espoused by the early American philosopher Alexander Bryan Johnson.[1] "The word iron names an associated sight and feel," Johnson wrote.

What then of the doctrinal side, the justification of our knowledge of truths about nature? Here, Hume despaired. By his identification of bodies with impressions he did succeed in construing some singular statements about bodies as indubitable truths, yes; as truths about impressions, directly known. But general statements, also singular statements about the future, gained no increment of certainty by being construed as about impressions.

On the doctrinal side, I do not see that we are farther along today than where Hume left us. The Humean predicament is the human predicament. But on the conceptual side there has been progress. There the crucial step forward was made already before Alexander Bryan Johnson's day, although Johnson did not emulate it.[ii] It was made by Bentham in his theory of fictions.[iii] Bentham's step was the recognition of contextual definition, or what he called paraphrasis. He recognized that to explain a term we do not need to specify an object for it to refer to, nor even specify a synonymous word or phrase; we need only show, by whatever means, how to translate all the whole sentences in which the term is to be used. Hume's and Johnson's desperate measure of identifying bodies with impressions ceased to be the only conceivable way of making sense of talk of bodies, even granted that impressions were the only reality. One could undertake to explain talk of bodies in terms of talk of impressions by translating one's whole sentences about bodies into whole sentences about impressions, without equating the bodies themselves to anything at all.

This idea of contextual definition, or recognition of the sentence as the primary vehicle of meaning, was indispensable to the ensuing developments in the foundations of mathematics. It was explicit in Frege, and it attained its full flower in Russell's

---

[i] Kurt Gödel (1906–78), Czech mathematical logician whose "On Formally Undecideable Propositions of *Principia Mathematica* and Related Systems" (1931) demonstrated the formal incompleteness of logics rich enough to contain arithmetic.

[ii] Alexander Bryan Johnson (1786–1867), early American philosopher of language.
[iii] Jeremy Bentham (1748–1867), inventor of Utilitarianism, Philosophical Radical, and critic of legal "fictions."

doctrine of singular descriptions as incomplete symbols.[iv]

Contextual definition was one of two resorts that could be expected to have a liberating effect upon the conceptual side of the epistemology of natural knowledge. The other is resort to the resources of set theory as auxiliary concepts. The epistemologist who is willing to eke out his austere ontology of sense impressions with these set-theoretic auxiliaries is suddenly rich: he has not just his impressions to play with, but sets of them, and sets of sets, and so on up. Constructions in the foundations of mathematics have shown that such set-theoretic aids are a powerful addition; after all, the entire glossary of concepts of classical mathematics is constructible from them. Thus equipped, our epistemologist may not need either to identify bodies with impressions or to settle for contextual definition; he may hope to find in some subtle construction of sets upon sets of sense impressions a category of objects enjoying just the formula properties that he wants for bodies.

The two resorts are very unequal in epistemological status. Contextual definition is unassailable. Sentences that have been given meaning as wholes are undeniably meaningful, and the use they make of their component terms is therefore meaningful, regardless of whether any translations are offered for those terms in isolation. Surely Hume and A. B. Johnson would have used contextual definition with pleasure if they had thought of it. Recourse to sets, on the other hand, is a drastic ontological move, a retreat from the austere ontology of impressions. There are philosophers who would rather settle for bodies out right than accept all these sets, which amount, after all, to the whole abstract ontology of mathematics.

This issue has not always been clear, however, owing to deceptive hints of continuity between elementary logic and set theory. This is why mathematics was once believed to reduce to logic, that is, to an innocent and unquestionable logic, and to inherit these qualities. And this is probably why Russell was content to resort to sets as well as to contextual definition when in *Our Knowledge of the External World* and elsewhere he addressed himself to the epistemology of natural knowledge, on its conceptual side.

To account for the external world as a logical construct of sense data – such, in Russell's terms, was the program. It was Carnap, in his *Der logische Aufbau der Welt* of 1928, who came nearest to executing it.[v]

This was the conceptual side of epistemology; what of the doctrinal? There the Humean predicament remained unaltered. Carnap's constructions, if carried successfully to completion, would have enabled us to translate all sentences about the world into terms of sense data, or observation, plus logic and set theory. But the mere fact that a sentence is *couched* in terms of observation, logic, and set theory does not mean that it can be *proved* from observation sentences by logic and set theory. The most modest of generalizations about observable traits will cover more cases than its utterer can have had occasion actually to observe. The hopelessness of grounding natural science upon immediate experience in a firmly logical way was acknowledged. The Cartesian quest for certainty had been the remote motivation of epistemology, both on its conceptual and its doctrinal side; but that quest was seen as a lost cause. To endow the truths of nature with the full authority of immediate experience was as forlorn a hope as hoping to endow the truths of mathematics with the potential obviousness of elementary logic.

What then could have motivated Carnap's heroic efforts on the conceptual side of epistemology, when hope of certainty on the doctrinal side was abandoned? There were two good reasons still. One was that such constructions could be expected to elicit and clarify the sensory evidence for science, even if the inferential steps between sensory evidence and scientific doctrine must fall short of certainty. The other reason was that such constructions would deepen our understanding of our discourse about the world, even apart from questions of evidence; it would make all cognitive discourse as clear as observation terms and logic and, I must regretfully add, set theory.

It was sad for epistemologists, Hume and others, to have to acquiesce in the impossibility of strictly deriving the science of the external world from sensory evidence. Two cardinal tenets of empiricism remained unassailable, however, and so

---

[iv] Gottlob Frege (1848–1925), philosopher of mathematics, language, and the central innovator of modern logic, and Betrand Russell (1872–1970), founder of twentieth-century analytic philosophy and author, with Alfred North Whitehead, of *Principia Mathematica*.

[v] *The Logical Structure of the World* (1928) by Rudolf Carnap (1891–1970), member of the Vienna Circle and influential logical positivist.

remain to this day. One is that whatever evidence there *is* for science *is* sensory evidence. The other, to which I shall recur, is that all inculcation of meanings of words must rest ultimately on sensory evidence. Hence the continuing attractiveness of the idea of a *logischer Aufbau* in which the sensory content of discourse would stand forth explicitly.

If Carnap had successfully carried such a construction through, how could he have told whether it was the right one? The question would have had no point. He was seeking what he called a *rational reconstruction*. Any construction of physicalistic discourse in terms of sense experience, logic, and set theory would have been seen as satisfactory if it made the physicalistic discourse come out right. If there is one way there are many, but any would be a great achievement.

But why all this creative reconstruction, all this make-believe? The stimulation of his sensory receptors is all the evidence anybody has had to go on, ultimately, in arriving at his picture of the world. Why not just see how this construction really proceeds? Why not settle for psychology? Such a surrender of the epistemological burden to psychology is a move that was disallowed in earlier times as circular reasoning. If the epistemologist's goal is validation of the grounds of empirical science, he defeats his purpose by using psychology or other empirical science in the validation. However, such scruples against circularity have little point once we have stopped dreaming of deducing science from observations. If we are out simply to understand the link between observation and science, we are well advised to use any available information, including that provided by the very science whose link with observation we are seeking to understand.

But there remains a different reason, unconnected with fears of circularity, for still favoring creative reconstruction. We should like to be able to *translate* science into logic and observation terms and set theory. This would be a great epistemological achievement, for it would show all the rest of the concepts of science to be theoretically superfluous. It would legitimize them – to whatever degree the concepts of set theory, logic, and observation are themselves legitimate – by showing that everything done with the one apparatus could in principle be done with the other. If psychology itself could deliver a truly translational reduction of this kind, we should welcome it; but certainly it cannot, for certainly we did not grow up learning definitions of physicalistic language in terms of a prior language of set theory, logic, and observation.

Here, then, would be good reason for persisting in a rational reconstruction: we want to establish the essential innocence of physical concepts, by showing them to be theoretically dispensable.

The fact is, though, that the construction which Carnap outlined in *Der logische Aufbau der Welt* does not give translational reduction either. It would not even if the outline were filled in. The crucial point comes where Carnap is explaining how to assign sense qualities to positions in physical space and time. These assignments are to be made in such a way as to fulfill, as well as possible, certain desiderata which he states, and with growth of experience the assignments are to be revised to suit. This plan, however illuminating, does not offer any key to *translating* the sentences of science into terms of observation, logic, and set theory.

We must despair of any such reduction. Carnap had despaired of it by 1936, when, in "Testability and meaning,"[2] he introduced so-called *reduction forms* of a type weaker than definition. Definitions had shown always how to translate sentences into equivalent sentences. Contextual definition of a term showed how to translate sentences containing the term into equivalent sentences lacking the term. Reduction forms of Carnap's liberalized kind, on the other hand, do not in general give equivalences; they give implications. They explain a new term, if only partially, by specifying some sentences which are implied by sentences containing the term, and other sentences which imply sentences containing the term.

It is tempting to suppose that the countenancing of reduction forms in this liberal sense is just one further step of liberalization comparable to the earlier one, taken by Bentham, of countenancing contextual definition. The former and sterner kind of rational reconstruction might have been represented as a fictitious history in which we imagined our ancestors introducing the terms of physicalistic discourse on a phenomenalistic and set-theoretic basis by a succession of contextual definitions. The new and more liberal kind of rational reconstruction is a fictitious history in which we imagine our ancestors introducing those terms by a succession rather of reduction forms of the weaker sort.

This, however, is a wrong comparison. The fact is rather that the former and sterner kind of rational reconstruction, where definition reigned, embodied no fictitious history at all. It was nothing more nor less than a set of directions – or would have been, if successful – for accomplishing everything in terms of phenomena and set theory that we now accomplish in terms of bodies. It would have been a true reduction by translation, a legitimation by elimination. *Definire est eliminare.*[vi] Rational reconstruction by Carnap's later and looser reduction forms does none of this.

To relax the demand for definition, and settle for a kind of reduction that does not eliminate, is to renounce the last remaining advantage that we supposed rational reconstruction to have over straight psychology; namely, the advantage of translational reduction. If all we hope for is a reconstruction that links science to experience in explicit ways short of translation, then it would seem more sensible to settle for psychology. Better to discover how science is in fact developed and learned than to fabricate a fictitious structure to a similar effect.

The empiricist made one major concession when he despaired of deducing the truths of nature from sensory evidence. In despairing now even of translating those truths into terms of observation and logico-mathematical auxiliaries, he makes another major concession. For suppose we hold, with the old empiricist Peirce, that the very meaning of a statement consists in the difference its truth would make to possible experience.[vii] Might we not formulate, in a chapter-length sentence in observational language, all the difference that the truth of a given statement might make to experience, and might we not then take all this as the translation? Even if the difference that the truth of the statement would make to experience ramifies indefinitely, we might still hope to embrace it all in the logical implications of our chapter-length formulation, just as we can axiomatize an infinity of theorems. In giving up hope of such translation, then, the empiricist is conceding that the empirical meanings of typical statements about the external world are inaccessible and ineffable.

How is this inaccessibility to be explained? Simply on the ground that the experiential implications of a typical statement about bodies are too complex for finite axiomatization, however lengthy? No; I have a different explanation. It is that the typical statement about bodies has no fund of experiential implications it can call its own.

[vi] "To define is to eliminate," that is to reduce to something else.
[vii] The pragmatist Charles S. Peirce, here labelled an empiricist (or, as Justus Buchler suggested, a "public empiricist").

A substantial mass of theory, taken together, will commonly have experiential implications; this is how we make verifiable predictions. We may not be able to explain why we arrive at theories which make successful predictions, but we do arrive at such theories.

Sometimes also an experience implied by a theory fails to come off; and then, ideally, we declare the theory false. But the failure falsifies only a block of theory as a whole, a conjunction of many statements. The failure shows that one or more of those statements is false, but it does not show which. The predicted experiences, true and false, are not implied by any one of the component statements of the theory rather than another. The component statements simply do not have empirical meanings, by Peirce's standard; but a sufficiently inclusive portion of theory does. If we can aspire to a sort of *logischer Aufbau der Welt* at all, it must be to one in which the texts slated for translation into observational and logico-mathematical terms are mostly broad theories taken as wholes, rather than just terms or short sentences. The translation of a theory would be a ponderous axiomatization of all the experiential difference that the truth of the theory would make. It would be a queer translation, for it would translate the whole but none of the parts. We might better speak in such a case not of translation but simply of observational evidence for theories; and we may, following Peirce, still fairly call this the empirical meaning of the theories.

These considerations raise a philosophical question even about ordinary unphilosophical translation, such as from English into Arunta or Chinese. For, if the English sentences of a theory have their meaning only together as a body, then we can justify their translation into Arunta only together as a body. There will be no justification for pairing off the component English sentences with component Arunta sentences, except as these correlations make the translation of the theory as a whole come out right. Any translations of the English sentences into Arunta sentences will be as correct as any other, so long as the net empirical implications of the theory as a whole are preserved in translation. But it is to be expected that many different ways of translating the component sentences, essentially different individually, would deliver the same empirical implications for the theory as a whole; deviations in the translation of one component sentence could be compensated for in the translation of another component sentence. Insofar, there can be no ground for saying which of two glaringly unlike translations of individual sentences is right.[viii]

For an uncritical mentalist, no such indeterminacy threatens. Every term and every sentence is a label attached to an idea, simple or complex, which is stored in the mind. When on the other hand we take a verification theory of meaning seriously, the indeterminacy would appear to be inescapable.[ix] The Vienna Circle espoused a verification theory of meaning but did not take it seriously enough. If we recognize with Peirce that the meaning of a sentence turns purely on what would count as evidence for its truth, and if we recognize with Duhem that theoretical sentences have their evidence not as single sentences but only as larger blocks of theory, then the indeterminacy of translation of theoretical sentences is the natural conclusion.[x] And most sentences, apart from observation sentences, are theoretical. This conclusion, conversely, once it is embraced, seals the fate of any general notion of propositional meaning or, for that matter, state of affairs.

Should the unwelcomeness of the conclusion persuade us to abandon the verification theory of meaning? Certainly not. The sort of meaning that is basic to translation, and to the learning of one's own language, is necessarily empirical meaning and nothing more. A child learns his first words and sentences by hearing and using them in the presence of appropriate stimuli. These must be external stimuli, for they must act both on the child and on the speaker from whom he is learning. Language is socially inculcated and controlled; the inculcation and control turn strictly on the keying of sentences to shared stimulation. Internal factors may vary *ad libitum*[xi] without prejudice to communication as long as the keying of language to external stimuli is undisturbed. Surely one has no choice but to be an empiricist so far as one's theory of linguistic meaning is concerned.

What I have said of infant learning applies equally to the linguist's learning of a new language in the field. If the linguist does not lean on related languages for which there are previously accepted translation practices, then obviously he has no data but the concomitances of native utterance and ob-servable stimulus situation. No wonder there is indeterminacy of translation – for of course only a small fraction of our utterances report concurrent external stimulation. Granted, the linguist will end up with unequivocal translations of everything; but only by making many arbitrary choices – arbitrary even though unconscious – along the way. Arbitrary? By this I mean that different choices could still have made everything come out right that is susceptible in principle to any kind of check.

Let me link up, in a different order, some of the points I have made. The crucial consideration behind my argument for the indeterminacy of translation was that a statement about the world does not always or usually have a separable fund of empirical consequences that it can call its own. That consideration served also to account for the impossibility of an epistemological reduction of the sort where every sentence is equated to a sentence in observational and logico-mathematical terms. And the impossibility of that sort of epistemological reduction dissipated the last advantage that rational reconstruction seemed to have over psychology.

Philosophers have rightly despaired of translating everything into observational and logico-mathematical terms. They have despaired of this even when they have not recognized, as the reason for this irreducibility, that the statements largely do not have their private bundles of empirical consequences. And some philosophers have seen in this irreducibility the bankruptcy of epistemology. Carnap and the other logical positivists of the Vienna Circle had already pressed the term "metaphysics" into pejorative use, as connoting meaninglessness; and the term "epistemology" was next. Wittgenstein and his followers, mainly at Oxford, found a residual philosophical vocation in therapy: in curing philosophers of the delusion that there were epistemological problems.

But I think that at this point it may be more useful to say rather that epistemology still goes on, though in a new setting and a clarified status. Epistemology, or something like it, simply falls into place as a chapter of psychology and hence of natural science. It studies a natural phenomenon, viz., a physical human subject. This human subject is accorded a certain experimentally controlled input – certain patterns of irradiation in assorted frequencies, for instance – and in the fullness of time the subject delivers as output a description of the three-dimensional external world and its history. The relation between the meager input and the torrential output is a relation that we are prompted to

---

[viii]   Quine argued for this "indeterminacy of translation" in *Word and Object*.

[ix]   A verification theory, such as that of the Vienna Circle of Logical Positivists, held that only statements whose verification conditions could be imagined have meaning.

[x]   Pierre Duhem (1861–1916), French philosopher of science, whose holism influenced Quine.

[xi]   Freely.

study for somewhat the same reasons that always prompted epistemology; namely, in order to see how evidence relates to theory, and in what ways one's theory of nature transcends any available evidence.

Such a study could still include, even, something like the old rational reconstruction, to whatever degree such reconstruction is practicable; for imaginative constructions can afford hints of actual psychological processes, in much the way that mechanical simulations can. But a conspicuous difference between old epistemology and the epistemological enterprise in this new psychological setting is that we can now make free use of empirical psychology.

The old epistemology aspired to contain, in a sense, natural science; it would construct it somehow from sense data. Epistemology in its new setting, conversely, is contained in natural science, as a chapter of psychology. But the old containment remains valid too, in its way. We are studying how the human subject of our study posits bodies and projects his physics from his data, and we appreciate that our position in the world is just like his. Our very epistemological enterprise, therefore, and the psychology wherein it is a component chapter, and the whole of natural science wherein psychology is a component book – all this is our own construction or projection from stimulations like those we were meting out to our epistemological subject. There is thus reciprocal containment, though containment in different senses: epistemology in natural science and natural science in epistemology.

This interplay is reminiscent again of the old threat of circularity, but it is all right now that we have stopped dreaming of deducing science from sense data. We are after an understanding of science as an institution or process in the world, and we do not intend that understanding to be any better than the science which is its object. This attitude is indeed one that Neurath was already urging in Vienna Circle days, with his parable of the mariner who has to rebuild his boat while staying afloat in it.[xii]

One effect of seeing epistemology in a psychological setting is that it resolves a stubborn old enigma of epistemological priority. Our retinas are irradiated in two dimensions, yet we see things as three-dimensional without conscious inference.

Which is to count as observation – the unconscious two-dimensional reception or the conscious three-dimensional apprehension? In the old epistemological context the conscious form had priority, for we were out to justify our knowledge of the external world by rational reconstruction, and that demands awareness. Awareness ceased to be demanded when we gave up trying to justify our knowledge of the external world by rational reconstruction. What to count as observation now can be settled in terms of the stimulation of sensory receptors, let consciousness fall where it may.

The Gestalt psychologists' challenge to sensory atomism, which seemed so relevant to epistemology forty years ago, is likewise deactivated.[xiii] Regardless of whether sensory atoms or Gestalten are what favor the forefront of our consciousness, it is simply the stimulations of our sensory receptors that are best looked upon as the input to our cognitive mechanism. Old paradoxes about unconscious data and inference, old problems about chains of inference that would have to be completed too quickly – these no longer matter.

In the old anti-psychologistic days the question of epistemological priority was moot. What is epistemologically prior to what? Are Gestalten prior to sensory atoms because they are noticed, or should we favor sensory atoms on some more subtle ground? Now that we are permitted to appeal to physical stimulation, the problem dissolves; A is epistemologically prior to B if A is causally nearer than B to the sensory receptors. Or, what is in some ways better, just talk explicitly in terms of causal proximity to sensory receptors and drop the talk of epistemological priority.

Around 1932 there was debate in the Vienna Circle over what to count as observation sentences, or *Protokollsätze*.[3] One position was that they had the form of reports of sense impressions. Another was that they were statements of an elementary sort about the external world, e.g., "A red cube is standing on the table." Another, Neurath's, was that they had the form of reports of relations between percipients and external things: "Otto now sees a red cube on the table." The worst of it was that there seemed to be no objective way of settling the matter: no way of making real sense of the question.

[xiii] They held that sensory "wholes" could not be analyzed into parts without residue.

Let us now try to view the matter unreservedly in the context of the external world. Vaguely speaking, what we want of observation sentences is that they be the ones in closest causal proximity to the sensory receptors. But how is such proximity to be gauged? The idea may be rephrased this way: observation sentences are sentences which, as we learn language, are most strongly conditioned to concurrent sensory stimulation rather than to stored collateral information. Thus let us imagine a sentence queried for our verdict as to whether it is true or false; queried for our assent or dissent. Then the sentence is an observation sentence if our verdict depends only on the sensory stimulation present at the time.

But a verdict cannot depend on present stimulation to the exclusion of stored information. The very fact of our having learned the language evinces much storing of information, and of information without which we should be in no position to give verdicts on sentences however observational. Evidently then we must relax our definition of observation sentence to read thus: a sentence is an observation sentence if all verdicts on it depend on present sensory stimulation and on no stored information beyond what goes into understanding the sentence.

This formulation raises another problem: how are we to distinguish between information that goes into understanding a sentence and information that goes beyond? This is the problem of distinguishing between analytic truth, which issues from the mere meanings of words, and synthetic truth, which depends on more than meanings. Now I have long maintained that this distinction is illusory.[xiv] There is one step toward such a distinction, however, which does make sense: a sentence that is true by mere meanings of words should be expected, at least if it is simple, to be subscribed to by all fluent speakers in the community. Perhaps the controversial notion of analyticity can be dispensed with, in our definition of observation sentence, in favor of this straightforward attribute of community-wide acceptance.

This attribute is of course no explication of analyticity. The community would agree that there have been black dogs, yet none who talk of analyticity would call this analytic. My rejection of the analyticity notion just means drawing no line between what goes into the mere understanding of the

sentences of a language and what else the community sees eye-to-eye on. I doubt that an objective distinction can be made between meaning and such collateral information as is community-wide.

Turning back then to our task of defining observation sentences, we get this: an observation sentence is one on which all speakers of the language give the same verdict when given the same concurrent stimulation. To put the point negatively, an observation sentence is one that is not sensitive to differences in past experience within the speech community.

This formulation accords perfectly with the traditional role of the observation sentence as the court of appeal of scientific theories. For by our definition the observation sentences are the sentences on which all members of the community will agree under uniform stimulation. And what is the criterion of membership in the same community? Simply general fluency of dialogue. This criterion admits of degrees, and indeed we may usefully take the community more narrowly for some studies than for others. What count as observation sentences for a community of specialists would not always so count for a larger community.

There is generally no subjectivity in the phrasing of observation sentences, as we are now conceiving them; they will usually be about bodies. Since the distinguishing trait of an observation sentence is intersubjective agreement under agreeing stimulation, a corporeal subject matter is likelier than not.

The old tendency to associate observation sentences with a subjective sensory subject matter is rather an irony when we reflect that observation sentences are also meant to be the intersubjective tribunal of scientific hypotheses. The old tendency was due to the drive to base science on something firmer and prior in the subject's experience; but we dropped that project.

The dislodging of epistemology from its old status of first philosophy loosed a wave, we saw, of epistemological nihilism. This mood is reflected somewhat in the tendency of Polányi, Kuhn, and the late Russell Hanson to belittle the role of evidence and to accentuate cultural relativism.[xv] Hanson ventured even to discredit the idea of observation, arguing that so-called observations vary from observer to observer with the amount

---

[xiv] Quine denied that distinction in his famous essay, "Two Dogmas of Empiricism."

[xv] Three philosophers of science: the Hungarian Michael Polányi (1891–1976), and Americans Thomas Kuhn and Norwood Russell Hanson (1924–67).

of knowledge that the observers bring with them. The veteran physicist looks at some apparatus and sees an x-ray tube. The neophyte, looking at the same place, observes rather "a glass and metal instrument replete with wires, reflectors, screws, lamps, and pushbuttons."[4] One man's observation is another man's closed book or flight of fancy. The notion of observation as the impartial and objective source of evidence for science is bankrupt. Now my answer to the x-ray example was already hinted a little while back: what counts as an observation sentence varies with the width of community considered. But we can also always get an absolute standard by taking in all speakers of the language, or most.[5] It is ironical that philosophers, finding the old epistemology untenable as a whole, should react by repudiating a part which has only now moved into clear focus.

Clarification of the notion of observation sentence is a good thing, for the notion is fundamental in two connections. These two correspond to the duality that I remarked upon early in this lecture: the duality between concept and doctrine, between knowing what a sentence means and knowing whether it is true. The observation sentence is basic to both enterprises. Its relation to doctrine, to our knowledge of what is true, is very much the traditional one: observation sentences are the repository of evidence for scientific hypotheses. Its relation to meaning is fundamental too, since observation sentences are the ones we are in a position to learn to understand first, both as children and as field linguists. For observation sentences are precisely the ones that we can correlate with observable circumstances of the occasion of utterance or assent, independently of variations in the past histories of individual informants. They afford the only entry to a language.

The observation sentence is the cornerstone of semantics. For it is, as we just saw, fundamental to the learning of meaning. Also, it is where meaning is firmest. Sentences higher up in theories have no empirical consequences they can call their own; they confront the tribunal of sensory evidence only in more or less inclusive aggregates. The observation sentence, situated at the sensory periphery of the body scientific, is the minimal verifiable aggregate; it has an empirical content all its own and wears it on its sleeve.

The predicament of the indeterminacy of translation has little bearing on observation sentences. The equating of an observation sentence of our language to an observation sentence of another language is mostly a matter of empirical generalization; it is a matter of identity between the range of stimulations that would prompt assent to the one sentence and the range of stimulations that would prompt assent to the other.[6]

It is no shock to the preconceptions of old Vienna to say that epistemology now becomes semantics. For epistemology remains centered as always on evidence, and meaning remains centered as always on verification; and evidence is verification. What is likelier to shock preconceptions is that meaning, once we get beyond observation sentences, ceases in general to have any clear applicability to single sentences; also that epistemology merges with psychology, as well as with linguistics.

This rubbing out of boundaries could contribute to progress, it seems to me, in philosophically interesting inquiries of a scientific nature. One possible area is perceptual norms. Consider, to begin with, the linguistic phenomenon of phonemes. We form the habit, in hearing the myriad variations of spoken sounds, of treating each as an approximation to one or another of a limited number of norms – around thirty altogether – constituting so to speak a spoken alphabet. All speech in our language can be treated in practice as sequences of just those thirty elements, thus rectifying small deviations. Now outside the realm of language also there is probably only a rather limited alphabet of perceptual norms altogether, toward which we tend unconsciously to rectify all perceptions. These, if experimentally identified, could be taken as epistemological building blocks, the working elements of experience. They might prove in part to be culturally variable, as phonemes are, and in part universal.

Again there is the area that the psychologist Donald T. Campbell calls evolutionary epistemology.[7] In this area there is work by Hüseyin Yilmaz, who shows how some structural traits of color perception could have been predicted from survival value.[8] And a more emphatically epistemological topic that evolution helps to clarify is induction, now that we are allowing epistemology the resources of natural science.

Author's Notes

1   A. B. Johnson, *A Treatise on Language* (New York, 1836; Berkeley, 1947).
2   *Philosophy of Science* 3 (1936), 419–71; 4 (1937), 1–40.
3   Carnap and Neurath in *Erkenntnis* 3 (1932), 204–28.
4   N. R. Hanson, "Observation and interpretation," in S. Morgenbesser, ed., *Philosophy of Science Today* (New York: Basic Books, 1966).
5   This qualification allows for occasional deviants such as the insane or the blind. Alternatively, such cases might be excluded by adjusting the level of fluency of dialogue whereby we define sameness of language. (For prompting this note and influencing the development of this paper also in more substantial ways I am indebted to Burton Dreben [the very influential and Socratic Wittgensteinian, Burton Dreben (1928–99), late of Harvard and Boston Universities].)
6   Cf. Quine, *Word and Object*, pp. 31–46, 68.
7   D. T. Campbell, "Methodological suggestions from a comparative psychology of knowledge processes," *Inquiry* 2 (1959), 152–82.
8   Hüseyin Yilmaz, "On color vision and a new approach to general perception," in E. E. Bernard and M. R. Kare, eds., *Biological Prototypes and Synthetic Systems* (New York: Plenum, 1962); "Perceptual invariance and the psychophysical law," *Perception and Psychophysics* 2 (1967), 533–8.

52

"The Virtues, the Unity of a Human Life, and the Concept of a Tradition"

Alasdair MacIntyre

Philosopher Alasdair MacIntyre (1929–) agrees with postmodernists on the disability of the modern consciousness or Enlightenment, but disagrees on the solution, choosing to renovate the premodern rather than splurge on a brand new postmodernism. Enlightened liberalism has regarded cultural tradition as, at best, a nuisance, at worst a regressive force. But, MacIntyre insists in his 1981 book *After Virtue*, traditions provide the ultimate vocabularies for the narratives that constitute the only source of intelligibility for human agency. Man is a story-telling animal. Rational deliberation itself is impossible outside of a cultural tradition. By denying the legitimacy of traditional narratives modern liberal societies condemn all public deliberation to clashing pronouncements of subjective preferences incapable of adjudication. MacIntyre's hope lies in a rehabilitation of the virtue ethics of Aristotle which, unlike the attempted universalism of Kantian ethics and Utilitarianism, accepts an intrinsically social moral psychology tied to an ultimate cultural *telos*.

Any contemporary attempt to envisage each human life as a whole, as a unity, whose character provides the virtues with an adequate *telos* encounters two different kinds of obstacle, one social and one philosophical. The social obstacles derive from the way in which modernity partitions each human life into a variety of segments, each with its own norms and modes of behavior. So work is divided from leisure, private life from public, the corporate from the personal. So both childhood and old age have been wrenched away from the rest of human life and

made over into distinct realms. And all these separations have been achieved so that it is the distinctiveness of each and not the unity of the life of the individual who passes through those parts in terms of which we are taught to think and to feel.

The philosophical obstacles derive from two distinct tendencies, one chiefly, though not only, domesticated in analytical philosophy and one at home in both sociological theory and in existentialism. The former is the tendency to think atomistically about human action and to analyze complex actions and transactions in terms of simple components. Hence the recurrence in more than one context of the notion of "a basic action." That particular actions derive their character as parts of larger wholes is a point of view alien to our dominant ways of thinking and yet one which it is necessary at least to consider if we are to begin to understand how a life may be more than a sequence of individual actions and episodes.

Equally the unity of a human life becomes invisible to us when a sharp separation is made either between the individual and the roles that he or she plays – a separation characteristic not only of Sartre's existentialism, but also of the sociological theory of Ralf Dahrendorf – or between the different role – and quasi-role – enactments of an individual life so that life comes to appear as nothing but

Alasdair MacIntyre, "The Virtues, the Unity of a Human Life and the Concept of a Tradition," chapter 15 (pp. 204–25) from *After Virtue: A Study in Moral Theory*. Notre Dame, Ind.: University of Notre Dame Press, 1984.

a series of unconnected episodes – a liquidation of the self characteristic, as I noticed earlier, of Goffman's sociological theory. I already, also suggested [in Chapter 3] that both the Sartrian and the Goffmanesque[i] conceptions of selfhood are highly characteristic of the modes of thought and practice of modernity. It is perhaps therefore unsurprising to realize that the self as thus conceived cannot be envisaged as a bearer of the Aristotelian virtues.

For a self separated from its roles in the Sartrian mode loses that arena of social relationships in which the Aristotelian virtues function if they function at all. The patterns of a virtuous life would fall under those condemnations of conventionality which Sartre put into the mouth of Antoine Roquentin in La Nausée and which he uttered in his own person in L'Etre et le néant.[ii] Indeed the self's refusal of the inauthenticity of conventionalized social relationships becomes what integrity is diminished into in Sartre's account.

At the same time the liquidation of the self into a set of demarcated areas of role-playing allows no scope for the exercise of dispositions which could genuinely be accounted virtues in any sense remotely Aristotelian. For a virtue is not a disposition that makes for success only in some one particular type of situation. What are spoken of as the virtues of a good committee man or of a good administrator or of a gambler or a pool hustler are professional skills professionally deployed in those situations where they can be effective, not virtues. Someone who genuinely possesses a virtue can be expected to manifest it in very different types of situation, many of them situations where the practice of a virtue cannot be expected to be effective in the way that we expect a professional skill to be. Hector exhibited one and the same courage in his parting from Andromache and on the battlefield with Achilles; Eleanor Marx exhibited one and the same compassion in her relationship with her father, in her work with trade unionists and in her entanglement with Aveling. And the unity of a virtue in someone's life is intelligible only as a characteristic of a unitary life, a life that can be conceived and evaluated as a whole. Hence just as in the discussion of the changes in and fragmentation of morality which accompanied the rise of modernity in the earlier parts of this book, each

stage in the emergence of the characteristically modern views of the moral judgment was accompanied by a corresponding stage in the emergence of the characteristically modern conceptions of selfhood; so now, in defining the particular premodern concept of the virtues with which I have been preoccupied, it has become necessary to say something of the concomitant concept of selfhood, a concept of a self whose unity resides in the unity of a narrative which links birth to life to death as narrative beginning to middle to end.

Such a conception of the self is perhaps less unfamiliar than it may appear at first sight. Just because it has played a key part in the cultures which are historically predecessors of our own, it would not be surprising if it turned out to be still an unacknowledged presence in many of our ways of thinking and acting. Hence it is not inappropriate to begin by scrutinizing some of our most taken-for-granted, but clearly correct conceptual insights about human actions and selfhood in order to show how natural it is to think of the self in a narrative mode.

It is a conceptual commonplace, both for philosophers and for ordinary agents, that one and the same segment of human behavior may be correctly characterized in a number of different ways. To the question "What is he doing?" the answers may with equal truth and appropriateness be "Digging," "Gardening," "Taking exercise," "Preparing for winter" or "Pleasing his wife." Some of these answers will characterize the agent's intentions, others unintended consequences of his actions, and of these unintended consequences some may be such that the agent is aware of them and others not. What is important to notice immediately is that any answer to the questions of how we are to understand or to explain a given segment of behavior will presuppose some prior answer to the question of how these different correct answers to the question "What is he doing?" are related to each other. For if someone's primary intention is to put the garden in order before the winter and it is only incidentally the case that in so doing he is taking exercise and pleasing his wife, we have one type of behavior to be explained; but if the agent's primary intention is to please his wife by taking exercise, we have quite another type of behavior to be explained and we will have to look in a different direction for understanding and explanation.

In the first place the episode has been situated in an annual cycle of domestic activity, and the behavior embodies an intention which presupposes a particular type of household-cum-garden setting

---

[i] Erving Goffman (1922–82), sociologist famous for studying the relation of personal identity to social roles.
[ii] Sartre's novel, Nausea, and his most important philosophical work, Being and Nothingness, respectively.

with the peculiar narrative history of that setting in which this segment of behavior now becomes an episode. In the second instance the episode has been situated in the narrative history of a marriage, a very different, even if related, social setting. We cannot, that is to say, characterize behavior independently of intentions, and we cannot characterize intentions independently of the settings which make those intentions intelligible both to agents themselves and to others.

I use the word 'setting' here as a relatively inclusive term. A social setting may be an institution, it may be what I have called a practice, or it may be a milieu of some other human kind. But it is central to the notion of a setting as I am going to understand it that a setting has a history, a history within which the histories of individual agents not only are, but have to be, situated, just because without the setting and its changes through time the history of the individual agent and his changes through time will be unintelligible. Of course one and the same piece of behavior may belong to more than one setting. There are at least two different ways in which this may be so.

In my earlier example the agent's activity may be part of the history both of the cycle of household activity and of his marriage, two histories which have happened to intersect. The household may have its own history stretching back through hundreds of years, as do the histories of some European farms, where the farm has had a life of its own, even though different families have in different periods inhabited it; and the marriage will certainly have its own history, a history which itself presupposes that a particular point has been reached in the history of the institution of marriage. If we are to relate some particular segment of behavior in any precise way to an agent's intentions and thus to the settings which that agent inhabits, we shall have to understand in a precise way how the variety of correct characterizations of the agent's behavior relate to each other first by identifying which characteristics refer us to an intention and which do not and then by classifying further the items in both categories.

Where intentions are concerned, we need to know which intention or intentions were primary, that is to say, of which it is the case that, had the agent intended otherwise, he would not have performed that action. Thus if we know that a man is gardening with the self-avowed purposes of healthful exercise and of pleasing his wife, we do not yet know how to understand what he is doing until we know the answer to such questions as whether he would con-

tinue gardening if he continued to believe that gardening was healthful exercise, but discovered that his gardening no longer pleased his wife, *and* whether he would continue gardening, if he ceased to believe that gardening was healthful exercise, but continued to believe that it pleased his wife, *and* whether he would continue gardening if he changed his beliefs on both points. That is to say, we need to know both what certain of his beliefs are and which of them are causally effective; and, that is to say, we need to know whether certain contrary-to-fact hypothetical statements are true or false. And until we know this, we shall not know how to characterize correctly what the agent is doing.

Consider another equally trivial example of a set of compatible correct answers to the question "What is he doing?" "Writing a sentence"; "Finishing his book"; "Contributing to the debate on the theory of action"; "Trying to get tenure." Here the intentions can be ordered in terms of the stretch of time to which reference is made. Each of the shorter-term intentions is, and can only be made, intelligible by reference to some longer-term intentions; and the characterization of the behavior in terms of the longer-term intentions can only be correct if some of the characterizations in terms of shorter-term intentions are also correct. Hence the behaviour is only characterized adquately when we know what the longer and longest-term intentions invoked are and how the shorter-term intentions are related to the longer. Once again we are involved in writing a narrative history.

Intentions thus need to be ordered both causally and temporally and both orderings will make references to settings, references already made obliquely by such elementary terms as "gardening," "wife," "book," and "tenure." Moreover the correct identification of the agent's beliefs will be an essential constituent of this task; failure at this point would mean failure in the whole enterprise. (The conclusion may seem obvious; but it already entails one important consequence. There is no such thing as 'behaviour', to be identified prior to and independently of intentions, beliefs and settings. Hence the project of a science of behavior takes on a mysterious and somewhat outré character. It is not that such a science is impossible; but there is nothing for it to be but a science of uninterpreted physical movement such as B.F. Skinner aspires to.[iii] It is no part of my taks here to examine Skinner's problems; but it is

iii   B. F. Skinner (1904–90), famous American behaviorist psychologist.

worth noticing that it is not at all clear what a scientific experiment could be, if one were a Skinnerian; since the conception of an experiment is certainly one of intention- and belief-informed behavior. And what would be utterly doomed to failure would be the project of a science of, say, *political* behavior, detached from a study of intentions, beliefs and settings. It is perhaps worth noting that when the expression "the behavioral sciences" was given its first influential use in a Ford Foundation Report of 1953, the term "behavior" was defined so as to include what were called "such subjective behavior as attitudes, beliefs, expectations, motivations and aspirations" as well as "overt acts." But what the Report's wording seems to imply is that it is cataloguing two distinct sets of items, available for independent study. If the argument so far is correct, then there is only one set of items.)

Consider what the argument so far implies about the interrelationships of the intentional, the social and the historical. We identify a particular action only by invoking two kinds of context, implicitly if not explicitly. We place the agent's intentions, I have suggested, in causal and temporal order with reference to their role in his or her history; and we also place them with reference to their role in the history of the setting or settings to which they belong. In doing this, in determining what causal efficacy the agent's intentions had in one or more directions, and how his short-term intentions succeeded or failed to be constitutive of long-term intentions, we ourselves write a further part of these histories. Narrative history of a certain kind turns out to be the basic and essential genre for the characterization of human actions.

It is important to be clear how different the standpoint presupposed by the argument so far is from that of those analytical philosophers who have constructed accounts of human actions which make central the notion of "a" human action. A course of human events is then seen as a complex sequence of individual actions, and a natural question is: How do we individuate human actions? Now there are contexts in which such notions are at home. In the recipes of a cookery book for instance actions are individuated in just the way that some analytical philosophers have supposed to be possible of all actions. "Take six eggs. Then break them into a bowl. Add flour, salt, sugar, etc." But the point about such sequences is that each element in them is intelligible as an action only as a-possible-element-in-a-sequence. Moreover even such a sequence requires a context to be intelligible. If in the middle of my lecture on Kant's ethics I suddenly broke six eggs into a bowl and added flour and sugar, proceeding all the while with my Kantian exegesis, I have *not*, simply in virtue of the fact that I was following a sequence prescribed by Fanny Farmer, performed an intelligible action.

To this it might be retorted that I certainly performed an action or a set of actions, if not an intelligible action. But to this I want to reply that the concept of an intelligible action, is a more fundamental concept than that of an action as such. Unintelligible actions are failed candidates for the status of intelligible action; and to lump unintelligible actions and intelligible actions together in a single class of actions and then to characterize action in terms of what items of both sets have in common is to make the mistake of ignoring this. It is also to neglect the central importance of the concept of intelligibility.

The importance of the concept of intelligibility is closely related to the fact that the most basic distinction of all embedded in our discourse and our practice in this area is that between human beings and other beings. Human beings can be held to account for that of which they are the authors; other beings cannot. To identify an occurrence as an action is in the paradigmatic instances to identify it under a type of description which enables us to see that occurrence as flowing intelligibly from a human agent's intentions, motives, passions and purposes. It is therefore to understand an action as something for which someone is accountable, about which it is always appropriate to ask the agent for an intelligible account. When an occurrence is apparently the intended action of a human agent, but nonetheless we cannot so identify it, we are both intellectually and practically baffled. We do not know how to respond; we do not know how to explain; we do not even know how to characterize minimally as an intelligible action; our distinction between the humanly accountable and the merely natural seems to have broken down. And this kind of bafflement does indeed occur in a number of different kinds of situation; when we enter alien cultures or even alien social structures within our own culture, in our encounters with certain types of neurotic or psychotic patient (it is indeed the unintelligibility of such patients' actions that leads to their being treated as patients; actions unintelligible to the agent as well as to everyone else are understood – rightly – as a kind of suffering), but also in everyday situations. Consider an example.

I am standing waiting for a bus and the young man standing next to me suddenly says: "The name of the common wild duck is *Histrionicus histrionicus histrionicus*." There is no problem as to the meaning of the sentence he uttered: the problem is, how to answer the question, what was he doing in uttering it? Suppose he just uttered such sentences at random intervals; this would be one possible form of madness. We would render his action of utterance intelligible if one of the following turned out to be true. He has mistaken me for someone who yesterday had approached him in the library and asked: "Do you by any chance know the Latin name of the common wild duck?" *Or* he has just come from a session with his psychotherapist who has urged him to break down his shyness by talking to strangers. "But what shall I say?" "Oh, anything at all." *Or* he is a Soviet spy waiting at a prearranged rendez-vous and uttering the ill-chosen code sentence which will identify him to his contact. In each case the act of utterance becomes intelligible by finding its place in a narrative.

To this it may be replied that the supplying of a narrative is not necessary to make such an act intelligible. All that is required is that we can identify the relevant type of speech act (e.g. "He was answering a question") or some purpose served by his utterance (e.g. "He was trying to attract your attention"). But speech acts and purposes too can be intelligible or unintelligible. Suppose that the man at the bus stop explains his act of utterance by saying "I was answering a question." I reply: "But I never asked you any question to which that could have been the answer." He says, "Oh, I know *that*." Once again his action becomes unintelligible. And a parallel example could easily be constructed to show that the mere fact that an action serves some purposes of a recognized type is not sufficient to render an action intelligible. Both purposes and speech-acts require contexts.

The most familiar type of context in and by reference to which speech-acts and purposes are rendered intelligible is the conversation. Conversation is so all-pervasive a feature of the human world that it tends to escape philosophical attention. Yet remove conversation from human life and what would be left? Consider then what is involved in following a conversation and finding it intelligible or unintelligible. (To find a conversation intelligible is not the same as to understand it; for a conversation which I overhear may be intelligible, but I may fail to understand it.) If I listen to a conversation between two other people my ability to grasp the thread of the conversation will involve an ability to bring it under some one out of a set of descriptions in which the degree and kind of coherence in the conversation is brought out: "a drunken, rambling quarrel," "a serious intellectual disagreement," "a tragic misunderstanding of each other," "a comic, even farcial miscontrual of each other's motives," "a penetrating interchange of views," "a struggle to dominate each other," "a trivial exchange of gossip."

The use of words such as "tragic," "comic," and "farcial" is not marginal to such evaluations. We allocate conversations to genres, just as we do literary narratives. Indeed a conversation is a dramatic work, even if a very short one, in which the participants are not only the actors, but also the joint authors, working out in agreement or disagreement the mode of their production. For it is not just that conversations belong to genres in just the way that plays and novels do; but they have beginnings, middles and endings just as do literary works. They embody reversals and recognitions; they move towards and away from climaxes. There may within a longer conversation be digressions and subplots, indeed digressions within digressions and subplots within subplots.

But if this is true of conversations, it is true also *mutatis mutandis* of battles, chess games, courtships, philosophy seminars, families at the dinner table, businessmen negotiating contracts – that is, of human transactions in general. For conversation, understood widely enough, is the form of human transactions in general. Conversational behavior is not a special sort or aspect of human behavior, even though the forms of language-using and of human life are such that the deeds of others speak for them as much as do their words. For that is possible only because they are the deeds of those who have words.

I am presenting both conversations in particular then and human actions in general as enacted narratives. Narrative is not the work of poets, dramatists and novelists reflecting upon events which had no narrative order before one was imposed by the singer or the writer; narrative form is neither disguise nor decoration. Barbara Hardy has written that "we dream in narrative, day-dream in narrative, remember, anticipate, hope, despair, believe, doubt, plan, revise, criticize, construct, gossip, learn, hate and love by narrative" in arguing the same point.[iv]

[iv] Barbara Hardy, "Towards a Poetics of Fiction," *Novel*, 2, 1968: 5–14.

At the beginning of this chapter I argued that in successfully identifying and understanding what someone else is doing we always move towards placing a particular episode in the context of a set of narrative histories, histories both of the individuals concerned and of the settings in which they act and suffer. It is now becoming clear that we render the actions of others intelligible in this way because action itself has a basically historical character. It is because we all live out narratives in our lives and because we understand our own lives in terms of the narratives that we live out that the form of narrative is appropriate for understanding the actions of others. Stories are lived before they are told – except in the case of fiction.

This has of course been denied in recent debates. Louis O. Mink, quarrelling with Barbara Hardy's view, has asserted: "Stories are not lived but told. Life has no beginnings, middles, or ends; there are meetings, but the start of an affair belongs to the story we tell ourselves later, and there are partings, but final partings only in the story. There are hopes, plans, battles and ideas, but only in retrospective stories are hopes unfulfilled, plans miscarried, battles decisive, and ideas seminal. Only in the story is it America which Columbus discovers and only in the story is the kingdom lost for want of a nail".[v]

What are we to say to this? Certainly we must agree that it is only retrospectively that hopes can be characterized as unfulfilled or battles as decisive and so on. But we so characterize them in life as much as in art. And to someone who says that in life there are no endings, or that final partings take place only in stories, one is tempted to reply, "But have you never heard of death?" Homer did not have to tell the tale of Hector before Andromache could lament unfulfilled hope and final parting.[vi] There are countless Hectors and countless Andromaches whose lives embodied the form of their Homeric namesakes, but who never came to the attention of any poet. What is true is that in taking an event as a beginning or an ending we bestow a significance upon it which may be debatable. Did the Roman republic end with the death of Julius Caesar, or at Philippi, or with the founding of the principate? The answer is surely that, like Charles II, it was a long time a-dying; but this answer implies the reality of its ending as much as

do any of the former. There is a crucial sense in which the principate of Augustus, or the taking of the oath in the tennis court, or the decision to construct an atomic bomb at Los Alamos constitute beginnings; the peace of 404 BC, the abolition of the Scottish Parliament and the battle of Waterloo equally constitute endings; while there are many events which are both endings and beginnings.[vii]

As with beginnings, middles and endings, so also with genres and with the phenomenon of embedding. Consider the question of to what genre the life of Thomas Becket belongs, a question which has to be asked and answered before we can decide how it is to be written. (On Mink's paradoxical view this question could not be asked until *after* the life had been written.) In some of the medieval versions, Thomas's career is presented in terms of the canons of medieval hagiography. In the Icelandic *Thomas Saga* he is presented as a saga hero. In Dom David Knowles's modern biography the story is a tragedy, the tragic relationship of Thomas and Henry II, each of whom satisfies Aristotle's demand that the hero be a great man with a fatal flaw. Now it clearly makes sense to ask who is right, if anyone: the monk William of Canterbury, the author of the saga, or the Cambridge Regius Professor Emeritus? The answer appears to be clearly the last. The true genre of the life is neither hagiography nor saga, but tragedy. So of such modern narrative subjects as the life of Trotsky or that of Lenin, of the history of the Soviet Communist Party or the American presidency, we may also ask: To what genre does their history belong? And this is the same question as: What type of account of their history will be both true and intelligible?

Or consider again how one narrative may be embedded in another. In both plays and novels there are well-known examples: the play within the play in *Hamlet*, Wandering Willie's Tale in *Redgauntlet*, Aeneas' narrative to Dido in book 2 of the *Aeneid*, and so on.[viii] But there are equally well-known examples in real life. Consider again the way in which the career of Becket as archbishop and chancellor is embedded within the reign of Henry II, or the way in which the tragic life of Mary Stuart is embedded in that of Elizabeth I, or

[v] Louis O. Mink, "History and Fiction as Modes of Comprehension," *New Literary History*, 1, 1970: 541–58.
[vi] In the *Iliad*.

[vii] Augustus Caesar, Roman Emperor (27 BC–AD 14); in the French Revolution a republican National Assembly was first declared on a tennis court; the Peloponnesian War ended in 404 BC; the Scottish Parliament ended in 1707; in 1815 Napoleon was defeated at Waterloo.
[viii] *Redgauntlet* by Sir Walter Scott (1771–1832), *Aeneid* by Virgil (70–19 BC).

the history of the Confederacy within the history of the United States. Someone may discover (or not discover) that he or she is a character in a number of narratives at the same time, some of them embedded in others. Or again, what seemed to be an intelligible narrative in which one was playing a part may be transformed wholly or partly into a story of unintelligible episodes. This last is what happened to Kafka's character K. in both *The Trial* and *The Castle*. (It is no accident that Kafka could not end his novels, for the notion of an ending like that of a beginning has its sense only in terms of intelligible narrative.)

I spoke earlier of the agent as not only an actor, but an author. Now I must emphasize that what the agent is able to do and say intelligibly as an actor is deeply affected by the fact that we are never more (and sometimes less) than the co-authors of our own narratives. Only in fantasy do we live what story we please. In life, as both Aristotle and Engels noted, we are always under certain constraints. We enter upon a stage which we did not design and we find ourselves part of an action that was not of our making. Each of us being a main character in his own drama plays subordinate parts in the dramas of others, and each drama constrains the others. In my drama, perhaps, I am Hamlet or Iago or at least the swineherd who may yet become a prince, but to you I am only A Gentleman or at best Second Murderer, while you are my Polonius or my Gravedigger, but your own hero. Each of our dramas exerts constraints on each other's, making the whole different from the parts, but still dramatic.

It is considerations as complex as these which are involved in making the notion of intelligibility the conceptual connecting link between the notion of action and that of narrative. Once we have understood its importance the claim that the concept of an action is secondary to that of an intelligible action will perhaps appear less bizarre and so too will the claim that the notion of 'an' action, while of the highest practical importance, is always a potentially misleading abstraction. An action is a moment in a possible or actual history or in a number of such histories. The notion of a history is as fundamental a notion as the notion of an action. Each requires the other. But I cannot say this without noticing that it is precisely this that Sartre denies – as indeed his whole theory of the self, which captures so well the spirit of modernity, requires that he should. In *La Nausée*, Sartre makes Antoine Roquentin argue not just what Mink argues, that narrative is very different from life, but that to present human life in

the form of a narrative is always to falsify it. There are not and there cannot be any true stories. Human life is composed of discrete actions which lead nowhere, which have no order; the story-teller imposes on human events retrospectively an order which they did not have while they were lived. Clearly if Sartre/Roquentin is right – I speak of Sartre/Roquentin to distinguish him from such other well-known characters as Sartre/Heidegger and Sartre/Marx – my central contention must be mistaken. There is nonetheless an important point of agreement between my thesis and that of Sartre/Roquentin. We agree in identifying the intelligibility of an action with its place in a narrative sequence. Only Sartre/Roquentin takes it that human actions are as such unintelligible occurrences: it is to a realization of the metaphysical implications of this that Roquentin is brought in the course of the novel and the practical effect upon him is to bring to an end his own project of writing an historical biography. This project no longer makes sense. Either he will write what is true or he will write an intelligible history, but the one possibility excludes the other. Is Sartre/Roquentin right?

We can discover what is wrong with Sartre's thesis in either of two ways. One is to ask: what would human actions deprived of any falsifying narrative order be like? Sartre himself never answers this question; it is striking that in order to show that there are no true narratives, he himself writes a narrative, albeit a fictional one. But the only picture that I find myself able to form of human nature *an-sich*,[ix] prior to the alleged misinterpretation by narrative, is the kind of dislocated sequence which Dr Johnson offers us in his notes of his travels in France: "There we waited on the ladies – Morville's. – Spain. Country towns all beggars. At Dijon he could not find the way to Orleans. – Cross roads of France very bad. – Five soldiers. – Women. – Soldiers escaped. – The Colonel would not lose five men for the sake of one woman. – The magistrate cannot seize a soldier but by the Colonel's permission, etc., etc."[x] What this suggests is what I take to be true, namely that the characterization of actions allegedly prior to any narrative form being imposed upon them will always turn out to be the presentation of what are

---

[ix] In–itself.

[x] See Philip Hobsbaum, *A Reader's Guide to Charles Dickens* (New York, 1973), p. 32.

plainly the disjointed parts of some possible narrative.

We can also approach the question in another way. What I have called a history is an enacted dramatic narrative in which the characters are also the authors. The characters of course never start literally *ab initio*; they plunge *in medias res*, the beginnings of their story already made for them by what and who has gone before. But when Julian Grenfell or Edward Thomas went off to France in the 1914–18 war they no less enacted a narrative than did Menelaus or Odysseus when *they* went off.[xi] The difference between imaginary characters and real ones is not in the narrative form of what they do; it is in the degree of their authorship of that form and of their own deeds. Of course just as they do not begin where they please, they cannot go on exactly as they please either; each character is constrained by the actions of others and by the social settings presupposed in his and their actions, a point forcibly made by Marx in the classical, if not entirely satisfactory account of human life as enacted dramatic narrative, *The Eighteenth Brumaire of Louis Bonaparte*.

I call Marx's account less than satisfactory partly because he wishes to present the narrative of human social life in a way that will be compatible with a view of the life as law-governed and predictable in a particular way. But it is crucial that at any given point in an enacted dramatic narrative we do not know what will happen next. The kind of unpredictability for which I argued [in Chapter 8] is required by the narrative structure of human life, and the empirical generalizations and explorations which social scientists discover provide a kind of understanding of human life which is perfectly compatible with that structure.

This unpredictability coexists with a second crucial characteristic of all lived narratives, a certain teleological character. We live out our lives, both individually and in our relationships with each other, in the light of certain conceptions of a possible shared future, a future in which certain possibilities beckon us forward and others repel us, some seem already foreclosed and others perhaps inevitable. There is no present which is not informed by some image of some future and an image of the future which always presents itself in the form of a

telos – or of a variety of ends or goals – towards which we are either moving or failing to move in the present. Unpredictability and teleology therefore coexist as part of our lives; like characters in a fictional narrative we do not know what will happen next, but nonetheless our lives have a certain form which projects itself towards our future. Thus the narratives which we live out have both an unpredictable and a partially teleological character. If the narrative of our individual and social lives is to continue intelligibly – and either type of narrative may lapse into unintelligibility – it is always both the case that there are constraints on how the story can continue *and* that within those constraints there are indefinitely many ways that it can continue.

A central thesis then begins to emerge: man is in his actions and practice, as well as in his fictions, essentially a story-telling animal. He is not essentially, but becomes through his history, a teller of stories that aspire to truth. But the key question for men is not about their own authorship; I can only answer the question "What am I to do?" if I can answer the prior question "Of what story or stories do I find myself a part?" We enter human society, that is, with one or more imputed characters – roles into which we have been drafted – and we have to learn what they are in order to be able to understand how others respond to us and how our responses to them are apt to be construed. It is through hearing stories about wicked stepmothers, lost children, good but misguided kings, wolves that suckle twin boys, youngest sons who receive no inheritance but must make their own way in the world and eldest sons who waste their inheritance on riotous living and go into exile to live with the swine, that children learn or mislearn both what a child and what a parent is, what the cast of characters may be in the drama into which they have been born and what the ways of the world are. Deprive children of stories and you leave them unscripted, anxious stutterers in their actions as in their words. Hence there is no way to give us an understanding of any society, including our own, except through the stock of stories which constitute its initial dramatic resources. Mythology, in its original sense, is at the heart of things. Vico[xii] was right and so was Joyce. And so too of course is that moral tradition from heroic society to its medieval heirs according

---

[xi] English writers Julian Grenfell (1888–1915) and Edward Thomas (1878–1917) died in the war; Menelaus, King of Sparta, served Greece in the Trojan War, as did Odysseus, hero of Homer's *Odyssey*.

[xii] The Italian philosopher Giambattista Vico (1668–1744) argued against the rationalism of his day for the ineliminability of mythical thought.

to which the telling of stories has a key part in educating us into the virtues.

I suggested earlier that "an" action is always an episode in a possible history: I would now like to make a related suggestion about another concept, that of personal identity. Derek Parfit and others have recently drawn our attention to the contrast between the criteria of strict identity, which is an all-or-nothing matter (*either* the Tichborne claimant *is* the last Tichborne heir *or* he is not; *either* all the properties of the last heir belong to the claimant *or* the claimant is not the heir — Leibniz's Law applies)[xiii] and the psychological continuities of personality which are a matter of more or less. (Am I the same man at fifty as I was at forty in respect of memory, intellectual powers, critical responses? More or less.) But what is crucial to human beings as characters in enacted narratives is that, possessing only the resources of psychological continuity, we have to be able to respond to the imputation of strict identity. I am forever whatever I have been at any time for others — and I may at any time be called upon to answer for it — no matter how changed I may be now. There is no way of *founding* my identity — or lack of it — on the psychological continuity or discontinuity of the self. The self inhabits a character whose unity is given as the unity of a character. Once again there is a crucial disagreement with empiricist or analytical philosophers on the one hand and with existentialists on the other.

Empiricists, such as Locke or Hume, tried to give an account of personal identity solely in terms of psychological states or events. Analytical philosophers, in so many ways their heirs as well as their critics, have wrestled with the connection between those states and events and strict identity understood in terms of Leibniz's Law. Both have failed to see that a background has been omitted, the lack of which makes the problems insoluble. That background is provided by the concept of a story and of that kind of unity of character which a story requires. Just as a history is not a sequence of actions, but the concept of an action is that of a moment in an actual or possible history abstracted for some purpose from that history, so the characters in a history are not a collection of persons, but the concept of a person is that of a character abstracted from a history.

What the narrative concept of selfhood requires is thus twofold. On the one hand, I am what I may justifiably be taken by others to be in the course of living out a story that runs from my birth to my death; I am the *subject* of a history that is my own and no one else's, that has its own peculiar meaning. When someone complains — as do some of those who attempt or commit suicide — that his or her life is meaningless, he or she is often and perhaps characteristically complaining that the narrative of their life has become unintelligible to them, that it lacks any point, any movement towards a climax or a *telos*.[xiv] Hence the point of doing any one thing rather than another at crucial junctures in their lives seems to such a person to have been lost.

To be the subject of a narrative that runs from one's birth to one's death is, I remarked earlier, to be accountable for the actions and experiences which compose a narratable life. It is, that is, to be open to being asked to give a certain kind of account of what one did or what happened to one or what one witnessed at any earlier point in one's life than the time at which the question is posed. Of course someone may have forgotten or suffered brain damage or simply not attended sufficiently at the relevant time to be able to give the relevant account. But to say of someone under some one description ("The prisoner of the Chateau d'If") that he is the same person as someone characterized quite differently ("The Count of Monte Cristo") is precisely to say that it makes sense to ask him to give an intelligible narrative account enabling us to understand how he could at different times and different places be one and the same person and yet be so differently characterized. Thus personal identity is just that identity presupposed by the unity of the character which the unity of a narrative requires. Without such unity there would not be subjects of whom stories could be told.

The other aspect of narrative selfhood is correlative: I am not only accountable, I am one who can always ask others for an account, who can put others to the question. I am part of their story, as they are part of mine. The narrative of any one life is part of an interlocking set of narratives. Moreover this asking for and giving of accounts itself plays an important part in constituting narratives. Asking you what you did and why, saying what I did and why, pondering the differences between your account of what I did and my account of what I did, and *vice versa*, these are essential constituents

[xiii] There was a false claim to the Tichborne estates in England in the nineteenth century; G. W. Leibniz held that two things are identical only if "indiscernible."

[xiv] Goal.

of all but the very simplest and barest of narratives. Thus without the accountability of the self those trains of events that constitute all but the simplest and barest of narratives could not occur; and without that same accountability narratives would lack that continuity required to make both them and the actions that constitute them intelligible.

It is important to notice that I am not arguing that the concepts of narrative or of intelligibility or of accountability are *more* fundamental than that of personal identity. The concepts of narrative, intelligibility and accountability presuppose the applicability of the concept of personal identity, just as it presupposes their applicability and just as indeed each of these three presupposes the applicability of the two others. The relationship is one of mutual presupposition. It does follow of course that all attempts to elucidate the notion of personal identity independently of and in isolation from the notions of narrative, intelligibility and accountability are bound to fail. As all such attempts have.

It is now possible to return to the question from which this enquiry into the nature of human action and identity started: In what does the unity of an individual life consist? The answer is that its unity is the unity of a narrative embodied in a single life. To ask "What is the good for me?" is to ask how best I might live out that unity and bring it to completion. To ask "What is the good for man?" is to ask what all answers to the former question must have in common. But now it is important to emphasize that it is the systematic asking of these two questions and the attempt to answer them in deed as well as in word which provide the moral life with its unity. The unity of a human life is the unity of a narrative quest. Quests sometimes fail, are frustrated, abandoned or dissipated into distractions; and human lives may in all these ways also fail. But the only criteria for success or failure in a human life as a whole are the criteria of success or failure in a narrated or to-be-narrated quest. A quest for what?

Two key features of the medieval conception of a quest need to be recalled. The first is that without some at least partly determinate conception of the final *telos* there could not be any beginning to a quest. Some conception of the good for man is required. Whence is such a conception to be drawn? Precisely from those questions which led us to attempt to transcend that limited conception of the virtues which is available in and through practices. It is in looking for a conception of *the* good which will enable us to order other goods, for

a conception of *the* good which will enable us to extend our understanding of the purpose and content of the virtues, for a conception of *the* good which will enable us to understand the place of integrity and constancy in life, that we initially define the kind of life which is a quest for the good. But secondly it is clear the medieval conception of a quest is not at all that of a search for something already adequately characterized, as miners search for gold or geologists for oil. It is in the course of the quest and only through encountering and coping with the various particular harms, dangers, temptations and distractions which provide any quest with its episodes and incidents that the goal of the quest is finally to be understood. A quest is always an education both as to the character of that which is sought and in self-knowledge.

The virtues therefore are to be understood as those dispositions which will not only sustain practices and enable us to achieve the goods internal to practices, but which will also sustain us in the relevant kind of quest for the good, by enabling us to overcome the harms, dangers, temptations and distractions which we encounter, and which will furnish us with increasing self-knowledge and increasing knowledge of the good. The catalogue of the virtues will therefore include the virtues required to sustain the kind of households and the kind of political communities in which men and women can seek for the good together and the virtues necessary for philosophical enquiry about the character of the good. We have then arrived at a provisional conclusion about the good life for man: the good life for man is the life spent in seeking for the good life for man, and the virtues necessary for the seeking are those which will enable us to understand what more and what else the good life for man is. We have also completed the second stage in our account of the virtues, by situating them in relation to the good life for man and not only in relation to practices. But our enquiry requires a third stage.

For I am never able to seek for the good or exercise the virtues only *qua* individual. This is partly because what it is to live the good life concretely varies from circumstance to circumstance even when it is one and the same conception of the good life and one and the same set of virtues which are being embodied in a human life. What the good life is for a fifth-century Athenian general will not be the same as what it was for a medieval nun or a seventeenth-century farmer. But it is not just that different individuals live in different social circumstances; it is also that we all approach our own circumstances as bearers of a particular social identity. I am someone's son or daughter, someone else's cousin or uncle, I am a citizen of this or that city, a member of this or that guild or profession; I belong to this clan, that tribe, this nation. Hence what is good for me has to be the good for one who inhabits these roles. As such, I inherit from the past of my family, my city, my tribe, my nation, a variety of debts, inheritances, rightful expectations and obligations. These constitute the given of my life, my moral starting point. This is in part what gives my life its own moral particularity.

This thought is likely to appear alien and even suprising from the standpoint of modern individualism. From the standpoint of individualism I am what I myself choose to be. I can always, if I wish to, put in question what are taken to be the merely contingent social features of my existence. I may biologically be my father's son; but I cannot be held responsible for what he did unless I choose implicitly or explicitly to assume such responsibility. I may legally be a citizen of a certain country; but I cannot be held responsible for what my country does or has done unless I choose implicitly or explicitly to assume such responsibility. Such individualism is expressed by those modern Americans who deny any responsibility for the effects of slavery upon black Americans, saying "I never owned any slaves." It is more subtly the standpoint of those other modern Americans who accept a nicely calculated responsibility for such effects measured precisely by the benefits they themselves as individuals have indirectly received from slavery. In both cases "being an American" is not in itself taken to be part of the moral identity of the individual. And of course there is nothing peculiar to modern Americans in this attitude: the Englishman who says, "*I* never did any wrong to Ireland; why bring up that old history as though it had something to do with *me*?" or the young German who believes that being born after 1945 means that what Nazis did to Jews has no moral relevance to his relationship to his Jewish contemporaries, exhibit the same attitude, that according to which the self is detachable from its social and historical roles and statuses. And the self so detached is of course a self very much at home in either Sartre's or Goffman's perspective, a self that can have no history. The contrast with the narrative view of the self is clear. For the story of my life is always embedded in the story of those communities from which I derive my

identity. I am born with a past; and to try to cut myself off from that past, in the individualist mode, is to deform my present relationships. The possession of an historical identity and the possession of a social identity coincide. Notice that rebellion against my identity is always one possible mode of expressing it.

Notice also that the fact that the self has to find its moral identity in and through its membership in communities such as those of the family, the neighborhood, the city and the tribe does not entail that the self has to accept the moral *limitations* of the particularity of those forms of community. Without those moral particularities to begin from there would never be anywhere to begin; but it is in moving forward from such particularity that the search for the good, for the universal, consists. Yet particularity can never be simply left behind or obliterated. The notion of escaping from it into a realm of entirely universal maxims which belong to man as such, whether in its eighteenth-century Kantian form or in the presentation of some modern analytical moral philosophies, is an illusion and an illusion with painful consequences. When men and women identify what are in fact their partial and particular causes too easily and too completely with the cause of some universal principle, they usually behave worse than they would otherwise do.

What I am, therefore, is in key part what I inherit, a specific past that is present to some degree in my present. I find myself part of a history and that is generally to say, whether I like it or not, whether I recognize it or not, one of the bearers of a tradition. It was important when I characterized the concept of a practice to notice that practices always have histories and that at any given moment what a practice is depends on a mode of understanding it which has been transmitted often through many generations. And thus, insofar as the virtues sustain the relationships required for practices, they have to sustain relationships to the past – and to the future – as well as in the present. But the traditions through which particular practices are transmitted and reshaped never exist in isolation for larger social traditions. What constitutes such traditions?

We are apt to be misled here by the ideological uses to which the concept of a tradition has been put by conservative political theorists. Characteristically such theorists have followed Burke in contrasting tradition with reason and the stability of tradition with conflict. Both contrasts obfuscate. For all reasoning takes place within the context of some traditional mode of thought, transcending through criticism and invention the limitations of what had hitherto been reasoned in that tradition; this is as true of modern physics as of medieval logic. Moreover when a tradition is in good order it is always partially constituted by an argument about the goods the pursuit of which gives to that tradition its particular point and purpose.

So when an institution – a university, say, or a farm, or a hospital – is the bearer of a tradition of practice or practices, its common life will be partly, but in a centrally important way, constituted by a continuous argument as to what a university is and ought to be or what good farming is or what good medicine is. Traditions, when vital, embody continuities of conflict. Indeed when a tradition becomes Burkean, it is always dying or dead.

The individualism of modernity could of course find no use for the notion of tradition within its own conceptual scheme except as an adversary notion; it therefore all too willingly abandoned it to the Burkeans, who, faithful to Burke's own allegiance, tried to combine adherence in politics to a conception of tradition which would vindicate the oligarchical revolution of property of 1688 and adherence in economics to the doctrine and institutions of the free market. The theoretical incoherence of this mismatch did not deprive it of ideological usefulness. But the outcome has been that modern conservatives are for the most part engaged in conserving only older rather than later versions of liberal individualism. Their own core doctrine is as liberal and as individualist as that of self-avowed liberals.

A living tradition then is an historically extended, socially embodied argument and an argument precisely in part about the goods which constitute that tradition. Within a tradition the pursuit of goods extends through generations, sometimes through many generations. Hence the individual's search for his or her good is generally and characteristically conducted within a context defined by those traditions of which the individual's life is a part, and this is true both of those goods which are internal to practices and of the goods of a single life. Once again the narrative phenomenon of embedding is crucial: the history of a practice in our time is generally and characteristically embedded in and made intelligible in terms of the larger and longer history of the tradition through which the practice in its present form was conveyed to us; the history of each of our own lives is generally and characteristically embedded in and made intelligible in terms of the larger and longer histories of a number of traditions. I have to say 'generally and characteristically' rather than 'always', for traditions decay, disintegrate and disappear. What then sustains and strengthens traditions? What weakens and destroys them?

The answer in key part is: the exercise or the lack of exercise of the relevant virtues. The virtues find their point and purpose not only in sustaining those relationships necessary if the variety of goods internal to practices are to be achieved and not only in sustaining the form of an individual life in which that individual may seek out his or her good as the good of his or her whole life, but also in sustaining those traditions which provide both practices and individual lives with their necessary historical context. Lack of justice, lack of truthfulness, lack of courage, lack of the relevant intellectual virtues – these corrupt traditions, just as they do those institutions and practices which derive their life from the traditions of which they are the contemporary embodiments. To recognize this is of course also to recognize the existence of an additional virtue, one whose importance is perhaps most obvious when it is least present, the virtue of having an adequate sense of the traditions to which one belongs or which confront one. This virtue is not to be confused with any form of conservative antiquarianism; I am not praising those who choose the conventional conservative role of *laudator temporis acti*.[xv] It is rather the case that an adequate sense of tradition manifests itself in a grasp of those future possibilities which the past has made available to the present. Living traditions, just because they continue a not-yet-completed narrative, confront a future whose determinate and determinable character, so far as it possesses any, derives from the past.

In practical reasoning the possession of this virtue is not manifested so much in the knowledge of a set of generalizations or maxims which may provide our practical inferences with major premises; its presence or absence rather appears in the kind of capacity for judgment which the agent possesses in knowing how to select among the relevant stack of maxims and how to apply them in particular situations. Cardinal Pole possessed it, Mary Tudor did not; Montrose possessed it, Charles I did not. What Cardinal Pole and the Marquis of Montrose possessed were in fact those virtues which enable their possessors to pursue

---

[xv] Eulogizer of times gone by.

both their own good and the good of the tradition of which they are the bearers even in situations defined by the necessity of tragic, dilemmatic choice.[xvi] Such choices, understood in the context of the tradition of the virtues, are very different from those which face the modern adherents of rival and incommensurable moral premises in the debates about which I wrote [in Chapter 2]. Wherein does the difference lie?

It has often been suggested – by J. L. Austin, for example – that *either* we can admit the existence of rival and contingently incompatible goods which make incompatible claims to our practical allegiance *or* we can believe in some determinate conception of *the* good life for man, but that these are mutually exclusive alternatives. No one can consistently hold both these views. What this contention is blind to is that there may be better or worse ways for individuals to live through the tragic confrontation of good with good. And that to know what the good life for man is may require knowing what are the better and what are the worse ways of living in and through such situations. Nothing *a priori* rules out this possibility; and this suggests that within a view such as Austin's there is concealed an unacknowledged empirical premise about the character of tragic situations.

One way in which the choice between rival goods in a tragic situation differs from the modern choice between incommensurable moral premises is that *both* of the alternative courses of action which confront the individual have to be recognized as leading to some authentic and substantial good. By choosing one I do nothing to diminish or derogate from the claim upon me of the other; and therefore, whatever I do, I shall have left undone what I ought to have done. The tragic protagonist, unlike the moral agent as depicted by Sartre or Hare,[xvii] is not choosing between allegiance to one moral principle rather than another, nor is he or she deciding upon some principle of priority between moral principles. Hence the "ought" involved has a different meaning and force from that of the "ought" in moral principles understood in a modern way. For the tragic protagonist cannot do everything that he or she ought to do. This "ought", unlike Kant's, does not imply "can."

Moreover any attempt to map the logic of such "ought" assertions on to some modal calculus so as to produce a version of deontic logic has to fail. (See, from a very different point of view, Bas C. Van Fraasen 1973.[xviii])

Yet it is clear that the moral task of the tragic protagonist may be performed better or worse, independently of the choice between alternatives that he or she makes – *ex hypothesi* he or she has no *right* choice to make.[xix] The tragic protagonist may behave heroically or unheroically, generously or ungenerously, gracefully or gracelessly, prudently or imprudently. To perform his or her task better rather than worse will be to do both what is better for him or her *qua* individual and *qua* parent or child or *qua* citizen or member of a profession, or perhaps *qua* some or all of these. The existence of tragic dilemmas casts no doubt upon and provides no counterexamples to the thesis that assertions of the form "To do this in this way would be better for X and/or for his or her family, city or profession" are susceptible of objective truth and falsity, any more than the existence of alternative and contingently incompatible forms of medical treatment casts doubt on the thesis that assertions of the form "To undergo his medical treatment in this way would be better for X and/or his or her family" are susceptible of objective truth and falsity. (See, from a different point of view, the illuminating discussion in Samuel Guttenplan[xx]).

The presupposition of this objectivity is of course that we can understand the notion of "good for X" and cognate notions in terms of some conception of the unity of X's life. What is better or worse for X depends upon the character of that intelligible narrative which provides X's life with its unity. Unsurprisingly it is the lack of any such unifying conception of a human life which underlies modern denials of the factual character of moral judgments and more especially of those judgments which ascribe virtues or vices to individuals.

I argued earlier that every moral philosophy has some particular sociology as its counterpart. What I have tried to spell out in this chapter is the kind of understanding of social life which the tradition of the virtues requires, a kind of understanding very different from those dominant in the culture of

---

[xvi] Reginald Pole (1500–58) English cardinal in the reign of Mary Tudor (1553–8); Marquess of Montrose (1612–50), Scottish general who changed sides to support Charles I, King 1625–49.

[xvii] Rom Hare, contemporary moral philosopher.

[xviii] "Values and the Heart's Command," *Journal of Philosophy*, 70, 1973: 5–19.

[xix] "*Ex hypothesi*" – according to what is assumed.

[xx] Samuel Guttenplan, "Moral Realism and Moral Dilemmas," *Proceedings of the Aristotelian Society*, 1979–80: 61–80.

bureaucratic individualism. Within that culture conceptions of the virtues become marginal and the tradition of the virtues remains central only in the lives of social groups whose existence is on the margins of the central culture. Within the central cultural of liberal or bureaucratic individualism new conceptions of the virtues emerge and the concept of a virtue is itself transformed. To the history of that transformation I therefore now turn; for we shall only understand the tradition of the virtues fully if we understand to what kinds of degeneration it has proved liable.

From "The Cultural Logic of Late Capitalism"

Fredric Jameson

Professor of comparative literature, Fredric Jameson (1934–) has commented widely on contemporary literature, art, and culture. In the following essay, originally published in 1984, Jameson presents a Marxist critique of postmodernism as an expression of the current state of capitalist society, "late capitalism." The phenomena that postmodernists interpret as signaling a discontinuity with modernity Jameson sees instead as symptoms of underlying political-economic realities that are continuous with earlier phases of capitalism. Far from treating cultural phenomena in the non-economic style of postmodernism, Jameson suggests that the hallmark of postmodern culture is the absorption of culture by multinational capital, the final overcoming of the partial independence that art and theory had been permitted by earlier forms of capitalism. He is a harsh critic of postmodern theory for celebrating, rather than criticizing, these developments.

The last few years have been marked by an inverted millenarianism in which premonitions of the future, catastrophic or redemptive, have been replaced by senses of the end of this or that (the end of ideology, art, or social class; the "crisis" of Leninism, social democracy, or the welfare state, etc., etc.); taken together, all of these perhaps constitute what is increasingly called postmodernism. The case for its existence depends on the hypothesis of some radical break or *coupure*, generally traced back to the end of the 1950s or the early 1960s.

As the word itself suggests, this break is most often related to notions of the waning or extinction of the hundred-year-old modern movement (or to its ideological or aesthetic repudiation). Thus abstract expressionism in painting, existentialism in philosophy, the final forms of representation in the novel, the films of the great *auteurs*, or the modernist school of poetry (as institutionalized and canonized in the works of Wallace Stevens) all are now seen as the final, extraordinary flowering of a high-modernist impulse which is spent and exhausted with them. The enumeration of what follows, then, at once becomes empirical, chaotic, and heterogeneous: Andy Warhol and pop art, but also photorealism, and beyond it, the "new expressionism";[i] the moment, in music, of John Cage, but also the synthesis of classical and "popular" styles found in composers like Phil Glass and Terry Riley, and also punk and new wave rock (the Beatles and the Stones now standing as the high-modernist moment of that more recent and rapidly evolving tradition); in film, Godard, post-Godard, and experimental cinema and video, but also a whole new type of commercial film (about which more below); Burroughs, Pynchon, or Ishmael Reed, on the one hand, and the French *nouveau roman*[ii] and its suc-

---

[i] Neo-Expressionism, a predominantly German style of painting from the 1960s to mid-1980s (e.g. see the work of Georg Baselitz).

[ii] Literally, "new novel," this refers to the French anti-novel of the 1950s and 1960s.

Fredric Jameson, pp. 1–6, 32–8, 45–51, and 54 from "The Cultural Logic of Late Capitalism," chapter 1 in *Postmodernism, Or, The Cultural Logic of Late Capitalism.* Durham: Duke University Press, 1991.

cession, on the other, along with alarming new kinds of literary criticism based on some new aesthetic of textuality or *écriture* . . .[iii] The list might be extended indefinitely; but does it imply any more fundamental change or break than the periodic style and fashion changes determined by an older high-modernist imperative of stylistic innovation?

It is in the realm of architecture, however, that modifications in aesthetic production are most dramatically visible, and that their theoretical problems have been most centrally raised and articulated; it was indeed from architectural debates that my own conception of postmodernism – as it will be outlined in the following pages – initially began to emerge. More decisively than in the other arts or media, postmodernist positions in architecture have been inseparable from an implacable critique of architectural high modernism and of Frank Lloyd Wright or the so-called international style (Le Corbusier, Mies, etc), where formal criticism and analysis (of the high-modernist transformation of the building into a virtual sculpture, or monumental "duck,"[iv] as Robert Venturi puts it)[1] are at one with reconsiderations on the level of urbanism and of the aesthetic institution. High modernism is thus credited with the destruction of the fabric of the traditional city and its older neighborhood culture (by way of the radical disjunction of the new Utopian high-modernist building from its surrounding context), while the prophetic elitism and authoritarianism of the modern movement are remorselessly identified in the imperious gesture of the charismatic Master.

Postmodernism in architecture will then logically enough stage itself as a kind of aesthetic populism, as the very title of Venturi's influential manifesto, *Learning from Las Vegas*, suggests. However, we may ultimately wish to evaluate this populist rhetoric,[2] it has at least the merit of drawing our attention to one fundamental feature of all the postmodernisms enumerated above: namely, the effacement in them of the older (essentially high-modernist) frontier between high culture and so-called mass or commerical culture, and the emergence of new kinds of texts infused with the forms, categories, and contents of that very culture indus-

try so passionately denounced by all the ideologues of the modern, from Leavis[v] and the American New Criticism[vi] all the way to Adorno and the Frankfurt School. The postmodernisms have, in fact, been fascinated precisely by this whole "degraded" landscape of schlock and kitsch, of TV series and *Reader's Digest* culture, of advertising and motels, of the late show and the grade-B Hollywood film, of so-called paraliterature, with its airport paperback categories of the gothic and the romance, the popular biography, the murder mystery, and the science fiction or fantasy novel: materials they no longer simply "quote," as a Joyce or a Mahler might have done, but incorporate into their very substance.

Nor should the break in question be thought of as a purely cultural affair: indeed, theories of the postmodern – whether celebratory or couched in the language of moral revulsion and denunciation – bear a strong family resemblance to all those more ambitious sociological generalizations which, at much the same time, bring us the news of the arrival and inauguration of a whole new type of society, most famously baptized "postindustrial society" (Daniel Bell) but often also designated consumer society, media society, information society, electronic society or high tech, and the like. Such theories have the obvious ideological mission of demonstrating, to their own relief, that the new social formation in question no longer obeys the laws of classical capitalism, namely, the primacy of industrial production and the omnipresence of class struggle. The Marxist tradition has therefore resisted them with vehemence, with the signal exception of the economist Ernest Mandel, whose book *Late Capitalism* sets out not merely to anatomize the historic originality of this new society (which he sees as a third stage or moment in the evolution of capital) but also to demonstrate that it is, if anything, a *purer* stage of capitalism than any of the moments that preceded it. I will return to this argument later; suffice it for the moment to anticipate a point that will be argued [in chapter 2], namely, that every position on postmodernism in culture – whether apologia or stigmatization – is also at one and the same time, and *necessarily*, an implicitly or explicitly political stance on the nature of multinational capitalism today.

[iii] Writing.

[iv] A category of building-as-sculpture, formulated by Robert Venturi in his *Learning from Las Vegas*. The term is taken from a photograph of a duck-shaped drive-in on Long Island in Peter Blake's *God's Own Junkyard: The Planned Deterioration of America's Landscape*.

[v] Frank Leavis (1895–1978) evaluated literature according to the author's moral standing.

[vi] Post-World War I critical school advocating purely internal analysis of literary texts.

A last preliminary word on method: what follows is not to be read as stylistic description, as the account of one cultural style or movement among others. I have rather meant to offer a periodizing hypothesis, and that at a moment in which the very conception of historical periodization has come to seem most problematical indeed. I have argued elsewhere that all isolated or discrete cultural analysis always involves a buried or repressed theory of historical periodization; in any case, the conception of the "genealogy" largely lays to rest traditional theoretical worries about so-called linear history, theories of "stages," and teleological historiography. In the present context, however, lengthier theoretical discussion of such (very real) issues can perhaps be replaced by a few substantive remarks.

One of the concerns frequently aroused by periodizing hypotheses is that these tend to obliterate difference and to project an idea of the historical period as massive homogeneity (bounded on either side by inexplicable chronological metamorphoses and punctuation marks). This is, however, precisely why it seems to me essential to grasp postmodernism not as a style but rather as a cultural dominant: a conception which allows for the presence and coexistence of a range of very different, yet subordinate, features.

Consider, for example, the powerful alternative position that postmodernism is itself little more than one more stage of modernism proper (if not, indeed, of the even older romanticism); it may indeed be conceded that all the features of postmodernism I am about to enumerate can be detected, full-blown, in this or that preceding modernism (including such astonishing genealogical precursors as Gertrude Stein, Raymond Roussel, or Marcel Duchamp, who may be considered outright postmodernists, avant la lettre).[vii] What has not been taken into account by this view, however, is the social position of the older modernism, or better still, its passionate repudiation by an older Victorian and post-Victorian bourgeoisie for whom its forms and ethos are received as being variously ugly, dissonant, obscure, scandalous, immoral, subversive, and generally "antisocial." It will be argued here, however, that a mutation in the sphere of culture has rendered such attitudes archaic. Not

only are Picasso and Joyce no longer ugly; they now strike us, on the whole, as rather "realistic," and this is the result of a canonization and academic institutionalization of the modern movement generally that can be traced to the late 1950s. This is surely one of the most plausible explanations for the emergence of postmodernism itself, since the younger generation of the 1960s will now confront the formerly oppositional modern movement as a set of dead classics, which "weigh like a nightmare on the brains of the living," as Marx once said in a different context.

As for the postmodern revolt against all that, however, it must equally be stressed that its own offensive features – from obscurity and sexually explicit material to psychological squalor and overt expressions of social and political defiance, which transcend anything that might have been imagined at the most extreme moments of high modernism – no longer scandalize anyone and are not only received with the greatest complacency but have themselves become institutionalized and are at one with the official or public culture of Western society.

What has happened is that aesthetic production today has become integrated into commodity production generally: the frantic economic urgency of producing fresh waves of ever more novel-seeming goods (from clothing to airplanes), at ever greater rates of turnover, now assigns an increasingly essential structural function and position to aesthetic innovation and experimentation. Such economic necessities then find recognition in the varied kinds of institutional support available for the newer art, from foundations and grants to museums and other forms of patronage. Of all the arts, architecture, is the closest constitutively to the economic, with which, in the form of commissions and land values, it has a virtually unmediated relationship. It will therefore not be surprising to find the extraordinary flowering of the new postmodern architecture grounded in the patronage of multinational business, whose expansion and development is strictly contemporaneous with it. Later I will suggest that these two new phenomena have an even deeper dialectical interrelationship than the simple one-to-one financing of this or that individual project. Yet this is the point at which I must remind the reader of the obvious; namely, that this whole global, yet American, postmodern culture is the internal and superstructural expression of a whole new wave of American military and economic domination throughout the world: in this

vii "Before the word." Gertrude Stein (1874–1946), American writer and poet; Raymond Roussel (1877–1933), French writer; Marcel Duchamp (1887–1968), French painter.

sense, as throughout class history, the underside of culture is blood, torture, death, and terror.

The first point to be made about the conception of periodization in dominance, therefore, is that even if all the constitutive features of postmodernism were identical with and coterminous to those of an older modernism – a position I feel to be demonstrably erroneous but which only an even lengthier analysis of modernism proper could dispel – the two phenomena would still remain utterly distinct in their meaning and social function, owing to the very different positioning of postmodernism in the economic system of late capital and, beyond that, to the transformation of the very sphere of culture in contemporary society.

This point will be further discussed at the conclusion of this book. I must now briefly address a different kind of objection to periodization, a concern about its possible obliteration of heterogeneity, one most often expressed by the Left. And it is certain that there is a strange quasi-Sartrean irony – a "winner loses" logic – which tends to surround any effort to describe a "system," a totalizing dynamic, as these are detected in the movement of contemporary society. What happens is that the more powerful the vision of some increasingly total system or logic – the Foucault of the prisons book is the obvious example – the more powerless the reader comes to feel. Insofar as the theorist wins, therefore, by constructing an increasingly closed and terrifying machine, to that very degree he loses, since the critical capacity of his work is thereby paralyzed, and the impulses of negation and revolt, not to speak of those of social transformation, are increasingly perceived as vain and trivial in the face of the model itself.

I have felt, however, that it was only in the light of some conception of a dominant cultural logic or hegemonic norm that genuine difference could be measured and assessed. I am very far from feeling that all cultural production today is "postmodern" in the broad sense I will be conferring on this term. The postmodern is, however, the force field in which very different kinds of cultural impulses – what Raymond Williams has usefully termed "residual" and "emergent" forms of cultural production – must make their way.[viii] If we do not achieve some general sense of a cultural dominant, then we

fall back into a view of present history as sheer heterogeneity, random difference, a coexistence of a host of distinct forces whose effectivity is undecidable. At any rate, this has been the political spirit in which the following analysis was devised: to project some conception of a new systematic cultural norm and its reproduction in order to reflect more adequately on the most effective forms of any radical cultural politics today.

The exposition will take up in turn the following constitutive features of the postmodern: a new depthlessness, which finds its prolongation both in contemporary "theory" and in a whole new culture of the image or the simulacrum; a consequent weakening of historicity, both in our relationship to public History and in the new forms of our private temporality, whose "schizophrenic" structure (following Lacan[ix]) will determine new types of syntax or syntagmatic relationships in the more temporal arts; a whole new type of emotional ground tone – what I will call "intensities" – which can best be grasped by a return to older theories of the sublime; the deep constitutive relationships of all this to a whole new technology, which is itself a figure for a whole new economic world system; and, after a brief account of postmodernist mutations in the lived experience of built space itself, some reflections on the mission of political art in the bewildering new world space of late or multinational capital.

Now we need to complete this exploratory account of postmodernist space and time with a final analysis of that euphoria or those intensities which seem so often to characterize the newer cultural experience. Let us reemphasize the enormity of a transition which leaves behind it the desolation of Hopper's buildings or the stark Midwest syntax of Sheeler's forms,[x] replacing them with the extraordinary surfaces of the photorealist cityscape, where even the automobile wrecks gleam with some new hallucinatory splendor. The exhilaration of these new surfaces is all the more paradoxical in that their essential content – the city itself – has deteriorated or disintegrated to a degree surely still inconceivable in the early years of the twentieth century, let alone in the previous era. How urban squalor can be a delight to the eyes when expressed in

---

viii   Prominent English critic and man of the left, Raymond Williams (1922–88) distinguished the *emergent* (or novel) from the *residual* (anachronistic) dominant cultural elements of a given historical period.

ix   French psychoanalyst Jacques Lacan (1901–81).
x   American artists Edward Hopper (1882–1967), painter of stark urban scenes, and Charles Sheeler (1883–1965), who abstractly rendered industrial forms.

commodification, and how an unparalleled quantum leap in the alienation of daily life in the city can now be experienced in the form of a strange new hallucinatory exhilaration – these are some of the questions that confront us in this moment of our inquiry. Nor should the human figure be exempted from investigation, although it seems clear that for the newer aesthetic the representation of space itself has come to be felt as incompatible with the representation of the body: a kind of aesthetic division of labor far more pronounced than in any of the earlier generic conceptions of landscape, and a most ominous symptom indeed. The privileged space of the newer art is radically antianthropomorphic, as in the empty bathrooms of Doug Bond's work. The ultimate contemporary fetishization of the human body, however, takes a very different direction in the statues of Duane Hanson: what I have already called the simulacrum, whose peculiar function lies in what Sartre would have called the *derealization* of the whole surrounding world of everyday reality. Your moment of doubt and hesitation as to the breath and warmth of these polyester figures, in other words, tends to return upon the real human beings moving about you in the museum and to transform them also for the briefest instant into so many dead and flesh-colored simulacra in their own right. The world thereby momentarily loses its depth and threatens to become a glossy skin, a stereoscopic illusion, a rush of filmic images without density. But is this now a terrifying or an exhilarating experience?

It has proved fruitful to think of such experiences in terms of what Susan Sontag, in an influential statement, isolated as "camp." I propose a somewhat different cross-light on it, drawing on the equally fashionable current theme of the "sublime," as it has been rediscovered in the works of Edmund Burke and Kant; or perhaps one might want to yoke the two notions together in the form of something like a camp or "hysterical" sublime.[xi] The sublime was for Burke an experience bordering on terror, the fitful glimpse, in astonishment, stupor, and awe, of what was so enormous as to crush human life altogether: a description then refined by Kant to include the question of representation itself, so that the object of the sublime becomes not only a matter of sheer power and of the

physical incommensurability of the human organism with Nature but also of the limits of figuration and the incapacity of the human mind to give representation to such enormous forces. Such forces Burke, in his historical moment at the dawn of the modern bourgeois state, was only able to conceptualize in terms of the divine, while even Heidegger continues to entertain a phantasmatic relationship with some organic precapitalist peasant landscape and village society, which is the final form of the image of Nature in our own time.

Today, however, it may be possible to think all this in a different way, at the moment of a radical eclipse of Nature itself: Heidegger's "field path" is, after all, irredeemably and irrevocably destroyed by late capital, by the green revolution, by neocolonialism and the megalopolis, which runs its superhighways over the older fields and vacant lots and turns Heidegger's "house of being" into condominiums, if not the most miserable unheated, rat-infested tenement buildings. The *other* of our society is in that sense no longer Nature at all, as it was in precapitalist societies, but something else which we must now identify.

I am anxious that this other thing not overhastily be grasped as technology per se, since I will want to show that technology is here itself a figure for something else. Yet technology may well serve as adequate shorthand to designate that enormous properly human and anti-natural power of dead human labor stored up in our machinery – an alienated power, what Sartre calls the counterfinality of the practico-inert, which turns back on and against us in unrecognizable forms and seems to constitute the massive dystopian horizon of our collective as well as our individual praxis.

Technological development is however on the Marxist view the result of the development of capital rather than some ultimately determining instance in its own right. It will therefore be appropriate to distinguish several generations of machine power, several stages of technological revolution within capital itself. I here follow Ernest Mandel, who outlines three such fundamental breaks or quantum leaps in the evolution of machinery under capital:

> The fundamental revolutions in power technology – the technology of the production of motive machines by machines – thus appears as the determinant moment in revolutions of technology as a whole. Machine production of steam-driven motors since 1848; machine pro-

---

[xi] The distinction between the beautiful and the sublime is traditional in aesthetic theory, the former often being understood as what is well-formed and pleasing, the latter as what is awesome, beyond comprehension.

duction of electric and combustion motors since the 90s of the 19th century; machine production of electronic and nuclear-powered apparatuses since the 40s of the 20th century – these are the three general revolutions in technology engendered by the capitalist mode of production since the "original" industrial revolution of the later 18th century.[3]

This periodization underscores the general thesis of Mandel's book *Late Capitalism*; namely, that there have been three fundamental moments in capitalism, each one marking a dialectical expansion over the previous stage. These are market capitalism, the monopoly stage or the stage of imperialism, and our own, wrongly called postindustrial, but what might better be termed multinational, capital. I have already pointed out that Mandel's intervention in the postindustrial debate involves the proposition that late or multinational or consumer capitalism, far from being inconsistent with Marx's great nineteenth-century analysis, constitutes, on the contrary, the purest form of capital yet to have emerged, a prodigious expansion of capital into hitherto uncommodified areas. This purer capitalism of our own time thus eliminates the enclaves of precapitalist organization it had hitherto tolerated and exploited in a tributary way. One is tempted to speak in this connection of a new and historically original penetration and colonization of Nature and the Unconscious: that is, the destruction of precapitalist Third World agriculture by the Green Revolution, and the rise of the media and the advertising industry. At any rate, it will also have been clear that my own cultural periodization of the stages of realism, modernism, and postmodernism is both inspired and confirmed by Mandel's tripartite scheme.

We may therefore speak of our own period as the Third Machine Age; and it is at this point that we must reintroduce the problem of aesthetic representation already explicitly developed in Kant's earlier analysis of the sublime, since it would seem only logical that the relationship to and the representation of the machine could be expected to shift dialectically with each of these qualitatively different stages of technological development.

It is appropriate to recall the excitement of machinery in the moment of capital preceding our own, the exhilaration of futurism, most notably, and of Marinetti's celebration of the machine gun and the motorcar. These are still visible emblems, sculptural nodes of energy which give tangibility and figuration to the motive energies of that earlier moment of modernization. The prestige of these great streamlined shapes can be measured by their metaphorical presence in Le Corbusier's buildings, vast Utopian structures which ride like so many gigantic steamship liners upon the urban scenery of an older fallen earth.[4] Machinery exerts another kind of fascination in the works of artists like Picabia and Duchamp,[xii] whom we have no time to consider here; but let me mention, for completeness' sake, the ways in which revolutionary or communist artists of the 1930s also sought to reappropriate this excitement of machine energy for a Promethean reconstruction of human society as a whole, as in Fernand Léger and Diego Rivera.

It is immediately obvious that the technology of our own moment no longer possesses this same capacity for representation: not the turbine, nor even Sheeler's grain elevators or smokestacks, not the baroque elaboration of pipes and conveyor belts, nor even the streamlined profile of the railroad train – all vehicles of speed still concentrated at rest – but rather the computer, whose outer shell has no emblematic or visual power, or even the casings of the various media themselves, as with that home appliance called television which articulates nothing but rather implodes, carrying its flattened image surface within itself.

Such machines are indeed machines of reproduction rather than of production, and they make very different demands on our capacity for aesthetic representation than did the relatively mimetic idolatry of the older machinery of the futurist moment, of some older speed-and-energy sculpture. Here we have less to do with kinetic energy than with all kinds of new reproductive processes; and in the weaker productions of postmodernism the aesthetic embodiment of such processes often tends to slip back more comfortably into a mere thematic representation of content – into narratives which are *about* the processes of reproduction and include movie cameras, video, tape recorders, the whole technology of the production and reproduction of the simulacrum. (The shift from Antonioni's modernist *Blow-Up* to DePalma's postmodernist *Blowout* is here paradigmatic.) When Japanese architects, for example, model a building on the decorative imitation of

xii French painters Francis Picabia (1879–1953) and Marcel Duchamp were associated with abstraction, Surrealism, and Dadaism.

stacks of cassettes, then the solution is at best the-matic and allusive, although often humorous.

Yet something else does tend to emerge in the most energetic postmodernist texts, and this is the sense that beyond all thematics or content the work seems somehow to tap the networks of the repro-ductive process and thereby to afford us some glimpse into a postmodern or technological sub-lime, whose power or authenticity is documented by the success of such works in evoking a whole new postmodern space in emergence around us. Architecture therefore remains in this sense the privileged aesthetic language; and the distorting and fragmenting reflections of one enormous glass surface to the other can be taken as paradigmatic of the central role of process and reproduction in postmodernist culture.

As I have said, however, I want to avoid the implication that technology is in any way the "ul-timately determining instance" either of our pre-sent-day social life or of our cultural production: such a thesis is, of course, ultimately at one with the post-Marxist notion of a postindustrial society. Rather, I want to suggest that our faulty represen-tations of some immense communicational and computer network are themselves but a distorted figuration of something even deeper, namely, the whole world system of a present-day multinational capitalism. The technology of contemporary soci-ety is therefore mesmerizing and fascinating not so much in its own right but because it seems to offer some privileged representational short hand for grasping a network of power and control even more difficult for our minds and imaginations to grasp: the whole new decentered global network of the third stage of capital itself. This is a figural process presently best observed in a whole mode of contemporary entertainment literature – one is tempted to characterize it as "high-tech paranoia" – in which the circuits and networks of some puta-tive global computer hookup are narratively mobil-ized by labyrinthine conspiracies of autonomous but deadly interlocking and competing information agencies in a complexity often beyond the capacity of the normal reading mind. Yet conspiracy theory (and its garish narrative manifestations) must be seen as a degraded attempt – through the figuration of advanced technology – to think the impossible totality of the contemporary world system. It is in terms of that enormous and threatening, yet only dimly perceivable, other reality of economic and social institutions that, in my opinion, the post-modern sublime can alone be adequately theorized.

Such narratives, which first tried to find expres-sion through the generic structure of the spy novel, have only recently crystallized in a new type of science fiction, called *cyberpunk*, which is fully as much an expression of transnational corporate real-ities as it is of global paranoia itself: William Gib-son's representational innovations, indeed, mark his work as an exceptional literary realization within a predominantly visual or aural postmodern production.

The conception of postmodernism outlined here is a historical rather than a merely stylistic one. I cannot stress too greatly the radical distinction between a view for which the postmodern is one (optional) style among many others available and one which seeks to grasp it as the cultural dominant of the logic of late capitalism: the two approaches in fact generate two very different ways of conceptual-izing the phenomenon as a whole: on the one hand, moral judgments (about which it is indifferent whether they are positive or negative), and, on the other, a genuinely dialectical attempt to think our present of time in History.

Of some positive moral evaluation of postmod-ernism little needs to be said: the complacent (yet delirious) camp-following celebration of this aes-thetic new world (including its social and economic dimension, greeted with equal enthusiasm under the slogan of "postindustrial society") is surely unacceptable, although it may be somewhat less obvious that current fantasies about the salvational nature of high technology, from chips to robots – fantasies entertained not only by both left and right governments in distress but also by many intellec-tuals – are also essentially of a piece with more vulgar apologias for postmodernism.

But in that case it is only consequent to reject moralizing condemnations of the postmodern and of its essential triviality when juxtaposed against the Utopian "high seriousness" of the great mod-ernisms: judgments one finds both on the Left and on the radical Right. And no doubt the logic of the simulacrum, with its transformation of older real-ities into television images, does more than merely replicate the logic of late capitalism; it reinforces and intensifies it. Meanwhile, for political groups which seek actively to intervene in history and to modify its otherwise passive momentum (whether with a view toward channeling it into a socialist transformation of society or diverting it into the regressive reestablishment of some simpler fantasy past), there cannot but be much that is deplorable

and reprehensible in a cultural form of image ad-
diction which, by transforming the past into visual
mirages, stereotypes, or texts, effectively abolishes
any practical sense of the future and of the collective project, thereby abandoning the thinking of
future change to fantasies of sheer catastrophe and
inexplicable cataclysm, from visions of "terrorism"
on the social level to those of cancer on the personal. Yet if postmodernism is a historical phenomenon, then the attempt to conceptualize it in terms
of moral or moralizing judgments must finally be
identified as a category mistake. All of which becomes more obvious when we interrogate the position of the cultural critic and moralist; the latter,
along with all the rest of us, is now so deeply
immersed in postmodernist space, so deeply suffused and infected by its new cultural categories,
that the luxury of the old-fashioned ideological
critique, the indignant moral denunciation of the
other, becomes unavailable.

The distinction I am proposing here knows
one canonical form in Hegel's differentiation
of the thinking of individual morality or moralizing
(*Moralität*) from that whole very different realm of
collective social values and practices (*Sittlichkeit*).[5]
But it finds its definitive form in Marx's demonstration of the materialist dialectic, most notably
in those classic pages of the *Manifesto* which teach
the hard lesson of some more genuinely dialectical
way to think historical development and change.
The topic of the lesson is, of course, the historical
development of capitalism itself and the deployment of a specific bourgeois culture. In a well-
known passage Marx powerfully urges us to do
the impossible, namely, to think this development
positively *and* negatively all at once; to achieve, in
other words, a type of thinking that would be
capable of grasping the demonstrably baleful features of capitalism along with its extraordinary
and liberating dynamism simultaneously within a
single thought, and without attenuating any of the
force of either judgment. We are somehow to lift
our minds to a point at which it is possible to
understand that capitalism is at one and the same
time the best thing that has ever happened to the
human race, and the worst. The lapse from this
austere dialectical imperative into the more comfortable stance of the taking of moral positions in
inveterate and all too human: still, the urgency of
the subject demands that we make at least some
effort to think the cultural evolution of late capitalism dialectically, as catastrophe and progress all
together.

Such an effort suggests two immediate questions, with which we will conclude these reflections. Can we in fact identify some "moment of
truth" within the more evident "moments of falsehood" of postmodern culture? And, even if we can
do so, is there not something ultimately paralyzing
in the dialectical view of historical development
proposed above; does it not tend to demobilize us
and to surrender us to passivity and helplessness by
systematically obliterating possibilities of action
under the impenetrable fog of historical inevitability? It is appropriate to discuss these two (related)
issues in terms of current possibilities for some
effective contemporary cultural politics and for
the construction of a genuine political culture.

To focus the problem in this way is, of course,
immediately to raise the more genuine issue of the
fate of culture generally, and of the function of
culture specifically, as one social level or instance,
in the postmodern era. Everything in the previous
discussion suggests that what we have been calling
postmodernism is inseparable from, and unthinkable without the hypothesis of, some fundamental
mutation of the sphere of culture in the world of
late capitalism, which includes a momentous modification of its social function. Older discussions of
the space, function, or sphere of culture (mostly
notably Herbert Marcuse's classic essay "The Affirmative Character of Culture") have insisted on
what a different language would call the "semiautonomy" of the cultural realm: its ghostly, yet Utopian, existence, for good or ill, above the practical
world of the existent, whose mirror image it throws
back in forms which vary from the legitimations of
flattering resemblance to the contestatory indict-
ments of critical satire or Utopian pain.

What we must now ask ourselves is whether it is
not precisely this semiautonomy of the cultural
sphere which has been destroyed by the logic of
late capitalism. Yet to argue that culture is today no
longer endowed with the relative autonomy it once
enjoyed as one level among others in earlier
moments of capitalism (let alone in precapitalist
societies) is not necessarily to imply its disappearance or extinction. Quite the contrary; we must go
on to affirm that the dissolution of an autonomous
sphere of culture is rather to be imagined in terms
of an explosion: a prodigious expansion of culture
throughout the social realm, to the point at which
everything in our social life – from economic
value and state power to practices and to the
very structure of the psyche itself – can be said to
have become "cultural" in some original and yet

untheorized sense. This proposition is, however, substantively quite consistent with the previous diagnosis of a society of the image or the simulacrum and a transformation of the "real" into so many pseudoevents.

It also suggests that some of our most cherished and time-honored radical conceptions about the nature of cultural politics may thereby find themselves outmoded. However distinct those conceptions – which range from slogans of negativity, opposition, and subversion to critique and reflexivity – may have been, they all shared a single, fundamentally spatial, presupposition, which may be resumed in the equally time-honored formula of "critical distance." No theory of cultural politics current on the Left today has been able to do without one notion or another of a certain minimal aesthetic distance, of the possibility of the positioning of the cultural act outside the massive Being of capital, from which to assault this last. What the burden of our preceding demonstration suggests, however, is that distance in general (including "critical distance" in particular) has very precisely been abolished in the new space of postmodernism. We are submerged in its henceforth filled and suffused volumes to the point where our now postmodern bodies are bereft of spatial coordinates and practically (let alone theoretically) incapable of distantiation; meanwhile, it has already been observed how the prodigious new expansion of multinational capital ends up penetrating and colonizing those very precapitalist enclaves (Nature and the Unconscious) which offered extraterritorial and Archimedean footholds for critical effectivity. The shorthand language of co-optation is for this reason omnipresent on the left, but would now seem to offer a most inadequate theoretical basis for understanding a situation in which we all, in one way or another, dimly feel that not only punctual and local countercultural forms of cultural resistance and guerrilla warfare but also even overtly political interventions like those of The Clash[xiii] are all some how secretly disarmed and reabsorbed by a system of which they themselves might well be considered a part, since they can achieve no distance from it.

What we must now affirm is that it is precisely this whole extraordinarily demoralizing and depressing original new global space which is the "moment of truth" of postmodernism. What has

[xiii] An English punk-based but mainstream rock band, active in the late 1970s and early 1980s.

been called the postmodernist "sublime" is only the moment in which this content has become most explicit, has moved the closest to the surface of consciousness as a coherent new type of space in its own right – even though a certain figural concealment or disguise is still at work here, most notably in the high-tech thematics in which the new spatial content is still dramatized and articulated. Yet the earlier features of the postmodern which were enumerated above can all now be seen as themselves partial (yet constitutive) aspects of the same general spatial object.

The argument for a certain authenticity in these otherwise patently ideological productions depends on the prior proposition that what we have been calling postmodern (or multinational) space is not merely a cultural ideology or fantasy but has genuine historical (and socioeconomic) reality as a third great original expansion of capitalism around the globe (after the earlier expansions of the national market and the older imperialist system, which each had their own cultural specificity and generated new types of space appropriate to their dynamics). The distorted and unreflexive attempts of newer cultural production to explore and to express this new space must then also, in their own fashion, be considered as so many approaches to the representation of (a new) reality (to use a more antiquated language). As paradoxical as the terms may seem, they may thus, following a classic interpretive option, be read as peculiar new forms of realism (or at least of the mimesis of reality), while at the same time they can equally well be analyzed as so many attempts to distract and divert us from that reality or to disguise its contradictions and resolve them in the guise of various formal mystifications.

As for that reality itself, however – the as yet untheorized original space of some new "world system" of multinational or late capitalism, a space whose negative or baleful aspects are only too obvious – the dialectic requires us to hold equally to a positive or "progressive" evaluation of its emergence, as Marx did for the world market as the horizon of national economies, or as Lenin did for the older imperialist global network. For neither Marx nor Lenin was socialism a matter of returning to smaller (and thereby less repressive and comprehensive) systems of social organization; rather, the dimensions attained by capital in their own times were grasped as the promise, the framework, and the precondition for the achievement of some new and more comprehensive socialism. Is this not the case with the yet more global and totalizing space of the new world system, which demands the intervention and elaboration of an internationalism of a radically new type? The disastrous realignment of socialist revolution with the older nationalisms (not only in Southeast Asia), whose results have necessarily aroused much serious recent left reflection, can be adduced in support of this position.

But if all this is so, then at least one possible form of a new radical cultural politics becomes evident, with a final aesthetic proviso that must quickly be noted. Left cultural producers and theorists – particularly those formed by bourgeois cultural traditions issuing from romanticism and valorizing spontaneous, instinctive, or unconscious forms of "genius," but also for very obvious historical reasons such as Zhdanovism[xiv] and the sorry consequences of political and party interventions in the arts – have often by reaction allowed themselves to be unduly intimidated by the repudiation, in bourgeois aesthetics and most notably in high modernism, of one of the age-old functions of art – the pedagogical and the didactic. The teaching function of art was, however, always stressed in classical times (even though it there mainly took the form of moral lessons), while the prodigious and still imperfectly understood work of Brecht reaffirms, in a new and formally innovative and original way, for the moment of modernism proper, a complex new conception of the relationship between culture and pedagogy. The cultural model I will propose similarly foregrounds the cognitive and pedagogical dimensions of political art and culture, dimensions stressed in very different ways by both Lukács and Brecht[xv] (for the distinct moments of realism and modernism, respectively).

[xiv] The USSR's policy of strict control of the arts following World War II, named after its executor, A. A. Zhdanov.
[xv] György Lukács (1885–1971), Hungarian philosopher who authored an idealist reinterpretation of Marxism, and Bertolt Brecht (1898–1956), radical German playwright, who employed "distancing-effects" to prevent suspension of disbelief.

We cannot, however, return to aesthetic practices elaborated on the basis of historical situations and dilemmas which are no longer ours. Meanwhile, the conception of space that has been developed here suggests that a model of political culture appropriate to our own situation will necessarily have to raise spatial issues as its fundamental organizing concern. I will therefore provisionally define the aesthetic of this new (and hypothetical) cultural form as an aesthetic of cognitive mapping. . . .

An aesthetic of cognitive mapping – a pedagogical political culture which seeks to endow the individual subject with some new heightened sense of its place in the global system – will necessarily have to respect this now enormously complex representational dialectic and invent radically new forms in order to do it justice. This is not then, clearly, a call for a return to some older kind of machinery, some older and more transparent national space, or some more traditional and reassuring perspectival or mimetic enclave: the new political art (if it is possible at all) will have to hold to the truth of postmodernism, that is to say, to its fundamental object – the world space of multinational capital – at the same time at which it achieves a breakthrough to some as yet unimaginable new mode of representing this last, in which we may again begin to grasp our positioning as individual and collective subjects and regain a capacity to act and struggle which is at present neutralized by our spatial as well as our social confusion. The political form of postmodernism, if there ever is any, will have as its vocation the invention and projection of a global cognitive mapping, on a social as well as a spatial scale.

Author's Notes

1 Robert Venturi and Denise Scott-Brown, *Learning from Las Vegas* (Cambridge, Mass., 1972).
2 The originality of Charles Jencks's pathbreaking *Language of Post-Modern Architecture* (1977) lay in its well-

nigh dialectical combination of postmodern architecture and a certain kind of semiotics, each being appealed to to justify the existence of the other. Semiotics becomes appropriate as a mode of analysis of the newer architecture by virtue of the latter's populism, which does emit signs and messages to a spatial "reading public," unlike the monumentality of the high modern. Meanwhile, the newer architecture is itself thereby validated, insofar as it is accessible to semiotic analysis and thus proves to be an essentially aesthetic object (rather than the transaesthetic constructions of the high modern). Here, then, aesthetics reinforces an ideology of communication (about which more will be observed in the concluding chapter), and vice versa. Besides Jencks's many valuable contributions, see also

Heinrich Klotz, *History of Postmodern Architecture* (Cambridge, Mass., 1988); Pier Paolo Portoghesi, *After Modern Architecture* (New York, 1982).

3   Ernest Mandel, *Late Capitalism* (London, 1978), p. 118.

4   See, particularly on such motifs in Le Corbusier, Gert Kähler, *Architektur als Symbolverfall: Das Dampfermotiv in der Baukunst* (Brunswick, 1981).

5   See my "Morality and Ethical Substance," in *The Ideologies of Theory*, vol. I (Minneapolis, 1988).

54

"An Alternative Way Out of the Philosophy of the Subject: Communicative versus Subject-Centered Reason"

Jürgen Habermas

Former assistant to Theodor Adorno and heir to the Frankfurt School legacy, philosopher, Jürgen Habermas (1929–) made a mammoth contribution to the debate over modernity with his two-volume *Theory of Communicative Action* (German original, 1981; English, 1984 and 1987), based largely on his notion of "communicative reason." Weber, Adorno, and Horkheimer had neglected the communicative essence of rationality in favor of the purely instrumental rationality that led to the "Dialectic of Enlightenment." For Habermas, as he titled a 1980 lecture, "Modernity" is not misguided, but "an Unfinished Project." His reformulation of modernity is based on the two insights that: (a) rationality is inherently linguistic and discursive, hence social; and (b) discourse requires that interlocutors assume the possibility of sincere, truth-governed speech. This means that participants in discourse cannot regard all of discourse as merely a matter of power and self-interest. Consequently, Habermas rejects the pessimism of Adorno and Horkheimer, as well as the postmodern denial of the transcendence of norms: there remains, he claims, "a moment of unconditionality," of truth and freedom in human relations, despite the inroads of the late modern "system" of money and power. In the following selection from 1985, Habermas laments the traditional dependence of both modern thought and its postmodern critics on a "subjectivist," non-social conception of rationality.

The aporias[i] of the theory of power leave their traces behind in the selective readings of genealogical historiography, whether of modern penal procedure or of sexuality in modern times. Unsettled methodological problems are reflected in empirical deficits. Foucault did indeed provide an illuminating critique of the entanglement of the human sciences in the philosophy of the subject: These sciences try to escape from the aporetic tangles of contradictory self-thematization by a subject seeking to know itself, but in doing so they become all the more deeply ensnared in the self-reifications of scientism. However, Foucault did not think through the aporias of his own approach well enough to see how his theory of power was overtaken by a fate similar to that of the human sciences rooted in the philosophy of the subject. His theory tries to rise above those pseudo-sciences to a more rigorous objectivity, and in doing so it gets caught all the more hopelessly in the trap of a presentist historiography, which sees itself compelled to a relativist self-denial and can give no account of the normative foundations of its own

---

[i] *Aporia* is a Greek term meaning an undecidable issue.

Jürgen Habermas, "An Alternative Way out of the Philosophy of the Subject: Communicative versus Subject-Centered Reason," pp. 294–326 from *The Philosophical Discourse of Modernity* (trans. Frederick Lawrence). Cambridge, Mass: The MIT Press, 1987.

Jürgen Habermas

rhetoric. To the objectivism of self-mastery on the part of the human sciences there corresponds a subjectivism of self-forgetfulness on Foucault's part. Presentism, relativism, and cryptonormativism are the consequences of his attempt to preserve the transcendental moment proper to generative performances in the basic concept of power while driving from it every trace of subjectivity. This concept of power does not free the genealogist from contradictory self-thematizations.

Hence it would be a good idea to return once again to the unmasking of the human sciences through the critique of reason, but this time in full awareness of a fact that the successors of Nietzsche stubbornly ignore. They do not see that the philosophical counterdiscourse which, from the start, accompanied the philosophical discourse of modernity initiated by Kant already drew up a counterreckoning for subjectivity as the principle of modernity.[1] The basic conceptual aporias of the philosophy of consciousness, so acutely diagnosed by Foucault in the final chapter of *The Order of Things*, were already analyzed by Schiller, Fichte, Schelling,[ii] and Hegel in a similar fashion. To be sure, the solutions they offer are quite different. But if, now, the theory of power also fails to provide a way out of this problematic situation, it behooves us to retrace the path of the philosophical discourse of modernity back to its starting point – in order to examine once again the directions once suggested at the chief crossroads. This is the intention behind these lectures. You will recall that I marked the places where the young Hegel, the young Marx, and even the Heidegger of *Being and Time* and Derrida in his discussion with Husserl stood before alternative paths they did not choose.

With Hegel and Marx, it would have been a matter of not swallowing the intuition concerning the ethical totality back into the horizon of the self-reference of the knowing and acting subject, but of explicating it in accord with the model of unconstrained consensus formation in a communication community standing under cooperative constraints. With Heidegger and Derrida it would have been a matter of ascribing the meaning-creating horizons of world interpretation not to a Dasein heroically projecting itself or to a background occurrence that shapes structures, but rather to communicatively structured lifeworlds that reproduce themselves via

the palpable medium of action oriented to mutual agreement. At these places, I have already *suggested* that the paradigm of the knowledge of objects has to be replaced by the paradigm of mutual understanding between subjects capable of speech and action. Hegel and Marx did not achieve this paradigm-change; in their attempt to leave behind the metaphysics of subjectivity, Heidegger and Derrida likewise remain caught up in the intention of *Ursprungsphilosophie*.[iii] From the point where he gave a threefold analysis of the compulsion to an aporetic doubling on the part of the self-referential subject, Foucault veered off into a theory of power that has shown itself to be a dead end. He follows Heidegger and Derrida in the abstract negation of the self-referential subject, inasmuch as, put briefly, he declares "man" to be nonexistent. But unlike them, he no longer attempts to compensate, by way of temporalized originary powers, for the lost order of things that the metaphysically isolated and structurally overburdened subject tries in vain to renew from its own forces. In the end, the transcendental-historicist "power," the single constant in the ups and downs of overwhelming and overwhelmed discourses, proves to be only an equivalent for the "life" of the hoary *Lebensphilosophie*.[iv] A more viable solution suggests itself if we drop the somewhat sentimental presupposition of metaphysical homelessness, and if we understand the hectic to and fro between transcendental and empirical modes of dealing with issues, between radical self-reflection and an incomprehensible element that cannot be reflectively retrieved, between the productivity of a self-generating species and a primordial element prior to all production – that is to say, when we understand the puzzle of all these doublings for what it is: a symptom of exhaustion. The paradigm of the philosophy of consciousness is exhausted. If this is so, the symptoms of exhaustion should dissolve with the transition to the paradigm of mutual understanding.

If we can presuppose for a moment the model of action oriented to reaching understanding that I have developed elsewhere,[2] the objectifying attitude in

---

ii Three German idealist philosophers: Friedrich Schiller (1759–1805), Johann Fichte and Friedrich Schelling (1775–1854).

iii Philosophy of origins.

iv Also *Philosophie des Lebens*, philosophy of Life. Although he did not invent the term, German philosopher of the human sciences Wilhelm Dilthey (1833–1911) most prominently employed it to mean a philosophy of the living, historical, cultural human subject. The term was later applied to very diverse philosophical movements, including Bergson's "process" philosophy and Husserl's phenomenology.

which the knowing subject regards itself as it would entities in the external world is no longer privileged. Fundamental to the paradigm of mutual understanding is, rather, the performative attitude of participants in interaction, who coordinate their plans for action by coming to an understanding about something in the world. When ego carries out a speech act and alter takes up a position with regard to it, the two parties enter into an interpersonal relationship. The latter is structured by the system of reciprocally interlocked perspectives among speakers, hearers, and non-participants who happen to be present at the time. On the level of grammar, this corresponds to the system of personal pronouns. Whoever has been trained in this system has learned how, in the performative attitude, to take up and to transform into one another the perspectives of the first, second, and third persons.

Now this attitude of participants in linguistically mediated interaction makes possible a different relationship of the subject to itself from the sort of objectifying attitude that an observer assumes toward entities in the external world. The transcendental-empirical doubling of the relation to self is only unavoidable so long as there is no alternative to this observer perspective; only then does the subject have to view itself as the dominating counterpart to the world as a whole or as an entity appearing within it. No mediation is possible between the extramundane stance of the transcendental I and the intramundane stance of the empirical I. As soon as linguistically generated intersubjectivity gains primacy, this alternative no longer applies. Then ego stands within an interpersonal relationship that allows him to relate to himself as a participant in an interaction from the perspective of alter. And indeed this reflection undertaken from the perspective of the participant escapes the kind of objectification inevitable from the reflexively applied perspective of the observer. Everything gets frozen into an object under the gaze of the third person, whether directed inwardly or outwardly. The first person, who turns back upon himself in a performative attitude from the angle of vision of the second person, can *recapitulate* the acts it just carried out. In place of reflectively objectified knowledge – the knowledge proper to self-consciousness – we have a recapitulating reconstruction of knowledge already employed.

What earlier was relegated to transcendental philosophy, namely the intuitive analysis of self-consciousness, now gets adapted to the circle of reconstructive sciences that try to make explicit,

from the perspective of those participating in discourses and interactions, and by means of analyzing successful or distorted utterances, the pretheoretical grasp of rules on the part of competently speaking, acting, and knowing subjects. Because such reconstructive attempts are no longer aimed at a realm of the intelligible beyond that of appearances, but at the actually exercised rule-knowledge that is deposited in correctly generated utterances, the ontological separation between the transcendental and the empirical is no longer applicable. As can be shown in connection with Jean Piaget's genetic structuralism, reconstructive and empirical assumptions can be brought together in one and the same theory.[3] In this way, the spell of an unresolved back-and-forth between two aspects of self-thematization that are as inevitable as they are incompatible is broken. Consequently, we do not need hybrid theories any more to close the gap between the transcendental and the empirical.

The same holds true for the doubling of the relation to self in the dimension of making the unconscious conscious. Here, according to Foucault, the thought of subject philosophy oscillates back and forth between heroic exertions bent on reflectively transforming what is in-itself into what is for-itself, and the recognition of an opaque background that stubbornly escapes the transparency of self-consciousness. If we make the transition to the paradigm of mutual understanding, these two aspects of self-thematization are no longer incompatible. Insofar as speakers and hearers straightforwardly achieve a mutual understanding about something in the world, they move within the horizon of their common lifeworld; this remains in the background of the participants – as an intuitively known, unproblematic, and unanalyzable, holistic background. The speech situation is the segment of a lifeworld[v] tailored to the relevant theme; it both forms a *context* and furnishes *resources* for the process of mutual understanding. The lifeworld forms a horizon and at the same time offers a store of things taken for granted in the given culture from which communicative participants draw consensual interpretative patterns in their efforts at interpretation. The solidarities of groups integrated by values and the competences of socialized individuals belong, as do culturally ingrained background assumptions, to the components of the lifeworld.

v   Husserl's notion of the pre-theoretical world of experience.

In order to be able to make these kinds of statements, we naturally have to undertake a change in perspective: We can only get insight into the lifeworld *a tergo*.[vi] From the straightforward perspective of acting subjects oriented to mutual understanding, the lifeworld that is always only "co-given" has to evade thematization. As a totality that makes possible the identities and biographical projects of groups and individuals, it is present only prereflectively. Indeed, the practically employed rule-knowledge sedimented in utterances can be reconstructed from the perspective of participants, but not the ever-receding context and the always-in-the-background resources of the lifeworld as a whole. We need a *theoretically constituted perspective* to be able to treat communicative action as the medium through which the lifeworld as a whole is reproduced. Even from this vantage point, only formal-pragmatic statements are possible, statements related to the structures of the lifeworld in general, and not to determinate lifeworlds in their concrete historical configurations. Of course, interaction participants then no longer appear as originators who master situations with the help of accountable actions, but as the products of the traditions in which they stand, of the solidary groups to which they belong, and of the socialization processes within which they grow up. This is to say that the lifeworld reproduces itself to the extent that these three functions, which transcend the perspectives of the actors, are fulfilled: the propagation of cultural traditions, the integration of groups by norms and values, and the socialization of succeeding generations. But what comes into view in this manner are the properties of communicatively structured lifeworlds *in general*.

Whoever wants to become reflectively aware of the individual totality of any individual biography or of a particular way of life has to recur to the perspective of the participants, give up the intention of rational reconstruction, and simply proceed historically. Narrative tools can, if necessary, be stylized into a dialogically conducted self-critique, for which the analytic conversation between doctor and patient offers a suitable model. This self-critique, which is aimed at eliminating pseudo-nature, that is, the pseudo-aprioris made up of unconsciously motivated perceptual barriers and compulsions to action, is related to the narratively recollected entirety of a course of life or way of life. The analytic dissolution of hypostatizations, of self-engendered objective illusions, is due to an experience of reflection. But its liberating force is directed toward *single* illusions: It cannot make transparent the *totality* of a course of life in the process of individuation or of a collective way of life.

The two heritages of self-reflection that get beyond the limits of the philosophy of consciousness, have different aims and scopes. *Rational reconstruction* subscribes to the program of heightening consciousness, but is directed toward anonymous rule systems and does not refer to totalities. In contrast, *methodically carried out self-critique* is related to totalities, and yet in the awareness that it can never completely illuminate the implicit, the prepredicative, the not focally present background of the lifeworld.[4] As can be shown through the example of psychoanalysis, as interpreted in terms of communication theory,[5] the two procedures of reconstruction and of self-critique can still be brought together within the framework of one and the same theory. These two aspects of self-thematization on the part of the knowing subject are also not irreconcilable; in this respect, too, hybrid theories that overcome contradictions by force are superfluous.

Something similar holds true of the third doubling of the subject as an originally creative actor simultaneously alienated from its origin. If the formal-pragmatic concept of the lifeworld is going to be made fruitful for the purposes of social theory, it has to be transformed into an empirically usable concept and integrated with the concept of a self-regulating system into a two-level concept of society. Furthermore, a careful separation between problems of developmental logic and those of developmental dynamics is necessary so that social evolution and social history can be methodically discriminated from each other and related to each other. Finally, social theory has to remain aware of the context of its own emergence and of its position in the contemporary context; even basic concepts that are starkly universalist have a temporal core.[6] If, with the aid of these operations, one succeeds in steering between the Scylla of absolutism and the Charybdis of relativism,[7] we are no longer faced with the alternatives of the conception of world history as a process of self-generation (whether of the spirit or of the species), on the one hand, and, on the other hand, the conception of an impenetrable dispensation that makes the power of lost origins felt through the negativity of withdrawal and deprival.

I cannot go into these complicated interconnections here. I only wanted to suggest how a para-

---

[vi] *A tergo* means "from the rear."

digm-change can render objectless those dilemmas out of which Foucault explains the perilous dynamics of a subjectivity that is bent on knowledge and falls prey to pseudo-sciences. The change of paradigm from subject-centered to communicative reason also encourages us to resume once again the counterdiscourse that accompanied modernity from the beginning. Since Nietzsche's radical critique of reason cannot be consistently carried out along the lines of a critique of metaphysics or of a theory of power, we are directed toward a *different* way out of the philosophy of the subject. Perhaps the grounds for the self-critique of a modernity in collapse can be considered under other premises such that we can do justice to the motives, virulent since Nietzsche, for a precipitous leavetaking of modernity. It must be made clear that the purism of pure reason is not resurrected again in communicative reason.

During the last decade, the radical critique of reason has become fashionable. A study by Hartmut and Gernot Böhme, who take up Foucault's idea of the rise of the modern form of knowledge in connection with the work and biography of Kant, is exemplary in theme and execution. In the style of a historiography of science expanded by cultural and social history, the authors take a look, so to speak, at what goes on behind the back of the critique of pure and of practical reason. For example, they seek the real motives for the critique of reason in the debate with the spiritual clairvoyant, Swedenborg, in whom Kant is supposed to have recognized his dark twin, his repressed counterimage. They pursue these motives into the sphere of the personal, into the, as it were, abstract conduct (turned away from everything sexual, bodily, and imaginative) of a scholarly life marked by hypochondria, crotchetiness, and immobility. The authors marshal before our eyes the "costs of reason" in terms of psychohistory. They undertake this cost/benefit accounting ingenuously with psychoanalytic arguments and document it with historical data, though without being able to specify the place at which such arguments could claim any weight – if indeed the thesis they are concerned with is supposed to make sense.

Kant had carried out his critique of reason from reason's own perspective, that is to say, in the form of a rigorously argued self-limitation of reason. If, now, the production costs of this self-confining reason (which places anything metaphysical off limits) are to be made clear, we require a horizon of reason reaching beyond this drawing of bound-

aries in which the transcending discourse that adds up the bill can operate. This further radicalized critique of reason would have to postulate a more far-reaching and *comprehensive* reason. But the Böhme brothers do not intend to cast out the devil by Beelzebub; instead, with Foucault, they see in the transition from an exclusive reason (in the Kantian mold) to a comprehensive reason merely "the completion of the power-technique of exclusion by the power-technique of permeation."[8] If they were to be consistent, their own investigation of the other of reason would have to occupy a position utterly heterogeneous to reason – but what does consistency count for in a place that is a priori inaccessible to rational discourse? In this text, the paradoxes repeatedly played out since Nietzsche leave behind no recognizable traces of unrest. This methodological enmity toward reason may have something to do with the type of historical innocence with which studies of this kind today move in the no-man's-land between argumentation, narration, and fiction.[9] The New Critique of Reason suppresses that almost 200-year-old counterdiscourse inherent in modernity itself which I am trying to recall in these lectures.

The latter discourse set out from Kantian philosophy as an unconscious expression of the modern age and pursued the goal of enlightening the Enlightenment about its own narrow-mindedness. The New Critique of Reason denies the continuity with this counterdiscourse, within which it nevertheless still stands: "No longer can it be a matter of completing the project of modernity (Habermas); it has to be a matter of revising it. Also, the Enlightenment has not remained incomplete, but unenlightened."[10] The intention of revising the Enlightenment with the very tools of the Enlightenment is, however, what united the critics of Kant from the start – Schiller with Schlegel, Fichte with the Tübingen seminarians. Further on we read: "Kant's philosophy was initiated as the enterprise of drawing boundaries. But nothing was said about the fact that drawing boundaries is a dynamic process, that reason retreated to firm ground and abandoned other areas, that drawing boundaries means self-inclusion and exclusion of others." At the start of our lectures, we saw how Hegel, along with Schelling and Hölderlin, saw as so many provocations the philosophy of reflection's achievements of delimitation – the opposition of faith and knowledge, of infinite and finite, the separation of spirit and nature, of understanding and sensibility, of duty and inclination. We saw how they tracked the estrangement of an overblown subjective reason from internal and external nature right into the "positivities" of the demolished *Sittlichkeit*[vii] of everyday political and private life. Indeed, Hegel saw the vanishing of the power of reconciliation from the life of mankind as the source of an objective need for philosophy. At any rate, he interpreted the boundaries drawn by subject-centered reason not as exclusions from but as dichotomies within reason, and ascribed to philosophy an access to the totality *that encompasses within itself* subjective reason and its other. Our authors' distrust is directed against this, when they continue: "Whatever reason is, however, remains unclear as long as its other is not thought along with it (in its irreducibility). For reason can be deceived about itself, take itself to be the whole (Hegel), or pretend to comprehend the totality."

This is just the objection that the Young Hegelians once made good against the master. They brought a suit against absolute reason in which the other of reason, what is always prior to it, was supposed to be rehabilitated in its own proper right. The concept of a *situated reason* issued from this process of desublimation; its relationship to the historicity of time, to the facticity of external nature, to the decentered subjectivity of internal nature, and to the material character of society was defined neither by inclusion nor by exclusion, but by a praxis of projecting and developing essential powers that takes place under conditions "not themselves chosen." Society is portrayed as practices in which reason is embodied. This praxis takes place in the dimension of historical time; it mediates the inner nature of needful individuals with an external nature objectified by labor, within the horizon of a surrounding cosmic nature. This social practice is the place where a historically situated, bodily incarnated reason, confronted by external nature, is concretely mediated with its other. Whether this mediating practice is successful depends on its internal constitution, on the degrees of bifurcation and of reconciliation in the socially institutionalized context of life. What was called the system of egoism and divided ethical totality in Schiller and Hegel is transformed by Marx into a society split into social classes. Just as in Schiller and in the young Hegel, the social bond – that is, the community-forming and solidarity-building force of unalienated cooperation and living together – ultimately decides whether reason embodied in

[vii] Community *mores* or customs.

social practices is in touch with history and nature. It is the dichotomized society itself that exacts the repression of death, the leveling of historical consciousness, and the subjugation of both internal and external nature.

Within the context of the philosophy of history, the praxis philosophy of the young Marx has the significance of disconnecting Hegel's model of diremption from an *inclusive* concept of reason that incorporated even the other of reason in its totality. The reason of praxis philosophy is understood as finite; nevertheless it remains tied to a *comprehensive* reason – in the form of a critical social theory – insofar as it realizes that it could not identify the historical limits of subject-centered reason – as embodied in bourgeois social relations – without transcending them. Whoever fastens obstinately upon the model of exclusion has to be closed to this Hegelian insight, which, as is evident in Marx, can be had without paying the price of abolutizing the spirit. From such a restricted perspective, the Hegelian defect attending the birth of post-Hegelian theory is still also effective "where reason is criticized as instrumental, repressive, narrow: in Horkheimer and Adorno. Their critique still takes place in the name of a superior reason, namely, the comprehensive reason, to which the intention of totality is conceded, though it was always disputed when it came to real reason. There is no comprehensive reason. One should have learned from Freud or even from Nietzsche that reason does not exist apart from its other and that – functionally considered – it becomes necessary in virtue of this other."[11]

With this assertion, the Böhme brothers call to mind the place where Nietzsche, having recourse to the Romantic heritage, once set a totalizing critique of reason in opposition to an intrinsically dialectical Enlightenment. The dialectic of enlightenment would indeed only have played itself out if reason were robbed of any transcendent force and, in virtual impotence, remained confined, in the madness of its autonomy, to those boundaries that Kant had defined for understanding and for any state based on understanding: "That the subject of reason wants to owe no one and nothing outside itself is its ideal and its insanity at once."[12] Only if reason shows itself to be essentially narcissistic – an identifying, only seemingly universal power, bent upon self-assertion and particular self-aggrandizement, subjugating everything around it as an object – can the other of reason be thought for its part as a spontaneous, creative power that is at the ground of Being, a power that is simultaneously vital and unperspicuous, that is no longer illuminated by any spark of reason. Only reason as reduced to the subjective faculty of understanding and purposive activity corresponds to the image of an *exclusive* reason that further uproots itself the more it strives triumphally for the heights, until, withered, it falls victim to the power of its concealed heterogeneous origin. The dynamism of self-destruction, in which the secret of the dialectic of enlightenment supposedly comes to light, can only function if reason cannot produce anything from itself except that naked power to which it actually hopes to provide an alternative, namely the unforced force of a better insight.

This move explains, moreover, the drastic leveling of Kant's architectonic of reason that results from the Nietzsche-inspired reading of Kant; it has to obliterate the connection of the critiques of pure and practical reason with the critique of judgment, so as to reduce the former to a theory of alienated, external nature and the latter to a theory of domination over internal nature.[13]

Whereas the *diremption model* of reason distinguishes solidary social practice as the locus of a historically situated reason in which the threads of outer nature, inner nature, and society converge, in the *exclusion model* of reason the space opened up by utopian thought gets completely filled in with an irreconcilable reason reduced to bare power. Here social practice only serves as the stage upon which disciplinary power finds ever new scenarios. It is haunted by a reason denied the power to gain access, without coercion, to what is prior to it. In its putative sovereignty, reason that has evaporated into subjectivity becomes the plaything of unmediated forces working upon it, as it were, mechanically – forces of the internal and external nature that have been excluded and rendered into objects.

The other of this self-inflated subjectivity is no longer the dirempted totality, which makes itself felt primarily in the avenging power of destroyed reciprocities and in the fateful causality of distorted communicative relationships, as well as through suffering from the disfigured totality of social life, from alienated inner and outer nature. In the model of exclusion, this complicated structure of a subjective reason that is socially divided and thereby torn away from nature is peculiarly de-differentiated: "The other of reason is nature, the human body, fantasy, desire, the feelings – or better: all this insofar as reason has not been able to appropriate it."[14] Thus, it is directly the vital forces of a

split-off and repressed subjective nature, it is the sorts of phenomena rediscovered by Romanticism – dreams, fantasies, madness, orgiastic excitement, ecstacy – it is the aesthetic, body-centered experiences of a decentered subjectivity that function as the placeholders for the other of reason. To be sure, early Romanticism still wanted to establish art, in the form of a new mythology, as a public institution in the midst of social life; it wanted to elevate the excitement radiating from this into an equivalent for the unifying power of religion. Nietzsche was the first to transfer this potential for excitement into the beyond of modern society and of history overall. The modern origin of aesthetic experience heightened in an avant-garde fashion remains concealed.

The potential for excitement, stylized into the other of reason, becomes at once esoteric and pseudonymous; it comes up under different names – as Being, as the heterogeneous, as power. The cosmic nature of the metaphysicians and the God of the philosophers become blurred into an enchanting reminiscence, a moving remembrance on the part of the metaphysically and religiously isolated subject. The order from which this subject has emancipated himself – which is to say, internal and external nature in their unalienated form – appears now only in the past tense, as the archaic origin of metaphysics for Heidegger, as a turning point in the archeology of the human sciences for Foucault – and also, somewhat more fashionably, as follows: "Separated from the body, whose libidinous potencies could have supplied images of happiness, separated from a maternal nature, which embraced the archaic *image* of symbiotic wholeness and nurturing protection, separated from the feminine, mingling with which belonged to the primal images of happiness – the philosophy of a reason robbed of all images generated only a grandiose consciousness of the superiority in principle of the intelligible over nature and over the lowliness of the body and the woman. . . . Philosophy attributed to reason an omnipotence, infinity, and future perfection, whereas *the lost childlike relationship to nature* did not appear."[15]

Nonetheless, these recollections of origins by the modern subject serve as points of reference for responses to the question that the more consistent among Nietzsche's followers did not try to evade. As long as we speak in narrative form of the other of reason (whatever it might be called), and as long as this factor that is heterogeneous to discursive thought comes up in portrayals of the history of philosophy and science as a name without any further qualifications, the pose of innocence cannot make up for this underselling of the critique of reason inaugurated by Kant. In Heidegger and Foucault, subjective nature as the placeholder for the other has disappeared, because it can no longer be declared the other of reason once it is brought into scientific discourse as the individual or collect-ive unconscious in the concepts of Freud or Jung, of Lacan or Lévi-Strauss.[viii] Whether in the form of meditative thought or of genealogy, Heidegger and Foucault want to initiate a *special discourse* that claims to operate *outside* the horizon of reason with-out being utterly irrational. To be sure, this merely shifts the paradox.

Reason is supposed to be criticizable in its his-torical forms from the perspective of the other that has been excluded from it; this requires, then, an ultimate act of self-reflection that surpasses itself, and indeed an act of reason for which the place of the *genitivus subjectivus*[ix] would have to be occupied by the other of reason. Subjectivity, as the relation-to-self of the knowing and acting subject, is repre-sented in the bipolar relationship of self-reflection. This figure is retained, and yet subjectivity is sup-posed to appear only in the place reserved for the object. Heidegger and Foucault elaborate this para-dox in a structurally similar way, inasmuch as they *generate* what is heterogeneous to reason by way of a self-exiling of reason, a banishing of reason from its own territory. This operation is understood as an unmasking reversal of the self-idolizing that sub-jectivity carries on and at the same time conceals from itself. In the process, it ascribes attributes to itself that it borrows from the shattered religious and metaphysical concepts of order. Conversely, the other they seek, which is heterogeneous to reason and still related to it as its heterogeneous factor, results from a radical finitizing of the abso-lute for which subjectivity had falsely substituted itself. As we have seen, Heidegger chooses time as the dimension of finitizing and conceives the other of reason as an anonymous, primordial power, set aflow temporally; Foucault chooses the dimension of spatial centering in the experience of one's own body and conceives the other of reason as the an-onymous source of the empowerment of inter-actions tied to the body.

[viii]   Carl Jung (1875–1961), Swiss psychiatrist, modified Freud's theory.
[ix]   Generating subject.

We have seen that this elaboration of the paradox by no means amounts to its solution; the paradox is withdrawn into the special status of extraordinary discourse. Just as meditative thought pertains to a mystified Being, genealogy pertains to power. Meditative thought is supposed to open up a privileged access to metaphysically buried truth; genealogy is supposed to take the place of the ap-parently degenerate human sciences. Whereas Hei-degger remains reticent about the kind of privilege that is his – so that one is not sure of how the genre of his late philosophy could be judged in any sense – Foucault has carried out his work unpretentiously to the very last, in the awareness of being unable to dodge his methodological aporias.

The spatial metaphor of inclusive and exclusive reason reveals that the supposedly radical critique of reason remains tied to the presuppositions of the philosophy of the subject from which it wanted to free itself. Only a reason to which we ascribe a "power of the keys" could either include or ex-clude. Hence, inside and outside are linked with domination and subjugation; and the overcoming of reason-as-powerholder is linked with breaking open the prison gates and vouchsafing release into an indeterminate freedom. Thus, the other of reason remains the mirror image of reason in power. Surrender and letting-be remain as chained to the desire for control as the rebellion of counter-power does to the oppression of power. Those who would like to leave all paradigms behind along with the paradigm of the philosophy of consciousness, and go forth into the clearing of postmodernity, will just not be able to free themselves from the con-cepts of subject-centered reason and its impres-sively illustrated topography.

Since early Romanticism, limit experiences of an aesthetic and mystical kind have always been claimed for the purpose of a rapturous transcend-ence of the subject. The mystic is blinded by the light of the absolute and closes his eyes; aesthetic ecstasy finds expression in the stunning and dizzy-ing effects of (the illuminating) shock. In both cases, the source of the experience of being shaken up evades any specification. In this indeterminacy, we can make out only the silhouette of the para-digm under attack – the outline of what has been deconstructed. In this constellation, which persists from Nietzsche to Heidegger and Foucault, there arises a readiness for excitement without any proper object; in its wake, subcultures are formed which simultaneously allay and keep alive their excitement in the face of future truths (of which they have been notified in an unspecified way) by means of cultic actions without any cultic object. This scurrilous game with religiously and aesthetically toned ecstasy finds an audience especially in circles of intellectuals who are prepared to make their *sacrificium intellectus*[x] on the altar of their needs of orientation.

But here, too, a paradigm only loses its force when it is negated in a *determinate* manner by a *different* paradigm, that is, when it is devalued in an *insightful* way; it is certainly resistant to any simple invocation of the extinction of the subject. Even the furious labor of deconstruction has identifiable consequences only when the paradigm of self-consciousness, of the relation-to-self of a subject knowing and acting in isolation, is replaced by a different one – by the paradigm of mutual understanding, that is, of the intersubjective relationship between individuals who are socialized through communication and reciprocally recognize one another. Only then does the critique of the domineering thought of subject-centered reason emerge in a *determinate* form – namely, as a critique of Western "logocentrism," which is diagnosed not as an excess but as a deficit of rationality. Instead of overtrumping modernity, it takes up again the counterdiscourse inherent in modernity and leads it away from the battle lines between Hegel and Nietzsche, from which there is no exit. This critique renounces the high-flown originality of a return to archaic origins; it unleashes the subversive force of modern thought itself against the paradigm of the philosophy of consciousness that was installed in the period from Descartes to Kant.

The critique of the Western emphasis on logos[xi] inspired by Nietzsche proceeds in a destructive manner. It demonstrates that the embodied, speaking and acting subject is not master in its own house; it draws from this the conclusion that the subject positing itself in knowledge is in fact dependent upon something prior, anonymous, and transsubjective – be it the dispensation of Being, the accident of structure-formation, or the generative power of some discourse formation. The logos of an omnipotent subject thus appears as a misadventure of misguided specialization, which is as rich in consequences as it is wrongheaded. The hope awakened by such post-Nietzschean analyses has constantly the same quality of expectant indeterminacy. Once the defenses of subject-centered reason are razed, the logos, which for so long had held together an interiority protected by power, hollow within and aggressive without, will collapse into itself. It has to be delivered over to its other, whatever that may be.

A different, less dramatic, but step-by-step testable critique of the Western emphasis on logos starts from an attack on the abstractions surrounding logos itself, as free of language, as universalist, and as disembodied. It conceives of intersubjective understanding as the telos inscribed into communication in ordinary language, and of the logocentrism of Western thought, heightened by the philosophy of consciousness, as a systematic *foreshortening* and *distortion* of a potential always already operative in the communicative practice of everyday life, but only selectively exploited. As long as Occidental self-understanding views human beings as distinguished in their relationship to the world by their monopoly on encountering entities, knowing and dealing with objects, making true statements, and implementing plans, reason remains confined ontologically, epistemologically, or in terms of linguistic analysis to only one of its dimensions. The relationship of the human being to the world is cognitivistically reduced: Ontologically, the world is reduced to the world of entities as a whole (as the totality of objects that can be represented and of existing states of affairs); epistemologically, our relationship to that world is reduced to the capacity to know existing states of affairs or to bring them about in a purposive-rational fashion; semantically, it is reduced to fact-stating discourse in which assertoric sentences are used – and no validity claim is admitted besides propositional truth, which is available *in foro interno*.[xii]

Language philosophy – from Plato to Popper – has concentrated this logocentrism into the affirmation that the linguistic function of representing states of affairs is the sole human monopoly.[xiii] Whereas human beings share the so-called appellative and expressive functions (Bühler) with animals, only the representative function is supposed to be constitutive of reason.[16] However, evidence from more recent ethology, especially experiments with the artificially induced acquisition of language by chimpanzees, teaches us that it is not the use of propositions per se, but only the *communicative use*

---

[x]   Sacrifice of the intellect.
[xi]   Rational discourse, logic.

[xii]   Sir Karl Popper, English philosopher. Below, Karl Bühler (1879–1963) was a German psychologist.
[xiii]   Before an inner tribunal.

of propositionally differentiated language that is proper to our sociocultural form of life and is constitutive for the level of a genuinely social reproduction of life. In terms of language philosophy, the equiprimordiality and equal value of the three fundamental linguistic functions come into view as soon as we abandon the analytic level of the judgment or the sentence and expand our analysis to speech acts, precisely to the communicative use of sentences. Elementary speech acts display a structure in which three components are mutually combined: the propositional component for representing (or mentioning) states of affairs; the illocutionary component for taking up interpersonal relationships; and finally, the linguistic components that bring the intention of the speaker to expression. The clarification, in terms of speech-act theory, of the complex linguistic functions of representation, the establishment of interpersonal relationships, and the expression of one's own subjective experiences has far-reaching consequences for (a) the theory of meaning, (b) the ontological presuppositions of the theory of communication, and (c) the concept of rationality itself. Here I will only point out these consequences to the extent that they are directly relevant to (d) a *new orientation* for the critique of instrumental reason.

(a) Truth-condition semantics,[xiv] as it has been developed from Frege to Dummett and Davidson,[xv] proceeds – as does the Husserlian theory of meaning – from the logocentric assumption that the truth reference of the assertoric sentence (and the indirect truth reference of intentional sentences related to the implementation of plans) offers a suitable point of departure for the explication of the linguistic accomplishment of mutual understanding generally. Thus, this theory arrives at the principle that we understand a sentence when we know the conditions under which it is true. (For understanding intentional and imperative sentences it requires a corresponding knowledge of "conditions for success."[17]) The pragmatically expanded theory of meaning overcomes this fixation on the fact-mirroring function of language. Like truth-condition semantics, it affirms an internal connection between meaning and validity, but it does not reduce this to the validity proper

to truth. Correlative to the three fundamental functions of language, each elementary speech act as a whole can be contested under three different aspects of validity. The hearer can reject the utterance of a speaker *in toto* by either disputing the *truth* of the proposition asserted in it (or of the existential presuppositions of its propositional content), or the *rightness* of the speech act in view of the normative context of the utterance (or the legitimacy of the presupposed context itself), or the *truthfulness* of the intention expressed by the speaker (that is, the agreement of what is meant with what is stated). Hence, the internal connection of meaning and validity holds for the *entire spectrum* of linguistic meanings – and not just for the meaning of expressions that can be expanded into assertoric sentences. It holds true not only for constative[xvi] speech acts, but for any given speech act, that we understand its meaning when we know the conditions under which it can be accepted as valid.

(b) If, however, not just constative but also regulative and expressive speech acts can be connected with validity claims and accepted as valid or rejected as invalid, the basic, ontological framework of the philosophy of consciousness (which has remained normative for linguistic philosophy as well, with exceptions such as Austin)[xvii] proves to be too narrow. The "world" to which subjects can relate with their representations or propositions was hitherto conceived of as the totality of objects or existing states of affairs. The objective world is considered the correlative of all true assertoric sentences. But if normative rightness and subjective truthfulness are introduced as validity claims analogous to truth, "worlds" analogous to the world of facts have to be postulated for legitimately regulated interpersonal relationships and for attributable subjective experiences – a "world" not only for what is "objective," which appears to us in the attitude of the third person, but also one for what is normative, to which we feel obliged in the attitude of addresses, as well as one for what is subjective, which we either disclose or conceal to a public in the attitude of the first person. With any speech act, the speaker takes up a relation to something in the objective world, something in a common social world, and something in his own subjective world. The legacy of logocentrism is still noticeable in the

---

xiv The study of the meanings of utterances that are either true or false.

xv German logician Gottlob Frege (1848–1925); Michael Dummett and Donald Davidson are contemporary philosophers of language.

xvi Utterances intended to state what is true.

xvii Premier Oxford "ordinary language" philosopher J. L. (John Longshaw) Austin (1911–60).

terminological difficulty of expanding the ontological concept of "world" in this way.

The phenomenological concept (elaborated by Heidegger in particular) of a referential context, a lifeworld, that forms the unquestioned context for processes of mutual understanding – behind the backs of participants in interaction, so to speak – needs a corresponding expansion. Participants draw from this *lifeworld* not just consensual patterns of interpretation (the background knowledge from which propositional contents are fed), but also normatively reliable patterns of social relations (the tacitly presupposed solidarities on which illocutionary acts are based) and the competences acquired in socialization processes (the background of the speaker's intentions).

(c) "Rationality" refers in the first instance to the disposition of speaking and acting subjects to acquire and use fallible knowledge. As long as the basic concepts of the philosophy of consciousness lead us to understand knowledge exclusively as knowledge of something in the objective world, rationality is assessed by how the isolated subject orients himself to representational and propositional contents. Subject-centered reason finds its criteria in standards of truth and success that govern the relationships of knowing and purposively acting subjects to the world of possible objects or states of affairs. By contrast, as soon as we conceive of knowledge as communicatively mediated, rationality is assessed in terms of the capacity of responsible participants in interaction to orient themselves in relation to validity claims geared to intersubjective recognition. Communicative reason finds its criteria in the argumentative procedures for directly or indirectly redeeming claims to propositional truth, normative rightness, subjective truthfulness, and aesthetic harmony.[18]

Thus, a procedural concept of rationality can be worked out in terms of the interdependence of various forms of argumentation, that is to say, with the help of a pragmatic logic of argumentation. This concept is richer than that of purposive rationality, which is tailored to the cognitive-instrumental dimension, because it integrates the moral-practical as well as the aesthetic-expressive domains; it is an explicitation of the rational potential built into the validity basis of speech. This communicative rationality recalls older ideas of logos, inasmuch as it brings along with it the connotations of a noncoercively unifying, consensus-building force of a discourse in which the participants overcome their at first subjectively

biased views in favor of a rationally motivated agreement. Communicative reason is expressed in a decentered understanding of the world.

(d) From this perspective, both cognitive-instrumental mastery of an objectivated nature (and society) and narcissistically overinflated autonomy (in the sense of purposively rational self-assertion) are derivative moments that have been rendered independent from the communicative structures of the lifeworld, that is, from the intersubjectivity of relationships of mutual understanding and relationships of reciprocal recognition. Subject-centered reason is the *product of division and usurpation*, indeed of a social process in the course of which a subordinated moment assumes the place of the whole, without having the power to assimilate the structure of the whole. Horkheimer and Adorno have, like Foucault, described this process of a self-overburdening and self-reifying subjectivity as a world-historical process. But both sides missed its deeper irony, which consists in the fact that the communicative potential of reason first had to be released in the patterns of modern lifeworlds before the unfettered imperatives of the economic and administrative subsystems could react back on the vulnerable practice of everyday life and could thereby promote the cognitive-instrumental dimension to domination over the suppressed moments of practical reason. The communicative potential of reason has been simultaneously developed and distorted in the course of capitalist modernization.

The paradoxical contemporaneity and interdependence of the two processes can only be grasped if the false alternative set up by Max Weber, with his opposition between substantive and formal rationality, is overcome. Its underlying assumption is that the disenchantment of religious-metaphysical world views robs rationality, along with the contents of tradition, of all substantive connotations and thereby strips it of its power to have a structure-forming influence on the lifeworld beyond the purposive-rational organization of means. As opposed to this, I would like to insist that, despite its purely procedural character as disburdened of all religious and metaphysical mortgages, communicative reason is directly implicated in social life-processes insofar as acts of mutual understanding take on the role of a mechanism for coordinating action. The network of communicative actions is nourished by resources of the lifeworld and is at the same time the *medium* by which concrete forms of life are reproduced.

Hence, the theory of communicative action can reconstruct Hegel's concept of the ethical context of life (independently of premises of the philosophy of consciousness). It disenchants the unfathomable causality of fate, which is distinguished from the destining of Being by reason of its *inexorable immanence*. Unlike the "from-time-immemorial" character of the happening of Being or of power, the pseudo-natural dynamics of impaired communicative life-contexts retains something of the character of a destining for which one is *"at fault" oneself* – though one can speak of "fault" here only in an intersubjective sense, that is, in the sense of an involuntary product of an entanglement that, however things stand with individual accountability, communicative agents would have to ascribe to communal responsibility. It is not by chance that suicides set loose a type of shock among those close to them, which allows even the most hardhearted to discover something of the *unavoidable communality* of such a fate.

In the theory of communicative action, the feedback process by which lifeworld and everyday communicative practice are intertwined takes over the mediating role that Marx and Western Marxism had reserved to social practice. In this social practice, reason as historically situated, bodily incarnated, and confronted by nature was supposed to be mediated with its other. If communicative action is now going to take over the same mediating function, the theory of communicative action is going to be suspected of representing just another version of praxis philosophy. In fact, both are supposed to take care of the same task: to conceive of rational practice as reason concretized in history, society, body, and language.

We have traced the way praxis philosophy substituted labor for self-consciousness and then got caught in the fetters of the production paradigm. The praxis philosophy renewed by phenomenology and anthropology, which has at its disposal the tools of the Husserlian analysis of the lifeworld, has learned from the critique of Marxian productivism. It relativizes the status of labor and joins in the aporetic attempts to accommodate the externalization of subjective spirit, the temporalization, socialization, and embodiment of situated reason, within *other* subject–object relationships. Inasmuch as it makes use of phenomenological-anthropological tools of thought, praxis philosophy renounces originality precisely at the point where it cannot afford to: in specifying praxis as a rationally structured

process of mediation. It is once again subjected to the dichotomizing basic concepts of the philosophy of the subject: *History* is projected and made by subjects who find themselves in turn already projected and made in the historical process (Sartre); *society* appears to be an objective network of relations that is either set, as a normative order, above the heads of subjects with their transcendentally prior mutual understandings (Alfred Schütz) or is generated by them, as instrumental orders, in the battle of reciprocal objectifications (Kojève); the subject either finds itself centered in its *body* (Merleau-Ponty) or is related eccentrically to itself, regarding its body as an object (Plessner).[xviii] Thought that is tied to the philosophy of the subject cannot bridge over these dichotomies but, as Foucault so acutely diagnosed, oscillates helplessly between one and the other pole.

Not even the linguistic turn of praxis philosophy leads to a paradigm change. Speaking subjects are either masters or shepherds of their linguistic systems. Either they make use of language in a way that is creative of meaning, to disclose their world innovatively, or they are always already moving around within a horizon of world-disclosure taken care of for them by language itself and constantly shifting behind their backs – language as the medium of creative practice (Castoriadis) or as differential event (Heidegger, Derrida).

Thanks to the approach of linguistic philosophy, Cornelius Castoriadis, with his theory of the imaginary institution, can boldly advance praxis philosophy.[xix] In order to give back again to the concept of social practice its revolutionary explosiveness and normative content, he conceives of action no longer expressivistically, but poetically-demiurgically, as the originless creation of absolutely new and unique patterns, whereby each of them discloses an incomparable horizon of meaning. The guarantee of the rational content of modernity – or self-consciousness, authentic self-realization, and self-determination in solidarity – is represented as an imaginary force creative of language. This, of course, comes uncomfortably close to a Being operating without reason. In the end,

---

[xviii] Alexander Kojève (1902–68), twentieth-century French Hegelian philosopher, and three phenomenologists: Alfred Schütz (1899–1959), Maurice Merleau-Ponty (1908–61), contemporary Helmuth Plessner.
[xix] Cornelius Castoriadis, contemporary Greek-born French political philosopher.

there is only a rhetorical difference between voluntaristic "institution" and fatalistic "dispensation."

According to Castoriadis, society is split (like transcendental subjectivity) into the generating and the generated, the instituting and the instituted, whereby the stream of the imaginary, as originative of meaning, flows into changing linguistic world views. This ontological creation of absolutely new, constantly different and unique totalities of meaning occurs like a dispensation of Being; one cannot see how this *demiurgic setting-in-action* of historical truths could be transposed into the *revolutionary project* proper to the practice of consciously acting, autonomous, self-realizing individuals. Autonomy and heteronomy are ultimately supposed to be assessed in terms of the authenticity of the self-transparency of a society that does not hide its imaginary origin beneath extrasocietal projections and knows itself explicitly as a self-instituting society. But who is the subject of this knowledge? Castoriadis acknowledges no reason for revolutionizing reified society except the existentialist resolve: "because we will it." Thus, he has to allow himself to be asked who this "we" of the radical willing might be, if indeed the socialized individuals are merely "instituted" by the "social imaginary." Castoriadis ends where Simmel began: with *Lebensphilosophie*.[xx]

This results from the concept of language Castoriadis borrows from hermeneutics as well as from structuralism. Castoriadis proceeds – as do Heidegger, Derrida, and Foucault, in their own ways – from the notion that an ontological difference exists between language and the things spoken about, between the constitutive understanding of the world and what is constituted in the world. This difference means that language discloses the horizon of meaning within which knowing and acting subjects interpret states of affairs, that is, encounter things and people and have experiences in dealing with them. The world-disclosing function of language is conceived on analogy with the generative accomplishments of transcendental consciousness, prescinding, naturally, from the sheerly formal and supratemporal character of the latter. The linguistic world view is a concrete and historical a priori; it fixes interpretative perspectives that are substantive and variable and that cannot be gone behind. This constitutive world-understanding changes independently of what subjects experience

concerning conditions in the world interpreted in the light of this preunderstanding, and independently of what they can *learn* from their practical dealings with anything in the world. No matter whether this metahistorical transformation of linguistic world views is conceived of as Being, différance,[xxi] power, or imagination, and whether it is endowed with connotations of a mystical experience of salvation, of aesthetic shock, of creaturely pain, or of creative intoxication: What all these concepts have in common is the peculiar uncoupling of the horizon-constituting productivity of language from the consequences of an intramundane practice that is wholly prejudiced by the linguistic system. Any interaction between world-disclosing language and learning processes in the world is excluded.

In this respect, praxis philosophy had distinguished itself sharply from every kind of linguistic historicism. It conceived of social production as the self-generative process of the species, and the transformation of external nature achieved through labor as an impulse to a learning self-transformation of our own nature. The world of ideas, in light of which socialized producers interpret a pregiven, historically formed nature, changes in turn as a function of the learning processes connected with their transformative activity. By no means does this *innerworldly praxis* owe its *world-building effects* to a mechanical dependence of the superstructure upon the basis, but to two simple facts: The world of ideas is what first makes possible determinate interpretations of a nature that is then cooperatively worked upon; but it is affected in turn by the learning processes set in motion by social labor. Contrary to linguistic historicism, which hypostatizes the world-disclosing force of language, historical materialism takes into account (as do, later on, pragmatism and genetic structuralism) a dialectical relationship between the world-view structures that make intermundane practice possible by means of a prior understanding of meaning, on the one hand, and, on the other, learning processes deposited in the transformation of world-view structures.

This reciprocal causality goes back to an intrinsic connection between meaning and validity, which nevertheless does not eliminate the difference between the two. Meaning could not exhaust validity. Heidegger jumped to conclusions in

---

[xx]   Georg Simmel (1858–1918), German sociologist.

[xxi]   Derrida's term for the differing-deferring intrinsic to all signs.

identifying the disclosure of meaning-horizons with the truth of meaningful utterances; it is only the *conditions* for the validity of utterances that change with the horizon of meaning – the changed understanding of meaning has to prove itself in experience and in dealing with what can come up within its horizon. And yet praxis philosophy is unable to exploit the superiority it possesses in this respect, because, as we have seen, with its paradigm of production it screens out of the validity spectrum of reason every dimension except those of truth and efficiency. Accordingly, what is learned in innerworldly practice can only accumulate in the development of the forces of production. With this productivist conceptual strategy, the normative content of modernity can no longer be grasped; it can at most be tacitly used to circle about a purposive rationality that has grown into a totality in the exercise of an accusatory negative dialectics.

This unfortunate consequence may be what moved Castoriadis to entrust the rational content of socialism (that is, of a form of life that is supposed to make autonomy and self-realization in solidarity possible) to a demiurge creative of meaning, which brushes aside the difference between meaning and validity and no longer relies upon the profane verification of its creations. A totally different perspective results when we transfer the concept of praxis from labor to communicative action. Then we recognize the interdependences between world-disclosing systems of language and intramundane learning proceses along the entire spectrum of validity: Learning processes are no longer channeled only into processes of social labor (and ultimately into cognitive-instrumental dealings with an objectified nature). As soon as we drop the paradigm of production, we can affirm the internal connection between meaning and validity for the whole reservoir of meaning – not just for the segment of meaning of linguistic expressions that play a role in assertoric and intentional sentences. In communicative action, which requires taking yes/no positions on claims of rightness and truthfulness no less than reactions to claims of truth and efficiency, the background knowledge of the lifeworld is submitted to an ongoing test across its entire breadth. To this extent, the concrete a priori of world-disclosing language systems is exposed – right down to their widely ramifying ontological presuppositions – to an indirect revision in the light of our dealings with the intramundane.

This does not mean that the internal connection between meaning and validity is to be undone

now from the other side. The potency to create meaning, which in our day has largely retreated into aesthetic precincts, retains the contingency of genuinely innovative forces.

There is a more serious question: whether the concepts of communicative action and of the transcending force of universalistic validity claims do not reestablish an idealism that is incompatible with the naturalistic insights of historical materialism. Does not a lifeworld that is supposed to be reproduced only via the medium of action oriented to mutual understanding get cut off from its material life processes? Naturally, the lifeworld is materially reproduced by way of the results and consequences of the goal-directed actions with which its members intervene in the world. But these instrumental actions are interlaced with communicative ones insofar as they represent the execution of plans that are linked to the plans of other interaction participants by way of common definitions of situations and processes of mutual understanding. Along these paths, the solutions to problems in the sphere of social labor are also plugged into the medium of action oriented by mutual understanding. The theory of communicative action takes into account the fact that the symbolic reproduction of the lifeworld and its material reproduction are internally interdependent.

It is not so simple to counter the suspicion that with the concept of action oriented to validity claims the idealism of a pure, nonsituated reason slips in again, and the dichotomies between the realms of the transcendental and the empirical are given new life in another form.

There is no pure reason that might don linguistic clothing only in the second place. Reason is by its very nature incarnated in contexts of communicative action and in structures of the lifeworld.[19] To the extent that the plans and actions of different actors are interconnected in historical time and across social space through the use of speech oriented toward mutual agreement, taking yes/no positions on criticizable validity claims, however implicitly, gains a key function in *everyday* practice. Agreement arrived at through communication, which is measured by the intersubjective recognition of validity claims, makes possible a networking of social interactions and lifeworld contexts. Of course, these validity claims have a Janus[xxii] face: As claims, they transcend any local

---

[xxii] A Roman god with two faces.

context; at the same time, they have to be raised here and now and be de facto recognized if they are going to bear the agreement of interaction participants that is needed for effective cooperation. The transcendent moment of *universal* validity bursts every provinciality asunder; the obligatory moment of accepted validity claims renders them carriers of a *context-bound* everyday practice. Inasmuch as communicative agents reciprocally raise validity claims with their speech acts, they are relying on the potential of assailable grounds. Hence, a moment of *unconditionality* is built into *factual* processes of mutual understanding – the validity laid claim to is distinguished from the social currency of a de facto established practice and yet serves it as the foundation of an existing consensus. The validity claimed for propositions and norms transcends spaces and times, *"blots out" space and time*; but the claim is always raised *here and now*, in specific contexts, and is either accepted or rejected with factual consequences for action. Karl-Otto Apel speaks in a suggestive way about the entwinement of the real communication community with an ideal one.[20]

The communicative practice of everyday life is, as it were, reflected in itself. This "reflection" is no longer a matter of the cognitive subject relating to itself in an objectivating manner. The stratification of discourse and action built into communicative action takes the place of this prelinguistic and isolated reflection. For factually raised validity claims point directly or indirectly to arguments by which they can be worked out and in some cases resolved. This argumentative debate about hypothetical validity claims can be described as the reflective form of communicative action: a relation-to-self that does without the compulsion to objectification found in the basic concepts of the philosophy of the subject. That is to say, the "vis-à-vis" of proponents and opponents reproduces at a reflective level that basic form of intersubjective relationship which always mediates the self-relation of the speaker through the performative relation to an addressee. The tense interconnection of the ideal and the real is also, and especially clearly, manifest in discourse itself. Once participants enter into argumentation, they cannot avoid supposing, in a reciprocal way, that the conditions for an ideal speech situation have been sufficiently met. And yet they realize that their discourse is never definitively "purified" of the motives and compulsions that have been filtered out. As little as we can do without the supposition of a purified discourse, we have equally to make do with "unpurified" discourse.

At the end of the fifth lecture, I indicated that the internal connection between contexts of justification and contexts of discovery, between validity and genesis, is never utterly severed. The task of justification, or, in other words, the critique of validity claims carried out from the perspective of a participant, cannot ultimately be separated from a genetic consideration that issues in an ideology critique – carried out from a third-person perspective – of the mixing of power claims and validity claims. Ever since Plato and Democritus,[xxiii] the history of philosophy has been dominated by two opposed impulses: One relentlessly elaborates the transcendent power of abstractive reason and the emancipatory unconditionality of the intelligible, whereas the other strives to unmask the imaginary purity of reason in a materialist fashion.

In contrast, dialectical thought has enlisted the subversive power of materialism to undercut these false alternatives. It does not respond to the banishment of everything empirical from the realm of ideas merely by scornfully reducing relationships of validity to the powers that triumph behind their back. Rather, the theory of communicative action regards the dialectic of knowing and not knowing as embedded within the dialectic of successful and unsuccessful mutual understanding.

Communicative reason makes itself felt in the binding force of intersubjective understanding and reciprocal recognition. At the same time, it circumscribes the universe of a common form of life. Within this universe, the irrational cannot be separated from the rational in the same way as, according to Parmenides, ignorance could be separated from the kind of knowledge that, as the absolutely affirmative, rules over the "nothing." Following Jacob Böhme and Isaac Luria, Schelling correctly insisted that mistakes, crimes, and deceptions are not simply without reason; they are forms of manifestation of the inversion of reason.[xxiv] The violation of claims to truth, correctness, and sincerity affects the whole permeated by the bond of reason. There is no escape and no refuge for the few who are in the truth and are supposed to take their leave of the many who stay behind in the

xxiii   Greek Atomist philosopher (ca.460–ca.370 BC).
xxiv   Jacob Böhme (1575–1624), German mystic and philosopher; Isaac Luria (1534–72), cabalist (Jewish mystic).

Jürgen Habermas

darkness of their blindness, as the day takes leave of the night. Any violation of the structures of rational life together, to which all lay claim, affects everyone equally. This is what the young Hegel meant by the ethical totality that is disrupted by the deed of the criminal and that can only be restored by insight into the indivisibility of suffering due to alienation. The same idea motivates Klaus Heinrich in his confrontation of Parmenides with Jonah.[xxv]

In the idea of the convenant made by Yahweh with the people of Israel, there is the germ of the dialectic of betrayal and avenging force: "Keeping the covenant with God is the symbol of fidelity; breaking this covenant is the model of betrayal. To keep faith with God is to keep faith with life-giving Being itself – in oneself and others. To deny it in any domain of being means breaking the covenant with God and betraying one's own foundation. ... Thus, betrayal of another is simultaneously betrayal of oneself; and every protest against betrayal is not just protest in one's own name, but in the name of the other at the same time.... The idea that each being is potentially a 'covenant partner' in the fight against betrayal, including anyone who betrays himself and me, is the only counterbalance against the stoic resignation already formulated by Parmenides when he made a cut between those who know and the mass of the ignorant. The concept of 'enlightenment' familiar to us is unthinkable without the concept of a potentially universal confederation against betrayal."[21] Peirce and Mead[xxvi] were the first to raise this religious motif of a confederation to philosophical status in the form of a consensus theory of truth and a communication theory of society. The theory of communicative action joins itself with this pragmatist tradition; like Hegel in his early fragment on crime and punishment, it, too, lets itself be guided by an intuition that can be expressed in the concepts of the Old Testament as follows: In the restlessness of the real conditions of life, there broods an ambivalence that is due to the dialectic of betrayal and avenging force.[22]

In fact, we can by no means always, or even only often, fulfill those improbable pragmatic presuppositions from which we nevertheless set forth in day-to-day communicative practice – and, in the

sense of transcendental necessity, from which we *have to* set forth. For this reason, sociocultural forms of life stand under the structural restrictions of a communicative reason *at once claimed and denied*.

The reason operating in communicative action not only stands under, so to speak, external, situational constraints; its own conditions of possibility necessitate its branching out into the dimensions of historical time, social space, and body-centered experiences. That is to say, the rational potential of speech is interwoven with the *resources* of any particular given lifeworld. To the extent that the lifeworld fulfills the resource function, it has the character of an intuitive, unshakeably certain, and holistic knowledge, which cannot be made problematic at will – and in this respect it does not represent "knowledge" in any strict sense of the word. This amalgam of background assumptions, solidarities, and skills bred through socialization constitutes a conservative counterweight against the risk of dissent inherent in processes of reaching understanding that work through validity claims.

As a resource from which interaction participants support utterances capable of reaching consensus, the lifeworld constitutes an equivalent for what the philosophy of the subject had ascribed to consciousness in general as synthetic accomplishments. Now, of course, the generative accomplishments are related not to the form but to the content of possible mutual understanding. To this extent, *concrete* forms of life replace transcendental consciousness in its function of creating unity. In culturally embodied self-understandings, intuitively present group solidarities, and the competences of socialized individuals that are brought into play as know-how, the reason expressed in communicative action is mediated with the traditions, social practices, and body-centered complexes of experience that coalesce into *particular* totalities. These particular forms of life, which only emerge in the plural, are certainly not connected with each other only through a web of family resemblances; they exhibit structures common to lifeworlds in general. But these universal structures are only stamped on particular life forms through the medium of action oriented to mutual understanding by which they have to be reproduced. This explains why the importance of these universal structures can increase in the course of historical processes of differentiation. This is also the key to the rationalization of the lifeworld and to

[xxv] Parmenides, the ancient Greek philosopher (b. 515 BC), and the Biblical Jonah, swallowed and regurgitated by a whale.
[xxvi] American philosopher George Herbert Mead (1863–1931).

the successive release of the rational potential contained in communicative action. This historical tendency can account for the normative content of a modernity threatened by self-destruction without drawing upon the constructions of the philosophy of history.

Author's Notes

1 See the unique lecture delivered by Foucault in 1983 on Kant's "What Is Enlightenment?," in Paul Rabinow (ed.), *The Foucault Reader* (New York, 1984), pp. 32–50. I refer to this in my evocation in the *t a z* (2 July 1984).

2 Jürgen Habermas, "Remarks on the Concept of Communicative Action," in G. Seebass and R. Tuomela (eds), *Social Action* (Dordrecht, 1985), pp. 151–78.

3 Jürgen Habermas, "Interpretive Social Science and Hermeneuticism," in N. Haan, R. Bellah, P. Rabinow, and W. Sullivan (eds), *Social Science as Moral Inquiry* (New York, 1983), pp. 251–70.

4 Jürgen Habermas, "A Postscript to *Knowledge and Human Interests*", *Philosophy of Social Science*, 3 (1973): 157–89. Also H. Dahmer, *Libido und Gesellschaft* (Frankfurt, 1982), pp. 8ff.

5 Jürgen Habermas, "The Hermeneutic Claim to University," in J. Bleicher (ed.), *Contemporary Hermeneutics* (London and Boston, 1980), pp. 181–211.

6 Jürgen Habermas, *Theorie des kommunikativen Handelns*, vol. 2 (Frankfurt, 1981), pp. 589ff. English: *Theory of Communicative Action*, vol. 2: *System and Lifeworld: A Critique of Functionalist Reason* (Boston, 1987).

7 Cf. Richard J. Bernstein, *Beyond Objectivism and Relativism* (Philadelphia, 1983).

8 H. Böhme and G. Böhme, *Das Andere der Vernunft* (Frankfurt, 1983), p. 326.

9 See the excursus following lecture VII.

10 Böhme and Böhme, *Das Andere der Vernunft*, p. 11.

11 Ibid., p. 18.

12 Ibid., p. 19.

13 Whereas Schiller and Hegel want to see the moral idea of self-legislation realized in an aesthetically reconciled society or in the totality of the context of ethical life, the Böhmes can see only the work of disciplinary power in moral autonomy: "If one wanted to envision the inner judicial process conducted in the name of the moral law with regard to maxims, one would have to recur to the Protestant examination of conscience, which displaced the model of the witch trial into the interiority of humans; or better still, go forward into the cool, hygienic interrogation rooms and the silent, elegant computer arsenals of the police gone scientific, whose ideal is the categorical imperative – the uninterrupted apprehension and control of everything particular and resistant, right into the interiority of the human being." (Böhme and Böhme, *Das Andere der Vernunft*, p. 349).

14 Ibid., p. 13.

15 Ibid., p. 23.

16 Karl-Otto Apel, "Die Logosauszeichnung der menschlichen Sprache. Die philosophische Tragweite der Sprechakttheorie" (1984), manuscript.

17 Ernst Tugendhat, *Einführung in die sprachanalytische Philosophie* (Frankfurt, 1976).

18 Albrecht Wellmer has shown that the harmony of a work of art – aesthetic truth, as it is called – can by no means be reduced, without further ado, to authenticity or sincerity: see his "Truth, Semblance and Reconciliation," *Telos*, 62 (1984/85): 89–115.

19 J. H. Hamann, "Metakritik über den Purismus der Vernunft," in J. Simon (ed.), *Schriften zur Sprache* (Frankfurt, 1967), pp. 213ff.

20 Karl-Otto Apel, *Towards a Transformation of Philosophy* (London, 1980), pp. 225ff. See also my response to Mary Hesse in John Thompson and David Held (eds), *Habermas: Critical Debates* (Cambridge, MA, and London, 1982), pp. 276ff.

21 K. Heinrich, *Versuch über die Schwierigkeit nein zu sagen* (Frankfurt, 1964), p. 20; see also his *Parmenides und Jona* (Frankfurt, 1966).

22 H. Brunkhorst, "Kommunikative Vernunft und rächende Gewalt," *Sozialwissenschaftliche Literatur-Rundschau*, 8/9 (1983): 7–34.

55

"Is There Still Anything to Say about Reality and Truth?"

Hilary Putnam

American philosopher Hilary Putnam (1926–) has been a major contributor to the philosophy of mind, language, and knowledge in recent decades. An earlier proponent of a "functionalist" approach to mind and reference, Putnam later argued for an "internal" or "pragmatic realism," influenced by Peirce and James, for which the dependence of reference on humanly constructed theory does not undermine a realist account of truth. As he explains in the following 1985 lecture, for Putnam there can be no truth about the world that holds independent of a conceptual scheme; but given any such scheme, reference is fixed and not merely "conventional." As such, his opposition to Richard Rorty's postmodernism is instructive. Both reject foundationalism on the basis of pragmatism. For Putnam, however, having abandoned the hope for a "God's eye view" of reality, pragmatism leaves us with a chastened, but still realist and philosophical, account of truth.

The man on the street, Eddington reminded us, visualizes a table as 'solid' – that is, as *mostly* solid matter.[i] But physics has discovered that the table is mostly empty space: that the distance between the particles is immense in relation to the radius of the electron or the nucleus of one of the atoms of which the table consists. One reaction to this state of affairs, the reaction of Wilfrid Sellars,[1] is to deny that there are tables at all as we ordinarily conceive them (although he chooses an ice cube rather than a

[i] Arthur Stanley Eddington (1882–1944), British Physicist and astronomer.

table as his example). The commonsense conception of ordinary middle-sized material objects such as tables and ice cubes (the 'manifest image') is simply *false* in Sellars's view (although not without at least some cognitive value – there are real objects that the 'tables' and 'ice cubes' of the manifest image 'picture', according to Sellars, even if these real objects are not the layman's tables and ice cubes). I don't agree with this view of Sellars's, but I hope he will forgive me if I use it, or the phenomenon of its appearance on the philosophical scene, to highlight certain features of the philosophical debate about 'realism'.

First of all, this view illustrates the fact that Realism with a capital 'R' doesn't always deliver what the innocent expect of it. If there is any appeal of Realism which is wholly legitimate it is the appeal to the commonsense feeling that *of course* there are tables and chairs, and any philosophy that tell us that there really aren't – that there are really only sense data, or only 'texts', or whatever, is more than slightly crazy. In appealing to this commonsense feeling, Realism reminds me of the Seducer in the old-fashioned melodrama. In the melodramas of the 1890s the Seducer always promised various things to the Innocent Maiden which he failed to deliver when the time came. In this case the Realist (the evil Seducer) promises common sense (the Innocent Maiden) that he will rescue her from her enemies

Hilary Putnam, "Is There Still Anything to Say About Reality and Truth," Lecture One, pp. 3–21 from *The Many Faces of Realism*. LaSalle, Ill.: Open Court Publishing Inc., 1987.

(Idealists, Kantians and Neo-Kantians, Pragmatists, and the fearsome self-described "Irrealist" Nelson Goodman) who (the Realist says) want to deprive her of her good old ice cubes and chairs.[ii] Faced with this dreadful prospect, the fair Maiden naturally opts for the company of the commonsensical Realist. But when they have travelled together for a little while the 'Scientific Realist' breaks the news that what the Maiden is going to get *isn't* her ice cubes and tables and chairs. In fact, all there *really* is – the Scientific Realist tells her over breakfast – is what 'finished science' will say there is – whatever that may be. She is left with a promissory note for She Knows Not What, and the assurance that even if there *aren't* tables and chairs, still there are some *Dinge an sich*[iii] that her 'manifest image' (or her 'folk physics', as some Scientific Realists put it) 'picture'. Some will say that the lady has been had.

Thus, it is clear that the name 'Realism' can be claimed by or given to at least two very different philosophical attitudes (and, in fact, to many). The philosopher who claims that only scientific objects 'really exist' and that much, if not all, of the commonsense world is mere 'projection' claims to be a 'realist', but so does the philosopher who insists that there *really are* chairs and ice cubes (and some of these ice cubes really are *pink*), and these two attitudes, these two images of the world, can lead to and have led to many different programs for philosophy.

Husserl[2] traces the first line of thought, the line that denies that there 'really are' commonsense objects, back to Galileo, and with good reason. The present Western worldview depends, according to Husserl, on a new way of conceiving 'external objects' – the way of mathematical physics. An external thing is conceived of as a congeries of particles (by atomists) or as some kind of extended disturbance (in the seventeenth century, a 'vortex', and later a collection of 'fields'). Either way, the table in front of me (or the object that I 'picture as' a table) is described by 'mathematical formulas', as Husserl says. And this, he points out, is what above all came into Western thinking with the Galilean revolution: the idea of the 'external world' as something whose true description, whose description 'in itself', consists of mathematical formulas.

It is important to this way of thinking that certain familiar properties of the table – its size and shape and location – are 'real' properties, describable, for

example, in the language of Descartes' analytic geometry. Other properties, however, the so-called 'secondary' properties, of which *color* is a chief example, are *not* treated as real properties in the same sense. No 'occurrent' (non-dispositional) property of that swarm of molecules (or that space–time region) recognized in mathematical physics can be said to be what we all along called its *color*.

What about dispositional properties? It is often claimed that color is simply a function of *reflectancy*, that is, of the disposition of an object (or of the surface of an object) to selectively absorb certain wavelengths of incident light and reflect others. But this doesn't really do much for the reality of colors. Not only has recent research shown that this account is much too simple (because changes of reflectancy across edges turn out to play an important role in determining the colors we see), but reflectancy itself does not have one uniform physical explanation. A red star and a red apple and a reddish glass of colored water are red for quite different physical reasons. In fact, there may well be an infinite number of different physical conditions which could result in the disposition to reflect (or emit) red light and absorb light of other wavelengths. A dispositional property whose underlying non-dispositional 'explanation' is so very non-uniform is simply incapable of being represented as a mathematical function of the dynamical variables. And these – the dynamical variables – are the parameters that this way of thinking treats as the 'characteristics' of 'external' objects.

Another problem[3] is that *hues* turn out to be much more subjective than we thought. In fact, any shade on the color chart in the green part of the spectrum will be classed as 'standard green' by some subject – even if it lies at the extreme 'yellow-green' end or the extreme 'blue-green' end.

In sum, no 'characteristic' recognized by this way of thinking – no 'well-behaved function of the dynamical variables' – corresponds to such a familiar property of objects as *red* or *green*. The idea that there is a property all red objects have in common – the same in all cases – and another property all green objects have in common – the same in all cases – is a kind of illusion, on the view we have come more and more to take for granted since the age of Descartes and Locke.

However, Locke and Descartes did give us a sophisticated substitute for our pre-scientific notion of color; a substitute that has, perhaps, come to seem mere 'post-scientific common sense' to most people. This substitute involves the idea of

---

[ii]   Nelson Goodman (1906–98), American philosopher and author of *Ways of World Making*.
[iii]   Thing in itself.

a sense datum (except that, in the seventeenth and eighteenth century vocabulary, sense data were referred to as 'ideas' or 'impressions'). The red sweater I see is not red in the way I thought it was (there is no 'physical magnitude' which is its redness), but it does have a disposition (a Power, in the seventeenth and eighteenth century idiom) to affect me in a certain way – to cause me to have sense data. And these, the sense data, do truly have a simple, uniform, non-dispositional sort of 'redness'.

This is the famous picture, the dualistic picture of the physical world and its primary qualities, on the one hand, and the mind and its sense data, on the other, that philosophers have been wrangling over since the time of Galileo, as Husserl says. And it is Husserl's idea – as it was the idea of William James, who influenced Husserl – that this picture is disastrous.

But why should we regard it as disastrous? It was once shocking, to be sure, but as I have already said it is by now widely accepted as 'post-scientific common sense'. What is *really* wrong with this picture?

For one thing, *solidity* is in much the same boat as color. If objects do not have color as they 'naively' seem to, no more do they have solidity as they 'naively' seem to.[4] It is this that leads Sellars to say that such commonsense objects as ice cubes do not really exist at all. What *is* our conception of a typical commonsense object if not of something solid (or liquid) which exhibits certain colors? What there really are, in Sellars's scientific metaphysics, are objects of mathematical physics, on the one hand, and 'raw feels', on the other. This is precisely the picture I have just described as "disastrous"; it is the picture that denies precisely the common man's kind of realism, his realism about tables and chairs.

The reply to me (the reply a philosopher who accepts the post-Galilean picture will make) is obvious: 'You are just nostalgic for an older and simpler world. This picture works; our acceptance of it is an "inference to the best explanation". We cannot regard it as an objection to a view that it does not preserve everything that laymen once falsely believed.'

If it is an inference to the best explanation, it is a strange one, however. How does the familiar explanation of what happens when I 'see something red' go? The light strikes the object (say, a sweater), and is reflected to my eye. There is an image on the retina (Berkeley knew about images on the retina, and so did Descartes, even if the wave aspect of

light was not well understood until much later). There are resultant nerve impulses (Descartes knew there was some kind of transmission along the nerves, even if he was wrong about its nature – and it is not clear we know its nature either, since there is again debate about the significance of chemical, as opposed to electrical, transmissions from neuron to neuron.) There are events in the brain, some of which we understand thanks to the work of Hubel and Wiesel, David Marr, and others. And then – this is the mysterious part – there is somehow a 'sense datum' or a 'raw feel'. *This* is an *explanation*?

An 'explanation' that involves connections of a kind we do not understand at all ("nomological danglers", Herbert Feigl called them[5]) and concerning which we have not even the sketch of a theory is an explanation through something more obscure than the phenomenon to be explained. As has been pointed out by thinkers as different from one another as William James, Husserl, and John Austin, every single part of the sense datum story is supposition – theory – and theory of a most peculiar kind. Yet the epistemological role 'sense data' are supposed to play by traditional philosophy required them to be what is 'given', to be *what we are absolutely sure of independently of scientific theory*. The kind of scientific realism we have inherited from the seventeenth century has not lost all its prestige even yet, but it has saddled us with a disastrous picture of the world. It is high time we looked for a different picture.

Intrinsic Properties: Dispositions

I want to suggest that the problem with the 'Objectivist' picture of the world (to use Husserl's term for this kind of scientific realism) lies deeper than the postulation of 'sense data'; sense data are, so to speak, the visible symptoms of a systemic disease, like the pock marks in the case of smallpox. The deep systemic root of the disease, I want to suggest, lies in the notion of an 'intrinsic' property, a property something has 'in itself', apart from any contribution made by language or the mind.

This notion, and the correlative notion of a property that is merely 'appearance', or merely something we 'project' onto the object, has proved extremely robust, judging by its appeal to different kinds of philosophers. In spite of their deep disagreements, all the strains of philosophy that accepted the seventeenth-century circle of problems – subjective idealists as well as dualists and materialists – accepted the distinction, even if they disagreed over its application. A subjective idealist would say that there are only sense data (or minds and sense data, in some versions), and that 'red' is an intrinsic property of these objects, while persistence (being there even when we don't look) is something we 'project'; a dualist or a materialist would say the 'external' objects have persistence as an intrinsic property, but red is, in their case, something we 'project'. But all of these philosophers *have* the distinction. Even Kant, who expresses serious doubts about it in the first Critique (to the point of saying that the notion of a "Ding an sich" *may* be "empty"), makes heavy use of it in the second Critique.

Putting aside the Berkeleyan view (that there aren't really any external objects at all)[iv] as an aberrant form of the seventeenth-century view, we may say that the remaining philosophers all accept the account of 'redness' and 'solidity' that I have been describing; these are not 'intrinsic properties' of the external things we ascribe them to, but rather (in the case of external things) dispositions to affect us in certain ways – to produce certain sense data in us, or, the materialist philosophers would say, to produce certain sorts of 'states' in our brains and nervous systems. The idea that these properties are 'in' the things themselves, as intrinsic properties, is a spontaneous 'projection'.

The Achilles' Heel of this story is the notion of a disposition. To indicate the problems that arise – they have preoccupied many first-rate philosophical minds, starting with Charles Peirce's – let me introduce a technical term (I shall not introduce much terminology in this lecture, I promise!). A disposition that something has to do something *no matter what*, I shall call a *strict disposition*. A disposition to do something under 'normal conditions', I shall call an *'other things being equal' disposition*. Perhaps it would be wise to give examples.

The disposition of bodies with non-zero rest mass to travel at sub-light speeds is a *strict* disposition; it is physically impossible for a body with non-zero rest mass to travel at the speed of light. Of course, the notion of a 'strict disposition' presupposes the notion of 'physical necessity', as this

example illustrates, but this is a notion I am allowing the 'scientific realist', at least for the sake of argument. What of the disposition of sugar to dissolve in water?

This is not a strict disposition, since sugar which is placed in water which is already saturated with sugar (or even with other appropriate chemicals) will not dissolve. Is the disposition of sugar to dissolve in *chemically pure water*, then, a strict disposition?

This is also not a strict disposition; the first counterexample I shall mention comes from thermodynamics. Suppose I drop a sugar cube in water and the sugar cube dissolves. Consider sugar which is in water, but in such a way that while the situation is identical with the situation I just produced (the sugar is dissolved in the water) with respect to the position of each particle, and also with respect to the numerical value of the momentum of each particle, all the momentum vectors have the exactly opposite directions from the ones they now have. This is a famous example: what happens in the example is that the sugar, instead of staying dissolved, simply forms a sugar cube which spontaneously leaps out of the water! Since every normal state (every state in which sugar dissolves) can be paired with a state in which it 'undissolves', we see that there are infinitely many physically-possible conditions in which sugar 'undissolves' instead of staying in solution. Of course, these are all states in which entropy decreases; but that is not impossible, only extremely improbable!

Shall we say, then, that sugar has a strict disposition to dissolve unless the condition is one in which an entropy decrease takes place? No, because if sugar is put in water and there is immediately a flash freeze, the sugar will not dissolve if the freezing takes place fast enough. . . .

The fact is that what we can say is that under *normal* conditions sugar will dissolve if placed in water. And there is no reason to think that all the various abnormal conditions (including bizarre quantum mechanical states, bizarre local fluctuations in the space–time, etc.) under which sugar would not dissolve if placed in water could be summed up in a closed formula in the language of fundamental physics.

This is exactly the problem we previously observed in connection with redness and solidity! If the 'intrinsic' properties of 'external' things are the ones that we can represent by formulas in the language of fundamental physics, by 'suitable functions of the dynamical variables', then *solubility*

[iv] George Berkeley (1685–1753), Irish philosopher who denied the existence of matter on empiricist grounds.

is also not an 'intrinsic' property of any external thing. And, similarly, neither is any 'other things being equal' disposition. The Powers, to use the seventeenth-century language, have to be set over against, and carefully distinguished from, the properties the things have 'in themselves'.

Intrinsic Properties: Intentionality

Well, what of it? Why should we not say that dispositions (or at least 'other things being equal' dispositions, such as solubility) are also not 'in the things themselves' but rather something we 'project' onto those things? Philosophers who talk this way rarely if ever stop to say what *projection* itself is supposed to be. Where in the scheme does the ability of the mind to 'project' anything onto anything come in?

Projection is thinking of something as having properties it does not have, but that we can imagine (perhaps because something else we are acquainted with really does have them), without being conscious that this is what we are doing. It is thus a species of *thought* – thought about something. Does the familiar 'Objectivist' picture have anything to tell us about thought (or, as philosophers say, about 'intentionality', that is, about *aboutness*)?

Descartes certainly intended that it should. His view was that there are two fundamental substances – mind and matter – not one, and, correspondingly there should be two fundamental sciences: physics and psychology. But we have ceased to think of mind as a separate 'substance' at all. And a 'fundamental science' of psychology which explains the nature of thought (including how thoughts can be true or false, warranted or unwarranted, about something or not about something) never did come into existence, contrary to Descartes' hopes. So to explain the features of the commonsense world, including color, solidity, causality – I include causality because the commonsense notion of 'the cause' of something is a 'projection' if dispositions are 'projections'; it depends on the notion of 'normal conditions' in exactly the same way – in terms of a mental operation called 'projection' is to explain just about every feature of the commonsense world in terms of *thought*.

But wasn't that what idealists were accused of doing? This is the paradox that I pointed out at the beginning of this lecture. So far as the commonsense world is concerned (the world we experience ourselves as *living* in, which is why Husserl called it the *Lebenswelt*), the effect of what is called 'realism' in philosophy is to deny objective reality, to make it all simply *thought*. It is the philosophers who in one way or another stand in the Neo-Kantian tradition – James, Husserl, Wittgenstein – who claim that commonsense tables and chairs and sensations and electrons are *equally real*, and not the metaphysical realists.

Today, some metaphysical realists would say that we don't need a perfected science of psychology to account for thought and intentionality, because the problem is solved by some philosophical theory; while others claim that a perfected 'cognitive science' based on the 'computer model' will solve the problem for us in near or distant future. I obviously do not have time to examine these suggestions closely today, but I shall indicate briefly why I believe that none of them will withstand close inspection.

Why Intentionality is so Intractable

The problem, in a nutshell, is that thought itself has come to be treated more and more as a 'projection' by the philosophy that traces its pedigree to the seventeenth century. The reason is clear: we have not succeeded in giving the theory that thought is just a primitive property of a mysterious 'substance', mind, any content. As Kant pointed out in the first Critique, we have no theory of this substance or its powers and no prospect of having one. If *unlike* the Kant of the first Critique (as I read the *Critique of Pure Reason*), we insist on sticking to the fundamental 'Objectivist' assumptions, the only line we can then take is that *mental phenomena must be highly derived physical phenomena in some way*, as Diderot and Hobbes had already proposed. By the 'fundamental Objectivist assumptions', I mean (1) the assumption that there is a clear distinction to be drawn between the properties things have 'in themselves' and the properties which are 'projected by us' and (2) the assumption that the fundamental science – in the singular, since only physics has that status today – tells us what properties things have 'in themselves'. (Even if we were to assume, with Wilfrid Sellars, that 'raw feels' – fundamental sensuous qualities of experience – are not going to be reduced to physics, but are in some way going to be added to fundamental science in some future century, it would not affect the situation much; Sellars does not anticipate that *intentionality* will turn out to be something we have to add to physics in the same way, but rather supposes that a theory of the 'use of words' is all that is needed to account for it.)

Modern Objectivism has simply become Materialism. And the central problem for Materialism is 'explaining the emergence of mind'. But if 'explaining the emergence of mind' means solving Brentano's problem, that is, saying in *reductive* terms what 'thinking there are a lot of cats in the neighborhood' *is*, and what 'remembering where Paris is' *is*, etc., why should we now think *that's* possible? If reducing color or solidity or solubility to fundamental physics has proved impossible, why should this vastly more ambitious reduction program prove tractable?

Starting in the late 1950s, I myself proposed a program in the philosophy of mind that has become widely known under the name 'Functionalism'. The claim of my 'Functionalism' was that thinking beings are *compositionally plastic* – that is, that there is no one physical state or event (i.e., no necessary and sufficient condition expressible by a finite formula in the language of first-order fundamental physics) for being even a *physically possible* (let alone 'logically possible' or 'metaphysically possible') occurrence of a thought with a given propositional content, or of a feeling of anger, or of a pain, etc. *A fortiori*, propositional attitudes, emotions, feelings, are not *identical* with brain states, or even with more broadly characterized physical states. When I advanced this claim, I pointed out that thinking of a being's mentality, affectivity, etc., as aspects of its *organization to function* allows one to recognize that all sorts of logically possible 'systems' or beings could be conscious, exhibit mentality and affect, etc., in exactly the same sense without having the same matter (without even consisting of 'matter' in the sense of elementary particles and electromagnetic fields at all). For beings of many different physical (and even 'non-physical') constitutions could have the same functional organization. The thing we want insight into is the nature of human (and animal) functional organization, not the nature of a mysterious 'substance', on the one hand, or merely additional physiological information on the other.

I also proposed a theory as to what our organization to function is, one I have now given up –

this was the theory that our functional organization is that of a Turing machine.[v] I have given this up because I believe that there are good arguments to show that mental states are not only compositionally plastic but also *computationally plastic*. What I mean by this is that physically possible creatures who believe that there are a lot of cats in the neighborhood, or whatever, may have an *indefinite number of different 'programs'*. The hypothesis that there is a necessary and sufficient condition for the presence of a given belief in computational (or computational *cum* physical) terms is unrealistic in just the way that the theory that there is a necessary and sufficient condition for the presence of a table in phenomenalistic terms is unrealistic. Such a condition would have to be infinitely long, and not constructed according to any effective rule, or even according to a non-effective prescription that we could state without using the very terms to be reduced. I do not believe that even all *humans* who have the same belief (in different cultures, or with different bodies of knowledge and different conceptual resources) have in common a physical *cum* computational feature which could be 'identified with' that belief. The 'intentional level' is simply not reducible to the 'computational level' any more than it is to the 'physical level'.[6]

If this is right, then the Objectivist will have to conclude that intentionality *too* must be a mere 'projection'. But how can any philosopher think this suggestion has even the semblance of making sense? As we saw, the very notion of 'projection' *presupposes* intentionality!

Strange to say, the idea that thought *is* a mere projection is being defended by a number of philosophers in the United States and England, in spite of its absurdity. The strength of the 'Objectivist' tradition is so strong that some philosophers will abandon the deepest intuitions we have about ourselves-in-the-world, rather than ask (as Husserl and Wittgenstein did) whether the whole picture is not a mistake. Thus it is that in the closing decades of the twentieth century we have intelligent philosophers[7] claiming that intentionality itself is something we project by taking a 'stance' to some parts of the world (as if 'taking a stance'

[v]   Alan Turing (1912–54), whose attempt to define a mechanical method to address the question of mathematical decidability, "On Computable Numbers with an Application to the *Entscheidungs* Problem" (1936), later called the "Turing Machine," founded computer science.

were not itself an intentional notion!), intelligent philosophers claiming that no one really has propositional attitudes (beliefs and desires), that 'belief' and 'desire' are just notions from a false theory called 'folk psychology', and intelligent philosophers claiming there is no such property as 'truth' and no such relation as reference, that 'is true' is just a phrase we use to 'raise the level of language'. One of these – Richard Rorty – a thinker of great depth – sees that he is committed to rejecting the intuitions that underly every kind of realism[8] (and not just metaphysical realism), but most of these thinkers write as if they were *saving* realism (in its Materialist version) by abandoning intentionality! It's as if it were all right to say 'I don't deny that there is an external world; I just deny that we *think* about it'! Come to think of it, this is the way Foucault wrote, too. The line between relativism *à la française* and Analytic Philosophy seems to be thinner than anglophone philosophers think! Amusingly enough, the dust-jacket of one of the lattest attacks on 'folk psychology'[9] bears an enthusiastic blurb in which a reviewer explains the importance of the book inside the dust-jacket by saying that most people *believe* that there are such things as beliefs!

"The Trail of the Human Serpent is Over All"

If seventeenth-century Objectivism has led twentieth-century philosophy into a blind alley, the solution is neither to fall into extreme relativism, as French philosophy has been doing, nor to deny our commonsense realism. There *are* tables and chairs and ice cubes. There are also electrons and space–time regions and prime numbers and people who are a menace to world peace and moments of beauty and transcendence and many other things. My old-fashioned story of the Seducer and the Innocent Maiden was meant as a double warning, a warning against giving up commonsense realism and, simultaneously, a warning against supposing that the seventeenth-century talk of 'external world' and 'sense impressions', 'intrinsic properties', and 'projections', etc., was in any way a Rescuer of our commonsense realism. Realism with a capital 'R' is, sad to say, the foe, not the defender, of realism with a small 'r'.

If this is hard to see, it is because the task of overcoming the seventeenth-century world picture

is only begun. I asked – as the title of this lecture – whether there is still anything to say, anything really new to say, about reality and truth. If 'new' means 'absolutely unprecedented', I suspect the answer is 'no'. But if we allow that William James might have had something 'new' to say – something new to *us*, not just new to his own time – or, at least, might have had a program for philosophy that is, in part, the right program, even if it has not been properly worked out yet (and may never be completely 'worked out'); if we allow that Husserl and Wittgenstein and Austin may have shared something of the same program, even if they too, in their different ways, failed to state it properly; then there is still something new, something *unfinished and important* to say about reality and truth.[vi] And that is what I believe.

The key to working out the program of preserving commonsense realism while avoiding the absurdities and antinomies of metaphysical realism in all its familiar varieties (Brand X: Materialism; Brand Y: Subjective Idealism; Brand Z: Dualism. . . . . . .) is something I have called *internal realism*. (I should have called it pragmatic realism!) Internal realism is, at bottom, just the insistence that realism is *not* incompatible with conceptual relativity. One can be *both* a realist *and* a conceptual relativist. Realism (with a small 'r') has already been introduced; as was said, it is a view that takes our familiar commonsense scheme, as well as our scientific and artistic and other schemes, at face value, without helping itself to the notion of the thing 'in itself'. But what is conceptual relativity?

Conceptual relativity sounds like 'relativism', but has none of the 'there is no truth to be found . . . "true" is just a name for what a bunch of people can agree on' implications of 'relativism'. A simple example will illustrate what I mean. Consider 'a world with three individuals' (Carnap often used examples like this when we were doing inductive logic together in the early nineteen-fifties), $x1$, $x2$, $x3$. How many *objects* are there in this world?

Well, I *said* "consider a world with just three individuals", didn't I? So mustn't there be three objects? Can there be non-abstract entities which are not 'individuals'?

One possible answer is 'no'. We can identify 'individual', 'object', 'particular', etc., and find no

---

[vi] J. L. Austin (1911–60), Oxford "ordinary language" philosopher.

absurdity in a world with just three objects which are independent, unrelated 'logical atoms'. But there are perfectly good logical doctrines which lead to different results.

Suppose, for example, that like some Polish logicians, I believe that for every two particulars there is an object which is their sum. (This is the basic assumption of 'mereology', the calculus of parts and wholes invented by Lezniewski.)[vii] If I ignore, for the moment, the so-called 'null object', then I will find that the world of 'three individuals' (as Carnap might have had it, at least when he was doing inductive logic) actually contains *seven* objects:

World 1	World 2
x1, x2, x3	x1, x2, x3, x1 + x2, x1 + x3, x2 + x3, x1 + x2 + x3
(A world à la Carnap)	('Same' world à la Polish logician)

Some Polish logicians would also say that there is a 'null object' which they count as a part of every object. If we accepted this suggestion, and added this individual (call it **O**), then we would say that Carnap's world contains *eight* objects.

Now, the classic metaphysical realist way of dealing with such problems is well-known. It is to say that there is a single world (think of this as a piece of dough) which we can slice into pieces in different ways. But this 'cookie cutter' metaphor founders on the question, 'What are the "parts" of this dough?' If the answer is that O, x1, x2, x3, x1 + x2, x1 + x3, x2 + x3, x1 + x2 + x3 are all the different 'pieces', then we have not a *neutral* description, but rather a *partisan* description – just the description of the Warsaw logician! And it is no accident that metaphysical realism cannot really recognize the phenomenon of conceptual relativity – for that phenomenon turns on the fact that *the logical primitives themselves, and in particular the notions of object and existence, have a multitude of different uses rather than one absolute 'meaning'.*

An example which is historically important, if more complex than the one just given, is the ancient dispute about the ontological status of the Euclidean plane. Imagine a Euclidean plane. Think of the

points in the plane. Are these *parts* of the plane, as Leibniz thought? Or are they 'mere limits', as Kant said?

If you say, in *this* case, that these are 'two ways of slicing the same dough', then you must admit that what is a *part* of space, in one version of the facts, is an abstract entity (say, a set of convergent spheres – although there is not, of course, a *unique* way of construing points as limits) in the other version. But then you will have conceded that which entities are 'abstract entities' and which are 'concrete objects', at least, is version-relative. Metaphysical realists to this day continue to argue about whether points (space–time points, nowadays, rather than points in the plane or in three-dimensional space) are individuals or properties, particulars or mere limits, etc. My view is that God himself, if he consented to answer the question, 'Do points really exist or are they mere limits?', would say 'I don't know'; not because His omniscience is limited, but because there is a limit to how far questions make sense.

One last point before I leave these examples: *given* a version, the question, 'How many objects are there?' has an answer, namely 'three' in the case of the first version ('Carnap's World') and 'seven' (or 'eight') in the case of the second version ('The Polish Logician's World'). Once we make clear how we are using 'object' (or 'exist'), the question 'How many objects exist?' has an answer that is not at all a matter of 'convention'. That is why I say that this sort of example does not support *radical* cultural relativism. Our concepts may be culturally relative, but it does not follow that the truth or falsity of everything we say using those concepts is simply 'decided' by the culture. But the idea that there is an Archimedean point, or a use of 'exist' inherent in the world itself, from which the question 'How many objects *really* exist?' makes sense, is an illusion.

If this is right, then it may be possible to see how it can be that what is in one sense the 'same' world (the two versions are deeply related) can be described as consisting of 'tables and chairs' (and these described as colored, possessing dispositional properties, etc.) in one version *and* as consisting of space–time regions, particles and fields, etc., in other versions. To require that all of these *must* be reducible to a single version is to make the mistake of supposing that 'Which are the real objects?' is a question that makes sense *independently of our choice of concepts.*

vii   Stanislaw Lezniewski (1886–1939), member of the Lvov-Warsaw school of logic (with Tarski and Lukasiewicz), and creator of "mereology," the logic of wholes and parts.

What I am saying is frankly programmatic. Let me close by briefly indicating where the program leads, and what I hope from it.

Many thinkers have argued that the traditional dichotomy between the world 'in itself' and the concepts we use to think and talk about it must be given up. To mention only the most recent examples, Davidson has argued that the distinction between 'scheme' and 'content' cannot be drawn; Goodman has arugued that the distinction between 'world' and 'versions' is untenable; and Quine has defended 'ontological relativity'. Like the great pragmatists, these thinkers have urged us to reject the spectator point of view in metaphysics and epistemology. Quine has urged us to accept the existence of abstract entities on the ground that these are indispensable in mathematics,[10] and of microparticles and space–time points on the ground that these are indispensable in physics; and what better justification is there for accepting an ontology than its indispensibility in our scientific practice? he asks. Goodman has urged us to take seriously the metaphors that artists use to restructure our worlds, on the ground that these are an indispensible way of understanding our ex-perience. Davidson has rejected the idea that talk of propositional attitudes is 'second class', on similar grounds.[viii] These thinkers have been somewhat hesitant to forthrightly extend the same approach to our moral images of ourselves and the world. Yet what can giving up the spectator view in philosophy mean if we don't extend the pragmatic approach to the most indispensible 'versions' of ourselves and our world that we possess? Like William James (and like my teacher Morton White[11]) I propose to do exactly that. [In the remaining lectures], I shall illustrate the standpoint of pragmatic realism in ethics by taking a look at some of our moral images, and particularly at the ones that underlie the central democratic value of *equality*. Although reality and truth are old, and to superficial appearances 'dry', topics, I shall try to convince you in the course of these lectures that it is the persistence of obsolete assumptions about these 'dry' topics that sabotages philosophical discussion about all the 'exciting' topics, not to say the possibility of doing justice to the reality and mystery of our commonsense world.

[viii]   American philosopher of language Donald Davidson (1917–).

Author's Notes

1   *Science, Perception, and Reality*, Atlantic Highlands, NJ: Humanities Press, 1963.

2   *The Crisis of the European Sciences and Transcendental Phenomenology*, translated by David Carr, Evanston: Northwestern University Press, 1970.

3   See C. L. Hardin's 'Are "Scientific" Objects Colored?', in *Mind*, XCIII, No. 22 (October 1964), 491–500.

4   The commonsense notion of 'solidity' should not be confused with the physicist's notion of being in 'the solid state'. For example, a sand dune is in the 'solid state' but is not solid in the ordinary sense of the term, while a bottle of milk may be solid, but most of its contents are not in the solid state.

5   'The "Mental" and the "Physical"', in *Minnesota Studies in the Philosophy of Science*, vol. II, *Concepts, Theories and the Mind–Body Problem*, ed. by Feigl, Scriven, and Maxwell, Minneapolis: University of Minnesota Press, 1958, 370–497.

6   This is argued in my *Representation and Reality*, Cambridge, MA: MIT Press, 1988.

7   D. C. Dennett, *Content and Consciousness*, Atlantic Highlands, NJ: Humanities Press, 1969.

8   *Philosophy and the Mirror of Nature*, Princeton: Princeton University Press, 1979.

9   Stephen Stich, *From Folk Psychology to Cognitive Science: The Case Against Belief*, Cambridge, MA: MIT Press, 1983.

10   'On What There Is', reprinted in *From a Logical Point of View*, Cambridge, MA: Harvard 1953.

11   White has advocated doing this early and late (*Toward Reunion in Philosophy*, Cambridge, MA: Harvard University Press, 1956; *What Is and What Ought to Be Done*, Oxford: Oxford University Press, 1981).

Select Bibliography

It is both impossible and inadvisable to attempt a comprehensive bibliography of works that deal with postmodernism and its relation to modernism and/or modernity. The topic's interdisciplinary nature would make for an immense list of marginally related works (unless only those that prominently use the terms "postmodern," "modernity," etc., are included, but that would exclude many relevant texts). Too many different kinds of phenomena and too many disciplines are involved in the subject. The following bibliography aims merely to aid those readers who seek some additional reading. It includes only works that I consider especially interesting or useful for students, and, with rare exceptions, only works available in English. It is organized into four parts: the first contains general introductions to or commentaries on postmodernism; the second, works of interest for tracing the history of the concept of the "postmodern" and the related term "post-industrial"; the third, some important works on modernity and/or modernism; and the fourth, the titles selected in this volume with other relevant works by their authors. For the sake of simplicity there is no redundancy among the four parts; works relevant to multiple sections appear only once. Consequently, interested readers ought to peruse all four.

1 Works on Postmodernism

Best, Stephen and Douglas Kellner. *Postmodern Theory: Critical Interrogations*. New York: Guilford, 1991.

Descombes, Vincent. *Modern French Philosophy*, trans. L. Schott-Fox and J. M. Harding. New York: Cambridge University Press, 1980.

Dews, Peter. *Logics of Disintegration: Post-Structuralist Thought and the Claims of Critical Theory*. New York: Verso, 1987.

Foster, Hal. *The Anti-Aesthetic: Essays on Postmodern Culture*. Port Townsend, Wash.: Bay Press, 1983.

Harvey, David. *The Condition of Postmodernity: An Enquiry into the Origins of Cultural Change*. Oxford and New York: Blackwell, 1989.

Jencks, Charles, *The Post-Modern Reader*. London: Academy Editions, 1992.

Klotz, Heinrich. *The History of Postmodern Architecture*, trans. Radka Donnell. Cambridge, MA: MIT Press, 1988.

Macksey, Richard and Eugenio Donato. *The Structuralist Controversy: The Languages of Criticism and the Sciences of Man*. Baltimore: Johns Hopkins University Press, 1972.

Portoghesi, Paolo. *Postmodern, The Architecture of Postindustrial Society*, trans. Ellen Shapiro. New York: Rizzoli, 1983.

Rose, Margaret. *The Post-Modern and the Post-Industrial: A Critical Analysis*. Cambridge: Cambridge University Press, 1991.

Rosenau, Pauline Marie. *Post-Modernism and the Social Sciences: Insights, Inroads, and Intrusions*. Princeton, NJ: Princeton University Press, 1992.

Sim, Stuart. *The Routledge Critical Dictionary of Postmodern Thought*. New York: Routledge, 1999.

2 Works of Historical Interest

Bell, Bernard Iddings. *Religion For Living: A Book for Postmodernists*. London: The Religious Book Club, 1939.

Bell, Daniel. *The Cultural Contradictions of Capitalism*. New York: Basic Books, 1976.

De Onis, Federico. *Antologia de la Poesia española e his-panoamericana: 1882–1932*. Madrid: 1934.

Etzioni, Amitai. *The Active Society: A Theory of Societal and Political Processes*. New York: Free Press, 1968.

Fiedler, Leslie. "The New Mutants," in *The Collected Essays of Leslie Fiedler*, vol. II. New York: Stein and Day, 1971, pp. 379–99.

Hassan, Ihab. *The Dismemberment of Orpheus: Toward a Postmodern Literature*. Madison: University of Wisconsin Press, 1971.

Hebdige, Dick. *Hiding in the Light: on Images and Things*. New York: Routledge, 1988.

Howe, Irving. *The Decline of the New*. New York: Harcourt, Brace and World, 1970, pp. 190–207.

Hudnut, Joseph. "The Post-Modern House." *Architectural Record*, 97, May 1945, pp. 70–5.

Jacobs, Jane. *The Death and Life of Great American Cities*. New York: Random House, 1961.

Jencks, Charles. "The Rise of Post-Modern Architecture." *Architectural Association Quarterly*, Summer, 1976, 7:4, pp. 7–14.

Levin, Harry. "What was Modernism?" in *Refractions: Essays in Comparative Literature*. New York: Oxford University Press, 1966, pp. 271–95.

McLuhan, Marshall. *Understanding Media: The Extensions of Man*. New York: McGraw-Hill, 1964.

Mills, C. Wright. *The Sociological Imagination*. New York: Oxford University Press, 1959.

Pannwitz, Rudolf. *Die Krisis der Europaeischen Kultur*. Nürnberg: Hans Carl, 1917.

Penty, Arthur J. and Ananda K. Coomaraswamy. *Essays in Post-Industrialism: A Symposium of Prophecy Concerning the Future of Society*. London: 1914.

Reisman, David. "Leisure and Work in Post-Industrial Society," in *Mass Leisure*, ed. E. Larrabee and R. Meyershon. Glencoe, Ill.: Free Press, 1958, pp. 363–85.

Touraine, Alaine. *The Post-Industrial Society*, trans. Leonard F. X. Mayhew. New York: Random House, 1971; original, 1969.

Toynbee, Arnold J. *A Study of History*. London: Oxford University Press, 1939 and 1954, vols. V and VIII.

3 Works on Modernity and Modernism

Bauman, Zygmunt. *Modernity and the Holocaust*. Ithaca: Cornel University, 2001.

Berger, Peter, Brigitte Berger, and Hansfried Kellner. *The Homeless Mind: Modernization and Consciousness*. New York: Vintage, 1974.

Berman, Marshall. *All That Is Solid Melts Into Air: The Experience of Modernity*. New York: Viking Penguin, 1988.

Bernstein, Richard. *Habermas and Modernity*. Cambridge, MA: MIT Press, 1985.

Blumenberg, Hans. *The Legitimacy of the Modern Age*, trans. Robert Wallace. Cambridge, MA: MIT Press, 1983.

Cahoone, Lawrence. *The Dilemma of Modernity: Philosophy, Culture, and Anti-Culture*. Albany: State University of New York Press, 1988.

Durkheim, Emile. *The Division of Labour in Society*. New York: Free Press, 1964.

Frisby, David. *Fragments of Modernity: Theories of Modernity in the work of Simmel, Kracauer, and Benjamin*. Cambridge, MA: MIT Press, 1986.

Gehlen, Arnold. *Man in the Age of Technology*, trans. Patricia Lipscomb. New York: Columbia, 1980.

Gellner, Ernest. *Plough, Sword, and Book: The Structure of Human History*. Chicago: University of Chicago, 1988.

Giddens, Anthony. *The Consequences of Modernity*. Stanford: Stanford University Press, 1990.

Hughes, Robert. *The Shock of the New*. New York: Knopf, 1981.

Latour, Bruno. *We Have Never Been Modern*, trans. Catherine Porter. Cambridge, MA: Harvard University, 1993.

Levy Jr., Marion. *Modernization: Latecomers and Survivors*. New York: Basic Books, 1972.

——*Modernization and the Structure of Societies*, vols. 1 and 2. Princeton, NJ: Princeton University Press, 1966.

Mumford, Lewis. *The Myth of the Machine: The Pentagon of Power*. New York: Harcourt, Brace, Jovanovich, 1970.

Nisbet, Robert. *The Quest for Community: A Study in the Ethics of Order and Freedom*. San Francisco: Institute for Contemporary Studies, 1990.

Parsons, Talcott. *Societies: Evolutionary and Comparative Perspectives*. Englewood Cliffs, NJ: Prentice-Hall, 1966.

——*Structure and Process in Modern Societies*. Glencoe, Ill.: Free Press, 1960.

Pippin, Robert. *Modernism as a Philosophical Problem: On the Dissatisfactions of European High Culture*. Cambridge: Basil Blackwell, 1991.

Polanyi, Karl. *The Great Transformation: The Political and Economic Origins of Our Time*. Boston: Beacon Press, 1957.

Rosenberg, Harold. *The Tradition of the New*. New York: Horizon, 1959.

Rorty, Richard. *Philosophy and the Mirror of Nature*. Princeton, NJ: Princeton University Press, 1979.

Rosen, Stanley. *The Ancients and the Moderns: Rethinking Modernity*. New Haven: Yale University, 1989.

Sandel, Michael. *Liberalism and its Critics*. New York: New York University Press, 1984.

Sennett, Richard. *The Fall of Public Man: On the Social Psychology of Capitalism*. New York: Vintage, 1974.

Simmel, Georg. *The Philosophy of Money*, trans. Tom Bottomore and David Frisby. Boston: Routledge & Kegan Paul, 1978.

Spengler, Oswald. *The Decline of the West*, trans. Charles Atkinson. New York: Knopf, 1932. [abridged edn.: ed. Helmut Werner, trans. Charles Atkinson. New York: Modern Library, 1965.]

Strauss, Leo. *Natural Right and History*. Chicago: University of Chicago Press, 1953.

Taylor, Charles. *Sources of the Self: the Making of the Modern Identity*. Cambridge, MA: Harvard University Press, 1989.

Tönnies, Ferdinand. *Community and Society*, trans. and ed. Charles Loomis. East Lansing, Mich.: Michigan State University Press, 1957.

Toulmin, Stephen. *Cosmopolis: The Hidden Agenda of Modernity*. New York: Free Press, 1990.

Yack, Bernard. *Fetishism of Modernities: Epochal Self-Consciousness in Contemporary Social and Political Thought*. Notre Dame: Notre Dame University, 1997.

4   Writers Selected in this Volume

Baudelaire, Charles. "The Painter of Modern Life," trans. Jonathan Mayne, in *The Painter of Modern Life and Other Essays*. London: Phaidon, 1964.

Baudrillard, Jean. *Symbolic Exchange and Death*, trans. Iain H. Grant. London: Sage, 1993.

——*Selected Writings*, ed. Mark Poster. Stanford: Stanford University Press, 1988.

Bell, Daniel. *The Coming of Post-Industrial Society*. New York: Basic Books, 1976; original, 1973.

—— *The End of Ideology*. Glencoe, Ill.: Free Press, 1960.

Bordo, Susan. "Feminism, Postmodernism, and Gender-Scepticism," in *Feminism/Postmodernism*, ed. Linda Nicholson. New York: Routledge, 1990, pp. 133–56.

—— *The Flight to Objectivity: Essays on Cartesianism and Culture*. Albany: State University of New York Press, 1987.

Burke, Edmund. *Reflections on the Revolution in France*. ed. J. G. A. Pocock. Indianapolis: Hackett, 1987.

Butler, Judith. *Gender Trouble*. New York: Routledge, 1999.

——*Bodies That Matter: On the Discursive Limits of Sex*. New York: Routledge, 1993.

—— "Contingent Foundations: Feminism and the Question of 'Postmodernism'," from Judith Butler and Joan Scott, *Feminists Theorize the Political*. New York: Routledge, 1992.

Condorcet, Marie Jean Antoine Nicolas Caritat, marquis de. *Sketch for an Historical Picture of the Progress of the Human Mind*, trans. June Barraclough. New York: Hyperion, rpt of 1955 Noonday Press edn.

Darwin, Charles. *Origin of Species*. Oxford: Oxford University, 1996.

—— *The Descent of Man*. Princeton: Princeton University, 1981.

de Saussure, Ferdinand. *Course in General Linguistics*, trans. Wade Baskin. New York: McGraw-Hill, 1966.

Deleuze, Gilles and Félix Guattari. *A Thousand Plateaus: Capitalism and Schizophrenia*, trans. Brian Massumi. Minneapolis: University of Minnesota Press, 1987.

——*Anti-Oedipus: Capitalism and Schizophrenia*, trans. Helen Lane, Mark Seem, and Robert Hurley. New York: Viking Penguin, 1977.

Derrida, Jacques. *A Derrida Reader: Between the Blinds*, ed. Peggy Kamuf. New York: Columbia University Press, 1991.

——*Margins of Philosophy*, trans. Alan Bass. Chicago: University of Chicago, 1984.

——*Of Grammatology*, trans. Gayatri Chakravorty Spivak. Baltimore: Johns Hopkins University Press, 1974.

——"*Differance*." trans. David B. Allison, in *Speech and Phenomena And Other Essays on Husserl's Theory of Signs*. Evanston: Northwestern University, 1973.

Descartes, René. *Meditations on First Philosophy*, trans. Elizabeth Haldane and G. R. T. Ross, in *The Philosophical Works of Descartes*, vol. I. Cambridge: Cambridge University Press, 1975.

Foster, Hal. *The Anti-Aesthetic: Essays in Postmodern Culture*. New York: The New Press, 1999.

——*Recordings: Art, Spectacle, Cultural Politics*. New York: The New Press, 1985.

Foucault, Michel. *The Foucault Reader*, ed. Paul Rabinow. New York: Pantheon, 1984.

——"Nietzsche, Genealogy, History," trans. Donald Bouchard and Sherry Simon, in *Language, Counter-Memory, Practise: Selected Essays and Interviews*, ed. Donald Bouchard. Ithaca, NY: Cornell University Press, 1977, pp. 139–64.

——"Truth and Power," trans. Colin Gordon, in *Power/Knowledge: Selected Interviews and Other Writings 1972–77*, ed. Colin Gordon. New York: Pantheon, 1972, pp. 131–3.

Freud, Sigmund. *Civilization and its Discontents*, trans. James Strachey. New York: Norton, 1961.

Giroux, Henry A. *Postmodernism, Feminism, and Cultural Politics: Redrawing Educational Boundaries*. Albany: State University of New York Press, 1991.

Griffin, David Ray. *The Reenchantment of Science*. Albany: State University of New York Press, 1988.

Habermas, Jürgen. *The Philosophical Discourse of Modernity*, trans. Frederick Lawrence. Cambridge, MA: MIT Press, 1987.

—— *Theory of Communicative Action*, 2 vols, trans. Thomas McCarthy. Boston: Beacon, 1984, 1987.

——"Modernity versus Postmodernity." *New German Critique*, no. 22, 1981, pp. 3–14.

Hall, David. "Modern China and the Postmodern West," in *Culture and Modernity: East–West Philosophic Perspectives*, ed. Eliot Deutsch. Honolulu: University of Hawaii Press, 1991, pp. 57–67.

Haraway, Donna. *Simians, Cyborgs, and Women: The Reinvention of Nature*. New York: Routledge, 1991.

—— "A Manifesto for Cyborgs: Science, Technology, and Socialist Feminism in the 1980s," in Linda Nicholson, *Feminism/Postmodernism*. New York: Routledge, 1990.

Harding, Sandra. *The Science Question in Feminism*. Ithaca, NY: Cornell University Press, 1986.

Hassan, Ihab. *The Postmodern Turn: Essays in Postmodern Theory and Culture*. Columbus: Ohio State University Press, 1987.

Hassan, Ihab. *Paracriticisms: Seven Speculations of the Times.* Urbana: University of Illinois Press, 1975.

Hegel, Georg Wilhelm Friedrich. *Phenomenology of Spirit,* trans. A. V. Miller. Oxford: Oxford University Press, 1977.

——*The Philosophy of History,* trans. J. Sibree. New York: Dover, 1956.

Heidegger, Martin. "Letter on Humanism," in *Martin Heidegger: Basic Writings,* ed. David Farrell Krell, trans. Frank A. Capuzzi, with J. Glenn Gray and David Farrell Krell. New York: Harper and Row, 1977, pp. 193–242.

——"The Question Concerning Technology," in *Martin Heidegger: Basic Writings,* pp. 287–317.

——"The End of Philosophy and the Task of Thinking," in *Martin Heidegger: Basic Writings,* pp. 373–92.

Horkheimer, Max and Theodor Adorno. *Dialectic of Enlightenment,* trans. John Cumming. New York: Seabury, 1972.

Hume, David. *A Treatise on Human Nature.* Oxford: Oxford University, 1975.

Husserl, Edmund. *The Crisis of European Sciences and Transcendental Phenomenology,* trans. David Carr. Evanston: Northwestern University Press, 1970.

Irigary, Luce. *Speculum of the Other Woman,* trans. Gillian C. Gill. Ithaca: Cornell University, 1985.

——"The Sex Which is Not One," trans. Claudia Reeder, in *New French Feminisms,* ed. Elaine Marks and Isabelle de Courtivron. New York: Schoken, 1981.

Jameson, Fredric. *Postmodernism, Or, The Cultural Logic of Late Capitalism.* Durham: Duke University Press, 1991.

Jencks, Charles. *The Language of Post-Modern Architecture.* New York: Rizzoli, 1984.

——*What Is Post-Modernism?* London: Academy Editions, 1986.

Kant, Immanuel. "An Answer to the Question: 'What is Enlightenment?' " in *Kant's Political Writings,* trans. H. B. Nisbet, ed. Hans Reiss. Cambridge: Cambridge University Press, 1970, pp. 54–60.

——*Critique of Pure Reason.* New York: St. Martin's, 1965.

Kuhn, Thomas. *The Structure of Scientific Revolutions.* Chicago: University of Chicago Press, 1962.

Lacan, Jacques. *The Ethics of Psychoanalysis, 1959–1960.* New York: W. W. Norton & Co., 1997.

——"The mirror stage as formative of the function of the I as revealed in psychoanalytic experience." in *Écrits: A Selection.* trans. Alan Sheridan. New York: W. W. Norton & Company, 1977.

Le Corbusier (né Charles-Édouard Jeanneret). *Towards a New Architecture,* trans. Frederick Etchells. New York: Dover, 1986.

Levinas, Emmanuel. *The Levinas Reader,* edited by Sean Hand. Oxford: Blackwell, 1990.

——*Collected Philosophical Papers,* edited by Alphonso Lingis. Dordrecht: Nijhoff, 1987.

Luhmann, Niklas, *Social Systems,* trans. John Bednarz and Dirk Baecker. Stanford: Stanford University, 1995.

——"The Cognitive Program of Constructivism and a Reality that Remains Unknown," in Wolfgang Krohn, Guenter Kueppers and Helga Nowotny, *Selforganization: Portrait of a Scientific Revolution.* Dordrecht: Kluwer Academic Publishers, 1990.

Lyotard, Jean-François. *Toward the Postmodern,* ed. Robert Harvey and Mark Roberts. Atlantic Highlands, NJ: Humanities, 1993.

——*The Postmodern Condition: A Report on Knowledge,* trans. Geoff Bennington and Brian Massumi. Minneapolis: Minnesota University Press, 1984.

MacIntyre, Alasdair. *Three Rival Versions of Moral Enquiry: Encyclopedia, Genealogy, and Tradition.* Notre Dame, Ind.: University of Notre Dame Press, 1990.

——*Whose Justice? Which Rationality?* Notre Dame, Ind.: University of Notre Dame Press, 1988.

——*After Virtue.* Notre Dame, Ind.: University of Notre Dame Press, 1984.

Marinetti, Filippo Tommaso. "The Founding and Manifesto of Futurism," trans. R. W. Flint and Arthur W. Coppotelli, in *Marinetti: Selected Writings,* ed. R. W. Flint. New York: Farrar, Straus, Giroux, 1972.

Marx, Karl and Friedrich Engels. *Manifesto of the Communist Party,* trans. Samuel Moore, in Robert Tucker, *The Marx–Engels Reader.* New York: Norton, 1978.

Nietzsche, Friedrich. "On Truth and Lies in a Non-Moral Sense." in *Philosophy and Truth,* ed. by Daniel Brazeale. New York: Humanities Press, 1979.

——*The Gay Science,* trans. with commentary by Walter Kaufmann. New York: Random House, 1974.

——"How the True World finally became a Fable," in *Twilight of the Idols,* trans. and edited by Walter Kaufmann, in *The Portable Nietzsche.* New York: Viking, 1968.

——*The Will to Power,* ed. Walter Kaufmann, trans. Walter Kaufmann and R. J. Hollingdale. New York: Random House, 1967.

——*Beyond Good and Evil,* trans. with commentary by Walter Kaufmann. New York: Random House, 1966.

Peirce, Charles S. "How to Make Our Ideas Clear." *Collected Papers of Charles Sanders Peirce,* vol. V, ed. Charles Hartshorne and Paul Weiss. Cambridge, MA: Harvard University Press, 1965.

Putnam, Hilary. *The Many Faces of Realism.* LaSalle, Illinois: Open Court, 1987.

——*Reason, Truth, and History.* Cambridge: Cambridge University, 1981.

Quine, W. V. *From a Logical Point of View: Nine Logico-Philosophical Essays.* Cambridge, MA: Harvard University, 1980.

——*Ontological Relativity and Other Essays.* New York: Columbia University, 1969.

——*Word and Object.* Cambridge, MA: MIT, 1964.

Rorty, Richard. *Essays on Heidegger and Others.* Cambridge: Cambridge University Press, 1991.

——"Solidarity or Objectivity?" in *Objectivity, Relativism, and Truth.* Cambridge: Cambridge University Press, 1991, pp. 21–34.

——Contingency, Irony, and Solidarity. New York: Cambridge University Press, 1989.

——Consequences of Pragmatism: Essays, 1972–1980. Minneapolis: University of Minnesota Press, 1982.

Rousseau, Jean-Jacques. Discourse on the Sciences and the Arts, in The Basic Political Writings of Jean-Jacques Rousseau, trans. Donald Cress. Indianapolis: Hackett, 1987.

——Discourse on the Foundations and Origin of Inequality Among Men, in The Basic Political Writings of Jean-Jacques Rousseau.

Sartre, Jean-Paul. Being and Nothingness, trans. Hazel E. Barnes. Washington Square: New York, 1993.

——"Existentialism," trans. Bernard Frechtman, in Existentialism and Human Emotions. New York: Citadel, 1985.

Smith, Adam. The Theory of Moral Sentiments, Glasgow Edition. Indianapolis: Liberty Fund, 1984.

——An Inquiry into the Nature and Causes of the Wealth of Nations, Glasgow Edition. Indianapolis: Liberty Fund, 1982.

Spivak, Gayatri Chakravorty. "Can the Subaltern Speak?" in Marxism and the Interpretation of Culture, ed. Cary Nelson and Lawrence Grossberg. Urbana: University of Illinois, 1988.

——In Other Worlds: Essays in Cultural Politics. New York: Routledge, Kegan, & Paul, 1988.

Taylor, Mark. C. Erring: A Postmodern A/theology. Chicago: University of Chicago Press, 1984.

Venturi, Robert. Complexity and Contradiction in Architecture. New York: Museum of Modern Art, 1966.

——with Denise Scott Brown and Steven Izenour. Learning from Las Vegas. Cambridge, MA: MIT Press, 1972.

Weber, Max. The Protestant Ethic and the Spirit of Capitalism, trans. Talcott Parsons. New York: Scribner, 1958.

——"Science as a Vocation," in From Max Weber: Essays in Sociology, trans. and ed. H. H. Gerth and C. Wright Mills. New York: Oxford University Press, 1946.

Cornel, West, Race Matters. New York: Vintage, 1994.

——The American Evasion of Philosophy: A Genealogy of Pragmatism. Madison: University of Wisconsin, 1989.

——"A Genealogy of Modern Racism," in Prophesy Deliverance! An Afro-American Revolutionary Christianity. Philadelphia: Westminister John Knox Press, 1982.

Wittgenstein, Ludwig. "Lecture on Ethics." The Philosophical Review, 74, no. 1, January 1965, pp. 3–12.

——Tractatus Logico-Philosophicus, trans. D. F. Pears and B. F. McGuinness. London: Routledge and Kegan Paul, 1961.

Young, Iris Marion. Justice and the Politics of Difference. Princeton: Princeton University, 1990.

——Throwing Like a Girl and Other Essays in Feminist Philosophy and Social Theory. Bloomington: Indiana University, 1990.

Index

Note: Page numbers in bold type indicate a main reference.

Index

Index

Hall, David, 223, **512–18**
Hanson, Duane, 568
Hanson, Norwood Russell, 547–8
Haraway, Donna, 223, **464–81**
Harding, Sandra, **342–52**, 358, 493 n.26, 494 n.41
Hardy, Barbara, 554, 555
Hare, Rom, 562
Harth, Erica, 366 n.1
Hartsock, Nancy, **344–7**, 350
Harvey, William, 367 n.8
Hassan, Ihab, 223, **410–20**
Havel, Vaclav, 383
Hawthorne, Nathaniel, 4
Heckscher, August, 404
Heelan, Patrick, 366
Hegel, Georg Wilhelm Friedrich, 11, 75, 251, 392, 583
    on absolute freedom, 70–4
    death of God, 435
    definition of *existentia*, 179
    Encyclopaedia, 226, **261–2**
    estrangement of man, 185
    ethics, 571, 586, 590, 591 n.13
    on history, 183, 526
    irrationalism, 166
    legitimation of knowledge, **261–2**, 264
    Marx and, 18, 580
    master and slave, 349, 350
    naming of philosophy, 194
    negativity, 159–60, **232**, 329
    Phenomenology of Spirit, 185, 274 n.19
    on subjectivity, 576, 579–80
Heidegger, Martin, 335, 525, 526, 530, 532
    Being/beings distinction, 174, 226, 237–8
    Dasein concept, 174, **179**, 180, 181, 183–4, 189, 192, 576
    on ek-sistence, **178–83**, 185–6, 189, 192, 193
    on ethics and ontology, 190–2
    etymologies, 523
    forlornness (*Verlassenheit*), 171
    on homelessness, 184–5
    on humanism, 86, **174–94**
    influence on Gadamer, 452
    on language, 174, 175, **176–7**, 179–80, 182, 183, 186, 193, 586, 587
    on metaphysics, 175, **178**, 181–2, 183, 184, 185, 186–7, 189, 194, 581
    Nazism, 174, 263, 452
    on nihilation, 192–3
    phenomenology and, 85, 86, 149, 174, 585
    on presence, 233, **237–9**, 240
    Sartre's existentialism and, 86, 169, 174, 177, **180–1**, 182–3, 185
    on science, 301
    speech on knowledge legitimation, 263–4

    on thinking, **174–6**, 182–3, 186, 188, 189, 191–2, 193–4
    view of nature, 86, 179, 568, 582
Heinrich, Klaus, 590
Heisenberg, Werner, 86
Heller, Erich, 414
Hemingway, Ernest, 9, 86, 420
Heraclitus, 190–1
Herbert, William, 89
hermeneutics, 587
Herodotus, 115 n, 307, 448
Hervey, Charles, 336
Hesse, Mary, 450, 491 n.1
Heusch, Luc de, 280, 292 n.5
hieroglyphist prejudice, 327, 330
Hillman, James, 357, 358
Hinduism, 7, 199, 321
    sati, 330, **331–8**
Hirsch, E. D. Jr., 385
history
    Being and, 183
    change and, 411
    effective, 246–8
    of feminism, **350–2**, 363–4
    genealogy and, 242–3, 248–9
    individual and, 552, **560–1**
    Marx's view, 425
    projection and, 586
    religion and, 436
    of science, 201–8
    Thompson on end of, 383–4
    truth and, 243
    uses of, 249–51
Hobbes, Thomas, 155, 164, 596
Hölderlin, Johann Christian Friedrich, 177, 184, 185, 192, 579
Hollein, Hans, 460
Holzer, Jenny, 313, **314–15**
homelessness, 184–5
Homer, 555, 557
homophobia, **378**, 379, 381
hooks, bell, 388
Hopper, Edward, 567
Horace, 45, 55
Horkheimer, Max, 86, **159–67**, 575, 580, 585
Howe, Irving, 6
Hubel, David, 594
Hudnut, Joseph, 6, 458
Hull, Clark, 483, 484
humanism, 10, 301
    existentialism and, 172–3
    Heidegger on, 86, **174–94**
    history of, 177–8
    science and, 6
Humboldt, Wilhelm von, 261